Fodor's 98

USA

The complete guide, thoroughly up-to-date

Packed with details that will make your trip

The must-see sights, off and on the beaten path

What to see, what to skip

Smart lodging and dining options

Essential local do's and taboos

Transportation tips, distances and directions

Key contacts, savvy travel tips

When to go, what to pack

Clear, accurate, easy-to-use maps

Fodor's Travel Publications, Inc.
New York • Toronto • London • Sydney • Auckland
www.fodors.com/

Fodor's USA

EDITORS: Matthew Lore and Amy McConnell

Editorial Contributors: Robert Andrews, Glen Berger, David Brown, Linda Cabasin, Steve Crohn, Audra Epstein, Andrea Lehman, David Low, Danny Mangin, Chelsea Mauldin, Rebecca Miller, Anastasia Mills, Heidi Sarna, Helayne Schiff, Mary Ellen Schultz, M.T. Schwartzman (Gold Guide Editor), Dinah A. Spritzer, Susan Winsten, Sara Wood

Editorial Production: Tracy Patruno

Maps: David Lindroth, *cartographer;* Steven K. Amsterdam and Bob Blake, *map editors*

Design: Fabrizio La Rocca, *creative director;* Guido Caroti, *associate art director;* Jolie Novak, *photo editor*

Production/Manufacturing: Mike Costa

Cover Photograph: Richard Nowitz

Copyright

Special Sales

Fodor's Travel Publications are available at special discounts for bulk purchases for sales promotions or premiums. Special editions, including personalized covers, excerpts of existing guides, and corporate imprints, can be created in large quantities for special needs. For more information, contact your local bookseller or write to Special Markets, Fodor's Travel Publications, 201 East 50th Street, New York, NY 10022. Inquiries from Canada should be directed to your local Canadian bookseller or sent to Random House of Canada, Ltd., Marketing Department, 1265 Aerowood Drive, Mississauga, Ontario L4W 1B9. Inquiries from the United Kingdom should be sent to Fodor's Travel Publications, 20 Vauxhall Bridge Road, London SW1V 2SA.

PRINTED IN THE UNITED STATES OF AMERICA

10 9 8 7 6 5 4 3 2 1

CONTENTS

🌐 *Italic entries are maps.*

Contents

ON THE ROAD WITH FODOR'S

WE'RE ALWAYS THRILLED to get letters from readers, especially one like this:

It took us an hour to decide what book to buy and we now know we picked the best one. Your book was wonderful, easy to follow, very accurate, and good on pointing out eating places, informal as well as formal. When we saw other people using your book, we would look at each other and smile.

In the creation of *USA '98*, we at Fodor's have made every effort to capture the best of our national heritage and to convey the excitement of the contemporary American scene. It's good to remember how much of our landscape remains essentially unchanged from the days when the earliest explorers stepped ashore. Flowers continue to bloom each spring in the deserts of the Southwest, the oceans go on pounding the coasts of Oregon and Maine, and the Great Plains still stretch as far as the eye can see beneath endless arches of sky. From the Grand Canyon to the Hudson Highlands, you can still see much of what the early settlers saw, and with the same sense of wonder and awe.

NEW THIS YEAR

This year, Fodor's joins Rand McNally, the world's largest commercial mapmaker to bring you a detailed color map of the USA. Just detach it along the perforation and drop it in your tote bag.

We're also proud to announce that the American Society of Travel Agents has endorsed Fodor's as its guidebook of choice. ASTA is the world's largest and most influential travel trade association, operating in more than 170 countries, with 27,000 members pledged to adhere to a strict code of ethics reflecting the Society's motto, "Integrity in Travel." ASTA shares Fodor's devotion to providing smart, honest travel information and advice to travelers, and we've long recommended that our readers consult ASTA member agents for the experience and professionalism they bring to the table.

ON THE WEB

Be sure to check out Fodor's Web site (www.fodors.com/) for information on major destinations around the world and travel-savvy interactive features. The Web site also lists the 80-plus stations nationwide that carry the Fodor's Travel Show, a live call-in radio program that airs every weekend. Tune in to hear guests discuss their wonderful adventures—or call in to get answers for your most pressing travel questions.

FODOR'S CHOICE

No two people will agree on what makes a perfect vacation, but it's fun and helpful to know what others think. We hope you'll have a chance to experience some of Fodor's Choices yourself while traveling in the United States. For detailed information about each entry, refer to the appropriate chapters in this guidebook.

Natural Wonders

Northeast
Niagara Falls (NY)

Mid-Atlantic
Delaware Water Gap (PA/NJ)
Natural Bridge (Natural Bridge, VA)

Southeast
Everglades (FL)
Okefenokee (GA)

Mississippi Valley
Buffalo National River (AR)
Mammoth Cave (KY)
Bayou Teche (Acadiana, LA)

Midwest
Pictured Rocks National Lakeshore (Munising, MI)
Boundary Waters (MN)
Apostle Islands National Lakeshore (WI)

Great Plains
Badlands (ND/SD)

Southwest
Grand Canyon (AZ)
Palo Duro Canyon (TX)
Bryce and Zion canyons (UT)

Rockies
Glacier National Park (MT)
Old Faithful Geyser (Yellowstone, WY)

West Coast

El Capitan and Half Dome
(Yosemite National Park, CA)

Joshua Tree National Park (CA)

Muir Woods (Mill Valley, CA)

Crater Lake (OR)

Hoh Rain Forest
(Olympic Peninsula, WA)

Pacific

Mt. McKinley (AK)

Kilauea Volcano (The Big Island, HI)

Historic Buildings and Sites

Northeast

African Meeting House (Boston, MA)

Bunker Hill (Boston, MA)

Old North Church (Boston, MA)

Historic Deefield (Deerfield, MA)

Plimoth Plantation (Plymouth, MA)

Ellis Island (New York, NY)

Statue of Liberty (New York, NY)

Hunter House (Newport, RI)

Mid-Atlantic

Antietam National Battlefield
(Sharpsburg, MD)

Washington Crossing State Park
(Titusville, NJ)

Independence National Historical Park
(Philadelphia, PA)

Gettysburg National Military Park
(Gettysburg, PA)

Monticello (Charlottesville, VA)

Washington Monument
(Washington, DC)

Frederick Douglass National Historic
Site (Washington, DC)

Vietnam Memorial (Washington, DC)

The White House (Washington, DC)

Harper's Ferry National Park
(Harper's Ferry, WV)

Southeast

Civil Rights Memorial
(Montgomery, AL)

Birmingham Civil Rights Institute
(Birmingham, AL)

Andersonville National Historic Site
(Andersonville, GA)

Johnston-Hay House (Macon, GA)

Old Salem (Winston-Salem, NC)

Wright Brothers National Memorial
(Kill Devil Hills, NC)

Biltmore House (Asheville, NC)

Ft. Sumter National Monument
(Charleston, SC)

Drayton Hall (Charleston, SC)

Mississippi Valley

Old State House (Little Rock, AR)

Old Washington Historic State Park
(Washington, AR)

Shaker Village of Pleasant Hill
(Harrodsburg, KY)

Old Ursuline Convent
(New Orleans, LA)

Rosalie (Natchez, MS)

Midwest

Sears Tower (Chicago, IL)

George Rogers Clark National
Historical Park (Vincennes, IN)

Great Plains

George Washington Carver National
Monument (MO)

Liberty Memorial (Kansas City, MO)

Mt. Rushmore National Memorial (SD)

Southwest

Mission Ysleta (near El Paso, TX)

Palace of the Governors (Santa Fe, NM)

Salt Lake Mormon Tabernacle and
Temple (Salt Lake City, UT)

Rockies

Little Bighorn Battlefield National
Monument (MT)

West Coast

Olvera Street (Los Angeles, CA)

Fort Clatsop National Memorial
(Astoria, OR)

Hearst Castle (San Simeon, CA)

Sutter's Mill (Coloma, CA)

Pacific

Iolani Palace (Honolulu, HI)

The Pacific Ketchikan Totem Parks
(Ketchikan, AK)

Museums

Northeast

Wadsworth Atheneum (Hartford, CT)

Museum of Fine Arts (Boston, MA)

Isabella Stewart Gardner Museum
(Boston, MA)

Hood Museum of Art(Hanover, NH)

Frick Collection (New York, NY)

Metropolitan Museum of Art
(New York, NY)

Museum of Modern Art
(New York, NY)

Mid-Atlantic

B&O Railroad Museum
(Baltimore, MD)

Walters Art Gallery (Baltimore, MD)

Chesapeake Bay Maritime Museum
(St. Michaels, MD)

Barnes Foundation (Philadelphia, PA)

Smithsonian Institution
(Washington, DC)

Phillips Collection (Washington, DC)

Southeast

Ringling Museum of Art (Sarasota, FL)

Morris Museum of Art (Augusta, GA)

Museum of Early Southern Decorative
Arts (Winston-Salem, NC)

Mississippi Valley

Louisville Slugger Museum
(Louisville, KY)

Midwest

Walker Art Center (Minneapolis, MN)

Art Institute (Chicago, IL)

Milwaukee Public Museum
(Milwaukee, WI)

Great Plains

Mark Twain Home and Museum
(Hannibal, MO)

Nelson-Atkins Museum of Art
(Kansas City, MO)

Southwest

Heard Museum (Phoenix, AZ)

Museum of International Folk Art
(Santa Fe, NM)

Kimbell Art Museum (Fort Worth, TX)

Rockies

Buffalo Bill Historical Center
(Cody, WY)

West Coast

San Francisco Museum of Modern Art
(CA)

Los Angeles County Museum of Art
(CA)

Seattle Art Museum (Seattle, WA)

Pacific

Alaska State Museum (Juneau, AK)

Neighborhoods

Northeast

Beacon Hill (Boston, MA)

Brooklyn Heights (New York, NY)

Mid-Atlantic

Fells Point (Baltimore, MD)

Victorian Cape May (Cape May, NJ)

Society Hill (Philadelphia, PA)

Old Town (Alexandria, VA)

Georgetown (Washington, DC)

Southeast

South Beach (Miami Beach, FL)

Buckhead and Druid Hills
(Atlanta, GA)

Mississippi Valley

Old Louisville (Louisville, KY)

French Quarter (New Orleans, LA)

Midwest

Lincoln Park (Chicago, IL)

Summit Avenue/Ramsey Hill
(St. Paul, MN)

German Village (Columbus, OH)

Southwest

Plaza (Santa Fe, NM)

Deep Ellum (Dallas, TX)

West Coast

North Beach (San Francisco, CA)

Rodeo Drive (Beverly Hills, CA)

Pioneer Square (Seattle, WA)

Parks and Gardens

Northeast

Acadia National Park (Bar Harbor, ME)

Public Garden (Boston, MA)

Central Park (New York, NY)

Mid-Atlantic

Winterthur Gardens (Winterthur, DE)

Sherwood Gardens (Baltimore, MD)

Longwood Gardens
(Brandywine Valley, PA)

Dumbarton Oaks (Washington, DC)

Southeast

Bellingrath Gardens and Home
(Mobile, AL)

Town squares (Savannah, GA)

Biltmore Estate Gardens
(Asheville, NC)

Magnolia Plantation (Charleston, SC)

Middleton Place (Charleston, SC)

Mississippi Valley

Cheekwood–Tennessee Botanical
Gardens and Museum of Art
(Nashville, TN)

Midwest

Lincoln Park (Chicago, IL)

Great Plains

International Peace Garden (ND)

Southwest

Arizona–Sonora Desert Museum
(Tucson, AZ)

Water Gardens Park (Fort Worth, TX)

West Coast

Golden Gate Park (San Francisco, CA)

Balboa Park (San Diego, CA)

Washington Park International Rose
Test Garden and Japanese Gardens
(Portland, OR)

Beaches

Northeast
Cape Cod National Seashore (MA)

Jones Beach (Long Island, NY)

Mansion Beach (Block Island, RI)

Mid-Atlantic
Assateague Island (MD/VA)

Island Beach State Park (NJ)

Southeast
Gulf State Park (AL)

Grayton Beach State Recreation Area (Seaside, FL)

Cumberland Island National Seashore (GA)

Cape Hatteras National Seashore (NC)

Hilton Head Island (SC)

Mississippi Valley
Gulf Islands National Seashore (Ocean Springs, MS)

Midwest
Indiana Dunes National Lakeshore (IN)

Great Plains
Lake McConaughy State Recreation Area (NE)

Southwest
Lake Powell (UT)

Padre Island National Seashore (TX)

West Coast
Point Reyes National Seashore (CA)

Corona del Mar (CA)

Pismo State Beach (CA)

Cannon Beach (OR)

Pacific
Kauanoa Beach (The Big Island, HI)

Wailea's five crescent beaches (Maui, HI)

Amusement and Theme Parks

Northeast
Coney Island (NY)

Mid-Atlantic
Adventure World (Mitchellville, MD)

Six Flags Great Adventure (Jackson, NJ)

Sesame Place (Langhorne, PA)

Southeast
Walt Disney World (Orlando, FL)

Mississippi Valley
Opryland USA (Nashville, TN)

Midwest
Six Flags Great America (Gurnee, IL)

Cedar Point Amusement Park (Sandusky, OH)

Great Plains
Silver Dollar City (Branson, MO)

Worlds of Fun (Kansas City, MO)

Southwest
Astroworld/Waterworld (Houston, TX)

West Coast
Disneyland (Anaheim, CA)

Universal Studios (Universal City, CA)

Pacific
Alaskaland Park (Fairbanks, AK)

Restaurants

Northeast
Hurricane (Ogunquit, ME; $$–$$$)

Lespinasse (New York, NY; $$$$)

Al Forno (Providence, RI; $$$)

Mid-Atlantic
Tio Pepe (Baltimore, MD; $$$)

Le Bec-Fin (Philadelphia, PA; $$$$)

Meskerem (Washington, DC; $)

Red Fox (Snowshoe, WV; $$$–$$$$)

Southeast
Highlands Bar & Grill (Birmingham, AL; $$$)

Louie's Back Yard (Key West, FL; $$$)

Bacchanalia (Atlanta, GA; $$$)

Elizabeth on 37th (Savannah, GA; $$$$)

Mississippi Valley
Lilly's (Louisville, KY; $$$)

Commander's Palace (New Orleans, LA; $$$$)

Nola (New Orleans, LA; $$)

Midwest
Charlie Trotter's (Chicago, IL; $$$$)

Lelli's Inn (Detroit, MI; $$)

Sanford (Milwaukee, WI; $$)

Great Plains
Stroud's (Kansas City, MO; $)

Mandan Drug (Mandan, ND; $)

Cattlemen's Steak House (Oklahoma City, OK; $$)

Southwest
Calle Doce (Dallas, TX; $$)

Christopher's (Phoenix, AZ; $$$)

Glitretind (Park City, UT; $$$$)

Rockies
Strings (Denver, CO; $$$)

West Coast
Stars (San Francisco, CA; $$$)

Granita (Malibu, CA; $$–$$$)

Pacific
The Double Musky
(Anchorage, AK; $$–$$$)

A Pacific Café (Kaua'i, HI; $$$)

Hotels

Northeast
Wyndham Copley Plaza
(Boston, MA; $$$$)

Charlotte Inn (Edgartown, MA; $$$$)

The Carlyle (New York, NY; $$$$)

The Mark (New York, NY; $$$$)

Inn at Castle Hill (Newport, RI; $$$$)

Mid-Atlantic
Harbor Court (Baltimore, MD; $$$$)

The Homestead (Hot Springs, VA; $$$$)

Hay-Adams Hotel
(Washington, DC; $$$$)

The Greenbrier
(White Sulphur Springs, WV; $$$$)

Southeast
Registry Resort (Naples, FL; $$$$)

Ritz-Carlton, Buckhead
(Atlanta, GA; $$$$)

Grove Park Inn (Asheville, NC; $$$$)

John Rutledge House Inn
(Charleston, SC; $$$$)

Mississippi Valley
The Seelbach (Louisville, KY; $$$)

Windsor Court Hotel
(New Orleans, LA; $$$$)

Midwest
The Drake (Chicago, IL; $$$$)

Pfister Hotel (Milwaukee, WI; $$$$)

Great Plains
Island Guest Ranch (Ames, OK; $$$)

Southwest
Cliff Lodge at Snowbird Resort
(Snowbird, UT; $$$$)

The Boulders (Carefree, AZ; $$$$)

Menger Hotel (San Antonio, TX; $$$)

Rockies
Oxford (Denver, CO; $$$)

Old Faithful Inn
(Yellowstone, WY; $$–$$$$)

West Coast
Sherman House
(San Francisco, CA; $$$$)

Ritz-Carlton Laguna Niguel
(Dana Point, CA; $$$$)

Stephanie Inn
(Cannon Beach, OR; $$$–$$$$)

Pacific
Camp Denali
(Denali National Park, AK; $$$$)

Princeville Hotel (Kaua'i, HI; $$$$)

HOW TO USE THIS BOOK

Organization

Chapter 1 is the **Gold Guide,** an easy-to-use section divided alphabetically by topic. Under each listing you'll find tips and information that will help you accomplish what you need to in the USA. You'll also find addresses and telephone numbers of organizations and companies that offer destination-related services and detailed information and publications.

The next chapter, **Special-Interest Vacations,** tells you the best places in the country to pursue your favorite hobby or sport. The **10 regional chapters** that follow begin with the Northeast and zigzag across the country to the Pacific. Each chapter introduction includes a list of that region's best festivals and seasonal events—all great opportunities to see a destination at its best. Within each region, states are listed alphabetically; within each state are sections on the major cities, the most popular tourist areas, and worthwhile but less-known destinations grouped together under the heading "Elsewhere in [state name]."

Icons and Symbols

★   Our special recommendations

✕   Restaurant

🏠   Lodging

✕🏠   Lodging establishment whose restaurant warrants a detour

☞   Sends you to another section of the guide for more info

✉   Address

☎   Telephone number

FAX   Fax number

🎫   Admission over $20

Admission Prices

Free sights are noted as such. We note only admission prices in excess of $20 for adults. Where no information is given, the admission fee is a suggested donation or less than $20 for adults. Call ahead for specific entrance fee information. Substantially reduced fees are almost always available for children, students, and senior citizens.

Restaurant and Hotel Criteria and Price Categories

Restaurants and lodging establishments are chosen with a view to giving you the cream of the crop in each location and in each price range. Price categories are as follows:

For restaurants:

CHART 1	(A)	(B)
CATEGORY	MAJOR CITY OR RESORT*	OTHER AREAS*
$$$$	over $50	over $30
$$$	$30–$50	$20–$30
$$	$15–$30	$10–$20
$	under $15	under $10

Rates are per person for a 3-course meal excluding drinks, tips, and taxes.

For hotels:

CHART 2	(A)	(B)
CATEGORY	MAJOR CITY OR RESORT*	OTHER AREAS*
$$$$	over $200	over $100
$$$	$125–$200	$75–$100
$$	$75–$125	$50–$75
$	under $75	under $50

Rates are for a standard double room for two, excluding tax and service charges.

We always list the facilities that are available—but we don't specify whether they cost extra: When pricing accommodations, always ask what's included.

Assume that hotels operate on the **European Plan** (EP, with no meals) unless we note that they use the **Full American Plan** (FAP, with all meals), the **Modified American Plan** (MAP, with breakfast and dinner daily), or the **Continental Plan** (CP, with a Continental breakfast daily).

Restaurant Reservations and Dress Codes

Reservations are always a good idea; we note only when they're essential or when they are not accepted. Even restaurants with a no-reservations policy will often book tables for groups of 6 or more. Book as far ahead as you can, and reconfirm when you get to town. Unless otherwise noted, the restaurants listed are open daily for lunch and dinner. We mention dress only when men are required to wear a jacket or a jacket and tie. Look for an overview of local habits *under* Dining *in* Chapter 1, The Gold Guide.

Credit Cards

The following abbreviations are used: **AE,** American Express; **D,** Discover; **DC,** Diners Club; **MC,** MasterCard; and **V,** Visa.

DON'T FORGET TO WRITE

You can use this book in the confidence that all prices and opening times are based on information supplied to us at press time; Fodor's cannot accept responsibility for any errors. Time inevitably brings changes, so always confirm information when it matters—especially if you're making a detour to visit a specific place. In addition, when making reservations be sure to mention if you have a disability or are traveling with children, if you prefer a private bath or a certain type of bed, or if you have specific dietary needs or any other concerns.

Were the restaurants we recommended as described? Did our hotel picks exceed your expectations? Did you find a museum we recommended a waste of time? If you have complaints, we'll look into them and revise our entries when the facts warrant it. If you've discovered a special place that we haven't included, we'll pass the information along to our correspondents and have them check it out. So send us your feedback, positive *and* negative: e-mail us at editors@fodors.com (specifying the name of the book on the subject line) or write the USA editor at Fodor's, 201 East 50th Street, New York, New York 10022. Have a wonderful trip!

Karen Cure
Editorial Director

The United States

CANADA

Vancouver
Victoria
Calgary

BRITISH COLUMBIA
ALBERTA
SASKATCHEWAN
MANITOB

Regina

Winnipeg

Seattle
Olympia

Trans-Canada Hwy.

Columbia R.

WASHINGTON
Spokane
Great Falls
Missouri R.

NORTH DAKOTA
Farg

Portland
Salem

Helena

MONTANA

OREGON

IDAHO

Billings

Bismarck

SOUTH DAKOTA

Boise
Snake R.

Pierre

Missouri R.

WYOMING

NEBRASKA

Carson City
Sacramento

NEVADA
Salt Lake City
Cheyenne
Linc

San Francisco

UTAH
Denver

Fresno

Colorado Springs
COLORADO

KANSA

Las Vegas

Colorado R.

CALIFORNIA

Santa Barbara
Los Angeles

Flagstaff

Santa Fe

OKLAHOMA
Oklahoma City

Albuquerque
Amarillo

ARIZONA

NEW MEXICO

San Diego
Phoenix

Tucson

PACIFIC OCEAN

BAJA CALIFORNIA
SONORA

El Paso
Dal

CHIHUAHUA

Rio Grande

TEXAS

Austin

San Antonio

ARCTIC OCEAN

RUSSIA

Bering Strait

ALASKA

MEXICO

Bering Sea

Nome
Fairbanks

CANADA

COAHUILA

ALEUTIAN ISLANDS

Anchorage

Juneau

PACIFIC OCEAN

0   400 miles
0   400 km

N

NUEVO LEON

Honolulu
Oahu   Maui
HAWAII
Hawaii
PACIFIC OCEAN

Amtrak Rail Passenger System

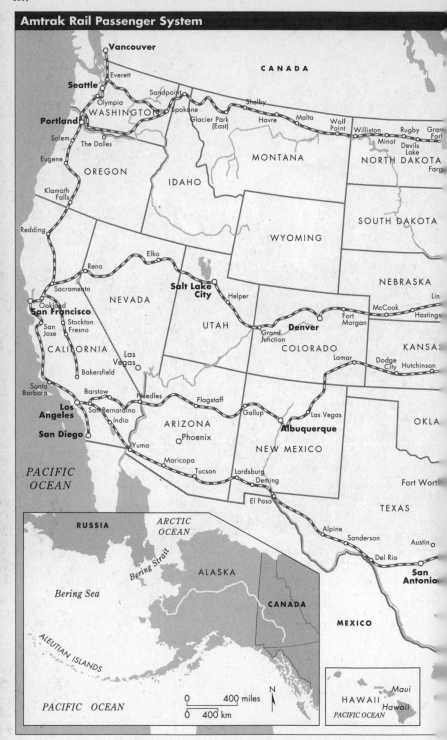

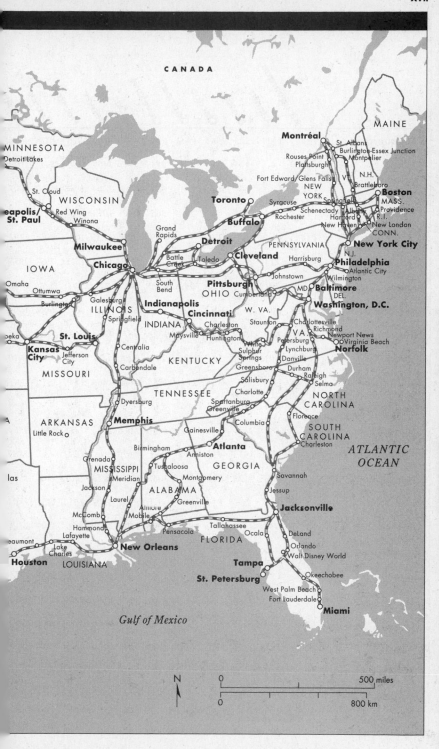

CANADA

MINNESOTA
Detroit Lakes

St. Cloud

WISCONSIN
Red Wing
eapolis/
St. Paul   Winona

IOWA

Omaha   Ottumwa
Burlington
ILLINOIS
Galesburg
Springfield
oeka
St. Louis
Kansas   Jefferson
City   City
Centralia
MISSOURI   Carbondale

ARKANSAS
Little Rock

las

MINNESOTA

Milwaukee
Chicago

Grand
Rapids
Battle
Creek
South
Bend
Indianapolis
INDIANA
Charleston
Maysville
KENTUCKY

TENNESSEE
Dyersburg

Memphis

Grenada
MISSISSIPPI
Meridian
Jackson
Laurel

McComb
Hammond
Lafayette
eaumont   Lake
Charles
Houston   New Orleans
LOUISIANA

Toronto

Detroit
Toledo   Cleveland
OHIO
Cincinnati
Huntington

Birmingham
Tuscaloosa
ALABAMA
Montgomery
Greenville
Elmore
Mobile
Pensacola
Tallahassee

Buffalo

Pittsburgh
Cumberland

W. VA.
Staunton
White
Sulphur
Springs
Greensboro
Salisbury
Charlotte
Spartanburg
Greenville
Columbia
Gainesville

Atlanta
GEORGIA

Anniston

Montréal
St. Albans
Burlington-Essex Junction
Rouses Point   Montpelier
Plattsburgh
Fort Edward/Glens Falls   VT.
NEW   Brattleboro
YORK   N.H.
Syracuse   Springfield   Boston
Schenectady Albany   MASS.
Rochester   Providence
Hartford   R.I.
New Haven   New London
CONN.

Harrisburg   New York City
NJ.
Johnstown   Philadelphia
Atlantic City
MD   Wilmington
Baltimore
DEL.
Washington, D.C.

Charlottesville
Richmond
VA.   Newport News
Petersburg   Virginia Beach
Lynchburg   Norfolk
Danville
Durham
Raleigh
Selma
NORTH
CAROLINA
Florence
SOUTH
CAROLINA
Charleston

ATLANTIC
OCEAN

Savannah

Jessup

Jacksonville

Ocala   DeLand
FLORIDA   Orlando
Walt Disney World
Tampa
St. Petersburg   Okeechobee
West Palm Beach
Fort Lauderdale
Miami

Gulf of Mexico

N

0   500 miles

0   800 km

PENNSYLVANIA

Grand
Rapids

Galesburg

Mileages Between Major U.S. Cities

	Albuquerque	Atlanta	Boston	Chicago	Cincinnati	Cleveland	Dallas	Denver	Houston	Kansas City	Los An...
Albuquerque	—	1409	2225	1343	1402	1608	666	446	876	818	790
Atlanta	1409	—	1105	703	466	715	791	1404	800	801	2199
Boston	2225	1105	—	1018	861	657	1765	2006	1857	1414	3007
Chicago	1343	703	1018	—	296	365	940	1013	1107	511	2014
Cincinnati	1402	466	861	296	—	249	943	1195	1079	592	2192
Cleveland	1608	715	657	365	249	—	1193	1354	1328	797	2355
Dallas	666	791	1765	940	943	1193	—	825	241	523	1440
Denver	446	1404	2006	1013	1195	1354	825	—	1075	606	1004
Houston	876	800	1857	1107	1079	1328	241	1075	—	764	1545
Kansas City	818	801	1414	511	592	797	523	606	764	—	1610
Los Angeles	790	2199	3007	2014	2192	2355	1440	1004	1545	1610	—
Memphis	1004	401	1309	533	487	736	456	1113	592	474	1798
Miami	2009	695	1524	1388	1149	1251	1342	2088	1215	1485	2759
Minneapolis	1255	1121	1435	417	713	782	962	916	1202	437	1889
New Orleans	1178	473	1529	928	818	1067	511	1273	350	842	1894
New York	2002	878	226	814	634	463	1538	1802	1630	1192	2803
Orlando	1770	446	1314	1149	912	1041	1104	1850	976	1247	2521
Philadelphia	1949	779	326	798	581	437	1462	1742	1554	1139	2738
Phoenix	463	1859	2687	1805	1865	2071	1068	832	1173	1280	372
Portland, OR	1411	2599	3046	2126	2370	2466	2009	1241	2205	1796	963
St. Louis	1050	555	1175	293	352	558	647	852	819	249	1840
Salt Lake	646	1876	2396	1403	1647	1743	1290	518	1500	1073	689
San Francisco	1095	2505	3125	2132	2376	2472	1761	1247	1923	1802	381
Seattle	1463	2651	3085	2067	2328	2432	2117	1293	2274	1848	113€
Washington, DC	1875	641	462	733	488	377	1323	1649	1415	1045	266£

Memphis	Miami	Minneapolis	New Orleans	New York	Orlando	Philadelphia	Phoenix	Portland, OR	St. Louis	Salt Lake	San Francisco	Seattle	Washington, DC
1008	2009	1255	1178	2002	1770	1949	463	1411	1050	646	1095	1463	1875
401	685	1121	473	878	446	779	1859	2599	555	1876	2505	2651	641
1309	1524	1435	1529	226	1314	326	2687	3046	1175	2396	3125	3085	462
533	1388	417	928	814	1149	798	1805	2126	293	1403	2132	2067	733
487	1149	713	818	634	912	581	1865	2370	352	1647	2376	2328	488
736	1251	782	1067	453	1041	437	2071	2466	558	1743	2472	2432	377
456	1342	962	511	1538	1104	1462	1068	2009	647	1290	1761	2177	1323
1113	2088	916	1273	1802	1850	1742	832	1241	852	518	1247	1293	1649
592	1215	1202	350	1630	976	1554	1173	2205	819	1500	1923	2274	1415
474	1485	437	842	1192	1247	1139	1280	1796	249	1073	1802	1848	1045
1798	2759	1889	1894	2803	2521	2738	372	963	1840	689	381	1136	2665
—	1045	848	398	1082	807	1006	1471	2276	286	1553	2104	2328	867
1045	—	1805	887	1298	245	1203	2387	3284	1239	2561	3137	3336	1066
848	1805	—	1243	1231	1567	1215	1718	1737	575	1264	1994	1651	1150
398	887	1243	—	1302	649	1226	1512	2505	681	1802	2272	2574	1087
1082	1298	1231	1302	—	1088	95	2465	2915	952	2192	2921	2881	237
807	245	1567	649	1088	—	994	2149	3046	1061	2322	2899	3098	856
1006	1203	1215	1226	95	994	—	2412	2899	899	2176	2905	2751	142
1471	2387	1718	1512	2465	2149	2412	—	1333	1513	673	750	1489	2337
2276	3284	1737	2505	2915	3046	2899	1333	—	2048	765	634	173	2835
286	1239	575	681	952	1061	899	1513	2048	—	1324	2054	2100	806
553	2561	1264	1802	2192	2322	2176	673	765	1324	—	735	817	2111
2104	3137	1994	2272	2921	2899	2905	750	634	2054	735	—	807	2841
328	3336	1651	2574	2881	3098	2751	1489	173	2100	817	807	—	2800
867	1066	1150	1087	237	856	142	2337	2835	806	2111	2841	2800	—

1 The Gold Guide

Smart Travel Tips A to Z

Basic Information on Traveling in the United States, Savvy Tips to Make Your Trip a Breeze, and Companies and Organizations to Contact

SMART TRAVEL TIPS A TO Z

A
AIR TRAVEL

MAJOR AIRLINE OR LOW-COST CARRIER?

Most people choose a flight based on price. Yet there are other issues to consider. Major airlines offer the greatest number of departures; smaller airlines—including regional, low-cost and no-frill airlines—usually have a more limited number of flights daily. Major airlines have frequent-flyer partners, which allow you to credit mileage earned on one airline to your account with another. Low-cost airlines offer a definite price advantage and fewer restrictions, such as advance-purchase requirements. Safety-wise, low-cost carriers as a group have a good history, but **check the safety record before booking** any low-cost carrier; call the Federal Aviation Administration's Consumer Hotline (☞ Airline Complaints, *below*).

➤ MAJOR AIRLINES: **Air Canada** (☎ 800/776–3000). **Alaska** (☎ 800/426–0333). **American** (☎ 800/433–7300). **America West** (☎ 800/235–9292). **Continental** (☎ 800/525–0280). **Delta** (☎ 800/221–1212). **Northwest Airlines** (☎ 800/225–2525). **TWA** (☎ 800/221–2000). **United** (☎ 800/241–6522). **US Airways** (☎ 800/428–4322).

➤ SMALLER CARRIERS: **Aloha** (☎ 800/367–5250). **Hawaiian** (☎ 800/367–5320). **IslandAir** (☎ 800/323–3345). **Mesa** (☎ 800/637–2247). **SkyWest** (☎ 800/453–9417). **Southwest** (☎ 800/435–9792).

➤ FROM THE U.K.: **American** (☎ 0345/789–789). **British Airways** (☎ 0345/222–111). **Continental** (☎ 0800/776–464 toll-free or 01293/776–464). **Delta** (☎ 0800/414–767). **Northwest** (☎ 0990/561–000). **TWA** (☎ 0800/222–222). **United** (☎ 0800/888–555). **Virgin Atlantic** (☎ 01293/747–747). Most serve at least the New York area plus their own U.S. hubs. British Airways serves the largest number of U.S. cities—an impressive 17 destinations, including Atlanta, Boston, Charlotte, Chicago, Dallas, Detroit, Houston, Los Angeles, Miami, New York, Orlando, Philadelphia, Pittsburgh, San Francisco, Seattle, and Washington, DC. A few cities not served by British Airways can be reached by connections with other major carriers.

➤ FROM AUSTRALIA: **Air New Zealand** (☎ 1800/221–111). **Continental** (☎ 02/9249–0111 in Sydney, 03/9602–4899 in Melbourne).

GET THE LOWEST FARE

The least-expensive airfares to the U.S. are priced for round-trip travel. Major airlines usually require that you **book in advance and buy the ticket within 24 hours,** and you may have to **stay over a Saturday night.** It's smart to **call a number of airlines, and when you are quoted a good price, book it on the spot**—the same fare may not be available on the same flight the next day. Airlines generally allow you to change your return date for a fee $25–$50. If you don't use your ticket you can apply the cost toward the purchase of a new ticket, again for a small charge. However, most low-fare tickets are nonrefundable. To get the lowest airfare, **check different routings.** If your destination or home city has more than one gateway, compare prices to and from different airports. Also price off-peak flights, which may be significantly less expensive.

To save money on flights from the United Kingdom and back, **look into an APEX or Super-PEX ticket.** APEX tickets must be booked in advance and have certain restrictions. Super-PEX tickets can be purchased at the airport on the day of departure—subject to availability.

On flights within the United States, most airlines offer non-U.S. residents discounted Visit USA fares, with savings of 25%–30%, provided the arrangements are made outside the United States. Many airlines, including America West, American, Delta, Hawaiian, Northwest, TWA, and United, also have air-pass programs that give you a fixed number of domestic flights for a flat fee (these also must be booked before you come to America). Check details with the airline or a travel agent.

DON'T STOP UNLESS YOU MUST

When you book, **look for nonstop flights** and **remember that "direct" flights stop at least once.** Try to **avoid connecting flights,** which require a change of plane. Two airlines may jointly operate a connecting flight, so ask if your airline operates every segment—you may find that your preferred carrier flies you only part of the way.

USE AN AGENT

Travel agents, especially those who specialize in finding the lowest fares (☞ Discounts & Deals, *below*), can be especially helpful when booking a plane ticket. When you're quoted a price, **ask your agent if the price is likely to get any lower.** Good agents know the seasonal fluctuations of airfares and can usually anticipate a sale or fare war. However, waiting can be risky: The fare could go *up* as seats become scarce, and you may wait so long that your preferred flight sells out. A wait-and-see strategy works best if your plans are flexible, but if you must arrive and depart on certain dates, don't delay.

AVOID GETTING BUMPED

Airlines routinely overbook planes, knowing that not everyone with a ticket will show up, but sometimes everyone does. When that happens, airlines ask for volunteers to give up their seats. In return these volunteers usually get a certificate for a free flight and are rebooked on the next flight out. If there are not enough volunteers the airline must choose who will be denied boarding. The first to get bumped are passengers who checked in late and those flying on discounted tickets, **so get to the gate and check in as early as possible,** especially during peak periods.

Always **bring a photo ID to the airport.** You may be asked to show it before you are allowed to check in.

ENJOY THE FLIGHT

For more legroom, **request an emergency-aisle seat**; don't, however, sit in the row in front of the emergency aisle or in front of a bulkhead, where seats may not recline.

If you don't like airline food, **ask for special meals when booking.** These can be vegetarian, low-cholesterol, or kosher, for example.

COMPLAIN IF NECESSARY

If your baggage goes astray or your flight goes awry, complain right away. Most carriers require that you file a claim immediately.

➤ AIRLINE COMPLAINTS: U.S. Department of Transportation **Aviation Consumer Protection Division** (✉ C-75, Washington, DC 20590, ☎ 202/366–2220). **Federal Aviation Administration (FAA) Consumer Hotline** (☎ 800/322–7873).

AIRPORTS & TRANSFERS

The major gateways to the U.S. include New York, Miami, Chicago, and Los Angeles.

Flying time from London is 7 hours to New York; 8 hours, 40 minutes to Chicago; 9 hours, 45 minutes to Miami; and 11 hours to Los Angeles.

Flying time from Sydney is 21–22 hours to New York; and 13 hours, 25 minutes to Los Angeles on a direct flight. Flights from Melbourne add about 3 hours of flying time.

Flying time from Toronto is 1½ hours to New York and 4½ hours to Los Angeles. Flying time from Vancouver is 2½ hours to Los Angeles, 4 hours to Chicago.

➤ AIRPORT INFORMATION: See Arriving and Departing by Plane under New York City (☞ New York *in* Chapter 3), Miami (☞ Florida *in* Chapter 5), Chicago (☞ Illinois *in* Chapter 7), and Los Angeles (☞ California *in* Chapter 11) for specific information about airports in these cities, or the appropriate Arriving and Departing by Plane section under whatever city or region you are planning to fly into.

B

BUS TRAVEL

Aside from the two coasts and the major cities, long-distance buses (motor coaches) serve more of the United States than trains do. Various regional bus companies serve their areas of the country; the most extensive long-haul service is provided by Greyhound Lines. Generally no reservations are needed—**buy your tickets before boarding** (allow 15 minutes in advance in small towns, up to 45 minutes in larger cities). Long-distance buses often feature reclining seats, individually controlled reading lights, rest rooms, and air-conditioning and heating.

➤ BUS LINES: **Greyhound Lines** (☎ 800/231–2222, TTY 800/752–4841).

BUS PASSES

Visitors from overseas receive as much as 50% savings on Greyhound by purchasing the International Ameripass through their travel agent prior to arriving in the United States. The cost is $109 for a 4-day pass, $129 for 5 days, $159 for 7 days, $239 for 15 days, $319 for 30 days, and $499 for 60 days. In the United States, the pass can be obtained only in New York City, from Greyhound International; you must show a valid non-U.S. passport. U.S. citizens can also buy Greyhound's Ameripass for unlimited travel; the cost is $179 for 7 days, $289 for 15 days, $399 for 30 days, $599 for 60 days.

➤ DISCOUNT PASSES: The **International Ameripass** is available through certain travel agents or, in New York City, from Greyhound International (✉ 625 8th Ave., New York, NY 10018, ☎ 212/971–0492 or 800/246–8572). U.S. citizens can buy Greyhound's **Ameripass** (☎ 800/231–2222).

CHILDREN

On Greyhound buses, one child under age 2 travels free on an adult's lap, and children 2–11 accompanied by an adult pay 50% of the adult fare. Again, call ahead for specifics, as special fares have restrictions.

SENIOR CITIZENS

Greyhound offers a 15% discount on regular fares for passengers 55 and older; there are restrictions, so be sure to call local numbers for specific information.

TRAVELERS WITH DISABILITIES

Greyhound offers no special fares or facilities for passengers with disabilities, but an attendant is entitled to ride for free. If you will be traveling alone and need special assistance, call Greyhound at least 48 hours before departure.

BUSINESS HOURS

Banks are generally open weekdays 9 AM–3 PM, post offices weekdays 8 AM–5 PM; many branches operate Saturday morning hours. Business hours tend to be weekdays 9–5, a little later on the East Coast and earlier the farther west you go. Many stores may not open until 10 or 11, but they remain open until 6 or 7; most carry on brisk business on Saturday as well. Large suburban shopping malls, the focus of most Americans' shopping activity, are generally open seven days a week, with evening hours every day except Sunday. All across the country, so-called convenience stores sell food and sundries until about 11 PM. Along the highways and in major cities you can usually find all-night diners, supermarkets, drugstores, and convenience stores, as Americans increasingly expect 24-hour service.

C

CAMERAS, CAMCORDERS, & COMPUTERS

Always **keep your film, tape, or computer disks out of the sun.** Carry an extra supply of batteries, and **be prepared to turn on your camera, camcorder, or laptop** to prove to security personnel that the device is real. Always **ask for hand inspection of film,** which becomes clouded after successive exposure to airport X-ray machines, and **keep videotapes and computer disks away from metal detectors.**

➤ PHOTO HELP: **Kodak Information Center** (☎ 800/242–2424). *Kodak Guide to Shooting Great Travel Pictures,* available in bookstores or from Fodor's Travel Publications (☎ 800/533–6478); $16.50 plus $4 shipping.

CAR RENTAL

➤ MAJOR AGENCIES: **Alamo** (☎ 800/327–9633). **Avis** (☎ 800/331–1212). **Budget** (☎ 800/527–0700). **Courtesy** (☎ 800/252–9756). **Dollar** (☎ 800/800–4000). **Enterprise** (☎ 800/325–8007). **Hertz** (☎ 800/654–3131). **National** (☎ 800/328–4567). Rent-

A-Wreck (☎ 800/535–1391). **Sears** (☎ 800/527–0770). **Thrifty** (☎ 800/367–2277). **Ugly Duckling** (☎ 800/843–3825).

CUT COSTS

To get the best deal, **book through a travel agent who is willing to shop around.** When pricing cars, **ask about the location of the rental lot.** Some off-airport locations offer lower rates, and their lots are only minutes from the terminal via complimentary shuttle. You also may want to **price local car-rental companies,** whose rates may be lower still, although their service and maintenance may not be as good as those of a name-brand agency. Remember to ask about required deposits, cancellation penalties, and drop-off charges if you're planning to pick up the car in one city and leave it in another.

Also **ask your travel agent about a company's customer-service record.** How has it responded to late plane arrivals and vehicle mishaps? Are there often lines at the rental counter, and, if you're traveling during a holiday period, does a confirmed reservation guarantee you a car?

Be sure to **look into wholesalers,** companies that do not own fleets but rent in bulk from those that do and often offer better rates than traditional car-rental operations. Prices are best during off-peak periods.

➤ RENTAL WHOLESALERS: The **Kemwel Group** (☎ 914/835–5555 or 800/678–0678, FAX 914/835–5126).

NEED INSURANCE?

When driving a rented car you are generally responsible for any damage to or loss of the vehicle. You also are liable for any property damage or personal injury that you may cause while driving. Before you rent, **see what coverage you already have** under the terms of your personal auto-insurance policy and credit cards.

For about $14 a day, rental companies sell protection, known as a collision- or loss-damage waiver (CDW or LDW) that eliminates your liability for damage to the car; it's always optional and should never be automatically added to your bill.

Some states, including California and Nevada, have capped the price of CDW and LDW. New York and Illinois have outlawed the sale of CDW and LDW altogether.

In Arizona, Maryland, Massachusetts, and Utah, the car-rental company must pay for damage to third parties up to a preset legal limit. Once that limit is reached your personal auto or other liability insurance kicks in. However, **make sure you have enough coverage to pay for the car.** If you do not have auto insurance or an umbrella policy that covers damage to third parties, purchasing CDW or LDW is highly recommended.

BEWARE SURCHARGES

Before you pick up a car in one city and leave it in another, **ask about drop-off charges or one-way service fees,** which can be substantial. Note, too, that some rental agencies charge extra if you return the car before the time specified on your contract. To avoid a hefty refueling fee, **fill the tank just before you turn in the car,** but be aware that gas stations near the rental outlet may overcharge.

MEET THE REQUIREMENTS

In the United States you must be 21 to rent a car, and rates may be higher if you're under 25. You'll pay extra for child seats (about $3 per day), which are compulsory for children under five, and for additional drivers (about $2 per day). Residents of the U.K. will need a reservation voucher, a passport, a U.K. driver's license, and a travel policy that covers each driver, in order to pick up a car.

CHILDREN & TRAVEL

CHILDREN IN THE U.S.

Be sure to plan ahead and **involve your youngsters** as you outline your trip. When packing, include things to keep them busy en route. On sightseeing days try to schedule activities of special interest to your children. If you are renting a car don't forget to **arrange for a car seat** when you reserve. Most hotels in the U.S. allow children under a certain age to stay in their parents' room at no extra charge, but others charge them as extra adults; be sure to **ask about the cutoff age for children's discounts.**

THE GOLD GUIDE / SMART TRAVEL TIPS

THE GOLD GUIDE / SMART TRAVEL TIPS

FLYING

As a general rule, infants under two not occupying a seat fly free. If your children are two or older **ask about children's airfares.**

In general the adult baggage allowance applies to children paying half or more of the adult fare.

According to the FAA it's a good idea to use safety seats aloft for children weighing less than 40 pounds. Airlines, however, can set their own policies: U.S. carriers allow FAA-approved models but usually require that you buy a ticket, even if your child would otherwise ride free, since the seats must be strapped into regular seats. Airline rules vary regarding their use, so it's important to **check your airline's policy about using safety seats during takeoff and landing.** Safety seats cannot obstruct any of the other passengers in the row, so get an appropriate seat assignment as early as possible.

When making your reservation, **request children's meals or a free-standing bassinet** if you need them; the latter are available only to those seated at the bulkhead, where there's enough legroom. Remember, however, that bulkhead seats may not have their own overhead bins, and there's no storage space in front of you—a major inconvenience.

GROUP TRAVEL

If you're planning to take your kids on a tour, look for companies that specialize in family travel.

➤ FAMILY-FRIENDLY TOUR OPERATORS: **Grandtravel** (✉ 6900 Wisconsin Ave., Suite 706, Chevy Chase, MD 20815, ☎ 301/986–0790 or 800/247–7651) for people traveling with grandchildren ages 7–17. **Families Welcome!** (✉ 92 N. Main St., Ashland, OR 97520, ☎ 541/482–6121 or 800/326–0724, FAX 541/482–0660). **Rascals in Paradise** (✉ 650 5th St., Suite 505, San Francisco, CA 94107, ☎ 415/978–9800 or 800/872–7225, FAX 415/442–0289).

CONSUMER PROTECTION

Whenever possible, **pay with a major credit card** so you can cancel payment if there's a problem, assuming that you can provide documentation. This is a good practice whether you're buying travel arrangements before your trip or shopping at your destination.

If you're doing business with a particular company for the first time, **contact your local Better Business Bureau and the attorney general's offices** in your state and the company's home state, as well. Have any complaints been filed?

Finally, if you're buying a package or tour, always **consider travel insurance** that includes default coverage (☞ Insurance, *above*).

➤ LOCAL BBBS: **Council of Better Business Bureaus** (✉ 4200 Wilson Blvd., Suite 800, Arlington, VA 22203, ☎ 703/276–0100, FAX 703/525–8277).

CUSTOMS & DUTIES

ENTERING THE U.S.

Visitors age 21 and over may import the following into the United States: 200 cigarettes or 50 cigars or 2 kilograms of tobacco, 1 liter of alcohol, and gifts worth $100. Prohibited items include meat products, seeds, plants, and fruits. **Absolutely avoid carrying illegal drugs.**

ENTERING CANADA

If you've been out of Canada for at least seven days you may bring in C$500 worth of goods duty-free. If you've been away for fewer than seven days but more than 48 hours, the duty-free allowance drops to C$200; if your trip lasts 24–48 hours, the allowance is C$50. You may not pool allowances with family members. Goods claimed under the C$500 exemption may follow you by mail; those claimed under the lesser exemptions must accompany you.

Alcohol and tobacco products may be included in the seven-day and 48-hour exemptions but not in the 24-hour exemption. If you meet the age requirements of the province or territory through which you reenter Canada you may bring in, duty-free, 1.14 liters (40 imperial ounces) of wine or liquor *or* 24 12-ounce cans or bottles of beer or ale. If you are 16 or older you may bring in, duty-free, 200 cigarettes and 50 cigars; these items must accompany you.

You may send an unlimited number of gifts worth up to C$60 each duty-free to Canada. Label the package UNSOLICITED GIFT—VALUE UNDER $60. Alcohol and tobacco are excluded.

➤ INFORMATION: **Revenue Canada** (✉ 2265 St. Laurent Blvd. S, Ottawa, Ontario K1G 4K3, ☎ 613/993–0534, 800/461–9999 in Canada).

ENTERING THE U.K.

From countries outside the EU, including the United States, you may import, duty-free, 200 cigarettes or 50 cigars; 1 liter of spirits or 2 liters of fortified or sparkling wine or liqueurs; 2 liters of still table wine; 60 milliliters of perfume; 250 milliliters of toilet water; plus £136 worth of other goods, including gifts and souvenirs.

➤ INFORMATION: **HM Customs and Excise** (✉ Dorset House, Stamford St., London SE1 9NG, ☎ 0171/202–4227).

D

DINING

Breakfast is served anywhere from 6 to 11, lunch 11 to 2, dinner from 5 until late. Like business hours in general, mealtimes tend to become earlier when you leave the cities and as you go farther west.

DISABILITIES & ACCESSIBILITY

ACCESS IN THE U.S.

When discussing accessibility with an operator or reservationist, **ask hard questions.** Are there any stairs, inside or out? Are there grab bars next to the toilet *and* in the shower/tub? How wide is the doorway to the room? To the bathroom? For the most extensive facilities meeting the latest legal specifications, **opt for newer accommodations,** which are more likely to have been designed with access in mind. Older buildings or ships may offer more limited facilities. Be sure to **discuss your needs before booking.**

➤ COMPLAINTS: **Disability Rights Section** (✉ U.S. Department of Justice, Box 66738, Washington, DC 20035–6738, ☎ 202/514–0301 or 800/514–0301, FAX 202/307–1198, TTY 202/514–0383 or 800/514–0383) for general complaints. **Aviation Consumer Protection Division** (☞ Air Travel, *above*) for airline-related problems. **Civil Rights Office** (✉ U.S. Department of Transportation, Departmental Office of Civil Rights, S-30, 400 7th St. SW, Room 10215, Washington, DC, 20590, ☎ 202/366–4648) for problems with surface transportation.

➤ PUBLICATIONS: *Great American Vacations for Travelers with Disabilities,* available in bookstores or from Fodor's Travel Publications (☎ 800/533–6478); $19.50 plus $4 shipping.

TRAVEL AGENCIES & TOUR OPERATORS

The Americans with Disabilities Act requires that travel firms serve the needs of all travelers. That said, you should note that some agencies and operators specialize in making travel arrangements for individuals and groups with disabilities.

➤ TRAVELERS WITH MOBILITY PROBLEMS: **Access Adventures** (✉ 206 Chestnut Ridge Rd., Rochester, NY 14624, ☎ 716/889–9096), run by a former physical-rehabilitation counselor. **CareVacations** (✉ 5019 49th Ave., Suite 102, Leduc, Alberta T9E 6T5, ☎ 403/986–6404, 800/648–1116 in Canada) has group tours and is especially helpful with cruise vacations. **Hinsdale Travel Service** (✉ 201 E. Ogden Ave., Suite 100, Hinsdale, IL 60521, ☎ 630/325–1335), a travel agency that benefits from the advice of wheelchair traveler Janice Perkins. **Wheelchair Journeys** (✉ 16979 Redmond Way, Redmond, WA 98052, ☎ 425/885–2210 or 800/313–4751), for general travel arrangements.

➤ TRAVELERS WITH DEVELOPMENTAL DISABILITIES: **New Directions** (✉ 5276 Hollister Ave., Suite 207, Santa Barbara, CA 93111, ☎ 805/967–2841, FAX 805/964–7344). **Sprout** (✉ 893 Amsterdam Ave., New York, NY 10025, ☎ 212/222–9575 or 888/222–9575, FAX 212/222–9768).

DISCOUNTS & DEALS

Be a smart shopper and **compare all your options before making a choice.** A plane ticket bought with a promotional coupon may not be cheaper than the least expensive fare from a discount ticket agency. For high-price travel purchases, such as packages or tours, keep in mind that what you get is just as important as what you save. Just because something is cheap doesn't mean it's a bargain.

LOOK IN YOUR WALLET

When you use your credit card to make travel purchases you may get free travel-accident insurance, collision-damage insurance, and medical or legal assistance, depending on the card and the bank that issued it. American Express, MasterCard, and Visa provide one or more of these services, so **get a copy of your credit card's travel-benefits policy.** If you are a member of the American Automobile Association (AAA) or an oil-company-sponsored road-assistance plan, always **ask hotel or car-rental reservationists about auto-club discounts.** Some clubs offer additional discounts on tours, cruises, or admission to attractions. And don't forget that auto-club membership entitles you to free maps and trip-planning services.

DIAL FOR DOLLARS

To save money, **look into "1-800" discount reservations services,** which use their buying power to get a better price on hotels, airline tickets, even car rentals. When booking a room, always **call the hotel's local toll-free number** (if one is available) rather than the central reservations number—you'll often get a better price. Always ask about special packages or corporate rates.

➤ AIRLINE TICKETS: ☎ 800/FLY–4–LESS. ☎ 800/FLY–ASAP.

➤ HOTEL ROOMS: **Accommodations Express** (☎ 800/444–7666). **Central Reservation Service** (CRS; ☎ 800/548–3311). **Hotel Reservations Network** (HRN; ☎ 800/964–6835). **Players Express Vacations** (☎ 800/458–6161). **Quickbook** (☎ 800/789–9887). **Room Finders USA** (☎ 800/473–7829). **RMC Travel** (☎ 800/245–5738). **Steigenberger Reservation Service** (☎ 800/223–5652).

SAVE ON COMBOS

Packages and guided tours can both save you money, but don't confuse the two. When you buy a package your travel remains independent, just as though you had planned and booked the trip yourself. Fly-drive

packages, which combine airfare and car rental, are often a good deal.

JOIN A CLUB?

Many companies sell discounts in the form of travel clubs and coupon books, but these cost money. You must use participating advertisers to get a deal, and only after you recoup the initial membership cost or book price do you begin to save. If you plan to use the club or coupons frequently you may save considerably. Before signing up, find out what discounts you get for free.

➤ DISCOUNT CLUBS: **Entertainment Travel Editions** (✉ Box 1068, Trumbull, CT 06611, ☎ 800/445–4137); $28–$53, depending on destination. **Great American Traveler** (✉ Box 27965, Salt Lake City, UT 84127, ☎ 800/548–2812); $49.95 per year. **Moment's Notice Discount Travel Club** (✉ 7301 New Utrecht Ave., Brooklyn, NY 11204, ☎ 718/234–6295); $25 per year, single or family. **Privilege Card International** (✉ 201 E. Commerce St., Suite 198, Youngstown, OH 44503, ☎ 330/746–5211 or 800/236–9732); $74.95 per year. **Sears's Mature Outlook** (✉ Box 9390, Des Moines, IA 50306, ☎ 800/336–6330); $14.95 per year. **Travelers Advantage** (✉ CUC Travel Service, 3033 S. Parker Rd., Suite 1000, Aurora, CO 80014, ☎ 800/548–1116 or 800/648–4037); $49 per year, single or family. **Worldwide Discount Travel Club** (✉ 1674 Meridian Ave., Miami Beach, FL 33139, ☎ 305/534–2082); $50 per year family, $40 single.

DRIVING

RULES OF THE ROAD

Driving in the U.S. is done on the right side of the road. Speed limits vary and are sign-posted along roads and highways. **Adhere to speed limits.** Recent federal legislation allows each state to set individual speed limits; they may range from 55 miles per hour to unlimited speeds in the Great Plains states. Watch for lower speed limits on back roads. Except for limited-access roads, highways usually post a lower speed limit in towns, so slow down when houses and buildings start to appear. Most states require front-seat passengers to wear seat belts, and in all states **children**

under age 4 must ride in approved child-safety seats.

In some communities, it is permissible to make a right turn at a red light once the car has come to a full stop and there is no oncoming traffic. When in doubt about local laws, however, wait for the green light.

Beware of weekday rush-hour traffic—anywhere from 7 AM to 10 AM and 4 PM to 7 PM—around major cities. To encourage car sharing, some crowded expressways may reserve an express lane for cars carrying more than one passenger. In downtown areas, watch signs carefully—there are lots of one-way streets, "no-left-turn" intersections, and blocks closed to car traffic, all in the name of easing congestion.

HIGHWAYS

The fastest routes are usually the interstate highways, each numbered with a prefix "I–". Even numbers (I–80, I–40, and so on) are east–west roads; odd numbers (I–91, I–55, and so on) run north–south. These are fully signposted, limited-access highways, with at least two lanes in each direction. In some cases they are toll roads (the Pennsylvania Turnpike is I–76; the Massachusetts Turnpike is I–90). Near large cities, interstates usually intersect with a circumferential loop highway (I–295, and so on) that carries traffic around the city.

Another highway system is the U.S. highway (designated U.S. 1, and so on); they are not necessarily limited access, but well paved and usually multilane. State highways are also well paved and often have more than one lane in each direction. Large cities usually have a number of limited-access expressways, freeways, and parkways, referred to by names rather than numbers (the Merritt Parkway, the Kennedy Expressway, the Santa Monica Freeway).

AUTO CLUBS

Consider joining the American Automobile Association (AAA), a federation of state auto clubs that offers maps, route planning, and emergency road service to its members; members of Britain's Automobile Association (AA) are granted reciprocal privileges. Check local phone directories under AAA for the nearest club or contact the national organization.

➤ IN THE U.S.: **American Automobile Association** (✉ 1000 AAA Dr., Heathrow, FL 32746–5063, ☎ 800/564–6222).

➤ IN THE U.K.: **Automobile Association** (AA; ☎ 0990/500–600), **Royal Automobile Club** (RAC; ☎ 0990/722–722 for membership, 0345/121–345 for insurance).

E

ELECTRICITY

Overseas visitors will need to bring adapters to convert their personal appliances to the U.S. standard: AC, 110 volts/60 cycles, with a plug of two flat pins set parallel to one another.

EMERGENCIES

In most communities, **dial 911** in an emergency to reach the police, fire, or ambulance services. If your car breaks down on an interstate highway, try to pull over onto the shoulder of the road and either wait for the state police to find you or, if you have other passengers who can wait in the car, walk to the nearest emergency roadside phone and call the state police. If you carry a cellular or car telephone, *55 is the emergency number to call. When calling for help, note your location according to the small green mileage markers posted along the highway. Other highways are also patrolled but may not have emergency phones or mileage markers. If you are a member of the AAA auto club (☞ Driving, *above*), look in a local phone book for the AAA emergency road-service number.

F

FAX MACHINES

You can usually make hotel reservations via fax, and you can probably send a fax on the hotel's machine while staying there, especially if the hotel caters to business travelers. If your hotel isn't helpful or charges exorbitantly for this service, look for fax service at local photocopying stores; the charge may be as much as $2–$3 a page, more for overseas.

G

GAY & LESBIAN TRAVEL

➤ Tour Operators: **R.S.V.P. Travel Productions** (✉ 2800 University Ave. SE, Minneapolis, MN 55414, ☎ 612/379–4697 or 800/328–7787), for cruises and resort vacations for gays. **Olivia** (✉ 4400 Market St., Oakland, CA 94608, ☎ 510/655–0364 or 800/631–6277), for cruises and resort vacations for lesbians. **Toto Tours** (✉ 1326 W. Albion Ave., Suite 3W, Chicago, IL 60626, ☎ 773/274–8686 or 800/565–1241, ℻ 773/274–8695), for groups.

➤ Gay- and Lesbian-Friendly Travel Agencies: **Advance Damron** (✉ 1 Greenway Plaza, Suite 800, Houston, TX 77046, ☎ 713/682–2002 or 800/695–0880, ℻ 713/888–1010). **Club Travel** (✉ 8739 Santa Monica Blvd., West Hollywood, CA 90069, ☎ 310/358–2200 or 800/429–8747, ℻ 310/358–2222). **Islanders/Kennedy Travel** (✉ 183 W. 10th St., New York, NY 10014, ☎ 212/242–3222 or 800/988–1181, ℻ 212/929–8530). **Now Voyager** (✉ 4406 18th St., San Francisco, CA 94114, ☎ 415/626–1169 or 800/255–6951, ℻ 415/626–8626). **Yellowbrick Road** (✉ 1500 W. Balmoral Ave., Chicago, IL 60640, ☎ 773/561–1800 or 800/642–2488, ℻ 773/561–4497). **Skylink Women's Travel** (✉ 3577 Moorland Ave., Santa Rosa, CA 95407, ☎ 707/585–8355 or 800/225–5759, ℻ 707/584–5637), serving lesbian travelers.

➤ Publication: *Fodor's Gay Guide to the USA,* available in bookstores or from Fodor's Travel Publications (☎ 800/533–6478); $19.50 plus $4 shipping.

I

INSURANCE

Travel insurance is the best way to **protect yourself against financial loss.** The most useful policies are trip-cancellation-and-interruption, default, medical, and comprehensive insurance.

Without insurance you will lose all or most of your money if you cancel your trip, regardless of the reason. It's essential that you **buy trip-cancellation-and-interruption insurance,** particularly if your airline ticket, cruise, or package tour is nonrefundable and cannot be changed. When considering how much coverage you need, look for a policy that will cover the cost of your trip plus the nondiscounted price of a one-way airline ticket, should you need to return home early. Also **consider default or bankruptcy insurance,** which protects you against a supplier's failure to deliver.

Citizens of the United Kingdom can buy an annual travel-insurance policy valid for most vacations during the year in which it's purchased. If you are pregnant or have a preexisting medical condition, make sure you're covered. According to the Association of British Insurers, a trade association representing 450 insurance companies, it's wise to buy extra medical coverage when you visit the United States.

If you have purchased an expensive vacation, comprehensive insurance is a must. **Look for comprehensive policies that include trip-delay insurance,** which will protect you in the event that weather problems cause you to miss your flight, tour, or cruise. A few insurers sell waivers for preexisting medical conditions. Companies that offer both features include Access America, Carefree Travel, Travel Insured International, and Travel Guard (☞ *below*).

Always **buy travel insurance directly from the insurance company;** if you buy it from a travel agency or tour operator that goes out of business you probably will not be covered for the agency or operator's default, a major risk. Before you make any purchase, **review your existing health and home-owner's policies** to find out whether they cover expenses incurred while traveling.

➤ Travel Insurers: In the U.S., **Access America** (✉ 6600 W. Broad St., Richmond, VA 23230, ☎ 804/285–3300 or 800/284–8300), **Carefree Travel Insurance** (✉ Box 9366, 100 Garden City Plaza, Garden City, NY 11530, ☎ 516/294–0220 or 800/323–3149), **Near Travel Services** (✉ Box 1339, Calumet City, IL 60409, ☎ 708/868–6700 or 800/654–6700), **Travel Guard International** (✉ 1145 Clark St., Stevens Point, WI 54481, ☎ 715/345–0505 or 800/826–1300), **Travel Insured International** (✉ Box 280568, East Hartford, CT 06128–0568, ☎ 860/528–7663 or 800/243–3174), **Travelex Insurance Services** (✉ 11717 Burt St., Suite 202, Omaha, NE 68154-1500, ☎ 402/445–8637 or 800/228–9792, FAX 800/867–9531), **Wallach & Company** (✉ 107 W. Federal St., Box 480, Middleburg, VA 20118, ☎ 540/687–3166 or 800/237–6615). In Canada, **Mutual of Omaha** (✉ Travel Division, 500 University Ave., Toronto, Ontario M5G 1V8, ☎ 416/598–4083, 800/268–8825 in Canada). In the U.K., **Association of British Insurers** (✉ 51 Gresham St., London EC2V 7HQ, ☎ 0171/600–3333).

L

LIQUOR LAWS

Liquor laws vary from state to state, affecting such matters as bar and liquor-store opening times and whether restaurants can sell liquor by the glass or only by the bottle. A few states—mostly in the South or Midwest—allow each county to choose its own policy, resulting in so-called dry counties, where no alcoholic beverages are sold, next to counties where the bars do a roaring business.

The drinking age is 21 in all states, and you should **be prepared to show identification** in order to be served. Restaurants must obtain a license to sell alcoholic beverages on the premises, so some inexpensive establishments, or places that have recently opened, may not sell drinks at all or may sell only beer or wine. In most of these restaurants, however, you can bring your own beer or wine with you to drink with your meal. In this book, we note such a policy as BYOB (bring your own bottle).

Local laws against driving while intoxicated are growing stricter. Many bars now serve nonalcoholic drinks for the "designated driver," so at least one person in a group is sober enough to drive everyone else safely home.

LODGING

A wide variety of lodging facilities is available in the U.S., from gilded suites with marble bathrooms and sweeping views to bare-bones rooms with concrete walls and plastic furniture. An ultralavish hotel or resort room can easily run $500-plus a night, while a spartan roadside motel in a small town could cost $20–$30 per night. Prices vary dramatically depending on location and level of luxury. Whether you're looking for the best, the cheapest or something in between, there are ample accommodation options to choose from.

Motels are geared to motorists, with locations close to highways and convenient parking. **Airport hotels,** within a few minutes' drive of major airports, are geared to plane travelers in transit, with a strong business-travel clientele; noise may be a problem, although the best ones are excellently soundproofed. **Convention hotels** have hundreds of guest rooms, warrens of meeting rooms (usually on separate floors), and big ballrooms used for exhibits and banquets; when a large convention is staying at one, other guests sometimes feel overwhelmed. Other **downtown hotels** cater more to individual guests and may offer more in the way of health facilities and à la carte restaurants. **Suburban hotels** in many cities attract travelers who want to be close to the circumferential highway and to suburban office parks, shopping malls, or theme parks; they may be larger and more upscale than motels, offering more restaurants, health facilities, and other amenities. **Resorts** tend to be destinations in and of themselves—complete with golf courses, tennis courts, beaches, several restaurants, on-site entertainment, and so on. The setting usually emphasizes a particular outdoor activity, whether skiing, water sports, or golf. One variation on this is the **dude ranch,** where paying guests sample horseback riding, hiking, lake fishing, cookouts, and such western-style activities as rodeos. **Country inns and bed-and-breakfasts** are generally charming older properties that, unlike European B&Bs, tend to be pricey and upscale. They may not have private bathrooms, an in-room phone, or TVs, and as they are frequently meticulously furnished with antiques, they may not be the best place to take young children. There is often an inviting common room where guests can gather for quiet conversation in front of a roaring fireplace or nestle in the folds of a big, soft chair with a good book. Breakfast is usually included in the room rate, but verify this when you make a reservation. For recommendations, see *Fodor's Best Bed & Breakfasts* books for various regions of the country. At the budget end of the scale, **YMCAs and youth hostels** offer somewhat more spartan accommodations, often dormitory style, and limited amenities.

APARTMENT & VILLA RENTALS

If you want a home base that's roomy enough for a family and comes with cooking facilities, **consider a furnished rental.** These can save you money; however, some rentals are luxury properties, economical only when your party is large. Home-exchange directories list rentals (often second homes owned by prospective house swappers), and some services search for a house or apartment for you (even a castle if that's your fancy) and handle the paperwork. Some send an illustrated catalog; others send photographs only of specific properties, sometimes at a charge. Up-front registration fees may apply.

➤ RENTAL AGENTS: **Europa-Let/Tropical Inn-Let** (✉ 92 N. Main St., Ashland, OR 97520, ☎ 541/482–5806 or 800/462–4486, FAX 541/482–0660). **Hometours International** (✉ Box 11503, Knoxville, TN 37939, ☎ 423/690–8484 or 800/367–4668). **Property Rentals International** (✉ 1008 Mansfield Crossing Rd., Richmond, VA 23236, ☎ 804/378–6054 or 800/220–3332, FAX 804/379–2073). **Rent-a-Home International** (✉ 7200 34th Ave. NW, Seattle, WA 98117, ☎ 206/789–9377 or 800/488–7368, FAX 206/789–9379). **Vacation Home Rentals Worldwide** (✉ 235 Kensington Ave., Norwood, NJ 07648, ☎ 201/767–9393 or 800/633–3284, FAX 201/767–5510). **Hideaways International** (✉ 767 Islington St., Portsmouth, NH 03801, ☎ 603/430–4433 or 800/843–4433, FAX 603/430–4444) is a travel club whose members arrange rentals among themselves; yearly membership is $99.

CAMPING

Some of the most reasonably priced campgrounds with the most compelling sites operate under the auspices of the National Park system (☞ National Parks, *below*). If, however, you opt for private commercial operations, your best source for nationwide information on both public and private parks is the National Association of RV Parks and Campgrounds.

An overnight stay at a commercial campground can cost from $15 to $30, depending on three factors: the amenities offered, the location, and the time of year. Tent camping, of course, is the least expensive form of accommodation; if you want water, electric, and sewage hook-ups, you move into the higher end of the price range.

Many private campgrounds are not open year-round, so it's important to **call ahead.** You can make reservations over the phone and, customarily, a one-night deposit is required. The peak summer months of June, July, and August are very busy at the more desirable locations; the sooner you book, the more you can count on being awarded an attractive site.

➤ INFORMATION: **National Association of RV Parks and Campgrounds** (✉ 8605 Westwood Center Dr., Suite 201, Vienna, VA 22182, ☎ 800/477–8669); call for a free copy of the "Go Camping America Planner."

➤ PUBLICATIONS: In *Woodall's 1996 North American Edition: Campground Directory* ($17.95; at your local bookstore), all private parks in the United States and Canada are listed, quality inspected, and rated. Look for the annually updated directories published by the **American Automobile Association** for similar assessments. **Fodor's** (☎ 800/533–6478) publishes two guides that provide in-depth coverage of campgrounds around the country: *National Parks of the West* ($17.50) and *National Parks and Seashores of the East* ($17); both are available in bookstores.

HOME EXCHANGES

If you would like to exchange your home for someone else's, **join a home-exchange organization,** which will send you its updated listings of available exchanges for a year and will include your own listing in at least one of them. Making the arrangements is up to you.

➤ EXCHANGE CLUBS: **HomeLink International** (✉ Box 650, Key West, FL 33041, ☎ 305/294–7766 or 800/638–3841, FAX 305/294–1148) charges $83 per year.

HOTELS

Hotel chains dominate the lodging landscape in the United States. Some of the large chains, such as Holiday Inn, Hilton, Hyatt, Marriott, and Ramada, are even further subdivided into chains of budget properties, all-suite properties, downtown hotels, or luxury resorts, each with a different name. While some chain hotels may have a standardized look to them, this "cookie-cutter" approach also means that you can rely on the same level of comfort and efficiency at all properties in a well-managed chain, and at a chain's premier properties—its so-called flagship hotels—decor and services may be outstanding.

Most hotels will hold your reservation until 6 PM; **call ahead if you plan to arrive late.** Hotels will be more willing to hold a late reservation for you if you reserve with a credit-card number.

When you call to make a reservation, **ask all the necessary questions up front.** If you are arriving with a car, ask if the hotel has a parking lot or covered garage and whether there is an extra fee for parking. If you like to eat your meals in, ask if the hotel has a restaurant or whether it has room service (most do, but not necessarily 24 hours a day—and be forewarned that it can be expensive). Most hotels have in-room telephones, but double-check this at inexpensive properties and bed-and-breakfasts. Most hotels and motels have in-room TVs, often with cable movies (usually pay-per-view), but verify this if you like to watch TV. If you want an in-room crib for your child, there will probably be an additional charge.

➤ HOTEL TOLL-FREE PHONE NUMBERS:
Adam's Mark (☎ 800/444–2326).
Best Western (☎ 800/528–1234).
Choice (☎ 800/221–2222).
Clarion (☎ 800/252–7466).
Colony (☎ 800/777–1700).
Comfort (☎ 800/228–5150).
Days Inn (☎ 800/325–2525).
Doubletree (☎ 800/528–0444).
Embassy Suites (☎ 800/362–2779).

Fairfield Inn (☎ 800/228–2800).
Forte (☎ 800/225–5843).
Four Seasons (☎ 800/332–3442).
Guest Quarters Suites (☎ 800/424–2900).
Hilton (☎ 800/445–8667).
Holiday Inn (☎ 800/465–4329).
Howard Johnson (☎ 800/654–4656).
Hyatt & Resorts (☎ 800/233–1234).
Inter-Continental (☎ 800/327–0200).
La Quinta (☎ 800/531–5900).
Marriott (☎ 800/228–9290).
Meridien (☎ 800/543–4300).
Nikko International (☎ 800/645–5687).
Omni (☎ 800/843–6664).
Quality Inn (☎ 800/228–5151).
Radisson (☎ 800/333–3333).
Ramada (☎ 800/228–2828).
Red Lion (☎ 800/547–8010).
Renaissance Hotels International (☎ 800/468–3571).
Ritz-Carlton (☎ 800/241–3333).
Sheraton and ITT Sheraton (☎ 800/325–3535).
Sleep Inn (☎ 800/221–2222).
Westin Hotels & Resorts (☎ 800/228–3000).
Wyndham Hotels & Resorts (☎ 800/822–4200).

MOTELS

➤ MOTEL TOLL-FREE PHONE NUMBERS:
Budget Hosts Inns (☎ 800/283–4678).
Econo Lodge (☎ 800/553–2666).
Friendship Inns (☎ 800/453–4511).
Motel 6 (☎ 800/466–8356).
Rodeway (☎ 800/228–2000).
Super 8 (☎ 800/848–8888).

M
MAIL

Every address in the United States belongs to a specific zip-code district, and each zip code has five digits. Some addresses include a second sequence of four numbers following the first five numbers, but although this speeds mail delivery for large organizations, it is not necessary to use it. Each zip-code district has at least one post office, where you can buy stamps and aerograms, send parcels, or conduct other postal business. Occasionally you may find small stamp-dispensing machines in airports, train stations, bus terminals, large office buildings, hotel lobbies, drugstores, or grocery stores, but don't count on it. Most Americans go to the post office to buy their stamps, and the lines can be long.

Official mailboxes are either the stout, royal blue steel bins on city sidewalks or mail chutes on the walls of post offices or in large office buildings. A schedule posted on mailboxes and mail slots should indicate when the mail is picked up.

POSTAL RATES

First-class letters weighing up to 1 ounce can be sent anywhere within the United States with a 32¢ stamp; each additional ounce costs 23¢. Postcards need a 20¢ stamp. A half-ounce airmail letter overseas takes 60¢, an airmail postcard 50¢, and a surface-rate postcard 35¢. For Canada, you'll need a 46¢ stamp for a 1-ounce letter, 40¢ for a postcard. For Mexico, you'll need 40¢ for a half-ounce letter, 35¢ for a postcard. For 50¢, you can buy an aerogram—a single sheet of lightweight blue paper that folds into its own envelope, already stamped for overseas airmail delivery.

RECEIVING MAIL

If you wish to receive mail while traveling in the USA, **have it sent c/o General Delivery** at the city's main post office (be sure to use the right zip code). It should be held there for up to 30 days. You must pick it up in person, and bring identification with you. American Express offices in the United States do not hold mail.

MONEY

The basic unit of U.S. currency is the dollar, which is subdivided into 100 cents. Coins are the copper penny (1¢) and four silver coins: the nickel (5¢), the dime (10¢), the quarter (25¢), and the half-dollar (50¢). Silver $1 coins are rarely seen in circulation. Paper money comes in denominations of $1, $5, $10, $20, $50, and $100. All these bills are the same size and green color; they are distinguishable only by the dollar amount indicated on them and by different pictures of famous American people and monuments.

ATMS

Before leaving home, **make sure that your credit cards have been programmed for ATM use.**

➤ ATM LOCATIONS: **Cirrus** (☎ 800/424–7787). **Plus** (☎ 800/843–7587).

BANKS

In general, U.S. banks will not cash a personal check for you unless you have an account at that bank (it doesn't have to be at that branch). Only in major cities are large bank branches equipped to exchange foreign currencies. Therefore, it's best to rely on credit cards, cash machines, and traveler's checks to handle expenses while you're traveling.

CREDIT CARDS

MasterCard is the U.S. equivalent of the Access card in Britain or the EuroCard in other European countries. Visa is the equivalent of the BarclayCard in Britain or the ChargeEx card in Canada. The American Express card is widely accepted in the U.S. Charges incurred in the United States will appear on your regular monthly bill, converted to your own currency at the exchange rate applicable on the day the charge was entered.

EXCHANGING CURRENCY

In the United States, it is not as easy to find places to exchange currency as it is in European cities. In major international cities, such as New York and Los Angeles, currency may be exchanged at some bank branches, as well as at currency-exchange booths in airports and at foreign-currency offices such as American Express Travel Service and Thomas Cook (check local directories for addresses and phone numbers). The best strategy is to **buy traveler's checks in U.S. dollars** before you come to the United States; although the rates may not be as good abroad, the time saved by not having to search constantly for exchange facilities far outweighs any financial loss.

For the most favorable rates, **change money at banks.** You won't do as well at exchange booths in airports, rail, and bus stations, or in hotels, restaurants, and stores, although you may find their hours more convenient. To avoid lines at airport exchange booths, **get a small amount of currency before you leave home.**

At press time, the exchange rate was $1.64 to the pound sterling, 73¢ to the Canadian dollar, and 79¢ to the Australian dollar.

MONEY ORDERS, FUNDS TRANSFERS

Any U.S. bank is equipped to accept transfers of funds from foreign banks. It helps if you can plan specific dates to pick up money at specific bank branches. Your home bank can supply you with a list of its correspondent banks in the United States.

If you have more time, and you have a U.S. address where you can receive mail, you can have someone send you a certified check, which you can cash at any bank, or a postal money order (for as much as $700, obtained for a fee of up to 85¢ at any U.S. post office and redeemable at any other post office). From overseas, you can have someone go to a bank to send you an international money order (also called a bank draft), which will cost a $15–$20 commission plus airmail postage. Always bring two valid pieces of identification, preferably with photos, to claim your money.

N

NATIONAL PARKS

You may be able to **save money on park entrance fees** by getting a discount pass. The Golden Eagle Pass ($50) gets you and your companions free admission to all parks for one year. (Camping and parking are extra.) Both the Golden Age Passport, for U.S. citizens or permanent residents age 62 and older, and the Golden Access Passport, for travelers with disabilities, entitle holders to free entry to all national parks plus 50% off fees for the use of many park facilities and services. Both passports are free; you must show proof of age and U.S. citizenship or permanent residency (such as a U.S. passport, driver's license, or birth certificate) or proof of disability. All three passes are available at all national park entrances. Golden Eagle and Golden Access passes are also available by mail.

➤ PASSES BY MAIL: **National Park Service** (✉ Department of the Interior, Washington, DC 20240).

P

PACKING FOR
THE UNITED STATES

The American lifestyle is generally casual: Women may wear slacks and men may go without a jacket and tie virtually anywhere, except expensive restaurants in larger cities. If you prefer to dress up for dinner or the theater, though, go right ahead. As a rule, people in the Northeast dress more formally, while people in such places as Florida, Texas, and southern California are more informal. In beach towns, many hotels and restaurants post signs announcing that they will not serve customers who are shoeless, shirtless, or dressed in bathing suits or other skimpy attire, so tote along some shoes and cover-ups.

The United States has a wide range of climates. When deciding what weather to dress for, **read the "When to Go" sections in chapter introductions** for each region you'll be visiting. One caveat: Even in warm destinations, you may want an extra layer of clothing to compensate for overactive air-conditioning or to protect against brisk ocean breezes. Although you can count on all modern buildings being well heated in winter, historic inns and hunting lodges in rugged climates—New England, the Great Lakes states, the Rockies, or the Pacific Northwest—may be poorly insulated, drafty, or heated only by wood-burning fireplaces. It's charming, but you'll need warmer clothing.

If you'll be sightseeing in historic cities, you'll spend a lot of time walking, so **bring sturdy, well-fitting, flat-heeled shoes.** Don't forget deck shoes if you want to go sailing and sandals for walking across the burning-hot sand of southern beaches. If you plan to hike in the country, pack shoes or boots with strong flexible soles and wear long pants to protect your legs from brambles and insect bites.

Bring sunscreen lotion if you expect to be out in the sun, because prices may be high at beachside stores. These days most upscale hotels provide a basket of toiletries—soaps, shampoo, conditioner, bath gel—but if you are picky about the brand you use, bring your own. Hand-held hair dryers are sometimes provided, but don't rely on this. You can generally request an iron and ironing board from the front desk.

Bring an extra pair of eyeglasses or contact lenses in your carry-on luggage, and if you have a health problem, **pack enough medication** to last the entire trip. It's important that you **don't put prescription drugs or valuables in luggage to be checked**: It might go astray.

LUGGAGE

In general you are entitled to check two bags on flights within the United States. A third piece may be brought on board, but it must fit easily under the seat in front of you or in the overhead compartment.

Airline liability for baggage is limited to $1,250 per person on flights within the United States. On international flights it amounts to $9.07 per pound or $20 per kilogram for checked baggage (roughly $640 per 70-pound bag) and $400 per passenger for unchecked baggage. Insurance for losses exceeding these amounts can be bought from the airline at check-in for about $10 per $1,000 of coverage; note that this coverage excludes a rather extensive list of items, which is shown on your airline ticket.

Before departure, **itemize your bags' contents** and their worth, and label the bags with your name, address, and phone number. (If you use your home address, cover it so that potential thieves can't see it readily.) Inside each bag, **pack a copy of your itinerary.** At check-in, **make sure that each bag is correctly tagged** with the destination airport's three-letter code. If your bags arrive damaged or fail to arrive at all, file a written report with the airline before leaving the airport.

PASSPORTS & VISAS

AUSTRALIAN CITIZENS

Australian citizens are required to have a valid passport and visa to enter the United States.

➤ INFORMATION: **Embassy of Australia** (✉ 1601 Massachusetts Ave. NW, Washington, DC 20036, ☎ 202/797–3000). Consulates are in Chicago, Honolulu, Los Angeles, and New York.

CANADIANS

A passport is not required to enter the United States.

U.K. CITIZENS

British citizens need a valid passport to enter the United States. If you are

staying for fewer than 90 days on vacation, with a return or onward ticket, you probably will not need a visa. However, you will need to fill out the Visa Waiver Form, 1-94W, supplied by the airline.

➤ INFORMATION: **London Passport Office** (☎ 0990/21010) for fees and documentation requirements and to request an emergency passport. U.S. Embassy Visa Information Line (☎ 01891/200–290) for U.S. visa information; calls cost 49p per minute or 39p per minute cheap rate. U.S. Embassy Visa Branch (✉ 5 Upper Grosvenor St., London W1A 2JB) for U.S. visa information; send a self-addressed, stamped envelope. Write the U.S. **Consulate General** (✉ Queen's House, Queen St., Belfast BTI 6EO) if you live in Northern Ireland.

S
SENIOR-CITIZEN TRAVEL

To qualify for age-related discounts, **mention your senior-citizen status up front** when booking hotel reservations (not when checking out) and before you're seated in restaurants (not when paying the bill). Note that discounts may be limited to certain menus, days, or hours. When renting a car, **ask about promotional car-rental discounts,** which can be cheaper than senior-citizen rates.

➤ EDUCATIONAL TRAVEL PROGRAMS: **Elderhostel** (✉ 75 Federal St., 3rd floor, Boston, MA 02110, ☎ 617/426–7788).

STUDENTS

➤ STUDENT IDS AND SERVICES: **Council on International Educational Exchange** (✉ CIEE, 205 E. 42nd St., 14th floor, New York, NY 10017, ☎ 212/822–2600 or 888/268–6245, FAX 212/822–2699), for mail orders only, in the United States. **Travel Cuts** (✉ 187 College St., Toronto, Ontario M5T 1P7, ☎ 416/979–2406 or 800/667–2887) in Canada.

➤ HOSTELING: **Hostelling International—American Youth Hostels** (✉ 733 15th St. NW, Suite 840, Washington, DC 20005, ☎ 202/783–6161, FAX 202/783–6171). **Hostelling International—Canada** (✉ 400-205 Catherine St., Ottawa, Ontario K2P

1C3, ☎ 613/237–7884, FAX 613/237–7868). **Youth Hostel Association of England and Wales** (✉ Trevelyan House, 8 St. Stephen's Hill, St. Albans, Hertfordshire AL1 2DY, ☎ 01727/855215 or 01727/845047, FAX 01727/844126). Membership in the U.S., $25; in Canada, C$26.75; in the U.K., £9.30.

➤ STUDENT TOURS: **Contiki Holidays** (✉ 300 Plaza Alicante, Suite 900, Garden Grove, CA 92840, ☎ 714/740–0808 or 800/266–8454, FAX 714/740–0818).

T

TAXES

HOTEL

Many states and cities levy hotel taxes, usually as a percentage of the room rate. For example, in New York City, which already has an 8¼% sales tax, the progressive hotel tax can raise the tariff as much as 13% more, to 21¼%. When you make room reservations, **ask how much tax will be added to the basic rate.**

SALES

There is no U.S. value-added tax, but sales taxes are set by most individual states, and they can range anywhere from 3% to 8¼%. In some states, localities are permitted to add their own sales taxes as well. Exactly what is taxable, however, varies from place to place. In some areas, food and other essentials are not taxable, although you might pay tax for restaurant food. Luxury items such as cigarettes and alcohol are sometimes subject to an extra tax (known colloquially as a "sin tax"), as is gasoline, on the theory that car users should provide funds used to improve local roads.

TELEPHONES

All U.S. telephone numbers consist of 10 digits—the three-digit area code, followed by a seven-digit local number. If you're calling a number from another area-code region, dial "1" then all 10 digits. If you're calling from a distance but within the same area code, dial "1" then the last seven digits. For calls within the same local calling area, just dial the seven-digit number. A map of U.S. area codes is printed in the front of most local telephone directories; throughout this book, we have listed each phone number in full, including its area code.

Three special prefixes, "800," "888," and "900," are not area codes but indicators of particular kinds of service. "800" and "888" numbers can be dialed free from anywhere in the country—usually they are prepaid commercial lines that make it easier for consumers to obtain information, products, or services. The "900" numbers charge you for making the call and generally offer some kind of entertainment, such as horoscope readings, sports scores, or sexually suggestive conversations. These services can be very expensive, so **know what you're getting into before you dial a "900" number.**

CREDIT-CARD CALLS

U.S. telephone credit cards are not like the magnetic cards used in some European countries, which pay for calls in advance; they simply represent an account that lets you charge a call to your home or business phone. On any phone, you can make a credit-card call by punching in your individual account number or by telling the operator that number. Certain specially marked pay phones (usually found in airports, hotel lobbies, and so on) can be used only for credit-card calls. To get a credit card, contact your long-distance telephone carrier, such as AT&T, MCI, or Sprint.

LONG DISTANCE

International calls can be direct-dialed from most phones; dial "011," followed by the country code and then the local number (the front pages of many local telephone directories include a list of overseas country codes). To have an operator assist you, dial "0" and ask for the overseas operator.

AT&T, MCI, and Sprint long-distance services make calling home relatively convenient and let you avoid hotel surcharges. Typically you dial an 800 number.

➤ To OBTAIN ACCESS CODES: **AT&T USADirect** (☎ 800/874–4000). **MCI Call USA** (☎ 800/444–4444). **Sprint Express** (☎ 800/793–1153).

OPERATOR ASSISTANCE

For assistance from an operator, dial "0". To find out a telephone number, call directory assistance, 555–1212 in every locality. These calls are free even from a pay phone. If you want to charge a long-distance call to the person you're calling, you can call collect by dialing "0" instead of "1" before the 10-digit number, and an operator will come on the line to assist you (the party you're calling, however, has the right to refuse the call).

PUBLIC PHONES

Instructions for pay telephones should be posted on the phone, but generally you insert your coins—anywhere from 10¢ to 30¢ for a local call—in a slot and wait for the steady hum of a dial tone before dialing the number you wish to reach. If you dial a long-distance number, the operator will come on the line and tell you how much more money you must insert for your call to go through.

TIPPING

Tipping is a way of life in the United States, and some individuals may even be rude if you don't give them the amount of tip they expect. At restaurants, a 15% tip is standard for waiters; up to 20% may be expected at more expensive establishments. The same goes for taxi drivers, bartenders, and hairdressers. Coat-check facilities usually expect $1; bellhops and porters should get about 50¢ per bag; hotel maids in upscale hotels should get about $1 per day of your stay. On package tours, conductors and drivers usually get about $2–$3 per day from each group member; check whether this has already been figured into your cost. For local sightseeing tours, you may individually tip the driver-guide $1 if he or she has been helpful or informative. Ushers in theaters do not expect tips.

TOUR OPERATORS

Buying a prepackaged tour or independent vacation can make your trip to the U.S. less expensive and more hassle-free. Because everything is prearranged you'll spend less time planning.

Operators that handle several hundred thousand travelers per year can use their purchasing power to give you a good price. Their high volume may also indicate financial stability. But some small companies provide more personalized service; because they tend to specialize, they may also be more knowledgeable about a given area.

A GOOD DEAL?

The more your package or tour includes, the better you can predict the ultimate cost of your vacation. Make sure you know exactly what is covered, and **beware of hidden costs.** Are taxes, tips, and service charges included? Transfers and baggage handling? Entertainment and excursions? These can add up.

If the package or tour you are considering is priced lower than in your wildest dreams, **be skeptical.** Also, **make sure your travel agent knows the accommodations** and other services. Ask about the hotel's location, room size, beds, and whether it has a pool, room service, or programs for children, if you care about these. Has your agent been there in person or sent others you can contact?

BUYER BEWARE

Each year consumers are stranded or lose their money when tour operators—even very large ones with excellent reputations—go out of business. So **check out the operator.** Find out how long the company has been in business, and ask several agents about its reputation. **Don't book unless the firm has a consumer-protection program.**

Members of the National Tour Association and United States Tour Operators Association are required to set aside funds to cover your payments and travel arrangements in case the company defaults. Nonmembers may carry insurance instead. Look for the details, and for the name of an underwriter with a solid reputation, in the operator's brochure. Note: When it comes to tour operators, **don't trust escrow accounts.** Although the Department of Transportation watches over charter-flight operators, no regulatory body prevents tour operators from raiding the till. You may want to protect yourself by buying travel insurance that includes a tour-operator default provision. For more information, *see* Consumer Protection, *above*.

It's also a good idea to choose a company that participates in the American Society of Travel Agent's Tour Operator Program (TOP). This gives you a forum if there are any disputes between you and your tour operator; ASTA will act as mediator.

➤ TOUR-OPERATOR RECOMMENDATIONS: **National Tour Association** (✉ NTA, 546 E. Main St., Lexington, KY 40508, ☎ 606/226–4444 or 800/ 755–8687). **United States Tour Operators Association** (✉ USTOA, 342 Madison Ave., Suite 1522, New York, NY 10173, ☎ 212/599–6599, FAX 212/599–6744). **American Society of Travel Agents** (☞ Travel Agencies, *below*).

USING AN AGENT

Travel agents are excellent resources. In fact, large operators accept bookings made only through travel agents. But it's a good idea to **collect brochures from several agencies,** because some agents' suggestions may be influenced by relationships with tour and package firms that reward them for volume sales. If you have a special interest, **find an agent with expertise in that area**; ASTA (☞ Travel Agencies, *below*) has a database of specialists worldwide. Do some homework on your own, too: Local tourism boards can provide information about lesser-known and small-niche operators, some of which may sell only direct.

SINGLE TRAVELERS

Prices for packages and tours are usually quoted per person, based on two sharing a room. If traveling solo, you may be required to pay the full double-occupancy rate. Some operators eliminate this surcharge if you agree to be matched with a roommate of the same sex, even if one is not found by departure time.

GROUP TOURS

Among companies that sell tours to the U.S., the following are nationally known, have a proven reputation, and offer plenty of options. The classifications used below represent different price categories, and you'll probably encounter these terms when talking to a travel agent or tour operator. The

key difference is usually in accommodations, which run from budget to better, and better-yet to best.

➤ DELUXE: **Globus** (✉ 5301 S. Federal Circle, Littleton, CO 80123-2980, ☎ 303/797–2800 or 800/ 221–0090, FAX 303/347–2080). **Maupintour** (✉ 1515 St. Andrews Dr., Lawrence, KS 66047, ☎ 913/ 843–1211 or 800/255–4266, FAX 913/ 843–8351). **Tauck Tours** (✉ Box 5027, 276 Post Rd. W, Westport, CT 06881-5027, ☎ 203/226–6911 or 800/468–2825, FAX 203/221–6828).

➤ FIRST-CLASS: **Brendan Tours** (✉ 15137 Califa St., Van Nuys, CA 91411, ☎ 818/785–9696 or 800/ 421–8446, FAX 818/902–9876). **Collette Tours** (✉ 162 Middle St., Pawtucket, RI 02860, ☎ 401/728– 3805 or 800/832–4656, FAX 401/ 728–1380). **Gadabout Tours** (✉ 700 E. Tahquitz Canyon Way, Palm Springs, CA 92262-6767, ☎ 619/ 325–5556 or 800/952–5068). **Mayflower Tours** (✉ Box 490, 1225 Warren Ave., Downers Grove, IL 60515, ☎ 630/960–3793 or 800/ 323–7604, FAX 630/960–3575).

➤ BUDGET: **Cosmos** (☞ Globus, *above*).

PACKAGES

Like group tours, independent vacation packages are available from major tour operators and airlines. The companies listed below offer vacation packages in a broad price range.

➤ AIR/HOTEL/CAR: **American Airlines Fly AAway Vacations** (☎ 800/321– 2121). **Continental Vacations** (☎ 800/634–5555). **Delta Dream Vacations** (☎ 800/872–7786). **United Vacations** (☎ 800/328–6877). **US Airways Vacations** (☎ 800/455– 0123).

➤ AIR/HOTEL: **American Airlines Fly AAway Vacations** (☎ 800/321– 2121). **Continental Vacations** (☎ 800/634–5555). **Delta Dream Vacations** (☎ 800/872–7786). **TWA Getaway Vacations** (☎ 800/438– 2929). **United Vacations** (☎ 800/ 328–6877). **US Airways Vacations** (☎ 800/455–0123).

➤ HOTEL ONLY: **SuperCities** (✉ 139 Main St., Cambridge, MA 02142, ☎ 800/333–1234).

➤ CUSTOM PACKAGES: **Amtrak's Great American Vacations** (☎ 800/321–8684).

➤ FROM THE U.K.: **Trailfinders** (✉ 42–50 Earls Court Rd., London W8 6FT, ☎ 0171/937–5400; ✉ 58 Deansgate, Manchester M3 2FF, ☎ 0161/839–6969). **Travel Cuts** (✉ 295A Regent St., London W1R 7YA, ☎ 0171/637–3161); ☞ Students, *above*. **Flight Express Travel** (✉ 77 New Bond St., London W1Y 9DB, ☎ 0171/409–3311).

THEME TRIPS

For a complete list of operators, *see* Chapter 2, Special-Interest Vacations.

TRAIN TRAVEL

Amtrak is the national passenger rail service. It runs a limited number of routes; the northeast coast from Boston down to Washington, D.C., is generally well served. Chicago is a major rail terminus as well.

Some trains travel overnight, and you can sleep in your seat or book a roomette at additional cost. Most trains have diner cars with acceptable food, but you may prefer to bring your own. Excursion fares, when available, may save you nearly half the round-trip fare.

➤ RESERVATIONS: **Amtrak** (☎ 800/872–7245).

CHILDREN

Children under 2 ride free (one child per adult) if they don't occupy a seat; children 2–15 accompanied by a fare-paying adult pay half-price (two children per adult); children 15 and over pay the full adult fare.

SENIOR CITIZENS

Senior citizens (over 62) are entitled to a 15% discount on the lowest available fares.

TRAVELERS WITH DISABILITIES

Amtrak requests 48 hours' advance notice to provide redcap service, special seats, or wheelchair assistance at stations equipped to provide these services.

Passengers with disabilities receive 25% off an adult one-way fare. A special fare for children under 15 with disabilities (38% off an adult one-way fare) is also available.

DISCOUNT PASSES

The USA Railpass allows overseas visitors 15 or 30 days of unlimited nationwide travel for $355 or $440 (peak season, May 2–Aug. 21) and $245–$350 (off peak, Aug. 22–May 1), respectively. Fifteen- and 30-day regional rail passes can be purchased by non-U.S. citizens for the Far West ($205/$265, peak season; $185/$235, off peak), Western ($265/$330, peak; $215/$290), Eastern ($205/$265, peak; $185/$240), and Northeast ($175/$205, peak; $155/$195) areas of the United States; 30-day passes are also offered for rail travel along the East Coast and West Coast (each is $235, peak; $205) regions of the country. You can purchase these railpasses in the United States at any Amtrak station, but to qualify you must show a valid non-U.S. passport.

TRAVEL AGENCIES

A good travel agent puts your needs first. Look for an agency that has been in business at least five years, emphasizes customer service, and has someone on staff who specializes in your destination. In addition, **make sure the agency belongs to the American Society of Travel Agents** (ASTA). If your travel agency is also acting as your tour operator, *see* Tour Operators, *above*.

➤ LOCAL AGENT REFERRALS: **American Society of Travel Agents** (✉ ASTA, ☎ 800/965–2782 for 24-hr hot line, FAX 703/684–8319). **Alliance of Canadian Travel Associations** (✉ 1729 Bank St., Suite 201, Ottawa, Ontario K1V 7Z5, ☎ 613/521–0474, FAX 613/521–0805). **Association of British Travel Agents** (✉ 55–57 Newman St., London W1P 4AH, ☎ 0171/637–2444, FAX 0171/637–0713).

TRAVEL GEAR

Travel catalogs specialize in useful items, such as compact alarm clocks and travel irons, that can **save space when packing.**

➤ MAIL-ORDER CATALOGS: **Magellan's** (☎ 800/962–4943, FAX 805/568–5406). **Orvis Travel** (☎ 800/541–3541, FAX 540/343–7053). **TravelSmith** (☎ 800/950–1600, FAX 800/950–1656).

U

U.S. GOVERNMENT

The U.S. government can be an excellent source of inexpensive travel information. When planning your trip, **find out what government materials are available.**

➤ ADVISORIES: **U.S. Department of State American Citizens Services Office** (✉ Room 4811, Washington, DC 20520); enclose a self-addressed, stamped envelope. **Interactive hot line** (☎ 202/647–5225, FAX 202/647–3000). **Computer bulletin board** (☎ 202/647–9225).

➤ PAMPHLETS: **Consumer Information Center** (✉ Consumer Information Catalogue, Pueblo, CO 81009, ☎ 719/948–3334) for a free catalog that includes travel titles.

V

VISITOR INFORMATION

State tourism offices, city tourist bureaus, and local chambers of commerce, which are usually the best sources of information about their communities, are listed throughout this book at the beginning of each state, city, or regional section.

➤ IN CANADA: **Travel USA** (☎ 905/890–5662 or 800/268–3482 in Ontario).

➤ IN THE U.K.: There is no single tourist organization for the United States; U.S. states have their own agencies. Call **Visit USA** (☎ 0891/600–530) for contact addresses and telephone numbers; calls cost 50p per minute peak times, 45p per minute all other times.

W

WHEN TO GO

Although there is no country-wide tourist "season," various regions may have high and low seasons that are reflected in airfares and hotel rates. Unless the weather is a real drawback (as in Alaska in the winter or Miami in August), **visit areas during their off-season to save money and avoid crowds.** For climate information in specific regions of the country, **read the "When to Go" sections in chapter introductions.**

2 Special-Interest Vacations

Sports and the Outdoors

Spiritual and Physical Fitness Vacations

Education and Culture

By Karen Cure

Updated by
Heidi Spangler
Sarna

YOU CAN SEE THE UNITED STATES in many ways, but you'll have the most fun seeing it in the company of like-minded travelers while doing what you like to do best. The following pages suggest what's available; contact state tourism departments for other ideas.

Group Trips

Want a vacation-immersion in archeobotany? How about studying the natural history of New York's Finger Lakes, or whooping cranes, or bald eagles? Have you always wanted someone to teach you kayaking? Or yearned to ride-and-roll the white water down the Colorado? Whatever your interest, you'll find a program or an organization sponsoring group trips in the field.

How to Choose

Either pick a destination, or determine the special type of travel you are interested in and let the destination choose you. Then gather names of outfitters or resorts in your area of interest and contact them. For trips, ask about group size and composition (singles, couples, families, and so on), daily schedules, required gear, and any specifics of the activity. When looking into resorts, consider size, facilities, activities, and style. For courses and workshops, also find out about lodging arrangements, instructors' qualifications, and diversions for nonparticipating traveling companions. In every case, inquire about costs—what's included (meals, equipment), what's extra, how you pay, and how you get a refund if necessary. Check references.

Sports and the Outdoors

Monuments and museums aside, the nation's deep forests, mighty waters, and wide-open spaces are some of its most distinctive assets. Whether by bicycle or boat, on horseback or skis, or with your own two feet, a sports- or outdoors-oriented vacation will undoubtedly give you a new appreciation of the country's natural wonders.

Group Trips

Knowledgeable leaders make group trips the safest way to develop or add to your wilderness experience. Because you overnight in campgrounds or simple accommodations, costs are often modest. Some trips are organized for their members by conservation-minded nonprofit groups, such as the **Appalachian Mountain Club** (⊠ 5 Joy St., Boston, MA 02108, ☎ 617/523–0636) and the **Sierra Club** (⊠ 730 Polk St., San Francisco, CA 94109, ☎ 415/776–2211). On Sierra Club trips, members volunteer as leaders, participants do camp chores, and costs stay low. Trips sponsored by the **National Audubon Society** (⊠ Nature Odysseys, 700 Broadway, New York, NY 10003, ☎ 212/979–3066, FAX 212/353–0190) focus on birds and other wildlife.

Private firms offering outdoors-oriented trips include **American Wilderness Experience** (⊠ Box 1486, Boulder, CO 80306, ☎ 800/444–0099, FAX 303/444–3999), adventure-travel pioneer **Mountain Travel Sobek** (⊠ 6420 Fairmount Ave., El Cerrito, CA 94530-3606, ☎ 800/227–2384, FAX 510/525–7710), and for the Southeast, **Nantahala Outdoor Center** (⊠ 13077 Hwy. 19W, Bryson City, NC 28713, ☎ 704/488–6737).

Bookings and Information

Pat Dickerman, in business since 1949, matches travelers with congenial operators in her books *Adventure Travel North America* and *Farm, Ranch, and Country Vacations* ($16.95 and $19.95 respectively, plus $3 postage, from Adventure Guides, Inc., or Farm & Ranch Vacations,

Inc., ✉ 7550 E. McDonald Dr., Scottsdale, AZ 85250, ☎ 800/252–7899). Fodor's publishes *Great American Sports and Adventure Vacations* ($17.50; available in bookstores, or call ☎ 800/533–6478), covering 30 activities with details on more than 500 schools, workshops, and tours throughout the United States. The twice-yearly *Specialty Travel Index* (✉ 305 San Anselmo Ave., Suite 313, San Anselmo, CA 94960, ☎ 800/442–4922, ℻ 415/459–4974; $10 annually) has ads for everything from fishing and mountain-bike trips to gambling and shopping trips. Specialty magazines available on newsstands are full of ideas; the following sections suggest other resources.

Bicycling

Biking the nation's byways, you'll discover a bewitching hodgepodge of farms and factories, forests and strip malls, antique mansions and trailer parks. The leisurely pace makes it easy to stop to admire a cottage garden or get ice cream at a local stand.

DISTINCTIVELY AMERICAN CYCLING

Clapboard houses, salty seacoasts, and pine-and-hardwood forests beckon cyclists to **New England.** Particularly noteworthy are the Maine coast; Vermont's green and bucolic Northeast Kingdom; the forests and farms along the banks of New Hampshire's Connecticut River; Massachusetts's beach-ringed Martha's Vineyard and moor-covered Nantucket Island; northwestern Connecticut's hilly terrain, dotted with old houses and charming inns; mansion-laden Newport, Rhode Island; and the mountains and country roads of New York state's Catskills and Adirondack mountain regions.

The flat to mildly rolling landscape yields a bounty of scenic nooks and crannies in corners of the **mid-Atlantic states,** such as Pennsylvania's Lancaster County, full of peaceful byroads and Amish farms; the manicured emerald lawns of northern Virginia's horse country; Maryland's Eastern Shore, with its long Atlantic beaches and marshy backwaters; and the woods-edged towpath of the old C&O Canal, near Washington, D.C.

In the **Rockies** cyclists are mad for rugged, fat-tired mountain bikes—common sights in the rugged, piney high country, near Durango, Colorado, and on the sandstone cliff top that is the Slickrock Trail, near Moab, Utah, where the landscape is the color of sunset.

In **California** the pedaling is good on the roads through the vineyards of the Napa Valley and on the rock-bound Monterey Peninsula, while Highway 1, which teeters on the cliff tops above the Pacific, is the trip of a lifetime. Traveling by bike is also a great way to experience **Hawaii.**

More than 17,000 mi of abandoned railroad beds nationwide are slated to become bike trails; contact **Rails to Trails Conservancy** (✉ 1400 16th St. NW, Suite 300, Washington, DC 20036, ☎ 202/797–5400, ℻ 202/939–3381) for information on the almost 9,000 mi converted so far.

MOUNTAIN BIKING

Climbing steep inclines, fording streams, and darting over dirt trails are all part of the exhilaration of mountain biking, now a subculture all its own. Look for designated trail systems in city, county, and state parks; in addition, many ski resorts open their slopes, trails, and chairlifts to mountain bikers during the off-season. *See* Resources, *below,* for organized tours.

WITH A GROUP

Packages from bicycle-tour operators include basic-to-sumptuous lodging and often meals, along with escorts, "sag wagons" to carry luggage and weary pedalers, and optional rental bikes and helmets. They also supply maps that pinpoint easy-to-strenuous routes between overnights—you choose the one that suits you and pedal at your own pace. A good source is **Adventure Cycling** (⊠ Box 8308, Missoula, MT 59807, ☎ 406/721–1776), the country's largest nonprofit recreational-cycling organization.

RESOURCES

Adventure Cycling (☞ *above*) has helpful trip-planning information for members ($28 annually). *Bicycling* magazine (☎ 800/666–2806) lists specialist operators, such as the active **Backroads Bicycle Touring** (⊠ 1516 5th St., Berkeley, CA 94710, ☎ 510/527–1555 or 800/462–2848); **Brooks Country Cycling Tours** (⊠ 140 W. 83rd St., New York, NY 10024, ☎ 212/874–5151), which roams up and down the East Coast and packages trips with transportation to and from Manhattan; **Timberline Bicycle Tours** (⊠ 7975 E. Harvard St., No. J, Denver, CO 80231, ☎ 303/ 759–3804 or 800/417–2453, ₣Aₓ 303/368–1651), which concentrates on the West; and **Vermont Bicycle Touring** (⊠ Box 711, Bristol, VT 05433, ☎ 802/453–4811 or 800/245–3868), which has won many fans with its trips over country roads and overnight stops at local inns. For organized mountain-biking tours in the national parks of the West, contact **Backcountry Tours** (⊠ Box 4029, Bozeman, MT 59772, ☎ 800/ 575–1540 or 406/586–3556).

Canoeing and Kayaking

Paddling along the ocean's edge, across freshwater lakes, or down free-flowing streams gives a traveler a view of the wilderness that's hard to come by any other way. Moving almost soundlessly, canoes and kayaks seldom disturb wildlife feeding at the water's edge, and paddlers encounter birds and animals alike, practically eye to eye. The choice of craft is up to you: Canoes are more comfortable and give you more room to carry gear (and easier access to it); kayaks are more stable—important when you're maneuvering among boulders on white water.

DISTINCTIVELY AMERICAN CANOEING

You don't have to be an expert to tackle America's most beautiful paddling waters. Many are within the skills of beginners—though wind, heavy rainfall, or spring runoff can present challenges.

In the East canoeists head for **Maine's wild Allagash River** and the adjacent stream- and portage-connected lakes or to the island-flecked lakes in **New York's Adirondack Mountains,** where log lean-tos shelter campers on the mainland and on pristine islands. Lush hardwood forests edge white-water torrents in **West Virginia.** In the South the still waters of **Florida's Everglades National Park** and **Georgia's Okefenokee National Wildlife Refuge** access water-based "prairies" and mangrove swamps. The water in parts of the Okefenokee—stained black by leachings from vegetation—mirrors the verdant foliage overhead.

In the Midwest, Voyageurs National Park and the Superior National Forest and its Boundary Waters Canoe Area Wilderness showcase the woods of **northern Minnesota,** crossed by rivers and streams and scattered with lakes; in some areas no motorized vehicles are permitted, and you could explore for months without backtracking. **Missouri's Ozark National Scenic Riverways** and **Arkansas's Buffalo National River**—bluff-edged blends of rapids, fast water, and still pools—are just two of six National Rivers administered by the National Park Service (⊠ Box 37127, Washington, DC 20013-7127, ☎ 202/208–4747); the service also administers nine National Wild and Scenic Rivers.

RESOURCES

The century-old **American Canoe Association** (⊠ 7432 Alban Station Blvd., Suite B226, Springfield, VA 22150, ☎ 703/451–0141) has lists of canoeing clubs, schools, books, and trips ($25 annually). Consult *Canoe and Kayak* (☎ 206/827–6363) and *Paddler* (☎ 208/939–4500) magazines for other ideas.

River Rafting

The spray soaks your clothes and stings your face, the roar drowns out your screams—nothing reveals nature's power like white water. By comparison, the quiet stretches are all the more peaceful, the campfires more glowing. It's no wonder river rafting is so popular.

DISTINCTIVELY AMERICAN RAFTING

Rafting the **Colorado** through the Grand Canyon may be the ultimate American river experience, with its hundred-odd devilishly named rapids and glowing canyon scenery. However, it gets a run for its money from the river's demanding **Cataract Canyon** section, in Utah's Canyonlands National Park; Idaho's **Salmon** (both the Main Fork, the stream that Lewis and Clark called the River of No Return, and its Middle Fork, with 80 stretches of white water); and Idaho's sometimes-hellish **Selway.** Long, smooth stretches between rapids make Oregon's **Rogue,** a National Wild and Scenic River, especially good for families.

In the East the most famous white-water rafting stream may be Georgia's **Chattooga,** where *Deliverance* was filmed. But river rats know West Virginia as the country's most concentrated area of challenging and diverse white water. A case in point is the powerhouse **New River** (actually the oldest river on the continent), which roars through a gorge so deep it's known as the Grand Canyon of the East.

RAFT TRIPS

Commercial outfitters make even the rowdiest white water accessible to the inexperienced. They also supply gear, food, and appropriate permits—all you have to do is show up (and hold on!). Some outfitters use motorized rafts, some only oar power; some request paddling help, whereas others prohibit it. Find out what's expected before you book.

RESOURCES

State tourism offices and **America Outdoors** (✉ Box 10847, Knoxville, TN 37939, ☎ 423/558–3595), a trade organization, have names of outfitters. **OARS** (Outdoor Adventure River Specialists; ✉ Box 67, Angels Camp, CA 95222, ☎ 209/736–4677), established in 1972, and the nonprofit **American River Touring Association** (✉ 24000 Casa Loma Rd., Groveland, CA 95321, ☎ 209/962–7873 or 800/323–2782, ℻ 209/962–4819) have extensive programs, as does **Dvoák Kayak & Rafting Expeditions** (✉ 17921 U.S. 285, Nathrop, CO 81236, ☎ 719/539–6851 or 800/824–3795), the outfitter that introduced you-paddle trips. *Paddler* magazine (☎ 208/939–4500) covers guided trips and paddling schools.

Climbing and Mountaineering

Every year scores of hardy hikers visit the nation's highest peaks and leave invigorated by the view and exhilarated by their accomplishment. Rock-climbing skills put just that many more summits within reach on longer mountaineering expeditions.

DISTINCTIVELY AMERICAN CLIMBS

Routes on Colorado's 14,255-ft **Longs Peak,** Maine's 5,267-ft **Mt. Katahdin,** New Hampshire's 6,288-ft **Mt. Washington,** and New York's 5,344-ft **Mt. Marcy** are within the abilities of well-conditioned hikers. Many other peaks require rock-climbing skills—or expert guiding. In the West the most famous of these may be 20,320-ft **Mt. McKinley,** the Great One, in Alaska's Denali National Park; but the 13,770-ft hunk of granite known as the **Grand Teton,** in Wyoming's eponymous national park, and the granite walls and domes of California's **Yosemite** have comparable charisma. Easterners find challenges in New York's **Adirondacks** and **Shawangunks.**

SCHOOLS AND GUIDED ASCENTS

For extra excitement in national parks and forests, try a day at the **Colorado Mountain School** (✉ Box 2062, Estes Park, CO 80517, ☎ 970/586–5758), in Rocky Mountain National Park; **Exum Mountain Guides** (✉ Box 56, Moose, WY 83012, ☎ 307/733–2297), in the Tetons; and **Yosemite Mountaineering School** (✉ Yosemite National Park, Yosemite, CA 95389, ☎ 209/372–1244 or 209/372–1335 in summer). Offering a good mix of guided climbs and lessons at beginner-to-advanced levels are the **American Alpine Institute** (✉ 1515 12th St., Bellingham, WA 98225, ☎ 360/671–1505), **Fantasy Ridge Mountain Guides** (✉ Box 1679, Telluride, CO 81435, ☎ 970/728–3546), **Sierra Wilderness Seminars** (✉ 369-B 3rd St., Suite 347, San Raphael, CA 94901, ☎ 415/455–9358, FAX 415/455–9359); and in the East, **Adirondack Alpine Adventures** (✉ Box 179, Keene, NY 12942, ☎ 518/576–9881), the southern Appalachians' **Nantahala Outdoor Center** (✉ 13077 Hwy. 19W, Bryson City, NC 28713, ☎ 704/488–6737), the White Mountains' **Eastern Mountain Sports** (✉ Main St., Box 514, North Conway, NH 03860, ☎ 603/356–5433), and the Shawangunks' **Mountain Skills Climbing School** (✉ 595 Peak Rd., Stone Ridge, NY 12484, ☎ 914/687–9643).

RESOURCES

The **American Mountain Guides Association** (✉ 710 10th St., Suite 101, Golden, CO 80401, no phone) can provide a list of more than 100 qualified guides and services. Contact the **American Alpine Club** (✉ 710 10th St., Suite 100, Golden, CO 80401, ☎ 303/384–0110, FAX 303/384–0111) for information on all facets of climbing.

Fishing

The challenge of filling up a stringer isn't the only reason angling is the country's single most popular sport. There's also the prospect of a fresh-fish dinner. And the quiet hours spent by the water are their own reward.

DISTINCTIVELY AMERICAN ANGLING

Surf casting on Atlantic-pounded beaches and jetties yields good sport from Cape Cod to southern Florida. **Deep-sea fishing** gives you a good dose of the local culture. You can charter anything from a creaky wooden boat to a state-of-the-art yacht or join the often rough-and-ready crowd aboard party boats, where anglers pay by the head. Ocean City, Maryland, thinks of itself as the world's white-marlin capital, but marlin is prime quarry in Hawaii, too, where a whole fleet of boats leaves Kona every morning. There are huge sportfishing fleets in the Florida Panhandle, at small towns such as Destin and Fort Walton Beach; and in the Florida Keys, particularly Islamorada, Marathon, and Key West, where you might catch a long, gleaming needle-nose tarpon. **Fishing for snook,** a wily, scrappy, bony fish, is great sport—the Florida west-coast town of Naples is a hotbed—as is **casting for bonefish** in shallow saltwater flats.

In fresh water **trout fishing** is a whole angling subculture on such celebrated streams as Vermont's Battenkill, New York's Beaverkill, Arkansas's White River, and many rivers in Michigan and the northern Rockies. In Missouri **river fishing** is for bass in clear, slow, bluff-and forest-edged streams; in Idaho it's for steelhead and chinook in waters like the Salmon, Snake, and Clearwater; and in Oregon it's for steelhead, with huge runs in winter.

Other anglers prefer **lake fishing** and take motorboats or canoes in search of their quarry: lake trout and landlocked salmon in deep waters such as Maine's Moosehead and New Hampshire's Winnepesaukee; crappie and largemouth bass on such man-made lakes in the South and Midwest as Kentucky's Lake Barkley and Kentucky Lake and South Carolina's Lakes Marion and Moultrie. Northern Minnesota woodlands are as famous for yielding creels of scrappy walleye and northern pike and large- and smallmouth bass as for canoeing.

In a class by itself, **fishing in Alaska** is legendary: in the southeast panhandle for salmon (including sockeye, humpback, calico, king, and coho) and in the Interior and South Central regions for grayling. Good fishing is often right beside a highway; but fly-in trips to remote lakes and streams are common.

To plan a trip, decide what kind of fishing you want to do, then pick a destination. A letter to appropriate state fish and wildlife departments and a follow-up phone call are the first steps to a good creel. Or choose a fishing lodge in an area you want to visit, and let the pros find the fish. Bait-and-tackle shops or sporting goods stores, thriving wherever there are waters to fish, will know what's biting where and sell necessary licenses (usually required only by states and necessary only for freshwater fishing).

SCHOOLS

To hone your fishing skills, spend time at the **Joan and Lee Wulff Fishing Schools** (⌧ HCR1, Box 70, Lew Beach, NY 12758, ☎ 914/439–4060) or **Bud Lilly's Trout Shop** (⌧ Box 530, 39 Madison Ave., West Yellowstone, MT 59758, ☎ 406/646–7801), both founded by veteran anglers, or at **Orvis Fly Fishing Schools** (⌧ Historic Rte. 7A, Manchester, VT 05254, ☎ 802/362–3622), sponsored by the noted equipment maker.

RESOURCES

Fishing lodges dedicated to the care and feeding of anglers advertise in the magazines *Field & Stream* (☎ 212/779–5000), *Fishing World* (☎ 612/936–9333), and *Fly Fisherman* (☎ 717/657–9555).

Golf

Although most top courses are at private clubs, U.S. resorts offer challenges for itinerant players, not to mention the chance to enjoy some of the country's lushest scenery.

DISTINCTIVELY AMERICAN GOLFING

The Masters Tournament, held annually at the Augusta National Golf Club in Augusta, Georgia, has made the Southeast famous among golfers. Although that course is not open to the public, golfers can enjoy southern graciousness along with equally verdant, beautifully tended layouts at another American golf center—**Pinehurst, North Carolina,** home of the Pinehurst Hotel (⌧ Box 4000, Pinehurst, NC 28374, ☎ 800/487–4653) and no fewer than eight golf courses. Two southeastern old-line mountain resorts offer an equally sharp picture of golfing America: the **Homestead** (⌧ U.S. 220, Box 2000, Hot Springs, VA 24445, ☎ 540/839–1766 or 800/838–1766) and the **Greenbrier Hotel** (⌧ White Sulphur Springs, WV 24986, ☎ 304/536–1110). On **Hilton Head Island, South Carolina,** the beach scene meets the golf culture, and the hybrid attracts golfers from all over the country.

Golf-loving Japanese businessmen bought the world-class **Pebble Beach Golf Links** (⌧ 17-Mile Dr., Pebble Beach, CA 93953, ☎ 408/624–3811 or 800/654–9300) with a view to making a virtually private enclave of this California institution flung along the ragged edge of the rocky Monterey Peninsula; but public outcry has ensured it will continue to show off the best side of U.S. golfing to itinerant players. For sheer numbers, golf enthusiasts look south to **San Diego,** home of six dozen courses. Courses like the Gold, at the posh **Wigwam Resort** (⊠ Box 278, 300 E. Indian School La., Litchfield Park, AZ 85340, ☎ 602/935–3811 or 800/327–0396), have brought Arizona the fame once reserved for California. Elegant Hawaii resorts such as **Mauna Kea** (⊠ 62-100 Mauna Kea Beach Dr., Kamuela, HI 96743, ☎ 808/882–7222), **Mauna Lani Bay Hotel and Bungalows** (⊠ 68–1310 Mauna Lani Dr., Kohala Coast, HI 96743, ☎ 808/885–6655), and **Princeville Hotel** (⊠ Box 3040, Princeville, HI 96722, ☎ 808/826–3040) mix challenges with verdant coastline scenery and attract a golf-loving crowd from all over the country.

GOLF CLINICS

Most resort pros also teach. Then there are golf clinics, where golfers spend whole vacations working on their swing: the **Golf Digest Instruction Schools** (⊠ 5520 Park Ave., Box 395, Trumbull, CT 06611-0395, ☎ 203/373–7130 or 800/243–6121), with programs year-round at resorts nationwide, and the **Craft-Zavichas Golf School** (⊠ 600 Dittmer Ave., Pueblo, CO 81005, ☎ 719/564–4449 or 800/858–9633).

RESOURCES

The *Guide to Golf Schools & Camps* (Shaw Guides Publishers, ⊠ Box 1295, New York, NY 10023, ☎ 212/799–6464 or 800/247–6553) was last published in 1993 ($16.95 plus $3 shipping).

Hiking and Backpacking

The United States has enough forests and trails to wear out a lifetime of hiking boots. If you've graduated from short walks in local parks, you're ready to tackle the wide-open spaces of national parks and forests.

DISTINCTIVELY AMERICAN BACKPACKING

The Rockies showcase snowcapped mountains, high-country lakes, and mixed conifer-hardwood forests. Key destinations include national forests such as the huge, wild, and varied **Nez Perce** (⊠ Rte. 2, Box 475, Grangeville, ID 83530, ☎ 208/983–1950) and trail-crossed national parks such as Colorado's **Rocky Mountain National Park** (⊠ Estes Park, CO 80517, ☎ 970/586–1206), northern Wyoming's **Grand Teton National Park** (⊠ Drawer 170, Moose, WY 83012, ☎ 307/739–3300), and **Yellowstone National Park** (⊠ Box 168, Yellowstone National Park, WY 82190, ☎ 307/344–7381) to the north. For a unique experience in **Glacier National Park** (⊠ Belton Chalets, Box 188, West Glacier, MT 59936, ☎ 406/888–7800), book a night in one of its spartan pair of World War I–era chalets, accessible only by trail. The Sierras have an entirely different mountain landscape, with granite peaks, lichen-splotched granite boulders, and pine and fir forests; in **Yosemite National Park** you don't even have to carry camping gear if you stay in one of the five High Sierra Camps. They cost $78 per night for motel room and $43–$66 for cabins (⊠ Yosemite Park Reservations, 5410 E. Home Ave., Fresno, CA 93727, ☎ 209/252–4848).

In the East backpackers tramp the Appalachians, ancient mountains with rounded summits, hardwood forests, and many a killer grade. In the Appalachians' bare, windswept **White Mountains' Presidential Range,** the Appalachian Mountain Club runs no-frills hikers' huts, which cost $50 nightly by reservation through the AMC (⊠ Box 298, Gorham, NH 03581, ☎ 603/466–2727, ℻ 603/466–3871). The **Great Smoky Mountains National Park** (⊠ Gatlinburg, TN 37738, ☎ 423/436–1200), which preserves another range of the Appalachians and is crossed by some 800 mi of trails, shows off a gentler side of these old mountains, splendid in spring when the dogwood is in bloom and in fall when the foliage is at its peak.

Backpacking is less common in some areas in the middle of the country, except in Arkansas reserves such as the **Ouachita National Forest** (⊠ Box 1270, Hot Springs, AR 71902, ☎ 501/321–5202, ℻ 501/321–5353) and the **Ozark–St. Francis National Forest** (⊠ 605 W. Main St., Russellville, AR 72801, ☎ 501/968–2354). For hikers in **northern Michigan and Minnesota,** the draw is often the superior fishing in waters accessible only on foot. Try **Isle Royale National Park** (⊠ 800 E. Lakeshore Dr., Houghton, MI 49931, ☎ 906/482–0984) and **Superior National Forest** (⊠ Box 338, Duluth, MN 55801, ☎ 218/720–5324).

LONG TRAILS

Veteran hikers aspire to walk the length of the 2,147-mi Maine-to-Georgia **Appalachian Trail** (⊠ Appalachian Trail Conference, Box 807, Harpers Ferry, WV 25425, ☎ 304/535–6331), Vermont's 265-mi **Long Trail** (⊠ Green Mountain Club, R.R. 1, Box 650, Waterbury Center, VT 05677, ☎ 802/244–7037), the 2,700-mi **Continental Divide Trail** (⊠ Box 30002, Bethesda, MD 20824, no phone), and the 2,638-mi **Pacific Crest Trail Association** (⊠ 5325 Elk Horn Blvd., No. 256, Sacramento, CA 95842, ☎ 800/817–2243).

OFFBEAT GUIDED TRIPS

If you don't have the experience to tackle a long backpacking trip on your own, go with a group. In the West you have the option of llama treks, where the sturdy, gentle animals carry gear. In the East inn-to-inn trips put country comfort at trail's end—and innkeepers transport your gear between stops. Contact **Country Inns Along the Trail** (⊠ R.D. 3, Box 3115, Brandon, VT 05733, ☎ 802/247–3300) or **Knapsack Tours** (⊠ 5961 Zinn Dr., Oakland, CA 94611, ☎ 510/339–0160). **Vermont Walking Tours** (⊠ Box 31, Craftsbury Common, VT 05827, ☎ 802/586–7767) specializes in back-roads walks in the Green Mountain State's unspoiled Northeast Kingdom.

RESOURCES

Fodor's Sports: Hiking ($12) covers other trips and trails. Magazines such as *Outside* (☎ 505/989–7100) and *Walking* (☎ 617/266–3322) list many group trips.

Horseback: Pack Trips and Dude Ranches

Seeing the country from the back of a horse has many advantages. You can cover more ground than you would on foot yet still penetrate deep into the wilderness. Best of all, you don't have to carry your gear.

PACK TRIPS

The horse fancier's version of guided backpacking trips, pack trips mix days of traveling between base camps and layover days filled with hiking, fishing, loafing, and eating. Western hospitality prevails, and experience is seldom required. Some outfitters schedule trips in advance, while others do custom trips; daily cost is $85–$175. When choosing, ask about the ratio of traveling to layover days, daily distances covered, and the extent of horse care you're expected to provide.

If this appeals to you, look into American Forests' **Trail Riders of the Wilderness** program (☞ Group Trips, *above*) or contact local specialists; for names, consult state tourism offices or Pat Dickerman's **Adventure Travel** (☞ Bookings and Information, *above*).

INN-TO-INN RIDES

Eastern horse lovers relish the inn-to-inn rides of **Kedron Valley Stables** (⊠ Box 368, South Woodstock, VT 05071, ☎ 802/457–1480 or 800/225–6301, ℻ 802/457–3029) and **Vermont Icelandic Horse Farm** (⊠ Box 577, Waitsfield, VT 05673, ☎ 802/496–7141, ℻ 802/496–5390).

DUDE RANCHES

Some are spiffy, upscale resorts, such as **Rancho de los Caballeros** (⊠ 1551 S. Vulture Mine Rd., Wickenburg, AZ 85390, ☎ 520/684–5484, FAX 520/684–2267), where riding is combined with top-notch tennis and golf. Others, such as **Lone Mountain** (⊠ Box 69, Big Sky, MT 59716, ☎ 406/995–4644), also offer rafting trips, fishing excursions, and other outdoor activities. At working ranches like **G Bar M** (⊠ Box 29, Clyde Park, MT 59018, ☎ 406/686–4687), pitching in is part of the fun. All offer a healthy dose of horse-related activities, such as pack trips, breakfast cookout rides, and horseback picnics. Rates range from $700 weekly to more than twice that.

Pat Dickerman's *Farm, Ranch and Country Vacations* (☞ Bookings and Information, *above*) is a good source; for other listings contact the **Colorado Dude and Guest Ranch Association** (⊠ Box 300, Tabernash, CO 80478, ☎ 303/887–3128), the **Dude Ranchers Association** (⊠ Box 471, LaPorte, CO 80535, ☎ 970/223–8440, FAX 970/223–0201), and **Old West Dude Ranch Vacations** (⊠ c/o American Wilderness Experiences, Box 1486, Boulder, CO 80306, ☎ 800/444–3833, FAX 303/444–3999), as well as state tourism offices. Gene Kilgore's *Ranch Vacations* (⊠ Box 629000, El Dorado Hills, CA 95762, ☎ 800/637–8100) lists 240 ranches in the United States and western Canada ($22.95 plus $7.95 shipping).

Nature and Wildlife Education

Spotting moose and seals and focusing your binoculars on trumpeter swans are among the pleasures of outdoor activities. Specialized programs and tours help you understand what you see.

NATURE CAMPS

Naturalists on hikes, in classrooms, and around evening campfires offer insights into nature and its interdependencies at several summer programs. The half-century-old **Audubon Ecology Camps** (⊠ 613 Riversville Rd., Greenwich, CT 06831, ☎ 203/869–2017) attract people of all ages to one-week summer sessions held in Wyoming's Wind River Range; on a 300-acre Maine island; and at a Greenwich, Connecticut, nature sanctuary. Accommodations are simple but comfortable. These are almost as well known among outdoors lovers as those offered by the **Sierra Club National Outing Program** (⊠ 85 2nd St., San Francisco, CA 94105, ☎ 415/977–5500), including wilderness camps in the Sierras, the Rockies, the Smokies, and other wild places, where club members spend a week or two among similarly conservation-minded vacationers, day-hiking into the surrounding countryside, helping with camp tasks under staff supervision, and paying relatively modest fees. Also look into **National Wildlife Federation Conservation Summits** (⊠ 8925 Leesburg Pike, Vienna, VA 22184, ☎ 703/790–4363), which mix nature, outdoor skills, and folk culture; and the **Chewonki Foundation** (⊠ R.R. 2, Box 1200, Wiscasset, ME 04578, ☎ 207/882–7323, FAX 207/882–4074), an environmentally oriented group with the twin objectives of nature education and personal growth, which numbers the late naturalist Roger Tory Peterson among its alumni.

IN THE NATIONAL PARKS

Participants learn about the environment through lectures, field courses, and photography and writing workshops at **Canyonlands Field Institute** (⊠ Box 68, Moab, UT 84532, ☎ 801/259–7750, FAX 801/259–2335), in Canyonlands National Park; the **Glacier Institute** (⊠ Box 7457, Kalispell, MT 59904, ☎ 406/755–1211); the **Olympic Park Institute** (⊠ 111 Barnes Point Rd., Port Angeles, WA 98363, ☎ 360/928–3720); **Point Reyes Field Seminars** (⊠ Point Reyes National Seashore, Point Reyes Station, CA 94956, ☎ 415/663–1200), at the Point Reyes National Seashore; and the **Yellowstone Institute** (⊠ Box 117, Yellowstone National Park, WY 82190, ☎ 307/344–2294).

NATURALIST-LED TOURS AND CRUISES

Guided by university professors, botanists, or zoologists, wildlife tours reveal dimensions of the American landscape that most vacationers never even suspect. Hiking and camping may be involved, but accommodations are often comfortable or even luxurious, and travel is by small cruise boat or van. Whale-watching is often a feature. Contact **Nature Expeditions International** (⊠ 6400 E. El Dorado Circle, Suite 210, Tucson, AZ 85715, ☎ 520/721–6712 or 800/869–0639).

WILDERNESS SKILLS PROGRAMS

Here you might learn winter camping, sea kayaking, rock climbing, minimum-impact camping, or river rafting; but it's the personal growth from mastering something new that attracts participants to the rigorous mental and physical challenges of **Outward Bound** (⊠ Rte. 9D, R2, Box 280, Garrison, NY 10524-9757, ☎ 914/424–4000 or 800/243–8520), the granddaddy of such programs, or the **National Outdoor Leadership School** (⊠ 288 Main St., Lander, WY 82520, ☎ 307/332–6973), originally founded to train trip leaders.

Sailing

The mighty U.S. coastline ranks among the nation's most stirring sights, and although roads provide access to much of it, seeing the coast from the water gives an undeniably better view.

DISTINCTIVELY AMERICAN SAILING

Nothing says United States quite like **Maine's rocky coast,** known to sailors all over the world for its scenery, good moorings, and abundant facilities. But there's comparable variety among the islands, coves, and shoreside towns of the **Chesapeake Bay** and **Long Island Sound.** The waters off **Newport, Rhode Island,** home of the Museum of Yachting, are light-years away from landlubber gridlock; the crowd is well heeled and tony. In the **Florida Keys** the winds are good, the waters teeming with marine life, and the shoreside life casual and laid-back. In the Midwest sailors relish the challenging **Great Lakes,** which are inland seas. **California** is sail-crazed; Sausalito, near San Francisco Bay, and Marina del Rey and Newport Beach, in the south, are boating centers. In northwestern Washington state the **San Juan Islands** offer their own barefoot life amid coves and beaches teeming with birds and animals. For the adventurous side of the sport, consider **Alaska**—extraordinary with its fjords, shoreline peaks and waterfalls, good fishing, and abundant wildlife.

CHARTERS

You can book craft either crewed (staffed to handle cooking and navigation) or bareboat (for experienced sailors only). Contact state visitor centers for lists of charter operators.

SCHOOLS

The pleasures of the sea mix with the satisfaction of acquiring a new skill at the nation's two principal sailing programs: the **Annapolis Sailing School** (⊠ Box 3334, Annapolis, MD 21403, ☎ 410/267–7205 or 800/638–9192), which has a branch in the U.S. Virgin Islands, and the **Offshore Sailing School** (⊠ 16731 McGregor Blvd., Suite 110, Fort Myers, FL 33908, ☎ 813/454–1700 or 800/221–4326), founded by former Olympian Steve Colgate and now offering programs on Florida's Captiva Island; in Newport, Rhode Island; in Stamford, Connecticut; and in Jersey City, New Jersey.

Consult *Fodor's Sports: Sailing* ($12) for more on great sailing destinations. Ads and information on charter operators can be found in the magazines *Sail* (☎ 617/964–3030), *Cruising World* (☎ 401/847–1588), and *Yachting* (☎ 212/779–5300).

The beating of sails in the wind, the smell of the sea, and the excitement of calling at scenic ports create an unbeatable camaraderie on cruises aboard the nation's fleet of tall ships—restorations or reconstructions of 19th-century craft that accommodate fewer than 30 passengers. Per-person fares are about $100 a day, much lower than those for larger cruise ships, and most people don't mind the spartan cabins and cold showers (or absence thereof), since it's easy to clean up at local marinas.

In the East, Rockland, Camden, and Rockport, Maine, are the bases for a dozen ships, mostly members of the **Maine Windjammer Association** (✉ Box 1144, Blue Hill, ME 04614, ☎ 800/807–9463). Also contact Maine's state tourism office. In the Midwest look into the **Traverse Tall Ship Company** (✉ 13390 S.W. Bay Shore Dr., Traverse City, MI 49684, ☎ 616/941–2000).

Skiing

Ski areas can be found even in such unlikely states as Indiana, but some of the best skiing in the world is in the Rockies. True, the typical ski area in the Alps has a greater vertical drop (as skiers call the difference in altitude between lift base and the highest lift-served point). But no other ski areas have comparable snow quality. Not only is snowfall (usually) abundant, but it is also dry and featherlight, and snow quality is consistent from top to bottom—a rarity in Europe. To enjoy it all, you don't have to be a hotdog mogul skier or one of the manic daredevils dubbed "extreme skiers": U.S. mountains have slopes you can ski no matter what your ability.

In the Rockies you'll find an affluent crowd in **Sun Valley,** Idaho; a certain former Colorado mining town known as **Aspen;** faux-alpine **Vail** not far away; and perhaps **Deer Valley,** Utah—relentlessly tasteful right down to the marble in the base lodge rest rooms. For mellow western charm in addition to abundant facilities, it's hard to beat **Breckenridge, Copper Mountain, Keystone,** and **Steamboat,** Colorado, or even **Park City,** Utah. Friendly, low-key spots like **Big Mountain,** near Whitefish, Montana, are practically unknown outside the West. The same can't be said of New Mexico's challenging **Taos;** Wyoming's one-of-a-kind **Jackson Hole;** Utah's cozy, rustic **Alta,** the sine qua non among powder skiers; and its mod cousin, **Snowbird.** Yet by comparison to the fame of the big Colorado resorts, theirs is limited.

Elsewhere in the West, California's Sierras get massive amounts of snow, and skiers come by the thousands to the resorts around crystal-clear Lake Tahoe, including **Squaw, Heavenly, Northstar,** and **Kirkwood.**

In the East narrow trails and icy conditions magnify the challenges, although slope grooming and snowmaking ease the sting at Vermont's **Stowe** and its Vermont cousins closer to the big cities: huge **Killington** and **Mt. Snow,** genteel **Stratton** and **Sugarbush.** New Hampshire resorts, such as **Waterville Valley,** are even more relaxed.

To choose, consider the area's personality, terrain, and convenience. Are there slope-side accommodations or do you need a car? Can you find the lodgings you want (motel, inn, B&B, dorm, or resort) at a price you can afford? Are there programs for kids? Families appreciate areas with centralized lift layouts, which make it easy to rendezvous for lunch or at day's end.

SKI SCHOOLS AND PACKAGES
Most ski areas offer instruction and packages. Some offer deals on multiday lift tickets; others add lessons, lodging, or meals. The best deals are midweek, particularly in areas with heavy weekend traffic.

RESOURCES
Ski (☎ 212/779–5000), *Ski Tripper* (☎ 703/772–7644), *Skiing* (☎ 212/779–5000), *Snow Country* (☎ 203/323–7000), and *Powder* (☎ 714/496–5922) magazines cover the field.

Ski Touring

Heavy snows that otherwise make the nation's meadows and forests inaccessible are no problem for those who can cross-country ski.

DISTINCTIVELY AMERICAN SKI TOURING
National and state park and forest trails are sometimes suitable for cross-country skiing, although rental equipment is not always available. At ski areas, valleys at the base and high ridges and plateaus often offer excellent sport.

For a once-in-a-lifetime experience, there's nothing like **Yellowstone National Park.** In winter waterfalls freeze into bizarre sculptures, steam billowing from the thermal features turns trees into hoary ghosts, and icicles glitter everywhere. Lodging, equipment, and instruction are available.

Elsewhere in the West there's abundant ski touring at several areas in and around Wyoming's **Grand Teton National Park** and California's **Yosemite National Park.** Idaho's **Sun Valley** has hundreds of skiable acres, and you can even helicopter up to the high country. Communities of cross-country fanatics flourish in Colorado at **Steamboat Springs** and **Vail,** and the trail system in **Aspen** is one of the nation's most extensive. Minnesota's **Superior National Forest** enjoys abundant snowfall and hundreds of miles of trails.

In the East prime areas include Massachusetts's **Berkshire Mountains,** full of parks, forests, and inns; New Hampshire's **Mt. Washington Valley;** and Vermont's **Stowe,** where dozens of miles of trails link restaurants, inns, and shops.

GROUP TRIPS
Rock-climbing schools (☞ Climbing and Mountaineering, *above*) often have cross-country skiing programs. For inn-to-inn tours, contact **Country Inns Along the Trail** (✉ R.D. 3, Box 3115, Brandon, VT 05733, ☎ 802/247–3300). Rugged hut-to-hut tours of Colorado's spectacular Tenth Mountain Trail are offered by **Paragon Guides** (✉ Box 130, Vail, CO 81658, ☎ 970/926–5299, FAX 970/926–5298).

RESOURCES
The **USIA Cross-Country Ski Areas Association** (✉ 259 Bolton Rd., Winchester, NH 03470, ☎ 603/239–4341) publishes a book ($3) detailing more than 500 cross-country areas and can send a list of those sponsoring overnight cross-country trips. Also read *Cross Country Skier* magazine (☎ 612/377–0312).

Tennis

If you have nonplaying companions, consider a full-scale resort with a heavy tennis program; otherwise consider sites where tennis is the only activity: tennis camps or clinics. Rather than trying to remake your game, most build on what you already have in order to send you home a better player.

CAMPS AND CLINICS

Staged year-round at resorts nationwide and at private schools in summer, these provide the most intense tennis experience, with up to five hours of play every day. Established in 1968, **Tennis Camps, Ltd.** (✉ 444 E. 82nd St., New York, NY 10028, ☎ 212/879–0225 or 800/223–2442) is a major player. The **Nick Bollettieri Tennis Academy** (✉ 5500 34th St. W, Bradenton, FL 34210, ☎ 813/755–1000 or 800/872–6425) and **Harry Hopman/Saddlebrook International Tennis** (✉ 5700 Saddlebrook Way, Wesley Chapel, FL 33543, ☎ 813/973–1111 or 800/729–8383) are both famed for turning prodigies into pros. For off-court luxury, the last word is **John Gardiner's**—both the exclusive California ranch (✉ Box 228, Carmel Valley, CA 93924, ☎ 408/659–2207) and its even posher desert cousin (✉ 5700 E. McDonald Dr., Scottsdale, AZ 85253, ☎ 602/948–2100). Former top players mastermind the friendly **John Newcombe's Tennis Ranch** (✉ Box 310–469, New Braunfels, TX 78131, ☎ 210/625–9105 or 800/444–6204), the **Van Der Meer Tennis University** (✉ Box 5902, Hilton Head Island, SC 29938, ☎ 803/785–8388 or 800/845–6138), and the high-tech **Vic Braden Tennis College** (✉ 23335 Avenida la Caza, Coto de Caza, CA 92679, ☎ 714/581–2990 or 800/422–6878).

RESORTS

Planned resort developments almost always have extensive facilities. At **Hilton Head Island, South Carolina,** two resorts alone offer more than five dozen courts—Sea Pines Plantation (✉ Box 7000, Hilton Head Island, SC 29938, ☎ 800/845–6131) and Palmetto Dunes (✉ Box 5606, Hilton Head Island, SC 29938, ☎ 803/785–7300 or 800/845–6130). Ski resorts usually have extensive tennis programs—among them are Bolton Valley, Killington, Stratton, and Sugarbush—and so do large resort hotels. A special case is the elegant Gulf Coast **Colony Beach & Tennis Resort** (✉ 1620 Gulf of Mexico Dr., Longboat Key, FL 34228, ☎ 914/383–6464 or 800/237–9443), devoted exclusively to tennis.

To choose, ask the pro shop about court fees, reservations procedures and availability, game-matching services, night play, guest tourneys, court-time limits, instruction, and the resort's court-to-room ratio (1 to 10 is fine; half that if there are many other activities).

RESOURCES

See *Tennis* magazine (☎ 212/789–3000) for listings of tennis resorts, camps, and clinics.

Spiritual and Physical Fitness Vacations

Providing meaningful recreation for both mind and body is the objective of hundreds of establishments across the United States. Totally unlike spas in the old, European sense—grand hotels that cosset those who come to sip the waters—American spas reflect current attitudes on diet and health. *Fodor's Healthy Escapes* ($16) lists 243 fitness-oriented camps, resorts, and programs starting at $35 a day, some all-inclusive packages and some à la carte.

Holistic Centers

The verdant Catskills' **New Age Health Spa** (✉ Rte. 55, Neversink, NY 12765, ☎ 914/985–7601 or 800/682–4348) helps guests balance body, soul, and mind via programs ranging from astrological consultations and aerobics to Zen meditation. Flotation tanks and massages supplement nutrition and counseling at old-timers such as the **Omega Institute** (✉ 260 Lake Dr., Rhinebeck, NY 12572, ☎ 914/266–4301 or 800/944–1001).

Spas for Luxury and Pampering

To those who say, "No pain, no gain," others reply, "No frills, no thrills" and seek out deluxe establishments for regimens of body wraps, saunas, Swiss showers, massages, manicures, and maybe a yoga class or two. On the cutting edge is **Canyon Ranch** (✉ 165 Kemble St., Lenox, MA 01240, ☎ 413/637–4100 or 800/742–9000; ✉ 8600 E. Rockcliff Rd., Tucson, AZ 85750, ☎ 520/749–9000 or 800/742–9000), where treatments are combined with outdoor activities such as hiking, biking, and tennis, as well as sophisticated spa cuisine. The women-only **Greenhouse** (✉ Box 1144, Arlington, TX 76004, ☎ 817/640–4000) is a study in elegant southern hospitality. Many luxury spas take the more active approach of the serene **Golden Door** (✉ Box 463077, Escondido, CA 92046, ☎ 619/744–5777), where individually planned programs include 6 AM hikes and exercise classes. **La Costa Resort & Spa** (✉ 2100 Costa del Mar Rd., Carlsbad, CA 92009, ☎ 619/438–9111 or 800/854–5000) is the megaresort of the breed. The **Spa at Doral** (✉ 8755 N.W. 36th St., Miami, FL 33178, ☎ 305/593–6030 or 800/331–7768) fuses a typically American program involving exercise and stress-management training with European treatments, such as warm mud packs for muscular problems.

Weight Management and Preventive Medicine Centers

Another type of American spa has extensive medical supervision. Examples include the well-rounded **Duke University Diet and Fitness Center** (✉ 804 W. Trinity Ave., Durham, NC 27701, ☎ 919/684–6331 or 800/362–8446); the **Cooper Institute for Aerobics Fitness** (✉ 12230 Preston Rd., Dallas, TX 75230, ☎ 972/701–8001 or 800/635–7050, FAX 972/991–4626), inspired by aerobics pioneer Dr. Kenneth H. Cooper; and the **Pritikin Longevity Centers** (✉ 1910 Ocean Front Walk, Santa Monica, CA 90405, ☎ 310/450–5433 or 800/421–9911; ✉ 5875 Collins Ave., Miami Beach, FL 33140, ☎ 305/866–2237 or 800/327–4914), which focus on the late Nathan Pritikin's belief that diet can reverse atherosclerosis.

Education and Culture

All travel stretches the observant voyager's mind. A number of programs—university-sponsored tours and continuing-education courses, as well as workshops in the arts—formalize this process. Equally educational are volunteer programs such as archaeological research or trail building. Although vacations organized around volunteer activities may not send you back home with a tan, they *are* likely to benefit you as well as the rest of the world.

Academic Tours and Programs

Once upon a time, **Chautauqua** (✉ Box 1098, Chautauqua, NY 14722, ☎ 716/357–6200) was unique among travel destinations because it offered language, history, crafts, hobbies, and music and other arts programs. Established in 1874, it now crams more than 300 courses into the nine-week July–August program on its lakeside campus.

VACATIONS ON COLLEGE CAMPUSES

At these you can expand your intellectual horizons in the spirit of Chatauqua and in the company of university professors and other inquisitive spirits at summer colleges sponsored by major colleges and universities. Typically, these programs require no tests, give no grades, admit nonalumni as well as alumni, keep costs low with simple dormitory lodging and cafeteria meals, and explore themes such as Victorian England or capitalism in China. They also fill up fast.

Summer schools for adults are currently offered in the East at **Cornell** (✉ 626 Thurston Ave., Ithaca, NY 14850, ☎ 607/255–6260); **Dartmouth** (✉ 308 Blunt Alumni Center, Hanover, NH 03755, ☎ 603/646–2454); **Johns Hopkins** (✉ 3400 N. Charles St., Baltimore, MD 21218, ☎ 410/516–7187); and **Penn State** (✉ 315 Keller Bldg., University Park, PA 16802, ☎ 814/863–3781). Comparable programs are run in the South at the **University of North Carolina at Chapel Hill** (✉ Vacation College Humanities Program, Campus Box 3425, 3 Bolin Heights, Chapel Hill, NC 27599-3425, ☎ 919/962–1544) and **Washington and Lee University** (✉ Office of Special Programs, Lexington, VA 24450, ☎ 540/463–8723), and in the Midwest at **Indiana University** (✉ Mini University, Indiana Memorial Union, Suite 400, Bloomington, IN 47405, ☎ 800/824–3044) and the **College of Wooster** (✉ Alumni Relations, Wooster, OH 44691, ☎ 330/263–2263).

Programs come and go, however, so it's best to pick a university you'd like to attend, then call its alumni office or its continuing education or adult education department to inquire about what's being offered.

ACADEMIC AND OTHER CULTURAL TOURS

Major U.S. museums sponsor dozens of study tours every year, most escorted by museum personnel, university professors, and other experts. Another option is the programs of independent operators; for extensive listings consult the *Guide to Academic Travel* ($19.95 postpaid from Shaw Guides Publishers, $16.95 plus $3 shipping [✉ Box 1295, New York, NY 10023, ☎ 212/799–6464 or 800/247–6553]), last published in 1992.

HISTORY TOURS

American architecture, social history, and culture are emphasized on tours led by the **National Trust for Historic Preservation** (✉ 1785 Massachusetts Ave. NW, Washington, DC 20036, ☎ 202/588–6000). Four- to 30-day trips have explored Virginia's grand houses and plantations, the heritage of the Maine coast, and Route 66. **Smithsonian Study Tours and Seminars** (✉ 1100 Jefferson Dr. SW, Washington DC, 20560, ☎ 202/357–4700) offers a variety of four- to six-day history seminar tours led by experts in the field. Subjects include the Civil War, Native American culture, and jazz music.

Cooking Schools

Those who love to cook, eat well, and enjoy fine wines have few better travel options than signing up for an intensive multiday cooking course at a hotel or cooking school. When choosing, be sure to find out the demonstration-to-participation ratio.

INTENSIVE COURSES AT COOKING SCHOOLS

Two- to five-day programs are widely available. Some are through professional schools such as the **Culinary Institute of America** (✉ 433 Albany Post Rd., Hyde Park, NY 12538, ☎ 914/451–1066 or 800/888–7850), the nation's major professional school, and the **California Culinary Academy** (✉ 625 Polk St., San Francisco, CA 94102, ☎ 415/771–3536).

Well-known chefs and cookbook authors sponsor other programs, notably **Julie Sahni's Indian Cooking** (✉ 101 Clark St., Brooklyn Heights, NY 11201, ☎ 718/625–3958, FAX 718/625–3456) and **Karen Lee Chinese Cooking Classes** (✉ 142 West End Ave., New York, NY 10023, ☎ 212/787–2227). Other options are at vineyards such as the **Robert Mondavi Winery** (✉ Box 106, Oakville, CA 94562, ☎ 707/944–2866).

PROGRAMS AT HOTELS, INNS, AND RESORTS
If your traveling companions would rather play golf or tennis than slave over a hot stove, look into short programs at such grand resorts as the **Greenbrier Hotel** (✉ 300 W. Main St., White Sulphur Springs, WV 24986, ☎ 304/536–1110 or 800/228–5049), where La Varenne's Anne Willan directs.

RESOURCES
Consult the *Guide to Cooking Schools* (Shaw Guides Publishers, ☎ 212/799–6464 or 800/247–6553) for extensive listings of both short- and long-term programs, as well as information on gourmet and wine tours ($19.95 plus $3 shipping).

Crafts Workshops

Short workshops in the crafts and fine arts are staged by major museums and at national parks such as Glacier, Yosemite, and Olympic. More extensive programs, lasting from one to several weeks and focusing on a range of crafts—from metal, wood, and ceramics to indigenous regional and Native American crafts—are held at colleges, crafts centers, and individual studios.

INTERDISCIPLINARY CRAFTS CENTERS
Dozens of weekend and weeklong courses in basketry, bookmaking, ceramics, woodworking, and other topics draw pros as well as beginners and intermediates to crafts centers such as **Anderson Ranch Arts Center** (✉ Box 5598, Snowmass Village, CO 81615, ☎ 970/923–3181, FAX 970/923–3871), in the Rocky Mountains near Aspen; the **Arrowmont School of Arts and Crafts** (✉ Box 567, Gatlinburg, TN 37738, ☎ 423/436–5860, FAX 423/430–4101), founded in 1945 on 70 acres just a mile from the Great Smoky Mountains National Park; and the **Haystack Mountain School of Crafts** (✉ Box 518, Deer Isle, ME 04627-0518, ☎ 207/348–2306), occupying a shingled, Atlantic-view studio complex on a Maine island. Several focus on traditional folk crafts; the oldest and most active are the **John C. Campbell Folk School** (✉ Rte. 1, Box 14A, Brasstown, NC 28902, ☎ 704/837–2775), whose campus is a National Historic District, and the **Penland School of Crafts** (✉ Penland Rd., Penland, NC 28765, ☎ 704/765–2359, FAX 704/765–7389), on 500 acres in the Blue Ridge Mountains.

SPECIALIZED PROGRAMS
You can study everything from basketry and wooden boatbuilding to papermaking, couture sewing, and weaving. For extensive listings of what's available, consult the *Guide to Art & Craft Workshops* (✉ Shaw Guides Publishers, Box 1295, New York, NY 10023, ☎ 212/799–6464 or 800/247–6553; $16.95 plus $3 shipping for 1991 edition).

Painting and Fine-Arts Workshops

Amateurs can get professional tutelage at intensive programs at inns, resorts, museums, fine-arts centers, and even crafts schools nationwide (☞ Crafts Workshops, *above*).

VARIED PROGRAMS
Diverse programs that embrace disciplines ranging from printmaking and watercolors to painting styles such as portraiture, still life, and landscape are available at schools such as the **Art Institute of Boston** (✉ Continuing Education, 700 Beacon St., Boston, MA 02215, ☎ 617/262–1223) and **Dillman's Sand Lake Lodge** (✉ Box 98, Lac du Flambeau, WI 54538, ☎ 715/588–3143), an old family-style summer resort in northern Wisconsin. Programs abound in Maine, among them the **Maine Coast Art Workshops** (✉ c/o Merle Donovan, Box 236, Port Clyde, ME 04855, ☎ 207/372–8200).

Some workshops concentrate on a specific medium, such as pastels or watercolors, or a specific style or theme—realism, western motifs, or seascapes, for instance. A comprehensive listing is in the *Guide to Art & Craft Workshops* (☞ Crafts Workshops, *above*).

RESOURCES

American Artist (☎ 212/764–7300) magazine lists a wide array of summer programs, such as those in its March issue.

Photography Workshops and Tours

Throughout the year amateurs and professionals sign up for workshops and tours designed both to polish their techniques and to take them to photogenic spots at the best possible times.

WORKSHOPS

Each workshop has a distinctive focus. Some cover theory and practice through fieldwork and seminars in both black-and-white and color photography; these look at the field as both a fine and an applied art that ranges from fashion shots to photojournalism. Established in 1971, the well-respected **Maine Photographic Workshops** (⊠ 2 Central St., Rockport, ME 04856, ☎ 207/236–8581, ℻ 207/236–2558), explores most aspects of photography, as do the well-respected if less picturesquely situated **International Center of Photography** (⊠ 1130 5th Ave., New York, NY 10128, ☎ 212/860–1776, ℻ 212/360–6490) and the **Visual Studies Workshop** (⊠ 31 Prince St., Rochester, NY 14607, ☎ 716/442–8676, ℻ 716/442–1992). The **Friends of Photography Workshops** (⊠ 250 4th St., San Francisco, CA 94103, ☎ 415/495–7000) carries on the tradition of and now encompasses the venerable Ansel Adams Workshop, founded in 1940.

GUIDED PHOTOGRAPHY TOURS

Specialized tours, accompanied by professional photographers and scheduled to catch photogenic spots at optimal times, are offered by many organizations, including **Close-Up Expeditions** (⊠ 858 56th St., Oakland, CA 94608, ☎ 510/654–1548 or 800/457–9553, ℻ 510/654–3043), the official Photographic Society of America tour operator; and **Photo Adventure Tours** (⊠ 2035 Park St., Atlantic Beach, NY 11509, ☎ 516/371–0067 or 800/821–1221, ℻ 516/371–1352).

RESOURCES

American Photo (☎ 212/767–6273) and *Popular Photography* (☎ 212/767–6000) magazines advertise tours and workshops. The *Guide to Photography Workshops & Schools* (⊠ Shaw Guides Publishers, Box 1295, New York, NY 10023, ☎ 212/799–6464 or 800/247–6553) has extensive listings of programs ($19.95 plus $3 shipping).

Volunteer Vacations

Although fees for the nation's hundreds of vacation volunteer programs may be partly tax-deductible, their allure has less to do with money than with the satisfaction that comes from giving something back to society, the excitement of an entirely new activity, and the intensity of the group experience. Will you enjoy it? Yes, if you're flexible and independent, can cope with the unexpected, have a sense of humor, and like to be a team player.

When choosing a program, be sure to ask about insurance, the number of participants and staff, and the standards by which project and leader were chosen.

FIELD RESEARCH

How about tagging dolphins or collecting subtropical plants? Scientists in need of enthusiastic, inexpensive labor for projects like these are happy to enlist help from vacationers, who pay a stipend to cover their own expenses and defray expedition costs. Organizations that match up scientists and vacationers include **Earthwatch** (⊠ Box 9104, 680 Mount Auburn St., Watertown, MA 02272, ☎ 617/926–8200), the oldest in the field; **Smithsonian Research Expeditions Program** (⊠ 490 L'Enfant Plaza SW, Room 4210, Washington, DC 20560, ☎ 202/287–3210); and the **University Research Expeditions Program** (UREP; ⊠ c/o University of California, 2223 Fulton St., Berkeley, CA 94720-7050, ☎ 510/642–6586), with University of California scientists.

ARCHAEOLOGICAL RESEARCH

It's hot, dirty, and strenuous—but you don't have to be an archaeologist to catch the excitement. Earthwatch and UREP (☞ Field Research, *above*) often list digs among their fieldwork opportunities. For other ideas consult the lists in the Archaeological Institute of America's *Fieldwork Opportunities Bulletin* ($11; ⊠ Kendall Hunt Publishing Co., Order Dept., Box 1840, Dubuque, IA 52004-1840, ☎ 800/228–0810).

TRAIL BUILDING AND MAINTENANCE

Helping state and national parks and forests maintain old trails, build new ones, and clean up and replant campgrounds is the mission of several private groups that welcome volunteers—among them the active **Sierra Club** (☞ Group Trips, *above*) and the **Appalachian Mountain Club** (⊠ Trails Conservation Corps, Box 298, Gorham, NH 03581, ☎ 603/466–2721). Many state parks or conservation departments use volunteers, as do the National Park Service, U.S. Fish and Wildlife Service, and U.S. Forest Service.

SOCIAL SERVICE

Building community centers, repairing churches, setting up youth programs, and serving in group homes are just a few activities of volunteer work camps. Contact clearinghouses such as the **Volunteers for Peace** (⊠ 43 Tiffany Rd., Belmont, VT 05730, ☎ 802/259–2759, ℻ 802/259–2922) and the **Council on International Educational Exchange** (⊠ 205 E. 42nd St., New York, NY 10017, ☎ 212/822–2600 or 800/268–6245).

RESOURCES

The **Points of Light Foundation** (⊠ 1737 H St. NW, Washington, DC 20006, ☎ 202/223–9186) and **Volunteers for Peace** (☞ Social Service, *above*) have listings of other volunteer opportunities.

3 The Northeast

Connecticut, Maine, Massachusetts, New Hampshire, New York, Rhode Island, Vermont

The two major metropolitan areas of the Northeast—New York and Boston—offer the best of modern city life, the hurly-burly and intensity that come with so many ambitious, worldly citizens pursuing their dreams. New York City—one of the world's leading financial and cultural capitals—belongs to the world as much as to the country. Boston, the country's oldest (and still leading) college town, has redefined itself as a hub of new service and high-tech industries. As distinguished as each metropolis is, neither entirely defines the region: Captured in a single wide-angle lens, the six states of New England and the massive bulk of New York State are decidedly un-urban, offering a bigger variety of landscapes and outdoor diversions per square mile than any other part of the country.

Beyond the hustle and bustle and the glitz and grime of New York City, the Northeast fans out in waves of increasingly soothing vistas, from the placid charms of the Connecticut River valley through the forests of Vermont and New Hampshire's Green and White mountains to the pristine hinterland of Maine's remote Allagash Wilderness Waterway. Similarly, the "wilderness" of upstate New York begins within an hour's drive of the Bronx: The Hudson River valley lures frazzled urban dwellers northward past the Catskill resorts to vast Adirondack Park—at 6.2 million acres, almost three times as large as Yellowstone

CANADA

QUÉBEC

Montréal

ONTARIO

Ottawa

Massena

Plattsburg
Potsdam
Saranac Lake
Lake
Placid

ADIRONDACK
FOREST
PRESERVE

Watertown

11

87

Toronto

Lake Ontario

Oswego

81

NEW YORK

Glens Falls

Niagara
Falls

Rochester

Oneida

Rome
Utica

Saratoga
Springs

Tonawanda

90

Auburn

Syracuse

90

Mohawk R.

Schenect

Buffalo

Batavia

Geneva

Albany

Five Fingers Lakes

Cortland

Lake Erie

Dunkirk

90

Hornell

Ithaca

81

Oneonta

CATSKILL
FOREST
PRESERVE

Hudson River

Jamestown

17

Olean

Wellsville

Elmira

Binghamton

88

Kingston

Poughkee

17

17

Monticello

87

Scranton

Middletown

PENNSYLVANIA

West
Point

Yonkers

0   100 miles

0   150 km

NEW
JERSEY

New

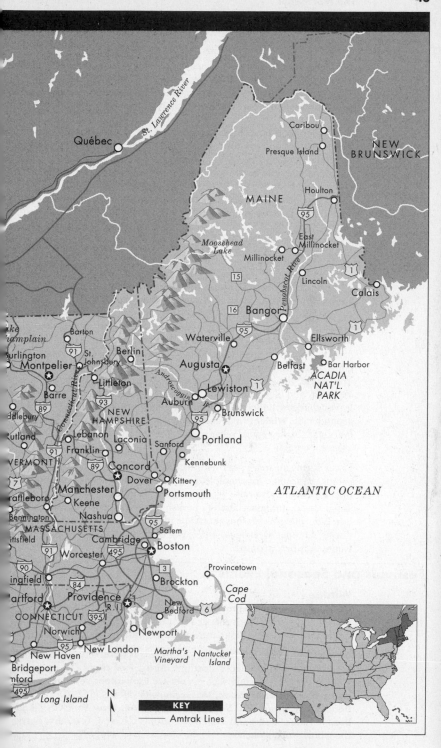

Québec

St. Lawrence River

Caribou

Presque Island

NEW BRUNSWICK

Houlton

MAINE

95

Moosehead Lake

East Millinocket

Millinocket

15

Lincoln

16

Bangor

95

Calais

Penobscot River

1

Barton

Waterville

Ellsworth

91

St. Johnsbury

Berlin

Belfast

Bar Harbor

Burlington

Montpelier

Augusta

ACADIA NAT'L. PARK

Littleton

Androscoggin R.

Lewiston

Barre

89

93

Auburn

1

NEW HAMPSHIRE

Brunswick

95

ddlebury

Connecticut River

Lebanon

Laconia

Portland

utland

Franklin

89

Sanford

Kennebunk

VERMONT

91

Concord

Dover

Kittery

Manchester

Keene

Portsmouth

raftleboro

Nashua

7

Bennington

95

Salem

ittsfield

MASSACHUSETTS

Cambridge

Boston

91

Worcester

495

3

ingfield

90

84

Brockton

Provincetown

artford

Providence

R.I.

Cape Cod

CONNECTICUT

395

New Bedford

6

Norwich

Newport

95

Martha's Vineyard

Nantucket Island

New London

New Haven

Bridgeport

nford

495

Long Island

N

KEY

Amtrak Lines

National Park. At the western end of the state, the wonders of Niagara Falls continue to attract droves of nature-loving, photo-snapping tourists from around the world.

The region was historically defined by the coastline, where the Pilgrims first established a toehold in the New World. Until it veers inland north of Yarmouth, Maine, I–95 skirts the inlets and harbors that sheltered the whaling and trading vessels of 17th- to 19th-century settlers—Mystic, Connecticut; Providence, Rhode Island; Cape Cod, Nantucket, and Plymouth, Massachusetts; and Portland, Maine. Beyond the interstate's exits, in between the living museums and tourist centers, is a region that offers a wealth of diversions—cerebral, spiritual, and athletic. Nowhere else in the country are the seasons so clearly defined. Every season brings its own recreations, whether fishing in New York and in Vermont's Lake Champlain, skiing in the White Mountains, camping on the Appalachian Trail, biking along Maine's rocky coast, sailing on Long Island Sound, applauding world-class musicians in the Berkshires, or watching whales cavort off Cape Cod.

When to Go

In the Northeast each season is distinct, and each has its own beauty. **Spring** blooms start in April along the southern coastal regions, beginning later the farther north you go. This tends to be the quietest period throughout the region because of rains and melting snows. **Summer,** which ranges from a hot 85°F in the southern region to a low 59°F in the north, attracts beach lovers to the islands and coastal regions, while those preferring cooler climes make for the lakes in New York State, the mists of Maine, or the mountains of Massachusetts, Vermont, and New Hampshire. **Autumn** is a kaleidoscope of colors as leaves change from green to burning gold. Temperatures will still be around 55°F. **Winter** brings snow and skiers to the mountain slopes in every state of the region (Vermont is the most popular), while the coastal areas hibernate.

Prices during an area's peak season climb accordingly—Newport hotel rooms in summer, for example, go for nearly double the late-autumn prices. Festivals also raise prices, such as the outdoor music festival at Tanglewood, in Massachusetts's Berkshire mountains. Reservations for hotels during peak seasons should be made well in advance, and travel during summer weekends, especially on Cape Cod's overburdened Route 6, is best avoided.

Festivals and Seasonal Events

Winter

EARLY DEC.➤ The **Nantucket Stroll** (☎ 508/228—1700), the best-known of the many Christmas-season celebrations held throughout the Cape, takes place the first Saturday of the month.

NEW YEAR'S EVE➤ The final day of the year is observed with festivals and entertainment in many locations during **First Night** Celebrations. Among the cities hosting such events are **Burlington, Vermont; Providence Rhode Island; Boston, Massachusetts** (☎ 617/542–1399); and **Danbury, Hartford,** and **Stamford, Connecticut. New York City**'s **Ball Drop in Times Square** (☎ 212/768–1560) is the New Year's Eve party the whole world watches.

MID-JAN.➤ Vermont's **Stowe Winter Carnival** (☎ 802/253–7321) is among the country's oldest such celebrations.

FEB.➤ Well-bred canines take over Madison Square Garden for the **Westminster Kennel Club Dog Show** (☎ 212/465–6000). In the invitational **Annual Empire State Building Run-Up** (☎ 212/736–3100), 125 runners scramble up the 1,576 stairs from the lobby of the Empire State Building to the 86th-floor observation deck.

Spring

MAR.➤ At **maple-sugaring festivals,** held throughout the month and into April, the sugarhouses of **Maine, New Hampshire, Vermont,** and **Massachusetts** demonstrate procedures like maple-tree tapping and sap boiling.

MAR. 17➤ All of **Boston** turns out for the **St. Patrick's Day Parade** (☎ 617/536–4100), while **New York City**'s boisterous version of the **parade** heads down 5th Avenue.

MID-APR.➤ On Patriot's Day in **Boston,** celebrants reenact **Paul Revere's ride** (☎ 617/536–4100) while the **Boston Marathon** (☎ 617/236–1652) fills the streets from Hopkinton to Back Bay.

LATE APR.➤ **Nantucket**'s four-day **Daffodil Festival** celebrates spring with a flower show, shop-window displays, and a procession of antique cars that ends with tailgate picnics at Siasconset.

EARLY MAY➤ New York's **Cherry Blossom Festival** (☎ 718/622–4433) is held at the Brooklyn Botanic Garden.

Summer

JUNE➤ Lincoln Center hosts the **Annual American Crafts Festival** (☎ 212/677–4627) on a couple of weekends during the month.

EARLY JUNE➤ The **Belmont Stakes** (☎ 718/641–4700, ext. 732), Thoroughbred racing's final Triple Crown event, takes place at Belmont Park, in **Elmont, New York.**

MID-JUNE➤ The **Festival of Historic Houses** (☎ 401/831–7440) celebrates the Colonial, Greek Revival, and Victorian homes of **Providence, Rhode Island**'s Benefit Street.

LATE JUNE➤ **Lesbian and Gay Pride Week** (☎ 212/807–7433) in **New York City** includes the world's largest lesbian and gay pride parade. The **New York Jazz Festival** (☎ 212/219–3006) showcases more than 200 groups spread in venues all over town. Besides classic acts, you'll find acid, Latin, and avant-garde jazz.

LATE JUNE–EARLY JULY➤ **Boston**'s annual weeklong Fourth of July celebration, **Harborfest** (☎ 617/227–1528), includes a concert synchronized to fireworks over the harbor.

LATE JUNE–AUG.➤ The **Jacob's Pillow Dance Festival** (☎ 413/243–0745), at **Becket, Massachusetts,** in the Berkshires, hosts performers from various dance traditions.

JULY–AUG.➤ The **Mid-Summer Night Swing** (☎ 212/875–5400) fills the Fountain Plaza of New York City's Lincoln Center with swinging couples and live music; swing lessons are given before the dance. The **Tanglewood Music Festival** (☎ 413/637–1600 or 617/638–9235), at **Lenox, Massachusetts,** the summer home of the Boston Symphony Orchestra, schedules top performers.

JULY 4➤ The **Fourth of July Parade** (☎ 401/245–0750) in **Bristol, Rhode Island,** is the oldest Independence Day parade in the country, attracting thousands of visitors and an array of bands and military units.

MID-JULY➣ Held in the picturesque village of **Wickford, Rhode Island,** the **Wickford Art Festival** (☎ 401/295–5566) is one of the oldest, largest, and most diversified art festivals on the East Coast. Rhode Island's **Newport Music Festival** (☎ 401/846–1133) brings together celebrated musicians for two weeks of concerts in Newport mansions.

LATE JULY➣ Forty wineries take part in the **Finger Lakes Wine Festival** (☎ 607/535–2481), which also brings hay rides, arts and crafts, food, and jazz, blues, and bluegrass music to **Watkins Glen, New York.**

EARLY AUG.➣ The **Maine Lobster Festival** (☎ 207/596–0376) is a public feast held on the first weekend of the month in **Rockland. Ben & Jerry's Folk Festival** (☎ 401/847–3700), held in Fort Adams State Park in **Newport, Rhode Island,** books top names like the Indigo Girls and Joan Baez.

MID-AUG.➣ A week later, also in **Newport,** the **JVC Jazz Festival** (☎ 401/847–3700)—first held at the Newport Casino in 1954 (and formerly called the Newport Jazz Festival), now held in Fort Adams State Park—is one of the nation's premier jazz events.

LATE AUG.➣ The **Cajun & Bluegrass Music and Dance Festival** (☎ 401/351–6312), at the Stepping Stone Ranch in **West Greenwich, Rhode Island,** attracts Cajun music fans from all over.

LATE AUG.–EARLY SEPT.➣ The **U.S. Open Tennis Tournament** (☎ 800/524–8440), in Flushing Meadow/Corona Park, Queens, is one of **New York City**'s premier annual sport events.

Autumn

EARLY SEPT.➣ Summer's close is met with dozens of Labor Day fairs, including the **Vermont State Fair,** in Rutland, and Rhode Island's **Providence Waterfront Festival.** The **Common Ground Country Fair,** in **Windsor, Maine,** is an organic farmer's delight.

EARLY OCT.➣ The big **Columbus Day Parade** (☎ 617/536–4100), in Boston, moves from East Boston to the North End, while south of Boston on the same Columbus Day weekend, you'll find the **Massachusetts Cranberry Harvest Festival** (☎ 508/295–5799 May–Oct.) in both Plymouth and neighboring South Carver's Edaville Cranberry Bog.

OCT.➣ The **Nantucket Cranberry Harvest** (☎ 508/228–1700) is a three-day celebration that includes bog and inn tours and a crafts fair.

EARLY NOV.➣ The **New York City Marathon** (☎ 212/860–4455) is the world's largest; it winds through all five boroughs of the city and finishes at Tavern on the Green in Central Park.

LATE NOV.➣ The **Macy's Thanksgiving Day Parade** (☎ 212/494–5432) is a **New York City** tradition; huge balloons float down Central Park West at 77th Street to Broadway and Herald Square.

Getting Around the Northeast

By Boat

In Rhode Island the **Block Island Ferry** (☎ 401/783–4613) has service from Providence, Newport, and Point Judith to Block Island. **Marine Atlantic** (☎ 800/341–7981) operates ferries between Yarmouth, Nova Scotia, and Bar Harbor, Maine. **Prince of Fundy Cruises** (☎ 800/341–7540) runs ferries between Yarmouth, Nova Scotia, and Portland, Maine, from May through October. **Casco Bay Lines** (☎ 207/774–7871) has ferries from Portland to the islands of Casco Bay. **Maine State Ferry Service** (☎ 207/596–2203) runs from Rockland to Vinalhaven and

Northhaven. For information about ferry service to Martha's Vineyard and Nantucket, *see* Massachusetts. The **Bridgeport and Port Jefferson Steamboat Company** (☎ 203/367–3043 or 516/473–0286) has ferries connecting the north shore of New York's Long Island to Bridgeport, Connecticut. **Cross Sound Ferry** (☎ 203/443–5281) connects New London, Connecticut, with Orient Point, New York, in northeastern Long Island.

By Bus

The major bus lines are **Greyhound Lines** (☎ 800/231–2222) and **Bonanza** (☎ 800/556–3815). **Peter Pan** (☎ 413/781–3320 or 800/237–8747) serves western Massachusetts and Connecticut.

By Car

The chief interstate through New England is I–95, which travels out of New York and along the Connecticut coast to Providence, Rhode Island, and into Boston, Massachusetts, before continuing up through New Hampshire and along the coast of Maine. From Boston I–89 goes through southern New Hampshire to central and northwestern Vermont and on into Canada. The New York State Thruway connects New York City to Albany and then veers northwest to Buffalo. I–87 runs between Albany and Montréal, Canada, and passes by Lake Champlain. Crossing the eastern region between Albany and Boston is the Massachusetts Turnpike (I–90). I–84 runs from Pennsylvania to Massachusetts and connects with I–684, which runs north from the New York metropolitan area, near the Connecticut border. Passing through Hartford is I–91, which links coastal Connecticut with New Hampshire and eastern Vermont.

By Plane

New York City has three major airports served by major domestic and international airlines: **John F. Kennedy International Airport** (☎ 718/244–4444), **LaGuardia Airport** (☎ 718/533–3400), and **Newark Airport** (call specific airlines for information). Upper New York State has the **Albany-Schenectady County Airport** (☎ 518/869–3021), which is served by most major airlines. Connecticut's **Bradley International Airport** (☎ 860/292–2000), outside Hartford, is also served by most major U.S. carriers. All the major domestic air carriers fly into Massachusetts's **Logan International Airport** (☎ 617/561–1800 or 800/235–6426), in Boston, as do several international carriers, such as British Airways. Vermont's main airport is **Burlington International Airport** (☎ 802/863–2874), served by six of the main airlines. For New Hampshire and southern Maine the major airport is **Portland International Airport** (☎ 207/774–7301), also served by several major U.S. airlines. Maine's other key airport is **Bangor International Airport** (☎ 207/947–0384), served by several major U.S. airlines.

By Train

Amtrak (☎ 800/872–7245) is the major long-distance train service for the region. Frequent trains make the run between New York, Stamford, New Haven, New London, Providence, and Boston. Fewer trains run between New York and Hartford. From Boston the *Lakeshore Limited* has train service west, stopping in Springfield and the Berkshires before continuing west to Chicago. The *Vermonter* starts in Washington, D.C., and ends in St. Albans, Vermont. Service to accommodate winter skiers has been initiated between New York and Rutland, Vermont.

Local trains of the region: **Metro North** (☎ 212/532–4900 or 800/638–7646 outside New York City) connects New York City and New

Haven with stops along the coast. The **Massachusetts Bay Transportation Authority** (☎ 617/722–3200) connects Boston with the north and south shores. Canada's **Via Rail** (☎ 800/561–9181) crosses northern Maine on its service between Montréal and Halifax. The **Long Island Railroad** (☎ 516/822–5477) runs from New York City to Montauk on its south-fork route and to Greenport on its north fork.

CONNECTICUT

Updated by
Michelle
Bodak

Capital	Hartford
Population	3,274,000
Motto	He Who Transplanted Still Sustains
State Bird	American robin
State Flower	Mountain laurel
Postal Abbreviation	CT

Statewide Visitor Information

Department of Tourism (✉ 865 Brook St., Rocky Hill 06067, ☎ 860/258–4355 or 800/282–6863 for brochure).

Scenic Drives

The narrow roads that wind through the **Litchfield Hills** in northwestern Connecticut offer scenic delights, especially in the spring and autumn. Each road bridge crossing the beautiful and historic **Merritt Parkway** (Route 15) between **Greenwich** and **Stratford** has its own architecturally significant design. The routes (Routes 57 to 53 to 107 to 302) that connect Exit 42 of the Merritt Parkway in **Westport** to Exit 10 of I–84 in **Newtown** take you by Colonial homesteads, over steep ridges, and alongside the **Saugatuck Reservoir.** In northeastern Connecticut, Route 169 from **Norwich** to **North Woodstock** has been designated a National Scenic Byway.

National and State Parks

National Park

The **Weir Farm National Historic Site** (✉ 735 Nod Hill Rd., Wilton 06897, ☎ 203/834–1896) is the first national park in the United States dedicated to the legacy of an American artist. Hikers and picnickers can take advantage of trails traversing the property's 60 wooded acres and tour J. Alden Weir's studio.

State Parks

One of the largest of Connecticut's 95 parks is the 4,000-acre **White Memorial Foundation** (✉ Rte. 202, Litchfield 06759, ☎ 860/567–0857), with its conservation center, wildlife sanctuary, and 35 mi of hiking, cross-country skiing, and horseback-riding trails. For information on state parks contact the **Department of Tourism** (☞ Statewide Visitor Information, *above*) or the **State Parks Bureau of Outdoor Recreation** (✉ 79 Elm St., Hartford 06106, ☎ 860/424–3200).

COASTAL CONNECTICUT

The state's 253-mi coast comprises a series of bedroom communities serving New York City and smaller towns linked to Connecticut's major cities of Stamford, Bridgeport, New Haven, and New London. Along with its Colonial heritage and 20th-century urban sprawl, the region has numerous nature centers and wilderness preserves for hiking and bird-watching, as well as restored 18th- and 19th-century townships and a wealth of marine and other museums dedicated to keeping Connecticut's past alive.

Visitor Information

Southeastern Connecticut: Connecticut's Mystic and More (✉ Box 89, New London 06320, ☎ 860/444–2206 or 800/863–6569). **Southwestern Connecticut:** Coastal Fairfield County Convention and Visitors Bureau (✉ 297 West Ave., The Gate Lodge–Matthews Park, Norwalk 06850, ☎ 203/854–7825 or 800/866–7925). **New Haven:** Greater New Haven Convention and Visitors District (✉ 1 Long Wharf Dr., Suite 7, New Haven 06511, ☎ 203/777–8550 or 800/332–7829).

Arriving and Departing

By Bus

Greyhound Lines (☎ 800/231–2222). **Bonanza Bus Lines** (☎ 800/556–3815). **Connecticut Transit** (☎ 203/327–7433) provides bus service in the Stamford, Hartford, and New Haven areas. **Southeast Area Transit** (☎ 860/886–2631) runs between East Lyme and Stonington.

By Car

The Merritt Parkway and I–95 are the principal highways on the coast between New York and New Haven. I–95 continues beyond New Haven into Rhode Island. From Hartford, I–91 goes south to New Haven.

By Ferry

The **Bridgeport and Port Jefferson Steamboat Company** (☎ 203/367–3043) has ferries connecting Bridgeport with the north shore of New York's Long Island. **Cross Sound Ferry** (☎ 860/443–5281) connects New London with northeastern Long Island's Orient Point.

By Plane

The state's chief airport is **Bradley International Airport** (☎ 860/627–3000), 12 mi north of Hartford, with scheduled daily flights by most major U.S. airlines. Along the coast, **Igor Sikorsky Memorial Airport** (☎ 203/576–7498), 4 mi south of Stratford, is served by US Airways Express. US Airways Express, Continental Express, and United Express fly into **Tweed/New Haven Airport** (☎ 203/946–8283), 5 mi southeast of New Haven.

By Train

Amtrak (☎ 800/872–7245) stops at Greenwich, Stamford, Bridgeport, New Haven, Hartford, New London, and Mystic. **Metro North** (☎ 212/532–4900 or 800/638–7646) runs between New York City and New Haven, with stops at many towns along the coast.

Exploring Coastal Connecticut

Greenwich, which borders New York state, is the epitome of affluent Fairfield County, with gourmet restaurants and chic boutiques. The **Bruce Museum** (✉ 1 Museum Dr., ☎ 203/869–0376), closed Monday, has wildlife dioramas, a small but worthwhile collection of American Impressionist paintings, and many exhibits about the area. In the northern part of town, the 485-acre **Audubon Center** (✉ 613 Riversville Rd., ☎ 203/869–5272) has 8 mi of secluded hiking trails and exhibits on the local environment. The small barn-red **Putnam Cottage** was built in about 1690 and was operated as Knapp's Tavern during the Revolutionary War. Inside are charts of battles and Colonial-era furnishings. ✉ 243 E. Putnam Ave., Rte. 1, ☎ 203/869–9697. Closed Mon.–Tues., Thurs., and Sat.

Cos Cob is a village within the township of Greenwich. The **Bush-Holley House,** built circa 1732, has paintings by Hassam and Twachtman, sculptures by John Rogers, and pottery by Leon Volkmar. ✉ 39 Strickland Rd., ☎ 203/869–6899. Closed late Dec.–Feb.

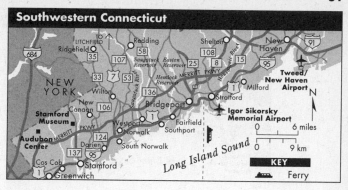

Southwestern Connecticut

Stamford's shoreline may be given over primarily to industry and commerce, but to the north some beautiful nature areas remain. The 118-acre **Stamford Museum and Nature Center** (⌧ 39 Scofieldtown Rd., ☎ 203/322–1646) is a 19th-century working farm and country store with exhibits of farm tools and local Native American life. Shows are offered at the center's observatory and planetarium. In the Champion International Corporation building, downtown, is the **Whitney Museum of American Art at Champion.** Exhibits of primarily 20th-century American painting and photography often include works from the Whitney's permanent collection in New York City. ⌧ *Atlantic St. and Tresser Blvd.,* ☎ *203/358–7630. Free. Closed Sun.–Mon.*

South Norwalk, affectionately dubbed SoNo, is off I–95's Exit 15. Just steps away from an avenue of restored art galleries, restaurants, and boutiques is the **Maritime Aquarium at Norwalk,** which has a huge aquarium, marine vessels, and an IMAX theater. ⌧ *10 N. Water St.,* ☎ *203/ 852–0700.*

Wilton, a well-preserved community with a wooded countryside and good antiques shopping, is just a brief detour away from the coast, up Routes 7 and 33 from Norwalk. Wilton has Connecticut's first national park, **Weir Farm National Historical Site** (☞ National and State Parks, *above*). **Ridgefield,** with its sweeping lawns and stately mansions, is where you'll find northwestern Connecticut atmosphere within an hour of Manhattan. Ridgefield is home to the **Aldrich Museum of Contemporary Art,** which has changing exhibits of cutting-edge works and one of the finest sculpture gardens in the Northeast. ⌧ *258 Main St.,* ☎ *203/438–4519. Closed Mon.*

Westport has long been an artistic and literary community and now is also a trendy hub of shops and eateries. **Sherwood Island State Park** (⌧ I–95 Exit 18, ☎ 203/226–6983) has the only beach (rocky though it may be) accessible year-round between Greenwich and New Haven.

The exclusive Colonial village of **Southport** is on the Pequot River. To get there from Sherwood Island, head east along Greens Farms Road. Greens Farms Road continues into **Fairfield,** the town almost destroyed in a raid by the British in 1779—four houses survived the attack and are still standing on Beach Road. In the northern part of town, the **Connecticut Audubon Society** (⌧ 2325 Burr St., ☎ 203/259–6305) maintains a 160-acre wildlife sanctuary.

Bridgeport, a city that has fallen on hard times, is unsafe at night and unappealing during the day. However, two attractions here warrant visiting. **Beardsley Park and Zoological Gardens** (⌧ 1875 Noble Ave., ☎ 203/576–8082) is Connecticut's only zoo. Here you'll find more than 350 animals as well as a South American rain forest and a

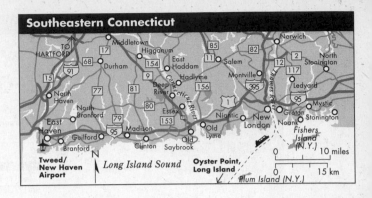

Southeastern Connecticut

carousel. The **Barnum Museum,** associated with onetime resident and mayor P. T. Barnum, has exhibits depicting the great showman's career and a scaled-down model of his famous creation, the three-ring circus. ☒ *820 Main St.,* ☎ *203/331–1104. Closed Mon.*

New Haven is a city of extremes: Although it's prosperous in the area around the common—encompassing the elite campus of Yale University and the numerous shops, museums, and restaurants of Chapel Street—20% of the city's residents live below the poverty level. Stay near the campus and city common, especially at night, and get a good map of the city. Knowledgeable guides give free one-hour walking tours of the **Yale University campus** (☒ 149 Elm St., ☎ 203/432–2300). The **Yale University Art Gallery** (☒ 1111 Chapel St., ☎ 203/432–0600), which is free and is closed Monday, has a collection that spans the centuries and the continents. The **Yale Center for British Art** (☒ 1080 Chapel St., ☎ 203/432–2800) has the most extensive collection of British artworks and rare books outside the United Kingdom; it's free and closed Monday. The **Peabody Museum of Natural History** (☒ 170 Whitney Ave., ☎ 203/432–5050) is the largest of its kind in New England.

The urban buildup that characterizes the Connecticut coast west of New Haven dissipates as you drive east on I–95 toward New London. **Old Saybrook** was once a lively shipbuilding and fishing town; today the bustle comes mostly from its many summer vacationers. On the other side of the Connecticut River from Old Saybrook is **Old Lyme.** The **Florence Griswold Museum** (☒ 96 Lyme St., ☎ 860/434–5542) once housed an art colony that included Childe Hassam. Now the mansion displays these artists' works, along with early furnishings and decorative items. The **Lyme Academy of Fine Arts** (☒ 84 Lyme St., ☎ 860/434–5232) shows works by students and other contemporary artists.

The seagoing community of **New London** has one of the finest deepwater ports on the Eastern seaboard. It is the home of the **U.S. Coast Guard Academy,** whose 100-acre cluster of traditional redbrick buildings includes a museum. The three-masted training bark *Eagle* may be boarded when in port. ☒ *15 Mohegan Ave.,* ☎ *860/444–8270. Free.*

In **Groton,** across the Thames River from New London, is the U.S. submarine base. The world's first nuclear-powered submarine, the *Nautilus,* was launched from here in 1954 and is now permanently berthed and open to visitors. Just outside the entrance to the base is the **U.S. Nautilus/Submarine Force Museum,** which contains submarine memorabilia, artifacts, and displays, including working periscopes and controls. ☒ *Crystal Lake Rd.,* ☎ *860/449–3174 or 860/449–3558. Free.*

Mystic, the celebrated whaling seaport, is a few miles east of Groton. **Mystic Seaport** (☒ 75 Greenmanville Ave., ☎ 860/572–0711)—the nation's largest maritime museum, on 17 riverfront acres—has 19th-century sailing vessels you can board, a maritime village with historic homes, steamboat cruises, small-boat rentals, and craftspeople who give demonstrations. At the **Mystic Marinelife Aquarium** (⊠ Off I–95 on Coogan Blvd., ☎ 860/536–3323) you can see more than 6,000 specimens and 50 live exhibits of sea life.

Little **Stonington Village** is a quiet fishing community clustered around white-spired churches. Past the historic buildings that surround the town green and border Water Street is the imposing **Old Lighthouse Museum,** where you'll find shipping, whaling, and early village displays. Climb to the top of the granite tower for a spectacular view of the sound and the ocean. ⊠ *7 Water St.,* ☎ *860/535–1440.*

Dining and Lodging

The **Covered Bridge B&B Reservation Service** (☎ 860/542–5944) and **Nutmeg B&B Agency** (☎ 860/236–6698) are reliable statewide services for B&Bs and small inns. **B&B, Ltd.** (☎ 203/469–3260) is a service for small bed-and-breakfasts, inns, and rooms rented in private homes. Rooms are costliest in summer and autumn. A 12% lodging tax is added to each bill. For price ranges *see* Charts 1 (B) and 2 (B) *in* On the Road with Fodor's.

Greenwich

$$$$ ✕ **Restaurant Jean–Louis.** Roses, Villeroy & Boch china, and crisp,
★ white tablecloths with lace underskirts complement extraordinary food, carefully served. Specialties include quail-and-vegetable ragout with foie gras sauce and, for dessert, lemon-and-pear gratin. ⊠ *61 Lewis St.,* ☎ *203/622–8450. Jacket required. AE, D, DC, MC, V. Closed Sun. No lunch Mon.–Thurs.*

$$$$ ✕⌂ **Homestead Inn.** Each bedroom is decorated with attractive furniture and period reproductions. The La Grange Restaurant (jacket required) serves outstanding classic French cuisine. ⊠ *420 Field Point Rd., 06830,* ☎ FAX *203/869–7500. 23 rooms. Restaurant, meeting rooms. CP. AE, DC, MC, V.*

Mystic

$$$$ ✕⌂ **Inn at Mystic.** The highlight of this inn, which sprawls over 15 hilltop acres and overlooks Pequotsepos Cove, is the five-bedroom Georgian Colonial mansion in which Lauren Bacall and Humphrey Bogart honeymooned. Almost as impressive are the rambling four-bedroom gatehouse and the unusually attractive motor lodge. The sunlighted Floodtide Restaurant serves traditional New England fare. ⊠ *Rtes. 1 and 27, 06355,* ☎ *860/536–9604 or 800/237–2415,* FAX *860/572–1635. 68 rooms. Restaurant, pool, tennis courts, dock, boating. AE, D, DC, MC, V.*

$$$$ ✕⌂ **Whaler's Inn and Motor Court.** In the heart of downtown, this group of white-clapboard buildings includes the original Victorian guest house, the sprawling main building, and the motor court across the parking lot. Decor is modern with nautical touches; there are some canopy beds, but mostly it's department-store maple. ⊠ *20 E. Main St., 06355,* ☎ *860/536–1506 or 800/243–2588 outside CT,* FAX *860/ 572–1250. 41 rooms. 3 restaurants, meeting rooms. AE, D, MC, V.*

New Haven

$ ✕ **Frank Pepe's.** The big ovens on the back wall bake pizzas that are served by smart-mouthed waitresses. On weekend evenings the wait for a table can be more than an hour, but the pizza—the sole item on the menu—is worth it. ⊠ *157 Wooster St.,* ☎ *203/865–5762. Reservations not accepted. No credit cards. Closed Tues. No lunch Mon. and Wed.–Thurs.*

$$$$ 🏨 **Three Chimneys Inn.** This 1870 Victorian mansion is one of the most
★ polished small inns in the state. Rooms have posh Georgian furnishings: mahogany four-poster beds, oversize armoires, Chippendale desks, and Oriental rugs. Three rooms have fireplaces. ⊠ *1201 Chapel St., 06511,* ☎ *203/789–1201,* ⅀ *203/776–7363. 10 rooms. Business services, meeting rooms. CP. AE, D, MC, V.*

New London

$$$$ 🏨 **Lighthouse Inn.** This is the quintessential grand seaside inn, with splendid views of Long Island Sound. Although rooms in the turn-of-the-century mansion are more expensive and have better views than the carriage-house rooms, furnishings in both are similar and include canopy beds and wing-back armchairs. ⊠ *6 Guthrie Pl., 06320,* ☎ *860/443–8411,* ⅀ *860/437–7027. 50 rooms. Restaurant, bar. AE, MC, V.*

North Stonington

$$$–$$$$ ✕🏨 **Randall's Ordinary.** Famed for its open-hearth cooking of authentic
★ Colonial dishes, the Ordinary (reservations essential for dinner) serves extraordinary lunches and three-course fixed-price dinners, served by staff in period costume. Accommodations are available in the John Randall House, where rooms are simply furnished with antiques, or in the converted barn. ⊠ *Rte. 2, Box 243, 06359,* ☎ *860/599–4540,* ⅀ *860/599–3308. 15 rooms. Restaurant. CP. AE, MC, V.*

Norwalk

$$$$ ✕🏨 **Silvermine Tavern.** The cozy rooms have wide-plank floors and
★ lie above the circa 1775 tavern and the separate country store. A low ceiling, Colonial decor, glowing candles, and many windows make the landmark restaurant an intimate setting for traditional New England favorites. ⊠ *194 Perry Ave., 06850,* ☎ *203/847–4558,* ⅀ *203/847–9171. 10 rooms. Restaurant. CP. AE, DC, MC, V. Closed Tues.*

Old Lyme

$$$–$$$$ ✕🏨 **Bee & Thistle Inn.** The innkeepers have furnished this two-story
★ 1756 Colonial on the Lieutenant River with period antiques and plenty of warm touches. Most rooms have canopy or four-poster beds. Outstanding American cuisine is served in one of the most romantic dining rooms around. ⊠ *100 Lyme St., 06371,* ☎ *860/434–1667 or 800/622–4946 outside CT,* ⅀ *860/434–3402. 11 rooms. Restaurant. AE, D, DC, MC, V. Closed Tues. and 1st ½ of Jan.*

Stamford

$$–$$$ ✕ **Fjord Fisheries.** Stamford's best fish house is in an unappealing concrete building about five minutes from Exit 6 on I–95; call for directions. A chatty yuppified bar is up front and in back is a small dining room. There are many preparations of fresh fish such as grouper, halibut, salmon, and trout. ⊠ *49 Brownhouse Rd.,* ☎ *203/325–0255. Reservations essential. AE, DC, MC, V. Closed Mon. No lunch.*

Westbrook

$$–$$$ ✕ **Aleia's.** This is an elegant dining room, with dark wainscoting and
★ bentwood chairs. It has a superb, eclectic menu with several nouvelle-inspired pasta, veal, and poultry dishes. ⊠ *1353 Boston Post Rd.,* ☎ *860/399–5050. AE, MC, V. Closed Mon. No lunch.*

$$$$ 🏨 **Water's Edge Inn & Resort.** With a spectacular setting on Long Island Sound, this traditional weathered gray-shingle compound is one of the Connecticut shore's premier resorts. Rooms in the main build-

ing, though not as large as the suites in surrounding outbuildings, have better views and nicer furnishings. ⊠ *1525 Boston Post Rd., 06498,* ☎ *860/399–5901 or 800/222–5901,* FAX *860/399–6172. 98 rooms. Restaurant, bar, indoor and outdoor pools, hot tub, health club, tennis court, volleyball, beach, meeting rooms. AE, D, DC, MC, V.*

Westport

$$$ ✕ **Mansion Clam House.** Here, the nautical atmosphere is casual, the service is friendly, and the oysters and Louisiana crawfish tails are outstanding. There are also a few chicken and steak entrées for the crustacean-shy. ⊠ *541 Riverside Ave.,* ☎ *203/454–7979. AE, MC, V.*

$$$$ ✕🏠 **Inn at National Hall.** The inn's redbrick building on the down-★ town banks of the Saugatuck River belies its whimsical, exotic interior. Each room is a study in innovative restoration, wall-stenciling, trompe l'oeil, and decorative design. Outstanding Continental dishes are served in the lushly decorated Restaurant Zanghi (reservations essential). ⊠ *2 Post Rd. W, 06880,* ☎ *203/221–1351 or 800/628–4255,* FAX *203/221–0276. 15 rooms. Restaurant, in-room VCRs, meeting room. Full breakfast. AE, DC, MC, V.*

Campgrounds

Riverdale Farm Campsites (⊠ 111 River Rd., Clinton, ☎ 860/669–5388). **Hammonasset Beach State Park** (⊠ I–95 Exit 62, Madison, ☎ 203/245–1817).

Nightlife and the Arts

Nightlife

Bars and clubs are sprinkled throughout southern Connecticut. The best of them are concentrated in **Westport, South Norwalk, New Haven's** Chapel West area, and along **New London's** Bank Street.

Foxwoods (☎ 860/885–3000), an enormous gambling and entertainment complex on the Mashantucket Pequots Reservation off Route 2 near Ledyard (8 mi north of Groton), is the world's largest casino. Here you can try your hand at poker, baccarat, slot machines, blackjack, and bingo. The new **Mohegan Sun** casino (☎ 860/848–5682), in Uncasville, offers more of the same, though on a smaller scale.

The Arts

The Connecticut coast's wealth of successful repertory and Broadway-style theaters includes the **Goodspeed Opera House** (⊠ East Haddam, ☎ 860/873–8668). The **Long Wharf Theatre** (⊠ New Haven, ☎ 203/787–4282) is known for its revivals of neglected classics. The **Shubert Performing Arts Center** (⊠ New Haven, ☎ 203/562–5666) presents an array of productions. **Stamford Center for the Arts** (☎ 203/325–4466) offers everything, from one-act plays to musicals. In summer the **Westport Playhouse** (☎ 203/227–4177) presents a series of first-rate plays. The **Yale Repertory Theatre** (⊠ New Haven, ☎ 203/432–1234) stages star-studded dramas.

Most towns along the coast have outdoor summer concerts and music festivals, and some have smaller regional theaters. Call area tourist offices for details (☞ Visitor Information, *above*).

Outdoor Activities and Sports

Fishing

Saltwater fishing is best from June through October; bass, bluefish, and flounder are popular catches. Boats are available from **Hel-Cat Dock** (⊠ Groton, ☎ 860/445–5991), **Tigra II Boat Charters** (⊠ Norwalk,

☎ 203/259–7719), **Brewer Yacht Charters** (✉ Westbrook, ☎ 203/421–0000), and **Captain John's Dock** (✉ Waterford, ☎ 860/443–7259).

Golf

Danbury's 18-hole **Richter Park Golf Course** (✉ 100 Aunt Hack Rd., ☎ 203/792–2550) is one of the top public courses in the country. Two other 18-hole courses are the **H. Smith Richardson Golf Course** (✉ 2425 Morehouse Hwy., Fairfield, ☎ 203/255–7300) and the Robert Trent Jones– and Gary Player–designed courses at the **Lyman Orchards Golf Club** (✉ Rte. 147, Middlefield, ☎ 860/349–8055).

Water Sports

Dodson Boat Yard (✉ 194 Water St., Stonington, ☎ 860/535–1507), **Longshore Sailing School** (✉ Longshore Club Park, Westport, ☎ 203/226–4646), and **Shaffer's Boat Livery** (✉ Mason's Island Rd., Mystic, ☎ 203/536–8713) rent sailboats and motorboats.

Shopping

Southwestern Connecticut

Route 7, which runs through **Wilton** and **Ridgefield,** has dozens of fine antiques sheds and boutiques. Of particular note is **Cannondale Village** (✉ Just off Rte. 7, Wilton, ☎ 203/762–2233), a pre–Civil War farm village turned shopping complex. Washington Street in **South Norwalk** (SoNo) has excellent galleries and crafts dealers. The **Stamford Town Center** (✉ 100 Greyrock Pl., ☎ 203/356–9700) houses 130 mostly upscale shops. Main Street in **Westport** is like an outdoor mall, with J. Crew, Ann Taylor, Coach, and dozens more fashionable shops. Downtown **New Canaan, Darien,** and **Greenwich** are also renowned for their swank brand-name stores and boutiques.

Southeastern Connecticut

The New Haven and New London areas have typical concentrations of shopping centers. **Clinton Crossing Premium Outlets** (✉ I–95 Exit 63, Clinton, ☎ 860/664–0700) has 70 upscale shops. **Westbrook Factory Stores** (✉ I–95 Exit 65, Westbrook, ☎ 860/399– 8656) has 55 outlets. Downtown **Mystic** has an interesting collection of boutiques and galleries. **Olde Mistick Village** (✉ I–95 Exit 90, Mystic, ☎ 860/536–1641), a re-created Colonial village, has crafts and souvenir shops. The **Tradewinds Gallery** (✉ 20 W. Main St., Mystic, ☎ 860/536–0119) specializes in antique prints and maps. The **Essex–Saybrook Antiques Village** (✉ 345 Middlesex Turnpike, Old Saybrook, ☎ 860/388–0689) has more than 125 dealers. **Old Lyme, Guilford,** and **Stonington** are also strong on antiques.

THE LITCHFIELD HILLS

Here, in the foothills of the Berkshires, is some of the most spectacular and unspoiled scenery in the state. Grand old inns—most of them fairly expensive—are plentiful, as are surprisingly sophisticated eateries. Rolling farmlands abut thick forests, and engaging trails traverse the state parks and forests. Two rivers, the Housatonic and the Farmington, attract anglers and canoeing enthusiasts, and there are two sizable lakes, Waramaug and Bantam. Most towns are anchored by sweeping town greens and stately homes and offer a glimpse of quiet New England village life as it probably existed two centuries ago.

Visitor Information

Litchfield Hills Travel Council (✉ Box 968, Litchfield 06759, ☎ 860/567–4506).

Exploring the Litchfield Hills

The mountainous northern towns of **Sharon, Lakeville, Salisbury,** and **Norfolk** are crisscrossed by scenic winding roads. Auto-racing fans come in summer to **Lime Rock Park** (⊠ Rte. 112, Lakeville, ☎ 860/435–2571), home to the best road racing in the Northeast.

Everything seems to exist on a larger scale in **Litchfield** than in neighboring towns: Enormous white Colonials line broad streets shaded by majestic elms, and serene Litchfield Green is surrounded by lovely shops and restaurants. Near the green is the **Tapping Reeve House and Law School** (⊠ 82 South St., ☎ 860/567–4501), America's first law school, which was founded in 1773. Alumni include six U.S. cabinet members, 26 U.S. senators, and more than 100 members of the U.S. House of Representatives. It's closed Monday and mid-October–mid-May. The **Litchfield Historical Society Museum** (⊠ Rtes. 63 and 118, ☎ 860/567–4501) has several well-laid-out galleries, an extensive reference library, and information on the town's many historic buildings. It's closed mid-November–mid-April. **White Flower Farm** (⊠ Rte. 63, ☎ 860/567–8789), where much of America shops in person or by mail for perennials and bulbs, is a restful stop.

To the south, the quiet villages of **Washington, Roxbury,** and **Bridgewater** offer a gentler landscape, in which numerous actors and writers seek refuge from the din of Manhattan and Hollywood. You can buy the ingredients for a gourmet picnic lunch—try the **Pantry** (⊠ Washington, ☎ 860/868–0258)—then laze on the shores of sparkling Lake Waramaug or enjoy a leisurely country drive along precipitous ridges, passing gracious farmsteads and meadows alive with wildflowers.

Dining and Lodging

Litchfield

$$$$ ✕ **West Street Grill.** This small, unpretentious dining room on Litchfield's quaint shopping street is the favorite of local glitterati, but all are warmly welcomed. If you start off with the grilled peasant bread with Parmesan aioli, you'll have a tough time making room for one of the imaginative grilled fish, poultry, and lamb dishes. ⊠ *43 West St. (Rte. 202),* ☎ *203/567–3885. AE, MC, V.*

New Preston

$$–$$$ ✕ **Doc's Restaurant.** Though in a small nondescript house across from Lake Waramaug, this place with mismatched chairs and tables covered with butcher's paper serves sophisticated northern Italian food, with a menu that changes daily and relies heavily on fresh local produce. You might choose a designer pizza, fresh pasta, or one of the vegetarian or game entrées. ⊠ *Rte. 45 and Flirtation Ave.,* ☎ *860/868–9415. Reservations essential. No credit cards. BYOB. Closed Mon.–Tues. No lunch Labor Day–Memorial Day.*

$$$$ ✕▦ **Boulders Inn.** This is the most idyllic and prestigious of the inns
★ along Lake Waramaug's uneven shoreline. The Boulders opened in 1940 but still looks like the private home it was at the turn of the century. Apart from the main house, a carriage house and several guest houses command panoramic views of the countryside and the lake. Rooms contain Victorian antiques, interesting odds and ends, and wood-burning fireplaces; four have double whirlpool baths. The Boulders' window-lined, stone-wall dining room (no lunch; call for dinner hours) is outstanding. ⊠ *E. Shore Rd. (Rte. 45), 06777,* ☎ *860/868–0541 or 800/552–6853,* ℻ *860/868–1925. 17 rooms. Restaurant, lake, tennis courts, boating. MAP. AE, MC, V.*

Norfolk

$$$$ ★ ᠍ **Greenwoods Gate.** This neatly preserved Colonial is possibly the state's foremost romantic hideaway. In each of the four suites, beds are covered in starched white linens. The Levi Thompson Suite is the most interesting: A short flight of stairs leads to a small sitting area with a cathedral ceiling; from here two additional staircases, which have solid cherry hand-tapered railings, lead to either side of an enormous master bed. A spacious two-bedroom suite with its own den and library is the inn's most popular accommodation. ⊠ *105 Greenwoods Rd. E (Rte. 44), 06058,* ☎ *860/542–5439. 4 suites. Full breakfast, afternoon tea, predinner wine and snacks. No credit cards.*

Washington

$$$$ ✕᠍ **Mayflower Inn.** Though certain suites at this inn will set you back $550 a night, the place is always booked well ahead (and with guests who are only a tad livelier than the Joshua Reynolds portrait in the living room). Streams and trails crisscross the 28-acre grounds. The inn is impeccably decorated: Guest rooms have fine antiques and four-poster canopy beds. The mouthwatering cuisine includes New York strip steak and Maine shellfish risotto. ⊠ *118 Woodbury Rd. (Rte. 47), 06793,* ☎ *860/868–9466,* ℻ *860/868–1497. 25 rooms. Restaurant, pool, tennis courts, health club, meeting rooms. AE, MC, V.*

Woodbury

$$$ ★ ✕ **Good News Café.** The emphasis here is on healthful, innovative fare: duck breast schnitzel with herbed sweet potato gnocchi is a tasty example. Or you can just bounce in for cappuccino and munchies—there's a separate room just for this purpose, decorated with a fascinating collection of vintage radios. ⊠ *694 Main St. S,* ☎ *203/266–4663. AE, MC, V. Closed Tues.*

Nightlife and the Arts

World-renowned artists and ensembles perform Friday and Saturday evening June–August at the **Norfolk Chamber Music Festival** (☎ 860/ 542–3000), at the Music Shed on the Ellen Battell Stoeckel Estate at the northwest corner of the Norfolk green. Students from the **Yale School of Music** perform Thursday evening and Saturday morning.

Outdoor Activities and Sports

Canoeing

Clarke Outdoors (⊠ West Cornwall, ☎ 860/672–6365) offers canoe and kayak rentals as well as 10-mi trips from Falls Village to Housatonic Meadow State Park.

Hiking

The Litchfield Hills area has terrific hiking terrain, with **Haystack Mountain, Dennis Hill** (⊠ Both on Rte. 272, Norfolk), and the 684-acre **Sharon Audubon Center** (⊠ Cornwall Bridge Rd., ☎ 860/364–0520) offering the region's best opportunities.

Ski Areas

Mohawk Mountain (⊠ Cornwall, ☎ 860/672–6100). **Ski Sundown** (⊠ New Hartford, ☎ 860/379–9851). **Woodbury Ski Area** (⊠ Woodbury, ☎ 203/263–2203).

Shopping

The best antiques and crafts shopping is along Route 6 in **Woodbury** and **Southbury,** Route 45 in **New Preston,** U.S. 7 in **Kent,** Route 128 in **West Cornwall,** and U.S. 202 in **Bantam.**

ELSEWHERE IN CONNECTICUT

The Connecticut River and Hartford

Arriving and Departing

Bradley International Airport is the main airport. **Amtrak, Greyhound,** and **Bonanza** provide service to the Hartford area (☞ Coastal Connecticut, *above*). By car take I–91 north from New Haven or I–84, which cuts diagonally southwest–northeast through the state. Head north along Route 9 from Old Saybrook for a scenic drive through this historic area.

What to See and Do

The Connecticut River valley meanders through rolling hills, offering a taste of Colonial history as well as sophisticated inns. Call the **Connecticut River Valley and Shoreline Visitors Council** (☒ 393 Main St., Middletown 06457, ☎ 860/347–0028 or 800/486–3346) for information. Also try the **Greater Hartford Tourism District** (☒ 234 Murphy Rd., Hartford 06114, ☎ 860/244–8181 or 800/793–4480).

Essex, on the west bank of the Connecticut River, is where the first submarine, the *American Turtle,* was built. A full-size reproduction is at the **Connecticut River Museum** (☒ Steamboat Dock, ☎ 860/767–8269). In **East Haddam** is the region's leading oddity: a 24-room oak-and-fieldstone hilltop castle that is part of **Gillette Castle State Park** (☒ 67 River Rd., off Rte. 82, ☎ 860/526–2336). East Haddam is also the home of the **Goodspeed Opera House** (☒ Rte. 82, ☎ 860/873–8668). The upper floors of this elaborate 1876 structure have served as a venue for theatrical performances for more than a century.

Hartford, known as the Insurance Capital of America, is the state capital as well. **Mark Twain** made his home here in an extravagant Victorian mansion (☒ 351 Farmington Ave., ☎ 860/493–6411). The Federal **Old State House** (☒ 800 Main St., ☎ 860/522–6766) was designed by Charles Bulfinch, architect of the U.S. Capitol. Admission is free.
★ Hartford's most noteworthy attraction is the **Wadsworth Atheneum** (☒ 600 Main St., ☎ 860/278–2670). Along with changing exhibits, its more than 50,000 works span 5,000 years of art, including paintings by the Hudson River School, the Impressionists, and 20th-century painters.

Dining and Lodging

$$$–$$$$ ✕ **Restaurant du Village.** A black wrought-iron gate beckons you away from the tony antiquaries of Chester's quaint Main Street to this classic little Colonial storefront, painted in historic Newport blue and adorned with flower boxes. Here you can sample exquisite classic French cuisine—escargots in puff pastry, filet mignon—while recapping the day's shopping coups. ☒ *59 Main St., Chester,* ☎ *860/526–5301. AE, MC, V. Closed Mon., and Tues. Oct.–Apr. No lunch.*

$$$ ✕🖫 **Griswold Inn.** The Gris, which has been offering rooms since 1776, sometimes goes overboard in its efforts to sustain its nautical character. Bedrooms have original beam ceilings and antique and reproduction furnishings. With its worn floorboard and exposed ceiling beams, the dining room is probably the most Colonial. The restaurant serves no-frills traditional American fare. ☒ *36 Main St., Essex 06426,* ☎ *860/767–1776,* ℻ *860/767–0481. 28 rooms. Dining room, taproom, meeting room. CP. AE, MC, V.*

$$$$ ✕🏨 **Copper Beech Inn.** A magnificent copper beech tree shades the imposing main building of this Victorian inn, which is furnished in period pieces. Each of the main house's four guest rooms has an old-fashioned tub; the nine rooms in the carriage house are more modern and have private decks. Seven acres of wooded grounds and groomed terraced gardens create an atmosphere of privileged seclusion. Country pâté and game dishes are the highlight of the distinctive country French menu in the romantic dining room (reservations essential; jacket and tie; closed Monday year-round and Tuesday January–March). ⊠ *46 Main St., Ivoryton 06442,* ☎ *860/767–0330,* ℻ *860/ 767–7840. 13 rooms. Restaurant, bar. CP. AE, DC, MC, V.*

$$$$ ✕🏨 **Goodwin Hotel.** Considering this grand city hotel's stately exte-
★   rior (a dark red, ornate classical facade), rooms are nondescript. Yet they are large and tastefully decorated and have Italian marble baths—and they're the best in town. The clubby, mahogany-panel Pierpont's Restaurant serves commendable new American fare. Along with an unsurprising selection of steak, chicken, and fish entrées, you can order unusual side dishes, such as celery-root chips. ⊠ *1 Haynes St., Hartford 06103,* ☎ *860/246–7500 or 800/922–5006,* ℻ *860/247–4576. 135 rooms. Restaurant, exercise room, meeting rooms. AE, D, DC, MC, V.*

MAINE

By Ed and
Roon Frost

Updated by
Hilary Nangle

Capital	Augusta
Population	1,243,000
Motto	I Direct
State Bird	Chickadee
State Flower	White pinecone and tassel
Postal Abbreviation	ME

Statewide Visitor Information

Maine Publicity Bureau (⊠ 325B Water St., Box 2300, Hallowell 04347, ☎ 207/623–0363 or 800/533–9595 outside ME, ℻ 207/623–0388). **Maine Innkeepers Association** (⊠ 305 Commercial St., Portland 04101, ☎ 207/773–7670).

Scenic Drives

Any road that offers views of Maine's dramatic **coastline** is usually worth exploring; *see* Exploring sections, *below,* for recommended coastal routes. For a leisurely inland excursion, try **Routes 37** and **35** from Bridgton north through the Waterfords to the charming resort village of Bethel, continuing north on **Route 26** past the Sunday River ski resort to Grafton Notch State Park and into northern New Hampshire.

National and State Parks

National Park

★ **Acadia National Park** (⊠ Box 177, Bar Harbor 04609, ☎ 207/288–3338), with fine stretches of shoreline and the highest mountains along the East Coast, offers camping, hiking, biking, and boating.

State Parks

More than two dozen state parks offer outdoor recreation along the coast and in less-traveled interior sections. For more information contact the **Bureau of Parks and Lands** (⊠ State House Station 22, Augusta 04333, ☎ 207/287–3821).

THE COAST: FROM KITTERY TO PEMAQUID POINT

Maine's southern coast has sandy beaches, historic towns, fine restaurants, and factory-outlet malls within an easy day's trip from many points in New England. Maine's largest city, Portland, is small enough to be seen in a day or two. Near Portland are Freeport, a mecca for shoppers, and Boothbay Harbor, the state's boating capital.

Visitor Information

Boothbay Harbor Region: Chamber of Commerce (⊠ Box 356, Boothbay Harbor 04538, ☎ 207/633–2353). **Freeport:** Merchants Association (⊠ Box 452, 04032, ☎ 207/865–1212). **Kennebunk-Kennebunkport:** Chamber of Commerce (⊠ 171 Port Rd., Kennebunk 04043, ☎ 207/967–0857). **Portland:** Greater Portland Chamber of Commerce (⊠ 145 Middle St., Portland, ☎ 207/772–2811). Additional information is available at the **Maine Publicity Bureau** (⊠ Rte. 1 [Exit 17 off I–95], Yarmouth, ☎ 207/846–0833; ⊠ Rte. 1 and I–95, Kittery, ☎ 207/439–1319).

Arriving and Departing

By Bus
Vermont Transit (☏ 207/772–6587), part of Greyhound Lines, links Portsmouth, New Hampshire, with Portland, Maine. **Concord Trailways** (☏ 800/639–3317) has daily year-round service between Boston and Bangor (via Portland), with a coastal route connecting towns between Brunswick and Searsport.

By Car
From Boston take U.S. 1 north to I–95, passing north through the short New Hampshire seacoast to Kittery, the first town in Maine. I–95 continues past Portland (I–295 gives access to the city) and Freeport (Exit 20 for the outlet stores). Pick up U.S. 1 in Brunswick to reach the coastal communities of Down East.

By Plane
Portland International Jetport (☏ 207/774–7301), 3 mi from Portland, has scheduled daily flights by major U.S. carriers.

Exploring the Coast from Kittery to Pemaquid Point

York County, and Kittery in particular, is probably better known these days for its outlet shopping than for its beaches. But those who crave the scenic coastline will appreciate the way Routes 103 and 1A hug the coastline and offer maritime scenery.

Route 1A north passes through fashionable **York Harbor** and the midriff-to-elbow summer cottages of **York Beach. Ogunquit,** a few miles north of the Yorks, is famed for its long white-sand beach and attractive galleries, shops, restaurants, and homes.

★ **Kennebunkport** is a picture-perfect town. Dock Square is the busy town center, lined with shops and galleries. **Ocean Avenue** follows the Kennebunk River to the sea, then winds around Cape Arundel.

Portland is a thriving seaport whose restaurants, coffee houses, and shops evoke a romantic mood. On Congress Square, the distinguished **Portland Museum of Art** has a strong collection of seascapes and landscapes by such masters as Winslow Homer, John Marin, Andrew Wyeth, and Marsden Hartley. ✉ *7 Congress Sq.,* ☏ *207/775–6148 or 207/773–2787. Closed Mon.*

★ Portland's **Old Port Exchange,** built following the Great Fire of 1866, was revitalized in the 1960s by artists and craftspeople. Now it is the city's shopping and dining hub, with boutiques, cafés, restaurants, and easy access to the waterfront. Allow a couple of hours to stroll on Market, Exchange, Middle, and Fore streets. Make the effort, too, to sample **Casco Bay** on a sunny day aboard one of the local ferries.

Freeport, 17 mi north of Portland, is the home of L. L. Bean, which attracts some 3.5 million shoppers a year. Nearby, like seedlings under a mighty spruce, more than 100 other outlets have sprouted (☞ Shopping, *below*).

Bath is farther up the coast. The **Maine Maritime Museum and Shipyard** has a collection to stir the nautical dreams of old salts and young. You can watch boatbuilders wield their tools on classic Maine boats at the restored shipyard. ✉ *243 Washington St.,* ☏ *207/443–1316.*

Wiscasset bills itself as "Maine's prettiest village" and lives up to it with historic homes, antiques shops, and museums overlooking the Sheepscot River.

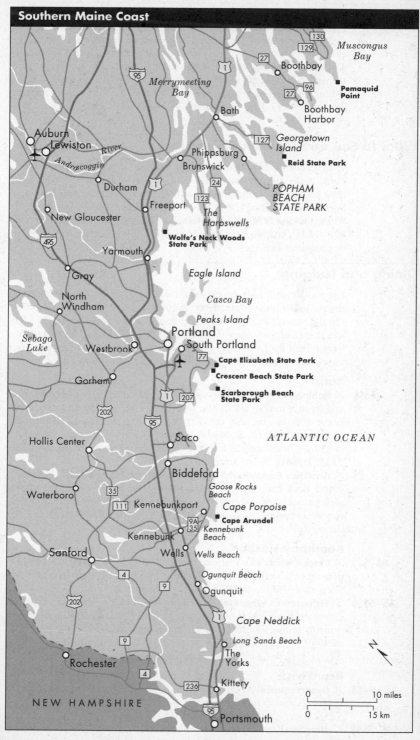

Southern Maine Coast

Muscongus Bay

130

129

27

Boothbay

96

27

Pemaquid Point

Boothbay Harbor

95

Merrymeeting Bay

1

Bath

127

Georgetown Island

Reid State Park

Auburn

Lewiston

Androscoggin River

Phippsburg

Brunswick

POPHAM BEACH STATE PARK

Durham

1

24

123

Freeport

The Harpswells

New Gloucester

Wolfe's Neck Woods State Park

495

Yarmouth

Eagle Island

Gray

Casco Bay

North Windham

Peaks Island

Sebago Lake

Portland

Westbrook

South Portland

77

Cape Elizabeth State Park

Gorham

Crescent Beach State Park

1

207

Scarborough Beach State Park

202

ATLANTIC OCEAN

95

Hollis Center

Saco

Biddeford

Goose Rocks Beach

Waterboro

35

Cape Porpoise

111

Kennebunkport

Cape Arundel

9A

35

Kennebunk Beach

Kennebunk

Sanford

Wells

Wells Beach

4

Ogunquit Beach

9

Ogunquit

202

Cape Neddick

1

Long Sands Beach

9

The Yorks

Rochester

4

Kittery

236

NEW HAMPSHIRE

95

Portsmouth

N

0   10 miles

0   15 km

Boothbay Harbor swells in summer with visitors and seasonal residents. Plan to wander the shops and waterfront or hop on an excursion boat
★ to **Monhegan Island** for the day. At **Pemaquid Point** be sure your camera stand is at the ready for a shot of a much-photographed lighthouse. At **Colonial Pemaquid Restoration** you'll see the excavations that have turned up thousands of artifacts from an early 17th-century English fishing and trading settlement and from even earlier Native American settlements. ⊠ *Rte. 130,* ☎ *207/677–2423. Closed Labor Day– Memorial Day.*

What to See and Do with Children

The old-fashioned pinball machines and hand-cranked moving pictures at the **Wells Auto Museum** (⊠ U.S. 1, Wells, ☎ 207/646–9064) fascinate kids. Trolley rides are the order of the day at the **Seashore Trolley Museum** (⊠ Log Cabin Rd., Kennebunkport, ☎ 207/967–2800). At the **Children's Museum of Maine** (⊠ 142 Free St., Portland, ☎ 207/ 828–1234), little ones can pretend they are lobster catchers, shopkeepers, or computer experts.

Dining and Lodging

For most visitors Maine means lobster, and lobster can be found on the menus of most Maine restaurants. Aficionados prefer to eat them "in the rough" at classic lobster pounds, where you choose your lobster in a pool and enjoy it at a picnic table. B&Bs and Victorian inns have joined the family-oriented motels of the coastal towns. For price ranges *see* Charts 1 (B) and 2 (B) *in* On the Road with Fodor's.

Bath

$$$$ ✕ **Robinhood Free Meetinghouse.** Chef Michael Gagne serves classic
★ and creative multiethnic cuisine in an 1855 Greek Revival meetinghouse. Begin with the artichoke strudel, move on to a classic veal saltimbocca or a confit of duck, and finish up with Gagne's signature, Obsession in Three Chocolates. ⊠ *Robinhood Road, Georgetown,* ☎ *207/371– 2188. D, MC, V. No lunch.*

$$ ✕ **Kristina's Restaurant & Bakery.** This frame house turned restaurant, with a deck built around a huge maple tree, bakes some of the finest pies, pastries, and cakes on the coast. Satisfying dinners are mainly new American cuisine. ⊠ *160 Centre St.,* ☎ *207/442–8577. D, MC, V. No dinner Sun.*

Boothbay Harbor

$$–$$$ ✕ **Black Orchid.** This trattoria serving classic Italian fare opens an outdoor area in summer, where you can select from a raw bar. ⊠ *5 By-Way,* ☎ *207/633–6659. AE, MC, V. No lunch.*

$$$–$$$$ 🏠 **Fisherman's Wharf Inn.** All rooms overlook the water at this modern motel built 200 ft out over the harbor. The large dining room has floor-to-ceiling windows. ⊠ *42 Commercial St., 04538,* ☎ *207/633– 5090 or 800/628–6872,* FAX *207/633-5092. 54 rooms. Dining room. AE, D, DC, MC, V. Closed late Oct.–May.*

Brunswick

$–$$ ✕ **Great Impasta.** At this storefront restaurant, try the seafood lasagna or match your favorite pasta and sauce. ⊠ *42 Maine St.,* ☎ *207/729– 5858. Reservations not accepted. AE, D, DC, MC, V.*

$$$–$$$$ 🏠 **Harpswell Inn.** Spacious lawns and neatly pruned shrubs surround this stately white-clapboard, dormered inn. Half the rooms have water views. There is no smoking in the inn, and only children over 10 are welcome. ⊠ *141 Lookout Point Rd., Harpswell 04079,* ☎ *207/833– 5509 or 800/843–5509. 15 rooms. MC, V.*

Freeport

$ ✕ **Harraseeket Lunch & Lobster Co.** At this bare-bones lobster pound beside the town landing, fried-seafood baskets and lobster dinners, eaten in the dining room or at picnic tables, are what it's all about. ⊠ *Main St., South Freeport,* ☎ *207/865–4888. Reservations not accepted. No credit cards. Closed mid-Oct.–Apr.*

$$$–$$$$ ✕▥ **Harraseeket Inn.** This inn, with elevators and whirlpools, has antique furniture and fireplaces in the common rooms; guest rooms have reproductions of Federal canopy beds and bright fabrics. In the formal dining room waiters prepare fettuccine Alfredo and flaming desserts at your table. ⊠ *162 Main St., 04032,* ☎ *207/865–9377 or 800/342–6423. 54 rooms. Restaurant, tavern. AE, D, DC, MC, V.*

Kennebunkport

$$$–$$$$ ✕▥ **White Barn Inn.** The rustic but elegant dining room of this inn serves
★ updated New England cuisine like steamed Maine lobster nestled on fresh fettuccine with carrots, ginger, snow peas, and a cognac-butter sauce. The lovely rooms have luxurious baths and are expensively appointed with a blend of hand-painted pieces and period furniture; some have fireplaces and whirlpool baths. ⊠ *Beach St., Box 560C, 04046,* ☎ *207/967–2321,* 𝔽𝔸𝕏 *207/967–1100. 25 rooms. Restaurant: jacket required for dinner; pool, bicycles. CP. AE, MC, V.*

$$$$ ▥ **Captain Lord Mansion.** This stately and sumptuously appointed 1812 Federal-style mansion with distinctive architecture that includes a suspended elliptical staircase, a widow's walk, gas fireplaces in 14 rooms, and near–museum quality decor, has a formal but not stuffy atmosphere. ⊠ *Box 800, 04046,* ☎ *207/967–3141,* 𝔽𝔸𝕏 *207/967–3172. 20 rooms. D, MC, V.*

Newcastle

$$$$ ✕▥ **Newcastle Inn.** This classic country inn overlooks the Damariscotta River. Guests spread out in the cozy pub, comfortable living room, and spacious sunporch overlooking the river; some rooms have fireplaces and whirlpools. The dining room (reservations essential) emphasizes Maine seafood such as local Pemaquid oysters, lobster, and Atlantic salmon. Choose from three- or five-course dinners. ⊠ *River Rd., Newcastle 04553,* ☎ *207/563–5685 or 800/832–8669. 14 rooms. 2 dining rooms, pub. Full breakfast; MAP available. AE, MC, V.*

Ogunquit

$$–$$$ ✕ **Hurricane.** Don't let its weather-beaten exterior deter you—this
★ small, comfortable seafood bar-and-grill offers first-rate cooking and spectacular views of the crashing surf. Start with lobster chowder or a napoleon of smoked salmon; entrées include rack of lamb, baked salmon-and-brie baklava, and shrimp scampi served over fresh pasta. ⊠ *Perkins Cove,* ☎ *207/646–6348. AE, D, DC, MC, V.*

Portland

$$$–$$$$ ✕ **Back Bay Grill.** Simple yet elegant, the grill is popular for its mel-
★ low jazz, a mural of Portland that's reflected by mirrors throughout, an impressive wine list, and carefully prepared food. ⊠ *65 Portland St.,* ☎ *207/772–8833. AE, D, DC, MC, V. Closed Sun.*

$$–$$$ ✕ **Street and Co.** At what may be the best seafood restaurant in Maine,
★ you enter through the kitchen, with all its wonderful aromas, and dine amid dried herbs and shelves of grocery staples. ⊠ *33 Wharf St.,* ☎ *207/775–0887. AE, MC, V. No lunch.*

$$$–$$$$ ✕▥ **Inn by the Sea.** On Greater Portland's most prime real estate, this all-suite inn is set back from the shoreline and has views of the ocean. The architecture is typically New England: One-bedroom suites have Chippendale furnishings; two-bedroom cottages are decorated in white pine and wicker. The dining room serves fine seafood and other regional

cuisine. ⊠ *40 Bowery Beach Rd., Cape Elizabeth (7 mi south of Portland) 04107,* ☎ *207/799–3134 or 800/888–4287,* 𝐅𝐀𝐗 *207/799–4779. 25 suites, 18 cottage condominiums. Restaurant, pool, tennis, croquet, bicycles, walking trails. AE, D, MC, V.*

$$$ 🏨 **Portland Regency Hotel.** This former 19th-century armory, the only major hotel in the center of the Old Port Exchange, has luxurious Victorian-style rooms, many with four-poster beds. ⊠ *20 Milk St., 04101,* ☎ *207/774–4200 or 800/727–3436. 103 rooms. Restaurant, health club, nightclub. AE, D, DC, MC, V.*

Scarborough

$$$$ ✕🏨 **Black Point Inn.** At the tip of a peninsula 12 mi south of Portland stands one of Maine's great old-time resorts. The inn is decorated with Early American and cherry-wood furniture, and the pastel colors of the rooms create an airiness throughout. On the grounds are beaches, a bird sanctuary, hiking trails, and sports facilities. The dining room has a menu strong in seafood. ⊠ *510 Black Point Rd., 04074,* ☎ *207/883–4126 or 800/258–0003,* 𝐅𝐀𝐗 *207/883–9976. 80 rooms. Restaurant, bar, indoor and outdoor pools, golf, tennis. AE, MC, V. Closed Dec.–Apr.*

The Yorks

$$$
★ ✕ **York Harbor Inn.** The dining room of this inn has country charm and great ocean views. Try the lobster-stuffed chicken breast with Boursin sauce or the angel-hair pasta with shrimp and scallops. Just save room for the crème caramel or any of the other wonderful desserts. ⊠ *Rte. 1A, York Harbor,* ☎ *207/363–5119 or 800/343–3869. AE, DC, MC, V. Jan.–mid-Apr., no lunch Sat.–Thurs., no dinner Mon.–Thurs.*

$$–$$$$ ✕🏨 **Dockside Guest Quarters and Restaurant.** On an 8-acre private island in the middle of York Harbor, the Dockside offers rooms in the Maine House, which has Early American antiques and a nautical theme. Four modern cottages have less character but bigger windows, and many have kitchenettes. Entrées in the esteemed dining room (closed Monday) may include scallop-stuffed shrimp Casino, steak au poivre with brandied mushroom sauce, and roast stuffed duckling. There's also a children's menu. ⊠ *York Harbor off Rte. 103; Box 205, York 03909,* ☎ *207/363–2868, 207/363–2722 for restaurant,* 𝐅𝐀𝐗 *207/363–1977. 21 rooms. Restaurant, badminton, croquet, dock, boating, bicycles. MC, V. Closed weekdays Nov.–late May.*

Nightlife and the Arts

Nightlife

Gritty McDuff's Brew Pub (⊠ 396 Fore St., Portland, ☎ 207/772–2739) is a tradition in these parts; fine ales are brewed on the premises. **Three Dollar Dewey's** (⊠ 446 Fore St., Portland, ☎ 207/772–3310) is an English-style alehouse, long a popular local nightspot. The **Café Club** (⊠ 38 Wharf St., ☎ 207/772–6976) is a wine and espresso bar with a light menu and desserts.

The Arts

Ogunquit Playhouse (⊠ Rte. 1, ☎ 207/646–5511), one of America's oldest summer theaters, mounts plays and musicals from late June to Labor Day. **Portland Performing Arts Center** (⊠ 25A Forest Ave., ☎ 207/744–0465) hosts music, dance, and theater. **Cumberland County Civic Center** (⊠ 1 Civic Center Sq., Portland, ☎ 207/775–3458) is a 9,000-seat auditorium where concerts are held. **Bowdoin Summer Music Festival** (⊠ Bowdoin College, ☎ 207/725–3322 for information, 207/725–3895 for tickets) is a six-week concert series featuring performances by students, faculty, and prestigious guest artists. **Maine State Music Theater** (⊠ Pickard Theater, Bowdoin College, ☎ 207/725–8769) stages musicals from mid-June through August.

Outdoor Activities and Sports

Boat Trips

From Perkins Cove in Ogunquit, **Finestkind** (☎ 207/646–5227) runs boats to Nubble Light and schedules lobstering trips. Boats offering whale-watching cruises and other excursions out of Kennebunkport include the *Elizabeth II,* the *Nautilus* (☎ 207/967–5595), and the *Indian* (☎ 207/967–5912).

In Portland, for tours of the harbor, Casco Bay, and the islands, try **Bay View Cruises** (☎ 207/761–0496), the *Buccaneer* (☎ 207/799–8188), or **Old Port Mariner Fleet** (☎ 207/775–0727). In Boothbay Harbor *Balmy Days II* (☎ 207/633–2284 or 800/298–2284) does day trips to Monhegan Island, and **Cap'n Fish's Boat Trips** (☎ 207/633–3244) offers sightseeing cruises throughout the region. From New Harbor, **Hardy Boat Cruises** (☎ 800/278–3346 or 207/677–2026) offers lighthouse and seal cruises and sails daily to Monhegan Island.

Canoeing

The **Maine Audubon Society** (☎ 207/781–2330) leads daily guided canoe trips in Scarborough Marsh (✉ Rte. 9, Scarborough), the largest salt marsh in Maine.

Deep-Sea Fishing

The *Ugly Anne* (✉ Perkins Cove, ☎ 207/646–7202) departs regularly. For half- and full-day fishing charters out of Portland, call *Devils Den* (☎ 207/761–4466).

Beaches

Kennebunk Beach is actually three beaches, with cottages and old Victorian boardinghouses nearby; for parking permits go to the Kennebunk Town Office (✉ 1 Summer St., ☎ 207/985–2102). **Goose Rocks,** north of Kennebunkport, is the largest area beach and a favorite of families with small children; the Kennebunkport Town Office (✉ Elm St., ☎ 207/967–4244) sells parking permits. **Ogunquit Beach** is a fine stretch at the mouth of the river that is protected from the surf. Families tend to camp at the ends, while the town's gay visitors go to the beach's middle.

Old Orchard Beach, with an amusement park reminiscent of Coney Island, is only a few miles north of Biddeford on Route 9.

At the end of Route 209 south of Bath, **Popham Beach State Park** (Phippsburg, ☎ 207/389–1335) has a good sand beach and picnic tables. **Reid State Park** (☎ 207/371–2303), on Georgetown Island off Route 127, has three beaches, bathhouses, picnic tables, and a snack bar.

Shopping

More than 100 **factory outlets** along U.S. 1 in Kittery sell clothing, shoes, glassware, and other products from top manufacturers. **Freeport** is a shopper's mecca. Across from its main store (✉ Rte. 1, ☎ 800/341–4341), an **L. L. Bean** factory outlet has seconds and discontinued merchandise at discount prices. Many of the 100 other in-town factory outlets are found in the **Fashion Outlet Mall** (✉ 2 Depot St.). Also try **Freeport Crossing** (✉ 200 Lower Main St.). More outlets crowd **Main Street** and **Bow Street.** The **Freeport Visitors Guide** (✉ Freeport Merchants Association, Box 452, 04032, ☎ 207/865–1212) has a complete listing of outlets; it's free.

Portland also has shopping. In the **Old Port Exchange** the better shops are concentrated along Fore and Exchange streets.

Wiscasset offers plenty of antiques shops in which to browse. Just south of town on Route 1 in Woolwich is the **Montsweag Flea Market,** a trash-and-treasure trove open Wednesday and Friday–Sunday.

THE COAST: PENOBSCOT BAY AND ACADIA

Purists hold that the Maine coast begins at Penobscot Bay, where water vistas are wider and bluer, with the shore a jumble of broken granite boulders, cobblestones, and gravel. East of Penobscot Bay, Acadia is the informal name for Mount Desert (pronounced like *dessert*) Island and environs. Mount Desert, Maine's largest island, harbors most of Acadia National Park, the state's principal tourist attraction. Camden, on Penobscot Bay, and Bar Harbor, on Mount Desert, both offer a range of accommodations and restaurants.

Visitor Information

Bar Harbor: Chamber of Commerce (⊠ 93 Cottage St., Box 158, 04609, ☎ 207/288–3393, 207/288–5103, or 800/288–5103). **Rockport, Camden, and Lincolnville:** Chamber of Commerce (⊠ Public Landing, Box 919, Camden 04843, ☎ 207/236–4404).

Arriving and Departing

By Car

U.S. 1 follows the west coast of Penobscot Bay, linking Rockland, Camden, and Ellsworth. From Ellsworth, Route 3 will take you onto Mount Desert Island.

By Plane

Bangor International Airport (☎ 207/947–0384), 30 mi north of Penobscot Bay, has daily flights by major U.S. carriers. **Knox County Regional Airport** (☎ 207/594–4131), 3 mi south of Rockland, has frequent flights to Boston. **Hancock County Airport** (☎ 207/667–7329), 8 mi northwest of Bar Harbor, is served by Colgan Air.

Exploring Penobscot Bay and Acadia

Tenants Harbor is a quintessential Maine fishing town—its harbor dominated by squat, serviceable lobster boats; its shores rocky and slippery; its town a scattering of clapboard houses, a church, and a general store. The fishing town of Port Clyde, south of Tenants Harbor, is the point of departure for the mail boat that serves **Monhegan Island.** The tiny, remote island, its high cliffs fronting the open sea, was discovered a century ago by some of America's finest painters. Day-trippers flock here for the scenery, the boat ride, and the artists' studios, which are occasionally open to visitors.

Rockland, home of the Seafood Festival (a.k.a. the Lobster Festival), ranks as the coast's commercial hub, with fishing boats moored alongside a growing flotilla of windjammers. The **William A. Farnsworth Library and Art Museum** is an excellent small museum specializing in American art, with a focus on Maine-related art. In 1998 as part of its 50th anniversary celebration, the museum plans to open a new gallery devoted to the Maine work of Andrew Wyeth and other members of the Wyeth family. ⊠ *532 Main St.,* ☎ *207/596–6457. Closed Mon. Oct.–May.*

★ In **Camden** mountains tower over the harbor, and the fashionable waterfront is home to the nation's largest windjammer fleet; such cruises are a superb way to explore the ports and islands of Penobscot Bay. The 5,500-acre **Camden Hills State Park** (☎ 207/236–3109), 2 mi north of Camden on U.S. 1, contains 20 mi of trails. Hike or take the toll road up Mt. Battie for a magnificent view over island-studded Penobscot Bay.

Searsport claims to be the antiques capital of Maine, with shops and a seasonal weekend flea market. Historic **Castine,** over which the French, the British, the Dutch, and the Americans fought, has two museums and the ruins of a British fort. But the finest thing about Castine is the town itself: the lively, welcoming town landing; the serene Federal and Greek Revival houses; and the town common.

Ellsworth has its own growing array of outlets including an L.L. Bean factory store. It is the gateway to Bar Harbor and Acadia, where you pick up Route 3 to Mount Desert Island. Although most of **Bar Harbor**'s grand mansions were destroyed in a 1947 fire, this busy resort town on the island's Frenchman Bay has retained its beauty. Shops, restaurants, and hotels are clustered along Main, Mount Desert, and Cottage streets.

★ The Hulls Cove approach to **Acadia National Park** (☞ National and State Parks, *above, and* Hiking, *below*) is northwest of Bar Harbor on Route 3. Though it is often clogged with traffic, the 27-mi Park Loop Road provides the best introduction to the park. The visitor center shows a free 15-minute film and has trail maps. The Ocean Trail is an easily accessible walk with some of Maine's most spectacular scenery. For a mountaintop experience without the effort of hiking, drive to the summit of **Cadillac Mountain,** the highest point on the eastern coast. The view from the bald summit is spectacular, especially at sunset.

What to See and Do with Children

Acadia Zoo (✉ Rte. 3, Trenton, ☎ 207/667–3244) has both wild and domesticated animals; it's closed from late December through April.

Dining and Lodging

For price ranges *see* Charts 1 (B) and 2 (B) *in* On the Road with Fodor's.

Bar Harbor

$$–$$$ × **George's.** Candles, flowers, and linens decorate the tables in four
★ small dining rooms in a romantic old house. The menu shows a distinct Mediterranean influence. ✉ *7 Stephen's La.,* ☎ *207/288–4505. AE, D, DC, MC, V. Closed Nov.–mid-June. No lunch.*

$$ × **Jordan Pond House.** Popovers and tea are a century-old tradition at this rustic restaurant in Acadia National Park, where you can sit on the terrace and admire the views. ✉ *Park Loop Rd.,* ☎ *207/276–3316. AE, D, MC, V. Closed late Oct.–May.*

$$$$ 🏠 **Inn at Canoe Point.** Seclusion and privacy are bywords of this snug 100-year-old Tudor-style house at Hulls Cove, 2 mi from Bar Harbor. The inn's large living room has huge windows on the water, a granite fireplace, and a waterfront deck where a full breakfast is served in summer. ✉ *Rte. 3, Box 216, 04609,* ☎ *207/288–9511. 5 rooms. D, MC, V. Closed winter.*

$$–$$$ 🏠 **Wonder View Inn.** Although the rooms are standard motel style, this establishment is distinguished by its extensive grounds and lovely views of Frenchman Bay. ✉ *Rte. 3, Box 25, 04609,* ☎ *207/288–3358,* ⑭ *207/288–2005. 79 rooms. Restaurant, pool. AE, D, MC, V. Closed late Oct.–mid-May.*

Camden

$$ ✕ **Waterfront Restaurant.** Come for a ringside seat on Camden Harbor; the best view is from the outdoor deck, open in warm weather. The fare is primarily seafood. ✉ *Bay View St.,* ☎ *207/236–3747. Reservations not accepted. AE, MC, V.*

$$$$ ✕⊞ **Whitehall Inn.** Camden's best-known inn was constructed in 1843 and is a white-clapboard ship-captain's home with a wide porch. Rooms are small and sparsely furnished, with dark-wood bedsteads and claw-foot bathtubs; some have ocean views. The dining room, open to the public for dinner and breakfast, serves traditional and creative American cuisine. ✉ *52 High St., Box 558, 04843,* ☎ *207/236–3391,* FAX *207/236–4427. 50 rooms. Tennis. MAP or B&B available. AE, MC, V. Closed mid-Oct.–late May.*

$$$$ ⊞ **Samoset Resort.** Next to the breakwater, on the Rockland-Rockport town line, is this sprawling ocean-side resort with excellent facilities. ✉ *220 Warrenton St., Rockport 04856,* ☎ *207/594–2511 or 800/341–1650 outside ME,* FAX *207/594–0722. 150 rooms. Restaurant, indoor and outdoor pools, golf, tennis, exercise room, racquetball. AE, D, DC, MC, V.*

Castine

$$$–$$$$ ✕⊞ **Castine Inn.** Upholstered easy chairs and fine prints and paintings are typical appointments in the light, airy guest rooms. The third floor has the best views: the harbor over the handsome formal gardens on one side, the village on the other. The dining room serves such New England staples as crab cakes with mustard sauce and chicken-and-leek potpie. ✉ *Main St. (Box 41), 04421,* ☎ *207/326–4365,* FAX *207/326–4570. 23 rooms. MC, V. Closed Nov.–mid-Apr.*

Hancock

$$$–$$$$ ✕ **Le Domaine.** On a rural stretch of U.S. 1, 9 mi east of Ellsworth, a French chef prepares *lapin pruneaux* (rabbit in a rich, brown prune sauce), sweetbreads with lemon and capers, and *coquilles* St. Jacques. The elegant but unintimidating dining room has hanging copper pots. ✉ *U.S. 1,* ☎ *207/422–3395 or 800/554–8498. AE, D, MC, V. Closed Nov.–mid-May. No lunch.*

Southwest Harbor

$$$$ ✕⊞ **Claremont Hotel.** Built in 1884, the yellow-clapboard Claremont commands a view of Somes Sound; croquet is played on the lawn, and cocktails and lunch are served at the Boat House in midsummer. The menu changes weekly in the large old-style dining room ($$, reservations essential, jacket required for dinner), open to the public for breakfast and dinner. ✉ *Off Clark Point Rd. (Box 137), Southwest Harbor 04679,* ☎ *207/244–5036 or 800/244–5036,* FAX *207/244–3512. 24 rooms, 12 cottages, 2 guest houses. Restaurant, tennis court, croquet, dock, boating, bicycles. MAP. No credit cards. Hotel closed mid-Oct.–mid-June, cottages closed Nov.–late May.*

Tenants Harbor

$$–$$$ ✕⊞ **East Wind Inn & Meeting House.** On a knob of land overlooking the harbor and the islands, the East Wind offers simple hospitality, a wraparound porch, and unadorned but comfortable guest rooms, suites, and efficiencies in three buildings. The inn is open to the public for breakfast, dinner, and Sunday brunch. ✉ *Rte. 131 (Box 149), 10 mi off Rte. 1, 04860,* ☎ *800/241–8439 or 207/372–6366,* FAX *207/372–6320. 24 rooms; 4 apartments/efficiencies. Restaurant. CP. AE, D, MC, V. Closed Jan.–Mar.*

Campgrounds

The two campgrounds in Acadia National Park—**Blackwoods** (☎ 800/365–2267) and **Seawall** (☎ 207/244–3600)—fill up quickly in summer. Nearby **Lamoine State Park** (☎ 207/667–4778) has a great location on Frenchman Bay.

The Arts

Bay Chamber Concerts (✉ Rockport Opera House, ☎ 207/236–2823) plays chamber music every Thursday night and some Friday nights in July and August and gives monthly concerts September through May. **Arcady Music Festival** (☎ 207/288–3151) has concerts on Mount Desert Island from late July through August. **Bar Harbor Festival** (✉ 59 Cottage St., ☎ 207/288–5744) has concerts in summer.

Outdoor Activities and Sports

Biking

The carriage paths that wind through **Acadia National Park** are ideal for biking; pick up a map from the Hulls Cove visitor center. Bikes can be rented in Bar Harbor from **Acadia Bike & Canoe** (✉ 48 Cottage St., ☎ 207/288–9605) and **Bar Harbor Bicycle Shop** (✉ 141 Cottage St., ☎ 207/288–3886).

Boat Trips

Port Clyde is the point of departure for the *Laura B.* (☎ 207/372–8848 for schedules), the mail boat that serves Monhegan Island. From Bar Harbor, the *Acadian Whale Watcher* (☎ 207/288–9794) runs whale-watching cruises, and the 65-ft *Chippewa* (☎ 207/288–4585) cruises past islands and lighthouses three times a day (including at sunset) in summer. The *Natalie Todd* (☎ 207/288–4585) offers weekend windjammer cruises. Camden and Rockland are the East Coast **windjammer** headquarters (contact ✉ Maine Windjammer Assoc., Box 1144, Blue Hill 04614, ☎ 800/807–9463; ✉ North End Shipyard Schooners, Box 482, Rockland 04841; ☎ 800/648–4544; ✉ Vessels of Windjammer Wharf, Box 1050, Rockland 04841). In Southwest Harbor, **Manset Yacht Service** (✉ Shore Rd., ☎ 207/244–4040) rents sailboats.

Hiking

Acadia National Park maintains nearly 200 mi of paths. Among the more rewarding hikes are the Precipice Trail to Champlain Mountain, the Great Head Loop, the Gorham Mountain Trail, and the path around Eagle Lake.

Shopping

The best shopping streets are Main and Bayview in **Camden.** Antiques shops (abundant in **Searsport**) are scattered around the outskirts of villages; yard sales abound in summer. Galleries and boutiques can be found in **Blue Hill** and **Deer Isle. Bar Harbor** is a good place to browse for gifts. For bargains head for the outlets along Route 3 in **Ellsworth.**

WESTERN LAKES AND MOUNTAINS

Less than 20 mi northwest of Portland, the lakes and mountains of western Maine stretch along the New Hampshire border to Quebec. The Sebago–Long Lake region has antiques stores and lake cruises on a 42-mi waterway. Kezar Lake, in a fold of the White Mountains, is a hideaway of the wealthy. Bethel, in the Androscoggin River valley, is a classic New England town, while the less-developed Rangeley Lakes area is a fishing paradise; both become ski country in winter.

Visitor Information

Bethel Area: Chamber of Commerce (✉ Box 439, Bethel 04217, ☎ 207/824–2282). **Bridgton–Lakes Region:** Chamber of Commerce (✉ Box 236, Bridgton 04009, ☎ 207/647–3472). **Rangeley Lakes Region:** Chamber of Commerce (✉ Box 317, Rangeley 04970, ☎ 207/864–5571 or 800/685–2537).

Arriving and Departing

By Car

U.S. 302 provides access to the region from I–95. U.S. 2, which runs east–west, links Bangor to Bethel.

Exploring the Western Lakes and Mountains

Sebago Lake State Park (☎ 207/693–6613 mid-June–Sept. or 207/693–6231 Oct.–mid-June) offers opportunities for swimming, picnicking, camping, boating, and fishing. To the north is **Naples,** with cruises and boat rentals on Long Lake. The **Songo Locks** connect the northern tip of Sebago Lake with Long Lake. **Bridgton,** near Highland Lake, has antiques shops in and around town. U.S. 302/Route 5 through Lovell and Route 37 through the Waterfords are scenic routes to **Bethel,** a town with white-clapboard houses, antiques stores, and a mountain vista at the end of every street. Keep this route in mind for your leaf-peeping days—and remember Maine flourishes in bright colors usually the first and second week of October, not in September.

The area from Bethel to **Rangeley Lake** is beautiful, too, particularly in autumn. In **Grafton Notch State Park** (☎ 207/824–2912) you can hike to stunning gorges and waterfalls and into the Baldpate Mountains. For a century **Rangeley** has lured people who fish and hunt to its more than 40 lakes and ponds. The town has a rough, wilderness feel to it; the best parts are tucked away in the woods and around the lake. **Rangeley Lake State Park** (☎ 207/864–3858) has superb scenery, swimming, picnicking, and boating. Campsites are set well apart.

In the shadow of Sugarloaf Mountain, **Kingfield** is prime ski country—a classic New England town with a general store, historic inns, and a white-clapboard church.

What to See and Do with Children

Sandy River & Rangeley Lakes Railroad (✉ Phillips, ☎ 207/639–3352) has a century-old train that travels through the woods. It is open the first and third Sunday of months from May through October; rides depart at 11, 1, and 3.

Dining and Lodging

Bethel has the largest concentration of inns and B&Bs, and its chamber of commerce has a **lodging reservations service** (☎ 207/824–3585). For price ranges *see* Charts 1 (B) and 2 (B) *in* On the Road with Fodor's.

Bethel

$$–$$$ ✗⊞ **Bethel Inn and Country Club.** Choice rooms in the old-fashioned hotel, sparsely furnished with colonial reproductions, have fireplaces and face the golf course and the mountains beyond. Condos on the fairway are a bit sterile. The dining room serves roast duck and prime rib. ✉ *Village Common (Box 49), 04217,* ☎ *207/824–2175 or 800/654–0125,* 🖷 *207/824–2233. 97 rooms. Restaurant, pool, tennis, golf, health club. AE, D, DC, MC, V.*

Kingfield

$$$–$$$$ ✕🖬 **Inn on Winter's Hill.** Designed in 1895 by the Stanley brothers, this Georgian mansion is renowned for Sunday brunches and New England dinners. The rooms of the renovated barn are brightly furnished. ✉ *R.R. 1 (Box 1272), 04947,* ☎ *207/265–5421 or 800/233–9687,* 🖷 *207/265–5424. 20 rooms. Restaurant, pool, tennis, cross-country skiing, ice-skating. AE, D, DC, MC, V.*

Rangeley

$$–$$$$ ✕🖬 **Rangeley Inn and Motor Lodge.** From Main Street you see only the massive blue three-story inn building (circa 1907), but behind it the newer motel wing commands Haley Pond, a lawn, and a garden. Some of the inn's sizable guest rooms have iron-and-brass beds; some have claw-foot tubs while others have whirlpool tubs. Motel units contain Queen Anne reproduction furniture. Gourmet meals are served in the spacious dining room with its Williamsburg brass chandeliers. ✉ *Main St. (Box 160), 04970,* ☎ *207/864–3341 or 800/666–3687,* 🖷 *207/864–3634. 51 rooms. Restaurant, bar, meeting room. MAP available. AE, D, MC, V. Closed Sun.–Wed. in winter.*

Outdoor Activities and Sports

Canoeing

The **Saco River** and **Rangeley** and **Mooselookmeguntic lakes** are favorites. For rentals try **Canal Bridge Canoes** (✉ Rte. 302, Fryeburg Village, ☎ 207/935–2605), **Oquossoc Cove Marina** (✉ Oquossoc, ☎ 207/864–3463), **Dockside Sports Center** (✉ Town Cove, Rangeley ☎ 207/864–2424), **River's Edge Sports** (✉ Rte. 4, Oquossoc, ☎ 207/864–5582), or **Saco River Canoe and Kayak** (✉ Rte. 5, Fryeburg, ☎ 207/935–2369).

Fishing

Fishing licenses (required) can be obtained at many sporting goods and hardware stores and at local town offices. The **Department of Inland Fisheries and Wildlife** (✉ 284 State St., Augusta 04333, ☎ 207/287–2871) has further information.

Water Sports

Sebago, Long, Rangeley, and Mooselookmeguntic are the most popular lakes for boating. Contact tourist offices for rentals.

Ski Areas

Sugarloaf/USA (✉ Kingfield 04947, ☎ 207/237–2000) has both downhill and cross-country trails. **Sunday River** (✉ Box 450, Bethel 04217, ☎ 207/824–3000) has 120 downhill trails.

ELSEWHERE IN MAINE

The North Woods

Arriving and Departing

Charter planes can be arranged from Bangor. Route 6 wends its way from I–95 to Greenville; Route 11 provides access from I–95 to Millinocket.

What to See and Do

Moosehead Lake, Maine's largest, offers rustic camps, restaurants, guides, and outfitters. Its 420 mi of shorefront are virtually uninhabited and mostly accessible only by floatplane or boat. **Greenville** is the largest town on the lake and the spot for canoe rentals, outfitters, and basic lodging. For information contact **Moosehead Lake Region Cham-**

ber of Commerce (⊠ Rtes. 6 and 15, Box 581, Greenville 04441, ☎ 207/695–2702).

Baxter State Park (⊠ 64 Balsam Dr., Millinocket 04462, ☎ 207/723–5140) is a 200,000-acre wooded wilderness. It surrounds **Katahdin,** Maine's highest mountain. There are 45 other mountains in the park, all accessible from a 150-mi trail network.

Even more remote is the **Allagash Wilderness Waterway,** a 92-mi corridor of lakes and rivers. **Ripogenus Dam,** 30 mi northwest of Millinocket on lumbering roads, is the most popular jumping-off point for Allagash trips. The **Maine Department of Conservation, Bureau of Parks and Lands** (⊠ State House Station 22, Augusta 04333, ☎ 207/289–3821) has information on camping and canoeing.

Dining and Lodging

$$–$$$$ ✕🖾 **The Birches Resort.** The living room in the main lodge of this family-oriented resort is dominated by a fieldstone fireplace. Log-cabin cottages have wood-burning stoves or fireplaces and sleep from 2 to 15. The dining room (closed December and April) overlooking the lake is open to the public for breakfast and dinner; the fare is pasta, seafood, and steak. ⊠ *Off Rte. 6/15 on Moosehead Lake (Box 41), Rockwood 04478,* ☎ *207/534–7305 or 800/825–9453,* ℻ *207/534–8835. 4 lodge rooms, 15 cottages. Dining room, hot tub, sauna, boating. AE, D, MC, V.*

$$$–$$$$ 🖾 **Chesuncook Lake House.** Guests can gain access to this 1864 lodge only by boat or floatplane, or in winter they can drive to within 3 mi and come in by snowmobile or cross-country skis. French-born Maggie McBurnie, who operates the inn with her husband, Bert, cooks all the meals—solid New England fare with a French touch. ⊠ *Rte. 76, Box 656, Chesuncook Lake Village 04441,* ☎ *207/745–5330 or 207/695–2821 for Folsom's Air Service. 4 rooms in main house, 3 housekeeping cottages. MAP for rooms in main house. Boating. No credit cards.*

$$$$ 🖾 **Lodge at Moosehead Lake.** All rooms in this luxurious mansion have
★   a whirlpool, fireplace, and hand-carved four-poster bed; most have lake views. The restaurant has a spectacular view of the lake. ⊠ *Lily Bay Rd., Greenville 04441,* ☎ *207/695–4400,* ℻ *207/695–2281. 8 rooms. D, MC, V.*

MASSACHUSETTS

Updated by
Dorothy
Antczak,
Michele
McPhee,
Kirsten Sadler,
Stephanie
Schorow, and
Mark Zanger

Capital   Boston
Population   6,092,000
Motto   By the Sword We Seek Peace,
          But Peace Only Under Liberty
State Bird   Chickadee
State Flower   Mayflower
Postal Abbreviation   MA

Statewide Visitor Information

Massachusetts Office of Travel and Tourism (✉ 100 Cambridge St., 13th floor, Boston 02202, ☎ 617/727–3201 or 800/447–6277).

Scenic Drives

Much of Cape Cod's **Route 6A,** from Sandwich to Orleans, is a National Historic District preserving traditional New England seacoast towns. **Routes 133 and 1A** on the North Shore, from Gloucester to Newburyport, cover some of the earliest settlements in the United States, established in the 1630s. In the Berkshires, the **Mohawk Trail,** running 63 mi along Route 2 between Greenfield and North Adams, is famous for its fall foliage, which peaks in late September and early October. In the southwest, **Route 23** from Great Barrington to Westfield yields wooded hills and rural towns.

National and State Parks

National Park

★ **Cape Cod National Seashore** (☞ Cape Cod and the Islands, *below*), a 30-mi stretch of dune-backed beach between Eastham and Provincetown, offers excellent swimming, bike riding, bird-watching, and nature walks.

State Parks

The **Department of Environmental Management** (✉ Division of Forests and Parks, 100 Cambridge St., Boston 02202, ☎ 617/727–3159) has information on all state parks, including the Heritage state parks, which have exhibits on the state's industrial history.

Mt. Greylock State Reservation (✉ Rockwell Rd., off Rte. 7, Lanesborough, ☎ 413/499–4262) has the state's highest peak. **Tolland State Forest** (✉ Rte. 8, Otis, ☎ 413/269–6002), in the Berkshires, has camping facilities and hiking trails. **Nickerson State Park** (✉ Rte. 6A, Brewster, ☎ 508/896–3491), on Cape Cod, has nearly 2,000 acres of forest with walking trails, trout-stocked ponds, and campsites.

BOSTON

New England's largest and most important city, and the cradle of American independence, Boston is more than 360 years old. Its most famous buildings are not merely civic landmarks but national icons; its greatest citizens—John Hancock, Paul Revere, and the Adamses— live at the crossroads of history and myth.

Boston is also New England's center of high finance and higher technology, a place of granite-and-glass towers rising along what were once rutted village lanes. Its enormous population of students, academics, artists, and young professionals makes the town a haven for the arts, international cinema, late-night bookstores, alternative music, and unconventional local politics.

Visitor Information

For general information and brochures, contact the **Greater Boston Convention and Visitors Bureau** (⊠ Box 490, Prudential Tower, 02199, ☎ 617/536–4100 or 800/888–5515), which runs a visitor center (closed weekends) near the Park Street station on the T Line. The **Boston Welcome Center** (⊠ 140 Tremont St., 02111, ☎ 617/451–2227) also has general information.

Boston magazine (on newsstands) and *Where: Boston* and *Panorama* (both free in hotels and visitor centers) list arts and entertainment events. The calendar of events in the *Boston Parents Paper* (☎ 617/522–1515), published monthly and distributed free throughout the city, is an excellent resource for parents and children. The *Boston Travel Planner,* available from the Greater Boston Convention and Visitors Bureau, contains a calendar of events, sports and regional activities, and information on hotel weekend packages.

Arriving and Departing

By Bus
Bonanza (⊠ 145 Dartmouth St., ☎ 617/720–4110 or 800/556–3815). **Greyhound Lines** (⊠ South Station, ☎ 800/231–2222). **Peter Pan Bus Lines** (⊠ 555 Atlantic Ave., ☎ 617/426–7838 or 800/237–8747). **Plymouth & Brockton Buses** (⊠ South Station, ☎ 508/746–0378).

By Car
Boston is the traffic hub of New England: I–95 (which is the same as Route 128 in parts) skirts the city along the coast, while I–90 heads west.

By Plane
Logan International Airport (☎ 617/567–5400 or 800/235–6426) has scheduled flights by most major domestic and foreign carriers. Only 3 mi and Boston Harbor separate the airport from downtown, but traffic is heavy. Cab fare to downtown is about $17, including tip. For 24-hour information on parking, bicycle access, and bus, subway, and water-shuttle transportation, call Logan's **Ground Transportation Desk** (☎ 800/235–6426). The **Massachusetts Bay Transportation Authority (MBTA) Blue Line** subway from the Airport station (85¢) goes downtown; free shuttle buses connect the station with airline terminals and run every 8–12 minutes from 5:30 AM to 1 AM.

By Train
South Station (⊠ Summer St. at Atlantic Ave., ☎ 617/345–7451) is served by Amtrak.

Getting Around Boston

Boston is meant for walking; a majority of its historic and architectural attractions are found in compact areas.

By Car
If possible avoid bringing a car into Boston; streets are narrow and twisting, drivers can be rude and unpredictable. Major public parking lots are at Government Center and Quincy Market; beneath Boston Common (entrance on Charles Street); beneath Post Office Square; at the Prudential Center; at Copley Place; and off Clarendon Street near the

John Hancock Tower. Rush hours are 6:30–9 AM and 3:30–6 PM; traffic becomes especially heavy at the Callahan Tunnel and at Tobin Bridge. Due to the massive Central Artery construction project, expected to continue past 2000, assume that traffic in the downtown and North End will be especially congested.

By Public Transportation

The **MBTA** (☎ 617/722–3200, TTY 617/722–5146), known as the T, operates subways, elevated trains, and trolleys along four connecting lines—Red, Blue, Green, and Orange. Trains run from 5:30 AM to about 12:30 AM daily; adult base fare is 85¢. Tourist passes are available for $9 for three days and $18 for seven days.

By Taxi

Cabs are not easily hailed; if you're in a hurry, try a hotel taxi stand or telephone for a cab. Fares run about $1.90 per mi, with a pickup fee of $1.50. Companies offering 24-hour service include **Checker** (☎ 617/536–7000), **Independent Taxi Operators Association** (☎ 617/426–8700), and **Cambridge Taxi** (☎ 617/547–3000).

Orientation Tours

By Boat

Boston Harbor Cruises (✉ 1 Long Wharf, ☎ 617/227–4320) has tours from mid-April through October.

By Bus and Trolley

Brush Hill/Gray Line (✉ 39 Dalton Ave., ☎ 617/236–2148) buses pick up passengers from several suburban and downtown hotels for a daily 9:30 AM departure of the 3½-hour Boston Adventure tour of Boston and Cambridge. They also offer tours to many other popular destinations in the state.

Old Town Trolley (✉ 329 W. 2nd St., ☎ 617/269–7010) takes you on a 1½-hour narrated tour of Boston with 17 stops. You can catch it at major hotels, Boston Common, Copley Place, or in front of the New England Aquarium on Atlantic Avenue. Summer only, the same company also offers an hour-long four-stop tour of Cambridge departing from Harvard Square.

Walking Tours

The 2½-mi **Freedom Trail** (☎ 617/242–5642) tour, which is marked on the sidewalk by a red line, winds past 16 of Boston's most important historic sites, beginning at the visitor center at Boston Common. **Harborwalk** is a self-guided tour that begins at the Old State House (✉ 206 Washington St.) and traces Boston's maritime history. Maps for both walks are available at the Boston Common Visitor Information Center. The **Black Heritage Trail** (☎ 617/742–5415), which begins on the Boston Common, winds through the Beacon Hill neighborhood.

Exploring Boston

Boston Common and Beacon Hill

★ **Boston Common,** the oldest public park in the United States and the site of festivals, political rallies, First Night New Year's activities, and family outings, is the heart of Boston. Near the Common at the Congregationalist **Park Street Church** (✉ 1 Park St., ☎ 617/523–3383), finished in 1810, Samuel Smith's hymn "America" was first sung in 1831. Next to the church is the **Old Granary Burial Ground,** where Revolutionary heroes Samuel Adams, John Hancock, and Paul Revere lie.

★ At the summit of Beacon Hill is Charles Bulfinch's magnificent neo-classical **State House,** its dome both sheathed in copper from Paul Revere's foundry and gilded after the Civil War. Tours are given weekdays. ⊠ *Beacon St. between Hancock and Bowdoin Sts.,* ☎ *617/727–3676. Closed weekends.*

★ With its brick row houses, most built between 1800 and 1850, the classic face of **Beacon Hill** is in a style never far from the early Federal norm. Here you'll find **Chestnut and Mt. Vernon streets,** distinguished not only for their individual houses but also for their general atmosphere and character. Mt. Vernon opens out on **Louisburg Square,** the heart of Beacon Hill. Once the home address of William Dean Howells and Louisa May Alcott, the square was an 1840s model for town house development. Today it's so perfectly preserved, Henry James would have no difficulty recognizing his whereabouts.

On the north slope of Beacon Hill is the 1806 **African Meeting House** (⊠ 8 Smith Ct., ☎ 617/742–1854), the oldest African-American church building in the United States and where the New England Anti-Slavery Society was formed in 1832. Today the site marks the end of the Black Heritage Trail, a walking tour. Information is available at the **Museum of Afro-American History.** ⊠ *46 Joy St.,* ☎ *617/742–1854.*

The North End and Charlestown
In the 17th century the **North End** *was* Boston, as much of the rest of the peninsula was still under water. During most of the 20th century the North End has been Italian Boston, full of restaurants, groceries, bakeries, churches, social clubs, cafés, and festivals honoring saints and food.

Off Hanover Street, the North End's main thoroughfare, is North Square and the **Paul Revere House,** the oldest house in Boston, built nearly a century before its illustrious tenant's midnight ride. The restored rooms exemplify Colonial Boston dwellings. ⊠ *19 North Sq.,* ☎ *617/523–1676 or 617/523–2338. Closed Mon., Jan.–Mar.*

★ Past North Square on Hanover Street is **St. Stephen's,** the only Charles Bulfinch–designed church still standing in Boston. The steeple of Christ Church, more commonly known as the **Old North Church** (⊠ 193 Salem St., ☎ 617/523–6676)—where Paul Revere hung the two lanterns to signal Cambridge residents on the night of April 18, 1775—can be seen on Tileston Street. The oldest church building in Boston, it was designed by William Price from a study of Christopher Wren's London churches.

Cross the Charlestown Bridge to reach the **USS Constitution,** nicknamed "Old Ironsides" for the strength of its oaken hull, which seemed to repel cannon fire. Launched in 1797, it is the oldest commissioned ship in the U.S. Navy and is moored at the Charlestown Navy Yard. During its service against the Barbary pirates and in the War of 1812, the ship never lost an engagement. ⊠ *Constitution Wharf,* ☎ *617/242–5670 or 617/426–1812 for Navy Yard Museum. Free.*

★ The Battle of Bunker Hill is one of America's most famous misnomers. The battle was actually fought on Breed's Hill, and this is where Solomon Willard's **Bunker Hill Monument**—a 221-ft shaft of Quincy granite—stands. It rises from the spot where on June 17, 1775, a citizens' militia—reputedly commanded not to fire "until you see the whites of their eyes"—inflicted more than 1,100 casualties on British regulars (who eventually did seize the hill). The views from the top are worth the 295-step ascent. ⊠ *Main St. to Monument St., then straight uphill;* ☎ *617/242–5641.*

Downtown Boston

Downtown is east of the Boston Common. There is little logic to the streets here because they were once village lanes; they are now lined with 40-story office towers. The granite **King's Chapel** (⊠ 58 Tremont St., at School St.), built in 1754, houses Paul Revere's largest and—in his own judgment—sweetest-sounding bell.

The **Old South Meeting House** (⊠ 310 Washington St., ☎ 617/482–6439), built in 1729, is Boston's second-oldest church. Many of the fiery town meetings that led to the Revolution were held here, including the one called by Samuel Adams concerning some dutiable tea that activists wanted returned to England.

A brightly colored lion and unicorn, symbols of British imperial power, adorn the facade of the **Old State House** (⊠ Washington and Court Sts.). This was the seat of the Colonial government from 1713 until the Revolution. The first floor is now a museum that traces Boston's Revolutionary War history. The site of the Boston Massacre is marked by a circle of stones in the traffic island in front of the building. A National Park Service visitor center is directly across from the Old State House on State Street. ⊠ 206 Washington St., ☎ 617/720–3290.

★ **Faneuil Hall,** erected in 1742 to serve as both a town meeting hall and a public market, is like a local Ark of the Covenant—it is where a part of Boston's spirit resides. It was here in 1772 that Samuel Adams first suggested that Massachusetts and the other colonies organize a Committee of Correspondence to maintain semiclandestine lines of communication in the face of hardening British repression. In national election years the hall usually hosts debates among contenders in the Massachusetts presidential primary. On the top floors are the headquarters and museum of the Ancient and Honorable Artillery Company of Massachusetts, the oldest militia in the nation (1638). Its status is now ceremonial, but it proudly displays its arms, uniforms, and other artifacts.

Nearby **Quincy Market** has served as a retail and wholesale distribution center for meat and produce for 150 years. Thanks to creative urban renewal in the mid-1970s, it now houses a mix of retail shops, restaurants, and offices. Some people consider it all hopelessly trendy, but the 50,000 visitors who come here each day seem to enjoy it. At the waterfront end of Quincy Market is **Marketplace Center,** another complex, which houses more shops, eateries, and boutiques.

The most glittering addition to Boston's waterfront can be found on **Rowes Wharf**—a 15-story redbrick Skidmore, Owings, and Merrill extravaganza of a building, gaily adorned with white trim and home to chic restaurants and shops.

One of the city's most popular attractions is the **New England Aquarium** (☎ 617/973–5200), on Central Wharf, which is immediately to the right of Long Wharf as you face the harbor. Here you'll find seals, penguins, a variety of sharks, and other sea creatures—some of which make their home in the aquarium's four-story, 187,000-gallon observation tank.

When you cross Fort Point Channel on the Congress Street Bridge, you encounter the *Beaver II,* a faithful replica of a Boston Tea Party ship, like the ones forcibly boarded and unloaded on the night Boston Harbor itself became a teapot. ⊠ Congress St. Bridge, ☎ 617/338–1773. Closed mid-Dec.–Feb.

Back Bay and the South End

Southwest of Boston Common is **Back Bay,** once a tidal flat that formed the south bank of a distended Charles River until it was filled

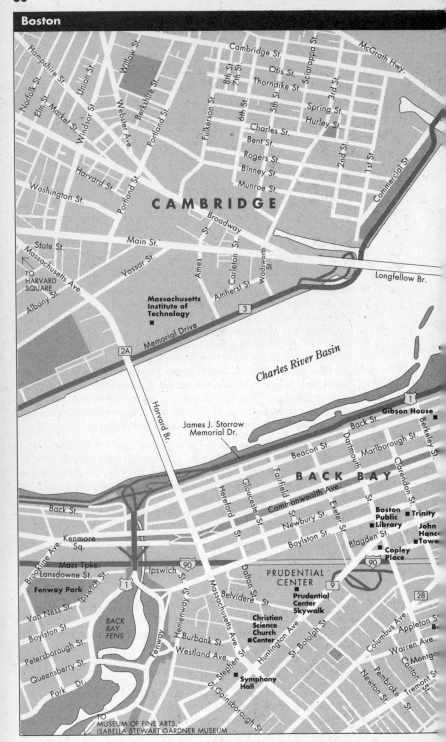

Hampshire St.
Norfolk St.
Union St.
Elm St.
Market St.
Windsor St.
Willow St.
Berkshire St.
Webster Ave.
Portland St.
Cambridge St.
8th St.
7th St.
6th St.
5th St.
Otis St.
Thorndike St.
Fulkerson St.
Sciarappa St.
3rd St.
McGrath Hwy.
Spring St.
Hurley St.
2nd St.
1st St.
Commercial St.

Washington St.
Harvard St.
Portland St.
Charles St.
Bent St.
Rogers St.
Binney St.
Munroe St.

CAMBRIDGE

Broadway

State St.
Main St.
Vassar St.
Ames St.
Carleton St.
Wadsworth St.
Longfellow Br.

Massachusetts Ave.
TO HARVARD SQUARE
Albany St.
Amherst St.
3

Massachusetts Institute of Technology ■

Memorial Drive

2A

Charles River Basin

Harvard Br.

James J. Storrow Memorial Dr.

Gibson House ■

Back St.
Berkeley St.
Marlborough St.
Clarendon St.

Beacon St.
Dartmouth St.

BACK BAY

Fairfield St.
Gloucester St.
Hereford St.
Commonwealth Ave.
Newbury St.
Exeter St.
Blagden St.

Back St.
Boston Public Library ■ ■**Trinity**

Kenmore Sq.
Boylston St.
John Hanc Towe

Brookline Ave.
Lansdowne St.
Mass Tpke.
Ipswich
90
Dalton St.
■**Copley Place**

Fenway Park
1
Ipswich St.
Belvidere St.

Van Ness St.
Hemenway St.
Massachusetts Ave.
PRUDENTIAL CENTER
9
28

Boylston St.
BACK BAY FENS
Burbank St.
St. Stephen St.
Huntington Ave.
St. Botolph St.
Prudential Center Skywalk ■
Columbus Ave.
Appleton S
B.
Warren Ave.

Petersborough St.
Fenway
Westland Ave.
Christian Science Church Center ■
Pembroke St.
Newton St.
Montg
Canton
Tremont

Queensberry St.
Park Dr.
St. Gainsborough St.
■**Symphony Hall**

TO MUSEUM OF FINE ARTS, ISABELLA STEWART GARDNER MUSEUM

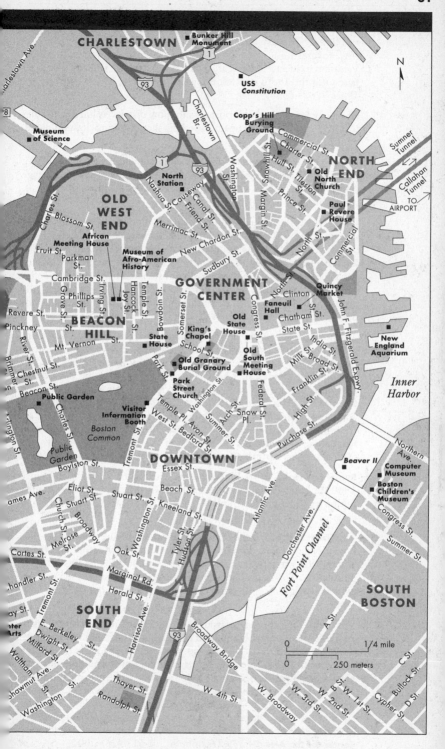

CHARLESTOWN

Bunker Hill
Monument

USS
Constitution

Copp's Hill
Burying
Ground

Charter St.
Old
North
Church

NORTH
END

Sumner Tunnel

Callahan Tunnel

TO AIRPORT

Museum
of Science

North
Station

Paul
Revere
House

OLD
WEST
END

African
Meeting House

Museum of
Afro-American
History

GOVERNMENT
CENTER

Quincy
Market

Clinton St.
Faneuil
Hall

Chatham St.

Fruit St.

Parkman
St.

Cambridge St.

Phillips
St.

BEACON
HILL

Mt. Vernon

State
House

King's
Chapel

Old
State
House

State St.

New
England
Aquarium

Revere St.

Pinckney

Chestnut
St.

Beacon St.

Public Garden

Visitor
Information
Booth

Boston
Common

Park
Street
Church

Old Granary
Burial Ground

Old
South
Meeting
House

Inner
Harbor

Public
Garden

Boylston St.

DOWNTOWN

Essex St.

Beaver II

Computer
Museum

Boston
Children's
Museum

Eliot St.
Stuart St.
Broadway
Melrose St.

Beach St.

Kneeland St.

Cortes St.

Oak St.

SOUTH
END

Marginal Rd.

Herald St.

E. Berkeley St.
Dwight St.
Milford St.

SOUTH
BOSTON

Thayer St.

Randolph St.

Broadway Bridge

Fort Point Channel

0   1/4 mile

0   250 meters

W. 4th St.

W. Broadway

W. 3rd St.

W. 2nd St.

A St.

B St.
C St.
D St.

as far as the Fens in the 19th century. Back Bay is a living museum of urban Victorian residential architecture. The **Gibson House** (1859) offers a representative look at how life was arranged in these tall, narrow, formal buildings. The house has been preserved with all its Victorian fixtures and furniture intact: A conservative Gibson scion lived here until the 1950s and left things as they were. ⊠ *137 Beacon St.,* ☎ *617/267–6338.*

Newbury Street, Boston's poshest shopping district, is lined with sidewalk cafés and dozens of upscale specialty shops offering clothing, china, antiques, and art.

From the 60th-floor observatory of the tallest building in New England, the 62-story **John Hancock Tower,** you'll have one of the best vantage points in the city. ⊠ *Observatory ticket office, Trinity Pl. and St. James Ave.,* ☎ *617/247–1977.*

One of the three monumental buildings that dominate **Copley Square** is the stately, bowfront Copley Plaza Hotel. **Trinity Church** is Henry Hobson Richardson's Romanesque Revival masterwork of 1877. And the **Boston Public Library** (☎ 617/536–5400) confirmed the status of McKim, Mead, and White as apostles of Renaissance Revival in 1895. The modern complex **Copley Place** comprises two major hotels (the Westin and the Marriott), dozens of shops and restaurants, and a cinema grouped on several levels around bright, open indoor spaces.

The headquarters of the **Christian Science Church Center** (⊠ 175 Huntington Ave., at Massachusetts Ave., ☎ 617/450–3790) presents a striking mixture of old and new architecture. Mary Baker Eddy's original granite First Church of Christ, Scientist (1894) and the domed Renaissance basilica added to the site in 1906 are now surrounded by the offices of the *Christian Science Monitor* and by I. M. Pei's 1973 complex of church administration buildings with its distinctive reflecting pool. Overlooking the Christian Science Church, the **Prudential Center Skywalk** (⊠ 800 Boylston St., ☎ 617/859–0648) is a 50th-floor observatory offering the best views of the city and suburbs.

Symphony Hall (⊠ 301 Massachusetts Ave., ☎ 617/266–1492), since 1900 the home of the Boston Symphony Orchestra, is another contribution of McKim, Mead, and White, though the acoustics rather than exterior design make this a special place.

The **South End,** eclipsed by the Back Bay more than a century ago, has now been gentrified, with upscale galleries and restaurants catering to young professionals, including a large concentration of Boston's gay population. The houses here continue the pattern established on Beacon Hill (in a uniformly bowfront style) but have more florid decoration.

The South End also has a strong African-American presence, particularly along Columbus Avenue and Massachusetts Avenue, which marks the beginning of the neighborhood of Roxbury. The early integration of the South End set the stage for its eventual transformation into a remarkably polyglot population. You are likely to hear Spanish spoken along Tremont Street, and there are Middle Eastern groceries along Shawmut Avenue. At the northeastern extreme of the South End, Harrison Avenue and Washington Street connect the area with Chinatown. On Tremont Street you'll find blocks of trendy restaurants and the **Boston Center for the Arts** (⊠ 539 Tremont St., ☎ 617/426–5000).

The Fens

After all the work that had gone into filling in the bay, it would have been little extra trouble to march row houses straight through to

Brookline. Happily, planners hired Frederick Law Olmsted to make the Fens into a park instead. Today's park consists of still, irregular, and reed-bound pools surrounded by broad meadows, trees, and flower gardens.

★ The **Museum of Fine Arts,** between Huntington Avenue and the Fenway, has holdings of American art surpassing those of all but two or three other U.S. museums; an extensive collection of Asian art; and European artwork from the 11th through the 20th centuries. Count on staying a while to have *any* hope of seeing even a smidgen of what is here. The west wing has a restaurant and a cafeteria. ⊠ *465 Huntington Ave.,* ☎ *617/267–9300.*

★ Encapsulating Boston's Golden Age, the **Isabella Stewart Gardner Museum** is a monument to one woman's taste—and a treasure trove of some 2,000 spectacular paintings, sculptures, furniture, and textiles, with an emphasis on Italian Renaissance and 17th-century Dutch masters. Friend to John Singer Sargent, Edith Wharton, and Henry James, Gardner shocked proper Bostonians with the flamboyance of her Venetian-style palazzo. The highlight of the collection—and according to some scholars, the greatest painting in America—is Titian's *Rape of Europa.* At the center of the building is a soaring courtyard planted with flowers. ⊠ *280 The Fenway,* ☎ *617/566–1401. Closed Mon.*

The Boston shrine known as **Fenway Park** is one of the smallest and oldest baseball parks in the major leagues. Built in 1912, it still has real grass on the field. **Kenmore Square** is home to fast food parlors, alternative rock clubs, an abundance of students from nearby Boston University, and the enormous neon CITGO sign, an area landmark.

Cambridge

In 1636 the country's first college was established in Cambridge, just across the Charles River from Boston. Two years later it was named in honor of John Harvard, a young Charlestown clergyman who had recently died, leaving the college his entire library and half his estate. **Harvard** remained the only college in the American colonies until 1693. The information office, in **Holyoke Center** (⊠ 1350 Massachusetts Ave., ☎ 617/495–1573), offers area maps and a free hour-long walking tour of Harvard Yard most days. North of Cambridge Common is **Radcliffe College,** founded in 1897; since 1975 Radcliffe students have shared classes and degrees with Harvard students.

Harvard University has three celebrated art museums, each a treasure in itself. The most famous is the **Fogg Art Museum.** Founded in 1895, it now owns 80,000 works of art from every major period and from every corner of the world. Its focus is primarily on European and American art, and it has notable collections of 19th-century French Impressionist and medieval Italian paintings. ⊠ *32 Quincy St.,* ☎ *617/ 495–9400.*

A ticket to the Fogg also gains you admission to Harvard's **Busch-Reisinger Museum** (☎ 617/495–9400), in Werner Otto Hall, which is entered through the Fogg. The collection specializes in Germanic and Central and Northern European art.

Fogg admission also gets you into the **Arthur M. Sackler Museum** (☎ 617/495–9400) across the street, which concentrates on ancient Greek and Roman, Egyptian, Islamic, Chinese, and other Eastern art.

The **Massachusetts Institute of Technology,** which borders the Charles River south of Harvard Square, boasts distinctive architecture by I. M. Pei and Eero Saarinen, plus several museums. Among them is the **MIT Museum,** where art and science meet. The **Information Center** (⊠ 77

Massachusetts Ave., Bldg. 7, ☎ 617/253–4795) offers free tours of the campus weekdays at 10 and 2.

Parks and Gardens

The **Back Bay Fens** mark the beginning of Boston's Emerald Necklace, a loosely connected chain of parks designed by Frederick Law Olmsted that extends along the Fenway, Riverway, and Jamaicaway to Jamaica Pond. At Jamaica Pond is the 265-acre **Arnold Arboretum** (⊠ 125 Arborway, Jamaica Plain, ☎ 617/524–1718). The **Franklin Park Zoo** (⊠ Columbia Rd. and Blue Hill Ave., Dorchester, ☎ 617/442–2002) is also here.

★ The **Boston Public Garden,** next to Boston Common, is the oldest botanical garden in the United States. Its pond has been famous since 1877 for its Swan Boats, which offer leisurely cruises during the warm months of the year.

The **Dr. Paul Dudley White Bikeway,** approximately 18 mi long, runs along both sides of the Charles River. The river's banks are also popular with joggers.

What to See and Do with Children

Across the Charles River from Beacon Hill, the **Museum of Science** has more than 450 exhibits covering astronomy, anthropology, medicine, computers, earth sciences, and more. The Charles Hayden Planetarium and the Mugar Omni Theater are also here. ⊠ *Science Park (on the Charles River Dam),* ☎ 617/723–2500.

The **Children's Museum** contains a multitude of hands-on exhibits, many designed to help children understand cultural diversity, their bodies, and the nature of disabilities. ⊠ *300 Congress St.,* ☎ 617/426–6500.

Dining

The choice of restaurants in Boston and Cambridge is wide and cosmopolitan, with bastions of tradition as well as nationally recognized spots featuring innovative young chefs. No matter what the style or cuisine, though, the main ingredient is still the bounty of the North Atlantic; the daily catch of fish and shellfish appears somewhere on virtually every menu. For price ranges *see* Chart 1 (A) *in* On the Road with Fodor's. Addresses below include a neighborhood reference.

$$$$ ✕ **Biba.** Arguably Boston's best restaurant and surely one of the most
★ original and high-casual restaurants in America, Biba is a place to see and be seen, from the vividness of the dining room's rambling mural to the huge street-level people-watching windows of the downstairs bar. The menu encourages inventive combinations, unusual cuts and produce, haute comfort food, and big postmodern desserts. Allow plenty of time for dining; service can be slow. ⊠ *272 Boylston St., Beacon Hill,* ☎ *617/426–7878. Reservations essential. D, DC, MC, V.*

$$$$ ✕ **Union Square Bistro.** A floor above the ethnic markets of Somerville's
★ Union Square, chef David Smoke McCluskey adds a regard for American foodstuffs and game based on his Native American heritage. Venison with a faux pemmican sauce made of black cherries and venison jerky and the best crab cakes in the league are served with heart. ⊠ *16 Bow St., Union Square, Somerville,* ☎ *617/628–3344. Reservations essential. AE, D, DC, MC, V. Brunch Sun.*

$$$ ✕ **East Coast Grill.** Owner-chef-author Chris Schlesinger serves up
★ dishes such as his renowned Jamaican jerk, North Carolina pulled pork, and *habanero*-laced Pasta from Hell with restrained spicing and inventive

grilling in an informal dining room. ✉ *1271 Cambridge St., Cambridge,* ☎ *617/491–6568. Reservations essential for 5 or more. AE, D, MC, V. Brunch Sun. No lunch.*

$$$ ✕ **Hamersley's Bistro.** Gordon Hamersley has earned a national rep-
★ utation thanks to his grilled mushroom-and-garlic sandwich and his cassoulet of duck confit, pork, and garlic sausage. His place has a full bar, a café area, and a larger dining room that's not much more formal than the bar. ✉ *553 Tremont St., South End,* ☎ *617/423–2700. D, MC, V.*

$$$ ✕ **Lala Rokh.** This delicious fantasia on Persian food and art transports
★ its patrons to the Azerbaijanian corner that is now northwestern Iran. Treasured Persian miniatures and medieval maps adorn the walls. The food includes exotically flavored specialties, and dishes such as pilaf, kebabs, *fesanjoon* (pomegranate-walnut sauce), and lamb stews. ✉ *97 Mount Vernon St., Beacon Hill,* ☎ *617/720–5511. AE, DC, MC, V. No lunch.*

$$$ ✕ **Legal Sea Foods.** The hallmark here is top-quality seafood; dishes
★ come to the table in whatever order they leave the kitchen, since freshness is of uppermost importance. The smoked bluefish pâté is one of the finest appetizers anywhere, and don't miss the chowder. ✉ *35 Columbus Ave., Park Sq.,* ☎ *617/426–4444;* ✉ *5 Cambridge Center, Kendall Sq.,* ☎ *617/864–3400;* ✉ *Logan Airport, Terminal C,* ☎ *617/569–4622. Reservations not accepted. AE, D, DC, MC, V.*

$$$ ✕ **Les Zygomates.** Taken straight from a French anatomy book, the
★ name refers to the human face muscles that enable you to smile—and this combination wine bar–bistro will do just that. Pan-seared catfish with house vinaigrette and the roasted rabbit leg stuffed with vegetables typify the taste. ✉ *129 South St., Downtown,* ☎ *617/542–5108. Reservations essential. AE, DC, MC, V. No lunch weekends.*

$$$ ✕ **Mamma Maria.** What happens when an Italian restaurant is commanded by an Irish chef? Chianti mashed potatoes. No joke. Despite the stereotypical name, Mamma Maria is one of the most elegant and romantic restaurants in the North End, from the homemade pasta to the innovative sauces and entrées to the North End's best desserts. ✉ *3 North Square, North End,* ☎ *617/523–0077. AE, DC, MC, V.*

$$ ✕ **Chau Chow.** *Chau chow* are the words meaning "people from Swa-
★ tow," in China's Fujian Province. The clams in black bean sauce, steamed sea bass, gray sole fried with its fins, or any dish with their famous ginger sauce won't disappoint. Chau Chow has expanded to a larger storefront called Grand Chau Chow, right across the street: It has live fish tanks, accepts credit cards, and looks a little nicer on the outside. ✉ *50 and 52 Beach St., Chinatown,* ☎ *617/426–6266. Cash only at Chau Chow; AE, DC, MC, V at Grand Chau Chow.*

$$ ✕ **Matt Murphy's Pub.** Among the dozens of Irish pubs in Boston, only Matt Murphy's is notable for its food as well as a well-drawn pint. The pub makes real poetry out of thick slabs of bread and butter, giant soups, fish-and-chips served in a twist of newspaper, shepherd's pie, and hot rabbit pie—all served in enormous portions. ✉ *14 Harvard St., Brookline Village,* ☎ *617/232–0188. No credit cards.*

$$ ✕ **Pomodoro.** This is a tiny gem of a trattoria, specializing in country
★ Italian favorites. It is owned and run by an Ireland native, Siobhan Carew, who single-handedly waits on the room. The walls are decorated with lacquered cutlery, and the wine list is exceptional. Best choice could well be the clam-and-tomato stew with herbed flat bread. ✉ *319 Hanover St., North End,* ☎ *617/367–4348. No credit cards.*

$ ✕ **Bartley's Burger Cottage.** It may be the perfect cuisine for student metabolism, but even aging Harvard dons can't resist the thick burgers, french fries, and onion rings served in this crowded restaurant with tiny tables. Veggie burgers provide a solid alternative for the health conscious. ⊠ *1246 Massachusetts Ave., Cambridge,* ☎ *617/354–6559. Reservations not accepted. No credit cards. Closed Sun.*

Lodging

Many of the city's most costly lodgings offer attractively priced weekend packages. Consult the *Boston Travel Planner* (☞ Visitor Information, *above*) for current rates. At many hotels children may stay free in their parents' room, or breakfast may be included in the rate.

Although Boston does not have a large number of B&Bs, there are several with daily rates between $55 and $120 per room. Reservations may be made through **Bed and Breakfast Associates Bay Colony** (⊠ Box 57166, Babson Park Branch, Boston 02157, ☎ 617/449–5302 or 800/347–5088, 🖷 617/449–5302).

For price ranges *see* Chart 2 (A) *in* On the Road with Fodor's.

$$$$ 🏨 **Boston Harbor Hotel at Rowes Wharf.** Surely the most exciting place
   ★   to stay in Boston, this elegant ocean-side hotel provides a dramatic entryway to the city for travelers arriving from Logan Airport via the water shuttle, which docks right at the door amid a slew of luxury yachts and powerboats. Guest rooms have either city or water views (both are dramatic), and some have balconies. ⊠ *70 Rowes Wharf, 02110,* ☎ *617/ 439–7000 or 800/752–7077,* 🖷 *617/330–9450. 254 rooms. Restaurant, bar, outdoor café, indoor lap pool, beauty salons, health club, concierge, business services, valet parking. AE, D, DC, MC, V.*

$$$$ 🏨 **Copley Plaza.** This stately bowfront, a classic among Boston hotels,
   ★   was built in 1912. Guest rooms have carpeting from England, custom furniture from Italy, and bathroom fixtures surrounded by marble tile. Since a 1996 takeover by the Fairmont hotel group, major top-to-bottom renovations of all rooms have begun and are slated to be completed by early 1998. ⊠ *138 St. James Ave., 02116,* ☎ *617/267–5300 or 800/996–3426,* 🖷 *617/267–7668. 424 rooms. 2 restaurants, 2 bars, barbershop, beauty salon. AE, D, DC, MC, V.*

$$$$ 🏨 **Ritz-Carlton.** Since 1927 this has been one of the most luxurious and
   ★   elegant hotels in Boston. The rooms are traditionally furnished; the suites in the older section have working fireplaces and views of the Public Garden. ⊠ *Arlington and Newbury Sts., 02117,* ☎ *617/536–5700 or 800/241–3333,* 🖷 *617/536–1335. 320 rooms. 3 restaurants, room service, beauty salon, exercise room, baby-sitting, laundry service, concierge, valet parking. AE, D, DC, MC, V.*

$$$–$$$$ 🏨 **Eliot Hotel.** Ambitious renovations have brought a new elegance and lots of marble to this nine-floor, European-style hotel. The luxurious all-suite accommodations have Italian marble bathrooms, living rooms with period furnishings, and stylish kitchenettes. The split-level, marble-clad lobby contains writing desks and a huge chandelier. ⊠ *370 Commonwealth Ave., 02215,* ☎ *617/267–1607 or 800/443–5468,* 🖷 *617/536–9114. 91 suites. Valet parking (fee). AE, D, DC, MC, V.*

$$$–$$$$ 🏨 **Lenox Hotel.** Extensive renovations have transformed the Lenox, built
   ★   in 1900, into a charming home-away-from-home with low-key elegance and first-class service. Both the heart of Newbury Street and a T stop are only one block away. The first 10 floors have Early American furnishings, while the top floor is decorated in the French provincial style. The lobby is handsome, trimmed in blues and golds and set off by a welcoming fireplace. ⊠ *710 Boylston St., 02116,* ☎ *617/536– 5300 or 800/225–7676,* 🖷 *617/266–7905. 215 rooms. Restaurant, pub, barbershop, exercise room, baby-sitting, concierge, parking (fee). AE, DC, MC, V.*

$$ 🏨 **Cambridge House Bed and Breakfast.** This gracious old home on the National Register of Historic Places has seven antiques-filled guest rooms and five more in its carriage house. Convenient to the T and buses, it also serves as a reservations center for host homes in metropolitan Boston. ⊠ *2218 Massachusetts Ave., Cambridge 02140,* ☎ *617/491–6300 or 800/232–9989,* ℻ *617/868–2848. 16 rooms. Parking. MC, V. No smoking, no pets.*

$$ ⌶ **Copley Square Hotel.** One of the best values in the city and popular with Europeans, this quirky, friendly hotel has rooms of various shapes and sizes outfitted with a host of amenities, including modems, windows you can open, safes, hair dryers, irons and ironing boards, and automatic coffeemakers. ⊠ *47 Huntington Ave., 02116,* ☎ *617/536–9000 or 800/225–7062,* ℻ *617/267–3547. 155 rooms. Restaurant, coffee shop. AE, D, DC, MC, V.*

$ ⌶ **Boston International Hostel.** Guests sleep in three- to five-person dormitories and must provide or rent linens or sleep sacks (sleeping bags not permitted). The maximum stay is three nights in summer, two weeks in off-season. In high season American Youth Hostel membership is required; it is possible to join here. ⊠ *12 Hemenway St., 02115,* ☎ *617/536–9455,* ℻ *617/424–6558. 205 beds. MC, V.*

Motels

⌶ **Best Western Terrace Motor Lodge** (⊠ 1650 Commonwealth Ave., 02135, ☎ 617/566–6260 or 800/242–8377, ℻ 617/731–3543), 73 rooms, parking; *$.* ⌶ **Harvard Square Hotel** (⊠ 110 Mt. Auburn St., Cambridge 02138, ☎ 617/864–5200 or 800/458–5886), 73 rooms, café; *$$–$$$.* ⌶ **Holiday Inn Logan Airport** (⊠ 225 McClellan Hwy., East Boston 02128, ☎ 617/569–5250 or 800/465–4329, ℻ 617/569–5159), 350 rooms, restaurant, bar, airport shuttle; *$$.* ⌶ **Susse Chalet Inn** (⊠ 211 Concord Turnpike, Cambridge 02140, ☎ 617/661–7800 or 800/258–1980, ℻ 617/868–8153,) 78 rooms, free parking, access to exercise room, CP; *$.*

Nightlife and the Arts

Thursday's *Boston Globe* calendar and the weekly *Boston Phoenix* provide contemporary listings of events for the coming week.

Nightlife

Quincy Market, Copley Square, and **Kenmore Square** in Boston and **Harvard Square** in Cambridge are centers of nightlife.

CAFÉS

Café Algiers (⊠ 40 Brattle St., ☎ 617/492–1557) is a genuine Middle Eastern café, with a choice of strong coffees and tea and pita lunches. The decor is plain, and the service is rather relaxed; go for conversation. **Other Side Cosmic Café** (⊠ 407 Newbury St., ☎ 617/536–9477) offers college-dorm ambience, a good cup of java, a fruit and vegetable juice bar, and no-frills soups and sandwiches. Both are open daily till midnight; no credit cards are accepted.

COMEDY

Comedy Connection (⊠ Faneuil Hall Marketplace, ☎ 617/248–9700) offers a mix of local and nationally known acts, seven nights a week (two shows Friday and Saturday), with a cover charge.

DISCO

Axis (⊠ 13 Lansdowne St., ☎ 617/262–2424) features high-energy disco and a giant dance floor. Sunday night is gay night, when it combines with Avalon next door, and dancers can circulate between the two. **Karma Club** (⊠ 11 Lansdowne St., Kenmore Square, ☎ 617/421–9678) is Boston's newest nightclub. Poufy couches, incense, and erotic music seduce a young, beautiful crowd.

JAZZ

Some top names in jazz perform at **Regattabar** (✉ Bennett and Eliot Sts., Cambridge, ☎ 617/876–7777), a spacious, elegant club in the Charles Hotel.

ROCK

The **Paradise** (✉ 967 Commonwealth Ave., ☎ 617/254–3939) is known for big-name alternative pop/rock shows.

The Arts

BosTix (✉ Faneuil Hall Marketplace and Copley Sq., ☎ 617/723–5181) sells half-price tickets for same-day performances and full-price advance tickets. With major credit cards, you can charge tickets for many events over the phone by calling **Ticketmaster** (☎ 617/931–2000).

DANCE

Dance Umbrella (✉ 380 Green St., Cambridge, ☎ 617/492–7578) produces major dance events around town. The **Boston Ballet** (✉ 19 Clarendon St., ☎ 617/695–6950) performs at the Wang Center.

MUSIC

Symphony Hall (✉ 301 Massachusetts Ave., ☎ 617/266–1492) is home to the Boston Symphony Orchestra and the Boston Pops. **Jordan Hall at the New England Conservatory** (✉ 30 Gainsborough St., ☎ 617/536–2412) is home to the Boston Philharmonic (☎ 617/868–6696) and visiting artists. Major pop and jazz acts often perform at **Berklee Performance Center** (✉ 136 Massachusetts Ave., ☎ 617/266–1400 or 617/266–7455). The **Orpheum Theatre** (✉ 1 Hamilton Pl., ☎ 617/482–0650) is another venue for major acts.

OPERA

Boston Lyric Opera Company (✉ 114 State St., ☎ 617/542–6772) presents three fully staged productions each season.

THEATER

First-rate Broadway tour and tryout theaters are clustered in the Theater District (near the intersection of Tremont and Stuart streets) and include the **Colonial Theatre** (✉ 106 Bolyston St., ☎ 617/426–9366). The **Wang Center for the Performing Arts** (✉ 270 Tremont St., ☎ 617/482–9393) is also in the Theater District. The **American Repertory Theatre** (✉ Loeb Drama Center, 64 Brattle St., Cambridge, ☎ 617/495–2668) produces classic and experimental works. The **Huntington Theatre Company** (✉ 264 Huntington Ave., ☎ 617/266–0800) stages new works and traditional repertory at Boston University.

Spectator Sports

Baseball: Boston Red Sox (✉ Fenway Park, ☎ 617/267–1700).

Basketball: Boston Celtics (✉ FleetCenter, ☎ 617/624–1000 or 617/931–2000 [Ticketmaster] for tickets).

Football: New England Patriots (✉ Foxboro Stadium, 45 min south of Boston, Foxboro, ☎ 800/543–1776).

Hockey: Boston Bruins (✉ FleetCenter, ☎ 617/624–1000 or 617/931–2000 [Ticketmaster] for tickets).

Shopping

Antiques, clothing, recorded music, and books keep cash registers ringing in Boston. Most Boston stores are in the area bounded by Quincy Market, the Back Bay, downtown, and Copley Square. There are few outlet stores but plenty of bargains, particularly in Filene's Basement and Chinatown's fabric district. Boston's two daily newspapers, the *Globe* and the *Herald,* are the best places to learn about sales.

Shopping Districts

Copley Place, an indoor shopping mall connecting two hotels, has 87 stores, restaurants, and cinemas that blend the elegant, the glitzy, and the overpriced. **Downtown Crossing,** between Summer and Washington streets, is a pedestrian mall with outdoor food and merchandise kiosks, street performers, and benches for people-watchers. **Faneuil Hall Marketplace** has crowds, small shops, and kiosks of every description. The busy food court of **Quincy Market** is also here. **Newbury Street** is where the funky and the trendy give way to the chic and the expensive. **Charles Street** on Beacon Hill is a mecca for antiques lovers from all over the country.

Harvard Square, in Cambridge, has more than 150 stores within a few blocks; it is a book lover's paradise. **CambridgeSide Galleria,** between Kendall Square and the Museum of Science in Cambridge, has about 100 shops.

Department Stores

Filene's (⊠ 426 Washington St., ☎ 617/357–2100; ⊠ CambridgeSide Galleria, Cambridge, ☎ 617/621–3800) carries name-brand men's and women's clothing. **Filene's Basement** (⊠ 426 Washington St., ☎ 617/542–2011), now an entity all its own, pioneered the idea of discounting; it reduces prices according to the number of days items have been on the rack.

Specialty Stores

Louis, Boston (⊠ 234 Berkeley St., ☎ 617/262–6100) is Boston's signature clothier, carrying elegantly tailored designs and subtly updated classics in everything from linen to tweeds. **Shreve, Crump & Low** (⊠ 330 Boylston St., ☎ 617/267–9100) is an old, well-respected store that carries the finest in jewelry, china, crystal, and silver.

Side Trip to Lexington and Concord

The events of April 19, 1775—the first military encounters of the American War of Independence—are very much a part of present-day Lexington and Concord. These two quintessential New England towns are also rich in literary history: Concord, for example, is the site of Walden Pond, immortalized by Thoreau. Several historic houses have been preserved and can be visited. The **visitor center** in Lexington (⊠ 1875 Massachusetts Ave., 02173, ☎ 617/862–1450) can direct you. The **Minute Man National Historical Park Visitors Center** (⊠ Off Rte. 2A, ☎ 617/862–7753) is another source of information.

Arriving and Departing

To reach Lexington and Concord by car from Boston, take Route 2A (Massachusetts Avenue) west from Cambridge or I–95/Route 128 north to the Lexington exit. Route 2A west will take you on to Concord. Both towns are about a half-hour drive from the metropolitan Boston area. The MBTA (☞ Getting Around Boston, *above*) operates buses to Lexington.

What to See and Do

Minuteman captain John Parker assembled his men on **Battle Green,** a 2-acre triangular piece of land, to await the arrival of the British, who were marching from Boston toward Concord to "teach rebels a lesson." Parker's role is commemorated in Henry Hudson Kitson's renowned sculpture, the **Minuteman statue.**

Buckman Tavern, built in 1690, is where the minutemen gathered the morning of April 19, 1775. ☒ *1 Bedford St.,* ☎ *617/862–5598. Closed Nov.–Mar.*

★ The **Museum of Our National Heritage** is a small but dynamic institution that does a superb job not only in displaying items and artifacts from all facets of American life but also in putting them to a social and political context. ☒ *33 Marrett Rd.,* ☎ *617/861–6559. Free.*

At the **Old North Bridge,** half a mile from Concord's center, the tables were turned on the British on the morning of April 19, 1775, by the Concord minutemen. Daniel Chester French's famous statue of **The Minuteman** (1875) honors the country's first freedom fighters.

The **Minute Man National Historical Park,** a two-parcel park with more than 800 acres straddling Lexington, Concord, and Lincoln, includes many of the sites central to Concord's role in the Revolution. The park is laced with hiking trails and crossed by Battle Road, which roughly follows the path the British took to and from Boston during the battle of Lexington and Concord. *North Bridge Visitor Center:* ☒ *174 Liberty St.,* ☎ *508/369–6993. Free.*

The 19th-century essayist and poet Ralph Waldo Emerson lived in the **Ralph Waldo Emerson House.** ☒ *28 Cambridge Turnpike, on Rte. 2A,* ☎ *508/369–2236. Closed mid-Oct.–mid-Apr.*

The **Concord Museum** has Emerson and Thoreau artifacts and one of the two lanterns hung at the Old North Church the night of April 18, 1775. ☒ *200 Lexington Rd.,* ☎ *508/369–9609.*

Louisa May Alcott's family home, **Orchard House,** is where the author wrote *Little Women.* ☒ *399 Lexington Rd.,* ☎ *508/369–4118. Closed Jan. 1–15.*

Nathaniel Hawthorne and Ralph Waldo Emerson both lived at the **Old Manse** but at different times. ☒ *Monument St.,* ☎ *508/369–3909. Closed Nov.–mid-Apr.*

Nathaniel Hawthorne also lived at **the Wayside.** ☒ *455 Lexington Rd. (Rte. 2A),* ☎ *508/369–6975. Closed Nov.–mid-Apr.*

Walden Pond is Henry David Thoreau's most famous residence. Thoreau published *Walden* (1854), a collection of essays on observations he made while living at this cabin in the woods. The site of that first cabin is staked out in stone. An authentically furnished full-size replica stands about a half mile from the original site, near the parking lot for the Walden Pond State Reservation. You can swim and hike here. ☒ *Rte. 126 (parking across from pond is $2 per vehicle),* ☎ *508/ 369–3254. Free.*

Side Trip to the North Shore

The North Shore extends from the northern suburbs to the Cape Ann region and beyond to the New Hampshire border. For information contact the **North of Boston Visitors and Convention Bureau** (☒ 248 Cabot St., Box 642, Beverly 01915, ☎ 508/921–4990).

Arriving and Departing

It's about 40 mi from Boston to Gloucester. The primary link between Boston and the North Shore is I–93 north to Route 128E, which then follows the line of the coast just inland as far north as Gloucester. The more scenic route is along coastal Route 1A (which leaves Boston via the Callahan Tunnel) to Route 127.

What to See and Do
Salem thrives on a history of witches, millionaires, and maritime trade. **Rockport** is crammed with crafts shops and artists' studios. **Gloucester** is the oldest seaport in America. **Newburyport** has a redbrick center and rows of clapboard Federal mansions.

Side Trip to the South Shore

Southeastern Massachusetts between Boston and the Cape is a region with strong historical associations.

Arriving and Departing
The most direct way to Fall River and New Bedford (themselves connected by I–195) is via Route 24, about a 45-minute drive; I–93 and Route 3 connect Boston with Plymouth, which is about an hour's drive. From Boston **MBTA** buses (☎ 617/722–3200) serve both Quincy and Braintree. **American Eagle** (☎ 508/993–5040) serves New Bedford. **Bonanza** (☎ 617/720–4110) serves Fall River. **Plymouth & Brockton Street Railway** buses (☎ 508/746–0378) call at Plymouth en route to Cape Cod.

What to See and Do
★ The great seafaring towns of **Fall River** and **New Bedford** offer marine museums and reminders of the area's industrial past. The **Plimoth Plantation** living history museum (✉ Rte. 3A Exit 4, ☎ 508/746–1622) re-creates the Pilgrims' 1627 village; it's closed December–March. At the waterfront is the *Mayflower II*, a replica of the ship that brought the Pilgrims from England. Nearby is **Plymouth Rock,** believed to be the very spot on which the Pilgrims first set foot in 1620 after unsuccessfully scouting the Provincetown area as a potential settlement.

CAPE COD AND THE ISLANDS

Separated from the mainland by the 17½-mi-long Cape Cod Canal, the Cape curves 70 mi from end to end. Every summer crowds are attracted to its charming villages of weathered-shingle houses and white-steepled churches and to its natural beauty of pinewoods, grassy marshes, and beaches backed by rolling dunes. To the south, Martha's Vineyard and Nantucket are resort islands ringed with beautiful sandy beaches; Nantucket preserves a near-pristine whaling-era town.

Visitor Information

Cape Cod: Chamber of Commerce (✉ Jct. Rtes. 6 and 132, Hyannis 02601, ☎ 508/362–3225); **information booths:** Sagamore Bridge rotary (☎ 508/888–2438) and Bourne Bridge on Route 28 (☎ 508/759–3814). **Martha's Vineyard:** Chamber of Commerce (✉ Box 1698, Beach Rd., Vineyard Haven 02568, ☎ 508/693–0085). **Nantucket:** Chamber of Commerce (✉ Pacific Club, 48 Main St., Nantucket 02554, ☎ 508/228–1700).

Arriving and Departing

By Bus
Plymouth & Brockton Street Railway (☎ 508/775–5524) has service from Boston and Logan Airport. **Bonanza** (☎ 508/548–7588 or 800/556–3815) connects Bourne, Falmouth, Woods Hole, and Hyannis with New York and points between.

By Car

From Boston take I–93 to Route 3 to the Sagamore Bridge. From New York take I–95 to Providence; change to I–195 and follow signs to the Cape.

By Ferry

Ferries connect Martha's Vineyard and Nantucket to the mainland from Woods Hole, Hyannis, Falmouth, and New Bedford. The **Steamship Authority** (☎ 508/477–8600), **Hy-Line Cruises** (☎ 508/778–2600), the **Island Queen** (☎ 508/548–4800), and the **Schamonchi** (☎ 508/997–1688) serve Martha's Vineyard; the **Steamship Authority** and **Hy-Line** serve Nantucket.

By Plane

Hyannis's **Barnstable Municipal Airport** is Cape Cod's air gateway, with flights from **Business Express/Delta Connection** (☎ 800/345–3400), **Cape Air** (☎ 800/352–0714), **Nantucket Airlines** (☎ 508/228–6252 or 800/635–8787 in MA), and **Northwest Airlink** (☎ 800/225–2525). **Provincetown Municipal Airport** is served by **Cape Air.**

By Train

Amtrak (☎ 800/872–7245) offers limited service in summer to Hyannis, with bus connections to Woods Hole.

Exploring Cape Cod and the Islands

U.S. 6 traverses the relatively unpopulated center of the Cape. Paralleling U.S. 6 but following the north coast is Route 6A, which passes through some of the Cape's old but well-preserved New England towns. The south shore, encompassing Falmouth, Hyannis, and Chatham and traced by Route 28, is heavily populated and the major center for tourism. The sparse outer portion of the Cape, from Orleans to Provincetown, is edged with white-sand beaches and nature preserves. At the Cape's southwestern corner is **Woods Hole,** an international center for marine research. The **Marine Biological Laboratory** (☎ 508/289–7623) offers tours by reservation. You can also visit the **Woods Hole Oceanographic Institute Exhibit Center** (✉ 15 School St., ☎ 508/289–2663). Before leaving Woods Hole, stop at **Nobska Light** for a splendid view of the Elizabeth Islands and the sea beyond.

The village green in **Falmouth** was a military training field in the 18th century and is today flanked by Colonial homes, fine inns, and an 1856 Congregational church with a bell made by Paul Revere. The **Falmouth Historical Society** (✉ Palmer Ave. at the Village Green, ☎ 508/548–4857) maintains two museums and conducts free walking tours of the town in season.

Quietly wealthy **Hyannis Port** is the site of the Kennedy family compound. **Hyannis** is the Cape's year-round commercial hub. The **John F. Kennedy Memorial Museum** (☎ 508/775–2201) has photographs and videos from the presidential years focusing on John F. Kennedy's ties to the Cape. It's in the Old Town Hall on busy Main Street.

At the southeastern tip of Cape Cod, **Chatham** is a seaside town relatively free of the development and commercialism found elsewhere, though it offers a downtown of traditional shops and fine inns. The view from **Chatham Lighthouse** is spectacular. Just off the coast is **Monomoy National Wildlife Refuge** (Headquarters: ✉ Morris Island, Chatham, ☎ 508/945–0594), a 2,750-acre preserve including Monomoy Island, which provides nesting grounds for 285 species of birds and waterfowl.

Sandwich, the oldest town on the Cape, was founded in 1637. Centered by a pond with a waterwheel-powered gristmill, this picturesque town remains famous for the colored glass produced here in the 19th century.

Off Route 130 is **Heritage Plantation,** a complex of museum buildings displaying classic and historic cars, antique military-related items, Currier & Ives prints, and other Americana—all set amid extensive gardens. ⊠ *Grove and Pine Sts., Sandwich,* ☎ *508/888–3300. Closed Nov.–mid-May.*

Barnstable, east of Sandwich on Route 6A, is a lovely town of large old houses. **Yarmouth** has a few attractions for children, including a zoo-aquarium and a miniature golf course. **Hallet's Store** (⊠ Rte. 6A, ☎ 508/362–3362), a working drugstore and soda fountain, is preserved as it was more than 100 years ago. **Dennis** is a town with a great beach (West Dennis Beach). **Scargo Hill,** the highest spot in the area at 160 ft, offers a spectacular view of Cape Cod Bay and Scargo Lake.

Brewster has numerous mansions originally built for sea captains in the 1800s. The **Cape Cod Museum of Natural History** has environmental and marine exhibits, and trails through 80 acres rich in wildlife. ⊠ *Rte. 6A, Brewster,* ☎ *508/896–3867.*

★ In **Orleans,** Nauset Beach is a 10-mi-long sweep of sandy beach and dunes open to off-road vehicles. The **Cape Cod National Seashore** preserves 30 mi of landscape along the lower Cape, including superb beaches and lighthouses. **Eastham** is a place for people who enjoy the outdoors. Just off Route 6 in Eastham, the **National Seashore's Salt Pond Visitor Center** has a museum with displays, tours, lectures, and films. ☎ *508/255–3421. Closed weekdays Jan.–Feb.*

Wellfleet was a Colonial whaling and codfishing port and is now home to fishermen, artists, and artisans. The **Wellfleet Bay Wildlife Sanctuary** (⊠ Off Rte. 6, South Wellfleet, ☎ 508/349–2615) is a 1,000-acre haven for a variety of wildlife and is a superb place for walking and bird-watching. **Truro** is popular with writers and artists for its high dunes and virtual lack of development. At the National Seashore's **Pilgrim Heights Area,** trails meander through terrain explored by the *Mayflower* crew before they moved on to Plymouth.

In **Provincetown,** which is filled with first-rate shops and galleries, Portuguese and American fishermen mix with painters, poets, writers, whale-watchers, and a large gay and lesbian community. The National Seashore's **Province Lands** (☎ 508/487–1256) allow access to Provincetown's spectacular beaches and dunes, as well as walking, biking, and horse trails; they are closed December–mid-April. The **Pilgrim Monument and Provincetown Museum** (⊠ High Pole Hill Rd., ☎ 508/487–1310), on a hill above the town center, commemorate the landing of the Pilgrims in 1620. From atop the 252-ft tower the panoramic view of the entire Cape is breathtaking.

Martha's Vineyard is connected by ferry year-round with Wood's Hole; in summer boats also leave from Hyannis, Falmouth, and New Bedford. On the island the honky-tonk town of **Oak Bluffs** has a warren of some 300 candy-color Victorian cottages. The main port of **Vineyard Haven** has a street of shops and a back street preserved to reflect the way it appeared in whaling days. Tidy and polished **Edgartown** has upscale boutiques, elegant sea-captains' houses, and beautiful flower gardens. **Chappaquiddick Island,** laced with nature preserves, is accessible by ferry from Edgartown. The dramatically striated red-clay **Gay Head Cliffs,** a major tourist sight, stand in a Wampanoag Indian township on the island's western tip.

Cape Cod

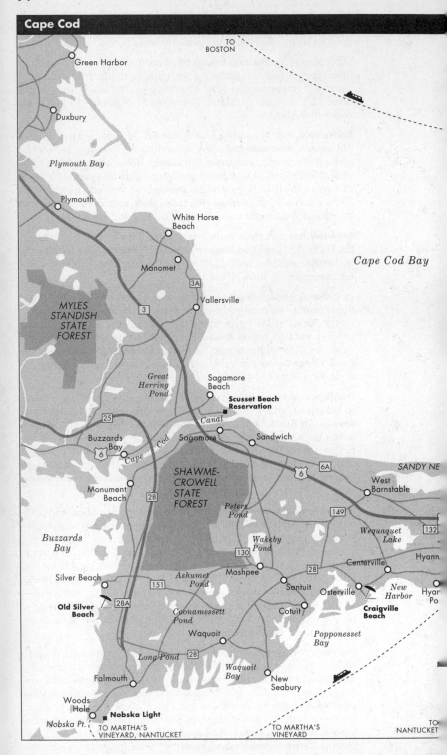

TO
BOSTON

Green Harbor

Duxbury

Plymouth Bay

Plymouth

White Horse
Beach

Cape Cod Bay

Manomet

3A

MYLES
STANDISH
STATE
FOREST

3

Vallersville

*Great
Herring
Pond*

Sagamore
Beach

**Scusset Beach
Reservation**

25

Canal

Buzzards
Bay

Sagamore

Sandwich

6

Cape Cod

6

6A

SANDY NE

West
Barnstable

Monument
Beach

SHAWME-
CROWELL
STATE
FOREST

28

*Peters
Pond*

149

132

*Wequaquet
Lake*

*Buzzards
Bay*

*Wakeby
Pond*

130

Mashpee

28

Centerville

Hyann

Silver Beach

151

*Ashumet
Pond*

Santuit

Osterville

*New
Harbor*

Hya
Po

**Old Silver
Beach**

28A

*Coonamessett
Pond*

Cotuit

**Craigville
Beach**

Waquoit

28

*Popponesset
Bay*

Long Pond

28

*Waquoit
Bay*

Falmouth

New
Seabury

Woods
Hole

Nobska Pt.

Nobska Light

TO MARTHA'S
VINEYARD, NANTUCKET

TO MARTHA'S
VINEYARD

TO
NANTUCKET

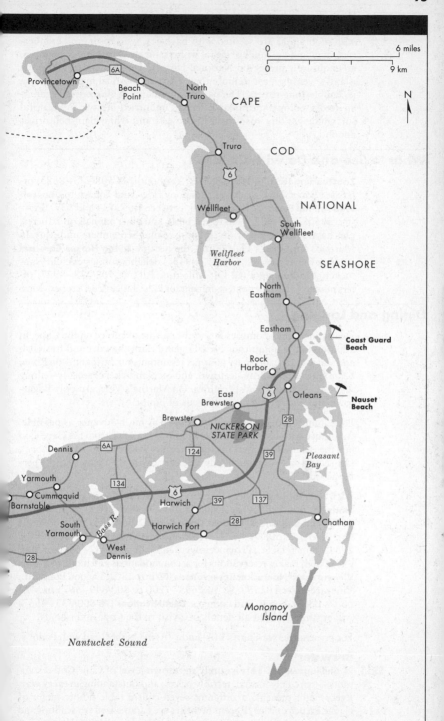

Nantucket, 30 mi out in the open Atlantic Ocean, is accessible by ferry year-round from Hyannis. Most of the 14 mi × 3 mi island is covered with moors that are scented with bayberry, wild roses, and cranberries; ringing it are miles of clean, white-sand beaches. **Nantucket town,** an exquisitely preserved National Historic District, encapsulates the island's whaling past in more than a dozen historical museums along its cobblestone streets. The beach community of **Siasconset** began as an actors' colony and today offers an unhurried lifestyle in beautiful surroundings; tiny rose-covered cottages and white-clamshell drives abound.

What to See and Do with Children

ZooQuarium (⊠ 674 Rte. 28, West Yarmouth, ☎ 508/775–8883) offers sea lion shows, a petting zoo, pony rides, and aquariums. **Bassett Wild Animal Farm** (⊠ Tubman Rd. between Rtes. 124 and 137, Brewster, ☎ 508/896–3224) has tigers, birds, and other animals on 20 acres, plus hayrides and pony rides; it is closed mid-September–mid-May. In Martha's Vineyard's Oak Bluffs, the historic **Flying Horses Carousel** (⊠ Oak Bluffs Ave., ☎ 508/693–9481) delights youngsters. On Nantucket, **J.J. Clammp's** (⊠ Off Milestone Rd., ☎ 508/228–8977) offers minigolf and other entertainment for kids; it is closed October–May.

Dining and Lodging

Hearty meat-and-potatoes fare is the cuisine of choice on the Cape, in addition to the ubiquitous New England clam chowder and fresh fish and seafood. Extraordinary gourmet restaurants can be found—on Route 6A in Brewster, in Provincetown, and on Nantucket especially—along with occasional ethnic specialties. On Martha's Vineyard only Edgartown and Oak Bluffs allow the sale of liquor.

For summer, lodgings should be booked as far in advance as possible. Assistance with last-minute reservations is available from the Cape Cod and the islands' chambers of commerce (☞ Visitor Information, *above*). Off-season rates are much reduced, and service then may be more personalized.

B&B reservations services include **House Guests Cape Cod and the Islands** (⊠ Box 1881, Orleans 02653, ☎ 508/896–7053 or 800/666–4678) and **Bed and Breakfast Cape Cod** (⊠ Box 341, West Hyannis Port 02672, ☎ 508/775–2772). **Provincetown Reservations System** (⊠ 293 Commercial St., Provincetown 02657, ☎ 508/487–4620 or 800/648–0364) makes reservations for accommodations and more. **Martha's Vineyard and Nantucket Reservations** (⊠ Box 1322, Lagoon Pond Rd., Vineyard Haven 02568, ☎ 508/693–7200 or 800/649–5671 in MA) books B&Bs, hotels, and cottages. **DestINNations** (☎ 800/333–4667) will arrange any and all details of a visit to the Cape and islands.

For price ranges *see* Charts 1 (A) and 2 (A) *in* On the Road with Fodor's.

Brewster

$$$$ ✕ **Chillingsworth.** This is surely the crown jewel of Cape Cod restau-
★ rants—extremely formal, terribly pricey, and outstanding in every way. Every night presents a different seven-course table d'hôte menu of classic French cuisine. Recent favorites are caramelized sea scallops and roast lobster. At dinner a more modest bistro menu is served in the Garden Room. ⊠ *2449 Main St. (Rte. 6A),* ☎ *508/896–3640. AE, DC, MC, V. Closed Mon., mid-June–mid-Oct.; closed weekdays, Memorial Day–mid-June and mid-Oct.–Memorial Day; closed Thanksgiving–Memorial Day.*

$$$–$$$$ **⊞ Captain Freeman Inn.** This splendid 1866 Victorian has 12-ft ceilings and windows as well as a spacious wraparound veranda. Guest rooms are furnished with antiques; suites have fireplaces and enclosed balconies with private hot tubs. ⊠ *15 Breakwater Rd., 02631,* ☎ *508/896–7481 or 800/843–4664,* ℻ *508/896–5618. 12 rooms. Pool, badminton, croquet, health club, bicycles. Full breakfast. AE, MC, V.*

Chatham

$$$$ **⊞ Chatham Bars Inn.** An oceanfront resort in the old style, this
★   Chatham landmark has a main building with a grand lobby and 26 cottages on 20 landscaped acres. Many rooms have private porches, some with lovely ocean views. There are three restaurants (reservations essential, no lunch, no dinner Sunday–Thursday, except holiday weekends November–March). ⊠ *Shore Rd., 02633,* ☎ *508/945–0096 or 800/527–4884,* ℻ *508/945–5491. 150 rooms, 26 cottages. 3 restaurants, bar, pool, tennis, beach, children's programs (July–Aug.). MAP available. AE, DC, MC, V.*

$$$–$$$$ **⊞ Captain's House Inn.** Finely preserved architectural details, tasteful
★   decor, delicious baked goods, and an overall feeling of warmth and quiet comfort are just part of what makes this one of the Cape's very best inns. The decor in the four inn buildings is mostly Williamsburg style; some rooms have fireplaces. Full breakfast and afternoon tea are included in the room rate. ⊠ *371 Old Harbor Rd., 02633,* ☎ *508/945–0127,* ℻ *508/945–0866. 19 rooms. Croquet, bicycles. AE, MC, V.*

Falmouth

$$$ **⊞ Mostly Hall.** Set in a landscaped yard, this imposing 1849 house has
★   a wraparound porch and a cupola. Corner rooms have leafy views, reading areas, antique pieces, and reproduction canopy beds. Full breakfasts and afternoon refreshments are complimentary and delicious. ⊠ *27 Main St., 02540,* ☎ *508/548–3786 or 800/682–0565. 6 rooms. Bicycles, library. AE, D, MC, V. Closed Jan.*

Hyannis

$$$–$$$$ **⊞ Tara Hyannis Hotel & Resort.** It's hard to beat the Tara's combination of landscaping, services, resort facilities, and location. Although the lobby is elegant, the rooms are bland, with pale colors and nondescript furnishings. All rooms have a private balcony or patio. ⊠ *West End Circle, 02601,* ☎ *508/775–7775,* ℻ *508/778–6039. 232 rooms. Restaurant, bar, indoor and outdoor pools, beauty salon, golf course, tennis courts, health club, children's program, business services. AE, D, DC, MC, V.*

Martha's Vineyard

$$$ **✕ Black Dog Tavern.** This island landmark (widely known for its T-shirts and other merchandise) serves basic chowders, pastas, fish, and steak, as well as more elaborate dishes. Waiting for a table is something of a tradition. Locals love an early breakfast on the glassed-in porch overlooking the harbor. ⊠ *Beach St. Ext., Vineyard Haven,* ☎ *508/693–9223. Reservations not accepted. AE, D, MC, V. BYOB.*

$$$$ **✕⊞ Charlotte Inn.** This 1865 inn, one of the best in New England, is
★   exquisitely furnished with English antiques, and original oil paintings and prints hang in the hallways. Some rooms have fireplaces; some, porches or verandas. Its L'étoile restaurant (reservations required, no lunch, closed January–mid-February and weekdays off-season) is excellent. ⊠ *27 S. Summer St., Edgartown 02539,* ☎ *508/627–4751,* ℻ *508/627–4652. 25 rooms. Restaurant. AE, MC, V.*

$$$–$$$$ **✕⊞ Inn at Blueberry Hill.** Exclusive and secluded, this 56-acre prop-
★   erty abutting a nature preserve has rooms that are simply and sparely furnished with Shaker-inspired island-made furniture; most have glass

doors that lead to terraces or private decks. The elegant restaurant features innovative, health-conscious cuisine. ⊠ *North Rd., Chilmark 02535,* ☎ *508/645–3322 or 800/356–3322,* ℻ *508/645–3799. 25 rooms; 1 to 3-room suites available. Restaurant, heated lap pool, hot tub, massage, hair salon, tennis court, health club, meeting room, business services. AE, MC, V. Closed Dec.–Apr.*

\$\$–\$\$\$ ✕🖪 **Lambert's Cove Country Inn.** Each room in the 1790 farmhouse has an individual flair, most with country cottage furnishings; rooms in the converted barn and carriage house have a more rustic look. There's a large wooden deck, and the intimate dining room is a superb place for a romantic dinner. ⊠ *Lambert's Cove Rd., West Tisbury (R.R.I, Box 422, Vineyard Haven, 02568),* ☎ *508/693–2298,* ℻ *508/693–7890. 16 rooms. Restaurant, tennis court. Full breakfast. AE, MC, V.*

Nantucket

\$\$\$\$ ✕ **Chanticleer.** A rose-covered cottage is the home of chef-owner Jean-Charles Berruet's renowned restaurant, where sumptuous classic French fare is prepared with the freshest island ingredients. Dinner is served in the formal French manor–style dining room with trompe l'oeil painting, in the greenhouse room, or in the upstairs grill room with fireplace. The wine cellar is legendary, and lunch in the rose garden is heavenly. ⊠ *9 New St., Siasconset,* ☎ *508/257–6231. Reservations essential. Jacket required at dinner. AE, MC, V. Closed Mon. and Columbus Day–Mother's Day.*

\$\$\$\$ ✕🖪 **Wauwinet.** Eight miles from town, this deluxe establishment has rooms decorated in country style with pine antiques and fine furnishings; some have spectacular views of the ocean. The restaurant is superb and sophisticated and serves lots of fresh seafood. ⊠ *120 Wauwinet Rd. (Box 2580), 02584,* ☎ *508/228–0145 or 800/426–8718,* ℻ *508/228–6712. 25 rooms, 5 cottages. Restaurant, bar, air-conditioning, tennis courts, croquet, boating, business services. Full breakfast, afternoon port and cheese. AE, DC, MC, V. Closed Nov.– May.*

\$–\$\$\$ 🖪 **Martin House Inn.** This nicely refurbished B&B in an 1803 house has mostly spacious rooms with four-poster or canopy beds, antique and country-cottage furnishings, and fresh flowers. Third-floor, shared-bath rooms are sunny and bright, with a quirky, under-the-eaves feel. The large living room with fireplace and the hammock swinging on the wide front porch invite lingering. ⊠ *61 Centre St. (Box 743), 02554,* ☎ *508/228–0678. 13 rooms. No smoking. CP. AE, MC, V.*

Provincetown

\$\$–\$\$\$ ✕ **Ciro's and Sal's.** Opened in 1950, this stage-set Italian restaurant—
★ raffia-covered Chianti bottles hanging from the rafters, Italian opera in the air—is still a star. Veal and pasta dishes are specialties. ⊠ *4 Kiley Ct.,* ☎ *508/487–0049. Reservations essential in summer and Sat. year-round. MC, V. Closed Mon.–Thurs. Nov.–Memorial Day. No lunch.*

\$\$–\$\$\$ ✕ **Front St.** In the cellar of a Victorian mansion, this intimate, bistro-
★ like restaurant is easy to miss . . . but don't! The rack of lamb, herb crusted and topped with cloves of roasted garlic, is the best on the Cape and is always offered in addition to a diverse Continental menu that changes every Friday. The wine list is extensive and award winning. ⊠ *230 Commercial St.,* ☎ *508/487–9715. AE, D, MC, V. Closed Jan.–Apr.*

\$\$\$–\$\$\$\$ 🖪 **Hargood House.** This apartment complex on the water, a short walk from the town center, is a great option for longer stays and families. Most units have decks and large water-view windows; all have kitchens and modern baths. ⊠ *493 Commercial St., 02657,* ☎ ℻ *508/487–9133. 19 apartments. Beach. AE, MC, V.*

\$\$–\$\$\$ 🖪 **Fairbanks Inn.** Just one block from Provincetown's busy Commercial Street, this comfortable inn has cozy rooms filled with antique and reproduction furnishings. Rooms in the 1776 main house have four-poster or canopy beds and Oriental rugs. Some rooms have kitchens or working fireplaces. ⊠ *90 Bradford St., 02657,* ☎ *508/487–0386. 13 rooms, 1 efficiency, 1 2-bedroom apartment. Air-conditioning. CP. AE, D, MC, V.*

$–$$$ ⛴ **The Masthead.** Families in particular are welcome at these unpretentious, homey seaside cottages and apartments. This is classic Provincetown: friendly and down-to-earth, with cooking facilities and a deck. The best and most expensive units overlook the water. ⊠ *31–41 Commercial St. (Box 577), 02657,* ☎ *508/487–0523 or 800/395–5095,* FAX *508/487–9251. 6 apartments, 4 cottages, 3 efficiencies, 8 rooms. Beach. AE, D, DC, MC, V.*

Campgrounds

Nickerson State Park (⊠ Rte. 6A, Brewster 02631, ☎ 508/896–3491 or 508/896–4615 for camping reservations), 418 sites, boating, biking, cross-country skiing (☞ National and State Parks, *above*). **Shawme–Crowell State Forest** (⊠ Rte. 130, Sandwich 02563, ☎ 508/888–0351), 280 sites, beach.

Nightlife and the Arts

Nightlife

Hyannis has many nightclubs and bars featuring live rock and jazz (Jazz Hot Line, ☎ 508/394–5277). Circuit Avenue in **Oak Bluffs** has rowdy bars and a year-round dance club. **Nantucket town** offers rock clubs, as well as restaurants with sedate piano bars.

The Arts

The Equity **Cape Playhouse** (⊠ Rte. 6A, Dennis, ☎ 508/385–3911) and the **Wellfleet Harbor Actors Theater** (⊠ W.H.A.T. box office: Main St., Wellfleet, ☎ 508/349–6835) present summer stock. The **Vineyard Playhouse** (⊠ 10 Church St., Vineyard Haven, ☎ 508/693–6450) offers Equity productions and community theater year-round. **Actor's Theatre of Nantucket** (⊠ Methodist Church, Centre and Main Sts., ☎ 508/228–6325) presents several Broadway-style plays each summer.

Outdoor Activities and Sports

Biking

Cape Cod Rail Trail, a 20-mi paved railroad right-of-way from Dennis to Wellfleet, is the Cape's premier bike path. On either side of the **Cape Cod Canal** is an easy 7-mi straight trail. The **Cape Cod National Seashore** and **Nickerson State Park** also maintain bicycle trails. On **Martha's Vineyard,** scenic well-paved paths follow the coast from Oak Bluffs to Edgartown and inland from Vineyard Haven to South Beach; some connect with rougher trails that weave through the state forest. Rural West Tisbury and Chilmark offer good biking past sheep, llama, and other farms. **Nantucket** has several miles-long bike paths that meander through the moorland. The more difficult, hilly trails have strategically placed benches and water fountains; an easier trail leads to Surfside Beach.

Fishing

Tuna, mako and blue sharks, bluefish, and bass are the main ocean catches. The necessary license to fish the Cape's freshwater ponds is available at tackle shops, such as **Eastman's Sport & Tackle** (⊠ 150 Main St., Falmouth, ☎ 508/548–6900) and **Truman's** (⊠ Rte. 28, West Yarmouth, ☎ 508/771–3470), which also rent gear. **Dick's Bait & Tackle** (⊠ New York Ave., Oak Bluffs, ☎ 508/693–7669), on Martha's Vineyard, and **Barry Thurston's Fishing Tackle** (⊠ Harbor Sq., ☎ 508/228–9595), on Nantucket, rent equipment and can point out the best fishing spots. Rental boats are available from **Cape Cod Boats** (⊠ Rte. 28 at Bass River Bridge, West Dennis, ☎ 508/394–9268), **Vineyard Boat Rentals** (⊠ Dockside Marketplace, Oak Bluffs Harbor, ☎ 508/693–8476), and **Nantucket Boat Rentals** (⊠ Slip 1, ☎ 508/325–1001).

Deep-sea fishing trips are operated by **Cap'n Bill & Cee Jay** (⊠ Macmillan Wharf, Provincetown, ☎ 508/487–4330 or 800/675–6723), **Hy-Line** (⊠ Ocean St. Dock, Hyannis, ☎ 508/790–0696), and **Patriot Party Boats** (⊠ Falmouth Harbor, ☎ 508/548–2626). On **Martha's Vineyard** the party boat *Skipper* (☎ 508/693–1238) leaves from Oak Bluffs Harbor. On **Nantucket** charters sail out of Straight Wharf.

Horseback Riding

Equine enthusiasts should contact **Deer Meadow Riding Stables** (⊠ Rte. 137, East Harwich, ☎ 508/432–6580), **Haland Stables** (⊠ Rte. 28A, West Falmouth, ☎ 508/540–2552), **Nelson's Riding Stable** (⊠ 43 Race Pt. Rd., Provincetown, ☎ 508/487–1112), **Misty Meadows Horse Farm** (⊠ Old County Rd., West Tisbury, Martha's Vineyard, ☎ 508/693–1870), or **South Shore Stable** (⊠ Across from airport off Edgartown Rd., West Tisbury, Martha's Vineyard, ☎ 508/693– 3770).

Water Sports

Arey's Pond Boat Yard (⊠ Off Rte. 28, Orleans, ☎ 508/255–0994) has a sailing school. **Cape Water Sports** (☎ 508/432–7079) has locations on several beaches for sailboat, canoe, and other rentals and lessons. Lessons and rentals are also available at **Wind's Up!** (⊠ Beach Rd., Vineyard Haven, ☎ 508/693–4252), on Martha's Vineyard, and at **Force 5 Water Sports** (⊠ Jetties Beach, ☎ 508/228–5358; ⊠ 37 Main St., ☎ 508/228–0700), on Nantucket.

Whale-Watching

The proximity of the Cape to the whales' feeding grounds at Stellwagen Bank (about 6 mi off the tip of Provincetown) affords the rare opportunity of spotting several species of whales, including minke, humpbacks, finbacks, and, occasionally, the endangered right whale. Whale-watching excursions are provided by **Hyannis Whale Watcher Cruises** (⊠ Millway, Barnstable, ☎ 508/362–6088 or 800/287–0374), *Dolphin Fleet* (⊠ Macmillian Wharf, Provincetown, ☎ 508/349–1900 or 800/826–9300), and *Ranger V* (Ticket office: ⊠ Bradford St., Provincetown, ☎ 508/487–3322 or 800/992–9333). Both boats out of Provincetown have naturalists on board.

Beaches

Beaches fronting on **Cape Cod Bay** generally have cold water and gentle waves. South-side beaches, on **Nantucket Sound,** have rolling surf
★ and are warmer. Open-ocean beaches on the **Cape Cod National Seashore** are cold, with serious surf. These beaches, backed by high dunes, are contiguous and have lifeguards and rest rooms. In summer parking lots can be full by 10 AM.

Shopping

Provincetown has many fine galleries. **Wellfleet** has emerged as a vibrant center for arts and crafts. There's a giant **flea market** (⊠ U.S. 6, Eastham-Wellfleet town line, ☎ 508/349–2520) on weekends and Monday holidays from April through October, plus Wednesday and Thursday in July and August. **Cape Cod Mall** (⊠ Rtes. 132 and 28, Hyannis, ☎ 508/771–0200), with 90 shops and counting, is the Cape's largest. **Antiques,** especially nautically related items, are popular Cape-wide.

On **Martha's Vineyard** there's only one department store, which is in Edgartown. **Edgartown,** the Vineyard's chief shopping town, has the best selection of antiques and crafts shops. The **West Tisbury Farmer's Market** (⊠ State Rd., West Tisbury), open Wednesday and Saturday in summer, is the largest in Massachusetts. **Nantucket**'s specialty is lightship baskets—expensive woven baskets, often decorated with scrimshaw or rosewood.

THE BERKSHIRES

Though only about a 2½-hour drive west from Boston or north from New York City, the Berkshires live up to storybook images of rural New England, with wooded hills, narrow winding roads, and compact charming villages. Summer offers a variety of cultural events, not the least of which is the Tanglewood festival of classical music, in Lenox. Fall brings a blaze of brilliant foliage. In winter the Berkshires are a popular ski area. Springtime visitors can enjoy maple-sugaring. The region can be crowded any weekend.

Visitor Information

Mohawk Trail Association (⊠ Box 722, Charlemont 01339, ☎ 413/664–6256). **Berkshire Visitors Bureau** (⊠ Berkshire Common Plaza, Pittsfield 01201, ☎ 413/443–9186 or 800/237–5747). **Lenox Chamber of Commerce** (⊠ Lenox Academy Bldg., 75 Main St., 01240, ☎ 413/637–3646).

Arriving and Departing

By Bus
Peter Pan Bus Lines (☎ 413/442–4451 or 800/237–8747) serves Lee and Pittsfield from Boston and Albany. **Bonanza Bus Lines** (☎ 800/556–3815) connects the Berkshires with Albany, New York City, and Providence.

By Car
The Massachusetts Turnpike (I–90) connects Boston with Lee and Stockbridge. The scenic Mohawk Trail (Route 2) parallels the northern border of Massachusetts. To reach the Berkshires from New York City, take either the New York Thruway (I–87) or the Taconic State Parkway. Within the Berkshires the main north–south road is Route 7.

By Plane
The closest airports are in Boston (☞ *above*), Albany, and New York City (☞ New York), and Hartford (☞ Connecticut). Small airports in Pittsfield and Great Barrington serve private planes.

Exploring the Berkshires

Williamstown is the northernmost Berkshires town, at the junction of Route 2 and U.S. 7. **Williams College** opened here in 1793, and the town still revolves around it. Gracious campus buildings lining the wide main street are open to visitors.

The **Sterling and Francine Clark Art Institute** is an outstanding small museum, with paintings by Renoir, Monet, and Degas. ⊠ *225 South St., Williamstown,* ☎ *413/458–9545. Closed Mon.*

The **Mohawk Trail,** a scenic 7-mi stretch of Route 2, follows a former Native American path east from Williamstown. **Mt. Greylock,** south of Williamstown off Route 7, is, at 3,491 ft, the highest point in the state. **Pittsfield,** county seat and geographic center of the region, has a lively small-town atmosphere. In 1850 outside Pittsfield, Herman Melville, the author of *Moby-Dick,* purchased a house he named **Arrowhead** (⊠ 780 Holmes Rd., ☎ 413/442–1793). The house, including the writer's desk, personal effects, and whaling trinkets, is open on a limited basis.

Hancock Shaker Village, 5 mi west of Pittsfield on Route 20, was founded in the 1790s as the third Shaker community in America. The religious community closed in 1960, and the site, complete with living quarters, round stone barn, and working crafts shops, is now a museum. ☎ 413/443–0188. *Closed Dec.–Mar.*

The village of **Lenox,** south of Pittsfield 5 mi on Route 7, epitomizes the Berkshires for many visitors. In the thick of the summer-cottage region, it's rich with old inns and majestic mansions. Novelist Edith Wharton's mansion, the **Mount,** is a perfect example of a turn-of-the-century classical American mansion. ⊠ *Plunkett St.,* ☎ 413/637–1899. *Closed Nov.–late May.*

Tanglewood is summer headquarters of the Boston Symphony. Thousands flock to the 200-acre estate every summer weekend to picnic on the lawns as musicians perform on the open-air stage (☞ The Arts *in* Nightlife and the Arts, *below*).

The archetypal New England small town of **Stockbridge** has a history of literary and artistic inhabitants, including painter Norman Rockwell and writers Norman Mailer and Robert Sherwood. The **Norman Rockwell Museum** (⊠ Rte. 183, ☎ 413/298–4100) boasts the world's largest collection of his original paintings.

Chesterwood was the summer home of sculptor Daniel Chester French, who created the *Minuteman* statue in Concord and the Lincoln Memorial in Washington, D.C. There are tours of the house and of his studio, where visitors can see the casts and models he used to make the Lincoln Memorial. ⊠ *Williamsville Rd. (off Rte. 183),* ☎ 413/298–3579. *Closed Nov.–Apr. except Veteran's Day weekend.*

Great Barrington is the largest town in the southern Berkshires and is a mecca for antiques hunters.

What to See and Do with Children

The **Jiminy Peak** ski resort (⊠ Corey Rd., Hancock, ☎ 413/738–5500) has an alpine slide and trout fishing in summer. The **Robbins-Zust Family Marionettes** (⊠ East Rd., Richmond, ☎ 413/698–2591) perform puppet shows in summer in different towns around the area.

Dining and Lodging

Lodging rates may include full or Continental breakfast. For price ranges *see* Charts 1 (B) and 2 (B) *in* On the Road with Fodor's.

Great Barrington

$$$ ✕ **Boiler Room Café.** In a turn-of-the-century clapboard house, eclec-
★   tic and sophisticated fare served in the three comfortable dining rooms may include a light New England seafood stew, grilled baby back ribs, or osso buco. ⊠ *405 Stockbridge Rd.,* ☎ 413/528–4280. MC, V. *Closed Sun.–Mon. except holidays.*

$ ✕ **20 Railroad St.** The exposed brick and subdued lighting lend atmosphere to this bustling restaurant. Specialties include sausage pie, burgers, and sandwiches. ⊠ *20 Railroad St.,* ☎ 413/528–9345. MC, V.

Lee

$$–$$$ 🏨 **The Morgan House.** Rooms in this 1817 inn have a sitting area, brightly painted wood furniture, four-poster beds, stenciled walls, and well-worn antiques. The lobby is papered with pages from old guest registers; among the signatures are those of George Bernard Shaw and Ulysses S. Grant. ✉ *33 Main St., 01238,* ☎ *413/243–0181. 11 rooms with bath, 5 rooms share 3 baths. 2 dining rooms, tavern. Full breakfast. AE, D, DC, MC, V.*

Lenox

$$$ ✕ **Gateways Inn.** Two dining rooms are hung with chandeliers and tapestries; working fireplaces soften the formal tone. Continental and southern Italian cuisine includes veal, salmon, and rack of lamb. ✉ *51 Walker St.,* ☎ *413/637–2532. AE, D, DC, MC, V. Closed Sun. Nov.– May.*

$$$$ 🏨 **Blantyre.** The castlelike Tudor architecture, vast public rooms, and 85 acres of beautiful grounds are impressive enough, but the guest rooms in the main house are also fabulous—huge and lavishly decorated. The stylishly prepared evening meal is wonderful. ✉ *16 Blantyre Rd. (off Rte. 7), 01240,* ☎ *413/637–3556 or 413/298–3806. 23 rooms. Restaurant, pool, tennis. AE, DC, MC, V.*

$$ 🏨 **Eastover.** This resort was opened by an ex–circus roustabout, and the tradition of noisy fun and informality continues. Accommodations include dormitory and motel-style rooms. There are loads of activities planned along with special weekends for couples, singles, and families. The resort is all-inclusive, and many guests never leave the vast grounds. ✉ *430 East St., off Rtes. 20 and 7 (Box 2160), 01240,* ☎ *413/637–0625,* 𝖥𝖠𝖷 *413/637–4939. 195 rooms. Dining room, indoor and outdoor pools, sauna, driving range, tennis courts, badminton, exercise room, horseback riding, volleyball, cross-country skiing, downhill skiing, tobogganing, mountain biking. AE, D, DC, MC, V.*

South Egremont

$$$ ✕🏨 **Egremont Inn.** The public rooms in this 1780 inn are enormous; the main lounge alone, with its vast open fireplace, is worth a visit. Bedrooms are small, with wide-board floors, uneven ceilings, four-poster beds, and claw-foot baths. The sunny main dining room serves Continental fare. ✉ *Old Sheffield Rd. (Box 418), 01258,* ☎ *413/528–2111,* 𝖥𝖠𝖷 *413/528–3284. 22 rooms. 3 dining rooms, lounge, pool, tennis courts. AE, MC, V.*

Stockbridge Area

$$$ ✕🏨 **Red Lion Inn.** An inn since 1773 and rebuilt after a fire in 1896, this landmark is now massive, with guest rooms in the main building and several annexes. Annex rooms are furnished with antiques. New England specialties are served in the elegant dining room. ✉ *Main St., 02162,* ☎ *413/298–5545. 118 rooms. Dining room, pool, exercise room. AE, D, DC, MC, V.*

$$ ✕🏨 **Historic Merrell Inn.** This old New England inn on the National Reg-
★ ister of Historic Places has some good-size bedrooms furnished with antiques and pencil-post beds. The breakfast room has an open fireplace. ✉ *Rte. 102, South Lee 01260,* ☎ *413/243–1794. 9 rooms. MC, V.*

Williamstown

$$ ✕ **Mezze Bistro & Bar.** A little bit of New York's SoHo is a welcome
★ surprise in the heart of this tiny college town. A large bar, birch walls, subtle lighting, and an airy beamed ceiling set a stylish stage for equally distinctive food. A changing seasonal menu highlights various American regions and celebrations. ✉ *84 Water St.,* ☎ *413/458–0123. AE, MC, V. Closed Mon. Oct.–Memorial Day. No lunch.*

$$$ 🖼 **Field Farm Guest House.** Built in 1948 on 254 acres, the house, which
★ resembles a modern museum, has large guest rooms with big windows
and expansive views of the grounds and pond. Much of the furniture
was handmade by the owner-collector, and there are sculptures in the
garden. Cross-country ski trails begin at the door of this unusual B&B.
⊠ *554 Sloan Rd. (off Rte. 43), Williamstown 01267,* ☎ *413/458–3135.
5 rooms. Dining room, pool, tennis courts. D, MC, V.*

Nightlife and the Arts

Listings appear daily in the *Berkshire Eagle* from June through Colum-
bus Day. *Berkshires Week* is the summer bible for events listings.
Weekly listings appear in the *Williamstown Advocate.* Major concerts
are listed in the Thursday *Boston Globe.*

Nightlife

The most popular local nightspot is the **Lion's Den** (☎ 413/298–5545),
at the Red Lion Inn in Stockbridge (☞ Dining and Lodging, *above*),
with nightly folk music and some contemporary local bands.

The Arts

DANCE

Jacob's Pillow Dance Festival, the oldest in the nation, mounts a 10-
week summer program every year. ⊠ *Rte. 20, Becket (Box 287, Lee
01238),* ☎ *413/243–0745 in season or 413/637–1322.*

MUSIC

The best-known music festival in New England is near Lenox, at **Tan-
glewood** (☞ Exploring the Berkshires, *above*), where the Boston Sym-
phony Orchestra (BSO) has its summer season, from June through
August. You can get a schedule by leaving your name and address, or
you can order tickets, both by calling the BSO's Symphonycharge (☎
617/266–1200). The **Berkshire Performing Arts Theater** (⊠ 40 Kem-
ble St., Lenox, ☎ 413/637–4718) attracts top-name artists in jazz, folk,
rock, and blues each summer.

THEATER

The **Berkshire Theatre Festival** (⊠ Rte. 102, Box 797, Stockbridge 01262,
☎ 413/298–5536) stages nightly performances in summer at a cen-
tury-old theater. The **Williamstown Theatre Festival** (⊠ Adams Memo-
rial Theatre, 1000 Main St., Box 517, Williamstown 01267, ☎ 413/
597–3400) presents classics and contemporary works each summer.

Outdoor Activities and Sports

Biking

The back roads of Berkshire County can be hilly, but the views and
the countryside are incomparable. Bikes can be rented from **Plaine's
Cycling Center** (⊠ 55 W. Housatonic St., Pittsfield, ☎ 413/499–0294).

Boating

The **Housatonic River** flows south from Pittsfield between the Berkshire
Hills and the Taconic Range toward Connecticut. Canoes and other
boats can be rented from the **Onota Boat Livery** (⊠ 455 Pecks Rd., Pitts-
field, ☎ 413/442–1724), on Onota Lake. **Main Street Sports and
Leisure** (⊠ 48 Main St., Lenox, ☎ 413/637–4407) rents canoes and
leads canoe trips on the Housatonic and other local lakes.

Fishing

The area's rivers, lakes, and streams abound with bass, pike, perch,
and trout. **Points North Fishing and Hunting Outfitters** (⊠ Rte. 8,
Adams, ☎ 413/743–4030) organizes summer fly-fishing schools.

Golf

Waubeeka Golf Links (⊠ Rte. 7, Williamstown, ☎ 413/458–5869) and the **Cranwell Resort and Hotel** (⊠ 55 Lee Rd., 02140, ☎ 413/637–1364 or 800/272–6935) have 18-hole courses open to the public.

Hiking

The **Appalachian Trail** goes through Berkshire County. Hiking is particularly rewarding in the higher elevations of **Mt. Greylock State Reservation** (☞ National and State Parks, *above*).

Ski Areas

Cross-Country

Brodie (⊠ Rte. 7, New Ashford 01237, ☎ 413/443–4752). **Butternut Basin** (⊠ Rte. 23, Great Barrington 01230, ☎ 413/528–2000).

Downhill

Berkshire East (⊠ Box 727, S. River Rd., Charlemont 01339, ☎ 413/339–6617). **Bousquet Ski Area** (⊠ Dan Fox Dr., Pittsfield 01201, ☎ 413/442–8316 or 413/442–2436). **Brodie** (☞ Cross-Country, *above*). **Butternut Basin** (☞ Cross-Country, *above*). **Jiminy Peak** (☞ What to See and Do with Children, *above*).

Shopping

Antiques

There are antiques stores throughout the Berkshires, but the greatest concentration is around Great Barrington, South Egremont, and Sheffield. For a list of storekeepers who belong to the **Berkshire County Antiques Dealers Association** and guarantee the authenticity of their merchandise, send a self-addressed, stamped envelope to R.D. 1, Box 1, Sheffield 01257.

Outlet Stores

Along Route 7 just north of Lenox are two factory-outlet malls, **Lenox House Country Shops** and **Brushwood Farms.**

ELSEWHERE IN MASSACHUSETTS

The Pioneer Valley

Arriving and Departing

I–91 runs north–south the entire length of the Pioneer Valley, from Greenfield to Springfield; I–90 links Springfield to Boston; and Route 2 connects Boston with Greenfield in the north. Amtrak stops in Springfield on routes from Boston and New York.

What to See and Do

The **Greater Springfield Convention and Visitors Bureau** (⊠ 34 Boland Way, Springfield 01103, ☎ 413/787–1548) provides information about the Pioneer Valley area.

In downtown Springfield four museums are situated at the museum quadrangle. The **Connecticut Valley Historical Museum** (☎ 413/263–6895) commemorates the history of the Pioneer Valley. The **George Walter Vincent Smith Art Museum** (☎ 413/263–6894) contains a private collection of Japanese armor, ceramics, and textiles. The **Museum of Fine Arts** (☎ 413/263–6885) has paintings by Gauguin and many other French Impressionists. The **Springfield Science Museum** (☎ 413/263–6875) has touchable displays in its Exploration Center, a planetarium, and dinosaur exhibits.

Riverside Park, just outside Springfield, is the largest amusement park in New England and has a giant roller coaster and picnic facilities. ⊠ *1623 Main St., Agawam,* ☎ *413/786–9300 or 800/370–7488. Closed Nov.–Mar.*

Home to a number of educational institutions, the valley is filled with cultural and historic attractions. **Deerfield** in the north has many historic buildings and is the site of the prestigious Deerfield Academy. The

★ Street in **Historic Deerfield** (⊠ Rte. 5, ☎ 413/774–5581) is a tree-lined avenue of 50 18th- and 19th-century houses maintained as a museum site; 14 of the preserved buildings are open to the public year-round. In **Amherst** are three of the valley's five major colleges—the University of Massachusetts, Amherst College, and Hampshire College. The **Emily Dickinson Homestead** (⊠ 280 Main St., ☎ 413/542–8161) is also here. **Northampton** is the site of Smith College as well as the one-time home of the 30th U.S. president, Calvin Coolidge. The village of **South Hadley** is best known for Mount Holyoke, founded in 1837 as the country's first women's college.

★ East of the southern end of the valley is **Old Sturbridge Village,** a living, working model of an early 1800s New England town, with more than 40 buildings on a 200-acre site. ⊠ *1 Old Sturbridge Village Rd., Sturbridge,* ☎ *508/347–3362.*

Dining and Lodging

AMHERST

$$$–$$$$ ✕🏨 **Lord Jeffery Inn.** This gabled brick inn sits on the green between the town center and the Amherst College campus. Many bedrooms have light floral decor; others are less formal, with simple cream walls and pastel woodwork. The large, elegant dining room has an open fireplace and serves such tempting items as roast rack of lamb and chateaubriand; a tavern serves lighter fare. ⊠ *30 Boltwood Ave., 01002,* ☎ *413/253–2576,* FAX *413/256–6152. 48 rooms. Restaurant, bar. AE, DC, MC, V.*

$$–$$$ 🏨 **The Allen House.** This 1886 inn is a glorious reproduction of the
★   aesthetic period of the Victorian era. Busy, colorful reproduction wall coverings reach to the high ceilings. The bedrooms have lace curtains and supremely comfortable beds with goose-down comforters. It's a short walk from the center of Amherst. ⊠ *599 Main St., 01002,* ☎ *413/253–5000. 7 rooms. Full breakfast, afternoon tea. AE, MC, V.*

NORTHFIELD

$$ 🏨 **Northfield Country House.** Truly remote, this big English manor house
★   is amid thick woodlands on a small hill. A wide staircase leads to the bedrooms, which have elegant, mostly antique furnishings; some rooms have fireplaces. ⊠ *181 School St., 01360,* ☎ *413/498–2692 or 800/498–2692. 4 rooms. Pool. Full breakfast. MC, V.*

NORTHAMPTON

$$ ✕ **Paul and Elizabeth's.** This classy natural foods restaurant serves such seasonal specials as butternut squash soup and Indian pudding, as well as Japanese tempura and innovative fish entrées. ⊠ *150 Main St.,* ☎ *413/584–4832. MC, V.*

NEW HAMPSHIRE

By Ed and
Roon Frost

Updated by
Paula J.
Flanders

Capital	Concord
Population	1,162,000
Motto	Live Free or Die
State Bird	Purple finch
State Flower	Purple lilac
Postal Abbreviation	NH

Statewide Visitor Information

New Hampshire Office of Travel and Tourism Development (✉ Box 1856, Concord 03302, ☎ 603/271–2343 or 800/386–4664). **Foliage hot line** (☎ 800/258–3608 or 800/262–660).

Scenic Drives

The **Kancamagus Highway** (Route 112) rolls through 32 mi of the White Mountains between Lincoln and Conway. **Route 113** between Holderness and South Tamworth, also 32 mi, is full of hills and curves, and winds between mountains and plains with open views of both. **Routes 12A and 12** parallel the Connecticut River along the Vermont border between Lebanon and Keene, with views of the river and the picturesque towns along the way.

National and State Parks

National Forest

The **White Mountain National Forest** (✉ U.S. Forest Service, 719 N. Main St., Laconia 03246, ☎ 603/528–8721) occupies 770,000 acres of northern New Hampshire (☞ The White Mountains, *below*).

State Parks

The **Division of Parks and Recreation** (✉ Box 1856, Concord 03302, ☎ 603/271–3556) maintains 75 state parks, beaches, and historic sites. Surrounded by privately held forests, **Monadnock State Park** (✉ Box 181, Jaffrey 03452, ☎ 603/532–8862) seems larger than its 5,000 acres.

THE SEACOAST

The southern end of New Hampshire's 18-mi coastline is dominated by Hampton Beach—5 mi of sand, midriff-to-elbow sunbathers, motels, arcades, carryouts, and a boardwalk. At the northern end is Portsmouth, with its beautifully restored historic area, a slew of one-of-a-kind restaurants, and the state's only working port. In between are dunes, beaches, salt marshes, and state parks where you can picnic, hike, swim, boat, and fish.

Visitor Information

Seacoast Council on Tourism (✉ 235 West Rd., Suite 10, Portsmouth 03801, ☎ 603/436–9800 or 800/221–5623). **Greater Portsmouth:** Chamber of Commerce (✉ 500 Market St. Ext., Portsmouth 03801, ☎ 603/436–1118). **Hampton Beach Area:** Chamber of Commerce (✉ 836 Lafayette Rd., Hampton 03842, ☎ 603/926–8717).

Arriving and Departing

By Bus
C&J (☏ 603/31–2424) **Concord Trailways** (☏ 800/639–3317). **Peter Pan Bus Lines** (☏ 603/889–2121). **Vermont Transit** (☏ 603/436–0163 or 800/451–3292).

By Car
I–95 provides access to the Hamptons (Exit 2), central Portsmouth (Exits 3–6), and Portsmouth harbor and historic district (Exit 7).

Exploring the Seacoast

The Atlantic is rarely out of sight from Route 1A, and there are plenty of spots for pulling over. In **North Hampton** factory outlets coexist with mansions. Take a leisurely drive past what the wealthy refer to as cottages, on **Millionaire's Row.** Or in summer stop to see the 2,000 rose-bushes at **Fuller Gardens** (⊠ 10 Willow Ave., ☏ 603/964–5414). **Rye** has great beaches. **Odiorne Point State Park** (⊠ Rte. 1A, ☏ 603/436–7406) has 230 acres of tidal pools and footpaths. The **Seacoast Science Center** (☏ 603/436–8043), in the park, has exhibits and an aquarium. From Rye Harbor inlet, **New Hampshire Seacoast Cruises** (☏ 603/964–5545 or 800/734–6488) takes whale-watching trips and trips to the Isles of Shoals, a Colonial fishing settlement.

★ **Portsmouth** is both a working port and a walkable city beloved by Boston trendsetters. The **Portsmouth Historical Society** (⊠ 43 Middle St., ☏ 603/436–8420) has a self-guided walking tour that includes seven historic houses.

Showcasing Portsmouth's architectural diversity is **Strawbery Banke,** a 10-acre village-museum whose 40 buildings date from 1695 to 1820. The gardens are splendid. ⊠ *Marcy St.,* ☏ *603/433–1100 or 603/433–1101. Closed Nov.–mid-Apr., except Thanksgiving weekend and 1st 2 weekends in Dec.*

Historic **Prescott Park** has a formal garden and lively fountains. The **Sheafe Warehouse Museum** (☏ 603/431–8748), within Prescott Park, displays decoys, ship models, and ship mastheads.

What to See and Do with Children

In Portsmouth start with the lively hands-on **Children's Museum** (⊠ 280 Marcy St., ☏ 603/436–3853). The **USS Albacore** (⊠ 600 Market St., ☏ 603/436–3680), a vintage submarine, is another Portsmouth attraction that appeals to kids.

Dining and Lodging

Portsmouth shines in warm weather, when restaurants along Bow and Ceres streets open their decks for sea breezes and harbor views. Make lodging reservations well in advance for summer stays in the area. For price ranges *see* Charts 1 (A) and 2 (A) *in* On the Road with Fodor's.

Hampton
$$$ 🏨 **Victoria Inn.** Built as a carriage house in 1875, this romantic bed-and-breakfast is decorated with wicker, chandeliers, and lace. Innkeepers Bill and Ruth Muzzey have named one room in honor of Franklin Pierce, the former U.S. president who for years summered in the home next door. ⊠ *430 High St. (½ mi from Hampton Beach), 03842,* ☏ *603/929–1437. 6 rooms. MC, V.*

Hampton Beach

$$ ✕ **Ron's Landing at Rocky Point.** This casually elegant restaurant serving fresh seafood and pasta has a second-floor porch that affords a sweeping ocean view. Try the seafood cioppino, a fisherman's stew. ✉ 379 Ocean Blvd., ☎ 603/929–2122. AE, D, DC, MC, V.

$$$ ✕🔳 **Ashworth by the Sea.** At this centrally located favorite of generations of beach goers, most rooms have decks. Some rooms have queen-size four-poster beds and glowing cherry-wood furnishings. ✉ 295 Ocean Blvd., 03842, ☎ 603/926–6762 or 800/345–6736, FAX 603/926–2002. 105 rooms. 3 restaurants, pool, beauty salon. AE, D, DC, MC, V.

Portsmouth

$$ ✕ **Blue Mermaid World Grill.** The stately exterior of this 1810 house ★ belies the hot Jamaican-style dishes that come from the wood-burning grill. The grilled Maine lobster with mango butter is a favorite. ✉ The Hill, ☎ 603/427–2583. AE, D, DC, MC, V.

$$ ✕ **Porto Bello.** In this second-story dining room overlooking the harbor, enjoy daily antipasti specials like grilled Portobello mushrooms and entrées such as spinach gnocchi and veal *carciofi*—a 4-ounce cutlet served with artichokes. ✉ 67 Bow St., 2nd floor, ☎ 603/431–2989. D, MC, V. Closed Sun.–Mon. No lunch Tues.

$$$ ✕🔳 **Sheraton Portsmouth Hotel.** Portsmouth's only luxury hotel has a nice harbor view and a central location. The main restaurant serves American cuisine, especially fresh seafood, in quiet surroundings. The Krewc Orleans restaurant serves Cajun specialties. ✉ 250 Market St., 03801, ☎ 603/431–2300 or 800/325–3535, FAX 603/433–5649. 177 rooms. 2 restaurants, bar, indoor pool, spa, exercise room, nightclub, meeting rooms. AE, D, DC, MC, V.

$$$ 🔳 **Sise Inn.** This elegant Queen Anne town house, full of chintz and ★ gleaming armoires, is convenient for waterfront strolls. No two rooms are alike; some have whirlpool baths. ✉ 40 Court St., 03801, ☎ FAX 603/433–1200 or ☎ 800/267–0525. 34 rooms. In-room VCRs, meeting rooms. CP. AE, DC, MC, V.

Nightlife and the Arts

Nightlife

Summer concerts draw crowds at the **Hampton Beach Casino Ballroom** (✉ 169 Ocean Beach Blvd., ☎ 603/926–4541). Catch jazz, folk, or blues at the **Press Room** (✉ 77 Daniel St., Portsmouth, ☎ 603/431–5186).

The Arts

Prescott Park Arts Festival (✉ 105 Marcy St., Portsmouth, ☎ 603/436–2848) kicks off with a Fourth of July concert and continues through Labor Day with music, dance, and an outdoor theater production four nights a week. The 1878 **Music Hall** (✉ 28 Chestnut St., Portsmouth, ☎ 603/436–2400) hosts touring events and an ongoing film series.

Outdoor Activities and Sports

Boating and Fishing

Rentals and charters are available from **Atlantic Fishing Fleet** in Rye Harbor (☎ 603/964–5220). **Al Gauron Deep Sea Fishing** (☎ 603/926–2469) and **Smith & Gilmore** (☎ 603/926–3503) are in Hampton Beach.

Shopping

Portsmouth is chockablock with crafts shops, galleries, and clothing boutiques. Stop at the **North Hampton Factory Outlet Center** (⊠ Rte. 1, ☎ 603/964–9050) for bargains.

THE LAKES REGION

The eastern half of central New Hampshire is scattered with beautifully preserved 18th- and 19th-century villages and sparkling lakes—Winnipesaukee (Smiling Water) is the largest—that echo with squeals and splashes all summer long.

Visitor Information

Greater Laconia Chamber of Commerce (⊠ 11 Veterans Sq., Laconia 03246, ☎ 603/524–5531 or 800/531–2347). **Lakes Region Association** (⊠ Box 589, Center Harbor 03226, ☎ 603/253–8555 or 800/605–2537). **Wolfeboro Chamber of Commerce** (⊠ Railroad Ave., Wolfeboro 03894, ☎ 603/569–2200 or 800/516–5324).

Arriving and Departing

By Bus

Concord Trailways (☎ 603/228–3300 or 800/639–3317 in New England) serves Meredith, Center Harbor, Moultonborough, and West Ossipee.

By Car

I–93 is the principal north–south artery. From the coast Route 11 goes to southern Lake Winnipesaukee; en route to the White Mountains, north–south Route 16 accesses spurs to the lakes.

Exploring the Lakes Region

Alton Bay, at Winnipesaukee's southernmost tip, has the lake's cruise-boat docks and a Victorian bandstand. In affluent Colonial **Gilford** there's a large state beach. The **Gunstock Recreation Area** (⊠ Rte. 11A, ☎ 603/293–4341) has swimming, hiking, and camping. In honky-tonk **Weirs Beach,** fireworks light up summer nights. Here you can board **lake cruisers** (☎ 603/366–5531). The **Winnipesaukee Railroad** (☎ 603/279–5253) carries passengers alongside the lake.

Commercial **Meredith,** on the northern tip of the most westerly of three bays on the north shore, has restaurants and shops. **Moultonborough** has a country store and several miles of lakeside shoreline. The 5,000-acre **Castle in the Clouds** estate (⊠ Rte. 171, ☎ 603/476–2352 or 800/729–2468) is anchored by an eccentric millionaire's former home. At the **Loon Center** (⊠ Lees Mills Rd., ☎ 603/476–5666), run by the Audubon Society, you can learn about the popular black-and-white birds whose calls haunt New Hampshire's lakes.

Contrasting with the busy southern Winnipesaukee towns are three lakeside villages where you can do lots of antiquing. **Center Sandwich** is pristine and historic. **Tamworth**'s birch-edged Chocorua Lake has been photographed so often that you may feel you've seen it before. **Ossipee,** divided into three villages, is known for its eponymous lake, which is great for fishing and swimming. Scenic, lake-hugging Route 109 leads from Moultonborough to **Wolfeboro,** an old-line resort. At **Canterbury Shaker Village** (⊠ Canterbury, ☎ 603/783–9511), southwest of Winnipesaukee, guided tours and crafts demonstrations depict 19th-century Shaker life.

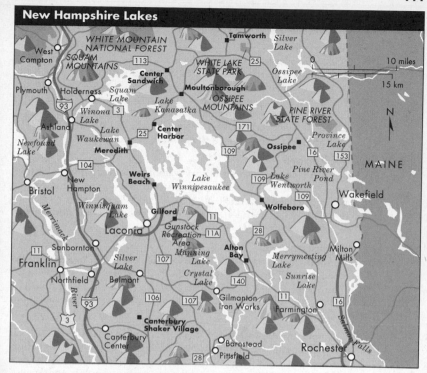

New Hampshire Lakes

What to See and Do with Children

Try Meredith's **Children's Museum and Shop** (⊠ 28 Lang St., ☎ 603/279–1007). Holderness's **Science Center of New Hampshire** (⊠ Junction of Rtes. 113 and 25, ☎ 603/968–7194) has lots of hands-on activities. **Amusement centers** like Funspot (☎ 603/366–4377), Surf Coaster (☎ 603/366–4991), and Water Slide (☎ 603/366–5161) line Route 3 in Weirs Beach.

Dining and Lodging

This is steak-and-prime-rib country, though there are exceptions. Reserve ahead in most any season for both meals and rooms because summer and fall are crowded, and many businesses close in winter. For price ranges *see* Charts 1 (B) and 2 (B) *in* On the Road with Fodor's.

Center Sandwich

$$$ ✕🏨 **Corner House Inn.** This quaint Victorian inn with comfortable, old-fashioned guest rooms upstairs serves home-cooked meals in dining rooms (closed Monday November–mid-June) cozy with local arts and crafts. Storytellers hold forth by the potbellied stove one night a week. ⊠ *Junction of Rtes. 109 and 113, 03227,* ☎ *603/284–6219,* 🖷 *603/284–6220. 3 rooms. Restaurant. AE, D, MC, V.*

Holderness

$$$$ ✕🏨 **Manor on Golden Pond.** This dignified inn has a dock on Squam ★ Lake, the setting for the movie *On Golden Pond.* Guests can stay in the main inn, carriage-house suites, or a housekeeping cottage. The five-course prix-fixe dinner includes such specialties as rack of lamb, filet mignon, and nonpareil apple pie. ⊠ *Rte. 3, 03245,* ☎ *603/968–3348 or 800/545–2141,* 🖷 *603/968–2116. 17 rooms in main house, 6 car-*

riage house rooms, 4 2-bedroom cottages. Restaurant, pub, pool, tennis courts, boating. AE, MC, V.

Tamworth

$$$$ ✕🏨 **Tamworth Inn.** This friendly B&B with romantic charm seems
★ straight from an old movie. Guest rooms are decorated with 19th-
century American pieces. The dining room (closed Sunday and Monday
in summer, Sunday–Tuesday in winter) serves American cuisine with a
French twist, such as provolone-and-pesto terrine. In summer you can
dine on the river-view porch. ✉ *Main St., 03886,* ☎ *603/323–7721 or
800/642–7352. 15 rooms. Restaurant, pub, pool. MC, V.*

Wolfeboro

$$$$ ✕🏨 **Wolfeboro Inn.** This landmark waterfront resort, partly dating from
★ the 19th century, has polished cherry and pine pieces and is abloom
with flowered chintz. ✉ *90 N. Main St., 03894,* ☎ *603/569–3016 or
800/451–2389,* 🖷 *603/569–5375. 49 rooms. 2 restaurants, bar,
beach, boating. AE, D, MC, V.*

Campgrounds

Gunstock Campground (✉ Gilford, ☎ 603/293–4344). **Yogi Bear's Jelly-
stone Park** (✉ Ashland, ☎ 603/968–9000). **White Lake State Park** (✉
Tamworth, ☎ 603/323–7350 or 603/271–3627 for reservations).

Nightlife and the Arts

The **Belknap Mill Society** (✉ Mill Plaza, Laconia, ☎ 603/524–8813)
has year-round concerts in an early 19th-century brick mill building.
Barnstormers (✉ Main St., Tamworth, ☎ 603/323–8500), New
Hampshire's oldest professional theater, performs in July and August.
The **M/S Mount Washington** (✉ Weirs Beach, ☎ 603/366–5531) has
moonlight cruises with dinner and dancing; it docks in Weirs Beach,
Alton Bay, and Wolfeboro.

Outdoor Activities and Sports

Biking

Not too hilly, the Lakes Region is fun for even inexperienced bikers—
though summer's heavy traffic can be a bit much. Lake's-edge roads
make for good pedaling.

Boating

Rent at **Thurston's,** in Weirs Beach (☎ 603/366–4811), or the **Mere-
dith Marina and Boating Center** (☎ 603/279–7921) or **Wild Meadow
Canoes and Kayaks** (☎ 603/253–7536 or 800/427–7536), both in
Meredith.

Fishing

Local waters yield trout; Winnipesaukee also has salmon. Hardy anglers fish from "ice bob" huts in winter. The **state fish and game department's local office** (✉ New Hampton, ☎ 603/744–5470) can tell
you where the action is.

Beaches

Most are private, so it's good to know about **Ellacoya State Beach,** in
Gilford, a smallish beach that's the area's major public strand. **Wentworth State Beach** is at Wolfeboro.

Shopping

Summer folk prowl area galleries and boutiques like the **Mill Falls Marketplace** (✉ Rte. 3, Meredith, ☎ 603/279–7006). The **League of New**

Hampshire Craftsmen runs a shop filled with one-of-a-kind items in Meredith (✉ Rte. 3, ☎ 603/279–7920). The **Old Country Store** in Moultonborough (✉ Rte. 25, ☎ 603/476–5750) has been purveying pickles and penny candy since 1781. Look for **antiques** in Wolfeboro, the Ossipees, and Center Sandwich.

THE WHITE MOUNTAINS

Northern New Hampshire is the home of New England's highest mountains and the 750,000-acre White Mountain National Forest. Rivers are born here, gorges slash the forests, and hikers, climbers, and Sunday drivers marvel at it all. Meanwhile, shoppers cheer for the bargain hunting in valley towns. Summers are busy, but foliage season draws the biggest crowds.

Visitor Information

Mt. Washington Valley: Visitors Bureau (✉ Box 2300, North Conway 03860, ☎ 603/356–5701 or 800/367–3364).

Arriving and Departing

By Bus

Concord Trailways (☎ 603/228–3300 or 800/639–3317 in New England) serves Littleton, Colbrook, Berlin, Conway, Meredith, Plymouth, and other towns.

By Car

North–south routes include I–93 and Route 3 in the west, Route 16 in the east. The Kancamagus Highway (Route 112) and Route 302 are the main east–west thoroughfares.

Exploring the White Mountains

One-street **North Conway** overflows with shops, restaurants, and inns. Trails from **Echo Lake State Park** (✉ Off Rte. 302, North Conway, ☎ 603/356–2672 in summer), in North Conway, lead up to White Horse and Cathedral ledges, both 1,000-ft cliffs overlooking the town in the west. The mountain lakes are good for swimming and the park road for New England woodland scenery; the picnicking is great.

Mountain-rimmed **Jackson** is picture-perfect, with its clapboard inns and shops. Dramatic **Pinkham Notch** is the departure point for hikes to the top of the Northeast's highest mountain, 6,288-ft Mt. Washington (be sure to carry warm clothing in case of sudden, nasty storms). In summer and fall you can corkscrew up via the **Mt. Washington Auto Road** (✉ Glen House, ☎ 603/466–3988), either in your own car or by guided van tour.

Crawford Notch State Park (✉ Rte. 302 at Twin Mountain, ☎ 603/374–2272) is good for a picnic and a hike to a waterfall. The steam-powered **Mt. Washington Cog Railway** has been running since 1869 (✉ Off Rte. 302, Bretton Woods, ☎ 603/846–5404 or 800/922–8825, ext. 7); reserve ahead.

Many famous literary figures have visited **Franconia.** You can visit poet **Robert Frost's home** (✉ Ridge Rd., ☎ 603/823–5510). **Franconia Notch** (☎ 603/823–5563) is known for the Old Man of the Mountains, a rock formation that looks like a human profile, and the 800-ft-long natural chasm known as the Flume.

The **Kancamagus Highway,** 32 mi of mountain scenery to the south (with bumper-to-bumper traffic during foliage season), starts in the re-

sort town of Lincoln and passes campgrounds, picnic spots, scenic overlooks, and trailheads en route to Conway.

What to See and Do with Children

Youngsters love the antique steam- and diesel-powered **Conway Scenic
Railroad** (⊠ Rtes. 16/302, North Conway, ☎ 603/356–5251 or 800/
232–5251). The water slides at the **Whale's Tale** (⊠ Rte. 3, ☎ 603/
745–8810), in Lincoln, are fun for the whole family. Two attractions
are on Route 16 in Glen. One is **Story Land** (☎ 603/383–4293), which
has life-size nursery-rhyme characters and themed rides. **Heritage New
Hampshire** (☎ 603/383–9776) features a simulated journey into New
England history.

Dining and Lodging

Reservations are essential in fall and during winter vacations. For
price ranges *see* Charts 1 (B) and 2 (B) *in* On the Road with Fodor's.

Dixville Notch

$$$$ ✕⊞ **The Balsams.** This elegant turn-of-the-century resort hotel on
★   15,000 acres is a real Victorian, built in 1866. Accommodations are
spare, bright, and homey, with floral-print wallpaper and lace curtains,
and the array of facilities gives you no reason to leave the grounds. At
the famous formal brunch (jacket and tie), the huge dining room overflows with elegantly presented bounty. ⊠ *Rte. 26, 03576,* ☎ *603/255–
3400 or 800/255–0600,* 𝐅𝐀𝐗 *603/255–4221. 212 rooms. Restaurant,
pool, golf, tennis, hiking, mountain biking, ice-skating, cross-country
skiing, downhill skiing, boating, children's programs. AE, D, MC, V.
Closed Apr.–mid-May, mid-Oct.–mid-Dec.*

Franconia

$$$–$$$$ ✕⊞ **Franconia Inn.** Guest rooms in this family resort have chintz and
canopy beds; some have whirlpool baths or fireplaces. ⊠ *Easton Rd.,
03580,* ☎ *603/823–5542 or 800/473–5299,* 𝐅𝐀𝐗 *603/823–8078. 34
rooms. Restaurant, pool, hot tub, tennis, croquet, horseback riding,
bicycles, ice-skating, cross-country skiing. AE, MC, V. Closed Apr.–
mid-May.*

Jackson

$$$$ ✕⊞ **Inn at Thorn Hill.** Dark furniture and rose-motif wallpaper pat-
★   terns recall the inn's origins as a home designed by Stanford White in
1895. Yet the comforts are strictly up-to-date, and the food—from a
frequently changing menu—is some of the area's best. Try the pan-fried
duck breast or the rib-eye steak stuffed with artichokes in the restau-
rant, which is closed weekdays in April. ⊠ *Thorn Hill Rd., 03846,* ☎
603/383–4242 or 800/289–8990, 𝐅𝐀𝐗 *603/383–8062. 19 rooms.
Restaurant, pub, pool, hot tub. MAP. AE, D, DC, MC, V.*

North Conway

$$–$$$ ✕ **Scottish Lion.** The tartan-carpeted dining rooms serve scones and De-
vonshire cream for breakfast, game and steak-and-mushroom pies for
lunch and dinner. Rumplethump potatoes are famous locally, and hot
oatcakes come with your meal. There are more than 50 varieties of
Scotch. ⊠ *Rte. 16,* ☎ *603/356–6381. AE, D, DC, MC, V.*

$$$$ ✕⊞ **Snowvillage Inn.** Rooms here are named after authors, and the
★   candlelighted dining room (reservations required) serves specialties
like roasted rack of lamb with herbs *d'Provence.* ⊠ *Box 68, Stuart Rd.,
03849,* ☎ *603/447–2818 or 800/447–4345,* 𝐅𝐀𝐗 *603/447–4345. 18
rooms. Restaurant, sauna, cross-country skiing. Full breakfast; MAP
available. AE, D, DC, MC, V.*

Nightlife and the Arts

Look into the **Mt. Washington Valley Theater Company** (⊠ Main St., North Conway, ☎ 603/356–5776). Catch some music at the **North Country Center for the Performing Arts** (⊠ Mill at Loon Mountain, Lincoln, ☎ 603/745–6032). Or sample the bars. The **Red Parka Pub** (⊠ Rte. 302, Glen, ☎ 603/383–4344) is favored by under-30s. The **Shannon Door Pub** (⊠ Rte. 16, Jackson, ☎ 603/383–4211) is the place to enjoy a Greek salad, Guinness on draft, and the area's best musicians. The **Wildcat Inn & Tavern** (⊠ Rte. 16A, Jackson, ☎ 603/383–4245) has live music and is popular with skiers.

Outdoor Activities and Sports

Biking

At **Great Glen Trails** (⊠ Rte. 16, Pinkham Notch, ☎ 603/466–2333), mountain bike rentals are available by the day and half day for use on their extensive network of trails on the slopes of Mt. Washington.

Fishing

Clear White Mountain streams yield trout and salmon; lakes and ponds have trout and bass. The **state fish and game department's regional office** (☎ 603/788–3164) has the latest information.

Hiking

The White Mountains are crisscrossed with footpaths. The Maine-to-Georgia **Appalachian Trail** crosses the state. The **Appalachian Mountain Club** (⊠ Pinkham Notch, ☎ 603/466–2727 for reservations or a free guide to huts, 603/466–2725 for trail information) operates spartan hikers' huts along the way, provides information, and suggests routes. The **White Mountains National Forest Office** (☎ 603/528–8721 or 800/283–2267) is a good source of hiking information. **New England Hiking Holidays–White Mountains** (⊠ Box 1648, North Conway 03860, ☎ 603/356–9696 or 800/869–0949) organizes guided inn-to-inn hikes.

Ski Areas

New Hampshire's best skiing is in the White Mountains. For the latest conditions (downhill or cross-country) statewide, call **SKI New Hampshire** (☎ 800/262–6660 or 800/258–3608).

Cross-Country

In Jackson nearly 100 mi of trails maintained by the **Jackson Ski Touring Foundation** (☎ 800/927–6697) string together inns, restaurants, and woodlands and connect to another 40 mi of trails maintained by the Appalachian Mountain Club (☞ Hiking *in* Outdoor Activities and Sports, *above*). **The Balsams** (☞ Dining and Lodging, *above*). **Bretton Woods** (⊠ Rte. 302, ☎ 603/278–5000). **Franconia Village Cross-country Center** (⊠ Easton Rd., Franconia, ☎ 603/823–5542). **Great Glen Trails** (☞ Biking *in* Outdoor Activities and Sports, *above*). **Waterville Valley** (⊠ Rte. 49, Waterville Valley, ☎ 603/236–8311 or 603/236–4144 for conditions).

Downhill

New Hampshire's biggest ski areas are medium-size compared with those in neighboring Vermont; their charm is in their low-key atmosphere. **Waterville Valley** (☞ Cross-Country, *above*). **Loon Mountain** (⊠ Kancamagus Hwy., Lincoln, ☎ 603/745–8111 or 603/745–8100 for conditions). **Attitash/Bear Peak** (⊠ Rte. 302, Bartlett, ☎ 603/374–2368 or 603/374–0946 for conditions). **Mt. Cranmore** (⊠ Box 1640, North Conway, ☎ 603/356–5544). **Wildcat** (⊠ Rte. 16, Pinkham

Notch, ☎ 603/466–3326 or 800/643–4521 for conditions). **Cannon** (✉ Franconia, ☎ 603/823–5563 or 603/823–7771 for conditions). **Balsams/Wilderness** and **Bretton Woods** (☞ Cross-Country, *above*) are small areas at grand old resort hotels.

Shopping

More than 150 outlets and shops line **Route 16** north of Conway. **Lincoln** offers factory outlets as well. Galleries throughout the region display local artisans' work.

WESTERN NEW HAMPSHIRE

The countryside east of the Connecticut River between the Massachusetts border and the White Mountains' foothills is a land of covered bridges, calendar-page villages, hardwood forests, jewel-like lakes, and lonely mountains. Cultural centers enliven workaday urban centers such as Manchester, Nashua, and the capital, Concord.

Visitor Information

Lake Sunapee: Business Association (✉ Box 400, Sunapee 03782, ☎ 603/763–2495 or 800/258–3530 in New England). **Monadnock:** Travel Council (✉ 48 Central Sq., Keene 03431, ☎ 603/352–1303). **Concord:** Chamber of Commerce (✉ 244 N. Main St., 03301, ☎ 603/224–2508). **Hanover:** Chamber of Commerce (✉ Box A-105, 03755, ☎ 603/643–3115). **Manchester:** Chamber of Commerce (✉ 889 Elm St., 03101, ☎ 603/666–6600). **Peterborough:** Chamber of Commerce (✉ Box 401, 03458, ☎ 603/924–7234).

Arriving and Departing

By Bus

Concord Trailways (☎ 800/639–3317) operates within the state and **Advance Transit** (☎ 802/295–1824) within the area.

By Car

I–89 cuts southeast–northwest into Vermont. North–south, I–93 provides scenic travel while I–91 follows the Connecticut River on its Vermont shore; in New Hampshire, Routes 12 and 12A are slow but beautiful. Route 4 winds between Lebanon and the coast.

Exploring Western New Hampshire

Concord, New Hampshire's capital, is undergoing an awakening. The Concord on Foot walking trail covers the historic district and includes the **Pierce Manse** (✉ 12 Penacook St., ☎ 603/224–9620 or 603/224–7668), once home to Franklin Pierce, the nation's 14th president. Visit the **Museum of New Hampshire History** to see exhibits from the days of the Abenaki Indians to the present. ✉ 6 Eagle Sq., ☎ 603/225–3381. *Closed Mon.*

Three governors were born in the quiet town of **Warner.** Now Warner is home to the **Kearsarge Indian Museum** (✉ Kearsarge Mountain Rd., ☎ 603/456–2600), where you'll find extensive exhibits on Native American crafts. It is closed mid-December–April. Mountains and parks set off bright, clear **Lake Sunapee.** You can cruise it on the M/V *Mt. Sunapee II* (✉ Sunapee Harbor, ☎ 603/763–4030). Or you can rise above it on a chairlift or picnic on a beach at quiet, woodsy **Mt. Sunapee State Park** (✉ Rte. 103, Newbury, ☎ 603/763–2356).

★ **Dartmouth College,** in Hanover, is a picture of redbrick and white clapboard around a village green. On Wheelock Street, its **Hood Museum of Art** (☎ 603/646–2808) houses works from Africa, Asia, Europe, and America. The modern **Hopkins Center** (☎ 603/646–2422) is a focal point for the local arts scene.

In modest **Cornish,** to the south of Hanover via Route 12A, you can cross four covered bridges. The **Saint-Gaudens National Historic Site** displays some of the artist's heroic, sensitive sculptures. ⊠ *Off Rte. 12A,* ☎ *603/675–2175. Closed late Oct.–late May.*

In **Charlestown** is the Fort at No. 4, a frontier outpost in Colonial times; today costumed guides demonstrate crafts. ⊠ *Rte. 11,* ☎ *603/826–5700. Closed late Oct.–late May.*

In **Monadnock State Park** (⊠ Rte. 124, Jaffrey, ☎ 603/532–8862) 20 trails ascend to the bald summit of 3,165-ft Mt. Monadnock, one of the world's most-climbed mountains. Near **Dublin,** where proper Bostonians summer and locals publish the *Old Farmer's Almanac,* you can exit Monadnock State Park onto Route 101. **Peterborough,** the model for Thornton Wilder's *Our Town,* is now a computer magazine–publishing center.

Beautifully preserved **Fitzwilliam,** spreading from the edges of an oval common, warrants a detour.

What to See and Do with Children

Reserve seats for shows at Concord's high-tech **Christa McAuliffe Planetarium** (⊠ 3 Institute Dr., ☎ 603/271–7827).

Dining and Lodging

For price ranges *see* Charts 1 (B) and 2 (B) *in* On the Road with Fodor's.

Bedford

$$$$ ✕⯐ **Bedford Village Inn.** Minutes from Manchester, this luxury inn has antique four-poster beds and Italian marble whirlpool baths; some rooms have fireplaces. ⊠ *2 Old Bedford Rd., 03110,* ☎ *603/472–2001 or 800/852–1166. 12 suites, 2 apartments. Restaurant, meeting rooms. AE, DC, MC, V.*

Chesterfield

$$$$ ✕⯐ **Chesterfield Inn.** The rooms in this inn, which is surrounded by
★ gardens, are spacious and tastefully decorated with fine antiques and period-style fabrics. Favorites from the dining room include crab cakes with *rémoulade* (a sauce made with olive oil, mustard, scallions, and spices) and duck with mango chutney. ⊠ *Rte. 9 (Box 115), 03443,* ☎ *603/256–3211 or 800/365–5515,* 𝖥𝖠𝖷 *603/256–6131. 13 rooms. Restaurant. Full breakfast. AE, D, DC, MC, V.*

Concord

$$–$$$ ✕ **Hermanos Cocina Mexicana.** Diners come from Boston for the Mex-
★ ican fare served here; expect a line. Don't eat too many nachos supreme made with blue-corn chips; you'll want room for Miguel's Dream (chocolate, cinnamon, pecans, and honey in a warm tortilla). ⊠ *11 Hills Ave.,* ☎ *603/224–5669. Reservations not accepted. MC, V.*

Cornish

$$$–$$$$ ⯐ **Chase House Bed & Breakfast.** This is the birthplace of Salmon P.
★ Chase, Abraham Lincoln's secretary of the treasury, a chief justice of the United States, and a founder of the Republican Party. Waverly fabrics, Colonial furnishings, and canopy beds add to the elegance through-

out. ✉ *Rte. 12A (1½ mi south of the Cornish-Windsor covered bridge), R.R. 2, Box 909, 03745,* ☎ *603/675–5391 or 800/401–9455,* FAX *603/ 675–5010. 8 rooms. Boating. Full breakfast. MC, V. No smoking. No children under 12.*

Hanover

$$$$
★
  ✕⬚ **Hanover Inn.** Three stories of white-trimmed brick, this embodiment of American traditional architecture, owned by Dartmouth College, is handsomely furnished with 19th-century antiques and reproductions. You can get regional American cuisine in the Daniel Webster Room, lighter bites in the Ivy Grill. ✉ *Box 151, The Green 03755,* ☎ *603/643–4300 or 800/443–7024,* FAX *603/646–3744. 92 rooms. 2 restaurants. AE, D, DC, MC, V.*

Nightlife and the Arts

Nightlife

Del Rossi's Trattoria (✉ Junction of Rtes. 137 and 101, Dublin, ☎ 603/ 563–7195) presents big names in jazz, bluegrass, folk, and blues. The **Colonial Theater** (✉ 95 Main St., Keene, ☎ 603/352–2033) has folk, rock, jazz, and movies.

The Arts

The arts flourish at the **Capitol Center for the Arts** (✉ 46 S. Main St., Concord, ☎ 603/225–1111). The **Palace Theatre** (✉ 80 Hanover St., Manchester, ☎ 603/668–5588) is the state performing arts center. **Monadnock Music** (✉ Peterborough, ☎ 603/924–7610) has concerts in July and August. Milford is home to the state's largest professional theater, the **American Stage Festival** (✉ Rte. 13N, ☎ 603/673–4005).

Outdoor Activities and Sports

Biking

Try **Route 10** along the Ashuelot River south of Keene; spurs lead to covered bridges. Contact the **Granite State Wheelmen** (✉ 16 Clinton St., Salem, no phone) for group rides. **Monadnock Bicycle Touring** (✉ Harrisville, ☎ 603/827–3925) offers inn-to-inn biking tours.

Boating

The Connecticut River, while usually safe after June 15, is not for beginners. Rent gear at **Northstar Canoe Livery** (✉ Rte. 12A, Balloch's Crossing, ☎ 603/542–5802).

Fishing

To find out where the action is on the area's 200 lakes and ponds, call the **Department of Fish and Game**'s regional office in Keene (☎ 603/ 352–9669).

Hiking

Networks of trails can be found in many state parks and forests, among them the **Mt. Sunapee** (✉ Newbury, ☎ 603/763–2356) and rugged **Pillsbury** (✉ Washington, ☎ 603/863–2860) state parks and **Fox State Forest** (✉ Hillsboro, ☎ 603/464–3453).

Shopping

Look for church fairs and artisans' studios marked by blue New Hampshire state signs. Antiques dealers sell "by chance or by appointment"; keep an eye peeled along Route 119 west of Fitzwilliam and along Route 101 east of Marlborough. Keene has malls and **Colony Mill Marketplace** (✉ 222 West St., ☎ 603/357–1240). You can buy outdoor gear at **Eastern Mountain Sports** (✉ Vose Farm Rd., ☎ 603/924–7231).

NEW YORK

Updated by
H. Borgeson,
M. Lore,
D. Low,
A. McConnell,
R. Miller,
A. Mills,
M. Mittelbach,
J. Paull,
J. Walman,
and S. Wolf

Capital	Albany
Population	18,185,000
Motto	Excelsior
State Bird	Bluebird
State Flower	Rose
Postal Abbreviation	NY

Statewide Visitor Information

New York State Division of Tourism (⊠ 1 Commerce Plaza, Albany 12245, ☏ 518/474–4116 or 800/225–5697).

Scenic Drives

The **Taconic Parkway,** particularly the stretch from Hopewell Junction to East Chatham, passes through rolling hills, orchards, woods, and pastures reminiscent of the English countryside. To make a dramatic loop around the Adirondacks' **High Peaks** region, pick up Route 73 off the Northway (I–87) at Exit 30, drive northwest through Lake Placid, proceed on Route 86 through Saranac Lake, then head southwest on Route 3 to Tupper Lake, due south on Route 30 to Long Lake, and east on Route 28N to North Creek. For information on the dozen officially designated scenic drives, call 800/225–5697.

National and State Parks

National Parks

The **Gateway National Recreation Area** (⊠ Floyd Bennett Field, Bldg. 69, Brooklyn 11234, ☏ 718/338–3338) extends through Brooklyn, Queens, Staten Island, and into New Jersey. It includes the **Jamaica Bay Wildlife Refuge,** a good spot to see migrating birds; **Jacob Riis Park,** where a boardwalk stretches along the surfy Atlantic; plus various beaches, parklands, and facilities for outdoor and indoor festivals. **Fire Island National Seashore** (⊠ 120 Laurel St., Patchogue 11772, ☏ 516/289–4810) offers Atlantic surf and beaches on a barrier island.

State Parks

New York has 150 state parks. The **Empire State Passport,** permitting unlimited entrance to the parks for a year (April–March), is available for $30 at most parks; you can also contact the **State Office of Parks and Recreation** (☏ 518/474–0456) or write for an application (⊠ Passport, State Parks, Albany 12238).

NEW YORK CITY

Whatever you're looking for in a big-city vacation, you'll find it in New York. The city has a rich history, from early Dutch settlers and the swearing in of George Washington as the first U.S. president to the arrival of millions of immigrants in the late 19th and early 20th centuries. Today's New York City is known around the world for its distinctive skyline, its first-rate museums and performing arts companies, and its status as the capital of finance, fashion, art, publishing, broadcasting, theater, and advertising. And, of course, New Yorkers themselves are world famous—if not always for their charm, at least for their panache, ethnic diversity, street smarts, and accents.

Beyond the list of must-see sights, from the Statue of Liberty to Times Square, from Central Park to the Metropolitan Museum of Art, New York has an indefinable aura all its own. It's a special intensity that comes from being in the big league, where everybody's chasing a dream and still keeping score. To paraphrase a slogan originally coined for the Plaza Hotel, you get the feeling that "nothing unimportant ever happens in New York."

Visitor Information

Convention and Visitors Bureau (⊠ 2 Columbus Circle, 10019, ☎ 212/397–8222 or 212/484–1200, FAX 212/484–1280).

Arriving and Departing

By Bus
The **Port Authority Terminal** (⊠ 40th to 42nd Sts., between 8th and 9th Aves., ☎ 212/564–8484) handles all long-haul and commuter bus lines. Among the bus lines serving New York are **Greyhound Lines** (☎ 212/971–6404 or 800/231–2222), **Bonanza Bus Lines** (for travel from New England, ☎ 800/556–3815), **Martz Trailways** (from northeastern Pennsylvania, ☎ 800/233–8604), and **New Jersey Transit** (New Jersey, ☎ 201/762–5100).

By Car
A complex network of **bridges and tunnels** provides access to Manhattan. I–95 enters via the George Washington Bridge. I–495 enters from Long Island via the Midtown Tunnel. From upstate the city is accessible via the New York (Dewey) Thruway (I–87).

By Plane
Virtually every major U.S. and foreign airline serves one or more of New York's three airports. **La Guardia** (☎ 718/533–3400) and **John F. Kennedy International** (☎ 718/244–4444) airports are in Queens. **Newark International Airport** (☎ 201/961–6000) is in New Jersey. Cab fare to midtown Manhattan runs $18–$23 plus tolls and tip from LaGuardia, $25–$30 plus tolls and tip from JFK, and $28–$30 plus tolls and tip from Newark. **Carey Transportation** (☎ 718/632–0500, 800/456–1012, or 800/284–0909) runs buses to midtown every 20–30 minutes from LaGuardia and every 20–30 minutes from JFK. The **Gray Line Airport Shuttle** (☎ 212/315–3006 or 800/451–0455) connects LaGuardia and JFK to Manhattan. **NJ Transit Airport Express** (☎ 201/762–5100) runs between Newark Airport and Manhattan's Port Authority Terminal. By public transportation, the **A train (subway)** to Howard Beach connects with a free airport shuttle bus to JFK.

By Train
MTA Metro North Railroad at Pennsylvania Station (⊠ 31st to 33rd Sts. between 7th and 8th Aves., ☎ 212/532–4900).

Getting Around New York City

New York is a city of neighborhoods best explored at a leisurely pace, up close, and on foot. Extensive public transportation easily bridges gaps between areas of interest.

By Car
If you're traveling by car, don't plan to use it much in Manhattan. Driving in the city can be a nightmare of gridlocked streets and aggressive fellow motorists. Free parking is almost nonexistent in midtown, and parking lots everywhere are exorbitant ($16 for three hours is not unusual in midtown).

By Public Transportation

The 714-mi **subway** system, the fastest and cheapest way to get around the city, serves Manhattan, Brooklyn, Queens, and the Bronx and operates 24 hours a day. Tokens cost $1.50 each, with reduced fares for people with disabilities and for senior citizens, and are sold in subway stations. MetroCards, purchased for a specific amount, are also available at all subway stations; to use one, swipe it through a reader at the turnstile; the fare is automatically deducted from the card's value. Transfers among subway lines are free at designated interchanges. Most **buses** follow easy-to-understand routes along the Manhattan grid, and some run 24 hours. Routes go up or down the north–south avenues, east and west on the major two-way crosstown streets: 96th, 86th, 79th, 72nd, 57th, 42nd, 34th, 23rd, and 14th. New bus stop signs were introduced in the fall of 1996 and should be in place throughout the city by 1998; look for a light blue sign (or green for an express bus) on a green pole. Bus fare is $1.50 in exact coins (no pennies or bills) or a subway token; a MetroCard can also be used on all city buses. If you need one, request a transfer—they're free—to a connecting bus line when paying the fare. For **24-hour bus and subway information** call 718/330–1234. Transfers between buses and subways are also free if you use a MetroCard. For subway or bus **maps** ask at token booths or write to the **New York City Transit Authority** (✉ Customer Assistance, 370 Jay St., Room 702, Brooklyn 11201).

By Taxi

Taxis (official, licensed ones are yellow) are usually easy to hail on the street, in front of major hotels, and by bus and train stations. The fare is $2.00 for the first ⅕ mi, 30¢ for each ⅕ mi thereafter, and 25¢ for each 75 seconds not in motion. A 50¢ surcharge is added to rides begun between 8 PM and 6 AM. Bridge and tunnel tolls are extra, and drivers expect a 15% tip. Barring performance above and beyond the call of duty, don't feel obliged to give more.

Orientation Tours

Boat Tour

From March to late December **Circle Line Cruises** (✉ Pier 83, west end of 42nd St., ☎ 212/563–3200) offers a three-hour, 35-mi circumnavigation of Manhattan.

Bus Tours

Gray Line New York Tours (✉ 1740 Broadway, ☎ 212/397–2620) offers a number of standard city bus tours in several languages, trolley tours, and day trips to Atlantic City. **New York Doubledecker Tours** (✉ Empire State Bldg., 350 5th Ave., Room 4503, ☎ 212/967–6008) covers the major attractions and allows you to hop on and off.

Walking Tours

Heritage Trails New York (☎ 212/767–0637) is a self-guided walking tour through the downtown area. **New York City Cultural Walking Tours** (☎ 212/979–2388) focuses on the city's architecture, landmarks, memorials, and outdoor art. The **Municipal Art Society** (☎ 212/935–3960) operates a series of bus and walking tours.

Exploring Manhattan

Midtown is the heart of New York City, so it makes sense to start your exploration there, then move on to the museum-rich Upper West and Upper East sides, then downtown to Chelsea, Greenwich Village, SoHo, Little Italy, and Chinatown, and finally to Lower Manhattan, the city's financial center.

Midtown

★ Many think the heart of midtown is **Rockefeller Center,** a complex of 19 buildings occupying nearly 22 acres of prime real estate between 5th and 7th avenues and 47th and 52nd streets. The outdoor ice rink, on the Lower Plaza between 49th and 50th streets, is the center's trademark. Open from October through April, the ice rink becomes an open-air café the rest of the year. In December the plaza is decorated with a huge Christmas tree. The Channel Gardens, connecting the rink to 5th Avenue, is a promenade with six pools surrounded by flower beds.

The backdrop for the Lower Plaza is Rockefeller Center's tallest tower, the 70-story **GE Building** (known as the RCA Building before GE acquired RCA in 1986). The 6,000-seat Art Deco **Radio City Music Hall** (✉ 6th Ave. at 50th St., ☎ 212/247–4777), is America's largest indoor theater. Originally a movie theater, which also presented live entertainment, Radio City produces major concerts, Christmas and Easter extravaganzas, awards presentations, and other special events, and is home of the fabled Rockettes chorus line. Its interior and bathrooms are worth a look even without a show.

The stretch of **5th Avenue** between Rockefeller Center and 59th Street glitters with world-famous shops, including Saks Fifth Avenue, Gucci, Steuben Glass, and Tiffany & Co. Gothic-style **St. Patrick's** (✉ 5th Ave. at 50th St., ☎ 212/753–2261), the Roman Catholic cathedral of New York, is dedicated to the patron saint of the Irish. The stone structure was begun in 1858, consecrated in 1879, and completed in 1906.

The **Museum of Television and Radio,** on 52nd Street between 5th and 6th avenues, has three galleries of photographs and artifacts documenting the history of broadcasting, all in a limestone building by Philip Johnson and John Burgee. The collection contains more than 60,000 television shows and radio programs, as well as several thousand commercials; you can watch your selections at individual consoles. ✉ *25 W. 52nd St., ☎ 212/621–6800 for general information and daily events, 212/621–6600 for other information. Closed Mon.*

★ The **Museum of Modern Art** (MoMA), on 53rd Street between 5th and 6th avenues, is a bright and airy four-story structure built around a secluded sculpture garden. All the greatest modern artists, from van Gogh to Picasso, Matisse to Andy Warhol, are represented. Afternoon and evening film showings are free with the price of admission. ✉ *11 W. 53rd St., ☎ 212/708–9480. Closed Wed.*

One of New York's principal energy centers, **Times Square** is southwest of the Museum of Modern Art. It's one of many New York City "squares" that are actually triangles formed by the angle of Broadway slashing across a major avenue—in this case it crosses 7th Avenue at 42nd Street. Known as the Crossroads of the World, the Great White Way, and the New Year's Eve Capital of America, it is perhaps best known as the Broadway Theater District. Most theaters considered Broadway theaters are actually on streets west of Broadway. Redevelopment on and around 42nd Street, long in the works, took off in 1996–97, as the Walt Disney Company opened a store and renovated the historic **New Amsterdam Theater** (✉ 214 W. 42nd St., ☎ 212/282–2900), opened in mid-1997. Times Square still isn't squeaky clean, but the reopening of the historic **New Victory Theater** (✉ 209 W. 42nd St., ☎ 212/239–6255), with productions by and for children, is another healthy sign.

Two crouching marble lions guard the entrance to the **New York Public Library**'s (☎ 212/930–0800) central research facility, between 40th and 42nd streets on 5th Avenue. This 1911 Beaux Arts masterpiece has frequent exhibits; its majestic **main reading room** is closed for ren-
★ ovations through mid-1999. Behind the library, **Bryant Park** has a sunny lawn strewn with hundreds of green café chairs in summer.

The headquarters of the **United Nations** (☎ 212/963–7713) is on a lushly landscaped riverside tract along 1st Avenue between 42nd and 48th streets, several blocks east of the main public library. A line of flagpoles with banners representing the current roster of 185 member nations stands before the striking 505-ft-high slab of the Secretariat Building. Tours depart from the General Assembly lobby.

At the southern end of midtown, the **Pierpont Morgan Library** is a small, patrician museum whose core is the famous banker's red-damask-lined study and his majestic personal library, with tiers of handsomely bound rare books, letters, and illuminated manuscripts; both rooms were completed in 1905. Rotating exhibitions from the permanent collection showcase drawings, prints, manuscripts, and books. ⊠ *29 E. 36th St., at Madison Ave.,* ☎ *212/685–0008. Closed Mon.*

★ The **Empire State Building** (⊠ 5th Ave. and 34th St., ☎ 212/736–3100), just two blocks southwest of the Pierpont Morgan Library, is no longer the world's tallest building, but it is certainly one of the world's best-loved skyscrapers. The Art Deco structure opened in 1931. Go to the concourse level to buy a ticket for the 86th- and 102nd-floor observation decks.

Upper West Side
One of New York's most desirable neighborhoods, the **Upper West Side** has boutiques and cafés lining Columbus Avenue and renovated brownstones standing proudly on the side streets. **Lincoln Center** (⊠ Broadway between 62nd and 66th Sts., ☎ 212/875–5000 for general information, 212/875–5351 for tour information), which spearheaded the revitalization of the Upper West Side, is today the area's cultural anchor. Flanking the central fountain are three major concert halls: **Avery Fisher Hall,** where the New York Philharmonic Orchestra performs; the glass-fronted **Metropolitan Opera House,** home of the Metropolitan Opera and the American Ballet Theatre; and the **New York State Theater,** the residence of the New York City Ballet and the New York City Opera. The **Vivian Beaumont Theater,** behind Lincoln Center's three main megabuildings, is a major New York dramatic venue. **Alice Tully Hall,** an acoustically near-perfect small concert hall, and the **Walter Reade Theater,** the city's poshest house for arty and obscure films, are both at Broadway and 65th Street.

The **American Museum of Natural History** (☎ 212/769–5200) is set on a four-block tract bounded by Central Park West, Columbus Avenue, and 77th and 81st streets. Its collection of 30 million artifacts includes a 94-ft replica of a blue whale, the 563-carat Star of India sapphire, and lots of dinosaur skeletons. The adjacent **Hayden Planetarium,** on 81st Street, is currently closed for rebuilding and won't be completed until 2000.

Founded in 1754, **Columbia University** is a wealthy, private university that is New York City's only Ivy League school. Bounded by 114th and 120th streets, Broadway, and Amsterdam Avenue, the campus is so effectively walled off from the city by buildings that it's easy to believe you're in a more rustic setting. Enter at 116th Street and Broadway for a look around. Close to Columbia University is the **Cathedral of St. John the Divine** (⊠ Amsterdam Avenue and 112th St., ☎ 212/

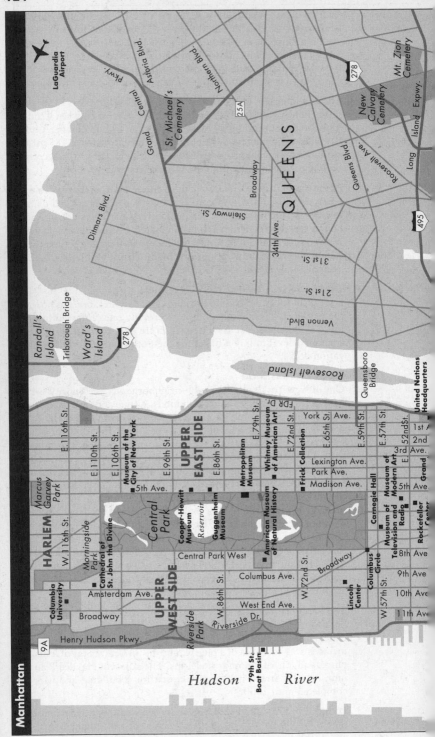

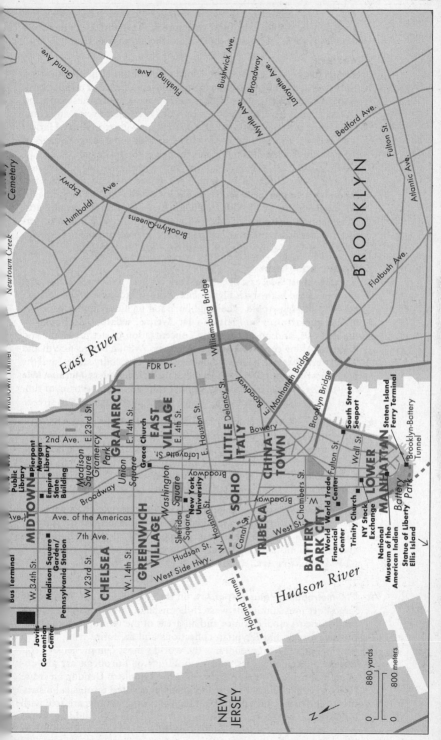

Newtown Creek

Grand Ave.

Flushing Ave.

Bushwick Ave.

Broadway

Lafayette Ave.

BROOKLYN

Bedford Ave.

Fulton St.

Atlantic Ave.

Humboldt Ave.

Expwy.

Brooklyn-Queens

Flatbush Ave.

Cemetery

East River

FDR Dr.

Williamsburg Bridge

E. Manhattan Br.

Brooklyn Bridge

South Street Seaport

Staten Island Ferry Terminal

Midtown Tunnel

GRAMERCY

EAST VILLAGE

LITTLE ITALY

CHINA-TOWN

LOWER MANHATTAN

Brooklyn-Battery Tunnel

E. 23rd St.

E. 14th St.

E. 4th St.

Grace Church

Delancy St.

E. Broadway

Bowery

Wall St.

Fulton St.

Battery

2nd Ave.

Madison Square

Gramercy Park

Union Square

Lafayette St.

E. Houston St.

Public Library

Pierpont Morgan Library

Empire State Building

Washington Square

New York University

SOHO

Broadway

Fulton St.

South Street Seaport

MIDTOWN

Broadway

Sheridan Square

Houston St.

Canal St.

TRIBECA

W. Chambers St.

World Trade Center

Trinity Church

NY Stock Exchange

Ave.

Ave. of the Americas

GREENWICH VILLAGE

W. Broadway

West St.

World Financial Center

National Museum of the American Indian

Statue of Liberty Ellis Island

Bus Terminal

W. 34th St.

7th Ave.

CHELSEA

W. 14th St.

Hudson St.

West Side Hwy.

BATTERY PARK CITY

Battery

Madison Square Garden/ Pennsylvania Station

W. 23rd St.

Holland Tunnel

Javits Convention Center

Hudson River

NEW JERSEY

880 yards

800 meters

0

0

316–7540), an immense limestone-and-granite church that, when finished, will be the largest Gothic structure in the world. Until then, you can have a rare, fascinating look at a cathedral in progress.

Harlem

Harlem has been the mecca for African-American culture for nearly a century. In the 1920s, during an astonishing confluence of talent known as the Harlem Renaissance, black novelists, playwrights, musicians, and artists gathered here. By the 1960s crowded housing, poverty, and crime had turned the neighborhood into a simmering ghetto. Today Harlem is on the way to restoring itself. Mixed in with some seedy remains of the past are old jewels like the refurbished Apollo Theatre (✉ 253 W. 125th St., ☎ 212/749–5838), where such music greats as Ella Fitzgerald and Duke Ellington brought black musicians into the limelight. **Schomburg Center for Research in Black Culture** contains more than 5 million items in its collection, including rare manuscripts, art and artifacts, motion pictures, records, and videotapes. Regular exhibits, performing arts programs, and lectures at the center contribute to Harlem's culture. ✉ 515 Lenox Ave., at 135th St., ☎ 212/491–2200.

Upper East Side

The **Upper East Side,** east of Central Park between 59th and 96th streets, epitomizes the high-style, high-society way of life most people associate with the Big Apple. The neighborhood includes singles bars and high-rise apartment buildings on 1st Avenue, sedate town houses in the east 60s, and an outstanding concentration of art museums and galleries. Along the **Madison Mile,** Madison Avenue between 59th and 79th streets, are patrician art galleries, unique specialty stores, and the boutiques of many of the world's major fashion designers. **Museum Mile** is a strip of cultural institutions, representing a broad spectrum of subjects and styles, on or near 5th Avenue between 70th and 104th streets.

★ The **Frick Collection,** housed in a Beaux Arts–style palace built by Pittsburgh coke and steel baron Henry Clay Frick, is the city's finest small art museum. Specializing in European works from the late 13th to the late 19th centuries, it has masterpieces by Rembrandt, Fragonard, Bellini, Turner, and Vermeer, among others. ✉ 1 E. 70th St., at 5th Ave., ☎ 212/288–0700. Closed Mon.

The **Whitney Museum of American Art,** a gray granite vault with cantilevering and startling trapezoidal windows that project outward, is devoted exclusively to 20th-century American works, from naturalism and impressionism to pop art, abstractionism, and whatever comes next. ✉ 945 Madison Ave., at 75th St., ☎ 212/570–3676. Closed Mon.–Tues.

★ The **Metropolitan Museum of Art,** on the edge of Central Park, is the largest art museum in the western hemisphere. Major displays cover prehistoric to modern times and all areas of the world, including impressive Greek and Egyptian collections and an entire wing devoted to tribal arts. The museum has the world's most comprehensive collection of American art, and its holdings of European art are unequaled outside Europe. Also here are the Temple of Dendur, an entire Roman temple (circa 15 BC), and galleries devoted to musical instruments and arms and armor. Walking tours and lectures are free with admission. The separate **Cloisters** (☎ 212/923–3700) building, transported stone by stone from France, overlooks the Hudson River in Fort Tryon Park at the top of Manhattan; it houses the museum's medieval collection. ✉ 5th Ave. at 82nd St., ☎ 212/879–5500. Closed Mon.

★ The **Guggenheim Museum,** designed by Frank Lloyd Wright and expanded and restored in 1992, is a six-story spiral rotunda that winds down past fine exemplars of modern art. Exhibits alternate between new artists and modern masters; the permanent collection includes more than 20 Picassos. ⊠ *1071 5th Ave., at 88th St.,* ☎ *212/423–3500. Closed Thurs.*

The **Cooper-Hewitt Museum,** a branch of the Smithsonian Institution, was once the residence of industrialist and philanthropist Andrew Carnegie. Changing exhibitions focus on various aspects of contemporary or historical design. Major holdings include drawings and prints, textiles, wall coverings, applied arts and industrial design, and contemporary design. ⊠ *2 E. 91st St.,* ☎ *212/860–6868. Closed Mon.*

The **Museum of the City of New York** brings the history of the Big Apple to life from its seafaring beginnings to yesterday's headlines, with period rooms, a video, clever displays of memorabilia, and a doll house collection. ⊠ *5th Ave. at 103rd St.,* ☎ *212/534–1672. Closed Mon.– Tues.*

Chelsea, Greenwich Village, and the East Village
Like its London namesake, **Chelsea** maintains a villagelike personality, with a number of quiet streets graced by lovingly renovated town houses. The neighborhood stretches from 5th Avenue west to the Hudson River and from 14th to 29th streets and is now home to an active gay community that frequents the lively stores and restaurants on 8th Avenue. In recent years the area has witnessed an economic boost with the opening of 6th Avenue superstores and the Chelsea Piers Sports and Entertainment Complex on the Hudson. Galleries have set up shop west of 10th Avenue from 20th to 29th streets.

★ With its narrow tree-lined streets, brick town houses, tiny green parks, and hidden courtyards, **Greenwich Village** is the closest thing to a small town in Manhattan. The Village is ideal for strolling, window-shopping, and café hopping; it extends from 14th Street south to Houston Street and from the Hudson River piers to 5th Avenue.

For generations the preferred haunt of writers, artists, musicians, and bohemians, the Village is known for the scores of famous Americans who lived and worked here and the cultural movements they defined. Perhaps those most synonymous with Greenwich Village are the avant-garde artists of this century, including abstract expressionist painters like Franz Kline and Mark Rothko, Beat writers and poets such as Jack Kerouac and Allen Ginsberg, and folk musicians and poets, notably Bob Dylan and Peter, Paul, and Mary.

You'll encounter all kinds of **historical buildings** in a walk through the Village. At different times Edna St. Vincent Millay and John Barrymore each lived at 75½ Bedford Street—at 9½ ft wide, New York's narrowest house. Theodore Dreiser wrote *An American Tragedy* at 16 St. Luke's Place. The houses at 127 and 129 MacDougal Street were built in 1829 for Aaron Burr, who held much of the land now part of the Village.

Washington Square, at the foot of 5th Avenue, is the best place to begin a walking tour of the Village. In the center of the square is the gleaming white Washington Arch, designed by Stanford White and built in 1889 to commemorate the 100th anniversary of George Washington's inauguration. Most buildings bordering the square belong to New York University. The surrounding area, around the intersection of Bleecker and MacDougal streets, attracts a young crowd to its shops, bars, jazz clubs, Off-Broadway theaters, cabarets, coffeehouses, fast-food stands, cafés, and unpretentious restaurants.

To the northwest, at **Sheridan Square,** is Christopher Street, the heart of New York's gay community and the location of many intriguing boutiques. West of 7th Avenue, the Village turns into a picture-book warren of twisting tree-lined streets, quaint houses, and tiny restaurants. The stretch of West 4th Street is particularly pleasant.

The **East Village,** east of 4th Avenue (Lafayette Street), has over the centuries housed Jewish, Ukrainian, and Puerto Rican immigrants; beatniks; hippies; punk rockers; artists of various stripes; and most recently, affluent young professionals. Soak up the eclectic atmosphere along St. Marks Place between 2nd and 3rd avenues and 9th Street between 2nd Avenue and Avenue A, with their veggie restaurants, alternative clothing boutiques, cafés, and offbeat shops.

SoHo, Little Italy, and Chinatown

SoHo (so named because it is the district *S*outh of *H*ouston [pronounced *How*-ston] Street, bounded by Broadway, Canal Street, and 6th Avenue) is synonymous with a gritty urban elegance—an amalgam of black-clad artists, hip young Wall Streeters, track-lighted loft apartments, art galleries, and restaurants with a minimalist approach to both food and decor.

West Broadway (paralleling Broadway four blocks to the west) is SoHo's main drag, with many shops and galleries. On Saturday, the big day for gallery hopping, it can be crowded but still great for people-watching. At **28–30** and **72–76 Greene Street** you'll find two fine examples of cast-iron architecture, of which SoHo has one of the world's greatest concentrations.

Walk one block east to Grand and Mulberry streets to enter **Little Italy,** an ever-shrinking enclave of Italian life. Mulberry Street, lined with tenement buildings, has long been the heart of Little Italy; now it's virtually the entire body. Between Broome and Canal streets, Mulberry consists entirely of restaurants, cafés, bakeries, food shops, and souvenir stores. Each September the Feast of San Gennaro turns the streets of Little Italy into a bright and turbulent Italian kitchen.

In recent years **Chinatown** has expanded beyond its traditional borders into Little Italy to the north and the Lower East Side, once a neighborhood of Jewish immigrants, to the south and east. Canal and Grand streets abound with crowded markets bursting with mounds of fresh seafood and strangely shaped vegetables in extraterrestrial shades of green. Food shops proudly display their wares, from almond cookies to roasted ducks.

Mott Street is Chinatown's principal business street. Narrow and twisting, crammed with souvenir shops and restaurants in funky pagoda-style buildings, and crowded with pedestrians at all hours of the day or night—Mott Street looks the way you'd expect Chinatown to look. Within a few dense blocks, hundreds of restaurants serve every imaginable type of Chinese cuisine, from simple fast-food noodles or dumplings to sumptuous Hunan, Szechuan, Cantonese, Mandarin, and Shanghai feasts.

Lower Manhattan

Lower Manhattan is compact and packed with attractions: narrow streets and immense skyscrapers, Wall Street and Colonial-era houses, South Street Seaport and Battery Park City. The city did not really expand beyond these precincts until the middle of the 19th century. Today Wall Street in many ways dominates Lower Manhattan; the thoroughfare is both an actual street and a shorthand name for the vast, powerful financial community that clusters around the New York and American stock exchanges.

Outside the **Staten Island Ferry Terminal,** at the southernmost tip of Manhattan, is a good place to start your exploration of Lower Manhattan. For great harbor views of the Statue of Liberty, Ellis Island, and the Lower Manhattan skyline, consider the free ferry ride to Staten Island. **Battery Park,** a verdant landfill loaded with monuments and sculpture and the point of embarkation for visits to the Statue of Liberty and Ellis Island, is a short walk up the Battery Park waterfront from the Staten Island Ferry Terminal. Buy your ticket for the ferry ride to the Statue of Liberty or Ellis Island at Castle Clinton (☎ 212/269–5755), inside the park; arrive early and be prepared to wait.

★ The **Statue of Liberty** (☎ 212/363–3200) has enjoyed a remarkable resurgence of popularity following its centennial restoration in 1986. Once on Liberty Island you may have to wait three hours to take the elevator 10 stories to the top of the pedestal. The strong of heart and limb can climb another 12 stories to the crown.

★ **Ellis Island** (☎ 212/363–3200), which reopened in 1990 after a $140 million restoration, was once the main East Coast federal immigration facility. Between 1892 and 1954, 17 million men, women, and children—the ancestors of more than 40% of the Americans living today—were processed here.

The **National Museum of the American Indian,** in a stunning Beaux Arts–style building, opened in 1995, is the first national museum dedicated solely to Native American culture, and its exhibits of fascinating objects from around the Americas are accompanied with good documentation. ✉ *1 Bowling Green,* ☎ *212/668–6624.*

Fraunces Tavern (✉ Broad and Pearl Sts., ☎ 212/425–1778) is a combination restaurant, bar, and museum occupying a Colonial house built in 1719 and restored in 1907. Best remembered as the site of George Washington's farewell address to his officers, which celebrated the British evacuation of New York in 1783, it contains two fully furnished period rooms and other displays on 18th- and 19th-century American history.

The **World Trade Center,** a 16-acre complex, contains New York's two tallest buildings (each 1,350 ft). Elevators to the observation deck on the 107th floor of 2 World Trade Center glide a quarter of a mile into the sky in only 58 seconds. The rock and soil excavated in order to construct the World Trade Center begat **Battery Park City,** 100 new acres of Manhattan on the Hudson River. It includes office buildings, high-rise apartment houses, town houses, a selection of shops, and the **World Financial Center,** a mammoth granite-and-glass complex designed by Cesar Pelli.

Wall Street's principal facility, the **New York Stock Exchange** has its august Corinthian main entrance around the corner from Wall Street, on Broad Street. A self-guided tour, a multimedia presentation, and staff members may help you interpret the chaos that seems to reign on the trading floor. ✉ *20 Broad St.,* ☎ *212/656–5168. Closed weekends.*

A regal **statue of George Washington** on Wall Street stands at the spot where he was sworn in as the first U.S. president in 1789. After the capital moved to Philadelphia in 1790, the original Federal Hall became New York's city hall but was demolished in 1812. The current **Federal Hall National Memorial** (✉ 26 Wall St., ☎ 212/825–6888), built in 1842, is a stately period structure that contains exhibits on New York and Wall Street; it is closed weekends. **Trinity Church** (✉ Broadway and Wall St.) was New York's first Anglican parish (1646). The graves of Alexander Hamilton and Robert Fulton are in the churchyard. The present structure (1846) ranked as the city's tallest building for most of the last half of the 19th century.

South Street Seaport is an 11-block historic district on the East River that encompasses a museum, shopping, historic ships, cruise boats, a multimedia presentation, and innumerable places to eat and drink. You can view the historic ships from Pier 16, which is the departure point for the one-hour Seaport Liberty Cruise (☎ 212/630–8888).

★ The **Brooklyn Bridge,** New York's oldest and best-known span, is just north of the South Street Seaport. When completed in 1883, it was the world's longest suspension bridge and the tallest structure in the city. Walking across the Brooklyn Bridge is a peak New York experience.

Parks and Gardens

★ **Central Park** was designed by landscape architects Frederick Law Olmsted and Calvert Vaux for 843 acres of land acquired by the city in 1856. Bounded by 59th and 110th streets, 5th Avenue, and Central Park West, the park contains grassy meadows, wooded groves, and formal gardens; paths for jogging, strolling, horseback riding, and biking; playing fields; a small zoo; an ice-skating rink; a carousel; an outdoor theater; and numerous fountains and sculptures.

The **Bronx Zoo** (☞ What to See and Do with Children, *below*) is in Bronx Park, along the Bronx River Parkway and bisected by Fordham Road. The **New York Botanical Garden** (☎ 718/817–8705), a 250-acre botanical treasury around the dramatic gorge of the Bronx River, is within Bronx Park. Its 40-acre forest, conservatory, museum, and outdoor gardens draw nature enthusiasts from around the world.

What to See and Do with Children

★ The **Bronx Zoo,** now officially known as the International Wildlife Conservation Park (⊠ Fordham Rd. and Bronx River Pkwy., ☎ 718/367–1010), is the nation's largest urban zoo, with more than 4,000 animals on 265 acres of woods, ponds, streams, and parkland. New York's **Aquarium for Wildlife Conservation** (⊠ W. 8th St. and Surf Ave., Coney Island, Brooklyn, ☎ 718/265–3474), just off the Coney Island Boardwalk, has more than 20,000 creatures on display, with dolphins and sea lions performing in periodic exhibitions.

Dining

By J. Walman

New York restaurants don't have to be expensive; savvy diners know how to keep costs within reason. Go for lunch or brunch instead of dinner. Order prix fixe instead of à la carte. Share several appetizers—skipping higher priced main courses. Or go ethnic: New York has restaurants specializing in almost any cuisine you can name (try Little India on 6th Street between 1st and 2nd avenues, Little Korea on West 32nd Street between 5th and 6th avenues, one of the ubiquitous storefront pasta parlors on the Upper East Side, or Chinatown, for starters). Be sure to make reservations on weekends. For price ranges *see* Chart 1 (A) *in* On the Road with Fodor's.

$$$$ ✕ **Chanterelle.** Soft peach walls, luxuriously spaced tables, and flaw-
★ less service set the stage for David Waltuck's inventions. Try his signature seafood sausage or just about anything else on the menu, which changes with the seasons. The cheese and wine selections are nonpareil. Lunch and dinner are prix fixe. ⊠ *2 Harrison St.,* ☎ *212/966–6960. Reservations essential. AE, DC, MC, V. No lunch Sun.–Mon.*

$$$$ ✕ **Daniel.** At Daniel Boulud's often celebrity-filled restaurant, whose
★ creation cost $1.9 million, lavish flower arrangements and antique mir-
rors adorn the main dining room along with exquisite table settings
by Limoges, gold-tinted walls, and red-checked banquettes. The cuisine (combining the contemporary with the classic) is among the best
in New York. Note the uncommon tuna tartare, with a touch of curry
and the restaurant's signature dish, black sea bass wrapped in a crispy
potato shell. ⊠ *20 E. 76th St.,* ☎ *212/288–0033. Reservations essential.
Jacket required. D, DC, MC, V. Closed Sun. No lunch Mon.*

$$$$ ✕ **Palio.** Named after the nearly 350-year-old Italian horse race that
★ celebrates the Assumption of the Virgin, this exceptional restaurant has
an impressive 13-ft mural by Sandro Chia, and a second-floor dining
room with luxuriously spaced tables set with Frette linen and Riedel
crystal. Here you'll experience authentic Italian cuisine—from a regional
six-course menu from Siena to one based on aged balsamic vinegar.
The wine selection and service are commensurate with the posh setting. ⊠ *151 W. 51st St.,* ☎ *212/245–4850. Reservations essential. Jacket
and tie. AE, DC, MC, V. Closed Sun. No lunch Sat.*

$$$$ ✕ **Rainbow Room.** This dinner-and-dancing room on the 65th floor
of 30 Rock remains a monument to glamour and fantasy. Tables clad
in silver lamé rise in tiers around a revolving dance floor lighted by an
immense chandelier; aubergine-color walls frame panoramic 50-mi views
seen through floor-to-ceiling windows. Revamped retro dishes including lobster Thermidor and oysters Rockefeller contrast with specialties utilizing Hudson River valley produce (such as cheeses, game,
and New York State fois gras), all prepared by executive chef Waldy
Malouf. ⊠ *30 Rockefeller Plaza,* ☎ *212/632–5000 or 212/632–
5100. Reservations essential. Jacket and tie. AE, DC, MC, V. Closed
Mon. (Sun.–Mon. in summer).*

$$$–$$$$ ✕ **Gramercy Tavern.** A 91-ft-long mural of fruit and vegetables wraps
around the bar, and although the look is reminiscent of an English tav-
ern, the food is decidedly new American. The section called the Tav-
ern, off the main dining room, offers some terrific plates from the
wood-burning grill (hanger steak sandwich, for one). An appealing se-
lection of cheese and a stellar wine list are offered here and in the main
room. ⊠ *42 E. 20th St., between Park Ave. S and Broadway,* ☎ *212/
477–0777. Reservations essential for main dining room. AE, DC, MC,
V. No lunch Sun.*

$$$–$$$$ ✕ **Windows on the World.** This monumental restaurant serving fine
★ contemporary cuisine on the World Trade Center's 107th floor reopened
in 1996 after a $25 million makeover. The complex now includes the
Greatest Bar on Earth, with a full multiethnic menu and dancing after
10 PM; the adjacent Skybox, a cigar-smoking oasis; and the intimate
60-seat Cellar in the Sky, where a seven-course dinner is served, ac-
companied by five wines. The 240-seat main dining room has artwork
by Milton Glaser, apricot-color fabric banquettes, and panoramic win-
dows with stunning views. ⊠ *1 World Trade Center, 107th floor,* ☎
*212/524–7011, 212/938–0030 for Cellar in the Sky. Reservations es-
sential. Jacket required. AE, DC, MC, V.*

$$$ ✕ **Nobu.** A curved wall of river-worn black pebbles, a 12-seat onyx-
★ faced sushi bar (perfect for single diners), bare-wood tables, birch
trees, and a hand-painted beech floor create drama as well as conversation. The hip clientele is as interesting as the kitchen, which is ruled
by chef Nobu Matsuhisa. It's difficult to decide in which direction to
go on his menu: rock-shrimp tempura; black cod with miso; new-style
sashimi—all are tours de force. ⊠ *105 Hudson St., off Franklin St.,*
☎ *212/219–0500 or 212/219–8095 for same-day reservations. Reservations essential. AE, DC, MC, V. Closed Sun. No lunch.*

$$$ ✕ **Water Club.** This glass-enclosed barge in the East River is decidedly dramatic, with its long wood-paneled bar, blazing fireplace, appetizing shellfish display, and panoramic water views. Food is ingeniously presented. The chef shows a fine hand with sautéed red snapper fillet with lobster dumplings, fennel, and saffron bouillon. ✉ *500 E. 30th St.,* ☎ *212/683–3333. Reservations essential. AE, DC, MC, V.*

$$–$$$ ✕ **Zoë.** At this colorful, high-ceiling SoHo eatery with terra-cotta columns and floor, the open kitchen produces impressive food such as grilled yellowfin tuna on wok-charred vegetables. Zoë also has an exceptionally well-organized wine list as well as a fine group of carefully tended wines by the glass. This is one of the better places in Manhattan for weekend brunch. ✉ *90 Prince St., between Broadway and Mercer St.,* ☎ *212/966–6722. Reservations essential. AE, DC, MC, V.*

$$ ✕ **Blue Water Grill.** Housed in what was once a bank, this popular spot
★ retains the original 1904 marble and molded ceiling. A copper-and-tile raw bar anchors one end of the sweeping room with its warm hues of indigo blue, sienna, and yellow. The menu is strong on seafood, served neat (chilled whole lobster; shrimp in the rough); in au courant "global" style (Moroccan-spiced red snapper, Maryland crab cakes); or in simple preparations from a wood-burning oven. ✉ *31 Union Sq. W, at 16th St.,* ☎ *212/675–9500. Reservations essential. AE, DC, MC, V.*

$$ ✕ **Duane Park Café.** This quiet TriBeCa restaurant can spoil you with its comfortable seating, excellent service, serious but fairly priced wines, and international menu. Look for marinated duck and arugula salad and crispy skate with the Japanese-inspired *ponzu* sauce. The pleasing design incorporates dark columns, a salmon color scheme, maple-veneer walls, and an abundance of cherry wood. ✉ *157 Duane St., between West Broadway and Hudson St.,* ☎ *212/732–5555. AE, D, DC, MC, V. Closed Sun. No lunch Sat.*

$$ ✕ **L'Absinthe.** The wonderful art nouveau bistro decor features etched
★ glass, huge gilt-framed mirrors, tile floors, and a few sidewalk tables. Chef-owner Jean-Michel Bergougnoux beautifully presents shellfish and cheese. Menu highlights include a fine foie gras terrine, slow-braised beef with carrots, poached free-range chicken in truffle broth, and for dessert, a thin, crisp apple tart or warm chocolate cake. ✉ *227 E. 67th St.,* ☎ *212/794–4950. Reservations essential. AE, MC, V.*

$$ ✕ **Park Avalon.** The flagship restaurant of Steven Hanson (owner of Blue Water Grill, ☞ *above*) has two dining levels, huge light fixtures with alabaster shades, massive mirrors, and a bar area with floor-to-ceiling wine cases and a dramatic display of lighted candles. Grilled free-range chicken with roasted garlic crust, sautéed broccoli rabe, and rosemary mashed potatoes is a standout. There are several low-fat desserts, including marvelously intense sorbets. ✉ *255 Park Ave. S, between 18th and 19th Sts.,* ☎ *212/533–2500. AE, DC, MC, V.*

$–$$ ✕ **Carmine's.** Despite the crowds it's worth lining up for these cavernous family-style eateries that serve up home-style meals at low prices. Dishes like rigatoni in broccoli, sausage, and white-bean sauce are so gargantuan you'll have enough for leftovers. ✉ *2450 Broadway,* ☎ *212/362–2200;* ✉ *200 W. 44th St.,* ☎ *212/221–3800. Reservations not accepted. AE. No lunch.*

$–$$ ✕ **Frico Bar.** Come here for a casual meal; there's an array of tempting snacks ranging from thin-crust pizza to the house specialty, *frico,* a crustless pizza of griddle-crisped cheese stuffed with potatoes and vegetables. As in Italy's Friulian countryside, wine comes on tap, along with 10 excellent beers. The restaurant has tile floors and its moon-and-star logo displayed on attractive wooden tables. ✉ *402 W. 43rd St., off 9th Ave.,* ☎ *212/564–7272. AE, DC, MC, V.*

$-$$ ✕ **Virgil's.** This massive barbecue roadhouse in the Theater District has clever neon-and-Formica decor. Start with stuffed jalapeños or buttermilk onion rings with blue-cheese dip. Then go for the Pig Out: a rack of pork ribs, Texas hot links, pulled pork, rack of lamb, chicken, and more. Wash it all down with beer from a good list. ⊠ *152 W. 44th St.,* ☎ *212/921–9494. Reservations essential. AE, MC, V.*

$ ✕ **Angry Monk.** Incense and exotic music greet you as you enter this Tibetan vegetarian eatery through velvet curtains. On the walls hang framed pictures of Tibetan farmworkers and ceremonial masks to cast away bad vibrations. Try the pureed soup of the day, cooked millet salad with mushrooms and tumeric, and sautéed bean curd with vegetables and clear bean-thread noodles. ⊠ *96 2nd Ave., between 5th and 6th Sts.,* ☎ *212/979–9202. AE, DC, MC, V. No lunch.*

$ ✕ **Boca Chica.** This raffish East Village restaurant has live music, danc-
★ ing, and assertive food from several Latin American nations. Try the soupy Puerto Rican chicken-and-rice stew known as *asopao,* the Cuban sandwiches, or the Bolivian corn topped with chicken. You may wish to sample a potent Brazilian *caipirinha* cocktail, with lime and rum, but don't trip over the boa constrictor by the bar. ⊠ *13 1st Ave.,* ☎ *212/473–0108. Reservations not accepted. AE, DC, MC, V.*

$ ✕ **French Roast.** This casual, around-the-clock spot with a Left Bank ambience charges bargain prices for some very good bistro dishes such as poached beef marrow finished with bread crumbs and served in broth. The *croque monsieur* (melted cheese sandwich, done in the style of French toast) is first-rate. Or just stop for coffee and dessert. ⊠ *458 6th Ave., at 11th St.,* ☎ *212/533–2233. AE, MC, V.*

$ ✕ **Hi-Life Restaurant and Lounge.** Young hip eaters wait in line to sit
★ down at one of the spacious half-moon-shaped booths at this bilevel art deco café. The draw? Soothing prices, huge portions, and some of the best martinis in town. Polish off sushi or something from the raw bar before you proceed to the filet mignon served with potato salad or heaping bowls of *pad thai* (noodles with chicken or shrimp). ⊠ *1340 1st Ave., at 72nd St.,* ☎ *212/249–3600;* ⊠ *477 Amsterdam Ave., at 83rd St.,* ☎ *212/787–7199. AE, DC, MC, V.*

$ ✕ **Ipanema.** Sample Brazil's exotic cuisine at this snug, modern restaurant with white- and peach-color walls covered with vivid oil paintings of Rio and Bahia. *Feijoada,* the national meal—black beans with smoked meats, collard greens, oranges, chili peppers, and a comforting grain called *farofa*—is good here. And don't miss the great drinks made with *cachaça* (Brazilian rum)—*batidas* (with coconut milk) and caipirinhas. ⊠ *13 W. 46th St.,* ☎ *212/730–5848. AE, DC, MC, V.*

$ ✕ **Joe's Shanghai.** At this modern, clean, and unadorned Chinese din-
★ ing spot, the specialty is *bun* (a tasty dumpling containing ground pork or crab and piping-hot broth). Also try Shanghai-fried flat noodles— long, winding doughy miracles in an intense brown sauce with stewed pork balls. ⊠ *9 Pell St.,* ☎ *212/233–8888. Reservations not accepted. No credit cards.*

$ ✕ **Mavalli Palace.** Service may be a bit slow, but the gentle prices and marvelous dishes more than compensate at this pretty Indian restaurant with exposed brick walls and blond-wood chairs. Magnificent crepes made with lentils and rice flour are wrapped around potatoes and a fiery chutney. Fresh onions top *uttappam,* a rice-and-lentil pancake. ⊠ *46 E. 29th St.,* ☎ *212/679–5535. AE, DC, MC, V. Closed Mon.*

$ ✕ **Republic.** Downtown epicureans on the run flock to this innovative Asian noodle emporium. At one of the two bluestone bars, you can simultaneously dine and enjoy the spectacle of chefs scurrying amid clouds of steam in the open kitchen. The large dining space also has sleek birch tables. The menu chiefly contains dishes of rice or noodles, stir-fried or served in savory broths. Beverages include cold, homemade flavored sakes, exotic juices, various wines, and domestic and Asian beers. ⊠ *37A Union Sq. W,* ☎ *212/627–7172. AE, DC, MC, V.*

$ ✕ **Turkish Kitchen.** This multilevel spot has Turkish carpets on the floors
★ and walls. Order anise-flavored *raki* as an aperitif with such *meze* (appetizers) as fried calamari with garlic sauce. Among entrées, try the succulent *doner* (vertically grilled lamb, sliced paper-thin). ⊠ *386 3rd Ave., between 27th and 28th Sts.,* ☎ *212/679–1810. AE, DC, MC, V. No lunch weekends.*

$ ✕ **Uncle Nick's.** At this inexpensive taverna you dine in a long room,
★ with a navy blue pipe-lined tin ceiling, an exposed kitchen, and a wood floor. Uncle Nick's owners, Tony and Mike Vanatakis, prepare each fish selection with simplicity and care. Be sure to try as many of the excellent appetizers as your tummy can handle, including crispy fried smelts, tender grilled baby octopus, and giant lima beans with tomatoes and herbs. ⊠ *747 9th Ave., between 50th and 51st Sts.,* ☎ *212/245–7992. MC, V.*

Lodging

Demand for hotel rooms in New York is currently outstripping supply as visitors pour into the city and new hotels are few and far between, so expect to pay more—much more—here than you would elsewhere for a comparable room.

Hundreds of **bed-and-breakfast rooms** are available in Manhattan and the outer boroughs, principally Brooklyn, and almost always cost well below $100 a night; some singles are available for under $50. Reservations may be made through **Abode** (⊠ Box 20022, 10021, ☎ 212/472–2000 or 800/835–8880), **Bed and Breakfast Network of New York** (⊠ 134 W. 32nd St., Suite 602, 10001, ☎ 212/645–8134), **City Lights Bed and Breakfast** (⊠ Box 20355, Cherokee Station, 10021, ☎ 212/737–7049, 𝖥𝖠𝖷 212/535–2755), **Inn New York** (⊠ 266 W. 71st St., 10023, ☎ 212/580–1900, 𝖥𝖠𝖷 212/580–4437), **Manhattan Home Stays** (⊠ Box 20684, Cherokee Station, 10021, ☎ 212/737–3868, 𝖥𝖠𝖷 212/265–3561), **New World Bed and Breakfast** (⊠ 150 5th Ave., Suite 711, 10011, ☎ 212/675–5600 or 800/443–3800, 𝖥𝖠𝖷 212/675–6366), or **Urban Ventures** (⊠ Box 426, 10024; ⊠ 38 W. 32nd St., 10001; ☎ 212/594–5650, 𝖥𝖠𝖷 212/947–9320). For price ranges *see* Chart 2 (A) *in* On the Road with Fodor's.

$$$$ ▦ **The Algonquin.** This beloved landmark hotel, where the Round Table group of writers and wits once met for lunch, still shelters celebrities, particularly literary types visiting nearby publishing houses or the *New Yorker* magazine offices. Rooms have homey, Victorian-style fixtures and furnishings; specialty suites are dedicated to Dorothy Parker, James Thurber, and *Vanity Fair.* ⊠ *59 W. 44th St., 10036,* ☎ *212/840–6800 or 800/548–0345,* 𝖥𝖠𝖷 *212/944–1618. 165 rooms. 2 restaurants, bar, lobby lounge, in-room safes, cabaret, library, business services, meeting rooms, free parking (weekends only). AE, D, DC, MC, V.*

$$$$ ▦ **The Carlyle.** European tradition and Manhattan swank shake hands
★ at New York's least hysterical grand hotel. Everything about this Madison Avenue landmark suggests refinement, starting with the Mark Hampton–designed rooms. Many guests head straight to the Bemelmans Bar, named after Ludwig Bemelmans, illustrator of the beloved children's book character Madeline and the "twelve little girls in two straight lines"; he created the murals here. ⊠ *35 E. 76th St., 10021,* ☎ *212/744–1600 or 800/227–5737,* 𝖥𝖠𝖷 *212/717–4682. 190 rooms. Restaurant, bar, café, kitchenettes, minibars, spa, meeting rooms. AE, DC, MC, V.*

$$$$ ⊞ **Luxury Collection.** At press time, the new name of this former Ritz-
★ Carlton property had not yet been decided. Everything about this
hotel is first-class, from the prestigious Central Park South address to
the very polished service to the fine art that covers virtually every wall.
Guest rooms are graced with rich brocades, polished woods, and marble bathrooms; some have breathtaking Central Park views. ✉ *112 Central Park S, 10019,* ☎ *212/757–1900 or 800/241–3333,* FAX *212/
757–9620. 214 rooms. Restaurant, bar, health club, business services,
meeting rooms. AE, D, DC, MC, V.*

$$$$ ⊞ **The Mark.** Find this friendliest of baby grand hotels one block north
★ of the Carlyle and steps from Central Park. Guest-room extras such
as Belgian bed linens and black-and-white marble bathrooms with deep
tubs make the Mark a serious contender among New York's elite hotels. ✉ *25 E. 77th St., 10021,* ☎ *212/744–4300 or 800/843–6275,*
FAX *212/744–2749. 180 rooms. Restaurant, lounge, in-room VCRs, minibars, health club, meeting rooms. AE, D, DC, MC, V.*

$$$$ ⊞ **St. Regis.** This 5th Avenue Beaux Arts landmark has ultrachic pub-
★ lic spaces: the celebrated restaurant, Lespinasse; the Astor Court tea
lounge, with its trompe l'oeil cloud ceiling; and the King Cole Bar, with
its famous Maxfield Parrish mural. Guest rooms, all serviced by but-
lers, are out of a period film, with high ceilings, crystal chandeliers, silk
wall coverings, Louis XV–style furnishings, and expensive amenities such
as Tiffany silver services. ✉ *2 E. 55th St., 10022,* ☎ *212/753–4500
or 800/759–7550,* FAX *212/787–3447. 213 rooms. Restaurant, bar,
lounge, in-room safes, minibars, beauty salon, massage, sauna, health
club, meeting rooms, business services. AE, D, DC, MC, V.*

$$$$ ⊞ **Soho Grand.** Starting from the first floor at SoHo's first hotel, the
★ grand staircase of translucent bottle glass and iron recalls the neighborhood's 19th-century cast-iron buildings. Upstairs in the Grand
Salon, 16-ft-high windows and overscaled furniture complement the
immense stone pillars that rise from below. Guest rooms have custom-
designed furnishings, including drafting-table-style desks, nightstands
that mimic sculptors' stands, and minibars made of old campaign
chests. ✉ *310 West Broadway, 10013,* ☎ *212/965–3000 or 800/
965–3000,* FAX *212/965–3244. 367 rooms. Restaurant, bar, lounge,
exercise room, meeting rooms.*

$$$–$$$$ ⊞ **The Mansfield.** Built in 1904, this small hotel is Victorian and club-
like. Turn-of-the-century details abound here: from the column-supported
coffered ceiling, warm ivory walls, and limestone floor in the lobby to
the guest rooms' black-marble bathrooms, ebony-stained floors and doors,
dark-wood blinds, and sleigh beds. ✉ *12 W. 44th St., 10036,* ☎ *212/
944–6050 or 800/255–5167,* FAX *212/764–4477. 123 rooms. In-room
VCRs, cinema, concert hall, library, free parking. AE, MC, V.*

$$$–$$$$ ⊞ **Manhattan East Suite Hotels.** Here's a group of good-value prop-
★ erties for the traveler who likes to combine full hotel service with in-
dependent pied-à-terre living. The four best are the **Beekman Tower**
(✉ 3 Mitchell Pl.), near the United Nations; the **Dumont Plaza** (✉ 150
E. 34th St.), on a direct bus line to the Javits Center; the **Surrey Hotel**
(✉ 20 E. 76th St.), near Madison Avenue boutiques and galleries; and
the **Southgate Tower** (✉ 371 7th Ave.), near Madison Square Garden
and Penn Station. *Sales office:* ✉ *500 W. 37th St., 10018,* ☎ *212/465–
3600 or 800/637–8483,* FAX *212/465–3663. AE, DC, MC, V.*

$$$–$$$$ ⊞ **Radisson Empire Hotel.** The Empire's English country–style lobby
is warm and inviting with its crimson carpet and hanging tapestry. Rooms
and suites are small but nicely furnished; all have textured teal carpets,
dark-wood furnishings, and high-tech electronics. This hotel is one of
the city's better buys, and you can't beat its location across from Lin-
coln Center. ✉ *44 W. 63rd St., at Broadway, 10023,* ☎ *212/265–7400*

or 800/333–3333, ⒻⒶⓍ 212/244–3382. 375 rooms. Restaurant, bar, in-room VCRs, minibars, meeting rooms. AE, D, DC, MC, V.

$$$ 🏨 **The Beverly.** This suite-dominated hotel's plush wood-paneled lobby, with a crystal chandelier, an original terrazzo floor, and Art Deco furniture, inspires confidence in what's upstairs. The spacious accommodations are popular with visitors to the nearby United Nations, Eurotourists, and business travelers. Corner suites cost slightly more but are especially grand. ⊠ *125 E. 50th St., 10022,* ☎ *212/753–2700 or 800/223–0945,* ⒻⒶⓍ *212/759–7300. 163 rooms. Restaurant, in-room safes, kitchenettes, beauty salon. Continental breakfast. AE, DC, MC, V.*

$$$ 🏨 **Hotel Wales.** In the tony neighborhood of Carnegie Hill this modestly priced hotel is a pleasant surprise. It occupies a landmark building that retains a turn-of-the-century mood. Bathrooms are miniscule, and guest rooms are slightly worse for wear, but fireplaces and fine oak woodwork make up for these faults. ⊠ *1295 Madison Ave., 10128,* ☎ *212/876–6000 or 800/528–5252,* ⒻⒶⓍ *212/860–7000. 86 rooms. Breakfast room, in-room VCRs. AE, MC, V.*

$$–$$$ 🏨 **Best Western Seaport Inn.** This thoroughly pleasant restored 19th-
★   century building is one block from the waterfront and close to South Street Seaport. With its cozy, library-like lobby, it has the feel of a Colonial sea captain's house, though the reasonably priced rooms are clearly those of a chain hotel—with dark wood, white walls, and floral nylon bedcovers. ⊠ *33 Peck Slip, 10038,* ☎ *212/766–6600 or 800/468–3569,* ⒻⒶⓍ *212/766–6615. 72 rooms. In-room safes, refrigerators, in-room VCRs. AE, D, DC, MC, V.*

$$ 🏨 **Broadway Bed & Breakfast.** In the heart of the Theater District, this
★   reasonably priced B&B is friendly and comfortable. The building, which dates from 1918, was completely renovated in 1995, and everything—from the freshly painted and carpeted rooms to the gleaming dark-wood stair banisters—is meticulously maintained. ⊠ *264 W. 46th St.,* ☎ *212/997–9200 or 800/826–6300,* ⒻⒶⓍ *212/768–2807. 40 rooms. Breakfast room. AE, D, DC, MC, V.*

$$ 🏨 **Herald Square Hotel.** Framed vintage magazine covers and sculpted cherubs lend character to this historic hotel, which is housed in the former *Life* magazine building. Rooms are basic and clean, with deep green carpets and floral-print bedspreads; all have TVs, phones with voice mail, and in-room safes. ⊠ *19 W. 31st St., 10001* ☎ *212/279–4017 or 800/727–1888,* ⒻⒶⓍ *212/643–9208. 127 rooms. In-room safes. AE, D, MC, V.*

$$ 🏨 **Hotel Beacon.** Once a Broadway residential building, this spiffy hotel has decent-size rooms with full kitchenettes—a real advantage, considering that some of New York's best gourmet stores, such as Zabar's and Fairway, are in the immediate area. The elegant cherry and walnut furnishings are less institutional than expected, the baths are modern and lighted with Hollywood dressing room–type bulbs, and your phone even comes with voice mail. ⊠ *2130 Broadway, at 75th St., 10023,* ☎ *212/787–1100 or 800/572–4969,* ⒻⒶⓍ *212/724–0839. 198 rooms. Kitchenettes, meeting room. AE, D, DC, MC, V.*

$$ 🏨 **Larchmont Hotel.** If you don't mind shared bathrooms and no room
★   service or concierge, the residential-style accommodations in this Beaux Arts brownstone are all anyone could ask for at this price. Rooms have a tasteful safari theme, with rattan furniture, ceiling fans, and framed animal or botanical prints. ⊠ *27 W. 11th St., 10011,* ☎ *212/989–9333,* ⒻⒶⓍ *212/989–9496. 77 rooms. Breakfast room, kitchen. Continental breakfast. AE, D, DC, MC, V.*

$$ 🏨 **Portland Square Hotel.** You can't beat this Theater District old-timer for value, with its clean, simple rooms, exercise facility (albeit tiny), and business services. James Cagney lived in the building, and—as the story goes—a few of his Radio City Rockette acquaintances lived upstairs. Rooms have green carpets and floral-print bedspreads; those on the east wing have oversize bathrooms. ⊠ *132 W. 47th St., 10036,* ☎ *212/382–0600 or 800/388–8988,* FAX *212/382–0684. 142 rooms. In-room safes, exercise room, coin laundry. AE, MC, V.*

$$ 🏨 **Washington Square Hotel.** This cozy Greenwich Village hotel has a true European feel, from the wrought iron and brass in the small, elegant lobby to the personal attention given by the staff. Rooms and baths are simple but pleasant. ⊠ *103 Waverly Pl., 10011,* ☎ *212/777–9515 or 800/222–0418,* FAX *212/979–8373. 150 rooms. Restaurant, bar, exercise room. Continental breakfast. AE, MC, V.*

$ 🏨 **Park Savoy.** Rooms here cost as little as $57 (rates go up to $126), and you're in close proximity to Central Park, Carnegie Hall, and the caviar at Petrossian. All of this more than makes up for the lack of room service, direct-dial phone, and cable TV channels. Room decor is eclectic (William Morris–pattern drapes, wine-color carpet, and rock-hard beds). The staff (okay, the guy at the desk) knows all the guests, and there's a lot of repeat business. ⊠ *158 W. 58th St., 10019,* ☎ *212/245–5755,* FAX *212/765–0668. 96 rooms. AE, MC, V.*

$ 🏨 **Vanderbilt YMCA.** Of the various Manhattan Y's offering accommodations, this has the best location and facilities. The rooms are little more than dormitory-style cells—even with only one or two beds to a room, you may feel crowded. The Turtle Bay neighborhood is safe and relatively convenient. ⊠ *224 E. 47th St., 10017,* ☎ *212/756–9600,* FAX *212/752–0210. 370 rooms. Restaurant, 2 indoor pools, sauna, exercise room, indoor track, coin laundry, meeting rooms. MC, V.*

Nightlife and the Arts

Full listings of entertainment and cultural events appear in the weekly magazines *New York* and *Time Out New York*; they include capsule summaries of plays and concerts, performance times, and ticket prices. The Arts & Leisure section of the Sunday *New York Times* lists and describes events but provides little service information. The Theater Directory in the daily *New York Times* advertises ticket information for Broadway and Off-Broadway shows. Listings of events also appear weekly in *The New Yorker* and the *Village Voice*, a weekly newspaper that probably has more nightclub ads than any other rag in the world. For the tattooed and pierced, *Paper* magazine's P.M. 'Til Dawn and bar sections have as good a listing as exists of the roving clubs and the best of the fashionable crowd's hangouts.

Nightlife

BAR-LOUNGES

Divine Bar (⊠ 244 E. 51st St., ☎ 212/319–9463) is an uptown spot with a SoHo feel, with its zebra-striped bar chairs, cigar area, and cozy, velvet couches upstairs. **Pravda** (⊠ 281 Lafayette St., ☎ 212/226–4696), a Russian-theme trendy bar, has more than 70 brands of vodka and nearly as many types of martinis. The **Screening Room** (⊠ 54 Varick St., ☎ 212/334–2100) offers good food, drinks, and movies all in one congenial TriBeCa space. **Spy** (⊠ 101 Greene St., ☎ 212/343–9000) provides a baroque parlor setting with plush couches and pretty people. **Wax** (⊠ 113 Mercer St., ☎ 212/226–6082) has bare wooden floors, rather uncomfortable settees, and candles creating a soft glow on the tables.

CABARET

At the intimate **Rainbow & Stars** (⊠ 30 Rockefeller Plaza, ☎ 212/632–5000) singers such as Maureen McGovern and Rosemary Clooney entertain, backed by a view of the twinkling lights of the city. The **Oak**

Room at the Algonquin Hotel (⊠ 59 W. 44th St., ☎ 212/840–6800) still offers yesteryear's charms. Just head straight for the long, narrow club-cum-watering-hole; you might find the hopelessly romantic singer Andrea Marcovicci or guitarist John Pizzarelli.

COMEDY CLUBS

Caroline's Comedy Club (⊠ 1626 Broadway, ☎ 212/757–4100), a high-gloss venue, features established names as well as comedians on the edge of stardom. **Original Improvisation** (⊠ 433 W. 34th St., ☎ 212/279–3446), one of New York's oldest comedy showcases, is where many big-name yucksters got their start.

DANCE CLUBS

Nell's (⊠ 246 W. 14th St., ☎ 212/675–1567) has an upstairs live-music jazz salon; downstairs is for dancing to music spun by a DJ. **Roseland** (⊠ 239 W. 52nd St., ☎ 212/247–0200) has ballroom dancing Thursday (music provided by a DJ) and Sunday (music by a live orchestra as well as a DJ). The **Rainbow Room** (⊠ 30 Rockefeller Plaza, ☎ 212/632–5000) serves dinner, and dancing to the strains of a live orchestra takes place on a floor right out of an Astaire-Rogers musical. **Webster Hall** (⊠ 125 E. 11th St., ☎ 212/353–1600), a fave among NYU students and similar species, boasts four floors and five eras of music.

JAZZ CLUBS

Many consider the **Blue Note** (⊠ 131 W. 3rd St., ☎ 212/475–8592) the jazz capital of the world. **Michael's Pub** (⊠ Parker Meridien Hotel, 118 W. 57th St., ☎ 212/758–2272) is where you can find Woody Allen moonlighting on the clarinet most Monday nights when he performs with his New Orleans Jazz Band. The **Village Vanguard** (⊠ 178 7th Ave. S, ☎ 212/255–4037) is a basement joint that has ridden the crest of every new wave in jazz for decades.

POP, ROCK, BLUES, AND COUNTRY

The **Bitter End** (⊠ 147 Bleecker St., ☎ 212/673–7030) has been giving a break to folk, rock, jazz, and country acts for more than 25 years. The **Bottom Line** (⊠ 15 W. 4th St., ☎ 212/228–7880), an intimate sit-down space, features folk and rock headliners. **Manny's Car Wash** (⊠ 1558 3rd Ave., ☎ 212/369–2583) has live blues every night, including powerhouse blues jams on Sunday. **Rodeo Bar** (⊠ 375 3rd Ave., ☎ 212/683–6500), a full-scale Texas roadhouse, never charges a cover for its country, rock, rockabilly, and blues bands. **Tramps** (⊠ 45 W. 21st St., ☎ 212/727–7788) has delivered bands like NRBQ, George Clinton, and Sponge for more then 25 years.

FOR SINGLES (UNDER 30)

At the **Ear Inn** (⊠ 326 Spring St., ☎ 212/226–9060) it's the artsy crowd that makes the place: The regular poetry readings are called Lunch for the Ear. **Hi-Life** (⊠ 477 Amsterdam Ave., ☎ 212/787–7199) is big with the Upper West Side's bon vivants. Make your way to **Merc Bar** (⊠ 151 Mercer St., ☎ 212/966–2727), in the heart of trendy SoHo. At **Telephone Bar** (⊠ 149 2nd Ave., ☎ 212/529–5000) you'll find imported English telephone booths and a polite, handsome crowd.

FOR SINGLES (OVER 30)

Jim McMullen's (⊠ 1341 3rd Ave., ☎ 212/861–4700) is a quintessential Upper East Side watering hole that has a busy bar decked out with bouquets of fresh flowers. **Pete's Tavern** (⊠ 129 E. 18th St., ☎ 212/473–7676) is a crowded, friendly saloon renowned as the place where O. Henry wrote "The Gift of the Magi." The **White Horse Tavern** (⊠ 567 Hudson St., ☎ 212/989–3956), famous with the literati, was patronized by Dylan Thomas.

For advice on the bar scene, health issues, and other assorted quandaries of the gay community, call the **Gay and Lesbian Switchboard** (☎ 212/777–1800) or stop by the **Lesbian and Gay Community Services Center** (⊠ 208 W. 13th St., ☎ 212/620–7310). Upstairs at the **Monster** (⊠ 80 Grove St., ☎ 212/924–3558), a crowd gathers and sings around the piano; downstairs, there's a disco. Tuesday night is boys' night at the **Roxy** (⊠ 515 W. 18th St., ☎ 212/645–5156), but girls "won't be turned away" from this huge roller-disco-cum-club. At the **Works** (⊠ 428 Columbus Ave., ☎ 212/799–7365), local Upper West Siders favor J. Crew. The wide-ranging crowd of women at **Crazy Nanny's** (⊠ 21 7th Ave. S, ☎ 212/366–6312) grooves to a house DJ on Wednesday and Friday and line dances to country-and-western on Thursday. **Henrietta Hudson** (⊠ 438 Hudson St., ☎ 212/924–3347) is a little more upscale than Crazy Nanny's and has a pool table. **Julie's** (⊠ 204 E. 58th St., ☎ 212/688–1294) is popular with a sophisticated-lady upper-crust crowd.

The Arts

DANCE

The **American Ballet Theatre** (☎ 212/362–6000) in Lincoln Center is the resident dance company of the Metropolitan Opera House. The **New York City Ballet** (☎ 212/870–5570) performs at Lincoln Center's New York State Theater; it reached world-class prominence under the direction of the late George Balanchine; Peter Martins is now ballet master-in-chief. **City Center** (⊠ 131 W. 55th St., ☎ 212/581–1212) hosts innovative dance companies, such as the Alvin Ailey and the Paul Taylor dance companies. The **Joyce Theater** (⊠ 8th Ave. at 19th St., ☎ 212/242–0800), home to the avant-garde Feld Ballet, schedules a potpourri of international dance troupes.

FILM

On any day of the year visitors to **New York movie theaters** will find all the major new releases, renowned classics, unusual foreign offerings, and experimental works. For information on schedules and theaters dial 212/777–FILM, the MovieFone, sponsored by WNEW 102.7 FM and the *New York Times*, or check the local newspapers. *New York, The New Yorker,* and *Time Out New York* magazines publish programs and reviews. The vast majority of Manhattan theaters are first-run houses. Among the **art film and revival houses** are the Walter Reade Theater (⊠ 70 Lincoln Plaza, Broadway at 65th St., ☎ 212/875–5600) and Film Forum (⊠ 209 W. Houston St., ☎ 212/727–8110); the Museum of Modern Art (☞ Midtown *in* Exploring New York City, *above*) also offers several film series every year.

MUSIC

Lincoln Center (☞ Upper West Side *in* Exploring New York City, *above*) has magnificent concert halls and theaters showcasing much of New York's serious music scene. Its Avery Fisher Hall (☎ 212/875–5030) is home to the New York Philharmonic Orchestra, the Mostly Mozart Festival, and visiting orchestras and soloists. **Carnegie Hall** (⊠ 154 W. 57th St., at 7th Ave., ☎ 212/247–7800), the city's most famous classical-music palace, is more than 100 years old. This is where Leonard Bernstein, standing in for New York Philharmonic conductor Bruno Walter, made his triumphant debut; where Jack Benny and Isaac Stern fiddled together; and where the Beatles played one of their first U.S. concerts.

OPERA

The **Metropolitan Opera House** (☎ 212/362–6000), at Lincoln Center, is a sublime setting for mostly classic operas performed by world-class stars. The **New York City Opera** (☎ 212/870–5570), at Lincoln

Center's State Theater, offers a diverse repertoire consisting of adventurous and rarely seen works as well as classic opera favorites.

THEATER

New York boasts nearly 40 Broadway theaters, three dozen Off-Broadway theaters, and 200 Off-Off-Broadway houses. Nearly all Broadway theaters are in the Theater District, most of which lies between Broadway and 8th Avenue, from 40th to 53nd streets. (The Vivian Beaumont Theatre is at Lincoln Center, Broadway at 65th Street.) Off- and Off-Off-Broadway theaters are scattered all over town, including Greenwich Village, the East Viilage, SoHo, the Upper West Side, and Theater Row, a strip of 42nd Street playhouses between 9th and 10th avenues.

The **TKTS booths** in Duffy Square (⊠ 47th St. and Broadway, ☎ 212/768–1818) and in the Wall Street area (⊠ 2 World Trade Center mezzanine, ☎ 212/768–1818) are New York's best-known discount source. TKTS sells day-of-performance tickets for Broadway and some Off-Broadway plays at discounts of 25% or 50% (plus $2.50 surcharge per ticket), depending on a show's popularity. The Broadway booth opens at 10 AM, the World Trade Center booth at 11 AM. TKTS accepts only cash or traveler's checks—no credit cards.

Spectator Sports

Baseball: New York Mets (⊠ Shea Stadium, Roosevelt Ave. off Grand Central Pkwy., Flushing, Queens, ☎ 718/507–8499). **New York Yankees** (⊠ Yankee Stadium, 161st St. and Jerome Ave., The Bronx, ☎ 212/293–6000).

Basketball: New York Knicks (⊠ Madison Square Garden, 4 Penn Plaza, ☎ 212/465–6741 or 212/465–5867 for Knicks Hot Line).

Football: New York Giants (⊠ Continental Airlines Sports Arena, Rte. 3, East Rutherford, NJ, ☎ 201/935–8111 or 201/935–3900). **New York Jets** (⊠ Continental Airlines Sports Arena, Rte. 3, East Rutherford, NJ, ☎ 516/560–8100 or 201/935–3900).

Hockey: New York Rangers(⊠ Madison Square Garden, 4 Penn Plaza, ☎ 212/465–6741 or 212/308–6977 for Rangers Hot Line).

Tennis: The annual **U.S. Open,** one of the four grand-slam events of tennis, is held in late August and early September at the USTA National Tennis Center in Flushing Meadows–Corona Park, Queens (☎ 718/760–6200).

Shopping

You can buy almost anything you might want or need at almost any time of day or night somewhere in New York City, but in general, major department stores and other shops are open every day and keep late hours on Thursday. Many of the upper-crust shops along upper 5th Avenue and the Madison Mile close on Sunday. Stores in such nightlife areas as SoHo and Columbus Avenue are usually open in the evenings. The bargain shops along Orchard Street on the Lower East Side are closed on Saturday, mobbed on Sunday. For specialty stores with several branches in the city we have listed the locations in the busier shopping neighborhoods.

Shopping Neighborhoods

Fifth Avenue from 49th to 58th streets contains many of the world's most famous—and expensive—stores, including several excellent jewelers and department stores. A cluster of chain stores along once-glamorous **57th Street** between Park and 6th avenues has opened in the past year; what these stores lack in elegance they almost make up for in sheer size. The area extending from **Herald Square** (✉ 6th Ave. and 34th St.) along 34th Street and up 5th Avenue to 40th Street includes several major department stores and a host of lower-price clothing stores. **Madison Mile,** the 20-block span along Madison Avenue between 59th and 79th streets, has many exclusive designer boutiques; the corridor has recently had a flurry of new store openings, many by big-name Italian designers. **SoHo**'s galleries, clothing boutiques, and avant-garde housewares shops stretch along West Broadway and radiate off Prince Street. The superstores along SoHo's lower Broadway and in **Chelsea** (extending from 14th Street to 29th Street, between 5th Avenue and the Hudson River) provide some great bargains; there's also a healthy mix of funky shops and galleries. **Columbus Avenue,** between 66th and 86th streets, features far-out European and down-home traditional fashions, and antiques and vintage stores. The **Lower East Side** is the place for clothing bargains. The **East Village** offers eclectic designer boutiques and shops.

Department Stores

Though it closed its original flagship Chelsea store in late 1997, **Barney's** (✉ 660 Madison Ave., ☎ 212/826–8900) is still selling chichi designers and home furnishings from its deluxe Madison Avenue store. **Bergdorf Goodman** (✉ 754 5th Ave., at 57th St., ☎ 212/753–7300) is where good taste reigns in an elegant and understated setting; the recently expanded men's store is across the street. **Bloomingdale's** (✉ 59th St. and Lexington Ave., ☎ 212/355–5900) is a New York institution, with a stupefying maze of cosmetic counters, mirrors, and black walls on the main floor. **Lord & Taylor** (✉ 424 5th Ave., at 38th St., ☎ 212/391–3344) is refined, well stocked, and never overwhelming. **Macy's** (✉ 34th St. and Broadway, ☎ 212/695–4400), the country's largest retail store, has huge housewares and gourmet-foods departments, as well as high fashion. **Saks Fifth Avenue** (✉ 611 5th Ave., at 50th St., ☎ 212/753–4000) has an outstanding selection of women's and men's designer outfits.

Specialty Stores

ANTIQUES

America Hurrah (✉ 766 Madison Ave., between 65th and 66th Sts., 3rd floor, ☎ 212/535–1930) is one of the country's premier dealers in Americana; it also stocks Native American work. At **Manhattan Art & Antiques Center** (✉ 1050 2nd Ave., between 55th and 56th Sts., ☎ 212/355–4400) more than 100 dealers stock three floors with antiques from around the world.

BOOKS

All the big national **chain bookstores** are here, with branches all over town—Barnes & Noble, B. Dalton, Borders, and Waldenbooks. **Corner Bookstore** (✉ 1313 Madison Ave., at 93rd St., ☎ 212/831–3554), a small, friendly shop, has been a favorite with local book lovers for years. **Gotham Book Mart** (✉ 41 W. 47th St., ☎ 212/719–4448) emphasizes literature and the performing arts in books and magazines. **Rizzoli Bookstore** (✉ 31 W. 57th St., ☎ 212/759–2424) is a hushed environment with a rich book selection. The downtown branch (✉ 454 West Broadway, ☎ 212/674–1616) has a quirky boutique section and espresso bar. **Shakespeare & Co.** (✉ 939 Lexington Ave., between 68th and 69th Sts., ☎ 212/570–0201; ✉ 716 Broadway at Washington Pl., ☎

212/529–1330) stocks the latest in just about every field. The somewhat scruffy **Strand** (⌧ 828 Broadway, at 12th St., ☎ 212/473–1452), North America's largest used-book store, offers more than 2 million volumes (including a rare-book collection).

MEN'S AND WOMEN'S WEAR

Calvin Klein (⌧ 654 Madison Ave., at 60th St., ☎ 212/292–9000) has a huge, stark store showcasing his latest design collection. **Gianni Versace** (⌧ 647 5th Ave., ☎ 212/317–0224; ⌧ 817 Madison Ave., between 68th and 69th Sts., ☎ 212/744–6868; ⌧ 816 Madison Ave., ☎ 212/744–5572) carries clothes with exuberant designs and colors that are never boring. **Giorgio Armani** (⌧ 760 Madison Ave., between 65th and 66th Sts., ☎ 212/988–9191) displays stunning cuts of clothes in a museumlike space. **Polo/Ralph Lauren** (⌧ 867 Madison Ave., at 72nd St., ☎ 212/606–2100) is in a grand, carefully renovated turn-of-the-century town house featuring high-style preppy wear. **Yohji Yamamoto** (⌧ 103 Grand St., ☎ 212/966–9066) has severe, beautifully cut designs from fashion's Zen master.

MUSIC STORES

Bleecker Bob's Golden Oldies (⌧ 118 W. 3rd St., ☎ 212/475–9677) is a Greenwich Village spot with all that good old rock on vinyl. **HMV** (⌧ 565 5th Ave., at 46th St., ☎ 212/681–6700; ⌧ 57 W. 34th St., ☎ 212/629–0900; ⌧ 2081 Broadway, at 72nd St., ☎ 212/721–5900) is a state-of-the-art music superstore that stocks hundreds of thousands of CDs, tapes, videos, and laser discs. **Tower Records and Videos** (⌧ 692 Broadway, at 4th St., ☎ 212/505–1500; ⌧ 1961 Broadway, at 66th St., ☎ 212/799–2500; ⌧ 725 5th Ave., basement level of Trump Tower, ☎ 212/838–8110) has a huge selection of music and videos at competitive prices. **Virgin Megastore Times Square** (⌧ 1540 Broadway, ☎ 212/921–1020), reportedly the largest music and entertainment store in the world, has a gigantic space with a café, movie theater, bookstore, and laser disc and video section—besides the rows and rows of CDs.

FOOD

Zabar's (⌧ 2245 Broadway, at 80th St., ☎ 212/787–2000) has long been a favorite with New York foodies, with everything from jams, cheeses, spices, and smoked fish to a superb selection of kitchen wares, all reasonably priced. Those who never venture north of 14th Street head for **Dean & DeLuca** (⌧ 560 Broadway, at Prince St., ☎ 212/431–1691), the SoHo trendsetter with a gleaming white space and an encyclopedic selection. The 15,000-square-ft **Williams-Sonoma Grande Cuisine** (⌧ 580 Broadway, at Houston St., ☎ 212/343–7330) carries tempting cookware and tableware, not to mention gourmet foods.

JEWELRY

Having recently passed the 150-year mark, **Cartier** (⌧ 653 5th Ave., ☎ 212/753–0111) still dazzles with extravagant gems. Every store is a jewelry shop in the **Diamond District** (⌧ 47th St. between 5th and 6th Aves.); be ready to haggle. **Fortunoff** (⌧ 681 5th Ave., at 54th St., ☎ 212/758–6660) draws crowds with its good prices on gold and silver jewelry and flatware. At legendary **Tiffany & Co.** (⌧ 727 5th Ave., at 57th St., ☎ 212/755–8000) prices can be extravagant, but there's always a selection of lower-price gift items, not to mention some of the most creative display windows on 5th Avenue.

Side Trips to Other Boroughs

The Bronx

The 250-acre **New York Botanical Garden,** built around the dramatic gorge of the Bronx River, is considered one of the leading botany centers of the world (☞ Parks and Gardens, *above*). Less than a mile from the botanical garden is the world-class **Bronx Zoo** (☞ What to See and Do with Children, *above*).

ARRIVING AND DEPARTING
For the zoo, take Metro North to the New York Botanical Garden, or take Subway D or 4 to Bedford Park Boulevard. For the botanical garden, take Subway 2 to Pelham Parkway and walk three blocks west to the zoo or take the Liberty Line BxM-11 express bus from mid-Manhattan (☎ 718/652–8400 for bus schedules, locations of stops, and fares).

Brooklyn

★ **Brooklyn Heights** was New York's first suburb, linked to the city first by ferry and later by the Brooklyn Bridge. In the 1940s and 1950s the Heights was an alternative to the bohemian haven of Greenwich Village—home to writers including Carson McCullers, W. H. Auden, Alfred Kazin, and Norman Mailer. In the late 1960s the neighborhood was designated as New York's first historic district. Some 600 buildings more than 100 years old, representing a wide range of American building styles, are lovingly preserved today. The **Plymouth Church of the Pilgrims** (✉ Orange St. between Henry and Hicks Sts., ☎ 718/624–4743) was the center of abolitionist sentiment in the years before the Civil War, thanks to the oratory of the eminent theologian Henry Ward Beecher. The church was a major stop on the Underground Railroad, which smuggled slaves to freedom. **Willow Street,** between Clark and Pierrepont streets, is one of Brooklyn Heights' prettiest and most architecturally varied blocks, with houses in the Queen Anne and Federal styles. Pierrepont Street ends at the **Brooklyn Heights Promenade,** a quiet sliver of park lined with benches offering a dramatic vista of the Manhattan skyline. Just off the promenade's south end, **Montague Street,** the commercial spine of the Heights, offers a flurry of shops, cafés, and restaurants of every ethnicity.

ARRIVING AND DEPARTING
Walk across the Brooklyn Bridge from lower Manhattan near city hall and return on Subway 2 or 3 from the Clark Street station, a few blocks southwest of the walkway terminus.

Queens

Astoria in Queens is one of New York's most vital ethnic neighborhoods; once German, then Italian, it is now heavily Greek and is filled with shops and restaurants reflecting the community. Astoria is the site
★ of the **American Museum of the Moving Image,** where a theater features clips from the works of leading Hollywood cinematographers; galleries offer interactive exhibits on filmmaking techniques; and the collection of movie memorabilia contains costumes worn by everyone from Marlene Dietrich to Robin Williams. ✉ *35th Ave. at 36th St., ☎ 718/784–0077. Closed Mon.*

ARRIVING AND DEPARTING
Take the N train from Manhattan to the Broadway stop. For the Museum of the Moving Image, walk five blocks along Broadway to 36th Street; turn right and walk two blocks to 35th Avenue.

LONG ISLAND

Long Island is not only the largest island on America's East Coast—1,682 square mi—but the most varied. From west to east, Long Island encompasses two Manhattan boroughs (Brooklyn and Queens), congested commuter towns, the farmland of the North Fork, and the world-famous villages of the Hamptons. It has arguably the nation's finest stretch of white-sand beach, as well as the notoriously clogged Long Island Expressway (LIE).

Visitor Information

Long Island Convention and Visitors Bureau (✉ 350 Vanderbilt Motor Pkwy., Suite 103, Hauppauge 11788, ☎ 516/951–3440 or 800/441–4601). **Visitor centers,** open late spring–early fall: ✉ Southern State Pkwy. between Exits 13 and 14, Valley Stream; LIE between Exits 52 and 53, Dix Hills–Deer Park; and Rte. 24, Flanders. **Fire Island Tourism Bureau** (✉ 49 N. Main St., Sayville 11782, ☎ 516/563–8448) is open Memorial Day through Labor Day.

Arriving and Departing

Although mass transit makes Long Island very accessible, a car is really necessary to explore all the island's nooks and crannies.

By Bus
Hampton Jitney (☎ 516/283–4600 or 800/936–0440 in New York City) links Manhattan and area airports with towns on the southeastern end of Long Island.

By Car
The **Midtown Tunnel** (I–495), **Queensborough Bridge** (Northern Boulevard, 25A), and the **Triborough Bridge** (I–278) connect Long Island with Manhattan. The **Throgs Neck Bridge** (I–295) and the **Whitestone Bridge** (I–678) provide access from the Bronx and New England.

By Plane
In addition to **John F. Kennedy International** and **LaGuardia** airports, in Queens (☞ Arriving and Departing *in* New York City), Long Island is served by **Long Island MacArthur Airport,** in Islip (☎ 516/467–3210 for airline information).

By Train
The **Long Island Railroad** (☎ 516/822–5477) has frequent service from Penn Station in Manhattan to all major towns on Long Island.

Exploring Long Island

The best way to get a feel for Long Island and explore its museums, stately mansions, nature preserves, and coastal villages is to avoid the traffic-choked LIE and take the more leisurely roads that parallel the coasts. On the North Shore your best bet is Route 25A; on the South Shore, Route 27 (Sunrise Highway).

The stretch of wealthy suburbs just outside New York City on the **North Shore** is known as the Gold Coast. Families like the Vanderbilts, Whitneys, and Roosevelts built mansions here in the late 19th and early 20th centuries, making this area on Long Island Sound a fashionable playground for the rich. It wasn't until after World War II that vast numbers of the middle class moved out to Long Island. However, some communities such as Oyster Bay still maintain their elite status even today.

Long Island's largest art museum, the **Nassau County Museum of Art** is housed in the former country residence of Henry Clay Frick and displays changing exhibits from Botticelli to Frida Kahlo. Outdoor sculptures dot the 145 acres of formal gardens and rolling fields. ✉ *1 Museum Dr., at Northern Blvd. (Rte. 25A), Roslyn Harbor,* ☎ *516/484–9337. Closed Mon.*

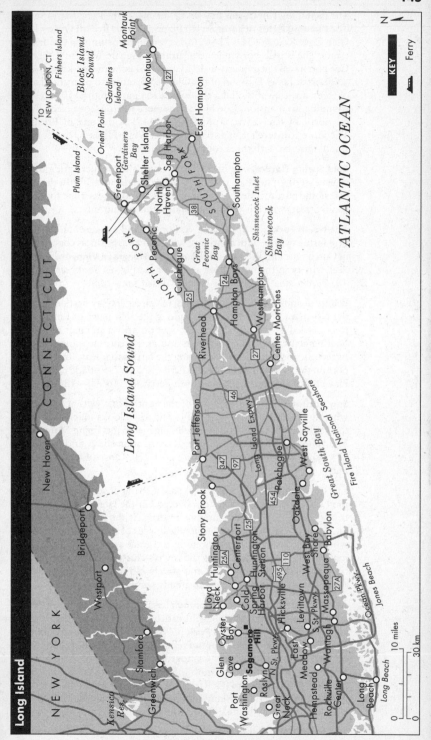

The quaint town of **Oyster Bay** sits on an inlet of the Long Island Sound. The **Planting Fields Arboretum** (✉ Planting Fields Rd. off Oyster Bay–Glen Cove Rd., ☎ 516/922–9200) is yet another stunning Gold Coast estate. The British-born marine-insurance magnate William Robertson Coe purchased the property in 1913 and worked with well-known landscape artist James Dawson of the Olmsted Brothers to plan grand allees of trees, azalea walks, and a rhododendron park on the 150 acres surrounding his mansion, Coe Hall. **Sagamore Hill** (✉ Cove Neck Rd., 1 mi north of Rte. 25A, ☎ 516/922–4447) is the site of President Theodore Roosevelt's Victorian summer White House. There's also a small museum with three rooms of exhibits.

Cold Spring Harbor, one of the Gold Coast's most enchanting towns, is just east of Oyster Bay. During its heyday in the mid-1800s, this town was home port to a fleet of whaling vessels. Take some time to browse Main Street, which is lined with shops and restaurants.

The **North Fork,** the upper part of Long Island's eastern tail, is beautiful farm country, with a thriving wine-growing business concentrated in Cutchogue and Peconic. Make a stop at **Hargrave Vineyard,** the pioneer winery in the region, for a tour or tasting. ✉ *South side of Rte. 48, Cutchogue,* ☎ *516/734–5158. Closed Jan.–Mar.*

Beautiful and historic **Shelter Island,** in Gardiners Bay nestled between the North and South forks, was among the first parts of Long Island to be settled by the British and is now primarily a summer resort and boating center. You can use the island as a scenic stepping-stone between one fork and the other, taking the ferries that leave from Greenport on the North Fork (✉ North Ferry, ☎ 516/749–0139) and North Haven on the South Fork (✉ South Ferry, ☎ 516/749–1200).

Sag Harbor, on the north shore of the South Fork, was an important whaling center from 1775 to 1871. The town looks much as it did in the 1870s, with stately homes of whaling merchants lining Main Street. The **Whaling Museum** displays logbooks, scrimshaw, and harpoons. ✉ *Garden and Main Sts.,* ☎ *516/725–0770. Closed Oct.–Memorial Day.*

The **Hamptons,** on the South Fork, are a string of seaside villages that the East Coast upper crust "discovered" in the late 19th century and transformed into elegant summer resorts. At the pinnacle of fashion and fame is **East Hampton;** despite the hordes of celebrities and tourists who descend each summer, it retains the grace and dignity of its Colonial heritage. Main Street has the town's classic white-frame Presbyterian church (built in 1860) and stately old homes and inns, which stand shoulder to shoulder with trendy shops and galleries.

At Long Island's eastern tip, **Montauk** has the double allure of extremity and the sea. Though the village is rather touristy, the beaches are unsurpassed. **Hither Hills State Park** (✉ Rte. 27, 12 mi east of Montauk village, ☎ 516/668–2461) preserves miles of rolling moors and forests of pitch pine and scrub oak. Campgrounds are available here but they book up quickly. You can climb the 137 steps that lead to the top of the **Montauk Lighthouse** (✉ Rte. 27, 6 mi east of village, ☎ 516/668–2544), a famous Long Island landmark. If you make the climb on a clear day, you may be able to see Rhode Island.

The **Long Island Game Farm** has baby animals for children to bottle-feed, a wild tiger show, and train rides. ✉ *Chapman Blvd., Manorville,* ☎ *516/878–6644. Closed mid-Oct.–mid-Apr.*

Fire Island, a slender 32-mi-long barrier island on Long Island's south shore, encompasses a designated national seashore with one of the few unspoiled stretches of seashore along the northeastern seaboard. Its half-dozen tiny communities include two longtime lesbian and gay enclaves.

Dining and Lodging

Long Island restaurants run the gamut from fast-food chains, pizzerias, and family-style eateries to ethnic restaurants and elegant country inns. Not surprisingly, the island draws on the bounty of the surrounding waters, especially on the east end, where commercial fishing remains a vital industry.

Recent years have brought all the major motel chains to Long Island. Resort hotels and small inns are concentrated in the Hamptons. In summer prices tend to double, if not triple, and there is often a minimum stay on weekends. For those who prefer the B&B route, most local chambers of commerce have information on B&Bs in their towns. For price ranges *see* Charts 1 (A) and 2 (A) *in* On the Road with Fodor's.

Amagansett

$$ ✕ **Honest Diner.** Just outside East Hampton, this trendy diner serves up large portions of good home cooking in a 1950s atmosphere. ✉ *74 Montauk Hwy.,* ☎ *516/267–3535. Reservations not accepted. AE. Closed late Oct.–Memorial Day.*

East Hampton

$$ ✕ **Babette's.** Towering banana trees give a tropical feel to the bright yellow, blue, and orange interior of this funky café. Although it's crowded in summer (especially for breakfast), the innovative fare here is worth the wait. There's a large selection of vegetarian dishes; try the smoked tempeh fajitas. ✉ *66 Newtown La.,* ☎ *516/329–5377. AE, MC, V. Closed late Feb.–Mar.*

$$$$ ✕🏨 **Maidstone Arms.** Dating to 1740, this inn is the coziest and most
★ comfortable in town. It also has one of the best locations—right across from a pond and a pristine park, surrounded by East Hampton's oldest streets and most beautiful houses. Beach parking permits are available for guests. An East Hampton mainstay, the inn's always-busy restaurant serves new American cuisine. A breakfast of delicious baked goods is included with the room. ✉ *207 Main St., 11937,* ☎ *516/324–5006,* FAX *516/324–5037. 16 rooms, 3 cottages. Restaurant, bar, room service. AE, MC, V.*

Greenport

$$$–$$$$ ✕ **Claudio's.** This family-run classic seafood restaurant has been around for more than 125 years; the fourth generation of the Claudio family is at the helm today. Forget fancy culinary creations: Go for the clams casino, fresh mussels, or fried calamari for starters, and the shrimp scampi or grilled swordfish as a main dish. You can also dine alfresco; the clam bar has tables overlooking Peconic Bay. ✉ *111 Main St.,* ☎ *516/477–0627. MC, V. Closed Jan.–mid-Apr.*

Montauk

$$–$$$ ✕ **Gosman's Dock.** This huge, somewhat touristy fish restaurant is jam-packed in the summer. It offers a spectacular location—at the entrance to Montauk Harbor—and the freshest possible fish, served indoors or out. You may have a long wait in peak season. ✉ *500 W. Lake Dr.,* ☎ *516/668–5330. Reservations not accepted. MC, V. Closed mid-Oct.–Apr.*

$$$$ ✕🏨 **Gurney's Inn Resort and Spa.** Long popular for its fabulous location, on a bluff overlooking 1,000 ft of private ocean beach, Gurney's has become even more famous in recent years for its European-style health-and-beauty spa. The large, luxurious rooms all have ocean views. ⊠ *290 Old Montauk Hwy., Montauk 11954,* ☎ *516/668–2345,* FAX *516/668–3576. 125 rooms. 2 restaurants, bar, indoor saltwater pool, beauty salon, spa, health club, recreation room, meeting rooms. AE, D, DC, MC, V.*

Sag Harbor

$$$$ ✕⊡ **The American Hotel.** If you can't get a room at this small hotel,
★ at least try to have lunch or dinner at its well-known restaurant. The dark wainscoted dining rooms are decorated with antique furniture and Oriental rugs. The bar is the sort where you'd want to sip brandy and light up a cigar. ⊠ *25 Main St., 11963,* ☎ *516/725–3535,* FAX *516/725–3573. 8 rooms. Restaurant, bar, air-conditioning. AE, D, DC, MC, V. No lunch weekdays.*

Shelter Island

$$$$ ⊡ **Ram's Head Inn.** This 1929 center-hall Colonial-style island retreat
★ makes for the perfect romantic getaway—far from the Hamptons' crowds. The inn overlooks 800 ft of beachfront, and sailboats and kayaks are available for guests' use. The dining room is regarded as one of the best on eastern Long Island. ⊠ *108 Ram Island Dr., Shelter Island 11965,* ☎ *516/749–0811,* FAX *516/749–0059. 17 rooms. Restaurant, tennis court, boating. AE, MC, V.*

Motels

⊡ **Ramada Inn East End** (⊠ 1830 Rte. 25, Riverhead 11901, ☎ 516/369–2200), 100 rooms, restaurant, bar, pool; *$$$$.* ⊡ **Drake Motor Inn** (⊠ 16 Penny La., Hampton Bays 11946, ☎ 516/728–1592), 15 rooms, pool; *$$–$$$$.*

Campground

Hither Hills State Park (☞ Exploring Long Island, *above*) has both tent and RV sites.

Nightlife and the Arts

Check the Friday edition of *Newsday,* the Long Island newspaper, which has a weekend supplement containing information about Long Island arts and entertainment, as well as the magazine *Long Island Monthly.*

Nightlife

The Long Island scene is lively, especially in the Hamptons. You can hear live music every night at **Stephen Talkhouse** (⊠ Main St., Amagansett, ☎ 516/267–3117), a fashionable hangout. **Oak Beach Inn** (⊠ Ocean Pkwy., Oak Beach, ☎ 516/587–0097) has a sing-along upstairs and a DJ on weekends. **Sonny's** (⊠ 3603 Merrick Rd., Seaford, ☎ 516/826–0973) features live jazz nightly.

The Arts

Jones Beach Marine Theatre (⊠ Jones Beach, Wantagh, ☎ 516/221–1000) hosts major outdoor concerts by contemporary pop artists May–September. **Nassau Coliseum** (⊠ 1255 Hempstead Turnpike, Uniondale, ☎ 516/794–9300) has major rock and pop concerts year-round. **Westbury Music Fair** (⊠ 590 Brush Hollow Rd., Westbury, ☎ 516/334–0800) features live concerts, shows, and theater.

Outdoor Activities and Sports

Participant Sports

BOATING

Oyster Bay Sailing School (⊠ Box 447, West End Ave., Oyster Bay 11771, ☎ 516/624–7900) offers classes and three- to five-day vacation packages from April through October.

Spectator Sports

Hockey: New York Islanders (⊠ Nassau Coliseum, Hempstead Turnpike, Uniondale, ☎ 516/794–4100).

Horse Racing: Belmont Park Race Track (⊠ Hempstead Turnpike, Elmont, ☎ 718/641–4700) is home to the third jewel in horse racing's triple crown, the Belmont Stakes, held in early June.

Beaches

★ **Jones Beach State Park** (⊠ Wantagh Pkwy., Wantagh, ☎ 516/785–1600), a wide, sandy stretch of ocean beach, is the most crowded but also the biggest and most fully equipped of Long Island's beaches, with a restaurant, concession stands, changing rooms, a boardwalk, a theater, and sports facilities. The **Robert Moses State Park** (⊠ Robert Moses Causeway, Babylon, ☎ 516/669–0449), on Fire Island, is an uncrowded, beautiful, sandy ocean beach. Parking at many of the Hamptons' beaches is difficult; a town permit is usually required.

Shopping

Long Island is known for its shopping malls. The **Roosevelt Field Mall** (⊠ Meadowbrook Pkwy., ☎ 516/742–8000), in **Garden City,** is the largest, with more than 200 stores including Bloomingdale's and Macy's. Branches of many New York City department stores are in Garden City (⊠ Franklin Ave.). **Manhasset's Miracle Mile,** along Route 25A, has department stores and designer boutiques such as one of Giorgio Armani's.

THE HUDSON VALLEY

The landscape along the Hudson River for the 140 mi from Westchester County to Albany, the state capital, is among the loveliest in America. Indeed, this natural beauty—dramatic palisades, pine forests, cool mountain lakes and streams—inspired an entire art movement: the Hudson River School, which originated in the 19th century. Still a rich agricultural region, the valley has scores of orchards, vineyards, and farm markets along country roads. Proximity to Manhattan makes this a viable destination for day trips, but the numerous country inns, B&Bs, and resorts make more leisurely journeys especially attractive.

Visitor Information

Albany County: Convention and Visitors Bureau (⊠ 52 S. Pearl St., Albany 12207, ☎ 518/434–1217 or 800/258–3582). **Columbia County:** Chamber of Commerce (⊠ 507 Warren St., Hudson 12534, ☎ 518/828–4417). **Dutchess County:** Tourism Promotion Agency (⊠ 3 Neptune Rd., Poughkeepsie 12601, ☎ 914/463–4000 or 800/445–3131). **Hudson River Valley:** Hudson Valley Tourism (⊠ Box 355, Salt Point 12578, ☎ 800/232–4782).

Arriving and Departing

By Boat
New York Waterways (☎ 800/533–3779) offers boat tours up the Hudson from Manhattan; one includes a stop at **Kykuit** (☞ Exploring the Hudson Valley, *below*).

By Bus
Adirondack Trailways (☎ 800/225–6815) has daily service between New York's Port Authority Bus Terminal and New Paltz, Kingston, Albany, and other Hudson Valley towns.

By Car

From New York City pick up the New York State Thruway (I–87), which parallels the west bank of the Hudson River, or the more scenic Taconic Parkway, which parallels the east bank. I–84 provides access to the region from southern New England.

By Plane

LaGuardia, John F. Kennedy, and **Newark** airports (☞ Arriving and Departing *in* New York City, *above*) are manageable distances from the Hudson Valley. In the Hudson Valley area itself, **Stewart International Airport** (☎ 914/564–2100), in Newburgh, is served by major airlines. Most major airlines fly into the **Albany County Airport** (☎ 518/869–3021), in Colonie.

By Train

Amtrak (☎ 800/872–7245) provides service to Hudson, Rhinecliff, Rensselaer (Albany), and points west and north of Poughkeepsie. **Metro-North** (☎ 212/532–4900) offers several sightseeing packages that include admission to the Hudson Valley's historic sites.

Exploring the Hudson Valley

U.S. 9 hugs the east bank of the Hudson, passing through many picturesque towns, including Tarrytown, Hyde Park, Rhinebeck, and Hudson. Route 9W hugs the west bank from Newburgh to Catskill.

Sunnyside, just minutes off the Tappan Zee Bridge, was the romantic estate of Washington Irving, author of *The Legend of Sleepy Hollow.* Guides in Victorian dress give tours regularly; the 17 rooms include Irving's library and many of his original furnishings. ⊠ *W. Sunnyside La. off U.S. 9, Tarrytown,* ☎ *914/631–8200. Closed Jan.–Feb., weekdays Mar., Tues. Apr.–Dec.*

Just north of Sunnyside is **Lyndhurst,** one of America's finest examples of Gothic Revival architecture. The mansion, designed in 1838, has been occupied by three noteworthy New Yorkers and their families: former New York City mayor William Paulding, merchant George Merritt, and railroad magnate Jay Gould. ⊠ *635 S. Broadway, off U.S. 9, Tarrytown,* ☎ *914/631–4481. Closed Mon. late Apr.–Oct., weekdays Nov.–mid-Apr.*

★ If you make reservations early enough (months in advance), you can visit **Kykuit,** the country house of the great American philanthropist John D. Rockefeller and his son John D. Rockefeller Jr. Two-hour tours of the house, art gallery, and gardens begin at the nearby **Philipsburg Manor,** an 18th-century farm and gristmill. ⊠ *U.S. 9, North Tarrytown,* ☎ *914/631–9491. Closed Nov.–late Apr.*

Harriman and **Bear Mountain state parks** (⊠ Off Palisades Pkwy., ☎ 914/786–2701) are the most famous parks of the vast Palisades interstate system. Outdoor activities include boating, swimming, hiking, fishing, and cross-country skiing on the parks' 54,000 acres.

West Point (⊠ U.S. 9W, 5 mi north of Bear Mountain State Park, West Point, ☎ 914/938–2638), America's oldest and most distinguished military academy, is on bluffs overlooking the Hudson River. Stop in the visitor center near the Thayer Gate entrance for a map of the grounds. Just next door in Olmstead Hall is the **West Point Museum,** which houses one of the world's foremost military collections.

Across the river from West Point, the small village of **Cold Spring-on-Hudson,** once one of the largest iron foundries in the United States, was founded in the 19th century. Take time to stroll its quiet streets

Hudson Valley

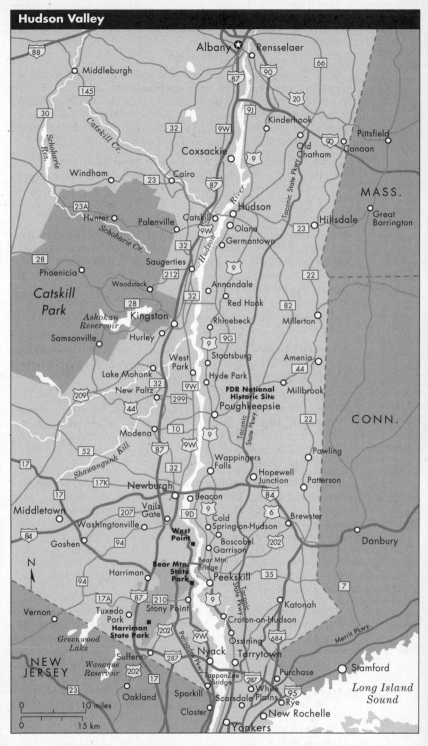

lined with antiques and crafts shops. **Boscobel,** in Garrison, is a restored Federal-style mansion surrounded by beautiful gardens that afford a breathtaking view of the Hudson River. ⊠ *Rte. 9D,* ☎ *914/265–3638. Closed Jan.–Feb., Tues. Mar.–Dec.*

Up the Hudson River north of Poughkeepsie at Hyde Park are the **Franklin Delano Roosevelt National Historic Site** and nearby Val-kill, the cottage where Eleanor Roosevelt lived from 1945 to 1962. The large Roosevelt family home contains original furnishings and a museum displaying personal documents. At **Val-kill,** set on 172 wooded acres, the tour includes the film biography *First Lady of the World.*

North of Hyde Park in Staatsburg is **Mills Mansion,** the opulent country estate of Ogden and Ruth Livingston Mills. You can see the interior by guided tour only. Hiking, picicking, and cross-country skiing on the grounds are encouraged. ⊠ *Old Post Rd., Staatsburg,* ☎ *914/ 889–8851. Closed Oct.–mid-Apr., Mon.–Tues. late Apr.–Sept.*

The country's most respected cooking school, the **Culinary Institute of America** (⊠ U.S. 9, Hyde Park, ☎ 914/471–6608), is housed in a former Jesuit seminary on grounds with stunning views of the Hudson. Founded in 1946, the institute has 2,000 students enrolled in 21-month programs on either culinary arts or baking and pastry arts. Facilities include 36 kitchens and bakeshops, plus eight instructional dining rooms, of which four are student-staffed restaurants open to the public (☞ Dining and Lodging, *below*).

Woodstock became a rock music legend after the 1969 concert (actually held 50 mi away, in Bethel). Today the town is a fun place for crafts shopping and people-watching.

Frederic Church, the leading artist of the Hudson River School, built **Olana,** a 37-room Moorish-style castle, on a hilltop with panoramic vistas of the valley. Persian carpets, decorative arts, and paintings, even some of his own works, are on display. The house is open only for guided tours made by reservation. ⊠ *Rte. 9G, Hudson,* ☎ *518/828–0135. Closed Nov.–Mar., Mon.–Tues. Apr.–Oct.*

A trip to Albany should start in the **Albany Urban Cultural Park Visitor Center** (⊠ 25 Quackenbush Sq., corner of Broadway and Clinton Ave., 12207, ☎ 518/434–6311), which has two permanent hands-on exhibits depicting Albany's past and present. It's an especially good stop for kids. The **Henry Hudson Planetarium** here presents star shows on Saturday at 11:30 AM and 12:30 PM and a free orientation film about Albany on weekdays at 11:30 AM. The center has a great brochure about its CityWalk tour, which will guide you knowledgeably through Albany's historic streets.

Albany's **Empire State Plaza** (☎ 518/474–2418) is a ¼-mi-long concourse with modern art and sculpture and a mix of government, business, and cultural buildings. The plaza includes the **Corning Tower,** with a free observation deck on the 42nd floor. The **New York State Museum** (⊠ Empire State Plaza, ☎ 518/474–5877), one of the oldest state museums in the country, has life-size exhibits depicting the state's natural and cultural history, including a reproduction of an Iroquois village with a full-size longhouse. It took more than 30 years (1867–99) to complete the **New York State Capitol** (⊠ Empire State Plaza, ☎ 518/474–2418), which incorporates many interesting architectural elements. Free guided tours are conducted daily on the hour.

Dining and Lodging

For price ranges *see* Charts 1 (B) and 2 (B) *in* On the Road with Fodor's.

Albany

$$$ ✕ **Ogden's.** On the ground floor of a 1903 brick-and-limestone build-
★ ing, this dining room has two-story arched windows built into 30-ft-
high ceilings. The menu focuses on Continental and new American
cuisine. ⊠ *42 Howard St., at Lodge St.,* ☎ *518/463–6605. AE, DC,
MC, V. Closed Sun. No lunch Sat.*

$$$$ ✕🏠 **Mansion Hill Inn.** Standard-issue rooms are eclipsed by the real
draw here—the intimate dozen-table restaurant (which doesn't serve
lunch). The dinner menu has an imaginative new American flair. If you
stay at the inn, your breakfast might include items such as blueberry
pancakes or frittatas. ⊠ *115 Philip St., at Park Ave., 12202,* ☎ *518/
465–2038,* 𝔽𝔸𝕏 *518/434–2313. 8 rooms. Restaurant. Full breakfast.
AE, D, DC, MC, V.*

$$$$ 🏠 **The State House.** During the day sunlight pours through the win-
★ dows of this late-19th-century town house that faces Washington Park.
Mahogany architectural accents complement the interior's hand-glazed
walls, high ceilings, fireplaces, and such touches as down comforters
and overstuffed chairs. Innkeeper Charles Kuhtic charmingly oversees
things. ⊠ *393 State St.,* ☎ *518/427–6063,* 𝔽𝔸𝕏 *518/465–8079. 4
rooms. In-room modem lines, library. D, MC, V.*

Bear Mountain

$$$ 🏠 **Bear Mountain Inn.** For more than 50 years this chalet-style resort
has been known for both its bucolic location (in Bear Mountain State
Park on the shores of Hessian Lake) and its warm hospitality. Rooms
are divided among a main inn and five lodges across the lake. In winter the lobby fireplaces make the lodges cozy; in summer there are great
spots nearby for picnicking. ⊠ *Rte. 9W, 10911,* ☎ *914/786–2731,*
𝔽𝔸𝕏 *914/786–2543. 61 rooms. Restaurant, lobby lounge, pool, hiking,
boating, ice-skating, playground. AE, D, MC, V.*

Cold Spring

$ ✕ **Marika's.** Duck into this tiny café for a sweet or savory treat—from
freshly baked bread pudding to spinach in puff pastry and Middle Eastern lamb pie. ⊠ *137 Main St.,* ☎ *914/265–4275. No credit cards.*

$$$$ ✕🏠 **Hudson House.** Clean and simple, this historic clapboard inn has
an Early American country feel with Shaker-style furnishings and wide-
plank floorboards. Tasty traditional American fare is served in the dining room. The inn is within walking distance of many antiques shops
and nearly sits on the Hudson River. ⊠ *2 Main St., 10516,* ☎ *914/
265–9355. 12 rooms. Restaurant. AE, MC, V.*

Hopewell Junction

$$$$ ✕🏠 **Le Chambord.** Owner Roy Benich has brought his finely tuned
aesthetic sense and prodigious energies to every aspect of this 1863
Georgian-style inn and restaurant. Nine guest rooms are in the main
house; 16 newer rooms are in Tara, an adjacent building on the property. Chef Leonard Mott's classic and contemporary French cuisine
is served under antique Waterford crystal chandeliers. ⊠ *2075 Rte.
52, 12533,* ☎ 𝔽𝔸𝕏 *914/221–1941 or 800/274–1941. 25 rooms. AE,
DC, MC, V.*

Hyde Park

$$–$$$ ✕ **Culinary Institute of America.** The institute (☞ Exploring the Hud-
son Valley, *above*) has four public restaurants. **Escoffier** features classic French cuisine. **American Bounty** offers American regional fare.
Caterina de Medici focuses on nouvelle Italian cooking; a four-course
prix-fixe menu is offered. **St. Andrew's Cafe** serves low-fat contemporary

American health food, from pizza to vegetarian dishes. Reservations are essential and are taken weekdays 9–5; reserve months in advance. ⊠ *433 Albany Post Rd., U.S. 9,* ☎ *914/471–6608. AE, DC, MC, V. Closed Sun., last 2 wks of July.*

New Paltz

$$$ 🏨 **Mohonk Mountain House.** In the middle of a 20,000-acre preserve, this awe-inspiring Victorian-era hotel, with its stone and shingled terraces, quiet parlors, and red-tiled turrets, perches on the edge of a quiet lake. Room rates include three hearty yet sadly uninspired meals in the large, bustling dining room as well as afternoon tea. Extensive hiking trails surround the hotel. ⊠ *1000 Mountain Rest Rd. [Exit 18 off the NY State Thruway], Lake Mohonk 12561,* ☎ *914/255–1000 or 800/772–6646,* 𝔽𝔸𝕏 *914/256–2161. 276 rooms. 3 dining rooms, 9-hole golf course, 6 tennis courts, basketball, boccie, croquet, hiking, horseback riding, shuffleboard, softball, volleyball, beach, boating, ice-skating, cross-country skiing, children's programs. AE, DC, MC, V.*

Rhinebeck

$$$–$$$$ ✕🏨 **Beekman Arms.** In all, 10 buildings make up this inn in the vil-
★   lage center: the original 1766 building, with its smallish though cheery and comfortable Colonial-style rooms (with modern baths); a motel-like building, behind the main inn; and, a block away, the mid-19th-century Delamater House, with Victorian-style rooms (a majority). The inn's restaurant, Larry Forgione's **Beekman 1766 Tavern,** which incorporates the old taproom, serves American regional fare. ⊠ *4 Mill St. (U.S. 9), 12572,* ☎ 𝔽𝔸𝕏 *914/876–7077 or* ☎ *914/871–1766 for restaurant. 59 rooms. AE, DC, MC, V.*

West Point

$$$–$$$$ 🏨 **Hotel Thayer.** On the grounds of the academy, this stately brick hotel, steeped in history and tradition, has been welcoming military and civilian guests for more than 60 years. Many guest rooms have views of the river and the West Point grounds. ⊠ *U.S. 9W, 10996,* ☎ *914/446–4731 or 800/247–5047,* 𝔽𝔸𝕏 *914/446–0338. 183 rooms. Restaurant, lounge. AE, D, DC, MC, V.*

Motels

🏨 **Days Inn Colonie Mall** (⊠ 16 Wolf Rd., Albany 12205, ☎ 518/459–3600 or 800/329–7466), 167 rooms, pool; *$$$.* 🏨 **Sheraton Civic Center Hotel** (⊠ 40 Civic Center Plaza, Poughkeepsie 12601, ☎ 914/485–5300 or 800/325–3535), 200 rooms, café, health club; *$$$–$$$$.* 🏨 **Roosevelt Inn** (⊠ 616 Albany Post Rd., Hyde Park 12538, ☎ 914/229–2443), 25 rooms, coffee shop (breakfast only); *$$.*

Nightlife and the Arts

The **Empire Center at the Egg** (⊠ Madison Ave. and S. Swan St., Albany, ☎ 518/473–1845) has music, dance, and theater performances. The **Palace Theater** (⊠ 19 Clinton Ave., Albany, ☎ 518/465–4663) is home to the Albany Symphony Orchestra.

Outdoor Activities and Sports

Fishing

The Hudson River estuary contains a remarkable variety of fish, most notably American shad, black bass, smallmouth and largemouth bass, and sturgeon. For information on licenses (required in fresh waters) and restrictions, as well as fishing hot spots and charts, contact the **New York State Department of Environmental Conservation** (⊠ 21 S. Putt Corners Rd., New Paltz 12561, ☎ 914/256–3000; ⊠ 50 Wolf Rd., Albany 12233, ☎ 518/457–3521).

Golf
Beekman Country Club (⊠ 11 Country Club Rd., Hopewell Junction, ☎ 914/226–7700) has 27 holes. **Dinsmore Golf Course** (⊠ Rte. 9, Staatsburg, ☎ 914/889–4082) has 18 holes.

Ski Areas

Cross-Country
Bear Mountain State Park (⊠ Bear Mountain, 10911, ☎ 914/786–2701) has 5 mi of trails. **Mills-Norrie State Park** (⊠ Old Post Rd., Staatsburg 12580, ☎ 914/889–4100) has 6 mi of trails with views of the Hudson River. **Olana State Historic Site** (⊠ Rte. 9G, Hudson, 12534, ☎ 518/828–0135) has 7 mi of trails. **Rockefeller State Park** (⊠ Rte. 117, North Tarrytown, 10591, ☎ 914/631–1470) has about 18 mi of trails.

THE CATSKILLS

The Catskill Mountains have a beauty and variety disproportionate to their modest size. Just a two- or three-hour drive from New York City, the area offers streams for fly-fishing, paths for hiking, cliffs for rock climbing, hills for skiing, and back roads for leisurely driving. Once known as the Borscht Belt for the resort complexes that catered to Jewish families from New York City, the region now tends to attract wilderness lovers and craftspeople.

Visitor Information

Catskill: Association for Tourism Services (CATS; ⊠ Box 449, Catskill 12414, ☎ 518/943–3223 or 800/882–2287). **Delaware County:** Chamber of Commerce (⊠ 97 Main St., Delhi 13753, ☎ 800/642–4443). **Greene County:** Promotion Department (⊠ Box 527, Catskill 12414, ☎ 518/943–3223 or 800/355–2287). **Sullivan County:** Office of Public Information (⊠ 100 North St., Box 5012, Monticello 12701, ☎ 914/794–3000 ext. 5010 or 800/882–2287).

Arriving and Departing

By Bus
Adirondack Trailways (☎ 800/225–6815) offers regular service from New York City and Albany to several Catskill communities, including Kingston, New Paltz, Hunter, and Fleischmanns. **Shortline** (☎ 800/631–8405) connects New York City with half a dozen Sullivan County communities, including Bloomingburg and Wurtsboro.

By Car
The northern Catskills can be reached off I–87 from Catskill (Route 23) and Kingston (Route 28). The resort region lies on both sides of Route 17 north from I–87 at Harriman or from I–84 at Middletown.

By Plane
Albany County Airport (☞ Arriving and Departing by Plane *in* the Hudson Valley, *above*) is an hour's drive from the heart of the Catskills. **Oneonta Municipal Airport** (☎ 607/431–1076) is in the northwest corner of the Catskills region.

Exploring the Catskills

In the northeastern section of the Catskills is the actual village of **Catskill,** which has its share of museums and quaint buildings. The **Catskill Game Farm,** in Catskill, is home to 2,000 birds and animals, including a large collection of rare hooved species, and has a petting zoo and a playground. ⊠ *400 Game Farm Rd. (off Rte. 32),* ☎ *518/678–9595. Closed Dec.–Apr.*

From the New York State Thruway (I–87), travel west on Route 28, and you'll be heading right toward the heart of the Catskills. If you're
★ the least bit hungry (or even if you're not), stop by the **Bread Alone bakery** (⊠ Rte. 28, Boiceville, ☎ 914/657–3328), where you can sample and purchase some organic hearth-baked breads, from currant buns to *pain levain* (European-style sourdough bread). In the area known as the **High Peaks** from Phoenicia north to the ski resort town of Hunter, Route 214 winds through **Stoney Clove,** a spectacular mountain cleft that has inspired countless tales of the supernatural. Another scenic route out of Phoenicia is across the Esopus River and south up lovely Woodland Valley to the well-marked trail to Slide Mountain, the highest peak in the Catskills.

Delaware County, newly discovered by big-city vacationers and second-home buyers, has gentler terrain than the High Peaks region. Fishers prize the east and west branches of the Delaware River, and the county's more than 500 farms offer honey, eggs, cider, and maple syrup at numerous roadside stands. **Roxbury,** on Route 30, has the kind of picture-perfect Main Street Norman Rockwell would have loved.

What to See and Do with Children

Delaware & Ulster Rail Ride (⊠ Rte. 28, Arkville, ☎ 607/652–2821), closed November–April, runs a one-hour scenic route between Arkville and Fleischmanns. In Catskill the **Ponderosa Ranch Fun Park** (⊠ 4620 Rte. 32, ☎ 518/678–9206) has the region's largest go-cart track, as well as miniature golf, bumper boats, and rodeos every Saturday night in summer. **Clyde Peeling's Reptiland** lets children see snakes and lizards up close. ⊠ *Rte. 32,* ☎ *518/678–3557. Closed Columbus Day–Memorial Day, weekdays Labor Day–Columbus Day.*

Dining and Lodging

Although the region offers some outstanding food, the most inspiring aspect of its restaurants is often the setting. The Catskills are best known for mammoth resort hotels, but there are plenty of B&Bs and country inns providing a personal touch, as well as ski-center condos and cabins in the woods. For price ranges *see* Charts 1 (B) and 2 (B) *in* On the Road with Fodor's.

Big Indian

$$ ✕ **Jake Moon.** The menu at this rustic country restaurant changes seasonally and features "Catskill Mountain cuisine"—fresh local produce, game, and fish. Large windows overlook Big Indian Valley. ⊠ *Rte. 28,* ☎ *914/254–5953. AE, D, DC, MC, V. Closed Tues.–Wed. No lunch.*

Catskill

$$ ✕ **La Conca D'Oro.** In 1984 chef-owner Alfonso Acampora brought his Italian culinary skills to the town of Catskill. Fare includes elk, boar, and pheasant prepared with a northern Italian accent. ⊠ *440 Main St.,* ☎ *518/943–3549. D, MC, V. Closed Tues. No lunch weekends.*

Elka Park

$$–$$$ ✕🏠 **Redcoat's Return.** The ambience at this spot in the northern Catskills is of an English country house complete with a cozy library—after all, the owners are British. The inn's dining room, with views of surrounding mountains, serves up British-influenced Continental dishes. ⊠ *Dale La., 12427,* ☎ 𝔽𝔸𝕏 *518/589–6379. 14 rooms. Restaurant. Continental breakfast. AE, MC, V.*

Hunter

$$$ ✕🖭 **Scribner Hollow Lodge.** This motor-lodge–like hotel has campy
theme rooms and many amenities, including a "grotto pool." The
restaurant, which serves eclectic new American dishes, overlooks the
mountains. ⊠ *Rte. 23A, 12442,* ☎ *518/263–4211 or 800/395–4683,*
℻ *518/263–5266. 38 rooms. Restaurant, indoor and outdoor pools,
hot tub, tennis court, meeting rooms. MAP. AE, D, MC, V.*

Kingston

$$ ✕ **Schneller's.** Schnitzels and wursts are served at this authentic Ger-
★ man tavern in Kingston's historic district. After your meal you may
want to stop in the meat market next door for some imported cheeses
or hickory-smoked bacon to take home. The outdoor beer garden is
splendid in summer. ⊠ *61 John St.,* ☎ *914/331–9800. No dinner Mon.–
Tues. AE, DC, MC, V.*

Shandaken

$$$ ✕🖭 **Auberge des 4 Saisons.** Best known for its first-rate French cui-
sine, this restaurant is also an inn; the rooms are very basic, with min-
imum furnishings. The food, however, is superb. ⊠ *Rte. 42, 12480,*
☎ *914/688–2223. AE, D, MC, V.*

Tannersville

$$$ ✕🖭 **Deer Mountain Inn.** This circa-1900 mansion on a 15-acre wooded
enclave is lushly packed with items that create a mountain ambience:
moose heads, boar heads, bearskin rugs, paintings of European mountain villages, and heavy overstuffed furniture. The dining room, bracketed by two huge stone fireplaces, offers American fare—trout, veal,
and seafood—with a European accent. ⊠ *Rte. 25 (Box 443), 12485,*
☎ ℻ *518/589–6268. 7 rooms. Restaurant. AE, MC, V.*

Windham

$$$ ✕ **La Griglia.** Elegant country dining here features northern Italian cui-
sine. A house specialty is the penne *pepperata* (with sautéed sun-dried
tomatoes, sweet red peppers, basil, and a touch of cream). The wine
list is one of the best in upstate New York. ⊠ *Rte. 296,* ☎ *518/734–
4499. AE, DC, MC, V. No lunch weekdays.*

$$–$$$$ ✕🖭 **Thompson House.** Guests are remembered by their first names at
★ this resort run for more than a century by five generations of the same
family. Guest rooms, some of which have four-poster beds and antiques,
are spread among six houses, including the Victorian Spruce Cottage.
⊠ *Rte. 296 (Box 129), 12496,* ☎ *518/734–4510,* ℻ *518/734–4525.
100 rooms; 15 in winter. Dining room, pool, 2 putting greens, 2 tennis courts, playground. MC, V. MAP. Closed Nov., Apr.*

Motel

🖭 **Hunter Inn** (⊠ *Rte. 23A, Hunter 12442,* ☎ *518/263–3777,* ℻ *518/
263–3981), 40 rooms, restaurant, pool, exercise room; $$$–$$$$.*

Nightlife and the Arts

Several well-established regional organizations offer a full menu of per-
forming arts year-round; in summer the cultural calendar is especially
busy. Contact the regional visitor centers for schedules. Hunter has some
lively nightspots during ski season and summer. The large resorts,
such as the Concord (☞ Dining and Lodging, *above*), offer dancing
and big-name acts.

Outdoor Activities and Sports

Canoeing

The 79-mi Upper Delaware Scenic and Recreational River is one of the finest streams for paddling in the region. For a list of trip planners and rental firms, contact the **Sullivan County Office of Public Information** (☞ Visitor Information, *above*).

Fishing

Trout are abundant in Catskill streams; smallmouth bass, walleye, and pickerel can be found in many lakes and in six reservoirs. For the "Catskill Fishing" brochure and map, write to **CATS** (☞ Visitor Information, *above*).

Golf

The region has nearly 50 golf courses, many of which are at the big resorts. For the "Golf Catskills" brochure, write to **CATS** (☞ Visitor Information, *above*).

Hiking

The **New York State Department of Environmental Conservation** (✉ 50 Wolf Rd., Albany 12233, ☎ 518/457–7433) puts out several brochures on Catskill Forest Preserve hiking trails.

Tubing

Town Tinker (✉ Bridge St., Phoenicia, ☎ 914/688–5553) rents tubes for beginner and advanced routes along the Esopus Creek between Shandaken and Mount Pleasant.

Spectator Sports

Horse Racing: Monticello Raceway (✉ Rtes. 17 and 17B, Monticello, ☎ 914/794–4100) offers year-round harness racing.

Ski Areas

For information on area slopes and trails, contact **Ski the Catskills** (✉ Box 135, Arkville 12406, ☎ 914/586–1944).

Cross-Country

Belleayre Mountain (☞ Downhill, *below*) has 5 mi of trails. **Mountain Trails Cross-Country Ski Center at Hyer Meadows,** in Tannersville (✉ Box 198, Rte. 23A, 12485, ☎ 518/589–5361), has 20 mi of groomed trails; rentals and lessons are available.

Downhill

Downhill ski areas in the Catskills have snowmaking capabilities. **Belleayre Mountain** (✉ Box 313, Highmount 12441, ☎ 914/254–5600), with 33 runs, 8 lifts, and a 1,404-ft vertical drop, is the only state-run ski facility in the Catskills. **Hunter Mountain** (✉ Box 295, Rte. 23A, Hunter 12442, ☎ 518/263–4223) has 48 runs, 13 lifts, and a 1,600-ft drop. **Ski Windham** (✉ C. D. Lane Rd., Windham 12496, ☎ 518/734–4300) has 33 runs, 7 lifts, and a 1,600-ft drop.

Shopping

Shopping is a major diversion in the Catskills, with a scattering of factory outlets, shopping villages, auctions, flea markets, crafts fairs, antiques shops, and galleries. **Woodbury Common Factory Outlets** (✉ Rte. 32, Exit 16 off I–87, Harriman, ☎ 914/928–6840) has more than 150 discount stores, including Gucci and Barney's.

SARATOGA SPRINGS AND THE NORTH COUNTRY

Saratoga Springs, about 30 mi north of Albany, is one of American high society's oldest summer playgrounds. The six-week Thoroughbred-racing season, starting in mid-July, is the high point of the year. Northwest of Saratoga, and in stark contrast, are the rugged mountains, immense forests, and abundant lakes and streams of Adirondack Park, the largest park expanse in the continental United States. The North Country—anchored by the resort towns of Lake Placid and Lake George—hums year-round. Hikers descend in the summer, autumn brings leaf peepers, and with the snow come many winter-sports enthusiasts.

Visitor Information

Greater Saratoga: Chamber of Commerce (⊠ 494 Broadway, Saratoga Springs 12866, ☎ 518/584–3255). **Lake Placid:** Visitors Bureau (⊠ 216 Main St., Olympic Center 12946, ☎ 518/523–2445 or 800/447–5224). **Saranac Lake:** Chamber of Commerce (⊠ 30 Main St., 12983, ☎ 518/891–1990 or 800/347–1992).

Arriving and Departing

By Car

The primary route through the region is the Northway (I–87), which links Albany and Montréal.

By Plane

The principal airports are in New York City (207 mi south of Lake George) and Montréal (177 mi north of Lake George). Other airports serving the region are in Albany, Syracuse, and Burlington, Vermont.

By Train

Amtrak (☎ 800/872–7245) operates the *Adirondack*, a daily train between New York and Montréal, with many North Country stops.

By Bus

Adirondack Trailways (☎ 914/339–4230 or 800/225–6815) provides bus service to Saratoga Springs, Lake Placid, Lake George, Chestertown, Bolton Landing (summer only), and many other area towns.

Exploring Saratoga Springs and the North Country

People have been frequenting **Saratoga Springs** for its medicinal properties since the late 18th century. In the late 19th century it emerged as one of North America's principal resorts, both for its spa waters and its gambling casino. It also became a horse-racing center in the 1890s, and August still brings crowds for the race meet and yearling sale.

You can still see mineral-water springs bubbling from the ground—22 are currently visible—at **Saratoga Spa State Park.** Listed on the National Register of Historic Places, this 2,000-acre park has walking paths to the springs. Mineral baths and massages are available at the Roosevelt and Lincoln Park bathhouses. You'll certainly find plenty to do here—there are tennis courts, swimming pools, and golf courses, among other things. ⊠ *Between Rtes. 9 and 50, 19 Roosevelt Dr., Saratoga Springs 12866,* ☎ *518/584–2000.*

Across from the Saratoga Race Course (☞ Spectator Sports, *below*), site of the renowned horse races, is the **National Museum of Racing.** Its centerpiece is the Hall of Fame, which has video clips of races featuring the horses and jockeys enshrined here. ⊠ *Union Ave.,* ☎ *518/584–0400.*

Yaddo (✉ Union Ave., ☎ 518/587–4886), once a private home, is now a highly regarded retreat for artists and writers. The 400-acre grounds and rose garden are open to the public.

The **National Museum of Dance** features rotating exhibits on the history and development of the art form, as well as the Hall of Fame, which honors dance luminaries. The studios allow visitors to watch or participate in a dance class. ✉ *99 S. Broadway,* ☎ *518/584–2225. Closed Labor Day–Memorial Day, Mon.*

The **Historical Society of Saratoga Springs** is housed in Canfield Casino—an 1870s Italianate building that was a gambling casino. The museum is devoted to the town's colorful history as a gambling center, and changing exhibits are displayed in a contemporary art gallery. ✉ *Congress Park, Broadway and Circular St.,* ☎ *518/584–6920. Closed Mon.–Tues. Oct.–Apr.*

In the Adirondack Mountain range, the 6-million-acre **Adirondack Park** encompasses 1,000 mi of rivers and more than 2,500 lakes and ponds. The southern sections are more developed, while the High Peaks region, in the north-central sector, offers the greatest variety of wilderness activities. *Visitor Interpretive Centers: ✉ Paul Smiths (north of Saranac Lake), Rte. 30, 1 mi north of Rte. 86 intersection,* ☎ *518/ 327–3000; ✉ Newcomb, Rte. 28N,* ☎ *518/582–2000.*

Lake George, 40 mi north of Saratoga, is a kitschy tourist town catering to families, with amusement parks, souvenir shops, and miniature golf. Cruises from the town dock are extremely popular from May through October; contact **Lake George Shoreline Cruises** (☎ 518/668–4644) and the **Lake George Steamboat Company** (☎ 518/668–5777).

Just south of town is **Great Escape Fun Park,** the North Country's largest amusement park. ✉ *U.S. 9,* ☎ *518/792–3500. Closed Labor Day– Memorial Day.*

★ Overlooking Blue Mountain Lake, the open-air **Adirondack Museum** has a day's worth of exhibits on the history, culture, and crafts of the region. The *New York Times* calls it "the best museum of its kind in the world." ✉ *Rte. 30,* ☎ *518/352–7311. Closed mid-Oct.–Memorial Day.*

Lake Placid, the hub of the northern Adirondacks, has a Main Street lined with shops and motels, two lakes in its backyard, and the **1932 and 1980 winter Olympics facilities** all around it. The Ice Arena and speed-skating oval are in the center of town; the ski jump is 2 mi out; Whiteface Mountain (scene of the downhill competitions) is a 10-minute drive away, on Route 86; and the bobsled run at Mt. Van Hoevenberg, on Route 73, is 15 minutes away. All sites are open to the public.

Self-guided tours can be made of the **John Brown Farm,** home and burial place of the famed abolitionist, who operated the farm for free blacks. ✉ *Off Rte. 73 past the Olympic ski jumps,* ☎ *518/523–3900. Closed Mon.–Tues. and Nov.–Apr.*

The serenity and mountain air of **Saranac Lake** (elevation: 1,600 ft) made it a health resort for the tubercular in the late 19th century. Ten miles west of Lake Placid, it is today the jumping-off point for canoe trips (☞ Outdoor Activities and Sports, *below*). Much of the lake is part of the **St. Regis Canoe Area,** which is off-limits to powerboats.

There is much more to the region called the **Thousand Islands** than the island-studded area of the St. Lawrence River. The name usually refers to an area defined by the Adirondacks to the east, the St. Lawrence to the north, and Lake Ontario to the west. Most of the region is flat or rolling farmland, but the economy is heavily dependent on the St. Lawrence Seaway. The scenic **Seaway Trail,** a combination of Routes 37, 12, and 12E, follows the river and the Lake Ontario shore. In summer huge cargo vessels pass through the **Eisenhower Lock,** in Massena; call ahead (☎ 315/769–2422) to find out when a ship is scheduled to pass through.

What to See and Do with Children

Those not big on hiking can sample the beauty of the Adirondack region at **Ausable Chasm** (⊠ U.S. 9 just north of Keeseville, ☎ 518/834–7454), where you can see massive stone formations. Kids will love the caves and gorge at **Natural Stone Bridge and Caves** (⊠ Exit 26 off I–87, near Pottersville, ☎ 518/494–2283). Another natural attraction, **High Falls Gorge,** has three dramatic waterfalls and a self-guided tour along the Ausable River. ⊠ *Off Rte. 86 near Wilmington,* ☎ *518/946–2278. Closed Labor Day–Memorial Day.*

Dining and Lodging

Saratoga is indisputably the North Country's culinary champion in quality and variety, with Lake Placid a distant second. Elsewhere expect large portions, home cooking, and a rustic atmosphere. Lodging runs the gamut from roadside motels to resorts. For information on B&Bs contact the **Adirondacks Bed and Breakfast Association** (☎ 518/623–2524). For price ranges *see* Charts 1 (B) and 2 (B) *in* On the Road with Fodor's.

Bolton Landing

$$$$ ✕▥ **Sagamore Resort.** This resort is on its own island in Lake George. The Adirondack-style rooms are spread among the main hotel and lakeside lodges. Each of the six dining rooms has its own atmosphere and cuisine, ranging from the formal, slightly nouvelle touches of Trillium (reservations essential, jacket required, no lunch) to the hearty burgers and steaks of Mr. Brown's Pub. ⊠ *110 Sagamore Rd., 12814,* ☎ *518/644–9400,* ℻ *518/644–2626. 350 rooms. 6 restaurants, air-conditioning, in-room VCRs, indoor pool, 18-hole golf course, 7 tennis courts, beauty salon, spa, health club, jogging, racquetball, beach, boating, convention center. AE, D, DC, MC, V.*

Chestertown

$$$$ ✕▥ **Friends Lake Inn.** Most of the inn's cozy guest rooms have moun-
★ tain or lake views. There's plenty to do in the area—cross-country skiing, hiking, swimming, or just relaxing in a big Adirondack-style chair on the inn's spacious lawn. The inn's regionally acclaimed restaurant serves new American cuisine. ⊠ *Friends Lake Rd., 12817,* ☎ *518/494–4751,* ℻ *518/494–4616. 14 rooms. Restaurant, hot tub, dock, cross-country skiing. Full breakfast, dinner. MC, V.*

Lake Placid

$$ ✕ **Artist's Cafe.** An enclosed lakeside deck and a comfortable dining room and bar make this a popular spot. Seafood, steaks, hearty soups, and imaginative sandwich combinations headline the menu. The paintings, by local artists, are for sale. ⊠ *1 Main St.,* ☎ *518/523–9493. AE, D, DC, MC, V.*

$ ✕ **Tail o' the Pup.** Conveniently located halfway between Lake Placid and Saranac Lake, this classic roadside restaurant specializes in savory barbecued items like chicken, ribs, and pork; waffle fries and cole slaw are perfect accompaniments. You can dine inside, at the outdoor picnic tables, or in your car—honk twice for service. ⊠ *Rte. 86, Ray Brook,* ☎ *518/891–5092. No credit cards.*

$$$$ ✕🏨 **Lake Placid Lodge.** Originally a rustic lodge built before the turn
★ of the century, this small hotel embodies the spirit of Lake Placid's past
and cossets guests with the comforts of luxurious amenities. Rooms
are furnished with twig and birch-bark furniture and Adirondack antiques; amenities include feather beds, terry-cloth robes, and soaking
tubs. All but five have granite fireplaces. The dining room's new American menu changes seasonally. ✉ *Whiteface Inn Rd. (Box 550), 12946,*
☎ *518/523–2573,* FAX *518/523–1124. 22 rooms. Restaurant, bar,
beach, hiking, boating, bicycles. AE, MC, V.*

$$$$ ✕🏨 **Lake Placid Resort Holiday Inn.** This friendly resort high on a hill
above Lake Placid's Main Street is by no means your typical Holiday
Inn: The service is personal, original art decorates public spaces, and amenities range from coffeemakers and microwaves in every room to a Scot-
tish-style links golf course. The lobby's floor-to-ceiling windows overlook
Mirror Lake and the mountains beyond. Many rooms have equally inspiring views. ✉ *1 Olympic Dr., Lake Placid 12946,* ☎ *518/523–2556,*
FAX *518/523–9410. 210 rooms. 4 restaurants, refrigerators, indoor pool,
beach, 2 18-hole golf courses, 9-hole putting green, 11 tennis courts, health
club, cross-country skiing, conference center. AE, D, DC, MC, V.*

$$$$ ✕🏨 **Mirror Lake Inn.** On the shores of Mirror Lake, this stately Adirondack inn is within walking distance of downtown Lake Placid. The atmosphere here is truly genteel. The elegant interior includes an antiques-filled
library and a living room with stone fireplaces and walnut floors. The
rooms are spread among several buildings; those on the lake have private balconies. The casual Cottage Restaurant, right on the lake, serves
imaginative sandwiches in addition to some heartier entrées. ✉ *5 Mirror Lake Dr., 12946,* ☎ *518/523–2544,* FAX *518/523–2871. 128 rooms.
2 restaurants, indoor and outdoor pools, tennis court, spa, beach, boating, fishing, cross-country skiing, meeting rooms. AE, D, DC, MC, V.*

Saranac Lake

$$$$ ✕🏨 **The Point.** Onetime home of William Avery Rockefeller, this all-
★ inclusive, elegantly rustic inn is the Adirondacks' and arguably one of
the country's most exclusive retreats. There are no signs pointing here;
you have to book a room in order to get the address. ✉ *HCR 1 (Box
65), 12983,* ☎ *518/891–5678 or 800/255–3530,* FAX *518/891–1152.
11 rooms. Dining room, bar, beach, boating, ice-skating, cross-country skiing. AE.*

Saratoga Springs

$$ ✕ **Eartha's Kitchen.** This small bistro is a local favorite, especially for
★ the mesquite-grilled seafood dishes from the ever-changing, eclectic menu.
The cinnamon bread pudding with brandy cream sauce is a house spe-
cialty. ✉ *60 Court St.,* ☎ *518/583–0602. Reservations essential. AE,
DC, MC, V. No lunch.*

$$–$$$ 🏨 **Adelphi Hotel.** This downtown Saratoga showplace is opulent, ex-
travagant, and fun. ✉ *365 Broadway, 12866,* ☎ *518/587–4688. 35
rooms. AE, MC, V.*

Motel

🏨 **Days Inn of Lake George** (✉ 1454 Rte. 9, Suite 1, Lake George 12845,
☎ 518/793–3196 or 800/325–2525), 110 rooms, restaurant, indoor
pool, valet service; *$$$–$$$$.*

Campgrounds

Adirondak Loj Wilderness Campground (✉ Off Rte. 73, Box 867,
Lake Placid 12946, ☎ 518/523–3441) provides information about
camping throughout the High Peaks region and operates a camp-
ground on Heart Lake, with 34 tent sites and 15 lean-tos, water, no
gas or electric, picnic tables, seasonal showers, and toilets.

The Arts

Adirondack Lakes Center for the Arts (✉ Rte. 28, Blue Mountain Lake, ☎ 518/352–7715) is a multipurpose arts center that presents art exhibits and concerts and has coffeehouses and workshops. The **Saratoga Performing Arts Center** (☎ 518/587–3330) hosts the New York City Opera, the New York City Ballet, the Philadelphia Orchestra, and the Newport Jazz Festival–Saratoga, as well as big-name pop stars, from June to September.

Outdoor Activities and Sports

Middle Earth Expeditions (✉ HCR 01, Box 37, Cascade Rd., Lake Placid 12946, ☎ 518/523–9572) leads tours and provides guides for individuals or groups in canoeing, white-water rafting, fishing, and backpacking. The friendly folks at **All Seasons Outfitters** (✉ 168 Lake Flower Ave., Saranac Lake, ☎ 518/891–6159) sell and rent gear for canoeing, cross-country skiing, snowshoeing, and hiking. They'll outfit an entire trip for you, including food.

Biking

Roadside signs mark several bike routes, most quite hilly, that wind through the North Country. For a map of routes in the area, contact the **Saranac Lake Chamber of Commerce** (☞ Visitor Information, *above*).

Canoeing

The 170-mi **Raquette River** and the **St. Regis Canoe Area,** east of Saranac Lake, are among the best and most popular canoe routes in the North Country.

Fishing

Brook and lake trout are taken year-round on the lakes and streams of the North Country. Licenses can be obtained at town or county clerk offices, sporting goods stores, and outfitters.

Golf

Among the more challenging courses are those at the **Whiteface Resort** (✉ Whiteface Inn Rd., Lake Placid, ☎ 518/523–2551), 18 holes; the **Sagamore Resort** (✉ 110 Sagamore Rd., Bolton Landing, ☎ 518/644–9400), 18 holes; and the **Saranac Inn Golf and Country Club** (✉ Upper Saranac Lake, ☎ 518/891–1402), 18 holes.

Hiking

The most popular area for hiking is the High Peaks region, accessible from the Lake Placid area in the north, Keene and Keene Valley in the east, and Newcomb in the south. For more information contact the **Adirondack Mountain Club** (✉ ADK, Box 867, Lake Placid 12946, ☎ 518/523–3441).

Rafting

Hudson River Rafting Company (✉ 1 Main St., North Creek, ☎ 800/888–7238) offers day trips on the Hudson, the Sacandaga, and the Black River from April to October.

Spectator Sports

Lake Placid summer and winter athletic competitions: Contact the **Olympic Authority** (☎ 518/523–1655 or 800/462–6236). Events include concerts, ski jumping, and figure-skating shows.

Horse Racing: The six-week Thoroughbred-racing season starts in mid-July at **Saratoga Race Course** (✉ Union Ave., Saratoga Springs, ☎ 518/584–6200). **Saratoga Harness Raceway** (✉ Nelson Ave., Saratoga Springs, ☎ 518/584–2110) has harness and Thoroughbred racing March–November.

Ski Areas

Cross-Country

Mt. Van Hoevenberg, on Route 73, has 30 mi of groomed tracks, which connect with the **Jackrabbit Trail,** a 33-mi network of ski trails through the High Peaks region connecting Lake Placid, Saranac Lake, and Paul Smiths. For information and conditions contact **Adirondack Ski Touring Council** (⊠ Box 843, Lake Placid 12946, ☎ 518/523–1365).

Downhill

Whiteface Mountain Ski Center (⊠ Wilmington 12997, 8 mi east of Lake Placid, ☎ 518/946–2223) has 65 runs, 10 lifts, a 3,251-ft vertical drop, and snowmaking.

Shopping

The region's maple syrup and sharp cheddar cheese make great gifts. **Blue Mountain Lake** and **Lake Placid** are good bets for crafts hunting. Look for baskets and pottery with pinecones painted on them, unique to the area; you'll also find an array of jewelry, leather work, and quilting. The **Adirondack Crafts Center** (⊠ Lake Placid Center for the Arts, 93 Saranac Ave., Lake Placid, ☎ 518/523–2062) is a year-round facility where more than 275 local artisans show their wares.

LEATHERSTOCKING COUNTRY AND THE FINGER LAKES

Visitor Information

Cooperstown: Chamber of Commerce (⊠ 31 Chestnut St., 13326, ☎ 607/547–9983). **Leatherstocking Country:** (⊠ 327 N. Main St., Herkimer 13350, ☎ 315/866–1500 or 800/233–8778). **Finger Lakes Association:** (⊠ 309 Lake St., Penn Yan 14527, ☎ 315/536–7488 or 800/548–4386).

Arriving and Departing

The Leatherstocking region is 200–300 mi from New York City via the New York State Thruway and Route 28 from Kingston. I–90 runs east–west through both Leatherstocking Country and the Finger Lakes, connecting Albany with Buffalo. I–88 runs northeast–southwest, leading to Binghamton.

Exploring Leatherstocking Country and the Finger Lakes

The early Yankees in their leather leggings gave the region its nickname; it is quintessential rural America, with gently rolling countryside, community chicken barbecues, and tree-shaded small towns. Cooperstown ★ is home to the **National Baseball Hall of Fame,** where displays, paintings, and audiovisual presentations honor the heroes, recall great moments, and trace the history of the game. ⊠ *Main St.,* ☎ *607/547–7200.*

Binghamton has the **Roberson Museum and Science Center,** comprising a restored 1910 historic house, a complex of museums, a planetarium, and a theater. ⊠ *30 Front St.,* ☎ *607/772–0660. Closed Mon.–Tues.*

Kids are especially fond of the wooded **Ross Park Zoo** (⊠ 60 Morgan Rd., ☎ 607/724–5461), where animals (including tigers and a timber wolf pack) live in natural environments. You can relive the old days of canal transport, including a ride in a horse-drawn canal boat, at **Erie Canal Village,** a reconstructed circa-1840 village. ⊠ *Rte. 49W, Rome,* ☎ *315/337–3999. Closed Labor Day–Apr.*

The 11 parallel **Finger Lakes,** from **Conesus Lake,** south of Rochester, to **Otisco Lake,** near Syracuse, stretch north to south like long, narrow fingers through the rolling countryside of western New York. The region's diverse terrain—waterfalls, gorges, rocky hillsides, lush forests— is the perfect backdrop for the area's many vineyards and wineries. The two largest lakes, **Seneca** and **Cayuga,** have wine trails; the visitor center has brochures that map them out. **Glenora Wine Cellars** (5435 Rte. 14, Dundee, ☎ 607/243–5513) is one of many wineries open for tours and tastings year-round.

About 5 mi west of the north end of Cayuga Lake is **Seneca Falls,** where on July 18, 1848, 300 people attended America's first women's rights convention, held at the Wesleyan Methodist Chapel (✉ 126 Falls St.). The **Women's Rights National Historical Park Visitor Center** (✉ 136 Falls St., ☎ 315/568–2991), next door, has informative exhibits.

The design studios and factory of the **MacKenzie-Childs, Ltd.** empire are housed in an old country house and barn on the eastern shore of Cayuga Lake. You can see artisans creating the company's signature majolica pottery, glassware, and trimmings on weekdays at 10 AM. ✉ *Rte. 90, Aurora,* ☎ *315/364–7123. Closed Sun.*

Ithaca, at the tip of Cayuga Lake, is the home of Cornell University. The town is more spectacular than most others in the Finger Lakes because of the deep gorges and more than 100 waterfalls that lace it.

Geneva, at the northern tip of Seneca Lake, seems like a town preserved in time. Its South Main Street, overlooking the lake, is lined with 19th-century houses and century-old trees. The picturesque campuses of Hobart and William Smith colleges are here, too.

The village of Watkins Glen is at the southern end of Seneca Lake adjoining the 669-acre **Watkins Glen State Park.** The 1½-mi gorge here is highlighted by rock formations and 18 waterfalls. It's a great spot for hiking. ✉ *Rte. 14,* ☎ *607/535–4511. Closed Nov.–May.*

The famous circuit **Watkins Glen International Raceway** (✉ Rte. 16, ☎ 607/535–2481) hosts world-class auto racing.

Rochester is the headquarters of the Eastman Kodak Company. The **George Eastman House,** onetime home of the company founder and photographic innovator, now houses the **International Museum of Photography,** the world's largest museum devoted to photographic art and technology. ✉ *900 East Ave.,* ☎ *716/271–3361. Closed Mon.*

It was here at **Susan B. Anthony's house** that the 19th-century women's rights advocate wrote *The History of Woman Suffrage.* The house is furnished in the style of the mid-1800s. ✉ *17 Madison St.,* ☎ *716/ 235–6124. Closed Sun.–Wed.*

In Corning the **Corning Museum of Glass** contains a world-class collection of glass, as well as a time-line exhibit describing 3,500 years of glassmaking, a library covering everything ever written about glass, and a self-guided tour of the Steuben glass factory. ✉ *1 Museum Way, off Rte. 17,* ☎ *607/974–8229.*

Dining and Lodging

For price ranges *see* Charts 1 (B) and 2 (B) *in* On the Road with Fodor's.

Geneva

$$$$ ✕🏠 **Geneva on the Lake.** Built in 1910, this impressive Renaissance-style palazzo was modeled after the Villa Lancelotti in Frascati, Rome. Originally a private residence, it has served as a monastery and an apart-

ment complex. Now part of a resort, the rooms here are spacious, some
have fireplaces, and almost all have a view of the lake and formal gardens. ⊠ *1001 Lochland Rd., Rte. 14S, 14456,* ☎ *315/789–7190,* FAX
*315/789–0322. 30 suites. Restaurant, refrigerators, pool, boating.
AE, D, MC, V.*

ELSEWHERE IN NEW YORK

Buffalo, Chautauqua, and Niagara Falls

Arriving and Departing

Access from the east, west, and south is primarily via I–90, the New
York State Thruway.

What to See and Do

Buffalo is a city of Victorian elegance, with many churches and strongly
ethnic neighborhoods. The **Albright-Knox Art Gallery** (⊠ 1285 Elmwood Ave., ☎ 716/882–8700) has a superb collection of modern art;
it is closed Monday.

The 50-mi drive from Silver Creek to Ripley, along the shores of Lake
Erie, is known as the **Chautauqua Wine Trail** and is dotted with five
wineries and numerous farm stands and antiques shops.

Niagara Falls, the most accessible and famous waterfall in the world,
is actually three cataracts: the **American** and **Bridal Veil** falls, in New
York, and **Horseshoe Falls,** in Ontario, Canada. More than 750,000
gallons of water flow each second in the summer.

For a good orientation to the falls, stop at the Niagara Visitor Center
in the **Niagara Reservation State Park** (⊠ Prospect Park, Niagara
Falls 14303, ☎ 716/278–1701), the oldest state park in the nation.
Goat Island provides the closest view of the American Falls; cross to
the Canadian side for the best view of Horseshoe Falls. The famous
Maid of the Mist boat ride lets you view the falls from the water.

For more information contact the **Greater Buffalo Convention and Visitors Bureau** (⊠ 107 Delaware Ave., Buffalo 14202, ☎ 716/852–0511
or 800/283–3256), the **Chautauqua County Vacationland Association**
(⊠ 4 N. Erie St., Mayville 14757, ☎ 716/753–1909 or 800/242–
4569), or the **Niagara Falls Official Information Center** (⊠ 4th and Niagara Sts., Niagara Falls 14301, ☎ 716/284–2000 or 800/338–7890).

Dining and Lodging

$$–$$$ ✕ **Red Coach Inn.** With a spectacular view of the upper rapids, this 1923
inn has an Old England atmosphere, plus wood-burning fireplaces and
an outdoor patio for summer dining. Specialties include prime rib, Boston
scrod, and seafood-sausage Mornay. ⊠ *2 Buffalo Ave., Niagara Falls,*
☎ *716/282–1459. AE, D, DC, MC, V.*

$$$ 🏨 **Days Inn Falls View.** A longtime landmark, this bustling property
has freshly painted rooms with floral fabrics. The top floors, with views
of the upper rapids, are best. ⊠ *201 Rainbow Blvd., Niagara Falls 14303,*
☎ *716/285–9321,* FAX *716/285–9760. 200 rooms. Dining room, bar.
AE, D, DC, MC, V.*

RHODE ISLAND

Updated by
K. D. Weaver

Capital	Providence
Population	990,000
Motto	Hope
State Bird	Rhode Island red hen
State Flower	Violet
Postal Abbreviation	RI

Statewide Visitor Information

Rhode Island Department of Economic Development, Tourism Division (⊠ 7 Jackson Walkway, Providence 02903, ☎ 401/277–2601 or 800/556–2484).

Scenic Drives

With 400 miles of shoreline, coastal scenes are Rhode Island's forte. The western end of its southern coastline from Watch Hill to Narragansett along **Routes 1 and 1A** (with a detour down to Galilee) takes you past state parks, forest areas, vast stretches of sandy beaches, and the marshes of Point Judith Pond. Two massive bridges on **Route 138** link Newport to Narragansett; this drive offers unbeatable views of Narragansett Bay. Route 77 runs through the idyllic towns of Tiverton and Little Compton. And nothing compares with the grand mansions along **Newport's Bellevue Avenue.**

State Parks

Rhode Island has 37 state parks and recreational grounds, with most along the south coast between Westerly and Jamestown. **Burlingame State Park, Charlestown Breachway, Fishermen's Memorial State Park, George Washington Camping Area,** and the **Ninigret Conservation Area** allow camping. For information about the state parks contact the Rhode Island Department of Economic Development (☞ Statewide Visitor Information, *above*).

THE SOUTH COAST

Visitor Information

South County: Tourism Council (⊠ 4808 Tower Hill Rd., Wakefield 02879, ☎ 401/789–4422 or 800/548–4662).

Arriving and Departing

By Bus
Greyhound Lines (☎ 800/231–2222). **Bonanza Bus Lines** (☎ 401/751–8800).

By Train
Amtrak (☎ 800/872–7245) stops at Westerly and Kingston.

Exploring the South Coast

Watch Hill is a pretty Victorian-era resort village with miles of beautiful beaches and a lighthouse. A **statue of Ninigret,** a 17th-century chief of the Rhode Island branch of the Niantic tribe, is on Bay Street. The **Flying Horse Carousel** is the oldest merry-go-round in America. ⊠ *Bay St. Closed Labor Day–mid-June.*

Napatree Point is one of the best long beach walks in Rhode Island. A walk to the end of Bay Street and a left onto Fort Road will lead you in the direction of the path.

South Kingstown, a town with many small Colonial villages, is full of crafts shops and galleries. The University of Rhode Island and fun-loving Matunuck Beach are here. **Wakefield** is a small mill town. At the old **Washington County Jail,** built in 1792, you can see jail cells, Colonial-period rooms, and a Colonial garden. ⊠ *1348 Kingstown Rd.,* ☎ *401/783–1328. Closed Mon., Wed., Fri., Sun., and Nov.–Apr.*

Narragansett was a posh resort in the late 19th century. **South County Museum** houses 20,000 artifacts dating from 1800. ⊠ *Anne Hoxie La. off Rte. 1A,* ☎ *401/783–5400. Closed Mon.–Tues. and Nov.–Apr.*

Just north of Narragansett is the picturesque village of **Wickford. Smith's Castle,** built in 1678, was the site of many orations by Roger Williams, Rhode Island's most famous historical figure. ⊠ *55 Richard Smith Dr., off U.S. 1 and 1A north,* ☎ *401/294–3521. Closed Mon.–Wed. and Oct.–Apr.*

Galilee, one of the busiest fishing ports on the East Coast, is where you catch the ferry to Block Island. Charter fishing trips and whale-watching are both popular with visitors. On Ocean Road are public beaches and, at land's end, the **Point Judith Lighthouse** (☎ 401/789–0444). The **Frances Fleet** offers whale-watching aboard the *Lady Frances.* ⊠ *2 State St.,* ☎ *401/783–4988 or 800/662–2824.* ⊒ *$30. Closed Oct.–May.*

What to See and Do With Children

Norman Bird Sanctuary (⊠ 583 3rd Beach Rd., Middletown, ☎ 401/846–2577) is a 450-acre sanctuary with nature trails, guided tours, and a small natural history museum.

Dining and Lodging

Narragansett

$$$–$$$$ ✕ **Basil's.** Basil's serves French and Continental cuisine in an intimate
★ setting. The specialty is veal topped with a light cream and mushroom sauce; other dishes include fish and duck à l'orange. ⊠ *22 Kingstown Rd.,* ☎ *401/789–3743. AE, DC, MC, V. Closed Mon.–Tues. and Oct.–June. No lunch.*

$$$ ✕ **Coast Guard House.** This restaurant, which dates to 1888, has candlelighted tables and picture windows that overlook the ocean on three sides. The menu offers a range of typical American fare—seafood, pasta, and meat entrées. Friday and Saturday nights see entertainment in the Oak Room and a DJ in the upstairs lounge. ⊠ *40 Ocean Rd.,* ☎ *401/789–0700. AE, D, DC, MC, V.*

$$–$$$ 🏨 **The Richards.** Imposing and magnificent, this English manor–style mansion has some rooms with antiques, floral-upholstered furniture, and fireplaces. From the wood-paneled common rooms downstairs, French windows allow views of a lush landscape. ⊠ *144 Gibson Ave., 02882,* ☎ *401/789–7746. 5 rooms. No credit cards.*

$$–$$$ 🏨 **Stone Lea.** This spacious house is more than 100 years old and is filled with period furniture. The atmosphere is rather stiff, but the location is wonderful, with a lawn that rolls down to the sea. Ocean-facing rooms have panoramic views, with the most striking from Numbers 1 and 7. ⊠ *40 Newton Ave., 02882,* ☎ *401/783–9546. 9 rooms. Billiards, piano. Full breakfast. No credit cards.*

Beaches

The southern coast of Rhode Island boasts mile after mile of beautiful, mostly sandy ocean beaches with clear, clean water. The best are at **Westerly, Charlestown, South Kingstown,** and **Narragansett.**

Shopping

On Route 1A in Charlestown is one of the most unusual shopping experiences in New England: The **Fantastic Umbrella Factory** (☎ 401/364–6616) has three rustic shops and a barn built around a spectacular wild garden. Flowers, greeting cards, kites, crafts, tapestries, jewelry, and goods from around the world are sold in the backyard bazaar. There is also an art gallery and a café that serves organic foods.

NEWPORT

Bounded on three sides by water, Newport is one of the great sailing cities of the world. It is also host to world-class music festivals, as well as international tennis tournaments. The city's first period of prosperity, the Golden Age, ran from 1720 to the 1770s. Many homes and shops built in that era still stand in the Colonial section of the city. In the 19th century during what became known as the Gilded Age, Newport was a summer playground for America's wealthiest families.

Visitor Information

Newport County: Convention and Visitors Bureau (✉ 23 America's Cup Ave., Newport 02840, ☎ 401/849–8048 or 800/326–6030).

Arriving and Departing

By Bus
Greyhound Lines (☎ 800/231–2222). **Bonanza Bus Lines** (☎ 401/751–8800).

By Plane
Newport State Airport (☎ 401/846–2200) is 3 mi northeast of Newport.

Exploring Newport

Colonial Newport has nearly 200 pre–Revolutionary War buildings. Thames Street is its main thoroughfare, while Washington Street has some of the city's finest examples of Colonial architecture.

★ The 1748 **Hunter House** is recognizable by the carved pineapple over the doorway, a symbol of hospitality. The elliptical arch in the central hall is a typical Newport detail. ✉ *54 Washington St.,* ☎ *401/847–1000. Closed Nov.–Mar., weekdays Apr. and Oct.*

The **Brick Market,** built in 1760, was designed by Peter Harrison, who was also responsible for the city's Touro Synagogue and Redwood Library. The building was first used as a theater, then as a town hall; today it houses the **Museum of Newport History** (☎ 401/841–8770). The **Colony House** (☎ 401/846–2980) faces the Brick Market on Washington Square. Built in 1739, it was the government's headquarters, and from its balcony the Declaration of Independence was read to Newporters. Tours are given by appointment.

Newport's oldest house, the **Wanton-Lyman-Hazard House,** has a two-room plan typical of the time. ✉ *17 Broadway,* ☎ *401/846–0813.*

The **White Horse Tavern,** in operation since 1687, has a large fireplace and cozy yet elegant tables that epitomize Newport's Colonial charm. ✉ *Marlborough St.,* ☎ *401/849–3600.*

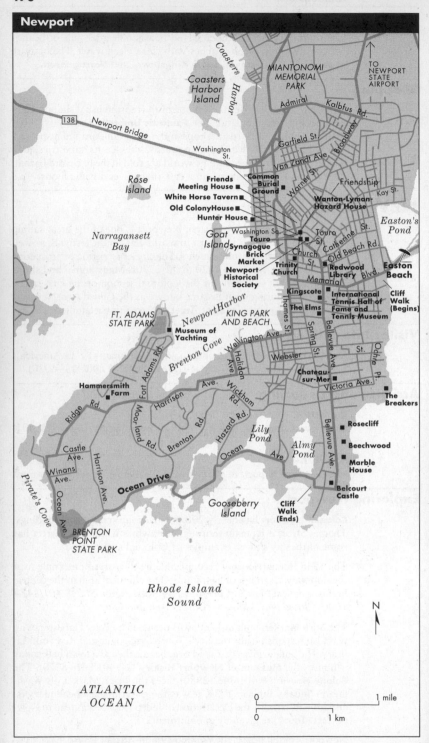

The **Friends Meeting House** (⊠ 29 Farewell St., ☎ 401/846–0813) was built in 1699 and is the oldest Quaker meeting house in America; tours are by appointment. **Touro Synagogue** (⊠ 85 Touro St., ☎ 401/847–4794), the oldest synagogue in the country, dedicated in 1763, is very simple on the outside but elaborate within.

The headquarters of the **Newport Historical Society** houses a small museum with a collection of Newport memorabilia, furniture, and maritime items. This, along with the Gateway Center, is a departure point for walking tours of Newport; call for times. ⊠ 82 Touro St., ☎ 401/846–0813. Closed Sat.–Mon.

Trinity Church (⊠ Queen Anne Sq., ☎ 401/846–0660), built in 1724, has a three-tier wineglass pulpit, the only one of its kind in America. The 1748 **Redwood Library** is the oldest library in continuous use in the United States. It houses a collection of paintings by early American artists. ⊠ 50 Bellevue Ave., ☎ 401/847–0292. Closed Sun.

The **Newport Art Museum and Art Association** exhibits Rhode Island art past and present. ⊠ 76 Bellevue Ave., ☎ 401/848–8200.

The **International Tennis Hall of Fame and Tennis Museum** is in a magnificent Stanford White building, the Newport Casino. ⊠ 194 Bellevue Ave., ☎ 401/849–3990.

Six Newport mansions are maintained by the **Preservation Society of Newport County** (☎ 401/847–1000). A combination ticket gives you a discount on individual admission prices. Each mansion gives guided tours that last about an hour. To avoid long lines on summer days, go early or tour the less popular mansions like the Elms, Kingscote, and Belcourt Castle.

Kingscote was built in 1839 for a plantation owner from Savannah, Georgia. It is furnished with antique furniture, glass and Asian art, and has a number of Tiffany windows. ⊠ Bowery St. off Bellevue Ave. Closed Nov.–Mar.; weekdays Apr. and Oct.

The Elms is one of Newport's most graceful mansions. Classical in design, it has a broad lawn, fountains, and formal gardens. ⊠ Bellevue Ave. Closed weekdays Nov.–Mar.

Chateau-sur-Mer, the first of Bellevue Avenue's stone mansions, is modest compared to the opulence of later "cottages." ⊠ Bellevue Ave. Closed weekdays Nov.–Apr.

★ **The Breakers** was built in 1893 for Cornelius Vanderbilt II. This 70-room palace took more than 2,500 workers two years to complete and required 40 servants to keep it running. ⊠ Ochre Point Ave. Closed weekdays Nov.–Mar.

Modeled on the Grand Trianon at Versailles, **Rosecliff** has a heart-shape staircase designed by Stanford White. Built in 1902, this 40-room mansion has appeared in several movies, including *The Great Gatsby* and *True Lies*. ⊠ Bellevue Ave. Closed Nov.–Mar.

The last of the Preservation Society's Bellevue Avenue properties is the **Marble House.** Known for its extravagant gold ballroom, this palace in marble was the gift of William Vanderbilt to his wife in 1892. ⊠ Bellevue Ave. Closed Nov.–Dec., weekdays Jan.–Mar.

At **Beechwood,** built for the Astors, actors in period costume play the parts of family members, servants, and household guests. ⊠ 580 Bellevue Ave., ☎ 401/846–3777. Closed Mon.–Thurs. Feb.–Apr.

Belcourt Castle was designed by Richard Morris Hunt, based on Louis XIII's hunting lodge. The castle contains an enormous collection of

European and Asian treasures. ⊠ *Bellevue Ave.,* ☎ *401/846–0669 or 401/849–1566. Closed weekdays Jan.*

Hammersmith Farm was the childhood summer home of Jacqueline Bouvier and the site of her wedding to John F. Kennedy. The house has a trove of Bouvier and Kennedy memorabilia. The gardens were designed by Frederick Law Olmsted. ⊠ *Ocean Dr. near Fort Adams,* ☎ *401/846–7346. Closed mid-Nov.–Feb., with special openings during Christmastime.*

Fort Adams State Park is a Revolutionary War–era fort (named after John Quincy Adams) and is now the site of the annual Newport jazz and folk festivals. The **Museum of Yachting,** on the grounds of Fort Adams Park, has four galleries of pictures. ⊠ *Ocean Dr.,* ☎ *401/847–1018. Closed Nov.–Apr.*

What to See and Do With Children

Old Colony & Newport Railway (⊠ 19 America's Cup Ave., ☎ 401/624–6951), a vintage diesel train, follows an 8-mi route along Narragansett Bay from Newport to Portsmouth's Green Animals Topiary Gardens.

Dining and Lodging

Traditional Rhode Island fare includes johnnycake, a sort of corn cake cooked on a griddle, and quahogs (pronounced *ko*-hawgs), local clams. Particularly popular are shore dinners, which include clam chowder, steamers, clam cakes, baked sausage, corn on the cob, lobster, watermelon, and Indian pudding (a steamed pudding made with cornmeal and molasses).

While the big chain hotels are represented in Rhode Island, many visitors prefer to stay in smaller inns and bed-and-breakfasts. For help with reservations, contact **Bed and Breakfast of Rhode Island, Inc.** (⊠ Box 3291, Newport 02840, ☎ 401/849–1298). Entering Newport from the direction of Providence, you will find more than a dozen motels where room rates are considerably lower than those downtown. Along the south shore there are many small motels on Routes 1 and 1A, especially in Westerly, and on the Post Road in North Kingstown. For price ranges *see* Charts 1 (A) and 2 (A) *in* On the Road with Fodor's.

$$$$ ✕ **Black Pearl.** Known to sailors throughout the world, this waterfront restaurant has a tavern for casual fare and a more formal dining room. Tuna with red-pepper sauce and oysters warmed with truffles and cream are two typical appetizers. Entrées may include swordfish or duck breast with green-peppercorn sauce. ⊠ *Bannister's Wharf,* ☎ *401/846–5264. Reservations essential. Jacket required. AE, DC, MC, V.*

$$$ ✕ **Scales & Shells.** A large blackboard serves as the menu at this ex-
★ cellent, informal though sometimes noisy restaurant. As many as 15 different types of extremely fresh fish are prepared in a display kitchen. ⊠ *527 Thames St.,* ☎ *401/848–9378. Reservations not accepted. No credit cards.*

$$ ✕ **Puerini's.** The aroma of garlic and basil wafts through this friendly
★ neighborhood restaurant. The long menu includes green noodles with chicken in Marsala wine sauce, tortellini with seafood, and *cavatelli* with four cheeses. ⊠ *24 Memorial Blvd.,* ☎ *401/847–5506. Reservations not accepted. No credit cards. Closed Mon. in winter. No lunch.*

$$$$ ▥ **Francis Malbone House.** This stately 1760 house, which is furnished
★ with period reproductions, has a resplendent courtyard with a foun-

tain. Some guest rooms have whirlpool tubs and fireplaces. The large corner rooms face either the garden or the street and harbor beyond; most rooms have working fireplaces. ⊠ *392 Thames St., 02840,* ☎ *401/846–0392. 18 rooms. Full breakfast. AE, MC, V.*

$$$$ 🏨 **Inn at Castle Hill.** On an ocean-side cliff at the mouth of Narragansett
★ Bay and 3 mi from the center of Newport, this rambling inn was built as a summer home in 1874, and much of the original furniture remains. The inn's Sunday brunches are famous—be sure to make reservations (also closed November–March). ⊠ *Ocean Dr., 02840,* ☎ *401/849–3800. 21 rooms. Restaurant, 3 beaches. CP. AE, MC, V.*

$$$ 🏨 **Ivy Lodge.** This grand Victorian (small by Newport's standards, but
★ mansionesque anywhere else) has gables and a Gothic turret. The defining feature is a Gothic 33-ft paneled oak entryway with a three-story turned baluster staircase and a wrought-iron chandelier. The wraparound front porch with cushioned wicker chairs is popular with summer guests. ⊠ *12 Clay St., 02840,* ☎ *401/849–6865. 8 rooms. AE, MC, V.*

$ 🏨 **Harbour Base Pineapple Inn.** This basic, clean motel is the least expensive lodging in Newport. All rooms have two double beds; some have kitchenettes. Close to the navy base and jai alai, it's a five-minute drive from downtown. ⊠ *372 Coddington Hwy., 02840,* ☎ *401/847–2600. 48 rooms. AE, D, DC, MC, V.*

Nightlife

For a sampling of Newport's lively nightlife, you need only stroll down **Thames Street** after dark. The **Newport Blues Cafe** (⊠ 286 Thames St., ☎ 401/841–5510) presents the best in live blues. For a classy bar, try the **Candy Store** (⊠ Bannister's Wharf, ☎ 401/849–2900), in the Clarke Cooke House restaurant. **Thames Street Station** (⊠ 337 America's Cup Ave., ☎ 401/849–9480) plays high-energy dance music and books live rock bands Monday through Thursday in summer. **One Pelham East** (⊠ 270 Thames St., ☎ 401/847–9460) draws a young crowd for progressive rock, reggae, and R&B.

Outdoor Activities and Sports

Biking
Ten Speed Spokes rents bikes (⊠ 18 Elm St., ☎ 401/847–5609).

Boating
Old Port Marine Services (⊠ Sayer's Wharf, ☎ 401/847–9109) offers harbor tours and daily and weekly crewed yacht charters. **Sail Newport** (⊠ Fort Adams State Park, ☎ 401/846–1983) rents sailboats by the hour. **Adventure Sports Rentals** (⊠ The Inn at Long Wharf, America's Cup Ave., ☎ 401/849–4820) rents waverunners, sailboats, kayaks, and canoes.

Beaches

Easton's Beach (⊠ Memorial Blvd.), also known as First Beach, is popular for its children's aquarium and other amusements. **Fort Adams State Park** (⊠ Ocean Dr.) has a small, sheltered beach with a picnic area, lifeguards, and beautiful views of Newport Harbor.

Shopping

Newport is a city for shoppers, though not for bargain hunters. Its specialties include antiques, traditional clothing, and marine supplies. Art galleries, antiques shops, and clothing boutiques line Thames, Franklin, and Spring streets. The **Brick Market** area between Thames Street and

America's Cup Avenue has some 50 shops with crafts, clothing, antiques, and toys. **Bowen's and Bannister's wharves** have shops with a nautical theme.

Side Trip to Block Island

Arriving and Departing

BY FERRY

Interstate Navigation Co. (✉ Galilee State Pier, Narragansett, ☎ 401/783–4613) has ferry service from Galilee to Block Island. From Memorial Day to October a passenger boat runs daily from Providence to Block Island via Newport. **Nelesco Navigation Co.** (✉ 2 Ferry St., New London, CT, ☎ 860/442–7891) offers car and passenger ferry service from New London to Block Island daily from June to September.

BY PLANE

Block Island State Airport (☎ 401/466-5511) is the state's second-busiest tarmac. New England Airlines offers regularly scheduled service to Block Island from **Westerly State Airport** (☎ 401/596–2460 or 800/243–2460).

What to See and Do

Newport (along with Galilee) is a jumping-off point for Block Island, 12 mi off the coast. Despite its popularity, the 11-square-mi island's beauty and privacy are intact. Its freshwater ponds are a haven for migrating birds; its harbors are a sanctuary for sailors; its beaches (especially Mansion Beach) are pristine and uncrowded; and its narrow roads and walking trails are ideal for relaxed exploring. The **Block Island Chamber of Commerce** (✉ Drawer D, Water St., 02807, ☎ 401/466–2982) can help with reservations at hotels and guest houses.

PROVIDENCE

Providence, Rhode Island's capital, is 30 mi north of Newport. Founded by Roger Williams in 1635 as a refuge for freethinkers and religious dissenters, the city is home to major forces in New England's intellectual and cultural life, like Brown University, the Rhode Island School of Design (RISD), and the Trinity Square Repertory Company. Historic walking-tour maps of the city are available at the Visitor Information Center (☞ Visitor Information, *below*).

Four Brown brothers had a major part in Providence's development in the 18th century. John Brown opened trade with China and aided the American Revolution. Joseph Brown's architectural designs changed the face of the city. Moses Brown founded the Quaker school that bears his name. Nicholas Brown rescued the failing Rhode Island College—known today as Brown University.

Visitor Information

Providence Visitor Information Center (✉ Clock Tower Building, Waterplace Park, ☎ 401/751–5069). **Greater Providence:** Convention and Visitors Bureau (✉ 30 Exchange Terr., 02903, ☎ 800/233–1636 or 401/274–1636).

Arriving and Departing

By Bus

Greyhound Lines (☎ 800/231–2222). **Bonanza Bus Lines** (☎ 401/751–8800). **Rhode Island Public Transit Authority** (☎ 401/781–9400, 401/847–0209 or 800/662–5088 in RI) provides local transportation in Providence and some service to other parts of the state.

By Car

I–95 cuts diagonally across the state and is the fastest route to Providence from Boston, coastal Connecticut, and New York City. I–195 links Providence with New Bedford and Cape Cod. U.S. 1 follows the coast east from Connecticut before turning north to Providence.

By Plane

The **Theodore Francis Green State Airport** (☎ 401/737–4000), 3 mi northeast of Warwick and 5 mi south of Providence, is served by major U.S. airlines and regional carriers.

By Train

Amtrak (☎ 800/872–7245) stops at Westerly, Kingston, and Providence's Union Station (✉ 100 Gaspee St.).

Exploring Providence

The **Providence Athenaeum,** established in 1753, is one of the oldest lending libraries in the world. It displays Rhode Island art and artifacts, as well as an original set of the folio *Birds of America* prints by John J. Audubon. ✉ *251 Benefit St.,* ☎ *401/421–6970. Closed Sun.*

The **Rhode Island School of Design Museum of Art** is small but comprehensive and exhibits textiles, Japanese prints, Paul Revere silver, 18th-century porcelain, French Impressionist paintings, and a mummy dating from circa 300 BC. ✉ *224 Benefit St.,* ☎ *401/454–6100. Free Sat. Closed Mon.*

Also on **Benefit Street**—known as the Mile of History—is a long row of small early Federal and 19th-century candy-color houses crammed shoulder to shoulder on a steep hill overlooking downtown Providence.

Market House (✉ Market Sq., between S. Water St. and S. Main St.) was designed by Joseph Brown. Tea was burned here in March 1775, and the upper floors were used as a barracks during the Revolutionary War. The **Arcade,** built in 1828, was America's first indoor shopping mall. Now a National Historic Landmark, the three-story Greek Revival Arcade still houses shops. ✉ *65 Weybosset St.,* ☎ *401/272–2340. Closed Sun.*

The **First Unitarian Church of Providence,** built in 1816, houses the largest bell ever cast in Paul Revere's foundry—a 2,500 pounder. ✉ *1 Benevolent St.,* ☎ *401/421–7970. Guided tours by appointment.*

The **Rhode Island State House** was built in 1900. Its dome is one of the world's largest, modeled after St. Peter's Basilica in Rome. On display is the original parchment charter granted by King Charles to the colony of Rhode Island in 1663. ✉ *82 Smith St.,* ☎ *401/277–2357. Closed weekends.*

Roger Williams was so integral to the concepts leading to the Declaration of Independence and the Constitution that the National Park Service dedicated the 4.5-acre **Roger Williams National Memorial** to his memory. Displays offer a quick course in the life and times of Rhode Island's founder. ✉ *282 N. Main St.,* ☎ *401/521–7266. Free.*

Just below the State House is the city's newest attraction, **Waterplace Park and Riverwalk,** a 4-acre park with Venetian-style footbridges, cobblestone walkways, and an amphitheater encircling a tidal pond on the Providence River. Completed in 1997, Waterplace Park is the crowning touch of the city's continuing revitalization efforts. ✉ *The Pavilion, 2 American Express Way,* ☎ *401/751–1177.*

The **John Brown House** was designed in 1786 by Joseph Brown for his brother. This three-story Georgian mansion has elaborate woodwork

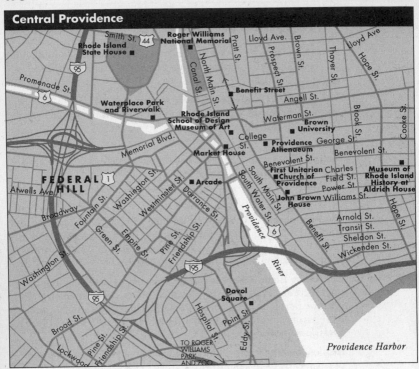

Central Providence

Providence Harbor

and furniture, silver, linens, Chinese porcelain, and an antique doll collection. ⊠ *52 Power St.,* ☎ *401/331–8575. Closed weekdays Jan.–Feb.*

At the **Museum of Rhode Island History at Aldrich House,** an 1822 Federal house, the Rhode Island Historical Society presents a variety of informative exhibits on the history, culture, and architecture of Rhode Island. ⊠ *110 Benevolent St.,* ☎ *401/331–8575. Closed Mon.*

What to See and Do with Children

Roger Williams Park and Zoo (⊠ Elmwood Ave., ☎ 401/785–3510) is a stunningly beautiful 430-acre Victorian park. The zoo is home to more than 900 animals and 150 different species; in the park you can have a picnic, feed the ducks in the lakes, ride a pony, or rent a paddleboat.

Dining and Lodging

$$$ ✕ **Al Forno.** This restaurant cemented Providence's reputation as one
★ of the culinary centers of New England. Out of the massive kitchen comes impeccable food, served by the best waitstaff in the city. The entrées, such as oven-roasted chicken cakes with applesauce, as well as sinful desserts like strawberry-and-rhubarb tart, are all made with fresh local ingredients. ⊠ *577 S. Main St.,* ☎ *401/273–9760. Reservations not accepted. AE, MC, V. Closed Sun.–Mon.*

$$$ ✕ **Pot au Feu.** As night falls, business-driven downtown Providence
★ clears out, and this bastion of French country cuisine lights up. For a quarter of a century Pot au Feu has worked to perfect the basics, like pâté de foie gras, beef bourguignonne, and potatoes au gratin. The downstairs Bistro offers a more casual dining experience. ⊠ *44 Custom House St.,* ☎ *401/273–8953. AE, DC, MC, V. Upstairs salon closed Sun.–Mon.*

$$ ╳ **Camille's.** Of all the Italian restaurants on Federal Hill, this is perhaps the most classical. Valet parking, black-tie service, and reproductions of early Renaissance murals lend sophistication to this fairly priced restaurant that serves traditional Florentine fare. ⊠ *71 Bradford St.,* ☎ *401/751–4812. Closed Sun. July–Aug.*

$$$ ⊞ **Providence Biltmore.** The Biltmore, completed in 1922, has a sleek
★ Art Deco exterior, Old World charm, and an external glass elevator that offers attractive views of Providence at night. The attentiveness of the staff, the downtown location, and a recent face-lift make this an appealing perch from which to explore the city. ⊠ *Kennedy Plaza, 02903,* ☎ *401/421–0700,* FAX *401/421–0210. 238 rooms. Restaurant. AE, DC, MC, V.*

$$$ ⊞ **Marriott.** Although it lacks the Biltmore's old-fashioned elegance, business travelers may prefer the Marriott's larger size and modern conveniences. ⊠ *Charles and Orms Sts., 02904,* ☎ *401/272–2400,* FAX *401/272–2400 . 345 rooms. Restaurant, indoor and outdoor pools, sauna, health club, meeting rooms, free parking. AE, D, DC, MC, V.*

$$ ⊞ **C.C. Ledbetter's.** The somber green exterior of this Benefit Street home belies its vibrant interior—the place is filled with two English springer spaniels, lively art, books, photographs, handmade quilts, and a homey blend of contemporary furnishings and antiques. ⊠ *326 Benefit St., 02903,* ☎ FAX *401/351–4699. 5 rooms. No credit cards.*

$$ ⊞ **Days Hotel on the Harbor.** This modern hotel offers a sense of openness once you get past its small lobby. Rooms have views of either the harbor or speeding traffic on I–95. ⊠ *220 India St., 02903,* ☎ *401/ 272–5577,* FAX *401/272–5577, ext. 199. 136 rooms. Restaurant, hot tub, exercise room, meeting rooms, airport shuttle, free parking. AE, D, DC, MC, V.*

Nightlife

Oliver's (⊠ 83 Benevolent St., ☎ 401/272–8795), a hangout for Brown University students, has a pool table and good pub food. The **Hot Club** (⊠ 575 S. Water St., ☎ 401/861–9007) is just that—a hip place with plants, a jukebox, and nice lighting. **Lupo's Heartbreak Hotel** (⊠ 239 Westminster St., ☎ 401/272–5876) is legendary for great rock and blues acts in an intimate club setting. **Snookers** (⊠ 145 Clifford St., ☎ 401/351–7665) is a classy billiards hall in the up-and-coming Jewelry District; in the same space is a hip lounge called the Green Room.

Outdoor Activities and Sports

Biking

For information on trails, call the **Department of Public Parks** (☎ 401/ 785–9450). The **East Bay Bicycle Path** is a 14½-mi paved trail linking Providence's India Point Park to Bristol.

Shopping

Wickenden Street has the greatest concentration of antiques stores, as well as several art galleries. The **Cat's Pajamas** (⊠ 227 Wickenden St., ☎ 401/751–8440) specializes in 1920s–1960s jewelry, linens, housewares, accessories, and small furnishings. **CAV** (⊠ 14 Imperial Pl., ☎ 401/751–9164) is a restaurant, bar, and coffeehouse in a revamped factory space that sells fine rugs, tapestries, prints, portraits, and antiques. **Tilden-Thurber** (⊠ 292 Westminster St., ☎ 401/272–3200) has high-end Colonial- and Victorian-era furniture and other antiques.

VERMONT

Updated by
Anne Peracca

Capital	Montpelier
Population	589,000
Motto	Freedom and Unity
State Bird	Hermit thrush
State Flower	Red clover
Postal Abbreviation	VT

Statewide Visitor Information

Vermont Travel Division (✉ 134 State St., Montpelier 05602, ☎ 802/828–3236 or 800/837–6668). **Vermont Chamber of Commerce** (✉ Box 37, Montpelier 05601, ☎ 802/223–3443).

Scenic Drives

Route 100 passes through small towns that serve ski areas, the eastern edge of Green Mountain National Forest, Mad River valley, and Stowe, then continues on to Canada.

National and State Parks

National Park

The 355,000-acre **Green Mountain National Forest** (✉ 231 N. Main St., Rutland 05701, ☎ 802/747–6700) runs through the center of the state, from Bristol south to the Massachusetts border.

State Parks

The 40 parks owned and maintained by the **Department of Forests, Parks, and Recreation** (✉ Waterbury 05676, ☎ 802/241–3655) offer nature and hiking trails, campsites, swimming, boating facilities, and fishing. Especially popular are the **Champlain Islands** sites: Burton Island, Kill Kare, and Sand Bar.

SOUTHERN VERMONT

Southern Vermont is the cradle of the state's tradition of independence and rebellion. Many of the towns with village greens and white-spired churches were founded in the early 18th century as frontier outposts and later became trading centers. In the western region the Green Mountain Boys fought off both the British and land-hungry New Yorkers. The influx of new residents in the past 20 years means the quaintness often comes with a patina of sophistication or funk; shoppers can find not only antiques but New Age crystals, Vermont-made salsa, and the highest-tech ski gear.

Visitor Information

Bennington: Chamber of Commerce (✉ Veterans Memorial Dr., 05201, ☎ 802/447–3311). **Brattleboro:** Chamber of Commerce (✉ 180 Main St., 05301, ☎ 802/254–4565). **Manchester and the mountains:** Chamber of Commerce (✉ 2 Main St., R.R. 2, Box 3451, 05255, ☎ 802/362–2100). **Rutland:** Chamber of Commerce, Convention and Visitors Division (✉ 256 N. Main St., 05701, ☎ 802/773–2747). **Woodstock:** Chamber of Commerce (✉ 4 Central St., Box 486, 05091, ☎ 802/457–3555).

Arriving and Departing

By Bus
Vermont Transit (☎ 802/864–6811 or 800/552–8737). **Bonanza Bus Lines** (☎ 800/556–3815).

By Car
I–91 runs north–south along the eastern edge of Vermont. U.S. 7 goes north–south through western Vermont, and Route 9 runs east–west across the state through Bennington and Brattleboro.

By Train
Amtrak (☎ 800/872–7245) stops at Brattleboro, Bellows Falls, Rutland, and White River Junction.

Exploring Southern Vermont

It was at **Bennington** that Ethan Allen formed the Green Mountain Boys, who helped capture Fort Ticonderoga in 1775. The **Bennington Battle Monument** (⊠ 15 Monument Ave., ☎ 802/447–0550), a 306-ft stone obelisk, commemorates General John Stark's defeat of the British in their attempt to capture Bennington's stockpile of supplies. It is closed late October–mid-April. Piled at the **Bennington Museum** (⊠ W. Main St. [Rte. 9], ☎ 802/447–1571) is a rich collection of Early American artifacts, including decorative arts and the folk art of Grandma Moses. Here you'll also find the only surviving automobile of Bennington's Martin Company, a 1925 Wasp.

Manchester has been a popular summer retreat since the mid-19th century, when Mary Todd Lincoln visited. Its tree-shaded marble sidewalks and stately old houses reflect the luxurious resort lifestyle of a century ago, while upscale factory-outlet stores appeal to the ski crowd. **Hildene** (⊠ Rte. 7A, 2 mi south of intersection with Rtes. 11 and 30, ☎ 802/362–1788), the 412-acre summer home of Abraham Lincoln's son Robert, has Georgian Revival symmetry and formal gardens and is closed late October–mid-May.

The **American Museum of Fly Fishing** displays the tackle of such noted anglers as Jimmy Carter, Winslow Homer, and Bing Crosby. ⊠ Rte. 7A, ☎ 802/362–3300. Closed weekends Nov.–Apr.

The steep 5¼-mi drive to the top of **Mt. Equinox** brings you to the **Saddle**, where the views are outstanding. ⊠ Rte. 7A, ☎ 802/362–1114. Closed Nov.–Apr.

In **Rutland** there are strips of shopping centers and a seemingly endless row of traffic lights. The **Chaffee Center for the Visual Arts** (⊠ 16 Main St., ☎ 802/775–0356) houses the work of more than 200 Vermont artists. At the **Vermont Marble Exhibit,** northwest of Rutland, visitors can watch the transformation of the rough stone into slabs, blocks, and gift items. ⊠ Off Rte. 3, Proctor, ☎ 802/459–3311. Closed Sun. Nov.–late May.

Woodstock is the quintessential quiet New England town, on the eastern side of Vermont on U.S. 4. Exquisitely preserved Federal houses surround the tree-lined village green. The **Vermont Institute of Natural Science's Raptor Center** has nature trails and 26 living species of birds of prey. ⊠ Church Hill Rd., ☎ 802/457–2779. Closed Sun. Nov.–Apr.

A half-mile north of the center of Woodstock, the reconstructed farmhouse, school, and general store at the **Billings Farm and Museum** demonstrate the daily activities of early Vermonters. ⊠ Rte. 12, ☎ 802/457–2355. Closed Jan.–May and weekdays Nov.–Dec.

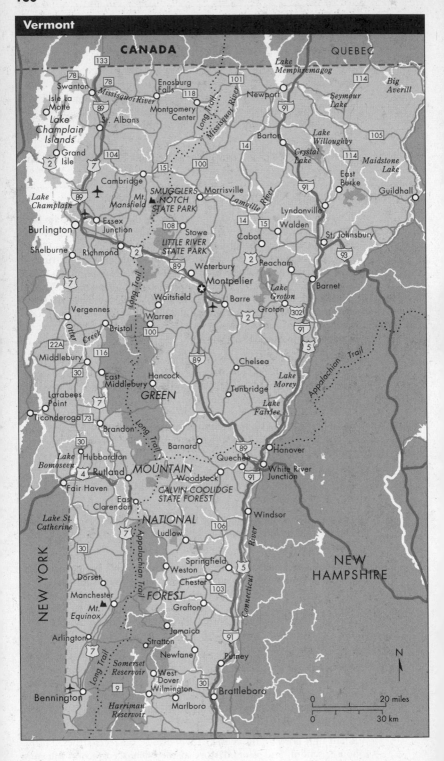

Vermont

The mile-long **Quechee Gorge** is visible from U.S. 4, but you can also scramble down one of the several descents. **Quechee** is perched astride the Ottauquechee River. On weekdays you can watch potters and glassblowers at **Simon Pearce** (⊠ Main St., ☎ 802/295–2711).

Dining and Lodging

For price ranges *see* Charts 1 (B) and 2 (B) *in* On the Road with Fodor's.

Bennington

$$$ ✕ **Main Street Café.** A few minutes from downtown, this small 1860 storefront café with tin ceilings draws raves for its northern Italian cuisine and chic but casual atmosphere. ⊠ *Rte. 67A, North Bennington,* ☎ *802/442–3210. AE, DC, MC, V. Closed Mon. No lunch.*

$$ ✕ **The Brasserie.** Chefs create hearty and creative fare using mostly local produce and organic foods. The decor is as clean-lined as the Bennington pottery sold in the same complex. ⊠ *324 County St.,* ☎ *802/447–7922. MC, V. Closed Tues.*

$$–$$$ 🏠 **South Shire Inn.** Canopy beds in plushly carpeted rooms, ornate plaster molding on the ceilings, and the mahogany fireplace in the library add up to turn-of-the-century grandeur in a quiet residential neighborhood. Most rooms have fireplaces; some have whirlpool baths. ⊠ *124 Elm St., 05201,* ☎ *802/447–3839,* 🆙 *802/442–3547. 9 rooms. AE, MC, V.*

$$ 🏠 **Molly Stark Inn.** This gem of a bed-and-breakfast makes you feel
★ as if you were staying with old friends. Blue-plaid wallpaper, gleaming hardwood floors, antique furnishings, and a wood stove in the brick alcove of the sitting room give a country charm to this 1860 Queen Anne Victorian. ⊠ *1067 E. Main St., 05201,* ☎ *802/442–9631 or 800/ 356–3076,* 🆙 *802/442–5224. 6 rooms. AE, D, MC, V.*

Manchester

$$–$$$ ✕ **Bistro Henry's.** Just outside town, this spacious restaurant attracts a devoted clientele for its authentic French bistro fare, extensive wine list, and attention to detail. Popular items are braised lamb shank with balsamic glazed onions served with garlic mashed potatoes and a Moroccan vegetable *tagine* (stew) with couscous. ⊠ *Rte. 11/30, Manchester,* ☎ *802/362–4982. AE, DC, MC, V. Closed Mon.*

$$ ✕ **Quality Restaurant.** The model for Norman Rockwell's *War News,* this family-owned spot serves sturdy New England standbys, such as hot, open-face roast beef or turkey sandwiches with gravy. ⊠ *Main St.,* ☎ *802/362–9839. AE, MC, V.*

$$$–$$$$ ✕🏠 **The Equinox.** This grand white-columned resort was a landmark on Vermont's tourism scene even before Abraham Lincoln's family began summering here. Rooms have pine furnishings, and the front porch is perfect for watching the passing parade. There's a medically supervised spa program and a falconry school. ⊠ *Rte. 7A, Manchester Village 05254,* ☎ *802/362–4700 or 800/362–4747,* 🆙 *802/362–4861. 155 rooms, 10 3-bedroom town houses. Restaurant, bar, 2 pools, golf course, tennis courts, health club. AE, D, DC, MC, V.*

$$$ 🏠 **1811 House.** Staying here is like staying at an elegant English country
★ house filled with antiques. The pub-style bar is decorated with horse brasses and equestrian paintings. No smoking is permitted. ⊠ *Rte. 7A, 05254,* ☎ *802/362–1811 or 800/432–1811. 11 rooms, 3 cottages. Lounge. AE, D, MC, V.*

$$ ⊡ **Barnstead Innstead.** This 1830s barn was transformed in 1968 into a handful of rooms that combine exposed beams and barn-board walls with modern plumbing and cheerful wallpaper. ✉ *Rte. 30, 05255,* ☎ *802/362–1619 or 800/331–1619,* FAX *802/362–1619. 14 rooms. Pool. AE, MC, V.*

Rutland

$$ ✕ **Back Home Cafe.** Wooden booths, black-and-white linoleum tile,
★ and exposed brick lend atmosphere at this second-story café where dinner might be chicken breast stuffed with roasted red peppers and goat cheese. There is often weekend entertainment. ✉ *21 Center St.,* ☎ *802/ 775–9313. AE, MC, V.*

$$ ⊡ **Comfort Inn.** Rooms at this chain hotel are a cut above the standard, with an upholstered wing chair and blond-wood furnishings. ✉ *19 Allen St., 05701,* ☎ *802/775–2200 or 800/432–6788,* FAX *802/775– 2694. 104 rooms. Restaurant, indoor pool, exercise room. CP. AE, D, DC, MC, V.*

$–$$ ⊡ **Inn at Rutland.** In this Victorian mansion an ornate oak staircase leads to rooms with such turn-of-the-century touches as botanical prints, elaborate ceiling moldings, and frosted glass. ✉ *70 N. Main St., 05701,* ☎ *802/773–0575 or 800/808–0575,* FAX *802/775–3506. 10 rooms. Hot tub. D, DC, MC, V.*

Woodstock

$$$ ✕ **The Prince and the Pauper.** Nouvelle French dishes with a Vermont
★ accent are served prix fixe in a romantically candlelighted Colonial setting. ✉ *24 Elm St.,* ☎ *802/457–1818. D, MC, V. No lunch.*

$$ ✕ **Bentleys.** Antique silk-fringed lamp shades and long lace curtains lend a tongue-in-cheek Victorian air to burgers, chili, homemade soups, and entrées like duck with raspberry puree. ✉ *3 Elm St.,* ☎ *802/457– 3232. AE, DC, MC, V.*

$$$–$$$$ ✕⊡ **Kedron Valley Inn.** One of the state's oldest hotels—built in the 1840s—has rooms decorated with family quilts and antiques. The motel units in back have exposed log walls. The dining room prepares dishes using classic French technique on Vermont ingredients. ✉ *Rte. 106, 05071,* ☎ *802/457–1473,* FAX *802/457–4469. 27 rooms. Restaurant, lounge, pond, beach. AE, D, MC, V. Closed Apr. and 10 days before Thanksgiving.*

$$$–$$$$ ✕⊡ **Woodstock Inn and Resort.** This massive facility presides over the village green like a dowager duchess. The rooms' standard modern ash furnishings are enlivened by patchwork quilts and original Vermont landscape paintings. The dining room (jacket and tie) serves nouvelle New England fare. ✉ *U.S. 4, 05091,* ☎ *802/457–1100 or 800/448– 7900,* FAX *802/457–6699. 146 rooms. Bar, dining room, indoor and outdoor pools, golf course, tennis, croquet, health club, cross-country skiing, downhill skiing. AE, MC, V.*

$$ ✕⊡ **Village Inn at Woodstock.** The rooms in this Victorian mansion are decorated simply with country antiques, chenille bedspreads, and fresh flowers. ✉ *U.S. 4, 05091,* ☎ *802/457–1255 or 800/722–4571,* FAX *802/457–3109. 8 rooms, 6 rooms with bath. Restaurant, lounge. AE, MC, V. Closed mid-Nov.*

Motels

⊡ **Aspen Motel** (✉ Box 548, Manchester Center 05255, ☎ 802/362– 2450, FAX 802/362–1348), 24 rooms, lobby lounge, pool; $$. ⊡ **Pond Ridge Motel** (✉ U.S. 4, Woodstock 05091, ☎ 802/457–1667), 21 rooms; $$. ⊡ **Harwood Hill Motel** (✉ Rte. 7A, Bennington 05201, ☎ 802/ 442–6278), 16 rooms, 3 cottages; $.

Campgrounds

The state park system runs nearly 40 campgrounds with more than 2,000 campsites. Contact the **Department of Forests, Parks, and Recreation** (⊠ Waterbury 05676, ☎ 802/244–8711). The official state map lists private campgrounds.

At **Green Mountain National Forest** (⊠ 231 N. Main St., 05701, ☎ 802/747–6700), you can reserve one campsite area in advance; the remaining areas are first-come, first-served.

Nightlife and the Arts

Like most things in Vermont, nightlife and the arts tend to be low-key. Most nightlife is concentrated at and around the ski resorts. Check local newspapers for listings. The **Marlboro Music Festival** (⊠ Marlboro Music Center, ☎ 802/254–2394 or 215/569–4690 Sept.–June) presents a broad range of chamber music in weekend concerts in July and August. **New England Bach Festival** (⊠ Brattleboro Music Center, ☎ 802/257–4523) is among the best classical music festivals in the country.

Outdoor Activities and Sports

Biking

Vermont Bicycle Touring (⊠ Box 711, Bristol 05443, ☎ 802/453–4811 or 800/245–3868) and **Mad River Bike Shop** (⊠ Rte. 100, Waitsfield, ☎ 802/496–9500) operate guided tours throughout Vermont.

Canoeing

The **Connecticut River** and the **Battenkill** offer easygoing canoe outings. Rentals are available from **Battenkill Canoe** (⊠ Rte. 7A, Arlington, ☎ 802/375–9559).

Fishing

The **Battenkill River** is famous for trout. **Orvis** (⊠ Rte. 7A, Manchester, ☎ 802/362–3900 or 800/235–9763) runs a fly-fishing school. The necessary fishing license is available through tackle shops, or call the **Department of Fish and Wildlife** (☎ 802/241–3700).

Golf

Equinox, in Manchester (☎ 802/362–4700), and **Haystack Country Club,** near Mt. Snow (☎ 802/464–8301), are public 18-hole courses.

Hiking and Backpacking

The southern half of the **Long Trail** is part of the **Appalachian Trail** and runs from just east of Rutland to the state's southern boundary. The **Green Mountain Club** (⊠ Rte. 100, R.R. 1, Box 650, Waterbury Center 05677, ☎ 802/244–7037) maintains the trail, staffs its huts in summer, and maps hiking elsewhere in Vermont.

Ski Areas

For up-to-date snow conditions in the state, call 802/229–0531. All downhill ski areas listed have snowmaking equipment.

Cross-Country

Mt. Snow/Haystack (⊠ 400 Mountain Rd., Mt. Snow 05356, ☎ 802/464–3333), 62 mi of trails. **Stratton** (⊠ Stratton Mountain 05155, ☎ 802/297–2200 or 800/843–6867), 20 mi of trails.

Downhill

Bromley (⊠ Box 1130, Manchester Center 05255, ☎ 802/824–5522), 39 runs, 9 lifts, 1,334-ft vertical drop. **Killington** (⊠ 400 Killington Rd., Killington 05751, ☎ 802/422–3333), 170 runs, gondola, 23 lifts, 3,150-ft drop. **Mt. Snow/Haystack** (⊠ 400 Mountain Rd., Mt. Snow 05356, ☎ 802/422–3333), 130 trails, 24 lifts, 1,700-ft drop. **Stratton** (⊠ Stratton Mountain 05155, ☎ 802/297–2200 or 800/843–6867), 90 slopes, gondola, 11 lifts, 2,000-ft drop.

Shopping

Antiques and traditional and contemporary crafts are everywhere. Particularly good is **U.S. 7** north of Manchester to Danby. The **Vermont Country Store** (⊠ Rte. 100, Weston, ☎ 802/824–3184) is more a way of life than a shop. It carries such forgotten items as Monkey Brand black tooth powder, Flexible Flyer sleds, and pickles in a barrel. **East Meets West** (⊠ Rte. 7, north of Rutland, ☎ 802/773–9030 or 800/443–2242) stocks arts and crafts of native peoples from around the world. The **Bennington Potters Yard** (⊠ 324 County St., ☎ 802/447–7531) has a huge selection of Bennington Pottery factory seconds. **Manchester,** with its designer names and factory outlets, has become to Vermont what Freeport is to Maine.

NORTHERN VERMONT

Northwestern Vermont is less populated and more mountainous than the southern part of the state. This region has the closest thing Vermont has to a seacoast, Lake Champlain; the state capital, Montpelier; and Burlington, Vermont's largest and most cosmopolitan city. Its recorded history dates from 1609, when Samuel de Champlain explored the lake now named for him.

In the northeastern part of the state, known as the Northeast Kingdom, the greatest pleasure is driving through pastoral scenery and discovering charming small towns such as Peacham, Barton, and Craftsbury Common. The area has been a beautiful backdrop for films, including *Ethan Frome* and *Spitfire Grill*.

Visitor Information

Central Vermont: Chamber of Commerce (⊠ Box 336, Barre 05641, ☎ 802/229–5711). **Lake Champlain:** Chamber of Commerce (⊠ 60 Main St., Suite 100, Burlington 05402, ☎ 802/863–3489). **Smugglers' Notch:** Chamber of Commerce (⊠ Box 364, Jeffersonville 05464, ☎ 802/644–2239). **St. Johnsbury Chamber of Commerce** (⊠ 30 Western Ave., 05819, ☎ 802/748–3678). **Stowe:** Area Association (⊠ Main St., Box 1320, Stowe 05672, ☎ 802/253–7321 or 800/247–8693).

Arriving and Departing

By Bus
Vermont Transit (☎ 802/864–6811 or 800/552–8737).

By Car
I–89 runs from White River Junction to Vermont's northwestern corner at the Canadian border. To get to the eastern part of the state, drive up I–91.

By Plane
Burlington Airport (⊠ South Burlington, ☎ 802/863–2874) is 4½ mi east of town off Route 2 and is served by major airlines. Private planes

land at **E. F. Knapp Airport** (☎ 802/223–2221), between Barre and Montpelier.

By Train

Amtrak (☎ 800/872–7245) stops at Montpelier, Waterbury, Essex Junction, and St. Albans.

Exploring Northern Vermont

On the western edge of Vermont, **Middlebury** is Robert Frost country; Vermont's former poet laureate spent 23 summers at a farm near here. The **Robert Frost Wayside Trail,** east of Middlebury on Route 125, winds through quiet woodland and has Frost quotations posted along the way.

★ **Shelburne,** a town on the banks of Lake Champlain, is known for two attractions. The 35 buildings of the 100-acre **Shelburne Museum** (⊠ U.S. 7, 5 mi south of Burlington, ☎ 802/985–3346) contain one of the largest Americana collections in the country. Exhibits include 18th- and 19th-century houses and furniture, fine and folk art, farm tools, carriages and sleighs, and an old side-wheel steamship. At the 1,400-acre **Shelburne Farms** (⊠ East of U.S. 7, 6 mi south of Burlington, ☎ 802/985–8686) visitors can see a working dairy farm, attend nature lectures, or stroll the grounds along a stretch of Lake Champlain's waterfront. The original landscaping, designed by Frederick Law Olmsted, the creator of New York's Central Park, gently channels the eye to expansive vistas.

Burlington is enlivened by the 20,000 students at the University of Vermont. **Church Street Marketplace**—with its down-to-earth shops, chic boutiques, and an appealing menagerie of sidewalk cafés, food and crafts vendors, and street performers—is an animated downtown focal point. There are narrated tours during the day as well as evening dinner-and-dance cruises on a replica of the paddle wheeler that once plied Lake Champlain, the *Spirit of Ethan Allen.* ⊠ *Burlington Boat House,* ☎ *802/862–9685. Closed mid-Oct.–May.*

Smugglers' Notch is the scenic, bouldered pass over Mt. Mansfield said to have given shelter to 18th-century outlaws. There are roadside picnic tables and a spectacular waterfall. Take Route 15 to Jeffersonville; then go south on narrow, twisting Route 108.

Stowe is best known as a venerable ski center. In summer you can take the 4½-mi toll road from Stowe to the top of Vermont's highest peak, **Mt. Mansfield.** At the road's end is a short and beautiful walk. Another way to ascend Mt. Mansfield is in the **gondola** that shuttles from the base of the ski area up 4,393 ft to the section known as the Chin, where there are scenic views and a restaurant. ⊠ *Entrance on Mountain Rd., 8 mi from Rte. 100,* ☎ *802/253–3000.* ☉ *June–late Oct., daily 10–5; Dec.–Apr., daily 8:30–4 for skiers; Oct. and May, weekends 10–5.*

The state capital of **Montpelier,** which has 10,000 residents, is the country's least populated seat of government. The impressive **Vermont State House** has a gleaming gold dome and columns 6 ft in diameter and fashioned from granite from neighboring Barre. ⊠ *State St.,* ☎ *802/828–2228. Closed Sun. and late Oct.–June.*

The **Vermont Museum,** on the ground floor of the Vermont Historical Society offices, has intriguing informative exhibits; its docents can answer New England trivia questions such as, "Why does the area have covered bridges?" ⊠ *109 State St.,* ☎ *802/828–2291. Closed Mon.*

The chief city of the Northeast Kingdom is **St. Johnsbury.** The **Fairbanks Museum and Planetarium** (⊠ Main and Prospect Sts., ☎ 802/

748–2372) engrosses visitors with its eclectic collections of plants, animals, and Vermontiana and a 50-seat planetarium. The **St. Johnsbury Athenaeum** is an architectural gem, with dark paneling, polished Victorian woodwork, and ornate circular staircases that rise to a gallery displaying photographer Albert Bierstadt's Domes of Yosemite. ⊠ *30 Main St.*, ☎ *802/748–8291. Closed Tues., Sun.*

What to See and Do with Children

The University of Vermont's **Morgan Horse Farm** has tours of the stables and paddocks. ⊠ *Follow signs off Rte. 23, 2½ mi from Middlebury,* ☎ *802/388–2011. Closed Nov.–Apr.*

Just south of Stowe is the mecca, the nirvana, the veritable Valhalla for ice cream lovers: **Ben & Jerry's Ice Cream Factory.** ⊠ *Rte. 100, 1 mi north of I–89,* ☎ *802/244–5641.*

Dining and Lodging

For price ranges *see* Charts 1 (B) and 2 (B) *in* On the Road with Fodor's.

Burlington

$$ ✕ **Isabel's.** Inspired American cuisine artfully presented is the hallmark
★   here. The menu changes weekly and has included seafood *alfredo* and eggplant Florentine. Weekend brunch is popular. ⊠ *112 Lake St.,* ☎ *802/865–2522. AE, DC, MC, V. No dinner Sun.–Mon. in winter.*

$–$$ ✕ **Sweet Tomatoes.** The Italian countryside turns up at this boister-
★   ous trattoria, which has a wood-fired oven, hand-painted ceramic pitchers, and crusty bread that comes with a bowl of oil and garlic for dunking. The menu includes caponata, *cavatappi* (pasta with roasted sweet sausage, tomatoes, and black olives), and pizza. ⊠ *83 Church St.,* ☎ *802/660–9533. AE, MC, V.*

$$–$$$$ ✕🏠 **Inn at Shelburne Farms.** Built at the turn of the century as the home
★   of William Seward and Lila Vanderbilt Webb, this Tudor-style inn overlooks Lake Champlain, the distant Adirondacks, and the sea of pastures on this 1,400-acre working farm. Each guest room is different, from the wallpaper to the period antiques. The seasonal menu in the elegant dining room might include Vermont venison tenderloin. ⊠ *Harbor Rd., Shelburne 05482,* ☎ *802/985–8498. 24 rooms. Restaurant, lake, tennis, boating, fishing, recreation rooms. AE, DC, MC, V. Closed mid-Oct.–mid-May.*

$ 🏠 **Marriott Fairfield Inn.** Clean, convenient, and entirely adequate, this hotel-cum-motel fills the niche for travelers in search of no-frills yet dependable accommodations. The spacious rooms, free local calls, and complimentary breakfast indicate a willingness to please. ⊠ *15 S. Park Dr., Colchester 05446,* ☎ 🅵🅰🆇 *802/655–1400. 117 rooms. Pool. CP. AE, D, DC, MC, V.*

Middlebury

$$$ ✕ **Woody's.** In addition to cool jazz, diner-deco light fixtures, and ab-
★   stract paintings, Woody's has a view of Otter Creek just below. The menu has nightly specials that might include Vermont lamb or a vegetarian grill; the seafood mixed grill is very popular. ⊠ *5 Bakery La.,* ☎ *802/388–4182. AE, DC, MC, V.*

$$$ ✕🏠 **Middlebury Inn.** Fluted cream-and-rose columns and a green-marble fireplace in the lobby speak of this 1827 inn's heritage. Rooms in the main building mix formal and country antiques; the 20 motel rooms have quilt hangings and floor-to-ceiling windows. The blue-and-white

Colonial dining room has an all-you-can-eat buffet on selected evenings. ⊠ *Court House Sq., 05753-0798,* ☏ *802/388–4961 or 800/842–4666,* ℻ *802/388–4563. 80 rooms. Restaurant, lounge. AE, D, DC, MC, V.*

Montpelier

$$$ ✕ **The Chef's Table** and the **Main Street Bar and Grill.** The staff at these sister restaurants are students at the New England Culinary Institute. At the Chef's Table, upstairs, the menu changes daily but always offers well-prepared, inventive dishes such as swordfish with spinach and cherry tomatoes. Downstairs at the Grill the atmosphere is more casual but the food no less delicious. ⊠ *118 Main St.,* ☏ *802/229–9202, 802/223–3188 for the Grill. AE, MC, V. Closed Sun.*

$$ ✕ **Horn of the Moon.** The bowls of honey and the bulletin board plastered with political notices hint at Vermont's prominent progressive contingent. This vegetarian restaurant's cuisine includes a little Mexican, a little Thai, a lot of flavor, and not too much tofu. ⊠ *8 Langdon St.,* ☏ *802/223–2895. No credit cards. Closed Mon.*

$$$ ✕⌂ **Inn at Montpelier.** This spacious early 1800s house has architectural detailing, antique four-posters, stately tapestry-upholstered wing chairs, and classical guitar on the stereo. ⊠ *147 Main St., 05602,* ☏ *802/223–2727,* ℻ *802/223–0722. 19 rooms. Restaurant. CP. AE, D, DC, MC, V.*

St. Johnsbury

$$$–$$$$ ✕⌂ **Rabbit Hill Inn.** The Irish pub next door is in contrast to this formal inn. Rooms are as stylistically different as they are consistently indulgent: Some have canopy beds, whirlpool baths, mountain views, and fireplaces. Eclectic, regional cuisine is served in the low-ceiling dining room—perhaps grilled sausage of Vermont pheasant with pistachios. ⊠ *Rte. 18, Lower Waterford 05848,* ☏ *802/748–5168 or 800/762–8669,* ℻ *802/748–8342. 21 rooms. Restaurant, pub, boating, hiking, cross-country skiing. Full breakfast, afternoon tea; MAP available. AE, MC, V. Closed 1st 3 wks in Apr., 1st 2 wks in Nov.*

$$–$$$ ✕⌂ **Wildflower Inn.** Guest rooms in the restored Federal-style main
★ house, as well as in the carriage houses, are decorated simply with both reproductions and contemporary furnishings; nearly all have incredible views of the property's 500 acres. Meals feature hearty country-style food, with homemade breads and vegetables from the garden. ⊠ *North of St. Johnsbury on Darling Hill Rd., Lyndonville 05851,* ☏ *802/626–8310 or 800/627–8310,* ℻ *802/626–3039. 22 rooms. Restaurant, pool, pond, hot tub, sauna, tennis court, fishing, ice-skating, cross-country skiing, sleigh rides, recreation room. Full breakfast, afternoon snacks. MC, V. Closed Apr. and Nov.*

Stowe

$$–$$$ ✕ **Villa Tragara.** A farmhouse interior has been converted into a num-
★ ber of intimate dining nooks where romance reigns. A specialty is fettuccine sautéed with baby shrimp, grilled vegetables, and shiitake and portobello mushrooms, topped with a lobster sauce. ⊠ *Rte. 100, 10 min south of Stowe,* ☏ *802/244–5288. AE, MC, V.*

$$$$ ✕⌂ **Topnotch at Stowe.** The lobby of this resort, one of the state's poshest, has floor-to-ceiling windows, a freestanding circular stone fireplace, and cathedral ceilings. Rooms have thick rust carpet and a barn-board wall or an Italian print. ⊠ *Mountain Rd., Stowe 05672,* ☏ *802/253–8585 or 800/451–8686. 100 rooms, 14 2- and 3-bedroom town houses. Restaurant, lounge, 2 pools, golf course, 12 tennis courts, aerobics, health club, horseback riding, cross-country skiing, sleigh rides. AE, DC, MC, V.*

$$$ ✕🖬 **10 Acres Lodge.** Rooms in the main inn are smaller than those in the newer building on the hill, but all are carefully decorated. Contemporary pottery complements antique horse brasses over the living-room fireplace. The intimate restaurant, which specializes in Continental cuisine, has a menu that changes daily. ⊠ *Barrows Rd. off Luce Hill Rd., 05672,* ☎ *802/253–7638 or 800/327–7357,* ℻ *802/253–4036. 16 rooms, 2 cottages. Restaurant, lounge, pool, hot tub, tennis courts, horseback riding, cross-country skiing. AE, D, MC, V.*

$$ 🖬 **Inn at the Brass Lantern.** Homemade cookies in the afternoon, a freshly filled basket of logs by the fireplace, and stenciled hearts along the wainscoting all speak of the care taken in renovating this 18th-century farmhouse. ⊠ *Rte. 100, 1 mi north of Stowe, 05672,* ☎ *802/253–2229. 9 rooms. AE, MC, V.*

Motels
🖬 **Econo Lodge** (⊠ 101 Northfield St., Montpelier 05602, ☎ 802/223–5258, ℻ 802/223–0716), 54 rooms, restaurant, CP; *$$.* 🖬 **Greystone Motel** (⊠ U.S. 7, Middlebury 05753, ☎ 802/388–4935), 11 rooms; *$$.*

Nightlife and the Arts

Nightlife
Burlington's nightlife caters to its college-age population, with pubs and a few dance spots. The **Vermont Pub and Brewery** (⊠ College and St. Paul Sts., Burlington, ☎ 802/865–0500) makes its own beers and seltzers. The **Metronome** (⊠ 188 Main St., Burlington, ☎ 802/865–4563) entertains with an eclectic mix of live music almost every night. **Nectar's** (⊠ 188 Main St., Burlington, ☎ 802/658–4771) is always jumping to the sounds of local bands and never charges a cover. **Comedy Zone** (⊠ Radisson Hotel, 60 Battery St., Burlington, ☎ 802/658–6500) provides the laughs in town on weekends.

The Arts
Burlington has the **Vermont Mozart Festival** (☎ 802/862–7352) and the **Flynn Theater for the Performing Arts** (☎ 802/863–8778), which schedules the Vermont Symphony Orchestra, theater, dance, big-name musicians, and lectures. Stowe has a summer **performing arts festival** (☎ 802/253–7792).

Outdoor Activities and Sports

Biking
In addition to the numerous back roads in the Champlain Valley, Stowe has a recreational path, and Burlington has a 9-mi path along its waterfront. Several operators offer guided tours through the state, among them **Vermont Bicycle Touring** (⊠ Box 711, Bristol 05443, ☎ 802/453–4811 or 800/245–3868) and **Mad River Bike Shop** (⊠ Rte. 100, Waitsfield, ☎ 802/496–9500).

Boating
The center for water activities in Vermont is Lake Champlain. There are marinas with rentals and charters available in or near Vergennes and Burlington. In Burlington the **North Beaches** border the northern edge of town and are popular for swimming and sailboarding. **Burlington Community Boathouse** (⊠ Foot of College St., Burlington Harbor, ☎ 802/865–3377) has sailboard and boat rentals (some captained) and lessons. **Marble Island Resort** (⊠ 150 Marble Island Rd., Colchester, ☎ 802/864–6800) rents sailboats, canoes, paddle boats, and aquacycles from April through June.

Fishing

Lake Champlain contains salmon, lake trout, bass, pike, and more. Marina services are offered by **Malletts Bay Marina** (⊠ 228 Lakeshore Dr., Colchester, ☎ 802/862–4072) and **Point Bay Marina** (⊠ Thompson's Point, Charlotte, ☎ 802/425–2431).

Golf

Public courses include **Ralph Myhre's** 18 holes, run by Middlebury College (⊠ Rte. 30, Middlebury, ☎ 802/443–5125), and 9 holes at **Montpelier Country Club** (⊠ U.S. 2 just south of U.S. 302, Montpelier, ☎ 802/223–7457).

Hiking and Backpacking

Aside from the **Long Trail** (The Green Mountain Club, ⊠ Rte. 100, R.R. 1, Box 650, Waterbury Center 05677, ☎ 802/244–7037), day hikes in northern Vermont include the **Little River** area in Mt. Mansfield State Forest, near Stowe, and **Stowe Pinnacle.** Local bookstores are a great source for Vermont day-hiking guidebooks.

Tennis

Stowe's **Grand Prix Tournament** is in early August (for information call the Stowe Area Association, ☎ 802/253–7321). Most resorts' courts are open only to guests. Tennis schools are offered at **Smugglers' Notch Tennis Camp** (⊠ Smugglers' Notch 05464, ☎ 802/644–8851) and **Sugarbush Tennis School** (⊠ Sugarbush Sports Center, R.R. 1, Box 350, Warren 05674, ☎ 802/583–2391 or 800/53–SUGAR).

Ski Areas

For statewide snow conditions call 802/229–0531. All downhill areas listed have snowmaking.

Cross-Country

Bolton Valley (⊠ Box 300, Bolton 05477, ☎ 802/434–2131) has 62 mi of trails. **Burke Mountain** has 37 mi of trails and a ski school. Alpine resorts that also have cross-country trails include **Jay Peak,** 25 mi; **Smugglers' Notch,** 23 mi; **Stowe,** 18 mi of groomed trails, 12 mi of back-country trails; and **Sugarbush,** 15 mi.

Downhill

Burke Mountain (⊠ Box 247, East Burke 05832, ☎ 802/626–3305 or 800/541–5480), 30 trails, 4 lifts, 2,000-ft vertical drop. **Jay Peak** (⊠ Rte. 242, Jay 05859, ☎ 802/988–2611 or 800/451–4449), 64 trails, 7 lifts, 2,153-ft vertical drop. **Mad River Glen** (⊠ Rte. 17, Waitsfield 05673, ☎ 802/496–3551), 33 runs, 3 lifts, 2,000-ft drop. **Smugglers' Notch** (⊠ Smugglers' Notch 05464, ☎ 802/644–8851 or 800/451–8752), 60 runs, 7 lifts, 2,610-ft drop. **Stowe** (⊠ 5781 Mountain Rd., Stowe 05672, ☎ 802/253–3000 or 800/253–4754 for lodging), 47 trails, 11 lifts, 2,360-ft drop. **Sugarbush** (⊠ R.R. 1, Box 350, Warren 05674, ☎ 802/583–2381 or 800/537–8427 for lodging), 112 trails, 18 lifts, 2,400- and 2,600-ft drops.

Shopping

The **Vermont State Craft Center at Frog Hollow** (⊠ Mill St., Middlebury, ☎ 802/388–3177; ⊠ Church St., Burlington, ☎ 802/863–6458) is a display of the work of more than 250 juried Vermont artisans. Burlington's **Church Street Marketplace** is a pedestrian thoroughfare lined with boutiques. Burlington's revitalized waterfront is home to the funky **Wing Building,** which houses many boutiques, a café, and an art gallery.

4 The Middle Atlantic States

Delaware, Maryland, New Jersey, Pennsylvania, Virginia, Washington, D.C., West Virginia

By Conrad Paulus

Updated by Nancy Serano

I n the closing decades of the 18th century, the major action in the New World was here, in 5 of the original 13 colonies. General George Washington's audacious crossing of the Delaware River made possible the colonists' victory in the Battle of Trenton; Virginia saw the war's final battles and surrender; the Constitution was hammered out in Philadelphia; Delaware ratified the Constitution and became the first state; and Maryland ceded land for the District of Columbia. Today the people of these states remember the past, proudly tending their historic monuments and welcoming visitors.

The Middle Atlantic countryside of rolling farmland and woods, ancient, soft-edged mountains, broad rivers, and green valleys is a livable land in a manageable climate—a land much walked through and fought over. Besides the Revolution, the region suffered many of the battles of the Civil War and today commemorates their sites. On its eastern edge (part of the densely populated urban corridor that runs from Boston to Richmond), you'll find the cities and most of the history. The international, multiracial population produces every possible cuisine, and you can buy anything on earth in the upscale boutiques, department stores, and antiques shops.

Beyond the smog on the New Jersey Turnpike are long beaches, casino-filled Atlantic City, and Victorian Cape May to the east; horse country, ski resorts, and Philadelphia to the west. The Eastern Shore's Delaware and Maryland beaches are sedate or swinging; Virginia Beach is both. And the seafood anywhere near the Chesapeake Bay is superb. Baltimore combines historic buildings with new restaurants and shops; Annapolis and Oxford are ports for boaters gunkholing around the

Chesapeake. Washington, D.C., the seat of government, is a wonderful showplace for visitors, with myriad treasures set off by cherry trees. Alexandria's historic district, in Virginia, and Georgetown's splendid town houses recall the capital's early years. In Williamsburg you'll hear echoes of the Revolution and sample 18th-century life.

West of the Tidewater, or the coastal region, the towns are smaller and farther apart. Continuing on a circuit past Richmond, with its glorious capitol, you'll come to Charlottesville, Thomas Jefferson's hometown; farther west rise the Blue Ridge Mountains and West Virginia's Appalachians, sprinkled with palatial 19th-century resorts. At the stunning confluence of the Shenandoah and Potomac rivers sits Harpers Ferry, where John Brown met his fate; and back in Pennsylvania are Gettysburg and Amish country. These are the habitats of the country auction, the wonderful local restaurant, and the farmhouse bed-and-breakfast—the secret places off the beaten track that you'll love to discover for yourself.

When to Go

In the cool early **spring** Washington's pink cherry blossoms are at their peak for a few spectacular days. The many equestrian events in Maryland and Virginia also herald the season. **Summer** is swampy in Washington, Baltimore, and Philadelphia, with temperatures in the 80s, yet thousands flock to all three for monuments or baseball. Ocean bathers head to the Jersey shore, Rehoboth, Ocean City, and Virginia Beach. The dazzling **autumn** foliage in Virginia's Shenandoah Valley draws hordes and also signals the opening of the orchestra, theater, and ballet seasons in the cities, most notably Philadelphia. In **winter**, when temperatures average in the 40s, workaday Washington grinds to a halt after just a sprinkling of snow, but Pennsylvania, Virginia, and West Virginia offer downhill and cross-country skiing, weather permitting.

Festivals and Seasonal Events

Winter

EARLY DEC.–JAN. 1➤ The **National Christmas Tree Lighting/Pageant of Peace** (☎ 202/619–7222), in **Washington, D.C.,** begins on the second Thursday in December, when the president lights the tree, and is followed by nightly choral performances at the Ellipse, a grassy area on the White House complex.

JAN. 1➤ The **Mummers Parade** (☎ 215/636–1666 or 215/336–3050 for Mummer's Museum), in **Philadelphia,** ushers in the year with some 20,000 sequined and feathered marchers between Broad Street and city hall.

LATE FEB.➤ **George Washington's Birthday** (☎ 703/838–5005) is celebrated in **Alexandria, Virginia,** with a parade and reenactment of a Revolutionary War skirmish at nearby Fort Ward.

Spring

LATE MAR.➤ **Maryland Days Weekend** (☎ 804/229–1607) of **St. Mary's City, Maryland,** commemorates the founding of the colony at its original birthplace.

EARLY APR.➤ The **National Cherry Blossom Festival** (☎ 202/547–1500) takes place in **Washington, D.C.,** with a parade, a marathon, and a Japanese lantern-lighting ceremony.

MID-APR.➤ The **Azalea Festival** (☎ 757/622–2312) in **Norfolk, Virginia,** features a parade, an air show, concerts, a ball, and the coronation of a queen from a NATO nation. Throughout **Virginia** during

The Middle Atlantic States

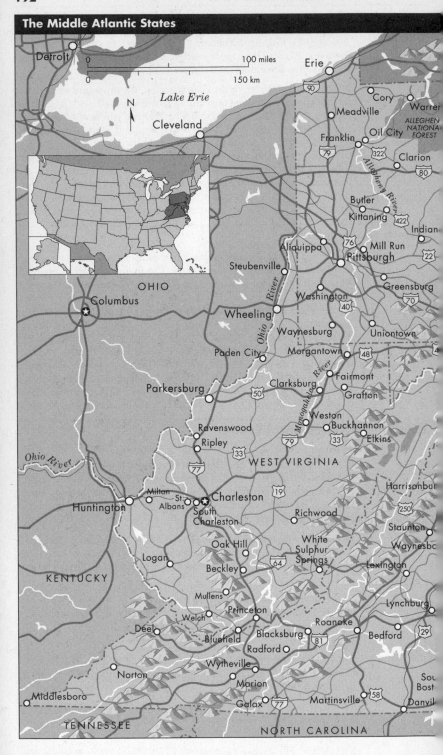

Detroit

0 | 100 miles
0 | 150 km

Lake Erie

N

Cleveland

Erie

90

Cory

Warre

Meadville

ALLEGHEN
NATIONA
FOREST

Franklin

Oil City

79

322

Clarion

80

Butler

Kittaning

422

Indian

Aliquippa

76

Mill Run

Pittsburgh

22

Steubenville

Greensburg

70

OHIO

Washington

40

Columbus

Wheeling

Waynesburg

Uniontown

Ohio River

Morgantown

48

Paden City

Clarksburg

Fairmont

Parkersburg

50

Grafton

Monongahela River

Ravenswood

Weston

Buckhannon

Ripley

79

33

Elkins

33

WEST VIRGINIA

77

19

Harrisonbur

Milton

Charleston

Richwood

250

Huntington

St.
Albans

South
Charleston

Staunton

Waynesbo

White
Sulphur
Springs

Lexington

Oak Hill

Logan

64

Beckley

KENTUCKY

Mullens

Lynchburg

Welch

Princeton

Roanoke

29

Deel

Blacksburg

81

Bedford

Bluefield

Radford

Norton

Wytheville

Sou
Bost

Marion

Middlesboro

Galax

77

Martinsville

58

Danvil

TENNESSEE

NORTH CAROLINA

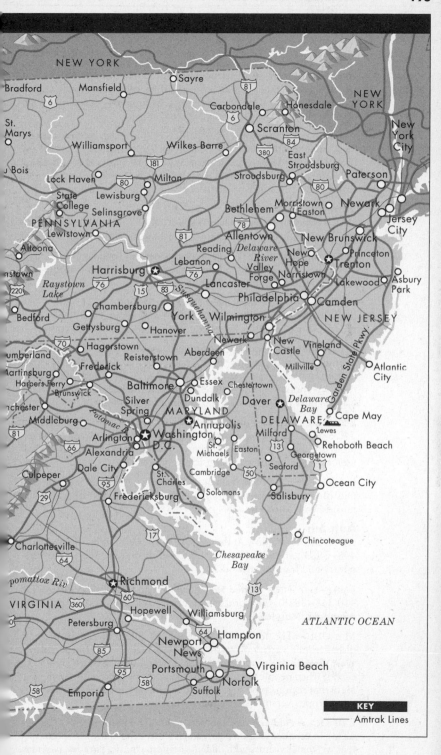

KEY
— Amtrak Lines

Historic Garden Week (☎ 804/644–7776), grand private homes open their doors to visitors.

EARLY MAY➤ **Old Dover Days** (☎ 302/734–1736) celebrates **Delaware**'s capital city with a parade, dancing, and tours of Colonial homes and gardens. The year 1998 marks the 20th annual **Point-to-Point Races** (☎ 302/888–4600 or 800/448–3883) at **Winterthur** outside **Wilmington, Delaware,** featuring steeplechase and pony races and an annual themed tailgate picnic competition.

LATE MAY➤ The **Preakness** (☎ 410/542–9400), held in **Baltimore, Maryland,** is the second event of horse racing's Triple Crown, after the Kentucky Derby and before the Belmont Stakes. The **Blue and Grey Reunion** (☎ 304/457–4265), in **Philippi, West Virginia,** is four days of music, food, crafts, and a costumed reenactment of the Civil War's first land battle.

Summer

LATE JUNE➤ The **Hampton Jazz Festival** (☎ 757/838–4203), in **Hampton, Virginia,** brings together top performers in various styles of jazz.

LATE JUNE–EARLY JULY➤ The **Festival of American Folklife** (☎ 202/357–2700), held on the Mall in **Washington, D.C.,** celebrates music, arts, crafts, and foods of regional cultures.

EARLY JULY➤ The **Philadelphia Freedom Festival** (☎ 215/636–1666 or 800/537–7676) includes parades, hot-air balloon races, ceremonies at Independence Hall, a restaurant festival, and July 4 fireworks.

JULY 4➤ **Independence Day** celebrations in **Baltimore** (☎ 410/837–4636) culminate in a major show of fireworks over the Inner Harbor. Celebrations in **Washington, D.C.** (☎ 202/619–7222), include a grand parade, a National Symphony Orchestra performance on the steps of the Capitol, and fireworks over the Washington Monument.

EARLY AUG.➤ The **Virginia Highlands Festival** (☎ 540/623–5266 or 540/676–2282), in **Abingdon,** offers crafts and farm animals on exhibit, antiques for sale, painting and writing workshops, hot-air balloon rides, and a variety of musicians in concert.

LATE AUG.➤ The **Wine Festival** in **The Plains, Virginia,** features tastings of vintages from 40 Virginia wineries, plus grape stomping and musical entertainment.

Autumn

LABOR DAY WEEKEND➤ At the **Crafts Festival** (☎ 302/888–4600 or 800/448–3883), at **Winterthur,** 200 high-quality craftspeople sell contemporary and traditional work.

EARLY–MID-OCT.➤ **United States Sailboat** and **Powerboat Shows** (☎ 410/268–8828), the world's largest events of their kind, take place in **Annapolis, Maryland.**

MID-OCT.➤ The **Taste of DC Festival** (☎ 202/789–7000) presents dishes from a variety of **Washington, D.C.,** eateries. In **Harpers Ferry, West Virginia,** the park service stages **Election Day 1860** (☎ 304/535–6299), when people portraying the presidential candidates on the ballot in that region come once again to debate the hot topics of their day: states' rights versus a strong federal union.

LATE OCT.➤ **Fiddler's and Sea Witch Weekend Festival** (☎ 302/227–2233), in **Rehoboth Beach, Delaware,** is a madcap Halloween spectacular that welcomes visitors with fiddler's contests, music, parades, hayrides, and the antics of masked marauders.

LATE OCT.–EARLY NOV.➤ New Hollywood and independent movies are screened at the **Virginia Film Festival** (☎ 804/982–5277), in **Charlottesville, Virginia,** fast becoming a major event in the film biz.

EARLY NOV.➤ Backyard inventors test out their homemade pumpkin-throwing machines at the **Punkin Chunkin** (☎ 800/515–9095), in **Lewes, Delaware;** the current record is 2,710 ft.

NOV.–DEC.➤ **Yuletide at Winterthur** (☎ 302/888–4600 or 800/448–3883) is a Christmas-theme tour of the treasure-filled rooms at this vast museum near **Wilmington, Delaware.**

Getting Around the Middle Atlantic States

By Bus
Greyhound Lines (☎ 800/231–2222) serves all these states. **NJ Transit** (☎ 201/762–5100 or 800/772–2222 for northern NJ; 215/569–3752 or 800/582–5946 for southern NJ) provides bus service to many areas of the Garden State.

By Car
I–95, the major East Coast artery, runs through all of these states except West Virginia. The New Jersey Turnpike, a toll road, fills in for I–95 in the Garden State. The 470-mi Pennsylvania Turnpike, also a toll road, runs from the Ohio border to Valley Forge, just outside Philadelphia. I–64 runs east–west, intersecting I–95 at Richmond, Virginia. At Staunton, Virginia, I–64 intersects I–81, which runs north–south through the Shenandoah Valley, toward West Virginia and Tennessee.

By Plane
American, Continental, Delta, Northwest, TWA, United, and US Airways, among others, serve **Philadelphia International Airport** (☎ 215/937–6937), **Greater Pittsburgh International Airport** (☎ 412/472–3525), **Baltimore–Washington International Airport** (☎ 410/859–7111), **Washington National Airport** (☎ 703/419–8000), and **Washington Dulles International Airport** (☎ 703/419–8000).

By Train
Amtrak (☎ 800/872–7245) serves the region both north–south and east–west, with major lines along the coast and inland lines through Pennsylvania, Virginia, and West Virginia. **NJ Transit** (☎ 201/762–5100 or 800/772–2222 for northern NJ; 215/569–3752 or 800/582–5946 for southern NJ), **Southeastern Pennsylvania Transportation Authority** (SEPTA; ☎ 215/580–7800), and **Maryland Area Rail Commuter** (MARC; ☎ 800/325–7245) provide service within their states.

DELAWARE

Updated by
Valerie
Helmbreck

Capital	Dover
Population	725,000
Motto	Liberty and Independence
State Bird	Blue hen
State Flower	Peach blossom
Postal Abbreviation	DE

Statewide Visitor Information

Delaware State Visitors Center (⊠ 406 Federal St., Dover 19901, ☎ 302/739–4266). **Delaware Tourism Office** (⊠ 99 Kings Hwy., Box 1401, Dover 19903, ☎ 302/739–4271 or 800/441–8846). **Visitor centers:** I–95, between Routes 896 and 273 (☎ 302/737–4059); at Delaware Memorial Bridge (☎ 302/571–6340); and north of Smyrna, on Route 13 North (☎ 302/653–8910).

Scenic Drives

From Wilmington's western edge, a **30-mi loop** follows winding Route 100 past well-screened estates, a state park, and the meandering Brandywine Creek; and then into Pennsylvania on a section of U.S. 1W, which takes you past several historical attractions; and finally back into Delaware, where you'll travel on Route 52 (locally called Château Country) to villages lined with antiques shops, to horse farms, and to Winterthur, a major du Pont estate turned museum. A drive south along **Route 9** from New Castle to Dover slides past tidal marshes and across creeks on one-lane bridges; side roads veer into bird sanctuaries or out to points of land with a view of Delaware Bay.

National and State Parks

National Parks

Bombay Hook National Wildlife Refuge (⊠ Rte. 9 east of Smyrna; R.D. 1, Box 147, Smyrna 19977, ☎ 302/653–6872) is more than 15,000 acres of ponds and fields filled between April and November with both resident and migrating waterfowl. **Prime Hook National Wildlife Refuge** (⊠ Country Rd. 236, just off Rte. 16; R.D. 3, Box 195, Milton 19968, ☎ 302/684–8419) is a smaller, well-developed preserve with boat ramps, canoe trails, and a boardwalk trail through marshes.

State Parks

A dozen parks run by the **Delaware Division of Parks and Recreation** (⊠ 89 Kings Hwy., Richardson and Robbins Bldg., Box 1401, Dover 19903, ☎ 302/739–4702) are set up for hiking, fishing, and picnicking. The chief inland parks, with freshwater ponds, add seasonal boat rentals to basic amenities.

Brandywine Creek State Park (⊠ Intersection of Rtes. 92 and 100, Box 3782, Greenville 19807, ☎ 302/577–3534), about 5 mi from Wilmington, is the state's best picnic park, with 800-plus acres of open fields and wooded grounds, a nature center, 12 mi of hiking trails, and perfect sledding slopes in winter. **Cape Henlopen** (⊠ 42 Henlopen Dr., Lewes 19958, ☎ 302/645–8983; ⊠ Seaside Nature Center, ☎ 302/654–6852), east of Lewes, has more than 150 campsites in pinelands. **Delaware Seashore** (⊠ 850 Inlet, Rehoboth Beach 19971, ☎ 302/227–2800; ⊠ Marina, ☎ 302/227–3071) has both ocean surf and calm bay waters, along with nearly 300 campsites with hookups. **Lums Pond**

State Park (✉ Rtes. 301 and 71 south of Newark; 1068 Howell School Rd., Bear 19701, ☎ 302/368–6989) has more than 70 campsites. **Trap Pond** (✉ Off Rte. 24 east of Laurel; R.D. 2, Box 331, Laurel 19956, ☎ 302/875–5153) includes part of the Great Cypress Swamp and has more than 140 rustic sites under a canopy of loblolly pines.

WILMINGTON

Wilmington, the state's commercial hub and largest city, was founded in 1638 as a Swedish settlement and successively taken over by the Dutch and the English. It has more recently been populated by employees at DuPont's company headquarters, credit card banks, and nearby poultry ranches. Now the city's—and the state's—long-standing pro-business policies have enticed corporations whose towers of granite and glass reflect (literally) the colonial stonework next door. These multinationals have imported many of their employees; at some recent but unmarked instant, the city became home to more newcomers than natives.

Two nearby towns—Newark, home of the University of Delaware, and New Castle, the state's beautifully restored colonial capital—are linked to Wilmington by a few miles of neighborhoods and strip malls and are important to the city's cultural, commercial, and social mix.

Visitor Information

Greater Wilmington: Convention and Visitors Bureau (✉ 1300 Market St., Suite 504, 19801, ☎ 302/652–4088 or 800/422–1181).

Arriving and Departing

By Bus
Greyhound Lines (✉ 318 N. Market St., ☎ 302/652–7391 or 800/231–2222).

By Car
Situated between Baltimore and Philadelphia, Wilmington is bisected by I–95 north–south and linked to small-town Pennsylvania by U.S. 202 and Routes 52 and 41.

By Plane
Philadelphia International Airport (☎ 215/492–3181), about 30 mi north of downtown Wilmington, is served by all major U.S. and international airlines. Taxi fare is about $25 to Wilmington. Door-to-door shuttle buses to the center of the city—**Airport Super Shuttle** (☎ 302/655–8878) or **Delaware Express Shuttle** (☎ 302/454–7634 or 800/648–5466)—cost $20 and $23 respectively and require reservations (24-hour advance notice is recommended).

By Train
Wilmington Train Station (✉ Martin Luther King Blvd. and French St., ☎ 302/429–6523) has **Amtrak** (☎ 800/872–7245) service, as well as **SEPTA** (☎ 215/580–7800) commuter service to Philadelphia.

Getting Around Wilmington

Downtown is compact enough to stroll, but visits to New Castle, Newark, or the museums and parks ringing Wilmington require a car. Downtown parking is moderately priced in garages and impossible to find on the streets in the jam-packed office district. Buses are geared to commuters, not explorers.

Exploring Wilmington

The four-block **Market Street Mall** marks the city center. The **Grand Opera House** (⊠ 818 Market St. Mall, ☎ 302/658–7897) is a working theater. Built by the Masonic Order in 1871 and restored in 1971, the four-story Grand's facade is cast iron painted white in French Second Empire style to mimic the old Paris Opera.

The **Old Town Hall Museum** (⊠ 512 Market St. Mall, ☎ 302/655–7161) is a two-story Georgian-style building with changing exhibits, a permanent display of regional decorative arts, and restored jail cells to tour. The hall and museum shop were restored as headquarters for the **Historical Society of Delaware**. A recent addition to Market Street Mall is the **Delaware History Museum** (☎ 302/656–0637), a restored 1940s Woolworth's building with three galleries and a changing exhibit of Delaware history.

The **Hercules Building** (⊠ 313 Market St., ☎ 302/594–5000), north of the mall, was built in the 1980s with ziggurat walls and a 20-ft-diameter clock. The core of the building is a 14-story atrium, with ground-level shops and a jungle of plants.

East of the mall and surrounded by some of the city's poorest neighborhoods, a monument to the 1638 landing of a Swedish expedition marks the first permanent settlement in the Delaware Valley. At the **Kalmar Nyckel Shipyard/Museum** volunteers have built a replica of the first vessel to land on these shores. ⊠ *1124 E. 7th St.,* ☎ *302/429–7447. Closed Sun., by appointment Sat.*

Old Swedes Church and the **Hendrickson House Museum** are worth a visit. The church, built in 1698, retains its original hipped roof and high wooden pulpit and is still regularly used for religious services. The farmhouse, built in 1690 by Swedish settlers, is furnished with period pieces. ⊠ *606 Church St.,* ☎ *302/652–5629. Free. Closed Tues., Thurs., Sun.*

Other Attractions

The **Delaware Art Museum,** a few miles west of the city center and I–95, houses a major collection of post-1840 American paintings and illustrations, including works by major figures such as Homer, Eakins, Hopper, Wyeth, Sloan, and illustrator Howard Pyle, as well as the foremost assemblage of English pre-Raphaelite paintings and decorative arts in the United States. ⊠ *2301 Kentmere Pkwy.,* ☎ *302/571–9590. Free Sat. 10 AM–1 PM. Closed Mon.*

Nemours Mansion and Gardens shows the Alfred du Pont family's preference for fine automobiles, European antiques, Louis XVI–style architecture, and formal French gardens. Adjacent to the renowned A. I. du Pont Hospital for Children, the estate is open only on weekends. ⊠ *1600 Rockland Rd.,* ☎ *302/651–6912. Reservations essential.*

The **Hagley Museum and Library,** one of three former du Pont family properties on the northwest edges of Wilmington, recalls the DuPont company's beginnings in 1802 as an explosives manufacturer. You can tour gunpowder mills, a 19th-century machine shop, and the family home and gardens, all set on 230 acres. ⊠ *Rte. 141,* ☎ *302/658–2400.*

Outside Wilmington

New Castle, 5 mi south of Wilmington on Route 9, is a barely commercialized gem of a town rich in lovingly restored colonial houses, cobblestone streets, and historic sites along the Delaware River. William

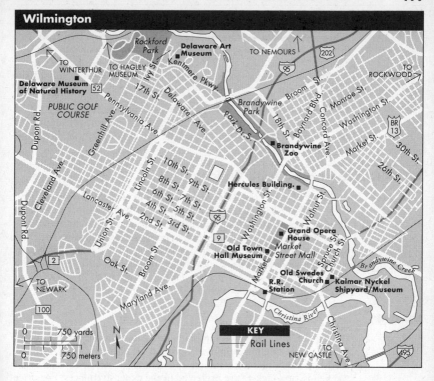

Wilmington

Penn's first landing in North America is noted in **Battery Park.** Two blocks west of the waterfront, the **New Castle Courthouse,** Delaware's colonial capital until 1777, is a pristine museum of state history, with three brick wings and a white cupola and spire. ✉ *211 Delaware St.,* ☎ *302/323–4453. Free. Closed Mon.*

New Castle's **George Read II House** was built in 1801 in Federal style by a signer of both the Declaration of Independence and the Constitution. Twelve rooms of the big brick house are open, including three furnished in period style. ✉ *42 The Strand,* ☎ *302/322–8411. Closed Mon., weekdays Jan.–Feb.*

★ **Winterthur Museum, Garden and Library** focuses on Henry Francis du Pont's passion for collecting furniture and decorative arts made or used in America from 1640 to 1860. The nine-story, 175-room hillside stucco mansion and museum wing shelter a world-class collection in period settings. There are three exhibition galleries and an elegant pavilion that houses the museum shop and glass-enclosed restaurant. The naturalistic gardens showcase native and exotic plants. ✉ *Rte. 52, Winterthur,* ☎ *302/888–4600 or 800/448–3883.*

Odessa is a tiny, mostly residential village set on the banks of the Appoquinimink River, about 23 mi south of Wilmington off Route 13. Originally a grain-shipping port, it stopped growing in the mid-19th century when disease attacked its peach crops and the railroad passed it by. Today this tiny community offers a bit of living history—until a few years ago, muskrat still topped the menu at the town's one-and-only restaurant. A branch of the Winterthur Museum includes four 18th- and 19th-century houses and the **Brick Hotel Gallery,** which houses rotating exhibits of American furniture and decorative arts. ☎ *302/378–4069. Closed Jan.–Feb.*

Parks and Gardens

In **Brandywine Creek State Park** (☞ National and State Parks, *above*), shady paths pass colonial stone walls and a tiny brick church that was built in 1740 and used for British wounded during the Revolutionary War. Lush Brandywine Creek and a millrace attract fishermen and splash-happy children.

Rockwood Museum, a 19th-century country estate with a Gothic manor house, displays unusual specimen plants on 6 acres of landscaped grounds and 62 acres of woodlands. ⊠ *610 Shipley Rd.,* ☎ *302/761–4340. Closed Mon.*

What to See and Do with Children

Children who visit the **Delaware Museum of Natural History** (⊠ Rte. 52 N, ☎ 302/658–9111), 5 mi northwest of Wilmington, can explore the mysteries of Australia's Great Barrier Reef and examine an African water hole and a 500-pound clam. The museum's hands-on, interactive discovery room allows children to use all their senses. Wilmington's **Brandywine Zoo** tucks outdoor exhibits into cliffs along Brandywine Creek. ⊠ *1001 N. Park Dr.,* ☎ *302/571-7747. Free Nov.–Mar. Exotic-animal house closed Nov.–Mar.*

Dining

During the '80s boom Wilmington's kitchens multiplied as new companies' globe-circling employees pushed for diversity. The most established restaurants are Italian and Asian. It's safest to reserve on weekends, and jackets are preferred in the expensive places. For price ranges *see* Chart 1 (B) *in* On the Road with Fodor's.

$$$ ✕ **Green Room.** French cuisine is served in a dramatic, wood-paneled
★   setting of 19th-century opulence. Lunch is served Monday through Saturday; dinner is only served on Saturday. The hotel's clubby **Brandywine Room**, with its original Wyeth paintings and continental cuisine, is open for dinner Sunday through Thursday. ⊠ *Hotel du Pont, 11th and Market Sts.,* ☎ *302/594–3154. Reservations essential. Jacket and tie for dinner. AE, D, DC, MC, V.*

$$$ ✕ **Harry's Savoy Grill.** Friendly service, great food, and a warm atmo-
★   sphere have made Harry's one of Delaware's most popular—and best—restaurants. Their *portobello* (mushroom) pizza is a wildly popular; in softshell crab season nobody does the little critters better. ⊠ *2020 Naamans Rd.,* ☎ *302/475–3000. AE, DC, MC, V.*

$$$ ✕ **Raffaele's.** In a town full of Italian restaurants, Raffaele's had stiff competition when it opened in 1996. But owner Ralph Papa knows his customers from years of serving them at his popular Italian grocery store up the block. Now they flock to this unpretentious spot for ravioli the size of a wallet, filled with mushrooms, spinach, and three cheeses and swimming in lobster broth. ⊠ *1934 W. 6th St.,* ☎ *302/658–3988. AE, DC, MC, V.*

$$ ✕ **Mirage.** In a colorful, contemporary space, young servers deliver such regional specialties as shrimp, duck, and roasted salmon. Chef Lisa Scolero's sauces, which include a maple glaze and a blue-cheese-and-honey concoction, change daily. This is the only fine-dining option in Newark and lures Wilmington visitors south. ⊠ *100 Elkton Rd., Newark,* ☎ *302/453–1711. AE, D, MC, V. Closed Sun. No lunch Sat.*

$$ ✕ **Tavola Toscana.** Chef-owner Dan Butler has built a devoted following in the past five years. The room's centerpiece is an antipasti station with shiny copper dishes hanging from an original iron sculpture overhead. Don't miss Butler's Milanese-style saffron-scented risotto or his superwide *pappardelle* with rabbit and thyme. ⊠ *1412 N. du Pont St.,* ☎ *302/ 654–8001. AE, DC, MC, V.*

$ ✕ **Di Nardo's.** This crowded, casual tavern—more plastic than rustic, with Formica tables and unpadded chairs—specializes in seafood. The catch of the day is always fresh, and the spicy (or ask for the plain, steamed variety) hard-shell crabs are famous. ⊠ *405 N. Lincoln St.,* ☎ *302/656–3685. AE, D, DC, MC, V.*

$ ✕ **India Palace.** The authentic Indian food served here includes spicy
★ curry dishes and clay-oven (tandoori) specialties. ⊠ *101 Maryland Ave. (Rte. 4),* ☎ *302/655–8772. AE, D, DC, MC, V.*

$ ✕ **Jessop's Tavern & Colonial Restaurant.** In a tiny space just steps from the town's waterfront park, Chef Jim Berman offers a taste of local history with a menu inspired by the English, Dutch, and Swedish founders of the region. The rich oyster chowder, double-crusted chicken pot pie, and crusty flat bread can be topped off with Berman's signature dessert, an English bread pudding. ⊠ *114 Delaware St., New Castle,* ☎ *302/322–6111. MC, V.*

Lodging

Most Wilmington-area hotels are designed for business travelers, with less emphasis on resort amenities and more on efficiency and value. For variety there are restored colonial inns (not modern adaptations) and a few bed-and-breakfasts. Two reservation services—**Bed & Breakfast of Delaware, Inc.** (⊠ 701 Landon Dr., Suite 200, Wilmington 19810, ☎ 302/479–9500) and **Guesthouses, Inc.** (⊠ Box 2137, West Chester, PA 19380, ☎ 800/950–9130)—help locate moderately priced lodgings. For price ranges *see* Chart 2 (B) *in* On the Road with Fodor's.

$$$ ▥ **Brandywine Guest Suites.** This former store, tucked into a nonde-
★ script downtown block, has dramatic contemporary architecture, suites with rich traditional furnishings, and a popular lounge. ⊠ *707 King St., 19801,* ☎ *302/656–9300,* ℻ *302/656–2459. 49 suites. Restaurant, bar. AE, DC, MC, V.*

$$$ ▥ **Christiana Hilton Inn.** This modern high-rise southwest of Wilmington is convenient to I–95. The rooms are furnished traditionally, but its restaurant, Ashley's, is notable. ⊠ *100 Continental Dr., Newark 19713,* ☎ *302/454–1500,* ℻ *302/454–0233. 266 rooms. 2 restaurants, bar, pool. AE, D, DC, MC, V.*

$$$ ▥ **Hotel du Pont.** This posh and popular downtown hotel has large rooms with living areas set off by mahogany dividers. The furnishings are 18th-century reproductions. ⊠ *11th and Market Sts., 19801,* ☎ *302/594–3100 or 800/441–9019,* ℻ *302/594–3108. 216 rooms. 3 restaurants, bar, spa. AE, D, DC, MC, V.*

$$$ ▥ **Inn at Montchanin Village.** Recently completed, the inn is actually
★ a collection of painstakingly restored 19th-century buildings that once housed DuPont powder mill workers. Each elegant guest unit is unique and appointed with antique reproduction furniture and luxurious linens. The village, in the heart of Chateau Country, also has an upscale and excellent restaurant, Krazy Kat's, where guests are served a complimentary breakfast. ⊠ *U.S. Rte. 100 and Kirk Road, Montchanin 19710,* ☎ *303/888–2133 or 800/369-2473,* ℻ *302/888–0389. 37 rooms. Restaurant, bar, gardens. AE, D, DC, MC, V.*

$ ▥ **Boulevard Bed & Breakfast.** This red tile–roofed B&B in the Triangle section of Wilmington is a citified, fancy, but reasonably priced six-bedroom dwelling. Outside, neo-Georgian elements and eccentric, fluted columns adorn the facade; inside, don't miss the Mueller tiles around the library fireplace. Proprietors Charles and Judy Powell serve a full breakfast on an enclosed side porch. ⊠ *1909 Baynard Blvd., 19802,* ☎ *302/656–9700. 6 rooms. AE, MC, V.*

$ ▥ **Fairfield Inn.** Close to the University of Delaware and about 9 mi west of Wilmington, this Marriott-owned inn is spartan but convenient. ⊠ *65 Geoffrey Dr., Newark 19713,* ☎ *302/292–1500. 135 rooms. Pool. AE, D, DC, MC, V.*

$ ▥ **Marriott Courtyard.** Centrally located in downtown Wilmington, this affordable establishment creates a Brandywine Valley ambience—lots of hunter green and cranberry red along with Wyeth reproductions. Many businesspeople stay here, but the Courtyard also specializes in wedding parties and family reunions. ⊠ *1102 West St., 19801,* ☎ *302/ 429–7600 or 800/321–2211,* ℻ *302/429–9167. 125 rooms. Restaurant, exercise room, 2 meeting rooms. AE, D, DC, MC, V.*

$ ▥ **Rodeway Inn.** No-smoking rooms and proximity to historic New Castle are two advantages of this traditional motor inn. ⊠ *111 S. DuPont Hwy., New Castle 19702,* ☎ *302/328–6246 or 800/321–6246,* ℻ *302/ 328–9493. 40 rooms. AE, D, DC, MC, V.*

Shopping

The anchor stores at Newark's **Christiana Mall** (⊠ Rte. 7 at I–95 Exit 4S, ☎ 302/731–9815), which has 130 stores, are Macy's and Strawbridge & Clothier. After a major renovation Wilmington's **Concord Mall** (⊠ 4737 Concord Pike, ☎ 302/478–9271) now has 95 stores and two department store biggies—Strawbridge & Clothier and Boscov's.

THE ATLANTIC COAST

Whether you have a day, a weekend, or the whole summer, a visit to Delaware's beaches will likely be a highlight of a trip to the First State. From Cape Henlopen State Park at the northern end to Fenwick Island at the southern border are 23 mi of Atlantic shoreline. The main route south gets you to shore points the fastest, but if you have time, drive scenic Route 9 (it runs from New Castle to Dover) between farm fields and stands of 10-ft-high grasses. The most scenic stretch of shoreline is south of Dewey Beach, where sand dunes and wide, white Atlantic beaches are just an arm's reach from Route 1.

Visitor Information

Bethany-Fenwick: Chamber of Commerce and Information Center (⊠ Rte. 1N, Fenwick Island; Box 1450, Bethany Beach 19930, ☎ 302/ 539–2100 or 800/962–7873). **Lewes:** Chamber of Commerce and Visitors Bureau (⊠ Savannah Rd. and Kings Hwy., Box 1, 19958, ☎ 302/ 645–8073). **Milton:** Chamber of Commerce (⊠ 104 Federal St., 19968, ☎ 302/684–1101). **Rehoboth Beach–Dewey Beach:** Chamber of Commerce (⊠ 501 Rehoboth Ave., Box 216, Rehoboth Beach 19971, ☎ 302/227–2233 or 800/441–1329).

Delaware Today magazine (☎ 302/656–1809 or 800/285–0400), published monthly, covers events and region-wide restaurants.

Arriving and Departing

By Bus
Greyhound Lines (☎ 800/231–2222) links Rehoboth Beach with Wilmington, New Castle, and Dover.

By Car
From the north exit I–95 to U.S. 13S at Wilmington. Take U.S. 113 at Dover and Route 1 at Milford. From the south the scenic route to Delaware's northern shores crosses Chesapeake Bay at Annapolis and continues east via U.S. 301/50; follows U.S. 50 to Route 404 at Wye

Mills, Maryland; then crosses Delaware on Routes 404, 18, and 9 to Route 1 at Lewes.

By Ferry

Cape May–Lewes Ferry (☎ 302/645–6346 or 302/645–6313) is a 70-minute ride from Cape May, New Jersey, to Lewes, Delaware.

Exploring the Atlantic Coast

There is ample public access to the Atlantic surf and to the 23 mi of sand, though crowds pour in from Washington, D.C., and points west on holidays and summer weekends. The Broadkill River, Rehoboth Bay, Indian River Bay, and Little Assawoman Bay offer sheltered waters.

Just west of the beaches are some of the state's historic villages and scenic bay-side parks (☞ National and State Parks, *above*). In **Milton,** once a major shipbuilding center at the head of the Broadkill River, the whole downtown area is a historic district of 18th- and 19th-century architecture, including old cypress-shingle houses. **Lewes,** a 1631 Dutch settlement at the mouth of Delaware Bay, cherishes its seafaring past with a marine museum and draws visitors with good restaurants, shops, and lodging that are away from the hectic beach resorts.

Coastal towns include **Rehoboth Beach,** the largest, with a busy boardwalk for noshing-strolling-shopping expeditions. Next door is **Dewey Beach,** popular with young singles. Adjacent **Bethany Beach, South Bethany,** and **Fenwick Island** (founded as a church camp and known for its fishing), south of the Indian River inlet, are quieter resorts.

Dining and Lodging

Once upon a time this sleepy resort area was home to a collection of basic motels and guest houses with restaurants that served up undistinguished fried seafood and burgers. But no more. Down-scale tourist businesses have been replaced by swank hotels and restaurants that cater to sophisticated visitors from nearby Washington, D.C., Baltimore, and Philadelphia. The dining renaissance has added dozens of exciting restaurants to the region along with a wide range of cuisines and a cadre of talented young chefs. Rehoboth Beach is the center of the culinary boom, which has spread as far north as Milford and southward to the state line at Fenwick Island. For price ranges *see* Charts 1 (B) and 2 (B) *in* On the Road with Fodor's.

Bethany Beach

$$$ ✗ **Sedona.** Among the showstoppers at this southwestern establishment are wild boar rubbed with a Thai mixture—ground cumin, spicy chilies, and garlic—and served with a side dish of tumbleweed onions and West Texas crab cakes with Santa Fe salsa. While upscale in its culinary intentions, Sedona cultivates a relaxed, casual atmosphere with a decor more Santa Fe and Albuquerque than Bethany or Dewey Beach. ✉ *26 Pennsylvania Ave.,* ☎ *302/539–1200. AE, D, DC, MC, V. Closed Jan.–Mar.*

Dewey Beach

$$$ ✗ **Rusty Rudder.** In this barnlike space with nautical decor overlooking Rehoboth Bay, the specialties are down-home service and local seafood, such as crab imperial. They offer a land-and-sea buffet, which includes seafood and chicken specialties, every Friday year-round and several times weekly during summer months. They also serve a Sunday brunch. ✉ *113 Dickinson St., on the bay,* ☎ *302/227–3888. AE, D, DC, MC, V.*

Lewes

$$ ✕ **Lazy Susan's.** For the fattest, sweetest steamed blue-shell crabs, this simple roadside eatery is the place. Eating inside can be stifling, and the outside deck has a prime view. . . of the highway, so order take-out and use your own wooden mallet and roll of paper towels. Call ahead to make sure the crabs are off the boat. ⊠ *Hwy. 1 at Tenley Court, Lewes,* ☎ *302/645–5115. MC, V.*

$$$ 🛏 **Inn at Canal Square.** Valued for its waterfront location and unusual accommodations, this inn has a full array of conventional rooms as well as the *Legend of Lewes,* a houseboat that floats peacefully at dockside and is equipped with a modern galley, two bedrooms, and two baths. (The houseboat is not recommended for landlubbers or families with children under 14.) ⊠ *122 Market St., 19958,* ☎ *302/645–8499 or 800/222–7902,* ﬂ𝖷 *302/645–7083. 18 rooms, 1 houseboat. Continental breakfast. AE, D, DC, MC, V.*

$$$ 🛏 **New Devon Inn.** The inn was built in 1926 and is listed in the Na-
★ tional Register of Historic Places. Each room's antique furnishings have a story, often documented by a local historian. The lobby and the parlor are treasuries of Early Americana. Ask about the self-guided biking inn-to-inn package. ⊠ *2nd and Market Sts., Box 516, 19958,* ☎ *302/645–6466,* ﬂ𝖷 *302/645–7196. 26 rooms. Restaurant, shops. AE, D, DC, MC, V.*

Milford

$$ ✕🛏 **Banking House Inn.** The country-French cooking in this restored
★ Victorian bank building uses a lighter approach than traditional French cuisine. Upstairs from the vivid Victoriana of the restaurant, the guest rooms—some with fireplaces—are traditionally decorated. ⊠ *112 N.W. Front St., 19963,* ☎ *302/422–5708. 3 rooms. Restaurant. Full breakfast. DC, MC, V.*

$ 🛏 **Traveler's Inn Motel.** Rooms in this two-story, balconied motel are plain, with two double beds and minimal furnishings (a hanging rack, no closet). ⊠ *1036 N. Walnut St., 19963,* ☎ *302/422–8089. 38 rooms. AE, MC, V.*

Rehoboth Beach

$$$$ ✕ **Blue Moon.** The decor is eye-popping, and the food is equally stimulating. Specialties include New Zealand mussels and sautéed skate. Chef Marla Sierzega visits Japan in the off-season; her travels are reflected in dishes like mahi-mahi with sake, ginger, scallion and *mirin* (sweet rice wine) broth and scallops wrapped in *nori* (dried seaweed) and surrounded by baby bok choy. The crowd is well heeled and appreciates the arty feel and mood of this always-busy restaurant. ⊠ *35 Baltimore Ave.,* ☎ *302/227–6515. AE, DC, MC, V.*

$$$ ✕ **LaLa Land.** In a tiny beach house, this magical restaurant welcomed
★ a new chef, Charles Theologus, to carry on its eclectic French-cum-Southwest-meets-Pacific Rim cuisine. Try the mignon of roasted eggplant or his tenderloin concoction with jalapeño-enhanced polenta. For a special treat ask to be seated in the bamboo-enclosed terrace. ⊠ *22 Wilmington Ave.,* ☎ *302/227–3887. AE, DC, MC, V.*

$$ ✕ **Dogfish Head Brewery.** Delaware's first brew pub, Dogfish Head is
★ owned by two young entrepreneurs who keep their clientele happy with a changing menu of in-house brews, pizzas, and musical performers. ⊠ *320 Rehoboth Ave.,* ☎ *302/226–2739. AE, MC, V.*

$$ ✕ **Sydney's Blues and Jazz.** New Orleans–influenced American cooking issues from the kitchen with such specialties as oysters Rockefeller, authentic gumbo and jambalaya, and a Cajun surf and turf. Wine flight tastings—samples of three wines served in small portions—are also offered. The innovative grazing menu is great for light eaters or those who like to sample several choices. ⊠ *25 Christian St.,* ☎ *302/227–1339. AE, D, DC, MC, V.*

$$ ✕ **Woody's Bar & Grill.** Casual but with an upscale air, Woody's is part of the recently renovated Dinner Bell Inn. Baked crab and artichoke dip, grilled pork chops with applejack brandy sauce and bread from the on-site bakery are filling and done well. ⊠ *2 Christian St.,* ☎ *302/ 227–2561. AE, D, MC, V.*

$ ✕ **Nicola's Pizza.** Home of the original Nic-O-Boli, this family-run pizzeria ships its trademarked neo-stromboli all over the world to demanding fans. The bustling shop is packed until the wee hours of the morning. ⊠ *8 N. 1st. St.,* ☎ *302/226–2654. MC, V.*

$ ✕ **Pierre's Pantry.** Pierre's does a fast takeout business and has tables for sit-down dining. The attractions are breakfast sandwiches (served all day), kosher items, Brooklyn bagels, fresh salads, and innovative offerings such as the Cajun chicken sandwich and the seven-vegetable sandwich. ⊠ *146 Rehoboth Ave.,* ☎ *302/227–7537. AE, MC, V.*

$$$ ☷ **Best Western Gold Leaf.** The rooms at this hotel, a half block from the beach and across the street from the bay, are traditionally furnished and pleasant. Some rooms have water views. ⊠ *1400 Hwy. 1, 19971,* ☎ *302/226–1100 or 800/422–8566,* ℻ *302/226–9785. 75 rooms. Pool, free parking. AE, D, DC, MC, V.*

$$$ ☷ **Boardwalk Plaza Hotel.** The most deluxe hotel on the boardwalk, the hotel sports grand Victorian decor everywhere. Rooms for guests with disabilities are available, and you can have your breakfast on the terrace right on the boardwalk. ⊠ *2 Olive Ave., 19971,* ☎ *302/227– 7169 or 800/332–3224. 84 rooms. Restaurant, pool, exercise room, parking. AE, D, MC, V.*

$$$ ☷ **Brighton Suites.** Each suite has a bedroom with king-size bed and a living room with refrigerator and wet bar. ⊠ *34 Wilmington Ave., 19971,* ☎ *302/227–5780 or 800/227–5788. 66 suites. Indoor pool, free parking. AE, D, DC, MC, V.*

$ ☷ **Atlantic Budget Inn.** Rooms in this two-story brick inn are crowded, with double or king-size beds and hanging clothes racks (no closets). ⊠ *4353 Hwy. 1, 19971,* ☎ *302/227–0401 or 800/245–2112. 74 rooms. AE, DC, MC, V.*

Outdoor Activities and Sports

Fishing

Charter boats for either deep-sea or bay (trout, bluefish) fishing can be booked for either day or half-day trips, including all the gear. Book through your hotel or try **Fisherman's Wharf** (☎ 302/645–8862 or 302/645–8541), in Lewes, or **Delaware Seashore State Park Marina** (☎ 302/422–8940), at the Indian River inlet.

Water Sports

Marinas on Rehoboth Bay and Delaware Bay (at Lewes) rent sailboards, sailboats, and motorboats. Catamarans are for rent at **Fenwick Island State Park** (⊠ ½ mi north of Fenwick Island on Rte. 1, ☎ 302/539– 9060), among others.

Shopping

On the Atlantic coast bargain hunters scour the shops at **Ocean Outlets** (⊠ Hwy. 1, Rehoboth Beach, ☎ 302/226–9223), a manufacturers' outlet center touting 110 stores that sprawl along both sides of the busy, four-lane highway. All stores sell products at a 20%–70% savings with, of course, no sales tax. Farther north, on the southbound side of the highway, the same owner operates the 35-unit **Rehoboth Outlet Center,** which is anchored by an L. L. Bean factory store. On the same road just north of Lewes is the **Lighthouse Outlet** (✉ 753 Hwy. 1., Lewes, ☎ 302/645–1207), which sells discounted fixtures and ceiling fans.

ELSEWHERE IN DELAWARE

Dover

Arriving and Departing

The north and south approaches to Dover are on U.S. 13; Route 10 links it with Goldsboro, Maryland; Route 1 heads toward Dover from the coast towns. **Blue Diamond Lines** (☎ 800/400–3800), a statewide public bus system, serves Wilmington, Newark, Middletown, Dover, and the Atlantic beaches, plus various intermediate points.

What to See and Do

An oasis of colonial preservation in a bustling government center, the **capitol complex** historic area is on a square laid out in 1722 according to William Penn's 1683 plan. Information about Delaware's historic sites and attractions is available at the **Delaware State Visitors Center** (✉ 406 Federal St., 19901 ☎ 302/739–4266); the Sewell C. Biggs Museum of American Decorative Arts occupies the building's upper floors. The **Dover Air Force Base,** southeast of town, (☎ 302/677–3376 for tours) and its C-5 Galaxies are visible from U.S. 13. Its museum has recently been renovated and is housed in a 20,000-square-ft hangar that's filled with planes and airlift memorabilia, including a Medal of Honor hall of fame. The hangar itself served as a rocket test center during World War II. The **John Dickinson Plantation** (✉ 340 Kitts Hummock Rd., ☎ 302/739–3277) offers visitors a glimpse of 18th-century plantation life in Kent County, Delaware.

A horse-drawn wagon, a crop duster, threshers, a corn house, and a privy are only part of the fascinating collection of tools and structures exhibited at the **Delaware Agricultural Museum and Village** (✉ 866 N. DuPont Hwy., ☎ 302/734–1618). A re-created 1890s village and farmstead, the operation is devoted to Delaware's rich agrarian past and present (agriculture is still the state's number-one industry).

Had enough culture? Then head straight for **Dover Downs International Speedway** (✉ North of Dover on Rte. 13, ☎ 302/674–4600 or 800/441–7223), where the grandstands can handle up to 5,000 spectators for stock car and harness racing. A casino was added in 1995.

Dining and Lodging

$$ ✕ **Where Pigs Fly.** With family-style food that's a notch above most, this is a kid- and wallet-friendly place. ✉ *617 Loockerman St., at U.S. 13,* ☎ *302/678–0586. AE, D, DC, MC, V.*

$$$ 🏨 **Sheraton Dover Hotel.** Convenient, comfortable, and well appointed, the Sheraton features spacious meeting rooms and a conference center. ✉ *1570 N. Du Pont Hwy., 19901.* ☎ *302/678–8500 or 800/325–3535,* FAX *302/678–9073. 153 rooms. Restaurant, pool, meeting rooms, free parking. AE, D, DC, MC, V.*

MARYLAND

By Francis X.
Rocca

Updated by
Gregory Tasker

Capital	Annapolis
Population	5,072,000
Motto	Manly Deeds, Womanly Words
State Bird	Baltimore oriole
State Flower	Black-eyed Susan
Postal Abbreviation	MD

Statewide Visitor Information

The **Maryland Division of Tourism and Promotion** (✉ 217 E. Redwood St., Baltimore 21202, ☎ 410/767–3400 or 800/543–1036) provides free publications and runs seven information centers.

Scenic Drives

Alternate U.S. Route 40, between Frederick and Hagerstown, rolls gently through farmlands and picturesque towns. In summer there are plenty of farm stands offering fresh fruit and produce. The area is especially attractive in early autumn, when the leaves begin to change. **I–68,** between Hancock and Cumberland in western Maryland, passes through a spectacular cut in the rocky crest of a mountain and then opens to sweeping views of the Appalachians. **U.S. 50/301,** at the eastern end of Kent Island on Maryland's Eastern Shore, traverses an elevated bridge that opened in 1991 and offers spectacular views of the inlet and the fishing boats, pleasure craft, and sailboats below.

National and State Parks

National Parks

National Park Service attractions include **Antietam National Battlefield**
★ **Site** (☎ 301/432–5124), **Assateague Island National Seashore** (☎ 410/641–1441), **Blackwater National Wildlife Refuge** (☎ 410/228–2677), **Catoctin Mountain Park** (☎ 301/663–9330), **Chesapeake and Ohio Canal National Historic Park** (☎ 301/739–4200), **Fort McHenry National Monument and Historic Shrine** (☎ 410/962–4290), and **Fort Washington Park** (☎ 301/763–4600).

State Parks

Maryland has 47 parks and forests on more than 280,000 acres of land. The Division of Tourism and Promotion (☞ Statewide Visitor Information, *above*) has information about each of the parks. **Swallow Falls State Park** (☎ 301/334–9180), along the north-flowing Youghiogheny River in extreme western Maryland, is the site of the scenic 63-ft Muddy Creek Falls. North of Baltimore **Gunpowder Falls State Park** (☎ 410/592–2897) is a 13,020-acre park in the picturesque Gunpowder River valley; it has more than 100 mi of hiking and biking trails. **Sandy Point State Park** (☎ 410/974–2149) sits on the western shore of the Chesapeake Bay and offers visitors sandy beaches, picnicking, fishing, and birdwatching. The **Department of Natural Resources** (☎ 410/974–3771) offers numerous programs, including guided canoe trips, hiking, backpacking, wildflower walks, forest walks, and guided mountain-bike trips.

BALTIMORE

Two decades ago Baltimore transformed itself and its once-dormant waterfront into a bustling tourist attraction, with shopping, restaurants, and the acclaimed National Aquarium. In the process the city became a model for urban redevelopment across the country. Celebrating its bicentennial in 1997, Baltimore found itself in the midst of another renaissance. A new stadium was in the works next to Camden Yards for the city's new NFL franchise, the aptly named Baltimore Ravens. On the other side of Inner Harbor, the Columbus Center Hall of Exploration, an entertainment complex devoted to marine life, was readying for opening in 1998. And Port Discovery, a children's museum being designed by the Walt Disney Co., was also slated for a 1998 debut. Away from its thriving harbor, Baltimore remains a city of historic neighborhoods, including Mount Vernon and Fells Point. It is a city steeped in history, too. Babe Ruth, Edgar Allen Poe, and H. L. Mencken and the "Star-Spangled Banner" are as synonymous with Baltimore as the Orioles and blue crabs.

Visitor Information

Baltimore Area Visitors Center (⌧ 301 E. Pratt St., 21202, ☎ 410/837–4636 or 800/282–6632). **Office of Promotion** (⌧ 200 W. Lombard St., 21201, ☎ 410/752–8632).

Arriving and Departing

By Bus
Greyhound Lines (⌧ 5625 O'Donnell St., ☎ 800/231–2222).

By Car
Baltimore is on I–95, the major East Coast artery.

By Plane
Baltimore-Washington International (BWI) Airport (☎ 410/859–7111), 10 mi south of town, is a destination for most major domestic and foreign carriers. Taxi fare to downtown is roughly $19. **Amtrak** and **Maryland Area Rail Commuter** (MARC; ☎ 800/325–7245) trains run between the airport station (10 minutes from the terminal via free shuttle bus) and Penn Station, about 20 minutes away. **BWI Super Shuttle** (☎ 410/724–0009) has van service to downtown and to most suburban hotels.

By Train
Amtrak serves Baltimore's Penn Station (⌧ Charles St. at Mt. Royal Ave., ☎ 800/872–7245). **Central Light Rail Line** (☎ 410/539–5000) provides service from Timonium, north of the city, through downtown and south to Glen Burnie.

Getting Around Baltimore

Most attractions are a walk or a short trolley ride (☞ Orientation Tours, *below*) from the Inner Harbor. **Water taxis** (☎ 410/563–3901) stop at Fells Point and at Inner Harbor locations. Beyond that a car is useful; the metro line is limited, and bus riding can mean lots of transfers (**Mass Transit Administration,** ☎ 410/539–5000).

Orientation Tours

From spring through fall **Baltimore Trolley Tours** (☎ 410/724–0077) runs 90-minute narrated tours of Baltimore's downtown attractions. The tours also stop at all downtown hotels. Passengers may get on and off an unlimited number of times in one day for one price. Tours are offered daily April–September.

Exploring Baltimore

The city fans out northward from the Inner Harbor, with newer attractions such as the National Aquarium and Oriole Park concentrated at the center and more historic neighborhoods and sites toward the edges. The major northbound artery is Charles Street; cross streets are labeled "East" or "West" relative to it.

Charles Street

Head north on Charles Street from Baltimore Street toward the impossible-to-miss Washington Monument. Restaurants and art galleries lend an urbane tone to this neighborhood, a mix of 19th-century brownstones and modern office buildings. A block west of Charles is the **Basilica of the Assumption** (⊠ Mulberry St. at Cathedral St., ☎ 410/727–3564), which was built in 1812 and is the oldest Catholic cathedral in the United States. Pope John Paul II visited this national shrine during a trip to Baltimore in October 1995.

★ At the **Walters Art Gallery** (⊠ N. Charles and Centre Sts., ☎ 410/547–2787), 30,000 objects from antiquity through the 19th century—encompassing Egyptology exhibits, medieval armor and artifacts, decorative arts and paintings—is housed in an Italianate palace. The adjacent Hackerman House has a magnificent gallery of Asian art.

The **Washington Monument** (⊠ Mt. Vernon Place, ☎ 410/396–0929), built in 1829, is a 178-ft marble column topped by a 16-ft statue of the first president. A 228-step spiral staircase within leads to a unique view of the city.

Surrounding the monument is **Mt. Vernon Square,** flanked by four block-long parks. Note the bronze sculptures in the parks and the elegant brownstones along East Mt. Vernon Place. The **Peabody Library** (⊠ 17 E. Mt. Vernon Pl., ☎ 410/659–8179) has a handsome reading room with a skylight in its five-story-high ceiling. At the **Maryland Historical Society** (⊠ 201 W. Monument St., ☎ 410/685–3750), the eclectic display of state memorabilia includes the original manuscript of the "Star-Spangled Banner."

The **Baltimore Museum of Art** (⊠ Charles and 31st Sts., ☎ 410/396–7101) displays works by Rodin, Matisse, Picasso, Cézanne, Renoir, and Gauguin. A new wing containing 20th-century art, including 15 Andy Warhol paintings, opened in late 1994. The 140-acre campus of **Johns Hopkins University** (⊠ Charles and 34th Sts., ☎ 410/516–5589) is next door to the museum. The main attraction on campus is **Homewood,** once the estate of Charles Carroll Jr., son of Charles Carroll of Carrollton, a signer of the Declaration of Independence. It has been restored to its 1800 appearance and is open to the public.

Inner Harbor and Environs

The **American Visionary Art Museum** (⊠ 800 Key Hwy., at Covington St., ☎ 410/244–1900), housed in a former whiskey distillery near Federal Hill, showcases "new frontiers" in art: the works of self-trained and self-taught artists. Its revolving exhibits include paintings, sculpture, reliefs, drawings, photographs, and a host of other objects created by farmers, housewives, those who have disabilities or are homeless, and others.

Harborplace (⊠ 200 E. Pratt St., ☎ 410/332–4191) comprises two glass-enclosed shopping malls with more than 100 specialty shops and gourmet markets. The Rouse Company's multilevel **Gallery,** across Pratt Street from Harborplace, offers upscale shopping and dining. Other waterfront attractions are nearby. At the **Maryland Science Center** (⊠ 601 Light St., ☎ 410/685–5225), the biggest draw is an **IMAX** movie

Baltimore

Broadway

1500 yards
1500 meters

N

Madison Square

Eden St.

Church Home Hospital

40

Monument St.

Old Town Mall

KEY
Rail Lines

Chase St.

Eager St.

Madison St.

Aisquith St.

Harford Ave.

McElderry St.

147

Johnson Square

Orleans St.

Main Post Office

State Penitentiary

45

Biddle St.

Greenmount Ave.

Enser St.

Hillen St.

Front St.

Low St.

Gay St.

83

The Fallsway

Gay

Guilford Ave.

Holliday

TO BALTIMORE MUSEUM OF ART, JOHNS HOPKINS UNIVERSITY

Chase St.

Calvert St.

Read St.

Peabody Library

Baltimore Sun Papers

Pleasant St.

Davis St.

Mercy Hospital

Saint Paul St.

Washington Monument

Saint Pau

Eager St.

Washington Pl.

Basilica of the Assumption

Charles St

Cathedral St.

Mt. Vernon Place

Walters Art Gallery

Centre St.

Enoch Pratt Main Library

Park Ave.

erty St.

Read St.

Franklin St.

Mulberry St.

Howard

Howard St.

Madison St.

Maryland Historical Society

Monument St.

Saratoga St.

Biddle St.

Eu aw St.

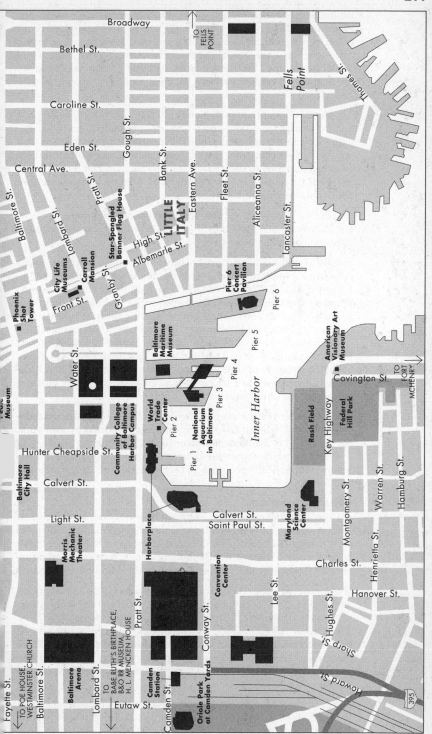

Broadway

Bethel St.

Caroline St.

Eden St.

Central Ave.

Gough St.

Bank St.

Eastern Ave.

Fleet St.

Aliceanna St.

Lancaster St.

TO FELLS POINT

Fells Point

Thames St.

Baltimore St.

Lombard St.

Pratt St.

Granby St.

High St.

LITTLE ITALY

Albemarle St.

Star-Spangled Banner Flag House

Carroll Mansion

City Life Museums

Phoenix Shot Tower

Front St.

Water St.

Community College of Baltimore Harbor Campus

Baltimore Maritime Museum

Pier 6 Concert Pavilion

Pier 6

Pier 5

Pier 4

Pier 3

World Trade Center

Pier 2

National Aquarium in Baltimore

Pier 1

Inner Harbor

American Visionary Art Museum

Covington St.

TO FORT McHENRY

Key Highway

Federal Hill Park

Rash Field

Hunter Cheapside St.

Calvert St.

Light St.

Baltimore City Hall

Morris Mechanic Theater

Harborplace

Calvert St.
Saint Paul St.

Maryland Science Center

Montgomery St.

Warren St.

Hamburg St.

Charles St.

Henrietta St.

Convention Center

Lee St.

Hanover St.

Hughes St.

Pratt St.

Baltimore Arena

TO BABE RUTH'S BIRTHPLACE, B&O RR MUSEUM, H. L. MENCKEN HOUSE

Camden Station

Conway St.

Sharp St.

Howard St.

395

Fayette St.

TO POE HOUSE, WESTMINSTER CHURCH

Baltimore St.

Lombard St.

Eutaw St.

Camden St.

Oriole Park at Camden Yards

Museum

theater with a five-story-high screen. There is also a planetarium. The **World Trade Center** (⊠ 401 Pratt St., ☎ 410/837−4515) is the world's tallest pentagonal building (30 stories); its 27th-floor observation deck—the **Top of the World**—offers a terrific view of the city. The World War II submarine USS *Torsk* and the lightship *Chesapeake* make up the **Baltimore Maritime Museum** (⊠ Piers 3 and 4, Pratt St., ☎ 410/ 396−5528).

The **National Aquarium in Baltimore** (⊠ Pier 3, ☎ 410/576−3800) is home to more than 5,000 species of marine life, including sharks, dolphins, beluga whales, and puffins. Escalators whisk visitors past a tank (which you can later walk through) with a recently refurbished coral reef and then to the rooftop "rain forest." On Pier 4 the **Marine Mammal Pavilion** offers performances by Atlantic bottle-nosed dolphins and themed exhibit areas.

East of Inner Harbor is the **Star-Spangled Banner Flag House** (⊠ Pratt and Albemarle Sts., ☎ 410/837−1793), where the flag that inspired the national anthem was woven.

Around a Lombard Street courtyard between Front and Albemarle streets is a complex of buildings known as the **City Life Museums** (⊠ 800 E. Lombard St., ☎ 410/396−3523). The recently opened **Morton K. Blaustein City Life Exhibition Center** provides a fascinating glimpse of Baltimore's urban and cultural history with a display of everyday objects, such as white vinyl reclining chairs from the 1950s and black gas stoves from the 1930s. Other highlights are a row house where actors perform short plays set in 1840 and the elegant town house of a signer of the Declaration of Independence. Also part of the complex is the **Phoenix Shot Tower,** at East Fayette and Front streets, where shot was made until the Civil War.

North of Inner Harbor on Holliday Street is the golden-domed **Baltimore city hall,** built in 1875 and completely supported by ironwork. Near city hall is the **Peale Museum** (⊠ 225 N. Holliday St., ☎ 410/ 396−1149), which shows paintings by Charles Willson Peale and his family and has been open since 1814, making it the oldest museum in the United States.

Other Attractions

★ A 10-minute trolley ride (or 12 minutes by water taxi) from the Inner Harbor takes you to **Fells Point,** once a thriving shipbuilding center and now a neighborhood of cobblestone streets and historic redbrick houses, many of them antiques shops, galleries, restaurants, and taverns. At Broadway and Thames streets is an operating tugboat pier.

West of Inner Harbor is the **H. L. Mencken House** (⊠ 1524 Hollins St., ☎ 410/396−7997), from which the "Sage of Baltimore" ruled American letters from the 1920s to the 1940s. The **Poe House** (⊠ 203 N. Amity St., ☎ 410/396−7932) is where Edgar Allan Poe wrote his first horror story. He lies buried at the **Westminster Church Grave** (⊠ W. Fayette and Greene Sts.). Bear in mind that neither Poe site is within walking distance of the Inner Harbor, and visitors should take safety precautions.

North of Inner Harbor is the **Great Blacks in Wax Museum** (⊠ 1601 E. North Ave., ☎ 410/563−6415), the first and only one of its kind in the United States. Rosa Parks, Frederick Douglass, Dr. Martin Luther King Jr., and Harriet Tubman are among the figures.

The 50,000-seat **Oriole Park at Camden Yards** (⊠ Camden and Howard Sts., ☎ 410/685−9800), opened in 1992, has a 700-square-ft video scoreboard, several restaurants, and a cocktail lounge. Its brick facade and asymmetric playing field evoke the big-league parks of the early 1900s. Built on the site of a former railroad depot, it is served by MARC trains from Washington, the Central Light Rail trains from the suburbs, and the local metro. Two blocks west of Oriole Park is **Babe Ruth's birthplace** (✉ 216 Emory St., ☎ 410/727–1539), where the baseball legend was born in 1895.

★ Locomotives and railroad cars are on display at the **B&O Railroad Museum** (✉ 901 W. Pratt St., ☎ 410/752–2490). One of the world's largest train museums, it sits on the site of the country's first railroad station.

At the end of the peninsula bounding the Patapsco River's northwestern branch is **Fort McHenry,** a star-shaped brick building famous for its role in the national anthem. The "star-spangled banner" that Francis Scott Key saw "by the dawn's early light" on September 14, 1814, was flying above this fort. ✉ *Fort Ave. (off Key Hwy.),* ☎ *410/ 962–4290. Boat rides from Inner Harbor, Memorial Day–Labor Day.*

Parks and Gardens

★ **Sherwood Gardens** (✉ Stratford Rd. and Greenway, 3 mi from Inner Harbor east of St. Paul St., ☎ 410/366–2572) is worth a special trip in late April and early May to see its 80,000 peaking tulips and azaleas. South of Inner Harbor is **Federal Hill Park** (✉ Battery St. and Key Hwy.), with an excellent view of the downtown skyline and a jogging track in adjacent **Rash Field.**

What to See and Do with Children

The 150 acres of the **Baltimore Zoo** are a year-round child pleaser. More than 1,200 animals, including polar bears, elephants, and penguins, call the zoo home. A $5.8 million Chimp Forest, in the zoo's African Region, opened in 1995. ✉ *Druid Park Lake Dr., I–83 Exit 7,* ☎ *410/ 366–5466.*

Dining

Seafood, especially Chesapeake Bay blue crab (steamed in the shell, fried in a crab cake, or baked with a white-cream-and-wine sauce), is the specialty, but every major cuisine is available, including the offerings of Baltimore's Greek and Italian neighborhoods. For price ranges *see* Chart 1 (B) *in* On the Road with Fodor's.

$$$ ✕ **Joy America Cafe.** Chef Peter Zimmer presides over Baltimore's most
★ creative kitchen in the unusual American Visionary Art Museum. In a spare, open dining room overlooking the harbor, Zimmer offers museum goers an appropriately unconventional seasonal menu that draws on the flavors of many countries, including dishes such as tropical fruit–barbecued halibut served with fresh peaches, bitter chocolate, and tomato-and-watermelon salsa. ✉ *American Visionary Art Museum, 800 Key Hwy.,* ☎ *410/244–6500. AE, DC, MC, V.*

$$$ ✕ **The Prime Rib.** Bustling and crowded, this dark, intimate dining room
★ just north of Mount Vernon Square is consistently ranked among the city's best. The traditional menu is headed by sterling prime rib and an even better filet mignon. The jumbo lump crab cakes are highly recommended. ✉ *1101 N. Calvert St.,* ☎ *410/539–1804. Reservations essential. Jacket and tie. AE, D, DC, MC, V.*

$$$ ✕ **Tio Pepe.** Paella à la Valenciana (chicken, sausage, shrimp, clams,
★ mussels, and saffron rice) is a specialty at this candlelighted cellar dining room, as is the lesser-known Basque red snapper—with clams, mussels, asparagus, and boiled egg. ✉ *10 E. Franklin St.,* ☎ *410/539–4675. Reservations essential. Jacket required. AE, D, DC, MC, V.*

$$ ✕ **Bertha's.** Mussels are the specialty here, served steamed (with a choice of eight butter-based sauces) or as a Turkish appetizer (stuffed with sweet-and-spicy rice). The decor is nautical. ⊠ *734 S. Broadway,* ☎ *410/327–5795. MC, V.*

$$ ✕ **Haussner's.** Since its opening in 1926 this has been one of Baltimore's favorite special-occasion spots. More than 80 freshly prepared items appear on the menu, and there are dozens of vegetables from which to choose. German dishes are the specialty of the house, but there is something—particularly the enormous desserts—to please everyone. The walls are adorned with hundreds of original paintings, including pieces by Gainsborough, Rembrandt, Bierstadt, Van Dyck, and Whistler. ⊠ *3244 Eastern Ave.,* ☎ *410/327–8365. Reservations not accepted at dinner. AE, D, DC, MC, V. Closed Sun.–Mon.*

$$ ✕ **O'Brycki's Crab House.** East of Inner Harbor, this 50-year-old Baltimore institution has a homey dining room with brick archways and early 1900s city scenes. Chesapeake Bay fare—steamed crabs and crab cakes—are the specialty, but you can also feast on other fresh seafood, steak, or chicken. ⊠ *1727 E. Pratt St.,* ☎ *410/732–6399. AE, D, DC, MC, V.*

$ ✕ **Burke's Cafe and Comedy Club.** Just a block from the Inner Harbor, convention center, and Baltimore Arena, Burke's has long been one of downtown's favorite casual dining spots. Though steak and seafood are on the menu, Burke's specialty is pub grub—frosty mugs, giant burgers, and platters of huge onion rings. It's a hit with the after-the-game crowd, tourists, and conventioneers alike. ⊠ *36 Light St., at Lombard St.,* ☎ *410/752–4189. AE, MC, V.*

$ ✕ **City Markets.** These are great for a stand-up or counter-side breakfast or lunch. Each offers different local favorites, including fresh Chesapeake Bay seafood, grilled wursts, homemade soups and salads, sushi, and Philadelphia cheese steaks (☞ Shopping, *below*).

$ ✕ **Donna's.** A good bet for both fresh-baked morning scones and after-theater espresso—it's open until 1 AM on Friday and Saturday—this Italian coffee bar also serves a variety of pastas, salads, and innovative sandwiches from midday on. ⊠ *1 Mt. Vernon Sq. (2 W. Madison St., at Charles St.),* ☎ *410/385–0180. AE, MC, V.*

Lodging

Staying around Inner Harbor means ready access to the major attractions. Away from the water, as far north as Mt. Vernon, are reminders of an older Baltimore and some relative bargains in accommodations. For price ranges *see* Chart 2 (A) *in* On the Road with Fodor's.

$$$$ 🏨 **Harbor Court.** This redbrick tower with an ersatz English-country-★ house interior (à la Ralph Lauren) has been Baltimore's most prestigious hotel since 1986. The priciest rooms have a harbor view. ⊠ *550 Light St., 21202,* ☎ *410/234–0550 or 800/824–0076,* ℻ *410/659–5925. 203 rooms. 2 restaurants, bar, indoor pool, sauna, exercise room. AE, D, DC, MC, V.*

$$$$ 🏨 **Renaissance Harborplace Hotel.** Across from the Inner Harbor shopping pavilions and the many waterfront tourist sights, the Renaissance Harborplace is the most conveniently located hotel in the city. The rooms are light and cheery. Rooms with a harbor view are the most popular. ⊠ *202 E. Pratt St., 21202,* ☎ *410/547–1200 or 800/468–3571,* ℻ *410/539–5780. 622 rooms. Restaurant, 2 bars, indoor pool, sauna, exercise room. AE, D, DC, MC, V.*

$$$ 🏨 **Celie's Waterfront Bed & Breakfast.** The spectacular setting—on Baltimore's historic waterfront in Fells Point—is matched by thoughtful details such as terry-cloth robes and clock radios that play ocean waves to soothe you to sleep. Two front rooms overlook the harbor and have

fireplaces and whirlpool tubs. Guests have access to a garden and a rooftop deck. ⊠ *1714 Thames St., 21231,* ☎ *410/522–2323,* FAX *410/522–2324. 7 rooms. AE, D, MC, V.*

$$$ 🏨 **Mr. Mole Bed & Breakfast.** Near Baltimore's cultural center, this 1870
★ brick row house has five suites beautifully decorated in various themes, from English country to whimsical scenes of nature. Breakfast is a mix of coffee cakes, pies, and Amish meats and cheeses. ⊠ *1601 Bolton St., 21217,* ☎ *410/728–1179,* FAX *410/728–3379. 5 suites. Free parking. AE, D, DC, MC, V.*

$$$ 🏨 **Sheraton Inner Harbor.** Just two blocks from Harborplace and Oriole Park, the Sheraton is the official hotel of the Baltimore Orioles. It's also within walking distance of most of the city's attractions and has the only Orthodox Union–certified kosher hotel kitchen in town. ⊠ *300 S. Charles St., 21201,* ☎ *410/962–8300,* FAX *410/962–8211. 357 rooms. Restaurant, bar, indoor pool, sauna, exercise room. AE, D, DC, MC, V.*

$$$ 🏨 **Tremont Hotel.** This small hostelry on a quiet downtown block has a level of service unsurpassed locally: The concierge will arrange free local transportation, and the staff will do guests' personal shopping. All rooms are suites with kitchens. ⊠ *8 E. Pleasant St., 21202,* ☎ *410/576–1200 or 800/873–6668,* FAX *410/244–1154. 58 suites. Restaurant, bar, kitchenettes. AE, D, DC, MC, V.*

$$–$$$ 🏨 **Clarion of Mount Vernon Square.** Formerly the Latham Hotel, a Baltimore landmark, the Clarion underwent a $1.2 million renovation in early 1996. The dark wood–paneled lobby remains, but upstairs is a new food court with Pizzeria Uno, Healthy Choice, and Nestlé Tollhouse Cafe. Rooms with views of Mt. Vernon Place and the Washington Monument are in demand. Some rooms have kitchenettes. ⊠ *612 Cathedral St., 21201,* ☎ *410/727–7101,* FAX *410/789–3312. 103 rooms. AE, D, DC, MC, V.*

$$ 🏨 **Tremont Plaza.** This plain, gray, 37-story tower has suites decorated
★ in gentle earth tones. All units have kitchens, and those numbered "06" have the best views. ⊠ *222 St. Paul Pl., 21202,* ☎ *410/727–2222 or 800/873–6668,* FAX *410/685–4215. 231 rooms. Restaurant, bar, deli, kitchenettes, pool, sauna, exercise room. AE, D, DC, MC, V.*

Motels

🏨 **Days Inn Inner Harbor** (⊠ 100 Hopkins Pl., 21201, ☎ 410/576–1000, FAX 410/576–9437), 252 rooms, restaurant, pool, bar; $$. 🏨 **Hampton Inn Hunt Valley** (⊠ 11200 York Rd., Hunt Valley 21031, ☎ 410/527–1500, FAX 410/771–0819), 126 rooms; $.

Nightlife and the Arts

Events listings appear in the Thursday *Baltimore Sun*, the monthly *Baltimore* magazine, and *City Paper*, a free weekly distributed in shops and from street-corner machines.

Nightlife

The harborside **Explorer's Lounge** (⊠ Harbor Court Hotel, ☎ 410/234–0550) serves up jazz and remarkable views. For blues and rock, **8x10** (⊠ 8 E. Cross St., ☎ 410/625–2000) is the spot. Move to the latest dance mixes at the **Baja Beach Club** (⊠ 55 Market Pl., ☎ 410/727–0468). Laughter is the predominant sound at **Winchester's Comedy Club** (⊠ Light and Water Sts., ☎ 410/576–8558). The talk is all sports at **Balls** (⊠ 200 W. Pratt St., ☎ 410/659–5844). The **Orioles Sports Bar** (⊠ Sheraton Inner Harbor Hotel, 300 S. Charles St., ☎ 410/962–8300) celebrates baseball and other sports with a decor that includes autographed baseballs, jerseys, and other memorabilia.

The **Fells Point** area is Baltimore's answer to D.C.'s Georgetown. Nightclubs, restaurants, pubs, coffeehouses, and small theaters line cobblestone streets around the foot of Broadway.

The Arts

Center Stage (⌧ 700 N. Calvert St., ☎ 410/332–0033) is the state theater of Maryland. Other venues include **Friedberg Hall** (⌧ Peabody Conservatory, E. Mt. Vernon Pl. and Charles St., ☎ 410/659–8124), **Lyric Opera House** (⌧ Mt. Royal Ave. and Cathedral St., ☎ 410/685–5086), **Meyerhoff Symphony Hall** (⌧ 1212 Cathedral St., ☎ 410/783–8000), **Morris A. Mechanic Theater** (⌧ Baltimore and Charles Sts., ☎ 410/625–1400), and **Pier Six Concert Pavilion** (⌧ Pier 6 at Pratt St., ☎ 410/752–8632). There are also numerous dinner theaters in the Baltimore suburbs; check newspapers for details.

Spectator Sports

Baseball: Orioles (⌧ Oriole Park at Camden Yards, Camden and Howard Sts., ☎ 410/685–9800).

Football: Ravens (⌧ 11001 Owings Mills Blvd., Owings Mills 21117, ☎ 410/261–7283 or 888/919–9797).

Shopping

The city's most diverse and colorful shopping areas are the **malls of Harborplace** and the **shops of Fells Point** (☞ Exploring Baltimore, *above*). There are more than three dozen first-rate **antiques shops on Antique Row** (⌧ 700 and 800 blocks, N. Howard St.; 200 block, W. Read St.). At **Kelmscott Bookshop** (⌧ 32 W. 25th St., ☎ 410/235–6810) you can browse among the enormous stock of rare books in the coziness of a converted town house. The city of Baltimore owns and leases space to a number of **indoor food markets:** At least 100 years old are **Belair Market** (⌧ Gay and Fayette Sts.), **Broadway Market** (⌧ Broadway and Fleet Sts.), **Cross Street Market** (⌧ Light and Cross Sts.), **Hollins Market** (⌧ Hollins and Arlington Sts.), **Lexington Market** (⌧ Lexington and Eutaw Sts.), and **Northeast Market** (⌧ Monument and Chester Sts.).

MARYLAND'S CHESAPEAKE

Maryland encompasses the top half of the Chesapeake Bay, where the attractions are, naturally, water-oriented: Annapolis is a world yachting capital, the Eastern Shore is a major duck-hunting ground, and Ocean City is a bustling Atlantic resort. Yet the bay-side towns are also rich in history, with many well-preserved 18th-century buildings.

Visitor Information

Annapolis and Anne Arundel County: Convention & Visitors Association (⌧ 26 West St., Annapolis 21401, ☎ 410/268–8687). **Calvert County:** Department of Economic Development (⌧ County Courthouse, 175 Main St., Prince Frederick 20678, ☎ 410/535–4583 or 800/331–9771). **Caroline County:** County Government (⌧ 109 Market St., Room 109, Denton 21629, ☎ 410/479–0660). **Cecil County:** Chamber of Commerce (⌧ 135 E. Main St., Elkton 21921, ☎ 410/392–3833 or 800/232–4595). **Charles County:** Division of Tourism (⌧ 8190 Port Tobacco Rd., Port Tobacco 20677, ☎ 800/766–3386). **Dorchester County:** Office of Tourism (⌧ 203 Sunburst Hwy., Cambridge 21613, ☎ 410/228–1000 or 800/522–8687). **Kent County:** Chamber of Commerce (⌧ 400 S. Cross St., Chestertown 21620, ☎

410/778–0416). **Ocean City:** Convention and Visitors Bureau (✉ Box 158, Ocean City 21842, ☎ 410/289–2800 or 800/626–2326). **Queen Anne's County:** Office of Tourism (✉ 3100 E. Main St., Grasonville 21638, ☎ 410/827–4810). **St. Mary's County:** Division of Tourism (✉ Box 653, Leonardtown 20650, ☎ 301/475–4411 or 800/327–9023). **St. Michaels:** Talbot County Chamber of Commerce (✉ 210 Marlboro, Suite 300, Easton 21601, ☎ 410/822–4606). **Somerset County:** Tourism Office (✉ Box 243, Princess Anne 21853, ☎ 410/651–2968 or 800/521–9189). **Wicomico County:** Convention and Visitors Bureau (✉ Box 2333, Salisbury 21802, ☎ 410/548–4914). **Worcester County:** Tourism Office (✉ 105 Pearl St., Snow Hill 21863, ☎ 410/632–3617).

Arriving and Departing

By Bus

Baltimore Mass Transit (☎ 410/539–5000) provides service—express on weekdays, local on weekends—between Annapolis and Baltimore. **Carolina Trailways** (☎ 410/727–5014) links Annapolis to Ocean City and intermediate points on the Eastern Shore.

By Car

To Annapolis: From Baltimore follow Route 3/97 to U.S. 50 (Rowe Blvd. exit). **To Southern Maryland:** From Annapolis take Route 2 south, which becomes Route 4 in Calvert County. **To the Eastern Shore:** From Baltimore or Annapolis cross the Bay Bridge (toll charged) northeast of Annapolis and stay on U.S. 50/301.

Exploring Maryland's Chesapeake

Annapolis

Start on the waterfront. Sailboats dock right at the edge of **Market Square,** where there is a visitor information booth. At **City Dock** look for the sidewalk plaque commemorating the arrival of Kunta Kinte, the African slave immortalized in Alex Haley's *Roots*.

At the **Historic Annapolis Foundation Museum Store and Welcome Center** (✉ 77 Main St., ☎ 410/268–5576) you can rent an audiocassette and let narrator Walter Cronkite be your guide on a walking tour of the Historic District.

On the riverside campus of the **United States Naval Academy** (✉ Gate 1, off King George St., ☎ 410/293–1000), known to West Pointers as the "country club on the Severn," the most prominent structure is the bronze-domed **U.S. Naval Chapel,** burial place of the Revolutionary War hero John Paul ("I have not yet begun to fight!") Jones. Outdoors, full-dress parades of midshipmen are a stirring sight.

Once briefly the capital of the United States, Annapolis has one of the finest collections of 18th- and 19th-century buildings in the country, including more than 50 **pre-Revolutionary structures.** Many of its stately brick buildings are still in use as homes, inns, shops, and restaurants. The three-story redbrick **Hammond-Harwood House** (✉ 19 Maryland Ave., ☎ 410/269–1714) is the only verified full-scale example of the work of William Buckland, colonial America's most prominent architect. Across the street the grand Georgian **Chase-Lloyd House** (✉ 22 Maryland Ave., ☎ 410/263–2723) was built by Samuel Chase, a signer of the Declaration of Independence. The 37-room redbrick 1765 **William Paca House** (✉ 186 Prince George St., ☎ 410/263–5553) was built by another signer of the Declaration of Independence and a governor of Maryland. **St. John's College** (✉ 60 College Ave., ☎ 410/263–2371) is the third-oldest college in the country and the home of a 600-year-old tree.

★ The **Maryland State House** (⊠ State Circle, ☎ 410/974–3400) is the oldest state capitol in continuous legislative use and the only one that has housed the U.S. Congress. Charles Willson Peale's painting *Washington at the Battle of Yorktown* hangs inside. Free 30-minute tours are offered seven days a week at 11 and 3.

Southern Maryland

Calvert County offers plenty of striking bay-side scenery. One standout sight is the imposing **Calvert Cliffs,** some 100 ft high, and several miles of surrounding beaches famous for the Miocene-period fossils that can be found along the water's edge. To see the cliffs and beaches, stop at **Calvert Cliffs State Park** (⊠ Rte. 2/4, Lusby, ☎ 301/872–5688). The fossils sites are about a 2-mi walk from the park entrance. For a glimpse of the Eastern Shore on a clear day, try the observation deck at the **Calvert Cliffs Nuclear Power Plant** (☎ 410/495–4600) next door. The **Battle Creek Cypress Swamp Sanctuary** (⊠ Rte. 2/4 to Rte. 506, ☎ 410/535–5327) is home to the northernmost naturally occurring stand of the ancient bald cypress tree in the United States.

Down at the tip of the peninsula is **Solomons,** a still-tranquil but increasingly fashionable sailing town. At Solomons' **Calvert Marine Museum** (⊠ Rte. 2/4 at Solomons Island Rd., ☎ 410/326–2042), boats from various epochs and a 19th-century screw-pile lighthouse are on display.

Across the Patuxent in St. Mary's County is **Historic St. Mary's City** (⊠ Rte. 5, ☎ 301/862–0990 or 800/762–1634), where the first colonists dispatched by Lord Baltimore under a grant by Charles I settled in 1634. Until 1694 this was the capital of Maryland. Reconstructions of 17th-century buildings and of the supply ship that accompanied the settlers are on view at this less spectacular but more peaceful version of Virginia's Colonial Williamsburg. The **Sotterley Plantation** (⊠ Rte. 235, ☎ 301/373–2280) is a fine example of Early American architecture, with the earliest known posted-beam structure in the United States: In place of a foundation, cedar timbers have been driven straight into the ground to support the house.

The Eastern Shore

The William Preston Lane, Jr., Memorial Bridge links Annapolis to the Eastern Shore, passing along the way through **Kent Island,** the bay's largest island. This is the site of the first English settlement in Maryland—agents of Virginia's governor set up a trading post here in 1631. Route 50 continues south past historic towns near the bay and then leads east to the Atlantic.

In the town of **Wye Mills,** on Route 662, stands the state tree, the 400-year-old, 95-ft-tall **Wye Oak,** and a working 17th-century gristmill that once ground grain for Washington's troops at Valley Forge. The affluent town of **Easton** has a 17th-century Quaker meetinghouse and an 18th-century courthouse.

On the Miles River is **St. Michaels** (on Route 33), once a shipbuilding ★ center and now a fashionable yachting destination. The **Chesapeake Bay Maritime Museum** has everything from a Native American dugout canoe to a modern sailboat, still under construction. Exhibitions of stuffed waterfowl, decoys, and guns are extensive. ⊠ *Navy Point,* ☎ *410/745–2916; closed weekdays Jan.–Mar.*

The **Oxford-Bellevue Ferry** has been running since 1683. Today it takes cars and pedestrians across the Tred Avon River from a spot 7 mi south of St. Michaels to the 17th-century town of Oxford. Few of the surviving buildings in **Oxford** date before the mid-1800s, but the bigger (and less charming) town of Cambridge, 15 mi to the southeast, has several from the 1700s. The area is well suited to cycling; many roads have special bike lanes.

Southwest of Cambridge is the **Blackwater National Wildlife Refuge** (⊠ Rte. 335, ☎ 410/228–2677), more than 22,000 acres of marshland, woodlands, and open fields inhabited by Canada geese, ospreys, and bald eagles. Visitors can travel by car, bicycle, or on foot. The Blackwater Refuge is a favorite of serious nature photographers.

On the Atlantic side of the peninsula is **Ocean City,** with 10 mi of whitesand beach and a flashy 27-block boardwalk. The Coastal Highway, with blocks of high-rise condos, runs down the center of town. More than 4 million vacationers flock here every summer.

What to See and Do with Children

Vintage aircraft are parked outside the **Naval Air Test and Evaluation Museum** (⊠ Rte. 235 and Shangri-la Dr., Lexington Park [western shore], ☎ 301/863–7418). Indoors you'll find failed contraptions on display, including the improbable Goodyear Inflatoplane. The **Godiah Spray Plantation** (⊠ Rosecroft Rd., St. Mary's City, ☎ 301/862–0990) offers authentic demonstrations of activities common to 17th-century plantation life, including planting, cooking, and building. **Trimper's Amusement Park** (⊠ Boardwalk and S. 1st St., Ocean City, ☎ 410/ 289–8617), with a huge roller coaster and other rides, celebrated its centennial in 1990.

Outdoor Activities and Sports

Biking

Viewtrail 100 is a 100-mi circuit in Worcester County, between Berlin and Pocomoke City. In **Ocean City** the right-hand lanes of Coastal Highway are for buses and bikes. Several boardwalk shops rent bikes.

Fishing

The principal catches are black drum, channel bass, flounder, bluefish, white perch, weakfish, croaker, trout, and largemouth bass. One-week **licenses** are sold at many sporting goods stores; one-year licenses, from the **Department of Natural Resources** (⊠ Box 1869, Annapolis 21404, ☎ 410/974–3211). **Rental equipment** is available at **Anglers** (⊠ 1456 Whitehall Rd., Annapolis, ☎ 410/757–3442). Bay **charters** are available through **Bunky's Charter Boats** (⊠ Solomons Island Rd., Solomons, ☎ 410/326–3241), the **Fishing Center** (⊠ Shantytown Rd., West Ocean City, ☎ 410/213–1121), and **Bahia Marina** (⊠ 22nd St. and the bay, Ocean City, ☎ 410/289–7438).

Golf

Eisenhower Golf Course (⊠ Generals Hwy., Crownsville, northwest of Annapolis, ☎ 410/222–7922) and the **Bay Club** (⊠ 9122 Libertytown Rd., Berlin, west of Ocean City, ☎ 410/641–4081) each have 18 holes. **Ocean City Golf and Yacht Club** (⊠ 11401 Country Club Dr., Berlin, ☎ 410/641–1779) has 36.

Sailing

Annapolis Sailing School (⊠ 601 6th St., ☎ 410/267–7205 or 800/ 638–9192) offers outfitting and instruction. **Schooner Woodwind** (⊠ 80 Compromise St., Annapolis, ☎ 410/263–8619) runs chartered cruises on a 74-ft yacht and rents sailboats. **Sailing, Etc.** (⊠ 5303 Coastal Hwy., Ocean City, ☎ 410/723–1144) has a wide range of sailboats for rent.

Beaches

Southern Maryland beaches are mainly for strolling and looking. Twelve miles east of **Annapolis**, Sandy Point State Park (⊠ Rte. 50, 12 mi east of Annapolis) is a good spot for fishing, swimming, or launching boats. There are no Chesapeake Bay beaches of any consequence on the **Eastern Shore**. South of **Ocean City**, the northern portion of Assateague Island National Seashore (☞ National and State Parks, *above*) is pristine.

Dining and Lodging

Restaurants in Annapolis and less-expensive southern Maryland, though reliable for seafood, do not warrant a special trip. Across the bay are innovative kitchens and classic crab houses. Lodging reservations are necessary as much as a year in advance of the Annapolis sailboat and powerboat shows in October, the Naval Academy commencement in May, and Easton's Waterfowl Festival in November. For price ranges *see* Charts 1 (B) and 2 (B) *in* On the Road with Fodor's.

Annapolis

$$$ ✕ **The Corinthian.** With cushioned armchairs, oil-lamp lighting, and a courtyard view, this hotel restaurant, the most formal in town, has the elegant feel of an old Maryland home. The distinctive crab cakes have an angel hair–pasta binder, and the New York strip has been aged three weeks. ⊠ *Loews Annapolis Hotel, 126 West St.,* ☎ *410/263–7777. AE, D, DC, MC, V.*

$$ ✕ **McGarvey's Saloon and Oyster Bar.** This casual saloon and restau-
★ rant is a popular hangout with locals, tourists, and sailors. The kitchen serves up standard American fare—burgers, steaks, seafood, and fun finger foods. ⊠ *8 Market Space, at northeast corner of Market House,* ☎ *410/263–5700. AE, MC, V.*

$$$ ✕ **Middleton's Tavern.** This waterfront building has served as a tav-
★ ern since 1750. Wooden tables bear blue-and-white-check tablecloths at night, and in winter fireplaces blaze in all four dining rooms. In the warmer months three dozen tables out front allow diners to watch the lively stream of pedestrian traffic at City Dock. The chef has perfected his own rich version of crab imperial, called crab Middleton. His Cuban black bean soup is a rare treat. ⊠ *2 Market Space,* ☎ *410/263– 3323. AE, D, MC, V.*

$$$ ⌂ **Annapolis Marriott Waterfront.** Amenities such as bathroom phones typify the pastel-and-floral-theme rooms, all of which face the water, the historic district, or—from private balconies—the bustle of City Dock. Pusser's Landing is a casual restaurant with a Caribbean flair, Jamaican and English fare, and a waterside setting. ⊠ *80 Compromise St., 21401,* ☎ *410/268–7555,* 🖷 *410/269–5864. 150 rooms. Restaurant, 2 bars. AE, D, DC, MC, V.*

$$–$$$ ⌂ **Gibson's Lodgings.** Three detached houses—two of them historic— stand together across the street from the United States Naval Academy. The inn has the character of a bed-and-breakfast; all rooms have brass or wood beds. Free parking in the courtyard is an advantage in the heart of a small city with heavy traffic. Room rates include Continental breakfast, served in the formal dining room of the 200-year-old Patterson House. ⊠ *110–114 Prince George St., 21401,* ☎ *410/268–5555,* 🖷 *410/268– 2775 (call first). 21 rooms. Dining room, free parking. AE, MC, V.*

Calvert County

$$ ✕ **CD Café.** Overlooking the Patuxent River and the main road into Solomons, this cozy café describes itself as a coffeehouse with a bistro flair; the menu is limited but inventive. A favorite is the pan-seared chicken breast with pecans, apples, onions and deglazed schnapps. The

homemade desserts are spectacular. ⊠ *14350 Solomons Island Rd., Solomons,* ☎ *410/326–3877. MC, V.*

$$ 🛏 **Back Creek Inn.** Rooms in this 19th-century wood-frame house have brass beds with colorful quilts and views of the water, a garden, or a quiet street. ⊠ *Calvert and Alexander Sts., Solomons 20688,* ☎ *410/326–2022. 6 rooms, cottage. Outdoor hot tub. MC, V. Closed mid-Dec.–mid-Feb.*

Ocean City

$$ ✕ **The Hobbit.** Murals and carved lamps portray J. R. R. Tolkien characters in this dining room with a two-angled view of Assawoman Bay. Veal with pistachios and sautéed catch of the day stand out on the menu. ⊠ *101 81st St.,* ☎ *410/524–8100. MC, V.*

$ ✕ **Lombardi's.** Cozy wooden booths and tables and walls decorated with photos provide the setting for thin-crust pizza, cheese steaks, and cold cut sandwiches. ⊠ *9203 Coastal Hwy.,* ☎ *410/524–1961. Reservations not accepted. MC, V. Closed Wed.*

$$$ ✕🛏 **Hotels at Fager's Island.** Ocean City's most prestigious guest address is actually two hotels linked by walkways over the street. The **Lighthouse Club** and the **Coconut Mallory** offer rooms with bedside Jacuzzis and balconies overlooking Assawoman Bay; some rooms also have fireplaces. Guests can dine in the hotels' restaurant, which has one of the state's most extensive wine lists. ⊠ *201 60th St., Ocean City 21842,* ☎ *410/723–6100 or 800/767–6060. 108 suites. Restaurant, 3 bars, pool, exercise room. AE, DC, MC, V.*

St. Mary's County

$$ ✕ **Evans Seafood.** Ask for a water view, then order lobster stuffed with crab imperial or the spicy hard-shell crab made from a secret recipe. ⊠ *Rte. 249, Piney Point,* ☎ *301/994–2299. MC, V. No lunch weekdays. Closed Mon.*

$$ 🛏 **Potomac View Farm.** Simple oak furniture and quilts fill this 19th-century wood-frame farmhouse. A mile away is an affiliated marina. Full breakfast is included. ⊠ *Rte. 249, Tall Timbers 20690,* ☎ *301/994–0418,* 🖷 *301/994–2613. 5 rooms, 1 cottage. At marina: restaurant, bar, pool, beach. AE, MC, V.*

St. Michaels

$$$ ✕ **208 Talbot.** An antiques-filled late-19th-century house is the setting
★ for regional cuisine. Maryland's own rockfish is sautéed with wild mushrooms in an oyster-cream sauce, and fresh bay oysters are served with a champagne-cream sauce, prosciutto, and pistachio nuts. Look for softshell crab in season. ⊠ *208 N. Talbot St.,* ☎ *410/745–3838. D, MC, V.*

$$ ✕ **Crab Claw.** Bang-them-yourself steamed blue crabs are first-rate at this harborside eatery. Spicy deep-fried hard crab is worth a try, too, as is the vegetable crab soup. ⊠ *Navy Point,* ☎ *410/745–2900. No credit cards. Closed Dec.–Feb.*

$$$$ ✕🛏 **Inn at Perry Cabin.** This early 19th-century farmhouse has been made
★ to resemble an English country house, with antiques and Laura Ashley in the bedrooms, a cozy library, spectacular gardens, and a formal dining room. Menu standouts are honey-and-tarragon-glazed lamb shank and marinated salmon on wilted arugula with pickled-onion sauce. ⊠ *308 Watkins La., 21663,* ☎ *410/745–2200 or 800/722–2949,* 🖷 *410/745–3348. 41 rooms. Restaurant, indoor pool. AE, DC, MC, V.*

$$ ✕🛏 **Robert Morris Inn.** Conveniently located near the Bellevue-Oxford Ferry terminal, this friendly inn offers a variety of accommodations, including efficiencies, river cottages, and simple bedrooms—some with bay windows, others with porches. The inn also is known for its excellent food, especially its crab cakes. ⊠ *314 N. Morris St. (Box 70),*

Oxford 21654, ☎ *410/226–5111,* ⒻⒶⓍ *410/226–5744. AE, MC, V. Restaurant closed Jan.–Mar.*

Motels

⌶ **Dunes Motel** (✉ 2700 Baltimore Ave., Ocean City 21842, ☎ 410/289–4414), 103 rooms, café, pool, wading pool; closed Dec.–mid-Feb.; *$$.* ⌶ **Holiday Inn Select Conference Center and Marina** (✉ 155 Holiday Dr., Box 1099, Solomons 20688, ☎ 410/326–6311 or 800/356–2009, ⒻⒶⓍ 410/326–1069), 326 rooms, restaurant, 2 bars, pool, sauna, 2 tennis courts, exercise room; *$$.* ⌶ **Best Western St. Michaels Motor Inn** (✉ Rte. 33 and Peaneck Rd., St. Michaels 21663, ☎ 410/745–3333, ⒻⒶⓍ 410/745–2906), 93 rooms, 2 pools; *$$.*

Nightlife and the Arts

Nightlife

Ocean City has plenty of places for dancing to rock—whether live or recorded; there is even an under-21 club, **Night Light** (✉ Boardwalk at Worcester St., ☎ 410/289–6313), for those too young to drink. Bars in Annapolis, Solomons, and St. Michaels are favored by the more subdued, and in many cases middle-aged, crowds.

The Arts

In summer the **U.S. Naval Academy Band** performs at Annapolis's City Dock on Tuesday evenings, and the **Starlight Series** takes place on Sunday evenings. **Ocean City** (☎ 410/289–2800 or 800/626–2326) sponsors free boardwalk concerts. When the **Colonial Players** (✉ 108 East St., Annapolis, ☎ 410/268–7373) go on vacation, the **Annapolis Summer Garden Theater** (✉ Compromise and Main Sts., ☎ 410/268–0809) takes over.

ELSEWHERE IN MARYLAND

Western Maryland

Arriving and Departing

From Baltimore I–70 runs westward through Frederick and up to the state's narrowest point, pinched between West Virginia and Pennsylvania. U.S. 40 passes through the Narrows into the Panhandle. From Hancock I–68—the new National Highway—is the quickest route to Cumberland, Deep Creek Lake, and several popular state parks and forests.

What to See and Do

In **Frederick** the visitor center (✉ 19 E. Church St., 21701, ☎ 301/663–8687 or 800/999–3613) has information on several historical and Civil War sites.

The **Barbara Fritchie House and Museum** (✉ 154 W. Patrick St., ☎ 301/698–0630) is where, according to legend and poetry, an old woman defied Stonewall Jackson by waving the Stars and Stripes.

Monocacy National Battlefield (✉ 4801 Urbana Pike, ☎ 301/662–3515) was the site of a little-known confrontation between 18,000 Confederates and 5,800 Union troops on July 9, 1864. The Union victory routed a Confederate invasion of Washington, D.C.

Mount Olivet Cemetery (✉ 515 S. Market St., ☎ 301/662–1164) is the final resting place of some of Maryland's most famous citizens, including Barbara Fritchie and Francis Scott Key, author of the "Star-Spangled Banner."

The **National Museum of Civil War Medicine** (✉ 48 E. Patrick St., ☎ 301/695–1864) is a repository of more than 3,000 medical artifacts, including the only known surviving Civil War surgeon's tent. The museum, still being developed, also is the starting point for a walking tour of Frederick's Civil War history.

★ Near Sharpsburg is **Antietam National Battlefield** (✉ Rte. 65, ☎ 301/432–5124), where Union troops repelled Lee's invasion in 1862. This day of fighting was the bloodiest confrontation of the Civil War, fought on a road now known as Bloody Lane. **Hagerstown** (✉ Hagerstown/Washington County Convention and Visitors Bureau, 16 Public Square, Hagerstown, 21740, ☎ 301/791–3130) was a frontier town founded by Germans in the early 18th century; several buildings from that period have been preserved, including the frontier home-fortress of Jonathan Hager, the town's founder.

The rolling, pastoral farmland west of Hagerstown gives way to rugged stretches of mountains—a landscape reminiscent of the more famous Blue Ridge chain to the south. In aptly named **Allegany County** (✉ Visitors Bureau, Mechanic and Harrison Sts., Cumberland 21502, ☎ 301/777–5905), the rugged Narrows provides an opening for U.S. 40, formerly called the National Road and taken by westward-bound settlers in the early years of the republic. This is one of western Maryland's most outdoorsy areas. **Garrett County** (✉ Promotion Council, 200 S. 3rd St., Oakland 21550, ☎ 301/334–1948) draws outdoors enthusiasts of all stripes, including skiers.

Dining and Lodging

$$$ ✕ **Brown Pelican.** Pelicans are an unusual theme for a restaurant an hour or so from Chesapeake Bay, but this dark, romantic rathskeller, with tablecloths and candlelight, has one of the finest menus in Frederick. Specialties are veal, seafood, and beef. ✉ *5 E. Church St., Frederick,* ☎ *301/695–5833. AE, D, DC, MC, V.*

$$$$ ✕⌂ **Stone Manor.** Secluded among rolling farmland outside Frederick, this 18th-century majestic stone home with 10 working fireplaces ★ is an elegant retreat and still part of a 114-acre working farm. Diners choose from a chef-selected five-course or four-course menu; featured dishes include wild game and fowl, seafood, and beef. ✉ *5820 Carroll Boyer Rd., Middletown 21769,* ☎ *301/473–5454. 5 suites. AE, MC, V. No lunch.*

$$$$ ✕⌂ **Turning Point Inn.** Rooms in this Edwardian-era home, once the residence of a prominent doctor, have a country decor; bowls of fresh fruit add a nice touch. Highlights of the excellent restaurant's menu include Chesapeake Bay seafood, roast duckling, and beef, and almost everything is prepared with local produce and herbs. ✉ *8406 Urbana Pike, Frederick 21701,* ☎ *301/874–2421. 5 rooms, 2 guest houses. D, MC, V. No lunch Mon. and Sat.*

NEW JERSEY

Updated by Jill
Sue Schensul

Capital	Trenton
Population	7,988,000
Motto	Liberty and Prosperity
State Bird	Eastern goldfinch
State Flower	Purple violet
Postal Abbreviation	NJ

Statewide Visitor Information

New Jersey Department of Commerce and Economic Development (⊠ Division of Travel and Tourism, 20 W. State St., CN-826, Trenton 08625-0826, ☎ 609/292–2470 or 800/537–7397, FAX 609/633–7418). There are seven **visitor information centers** at major destinations around the state. For information on state parks contact the **Department of Environmental Protection** (⊠ Division of Parks and Forestry, CN-404, Trenton 08625, ☎ 609/292–2797 or 800/843–6420).

Scenic Drives

For Hudson River views take the **Palisades Interstate Parkway** north from the George Washington Bridge to the state line or take **River Road** from Weehawken north to Fort Lee. Both **Route 23,** northwest from Newfoundland through High Point State Park, and **Route 15,** northwest from I–80, offer lakes, rural estates, and higher-elevation vistas. The back roads off **Routes 202** and **206** in central New Jersey pass by horse farms, antiques shops, and historic sites. Along the southern shore, **Ocean Drive** is a causeway that links barrier islands.

National and State Parks

National Parks

Sandy Hook Unit of Gateway National Recreation Area (⊠ Box 530, Highlands 07732, ☎ 732/872–0115) preserves sandbar ecology and fortifications built to protect New York Harbor. On the Delaware River boundary between New Jersey and Pennsylvania is the **Delaware Water Gap National Recreation Area** (⊠ Visitor Center, Kittatinny Point, off I–80; Bushkill, PA 18324, ☎ 908/496–4458; ☞ Pennsylvania), the largest national recreation area in the Northeast. The 40,000-acre **Edwin B. Forsythe National Wildlife Refuge's Brigantine Division** (⊠ Box 72, Great Creek Rd., Oceanville 08231, ☎ 609/652–1665) has an 8-mi wildlife drive, mainly through diverse coastal habitat, and two short, circular nature trails especially popular during spring and fall bird migrations.

State Parks

New Jersey has the third-largest state park system in the nation, with 36 parks, 11 forests, 4 recreation areas, 42 natural areas, 23 historic sites, 4 marinas, and 1 golf course. **Wharton State Forest** (⊠ Rte. 542, Hammonton 08037, ☎ 609/561–3262), New Jersey's largest, contains the **Batsto State Historic Site** (⊠ Rte. 542), a restored late-18th- and 19th-century Pinelands ironworking village, where traditional crafts are still demonstrated. **High Point State Park** is named after the state's tallest peak. Many of New Jersey's 19 **lighthouses** are preserved in state parks, including Barnegat Lighthouse, Cape May Point Lighthouse, and Sandy Hook Lighthouse (☞ Exploring the Jersey Shore, *below*).

THE JERSEY SHORE

The Jersey Shore is 127 mi of public beachfront stretching like a pointing finger along the Atlantic Ocean from the Sandy Hook Peninsula in the north to Cape May at the southern tip. There is no one description of what it's like "down the shore." Things change town by town and sometimes season by season (winter storms have a habit of rearranging beaches and boardwalks). Busy seaside resorts crammed with amusements (and families) sit next to quiet, primarily residential communities with undeveloped waterfronts, which in turn might be shoulder to shoulder with aging cities, restored Victorian districts, or anything in between. Unless you have "beachophobia," though, there's probably a place on the shore that's right for you.

The shore offers saltwater fishing from pier, bridge, dock, or boat (licenses not required); other water sports; bird-watching; and bicycling or strolling on the ubiquitous wood-plank or concrete boardwalks. In Atlantic City are the famed gambling casinos; in Cape May, Victorian bed-and-breakfasts.

Visitor Information

Atlantic City: Convention & Visitors Authority (⊠ 2314 Pacific Ave., 08401, ☎ 609/348–7100 or 800/262–7395, FAX 609/347–6577). **Cape May:** Chamber of Commerce (⊠ Box 556, 08204, ☎ 609/884–5508); Mid-Atlantic Center for the Arts (⊠ Box 340, 08204, ☎ 609/884–5404). **Cape May County:** Chamber of Commerce (⊠ Cape May Court House, Box 74, 08210, ☎ 609/465–7181, FAX 609/465–5017); Department of Tourism and Economic Development (⊠ Box 365, 08210, ☎ 609/886–0901). **Monmouth County:** Department of Promotion and Tourism (⊠ 25 E. Main St., Freehold 07728, ☎ 732/431–7476 or 800/523–2587, FAX 908/732–3696). **Ocean County:** Tourism Advisory Council (⊠ Box 2191, Toms River 08754, ☎ 732/929–2138 or 800/365–6933, FAX 732/506–5000). **Wildwoods:** Information Center (⊠ Box 609, Wildwood 08260, ☎ 609/522–1407 or 800/992–9732).

Arriving and Departing

By Plane

Philadelphia International (☞ Pennsylvania), **Newark International** (☎ 973/961–6000), and the **New York City airports** (☞ New York) are closest to Atlantic City and shore points. **Atlantic City International** (☎ 609/645–7895) serves the southern shore.

By Car

The main road serving the Jersey Shore is the Garden State Parkway, a north–south toll road that ends in Cape May. From New York City I–80 and the New Jersey Turnpike (toll) connect with the Garden State. From Philadelphia and southern New Jersey suburbs, take the Atlantic City Expressway (toll). From the south take the Delaware Memorial Bridge and continue north on the New Jersey Turnpike. Toms River, Barnegat, and Tuckerton are linked by U.S. 9.

By Train

Amtrak (⊠ 1 Atlantic City Expressway, near Kirkman Blvd., ☎ 800/872–7245) serves Atlantic City. **New Jersey Transit** (☎ 973/762–5100 for northern NJ or 800/772–2222 in NJ; ☎ 215/569–3752 for southern NJ or 800/582–5946 in NJ) operates local commuter service to Atlantic City from Philadelphia and to the shore towns in Monmouth and Ocean counties from New York City.

By Bus

New Jersey Transit (☞ By Train, *above*) offers bus service to most Jersey Shore towns. **Academy Lines** (☎ 732/291–1300) also runs buses between New York City and shore points. **Greyhound Lines** (☎ 609/345–6617 or 800/231–2222) serves Atlantic City. Ask Atlantic City casino hotels about direct service to their properties.

By Ferry

The **Cape May–Lewes Ferry** is a year-round 70-minute car ferry (800 passengers, 100 cars per ferry) across the Delaware Bay (☞ Delaware). ☎ *609/886–9699 or 800/643–3779, 800/717–7245 for reservations. AE, D, MC, V.*

Exploring the Jersey Shore

The **New Jersey Coastal Heritage Trail** (☎ 609/447–0103), under joint development by the National Park Service, the state of New Jersey, and other organizations, will connect significant natural and cultural resources along the shore. Five theme routes are planned. The first, maritime history, already has signs in place; coastal habitat is under development and at press time was scheduled for completion by mid-1997.

At the shore's north end the **Sandy Hook Unit of Gateway National Recreation Area** (☞ National and State Parks, *above*) is 4 mi east of Atlantic Highlands on Route 36. On this peninsula of barrier beach you can glimpse the New York City skyline, 19 mi across the harbor from North Beach; splash in the usually gentle, shallow surf; and explore sleepy **Fort Hancock**, established in 1895.

Just south on Route 36, **Long Branch** was founded in the 18th century as one of America's first resorts; over the years it has hosted seven presidents, from Grant to Wilson.

A century ago **Asbury Park** was the shore's toniest resort, but efforts to revive that glory have so far been disappointing. Nowadays it is known for its place in rock history; the young Bruce Springsteen performed here in the 1960s. By contrast, neighboring **Ocean Grove** was established in 1859 by Methodists as a camp meeting area and still retains that purpose. The dignified tone is echoed in its Victorian hotels and inns; relatively quiet beaches; a short, gameless boardwalk; and shops and cafés. Ocean Grove is also one of two shore towns that do not sell alcohol—the other is Ocean City, another Methodist town patterned after it. The imposing **Great Auditorium** (✉ Pilgrim Pathway, ☎ 732/775–0035) presents a summer schedule of concerts—from big bands to country, jazz, '50s and '60s oldies, and current pop.

In **Belmar** the **Municipal Marina** (✉ Rte. 35, ☎ 732/681–2266), on the Shark River, has party and charter boats that head for the ocean daily in search of blackfish, blues, fluke, tuna, and shark. Neighboring **Spring Lake** has an uncommercialized boardwalk, three spring-fed lakes with swans, a small town center, and a handful of romantic B&Bs. The more family-oriented **Point Pleasant Beach** has Jenkinson's Aquarium (✉ Ocean Ave., ☎ 732/899–1659), on the boardwalk at the Broadway Beach area, for rainy-day diversion.

On Barnegat Peninsula, the side-by-side resorts of **Seaside Heights** and **Seaside Park** have two major amusement piers plus water rides. Don't miss a turn on the antique Dentzel–Looff carousel. Just south but seemingly a world away is narrow **Island Beach State Park** (☎ 732/793–0506), 10 mi of ocean and bay beaches with almost no evidence of human habitation.

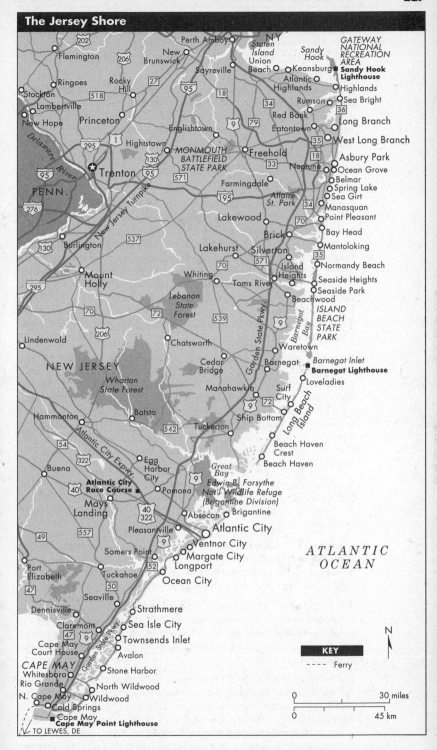

The Jersey Shore

Return inland over Barnegat Bay to **Toms River,** once a pirate and privateering port. The **Ocean County Museum** (✉ 26 Hadley Ave., ☎ 732/341–1880) contains Victorian artifacts and exhibits on the dirigibles that flew from the Lakehurst Naval Air Station, site of the 1937 *Hindenburg* tragedy.

Head south on U.S. 9 and east on Route 72 over Barnegat Bay to **Long Beach Island. Barnegat Lighthouse** (☎ 609/494–2016), known locally as Old Barne and completed in 1858, is at the northern tip of the island. To the south is **Beach Haven,** the island's commercial center, with Victorian houses set around the town square. In one of these houses you'll find the **Long Beach Island Museum** (✉ Engleside and Beach Aves., ☎ 609/492–0700), which conducts walking tours of the historic district from late June to early September.

Back on the mainland, the Garden State Parkway and U.S. 9 lead to **Atlantic City.** It was originally popular for seaside holidays in stone hotels and for promenades on the **Boardwalk,** the nation's first elevated wood walkway (1870), where saltwater taffy is still sold. Today more than 37 million people flood the town annually to gamble, dropping about $8 million daily in the **casinos.** (Be alert outside at night—the city has a high crime rate.) The dozen casino hotels are outrageous in design and entertainment—from the Mardi Gras festivity of the Showboat and the onion-shaped domes and other touches of whimsy of the Taj Mahal, on the ocean-side Boardwalk, to the pair of quieter marina casinos, on the bay.

Some of Atlantic City's famous ocean **amusement piers** can still be seen, but only the **Central Pier** (✉ St. James Pl. and Tennessee Ave.), on the boardwalk, retains its original 1884 appearance. The **Garden Pier** (✉ New Jersey Ave. and the Boardwalk) has been converted to an art center. The annual **Miss America Pageant** (☎ 609/345–7571) takes place in mid-September in the **Convention Center** (✉ 2301 Boardwalk, ☎ 609/348–7100). A new convention center opened in May 1997; at press time, the 500-room convention center hotel was under construction and slated to open in November 1997.

South of Atlantic City you'll find **Ocean City,** across Great Egg Harbor. Its **boardwalk** and boardwalk parades are family oriented, and summer-evening concerts at the **Music Pier** (✉ Moorlyn Terr.) are a tradition.

Savor a quiet walk on **Strathmere Beach.** Take time out to explore the **Wetlands Institute** (☎ 609/368–1211), in Stone Harbor, a research and education center on coastal ecology. The popular **Wings 'n Water Festival** is held here and in neighboring towns in early September.

Then head south along Ocean Drive to the little boroughs known as the **Wildwoods.** The best-known, the loudest, the kitschiest, and the wildest is **Wildwood** itself. Its 2-mi **boardwalk** has the single greatest concentration of outdoor amusement rides on the shore, including seven amusement piers.

★ For a change of pace and scenery, travel to the southern tip of the shore and the re-created world of Victorian **Cape May.** The state's oldest ocean resort, it was named for the Dutch captain who sighted it in 1620. Cape May today hosts myriad, mostly-for-grownups bed-and-breakfasts, many in elaborately gingerbreaded Victorian houses (some B&Bs and restaurants close January through March). In early October **Victorian Week** (☎ 609/884–5404) combines madcap frivolity with serious lectures on period history and restoration (make reservations well in advance). The July 4 celebration is vintage Americana, while Christmastime has Dickensian flair, with trolley, candlelight, and walking tours of houses decorated in traditional Victorian finery.

The Cape May area also attracts flocks of birds and bird-watchers, especially during the spring and fall migrations. A favorite birding locale is **Cape May Point State Park** (✉ Lighthouse Ave., ☎ 609/884–2159), site of the **Cape May Point Lighthouse** (☎ 609/884–5404 or 800/275–4278), built in 1859, which marks the end of the Jersey Shore. Another popular activity is whale-watching; several boats ply the Atlantic spring through fall, often coming upon pods of dolphins as well as whales. Not far from the lighthouse, **Sunset Beach** (✉ Sunset Blvd., Cape May Point) is the place to collect "Cape May diamonds," pebbles of pure quartz that wash up on the beach, and to watch the sun set over Delaware Bay.

What to See and Do with Children

The entire Jersey Shore is a children's playground, with its sandy beaches, usually gentle and shallow surf, and casual boardwalk snack bars. Towns with child-friendly **amusement parks** or **rides** include revitalized Keansburg, Seaside Park, Ocean City, Point Pleasant Beach, and Wildwood. **Lucy the Elephant** (✉ Atlantic and Decatur Aves., Margate, ☎ 609/823–6473), an elephant-shape building six stories high and a National Historic Landmark, has been drawing the curious of all ages since 1881.

★ **Six Flags Great Adventure,** a theme park bigger than Disneyland, comprises both an amusement park with a multitude of rides and a drive-through safari park. ✉ *Rte. 537, I–195 Exit 16, Jackson,* ☎ *732/928–2000 or 732/928–1821 for recording.* ✆ *$34; safari only $15; safari–theme park combination $37. Closed late Oct.–mid-Apr.*

Dining and Lodging

Although the restaurant fare ranges from cheap snacks to pricey haute cuisine, seafood is the Jersey Shore's biggest deal, with local catches featured on most menus. Ocean City and Ocean Grove do not allow the sale of liquor. For price ranges *see* Chart 1 (A) *in* On the Road with Fodor's.

Lodgings should be booked far in advance in summer. Beachfront rooms are more expensive. Rooms in Atlantic City casino hotels are the most popular, the most costly, and the most difficult to reserve, especially on weekends from mid-June to Labor Day. Chambers of commerce (☞ Visitor Information, *above*) can provide assistance. **Bed & Breakfast Adventures** (✉ 2310 Central Ave., Suite 132, North Wildwood 08260, ☎ 609/522–4000 or 800/992–2632, ℻ 609/522–6125) handles inns and private homes statewide. Also try the **Bed and Breakfast Innkeepers Association of New Jersey** (☎ 732/449–3535). For price ranges *see* Chart 2 (A) *in* On the Road with Fodor's.

Atlantic City

$$$$ ✕ **Le Palais.** Favorites such as shellfish-vegetable mélange Olga, rack
★ of lamb with rosemary and pine nuts, and individual dessert soufflés (order these at the start of the meal) are elegantly served in this lavish mirrored dining room hung with art. ✉ *Merv Griffin's Resorts Casino Hotel, N. Carolina Ave. and Boardwalk,* ☎ *609/344–6000 or 800/438–7424. AE, D, DC, MC, V. Closed Mon.–Tues.*

$$$ ✕ **Knife and Fork Inn.** Established in 1912 in its Tudor-accented Flemish tavern and owned by the same family since 1927, this local institution serves straightforward seafood and steaks. ✉ *Albany and Atlantic Aves.,* ☎ *609/344–1133. AE, D, DC, MC, V. Closed Nov.–Apr.*

$$–$$$ ✕ **Dock's Oyster House.** Owned and operated by the Dougherty family since 1897, the city's oldest restaurant serves seafood in a setting of wood and stained and engraved glass with nautical motifs. ⌧ *2405 Atlantic Ave.,* ☎ *609/345–0092. AE, DC, MC, V. Closed Jan.–Apr.*

$$ ✕ **Los Amigos.** South-of-the-border specialties such as Mexican pizza, burritos, and margaritas, served in the dimly lighted back room, are a good bet at this small bar and restaurant two blocks from the boardwalk casinos. ⌧ *1926 Atlantic Ave.,* ☎ *609/344–2293. AE, DC, MC, V.*

$ ✕ **Angelo's Fairmount Tavern.** The locals flock here for lots of good Italian fare served up by the Mancuso family, the owners since 1935. ⌧ *2300 Fairmount Ave.,* ☎ *609/344–2439. AE, MC, V. No lunch weekends.*
★

$ ✕ **White House Sub Shop.** It claims to have sold more than 17 million overstuffed sandwiches since 1946. Photo walls proclaim its celebrity fans. ⌧ *Mississippi and Arctic Aves.,* ☎ *609/345–1564 or 609/345–8599. Reservations not accepted. No credit cards.*

$$$–$$$$ ▥ **Bally's Park Place Casino Hotel & Tower.** Guests can stay in the art deco–style rooms of the historic Dennis Hotel, built in 1860, or in the newer 37-story tower, whose spacious, angular rooms have picture windows even in the marble-tile bathrooms. The spa facilities are exceptional. ⌧ *Park Place at Boardwalk, 08401,* ☎ *609/340–2000 or 800/ 225–5977,* ⅎ𝔸𝕏 *609/340–4713. 1,414 rooms. 8 restaurants, lounge, indoor pool, hot tubs, sauna, basketball, exercise room, racquetball, shops, cabaret. AE, D, DC, MC, V.*
★

$$$–$$$$ ▥ **Trump Marina Casino.** Blandly modern on the outside, this bayside marina—away from some of the boardwalk glitz—is airy and comfortable, with first-rate, friendly service. ⌧ *Huron Ave. and Brigantine Blvd., 08401,* ☎ *609/441–2000 or 800/777–8477,* ⅎ𝔸𝕏 *609/345–7604. 728 rooms. 8 restaurants, pool, hot tub, sauna, 4 tennis courts, health club, dock, nightclub, shops. AE, D, DC, MC, V.*

$$$ ▥ **Flagship Resorts.** This pleasant, modern, salmon-colored condo hotel is across from the boardwalk (facing Brigantine and the Absecon Inlet) and is quietly away from the casino action. Every room has a private terrace with a view. ⌧ *60 N. Main Ave., 08401,* ☎ *609/343–7447 or 800/647–7890,* ⅎ𝔸𝕏 *609/344–3545. 420 suites. Restaurant, bar, deli, pool, hot tub, health club. AE, D, DC, MC, V.*

$$ ▥ **Quality Inn Atlantic City.** A half block from the boardwalk, one of Atlantic City's best values has a 17-story modern guest wing set atop a Federal-style base. Rooms are decorated with handsome Colonial reproductions. Merv Griffin's casino is next door. ⌧ *S. Carolina and Pacific Aves., 08401,* ☎ *609/345–7070 or 800/356–6044,* ⅎ𝔸𝕏 *609/ 345–0633. 203 rooms. Restaurant, bar. AE, D, DC, MC, V.*
★

Cape May

$$–$$$ ✕ **Mad Batter.** The eclectic contemporary American cuisine—perhaps orange-and-almond French toast with strawberry dipping sauce for breakfast; a lunch of house-smoked maple chicken on a bed of mesculine greens; and, for dinner, crab *mappatello* (crabmeat, spinach, ricotta, and onions in a puff pastry)—is served in the skylighted Victorian dining room or outdoors on the porch or the garden terrace. ⌧ *19 Jackson St.,* ☎ *609/884–5970. D, MC, V. Closed 1st 3 wks in Jan.*
★

$$$–$$$$ ▥ **Queen Victoria.** In the center of the historic district, the inn's three restored Victorian houses are blessed with a genteel air and are decorated with items that pay homage to the queen and the period named for her. Rooms are furnished with antiques but have modern touches unusual for a B&B, including minirefrigerators in every room, whirl-

pool baths in many, and TVs in the suites. ⊠ *102 Ocean St., 08204,* ☎ *609/884–8702. 23 rooms. Bicycles, free parking. AE, MC, V.*

$$$ ☷ **The Mainstay.** This 1872 men's gambling club reincarnated as a B&B
★ captures the feel of another era with 14-ft ceilings, stenciling and historic wallpapers, and harmoniously arranged antiques, while another restored building across the street contains suites filled with modern amenities. ⊠ *635 Columbia Ave., 08204,* ☎ *609/884–8690. 16 rooms. Free parking. No credit cards.*

$$–$$$ ☷ **Chalfonte.** This authentic Victorian summer hotel is definitely one of a kind. Despite simple original furnishings, it attracts a loyal blue-blooded following. Interesting programs include evening entertainment; work weeks, during which students and other volunteers stay free at the hotel in return for help in upkeep; and a supervised children's dining room, where youngsters eat from a special menu while parents dine on the famous mostly southern home-style cooking. ⊠ *301 Howard St., 08204,* ☎ *609/884–8409,* FAX *609/884–4588. 78 rooms, 2 cottages. Restaurant, bar, dining room, playground, meeting room. MAP. MC, V. Closed Columbus Day–Memorial Day weekend.*

$$–$$$ ☷ **Manor House.** On a quiet tree-lined street two blocks from the beach, this guest house mixes antiques, stained glass, art, dashes of whimsy such as an old-fashioned barber's chair, and a wisecracking innkeeper. ⊠ *612 Hughs St., 08204,* ☎ *609/884–4710. 10 rooms. Valet parking. D, MC, V. Closed Jan.*

Spring Lake

$$$ ☷ **Seacrest by the Sea.** This 1885 Queen Anne Victorian is one of many in town. The rooms are furnished with feather beds and luxurious fabrics. Eight rooms have gas-log fireplaces; seven have ocean views. Try the buttermilk scones at the full buffet breakfast. ⊠ *19 Tuttle Ave.,* ☎ *732/449–9031,* FAX *732/974–0403. 12 rooms. AE, MC, V.*

$$–$$$ ☷ **Hollycroft.** Looking over Lake Como at the northern edge of town, this incongruous but beautiful B&B is a mountain lodge at the shore. A 16-ft ironstone fireplace; walls of knotty pine and, here and there, log or stone; and rooms decorated with collected treasures, stenciling, and good taste make this a charming getaway. ⊠ *North Blvd. (Box 448), 07762,* ☎ *732/681–2254. 8 rooms. Bicycles.*

Toms River

$$ ✕ **Old Time Tavern.** Italian dishes, steak, seafood, and sandwiches are the lures at this restaurant and tap room, and if you're an early bird, you can get soup-to-dessert meals at bargain prices. ⊠ *N. Main St. (Rte. 166 off Rte. 37),* ☎ *732/349–8778. AE, DC, MC, V.*

Motels

☷ **Ascot Motel** (⊠ Iowa and Pacific Aves., Box 1824, Atlantic City 08404, ☎ 609/344–5163 or 800/225–1476), 80 rooms, pool; *$$.* ☷ **Best Western Bayside Resort at Golf & Tennis World** (⊠ 8029 Black Horse Pike, W. Atlantic City 08232, ☎ 609/641–3546 or 800/999–9466, FAX 609/641–4329), 110 rooms, restaurant, 2 pools, 6 tennis courts, health club; *$$.* ☷ **Midtown–Bala Motor Inn** (⊠ Indiana and Pacific Aves., Atlantic City 08401, ☎ 609/348–3031 or 800/932–0534, FAX 609/347–6043), 300 rooms, restaurant, indoor and outdoor pools, free parking; *$$.* ☷ **Sandpiper** (⊠ Boulevard at 10th St., Ship Bottom 08008, ☎ 609/494–6909), 20 rooms, refrigerators, pool; closed Nov.–Apr.; *$–$$.*

Nightlife and the Arts

Garden State Arts Center (⊠ Garden State Pkwy. Exit 116, Holmdel, ☎ 732/442–9200) has a summer roster of performing arts groups, star acts, and ethnic festivals. Between the gambling action and the nationally famous nightclub acts, nightlife is fierce at the **Atlantic City casino hotels**; call the casino box offices for show reservations.

Outdoor Activities and Sports

Biking

Boardwalks are grand for biking if you don't mind dodging weekend walkers and joggers. The road around **Cape May Point** takes you past Cape May Point State Park and its lighthouse.

Canoeing

Try the many freshwater creeks, streams, and tributaries in the 1.1-million-acre **Pinelands National Reserve** (☎ 609/894–9342), the country's first national reserve, near Chatsworth.

Fishing

Monmouth County has more charter and party boats than any other area along the shore; most popular is the **Belmar Marina** (☞ Exploring the Jersey Shore, *above*). In Ocean County numerous party and charter boats sail from Point Pleasant and Long Beach Island. Fishing boats sail from state marinas in **Leonardo** (☎ 732/291–1333) and **Atlantic City** (☎ 609/441–8482).

Spectator Sports

Horse Racing: Before Atlantic City began staging big-name boxing events, horse racing was the shore's most popular spectator sport. **Monmouth Park** (⊠ Oceanport Ave., Oceanport, ☎ 732/222–5100) is the area's best-known track, with Thoroughbred races from late May through early September. The **Atlantic City Race Course** (⊠ 4501 Black Horse Pike, May's Landing, ☎ 609/641–2190) has Thoroughbred racing June–mid-August. **Freehold Raceway** (⊠ U.S. 9 and Rte. 33, Freehold, ☎ 732/462–3800) offers harness racing mid-August–May.

Beaches

From Memorial Day to Labor Day the **Water Information Hotline** (☎ 800/648–7263) supplies information about the shore's water quality and beach conditions. **Island Beach State Park** (☞ Exploring the Jersey Shore, *above*) is the most scenic natural beach on the Jersey Shore. Beaches usually charge a fee from Memorial Day or mid-June to Labor Day. Windsurfing is especially good in the calm waters of the open bays. Sailing, rowing, and powerboating are superb on sheltered Barnegat Bay in Ocean County.

Shopping

The **Englishtown Auction** (⊠ 90 Wilson Ave., ☎ 732/446–9644), a giant flea market held on weekends March–January plus selected holidays, covers 50 acres. Arrive at sunrise for the best buys.

ELSEWHERE IN NEW JERSEY

The Northwest Corner

Arriving and Departing

I–80 along with Routes 23 and 15, which run northwest from it, provide easy access from Manhattan to this area.

What to See and Do

This sparsely developed region of small lakes and low mountains attracts skiers in winter, while the rest of the year brings outdoorsy types who come to enjoy water sports on the Delaware River and Lake

Hopatcong, scenic roads, hikes on the Appalachian Trail, and historical sites from the 1700s and 1800s.

The state's highest elevation (1,803 ft) is in **High Point State Park** (☞ National and State Parks, *above*), 7 mi northwest of Sussex. Hugging
★ the river from I–80 to the northern tip of the state is the **Delaware Water Gap National Recreation Area** (☞ National and State Parks, *above*). **Waterloo Village** (✉ Waterloo Rd., Stanhope, ☎ 973/347–0900) is a restored Revolutionary War–era canal town. Staff members in period costume greet visitors and demonstrate traditional crafts. Children's activities, such as face painting and storytelling, are ongoing. Its summer concert series attracts renowned jazz, classical, rock, and country performers.

The most popular ski areas, clustered around the nondescript town of **McAfee,** are outfitted with artificial snowmaking equipment, have both day and evening skiing, are family oriented, and provide a mix of all-ability ski terrain. **Vernon Valley/Great Gorge** (✉ Rte. 94, Vernon, ☎ 973/827–2000) is the largest (14 chairlifts, 3 rope tows, 52 trails), with slopes on three mountains. In summer this resort becomes **Action Park,** filled with water-park activities and other action rides (motorbikes, an alpine slide, race cars). **Hidden Valley** (✉ Rte. 515, Vernon, ☎ 973/764–4200) is a lively alternative, with 3 chairlifts and 12 trails. **Craigmeur Ski Area** (✉ Rte. 513, Rockaway, ☎ 973/697–4500)—small (1 chairlift, 1 rope tow, 1 T-bar, 4 trails) and friendly—is best for rank beginners or families with younger children.

Along the Delaware

Arriving and Departing

From Manhattan the New Jersey Turnpike skirts the area, and U.S. 1 and I–195 are key access roads. From Philadelphia I–95 runs up the Pennsylvania side of the river, crossing north of Trenton, while I–295 and the New Jersey Turnpike parallel it on the Jersey side.

What to See and Do

Forming New Jersey's "other shore" (its border with Pennsylvania), the Delaware slowly changes from a relatively small, often rock-studded river in the north to a mighty, navigable river as it flows past Philadelphia and empties into Delaware Bay. The towns that line it change as well. Part of the way down the state, quaint towns like **Milford, Frenchtown, Stockton,** and, the largest of these, **Lambertville** hug the river below ridges and rolling hills beyond. Gracing the pastoral scenery are 18th-century buildings, galleries, antiques and crafts stores, excellent restaurants, and B&Bs and inns. Across the bridge from Lambertville is the popular, artsy town of **New Hope,** in Bucks County (☞ Pennsylvania). Inland a bit, **Flemington** is known for shopping of a different kind, thanks to a huge number of outlet stores. Flemington's **Liberty Village** (✉ Church St., ☎ 908/782–8550) contains more than 60 factory and designer outlets.

Follow the river south of Lambertville to find an area where George Washington actually did sleep for 10 critical days in 1776–77 (in fact, Washington and the Continental Army spent about one-third of the war in New Jersey). **Washington Crossing State Park** (✉ Rte. 546, Titusville, ☎ 609/737–0623) is the site of Washington's Christmas night
★ 1776 crossing (reenacted each Christmas). Follow Washington's trail south to the state capital, **Trenton,** previously a colonial pottery and manufacturing center, today a small city struggling with a quiet rebirth. One of Trenton's gems is **Chambersburg,** also known as the Burg, a residential neighborhood with dozens of superb Italian restaurants. Washington surprised the sleeping Hessians in the **Old Barracks** (✉ Barrack

St., ☎ 609/396–1776), now a museum. He followed his victory in Trenton with one in **Princeton,** just to the north. The two battles were the first major victories for the Continental Army. Princeton is now a pretty university town, with upscale shops and the governor's mansion, **Drumthwacket** (⊠ 354 Stockton St., ☎ 609/683–0057).

South of Trenton, the aging industrial town of **Camden** is enjoying some degree of revitalization along its waterfront. Central to the project is the **Thomas H. Kean New Jersey State Aquarium** (⊠ 1 Riverside Dr., ☎ 609/365–3300), built in 1992 and updated in 1995 with the award-winning **Ocean Base Atlantic exhibit,** which features interactive displays and an artful underwater effect extending beyond the tanks of more than 4,000 fish. Within walking distance along the waterfront is another new project, the $56 million **Blockbuster–Sony Music Entertainment Centre** (⊠ 1 Harbour Blvd., ☎ 609/365–1300). The state-of-the-art amphitheater accommodates 25,000 people, including 18,000 on the lawn; it is the first such venue to be converted to a year-round indoor theater. Camden also boasts **Walt Whitman's home** (⊠ 328–330 Mickle Blvd., ☎ 609/964–5383) and his tomb in the Harleigh Cemetery (⊠ Vesper and Haddon Aves.).

North Jersey

Arriving and Departing
From Manhattan take either the Lincoln Tunnel or the George Washington Bridge, and you're in North Jersey. I–80, to the north, and I–78, through Jersey City and Newark, connect with the New Jersey Turnpike, the Garden State Parkway, and I–287, which all run northeast–southwest through the region.

What to See and Do
Although Newark International Airport is all some travelers may experience of this part of the state, a wealth of activities is available for those who care to linger. Among the suburban bedroom communities of Manhattan-bound commuters are parks, performing arts venues, museums, great shopping, and some of the state's finest restaurants and accommodations.

Jersey City, at first glance merely gritty and urban, is nonetheless worth a visit—most obviously for its superb views of the broad Hudson River and the Manhattan skyline. It is the site of **Liberty State Park** (⊠ New Jersey Turnpike Exit 14B, ☎ 201/915–3400), where ferries leave for the **Statue of Liberty** and the **Ellis Island Immigration Museum** (☞ New York for both) on the site of the restored century-old former immigration facility, less than 2,000 ft offshore. Within Liberty State Park is the **Liberty Science Center** (⊠ 251 Phillip St., ☎ 201/200–1000), with three floors of hands-on and interactive exhibits plus an Omnimax theater (a domed screen 88 ft across and 125 ft high), as well as the restored, open-sided 1889 **Central Railroad of New Jersey Terminal,** now used for special events and exhibits. Or stroll along **Liberty Walk,** a promenade along the waterfront.

Its neighbor to the north, the "mile-square" city of **Hoboken,** boasts several claims to fame. It was the setting for the movie *On the Waterfront*; the birthplace of baseball, first played on Elysian Fields (at the site of the now-defunct Maxwell House plant) in 1846; and the hometown of Frank Sinatra. Though it's relationship with Old Blue Eyes has been a love-hate one—Sinatra spurned his hometown after being pelted with fruits at a concert there in 1952—his presence can be felt everywhere. A new plaque marks **Sinatra's birthplace** (⊠ 415 Monroe St.), destroyed by fire in 1967. **Frank Sinatra Way,** hugging the bank of the

Hudson River, commands some of the best views in town. Most of the long-standing businesses in town display faded photos of the singer. Music is also part of the draw for a new generation; yuppified **Washington Street** is the thoroughfare for the trendy and boisterous who drop in on its many music venues. **Maxwell's** (⌧ 1039 Washington St., ☎ 201/798–4064) is the granddaddy, featuring live, mostly alternative music every night. Hoboken has always been popular among artists, many of whom open their studios for an annual tour in October. Washington Street offers a suitably arty mix of boutiques, antiques shops, hole-in-the-wall restaurants and liquor stores, and fast-food chain restaurants. Parking is Manhattan-style impossible, especially on weekends.

Newark, the state's largest city, is making a valiant effort to emerge from many years of economic stagnation and urban decay. The new **New Jersey Performing Arts Center** (⌧ 1 Newark Ctr., between Military Park and the waterfront, ☎ 973/648–8989) was scheduled at press time to make its debut in the fall of 1997, with the 2,750-seat Prudential Hall, 500-seat Victoria Theater, two restaurants, parking facilities, and a landscaped plaza. The $180 million center is the new home to the New Jersey Symphony Orchestra. The **Newark Museum** (⌧ 49 Washington St., ☎ 973/596–6550) has outstanding fine arts, science, and industry collections; its recently restored Ballantine House, a National Historic Landmark, offers two floors of Victorian period rooms and decorative arts.

★ The **Edison National Historic Site** (⌧ Main and Lakeside Ave., West Orange, ☎ 973/736–0550), on the site of Thomas Alva Edison's former home, includes his main laboratory, machine shop and library, and replicas of many of his inventions.

In Millburn, the **Paper Mill Playhouse** (⌧ Brookside Dr., ☎ 973/376–4343) has long been regarded as one of the finest off-Broadway theaters, with a constantly changing slate of plays and musicals. In winter the New Jersey Ballet Company performs the *Nutcracker.*

To the west, outside suburban Morristown, is the **Morristown National Historical Park/Jockey Hollow** (⌧ Washington Pl., ☎ 973/539–2085), where George Washington and his Continental Army camped during the winter of 1779–80. The park includes the elegant Ford Mansion, once Washington's quarters, and the soldiers' log huts. From Morristown follow U.S. 202 south past antiques shops and farm stands. This is horse country, with estates and meadows edged with wood fencing, especially around **Bedminster.** Many horse farms are off U.S. 202 on Route 523. At the headquarters of the **U.S. Equestrian Team** (⌧ Rtes. 512 and 206, Gladstone, ☎ 908/234–1251), you can see the trophy room, which displays the team's Olympic medals, old photos, and other mementos. Competitions, including a major festival in June, are held throughout the year. **Far Hills** is the home of the U.S. Golf Association and its museum, **Golf House** (⌧ Rte. 512E, ☎ 908/234–2300).

The **Great Swamp National Wildlife Refuge** (⌧ Basking Ridge, ☎ 973/425–1222) always surprises visitors not expecting its 7,300 acres of wildlife sanctuary, crossed with 8½ mi of trails, blinds, and boardwalks.

For wildlife of a different sort, the **Meadowlands Racetrack,** at the Meadowlands Sports Complex (⌧ Rte. 3 and NJ Turnpike, East Rutherford, ☎ 201/935–8500), offers Thoroughbred racing in the fall, with harness racing and simulcasts from other tracks the rest of the year. Check local newspapers for gate times. **Pegasus** is the most upscale of the four restaurants on site. South of the track, in **Secaucus,** are acres and acres of **outlet shops** that put this otherwise unremarkable city on the map.

Dining and Lodging

$$$$ ✕ **Chez Madeline.** Tables at this romantic French spot are small and candlelighted; the mood is elegantly cozy. The menu changes often, but you might start with a napoleon puff pastry with wild mushrooms and asparagus and move on to chicken *à la niçoise* (with tomatoes, black olives, garlic, and anchovies). Five sinful desserts are proffered from a platter. Bring your own wine. ⊠ *Bedford Ave.,* ☎ *201/384–7637. Reservations required. DC, MC, V. Closed Sun.–Mon.*

$$–$$$ ✕ **Park & Orchard.** This extremely popular establishment has earned its marks with vegetarians, offering a variety of meatless dishes including meat-and-dairy-free lasagna. But nonvegetarians will appreciate the variety of non–red meat entrées. The place is cavernous, noisy, and always busy. Its wine list has won many awards; the house wines are usually terrific choices. Save room for the peanut butter pie. ⊠ *240 Hackensack St.,* ☎ *201/939–9393. Reservations not accepted, but call ahead for waiting list. AE, D, DC, MC, V.*

$$$$ ▥ **Hilton at Short Hills.** This is one of the state's finest hotels. Its gourmet restaurant, the Dining Room, receives raves for its Continental cuisine. Solace, the hotel's beautiful spa, is reason enough for a visit. The nearby Mall at Short Hills offers discriminating shoppers dozens of tony stores from which to choose. ⊠ *41 JFK Pkwy., 07078,* ☎ *973/379–0100,* ℻ *973/379–6870. 300 rooms. 2 restaurants, pool, spa, health club, laundry, concierge, business services, meeting rooms. AE, D, DC, MC, V.*

$$$$ ▥ **Clinton Inn Hotel.** Tucked into a pretty suburban neighborhood, the inn is especially popular for weddings and other special occasions, good food, and personalized service. ⊠ *145 Dean Dr.,* ☎ *201/871–3200 or 800/275–4411,* ℻ *201/871–3435. 112 rooms. Restaurant, exercise room. AE, DC, MC, V.*

$$$$ ✕ **The Manor.** Thousands of northern New Jersey youngsters have celebrated one or another occasion with their parents at this local institution, which offers American and Continental cuisine. Among the highlights are the paella, stir-fries, and the seafood buffet. ⊠ *111 Prospect Ave.,* ☎ *201/731–2360. Jacket and tie. Reservations required. AE, DC, MC, V. Closed Mon.*

PENNSYLVANIA

By Rathe Miller

Capital	Harrisburg
Population	12,056,000
Motto	Virtue, Liberty, and Independence
State Bird	Ruffed grouse
State Flower	Mountain laurel
Postal Abbreviation	PA

Statewide Visitor Information

Pennsylvania Department of Commerce, Office of Travel and Tourism (⊠ 453 Forum Bldg., Harrisburg 17120, ☎ 717/787–5453 or 800/847–4872). **Welcome centers** are on major highways around the state.

Scenic Drives

In Bucks County **River Road** wends 40 mi along the Delaware River, offering views of 18th- and 19th-century stone farmhouses, tucked-away villages, and fall foliage along wooded hills. In the Poconos **Route 209,** from Stroudsburg to Milford, passes untouched forests and natural waterfalls. The Lancaster County countryside, with its Amish farms and roadside stands, can best be seen along the side roads between **Routes 23** and **340.**

National and State Parks

National Parks

Pennsylvania has 17 national parks, historic sites, and monuments overseen by the **National Park Service** (⊠ 143 S. 3rd St., Philadelphia 19106, ☎ 215/597–7013), a few of which have camping. The **Delaware Water Gap National Recreation Area** (⊠ Bushkill 18324, ☎ 717/588–2451), a 40-mi-long preserve in the northeast corner of the state, has camping, fishing, river rafting, and tubing. The 500,000-acre **Allegheny National Forest** (⊠ Box 847, Warren 16365, ☎ 814/723–5150), in the northwestern part of the state, has hiking and cross-country skiing trails, three rivers suitable for canoeing, and outstanding stream fishing.

State Parks

Pennsylvania's 116 state parks include more than 7,000 campsites. The **Bureau of State Parks** (⊠ Rachel Carson State Bldg., Box 8551, Harrisburg 17105, ☎ 800/637–2757) provides information and campsite reservations. In the Poconos the heavily wooded **Hickory Run State Park** (⊠ R.D. 1, Box 81, White Haven 18661, ☎ 717/443–0400) offers fishing, camping, and Boulder Field, an area covered in rock formations dating to the Ice Age. The 19,400-acre **Ohiopyle State Park** (⊠ Box 105, Ohiopyle 15470, ☎ 412/329–8591) has camping, cross-country skiing, and a 27-mi hiking and biking trail along the Youghiogheny River. **Presque Isle State Park** (⊠ Rte. 832, Erie 16505, ☎ 814/833–7424), a 3,202-acre sandy peninsula that extends 7 mi into Lake Erie, is popular for fishing, swimming, and picnicking.

PHILADELPHIA

Almost a century after English Quaker William Penn founded Philadelphia in 1682, the city became the birthplace of the nation and the home of its first government. Today, for visitors and natives alike, Philadelphia is synonymous with Independence Hall, the Liberty Bell, cheese steaks and hoagies, ethnic neighborhoods, theaters, buoyant classical music—and city streets teeming with life. With close to 1.6 million people, Penn's "City of Brotherly Love" is the fifth-largest city in the country yet maintains the feel of a friendly small town.

Visitor Information

The **Philadelphia Visitors Center** (✉ 16th St. and John F. Kennedy Blvd., 19102, ☎ 215/636–1666 or 800/321–9563) is a good first stop for brochures, maps, discount coupons for tourist sites, and hotel and restaurant information. The gift shop stocks Philly-kitsch items.

Arriving and Departing

By Bus
Greyhound Lines (✉ 10th and Filbert Sts., ☎ 800/231–2222).

By Car
The main north–south highway through Philadelphia is I–95; to reach Center City, as the downtown area is called, take the Vine Street exit off I–95S or the Broad Street exit off I–95N. From the west the Schuylkill Expressway (I–76) has several exits to Center City. From the east the New Jersey Turnpike and I–295 provide access to either U.S. 30/I–676, which enters the city via the Benjamin Franklin Bridge, or New Jersey Route 42 and the Walt Whitman Bridge.

By Plane
Philadelphia International Airport (☎ 215/937–6937), 8 mi southwest of downtown, has scheduled flights on most major domestic and foreign carriers. A **SEPTA** (☞ Getting Around Philadelphia, *below*) rail line connects the airport with Center City stations; the trip takes 20 minutes and costs $5. Airport shuttle services, such as **Limelight Limousine** (☎ 215/782–8818) and **SuperShuttle** (☎ 215/551–6600), charge about $10 per person. Taxis cost about $20, plus tip.

By Train
Amtrak serves 30th Street Station (✉ 30th and Market Sts., ☎ 800/872–7245). **New Jersey Transit** (✉ 10th and Filbert Sts., ☎ 215/569–3752) trains connect with SEPTA (☞ Getting Around Philadelphia, *below*) trains at Trenton.

Getting Around Philadelphia

The traditional heart of the city is the intersection of Broad and Market streets, where city hall now stands. Market Street divides the city north and south. North–south streets are numbered, starting at the Delaware River with Front (1st) Street and increasing to the west. Most historical and cultural attractions are easy walks from the midtown area, which is safe during the day. After dark ask hotel personnel about the safety of places you're interested in visiting, but in general, cabs are safer than walking.

By Car
These narrow streets were designed for Colonial traffic of the four-legged kind, and driving can be difficult. On-street parking is often forbidden during rush hours (parking facilities include those at 41 N. 6th Street; 16th and Arch streets; and 10th and Locust streets). During rush hours avoid the major arteries leading into and out of the city, particularly I–95, U.S. 1, and the Schuylkill Expressway.

By Public Transportation
SEPTA (☎ 215/580–7800) operates an extensive network of buses, trolleys, subways, and commuter trains; the fare is $1.60, transfers 40¢

and exact change is required. Certain lines run 24 hours a day. SEPTA's **Day Pass,** good for a day's unlimited riding, can be purchased at the visitor center (☞ Visitor Information, *above*) for $5. Bus Route 76 connects the zoo in western Fairmount Park with Penn's Landing at the Delaware River. The purple **Phlash** buses do the downtown loop.

By Taxi

Cabs are plentiful during the day—especially along Broad Street and near hotels and train stations. At night and outside Center City, taxis are scarce, and you may have to call for service. Fares start at $1.80 and increase by $1.80 for every subsequent mile. The main companies are **Quaker City Cab** (☎ 215/728–8000), **United Cab** (☎ 215/425–7000), and **Yellow Cab** (☎ 215/922–8400).

Orientation Tours

Gray Line Tours (☎ 215/569–3666) offers a three-hour tour of historic and cultural areas. To combine lunch or dinner with a sightseeing cruise on the Delaware River, climb aboard the *Spirit of Philadelphia* (☎ 215/923–1419).

Boat Tours

The *Spirit of Philadelphia* (☎ 215/923–1419) and the *Liberty Belle* (☎ 215/629–1131) offer lunch, dinner, and moonlight cruises along the Delaware River. Both dock at Penn's Landing at the foot of Lombard Street.

Carriage Tours

Philadelphia Carriage Co. (☎ 215/922–6840), **'76 Carriage Co.** (☎ 215/923–8516), and **Society Hill Carriage Co.** (☎ 215/627–6128) offer tours of the historic area in antique horse-drawn carriages, narrated by costumed drivers.

Walking Tours

Audio Walk and Tour (✉ Norman Rockwell Museum, 6th and Sansom Sts., ☎ 215/925–1234) provides a cassette player and map for a city historic tour. From May through October **Centipede Tours** (☎ 215/735–3123) gives guided candlelight strolls through Old Philadelphia. The **Foundation for Architecture** (☎ 215/569–3187), which offers tours April through November, specializes in both theme and neighborhood tours.

Exploring Philadelphia

The *Calendar of Events* at the visitor center (☞ Visitor Information, *above*) lists Philadelphia's myriad free events and attractions. Several museums schedule a period when admission is free to all.

Historic District

Even if you're not a history buff, it's hard not to get excited by the "most historic square mile in America"—**Independence National Historical Park** (☎ 215/597–8974).

The **visitor center** (✉ 3rd and Chestnut Sts., ☎ 215/597–8974) has park rangers staffing the information desk and a shop with books and gifts related to Colonial times and the Revolutionary War. Note the mahogany wood carving on the pediment of the 1797 **First Bank of the United States,** the oldest bank building in the country. It is across the street from the visitor center. In **Carpenter's Court** (✉ Chestnut St. between 3rd and 4th Sts.) you'll find **Carpenter's Hall,** where the first Continental Congress convened in 1774, and the **New Hall Military Museum.**

You can almost hear "When in the course of human events . . ." when
★ you stand behind **Independence Hall** (⌧ Chestnut St. between 5th and
6th Sts.) on the spot where the Declaration of Independence was first
read to the public, and it's easy to imagine the impact those words and
this setting had on the colonists on July 8, 1776. Still an impressive
building, the hall opened in 1732 as the state house for the colony of
Pennsylvania. It was the site of many historic events: the Second Continental Congress, convened on May 10, 1775; the adoption of the Declaration of Independence a year later; the signing of the Articles of
Confederation in 1778; and the formal signing of the Constitution by
its framers on September 17, 1787. In front of the hall, next to the statue
of George Washington, note the plaques marking the spots where
Abraham Lincoln and John F. Kennedy stood and delivered speeches.
Tours of Independence Hall are given year-round; from early May to
Labor Day expect a wait.

Philadelphia's best-known symbol is the **Liberty Bell** (⌧ Market St. between 5th and 6th Sts.), currently housed in a glass-enclosed pavilion.
During the day park rangers relate the facts and the legends about the
2,080-pound bell. After hours you can press a button on the outside
walls to hear a recorded account of the bell's history. In its current home
you can still touch the bell and read its biblical inscription: PROCLAIM
LIBERTY THROUGHOUT ALL THE LAND UNTO ALL THE INHABITANTS THEREOF.
It's likely that the structure planned as its new home will limit access.
So touch it while you can!

Christ Church (⌧ 2nd St. north of Market St., ☎ 215/922–1695) is
where noted colonists, including 15 signers of the Declaration of Independence, worshiped. **Elfreth's Alley** (⌧ Off Front and 2nd Sts. between Arch and Race Sts.) is the oldest continuously occupied residential
street in America, dating from 1702; one house (⌧ 126 Elfreth's Alley,
☎ 215/574–0560) has been restored as a Colonial craftsman's home.
The **Betsy Ross House** (⌧ 239 Arch St., ☎ 215/627–5343) is still fun
to visit, although the story that she lived here and sewed the first
American flag in this house hangs by only a few threads of historical
evidence.

The **U.S. Mint** (⌧ 5th and Arch Sts., ☎ 215/597–7350), built in 1969,
is the largest mint in the world and stands two blocks from the first
U.S. mint, which opened in 1792. Tours and exhibits on coin making
are available.

The Waterfront and Society Hill

★ **Society Hill** was—and still is—Philadelphia's showplace. It is easily the
city's most charming and photogenic neighborhood. A treasure trove
of Federal brick row houses and quaint streets stretch from the Delaware
River to 6th Street. (The *Society* in the neighborhood's moniker refers
not to the wealthy Anglicans who first settled here but to the Free Society of Traders, a group of business investors who moved here on
William Penn's advice.) Many homes have been lovingly restored by
modern pioneers who have kept touches like chimney pots and brass
door knockers.

At Society Hill's eastern edge, the spot where William Penn stepped
ashore in 1682 is today a 37-acre park known as **Penn's Landing** (⌧
Delaware Riverfront from Lombard to Market St., ☎ 215/629–3237),
with festivals and concerts from spring to fall and an ice-skating rink
(☎ 215/925–7465) in winter.

The new $15 million **Independence Seaport Museum** (⌧ 211 S. Colum-
bus Blvd., ☎ 215/925–5439) has nautical artifacts, ship displays, and
kid-pleasing interactive exhibits.

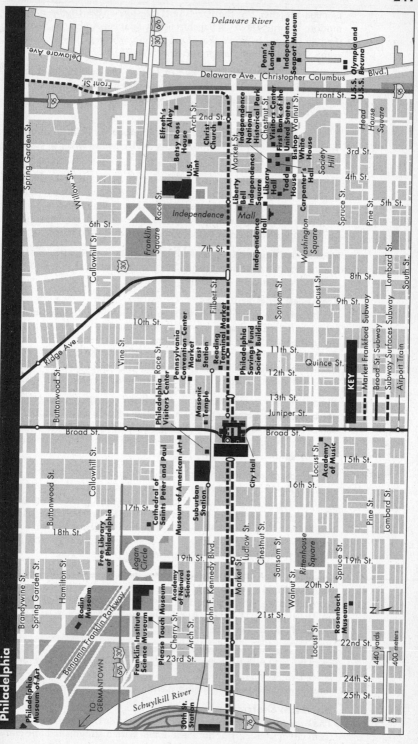

Philadelphia

Delaware River

Delaware Ave.

Front St.

Penn's Landing

Independence Seaport Museum

U.S.S. Olympia and U.S.S. Becuna

Delaware Ave. (Christopher Columbus Blvd.)

Front St.

Head House Square

Spring Garden St.

Willow St.

Elfreth's Alley

Arch St.

2nd St.

Market St.

Independence National Historical Park

Visitors Center

Chestnut St.

First Bank of the United States

Bishop White House

3rd St.

Betsy Ross House

Christ Church

4th St.

U.S. Mint

Library Hall

Todd House

Carpenter's Hall

Society Hill

5th St.

6th St.

Race St.

Callowhill St.

Franklin Square

Independence Mall

Independence Square

Liberty Bell

Independence Hall

Washington Square

Spruce St.

Pine St.

Ridge Ave.

7th St.

8th St.

9th St.

Sansom St.

Locust St.

Lombard St.

South St.

10th St.

Vine St.

Buttonwood St.

Filbert St.

Pennsylvania Convention Center

Reading Terminal Market

Philadelphia Savings Fund Society Building

11th St.

12th St.

Quince St.

KEY

Market Frankford Subway

Broad St. Subway

Subway Surfaces Subway

Airport Train

Philadelphia Race St. Visitors Center

East Station

Masonic Temple

13th St.

Juniper St.

Broad St.

Broad St.

Callowhill St.

Cathedral of Saints Peter and Paul

Museum of American Art

City Hall

Locust St.

15th St.

Academy of Music

16th St.

17th St.

Suburban Station

18th St.

Free Library of Philadelphia

Logan Circle

Pine St.

Lombard St.

Brandywine St.

Spring Garden St.

Hamilton St.

Rodin Museum

Cathedral of Saints Peter and Paul

Academy of Natural Sciences

John F. Kennedy Blvd.

19th St.

Ludlow St.

Chestnut St.

Sansom St.

Walnut St.

Rittenhouse Square

19th St.

20th St.

Buttonwood St.

Benjamin Franklin Parkway

Please Touch Museum

Cherry St.

Arch St.

20th St.

21st St.

Locust St.

Rosenbach Museum

22nd St.

Philadelphia Museum of Art

TO GERMANTOWN

Franklin Institute Science Museum

23rd St.

30th St. Station

Schuylkill River

24th St.

25th St.

440 yards

400 meters

Docked together are the handsomely restored **USS *Olympia,*** Commodore George Dewey's flagship in the Spanish-American War, and the **USS *Becuna,*** a World War II submarine, whose guides are sub veterans. ✉ *Penn's Landing at Spruce St.,* ☎ *215/922–1898.*

The ***Gazela of Philadelphia,*** built in 1883, is the last of a Portuguese fleet of cod-fishing ships and the oldest wooden square-rigger still sailing. ✉ *Penn's Landing between Walnut and Spruce Sts.,* ☎ *215/923–9030. Closed Oct.–May.*

You can take a 10-minute ride on the **Riverbus** (✉ Penn's Landing at Walnut St., ☎ 609/365–1400) across the Delaware River to Camden (☞ New Jersey).

The **Bishop White House** (✉ 309 Walnut St.), built in 1786 as the home of the rector of Christ Church, has been restored to Colonial elegance. The simply furnished **Todd House** (✉ 4th and Walnut Sts.) has been restored to its appearance in the 1790s, when its best-known resident, Dolley Payne Todd (later Mrs. James Madison), lived here.

Head House Square (✉ 2nd and Pine Sts.) was once an open-air Colonial marketplace. Today it is the site of crafts fairs, festivals, and other activities on summer weekends.

City Hall and Environs

At the geographic center of Penn's original city stands **city hall**—the largest city hall in the country and the tallest masonry-bearing building in the world. For a tour of the interior and a 360° view of the city from the Billy Penn statue, go to Room 121 via the northeast corner of the courtyard and ride the elevator to the top of the 548-ft tower. ✉ *Broad and Market Sts.,* ☎ *215/686–2840. Closed weekends.*

Philadelphia is the mother city of American Freemasonry, and the **Masonic Temple** is home to the Grand Lodge of Free and Accepted Masons of Pennsylvania. The seven lodge halls, each decorated according to a different architectural theme, make for a fun 45-minute tour. ✉ *1 N. Broad St.,* ☎ *215/988–1917.*

The **Academy of Music** (✉ Broad and Locust Sts., ☎ 215/893–1900 or 215/893–1930 for tickets), modeled on Milan's La Scala opera house, is home to the Philadelphia Orchestra and the Opera Company of Philadelphia. The **Philadelphia Savings Fund Society Building** (✉ 12th and Market Sts., ☎ 215/928–2000), built in 1930 and known locally as the PSFS Building, was one of the city's first skyscrapers and influential in the design of other American high-rises.

Opened in 1993, the **Pennsylvania Convention Center** (✉ 12th and Arch Sts., ☎ 215/418–4700 or 215/418–4989 for events) includes the restored Reading Train Shed. You can tour the $522 million complex on Tuesday and Thursday. It sits atop the not-to-be-missed **Reading Terminal Market** (☞ Dining, *below*).

★ The city's classiest park, **Rittenhouse Square** (✉ Walnut St. between 18th and 19th Sts.) frequently hosts art festivals. The **Rosenbach Museum** (✉ 2010 Delancey Pl., ☎ 215/732–1600) offers a one-hour tour of its sumptuous collection of antiques, paintings, rare books, and objets d'art.

Museum District

The **Benjamin Franklin Parkway** angles across the grid of city streets from city hall to Fairmount Park. Lined with distinguished museums, hotels, and apartment buildings, this 250-ft-wide boulevard inspired by the Champs-Elysées was built in the 1920s. Off the parkway you'll find the **Free Library of Philadelphia** (✉ 19th St., ☎ 215/686–5322), with more than 1 million volumes. The **Academy of Natural**

Sciences (⊠ 19th St., ☎ 215/299–1020), America's first museum of natural history, has a "Discovering Dinosaurs" exhibit and stuffed animals from around the world displayed in 35 natural settings. The **Rodin Museum** (⊠ 22nd St., ☎ 215/763–8100) has the largest collection of Auguste Rodin's works outside France, including masterworks like *The Kiss, The Thinker,* and *The Burghers of Calais.* The **Franklin Institute Science Museum** (⊠ 20th St., ☎ 215/448–1200) is as clever as its namesake; it includes many dazzling hands-on exhibits, a planetarium, and an Omniverse theater that shows science and nature documentaries with a 79-ft domed screen and 56-speaker high-tech sound system.

★ The crown jewel of the parkway is the **Philadelphia Museum of Art.** Modeled on a larger-scale version of ancient Greek temples, the 200 galleries house more than 300,000 works. The collections include paintings by Renoir, Picasso, Matisse, and Marcel Duchamp; Early American furniture; Amish and Shaker crafts; and reconstructions, including a 12th-century French cloister and a 16th-century Indian temple. *⊠ 26th St. and Benjamin Franklin Pkwy., ☎ 215/763–8100. Free Sun. 10–1. Closed Mon.*

Along both banks of the Schuylkill River is **Fairmount Park** (⊠ Accesses from Kelly Dr., West River Dr., and Belmont Ave., ☎ 215/685–0000), one of the largest city parks in the world, with woodlands, meadows, and rolling hills. Within its 4,500 acres you'll find tennis courts, ball fields, playgrounds, trails, an exercise course, the **Ellen Phillips Samuel Memorial Sculpture Garden,** and some fine Early American country houses (**Laurel Hill, Strawberry Mansion,** and others). **Boathouse Row,** 11 architecturally varied 19th-century buildings on the banks of the Schuylkill that are home to 13 rowing clubs, is best viewed from the West River Drive. In the northwest section of the park is the **Wissahickon,** a 5½-mi-long forested gorge carved out by Wissahickon Creek. At **Valley Green Inn** (☎ 215/247–1730), a restaurant halfway up the valley, you can dine on the porch and watch the ducks swimming in the creek.

The **Museum of American Art** is the oldest art institution in the United States. Its collection ranges from Winslow Homer and Benjamin West to Andrew Wyeth and Red Grooms. *⊠ Broad and Cherry Sts., ☎ 215/972–7600. Free Wed. 5–7:30.*

The Italian Renaissance–style **Cathedral of Saints Peter and Paul** (⊠ 18th and Race Sts., ☎ 215/561–1313), built between 1846 and 1864, is the basilica of the Roman Catholic archdiocese of Philadelphia.

Germantown

In 1683 Francis Pastorius led 13 Mennonite families out of Germany to seek religious freedom in the New World; they settled 6 mi northwest of Philadelphia in what is now **Germantown,** and many became Quakers. **Cliveden** (⊠ 6401 Germantown Ave., ☎ 215/848–1777), an elaborate country house built in 1763, was occupied by the British during the Revolution. On October 7, 1777, George Washington's attempt to dislodge them resulted in the Yankees' defeat in the Battle of Germantown. During the yellow fever epidemic of 1793–94, Washington lived in the **Deshler-Morris House** (⊠ 5442 Germantown Ave., ☎ 215/596–1748) to avoid the unhealthy air of sea-level Philadelphia. Contact the **Germantown Historical Society** (⊠ 5501 Germantown Ave., ☎ 215/844–1683) for information on all noteworthy sites in Germantown.

Other Attractions

The **University of Pennsylvania Museum** (⌧ 33rd and Spruce Sts., ☎ 215/898–4000) is one of the finest archaeology–anthropology museums in the world. The **Mutter Museum** (⌧ 19 S. 22nd St., ☎ 215/563–3737), a medical museum with a plethora of anatomical and pathological specimens, is best visited on an empty stomach! One of the world's great

★ collections of Impressionist and postimpressionist art is at the **Barnes Foundation,** 8 mi west of Center City. The Barnes reopened in 1995 after a national tour that dramatically increased public awareness of the collection. ⌧ *300 N. Latches La., Merion Station,* ☎ *610/667–0290. Closed Mon.–Wed.*

Parks and Gardens

Fairmount Park (☞ Exploring Philadelphia, *above*) is the city's largest, encompassing varied terrains as well as many cultural sites. The University of Pennsylvania's **Morris Arboretum** (⌧ Hillcrest Ave. between Germantown and Stenton Aves., Chestnut Hill, ☎ 215/247–5777) is 166 acres of romantically landscaped seclusion. America's first zoo, the **Philadelphia Zoological Gardens** (⌧ 34th St. and Girard Ave., ☎ 215/243–1100) is home to 1,600 animals on 42 acres.

What to See and Do with Children

The **Please Touch Museum** (⌧ 210 N. 21st St., ☎ 215/963–0667), designed for children ages seven and younger, encourages hands-on participation. The **Annenberg Center Theater for Children** (⌧ 37th and Walnut Sts., ☎ 215/898–6791) schedules productions from October

★ to May. **Sesame Place,** a 45-minute drive north of the city, is an amusement park for children ages 3–13, based on the popular public-television show. ⌧ *100 Sesame Rd., Langhorne,* ☎ *215/757–1100.* ▨ *$22.95.*

Dining

Philadelphia has become a first-rate restaurant town—one of the most exciting such cities in the United States. Here's a short list of a dozen distinctly Philadelphia sure bets. For price ranges *see* Chart 1 (A) *in* On the Road with Fodor's.

$$$$ ✕ **Le Bec-Fin.** The Fine Beak (or more loosely, "the Fine Palate") is ar-
★ guably the best restaurant in Philadelphia—and one of the best in the United States. The elegant mise-en-scène with crystal chandeliers and mirrors, the excellent (and rarely snooty) European service, and owner-chef Georges Perrier's obsessive perfectionism in creating the haute French menu all have their price: $102 prix fixe for dinner and $36 for lunch. ⌧ *1523 Walnut St.,* ☎ *215/567–1000. Reservations essential. Jacket and tie. AE, D, DC, MC, V. Closed Sun.*

$$$$ ✕ **The Fountain.** Nestled in the lavish yet dignified lobby of the Four
★ Seasons, with grand windows overlooking Logan Circle's Swann Fountain, this oasis offers predominantly local and American entrées, such as sautéed venison medallions in homemade pasta with fried leeks and juniper sauce. ⌧ *1 Logan Sq.,* ☎ *215/963–1500. Reservations essential. Jacket and tie. AE, D, DC, MC, V.*

$$$ ✕ **Cafe Nola.** The best Cajun-creole food in town is served in a lavishly restored 100-year-old bank building. House favorites include seafood jambalaya, coconut shrimp with orange sauce, and Cajun popcorn. ⌧ *603 S. 3rd St.,* ☎ *215/627–2590. AE, D, DC, MC, V.*

$$$ ✕ **Susanna Foo.** This is the most expensive—and arguably the best—
★ Chinese restaurant in town. A million-dollar renovation has enlarged and
beautified the already handsome room. Try the Eight Treasure quails;
top it off with the banana-chocolate mousse. ⊠ *1512 Walnut St.,* ☎ *215/
545–2666. Reservations essential. Jacket and tie. AE, DC, MC, V.*

$$$ ✕ **Tiramisù.** Owner-chef Albert Delbella describes his fare as "nouvelle
Jewish-Roman," but the only prerequisite needed to dine here is a love
of garlic, found in almost everything, from the matzo with olive oil to
the veal scallopini. The eponymous dessert (no garlic!) is delicious. ⊠
528 S. 5th St., ☎ *215/925–3335. AE, DC, MC, V.*

$$ ✕ **Restaurant School.** Managed and staffed entirely by students, this
restaurant offers French haute cuisine and European service in the glass-
enclosed atrium of a restored 1860 Victorian mansion—all for a mere
$15. ⊠ *4207 Walnut St.,* ☎ *215/222–4200. AE, D, DC, MC, V.
Closed Sun.–Mon.*

$$ ✕ **Sansom Street Oyster House.** This Philadelphia favorite serves first-
rate raw shellfish and grilled and blackened fish dishes. It's unpreten-
tiously paneled in dark wood, with uncovered tables. ⊠ *1516 Sansom
St.,* ☎ *215/567–7683. AE, D, DC, MC, V. Closed Sun.*

$$ ✕ **Victor Cafe.** The northern Italian cuisine of the DiStefano family gets
★ better all the time, but the big attraction here is the music: The servers
are all opera singers, and every few minutes one or more cuts loose
with an aria. ⊠ *1303 Dickinson St.,* ☎ *215/468–3040. Reservations
essential. AE, DC, MC, V.*

$ ✕ **Famous Delicatessen.** This is the closest thing in Philadelphia to a
classic New York deli. Boxes of tinfoil are kept handy to wrap up the
leftover halves of the overstuffed sandwiches. ⊠ *4th and Bainbridge
Sts.,* ☎ *215/922–3274. AE, DC, MC, V.*

$ ✕ **Joe's Peking Duck House.** Known for Peking duck and barbecued
pork, Joe's is one of the best of the more than 50 restaurants in Chi-
natown. ⊠ *925 Race St.,* ☎ *215/922–3277. No credit cards.*

$ ✕ **Reading Terminal Market.** A Philadelphia treasure, this potpourri
★ of 80 stalls, shops, and lunch counters offers a smorgasbord of cuisines,
including Chinese, Greek, Mexican, Japanese, soul food, Middle East-
ern, and Pennsylvania Dutch. ⊠ *12th and Arch Sts.,* ☎ *215/922–2317.
Closed Sun.*

Junk Food

"Philadelphia is the junk food capital of the world," says Mayor Ed
Rendell. Indeed, no Philadelphia dining experience would be complete
without tormenting your digestive system with at least one cheese
steak or hoagie. **Pat's** (⊠ 1237 E. Passyunk, ☎ 215/468–1546) serves
up Philadelphia's signature sandwich—a cheese steak, made of shred-
ded steak and cheese with sauce and fried onions. **Lee's** (⊠ 44 S. 17th
St., ☎ 215/564–1264) is hoagie heaven (be sure to ask for one with
oil, not mayo); the **Reading Terminal Market** (☞ Dining, *above*) sells
freshly baked soft pretzels with mustard—a Philly specialty. Stores all
over town sell TastyKakes, a local brand of prepackaged baked goods.
Philadelphia Favorites to Go (☎ 800/808–8646) will vacuum-pack and
send local treats anywhere in the United States.

Lodging

With the exception of the Army-Navy football game (around Thanks-
giving) and when big conventions are in town, it's easy to find a hotel
room. Most bed-and-breakfasts operate under the auspices of book-
ing agencies, such as **Bed and Breakfast, Center City** (⊠ 1804 Pine St.,
19103, ☎ 215/735–1137 or 800/354–8401), and **Bed and Breakfast
Connections** (⊠ Box 21, Devon 19333, ☎ 610/687–3565 or 800/448–
3619). For price ranges *see* Chart 2 (A) *in* On the Road with Fodor's.

$$$$ 🏨 **Four Seasons.** Built in 1983 and refurbished in 1996, this eight-
★ story hotel is the city's classiest and most expensive. Rooms are furnished in Federal style, and the best have romantic views overlooking
the fountains in Logan Circle. ⊠ *1 Logan Sq., 19103,* ☎ *215/963–
1500 or 800/332–3442,* FAX *215/963–9506. 371 rooms. 2 restaurants,
café, no-smoking floors, indoor pool, exercise room, concierge. AE,
D, DC, MC, V.*

$$$$ 🏨 **The Rittenhouse.** This 33-story luxury hotel takes full advantage of
★ its Rittenhouse Square location: Many rooms and both restaurants look
out over the city's most elegant park. ⊠ *210 W. Rittenhouse Sq.,
19103,* ☎ *215/546–9000 or 800/635–1042,* FAX *215/732–3364. 98
rooms. 2 restaurants, bar, tea garden, no-smoking floors, health club,
concierge. AE, D, DC, MC, V.*

$$$ 🏨 **Adam's Mark.** Guest rooms are small here, with an English-country
motif; request one on an upper floor facing south toward Fairmount Park
and the downtown skyline. The hotel's big attraction is the nighttime
activity at its nightclub, sports bar, and fine restaurant, the Marker. ⊠
City Ave. and Monument Rd., 19131, ☎ *215/581–5000 or 800/444–
2326,* FAX *215/581–5089. 480 rooms. 3 restaurants, bar, sports bar, 2
pools, exercise room. AE, D, DC, MC, V.*

$$$ 🏨 **Latham.** At this small, elegant hotel with a European accent and an
emphasis on personal service, guest rooms have marble-top bureaus
and French writing desks. ⊠ *17th St. at Walnut St., 19103,* ☎ *215/
563–7474 or 800/528–4261,* FAX *215/568–0110. 139 rooms. Restaurant, lounge. AE, D, DC, MC, V.*

$$$ 🏨 **Philadelphia Marriott.** At a cost of $200 million, this 23-story full-
service hotel opened in 1995 next door to the Pennsylvania Conven-
tion Center. The spacious guest rooms have large windows and pastel
colors. ⊠ *1201 Market St., 19107,* ☎ *215/625–2900 or 800/228–
9290,* FAX *215/625–6000. 1,200 rooms. Restaurants, sports bar, indoor
pool, health club, billiards. AE, D, DC, MC, V.*

$$$ 🏨 **The Warwick.** First opened in 1924, this 23-story hotel today at-
tracts a theatrical clientele. The lobby, adorned with gilded mirrors and
18-ft Palladian windows, is always busy. Capriccio, a European-style
café, serves desserts and espresso daily until late at night. ⊠ *1701 Locust St., 19103,* ☎ *215/735–6000 or 800/523–4210,* FAX *215/790–
7766. 200 rooms. Restaurant, nightclub. AE, DC, MC, V.*

$$ 🏨 **Clarion Suites.** This 1890 building in Chinatown was once the Bent-
wood Rocker Factory. Every guest room is a suite, and many have ex-
posed brick and wood beams. ⊠ *1010 Race St., 19107,* ☎ *215/
922–1730 or 800/628–8932,* FAX *215/922–1959. 96 suites. Parking
(fee). AE, D, DC, MC, V.*

$$ 🏨 **Society Hill Hotel.** Rooms in this 1832 former longshoreman's house
are furnished with brass beds and antiques. Continental breakfast,
brought to your room, includes freshly squeezed juice and newly baked
goodies. ⊠ *301 Chestnut St., 19106,* ☎ *215/925–1394,* FAX *215/925–
3780. 12 rooms. Restaurant, outdoor café, piano bar. AE, DC, MC, V.*

$$ 🏨 **Thomas Bond House.** Spend the night in the heart of the Old City,
★ the way Philadelphians did more than two centuries ago. Built in 1769,
this four-story house has rooms with marble fireplaces and four-poster
Thomasville beds—and 20th-century whirlpool baths. ⊠ *129 S. 2nd
St., 19106,* ☎ *215/923–8523 or 800/845–2663,* FAX *215/923–8504.
12 rooms. AE, D, DC, MC, V.*

$ 🏨 **Bank Street Hostel.** On the cusp of Olde City and Society Hill, this
clean, well-run establishment offers a dormitory arrangement that is
a downtown Philly lodging bargain. ⊠ *32 S. Bank St., 19106,* ☎ *215/
922–0222 or 800/392–4678,* FAX *215/922–4082. 70 beds. No credit
cards.*

$ 🏠 **Chamounix Mansion.** This youth hostel is on a wooded bluff over-looking the Schuylkill River (and, unfortunately, the Schuylkill Expressway). The 1802 estate is loaded with character; the drawbacks are dorm-style living and shared baths. ✉ *Chamounix Dr., 19131,* ☎ *215/878–3676 or 800/379–0017,* FAX *215/871–4313. 64 beds. MC, V. Closed mid-Dec.–mid-Jan.*

Nightlife and the Arts

Philadelphia magazine (at newsstands), *Calendar of Events* (free at the visitor center), the *Philadelphia Weekly* and the *City Paper* (weeklies available free from news boxes in Center City), and the *Inquirer* and the *Daily News* (the city's daily papers) list arts and entertainment events. The **Donnelley Directory Philadelphia Events Hotline** (☎ 610/337–7777, ext. 2116) is a recorded service providing information 24 hours a day. Tickets, often at a discount, for more than 75 performing and cultural organizations can be obtained at **UpStages** (✉ Liberty Pl., 16th and Chestnut Sts., ☎ 215/893–1145).

Nightlife

South Street from Front to 7th Street still attracts nighttime crowds, but the big noise is the **Delaware Waterfront** entertainment boom, with more than a dozen clubs opening in the past few years. In the northwestern part of the city, **Main Street** in **Manyunk** has joined **Germantown Avenue** in **Chestnut Hill** as an area in which to dine, shop, and stroll. On Wednesday night downtown shops and some museums stay open late; outside, street bands entertain smiling crowds. On the **First Friday** of every month 25 art galleries in Olde City stay open late. Call radio station WRTI's Jazz Line (☎ 610/337–7777, ext. 3234) and Concerts (☎ 215/568–3222) to learn what's happening around town.

BARS, LOUNGES, AND CABARETS

Egypt (✉ 520 N. Delaware Ave., ☎ 215/922–6500), one of Philly's hottest clubs, has dancing to music ranging from disco and pop to progressive. A loud, young crowd packs **Katmandu** (✉ Pier 25, Christopher Columbus Blvd., ☎ 215/629–1101), a large-capacity outdoor island restaurant and disco, every night until 2 from April 15 to early October. **Dirty Frank's** (✉ 347 S. 13th St., ☎ 215/732–5010) *is* dirty and attracts a motley crowd of writers, artists, students, and Philly characters. **Woody's** (✉ 202 S. 13th St., ☎ 215/545–1893) is the city's most popular gay bar. **Sisters** (✉ 1320 S. Chancellor St., ☎ 215/735–0735) is the city's premier lesbian bar. Head for **Zanzibar Blue** (✉ Broad and Walnut Sts., Park Hyatt Hotel, lower level, ☎ 215/732–5200) for top local and national names in jazz.

COMEDY

For 16 years **Comedy Cabaret** (✉ 126 Chestnut St., ☎ 215/625–5653) has presented national names and local talent.

MISCELLANEOUS

By day **Painted Bride Art Center** (✉ 230 Vine St., ☎ 215/925–9914) is an art gallery, by night a stage featuring performance art, readings, dance, and theater. Since 1975 the **Cherry Tree Music Co-op** (✉ 3916 Locust Walk, ☎ 215/386–1640) has staged Sunday-night folk concerts.

The Arts

CONCERTS

The **Philadelphia Orchestra** performs at the Academy of Music (✉ Broad and Locust Sts., ☎ 215/893–1900) in winter and at the Mann Music Center (✉ W. Fairmount Park, ☎ 215/878–7707) in summer. The **Philly Pops** (☎ 215/735–7506), conducted by Peter Nero, performs at the Academy of Music.

DANCE

The **Pennsylvania Ballet** (☎ 215/551–7014) dances at the Academy of Music from October to June. The **Philadelphia Dance Company** (☎ 215/387–8200) performs modern and jazz dance and ballet at the University of Pennsylvania's Annenberg Theater in spring and fall.

OPERA

The **Opera Company of Philadelphia** (☎ 215/928–2100) performs at the Academy of Music from October to May.

THEATER

Performances by touring companies and pre-Broadway productions can be seen at the **Merriam Theater** (✉ 250 S. Broad St., ☎ 215/732–5446), the **Forrest Theater** (✉ 1114 Walnut St., ☎ 215/923–1515), and the **Walnut Street Theater** (✉ 9th and Walnut Sts., ☎ 215/574–3550). The **Wilma Theater** (✉ Broad and Spruce Sts., ☎ 215/546–7824) does innovative work with American and European drama. **Freedom Theater** (✉ 1346 N. Broad St., ☎ 215/765–2793) is the oldest and most active black theater in Philadelphia.

Outdoor Activities and Sports

Golf

Of the six 18-hole courses in Philadelphia open to the public, **Cobbs Creek and Karakung** (✉ 7200 Landsdowne Ave., ☎ 215/877–8707) are the most challenging.

Ice-Skating

Skate outdoors with the Delaware River and Ben Franklin Bridge as a backdrop at the **Blue Cross RiverRink** (✉ Penn's Landing between Market and Chestnut Sts., ☎ 215/925–7465), open daily November to March.

Jogging and Running

Philly runners' favorite workout is the **river loop**—an 8.2-mi circuit starting at the Art Museum and heading up Kelly Drive along the Schuylkill River, then across Falls Bridge and back down West River Drive.

Spectator Sports

Baseball: Philadelphia Phillies (✉ Veterans Stadium, Broad St. and Pattison Ave., ☎ 215/463–1000).

Basketball: Philadelphia 76ers (✉ CoreStates Center, Broad St. and Pattison Ave., ☎ 215/336–3600).

Football: Philadelphia Eagles (✉ Veterans Stadium, ☎ 215/463–5500).

Hockey: Philadelphia Flyers (✉ CoreStates Center, ☎ 215/336–3600).

Horse Racing: Philadelphia Park (✉ Street Rd., Bensalem, ☎ 215/639–9000) has Thoroughbred racing year-round. For offtrack betting, the **Turf Club Center City** (✉ 1635 Market St., ☎ 215/246–1556) is open daily 11–11.

Shopping

There is no sales tax on clothing, medicine, or food bought in stores. Otherwise, Pennsylvania has a 6% sales tax, 7% in Philadelphia.

Shopping Districts

Walnut Street between Broad Street and Rittenhouse Square and the intersecting streets just north and south are filled with upscale boutiques and galleries. At 16th and Chestnut streets, the **Shops at Liberty Place** offer more than 70 stores and restaurants under a 90-ft glass-roof atrium. **Jewelers' Row,** centered on Sansom Street between 7th and 8th streets, is one of the world's oldest and largest markets of precious stones. Pine Street from 9th to 12th streets is **Antiques Row.** Along **South Street** are more than 300 unusual stores selling everything from New Age books and health food to avant-garde art. For local color visit the outdoor stalls and indoor stores of the **Italian Market,** on 9th Street between Christian and Washington streets.

Department Stores

Philadelphia's premier department store, John Wanamaker, was bought by the May Company in 1995, but Philadelphians still rendezvous at the eagle statue in the grand court of what is now **Lord & Taylor** (⊠ 13th and Market Sts., ☎ 215/422–2000). In 1996 Strawbridge and Clothier was also sold to the May Company and is now **Strawbridge's** (⊠ 8th and Market Sts., ☎ 215/629–6000), the anchor store for the **Gallery at Market East** (☎ 215/925–7162).

Specialty Stores

Architectural Antiques Exchange (⊠ 715 N. 2nd St., ☎ 215/922–3669) handles everything from embellishments of Victorian saloons and apothecary shops to stained and beveled glass. **Bauman Rare Books** (⊠ 1215 Locust St., ☎ 215/546–6466) has volumes from the 19th century and earlier on law, science, English literature, and travel. **Wine Reserve** (⊠ 205 S. 18th St., ☎ 215/560–4529) deals exclusively in fine wines and cognacs. **J. E. Caldwell** (⊠ Juniper and Chestnut Sts., ☎ 215/864–7800), since 1839 a local landmark for jewelry, is adorned with antique handblown crystal chandeliers by Baccarat. Philadelphia-born **Urban Outfitters** (⊠ 1801 Walnut St., ☎ 215/569–3131), now selling clothes, furnishings, and gifts to students in college towns across the country, opened its first store in this downtown Beaux Arts mansion.

Side Trip to the Brandywine Valley

Arriving and Departing

Take U.S. 1S from Philadelphia about 25 mi to the valley.

What to See and Do

The Brandywine River valley has inspired generations of Wyeths and du Ponts—the Wyeths to capture its peaceful harmony on canvas, the du Ponts to recontour the landscape with grand gardens, mansions, and mills. The **Brandywine River Museum** (⊠ U.S. 1 and Rte. 100, Chadds Ford, ☎ 610/388–7601), in a preserved 19th-century grist-★ mill, celebrates the Brandywine school of artists. **Longwood Gardens** (⊠ U.S. 1, Kennett Square, ☎ 610/388–6741), Pierre-Samuel du Pont's 350 acres of ultimate estate gardens, has an international reputation. The **Brandywine Battlefield State Park** (⊠ U.S. 1, Chadds Ford, ☎ 610/459–3342) is near the site of the British defeat of Washington and his troops on September 11, 1777. The region is dotted with antiques shops and cozy inns. The **Tourist Information Center for the Brandywine Valley** (⊠ 300 Greenwood Rd., Kennett Square 19348, ☎ 610/388–2900 or 800/228–9933) has information.

Side Trip to Bucks County

Arriving and Departing

From Philadelphia follow I–95 north to the Yardley exit, then go north on Route 32 toward New Hope. The trip takes one hour.

What to See and Do

Bucks County is known for antiques, covered bridges, and country inns. **New Hope** is a hodgepodge of art galleries, old stone houses, and shops along crooked little streets. William Penn's reconstructed Georgian-style mansion, **Pennsbury Manor** (⊠ Tyburn Rd. E off U.S. 13, Morrisville, ☎ 215/946–0400), presents living history demonstrations of 17th-century life. **Washington Crossing Historic Park** (⊠ Rtes. 532 and 32, ☎ 215/493–4076) is where George Washington and his troops crossed the river on Christmas night 1776. Contact the **Bucks County Tourist Commission** (⊠ 152 Swamp Rd., Doylestown 18901, ☎ 215/345–4552) or the **New Hope Information Center** (⊠ 1 W. Mechanic St., at Main St., 18938, ☎ 215/862–5880 or 215/862–5030) for more information.

Side Trip to Valley Forge

Arriving and Departing

By car take the Schuylkill Expressway (I–76) west from Philadelphia to Exit 25; then take Route 363 to North Gulph Road and follow the signs to Valley Forge National Historical Park, 18 mi from the city. **By bus** take SEPTA Route 125 from 16th Street and John F. Kennedy Boulevard.

What to See and Do

The monuments, huts, and headquarters on the 3,500 acres of rolling hills of the **Valley Forge National Historical Park** (⊠ Rtes. 23 and 363, Valley Forge, ☎ 610/783–1077) preserve the moment in American history when George Washington's Continental Army endured the bitter winter of 1777–78. The former home of John James Audubon, **Mill Grove** (⊠ Audubon and Paulings Rds., Audubon, ☎ 610/666–5593)
★ is now a museum displaying the naturalist's work. The **Wharton Esherick Museum** (⊠ Horseshoe Trail, Paoli, ☎ 610/644–5822) has more than 200 samples of this eccentric artist's paintings, furniture, and sculpture. With more than 450 stores, including nine department stores, the **Court and the Plaza** (⊠ Rte. 202 and N. Gulph Rd., King of Prussia, ☎ 610/265–5727) is the nation's second-largest shopping complex. For more information contact the **Valley Forge Convention and Visitors Bureau** (⊠ 600 W. Germantown Pike, Suite 130, Plymouth Meeting 19462, ☎ 610/834–1550 or 800/441–3549).

PENNSYLVANIA DUTCH COUNTRY

First of all, the Pennsylvania Dutch aren't Dutch; the name comes from *Deutsch* (German). In the 18th century this rolling farmland 65 mi west of Philadelphia became home to the Amish, the Mennonites, and other German and Swiss immigrants escaping religious persecution. Today their descendants continue to turn their backs on the modern world—and in doing so attract the world's attention. In summer buses jam Route 30, the main thoroughfare. But there is still charm on the back roads, where you will discover Amish farms, hand-painted signs advertising quilts, fields worked with mules, and horse-drawn buggies.

Visitor Information

Pennsylvania Dutch Convention and Visitors Bureau (⊠ 501 Greenfield Rd., Lancaster 17601, ☎ 717/299–8901 or 800/PA–DUTCH). **Mennonite Information Center** (⊠ 2209 Millstream Rd., Lancaster 17602, ☎ 717/299–0954).

Getting There

By Bus

Greyhound Lines (☎ 800/231–2222) has three runs daily from Philadelphia to Lancaster.

By Car

From Philadelphia (65 mi away) take the Schuylkill Expressway (I–76) west to the Pennsylvania Turnpike, exiting at Exit 20, 21, or 22.

By Train

Amtrak (☎ 800/872–7245) has service from Philadelphia to Lancaster.

Exploring Pennsylvania Dutch Country

Lancaster, a charming Colonial city, is the heart of Pennsylvania Dutch Country. The **Historic Lancaster Walking Tour** (☎ 717/392–1776), a two-hour stroll through the city, is conducted by guides who impart lively anecdotes about local architecture and history. **Central Market** (⊠ Penn Sq., ☎ 717/291–4723), one of the oldest covered markets in the country and now housed in an 1889 Romanesque structure, is where the locals shop for fresh produce, meats, and baked goods. The old city hall, reborn as the **Heritage Center of Lancaster County** (⊠ King and Queen St., ☎ 717/299–6440), shows the work of Lancaster County artisans and craftspeople.

Several furnished farmhouses offer simulated up-close looks at how the Amish live, including the **Amish Farm and House** (⊠ 2395 Lincoln Hwy. E, ☎ 717/394–6185). Abe, of **Abe's Buggy Rides** (⊠ Rte. 340, Bird-in-Hand, ☎ 717/392–1794), chats about the Amish during a 2-mi spin down country roads in an Amish family carriage. **Wheatland** (⊠ 1120 Marietta Ave. [Rte. 23], 1½ mi west of Lancaster, ☎ 717/392–8721), a restored 1828 Federal mansion, was the home of the only president from Pennsylvania, James Buchanan.

Train aficionados take note: **Strasburg** has a half-dozen museums and sights devoted to trains. The **Strasburg Railroad** (⊠ Rte. 741, ☎ 717/687–7522) is a scenic 9-mi round-trip excursion on a wooden coach pulled by a steam locomotive. The **Railroad Museum of Pennsylvania** (⊠ Rte. 741, ☎ 717/687–8628) displays colossal engines, railcars, and memorabilia documenting railroading in the state.

In **Ephrata** the 18th-century Protestants of the **Ephrata Cloister** (⊠ Rtes. 272 and 322, ☎ 717/733–6600) led an ascetic life, living examples of William Penn's "holy experiment." Guides now give tours of the restored medieval-style German buildings.

Lititz was founded by Moravians who settled in Pennsylvania to do missionary work among Native Americans. It's a lovely town with a tree-shaded main street of 18th-century cottages and shops. At the General Sutter Inn (⊠ 14 E. Main St., ☎ 717/626–2115) pick up the Historical Foundation's brochure that details a walking tour of the town.

Dining and Lodging

Like the German cuisine from which it's derived, Pennsylvania Dutch cooking is hearty. To sample such regional fare as ham, buttered noodles, chowchow, and shoofly pie, eat at one of the bustling family-style restaurants where diners sit with perhaps a dozen others and the food is passed around. A number of farm families open their homes to visitors, allowing them to observe and even participate in day-to-day farm life. For information contact the Convention and Visitors Bureau (☞ Visitor Information, *above*). For price ranges *see* Charts 1 (B) and 2 (B) *in* On the Road with Fodor's.

Bird-in-Hand

$ ✕ **Bird-in-Hand Family Restaurant.** This family-owned spot specializes in hearty Pennsylvania Dutch home cooking. ⊠ *Rte. 340 just west of N. Ronks Rd.,* ☎ *717/768–8266. MC, V. Closed Sun.*

Churchtown

$$–$$$ 🏠 **Churchtown Inn.** This restored 1735 fieldstone mansion overlook-
★   ing an Amish farm has cozy bedrooms with pencil-post, canopy, brass,
and high-back Victorian beds. A five-course breakfast is served in the
glass-enclosed garden room. ⊠ *2100 Main St., Narvon 17555,* ☎ *717/
445–7794. 9 rooms. D, MC, V.*

Ephrata

$$$ ✗ **The Restaurant at Doneckers.** Classic and country-French cuisine is
★   served downstairs amid Colonial antiques and upstairs in a country
garden. ⊠ *333 N. State St.,* ☎ *717/738–9501. AE, D, DC, MC, V.
Closed Wed.*

Lancaster

$$$$ 🏠 **Best Western Eden Resort Inn.** Spacious contemporary rooms and
attractive grounds contribute to the pleasant atmosphere here. The suites
have kitchens and fireplaces. ⊠ *222 Eden Rd. (U.S. 30 and Rte. 272),
17601,* ☎ *717/569–6444,* 🖷 *717/569–4208. 274 rooms. 2 restau-
rants, indoor pool, hot tub, nightclub. AE, D, DC, MC, V.*

Lititz

$$$–$$$$ 🏠 **Swiss Woods.** This comfortable, friendly European-style B&B on 30
★   acres looks like a Swiss chalet and offers contemporary country decor.
⊠ *500 Blantz Rd., 17543,* ☎ *717/627–3358 or 800/594–8018,* 🖷 *717/
627–3483. 7 rooms. Kitchenette, hot tub. No smoking. D, MC, V.*

Mount Joy

$$$ ✗ **Groff's Farm.** Hearty Mennonite farm fare, including chicken, rel-
ishes, and cracker pudding, is served in a restored 1756 farmhouse dec-
orated with country fabrics and fresh flowers. ⊠ *650 Pinkerton Rd.,*
☎ *717/653–2048. Reservations essential for dinner. AE, D, DC, MC,
V. Closed Sun.–Mon.*

$$$ 🏠 **Cameron Estate Inn.** Rooms in this sprawling Federal redbrick man-
sion on 15 wooded acres have Oriental rugs, antique and reproduc-
tion furniture, and canopy beds; seven have working fireplaces. ⊠ *1855
Mansion La., 17552,* ☎ *717/653–1773. 17 rooms. Restaurant. AE,
D, DC, MC, V.*

Strasburg

$$$ 🏠 **Historic Strasburg Inn.** This newly renovated Colonial-style inn is
★   set on 58 peaceful acres overlooking farmland. ⊠ *1 Historic Dr.,
17579,* ☎ *717/687–7691 or 800/872–0201,* 🖷 *717/687–6098. 101
rooms. 2 restaurants, pool, hot tub, exercise room, recreation room,
volleyball. Full breakfast. AE, D, DC, MC, V.*

Campgrounds

The Convention and Visitors Bureau (☞ Visitor Information, *above*)
has a list of area campgrounds. Two of the best are **Mill Bridge Village
and Campresort** (⊠ ½ mi south of U.S. 30 on S. Ronks Rd.; Box 86,
Strasburg 17579, ☎ 717/687–8181), both attached to a restored
18th-century village, and **Spring Gulch Resort Campground** (⊠ Rte. 897;
475 Lynch Rd., New Holland 17557, ☎ 717/354–3100).

Nightlife and the Arts

Dutch Apple Dinner Theater (⊠ 510 Centerville Rd., at U.S. 30, Lancaster, ☎ 717/898–1900) offers a buffet plus Broadway musicals and
comedies. Plays and concerts, as well as performances by the Lancaster
Symphony Orchestra and the Lancaster Opera, are presented at the
Fulton Opera House (⊠ 12 N. Prince St., Lancaster, ☎ 717/394–
7133), a restored 19th-century Victorian theater.

Outdoor Activities and Sports

Hot-Air Ballooning

Great Adventure Balloon Club (☎ 717/397–3623) offers a bird's-eye view of Pennsylvania Dutch Country.

Shopping

Antiques

Antiques malls are on Route 272 between Adamstown and Denver, 2 mi east of Pennsylvania Turnpike Exit 21; **Barr's Auctions** (☎ 717/336–2861), **Renninger's Antique and Collector's Market** (☎ 717/336–2177), and **Stoudt's Black Angus** (☎ 717/484–4385) all feature indoor and outdoor sales.

Crafts

Places to see fine local crafts include the **Weathervane Shop** at the Landis Valley Museum (✉ 2451 Kissel Hill Rd., Lancaster, ☎ 717/569–9312), the **Tin Bin** (✉ Valley Rd. and Rte. 501, Neffsville, ☎ 717/569–6210), and the 30-shop **Kitchen Kettle Village** (✉ Rte. 340, Intercourse, ☎ 717/768–8261). International crafts, ideal for Christmas gifts and stocking stuffers, can be found at the **Ten Thousand Villages** (✉ 240 N. Reading Rd., Ephrata, ☎ 717/721–8400), owned and operated by the Mennonite Central Committee.

Farmers Markets

In addition to Lancaster's **Central Market** (☞ Exploring Pennsylvania Dutch Country, *above*), the **Green Dragon Farmers Market and Auction** (✉ 955 N. State St., just off Rte. 272, Ephrata, ☎ 717/738–1117) is an old, traditional agricultural market with a country-carnival atmosphere, open Friday year-round.

Side Trip to Gettysburg

Arriving and Departing

From Lancaster take U.S. 30 east to Gettysburg (about 1½ hours).

What to See and Do

The battle of Gettysburg, fought in July 1863, was, along with Ulysses S. Grant's successful Vicksburg campaign, the turning point of the Civil
★ War. At the **Gettysburg National Military Park** (✉ Visitor center, 97 Taneytown Rd., ☎ 717/334–1124) you can follow the course of the fighting on a 750-square-ft electronic map or obtain brochures that will guide you along roads through the battleground. The **Gettysburg Travel Council** (✉ 35 Carlisle St., 17325, ☎ 717/334–6274) provides information on the region.

Side Trip to Hershey

Arriving and Departing

Take I–76 to Exit 20 and follow the signs—it's about 45 minutes from Lancaster.

What to See and Do

The streets have names like Cocoa Avenue, and the streetlights look like Hershey's Kisses at **Hersheypark** (✉ U.S. 422, ☎ 717/534–3090). At **Chocolate World** (✉ Park Blvd., ☎ 717/534–4900) you can take a 12-minute ride through the process of chocolate making. Contact the **Hershey Information Center** (✉ Hershey 17033, ☎ 800/437–7439).

Side Trip to Reading

Arriving and Departing

From Exit 22 off the Pennsylvania Turnpike take I–276 north and U.S. 422 west into downtown Reading, about an hour from Lancaster.

What to See and Do

Reading, a 19th-century industrial city, today promotes itself as the "outlet capital of the world." If you're in the mood for a diversion after a shopping spree, **Skyline Drive** is a meandering road with miles of unspoiled vistas and an expansive view of the city. The **Daniel Boone Homestead** (☎ 610/582–4900) is a renovation of the frontiersman's home. For information contact **Reading and Berks County Visitors Bureau** (✉ VF Factory Outlet Complex, Park Rd. and Hill Ave., Box 6677, Wyomissing 19610, ☎ 610/375–4085).

PITTSBURGH

At the point where the Monongahela and Allegheny rivers meet to form the Ohio River is a natural fortress first named Ft. Pitt and later Pittsburgh. Prosperity in coal, iron, and steel made the city a giant in the industrial age—and earned it its nickname of Smoky City. Today the smoke has cleared, and Pittsburgh—recently rated one of the "nation's most livable cities"—has been recast into an artful blend of turn-of-the-century architectural masterpieces and modern skyscrapers.

Visitor Information

Greater Pittsburgh: Convention and Visitors Bureau (✉ 4 Gateway Center, 15222, ☎ 800/366–0093). The same phone number connects to every **Visitor Information Center:** Downtown (✉ Gateway Center), Oakland (✉ Forbes Ave.), Mount Washington (✉ Grandview Ave.), and Airport (✉ Lower level near baggage claim). The Greater Pittsburgh Convention and Visitors Bureau operates a 24-hour **Activities Line** (☎ 800/366–0093), which lets you in on the events of the week.

Arriving and Departing

By Car

From the north or south take I–79 to I–279, which leads into downtown. From the east or west take the Pennsylvania Turnpike (I–76), then I–376 to the Grant Street exit.

By Plane

Greater Pittsburgh International Airport (☎ 412/472–3525), served by most major airlines, is 14 mi west of downtown; a cab ride there is about $30. **Airlines Transportation Co.** (☎ 412/471–8900) provides motor coach or van service to the major downtown hotels for $12 one-way and $20 round-trip.

By Train

Amtrak (✉ Liberty and Grant Sts., ☎ 800/872–7245).

By Bus

Greyhound Lines (✉ 11th St. and Liberty Ave., ☎ 800/231–2222).

Getting Around Pittsburgh

Port Authority Transit (☎ 412/231–5707) operates daily bus and trolley service. Within the central business district, the subway, called the T, is always free, and buses are free during the day. Two cable cars—the *Duquesne Incline,* from West Carson Street west on the Ohio River to the restaurant area of Grandview Avenue, and the *Monongahela In-*

cline, from Station Square on the Monongahela to Grandview Avenue—carry passengers from river level to the hilly south side of the city.

Exploring Pittsburgh

Downtown, an area framed by the three rivers and called the Golden Triangle, contains **Point State Park** (☞ Parks and Gardens, *below*) and major hotels, restaurants, and theaters. **PPG Place** (✉ Stanwix St. and 4th Ave., ☎ 412/434–3131), with its spires and towers evocative of a medieval castle, exemplifies the Pittsburgh renaissance. Several beautifully restored or maintained commercial and public buildings date from Pittsburgh's early boom days. The interior of the Flemish-Gothic **Two Mellon Bank Center** (✉ 5th Ave. and Grant St., ☎ 412/234–5000), formerly the Union Trust Building, has a glass rotunda. Daniel Burnham's Union Station is now the **Pennsylvanian** (✉ Grant St. and Liberty Ave., ☎ 412/391–6730); the **Oliver Building** (✉ 6th Ave. and Smithfield St., ☎ 412/281–8070) is also notable. H. H. Richardson's **Allegheny County Courthouse and Jail** (✉ 5th Ave. and Grant St., ☎ 412/355–5313), built in 1884, is one of the country's outstanding Romanesque buildings. **Station Square** (☎ 412/471–5808), on the Monongahela across the Smithfield Bridge, is a restored turn-of-the-century rail station with boutiques, restaurants (☞ Dining, *below*), and nightclubs.

★ East of downtown, **Oakland** is the headquarters of many of the city's cultural, educational, and medical landmarks. The **Carnegie** is an opulent cultural center, with the **Museum of Art**, the **Museum of Natural History**, the **Music Hall**, and the **Carnegie Library** all under one Beaux Arts roof. Don't miss the 19th-century French and American paintings; the Hall of Architecture, which re-creates in plaster some of the world's architectural masterpieces; the dinosaur collection; and the extravagant Music Hall lobby. ✉ *4400 Forbes Ave.,* ☎ *412/622–3131 or 412/622–3289 for tours.*

The **Frick Art and Historical Center** (✉ 7227 Reynolds St., ☎ 412/371–0606 or 412/371–0600) consists of **Clayton**, the turn-of-the-century home of Henry Clay Frick, which preserves the original furnishings and art; a **carriage museum;** and the **Frick Art Museum**, which possesses a small but choice collection of Old Master works. The **Andy Warhol Museum** (✉ 117 Sandusky St., ☎ 412/237–8300) devotes seven floors to the work of the native Pittsburgher and pop art icon.

The huge **Three Rivers Stadium** commands the north side of the Allegheny River. The **Carnegie Science Center** (✉ Allegheny Center, ☎ 412/237–3300) has a planetarium, an aquarium, hands-on science exhibits, and a four-story Omnimax theater.

Outside Pittsburgh

Northeast of Pittsburgh the **Laurel Highlands** region has Revolutionary War–era forts and battlefields, restored inns and taverns, and lush mountain scenery. The region is noted for white-water rafting, hiking, and skiing. Contact **Laurel Highlands, Inc.** (✉ Ligonier Town Hall, 120
★ E. Main St., Ligonier, ☎ 412/238–5661). **Fallingwater** is Frank Lloyd Wright's residential masterwork—a stone, concrete, and glass house dramatically cantilevered over a waterfall. ✉ *Rte. 381, Mill Run,* ☎ *412/329–8501. Closed Mon. Apr.–mid-Dec. and weekdays mid-Dec.–Mar.; reservations essential.*

Parks and Gardens

In the 36-acre **Point State Park** (☎ 412/471–0235) are the **Ft. Pitt Blockhouse** and **Ft. Pitt Museum** (☎ 412/281–9284). **Schenley Park** has a lake, trails, golf, and cross-country skiing. **Phipps Conservatory** (✉

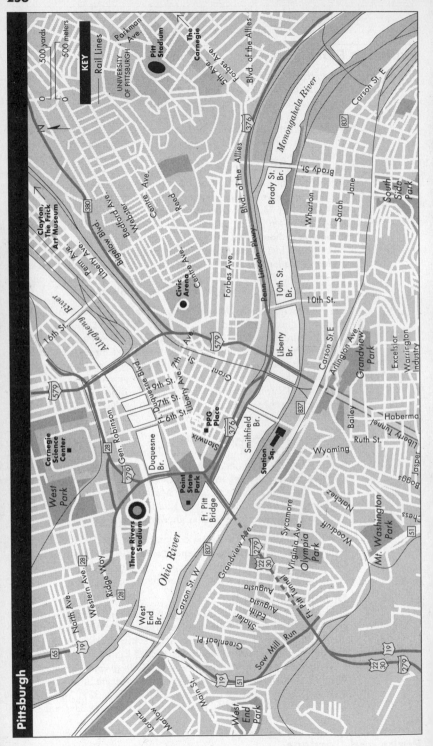

KEY

Rail Lines

500 yards
500 meters

UNIVERSITY OF PITTSBURGH

Pitt Stadium

Parkman Ave.

The Carnegie

5th Ave.
Forbes Ave.

Blvd. of the Allies

Monongahela River

Carson St. E

837

Clayton, The Frick Art Museum

Penn Ave.
Liberty Ave.

Bigelow Blvd.

380

Bedford Ave.
Webster
Centre Ave.
Reed

Brady St. Br.
Brady St.

Wharton

Jane

Sarah

South Side Park

Civic Arena

Centre Ave.

Forbes Ave.

Blvd. of the Allies

Penn Lincoln Pkwy.

10th St. Br.

10th St.

376

Allegheny River

16th St.

579

Liberty Br.

Carson St. E

Arlington Ave.

Grandview Park

Excelsior

Warrington Industry

579

Duquesne Blvd.
Gen. Robinson

28

Carnegie Science Center

West Park

279

5th Ave.
9th St.
7th St.
6th St.
Liberty Ave.
7th St.

Grant

Smithfield
Sixwix

PPG Place

837

Bailey

Haberma

Liberty Tunnel

Ruth St.

Wyoming

Jasper

Boggs

Duquesne Br.

Point State Park

Smithfield Br.

Station Sq.

Natchez

Woodruff

Mt. Washington Park

51

North Ave.

Western Ave.

Ridge Way

28

28

Three Rivers Stadium

Ft. Pitt Bridge

Ohio River

Carson St. W

837

Grandview Ave.

Sycamore

Virginia Ave.

Olympia Park

West End Br.

West End Park

Main St.

Lorenz

Merlow

Greenleaf Pl.

Shaler

Edith

Augusta

Augusta

Ft. Pitt Tunnel

279
22
30

Saw Mill Run

19
51

65

19

22
30
279

19

Schenley Park, ☎ 412/622–6914) is Henry Phipps's Victorian gardens—outdoors and under glass.

Dining

For price ranges *see* Chart 1 (B) *in* On the Road with Fodor's.

$$$ ✕ **Common Plea.** Many of the city's lawyers and judges dine in the three dining rooms here—one subdued, in dark wood; one flashy, with glass and mirrors; and a formal room with floor-to-ceiling wine cabinets and crystal chandeliers. Recommended are the fresh seafood and the veal dishes. ⊠ *310 Ross St.,* ☎ *412/281–5140. AE, DC, MC, V.*

$$$ ✕ **Grand Concourse/Gandy Dancer Saloon.** Set in a dazzlingly re-
★ stored Beaux Arts railroad terminal, the restaurant features seafood, homemade pastas, and gracious service. In the Saloon the emphasis is on raw-bar platters and lighter dishes. ⊠ *1 Station Sq., Carson and Smithfield Sts.,* ☎ *412/261–1717. AE, D, DC, MC, V.*

$$ ✕ **Georgetowne Inn.** Wraparound windows offer a majestic view from the Colonial-style dining rooms. The quality of the American food is exceptional; the low-key atmosphere makes this a good place for family dining. ⊠ *1230 Grandview Ave.,* ☎ *412/481–4424. AE, D, DC, MC, V. No lunch Sun.*

$ ✕ **Primanti Brothers.** What started out 50 years ago as a working-class bar is now a Pittsburgh favorite with six locations. The cheese steak comes with fries, coleslaw and tomato—all *in* the sandwich. ⊠ *46 18th St.,* ☎ *412/263–2142;* ⊠ *11 Cherry Way,* ☎ *412/566–8051;* ⊠ *Market Square,* ☎ *412/261–1599. No credit cards.*

Lodging

Choice hotels are limited in downtown Pittsburgh—and most are pricey. Nationally affiliated hotels are in Oakland and outlying suburban areas. For price ranges *see* Chart 2 (B) *in* On the Road with Fodor's.

$$$ 🏨 **Doubletree Hotel Pittsburgh.** The dramatically designed lobby leads to a 21-story tower housing rooms with contemporary decor. ⊠ *1000 Penn Ave., 15222,* ☎ *412/281–3700 or 800/367–8478,* FAX *412/227–4500. 616 rooms. Restaurant, lounge, pool, exercise room, meeting rooms, business center. AE, D, DC, MC, V.*

$$$ 🏨 **Westin William Penn.** Pittsburgh's grand hotel has a sumptuous lobby
★ with a coffered ceiling, intricate plasterwork, and crystal chandeliers. It is always filled with people relaxing over drinks or afternoon tea. The guest rooms are filled with light, and many are large enough for a couch and a wing chair. ⊠ *530 William Penn Pl., Mellon Sq., 15230,* ☎ *412/281–7100 or 800/228–3000,* FAX *412/553–5252. 595 rooms. 2 restaurants, lounge, beauty salon, exercise room, meeting rooms. AE, D, DC, MC, V.*

$$ 🏨 **Best Western Hotel University Center.** This modern nine-story hotel in the heart of Oakland provides easy access to the university and the museum district. ⊠ *3401 Blvd. of the Allies, 15213,* ☎ *412/683–6100 or 800/528–1234,* FAX *412/682–6115. 119 rooms. Restaurant, lounge, pool. AE, D, DC, MC, V.*

$$ 🏨 **Clubhouse Inn Pittsburgh.** At this garden-style hotel 9 mi from the
★ airport, guest rooms overlook a courtyard. The breakfast buffet is complimentary. ⊠ *5311 Campbells Run Rd., 15205,* ☎ *412/788–8400 or 800/258–2466,* FAX *412/788–2577. 152 rooms. Pool, spa, airport shuttle. AE, D, DC, MC, V.*

$$ \text{\$\$} \quad \text{⊞} \quad \textbf{The Priory.}$$ This European-style hotel is furnished with antiques and reproductions. A hearty Continental breakfast is served. ⊠ *614 Pressley St., 15212,* ☎ *412/231–3338,* ℻ *412/231–4838. 24 rooms. Meeting room. AE, D, DC, MC, V.*

$$ \text{\$\$} \quad \text{⊞} \quad \textbf{Ramada Plaza Suites and Conference Center.}$$ In the Golden Triangle, across from the Civic Arena and adjacent to the Steel Plaza subway station, the Ramada is a convenient, mid-price all-suite hotel whose spacious rooms have conventional hotel furnishings. Both full kitchens and kitchenettes are available. ⊠ *1 Bigelow Sq., 15219,* ☎ *412/281–5800 or 800/225–5858,* ℻ *412/281–8467. 311 suites. Restaurant, spa, laundry service, meeting rooms. AE, D, DC, MC, V.*

Nightlife and the Arts

Nightlife

Station Square (⊠ Carson at Smithfield St.) has **Chauncy's** (☎ 412/232–0601) for dining and dancing, the **FunnyBone Comedy Club** (☎ 412/281–3130), and **Jellyrolls** (☎ 412/391–7464), a piano bar.

The Arts

The **Pittsburgh Symphony Orchestra** appears at the Heinz Hall for the Performing Arts (⊠ 600 Penn Ave., ☎ 412/392–4800). The **Pittsburgh Opera** (☎ 412/281–0912) and the **Pittsburgh Ballet** (☎ 412/281–0360) are at the Benedum Center for the Performing Arts (⊠ 719 Liberty Ave., ☎ 412/456–6666). The **Point Park College Playhouse** (⊠ 222 Craft Ave., ☎ 412/621–4445) presents dance and theater, including shows for children.

Outdoor Activities and Sports

Jogging

Point State Park (☎ 412/471–0235) has an upper and a lower path, each forming a circuit of about a mile in length, with views of the skyline and the city's three rivers.

Golf

The **North Park Golf Course** (⊠ Kummer Rd., North Park, ☎ 412/935–1967) is one of the more than 50 courses within a 30-minute drive of downtown, all of which are open to the public.

Spectator Sports

Baseball: Pittsburgh Pirates (⊠ Three Rivers Stadium, 400 Stadium Circle, ☎ 412/321–2827).

Football: Pittsburgh Steelers (⊠ Three Rivers Stadium, ☎ 412/323–1200).

Hockey: Pittsburgh Penguins (⊠ Civic Arena, Center Ave. and Auditorium Pl., ☎ 412/333–7328).

Shopping

Pittsburgh's best downtown department stores, **Saks Fifth Avenue** (⊠ 513 Smithfield St., ☎ 412/263–4800) and **Kaufmann's** (⊠ 5th Ave. and Smithfield St., ☎ 412/232–2000), have recently been joined by **Lazurus** (⊠ 5th Ave. and Wood St., ☎ 412/655–6300). Nearby are the shopping complexes **Fifth Avenue Place, 1 Oxford Centre,** and **PPG Place.** In the **Strip District** (⊠ Between Liberty and Penn Aves. and 16th and 22nd Sts.) are streets lined with farmers' market stalls and sellers of imported food and dry goods. Antiques shops and art galleries are along Carson Street East on the **South Side.** The **Shops at Station Square** (☞ Exploring Pittsburgh, *above*) has 70 shops and restaurants.

ELSEWHERE IN PENNSYLVANIA

The Poconos

Getting There

I–80 leads to the Delaware Water Gap, I–84 to Milford. From the south U.S. 611 skirts the Delaware River and takes you into Stroudsburg, which is 98 mi from Philadelphia, 135 mi from Harrisburg, and 318 mi from Pittsburgh.

What to See and Do

The Poconos, in the northeastern corner of the state, encompass 2,400 square mi of mountainous wilderness bordering the Delaware River, with lakes, streams, waterfalls, resorts, and enchanting country inns. A backroads drive will turn up quaint villages such as **Jim Thorpe** (✉ Rte. 209), a late-Victorian mountain-resort town that has first-rate antiques shops and galleries. Winter brings downhill and cross-country skiing, skating, and snowmobiling; summer offers golf, boating, horseback riding, and hiking. The **Pocono Mountains Vacation Bureau** (✉ 1004 Main St., Stroudsburg 18360, ☎ 717/424–6050 or 800/762–6667) provides information.

Dining and Lodging

$$$$ ⊡ **French Manor.** Forget the heart-shaped bathtubs and other honeymoon hokeyness this area is known for—the French Manor is *the* most romantic spot in the Poconos. The chateau-style mansion, secluded on the top of a mountain, offers panoramic views, luxurious amenities, and excellent French cuisine. ✉ *Huckleberry Rd., South Sterling 18460,* ☎ *717/676–3244 or 800/523–8200,* 𝔽𝔸𝕏 *717/676–9786. 9 rooms. Restaurant. AE, D, DC, MC, V.*

$$$$ ⊡ **Sterling Inn.** Built in 1857 on an historic Indian site, the clapboard main house and cluster of cottages provide a bright country ambience. ✉ *Rte. 191, South Sterling 18460,* ☎ *717/676–3311 or 800/523–8200. 54 rooms. Restaurant, indoor pool, spa. AE, D, DC, MC, V.*

VIRGINIA

By Francis X.
Rocca

Updated by
Bruce Walker

Capital	Richmond
Population	6,676,000
Motto	Thus Always to Tyrants
State Bird	Cardinal
State Flower	Dogwood
Postal Abbreviation	VA

Statewide Visitor Information

Virginia Division of Tourism (⊠ 901 E. Byrd St., Richmond 23219, ☎ 804/786–2051 or 800/932–5827) can mail travel brochures and travel information to you. Call **Visit Virginia** (☎ 800/847–4882) for visitor information and a free state map. **Welcome centers** are in Bracey (on I–85), Bristol (I–81), Clearbrook (I–81), Covington (I–64), Fredericksburg (I–95), Lambsburg (I–77), Manassas (I–66), New Church (U.S. 13), Rocky Gap (I–77), and Skippers (I–95).

Scenic Drives

Skyline Drive, the **Blue Ridge Parkway,** and **Goshen Pass** offer spectacular mountain scenery (☞ Charlottesville and the Shenandoah Valley, *below*). A 25-mi drive north along **Route 20** from Charlottesville to Orange takes you through gently rolling green countryside, past horse farms and vineyards. For a stirring panorama of the famous buildings and monuments of Washington, D.C., drive north from Alexandria on the **George Washington Memorial Parkway.** Between Virginia Beach and the Eastern Shore stretches the 17½-mi **Chesapeake Bay Bridge-Tunnel,** where you are surrounded by sea without leaving your car; there are an observation pier and a restaurant along the way.

National and State Parks

National Parks

Shenandoah National Park (⊠ Rte. 4, Box 348, Luray 22835, ☎ 540/999–3500)—195,000 acres with a vertical change in elevation of 3,500 ft—offers hiking, horseback riding, and fishing. The 2.2-million-acre **George Washington and Jefferson National Forests** (⊠ 5162 Valleypointe Pkwy., Roanoke 24019, ☎ 540/265–5100) offer camping, boating, hiking, fishing, swimming, and horseback riding. **Mt. Rogers National Recreation Area** (⊠ Rte. 1, Box 303, Marion 24354, ☎ 540/783–5196) is a 116,000-acre expanse, including the state's highest point—5,729 ft above sea level.

State Parks

The **Department of Conservation and Recreation** (⊠ 203 Governor St., Richmond 23219, ☎ 804/786–1712) has information on Virginia's 28 state parks, which range in size from 500 to 4,500 acres. Two of the most popular are **Douthat State Park** (⊠ Rte. 1, Box 212, Millboro 24460, ☎ 757/862–8100) and **First Landing/Seashore State Park** (⊠ 2500 Shore Dr., Virginia Beach 23451, ☎ 757/481–2131).

CHARLOTTESVILLE AND THE SHENANDOAH VALLEY

Residents of Charlottesville, in the Piedmont region of rolling plains, call it "Mr. Jefferson's Country." They speak of the Sage of Monticello as if he were still writing, building, and governing. Yet aware as it is of its past, Charlottesville is anything but backward. Home to the state university and a fashionable retreat for tycoons and movie stars, it is one of America's most sophisticated small cities, often called the Santa Fe of the East.

In and along the Shenandoah Valley are small towns that were once frontier outposts; well-traveled driving routes with turnouts overlooking breathtaking scenery; many opportunities for outdoor recreation, on water and solid ground; and accommodations and restaurants to suit all tastes.

Visitor Information

Bath County: Chamber of Commerce (✉ Rte. 220, Box 718, Hot Springs 24445, ☎ 540/839–5409). **Roanoke Valley:** Convention and Visitors Bureau (✉ 114 Market St., Roanoke 24011, ☎ 540/342–6025 or 800/635–5535). **Shenandoah Valley:** Travel Association (✉ Box 1040, New Market 22844, ☎ 540/740–3132). **Charlottesville:** Charlottesville-Albemarle Convention and Visitors Bureau (✉ Box 161, 22902, ☎ 804/977–1783). **Lexington:** Visitor Center (✉ 102 E. Washington St., 24450, ☎ 540/463–3777). **Winchester:** Chamber of Commerce (✉ 1360 S. Pleasant Valley Rd., 22601, ☎ 540/662–4135 or 800/662–1360).

Arriving and Departing

By Bus
Greyhound Lines (☎ 800/231–2222) serves Charlottesville (✉ 310 W. Main St.), Lexington (✉ Classic Creations, 122 S. Main St.), Roanoke (✉ 26 Salem Ave.), and Staunton (✉ 1143 Richmond Rd.).

By Car
Charlottesville is where U.S. 29 (north–south) meets I–64. I–81 and U.S. 11 run north–south the length of the Shenandoah Valley and continue south into Tennessee. I–66 meets I–81 and U.S. 11 at the northern end of the valley; I–64 connects I–81 and U.S. 11 with Charlottesville. Route 39 into Bath County connects with I–81 just north of Lexington.

By Plane
Charlottesville-Albemarle Airport (☎ 804/973–8341) is 8 mi north of town on Route 29. **Roanoke Regional Airport** (☎ 540/362–1999) is 6 mi north of town on Route 581.

By Train
Amtrak (☎ 800/872–7245) has service to Charlottesville's Union Station (✉ 810 W. Main St.), to Clifton Forge (for the Homestead resort in Bath County), and to Staunton.

Exploring Charlottesville and the Shenandoah Valley

Charlottesville
★ Jefferson built his beloved **Monticello** on a "little mountain" over a period of 40 years, from 1769 to 1809. In details and overall conception Monticello was a revolutionary structure, a neoclassical repudiation of the Colonial style with all its political connotations. Throughout the house are Jefferson's inventions, including a seven-day clock and a two-pen contraption for copying letters as he wrote them. ✉ *Rte. 53,* ☎ *804/984–9800.*

The cozy rooms of **Ash Lawn–Highland,** James Monroe's modest presidential residence, evoke the fifth president—our first to spring from the middle class. Outside, sheep and peacocks roam the grounds of this working plantation. ⊠ *Rte. 795 (southwest of Rte. 53),* ☎ *804/293–9539.*

Historic Michie Tavern is an 18th-century building moved here in the 1920s from a neighboring location. The period rooms are a bit too tidy but otherwise convincing. ⊠ *Rte. 53,* ☎ *804/977–1234.*

There is little to see in downtown Charlottesville besides a pedestrian shopping mall that takes up six brick-paved blocks of Main Street. At the west end of town is the **University of Virginia** (☎ 804/924–1019), founded and designed by Thomas Jefferson and still widely acclaimed as the "proudest achievement in American architecture." Pavilions flank the lawn as it flows down from the Rotunda, a half-scale replica of Rome's Pantheon. Behind the pavilions, gardens and landscaping are laced with serpentine walls.

The Shenandoah Valley

At the top of the valley, and almost at the northernmost tip of the state, is **Winchester.** The town hosts parades and a beauty pageant during the **Shenandoah Apple Blossom Festival** every May (☎ 540/662–3863). September is apple time at pick-your-own orchards throughout the surrounding countryside. Because of its strategic location, the town has drawn more than its share of military action over the years. A young Colonel George Washington spent more than a year here during the French and Indian Wars; the log cabin in which he worked is now **George Washington's Office Museum** (⊠ 32 W. Cork St., ☎ 540/662–4412). **Stonewall Jackson's headquarters** is where the Confederate general planned the First Battle of Winchester (there were eventually three). ⊠ *415 N. Braddock St.,* ☎ *540/667–3242. Free.*

Belle Grove, just south of Middletown, is a grand 1790s limestone mansion designed with the help of Thomas Jefferson. It served as headquarters for the victorious Union general Philip Sheridan during the Battle of Cedar Creek (1864) and is today a working farm. Call ahead if you plan to visit—it sometimes closes for part of the winter. ⊠ *U.S. 11,* ☎ *540/869–2028.*

Shenandoah National Park (☞ National and State Parks, *above*), encompassing some 60 peaks, runs more than 80 mi along the Blue Ridge, south from Front Royal to Waynesboro. Mountain meadows open up to gorgeous views of the range. Hiking, camping, fishing, and horseback riding are all available. For information on seasonal activities pick up the free *Shenandoah Overlook* when you enter the park.

★   **Skyline Drive** winds 105 mi over the mountains of the park, affording panoramas of the valley to the west and the rolling country of the Piedmont to the east. On holidays and weekends in spring and fall, crowds slow down traffic to much less than the maximum of 35 mph. Many lodges, campsites, and eating places, and sometimes stretches of the drive itself, are closed from November through April.

Luray Caverns, the largest caves in the state, are just west of Skyline Drive. Water seepage over millions of years has created striking rock and mineral formations. Tours begin every 20 minutes. ⊠ *Rte. 211, Luray,* ☎ *540/743–6551.*

At **New Market,** the site of a costly Confederate victory late in the Civil War, the **New Market Battlefield Historical Park** has exhibits on the battle and the war. ⊠ *I–81 Exit 264,* ☎ *540/740–3102.*

In Staunton (pronounced *Stan-*ton) the **Woodrow Wilson Birthplace and Museum** (⊠ 24 N. Coalter St., ☎ 540/885–0897) has been restored to its appearance in 1856, when the 28th U.S. president was born here.

The **Museum of American Frontier Culture** (✉ 1250 Richmond Rd., ☎ 540/332–7850), just outside Staunton, is an outdoor living museum that re-creates early American agrarian life on four genuine 18th-century farmsteads, right down to the animals and the crops.

The 470-mi **Blue Ridge Parkway,** a continuation of Skyline Drive, runs south through the **George Washington National Forest** (☞ National and State Parks, *above*) to Great Smoky Mountains National Park in North Carolina and Tennessee. Less pristine than the drive, the parkway offers better, higher views—and free admission. **Peaks of Otter Recreation Area,** just off the Blue Ridge Parkway northeast of Roanoke, offers a 360-degree panorama.

In Lexington the sixth-oldest college in the country, **Washington and Lee University,** is named for the first U.S. president (an early benefactor) and the Confederate commander Robert E. Lee, who served as college president after the Civil War. Among the campus's white-columned redbrick buildings is the **Lee Memorial Chapel and Museum** (☎ 540/463–8768), where a saintly statue of the general shown recumbent behind the altar marks his tomb.

Next door to Washington and Lee University are the imposing neo-Gothic buildings of the **Virginia Military Institute,** since its founding in 1839 an all-male institution; a 1996 Supreme Court decision required it either to admit women or lose state funding. Here the **George C. Marshall Museum** (☎ 540/463–7103) preserves the memory of the general, secretary of state, and Nobel Peace Prize winner. On display at the **Institute Museum** (☎ 540/464–7232) is Stonewall Jackson's horse, stuffed and mounted. Near the Virginia Military Institute, the **Stonewall Jackson House** offers a glimpse of Jackson's private life (✉ 8 E. Washington St., ☎ 540/463–2552).

About 30 mi from Lexington, **Bath County** is the site of thermal springs once used for medical treatments and is still a popular resort area. Between Lexington and Bath County runs **Goshen Pass,** a stunning 3-mi stretch of Route 39 that follows the Maury River as it winds its way through the Alleghenies. The countryside is lush with rhododendrons in May.

★ **Natural Bridge,** south of Lexington, is a 215-ft-high, 90-ft-long arch that was created by the creek below gradually carving out the limestone. It really *is* a bridge, supporting U.S. 11. It's also part of a 150-acre park. ✉ *I–81, Exit 175 or 180A,* ☎ *540/291–2121 or 800/533–1410.*

Roanoke is a quiet and cheerful railroad hub. A restored downtown warehouse called **Center in the Square** (✉ Market Sq., ☎ 540/342–5700) houses a theater, a local historical museum, an art gallery, and a science museum with a planetarium. The **Virginia Museum of Transportation** (✉ 303 Norfolk Ave., ☎ 540/342–5670) houses dozens of original train cars and engines.

A restored plantation southeast of Roanoke, **Booker T. Washington National Monument** is the birthplace of the great black educator and a living museum of life under slavery. ✉ *Rte. 122,* ☎ *540/721–2094.*

About two hours east of Roanoke and less than two hours south of Charlottesville is **Appomattox Court House National Historical Park,** a village of about 30 buildings restored to their appearance on April 9, 1865, when Lee surrendered to Grant in the parlor of the McLean House here. A slide show supplements a self-guided tour, and costumed interpreters answer questions in summer. ✉ *Rte. 24,* ☎ *804/352–8987.*

What to See and Do with Children

At Charlottesville's **Virginia Discovery Museum** (⊠ 524 E. Main St., ☎ 804/977–1025) children can step inside a giant kaleidoscope or an authentic log cabin. The **Science Museum of Western Virginia** in Roanoke (⊠ Market Sq., ☎ 540/342–5710) offers interactive exhibits including computer games that entertain and inform youngsters on topics such as energy resources, oceanography, geology, and meteorology.

Dining and Lodging

Bed-and-breakfast reservations in the region can be made through **Blue Ridge Bed & Breakfast** (⊠ Rte. 2, Box 3895, Berryville 22611, ☎ 540/955–1246 or 800/296–1246) and **Guesthouses** (⊠ Box 5737, Charlottesville 22905, ☎ 804/979–7264). For price ranges *see* Charts 1 (B) and 2 (B) *in* On the Road with Fodor's.

Bath County

$$$$ ✕⊡ **The Homestead.** Famous since 1766 for its mineral waters, this
★ is one of the country's most luxurious resorts. The elegant, spacious guest rooms have traditional southern decor. The 16,000-acre property includes 100 mi of riding trails, 10 ski slopes, and 4 mi of streams stocked with rainbow trout. The formal dining room has nightly live dance music. Breakfast and dinner are included in the room rate. ⊠ *Rte. 220, Hot Springs 24445, ☎ 540/839–1766 or 800/838–1766,* 𝔽𝔸𝕏 *540/839–7670. 517 rooms. 10 restaurants, 2 outdoor pools, indoor pool, spa, 3 golf courses, 12 tennis courts, bowling, health club, horseback riding, boating, fishing, mountain bikes, ice-skating, skiing. AE, D, DC, MC, V.*

$$$$ ✕⊡ **Inn at Gristmill Square.** These five buildings (gristmill, miller's house, country store, blacksmith's house, and hardware store) are a State Historic Landmark; a walk-in wine cellar is set among the gears of the original waterwheel. Entrées may include breast of chicken stuffed with wild rice, sausage, apple, and pecans. Guest rooms have a rustic Colonial Virginia motif. ⊠ *Rte. 645 (Box 359), Warm Springs 24484, ☎ 540/839–2231,* 𝔽𝔸𝕏 *540/839–5770. 15 rooms, 1 apartment. Restaurant, pool, sauna, 3 tennis courts. D, MC, V.*

Blue Ridge Parkway

$$$ ⊡ **Doe Run Lodge.** The location on the crest of the Blue Ridge guarantees grand vistas of the Piedmont and proximity to golf, skiing, and hunting. Each chalet or villa has a fireplace and floor-to-ceiling windows. Book months in advance for the cabin, which dates to more than 100 years ago. ⊠ *Milepost 189, Blue Ridge Pkwy., Fancy Gap 24328, ☎ 540/398–2212 or 800/325–6189,* 𝔽𝔸𝕏 *540/398–2833. 48 units. Restaurant, bar, pool, sauna, 3 tennis courts, hiking, fishing. AE, MC, V.*

$$$ ⊡ **Wintergreen.** From December through March guests at this 11,000-acre resort may ski and golf on the same day; and there are plenty of sports options all year long. Accommodations range from studio mountain condos to six- and seven-bedroom houses, all-wood buildings that blend in with the leafy surroundings. ⊠ *Rte. 664 (Box 706), Wintergreen 22958, ☎ 804/325–2200 or 800/325–2200,* 𝔽𝔸𝕏 *804/325–8003. 330 units. 6 restaurants, bar, indoor pool, 5 outdoor pools, lake, massage, sauna, 2 golf courses, 25 tennis courts, exercise room, hiking, horseback riding, mountain bikes, cross-country skiing, downhill skiing. AE, D, MC, V.*

$ ⊡ **Rocky Knob Cabins.** These log cabins, hidden away in the woods near the spectacular Rock Castle Gorge, have kitchens but no bathtubs or phones. ⊠ *Milepost 174 (Box 5), Meadows of Dan 24120, ☎ 540/593–3503. 7 cabins. DC, MC, V. Closed Labor Day–Memorial Day.*

Charlottesville

$$–$$$ ✕ **C&O Restaurant.** A boarded-up storefront hung with an illuminated Pepsi sign conceals this stark-white formal dining room. Try the terrine *de campagne* (pâté of veal, venison, and pork). When available, *coquilles* St. Jacques is a staple of the changing menu. The informal bistro downstairs serves light meals. ✉ *515 E. Water St.,* ☎ *804/ 971–7044. Reservations essential upstairs. MC, V. Upstairs closed Sun.*

$$ ✕ **Eastern Standard.** Specialties served in the casual but subdued upstairs dining room include pan-seared tuna with ginger-kumquat salsa and loin of lamb with mint pesto. The lively downstairs bistro serves pastas and light fare. ✉ *West End Downtown Mall,* ☎ *804/295–8668. AE, D, MC, V. Upstairs closed Sun.–Mon. No lunch.*

$ ✕ **Crozet Pizza.** There are up to 35 toppings from which to choose, including snow peas and asparagus spears in season. The hardwood booths are always full, and on weekends takeout must be ordered hours in advance. ✉ *Rte. 240, Crozet, west of Charlottesville,* ☎ *804/823– 2132. No credit cards. Closed Sun.–Mon.*

$$$ ✕▥ **Boar's Head Inn.** Built around a restored early 19th-century gristmill set on two small lakes, the Boar's Head has simple but elegant guest rooms furnished chiefly with Victorian antiques. Some suites have fireplaces. In the Old Mill Room restaurant, the costumed staff serves items such as bison carpaccio and cider-marinated pork loin. ✉ *U.S. 250 W (Box 5307), 22905,* ☎ *804/296–2181 or 800/476–1988,* ℻ *804/972– 6024. 184 rooms. 2 restaurants, 3 pools, sauna, spa, golf course, 20 tennis courts, exercise room, squash, fishing, bicycles. AE, D, MC, V.*

$$$ ✕▥ **Silver Thatch Inn.** This 18th-century farmhouse has a Colonial America theme, and every guest room is unique. In the restaurant, provisioned by three organic farms, the fish is always fresh and the rabbits and chickens are locally raised. The wine cellar wins national awards. ✉ *3001 Hollymead Dr., 22911,* ☎ *804/978–4686,* ℻ *804/973– 6156. 7 rooms. Restaurant, pool. AE, DC, MC, V.*

$$ ✕▥ **English Inn.** Guests here are treated to the amenities of a fine hotel and the charm of a country inn. A complimentary buffet breakfast is offered in the Tudor-style dining room. Guest rooms are modern; suites have sitting rooms and reproduction antiques. Guests have access to a health club about a mile away. ✉ *2000 Morton Dr., 22903,* ☎ *804/971–9900 or 800/786–5400,* ℻ *804/977–8008. 88 rooms. Coffee shop, indoor pool, sauna, exercise room. AE, DC, MC, V.*

Lexington

$$$ ✕▥ **Maple Hall.** In this mid-19th-century plantation house on 56 acres, guest rooms are furnished with period antiques and modern amenities. The main dining room has a large decorative fireplace. Notable entrées include beef fillet with green-peppercorn sauce. ✉ *Rte. 5 (Box 223), 24450 (7 mi north of Lexington on Rte. 11),* ☎ *540/463–6693,* ℻ *540/463–7262. 21 rooms. Restaurant, pool, tennis court, hiking, fishing. MC, V.*

Roanoke

$$$ ✕ **La Maison du Gourmet.** The 12 dining rooms in this 1927 Georgian Colonial–style house range from grand to cozy, with additional dining in the formal garden and on two terraces. Filet mignon is flambéed at your table and served as steak Diane; the lamb is succulent and expertly grilled. ✉ *5732 Airport Rd.,* ☎ *540/366–2444. AE, D, DC, MC, V. Closed Mon. No lunch except by special appointment, no dinner Sun.*

$ ✕ **Texas Tavern.** The sign says, WE SERVE A THOUSAND, TEN AT A TIME. The tavern is often packed, especially at night, so you may have to wait for one of the 10 stools; but the tough-looking guys behind the counter will fill your order quickly. Chili is the specialty. No liquor is served.

✉ *114 Church Ave.,* ☎ *540/342–4825. Reservations not accepted. No credit cards.*

Staunton

$$ ✕ **Rowe's Family Restaurant.** This bright, booth-filled dining room has been operated by the same family since 1947. Specialties include Virginia ham, steak, chicken, and homemade pies (try the mincemeat). ✉ *I–81 Exit 222,* ☎ *540/886–1833. D, MC, V.*

$$$ ✕🛏 **Belle Grae Inn.** Dining rooms in this restored Victorian house are appointed with brass wall sconces and Oriental rugs; the menu is Continental, with a southern twist. Canopy beds, brass beds, and rocking chairs give the guest rooms a turn-of-the-century look. ✉ *515 W. Frederick St., 24401,* ☎ *540/886–5151,* FAX *540/886–6641. 16 rooms. Restaurant, breakfast room. AE, MC, V.*

$$ 🛏 **Frederick House.** Three restored town houses dating from 1810 make up this inn in the center of the historic district. Guest rooms are decorated with antiques. ✉ *28 N. New St., 24401,* ☎ *540/885–4220 or 800/334-5575. 14 rooms. Breakfast room. Full breakfast. AE, D, DC, MC, V. No smoking.*

Motels

🛏 **Holiday Inn Civic Center** (✉ 501 Orange Ave., Roanoke 24016, ☎ 540/342–8961, FAX 540/342–3813), 152 rooms, restaurant, bar, pool, free parking; $$. 🛏 **Roseloe Motel** (✉ Rte. 2, Box 590, Hot Springs 24445, ☎ 540/839–5373), 14 rooms, free parking; $.

Campgrounds

In Shenandoah National Park the **Big Meadows Campground** (☎ 540/999–3500 or 800/365–2267) accepts reservations. Other campsites in the park are available on a first-come, first-served basis; for information contact the park.

Nightlife and the Arts

Nightlife

In Charlottesville the large and comfortable **Miller's** (✉ 109 W. Main St., Downtown Mall, ☎ 804/971–8511) hosts blues and jazz musicians. At the **Homestead** in Hot Springs (☞ Dining and Lodging, *above*) there's nightly dancing to live music.

The Arts

CHARLOTTESVILLE

For details on performances at the University of Virginia, check the *Cavalier Daily.* **McGuffey Art Center** (✉ 201 2nd St. NW, ☎ 804/295–7973), which houses the studios of painters and sculptors, also hosts concerts and plays.

SHENANDOAH VALLEY

Garth Newel Music Center (✉ Hot Springs, ☎ 540/839–5018) hosts chamber music concerts on summer weekends. The **Theater at Lime Kiln** (✉ Lexington, ☎ 540/463–3074) is an outdoor rock-wall pit (the ruins of a lime kiln) where plays and concerts—folk, bluegrass, classical, and other nonrock music—are performed throughout the summer. **Roanoke Ballet Theatre** (☎ 540/345–6099) performs in spring and fall.

Outdoor Activities and Sports

Canoeing

Front Royal Canoe (✉ Rte. 340, ☎ 540/635–5440) and **Downriver Canoe** (✉ Rte. 613, ☎ 540/635–5526) are both near Front Royal.

Shenandoah River Outfitters (⊠ Rte. 684, ☎ 540/743–4159) is near Luray.

Fishing

To take advantage of the abundance of trout in some 50 streams of **Shenandoah National Park,** get a five-day Virginia fishing license, available in season (early April–mid-October) at concession stands along Skyline Drive.

Golf

Caverns Country Club Resort (⊠ Rte. 211, Luray, ☎ 540/743–6551). **Greene Hills Club** (⊠ Rte. 619, Stanardsville, ☎ 804/985–7328). The **Homestead** (⊠ Rte. 220, Hot Springs, ☎ 540/839–1766 or 800/838–1766). **Wintergreen Resort** (⊠ Rte. 664, Wintergreen, ☎ 804/325–2200 or 800/325–2200).

Hiking

The stretch of the **Appalachian Trail** running through Shenandoah National Park takes hikers along the Blue Ridge Skyline, offering stunning views of the Piedmont and the Shenandoah Valley in the distance; white-tailed deer often appear at arm's length. The main pathway's proximity to Skyline Drive and frequent parking lots make hike lengths flexible. For deep-wilderness hikes, 500 mi of marked side trails lead into the backcountry.

Tennis

Caverns Country Club Resort, the **Homestead,** and **Wintergreen Resort** (☞ Golf, *above*) also offer tennis.

Spectator Sports

Equestrian events: The **Virginia Horse Center** (⊠ Lexington, ☎ 540/463–2194) stages show jumping, hunter trials, and multibreed shows year-round.

Football, soccer, basketball, golf, tennis, and field hockey: The **University of Virginia** (☎ 804/924–8821) is nationally ranked in several varsity sports. The *Cavalier Daily* has listings.

Ski Areas

The **Homestead** (☞ Golf, *above*) has cross-country, downhill, and night skiing. **Massanutten Resort** (⊠ Rte. 644 off Rte. 33, McGaheysville, ☎ 540/289–9441) offers rentals and snowmaking. **Wintergreen Resort** (☞ Golf, *above*) maintains 17 slopes and trails.

Shopping

Lewis Glaser Quill Pens (⊠ 1700 Sourwood Pl., Charlottesville, ☎ 804/973–7783 or 800/446–6732) sells feather pens and pewter inkwells of the kind it has made for the U.S. Supreme Court and the British royal family. **Court Square Antiques** (⊠ 4th and Jefferson Sts., Charlottesville, ☎ 804/295–6244) carries a selection of quilts, furniture, and collectibles.

NORTHERN VIRGINIA

The affluent and cosmopolitan residents of this region look more to neighboring Washington, D.C., than to the rest of the state for direction. Yet they take pride in being Virginians and in protecting the historic treasures they hold in trust for the rest of the nation. Here are found some of America's most precious acreage, including Mount Vernon and the Civil War battlefield of Manassas (Bull Run). The enormous Potomac Mills Mall, in Prince William, is Virginia's most visited site. The gracious Old South lives on in the fox hunting and steeplechases of Loudoun County. On the nearby Northern Neck visitors can combine historic sightseeing with fishing and water sports.

Visitor Information

Fairfax County: Convention and Visitors Bureau (⊠ 8300 Boone Blvd., Suite 450, Vienna 22182, ☎ 703/790–3329). **Loudoun County:** Tourism Council (⊠ 108D South St. SE, Leesburg 22075, ☎ 703/777–0519 or 800/752–6118). **Northern Neck:** Travel Council (⊠ Box 312, Reedville 22539, ☎ 800/453–6167). **Alexandria:** Convention and Visitors Association (⊠ 221 King St., 22314, ☎ 703/838–4200). **Fredericksburg:** Visitor Center (⊠ 706 Caroline St., 22401, ☎ 540/373–1776 or 800/678–4748).

Arriving and Departing

By Bus

Greyhound Lines (☎ 800/231–2222) serves Fairfax (⊠ 4103 Rust St.), Arlington (⊠ 3860 S. Four Mile Run Dr.), Fredericksburg (⊠ 1400 Jefferson Davis Hwy.), and Springfield (⊠ 6583 Backlick Rd.).

By Car

I–95 runs north–south along the eastern side of the region. I–66 runs east–west. Fredericksburg is 50 mi south of Washington, D.C., on I–95. Route 3 runs the length of the Northern Neck.

By Plane

Two major airports serve both northern Virginia and the Washington, D.C., area. The busy **Washington National Airport** (☎ 703/419–8000), in Arlington, has scheduled daily flights by all major U.S. carriers. **Dulles International Airport** (☎ 703/419–8000), in Loudoun County 26 mi west of Washington, is a modern facility served by major U.S. airlines and many international carriers.

By Train

Amtrak (☎ 800/872–7245) stops in Alexandria (⊠ 110 Callahan Dr.) and Fredericksburg (⊠ Caroline St. and Lafayette Blvd.); some travelers find it easiest to arrive in the capital's Union Station (☞ Washington, D.C.).

Exploring Northern Virginia

★ George Washington's **Mount Vernon** is the most visited house museum in the country. The elegant, porticoed farmhouse, built beginning in 1754 from Washington's own plans, has been restored to its appearance during the years when the first president lived here (1759–75, 1783–89, and 1797–99). Washington and his wife, Martha, are buried here. ⊠ *Rte. 235 and George Washington Memorial Pkwy.,* ☎ *703/780–2000.*

Washington's nephew Lawrence Lewis lived at **Woodlawn** (⊠ U.S. 1, ☎ 703/780–4000), designed by the architect of the Capitol and begun in 1800. The formal gardens include a large collection of rare old-fashioned roses. Also on the grounds is the small **Pope-Leighey House,** designed by Frank Lloyd Wright and built in 1946.

South of Mount Vernon is the relatively unvisited but meticulously restored **Gunston Hall** (⊠ Gunston Rd., ☎ 703/550–9220), the circa-1755 Georgian-style plantation home of George Mason, one of the framers of the Constitution.

North of Mount Vernon, on the Potomac, is **Alexandria,** a suburb of Washington, D.C., with an identity based on more than two centuries

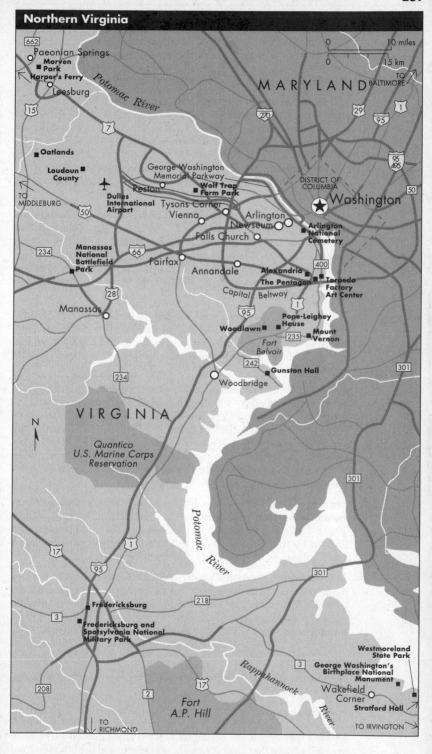

Northern Virginia

662 Paeonian Springs
Morven Park
Harper's Ferry
Leesburg

MARYLAND
TO BALTIMORE

0   10 miles
0   15 km

270
29
95
1

15
7

Oatlands

Loudoun County

George Washington Memorial Parkway
Wolf Trap Farm Park

DISTRICT OF COLUMBIA

95
495

50

TO MIDDLEBURG
50
Dulles International Airport
Reston
Tysons Corner
Vienna

★ Washington

Arlington
Newseum
Falls Church
Arlington National Cemetery

234
Manassas National Battlefield Park
66
Fairfax
Annandale

400
Alexandria
The Pentagon
Torpedo Factory Art Center

28
Capital Beltway
1

Manassas
95
Pope-Leighey House
Woodlawn
235
Mount Vernon

Fort Belvoir

234
242
Woodbridge
Gunston Hall

301

VIRGINIA

N

Quantico U.S. Marine Corps Reservation

301

17
1

Potomac River

301

95

Fredericksburg
3
Fredericksburg and Spotsylvania National Military Park

218

Westmoreland State Park
3
George Washington's Birthplace National Monument

208
2
17
Fort A.P. Hill

Rappahannock River

Wakefield Corner
Stratford Hall

TO RICHMOND

TO IRVINGTON

of history. **Old Town** is a neighborhood of 18th- and 19th-century town houses, most of them redbrick. Its major sights can be seen on foot within 20 blocks or so, and the area has scores of shops and restaurants. Parking is usually scarce, but the **Convention and Visitors Association** (☞ Visitor Information, *above*) provides a one-day pass that allows free parking at two-hour meters.

This visitor center—the best place to start a tour—is in the town's oldest structure, **Ramsay House** (✉ 221 King St., ☎ 703/838–4200), believed to have been built around 1724 in Dumfries (25 mi south) and moved here in 1749. The 1752 **Carlyle House** (✉ 121 N. Fairfax St., ☎ 703/549–2997), built by Scottish merchant John Carlyle, is still the grandest house in town. The **Old Presbyterian Meeting House** is another fine 18th-century reminder of the town's Scottish heritage. ✉ *321 S. Fairfax St., ☎ 703/549–6670. Free.*

George Washington frequented the **Stabler-Leadbeater Apothecary Shop** (✉ 105–107 S. Fairfax St., ☎ 703/836–3713), **Gadsby's Tavern Museum** (✉ 134 N. Royal St., ☎ 703/838–4242), and **Christ Church** (✉ 118 N. Washington St., ☎ 703/549–1450). Another member of Christ Church was Robert E. Lee; the **boyhood home of Robert E. Lee** (✉ 607 Oronoco St., ☎ 703/548–8454) is about three blocks from Christ Church.

The homes of less-famous residents help to fill out a picture of 18th- and 19th-century life. The block of Prince Street between Fairfax and Lee, lined by imposing three-story houses, is called **Gentry Row.** The cobblestone block of humbler residences between Lee and Union is called **Captain's Row.**

Alexandria's cultural heritage is honored at the **Lyceum** (✉ 201 S. Washington St., ☎ 703/838–4994), with displays of decorative arts and exhibits on local history. Works by local and national artists are shown at the **Athaeneum** (✉ 201 Prince St., ☎ 703/548–0035). At the **Torpedo Factory Art Center** (✉ 105 N. Union St., ☎ 703/838–4565), a renovated waterfront building where torpedoes were made during both world wars, more than 180 artists and craftspeople make and sell their wares. All three sites have free admission.

Farther away but visible from a distance is the 333-ft-high **George Washington Masonic National Memorial** (✉ 101 Callahan Dr., ☎ 703/683–2007). There is no admission to see relics of the first president and exhibits on the Masonic Order and to go to the top, which offers a spectacular view of Alexandria and nearby Washington.

★ The **Newseum,** the world's only museum dedicated exclusively to news, features a 126-ft-long wall of video monitors showing dozens of satellite news feeds from around the world and exhibits tracing the history of news gathering. Adjacent to the museum is **Freedom Park,** which honors journalists who have died in the line of duty. ✉ *1101 Wilson Blvd., Arlington, ☎ 703/284–3700 or 888/639–7386. Closed Mon.–Tues.*

For information on **Arlington National Cemetery** and the **Pentagon,** *see* Washington, D.C.

Fredericksburg, about an hour south of Washington, D.C., rivals Alexandria and Mount Vernon for associations with the Washington family. From ages 6–16 the future first president lived at Ferry Farm across the Rappahannock River. His sister Betty and her husband lived at **Kenmore** (✉ 1201 Washington Ave., ☎ 540/373–3381), a house whose plain facade belies a lavish interior. The home of Charles Washington, George's brother, later became the **Rising Sun Tavern** (✉ 1306

Caroline St., ☎ 540/371–1494), a watering hole for such revolutionaries as Patrick Henry and Thomas Jefferson. The **Mary Washington House** (✉ Charles and Lewis Sts., ☎ 540/373–1569) is a modest house George bought for his mother during her last years.

The future fifth president lived in Fredericksburg, and the **James Monroe Museum and Memorial Library** (✉ 908 Charles St., ☎ 540/654–1043) is in the tiny one-story building where he practiced law from 1787 to 1789.

At the **Hugh Mercer Apothecary Shop** (✉ Caroline and Amelia Sts., ☎ 540/373–3362), the guide's explicit descriptions of amputations, cataract operations, and tooth extractions can make latter-day visitors wince.

Four Civil War battlefields—Fredericksburg, Chancellorsville, the Wilderness, and the Spotsylvania Courthouse—make up the **Fredericksburg and Spotsylvania National Military Park.** All are within 17 mi of Fredericksburg, where a **visitor center** (✉ 1013 Lafayette Blvd. [U.S. 1], ☎ 540/371–0802) has an introductory slide show and exhibits.

Route 3 east of Fredericksburg takes you into the **Northern Neck,** a strip of land bounded by the Potomac and the Rappahannock rivers. At the top of the Neck is Westmoreland County, which produced both the Father of Our Country and one of the greatest tragic heroes of the Civil War.

George Washington's Birthplace National Monument, in Oak Grove, preserves the memory of the first president with a working farm and a reproduction of the original early 18th-century plantation house (the original burned down on Christmas Day 1779). Washington's family members are buried on the property. ✉ *Rte. 204,* ☎ *804/224–1732.*

Stratford Hall, the birthplace of Robert E. Lee, is an elegant original from the 1730s, built in the shape of an *H* with brick and timber produced on the site. Farmers still cultivate 1,600 of the original acres, and their yield, a variety of cereals, is for sale. Lunch is served in a log cabin from April through October. ✉ *Rte. 214,* ☎ *804/493–8038.*

At the far end of the Northern Neck is a jewel of Tidewater architecture: Irvington's **Christ Church** (✉ Junction of Rtes. 646 and 709, ☎ 804/438–6855), a redbrick sanctuary of cruciform design, built in 1732.

Twenty-six miles west of Washington is the monumentally important **Manassas National Battlefield Park,** or Bull Run, where the Confederacy won two major victories and Stonewall Jackson won his nickname. ✉ *Rte. 234 off I–66,* ☎ *703/361–1339.*

About an hour west of Washington is horse country. In **Loudoun County**'s fashionable towns of **Leesburg** and **Middleburg,** residents (many of them Yankee transplants) keep up the local traditions of fox hunts and steeplechases. The county visitor center in Leesburg (☞ Visitor Information, *above*) can suggest scenic drives.

Oatlands (✉ Rte. 15, 6 mi south of Leesburg, ☎ 703/777–3174) is a restored Greek Revival plantation house whose manicured fields host public and private equestrian events from spring through fall. The Greek Revival mansion at **Morven Park** (✉ Rte. 7, 1 mi north of Leesburg, ☎ 703/777–2414), a White House look-alike, contains two museums: one of horse-drawn carriages, the other of hounds and hunting.

What to See and Do with Children

Wolf Trap Farm Park (☞ Nightlife and the Arts, *below*) hosts mime, puppet, and animal shows as well as concerts, plays, and storytelling;

events are often free. Emus, monkeys, a zebra, giant tortoises, and domestic farm animals inhabit **Reston Animal Park** (⊠ 1228 Hunter Mill Rd., Vienna, ☎ 703/759–3636 or 703/759–3637).

Dining and Lodging

Old Town Alexandria's restaurants are many and varied, but they are also pricey and, on weekend nights, crowded. Arlington's Little Saigon, on and around Wilson Boulevard, has many excellent and affordable Vietnamese restaurants.

Lodging prices are high, but so are the standards of comfort and luxury. Bed-and-breakfasts tend to be more elegant here because many serve as romantic weekend hideaways for regular customers from Washington. For listings try **Bed & Breakfast Accommodations Ltd. of Washington, D.C.** (⊠ Box 12011, Washington, DC 20005, ☎ 202/328–3510). **Princely Bed & Breakfast** (⊠ Box 325, Port Haywood 23138, ☎ 804/725–9511 or 800/470–5588) lists accommodations in historic Old Town homes.

For price ranges *see* Charts 1 (A) and 2 (A) *in* On the Road with Fodor's.

Alexandria

$$ ✕ **Le Gaulois.** At this quiet country bistro whose white walls are hung with scenes of southern France, the specialties include pot-au-feu *gaulois* (a beef-and-chicken stew with whole vegetables) and cassoulet (a rich bean casserole with sausage and beef). ⊠ *1106 King St.,* ☎ *703/739–9494. AE, D, DC, MC, V. Closed Sun.*

$$ ✕ **Santa Fe East.** A recreation of old Santa Fe, with enclosed courtyards, exposed brick, and wood planking, Santa Fe East serves up neosouthwestern items such as shrimp empanadas, smoked duck quesadillas, and chile rellenos stuffed with goat cheese, rolled in blue cornmeal, and deep-fried. ⊠ *110 S. Pitt St.,* ☎ *703/548–6900. AE, DC, MC, V.*

$$ ✕ **Taverna Cretekou.** Inside, surrounded by whitewashed stucco walls
★ and brightly colored macramé tapestries, or outside in the canopied garden, diners enjoy such dishes as lamb *Exohikon* (baked in a pastry shell) and swordfish kebab. All the wines are Greek. ⊠ *818 King St.,* ☎ *703/548–8688. AE, D, MC, V. Closed Mon.*

$ ✕ **Hard Times Café.** Recorded country-and-western music and framed photographs of depression-era Oklahoma set the tone at this casual, always crowded hangout. Three kinds of chili are served—Texas (spicy), Cincinnati (mild), and vegetarian. ⊠ *1404 King St.,* ☎ *703/683–5340. Reservations not accepted. AE, MC, V.*

$$$$ 🛏 **Holiday Inn Old Town.** The mahogany-paneled lobby and the hunting prints in the guest rooms suggest a men's club. Marble bathtubs, modem-ready phones, and extraordinary service—an exercise bike will be brought to your room on request—make this an exceptional member of the chain. Free shuttle service to the airport and the Metro is provided. ⊠ *480 King St., 22314,* ☎ *703/549–6080 or 800/368–5047, ℻ 703/684–6508. 227 rooms. Restaurant, bar, indoor pool, barber shop, beauty salon, sauna, exercise room. AE, D, DC, MC, V.*

$$$$ 🛏 **Morrison House.** Butlers unpack for guests in rooms furnished with
★ four-posters, and tea is served every afternoon at this convincing Federal-style house (built in 1985). ⊠ *116 S. Alfred St., 22314,* ☎ *703/838–8000 or 800/367–0800, ℻ 703/684–6283. 45 rooms. 2 restaurants. AE, DC, MC, V.*

Arlington

$ ✕ **Queen Bee.** Arlington's Little Saigon area has many good Viet-
★ namese restaurants, but this is one of the best. Moist and delicately

flavored spring rolls and the Saigon pancake—accented with a mix of crab, pork, and shrimp—are two reasons that diners often wait in line for a table. ⊠ *3181 Wilson Blvd.,* ☎ *703/527–3444. AE, MC, V.*

$$$$ ⌂ **Ritz-Carlton Pentagon City.** This soundproofed enclave of luxury five minutes from the airport has Persian carpets in the lobby and silk wall-paper in the reproduction Federal bedrooms. All rooms have an over-stuffed chair and ottoman, Chippendale-style furniture, and silk bed coverings. Many rooms have a view of the monuments across the river in Washington. ⊠ *1250 S. Hayes St., 22202,* ☎ *703/415–5000,* FAX *703/415–5060. 345 rooms. Restaurant, bar, indoor pool, sauna, exercise room. AE, D, DC, MC, V.*

$$$ ⌂ **Marriott Crystal Gateway.** Black marble, blond wood, and lots of greenery distinguish this hostelry for big-budget business travelers and tourists who want to be pampered. ⊠ *1700 Jefferson Davis Hwy., 22202,* ☎ *703/920–3230 or 800/228–9290,* FAX *703/271–5212. 697 rooms. 3 restaurants, sports bar, indoor and outdoor pools, hot tub, sauna, exercise room, nightclub. AE, D, DC, MC, V.*

$$ ⌂ **Best Western Arlington.** The attraction here is convenience: easy access to I–395 and a free shuttle to the airport. The rooms are unex-ceptional and modern. ⊠ *2480 S. Glebe Rd., 22206,* ☎ *703/979–4400 or 800/426–6886,* FAX *703/685–0051. 325 rooms. Restaurant, pool, hot tub, exercise room, laundry service. AE, D, DC, MC, V.*

Fairfax

$$$$ ⌂ **Bailiwick Inn.** Each guest room in this 1812 house is furnished in the style of a famous Virginian and includes a feather bed and antiques or period reproductions. Some rooms have fireplaces; the bridal suite has a four-poster bed and a whirlpool bath. ⊠ *4023 Chain Bridge Rd., 22030,* ☎ *703/691–2266 or 800/366–7666,* FAX *703/934–2112. 14 rooms. AE, MC, V.*

Fredericksburg

$$$$ ✕ **Le Lafayette.** In this pre-Revolutionary Georgian house guests enjoy what could be called "Virginia French" food: alligator sausage with black beans, duckling with red currant sauce, and other novelties. ⊠ *623 Caroline St.,* ☎ *540/373–6895. AE, D, DC, MC, V. Closed Mon.*

$$ ✕ **Ristorante Renato.** This candlelighted Italian restaurant, an unusual find in the midst of a Colonial town, specializes in "Romeo and Juliet" (veal and chicken topped with mozzarella in a white-wine sauce) and shrimp scampi Napoli with lemon-butter sauce. ⊠ *422 Williams St.,* ☎ *540/371–8228. AE, MC, V.*

$$$ ⌂ **Richard Johnston Inn.** This three-story row house across from the visitor center has parking in the rear under magnolia trees. Guest rooms are furnished with a variety of 18th- and 19th-century antique reproductions; the suites open onto a courtyard. ⊠ *711 Caroline St., 22401,* ☎ *540/899–7606. 9 rooms. AE, MC, V.*

$ ⌂ **Best Western Johnny Appleseed.** This generic two-story, family-ori-ented hotel is five minutes from the battlefields. The most pleasant views are of the pool. ⊠ *543 Warrenton Rd. (U.S. 17 and I–95), 22406,* ☎ *540/373–0000 or 800/633–6443,* FAX *540/373–5676. 88 rooms. Restaurant, pool, playground. AE, D, DC, MC, V.*

Great Falls

$$$$ ✕ **L'Auberge Chez François.** White stucco, dark exposed beams, and ★ a garden just outside create a country-inn ambience 20 minutes from Tysons Corner. The Alsatian cuisine includes salmon soufflé with salmon-and-scallop mousse and white-wine or lobster sauce. ⊠ *332 Springvale Rd. (Rte. 674),* ☎ *703/759–3800. Reservations essential*

*4 wks in advance. Jacket required. AE, D, DC, MC, V. Closed Mon.
No lunch.*

Northern Neck

$$$$ ⊞ **Tides Inn.** At this 500-acre waterfront resort on a Rappahannock
tributary, all the rooms have water views. For an even closer look, guests
can take a dinner or luncheon cruise on one of the inn's two yachts.
Guests have access to a nearby fitness center. ⊠ *Box 480, Irvington
22480,* ☎ *804/438–5000 or 800/843–3746,* 𝔽𝔸𝕏 *804/438–5222. 111
rooms. 3 restaurants, bar, pool, 3 golf courses, 4 tennis courts, boating, children's programs. AE, D, DC, MC, V.*

Tysons Corner

$$ ✕ **Clyde's.** Quality is high, service is attentive, and the tone's always
lively in these art deco–style dining rooms. The long, eclectic menu
includes fresh fish, often in such preparations as trout Parmesan. ⊠
8332 Leesburg Pike, ☎ *703/734–1900. AE, D, DC, MC, V.*

Motel

⊞ **Hampton Inn** (⊠ 2310 William St., Fredericksburg 22401, ☎ 540/
371–0330, 𝔽𝔸𝕏 540/371–1753), 166 rooms, pool; *$$.*

Nightlife and the Arts

Nightlife

The **Birchmere** (⊠ 3901 Mount Vernon Ave., Alexandria, ☎ 703/
549–5919) has everything from rockabilly to bluegrass. **Murphy's
Irish Pub** (⊠ 713 King St., Alexandria, ☎ 703/548–1717) hosts Irish
and folk performers. **Two Nineteen** (⊠ 219 King St., Alexandria, ☎
703/549–1141) has jazz upstairs and a sports bar in the basement.
Clyde's (⊠ 8332 Leesburg Pike, Tysons Corner, ☎ 703/734–1900) attracts unattached professionals.

The Arts

The **Arts Council of Fairfax County** (☎ 703/642–0862) acts as a clearinghouse for information about performances and exhibitions throughout northern Virginia. **Wolf Trap Farm Park** (⊠ 1551 Trap Rd., Vienna,
☎ 703/255–1860 or 703/938–2404), one of the major performing arts
venues in the greater Washington area, presents top musical and dance
performers in a grand outdoor pavilion during the warmer months and
in 18th-century farm buildings the rest of the year.

Outdoor Activities and Sports

Biking

The 19-mi **Mount Vernon Bicycle Trail** (☎ 703/285–2598) runs along
the Potomac in George Washington Park and through Alexandria.
The 4¾-mi **Burke Lake Park Bicycle Trail** (☎ 703/323–6601), in Fairfax County, circles the lake. The Arlington Parks and Recreation Bureau (☎ 703/358–4747) offers a free map of the **county Bikeway System.**

Golf

Algonkian Park (⊠ 47001 Fairway Dr., Sterling, ☎ 703/450–4655)
and **Burke Lake Park** (⊠ Fairfax Station, ☎ 703/323–1641) have public courses. The **Tides Inn** (☎ 804/438–5501; ☞ Dining and Lodging,
above) offers 9- and 18-hole courses.

Water Sports

The Northern Neck gives sailors, water-skiers, and windsurfers access
to two rivers and the Chesapeake Bay. For information contact the **Northern Neck Travel Council** (☞ Visitor Information, *above*).

Shopping

Potomac Mills Mall (⊠ 2700 Potomac Mills Circle, I–95, Dale City) is the state's most visited attraction; Swedish furniture giant IKEA is one of 220 outlets. **Tysons Corner Center** (⊠ 1961 Chain Bridge Rd., junction of Rtes. 7 and 123) houses 240 retailers, including Bloomingdale's and Nordstrom. **Galleria at Tysons II** (⊠ 2001 International Dr.) has 125 retailers, including Saks Fifth Avenue and Neiman Marcus. **Tiffany & Co.** (⊠ 8045 Leesburg Pike, ☎ 703/893–7700) is a few minutes away from the Galleria at Tysons.

The old towns of Alexandria and Fredericksburg are dense with **antiques** shops, many quite expensive, that are particularly strong on the Federal and Victorian periods. The town visitor centers (☞ Visitor Information, *above*) have maps and lists of the stores.

RICHMOND AND TIDEWATER

Strictly speaking, Tidewater Virginia is the region east of the fall line of the rivers flowing into the Chesapeake Bay; but "Tidewater" has also come to stand for the so-called genteel Old South. Richmond, on the fall line of the James, straddles both the Tidewater region and the Piedmont region, with its rolling plains; so, too, it bridges Virginia past and present, with remnants of the Confederacy preserved amid the cultural and commercial bustle of a modern state capital. An hour southeast are two former capitals: Colonial Williamsburg, a restored 18th-century town; and Jamestown, Virginia's original capital, long deserted and all the more stirring for it. With Yorktown, where the Colonies won their independence, these pre-Revolutionary towns form the Historic Triangle.

Visitor Information

Metro Richmond: Visitors Center (⊠ 1710 Robin Hood Rd. [Exit 78 off I–95 and I–64], 23220, ☎ 804/358–5511); for mailed information, write to Sixth St. Marketplace, 5500 E. Marshall St., 22319, ☎ 804/782–2777 or 800/365–7272. **Petersburg:** Visitors Center (⊠ 425 Cockade Alley, 23803, ☎ 804/733–2400 or 800/368–3595). **Williamsburg:** Convention and Visitors Bureau (⊠ Box 3585, 23187, ☎ 757/253–0192 or 800/368–6511); Colonial Williamsburg (☎ 800/447–8679). **Yorktown:** Colonial National Historical Park (⊠ Box 210, 23690, ☎ 757/898–3400).

Arriving and Departing

By Bus

Greyhound Lines (☎ 800/231–2222) serves Richmond (⊠ 2910 N. Boulevard) and Williamsburg (⊠ 468 N. Boundary St.).

By Car

Richmond is at the intersection of I–95 and I–64; U.S. 1 runs north–south by the city. Petersburg is 20 mi south of Richmond on I–95. Williamsburg is west of I–64 and 51 mi southeast of Richmond; the Colonial Parkway joins it with Jamestown and Yorktown.

By Plane

Richmond International Airport (☎ 804/226–3000) is served by nine airlines. **Newport News–Williamsburg International Airport** (☎ 757/877–0924), in Newport News, and **Norfolk International Airport** (☎ 757/857–3351) also serve the region.

By Train

Amtrak (☎ 800/872–7245) serves Richmond (⊠ 7519 Staples Mill Rd.) and Williamsburg (⊠ 468 N. Boundary St.).

Exploring Richmond and Tidewater

Richmond

Most of Richmond's historic attractions lie north of the James River, which bisects the city in a sweeping curve. West of downtown are such gracious residential neighborhoods as Monument Avenue, with its statues of Civil War heroes. Streets fan out southwesterly from Park Avenue to form the gaslighted **Fan District,** a hip neighborhood of restored turn-of-the-century town houses.

The heart of old Richmond is the **Court End District,** which contains seven National Historic Landmarks, three museums, and 11 more buildings on the National Register of Historic Places—all within eight blocks. At any museum you will receive a self-guided walking tour with the purchase of a discount block ticket, good for all admission fees in this district. The 1790 **John Marshall House** (⊠ 9th and Marshall Sts., ☎ 804/648–7998), one of the Court End museums, was the home of the early U.S. chief justice. The **Museum and White House of the Confederacy** (⊠ 1201 E. Clay St., ☎ 804/649–1861) was the official residence of Confederate president Jefferson Davis; a newer building next door houses such relics as Robert E. Lee's sword.

★ The **Virginia State Capitol** (⊠ Capitol Sq., ☎ 804/786–4344), designed by Thomas Jefferson in 1785, contains a wealth of sculpture, including busts of the eight Virginia-born U.S. presidents and a life-size statue of George Washington. It was here that Lee accepted command of the Confederate forces.

Canal Walk, beginning at 12th and Main streets, follows the locks of the James River–Kanawha Canal proposed by George Washington. Plaques along the way note points of historic interest. The walk (less than a mile) continues over a footbridge to **Brown's Island,** the site of sculptures and outdoor concerts.

In the Church Hill Historic District, east of downtown, is **St. John's Episcopal Church** (⊠ 2401 E. Broad St., ☎ 804/648–5015). It was here on March 23, 1775, that Patrick Henry demanded of the Second Virginia Convention: "Give me liberty or give me death!"

The visitor center for **Richmond National Battlefield Park** (⊠ 3215 E. Broad St., ☎ 804/226–1981) provides a movie and a slide show about the three campaigns fought here, as well as maps for a self-guided tour; the park is free.

West of downtown you'll find the **Science Museum of Virginia** (⊠ 2500 W. Broad St., ☎ 804/367–6552, 804/367–1080, or 800/659–1727), housed in a massive, domed former train station. The planetarium, with its huge curved screen, doubles as a movie theater.

★ Aptly situated at the base of the artsy Fan District is the **Virginia Museum of Fine Arts** (⊠ The Boulevard and Grove Ave., ☎ 804/367–0844), whose collection includes paintings by Goya, Renoir, Monet, and van Gogh, as well as African masks, Roman statuaries, Asian icons, and five Fabergé eggs.

Just west of the Fan District stands **Agecroft Hall** (⊠ 4305 Sulgrave Rd., ☎ 804/353–4241), a 15th-century English house reassembled here in 1925 and surrounded by formal gardens and extensively furnished with Tudor and early Stuart art and furniture.

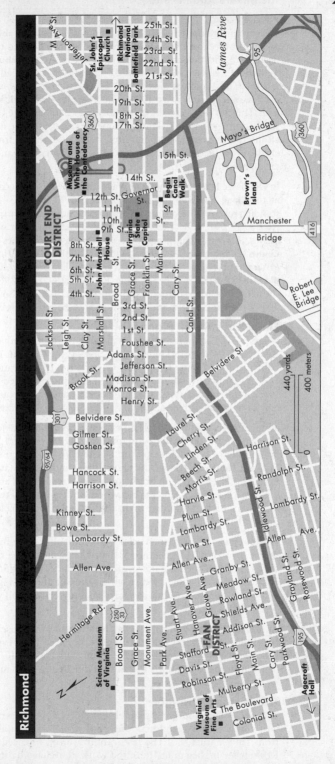

Richmond

Jefferson Ave.

21st St.

St. John's Episcopal Church ■

Richmond National Battlefield Park ■

25th St.
24th St.
23rd St.
22nd St.
21st St.
20th St.
19th St.
18th St.
17th St.

James River

I-95

Mayo's Bridge

360

Museum and White House of the Confederacy ■

15th St.

14th St.

Governor St.

Begin Canal Walk

Brown's Island

Manchester Bridge

416

COURT END DISTRICT

12th St.
11th
10th
9th St.
8th St.
7th St.
6th St.
5th St.
4th St.

St.

Main St.

John Marshall House ■

Virginia State Capitol ■

Grace St.
Franklin St.
Cary St.

Broad St.

3rd St.
2nd St.
1st St.
Foushee St.
Adams St.
Jefferson St.
Madison St.
Monroe St.
Henry St.

Canal St.

Robert E. Lee Bridge

Jackson St.

Leigh St.

Clay St.

Marshall St.

Brook St.

301

95/64

Belvidere St.

Gilmer St.
Goshen St.

Hancock St.

Harrison St.

Kinney St.

Bowe St.

Lombardy St.

Allen Ave.

Belvidere St.

Laurel St.
Cherry St.
Linden St.
Beech St.
Morris St.
Harvie St.
Plum St.
Lombardy St.
Vine St.

Harrison St.

Randolph St.

Lombardy St.

Idlewood St.

Allen   Ave.

440 yards
400 meters

Hermitage Rd.

250
33

195

Science Museum of Virginia ■

Broad St.
Grace St.
Monument Ave.

Park Ave.
Stuart Ave.
Hanover Ave.
Grove Ave.

FAN DISTRICT

Allen Ave.
Granby St.
Meadow St.
Rowland St.
Shields Ave.
Addison St.

Grayland St.
Rosewood St.

Stafford
Davis Ave.
Robinson St.

Floyd St.
Main St.
Cary St.
Parkwood St.

Agecroft Hall

Virginia Museum of Fine Arts ■

Mulberry St.
The Boulevard
Colonial St.

N

Petersburg

Twenty miles south of Richmond on I–95 lies **Petersburg,** the so-called last ditch of the Confederacy: Its fall in 1865 led to the fall of Richmond and the surrender at Appomattox. At **Petersburg National Battlefield** (✉ Rte. 36, ☎ 804/732–3531) you can tread the ground where 60,000 soldiers died. The 1,500-acre park, laced with miles of ★ .earthworks, includes two forts. The **Pamplin Park Civil War Site** (✉ 6523 Duncan Rd., Petersburg, ☎ 804/861–2408), where Union troops successfully penetrated General Robert E. Lee's defense line, includes an interpretive center and museum, a mile-long battle trail, 8-ft-high earthen fortifications, reconstructed soldier huts, and an 1812 plantation home.

In Old Town Petersburg the Civil War is examined from a local perspective at the **Siege Museum** (✉ 15 W. Bank St., ☎ 804/733–2404). Outstanding relics of antebellum Petersburg include the eccentric **Trapezium House** (✉ 244 N. Market St., ☎ 804/733–2404), built with no right angles. A 3-yard-long grand piano is among the antiques in the 1823 **Centre Hill Mansion** (✉ Centre Hill Ct., ☎ 804/733–2401), remodeled in Victorian style at the turn of this century. The pre-Revolutionary **Old Blanford Church** (✉ 319 S. Crater Rd., ☎ 804/733–2396) is today a Confederate shrine surrounded by the graves of 30,000 Southern dead. The Memorial Day tradition is said to have begun in this cemetery.

The James River Plantations

Southeast of Richmond on Route 5, along the north bank of the James River, lie four historical plantations. **Shirley,** the oldest in Virginia, has belonged to the same family, the Carters, for 10 generations. Robert E. Lee's mother was born here. The 1723 house is filled with family silver, ancestral portraits, and rare books. The hall staircase rises three stories with no visible supports. ✉ *Rte. 608,* ☎ *804/829–5121.*

Virginians say that the first Thanksgiving was celebrated not in Massachusetts but at the **Berkeley** plantation, on December 4, 1619. Benjamin Harrison, a signer of the Declaration of Independence, and William Henry Harrison, the short-lived ninth president, were born here. The 1726 Georgian brick house has been restored and furnished with period antiques, and the boxwood gardens are well tended. In addition to a restaurant, there are outdoor tables for picnickers. ✉ *Rte. 5,* ☎ *804/829–6018.*

Westover was home to the flamboyant colonel William Byrd II, member of the Colonial legislature and author of one of the region's first travel books (as well as a notorious secret diary). The 1735 house, celebrated for its moldings and carvings, is open only during April Garden Week, but the grounds and gardens can be visited all year. ✉ *Rte. 5,* ☎ *804/829–2882.*

At 300 ft, **Sherwood Forest** may be the longest frame house in the country. Built in 1720, it was the retirement home of John Tyler, the 10th U.S. president, and remains in his family. The house, furnished with heirloom antiques, and the five outbuildings are open daily. ✉ *Rte. 5,* ☎ *804/829–5377.*

The Historic Triangle

★ **Colonial Williamsburg** is a marvel: an improbably sanitary but otherwise convincing re-creation of the city that was the capital of Virginia from 1699 until 1780. The restoration project, financed by John D. Rockefeller Jr., began in 1926; the work of archaeologists and historians of the Colonial Williamsburg Foundation continues to this day. An extensive packet of information is available (☞ Visitor Information, *above*).

On Colonial Williamsburg's 173 acres, 88 original 18th- and early 19th-century structures, such as the **courthouse,** have been meticulously restored; another 50, including the **capitol** and the **governor's palace,** were reconstructed on their original sites. In all, 225 period rooms have been furnished from the foundation's collection of more than 100,000 pieces of furniture, pottery, china, glass, silver, pewter, textiles, tools, and carpeting. Period authenticity also governs the landscaping of the 90 acres of gardens and public greens.

All year hundreds of costumed interpreters, wearing bonnets or three-cornered hats, rove and ride through the cobblestone streets. Dozens of costumed craftspeople, such as the boot maker and the gunsmith, demonstrate and explain their trades inside their workshops; their wares are for sale nearby. Three taverns serve fare approximating that of 200 years ago. The restored area must be toured on foot, as all vehicles are banned between 8 AM and 6 PM. Free shuttle buses (available to ticket holders only) run continually to and from the visitor center and around the edge of the restored area. Vehicles for visitors with disabilities are permitted by prior arrangement. ⊠ *I–64 Exit 238,* ☎ *757/ 220–7645 or 800/447–8679.*

Jamestown Island, site of the first permanent English settlement in North America (1607) and the capital of Virginia until 1699, is now uninhabited. Foundation walls show the layout of the settlement, and push-button audio stations narrate the local history. The only standing structure is the ruin of a 1639 church tower. A 5-mi nature drive ringing the island is posted with historical markers. ⊠ *Colonial Pkwy.,* ☎ *757/229–1733.*

Adjacent to Jamestown Island is **Jamestown Settlement,** a living-history museum, with a reconstructed fort staffed by people dressed as colonists and an "Indian Village" inhabited by buckskin-clad interpreters. At the pier are reproductions of the *Godspeed,* the *Discovery,* and the *Susan Constant,* the ships that carried the settlers to the New World. ⊠ *Rte. 31 off Colonial Pkwy.,* ☎ *757/229–1607.*

At **Yorktown Battlefield** (⊠ Colonial Pkwy., ☎ 757/898–3400) in 1781 American and French forces surrounded British troops and forced an end to the American War of Independence. Today the museum here displays George Washington's original field tent; dioramas, illuminated maps, and a short movie tell the story. After a look from the observation deck, you can rent the taped audio tour and explore the battlefield (which is free) by car or join a free ranger-led walking tour.

The **Yorktown Victory Center,** next door to the Yorktown Battlefield, consists of a Continental Army encampment, with tents, a covered wagon, and interpreters—costumed as soldiers or female auxiliaries—who speak to visitors in the regional dialects of the time. Also on site are a small working tobacco farm and a museum focusing on the experience of ordinary people during the Revolution. ⊠ *Rte. 238 off Colonial Pkwy.,* ☎ *757/887–1776.*

Unlike Jamestown, **Yorktown** remains a living community, albeit a small one. Its **Main Street** is lined with preserved 18th-century buildings on a bluff overlooking the York River. The elegant **Nelson House** was the residence of a Virginia governor and signer of the Declaration of Independence. Along the Battlefield Tour Road is **Moore House,** where the terms of surrender were negotiated. Nelson and Moore houses are both open for tours in summer (☎ 757/898–3400). On adjacent Church Street, Grace Church, built in 1697, remains an active Episcopal congregation; its walls are made of marl (a mixture of clay, sand, and limestone containing fragments of seashells).

What to See and Do with Children

The 100-plus rides at **Paramount's Kings Dominion** (✉ I–95 Doswell exit, ☎ 804/876–5000), north of Richmond, include simulated white-water rafting and seven roller coasters. East of Williamsburg is **Busch Gardens Williamsburg** (✉ U.S. 60, ☎ 757/253–3350). Rides include an especially fast and steep roller coaster, while nine re-creations of European hamlets offer the cuisine and entertainment of different countries. Both amusement parks are closed November–March.

Dining and Lodging

The established upmarket dining rooms of Richmond are dependable, but keep an eye out for intriguing new bistros, often short-lived, in the Fan District. In Williamsburg remember that dining rooms within walking distance of the restored area are often crowded, and reservations are advised. Richmond's hotel rates are fair for its size, but standards of service lag behind those of many smaller communities. Williamsburg has a greater range of lodging choices for the money, but vacancies are scarce in summer. For price ranges *see* Charts 1 (B) and 2 (B) *in* On the Road with Fodor's.

Richmond

$$$ ✕ **La Petite France.** The emerald green walls are hung with English landscapes and portraits. Tuxedoed waiters serve lobster baked in puff pastry with whiskey sauce and Dover sole amandine, among other specialties. ✉ *2108 Maywill St.,* ☎ *804/353–8729. AE, DC, MC, V. Closed Sun.–Mon.*

$ ✕ **Joe's Inn.** The specialty at this Fan District hangout is Greek spaghetti, with feta and provolone baked on top; all the sandwiches are oversize. Regulars make newcomers feel right at home. ✉ *205 N. Shields Ave.,* ☎ *804/355–2282. AE, MC, V.*

$$$ ✕🏠 **Mr. Patrick Henry's.** Two houses circa 1858 were restored and joined
★ to create this restaurant (jacket and tie required) and inn. The three suites each have a fireplace. Antiques and fireplaces in the dining room contribute to the Colonial ambience, an English pub is in the basement, and there's a garden café. Menu favorites include crab cakes and crisp roast duck with bing cherry sauce. Breakfast is included for inn guests. ✉ *2300 E. Broad St.,* ☎ *804/644–1322. 3 suites. Restaurant, kitchenettes. AE, D, DC, MC, V. No dinner Sun.*

$$$$ 🏠 **Jefferson Hotel.** This 1895 National Historic Landmark has a grand
★ lobby, with a tall staircase straight out of *Gone with the Wind.* The rather small guest rooms have reproduction 19th-century furnishings. ✉ *Franklin and Adams Sts., 23220,* ☎ *804/788–8000 or 800/424–8014,* 🖷 *804/225–0334. 275 rooms. 2 restaurants, bar, health club. AE, D, DC, MC, V.*

$$$$ 🏠 **Omni Richmond.** Guest rooms in this luxury hotel have a contemporary look, but the marble lobby, with its equestrian statues and Romanesque vases, calls to mind a Venetian foyer. ✉ *100 S. 12th St., 23219,* ☎ *804/344–7000,* 🖷 *804/648–6704. 364 rooms. 3 restaurants, bar, indoor and outdoor pools, sauna, exercise room, indoor track, racquetball, squash, laundry service and dry cleaning. AE, D, DC, MC, V.*

$$$ 🏠 **Radisson Hotel.** Triangular rooms at the point of this wedge-shape hotel have views of the skyline and the river. A waterfall flows through the three-story atrium lobby. ✉ *555 E. Canal St., 23219,* ☎ *804/788–0900 or 800/333–3333,* 🖷 *804/788–7087. 306 rooms. Restaurant, bar, indoor pool, sauna, health club. AE, D, DC, MC, V.*

$ ⊞ **Massad House Hotel.** This modest Tudor-style hotel is five blocks from the capitol in the business district, a quiet area after 6 PM. Guest rooms are small, with stucco walls, and are well maintained. ⊠ *11 N. 4th St., 23219,* ☎ *804/648–2893,* FAX *804/780–0647. 62 rooms. Restaurant. MC, V.*

Williamsburg

$$$$ ✕ **Regency Room.** Crystal chandeliers, Asian silk-screen prints, and full
★ silver service set the tone. Chateaubriand is carved at the table; other specialties are lobster bisque and rich ice cream desserts. ⊠ *Williamsburg Inn, 136 E. Francis St.,* ☎ *757/229–1000. Reservations essential. Jacket and tie at dinner and Sun. brunch. AE, D, MC, V.*

$$$ ✕ **Le Yaca.** The country-French dining room is done in soft pastels with hardwood floors, candlelight, and a central open fireplace where leg of lamb roasts nightly on a spit. ⊠ *1915 Pocahontas Trail,* ☎ *757/220–3616. AE, DC, MC, V. Closed Sun. and early Jan.*

$$$ ✕ **The Trellis.** Hardwood floors, ceramic tiles, and green plants evoke Napa Valley and set the mood for world-class American cuisine. Save room for Death by Chocolate: seven layers of chocolate topped with cream sauce. ⊠ *Merchants Sq.,* ☎ *757/229–8610. AE, MC, V.*

$$ ✕ **The Cascades.** Bare polished-wood tables are piled with all-American fare: cheddar cheese soup, sugar-cured ham, fried chicken, and pecan pie. The daily Hunt Breakfast buffet includes fried chicken and oysters in season. ⊠ *104 Visitor Center Dr.,* ☎ *757/229–1000. AE, MC, V.*

$$$$ ⊞ **Embassy Suites.** Renovated in 1996, all rooms here are two-room suites, complete with two TVs, a minirefrigerator, and a microwave. The quiet hotel is on 11 wooded acres. ⊠ *152 Kingsgate Pkwy., 23185,* ☎ *757/229–6800,* FAX *757/220–3486. 168 suites. Indoor pool, hot tub, exercise room. Full breakfast. AE, D, DC, MC, V.*

$$$$ ⊞ **Williamsburg Hospitality House.** This four-story redbrick building, constructed in 1973, faces the College of William and Mary. Guest rooms are furnished with Chippendale reproductions; some face a cobblestone courtyard with a fountain. ⊠ *415 Richmond Rd., 23185,* ☎ *757/229–4020 or 800/932–9192,* FAX *757/220–1560. 309 rooms. Restaurant, bar, pool. AE, D, DC, MC, V.*

$$$ ⊞ **Williamsburg Inn.** This is the grandest local hotel, built in 1937 and
★ decorated in English Regency style. The surrounding Colonial houses, equipped with modern kitchens and baths, are also part of the inn. ⊠ *136 E. Francis St. (Box 1776), 23187-1776,* ☎ *757/229–1000 or 800/ 447–8679,* FAX *757/565–8797. 235 rooms. Restaurant, bar, pool, 2 golf courses, 8 tennis courts, health club. AE, D, MC, V.*

$$ ⊞ **Heritage Inn Motel.** Room furnishings include beds with two-poster headboards and an armoire concealing a TV. Though some rooms open directly onto the parking lot, this is still an unusually quiet, leafy site, and the pool is set in a garden. ⊠ *1324 Richmond Rd., 23185,* ☎ *757/ 229–6220 or 800/782–3800,* FAX *757/229–2774. 54 rooms. Pool. AE, DC, MC, V.*

Yorktown

$$ ✕ **Nick's Seafood Pavilion.** Atlantic seafood with a distinctly Mediterranean flavor, including such house specialties as lobster pilaf and seafood shish kebab, is served in ample portions at this simply decorated riverside restaurant. ⊠ *Water St.,* ☎ *757/887–5269. Reservations not accepted. AE, DC, MC, V.*

Motels

⊞ **The Woodlands** (⊠ 102 Visitor Center Dr., Williamsburg 23185, ☎ 757/229–1000 or 800/447–8679, FAX 757/565–8797), 315 rooms, restaurant, 3 pools, miniature golf, putting green, tennis court, playground; $$$. ☎ **Days Inn North** (⊠ 1600 Robin Hood Rd., Richmond 23220, ☎ 757/353–1287, FAX 757/355–2659), 99 rooms, restaurant, bar, pool; $$. ☎ **Duke of York Motel** (⊠ 508 Water St., Yorktown 23690, ☎ 757/898–3232, FAX 757/898–5922), 57 rooms, restaurant, pool; $$. ☎ **Governor Spottswood Motel** (⊠ 1508 Richmond Rd., Williamsburg 23185, ☎ 757/229–6444 or 800/368–1244, FAX 757/253–2410), 78 rooms, pool, playground; $.

Nightlife and the Arts

Nightlife

Bogart's (⊠ 203 N. Lombardy St., Richmond, ☎ 804/353–9280) is a cozy jazz club. **Chowning's Tavern** (⊠ Duke of Gloucester St., Williamsburg, ☎ 757/229–1000 or 800/447–8679) has lively "gambols," or Colonial games, with music and other entertainment, daily from 10 PM to 1 AM; a family version is offered from 7 PM to 9 PM.

The Arts

Barksdale Theatre (⊠ Hanover Tavern, Rte. 301, Hanover, ☎ 804/282–2620), founded in 1953, was the first dinner theater in the country. **Swift Creek Mill Playhouse** (17401 Jefferson Davis Hwy., Richmond, ☎ 804/748–5203), another dinner theater, is housed in a 17th-century gristmill. **TheatreVirginia** (⊠ 2800 Grove Ave., Richmond, ☎ 804/353–6161), an Equity theater maintained by the Virginia Museum of Fine Arts, has a strong repertory. The **Richmond Symphony** (☎ 804/788–1212) often features internationally known soloists. **Concert Ballet of Virginia,** in Richmond (⊠ 103 Main St., ☎ 804/780–1279), performs modern and experimental works. The **Richmond Ballet** (⊠ 614 N. Lombardy St., ☎ 804/359–0906) is the city's classical ballet company. The **Virginia Company** (Colonial Williamsburg, ☎ 757/220–7645 or 800/447–8679) offers rollicking 18th-century plays.

Outdoor Activities and Sports

Open to the public in Richmond—for free or at a nominal charge—are more than 150 tennis courts, 11 swimming pools, a golf driving range, and about 7 mi of fitness trails. The **Department of Parks, Recreation, and Community Facilities** (☎ 804/780–5733) has listings.

Biking

In Colonial Williamsburg ticket holders can rent bicycles at the **lodge** on South England Street; others can try **Bikesmith** (⊠ York St., ☎ 757/229–9858).

Golf

The **Crossings** (⊠ Junction of I–95 and I–295, Glen Allen, ☎ 804/266–2254), north of Richmond, has an 18-hole course open to the public. **Colonial Williamsburg** (☎ 757/220–7696) operates three courses. **Kingsmill Resort** (☎ 757/253–3906), east of Williamsburg near Busch Gardens, has three courses.

Rafting

From March through November **Richmond Raft** (☎ 757/222–7238) offers guided white-water rafting through the heart of the city (Class 3 and 4 rapids) and float trips upriver.

Tennis

Colonial Williamsburg (☎ 757/220–7794) has 10 tennis courts; **Kingsmill** (☎ 757/253–3945) has 15 courts open to the public; additional public courts in Williamsburg are at **Kiwanis Park,** on Long Hill Road, and **Quarterpath Park,** on Pocahontas Street.

Shopping

Fresh produce is for sale at Richmond's **Farmers' Market** (⊠ 17th and Main Sts.); art galleries, boutiques, and antiques shops are nearby. The **Colonial Williamsburg Craft House** (⊠ Merchants Sq., ☎ 757/220–7747) and the **Craft House Inn** (⊠ S. England St., ☎ 757/220–7749) sell approved reproductions of the antiques on display in the houses.

ELSEWHERE IN VIRGINIA

Hampton Roads, Virginia Beach, and the Eastern Shore

Visitor Information

Virginia Beach Visitor Information Center (⊠ 2100 Parks Ave., 23451, ☎ 757/437–4888 or 800/446–8038). **Chincoteague Chamber of Commerce** (⊠ Box 258, 23336, ☎ 757/336–6161). **Eastern Shore of Virginia Chamber of Commerce** (⊠ Box 460, Melfa 23410, ☎ 757/787–2460).

Arriving and Departing

Norfolk International and **Newport News–Williamsburg International airports** (☞ Richmond and Tidewater, *above*) are served by most major airlines. I–64 connects Richmond with Hampton Roads. U.S. 58 and Route 44 connect I–64 with Virginia Beach; U.S. 13 runs between Virginia Beach and the Eastern Shore via the Chesapeake Bay Bridge-Tunnel. **Greyhound Lines** (☎ 800/231–2222) serves Virginia Beach (⊠ 1017 Laskin Rd.) and various locations along U.S. 13 on the Eastern Shore.

What to See and Do

The cities of Newport News and Hampton on the north and Norfolk on the south flank the enormous port of **Hampton Roads,** where the James empties into the Chesapeake. In Newport News the **Mariner's Museum** (⊠ I–64 Exit 258A, ☎ 757/595–0368) displays tiny hand-carved models of ancient vessels and full-size specimens of more recent ones, including a gondola and a Chinese sampan. The very latest in transportation can be viewed in Hampton at the **Virginia Air and Space Center** (⊠ 600 Settlers Landing Rd., ☎ 757/727–0800), which opened in 1992; the exhibits include a lunar rock and an *Apollo* capsule. At Hampton's **Fort Monroe** (⊠ Rte. 258), the Casemate Museum (⊠ Casemate 20 Bernard Rd., ☎ 757/727–3391) tells the Civil War history of this moat-enclosed Union stronghold, which was the object of the battle between the *Monitor* and the *Merrimac* and later where President Jefferson Davis was imprisoned after the Confederacy's defeat.

Norfolk is best known for the **U.S. Naval Base** (⊠ Hampton Blvd., ☎ 757/444–7955 or 757/444–1577), home to about 115 ships of the Atlantic and Mediterranean fleets, including the nuclear-powered USS *Theodore Roosevelt*—the world's second-largest warship. The sights are gentler at the **Norfolk Botanical Gardens** (⊠ I–64 airport exit, ☎ 757/441–5831), with 175 acres of azaleas, camellias, and roses—plus a lone palm tree. The arts are preserved at the **Hermitage Foundation Museum** (⊠ 7637 North Shore Rd., ☎ 757/423–2052), a reconstructed Tudor mansion with a large collection of Asian art. The collections at the **Chrysler Museum** (⊠ 245 W. Olney Rd., ☎ 757/664–6200), one of America's major art museums, range from Gainsborough to Roy Lichtenstein. Of historical interest is the elegant **Moses Myers House** (⊠ 331 Bank St., ☎ 757/622–2787), built in 1792 by Norfolk's first Jewish resident. The **General Douglas MacArthur Memorial** (⊠ Bank St. and City Hall Ave., ☎ 757/441–2965), in the restored former city hall, is the burial place of the controversial war hero.

The heart of **Virginia Beach,** 6 mi of crowded public beach and a raucous 40-block boardwalk, has been a popular summer gathering place for many years. One advantage of the commercialism is easy access to sailing, surfing, and scuba renting. Almost 2 mi inland, at the southern end of Virginia Beach, is one of the state's most visited museums, the **Virginia Marine Science Museum** (✉ 717 General Booth Blvd., ☏ 757/425–3474), where visitors can use computers to predict the weather, bird-watch in a salt marsh, and take a simulated journey to the bottom of the sea. Also inland from the bay shore, and a throwback to much quieter times, is the 1680 **Adam Thoroughgood House** (✉ 1636 Parish Rd., ☏ 757/622–2787), said to be the oldest non-Spanish brick house in the country.

On the Eastern Shore U.S. 13 takes you past historic 17th- to 19th-century towns such as **Eastville,** with its 250-year-old courthouse. **Onancock** has a working general store established in 1842 and a wharf from which to catch that East Coast rarity: a sunset over the water (the bay, to be exact).

Assateague Island is a 37-mi-long wildlife refuge and recreational area that extends north into Maryland (☞ Maryland). Despite invasive tourism and overdevelopment, **Chincoteague Island** has had at least one tradition survive from a simpler time: Every July the wild ponies from Assateague are driven across the channel and placed at auction here; those unsold swim back home. All year long the fine beaches and natural beauty justify a visit to Chincoteague. On nearby **Wallops Island** is NASA's **Wallops Flight Facility** (✉ Rte. 175, ☏ 757/824–2298), where a museum tells the story of the space program on the site of early rocket launchings.

Dining and Lodging

For price ranges *see* Charts 1 (B) and 2 (B) *in* On the Road with Fodor's.

$$$ ✕ **Coastal Grill.** Chef-owner Jerry Bryan prepares American classics with an innovative twist. Spinach salad is paired with sautéed chicken livers and balsamic vinaigrette, New York strip steak comes with melted onions and horseradish cream, and the fresh seafood dishes are sublime. ✉ *1427 Great Neck Rd., Virginia Beach,* ☏ *804/496–3348. Reservations not accepted. AE, D, DC, MC, V. No lunch.*

$$$ ✕ **La Galleria.** In just a few years this restaurant has earned a reputa-
★   tion as one of the best in Norfolk. The decor includes large urns imported from Italy, Corinthian columns, and a long sculpted wall adorned with frames and half frames. Menu choices include a variety of excellent pastas. ✉ *120 College Pl., Norfolk,* ☏ *757/623–3939. AE, MC, V.*

$$–$$$ ✕ **Landmark Crab House.** The servings here are as generous as the view of the water. A creamy crab imperial, baked in a terrine, is the touted specialty; the crab cakes are a slightly drier alternative. Beef dishes, well represented on the regular menu, often appear as specials. A children's menu that includes hamburgers makes this a spot for family dining. ✉ *N. Main St., Chincoteague,* ☏ *757/336–5552. AE, D, DC, MC, V.*

$$ ✕ **Duck Inn.** This family seafood restaurant is near the water and within sight of the bridge-tunnel. The specialty of the house, a milk-based fisherman's chowder, contains shrimp, crabmeat, and mushrooms. Crab cakes are popular here, as is the nightly buffet. ✉ *3324 Shore Dr., Virginia Beach,* ☏ *757/481–0201. Reservations not accepted. AE, D, DC, MC, V.*

$$ ✕ **The Grate Steak.** Farm implements and unfinished pine walls decorate the four dining rooms. Diners may step up to a common barbecue pit and grill for themselves the steak, shrimp, or chicken of their choosing. The menu also includes fried shrimp, grilled tuna, and baby back pork ribs. ⊠ *1934 Coliseum Dr., Hampton,* ☎ *757/827–1886. AE, D, DC, MC, V. No lunch.*

$$$$ 🏨 **Norfolk Waterside Marriott.** This modern hotel next door to the convention center is connected by a walkway to the Waterside; it opened in late 1991. ⊠ *235 E. Main St., 23510,* ☎ *757/627–4200 or 800/ 228–9290,* FAX *757/628–6466. 404 rooms. 2 restaurants, piano bar, indoor pool, sauna, health club. AE, D, DC, MC, V.*

$$$ 🏨 **Omni Waterside Hotel.** Renovated in 1993, this hotel is adjacent to the Waterside Festival Market Place and offers views of the harbor from about half its rooms. The financial district is only a block away. Guests have access to a nearby health club. ⊠ *777 Waterside Dr., 23510,* ☎ *757/622–6664,* FAX *757/625–8271. 446 rooms. Restaurant, bar, pool. AE, D, DC, MC, V.*

WASHINGTON, D.C.

By John F. Kelly   **Population**   543,000
Updated by   **Official Bird**   Wood thrush
Bruce Walker   **Official Flower**   American Beauty rose

Washington, the District of Columbia, was founded in 1791 as the world's first planned national capital. It's a city of architectural splendors and unforgettable memorials, where the striking image of the Washington Monument is never far from sight and the stirring memories of a young democratic republic are never far from mind. Of course, the capital's attractions are more than monumental and governmental. Washington's museums, world-class theater, music, and parks and gardens make it an American showcase, its arms open to the world.

Visitor Information

Washington, D.C., Convention and Visitors Association information center (⊠ 1212 New York Ave. NW, 6th floor, 20005, ☎ 202/789–7000, FAX 202/789–7037). **Dial-A-Park** (☎ 202/619–7275), a recording of events at National Park Service attractions. The **White House Visitor Center** (⊠ 1450 Pennsylvania Ave. NW, 20230, ☎ 202/208–1631).

Arriving and Departing

By Bus
Greyhound Lines (⊠ 1005 1st St. NE, ☎ 800/231–2222) and **Peter Pan Trailways** (⊠ 1000 1st St. NE, ☎ 800/343–9999).

By Car
I–95 approaches Washington from the north and south, skirting east of the city as part of the Capital Beltway. I–495 is the western loop of the Beltway. I–395 connects D.C. with the Beltway to the south. Connecticut Avenue is the best approach from the north, dropping down from the Beltway in Maryland.

By Plane
Washington National Airport (☎ 703/419–8000), in Virginia 4 mi south of downtown Washington, has scheduled flights by most major domestic carriers. It is often cramped and crowded, but it's a convenient 20-minute Metro (short for Metrorail) ride from the city center ($1.10 or $1.40, depending on the time of day). Cab fare downtown averages $13, including tip. Many transcontinental and international flights arrive at **Dulles International Airport** (☎ 703/419–8000), a modern facility 26 mi west of Washington in Virginia. **Baltimore–Washington International (BWI) Airport** (☎ 410/859–7100) is in Maryland, about 25 mi northeast of Washington.

Bus service is provided to National and Dulles airports by the **Washington Flyer** (☎ 703/685–1400) and to National and BWI by the **Airport Connection** (☎ 301/441–2345).

By Train
Amtrak trains pull into Union Station (⊠ 50 Massachusetts Ave. NE, ☎ 800/872–7245).

Getting Around Washington, D.C.

Washington's best-known sights are a short walk—or a short Metro ride—from one another.

By Car

A car can be a drawback in Washington. Traffic is horrendous, especially at rush hours (6:30 AM–9:30 AM and 3:30 PM–7 PM). One-way and diagonal streets can make the city seem like a maze, and parking is an adventure. There is free, three-hour parking around the Mall on Jefferson Drive and Madison Drive, but good luck grabbing a spot! You can also park for free—in some spots all day—in areas south of the Lincoln Memorial, on Ohio and West Basin drives in West Potomac Park. Private lots are expensive.

By Public Transportation

The **Washington Metropolitan Area Transit Authority** (☎ 202/637–7000, TTY 202/638–3780) provides Metrorail and Metrobus service in the District and in the Maryland and Virginia suburbs. The base rail fare is $1.10. The final fare depends on the time of day and the distance you travel. All bus rides within the District are $1.10; $5 **Metro Tourist Pass** entitles you to one day of unlimited subway travel weekdays from 9:30 AM to midnight or all day any weekend or holiday (except July 4).

By Taxi

Taxis in the District operate on a zone system, with a one-zone fare of $4. Ask the driver for the total fare before you depart. Two major companies are **Capitol Cab** (☎ 202/546–2400) and **Diamond Cab** (☎ 202/387–6200). Maryland and Virginia taxis are metered and cannot take you between points within D.C.

Orientation Tours

Buses from **Tourmobile** (☎ 202/554–7950 or 202/554–5100) and **Old Town Trolley Tours** (☎ 301/985–3021) ply routes around the city's major attractions, allowing you to get on and off as often as you like. **Gray Line Tours** (☎ 301/386–8300) offers a four-hour motor coach tour of Washington, Embassy Row, and Arlington National Cemetery; four-hour tours of Mount Vernon and Alexandria; and a combination of both.

Walking Tour

Not a specific walking route but groups of sites within historic neighborhoods, the **Black History National Recreation Trail** (brochure available from National Park Service: ✉ 1100 Ohio Dr. SW, 20242, ☎ 202/619–7222) illustrates aspects of African-American history in Washington, from slavery days to the New Deal.

Exploring Washington, D.C.

The major museums and galleries of the Smithsonian Institution surround the Mall. The U.S. Capitol is at the east end, the city's major monuments are to the west, and the White House is just a stone's throw away. Start your visit here to see Washington the capital; then venture farther afield for Washington the city. Since virtually every major sight in Washington is appropriate to visit with children, child-friendly attractions are not specifically noted.

The Mall

The first museum built by the Smithsonian was architect James Renwick's Norman-style **Castle.** Today it's home to the **Smithsonian Information Center.** An orientation film inside provides an overview of the various Smithsonian offerings, and television monitors announce the day's special events. All museums on the Mall are free. ✉ *1000 Jefferson Dr. SW, ☎ 202/357–2700 for all Smithsonian museums, TTY 202/357–1729.*

Washington, D.C.

T St.

S St.

Vermont Ave.

R St.

Rhode Island Ave.

Q St.

O St.

SHAW/HOWARD U. Ⓜ

S St.

Florida Ave.

Lincoln Rd.

R St.

Q St.

O St.

NW ◀ ▶ **NE**

New Jersey Ave.

P St.

3rd St.

1st St.

9th St.

8th St.

7th St.

6th St.

5th St.

4th St.

1st St.

N St.

N St.

New York Ave.

M St.

M St.

North Capitol St.

1st St.

L St.

Massachusetts Ave.

50

Mt. Vernon Square

MT. VERNON Ⓜ

H St.

National Portrait Gallery, Museum of American Art

G St.

GALLERY PLACE Ⓜ

CHINA-TOWN

Pension Building (Nat'l Building Museum),

JUDICIARY SQUARE Ⓜ

New Jersey Ave.

Massachusetts Ave.

UNION STATION Ⓜ

Columbus Memorial Fountain

Ford's Theater

F St.

E St.

J. Edgar Hoover FBI Building

D St.

395

Navy Memorial

ARCHIVES / NAVY MEMORIAL Ⓜ

Pennsylvania Ave.

2nd St.

Louisiana Ave.

Supreme Court

National Archives

National Museum of Natural History

National Gallery of Art

U.S. Capitol

Castle/ Information Center

THE MALL

Jefferson Dr

National Air and Space Museum

Maryland Ave.

U.S. Botanical Garden

Independence Ave.

E. Capitol St.

Library of Congress (Jefferson Bldg.)

Arthur M. Sackler Gallery

Freer Gallery of Art

Arts and Industries Bldg.

Museum of African Art

Hirshhorn Museum

C St.

L'ENFANT PLAZA Ⓜ

D St.

Canal St.

D St.

Folger Shakespeare Library

FEDERAL CENTER S.W. Ⓜ

Dep't of Trans.

395

Southwest Fwy.

G St.

Virginia Ave.

New Jersey Ave.

CAPITOL SOUTH Ⓜ

E St.

0   500 yards

Case al Br.

Pentagon

Washington Navy Yard

0   500 meters

395

Fred. Douglass Nat'l Hist. Site

SW ◀ ▶ **SE**

A clutch of interesting museums surrounds the Castle. The **Freer Gallery of Art** (⊠ 12th St. and Jefferson Dr. SW) is a repository of Asian works that's also known for James McNeill Whistler's stunning painting *Peacock Room*. The **Arthur M. Sackler Gallery** (⊠ 1050 Independence Ave. SW) houses a collection including works from China, the Indian subcontinent, Persia, Thailand, and Indonesia. It is connected to the Freer Gallery by an underground tunnel. The **National Museum of African Art** (⊠ 950 Independence Ave. SW) is dedicated to the collection, exhibition, and study of the traditional arts of sub-Saharan Africa. The **Arts and Industries Building** (⊠ 900 Jefferson Dr. SW), just east of the Castle, is a treasure trove of Victoriana.

Walking counterclockwise around the Mall from the Castle, you'll come first to the cylindrical **Hirshhorn Museum and Sculpture Garden** (⊠ 7th St. and Independence Ave. SW), which exhibits modern art both indoors and in its outdoor sculpture garden.

★ The **National Air and Space Museum** is the most visited museum in the world. Twenty-three galleries tell the story of aviation, from our earliest attempts at flight to travels beyond this solar system. Sensational IMAX films are shown on the five-story screen of the museum's Langley Theater (admission charged), while images of celestial bodies are projected on a domed ceiling in the Albert Einstein Planetarium. ⊠ *Jefferson Dr. at 6th St. SW.*

★ The two **National Gallery of Art** buildings stand on the north side of the Mall. In its hundred-odd galleries, architect John Russell Pope's elegant, domed **West Building** presents masterworks of Western art from the 13th to the 20th centuries. I. M. Pei's angular **East Building,** with its stunning interior spaces, generally shows modern works. ⊠ *Madison Dr. and 4th St. NW,* ☎ *202/737–4215, TTY 202/842–6176.*

The **National Museum of Natural History** is filled with bones, fossils, stuffed animals, and other natural delights, including the popular Dinosaur Hall, the Hope Diamond, and a sea-life display featuring a living coral reef. ⊠ *Madison Dr. between 9th and 12th Sts. NW.*

Exhibits on the three floors of the **National Museum of American History** trace the social, political, and technological history of the United States. You'll find a 280-ton steam locomotive, a collection of first ladies' inaugural gowns, and a perenially popular pendulum. ⊠ *Madison Ave. between 12th and 14th Sts. NW.*

Alongside the city's many museums celebrating the best of humanity's accomplishments is one that illustrates what humans at their worst are ★ capable of. The **United States Holocaust Memorial Museum** tells the story of the 11 million Jews, Gypsies, homosexuals, political prisoners, and others killed by the Nazis between 1933 and 1945. Arrive early (by 9 AM to be safe) to get free, same-day, timed-entry tickets. Advance tickets are available through Protix (☎ 703/218–6500 or 800/400–9373) for a service charge. ⊠ *100 Raoul Wallenberg Pl. SW (15th St. and Independence Ave. SW),* ☎ *202/488–0400.*

The Monuments

Washington is a city of monuments. Those dedicated to the most famous Americans are west of the Mall on filled-in former marshy flats on the Potomac. Entrance to all monuments is free.

The tallest, of course, is the **Washington Monument,** toward the Mall's west end. Construction of the 555-ft obelisk was started in 1848, interrupted by the Civil War—the reason for the color change about a third of the way up—and completed in 1884. Pick up free timed-tickets at the kiosk on 15th Street for the elevator ride to the monument's top, where the view is unequaled. ⊠ *Constitution Ave. at 15th St. NW,* ☎ *202/426–6840.*

The exquisitely classical **Jefferson Memorial,** honoring America's third president, rests on the south bank of the **Tidal Basin.** One of the best views of the White House can be seen from the top steps of the memorial, John Russell Pope's reinterpretation of the Pantheon in Rome. ☎ *202/426–6821.*

★ Cherry trees, beautiful in their early April blossoms, ring the approach to the **Lincoln Memorial,** at the west end of the Mall. Henry Bacon's monument is considered by many to be the most moving spot in the city, its mood set by Daniel Chester French's somber statue of the seated president gazing over the **Reflecting Pool.** Visit this memorial at night for best effect. ☎ *202/426–6895.*

★ In Constitution Gardens, the **Vietnam Veterans Memorial**—a black granite V designed by Maya Ling, with sculpture by Frederick Hart—is another landmark that encourages introspection. The names of more than 58,000 Americans who died in Vietnam are etched on the face of the wall in the order of their deaths. The **Vietnam Women's Memorial** was dedicated on Veterans Day 1993 and sits southeast of the Vietnam Veterans Memorial. ⊠ *23rd St. and Constitution Ave. NW,* ☎ *202/634–1568.*

The President's Neighborhood

★ The **White House,** one of the world's most famous residences, has pride of place on Pennsylvania Avenue. The building was designed by Irishman James Hoban, who drew upon the Georgian design of Leinster Hall, near Dublin, and other Irish country houses. For a glimpse of some of the public rooms—including the East Room and the State Dining Room—get a ticket (one per person) at the White House Visitor Center (☞ *Visitor Information, above*); arrive by 8 AM to be safe. ⊠ *1600 Pennsylvania Ave. NW,* ☎ *202/619–7222 or 202/456–7041 for recorded information. Free. Closed Sun.–Mon.*

Lafayette Square is an intimate oasis in the midst of downtown Washington. It served as a campsite for soldiers of both the 1812 and Civil wars—in full view of presidents Madison and Lincoln across the way in the White House. At the top of the square, golden-domed **St. John's Episcopal Church** (⊠ *16th and H Sts. NW,* ☎ *202/347–8766*) is known as the Church of the Presidents. The opulent **Hay-Adams Hotel** (☞ *Lodging, below*), across 16th Street from St. John's, is a favorite with Washington insiders and visiting notables.

The first floor of the Federal-style redbrick **Decatur House** (⊠ *748 Jackson Pl. NW,* ☎ *202/842–0920*) is decorated as it was when occupied by naval hero Stephen Decatur in 1819. The green canopy at 1651 Pennsylvania Avenue marks the entrance to **Blair House,** the residence used by visiting heads of state. Flags from their respective countries fly from the outside lampposts when these dignitaries are in town to see the president. The busy, monumental, French Empire–style **Old Executive Office Building** (⊠ *17th St. and Pennsylvania Ave. NW*) houses many executive branch employees. Former vice president Dan Quayle had his office in here. The current second-in-command, Albert Gore Jr., is a little closer to the action—in the West Wing of the White House, just down the hall from the president.

While most of the Smithsonian museums are on the Mall, the **Renwick Gallery,** devoted to American decorative arts, is downtown. ⊠ *Pennsylvania Ave. and 17th St. NW. Free.*

One of the few large museums in Washington that are not part of the Smithsonian family is the **Corcoran Gallery of Art.** Its collection ranges from works by early American artists to late-19th- and early 20th-century paintings from Europe. A highlight is the entire 18th-century Grand Salon from the Hôtel d'Orsay in Paris. ⊠ *17th St. and New York Ave. NW,* ☎ *202/639–1700. Closed Tues.*

Despite its name, the **Octagon,** built in 1801, has six sides. The Treaty of Ghent, ending the War of 1812, was signed in an upstairs study. The building now houses exhibits relating to architecture, decorative arts, and Washington history. ⊠ *1799 New York Ave. NW,* ☎ *202/638–3105. Closed Mon.*

Memorial Continental Hall is the headquarters of the Daughters of the American Revolution. The 50,000-item collection of the **DAR Museum** includes fine examples of Colonial and Federal silver, china, porcelain, stoneware, earthenware, and glass. ⊠ *1776 D St. NW,* ☎ *202/879–3241. Free. Closed Sat.*

Another building with an excellent aerial view of the downtown area around the White House is the venerable **Hotel Washington.** The view from the rooftop **Sky Top Lounge,** which is open April–October, is one of the best in the city. ⊠ *515 15th St. NW,* ☎ *202/638–5900.*

The huge Greek Revival **Treasury Building** is in fact home to the Department of the Treasury. ⊠ *15th St. and Pennsylvania Ave. NW.*

The magazine comes to life at the **National Geographic Society's Explorers Hall.** Interactive exhibits encourage you to learn about the world. The centerpiece is a hand-painted globe, 11 ft in diameter, that floats and spins on a cushion of air, showing off different features of the planet. ⊠ *17th and M Sts. NW,* ☎ *202/857–7588. Free.*

Capitol Hill

Pierre L'Enfant, the French designer of Washington, called Capitol Hill (then known as Jenkins Hill) "a pedestal waiting for a monument."
★ That monument is the **U.S. Capitol,** the gleaming white-domed building in which elected officials toil. George Washington laid the cornerstone on September 18, 1793, and in November 1800 Congress moved down from Philadelphia. The Capitol has grown over the years and today contains some of the city's most inspiring art, from Constantino Brumidi's *Apotheosis of Washington,* the fresco at the center of the dome, to the splendid Statuary Hall. There are also live attractions: senators and representatives speechifying in their respective chambers. If you want to test your architectural eyes, spend a minute or two looking at the dome from afar: Does it fit or is it a bit too large? ⊠ *East end of the Mall,* ☎ *202/224–3121 or 202/225–6827.*

East of the Capitol are the three buildings that make up the **Library of Congress,** which contains 108 million items, of which only a quarter are books. The remainder includes manuscripts, prints, films, photographs, sheet music, and the largest collection of maps in the world. The green-domed **Jefferson Building** (⊠ *1st St. and Independence Ave. SE,* ☎ *202/707–8000*), with its grand octagonal Main Reading Room and mahogany readers' tables, is the centerpiece of the system.

The **Folger Shakespeare Library** is home to a world-class collection of Shakespeareana. Inside are a reproduction of an inn-yard theater and a gallery, designed in the manner of an Elizabethan great hall, that hosts exhibits from the library's collection of works by and about the Bard. ⊠ *201 E. Capitol St. SE,* ☎ *202/544–4600. Closed Sun.*

After being shunted around several locations, including a spell in a tavern, the **Supreme Court** got its own building in 1935. The impressive colonnaded white-marble temple was designed by Cass Gilbert. ⊠ *1st and E. Capitol Sts. NE,* ☎ *202/479–3000. Closed weekends.*

Union Station is now a shopping center as well as a train station. The Beaux Arts building's wonderful main waiting room is a perfect setting for the inaugural ball that's held here every four years. ✉ *50 Massachusetts Ave. NE.*

Old Downtown and Federal Triangle

Before the glass office blocks around 16th and K streets NW became the business center of town, Washington's mercantile hub was farther east. The open-air markets are gone, but some of the 19th-century character of Washington's east end remains. In the 1930s the humongous **Federal Triangle** complex was built to accommodate the expanding federal bureaucracy.

The massive redbrick **Pension Building** went up in the 1880s to house workers who processed the pension claims of veterans and their survivors. It is currently home to the **National Building Museum** (✉ F St. between 4th and 5th Sts. NW, ☎ 202/272–2448), devoted to architecture and related arts.

Judiciary Square is Washington's legal core, with local and district court buildings arrayed around it. At the center is the **National Law Enforcement Officers Memorial**, a 3-ft-high wall bearing the names of more than 15,000 American police officers killed in the line of duty since 1794. Washington's compact **Chinatown** is bordered roughly by G, H, 6th, and 8th streets NW.

The **National Portrait Gallery,** with its paintings and photographs of presidents and other notable Americans, and the **National Museum of American Art,** whose collection ranges from Colonial times to the present, are two more Smithsonian museums. Both are housed in the Greek Revival Old Patent Office Building (✉ 8th and G Sts. NW).

Ford's Theatre (✉ 511 10th St. NW, ☎ 202/426–6924), where Abraham Lincoln was assassinated by John Wilkes Booth on April 14, 1865, now houses a museum in the basement, which displays items connected with Lincoln's life and untimely death.

The Beaux Arts **Willard Hotel** (✉ 14th St. and Pennsylvania Ave. NW) is one of the most luxurious in Washington. As the story goes, its lobby is the origin of the term "lobbyist": U.S. President U. S. Grant would occasionally escape from the White House to have a brandy and cigar in the Willard's lobby, where interested parties would descend on him, trying to bend his ear.

The **Commerce Department Building** forms the base of **Federal Triangle.** Inside Commerce is the **National Aquarium,** the country's oldest public aquarium, featuring tropical and freshwater fish, moray eels, frogs, turtles, piranhas, even sharks. ✉ *14th St. and Pennsylvania Ave. NW,* ☎ *202/482–2825.*

The tour of the hulking **J. Edgar Hoover Federal Bureau of Investigation Building** outlines the work of the FBI and ends with a live-ammo firearms demonstration. From the end of March through June the wait to get inside may be as long as three hours. ✉ *10th St. and Pennsylvania Ave. NW (tour entrance on E St. NW),* ☎ *202/324–3447. No tours weekends.*

The Declaration of Independence, the Constitution, and the Bill of Rights are on display in the Rotunda of the **National Archives** (✉ Constitution Ave. between 7th and 9th Sts. NW, ☎ 202/501–5000).

The statue of a lone sailor staring out over the largest map in the world marks the site of the **Navy Memorial** (✉ 7th St. and Pennsylvania Ave.

NW). In summer the memorial's concert stage is the site of military-band performances (☎ 202/737–2300).

The **National Museum of Women in the Arts** displays the works of prominent female artists from the Renaissance to the present, including Georgia O'Keeffe, Mary Cassatt, Elisabeth Vigée-Lebrun, and Judy Chicago. ✉ *1250 New York Ave. NW,* ☎ *202/783–5000.*

Georgetown

At one time a tobacco port, this poshest of Washington neighborhoods is home to some of its wealthiest and best-known citizens. It's also the nucleus of the district's nightlife scene, with dozens of hot spots dotting Wisconsin Avenue and M Street, Georgetown's crossroads.

Downhill from the main bustle of G-town, the **Chesapeake & Ohio Canal** allows for a scenic getaway from the streets. Dug in the 19th century as an alternative to the rough and rocky Potomac, it used to carry lumber, coal, iron, and flour into northwest Maryland. Runners now tread its scenic towpath, and in summer mule-drawn barges ply its placid waters; tickets are available at the Foundry Mall (✉ 1057 Thomas Jefferson St. NW, ☎ 202/653–5190).

The Shops at Georgetown Park (✉ 3222 M St. NW, ☎ 202/298–5577), home to such high-ticket stores as F.A.O. Schwarz, Williams-Sonoma, and Polo–Ralph Lauren, is a multilevel shopping extravaganza that answers the question "If the Victorians had invented shopping malls, what would they look like?"

Georgetown University, the oldest Jesuit school in the country, has its campus at the western edge of the neighborhood. When seen from the Potomac or from Washington's high ground, the Gothic spires of the university's older buildings give it an almost medieval look.

Dumbarton Oaks, an estate comprising two museums—one of Byzantine works, the other of pre-Columbian art—is surrounded by 10 acres of stunning formal gardens designed by landscape architect Beatrix Farrand. *Art collections:* ✉ *1703 32nd St. NW,* ☎ *202/339–6401. Closed Mon. Gardens:* ✉ *31st and R Sts. NW.*

Other Attractions

The **Bureau of Engraving and Printing** is the birthplace of all paper currency in the United States. Although there are no free samples, the 30-minute guided tour—which takes you past presses that turn out $450 million worth of currency a day—is one of the city's most popular. ✉ *14th and C Sts. SW,* ☎ *202/874–3019. Closed weekends.*

The **Frederick Douglass National Historic Site** is at Cedar Hill, the Washington home of the noted abolitionist. The house displays mementos from Douglass's life and has a wonderful view of the Federal City, across the Anacostia River. ✉ *1411 W St. SE,* ☎ *202/426–5961.*

The 160-acre **National Zoological Park,** part of the Smithsonian Institution, is one of the foremost zoos in the world. Innovative compounds show animals in naturalistic settings, and the ambitious Amazonia recreates the ecosystem of a South American rain forest. ✉ *3001 Connecticut Ave. NW,* ☎ *202/673–4800.*

The **Phillips Collection** was the first permanent museum of modern art in the country. Holdings include works by Braque, Cézanne, Klee, Matisse, Renoir, and John Henry Twachtman. ✉ *1600 21st St. NW,* ☎ *202/387–2151. Closed Mon.*

It took 83 years to complete the Gothic Revival **Washington National Cathedral,** the sixth-largest cathedral in the world. Besides flying buttresses, a nave, transepts, and rib vaults that were built stone by stone, it is adorned with fanciful gargoyles created by skilled stone carvers. ⊠ *Wisconsin and Massachusetts Aves. NW,* ☎ *202/537–6200.*

The **Washington Navy Yard** is the navy's oldest shore establishment. A former shipyard and ordnance facility, the yard today is home to the **Navy Museum** and the **Marine Corps Museum,** which outline the history of those two services from their inception to the present. ⊠ *9th and M Sts. SE,* ☎ *202/433–4882.*

Arlington, Virginia

Though the attractions here are across the Potomac, it's well worth making them a part of your visit to the nation's capital. (For more suburban Virginia sites—including Mount Vernon and Old Town Alexandria—*see* Virginia.)

At **Arlington National Cemetery,** you can trace America's history through the aftermath of its battles. Dominating the cemetery is the Greek Revival **Arlington House,** onetime home of Robert E. Lee, which offers a breathtaking view across the Potomac to the Lincoln Memorial and the Mall. On a hillside below are the **Kennedy graves.** John Fitzgerald Kennedy is buried under an eternal flame. Jacqueline Bouvier Kennedy Onassis lies next to him. Robert Francis Kennedy is buried nearby, his grave marked by a simple white cross. The **Tomb of the Unknowns** is also in the cemetery. ⊠ *West end of Memorial Bridge,* ☎ *703/607–8052.*

Just north of Arlington Cemetery is the **United States Marine Corps War Memorial,** honoring Marines who have given their lives since the Corps was formed in 1775. The memorial statue, sculpted by Felix W. de Weldon, is based on Joe Rosenthal's Pulitzer Prize–winning photograph of six soldiers raising a flag atop Iwo Jima's Mt. Suribachi on February 19, 1945.

The **Pentagon,** headquarters of the Department of Defense, is an exercise in immensity: 23,000 military and civilian employees work here; it is as wide as three Washington Monuments laid end to end; and inside it contains 691 drinking fountains, 7,754 windows, and 17½ mi of corridors. Visitors can take a 75-minute tour on weekdays every half hour 9:30–3:30. A photo ID is required. ⊠ *Off I–395,* ☎ *703/695–1776.*

Parks and Gardens

The 444-acre **National Arboretum** blooms with all manner of plants, with clematis, peonies, rhododendrons, and azaleas among its showier inhabitants. The National Bonsai Collection, National Herb Garden, and an odd and striking hilltop construction of old marble columns from the U.S. Capitol are also well worth seeing. ⊠ *3501 New York Ave. NE,* ☎ *202/245–2726.*

Rock Creek Park (☎ *202/426–6829*) is a cool tongue of green jutting down into the center of Washington. Its 1,800 acres include picnic sites and biking, hiking, and equestrian trails that wend through groves of dogwood, beech, oak, and cedar.

The **United States Botanic Garden** (⊠ 1st St. and Maryland Ave. SW, ☎ *202/225–8333*), just below the Capitol, is a peaceful plant-filled conservatory that includes a cactus house, a fern house, and a subtropical house filled with orchids.

Dining

Washington's restaurants aren't exactly innovators, but neither are they blind to fashion. That means trends that started elsewhere—nouvelle cuisine, new American, southwestern—quickly show up in the capital. Good ethnic meals can be found in Adams-Morgan (lots of Ethiopian), Georgetown (Afghani to Indonesian), and Chinatown. For price ranges *see* Chart 1 (A) *in* On the Road with Fodor's.

$$$$ ✕ **Citronelle.** The essence of California chic, Citronelle's glass-front
★ kitchen allows diners to see all the action as chefs scurry to and fro. Appetizers include a tart of thinly sliced grilled scallops on puff pastry surrounded by a tomato vinaigrette. Loin of venison is served with an endive tart and garnished with dried apples. ⊠ *3000 M St. NW,* ☎ *202/625–2150. AE, DC, MC, V.*

$$$$ ✕ **Le Lion d'Or.** The superior entrées at this French restaurant include
★ lobster soufflé, ravioli with foie gras, and crepes with oysters and caviar. Don't forget to place an order for a dessert soufflé—it will leave you breathless. ⊠ *1150 Connecticut Ave. NW,* ☎ *202/296–7972. Reservations required. Jacket and tie. AE, DC, MC, V. Closed Sun. No lunch.*

$$$ ✕ **i Ricchi.** At this airy Tuscan restaurant, the spring-summer menu in-
★ cludes such offerings as rolled pork and rabbit roasted in wine and fresh herbs, while the fall-winter list brings grilled lamb chops and sautéed beef fillet. ⊠ *1220 19th St. NW,* ☎ *202/835–0459. AE, DC, MC, V. Closed Sun. No lunch Sat.*

$$$ ✕ **La Colline.** The menu here, at one of the city's best French restau-
★ rants, emphasizes seafood, with offerings ranging from simple grilled preparations to fricassees and food served au gratin with imaginative sauces. Other items include duck with orange sauce and veal with chanterelle mushrooms. ⊠ *400 N. Capitol St. NW,* ☎ *202/737–0400. AE, DC, MC, V. Closed Sun. No lunch Sat.*

$$$ ✕ **Occidental Grill.** Part of the stately Willard Hotel complex, this popular restaurant offers innovative dishes, attentive service, and lots of photos of politicians and other power brokers past and present. The menu changes frequently, but you can count on grilled poultry, fish, and steak, as well as salads and sandwiches. ⊠ *1475 Pennsylvania Ave. NW,* ☎ *202/783–1475. AE, MC, V.*

$$$ ✕ **Sam and Harry's.** The surroundings at this quintessential steak house are understated and genteel, with four private dining rooms available. The main attractions are porterhouse steak and filet mignon. ⊠ *1200 19th St. NW,* ☎ *202/296–4333. AE, D, DC, MC, V. Closed Sun. No lunch Sat.*

$$$ ✕ **Vincenzo al Sole.** Simply prepared seafood dishes, such as *merluzzo*
★ *alla calabrese* (roasted cod with capers and olives) and *branzino al salmoriglio* (grilled rockfish with oregano), reign here. The menu also includes meat and game dishes. ⊠ *1606 20th St. NW,* ☎ *202/667–0047. AE, DC, MC, V. Closed Sun. No lunch Sat.*

$$–$$$ ✕ **Bombay Club.** One block from the White House, the Bombay Club
★ tries to re-create a private club for 19th-century British colonials in India. The menu includes unusual seafood specialties and a large number of vegetarian dishes, but the real standouts are the breads and the seafood appetizers. ⊠ *815 Connecticut Ave. NW,* ☎ *202/659–3727. AE, DC, MC, V. No lunch Sat.*

$$ ✕ **Aditi.** Aditi's two-story dining room seems too elegant for a moderately priced Indian restaurant. Tandoori and curry dishes are expertly prepared and not aggressively spiced; if you want your food spicy, request it. Rice *biryani* entrées are good for lighter appetites. ⊠ *3299 M St. NW,* ☎ *202/625–6825. AE, D, DC, MC, V.*

$$ ✕ **Café Japone.** Café Japone's dark interior has an alternative-scene edge. Some nights you'll find karaoke; other nights there's a live jazz band. The sushi is not a rave, but it's good. Steamed wontons and crispy fried *age dofu* (tofu in a soy broth) are tasty appetizers. ⊠ *2032 P St. NW,* ☎ *202/223–1573. AE, DC, MC, V. No lunch.*

$$ ✗ **City Lights of China.** This restaurant always makes critics' lists. The
★ traditional Chinese fare is excellent. Less common specialties, such as lamb in a tangy peppery sauce and shark's fin soup, are deftly cooked as well. Jumbo shrimp with spicy salt are baked in their shells, then stir-fried with ginger and spices. ⊠ *1731 Connecticut Ave. NW,* ☎ *202/ 265-6688. AE, D, DC, MC, V.*

$$ ✗ **Hibiscus Café.** African masks and neon accents hang from the ceil-
★ ing of the modish restaurant, where weekend crowds are drawn by spicy jerk chicken, such blackened fish as grouper, shrimp curry, and flavorful soups (try the butternut-ginger bisque). ⊠ *3401 K St. NW,* ☎ *202/965– 7170. AE, D, MC, V. Closed Sun.–Mon. No lunch.*

$$ ✗ **Jaleo.** A lively Spanish bistro, Jaleo features a long list of hot and
★ cold tapas, although such entrées as grilled fish, seafood stew, and paella—which comes in three different versions—are just as tasty. For dessert, don't miss the crisp and buttery apple charlotte. ⊠ *480 7th St. NW,* ☎ *202/628–7949. AE, D, DC, MC, V.*

$$ ✗ **Old Glory.** Always teeming with visiting Texans, Georgetown students, and closet Elvis fans, Old Glory sticks to barbecued basics: sandwiches and platters of pulled and sliced pork, beef brisket, and smoked and pulled ribs and chicken. ⊠ *3139 M St. NW,* ☎ *202/337– 3406. AE, D, DC, MC, V.*

$ ✗ **Burma.** Batter-fried eggplant and squash are deliciously paired with
★ complex, peppery sauces at this exquisite jewel in Chinatown. Green Tea Leaf and other salads leave the tongue with a pleasant tingle. Such entrées as mango pork, tamarind fish, and Kokang chicken are equally satisfying. No item is over $10. ⊠ *740 6th St. NW,* ☎ *202/638–1280. AE, D, DC, MC, V. No lunch weekends.*

$ ✗ **The Islander.** Addie Green's tangy and spicy soup made with veg-
★ etables and marinated fish, her delicious *accra* cod fritters, nine varieties of dough-enveloped roti, and tropical herb-and-spice marinated calypso chicken will make you wish that this authentic Trinidadian roost were just around the corner from home. ⊠ *1762 Columbia Rd. NW, 2nd floor,* ☎ *202/234–4955. Closed Sun.–Mon.*

$ ✗ **Meskerem.** Among Adams-Morgan's many Ethiopian restaurants,
★ Meskerem is distinctive for a balcony where you can eat Ethiopian style: seated on leather floor cushions, with large woven baskets for tables. Stews served with *injera* (spongy flat bread) are made with teff, a grain grown only in Ethiopia and Idaho that imparts a distinctive sourness. ⊠ *2434 18th St. NW,* ☎ *202/462–4100. AE, DC, MC, V.*

$ ✗ **Peyote Café/Roxanne Restaurant.** Mexican influences on traditional southern food define the menus at these two connected restaurants, where you can order from both menus. Grilled rib-eye steak, grilled salmon, and Sweat Hot Fire Shrimp are specialties. ⊠ *2319 18th St. NW,* ☎ *202/462–8330. Reservations not accepted. AE, DC, MC, V. No lunch Mon.–Sat.*

$ ✗ **Sholl's Colonial Cafeteria.** Suited federal workers line up with tourists to grab a bite at this Washington institution, where favorites include chopped steak, liver and onions, and baked chicken and fish. Sholl's is famous for its apple, blueberry, and other fruit pies. ⊠ *1990 K St. NW,* ☎ *202/296–3065. No credit cards.*

Lodging

Many Washington hotels, particularly those downtown, offer special **reduced rates** and package deals on weekends, and some are available midweek; be sure to ask about them at the hotel of your choice. **Capi-**

tol Reservations books rooms at more than 70 better hotels in good locations at rates 20%–40% off; call 202/452–1270 or 800/847–4832 from 8:30 to 6:30 weekdays; it also offers group packages with tours and meals. **Washington D.C. Accommodations** will book rooms at any hotel in town, with discounts of 20%–40% available at about 90 locations; call 202/289–2220 or 800/554–2220 from 9 to 6 weekdays. To find reasonably priced accommodations in small guest houses and private homes, contact **Bed 'n' Breakfast Accommodations Ltd. of Washington, D.C.** (⊠ Box 12011, 20005, ☎ 202/328–3510, FAX 202/332–3885) or **Bed & Breakfast League, Ltd./Sweet Dreams & Toast** (⊠ Box 9490, 20016-9490, ☎ 202/363–7767, FAX 202/363–8396). For price ranges *see* Chart 2 (A) *in* On the Road with Fodor's.

$$$$ ⊞ **Four Seasons Hotel.** This contemporary hotel, conveniently situated
★ between Georgetown and Foggy Bottom, is a gathering place for Washington's elite. Guest rooms are traditionally furnished in light colors. The quieter rooms face the courtyard; others have a view of the C&O Canal. ⊠ *2800 Pennsylvania Ave. NW, 20007,* ☎ *202/342–0444,* FAX *202/342–1673. 196 rooms. 2 restaurants, bar, room service, pool, health club, nightclub, parking (fee). AE, DC, MC, V.*

$$$$ ⊞ **Hay-Adams Hotel.** The dignified reputation of this White House neigh-
★ bor has little need to call attention to itself, and it remains a choice for state policy-making meetings. Its elegance extends to guest rooms, where you might feel like you're in a mansion in disguise. ⊠ *1 Lafayette Sq., 20006,* ☎ *202/638–6600 or 800/424–5054,* FAX *202/638–2716. 143 rooms. Restaurant, lounge, room service, dry cleaning, parking (fee). AE, DC, MC, V.*

$$$$ ⊞ **Hyatt Regency on Capitol Hill.** Close to Union Station and the Mall, the elegant 11-story Hyatt Regency features a spectacular garden atrium. Suites on the south side have a view of the Capitol dome just a few blocks away, as does the rooftop Capitol View Club restaurant. ⊠ *400 New Jersey Ave. NW, 20001,* ☎ *202/737–1234 or 800/233–1234,* FAX *202/737–5773. 834 rooms. 2 restaurants, 2 bars, room service, pool, health club, parking (fee). AE, DC, MC, V.*

$$$$ ⊞ **Luxury Collection.** At press time, the new name of this former Ritz-
★ Carlton property had not yet been decided. Near Dupont Circle, the hotel is still exclusive and intimate, with an English hunt-club theme. Rooms have views of Embassy Row or Georgetown. ⊠ *2100 Massachusetts Ave. NW, 20008,* ☎ *202/293–2100,* FAX *202/835–2196. 206 rooms. Restaurant, bar, exercise room, concierge floor. AE, DC, MC, V.*

$$$$ ⊞ **Willard Inter-Continental.** The Willard is an opulent Beaux Arts feast
★ to the eye, as the main lobby with its great columns, huge chandeliers, and elaborately carved ceilings attests. The formal restaurant has won nationwide acclaim. ⊠ *1401 Pennsylvania Ave. NW, 20004,* ☎ *202/628–9100 or 800/327–0200,* FAX *202/637–7326. 341 rooms. 2 restaurants, 2 bars, minibars, room service, health club, laundry service and dry cleaning, shops, meeting rooms, parking (fee). AE, DC, MC, V.*

$$$ ⊞ **Hotel Washington.** Washingtonians bring visitors to the outdoor
★ rooftop bar here for cocktails and a renowned panorama that includes the White House grounds and Washington Monument. Some rooms look directly onto the White House lawn. ⊠ *515 15th St. NW, 20004,* ☎ *202/638–5900,* FAX *202/638–1594. 350 rooms. Restaurant, bar, deli, lobby lounge, room service, exercise room, laundry service and dry cleaning, business services. AE, DC, MC, V.*

$$$ ⊞ **Latham Hotel.** A small hotel in the city's liveliest neighborhood, this redbrick neocolonial is popular with Europeans, sports figures, and devotees of Georgetown. Rooms are sleek and updated. Some are underground; others have views of the C&O Canal or busy M Street. Its restaurant, Citronelle (☞ Dining, *above*), is considered one of Washington's best. ⊠ *3000 M St. NW, 20007,* ☏ *202/726–5000,* FAX *202/337–4250. 143 rooms. Restaurant, bar, room service, pool, parking (fee). AE, DC, MC, V.*

$$$ ▦ **Lincoln Suites.** A good value, this small hotel has a courteous staff, offers the basics in the midst of the K and L streets business district, and is close to the White House. Some rooms have a full kitchen, and all have a wet bar; king-size, queen-size, or extra-long double beds are available. ⊠ *1823 L St. NW, 20036,* ☏ *202/223–4320 or 800/424–2970,* FAX *202/223–8546. 99 rooms. Restaurant, room service, laundry service and dry cleaning, parking (fee). AE, DC, MC, V.*

$$$ ▦ **Phoenix Park Hotel.** Just steps from Union Station and four blocks from the Capitol, this high-rise has a wood-panel-and-brass Irishmen's-club theme and is the home of the Dubliner (☞ Nightlife and the Arts, *below*). Guest rooms are bright, traditionally furnished, and quiet. A new wing was completed in 1997, adding 61 rooms and suites, meeting rooms, and a ballroom. ⊠ *520 N. Capitol St. NW, 20001,* ☏ *202/638–6900 or 800/824–5419,* FAX *202/393–3236. 149 rooms. 2 restaurants, laundry service, parking (fee). AE, D, DC, MC, V.*

$$$ ▦ **Washington Hilton and Towers.** One of the city's busiest conven-
★ tion hotels, this high-rise also attracts travelers who like to be where the action is. The light-filled but compact guest rooms are furnished in standard modern hotel style and have marble bathrooms. ⊠ *1919 Connecticut Ave. NW, 20009,* ☏ *202/483–3000,* FAX *202/232–0438. 1,122 rooms. 3 restaurants, 2 bars, room service, pool, 3 tennis courts, health club, shops, parking (fee). AE, DC, MC, V.*

$$–$$$ ▦ **Hotel Tabard Inn.** Three Victorian town houses near Dupont Circle were linked in the 1920s to form an inn that is now the oldest continuously running hotel in Washington. Furnishings are broken-in Victorian and American Empire antiques; a Victorian-inspired carpet cushions the labyrinthine hallways. ⊠ *1739 N St. NW, 20036,* ☏ *202/785–1277,* FAX *202/785–6173. 42 rooms, 14 share bath. Restaurant. Continental breakfast. MC, V.*

$$ ▦ **Holiday Inn Capitol Hill.** For clean, comfortable, low-price rooms with high-price views, this is the place. A good value for budget-minded travelers, the Holiday Inn Capitol Hill offers the same magnificent views of the Capitol as the pricier Hyatt. Children under age 18 stay free. ⊠ *415 New Jersey Ave. NW, 20001,* ☏ *202/638–1616 or 800/638–1116,* FAX *202/638–0707. 341 rooms. Restaurant, bar, room service, pool, parking (fee). AE, D, DC, MC, V.*

$$ ▦ **Normandy Inn.** A small European-style hotel on a quiet street in the
★ exclusive embassy area of Connecticut Avenue, the Normandy is near restaurants and some of the most expensive residential real estate in Washington. Rooms are standard, functional, and comfortable; all have refrigerators. ⊠ *2118 Wyoming Ave. NW, 20008,* ☏ *202/483–1350 or 800/424–3729,* FAX *202/387–8241. 75 rooms. CP. Refrigerators, room service, parking (fee). AE, D, MC, V.*

$$ ▦ **Washington Courtyard by Marriott.** One of the city's best values for
★ budget travelers, Marriott's Washington Courtyard hotel is a good alternative for international tourists and businesspeople who can't find rooms at the Washington Hilton. Guest rooms on the west and south have good views. ⊠ *1900 Connecticut Ave. NW, 20009,* ☏ *202/332–9300 or 800/842–4211,* FAX *202/328–7039. 147 rooms. Restaurant, bar, pool, parking (fee). AE, DC, MC, V.*

$ ▦ **Washington International AYH-Hostel.** Eight- to 14-person dormitories and family rooms are available. In summer reservations are highly recommended; only groups need to reserve off-season. There is a common kitchen. Maximum stay is 29 days. ⊠ *1009 11th St. NW,*

20001, ☎ 202/737–2333, ℻ 202/737–1508. 250 beds. Shop, coin laundry. MC, V.

Nightlife and the Arts

Area arts and entertainment events are listed in the Weekend section of Friday's *Washington Post*, in the free *City Paper*, in *Washingtonian* magazine (on newsstands), and in *Where: Washington* (free in hotels).

Nightlife

Georgetown, Adams-Morgan, Dupont Circle, and **Capitol Hill** are the main nightlife centers in Washington.

BARS

The **Brickskeller** (⌧ 1523 22nd St. NW, ☎ 202/293–1885) sells more than 500 brands of beer—from Central American lagers to U.S.-microbrewed ales. The **Dubliner** (⌧ Phoenix Park Hotel, 520 N. Capitol St. NW, ☎ 202/737–3773) features snug paneled rooms, thick and tasty Guinness, and nightly live Irish entertainment.

CABARET

Two troupes offering political song and satire perform regularly in Georgetown clubs: the **Capitol Steps** (☎ 202/298–8222 or 703/683–8330) and **Gross National Product** (☎ 202/783–7212).

JAZZ

Blues Alley (⌧ Rear 1073 Wisconsin Ave. NW, ☎ 202/337–4141) books some of the biggest names in jazz. **One Step Down** (⌧ 2517 Pennsylvania Ave. NW, ☎ 202/331–8863) is an intimate, smoky space that's a favorite with hard-core devotees.

ROCK

The **Bayou** (⌧ 3135 K St. NW, ☎ 202/333–2897), in Georgetown, features live rock. The **9:30 Club** (⌧ 815 V St. NW, ☎ 202/393–0930) books an eclectic mix of local, national, and international artists, mostly playing so-called alternative rock.

The Arts

TicketPlace (⌧ Lisner Auditorium, 730 21st St. NW, ☎ 202/842–5387) sells half-price day-of-performance tickets; it is closed Sunday and Monday. **TicketMaster** (☎ 202/432–7328 or 800/551–7328) takes phone charges for events around the city. All manner of cultural events, from ballet to classical music, are offered at the **John F. Kennedy Center for the Performing Arts** (⌧ New Hampshire Ave. and Rock Creek Pkwy. NW, ☎ 202/467–4600 or 800/444–1324).

DANCE

Dance Place (⌧ 3225 8th St. NE, ☎ 202/269–1600) hosts a wide array of modern and ethnic dance. The **Washington Ballet** (☎ 202/362–3606) performs at the Kennedy Center and the Warner Theatre.

MUSIC

The **National Symphony Orchestra** (☎ 202/416–8100) performs at the Kennedy Center from September through June and during the summer at Wolf Trap Farm Park (☎ 703/255–1900; ☞ Virginia).

The **Armed Forces Concert Series** offers free military-band performances from June through August, nightly except Wednesday and Saturday, on the West Terrace of the Capitol and at the Sylvan Theater on the Washington Monument grounds. *☎ 202/767–5658 for Air Force, 703/696–3718 for Army, 202/433–4011 for Marines, 202/433–2525 for Navy.*

OPERA

The **Washington Opera** (☎ 202/416–7800 or 800/876–7372) presents seven operas each season in the Kennedy Center's Opera House and in Eisenhower Theater.

THEATER

Arena Stage (✉ 6th St. and Maine Ave. SW, ☎ 202/488–3300) has three theaters and is the city's most respected resident company. The historic **Ford's Theatre** (✉ 511 10th St. NW, ☎ 202/347–4833) is host mainly to musicals. The **National Theatre** (✉ 1321 Pennsylvania Ave. NW, ☎ 202/628–6161) presents tryouts and national touring companies of Broadway shows. The **Shakespeare Theatre** (✉ 450 7th St. NW, ☎ 202/393–2700) presents classics by the Bard. Many scrappy smaller companies—including the Source, the Studio, and the Woolly Mammoth—are clustered near 14th and P streets NW.

Spectator Sports

Basketball: Wizards (✉ USAirways Arena, 1 Harry S. Truman Dr., Landover, MD, ☎ 202/432–7328 or 800/551–7328 for tickets, 301/622–3865 for schedule).

Football: The **Redskins** have a new stadium in nearby Landover, Maryland (✉ New Redskin Stadium, ☎ 202/546–2222), with about 20,000 more seats than their old home at RFK Stadium, but all tickets are held by season-ticket holders. If you're willing to pay dearly, you can get tickets from brokers who advertise in the *Washington Post*.

Hockey: Capitals (✉ US Airways Arena, ☎ 202/432–7328, 800/551–7328 for tickets, 301/350–3400 for schedule).

Shopping

Shopping Districts

Georgetown (centered on Wisconsin Ave. and M St. NW) is probably Washington's densest shopping area, with specialty shops selling everything from antiques to designer fashions. **Adams-Morgan** (around 18th St. and Columbia Rd. NW) is a bit funkier, with used-book stores and vintage clothing shops and a bohemian atmosphere.

The **Shops at National Place** (✉ 13th and F Sts. NW, ☎ 202/783–9090) is a glittering three-story collection of stores, including a Sharper Image outlet store and clothing stores such as Powers & Goode and Oaktree. **Union Station** (✉ 50 Massachusetts Ave. NE, ☎ 202/371–9441) has clothing boutiques and special-interest shops. **Mazza Gallerie** (✉ 5300 Wisconsin Ave. NW, ☎ 202/966–6114) is an upmarket mall straddling the Maryland border that's anchored by the ritzy Neiman Marcus and a Filene's Basement.

Department Stores

With the closing in 1995 of the century-old Woodward & Lothrop chain, **Hecht's** (✉ 12th and G Sts. NW, ☎ 202/628–6661) is the sole downtown department store. It is near the Metro Center subway stop.

Specialty Stores

Every museum in Washington has a gift shop, and in each the range of items reflects the museum's collection and extends far beyond the mere souvenir. The largest is probably in the **National Museum of American History** (☞ Exploring Washington, D.C., *above*). The **Indian Craft Shop,** in the Department of the Interior (✉ 1849 C St. NW, ☎ 202/208–4056), sells a variety of handicrafts from more than a dozen Native American tribes.

WEST VIRGINIA

By Dale
Leatherman

Updated by
Therese S. Cox

Capital	Charleston
Population	1,826,000
Motto	Mountaineers Are Always Free
State Bird	Cardinal
State Flower	Rhododendron maximum
Postal Abbreviation	WV

Statewide Visitor Information

West Virginia Division of Tourism (✉ 2101 Washington St. E, Charleston 25305, ☎ 304/558–2200 or 800/225–5982, ℻ 304/558–0108).

Scenic Drives

In the eastern mountains a **National Scenic Byway** (W.Va. 39/55 and connecting W.Va. 150) roams between Richwood and U.S. 219/W.Va. 55 north of Edray, in the Monongahela National Forest. The **Midland Trail** follows historic U.S. 60, running east–west for 120 mi between White Sulphur Springs (location of the Greenbrier Resort) and Charleston, tracing the 200-year-old path through the Appalachians first used by buffalo and Native Americans. The **Coal Heritage Trail** leads from Beckley into the coalfields of Wyoming, McDowell, and Mercer counties along W.Va. 16 and U.S. 52.

National and State Parks

National Parks

Harpers Ferry National Historical Park (✉ Box 65, Harpers Ferry 25425, ☎ 304/535–6223) is situated at the picturesque confluence of the Potomac and Shenandoah rivers. The **New River Gorge National River** (☎ 304/465–0508), a 53-mi section of the New River, contains a wide variety of some of America's best white-water recreation. The **Monongahela National Forest** (✉ 200 Sycamore St., Elkins 26241, ☎ 304/636–1800) and **George Washington National Forest** (✉ Lee Ranger District, Rte. 4, Box 515, Edinburg, VA 22824, ☎ 703/984–4101, ℻ 703/984–8989) encompass 900,000 and 100,000 acres, respectively, near the Virginia border.

State Parks

West Virginia is unique in that 8 of its 35 state parks have fine lodges with restaurants and resort amenities, such as downhill skiing or championship golf courses. Most have cottages, cabins, and campsites with full hookups. **Cacapon Resort State Park** (✉ Rte. 1, Box 304, Berkeley Springs 25411, ☎ 304/258–1022 or 800/225–5982) is noted for its Robert Trent Jones golf course; amenities include 30 cottages and a 49-room lodge with restaurant. At **Canaan Valley Resort State Park** (✉ Rte. 1, Box 330, Davis 26260, ☎ 304/866–4121 or 800/225–5982) the 250-room lodge, 23 deluxe cabins, restaurant, and lounge are bustling year-round; the park has an alpine-skiing area, an 18-hole golf course, and outdoor and indoor pools and fitness center. **Pipestem Resort State Park** (✉ Box 150, Pipestem 25979, ☎ 304/466–1800 or 800/225–5982), southeast of Beckley, has two lodges (143 rooms) with restaurants, 25 deluxe cottages, and 82 campsites, as well as golf, indoor and outdoor pools, an aerial tramway, and cross-country skiing.

EASTERN WEST VIRGINIA

West Virginia's easternmost counties are replete with captivating, yet largely unsung, Colonial and Civil War history. The towns of Harpers Ferry, Berkeley Springs, Charles Town, Martinsburg, and Shepherdstown predate the Revolutionary War, bear the scars of the Civil War, and have remained largely untouched architecturally in the past 50 years. To the west the scene changes to one of rugged splendor in a swath of mountain land blessed with Canadian weather patterns—and the ski industry to prove it. In the spring the focus shifts to white-water rafting on some of the nation's most exciting rivers.

Visitor Information

Potomac Highlands: Jefferson County Visitor and Convention Bureau (✉ Box A, Harpers Ferry 25425, ☎ 304/535–2627 or 800/848–8687); Martinsburg/Berkeley County Convention and Visitors Bureau (✉ 208 S. Queen St., Martinsburg 25401, ☎ 304/264–8801 or 800/498–2386). **Southern West Virginia:** Convention and Visitors Bureau (✉ Box 1799, Beckley 25802, ☎ 304/252–2244, FAX 304/252–2252); Travel Berkeley Springs (✉ 304 Fairfax St., Berkeley Springs 25411, ☎ 304/258–9147 or 800/447–8797).

Arriving and Departing

By Bus
Greyhound Lines (☎ 800/231–2222) has terminals in major towns.

By Car
Three interstates traverse the region: I–64, between White Sulphur Springs and Beckley; I–77, Princeton to Charleston; and I–81, in the eastern panhandle. U.S. 340 enters Harpers Ferry from the east. From the west U.S. 50, I–79, and I–64 provide the best access.

By Plane
The region is served by Beckley's **Raleigh County Memorial Airport** (☎ 304/255–0476), Chantilly's **Dulles International Airport** (☎ 703/419–8000), Hagerstown's **Washington County Regional Airport** (☎ 301/791–3333), Lewisburg's **Greenbrier's Valley Airport** (☎ 304/645–3961), and Winchester's **Winchester Regional Airport** (☎ 540/662–5786).

By Train
Amtrak (☎ 800/872–7245) has stations in Harpers Ferry and Martinsburg.

Exploring Eastern West Virginia

Old and new mingle here in surprising harmony. In the eastern panhandle you can explore pre-Revolutionary buildings, shop for the latest in fashions, and relax in a Roman bath, all in the same day. To the west and south the mountain roads are scenic but sometimes narrow and limited to 40 mph. Do your driving in the daytime to enjoy the many overlooks and small towns reminiscent of the 1950s.

★ At the Panhandle's southeastern tip is **Harpers Ferry National Historical Park** (☞ National and State Parks, *above*), where the Shenandoah and Potomac rivers join. Hand-carved stone steps lead to the overlook where Thomas Jefferson proclaimed the view "worth a trip across the Atlantic." The township of Harpers Ferry grew around a U.S. armory built in 1740, and many buildings have been preserved.

Lining the cobblestone streets are shops and museums, where park employees in period costume demonstrate Early American skills and interpret the evolution of American firearms. Each second Saturday in October the park service stages Election Day 1860, when the presidential candidates on the slate in that region come once again to debate the hot topics of their day: states' rights versus a strong federal union. The **John Brown Wax Museum** depicts the abolitionist's raid on the town. ☎ *304/535–6342. Closed weekdays Dec.–Mar.*

Charles Town, named for George Washington's brother, who was an early resident, is irrevocably linked with Harpers Ferry, for it is where John Brown was hanged for treason. The Jefferson County Courthouse here houses a museum that includes among its artifacts the wagon that delivered Brown to his fate on the courthouse square.

In **Martinsburg** (☞ Shopping, *below*) two **pre–Civil War roundhouses** (circular buildings for housing and repairing locomotives) at the foot of Martin Street attract today's railroad buffs, though they're in poor condition. Downtown, pre–Civil War structures of Federal and Greek Revival style can be seen on John, Race, and North Spring streets.

Shepherdstown, on the Potomac River northwest of Harpers Ferry, is one of the region's oldest towns, established in 1730 as Mechlenberg. Today its quaint wooden storefronts and tree-lined brick streets form the framework for a collection of specialty shops, small inns, and restaurants that lure city folk from the Washington-Baltimore area.

Berkeley Springs was officially chartered in 1776 as the Town of Bath by George Washington and speculating friends, who envisioned the site of the ancient healing springs as a spa. The buoyant warm waters still flow freely, attracting a thriving community of massage therapists, practitioners of homeopathy, and artists. A variety of small inns, antiques shops, spa retreats, and services make it a year-round haven for relaxation. **Berkeley Springs State Park** (☎ 304/258–2711 or 800/225–5982) offers heated Roman baths and massages.

★ A southwesterly route leads through the Potomac Highlands, an area with boundless opportunity for outdoor recreation, to the **National Radio Astronomy Observatory,** in Green Bank, where huge radio telescopes listen for life in outer space. Bus tours and a slide presentation are available. ✉ *Rte. 28/92,* ☎ *304/456–2011. Closed weekdays Sept.–Oct. No tours Nov.–mid-May.*

Cass Scenic Railroad State Park encompasses an authentic turn-of-the-century lumber-company town and offers visitors a tow up to the second-highest peak in West Virginia in open railcars once used to haul logs off the mountain. Trains are drawn by geared Shay steam locomotives, built at the turn of the century to negotiate steep terrain. Massive flooding in the winter of 1996 affected the train schedule; call for specific information. ✉ *Rte. 66, Cass,* ☎ *304/456–4300 or 800/225–5982. Closed Nov.–mid-May.*

The **Lewisburg National Historic District** (✉ U.S. 219, ☎ 304/645–1000 or 800/833–2068) encompasses 236 acres and more than 60 18th-century buildings, many of native limestone or brick. At night gas lamps flicker on quaint storefronts and signs, and no overhead power lines spoil the image of a bygone era.

The mammoth **State Fair of West Virginia** (✉ 3 mi south of I–64 on Rte. 219, Lewisburg, ☎ 304/645–1090) each day offers livestock shows, harness racing, crafts, and famous entertainers. Each summer some of the foremost folk artists in the United States teach 90 week-long classes—like old-time fiddle playing, log-house construction, and white-oak rib basketry—at the **Augusta Heritage Workshops** (✉ 300 Sycamore St., Elkins 26241, ☎ 304/636–1800) at Davis & Elkins College. The engineering marvel of the New River Gorge Bridge, the world's longest steel arch span, is celebrated annually the third Saturday in October near Fayetteville. More than 200 food and crafts vendors sell their wares while festival goers watch parachutists leap hundreds of feet above the New River Gorge.

What to See and Do with Children

With its many outdoor sports, this area is one big natural amusement park. Rafting is suitable for children as young as five or six on specific sections of all commercially run rivers except the Gauley. All vacation and resort state parks offer free Junior Naturalist programs for children. **Potomac Eagle Scenic Rail Excursions** (⊠ Romney, ☎ 800/223–2453) takes passengers in vintage railcars into the wilderness of the South Branch of the Potomac River, where bald eagle sightings are common. The **Southern West Virginia Youth Museum** (⊠ New River Park, Beckley, ☎ 304/252–3730) offers a permanent village of reconstructed or relocated log structures that depict agricultural life in the area before the advent of mining. The **Beckley Exhibition Coal Mine** (☎ 304/256–1747) has 1,500 ft of restored passages open for guided tours; it's closed from November through Easter.

Dining and Lodging

Real West Virginia cooking is hearty, simple, and usually homemade from local ingredients—buckwheat cakes for breakfast, beef stew for lunch, brook trout or game for dinner—but more urbane fare is often available. As for accommodations, you can find everything from the Ritz to motels where "the light's always left on for you," but local bed-and-breakfasts (☎ 800/225–5982 for B&B listings and booklet) afford the best access to the state's greatest treasure: its people. For price ranges *see* Charts 1 (B) and 2 (B) *in* On the Road with Fodor's.

Berkeley Springs

$$ ✕ **Country Inn.** This restaurant's atmosphere suits its name—lots of natural wood and old prints. The best menu choices are crab cakes or lamb. ⊠ *207 S. Washington St.,* ☎ *304/258–2210 or 800/822–6630. AE, D, DC, MC, V.*

$$ 🏨 **Cacapon Resort State Park.** Locally crafted heavy oak pieces fur-
★ nish the main lodge's rooms and woodsy dining room, which overlook the golf course or Cacapon Ridge. Rustic cabins are tucked into the surrounding woods. ⊠ *Off U.S. 522, Rte. 1 (Box 304), Berkeley Springs, 25411,* ☎ *304/258–1022,* 𝖥𝖠𝖷 *304/258–5323. 49 rooms, 30 cabins. Restaurant, lake, golf course, tennis courts. AE, MC, V.*

Davis

$$ ✕ **Blackwater Falls State Park.** The stone-pillared dining room, furnished in handmade red oak, perches on the rim of the Blackwater Canyon. Diners' favorites are the breakfast bar, charbroiled chicken breast, and prime rib. ⊠ *Rte. 32 to Blackwater Falls State Park Rd.,* ☎ *304/259–5216,* 𝖥𝖠𝖷 *304/259–5881. AE, MC, V.*

$–$$ 🏨 **Canaan Valley Resort State Park.** The rooms here are motel style but spacious, and the resort's wooded setting is superb. ⊠ *Rte. 1, Box 330, 26260,* ☎ *304/866–4121 or 800/622–4121,* 𝖥𝖠𝖷 *304/866–2172. 250 rooms, 23 cabins. Restaurant, lounge, indoor and outdoor pools, golf course, downhill skiing, ice-skating. AE, D, DC, MC, V.*

Durbin

$$$ ✕🏨 **Cheat Mountain Club.** Originally an exclusive men's sports hide-
★ away, this 100-year-old hand-hewn-spruce log cabin is surrounded by

the 901,000-acre Monongahela National Forest and close to skiing, hiking, mountain biking, and hunting. The pine-paneled guest rooms on the lodge's second floor are functionally decorated and immaculately kept. Hearty homemade fare is on the restaurant's three daily menus. Prime rib and lemon-pepper pasta with lemon zest, olive oil, and garlic are typical dinner entrées. ⊠ *Rte. 250 (Box 28), Durbin 26264,* ☎ *304/456–4627,* FAX *304/456–3192. 9 rooms and 5-bed dormitory. FAP. Horseshoes, fishing, 2 meeting rooms. MC, V.*

Shepherdstown

$$–$$$　✕▥ **Bavarian Inn and Lodge.** In four alpine chalets overlooking the Potomac River, the Bavarian has luxurious rooms with canopy beds, fireplaces, and whirlpool tubs. The dining areas are decorated with antiques and fine china. The German and American cuisine includes wild pheasant, venison, and boar. ⊠ *Rte. 1 (Box 30), 25443,* ☎ *304/876–2551,* FAX *304/876–9355. 42 units. Restaurant, pool, tennis courts, bicycles. AE, DC, MC, V.*

Snowshoe/Slatyfork

$$$–$$$$　✕ **Red Fox Restaurant.** A cozy tavern room, plush seating, and greenhouse windows distinguish this restaurant, as do its extensive menu and exceptional service. The chefs use local meats, fish, herbs, and cheeses for such specialties as wild game pâtés or roast quail cooked with apples, country ham, sausages, and applejack brandy. ⊠ *Snowshoe Mountain Resort, off U.S. 219,* ☎ *304/572–2222. AE, D, MC, V.*

$–$$$　▥ **Snowshoe/Silver Creek Mountain Resort.** This resort can accommodate up to 9,000 guests; lodging varies from motel-style rooms to luxury condos. Snowshoe has an assortment of natural-wood structures in the forest fringing the ski slopes, and Silver Creek has lodgings in a high-rise. ⊠ *Off U.S. 219; 10 Snowshoe Rd., 26209,* ☎ *304/572–1000,* FAX *Ext. 268. 1,250 houses and condos, 302 lodge rooms. 22 restaurants, pubs and clubs, 4 indoor pools, 2 spas, golf course, tennis courts, exercise room, downhill skiing. AE, MC, V.*

Motel

▥ **Holiday Inn** (⊠ 301 Foxcroft Ave., Martinsburg 25401, ☎ 304/267–5500 or 800/862–6282), 120 rooms, restaurant, lounge, indoor and outdoor pools, tennis courts, health club, parking; $–$$.

Spas

For price ranges *see* Chart 2 (A) *in* On the Road with Fodor's.

$$$$　▥ **The Greenbrier.** One of the leading resorts in the country, this 6,500-acre spa is done in grand turn-of-the-century style. Massive white columns rise six stories against a white facade, while inside nine lobbies offer vast, chandeliered common areas. Every guest room is different, decorated in Dorothy Draper pastel prints. Gourmet cuisine features such dishes as farm-raised striped bass and rack of lamb. ⊠ *Off I–64, White Sulphur Springs 24986,* ☎ *304/536–1110 or 800/624–6070,* FAX *304/536–7854 or 304/536–7834. 640 units. 4 dining rooms, lounge, indoor-outdoor pool, 3 golf courses, tennis, health club, horseback riding. AE, DC, MC, V.*

$–$$$　▥ **Coolfont Resort & Spectrum Spa.** Accommodations are in modern chalets, rustic cabins, or lodge rooms. Special programs for losing weight, reducing stress, and stopping smoking are offered. The soup-salad-bread bar is exceptional, as are the daily buffet and the fresh brook trout. ⊠ *1777 Cold Run Valley Rd., Berkeley Springs 25411,* ☎ *304/258–4500 or 800/296–8768,* FAX *304/258–5499. 82 units. Restaurant, lounge, indoor pool, lake, tennis, health club. AE, D, DC, MC, V.*

Campgrounds

State park camping facilities and more than 100 commercial camp-grounds are listed in a camping booklet (☎ 800/225–5982).

Nightlife and the Arts

West Virginians celebrate everything—from potatoes and apple but-ter to the coming of spring—with festivals and fairs (☎ 800/225–5982). At Grandview State Park's **Theatre West Virginia** (☎ 304/256–6800 or 800/666–9142), you'll find the state's premier outdoor theatrical productions: *Honey in the Rock,* a Civil War story; *Hatfields and Mc-Coys,* depicting the famous feud; and a different musical each season.

Outdoor Activities and Sports

Biking

Rentals, instruction, and tours are available from **Blackwater Bikes** (⊠ Davis, ☎ 304/259–5286), the **Elk River Touring Center** (⊠ Slatyfork, ☎ 304/572–3771), and **Snowshoe Mountain Biking Centers** (⊠ Snow-shoe, ☎ 304/572–1000).

Canoeing

The **Greenbrier River** is one of the country's best paddling rivers. Area outfitters can put you on this and other waterways; for a list of oper-ators contact the Division of Tourism (☞ Visitor Information, *above*).

Fishing

Trout are abundant in faster streams, while bass, crappie, and walleye lurk in big rivers and lakes. Licenses are available at sporting and con-venience stores. Most rafting companies organize fishing trips. **Elk Mountain Outfitters** (⊠ Corner Rte. 66 and Rte. 219; Box 8, Slatyfork 26291, ☎ 304/572–3000) offers fly-fishing schools and guided trout expeditions.

Golf

Cacapon and **Canaan Valley Resort state parks** (☞ National and State Parks, *above*) offer 18 holes each; the **Greenbrier,** in White Sulphur Springs (☞ Spas *in* Dining and Lodging, *above*), 54 holes; **Locust Hill** (☎ 304/728–7300), in Charles Town, 18 holes; **Pipestem Resort State Park** (☞ National and State Parks, *above*), 27 holes; **Stonebridge** (☎ 304/263–4653 or 800/490–3470), in Martinsburg, 18 holes; the **Woods** (☎ 304/754–7977 or 800/248–2222), in Hedgesville, 27 holes.

Hiking

State and national parks have extensive trail systems. The **Appalachian Trail** (⊠ Harpers Ferry 25425, ☎ 304/535–6331) and the **Big Blue Trail** (⊠ Potomac Appalachian Trail Club, 118 Park St. SE, Vienna, VA 22180, ☎ 703/242–0965) run through this region.

Horseback Riding

Horseback riding along trails is available in most state parks. Stables at **Glade Springs Resort & Conference Center** (⊠ 3000 Lake Dr., Daniels 25832, ☎ 800/634–5233) offer a variety of activities, from short rides to overnight expeditions and wagon rides. **Swift Level** (⊠ Rte. 2, Box 269-A, Lewisburg 24901, ☎ 304/645–1155) is a horse farm offering multiday long-distance treks for experienced equestrians.

Rafting

The **New, Gauley,** and **Cheat** are West Virginia's most heavily traveled rivers, followed by the **Tygart** and **Shenandoah.** First-timers can tackle all but the Gauley. For information on more than 30 commercial out-fitters that run white-water excursions, contact the Division of Tourism (☞ Visitor Information, *above*).

Ski Areas

Cross-Country

Elk River Touring Center (☞ Biking *in* Outdoor Activities and Sports, *above*) and the **White Grass Ski Touring Center** (⊠ Rte. 1, Box 299, Davis 26260, ☎ 304/866–4114) offer rentals, instruction, and tours.

Downhill

Call 800/225–5982 for snow conditions at these ski areas: **Canaan Valley Resort State Park** (⊠ Davis), 34 slopes and trails, 3 chairlifts, vertical drop 850 ft, 1¼-mi run; **Snowshoe/Silver Creek** (⊠ Snowshoe), 53 trails, 11 chairlifts, vertical drop 1,500 ft, 1½-mi run; **Timberline** (⊠ Davis), 35 trails, 3 chairlifts, vertical drop 1,000 ft, 2-mi run, 200-ft half-pipe for snowboarders; and **Winterplace** (⊠ Flat Top), 27 trails, 5 chairlifts, vertical drop 603 ft, 1¼-mi run.

Shopping

Fairs and festivals are plentiful and are perfect places to shop for mountain handicrafts; check with the state visitor center for a calendar of events. The wares of 1,500 artists and craftspeople whose works have passed muster with a state jury are sold at **Tamarack** (⊠ 1 Tamarack Park, ☎ 304/256–6843), a sprawling center opened in 1996, just off I–77. **Berkeley Springs** is home to two large antiques consortiums and several independent dealers in glass, collectibles, and political memorabilia. **Harpers Ferry's Bolivar District** houses wall-to-wall antiques and specialty shops. **Martinsburg** offers antiques stores and several outlet malls, including the **Blue Ridge Outlet Center** (⊠ Stephen and Queen Sts., ☎ 304/263–7467 or 800/445–3993), which houses 60 select manufacturers and designers of quality goods.

WESTERN WEST VIRGINIA

The Charleston-Huntington area is a center of commerce and culture quite different from the mountain wilderness to the east and the farmland to the north. Skilled craftspeople, such as those who supplied the Kennedy White House with glassware, make their homes in this area in the central Ohio River valley. Its northern panhandle suffers from steel-industry troubles, but its fine old mansions and Victorian architecture are reminders of better times. Wheeling's Oglebay Park is a cultural jewel and one of the finest municipal parks in the nation.

Visitor Information

Charleston: Convention and Visitors Bureau (⊠ 200 Civic Center Dr., 25301, ☎ 304/344–5075 or 800/733–5469, FAX 304/344–1421). **Huntington:** Cabell-Huntington Convention and Visitors Bureau (⊠ Box 347, 25708, ☎ 304/525–7333 or 800/635–6329). **Wheeling:** Convention and Visitors Bureau (⊠ 1233 Main St., Suite 1000, 26003, ☎ 304/233–7709 or 800/828–3097, FAX 304/233–1320). **Northern West Virginia:** Convention and Visitors Bureau (⊠ 709 Beechurst Ave., Morgantown 26505, ☎ 304/292–5081 or 800/458–7373, FAX 304/291–1354).

Arriving and Departing

By Car

Major routes covering the region are I–64W; I–77 north–south; I–79 north–south; U.S. 50 between Clarksburg and Parkersburg; and I–70 crossing the northern panhandle at Wheeling.

By Plane

The region is served by Charleston's **Yeager Airport** (☎ 304/344–8033 or 800/241–6522), Huntington's **Tri-State Airport** (☎ 304/453–6165), Parkersburg's **Wood County Airport** (☎ 304/464–5115), Clarksburg/Fairmont's **Benedum Airport** (☎ 304/842–3400), and the **Morgantown Municipal Airport/Hart Field** (☎ 304/291–7461).

By Train

Amtrak (☎ 800/872–7245) provides service from White Sulphur Springs through Charleston to Huntington.

Exploring Western West Virginia

This area is heavily influenced by the early history and commerce of the Ohio River. Charleston, Parkersburg, and Huntington set an urban tone with museums, shopping malls, and cultural and entertainment centers, but the hustle is balanced by lazy days on the river. Moving north through valley farmland, you can watch glassblowers and other craftspeople at work. The boom of the 1890s is reflected throughout the area in grand mansions and nicely preserved Victorian architecture.

Charleston, first settled in 1794, has been the state capital since 1885 and is the hub of the Great Kanawha Valley. The Italian Renaissance **capitol,** designed by Cass Gilbert in 1932, is considered one of America's most beautiful state capitols. From the massive gilt dome, which rises 300 ft above the street, hangs a 2-ton chandelier of Czechoslovakian hand-cut crystal. ⊠ *1900 Kanawha Blvd. E,* ☎ *304/558–3809. Closed Sun. Labor Day–Memorial Day; no guided tours on weekends.*

Within the capitol complex is the **Cultural Center** (⊠ Greenbrier and Washington Sts., ☎ 304/558–0220), with its marble **Great Hall** and the **State Museum,** which traces West Virginia history. **Mountain Stage,** a live contemporary-music radio show, is taped here before an audience 6–8 most Sunday evenings; each show has a different emphasis, from world beat to jazz, blues, folk and rock. Prices vary with the performance. ☎ *800/723–4687 for information, 304/342–5757 for tickets.*

Overlooking the capitol is **Sunrise Museum,** comprising two historic mansions that house art galleries, a hands-on science center, and a planetarium. Outside are 16 acres of wooded grounds with gardens and trails. ⊠ *746 Myrtle Rd.,* ☎ *304/344–8035. Closed Mon.–Tues.*

Downtown are a large civic center and the pleasant **Charleston Town Center** shopping area (☞ Shopping, *below*). Eight styles of 19th-century architecture are represented in the **East End Historic District,** bordered by Bradford, Quarrier, and Michigan streets and Kanawha Boulevard.

Charleston takes pride in downtown **Haddad Riverfront Park,** which bustles the week before Labor Day during the annual Sternwheeler Regatta. The paddle wheeler **P. A. Denny** (☎ 304/348–0709 or 304/348–6419) offers cruises year-round.

It takes an hour by I–64 to reach metropolitan **Huntington,** the state's second-largest city, a river and rail town whose meticulously laid out streets are lined with stately turn-of-the-century houses. In the **9th Street West Historic District** the streets are brick, the houses Victorian frame bordered with wrought-iron fences. The **Huntington Museum of Art,** the state's largest museum, covers 52 acres and houses the Junior Art Museum, a celestial observatory, and an amphitheater. ⊠ *2033 McCay Rd.,* ☎ *304/529–2701. Free Wed. Closed Mon.*

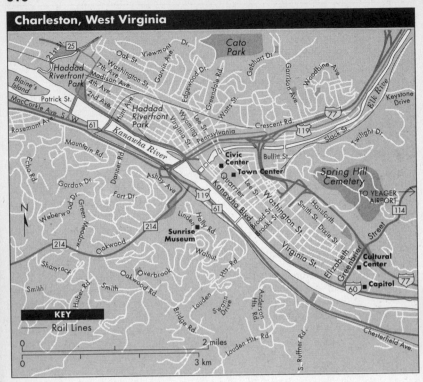

Charleston, West Virginia

KEY
Rail Lines

Near Huntington, at Milton, is the **Blenko Glass Visitor Center and Factory Outlet,** one of more than a dozen handblown-glass factories between Huntington and Parkersburg. ⊠ *Exit 28 off I–64 to U.S. 60,* ☎ *304/743–9081. No glassblowing weekends.*

Another thriving Ohio River town, Parkersburg has many restored turn-of-the-century houses, but its main attraction is **Blennerhassett Island Historical State Park.** In 1800 Harman Blennerhassett's magnificent island estate was the talk of the Northwest Territory, but he was later arrested with Aaron Burr for treason. Besides the Palladian-style mansion, you can visit a crafts village and take horse-drawn-wagon tours of the island, which is reached aboard a stern-wheeler. ⊠ *Blennerhassett Museum of Regional History, 2nd and Juliana Sts.,* ☎ *304/420–4800 or 800/225–5982. Island closed Nov.–Apr.*

In the heart of the state is the Mountain Lakes region, dotted with prime fishing areas (☞ Outdoor Activities and Sports, *below*) and a number of Civil War landmarks, such as **Carnifex Ferry Battlefield State Park.** The battle here dashed the South's hopes of controlling the Kanawha Valley. The **Patterson House,** which marked the line between Union and Confederate forces, has been restored as a museum. ⊠ *Rte. 2, Summersville at Carniflex Ferry Battlefield,* ☎ *304/872–0825. Museum closed Labor Day–Memorial Day.*

North of Clarksburg is **Morgantown,** both an industrial and educational center and known internationally for its glass. It is home of **West Virginia University,** where the world's first fully automated transportation system carries students between campuses. There's all the bustle of a college town here, plus the 1,700-acre **Cheat Lake,** which is served by three marinas (**Blosser's,** ☎ 304/594–2541; **Edgewater,** ☎ 304/594–2630; and **Sunset Harbor,** ☎ 304/594–1100).

In the northern panhandle, **Wheeling** was once the gateway to the West. Parks, museums, riverboat rides, and a wealth of restored Victorian houses—for instance, the **Design Co./Eckhart House** (☎ 304/232–5439) and **Victorian Wheeling Landmarks Foundation** (☎ 304/233–1600)—

★ are reminders of the old days. **Oglebay Resort** (☎ 304/243–4000 or 800/624–6988) is a 1,500-acre municipal park–resort with a hotel (☞ Dining and Lodging, *below*), a 65-acre petting zoo, planetarium, museum, indoor and outdoor swimming pools, naturalist programs for all ages, and two championship golf courses. From early November through late January both the park and downtown Wheeling explode into gigantic thematic displays for the premier **Winter Festival of Lights.**

What to See and Do with Children

Riverboating, fishing, and canoeing are prime attractions in this region. Charleston's **Sunrise Museum** and Wheeling's **Oglebay Park** (☞ Exploring Western West Virginia, *above*) are geared for children.

Dining and Lodging

For price ranges *see* Charts 1 (B) and 2 (B) *in* On the Road with Fodor's.

Morgantown

$$ ✕🏨 **Lakeview Resort and Conference Center.** This country club turned
★ resort sits on a dramatic cliff overlooking Cheat Lake. Comfortable motel-style rooms are accessed by a warren of halls and stairways. Restaurants have lake or golf course views, and the popular lounge features live entertainment on the weekend. Two golf courses and a $2 million fitness center boost the convention trade. Prime rib and poached salmon are the main attractions in the Reflections on the Lake Restaurant. The Grill Restaurant serves a light, healthy fare. ✉ *Rte. 6 (Box 88A), 26505,* ☎ *304/594–1111 or 800/624–8300,* 🕿 *304/594–9472. 187 rooms. 2 restaurants, lounge, 2 pools, lake, 2 golf courses, tennis courts, exercise room, jogging, racquetball. AE, D, DC, MC, V.*

St. Albans

$$ ✕ **Chilton House.** Fifteen miles west of Charleston, in a charming Vic-
★ torian house with seven gables, this restaurant overlooks the Coal River. Menu highlights include oysters Rockefeller, orange roughy with sesame sauce, and steak Diane flambé. ✉ *2 6th Ave.,* ☎ *304/722–2918. AE, D, MC, V. Closed Sun.*

Wheeling

$$–$$$ ✕🏨 **Stratford Springs.** This historic inn, composed of two turn-of-the-
★ century houses, is secluded on 30 wooded acres. The rooms are Colonial style, with cherry-wood or Amish furniture. Among the restaurants, which cater mainly to nonguests, the formal Stratford Room (jacket and tie) serves such dishes as stuffed strip steak and baby coho salmon. ✉ *355 Oglebay Dr., 26003,* ☎ *304/233–5100 or 800/521–8435,* 🕿 *304/232–6447. 6 rooms. 4 restaurants, pool, spa, exercise room. AE, MC, V.*

$$–$$$ 🏨 **Oglebay Resort and Conference Center.** Connected to the rustic lodge, which has a huge stone-floor lobby and a stone fireplace, are motel-style rooms and once-detached chalets. Nearby cabins sleeping 12 to 20 are rustic outside and ultramodern inside. ✉ *Rte. 88N,* ☎ *304/243–4000 or 800/624–6988,* 🕿 *304/243–4070. 204 lodge rooms, 16 suites, 50 deluxe cabins. Dining room, indoor and outdoor pools, lake, golf, tennis, horseback riding. AE, D, DC, MC, V.*

Motel

☷ **Charleston Marriott** (✉ 200 Lee St. E, Charleston 25301, ☎ 304/
345–6500 or 800/228–9290, FAX 304/353–3722), 354 rooms, 2 restau-
rants, lounge, indoor pool, tennis, health club; $$.

Campgrounds

The state tourism department (☞ Visitor Information, *above*) has list-
ings of commercial campgrounds as well as facilities in more than a
dozen state parks.

Nightlife and the Arts

Wheeling's **Capitol Music Hall** (✉ 1015 Main St., ☎ 800/624–5456),
home of WWVA radio's *Jamboree USA,* has live performances by
country music greats and two big-name jamborees in July and August.

Outdoor Activities and Sports

Canoeing

The area's many **lakes** (contact the Army Corps of Engineers, ☎ 304/
529–5211) are ideal for canoeing.

Fishing

Native trout are abundant in the faster streams and rivers, while bass,
crappie, and walleye lurk in the lakes. Licenses are available at sport-
ing and convenience stores. Rafting companies organize fishing trips.
Sutton Lake (✉ Sutton, ☎ 304/765–2705) and **Stonewall Jackson Lake**
(✉ Weston, ☎ 304/269–0523) are prime areas.

Golf

Coonskin Golf Course (✉ 2000 Coonskin Dr., Charleston, ☎ 304/341–
8013), 18 holes. **Lakeview Resort's Lakeview and Mountainview
courses** (✉ 1 Lakeview Dr., Morgantown, ☎ 304/594–1111 or 800/
624–8300), 36 holes. **Oglebay Park's Crispin and Speidel courses** (✉
Oglebay, Rte. 88N, Wheeling, ☎ 304/243–4000 or 800/624–6988),
36 holes. **Twin Falls Resort State Park Golf Course** (✉ Rte. 97, Mul-
lens, ☎ 304/294–4000 or 800/225–5982), 18 holes. **Worthington
Golf Club** (✉ 3414 Roseland Ave., Parkersburg, ☎ 304/428–4297),
18 holes.

Hiking and Backpacking

The **Allegheny Trail** (✉ 633 West Virginia Ave., Morgantown 26505,
☎ 304/296–5158) and the **Kanawha Trace** (✉ 733 7th Ave., Hun-
tington 25701, ☎ 304/523–3408) pass through state and national forests
and wilderness areas with rocky overlooks and thickets of rhododen-
dron and mountain laurel.

Rafting

The white waters of the **Cheat** and **Tygart** rivers flow through this re-
gion. Call 800/225–5982 for brochures on guided trips and a list of
more than 50 licensed outfitters.

Shopping

Antiques and local crafts, particularly handblown glass, are abundant
in this region. Venues vary from roadside shops to outdoor fairs to
sprawling glass-factory outlets (☞ Exploring Western West Virginia,
above). The largest showcase of West Virginia wares is displayed dur-
ing July 4th week at the **Mountain State Art & Craft Fair** (☎ 800/225–
5982), in Ripley. In downtown Charleston is the **Charleston Town
Center** (✉ Quarrier and Lee Sts., ☎ 304/345–9525), with 165 shops
adjacent to the Charleston Marriott Town Center.

5 The Southeast

Alabama, Florida, Georgia, North Carolina, South Carolina

By Conrad Paulus

Updated by Jane F. Garvey

From pine to palm, lapped by the Atlantic Ocean and the Gulf of Mexico, stretch North and South Carolina, Georgia, Florida, and Alabama. Celluloid stereotypes portray southerners as dreaming life away on the veranda, julep in hand, among the magnolias and Spanish moss. Certainly, there are verandas. Magnolias still bloom. Spanish moss drapes trees growing along coastal lowlands. And certainly, too, the Southeast retains its taste for history, especially its own, but nowadays the Southeast is clearly dealing in the present and planning for tomorrow as it vigorously competes with the rest of the country and, indeed, the world for business and economic development.

With the exception of Florida, all these states have both mountains (with resorts and sports) and seashore (with beaches and boating); in Florida the coast is never more than 50 mi away. It's a good thing, too, because the region's temperatures and humidity are fierce, although air-conditioning has transformed the summers. Southerners, chiefly wealthy ones, often sought refuge from the region's legendary heat in the highlands and piney woods of the Carolinas and northern Georgia. Today these areas are highly regarded resort destinations.

It's commonly held that following the Civil War the South entered a period of economic decay from which it has only recently emerged. In fact, huge fortunes—consider Coca-Cola—were made in the South after the war. It was the Great Depression that brought much economic disruption to the region. Post-depression poverty prevented much of the tearing down and rebuilding common in the rest of the East and forced people to make do with that outmoded old Empire and Victorian furniture they had hoped to replace with the new machine-made marvels.

The Southeast

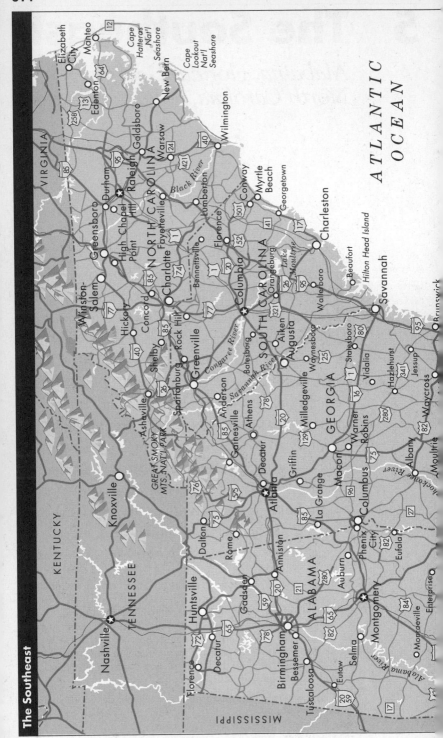

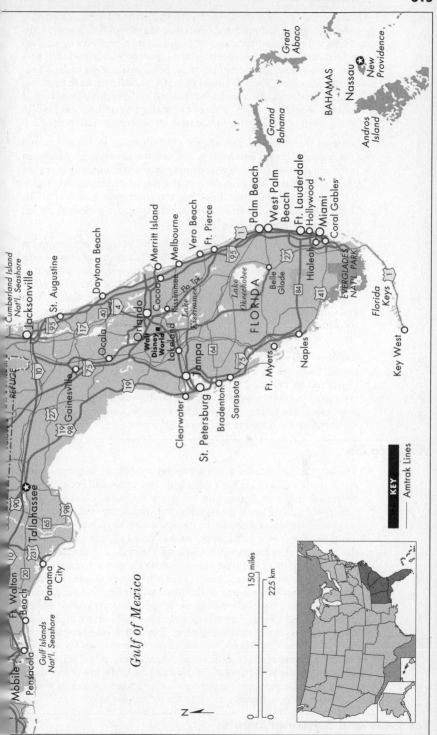

It also caused many of the classic homes to suffer decay and, sometimes, to be demolished. But much has been retained and restored. Today dozens of Greek Revival and Victorian mansions containing their original furnishings are open during special festival times to visitors, while others have become house museums open to the public on a regular basis. White-columned houses, some in advanced states of disrepair, have been rescued and restored, often converted into bed-and-breakfast inns, so that travelers may today sleep in those tall mahogany and walnut beds in which wealthy 19th-century plantation owners once slumbered.

Some of the cities are charmingly old-fashioned; in Savannah and Charleston, Edenton and Mobile, you can wander through houses on shady squares with brick courtyards and gardens of astonishing fecundity. There are modern cities, too: the dynamic research triangle of Raleigh–Durham–Chapel Hill; the booming transportation hub that is Atlanta; Birmingham, the steel town that today also is a medical center; and Miami, infused with Cuban culture.

Food in the Southeast today is as adventurous as regional fare can be: You may savor anything from fancy nouvelle cuisine to down-home country food and dishes drawn from the plantation tradition. And to come South and fail to taste barbecue, with all its subregional variations, is to miss the treat of a lifetime. But there's more. Spicy Cajun and Caribbean restaurants, authentic Asian and Mexican restaurants reflecting the tastes of new immigrants, and classic Italian and French fare all make dining in the Southeast a rich experience.

And there's always that well-regarded southern hospitality, perhaps inherited from the region's Celtic roots. "Y'all come, hear?" is an oft-heard, and oft-parodied, invitation. But it is usually extended in earnest. If you take it seriously and show up, you can bet you'll be greeted warmly. Southerners are an easygoing bunch—talkative, courteous, and witty, with a talent for laughing and enjoying life.

When to Go

The best times to visit the South are **spring** and **fall,** when temperatures are in the 70s and 80s. That's when golf and tennis buffs converge on the region en masse. Spring also brings the magnificent azaleas, magnolias, and other flora of the region to life, and visitors come to "ooh" and "aah" their way through the gardens and historic homes that traditionally open to the public at this time of year. Fall, when colors reach their peak in the mountains of Alabama, Georgia, and the Carolinas, draws thousands of leaf worshipers. Autumn is also a popular season for senior citizens to visit the region, taking advantage of smaller crowds and lower rates in beach and resort areas. **Winter** can be quite pleasant in the Southeast, especially in the more temperate, lower coastal regions of Georgia and Florida. In the higher elevations of western North Carolina and Georgia, temperatures often drop to freezing between mid-November and mid-March, producing ideal conditions for area ski resorts. **Summer** tends to be hot and muggy, with temperatures often soaring into the 90s, especially in Florida and at the lower elevations of Alabama, Georgia, and the Carolinas. That's when flatlanders (mountain slang for nonresidents) flock to the mountains to cool off.

Festivals and Seasonal Events

Festivals are a way of life in the Southeast. Even the smallest communities have planned celebrations around offbeat and often obscure themes, such as chitterlings (pronounced chitlins), hog-calling and -hollering contests, and the woolly worm.

Winter

EARLY NOV.–LATE DEC.➤ **Salem Christmas** (☎ 910/721–7300 or 888/653–7253) is celebrated in Old Salem, the restored 18th-century village once home to the Moravians, a Protestant sect, in **Winston-Salem, North Carolina.**

LATE NOV.–DEC.➤ **Christmas at Biltmore** (☎ 800/543–2961) brings six weeks of festive decorations, musical concerts, and candlelighted tours to this **North Carolina** estate.

EARLY DEC.➤ The **Atlanta Festival of Trees** (☎ 404/264–9348) celebrates the Christmas season with a parade and exhibit of elaborately decorated trees and wreaths.

MID-JAN.➤ **Art Deco Weekend** (☎ 305/539–3000) spotlights **Miami Beach**'s historic district with a street fair, a gala, and live entertainment.

LATE JAN.–EARLY FEB.➤ **Gasparilla Pirate Fest** (☎ 813/223–1111), in **Tampa, Florida,** celebrates Tampa's Hispanic heritage with a parade and other street festivities.

FEB.➤ **Black History Month** is observed throughout the South, with special events at many bookstores, universities, and other cultural venues, including **Tuskegee University** (☎ 334/727–8837), in **Tuskegee, Alabama,** and **Southern University** (☎ 504/771–3260), in **Baton Rouge, Louisiana.**

MID-FEB.➤ **Mardi Gras** in **Mobile, Alabama** (☎ 334/434–7304 or 800/252–3862), is an uproarious, pre-Lenten celebration similar to its more famous cousin in New Orleans. The **Miami Film Festival** (☎ 305/377–3456) screens 10 days of international, U.S., and local films. The **Florida Manatee Festival** (☎ 352/795–3149), in **Crystal River,** focuses on both the river and the endangered manatee.

FEB.–MAR.➤ The **Winter Equestrian Festival** (☎ 407/798–7000), at the Palm Beach Polo and Country Club in **West Palm Beach, Florida,** includes more than 1,000 horses and three grand prix equestrian events.

Spring

EARLY MAR.➤ The **Annual Sanibel Shell Fair** (☎ 813/472–2155), which runs for four days starting the first Thursday of the month, is the largest event of the year on **Sanibel Island, Florida.**

MID-MAR.➤ In South Carolina, the **Aiken Triple Crown** (☎ 803/641–1111), featuring Thoroughbred trials, harness races, and steeplechases, draws thousands of equestrian enthusiasts.

MID-MAR.–EARLY MAY➤ **Springtime Tallahassee** (☎ 904/224–5012) is a major cultural, sporting, and culinary event in Florida's capital.

MAR. 17➤ The **St. Patrick's Day Celebration** in **Savannah, Georgia** (☎ 800/444–2427), is one of the country's largest honoring Ireland's patron saint.

EARLY APR.➤ The **Master's Golf Tournament** (☎ 706/721–3276), in **Augusta, Georgia,** attracts top golf pros to this tournament of tournaments.

LATE APR.–EARLY MAY➤ Florida's **Daytona Beach Music Festival** (☎ 800/881–2473), held over four consecutive weekends, features concerts by marching, jazz, and stage bands, choirs, and orchestras.

MID-MAY–EARLY JUNE➤ **Spoleto Festival USA** (☎ 803/722–2764), a festival featuring world-renowned performers and artists, in **Charleston, South Carolina,** gets global attention.

LATE MAY➤ Over Memorial Day **Greenville, South Carolina,** celebrates **Freedom Weekend Aloft** (☎ 864/232–3700), the second-largest balloon rally in the country.

Summer

EARLY JUNE➤ The **Sun Fun Festival** (☎ 800/356–3016), in **Myrtle Beach, South Carolina,** features beauty-queen contests, sand sculpting, and other activities.

MID-JULY➤ The **Annual Highland Games and Gathering of the Scottish Clans** (☎ 704/733–1333 or 800/468–7325), held in the high meadows of **Grandfather Mountain in North Carolina,** is one of the largest Scottish celebrations in the world.

MID–LATE JULY➤ The **Hemingway Days Festival** (☎ 305/294–1136) holds look-alike contests as well as first-novel and short-story competitions in **Key West, Florida.**

LATE JULY➤ The **Folkmoot USA: North Carolina International Folk Festival** (☎ 704/452–2997), held in **Haywood County** and surrounding areas over a two-week period, spotlights dancers and singers from around the globe.

Autumn

MID-SEPT.➤ The **Arts Festival of Atlanta** (☎ 404/885–1125), held over nine days, is the largest arts-and-crafts festival in the Southeast. At the **Tuscumbia, Alabama**'s Music Hall of Fame, the annual **Harvest Jam** (☎ 205/381–4417 or 800/239–2643) draws top country musicians on the second Saturday of the month.

EARLY OCT.➤ The annual **Indian Key Festival** (☎ 305/664–4815), in Florida, celebrates the Key's history the first weekend of the month.

MID-OCT.➤ **Alabama's National Shrimp Festival** (☎ 800/745–7263), held in **Gulf Shores,** celebrates with seafood, arts and crafts, music, sky divers, and hot-air balloons. **Pig Jig** (☎ 912/268–8275), in **Vienna, Georgia,** attracts more than 100 entrants to compete for championships in several barbecue categories (ribs, shoulders, whole hog), plus hollering competitions, a beauty pageant, a parade, and plenty of music.

MID-NOV.➤ The annual **Miami Book Fair International** (☎ 305/237–3258), the largest book fair in the United States, is held on the Miami-Dade Community College Wolfson Campus.

Getting Around

By Boat

Traveling by boat along the Southeast's extensive waterways and rivers is quite a popular (and in some cases essential) mode of transportation. The **Intracoastal Waterway,** which extends from New England around Florida to the Gulf of Mexico, is filled with north–south traffic, and many of the region's major rivers are navigable. Ferries connect major islands and the mainlands of Alabama, the Carolinas, Georgia, and Florida. For more information on waterways and ferry schedules, contact the highway departments of individual states.

By Bus

The major intercity carrier is **Greyhound Lines** (☎ 800/231–2222).

By Car

More than a dozen interstate highways, including I–10, I–16, I–20, I–26, I–40, I–59, I–65, I–75, I–77, I–85, and I–95, crisscross the Southeast, linking major cities and providing easy access to other parts of the country. In some cases interstates and federal highways, such as U.S. 1 along the Florida Keys, link the region's many islands to the mainland. In other cases ferries (☞ By Boat, *above*) are the only means of transport. Scenic highways include South Carolina's Foothills Parkway and the Blue Ridge Parkway, the latter traversing the Virginia and North Carolina mountains. Interstate and federal highways are usually well maintained; some secondary roads are narrow, a few unpaved, and in mountain sections roads are often very curvy.

By Plane

The region is served by most major domestic airlines, including American, Continental, Delta, Northwest, Southwest, TWA, United, US Airways, and several foreign carriers. Some of the busiest airports in the nation and the world are in the Southeast, including Atlanta's **Hartsfield International Airport** (☎ 404/530–6600), **Miami International Airport** (☎ 305/876–7000), and **Orlando International Airport** (☎ 407/825–2352). Other major airports in the region are **Birmingham International Airport** (☎ 205/595–0533), in Alabama; **Charleston International Airport** (☎ 803/767–1100), in South Carolina; and **Charlotte–Douglas International Airport** (☎ 704/359–4000), in North Carolina.

By Train

Amtrak (☎ 800/872–7245) provides service to major southern cities including Charlotte, North Carolina; Charleston and Columbia, South Carolina; Atlanta and Savannah, Georgia; Miami and Orlando, Florida; and Birmingham and Mobile, Alabama.

ALABAMA

Updated by
Lynn Grisard
Fullman

Capital	Montgomery
Population	4,273,000
Motto	We Dare Defend Our Rights
State Bird	Yellowhammer
State Flower	Camellia
Postal Abbreviation	AL

Statewide Visitor Information

Alabama Bureau of Tourism and Travel (⊠ 401 Adams Ave., Box 4927, Montgomery 36103, ☎ 334/242–4169 or 800/252–2262). **Welcome centers:** I–59 near Valley Head, I–59 at Cuba, I–65 at Elkmont, I–10 north of Seminole, I–10 at Grand Bay, I–20 east of Heflin, I–85 at Lanett, U.S. 231 south of Dothan.

Scenic Drives

Lookout Mountain Parkway is a 100-mi scenic stretch in northeastern Alabama encompassing Routes 117, 89, and 176; markers indicate routes for side trips to Little River Canyon, DeSoto Falls, and Yellow Creek Falls. Maps are available at the welcome center off I–59 near the Georgia state line (☎ 205/635–6522). In and around Mobile, the well-marked **Azalea Trail** twines for 27 mi; the blooms are at their best in March and April.

State Parks

Alabama's 24 state parks include a wide variety of recreational activities and lodging accommodations. Visitors have the choice of resort lodges, hotels, campgrounds, chalets, and cabins, both modern and rustic. Several parks have marinas, golf courses, and tennis facilities. **DeSoto State Park,** in northern Alabama, has the spectacular Little River Canyon and falls. **Lake Guntersville State Park,** also in the northern part of the state, is home of the annual Eagle Awareness programs. **Gulf State Park,** near Gulf Shores, has one of the most popular beach areas along the Alabama coast. Contact **Alabama State Parks** (⊠ 64 N. Union St., Folsom Administrative Bldg., Suite 547, Montgomery 36130, ☎ 800/252–7275) for reservations or information on Alabama's state parks.

NORTH AND CENTRAL ALABAMA

This region encompasses the hilly Highlands around Birmingham, the state's largest city, and the state capital, Montgomery, with its antebellum history, 90 mi south of Birmingham.

Visitor Information

Birmingham: Convention and Visitors Bureau (⊠ 2200 9th Ave. N, 35203-1100, ☎ 205/458–8000 or 800/458–8085). **Montgomery:** Area Chamber of Commerce and Visitor Center (⊠ 401 Madison Ave., 36104, ☎ 334/240–9455 or 800/240–9452).

Arriving and Departing

By Bus

Greyhound Lines (⊠ 619 N. 19th St., Birmingham; 950 W. South Blvd., Montgomery; ☎ 800/231–2222) serves major towns.

By Car

I–59 runs northeast from Birmingham into Georgia and Tennessee and southwest into Mississippi. I–20 runs east–west through Birmingham. I–65 is the north–south route connecting Birmingham with Montgomery. I–85 leads southwest from Atlanta to Montgomery.

By Plane

Major airlines serve **Birmingham International Airport** (☎ 205/599–0500). Montgomery's **Dannelly Field** (☎ 334/281–5040) is served by many carriers.

By Train

Amtrak (☎ 800/872–7245) serves Birmingham and Mobile.

Exploring North and Central Alabama

Birmingham blossomed with the development of coal mines and the iron industry in the 19th century. Today its largest employer is the University of Alabama at Birmingham, home to one of the country's largest medical centers. The city has restored many of its 19th-century buildings and is a hospitable and beautiful metropolis.

The **Birmingham Museum of Art,** the Southeast's largest municipal museum, has some 18,000 works, from Italian Early Renaissance to contemporary American. ⊠ *8th Ave. and 21st St. N, ☎ 205/254–2565. Closed Mon.*

The **Alabama Sports Hall of Fame Museum** (⊠ Corner of 22nd St. N and Civic Center Blvd., ☎ 205/323–6665), adjacent to the Civic Center, displays memorabilia of such Alabama athletic heroes as coach Bear Bryant, Jesse Owens, Willie Mays, and Hank Aaron. The Kelly Ingram Park area, southwest of the Civic Center, contains the **16th Street Baptist Church** (⊠ 16th St. and 6th Ave. N, ☎ 205/251–9402), a civil rights landmark. Here numerous protests were staged during the 1960s and four black children lost their lives when a bomb planted by white supremacists exploded in 1963; there is a plaque in their memory. The ★ **Birmingham Civil Rights Institute** (⊠ 6th Ave. and 16th St. N, ☎ 205/328–9696) uses exhibits, multimedia presentations, music, and oral histories to document the civil rights movement from the 1920s to the present.

The **Jazz Hall of Fame,** two blocks from the Civil Rights Institute, has photos and memorabilia of the state's jazz greats, including Erskine Hawkins, Cleveland Eaton, and Frank Adams. ⊠ *4th Ave. and 17th St. N, ☎ 205/254–2720. Free. Closed Mon.*

The **Sloss Furnaces,** a massive ironworks, used ore dug from the hills around Birmingham when it was in operation between 1882 and 1971. Guided tours of this National Historic Landmark are given weekends. ⊠ *1st Ave. N and 32nd St., ☎ 205/324–1911. Closed Mon.*

The **Red Mountain Museum** (⊠ 2230 22nd St. S, ☎ 205/933–4153), south on U.S. 31, displays samples of rocks, fossils, and minerals found in the area. Sitting atop Red Mountain is **Vulcan** (⊠ Valley Ave. at U.S. 31S, ☎ 205/328–6198), the world's tallest cast-iron statue. From the enclosed observation deck you'll have a wonderful view of Birmingham.

★ **DeSoto Caverns,** 40 mi from Birmingham (head southeast on U.S. 280 to Childersburg, then east on Route 76), is a network of onyx caves used as a Native American burial ground 2,000 years ago. Rediscovered by Spanish explorer Hernando de Soto in 1540, the caverns later served as a Confederate gunpowder mining center and a Prohibition speakeasy. Tours of the stalagmite and stalactite formations end with a sound, water, and laser-light show in the 12-story Great Onyx Cathedral. ☎ *205/378–7252 or 800/933–2283.*

More than 300 Confederate veterans and their wives are buried in **Confederate Memorial Park,** southwest of Childersburg, off U.S. 31 near Mountain Creek. ⊠ *437 County Rd. 63, Marbury,* ☎ *205/755–1990.*

Montgomery, 90 mi south of Birmingham via I–65, is a city steeped in antebellum history. Today many of its old houses have been restored, and the city has become known as a cultural capital of the South. The **visitor center** (☞ Visitor Information, *above*) has a brief slide show. You can park your car at the center and visit many attractions on foot.

The handsome **state capitol** (⊠ Bainbridge St. at Dexter Ave., ☎ 334/242–3184), built in 1851, served as the first capitol for the Confederate States of America. The **Dexter Avenue King Memorial Baptist Church** (⊠ 454 Dexter Ave., ☎ 334/263–3970) is where Dr. Martin Luther King Jr. began his career as a minister in 1954; a basement mural depicts people and events associated with the civil rights movement. The first **White House of the Confederacy** (☎ 334/242–1861) stands at the corner of Washington Avenue and Union Street. Built in 1835, it contains many items that belonged to Jefferson Davis, the Confederate president, as well as Civil War artifacts.

★ The **Civil Rights Memorial** (⊠ 400 Washington Ave., ☎ 334/264–0286)—created by Maya Lin, designer of the Vietnam Veterans' Memorial, in Washington, D.C.—has a plaza and a pool from which water flows over a 40-ft black-granite wall. Inscribed on the wall are excerpts from King's "I have a dream . . ." speech. Adjacent are the names of many who gave their lives to the civil rights movement.

What to See and Do with Children

The **Birmingham Zoo** (⊠ 2630 Cahaba Rd., ☎ 205/879–0408) is one of the Southeast's largest zoos, with 800 animals. Opening in spring 1998, Birmingham's **Discovery 2000** (⊠ 216 19th St. N, ☎ 205/558–2000) is a hands-on science learning center with an IMAX theater.

Dining and Lodging

Throughout Alabama, Old South dishes—fried chicken, barbecue, roast beef, country-fried steak—prevail, though in recent years a number of upscale restaurants with more varied fare have opened in Birmingham and Montgomery. In Birmingham hotels and motels offer weekend specials but are often crowded during football season; the same holds true in Montgomery when the state legislature is in session. For price ranges *see* Charts 1 (B) and 2 (B) *in* On the Road with Fodor's.

Birmingham

$$$ ✕ **Highlands Bar and Grill.** Grand gourmet feasts prepared by owner-
★ chef Frank Stitt are served in a sophisticated setting accented with vintage French posters and brass. Delicacies include hickory-grilled Destin grouper with white-bean and grilled Portobello ragout and pot-au-feu composed of beef short ribs, savoy cabbage, and mushrooms. ⊠ *2011 11th Ave. S,* ☎ *205/939–1400. Reservations essential. AE, MC, V. Closed Sun.–Mon.*

$-$$ ✕ **Silvertron Cafe.** Since 1986 owner Alan Potts has been creating great dishes with chicken, Black Angus beef, orange roughy (a New Zealand fish), and pasta; his fresh sauces are notable. Tin ceilings, fresh flowers, and framed photos of early Birmingham set the mood. Save room for a Bailey's Brownie. ⊠ *3813 Clairmont Ave.,* ☎ *205/591–3707. AE, MC, V.*

$ ✕ **Irondale Cafe.** An inspiration for Fanny Flagg's book *Fried Green Tomatoes at the Whistlestop Cafe,* this is the place for fried chicken, country-fried steak, fried okra, cabbage, and those famed fried green tomatoes. It's not fancy, just good. ⊠ *1906 1st Ave. S, Irondale (7 mi east of Birmingham),* ☎ *205/956–5258. D, MC, V.*

$$$ ⊞ **Tutwiler.** This National Historic Landmark was built in 1913 as a
★ luxury apartment building and became a hotel in 1986. The elegant lobby has marble floors, chandeliers, antiques, and lots of flowers; guest rooms are furnished with reproductions of antiques. ⊠ *Park Pl. at 21st St. N, 35203,* ☎ *205/322–2100 or 800/845–1787,* ℻ *205/325–1183. 148 rooms. Restaurant, pub. AE, D, DC, MC, V.*

$$$ ⊞ **Wynfrey Hotel.** Rising 15 stories above the Riverchase Galleria mall, this deluxe hotel has an elegant lobby with an Italian marble floor, Chippendale-style furniture, an Oriental rug, an enormous floral arrangement, and a brass escalator. Rooms are done in English and French traditional styles. ⊠ *1000 Riverchase Galleria (U.S. 31S), 35244,* ☎ *205/987–1600 or 800/476–7006,* ℻ *205/987–9552. 341 rooms. Restaurant, café, lobby lounge, pool, hot tub, health club. AE, D, DC, MC, V.*

$$ ⊞ **Mountain Brook Inn.** An eight-story glass-walled hotel at the foot of Red Mountain has a marble-floor lobby and bilevel suites with spiral staircases. ⊠ *2800 U.S. 280, 35223,* ☎ *205/870–3100 or 800/523–7771,* ℻ *205/870–5938. 170 rooms. Restaurant, lobby lounge, pool. AE, D, DC, MC, V.*

Montgomery

$$ ✕ **Jubilee Seafood Company.** In a small café setting you'll find some of the finest and freshest seafood in town. ⊠ *1057 Woodley Rd., Cloverdale Plaza,* ☎ *334/262–6224. Reservations not accepted. AE, DC, MC, V. Closed Sun.–Mon.*

$$ ✕ **Sahara Restaurant.** At one of the city's finest restaurants Joe and
★ Mike Deep carry on a family tradition of friendly service. Broiled snapper and scampi and charbroiled steaks are done just right. ⊠ *511 E. Edgemont Ave.,* ☎ *334/262–1215. AE, D, DC, MC, V. Closed Sun.*

$ ✕ **Chris' Hot Dog Stand.** A Montgomery tradition for more than 75 years, this small eatery is always busy at lunchtime. Chris's famous sauce contains chili peppers, onions, and a variety of herbs that give his hot dogs a one-of-a-kind flavor. ⊠ *138 Dexter Ave.,* ☎ *334/265–6850. Reservations not accepted. No credit cards. Closed Sun.*

$ ⊞ **Red Bluff Cottage.** In this delightful cottage in the heart of downtown, guests can eat breakfast in the dining room or on a veranda overlooking the Alabama River. Rooms have ceiling fans and are furnished with antiques. There's a sitting room with fireplace and a music room–library where guests frequently congregate. ⊠ *551 Clay St., 36104,* ☎ *334/264–0056. 4 rooms. AE, D, MC, V.*

Motels

⊞ **Hampton Inn** (⊠ 1401 East Blvd., Montgomery 36117, ☎ 334/277–2400 or 800/426–7866), 106 rooms, pool; *$.* ⊞ **Motel Birmingham** (⊠ 7905 Crestwood Blvd., Birmingham 35210, ☎ 205/956–4440 or 800/338–9275, ℻ 205/956–3011), 242 rooms, pool; *$.*

The Arts

In Montgomery at the world-class **Alabama Shakespeare Festival** (⊠ Eastern Bypass Exit off I–85, ☎ 334/271–5353 or 800/841-4273), Shakespearean plays, contemporary dramas and comedies, and musicals are performed on two stages.

Shopping

Birmingham's **Riverchase Galleria** (☎ 205/985–3039), at the intersection of I–459 and U.S. 31S, is one of the largest shopping malls in the Southeast, with at least 200 stores. In **Boaz,** about 60 mi north of Birmingham, there are more than 140 outlet stores (☎ 800/746–7262).

MOBILE AND THE GULF COAST

In Mobile, a busy port and one of the oldest cities in Alabama, antebellum buildings survive as a bridge to the past, and azaleas bloom in profusion each spring. The country's first Mardi Gras was held here, and today the city still glories in its pre-Lenten parades and merrymaking. South of Mobile, across the bay, the area around Gulf Shores has 32 mi of white-sand beaches, including those on Pleasure and Dauphin islands. On the atmospheric eastern shore of Mobile Bay, live oaks are laced with Spanish moss, and sprawling clapboard houses with wide porches overlook the bay.

Visitor Information

Alabama Gulf Coast area–Gulf Shores/Orange Beach: Convention and Visitors Bureau (✉ Drawer 457, Gulf Shores 36542; ✉ 3150 Gulf Shores Pkwy., Gulf Shores 36542; ✉ 26650 Perdido Beach Blvd., Orange Beach 36561; ☎ 800/745–7263). **Mobile:** Department of Tourism (✉ 150 S. Royal St., 36602, ☎ 800/252–3862).

Arriving and Departing

By Bus
Greyhound Lines (☎ 800/231–2222) has stations in Mobile (✉ 2545 Government Blvd.) and Pensacola, Florida (✉ 505 W. Burgess Rd.).

By Car
I–10 leads west from Florida to Mobile and continues into Mississippi. I–65 leads south from Birmingham and Montgomery and ends at Mobile. Gulf Shores is connected with Mobile via I–10 and Route 59; Routes 180 and 182 are the main beach routes.

By Plane
Mobile Regional Airport (☎ 334/633–0313) is served by most major domestic carriers. Florida's **Pensacola Regional Airport** (☎ 904/435–1746), 40 mi east of Gulf Shores/Orange Beach, has service from many carriers.

By Train
Amtrak (☎ 800/872–7245) connects Mobile with the east and west coasts.

Exploring Mobile and the Gulf Coast

In 1711 **Fort Condé** was the name the French gave to the Colonial outpost that would one day expand and become Mobile. Indeed, the city's French origins survive in its creole cuisine. Fort Condé, too, survives, thanks to a $2.2 million reconstruction. One hundred fifty years after it was destroyed, remains of the fort were discovered during construction of the I–10 interchange. A reconstructed portion houses the city's **visitor center,** as well as a museum. Costumed guides conduct tours. ✉ *150 S. Royal St.,* ☎ *334/434–7304 or 800/252–3862.*

At the visitor center you can get information on the major annual events hosted by Mobile, the biggest of which is **Mardi Gras,** with balls, parties, and parades. The **Azalea Trail Festival** is held the last weekend of

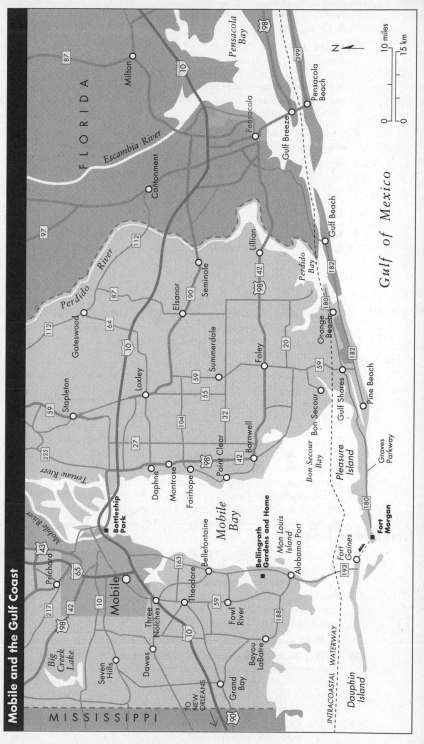

Mobile and the Gulf Coast

March. The **Historic Mobile Homes Tour,** also in March, opens private homes for tours.

Oakleigh (✉ 350 Oakleigh Pl., ☎ 334/432–1281), 1½ mi from Fort Condé, is a high-ceiling, half-timbered mansion, built between 1833 and 1838. It showcases fine period furniture, portraits, silver, jewelry, kitchen implements, toys, and more. Tickets include a tour of neighboring **Cox-Deasy House,** an 1850s cottage furnished with simple 19th-century pieces.

★ Mobile Bay, just east of downtown, is the site of the 155-acre **Battleship Park,** where the battleship USS *Alabama* is anchored. A tour gives a fascinating glimpse into the operation of the World War II vessel, which had a crew of 2,500. Anchored next to it is the USS *Drum,* a World War II submarine. Other exhibits include the B-52 bomber *Calamity Jane* and a P-51 Mustang fighter plane. ✉ *Battleship Pkwy.,* ☎ *334/433–2703.*

★ **Bellingrath Gardens and Home,** 20 mi south of Mobile, is the site of one of the world's most magnificent azalea gardens. Here, amid a 905-acre semitropical landscape, 65 acres of gardens bloom in all seasons: 200 species of azaleas in spring, 3,000 rosebushes in summer, 60,000 chrysanthemum plants in autumn, and fields of poinsettias in winter. Built by Coca-Cola bottling pioneer Walter D. Bellingrath, who started the gardens with his wife in 1917, the house contains one of the finest collections of antiques in the Southeast and also appears on the National Register of Historic Places. ✉ *12401 Bellingrath Gardens Rd., Theodore,* ☎ *334/973–2217.*

From Mobile take I–10 and Route 59 south to **Gulf Shores,** a family-oriented beach area with hotels, restaurants, and attractions. There's ample free parking along the white-as-snow beach, though the traffic is bumper to bumper at peak times. Star-shaped **Fort Morgan** (✉ Mobile Point, ☎ 334/540–7125) sits at the western tip of Pleasure Island, 20 mi west of Gulf Shores at the end of Route 180. The fort was built in the early 1800s to guard the entrance to Mobile Bay. In 1864 after Confederate torpedoes sank the ironclad *Tecumseh,* Union admiral David Farragut shouted, "Damn the torpedoes! Full speed ahead!" The rest of Farragut's fleet forced its way to the bay, and after the Civil War the fort's defenses were improved. The museum at the site tells the story.

Dining and Lodging

In Mobile and throughout the Gulf area, the specialty is fresh seafood, often prepared creole style, with peppery spices, crabmeat dressing, and sometimes a tomato-based sauce. The area's hotels and motels are comfortable and varied, offering the particular hospitality of the region alongside the comforts and amenities of nationwide chain hotels. For price ranges *see* Charts 1 (B) and 2 (B) *in* On the Road with Fodor's.

Gulf Shores

$$ ✕ **King Neptune's Seafood Restaurant.** Owners Al Sawyer and Diane Bush treat you like family at this low-key, down-home eatery where you sit at long tables equipped with rolls of paper towels. Besides local oysters served on the half shell and in award-winning recipes, favorites include steamed royal red shrimp, blue crab, and every variety of po'boy. ✉ *1137 Gulf Shores Pkwy., Hwy. 59 S,* ☎ *334/968–5464. Reservations not accepted. AE, MC, V.*

$$ ✕ **Original Oyster House.** Dining at this plant-filled restaurant over-
★ looking the bayou has become a local tradition. Oysters, plucked fresh from nearby Perdido Bay and served on the half shell, are the specialty of the house. The Cajun-style gumbo—a concoction of crab claws,

shrimp, amberjack, grouper, redfish, okra and other vegetables, and Cajun spices—has won 20 culinary awards. ⊠ *Bayou Village Shopping Center, Hwy. 59,* ☎ *334/948–2445. Reservations not accepted. AE, D, DC, MC, V.*

$$–$$$ 🏨 **Gulf Shores Plantation.** This 320-acre family resort, 8 mi east of Fort Morgan on the Gulf, offers condominiums with fully equipped kitchens in high-rises overlooking the beach. Abundant recreational activities are available. ⊠ *Hwy. 180W (Box 1299), 36547,* ☎ *334/540–5000 or 800/554–0344,* ℻ *334/540–6055. 524 units. Indoor and outdoor pools, 8 tennis courts. AE, MC, V.*

Mobile

$$$ ✕ **La Louisiana.** At this antiques-filled old house on the outskirts of
★ town, fresh seafood is prepared with a touch of French creole. The seafood gumbo comes heavy with shrimp, oysters, and okra. ⊠ *2400 Airport Blvd.,* ☎ *334/476–8130. AE, D, DC, MC, V. Closed Sun. No lunch.*

$$ ✕ **Roussos.** Just across the street from Fort Condé, this is one of the most popular seafood restaurants in the Mobile area. The outstanding service, the comfortable family atmosphere, and the excellent seafood—served fried, broiled, or Greek style—make Roussos a fun place. ⊠ *166 S. Royal St.,* ☎ *334/433–3322. AE, D, DC, MC, V.*

$$$ 🏨 **Radisson Admiral Semmes Hotel.** The hotel is popular with local politicians. Merrymakers appreciate its excellent location on the Mardi Gras parade route. Rooms are furnished in Queen Anne and Chippendale styles. ⊠ *251 Government St., 36602,* ☎ *334/432–8000 or 800/333– 3333,* ℻ *334/405–5942. 169 rooms. Restaurant, lobby lounge, pool, hot tub. AE, D, DC, MC, V.*

$–$$ 🏨 **Malaga Inn.** A delightful, romantic getaway, the Malaga has a lobby that is furnished with 19th-century antiques and opens onto a tropically landscaped central courtyard with a fountain. The large, airy rooms have massive antiques. ⊠ *359 Church St., 36602,* ☎ *334/438– 4701 or 800/235–1586,* ℻ *334/438–4701. 40 rooms. Restaurant, lounge, pool. AE, D, MC, V.*

Orange Beach

$$–$$$ ✕ **The Outrigger.** Perched at the tip of Alabama Point on Perdido Pass, this clean, contemporary restaurant has panoramic views of the water. The fried seafood (served with hush puppies) is hard to pass up, but fish also comes broiled or blackened. Hickory-smoked barbecued ribs and other meats are the specialty. ⊠ *27500 Perdido Beach Blvd.,* ☎ *334/981–6700. Reservations not accepted. AE, D, DC, MC, V.*

$$ ✕ **Dempsey's Restaurant.** The tropical setting at this lakeside dining room is enhanced by a 20-ft waterfall. ⊠ *24891 Perdido Beach Blvd.,* ☎ *334/981–6800. Reservations not accepted. AE, D, DC, MC, V.*

$$ ✕ **Franco's.** If you're homesick for Italian fare, try this popular restaurant whose specialties include stuffed mushrooms, veal and steak, and seafood fettuccine—all prepared with the freshest ingredients. ⊠ *26651 Perdido Beach Blvd.,* ☎ *334/981–9800. Reservations not accepted. AE, D, DC, MC, V.*

$ ✕ **Hazel's Family Restaurant.** This plain family-style restaurant with
★ a full menu serves a good, hearty breakfast (the biscuits are famous), soup-and-salad lunches, and buffet dinners with such seafood dishes as flounder Florentine. There's also a self-service bar serving soft ice cream. ⊠ *Gulf View Square Shopping Center, Rte. 182,* ☎ *334/981– 4628. Reservations not accepted. AE, D, DC, MC, V.*

$$$ ☷ **Perdido Beach Resort.** The exteriors of the eight- and nine-story tow-
ers of this Mediterranean-style hotel are stucco and red tile; the lobby
is tiled in terra-cotta and has mosaics by Venetian artists. Luxurious
rooms have beach views and balconies. ⊠ *27200 Perdido Beach Blvd.
(Box 400), 36561, ☎ 334/981–9811 or 800/634–8001, ℻ 334/981–
5670. 345 rooms. Restaurant, café, indoor-outdoor pool, hot tub,
sauna, 4 tennis courts, exercise room. AE, D, DC, MC, V.*

$$–$$$ ☷ **Original Romar House.** This unassuming beach cottage is full of sur-
  ★ prises—from the Caribbean-style upstairs sitting area to the Purple Par-
rot Bar to the luxurious Art Deco–style guest rooms. In the evening
wine and cheese are served. ⊠ *23500 Perdido Beach Blvd., 36561, ☎
334/981–6156 or 800/487–6627, ℻ 334/974–1163. 6 rooms. Hot
tub, bicycles. AE, MC, V.*

Point Clear

$$$ ✕☷ **Marriott's Grand Hotel.** Set within 550 acres of beautifully land-
  ★ scaped grounds on Mobile Bay, the Grand has been cherished since 1847.
Extensively refurbished by Marriott, it is one of the South's premier
resorts. Spacious rooms and cottages are traditionally furnished. The
food here is elegantly prepared and served, especially in the Bay View
Restaurant. ⊠ *U.S. Scenic 98, 36564, ☎ 334/928–9201 or 800/544–
9933, ℻ 334/928–1149. 306 rooms. 3 restaurants, lobby lounge,
pool, golf, 8 tennis courts, horseback riding, dock, boating, fishing,
bicycles, children's program. AE, D, DC, MC, V.*

Outdoor Activities and Sports

Biking

Gulf State Park Resort (☎ 334/948–7275 or 800/252–7275), in Gulf
Shores, rents bikes that must stay on site.

Canoeing

Sunshine Canoe Rentals (☎ 334/344–8664) runs canoe trips at Es-
catawpa River, 15 mi west of Mobile. The river has no rapids, so you
travel at a leisurely pace past lots of white sandbars.

Fishing

Fishing here is excellent. You can obtain a fishing license from most
bait shops. For information contact the **Department of Conservation
and Natural Resources** (☎ 334/242–3829). In Gulf Shores, **Gulf State
Park** (☞ State Parks, *above*) has fishing from an 825-ft pier; you can
also rent flat-bottom boats for lake fishing. Deep-sea fishing from
charter boats is very popular; **Orange Beach** has the **Moreno Queen**
(☎ 334/981–8499), which offers four- and six-hour fishing trips.
Orange Beach has 90 other charter boats from which to choose.

Water Sports

In Orange Beach **Fun Marina** (☎ 334/981–8587) rents Jet Skis, pon-
toon boats, and 16-ft bay-fishing boats. In Gulf Shores **Island Recreation Services** (☎ 334/948–7334) rents Jet Skis, bikes, body boards,
surfboards, and sailboats.

ELSEWHERE IN ALABAMA

Huntsville

Arriving and Departing

Huntsville is 100 mi north of Birmingham via I–65 and U.S. 72E.

What to See and Do

Huntsville has a clutch of attractions that include golf courses as well
as historic homes and a variety of museums. The **U.S. Space and Rocket**

Center here is home to the **U.S. Space Camp.** The center offers a bus tour of the NASA labs and shuttle test sites, hands-on exhibits in the museum, and an outdoor park filled with spacecraft. ✉ *1 Tranquillity Base,* ☎ *205/837–3400 or 800/637–7223.*

Alabama Constitution Village is the site of Alabama's Constitutional Convention of 1819. Demonstrations of skills such as woodworking, printing, cooking, and weaving are performed by craftspeople in period dress. The **Historic Huntsville Depot** offers a glimpse of railroad life in the early 19th century; it's a few blocks from the village. ✉ *109 Gates Ave.,* ☎ *205/535–6565 or 800/678–1819. Closed Jan.–Feb.*

Tuscumbia

Arriving and Departing
Tuscumbia is 120 mi northwest of Birmingham via I–65 and U.S. Alternate 72. Take Exit 310 off I–65 at Cullman.

What to See and Do
Tuscumbia and the adjoining towns of Florence, Sheffield, and Muscle Shoals form a quad-city area known throughout Alabama simply as the Shoals. Spreading out on both sides of the Tennessee River basin, this is an area rich in culture and history.

Ivy Green is the birthplace of author and lecturer Helen Keller, who was left unable to hear or see at the age of 19 months. With the help of her teacher, Anne Sullivan, she graduated from Radcliffe with honors in 1904 and became a champion for all those with similar disabilities. Tours are year-round. *The Miracle Worker,* the play about Keller's childhood and her relationship with Sullivan, is performed outdoors from late June through late July. First staged in 1961, it is the state's official drama. ✉ *300 W. North Commons,* ☎ *205/383–4066.*

At the **Alabama Music Hall of Fame and Museum,** you can wander through the history of Alabama's musical heritage—seeing the original contracts of Elvis Presley's deal with Sun Records, the actual touring bus of the rock band Alabama, and exhibits on the likes of Hank Williams, Lionel Richie, and Nat "King" Cole. The second weekend of September is the annual **Harvest Jam** festival, which draws performers and fans from across the country. ✉ *U.S. 72,* ☎ *205/381–4417 or 800/239–2643.*

FLORIDA

Updated by
Pam Acheson,
Andrea
Lehman, Gary
McKechnie,
Diane
Marshall, and
Rebecca Miller

Capital	Tallahassee
Population	14,400,000
Motto	In God We Trust
State Bird	Mockingbird
State Flower	Orange blossom
Postal Abbreviation	FL

Statewide Visitor Information

Florida Division of Tourism (✉ 126 Van Buren St., Tallahassee 32301, ☎ 904/487–1462). **Information centers:** on U.S. 301 at Hilliard, U.S. 231 near Graceville, I–75 near Jennings, I–10 at Pensacola, I–95 near Yulee, and in the lobby of the capitol in Tallahassee.

Scenic Drives

In **Everglades National Park** the 38-mi drive from the Main Visitor Center to Flamingo reveals a patchwork of ecosystems, including mangrove and cypress forests and saw-grass marshes. Although traffic jams abound during the winter tourist season, the **Overseas Highway** (U.S. 1) from Key Largo to Key West offers spectacular vistas of the Atlantic, Florida Bay, the Gulf of Mexico, and the myriad islands of the Keys. **Route 789,** along the Gulf Coast south from Holmes Beach in Bradenton to Lido Beach in Sarasota and from Casey Key south of Osprey to Nokomis Beach, passes over several picturesque barrier islands. Along the Atlantic coast the **Buccaneer Trail** (A1A) from Mayport to the old seaport town of Fernandina Beach passes through marshlands and along pristine beaches. **U.S. 98** winds east from historic Pensacola through the lush coastal landscape of the Panhandle.

National and State Parks

National Parks

Everglades and Biscayne national parks (☞ Elsewhere in Florida, *below*) are in Homestead, just south of Miami. In southwestern Florida **Big Cypress National Preserve** (✉ 20 mi east of Ochopee on U.S. 41; HCR 61, Box 110, Ochopee 33943, ☎ 941/695–2000 or 941/262–1066), noted for the bald and dwarf cypress trees that line its marshlands, is a sanctuary for alligators, bald eagles, and the endangered Florida panther.

Florida has three national forests. The 556,500-acre **Apalachicola National Forest** (✉ Rte. 65; Edward Ball Wakulla Spring State Park, Wakulla Spring Rd., Wakulla 32305, ☎ 904/653–9419) is popular for canoeing and hiking and has a recreational facility designed for people with disabilities. **Ocala National Forest** (✉ Forest Visitor Center, 10863 E. Hwy. 40, Silver Springs 34488, ☎ 904/625–7470) has lakes, springs, hiking trails, campgrounds, and historic sites. **Osceola National Forest** (✉ Osceola Ranger District, Box 70, Olustee 32072, ☎ 904/752–2577) is dotted with cypress swamps and offers good fishing and hunting. In addition, the state has five national monuments, two national seashores, and eight national wildlife refuges.

State Parks

The state administers hundreds of parks, nature preserves, and historic sites. Among these are **Blackwater River State Park** (✉ Rte. 1, Box 57C, Holt 32564, ☎ 904/623–2363), 40 mi northeast of Pensacola on I–10, popular with canoeists; **Delnor-Wiggins Pass State Recreation Area**

(⊠ 1100 Gulfshore Dr. N, Naples 33963, ☎ 813/597–6196), with miles of beaches, picnic areas, and fishing spots; **Florida Caverns State Park** (⊠ 3345 Caverns Rd., Mariana 32446, ☎ 904/482–9598), two hours north of Panama City on Route 167, comprising 1,783 acres of caves and nature trails; **Ft. Clinch State Park** (☞ Elsewhere in Florida, *below*); and the **St. Andrews State Recreation Area** (⊠ 4415 Thomas Dr., Panama City Beach 32408, ☎ 904/233–5140), in the Panhandle, encompassing 1,038 acres of beaches, pinewoods, and marshes for swimming, pier fishing, and dune hiking. For more information contact the **Florida Department of Natural Resources** (⊠ Marjory Stoneman Douglas Bldg., MS 525, 3900 Commonwealth Blvd., Tallahassee 32399-3000, ☎ 904/488–9872).

MIAMI

Because more than half of its population is Hispanic in origin, Miami is sometimes called the capital of Latin America. Indeed, Miami is a city of superlatives. This ever-growing metropolis has one of the busiest airports and cruise-ship ports in the world. More than 150 companies base their international operations in the city, and big-league sports are big news here. Undergirding all this energy and prosperity is a flourishing drug culture that fuels get-rich-quick lifestyles.

Visitor Information

Greater Miami: Convention and Visitors Bureau (⊠ 701 Brickell Ave., Suite 2700, 33131, ☎ 305/539–3063 or 800/283–2707). **Miami Beach:** Chamber of Commerce (⊠ 1920 Meridian Ave., 33139, ☎ 305/672–1270, FAX 305/538–4336). **South Dade County:** Visitors Information Center (⊠ 160 U.S. 1, Florida City 33034, ☎ 305/245–9180 or 800/388–9669, FAX 305/247–4335).

Arriving and Departing

By Bus
Greyhound Lines (☎ 800/231–2222) stops at four terminals in Greater Miami, including a terminal at the airport.

By Car
I–95, which runs north–south along Florida's east coast, flows into the heart of Miami. From the northwest I–75 leads to the city. Route 836 (also called East–West Expressway or Dolphin Expressway), connecting the airport to downtown (toll eastbound only, 25¢), continues across I–395 and the MacArthur Causeway to lower Miami Beach and the Art Deco District. Route 112 (Airport Expressway) connects the airport with midtown (toll eastbound only, 25¢) and continues across I–195 and the Julia Tuttle Causeway to mid–Miami Beach.

By Plane
Miami International Airport (MIA; ☎ 305/876–7000), 6 mi west of downtown via Route 836, is served by most major carriers and many minor ones. Cab fare downtown is $20–$27 plus tip. **SuperShuttle** (☎ 305/871–2000) vans transport passengers 24 hours a day between MIA and local hotels, the Port of Miami, and even individual residences. The cost to downtown hotels runs between $8–$11. **Bus service** (fare $1.25, transfer 25¢; exact change required) is available on the other side of the lower-level lanes in the center of the airport.

By Train
Amtrak (⊠ 8303 N.W. 37th Ave., ☎ 305/835–1221 or 800/872–7245).

Getting Around Miami

Greater Miami resembles Los Angeles in its urban sprawl and traffic congestion. You'll need a car to get from one area of the city to another. **Metromover** (☞ *below*), a light-rail mass-transit system, circles the heart of the city on twin elevated loops; use it to tour the downtown area. The Art Deco District in Miami Beach and the heart of Coconut Grove are best explored on foot.

By Car

Miami is laid out in quadrants: northwest, northeast, southwest, southeast. These meet at Miami Avenue, which separates east from west, and Flagler Street, which separates north from south. Avenues and courts run north–south; streets, terraces, and ways run east–west. Roads run diagonally, northwest–southeast. In Miami Beach avenues run north–south; streets, east–west. Streets in Coral Gables have names, not numbers.

By Public Transportation

The **Metro–Dade Transit Agency** (☎ 305/638–6700) runs the Metrorail, Metromover, and Metrobus. **Metrorail** (fare $1.25) runs from downtown Miami north to Hialeah and south along U.S. 1 to Dadeland. **Metromover** (fare 25¢), a separate system, has two loops that circle downtown Miami, linking major hotels, office buildings, and shopping areas. Metrobus (fare $1.25) stops are marked by blue-and-green signs with a bus logo and route information. Frequency of service varies widely.

By Taxi

Be on your guard when traveling by cab in Miami. Some drivers are rude and unhelpful and may take advantage of visitors unfamiliar with their destinations. To avoid this, connect with a consortium of drivers who have banded together to provide good service: This nameless group can be reached through its **dispatch service** (☎ 305/888–4444). If you have to use another company, try to be familiar with your route and destination. Major cab companies include **Central Taxicab Service** (☎ 305/532–5555), **Diamond Cab Company** (☎ 305/545–5555), **Metro Taxicab Company** (☎ 305/888–8888), **Miami–Dade Yellow Cab** (☎ 305/633–0503), and **Yellow Cab Company** (☎ 305/444–4444). The fare is $1.75 per mi, 25¢ a minute waiting time; there's no additional charge for up to five passengers, luggage, or tolls.

Orientation Tours

Boat Tours

Island Queen, Island Lady, and *Pink Lady* (☎ 305/379–5119) offer 90-minute narrated water tours of the Port of Miami and Millionaires' Row, departing from Bayside Marketplace.

Walking Tours

The **Miami Design Preservation League** (☎ 305/672–2014) runs a 90-minute tour of Miami Beach's Art Deco District at 10:30 AM Saturday, leaving from the Ocean Front Auditorium (✉ 1001 Ocean Dr.). Metro-Dade Community College history professor **Paul George** (☎ 305/858–6021) offers walking tours through downtown and other historic districts.

Exploring Miami

Downtown

★ Begin your tour of downtown Miami at the **Metro-Dade Cultural Center** (✉ 101 W. Flagler St.), a 3.3-acre postmodern Mediterranean-style complex by architect Philip Johnson. An elevated plaza provides a serene haven from the city's pulsation. Within the complex are several arts venues, including the **Miami Museum of Art** (MMA; ☎ 305/375–3000). In the tradition of the European Kunsthalle (exhibition gallery), this art museum has no permanent collection; throughout the year it organizes and borrows temporary exhibitions on diverse themes. The **Historical Museum of Southern Florida** (☎ 305/375–1492), also in the cultural center, has artifacts including Tequesta and Seminole ceramics and a 1920s streetcar. Another cultural center tenant, the **Main Public Library** (☎ 305/375–2665) has nearly 4 million holdings and art exhibits in its auditorium and second-floor lobby.

Between Biscayne Boulevard and Biscayne Bay is **Claude and Mildred Pepper Bayfront Park,** which Japanese sculptor Isamu Noguchi redesigned just before his death in 1989. It now includes a memorial to the *Challenger* astronauts, an amphitheater, and a fountain honoring the late Florida congressman Claude Pepper and his wife.

Bayside Marketplace (☎ 305/577–3344), between Bayfront Park and the entrance to the Port of Miami, is a massive waterside entertainment and shopping center that includes shops, outdoor cafés, and a food court. Street performers entertain throughout the day and evening, and free concerts, typically calypso, jazz, Latin, reggae, and rock, take place every day of the year.

At the **Freedom Tower** (✉ 600 Biscayne Blvd.), the Cuban Refugee Center processed more than 500,000 immigrating Cubans in the 1960s. Built in 1925 and restored to its original grandeur in 1988, this imposing Spanish Baroque–style structure was inspired by the Giralda, an 800-year-old bell tower in Seville, Spain.

South of downtown proper, several architecturally interesting condominiums rise between Brickell Avenue and Biscayne Bay. Israeli artist Yacov Agram painted the rainbow-hued exterior of **Villa Regina** (✉ 1581 Brickell Ave.). **Arquitectonica,** a nationally prominent architectural firm based in Miami, designed three buildings on Brickell Avenue: **the Palace** (✉ 1541 Brickell Ave.), **the Imperial** (✉ 1627 Brickell Ave.), and **the Atlantis** (✉ 2025 Brickell Ave.).

Miami Beach

Made up of 17 islands in Biscayne Bay, Miami Beach is officially a separate city from Miami. In recent years this city dubbed the American Riviera has revived its fortunes by renewing its **South Beach** area. Today South Beach revels in renewed world glory as a lure for models and millionaires. The hub of South Beach is the 1-square-mi **Art Deco District,** stretching along Ocean Drive and the most talked-about beachfront in America. About 650 significant buildings in the district are listed on the National Register of Historic Places (this is the nation's first 20th-century district to be honored as a district).

Begin your tour of the Art Deco District at the **Art Deco District Welcome Center** (✉ 1001 Ocean Dr., ☎ 305/531–3484). Proceed north past pastel-hued Art Deco hotels (outlined in brilliant neon at night) on your left and the palm-fringed beach on your right. The neighborhood's two main commercial streets are **Collins Avenue,** one block west of Ocean Drive, and, one block farther west, **Washington Avenue.** The latter is a colorful mix of Jewish, Cuban, Haitian, and more familiar American cultures, containing delicatessens, avant-garde stores, produce markets, shops selling religious artifacts, and many of the city's best restaurants. West of Washington Avenue is the **Lincoln Road Mall,** a popular pedestrian shopping street.

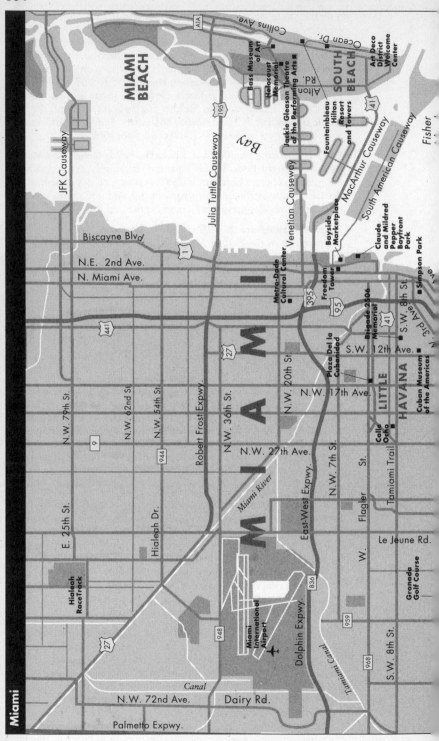

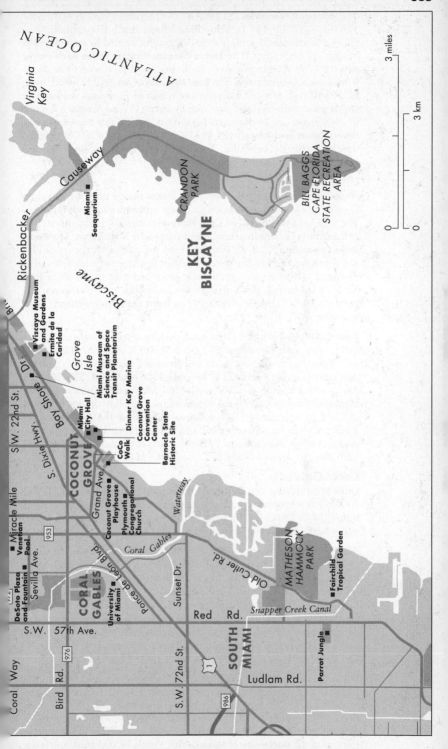

ATLANTIC OCEAN

Virginia
Key

Causeway

Rickenbacker

Miami
Seaquarium

CRANDON
PARK

KEY
BISCAYNE

BILL BAGGS
CAPE FLORIDA
STATE RECREATION
AREA

3 miles

3 km

Bill

Biscayne

Vizcaya Museum
and Gardens
Ermita de la
Caridad

Grove
Isle

S.W. 22nd St.

Bay Shore Dr.

S. Dixie Hwy.

Miami Museum of
Science and Space
Transit Planetarium

Miami
City Hall

Dinner Key Marina

Coconut Grove
Convention
Center

CoCo
Walk

COCONUT
GROVE

Barnacle State
Historic Site

Grand Ave.

Coconut Grove
Playhouse

Plymouth
Congregational
Church

Miracle Mile

Venetian
Pool

953

Ponce de Leon Blvd.

Coral Gables

Waterway

Sevilla Ave.

DeSoto Plaza
and Fountain

CORAL
GABLES

University
of Miami

S.W. 57th Ave.

Sunset Dr.

Coral Gables

Old Cutler Rd.

MATHESON
HAMMOCK
PARK

Fairchild
Tropical Garden

Red   Rd.

Snapper Creek Canal

Coral Way

Bird   Rd.

976

S.W. 72nd St.

1

SOUTH
MIAMI

Ludlam Rd.

986

Parrot Jungle

The **Holocaust Memorial** (✉ 1933–1945 Meridian Ave., ☎ 305/538–1663 or 305/538–1673), behind the Miami Beach Convention Center, is a monumental sculpture and a graphic record in memory of 6 million Jewish victims. The **Jackie Gleason Theater of the Performing Arts** (✉ 1700 Washington Ave., ☎ 305/673–7300) is where Gleason's television show originated. The **Bass Museum of Art** (✉ 2121 Park Ave., ☎ 305/673–7530) has a diverse collection of European works. The striking and triumphal archway that looms on Collins Avenue is a work of illusionary art by Richard Haas that depicts the **Fontainebleau Hilton Resort and Towers** (✉ 4441 Collins Ave., ☎ 305/538–2000), which actually sits behind it. The hotel is the largest in South Florida, with more than 1,200 rooms.

Little Havana

Some 35 years ago the tidal wave of Cubans fleeing the Castro regime flooded an older neighborhood just west of downtown with refugees. The area became known as **Little Havana**, although today more than half a million Cubans live throughout the greater Miami area. The **Plaza de la Cubanidad** (✉ S.W. 17th Ave.), on the southwest corner of Flagler Street and Teddy Roosevelt Avenue, is where redbrick sidewalks surround a fountain and monument inscribed with words from José Martí, a leader in Cuba's struggle for independence from Spain: LAS PALMAS SON NOVIAS QUE ESPERAN (The palm trees are girlfriends who will wait).

Calle Ocho (S.W. 8th St.) is the main commercial thoroughfare of Little Havana. Visit **Versailles** (✉ 3555 S.W. 8th St., ☎ 305/445–7614), a Cuban restaurant whose menu and decor will immerse you in Cuban-American popular culture. The **Brigade 2506 Memorial** (✉ S.W. 13th Ave.), which stands at Calle Ocho and Memorial Boulevard, commemorates the victims of the unsuccessful 1961 Bay of Pigs invasion of Cuba by an exile force. The **Cuban Museum of the Americas,** created by Cuban exiles to preserve and interpret their heritage, now includes exhibits from the entire Hispanic arts community. ✉ *1300 S.W. 12th Ave.,* ☎ *305/858–8006. Closed Sat.–Mon.*

Coral Gables

Developed during the 1920s by visionary George Merrick, Coral Gables has remained remarkably true to his dream of a planned community, with broad boulevards, Spanish-Mediterranean architecture, and a busy commercial downtown.

The heart of downtown Coral Gables stretches from Douglas Road (37th Avenue) to LeJeune Road (42nd Avenue). This four-block area, known as the **Miracle Mile,** has more than 150 shops and a concentration of fine restaurants. The **Granada Golf Course** (✉ 2001 Granada Blvd., ☎ 305/460–5367) is one of two public courses amid Coral Gables's largest historic district. **Coral Gables Merrick House and Gardens,** George Merrick's boyhood home, has been restored to its original 1920s appearance and contains family furnishings and artifacts. ✉ *907 Coral Way,* ☎ *305/460–5361. Closed Thurs.–Sat.*

On Granada Boulevard you'll find the **De Soto Plaza and Fountain,** a classical column on a pedestal, with water flowing from the mouths of four sculpted faces. The stunning **Venetian Pool** (✉ 2701 De Soto Blvd., ☎ 305/460–5356), on northeast-bound De Soto Boulevard, is a themed municipal pool created from a rock quarry. The 260-acre main campus of the **University of Miami,** with almost 14,000 students, is the largest private research university in the Southeast. Its **Lowe Art Mu-**

seum has a permanent collection of 8,000 works. ⊠ *1301 Stanford Dr.,* ☎ *305/284–3535. Closed Mon.*

Fine old homes and mature trees line **Sunset Drive,** the city-designated "historic and scenic road" to and through downtown South Miami. You can watch a trained-bird show, stroll among exotic plants and trees, and see a cactus garden at **Parrot Jungle** (⊠ 11000 S.W. 57th Ave., ☎ 305/666–7834), one of Miami's oldest and most popular attractions. Many of the 1,100 parrots, macaws, cockatoos, and other exotic birds fly free, but they'll come to you for seeds, sold from old-fashioned gumball machines.

Not far from Parrot Jungle is the 83-acre **Fairchild Tropical Garden** (⊠ 10901 Old Cutler Rd., ☎ 305/667–1651)—the largest tropical botanical garden in the continental United States. Old Cutler Road traverses Dade County's oldest and most scenic park, **Matheson Hammock Park** (⊠ 9610 Old Cutler Rd., ☎ 305/667–3035), which dates from the days of the Civilian Conservation Corps in the 1930s. The tide flushes a saltwater "atoll" pool through four gates at the park's popular bathing beach.

Coconut Grove

Coconut Grove is the oldest section of Miami, begun during the 1870s and annexed to the city in 1925. Its earliest settlers included New England intellectuals, bohemians, Bahamians, and—later—artists, writers, and scientists who established winter homes there. The Grove still reflects the pioneers' eclectic origins, with posh estates next to rustic cottages and starkly modern dwellings. The tone of Coconut Grove today is upscale and urban.

Before exploring the restaurants and shops of the Grove, you may want to visit the **Plymouth Congregational Church** (⊠ 3400 Devon Rd., ☎ 305/444–6521), a handsome coral-rock structure, which dates from 1917. Also on the 11-acre grounds are natural sunken gardens; the first schoolhouse in Dade County (one room), which was moved to this property; and the site of the original Coconut Grove water and electric works.
★ Main Highway brings you to the historic **Village of Coconut Grove,** a trendy commercial district with redbrick sidewalks and more than 300 restaurants, stores, and art galleries. Parking is often a problem, so be prepared to walk several blocks to the heart of the district.

In Coconut Grove's village center is **CocoWalk** (⊠ 3015 Grand Ave., ☎ 305/444–0777), a multilevel open mall of Mediterranean-style brick courtyards and terraces overflowing with restaurants, bars, and shops. The Spanish rococo–style apricot-hued **Coconut Grove Playhouse** (⊠ 3500 Main Hwy., ☎ 305/442–4000), dating from 1926, presents Broadway-bound plays, musical revues, and experimental productions. The **Barnacle State Historical Site,** a 19th-century pioneer residence, was built by Commodore Ralph Munroe in 1891. The house has a broad, sloping roof and deeply recessed verandas to channel sea breezes inside; many furnishings are original. ⊠ *3485 Main Hwy.,* ☎ *305/448–9445. Closed Mon.–Thurs.*

Dinner Key Marina (⊠ 3400 Pan American Dr., ☎ 305/579–6980) is Greater Miami's largest marina. Antiques, boat, and home furnishings shows are held annually at the 105,000-square-ft **Coconut Grove Convention Center** (⊠ 2700 S. Bayshore Dr., ☎ 305/579–3310). Not far from the Dinner Key Marina is **Miami City Hall** (⊠ 3500 Pan American Dr., ☎ 305/250–5357), a building decorated with nautical-motif Art Deco trim. It was built in 1934 as the terminal for the Pan American Airways seaplane base at Dinner Key.

South Miami

South Miami was a pioneer farming community that grew into a suburb while still managing to retain a small-town charm.

If you drive north on South Bayshore Drive from Coconut Grove, it becomes South Miami Avenue. At the next stoplight turn right on a private road that passes St. Kieran's Church to **Ermita de La Caridad** (Our Lady of Charity Shrine; ⊠ 3609 S. Miami Ave., ☎ 305/854–2404), a 90-ft-high conical shrine built to overlook the bay so that worshipers face Cuba. You can manipulate and marvel at the many hands-on sound, gravity, and electricity exhibits at the **Miami Museum of Science and Space Transit Planetarium** (⊠ 3280 S. Miami Ave., ☎ 305/854–4247), which also features traveling exhibits and virtual reality, life science demonstrations and Internet technology every day. Overlooking
★ Biscayne Bay on South Miami Avenue is **Vizcaya Museum and Gardens** (⊠ 3251 S. Miami Ave., ☎ 305/250–9133), an estate with an Italian Renaissance–style villa that was built in the early 20th century as the winter residence of Chicago industrialist James Deering. Today the house is a showplace of antiquities. If you continue north on South Miami Avenue past Vizcaya to 17th Road, you'll reach **Simpson Park** (⊠ 55 S.W. 17th Rd., ☎ 305/856–6801). Here you can enjoy a fragment of the dense jungle—marlberry, banyans, and black calabash—that once covered the entire 5 mi from downtown Miami to Coconut Grove.

Virginia Key and Key Biscayne

The waters of Government Cut and the Port of Miami separate densely populated Miami Beach from two of Greater Miami's playground islands, Virginia Key and Key Biscayne—the latter no longer the laid-back village where Richard Nixon set up his presidential vacation compound. Parks and stretches of dense mangrove swamp occupy much of both keys. To reach the keys, take the **Rickenbacker Causeway** across Biscayne Bay at Brickell Avenue and Southwest 26th Road, about 2 mi south of downtown Miami. The causeway links several islands in the bay.

The high-level **William M. Powell Bridge** rises 75 ft above the water to eliminate the need for a draw span. The panoramic view from the top encompasses the bay, keys, port, and downtown skyscrapers.

★ On Virginia Key, the **Miami Seaquarium** (⊠ 4400 Rickenbacker Causeway, ☎ 305/361–5705) features sea lion, dolphin, and killer whale performances and a 235,000-gallon tropical-reef aquarium.

The commercial center of Key Biscayne is a mix of shops and stores catering to neighborhood needs. At the key's south end is the **Bill Baggs Cape Florida State Recreation Area** (⊠ 1200 S. Crandon Blvd., ☎ 305/361–5811), with 1¼ mi of palm-topped white-sand beach.

What to See and Do with Children

Southwest of Dade County's urban core is the cageless 290-acre **Metrozoo** (⊠ 12400 S.W. 152nd St., ☎ 305/251–0400), where animals roam free on islands surrounded by moats. The **Gold Coast Railroad Museum** (⊠ 12450 Coral Reef Dr., ☎ 305/253–0063) displays a 1949 Silver Crescent dome car and the Ferdinand Magellan, the only Pullman car ever constructed specifically for U.S. presidents.

Dining

Miami has gained a world reputation for its fusion of tropical ingredients with a nouvelle-inspired remake of classical French cooking. The gourmet centers of the city are downtown Coral Gables and the Art

Deco District of Miami Beach, with pockets of fine dining also in ethnic neighborhoods, such as Little Havana, and in popular nightlife districts, such as Coconut Grove and Bayside downtown. For price ranges *see* Chart 1 (A) *in* On the Road with Fodor's.

$$$$ ✕ **Dominique's.** Woodwork and mirrors create an intimate setting for a unique experience in contemporary cuisine. Dine in either of two enclosed patios, both walled in glass to provide ocean views. The wine list is extensive. Sunday brunch is also served. ⊠ *Alexander Hotel, 5225 Collins Ave.,* ☎ *305/865–6500. AE, DC, MC, V.*

$$$ ✕ **Chef Allen's.** In an Art Deco setting of glass and neon, diners' gazes are drawn to the kitchen, visible through a large picture window, where chef Allen Susser creates new American masterpieces from a menu that changes nightly. Dishes such as honey-chilled roasted duck with stir-fried wild rice and green-apple chutney are almost too pretty to eat. ⊠ *19088 N.E. 29th Ave., North Miami Beach,* ☎ *305/935– 2900. AE, DC, MC, V. No lunch Sat.–Thurs.*

$$$ ✕ **Grand Cafe.** This upscale spot features a bilevel room with pink tablecloths and floral bouquets. International cuisine here means everything from pan-seared Florida crab cake to the cherry wood–smoked Chilean salmon. ⊠ *2669 S. Bay Shore Dr., Coconut Grove,* ☎ *305/858–9600. AE, DC, MC, V.*

$$$ ✕ **Mark's Place.** At this popular restaurant owner-chef Mark Militello
★ excels with regional fare prepared in an oak-burning oven from Genoa. The menu changes nightly, taking advantage of available fresh local produce. Entrées typically include several imaginative pizzas and pastas. ⊠ *2286 N.E. 123rd St., North Miami,* ☎ *305/893–6888. AE, DC, MC, V. No lunch.*

$$$ ✕ **Yuca.** This high-style Cuban eatery, decorated with striking mod
★ ern art prints and blond wood, attracts chic young Cubans and other fashionable types. Dazzling nouvelle tropical dishes include a traditional corn tamale filled with conch and plaintain-coated dolphin with a tamarind tartar sauce. ⊠ *501 Lincoln Rd.,* ☎ *305/532–9822. AE, DC, MC, V.*

$$ ✕ **Tony Chan's Water Club.** This beautiful dining room just off the lobby
★ of the high-rise Grand Prix Hotel looks onto a bay-side marina. The menu has more than 100 appetizers and entrées, including minced quail tossed with bamboo shoots, mushrooms wrapped in lettuce leaves, and pork chops sprinkled with green peppercorns in a black-bean-and-garlic sauce. ⊠ *1717 N. Bayshore Dr., Downtown Miami,* ☎ *305/374– 8888. AE, MC, V. No lunch weekends.*

$$ ✕ **Two Sisters.** Stiff competition among Coral Gables restaurants helps
★ keep the food here first-rate. The mood is understated, but the Pacific Rim–inspired dishes add pizzazz. Entrées such as stir-fried "tangled" shrimp with "jungle" curry, rice ribbons, and coconut glaze or jerk-marinated snapper with red-onion confit and ginger butter might make you consider a vacation in Polynesia. ⊠ *50 Alhambra Plaza, Coral Gables,* ☎ *305/441–1234. AE, MC, V.*

$–$$ ✕ **Las Tapas.** Tapas—Spanish foods in appetizer-size portions—give you a variety of tastes during a single meal. Full-size meals are also served at this Bayside Marketplace restaurant, typically packed at all hours. ⊠ *Bayside Marketplace, 401 Biscayne Blvd., Downtown Miami,* ☎ *305/372–2737. AE, D, DC, MC, V.*

$–$$ ✕ **Los Ranchos.** Carlos Somoza, owner of this beautiful bay-side establishment and a nephew of Nicaragua's deposed dictator Anastasio Somoza, sustains a tradition begun more than 30 years ago in Managua, when the original Los Ranchos instilled in Nicaraguan palates a love of Argentine-style beef—lean, grass-fed tenderloin with *chimichurri,* a green sauce of chopped parsley, garlic, oil, vinegar, and other spices. Specialties include chorizo, *cuajada con maduro* (skim cheese with fried bananas), and shrimp sautéed in butter and topped with a creamy jalapeño sauce. ⊠ *Bayside Marketplace, 401 Biscayne Blvd., Downtown Miami,* ☎ *305/375–8188 or 305/375–0666;* ⊠ *125 S.W. 107th Ave., Little Managua,* ☎ *305/221–9367;* ⊠ *Kendall Town & Country, 8505 Mills Dr., Kendall,* ☎ *305/596–5353;* ⊠ *Falls Shopping Center, 8888 S.W. 136th St., Suite 303, South Miami,* ☎ *305/238–6867;* ⊠ *2728 Ponce de León Blvd., Coral Gables,* ☎ *305/446–0050. AE, DC, MC, V.*

$ ✕ **Chez Moy.** This bustling restaurant with friendly staff is *the* choice in Little Haiti. Caribbean cuisine includes boiled spiced pork, conch with garlic and hot pepper, sugary fruit drinks, and sweet potato pie for dessert. ⊠ *1 N.W. 54th St., Little Haiti,* ☎ *305/757–5056. No credit cards. No smoking.*

$ ✕ **Hy-Vong Vietnamese Cuisine.** This tiny restaurant seating 36 is
★ popular with locals, who come for such Vietnamese dishes as barbecued pork with sesame seeds and fish sauce. Expect a wait if you come after 7 PM. ⊠ *3458 S.W. 8th St., Little Havana,* ☎ *305/446–3674. No credit cards. Closed Mon. and 2 wks in Aug. No lunch.*

$ ✕ **News Cafe.** This hip spot on Ocean Drive (open 24 hours) is always
★ packed with people-watchers and those who enjoy such eclectic dishes as huge fresh-fruit bowls, burgers, bagels, pâtés, and chocolate fondue. A bar is the newest addition. ⊠ *800 Ocean Dr., Miami Beach,* ☎ *305/538–6397. Reservations not accepted. AE, DC, MC, V.*

$ ✕ **Shorty's Bar-B-Q.** Miami's choice for barbecue and all the trimmings
★ since the 1950s, Shorty's serves meals family style at long picnic tables. ⊠ *9200 S. Dixie Hwy., Miami,* ☎ *305/670–7732;* ⊠ *11575 S.W. 40th St., Miami,* ☎ *305/227–3196;* ⊠ *5989 S. University Dr., Davie,* ☎ *954/ 680–9900. Reservations not accepted. MC, V (Davie location only).*

Lodging

Lodgings are concentrated in Miami Beach and downtown Miami, around the airport, and in Coral Gables, Coconut Grove, and Key Biscayne. For bed-and-breakfast accommodations contact **Bed & Breakfast Company, Tropical Florida** (⊠ Box 262, Miami 33243, ☎ 305/ 661–3270). Winter is peak season; summer is also busy but rates are lower. For price ranges (which reflect high-season rates), *see* Chart 2 (A) *in* On the Road with Fodor's.

$$$$ 🏨 **Alexander Hotel.** Every room here is a large suite with two baths
★ and a kitchen, ocean or bay view, and antique or reproduction furnishings. The hotel is renowned for service. ⊠ *5225 Collins Ave., Miami Beach 33140,* ☎ *305/865–6500 or 800/327–6121,* 䘠 *305/ 864–8525. 160 suites. Restaurant, coffee shop, 2 pools, spa, beach, boating. AE, D, DC, MC, V.*

$$$$ 🏨 **Delano Hotel.** Miami's hotel du jour, owned by New Yorker Ian Schrager, is home to the Madonna-owned Blue Door Restaurant and a grand lobby draped with massive, billowing white drapes. The stark whiteness of the beds, sheets, desks, and phones in the standard-size rooms makes them appear larger. Guests mutter about the lack of service, loud housekeepers, and the attitude of employees. ⊠ *1685 Collins Ave., 33139,* ☎ *305/672–2000 or 800/555–5001,* 䘠 *305/532–0099. 208 rooms. Restaurant, bar, pool, spa, health club. AE, D, DC, MC, V.*

$$$$ 🏨 **Grand Bay Hotel.** Artwork and fresh flowers enhance the elegant
★ lobby of this modern high-rise overlooking Biscayne Bay. The hotel's pyramid-like stepped profile gives each room facing the bay a private terrace. Guest rooms are filled with superb touches such as a canister of freshly sharpened pencils and an antique sideboard. ⊠ *2669 S. Bayshore Dr., Coconut Grove 33133,* ☎ *305/858–9600 or 800/327–*

2788, FAX 305/858–1532. 180 rooms. Restaurant, 2 bars, pool, beauty salon, hot tub, massage, saunas, health club. AE, DC, MC, V.

$$$$ ★ 🏨 **Sonesta Beach Resort & Tennis Club.** This hotel has always been one of Miami's best. Some rooms are in villas with full kitchens and screened-in pools. Don't miss the displays of modern art by notable painters and sculptors, especially three drawings by Andy Warhol of rock star Mick Jagger in the hotel's disco bar, Desires. ⊠ *350 Ocean Dr., Key Biscayne 33149,* ☎ *305/361–2021 or 800/766–3782,* FAX *305/361–3096. 300 rooms, 2 villas. 3 restaurants, bar, snack bar, pool, massage, steam rooms, 9 tennis courts, health club, beach, water sports. AE, DC, MC, V.*

$$$$ ★ 🏨 **Turnberry Isle Resort & Club.** Guests can choose from the newish Mediterranean-style annex, the intimate Marina Hotel, the Yacht Club on the Intracoastal Waterway, or the Country Club Hotel beside the golf course at this 300-acre resort and condominium complex in North Dade County. ⊠ *19999 W. Country Club Dr., Aventura 33180,* ☎ *305/ 932–6200 or 800/327–7028,* FAX *305/933–6560. 340 rooms. 7 restaurants, 5 lobby lounges, 4 pools, saunas, spa, steam rooms, 2 18-hole golf courses, 24 tennis courts, health club, racquetball, water sports, dive shop, boating, helipad. AE, D, DC, MC, V.*

$$$–$$$$ ★ 🏨 **Omni Colonnade Hotel.** The twin 13-story towers of this $65 million swank hotel, office, and shopping complex dominate downtown Coral Gables. Oversize rooms have sitting areas, built-in armoires, and traditional mahogany furnishings. ⊠ *180 Aragon Ave., Coral Gables 33134,* ☎ *305/441–2600 or 800/843–6664,* FAX *305/445–3929. 157 rooms. 2 restaurants, pool, 2 saunas, exercise room. AE, D, DC, MC, V.*

$$$–$$$$ 🏨 **Park Central.** Across the street from a glorious stretch of beach, this seven-story Art Deco hotel is a favorite of visiting fashion models and other trendsetters. The stylish guest rooms have mahogany furnishings. There is an espresso bar on site and a restaurant, Casablanca. ⊠ *640 Ocean Dr., Miami Beach 33139,* ☎ *305/538–1611 or 800/727–5236,* FAX *305/534–7520. 121 rooms. Restaurant, bar, pool, exercise room. AE, DC, MC, V.*

$$$ 🏨 **David William Hotel.** Easily the most affordable of the top Gables hotels, the 13-story DW (as aficionados call it) appears on the outside to be a 1960s retirement high-rise. However, the large rooms are very private; south-facing rooms have balconies, many have kitchens, and all have marble baths. The front-desk staff is excellent. Rooftop cabana guest rooms are the best bargains. ⊠ *700 Biltmore Way, Coral Gables 33134,* ☎ *305/445–7821 or 800/327–8770 outside FL,* FAX *305/ 445–5585. 106 rooms. Restaurant, bar, pool. AE, DC, MC, V.*

$$$ 🏨 **Essex House.** This restored Art Deco hotel was one of the finest lodgings of the era. Rooms—all soundproof—are small, as Art Deco accommodations typically are, but they're supplied with designer linens and feather-and-down pillows. ⊠ *1001 Collins Ave., Miami Beach 33139,* ☎ *305/534–2700 or 800/553–7739,* FAX *305/532–3827. 60 rooms. Breakfast room. AE, DC, MC, V.*

$$$ ★ 🏨 **Hotel Place St. Michel.** This, the finest small hotel in metropolitan Miami, is an intimate jewel in the heart of downtown. Art Nouveau chandeliers are suspended from vaulted lobby ceilings, and the scent of fresh flowers is circulated through the public spaces by paddle fans. Rooms, each a different size and individually furnished, contain English, French, and Scottish antiques. ⊠ *162 Alcazar Ave., Coral Gables 33134,* ☎ *305/444–1666 or 800/848–4683,* FAX *305/529–0074. 27 rooms. Restaurant, lobby lounge. AE, DC, MC, V.*

$$–$$$ 🏨 **Bay Harbor Inn.** Here's down-home hospitality in the county's most affluent area. The older of the inn's buildings is furnished in antiques; all rooms in the newer one face Indian Creek and have mid-century decor. A complimentary *Miami Herald* is provided for guests. ⊠ *9660 E. Bay Harbor Dr., Bay Harbor Islands 33154,* ☎ *305/868–4141,* FAX

305/867–9094. 38 rooms. 2 restaurants, lobby lounge, pool. Continental breakfast. AE, DC, MC, V.

$$ ☱ **Miami River Inn.** This hidden treasure is a 10-minute walk from the
★ heart of downtown. The turn-of-the-century inn consists of five clapboard buildings on a grassy, palm-studded compound. Don't be put off by the neighborhood—the setting is lovely, and rooms are filled with antiques. ⊠ *118 S.W. South River Dr., Miami 33130,* ☎ *305/325–0045,* FAX *305/325–9227. 40 rooms, 38 with bath. Pool. AE, D, DC, MC, V.*

$–$$ ☱ **Days Inn North Beach.** Dating from 1941, this seven-story hotel with modified Art Deco styling used to be the Broadmoor. It was—and still is—the pick of North Beach, across the road from a beautiful section of beach backed by grassy dunes. Rooms are undistinguished Days Inn–style with basic furnishings and fridges, but this is a good choice if you plan to use your room mostly for sleeping. ⊠ *7450 Ocean Terr., Miami Beach 33141,* ☎ *305/866–1631 or 800/325–2525,* FAX *305/868–4617. 93 rooms. Restaurant, bar. AE, D, DC, MC, V.*

Nightlife and the Arts

The best sources for events are the widely distributed free weeklies *Miami Today* and *New Times;* the *Miami Herald* publishes a Weekend section on Friday and a Lively Arts section on Sunday. If you read Spanish, rely on *El Nuevo Herald* (the Spanish version of the *Miami Herald*).

Nightlife

The liveliest scenes are in SoBe (Miami Beach's Art Deco District) and Coconut Grove, but clubs can be found in the suburbs, downtown, Little Havana, and Little Haiti.

BARS WITH MUSIC

Tobacco Road (⊠ 626 S. Miami Ave., Miami, ☎ 305/374–1198) holds Miami's oldest liquor license (Number 0001!) and is one of Miami's oldest bars, with excellent blues nightly. **Mac's Club Deuce** (⊠ 222 14th St., Miami Beach, ☎ 305/673–9537) is a funky—some might say weird—SoBe spot, where top international models come to shoot pool. **Bash** (⊠ 655 Washington Ave., ☎ 305/538–2274) is a grottolike bar with dance floors that reverberate to different sounds—sometimes reggae, sometimes Latin, but mostly loud disco.

DANCE CLUB

Amnesia (⊠ 136 Collins Ave., Miami Beach, ☎ 305/531–5535) feels like a luxurious amphitheater in the tropics—with a rain forest, what used to be called go-go dancers, and dancing in the rain when showers pass over the open-air club. It's open Thursday–Sunday.

NIGHTCLUBS

Some of the city's nightclubs offer a nostalgic look at the Miami of yore. **Les Violins Supper Club** (⊠ 1751 Biscayne Blvd., Miami, ☎ 305/371–8668) offers a live dance band and a wood dance floor. The bands at **Club Tropigala** (⊠ Fontainebleau Hilton, 4441 Collins Ave., Miami Beach, ☎ 305/672–7469)—whose four-tier round room is decorated with orchids, banana leaves, and philodendrons to resemble a tropical jungle—play standards as well as Latin music for dancing.

The Arts

BALLET

Miami City Ballet (⊠ 905 Lincoln Rd., Miami Beach, ☎ 305/532–7713 or 305/532–4880) is an acclaimed troupe under the direction of Edward Villella. You can watch rehearsals through a massive bay window.

MUSIC

New World Symphony (✉ 541 Lincoln Rd., Miami Beach 33139, ☎ 305/673–3331), conducted by Michael Tilson Thomas, is also a national orchestral academy for young musicians. **Concert Association of Florida** (✉ 555 Hank Meyer Blvd., at 17th St., Miami Beach 33139, ☎ 305/532–3491) is the South's largest presenter of classical artists, dance, and music.

OPERA

Florida Grand Opera (✉ 1200 Coral Way, Miami, ☎ 305/854–1643) presents five operas a year at the Dade County Auditorium.

THEATER

The **Coconut Grove Playhouse** (✉ 3500 Main Hwy., ☎ 305/442–4000) stages Broadway-bound plays and musical revues as well as experimental productions. **Colony Theater** (✉ 1040 Lincoln Rd., Miami Beach, ☎ 305/674–1026), once a movie theater, is now a city-owned 465-seat performing arts center featuring dance, drama, music, and experimental cinema. **Jackie Gleason Theater of the Performing Arts** (✉ 1700 Washington Ave., Miami Beach, ☎ 305/673–7300) is home of the Broadway Series and other stage events. **Teatro de Bellas Artes** (✉ 2173 S.W. 8th St., Miami, ☎ 305/325–0515), a 255-seat theater on Calle Ocho, presents Spanish plays and musicals year-round.

Outdoor Activities and Sports

Diving

Summer diving conditions in Greater Miami have been compared with those in the Caribbean. Winter can bring rough, cold waters. Fowey, Triumph, Long, and Emerald reefs are shallow 10- to 15-ft dives good for snorkelers and beginning divers. **Divers Paradise of Key Biscayne** (✉ 4000 Crandon Blvd., Key Biscayne, ☎ 305/361–3483) offers dive charters, rentals, and instruction. The **Diving Locker** (✉ 223 Sunny Isles Blvd., North Miami Beach, ☎ 305/947–6025) offers three-day and three-week certification courses, wreck and reef dives aboard the *Native Diver,* and a full complement of sales, service, and repairs. In Miami, **Bubbles Dive Center** (✉ 2671 S.W. 27th Ave., ☎ 305/856–0565) is an all-purpose dive shop.

Golf

Dade County has more than 30 private and public golf courses (☎ 305/857–6868 for county information, 305/575–5256 for Miami information, 305/673–7730 for Miami Beach information).

Sailing

The center of sailing in Greater Miami remains at the **Dinner Key** and the **Coconut Grove** waterfronts, although moorings and rentals are found elsewhere on the bay and up the Miami River.

Tennis

Greater Miami has more than 60 private and public tennis centers. All public courts charge nonresidents an hourly fee. **Biltmore Tennis Center** (✉ 1150 Anastasia Ave., Coral Gables, ☎ 305/460–5360) has 10 hard courts. **Flamingo Tennis Center** (✉ 1000 12th St., Miami Beach, ☎ 305/673–7761) has 19 clay courts. **Tennis Center at Crandon Park** (✉ 7300 Crandon Blvd., Key Biscayne, ☎ 305/365–2300), which hosts the annual Lipton Championships in March, provides 2 grass, 8 clay, and 17 hard courts.

Windsurfing

You can rent windsurfing equipment at **Sailboards Miami** (✉ Key Biscayne, ☎ 305/361–7245), on Hobie Island just past the tollbooth for the Rickenbacker Causeway to Key Biscayne.

Spectator Sports

Baseball: Florida Marlins (✉ Pro Player Stadium, 2269 N.W. 199th St., Miami, ☎ 305/626–7400 or 305/620–2578).

Basketball: Miami Heat (✉ Miami Arena, 1 S.E. 3rd Ave., Miami, ☎ 305/577–4328).

Football: Miami Dolphins (✉ Pro Player Stadium, 2269 N.W. 199th St., Miami, ☎ 305/620–2578).

Jai Alai: Miami Jai Alai (✉ 3500 N.W. 37th Ave., Miami, ☎ 305/633–6400; Nov.–Apr. and mid-May–late Sept.) is the oldest fronton in America. This is the fastest game on earth: pelotas—hard balls thrown from handheld baskets called cestas—travel at speeds of more than 170 mph. You can bet on a team to win or on the order in which teams will finish.

Beaches

Millions visit Dade County's beaches annually. **Miami Beach** extends continuously for 10 mi. A boardwalk runs from 23rd to 44th streets, and along this stretch various groups tend to congregate in specific areas. From 1st to 15th streets senior citizens often gather early in the day. **Lummus Park,** the stretch of beach opposite the Art Deco District, between 5th and 15th streets, attracts all ages. Volleyball, in-line skating along the paved upland path, and children's playgrounds make this a popular area for families. Gays frequent the beach between 11th and 13th streets. Sidewalk cafés parallel the entire beach area, which makes it easy to come ashore for everything from burgers to quiche. Families and anybody else who likes things quiet prefer **North Beach,** along Ocean Terrace between 72nd and 75th streets.

Two of metropolitan Miami's best beaches are on Key Biscayne. Nearest the causeway is the 3½-mi county beach in **Crandon Park** (✉ 4000 Crandon Blvd., ☎ 305/361–5421), popular with young couples and families. **Bill Baggs Cape Florida State Recreation Area** (✉ 1200 S. Crandon Blvd., ☎ 305/361–5811) has beaches, boardwalks, and nature trails among many other appealing features.

Shopping

Malls, an international free zone, and specialty shopping districts are the attractions in Miami. Many shopping areas have an ethnic flavor.

Shopping Districts

More than 500 garment manufacturers sell their clothing in more than 30 factory outlets and discount fashion stores in the **Fashion District,** east of I–95 along 5th Avenue from 25th to 29th streets. Most stores in the district are open Monday through Saturday 9–5. The **Miami Free Zone** (✉ 2305 N.W. 107th Ave., ☎ 305/591–4300) is a vast international wholesale trade center, where you can buy goods duty-free for export or pay duty on goods released for domestic use. More than 140 companies sell products from more than 100 countries, including clothing, computers, cosmetics, electronics, liquor, and perfumes. At **Cauley Square** (✉ 22400 Old Dixie Hwy., Goulds, ☎ 305/258–3543)—a complex of clapboard, coral-rock, and stucco buildings that housed railroad workers at the turn of the century—shops primarily sell antiques and crafts. To get there, exit U.S. 1 at S.W. 224th Street; it's usually closed on Sunday.

WALT DISNEY WORLD™ AND THE ORLANDO AREA

Once upon a time about the only things to see in Orlando were Walt Disney World and Mickey Mouse. Today, however, cosmopolitan Orlando is an international business center and tourist mecca. Many other attractions, interesting shopping areas, and a varied nightlife make the area an exciting, if sometimes frenetic and crowded, vacation destination. Away from the tourist areas, hundreds of spring-fed lakes surrounded by graceful oaks recall Orlando's bucolic past. About an hour's drive from the city, on the Atlantic coast, are the Cocoa Beach area and the Kennedy Space Center, Spaceport USA.

Visitor Information

Kissimmee/St. Cloud: Convention and Visitors Bureau (✉ 1925 E. Irlo Bronson Memorial Hwy., Kissimmee 34744, ☎ 407/363–5800, 407/847–5000, or 800/327–9159). **Orlando/Orange County:** Convention and Visitors Bureau (✉ 8445 International Dr., Orlando 32819, ☎ 407/363–5871).

Arriving and Departing

By Bus
Greyhound Lines (☎ 800/231–2222) provides service from major Florida cities and from outside the state.

By Car
From Jacksonville take I–95 south, then I–4 from Port Orange. From Tampa/St. Petersburg take I–4 east. From Miami take I–95 north and connect with Florida's Turnpike going northbound at White City. From Atlanta take I–75 south and connect with Florida's Turnpike.

By Plane
Orlando International Airport (✉ 6086 McCoy Rd., off the Bee Line Expressway, ☎ 407/825–2000) is served by major U.S. airlines as well as many foreign airlines.

By Train
Amtrak (☎ 800/872–7245) operates the *Silver Star* and the *Silver Meteor* to Florida. Both stop at Winter Park, Orlando, and Kissimmee.

Exploring Walt Disney World™ and the Orlando Area

Walt Disney World™

★ The focal point of an Orlando vacation is **Walt Disney World** (✉ Box 10040, Lake Buena Vista 32830, ☎ 407/824–4321), a collection of theme parks and attractions connected by extensive bus, monorail, motor-launch, and ferry systems (free if you stay at an on-site resort or if you hold a three-park ticket). Admission is not cheap: A one-day adult ticket costs $40.81 (at press time, spring 1997) and admits you to only one of the parks: Magic Kingdom, Epcot, Disney-MGM, or when it opens, Disney's Animal Kingdom. Your best bet, even if you plan to stay only two or three days, may be to purchase a Four-Day Park Hopper Pass ($152.64 for adults), or a Five-Day World Hopper Pass ($207.76 for adults); both admit you to all three parks, allow you to visit more than one on any given day, and include unlimited use of Disney transport.

THE MAGIC KINGDOM

The Magic Kingdom is divided into seven lands. Stories are told of tourists who spend an entire day in one land, thinking they have seen the entire park; don't let that happen to you. To get a great overview of the Kingdom, hop aboard the **Walt Disney World Railroad** and take a 1½-mi ride around the perimeter of the park. You can board at the Victorian-style station by the park entrance. Other stations are in Frontierland and at Mickey's Toontown Fair, on the border between Tomorrowland and Fantasyland.

Sprawling before you when you enter the Magic Kingdom is **Main Street**—a shop-filled boulevard with Victorian-style stores and dining spots. Stop at **City Hall** (on your left as you enter) to get information or to snap a picture with the Disney characters who frequent the spot. A cinema that runs vintage Disney cartoons is another attraction here. If you walk two blocks along Main Street, you'll enter Central Plaza, with Cinderella Castle rising directly in front of you. This is the hub of the Kingdom; all the lands radiate from it.

Adventureland is a mishmash of tropical and swashbuckling attractions that are among the most crowded in the Magic Kingdom. Visit as late in the afternoon as possible or, better yet, in the evening. The **Swiss Family Robinson Treehouse** (popular; all ages) is a good way to get both exercise and a panoramic view of the park. Visitors walk single file up the many-staired tree, a trip that can take up to a half hour. The **Jungle Cruise** (very popular; all ages) takes visitors along the Nile, the Mekong, the Congo, and the Amazon rivers. The tour guide's narration is corny but nevertheless brings laughs. **Pirates of the Caribbean** (very popular; all ages, although very young children might be scared) is a journey through a world of pirate strongholds and treasure-filled dungeons. The Audio-Animatronic pirates are first-rate.

Frontierland's major draw is **Big Thunder Mountain Railroad** (very popular; all but young children), a scream-inducing roller coaster. Children must be at least 3′4″. Try to go in the evening when the mountain is lighted up and lines are relatively short. **Splash Mountain** (very popular; all but young children), an elaborate water-flume ride, is based on Disney's 1946 film *Song of the South*. The ride includes characters from the movie, and you'll hear some of the songs as well. An eight-person hollowed-out log takes you on a half-mile journey that passes through Brer Rabbit's habitat. The final plunge is down Chickapin Hill—the world's longest and sharpest flume drop—at speeds of up to 40 mph.

Liberty Square is a journey back to Colonial America. The **Hall of Presidents** is a 30-minute multimedia tribute to the Constitution and the nation's 42 presidents. The star attraction here is Disney's special-effects extravaganza, the **Haunted Mansion** (popular; all but young children). Scary but not terrifying, this ride on a "doom buggie" takes you past a plethora of dust, cobwebs, tombstones, and creepy characters.

Fantasyland is, as the map says, "where storybook dreams come true." Fanciful gingerbread houses, gleaming gold turrets, and streams sparkling with shiny pennies dot the landscape, and its rides are based on Disney's animated movies. The first attraction on the left as you enter Fantasyland is **Legend of the Lion King.** Unlike many other stage shows in the Magic Kingdom, this one showcases not humans but "humanimals," Disneyspeak for bigger-than-life-size figures manipulated by human "animateers" hidden from audience view (the adult Simba, for example, is nearly 8 ft tall). The preshow consists of the "Circle of Life" overture from the film. Other attractions include the rides **Dumbo the Flying Elephant, Peter Pan's Flight,** a much-improved **Snow White's Adventures,** and the **Mad Tea Party.** Kids of all ages love the antique **Cinderella's Golden Carousel,** which encapsulates the entire Disney experience in its 90 prancing horses. Small children adore **It's a Small World,** a boat ride accompanied by its now-famous theme song of international brotherhood.

Mickey's Toontown Fair was built in 1988 in a quiet niche of Fantasyland to celebrate Mickey Mouse's 60th birthday. Now an official Magic Kingdom land, it is filled with all manner of things child size. Kids can visit **Mickey and Minnie's country houses, Goofy's Wiseacres Farm,** and **Toon Park,** a spongy green meadow filled with foam topiary in the shapes of goats, cows, pigs, and horses. This is a good opportunity for weary parents to rest their feet while children run around.

The new **Tomorrowland** made its long-awaited debut in 1995. **Space Mountain** (very popular; all but young children) is still here, and the needlelike spires of this space-age roller coaster are a Magic Kingdom landmark. Although the ride's speed never exceeds 28 mph, the experience in the dark, with everyone screaming, is thrilling, even for hardcore roller coaster fans. To see the interior without taking the ride, hop aboard the **Tomorrowland Transit Authority (TTA).** Despite a disappointing lack of truly special effects, **Alien Encounters** (very popular; all ages) provides an eerie experience with another world.

EPCOT

Visitors familiar with the Magic Kingdom find something entirely different at Epcot, a rare paradox—an educational theme park—and a very successful one, too.

Future World is two concentric circles of pavilions. In the inner core are the **Spaceship Earth** geosphere—the giant, golf-ball-shape Epcot icon whose ride explores the development of human communication—and just beyond it, the Innoventions exhibit and Innoventions Plaza. Making up the circle's outer ring are seven corporate-sponsored pavilions containing both rides and interactive displays on topics such as technology, motion, the seas, the land, and imagination.

The 40-acre **World Showcase Lagoon** is 1⅓ mi around, but in that space you can circumnavigate the globe—or at least explore it. Eleven pavilions present a Disney version of life in various countries through native food, entertainment, and wares. Models of some of the world's best-known monuments, such as the Eiffel Tower, a Mayan temple, and a majestic Japanese pagoda, are painstakingly re-created. During the day these structures are impressive enough, but at night when the darkness inhibits one's ability to judge their size, you feel as though you are seeing the real thing. It's a wonderful illusion, indeed.

Except for the boat rides in Mexico and Norway, the Showcase doesn't offer amusement-park-type rides. Instead, it features breathtaking films, ethnic art, cultural entertainment, Audio-Animatronic presentations, and dozens of fine shops and restaurants featuring national specialties. The most enjoyable diversions in World Showcase are not inside the national pavilions but in front of them: Throughout the day each pavilion offers some sort of live street show featuring comedy, song, or dance routines and demonstrations of folk arts and crafts.

DISNEY-MGM STUDIOS THEME PARK

The **Backstage Studio Tour,** a combination tram ride and walking tour, takes you on a 25-minute tour of the back-lot building blocks of movies: set design, costumes, props, lighting, and special effects—at the de rigueur Catastrophe Canyon, in which your tram starts bouncing up and down in a simulated earthquake, an oil tanker explodes in gobs of smoke and flame, and a water tower crashes to the ground, touching off a flash flood.

One of the funniest attractions at the theme park is the **Magic of Disney Animation,** a 30-minute self-guided tour that takes visitors step by step through the Disney animation process by looking over the artists' shoulders from a raised, glass-enclosed walkway.

Star Tours is a flight-simulator thrill ride. Created under the direction of George Lucas, the five 40-seat theaters become spaceships, and you're off to the moon of Endor. A word of caution: The ride can be rough.

The **Walt Disney Theater** usually runs *The Making of . . .* , a behind-the-scenes look at Disney's latest smash hit. Produced for the Disney Channel, programs have included *The Lion King, Toy Story,* and *The Hunchback of Notre Dame.*

The **Indiana Jones Epic Stunt Spectacular,** presented in a 2,200-seat amphitheater, is a 30-minute show featuring the stunt choreography of veteran coordinator Glenn Randall (*Raiders of the Lost Ark, Indiana Jones and the Temple of Doom, E.T.,* and *Jewel of the Nile* are among his credits).

At the 13-story **Twilight Zone Tower of Terror,** reputedly the now-abandoned Hollywood Tower Hotel, you board a giant elevator and head upward past seemingly deserted hallways. Suddenly, the creaking vehicle plunges in a terrifying 130-ft free-fall drop, and then it does it all over again! The ride is for older children and adults.

OTHER ATTRACTIONS

Blizzard Beach promises the seemingly impossible—a seaside playground with an alpine theme; admission is $26.45. **Discovery Island** is a nature sanctuary with bird shows. **River Country,** the first of Walt Disney World's water parks, is a rustic and rugged ol'-fashioned swimmin' hole. **Typhoon Lagoon,** also $26.45, four times the size of River Country, contains everything from an artificial coral reef with tropical fish (closed in winter) to a lazy river that circles the entire park.

The Orlando Area

Universal Studios Florida is the largest working film studio outside Hollywood. Visitors view live shows, participate in movie-themed attractions, and tour back-lot sets. The tour showcases the special-effects magic of creative consultant Steven Spielberg and the animation wizardry of Hanna-Barbera. Take Exit 29 off I–4, and follow the signs. ⊠ *1000 Universal Studios Plaza, Orlando,* ☏ *407/363–8000.* ⊡ *$37 adults, $30 children 3–9.*

Performing dolphins, killer whales, and a walk-through Plexiglas tunnel that lets you see a collection of predatory sea creatures such as sharks and barracudas capture your attention at **Sea World.** The park also has penguins, tropical fish, manatees, seals and sea lions, and other educational diversions. Take Exit 28 off I–4 and follow signs. ⊠ *7007 Sea Harbor Dr., Orlando,* ☏ *407/351–3600.* ⊡ *$39.95 adults, $32.80 children 3–9.*

Beautiful **Cypress Gardens** offers walks through exotic gardens, bird shows, and the famous waterskiing revue. Take I–4 to the U.S. 27S exit and follow signs. ⊠ *Off Rte. 540 east of Winter Haven,* ☏ *941/324–2111 or 800/237–4826.* ⊡ *$26.95 adults, $16.45 children 6–12.*

Splendid China—12 mi southwest of Orlando—is a theme park with more than 60 scaled-down replicas of China's greatest landmarks. Among the painstakingly crafted models are the Great Wall, the Imperial Palace of Beijing's Forbidden City, and Suzhou Gardens, a re-creation of a 14th-century Chinese village. ⊠ *3000 Splendid China Blvd., Kissimmee,* ☏ *407/397–8800 or 800/244–6226.* ⊡ *$23.55 adults, $13.90 children 5–12, $21.50 senior citizens.*

Orlando Area

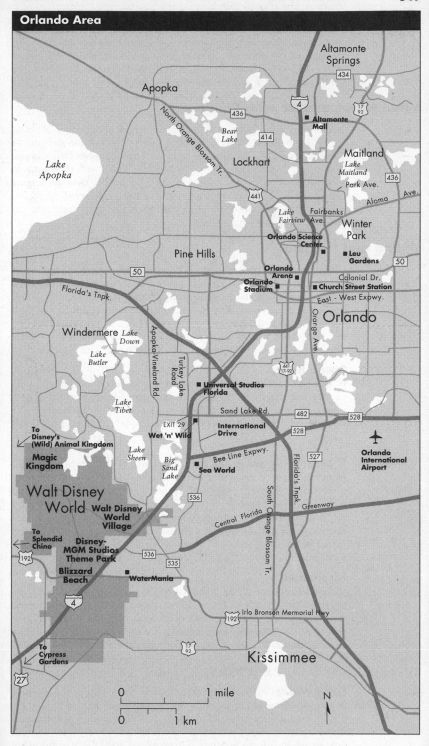

Altamonte Springs

Apopka

Lake Apopka

North Orange Blossom Tr.

Bear Lake

Lockhart

Maitland

Lake Maitland

Park Ave.

Aloma Ave.

Fairbanks Ave.

Lake Fairview

Winter Park

Pine Hills

Orlando Science Center

Leu Gardens

Orlando Arena

Colonial Dr.

Orlando Stadium

Church Street Station

Florida's Tnpk.

East - West Expwy.

Orlando

Orange Ave.

Windermere

Lake Down

Lake Butler

Apopka-Vineland Rd.

Turkey Lake Road

Lake Tibet

Universal Studios Florida

Sand Lake Rd.

EXIT 29

Wet 'n' Wild

International Drive

To Disney's (Wild) Animal Kingdom

Magic Kingdom

Lake Sheen

Big Sand Lake

Bee Line Expwy.

Sea World

Florida's Tnpk.

Orlando International Airport

Walt Disney World

Walt Disney World Village

Central Florida Greenway

South Orange Blossom Tr.

To Splendid China

Disney-MGM Studios Theme Park

Blizzard Beach

WaterMania

Irlo Bronson Mermorial Hwy

To Cypress Gardens

Kissimmee

Altamonte Mall

0 ___ 1 mile

0 ___ 1 km

N

In the Cocoa Beach area, 47 mi east of Orlando via Route 50 or the Bee Line Expressway, is **Spaceport USA.** Here the wonders of space travel unfold through superb film presentations and bus tours of spacecraft hangars and launch sites. ⊠ *Kennedy Space Center,* ☎ *407/452–2121 or 800/432–2153 outside FL.* ⊡ *Free, but admission charged for films and tours. Closed certain launch dates.*

What to See and Do with Children

In addition to the Disney parks (☞ Exploring Walt Disney World and the Orlando Area, *above*), the area offers children the delights of **Gatorland** (⊠ 14501 S. Orange Blossom Trail, between Orlando and Kissimmee, ☎ 407/855–5496 or 800/393–5297), with thousands of alligators, crocodiles, and other Florida wildlife. The **Orlando Science Center** (⊠ 777 E. Princeton St., ☎ 407/514–2000) moved in 1997 to a new 193,000-square-ft building with themed display halls and numerous exciting interactive exhibits.

Dining and Lodging

Dining is an adventure in the Orlando area, where international cuisines, fresh fish and seafood, and such exotic local dishes as grilled alligator tail tempt the hungry. Besides hotels in Walt Disney World, you'll find accommodations in Orlando; Kissimmee, just east of Walt Disney World; and other outlying towns. Lodging options include luxury hotels and resorts, family resorts, and motel chains. For price ranges *see* Charts 1 (B) and 2 (A) *in* On the Road with Fodor's.

Cocoa Beach

$$$ ✕ **Mango Tree Restaurant.** Dine in elegance amid orchid gardens, with piano music playing in the background. Broiled grouper topped with scallops, shrimp, and hollandaise sauce is a menu favorite. ⊠ *118 N. Atlantic Ave.,* ☎ *407/799–0513. AE, MC, V. Closed Mon. No lunch.*

$$–$$$ 🏨 **Inn at Cocoa Beach.** The spacious rooms in this charming oceanfront inn are each decorated differently, but all have some combination of reproduction 18th- and 19th-century armoires, four-poster beds, and comfortably upholstered chairs and sofas, as well as balconies or patios with ocean views. Included in the rate are a sumptuous Continental breakfast and wine and cheese in the evening. ⊠ *4300 Ocean Beach Blvd., 32931,* ☎ *407/799–3460 or 800/343–5307 outside FL. 50 rooms. Pool, beach. AE, D, DC, MC, V.*

Kissimmee

$ 🏨 **Sevilla Inn.** One of the best buys in the Orlando area, this family-operated motel, built in 1985 and expanded in 1990, has stucco and wood on the outside and up-to-date rooms inside. The tropically landscaped pool area looks like something you'd find at a much fancier resort. ⊠ *4640 W. Irlo Bronson Memorial Hwy., 34746,* ☎ *407/ 396–4135 or 800/367–1363,* 🖷 *407/396–4942. 46 rooms. Pool, coin laundry. AE, D, MC, V.*

Lake Wales

$$$$ ✕ **Chalet Suzanne.** Expanded bit by quirky bit since it opened in the 1930s, this unlikely inn looks like a small Swiss village right in the middle of orange groves. The menu has such items as shrimp curry, broiled grapefruit, and crepes Suzanne. This makes a good place to stop after a visit to Cypress Gardens. ⊠ *3800 Chalet Suzanne Dr.,* ☎ *941/676– 6011. AE, DC, MC, V. Closed Mon. in summer.*

Orlando

$$-$$$ ✕ **Chatham's Place.** The office exterior belies what's inside—a small,
★   unpretentious restaurant that is one of Orlando's finest. Enjoy such tantalizing entrées as black grouper with pecan butter and grilled duck breast. ⊠ *7575 Dr. Phillips Blvd.*, ☎ *407/345–2992. AE, D, DC, MC, V.*

$$ ✕ **Planet Hollywood.** You'll find movie memorabilia, like the bus that was used in the movie *Speed* and the leather jacket worn by Schwarzenegger in *The Terminator,* housed in this popular restaurant. Memorabilia rotates between the Orlando Planet and its many sister restaurants around the country. The wait is about two hours most evenings. ⊠ *Pleasure Island,* ☎ *407/827–7827. Reservations not accepted. AE, DC, MC, V.*

$$$–$$$$ ⊞ **Peabody Orlando.** The bland facade gives no hint of this 27-story
★   hotel's beautifully decorated interior, with marble floors, fountains, and modern art. Many rooms have views of Walt Disney World, but the real show is watching the Peabody's ducks waddle their way to the marble fountain, where they pass the day. ⊠ *9801 International Dr., 32819,* ☎ *407/352–4000 or 800/732–2639,* ℻ *407/351–9177. 891 rooms. 3 restaurants, 2 lobby lounges, pool, wading pool, hot tub, spa, golf privileges, 4 tennis courts, health club, baby-sitting, concierge. AE, D, DC, MC, V.*

$$$ ⊞ **Grosvenor Resort.** This colonial-style hotel, with comfortable rooms, plentiful amenities and recreational facilities, and spacious public areas, is one of the best deals in the area. ⊠ *1850 Hotel Plaza Blvd., Lake Buena Vista 32830,* ☎ *407/828–4444 or 800/624–4109,* ℻ *407/ 828–8192. 633 rooms. 2 restaurants, lobby lounge, 2 pools, wading pool, hot tub, 2 tennis courts, basketball, volleyball, playground, coin laundry, laundry service. AE, DC, MC, V.*

Walt Disney World™

For restaurants within Walt Disney World, reservations are especially easy to make, thanks to its central reservations lines, 407/939–3463 and 407/560–7277. In addition, the WorldKey Information Center can be used for the very popular restaurants of Epcot. Reserve early in the day before beginning your sightseeing.

World Showcase, in **Epcot,** offers some of the best dining in the Orlando area, with specialties from various nations that will appeal to every taste. **L'Originale Alfredo di Roma Ristorante** ($$$), in Italy of course, is known for its namesake dish, fettuccine Alfredo, sauced with cream, butter, and loads of freshly grated Parmesan cheese and served by singing waiters. The **Rose and Crown** pub ($$), in the United Kingdom, offers hearty portions of fish-and-chips with a Guinness stout. **Marrakesh** ($$–$$$) delights the palate with fare that's more exotic to most American palates, such as Moroccan couscous.

Although hotels and resorts on Disney property cost more than comparable facilities elsewhere, there are many perks to staying at one of them, including unlimited free transportation to all Walt Disney World parks. Book all Disney hotels—including the following—through **Walt Disney World Central Reservations** (☎ 407/934–7639).

$$$$ ⊞ **Grand Floridian.** With its brick chimneys, gabled roof, sweeping ve-
★   randas, and stained-glass domes, this resort exudes Victorian charm yet has all the conveniences of a modern hotel. Water sports are a focal point at the marina. ☎ *407/824–3000,* ℻ *407/824–3186. 990 rooms. 6 restaurants, 3 lobby lounges, pool, beauty salon, hot tub, 2 tennis courts, health club, beach, boating, baby-sitting, children's programs, playground, coin laundry, laundry service, concierge. AE, MC, V.*

$$ ⊞ **Caribbean Beach Resort.** On a 42-acre tropical lake, this resort has several villages named after Caribbean islands, each with its own pool,

but all share a white-sand beach. Facilities include a food court, a tropical lounge, and an island in the lagoon with bike paths, trails, and play areas. ☎ 407/934–3400, ꜰᴀx 407/934–3288. *2,112 rooms. Restaurant, food court, lobby lounge, 7 pools, wading pool, hot tub, jogging, beach, boating, bicycles, baby-sitting, playground, coin laundry, laundry service. AE, MC, V.*

Motels

U.S. 192 is crammed with motels offering the basics at affordable prices in a location near Walt Disney World. Rates range from inexpensive to moderate, and most have a pool but few other extras. Among these are **Best Western, Quality Suites,** and **Residence Inn** (☞ Toll-Free Numbers *in* The Gold Guide).

Campgrounds

Fort Wilderness Campground Resort (✉ Walt Disney World Central Reservations; ☞ Walt Disney World, *above*) is 700 acres of forests, streams, and small lakes within Walt Disney World. You can rent a trailer or bring your own to campsites equipped with electrical outlets, outdoor grills, running water, and waste disposal. Tent sites with water and electricity but no sewage are also available.

Nightlife and the Arts

Nightlife

Inside Walt Disney World every hotel has its quota of bars and lounges. Nightly shows include the laser show **IllumiNations** at Epcot and the **Polynesian Luau** at the Polynesian Resort (☎ 407/934–7639). **Pleasure Island** has seven clubs, a few restaurants, shops, and a 10-screen AMC cinema. In Orlando **Church Street Station** (✉ 129 W. Church St., ☎ 407/422–2434) is a popular entertainment complex in an authentic 19th-century setting. **Medieval Times** (✉ 4510 W. Irlo Bronson Memorial Hwy. [U.S. 192], Kissimmee, ☎ 407/239–0214 or 800/229–8300) has a dinner show with knights, nobles, and maidens.

The Arts

Carr Performing Arts Centre (✉ 401 W. Livingston St., Orlando, ☎ 407/849–2020) routinely features dance, music, and theater performances. **Orange County Convention and Civic Center** (✉ South end of International Dr., Orlando, ☎ 407/345–9800) presents big-name performers. The **Civic Theater of Central Florida** (✉ 1001 E. Princeton St., Orlando, ☎ 407/896–7365) presents a variety of shows.

Outdoor Activities and Sports

Biking

The Orlando area has a collection of city-constructed bike paths through downtown, and there are a few places suitable for cycling in the Winter Park area. Serious cyclists head to the rolling hills of nearby Lake County.

Golf

Cypress Creek Country Club (✉ 5353 Vineland Rd., Orlando, ☎ 407/351–2187) is a demanding 18-hole course with 16 water holes and lots of trees. **Grenelefe Golf & Tennis Resort** (✉ 3200 Rte. 546, Haines City, ☎ 941/422–7511 or 800/237–9549) has three excellent 18-hole courses, of which the toughest is the 7,325-yard West Course. **Timacuan Golf & Country Club** (✉ 550 Timacuan Blvd., Lake Mary, ☎ 407/321–0010) has a front nine that's open, with lots of sand, and a back nine that's heavily wooded. There are five championship courses within **Walt Disney World.**

Horseback Riding

Fort Wilderness Campground (⊠ Walt Disney World, ☎ 407/824–2832) offers tame trail rides through backwoods.

Spectator Sports

Basketball: The NBA **Orlando Magic** (⊠ 600 W. Amelia St., 2 blocks west of I–4 Amelia St. exit, Orlando, ☎ 407/839–3900) play in Orlando Arena.

Beaches and Water Sports

A plethora of water sports is available in the Orlando area. Marinas at resorts in **Walt Disney World** rent all types of boats, from canoes and catamarans to pedal boats. Just north of the Kennedy Space Center, the **Canaveral National Seashore** (⊠ Between New Smyrna Beach and Titusville, ☎ 904/428–3384) has 24 mi of unspoiled, uncrowded beaches with facilities for swimming and boating.

Shopping

Altamonte Mall (⊠ 451 Altamonte Ave., Altamonte Springs) is a two-level mall with major department stores and 165 specialty shops. The festive **Mercado Mediterranean Village** (⊠ 8445 International Dr., Orlando) has specialty shops and a large food court with cuisines from around the world. **Flea World** (⊠ 3 mi east of I–4 Exit 50 on Lake Mary Blvd., then 1 mi south on U.S. 17–92, between Orlando and Sanford) has more than 1,600 booths selling new merchandise from citrus products to auto parts.

THE FLORIDA KEYS

The string of 31 islands—or keys—placed like a comma between the Atlantic Ocean and the Gulf of Mexico at the southern tip of Florida presents a paradox to the visitor. On the one hand, the Keys are natural wonders of lush vegetation, tropical birds, and wildlife, washed by waters teeming with more than 600 kinds of fish; a place where swimming, fishing, and boating are a way of life. On the other hand, the Keys are a highly commercialized tourist attraction that has brought a clutter of unsightly billboards, motels, and shopping malls to U.S. 1 (also known as the Overseas Highway), which links the islands to the mainland. Although the 110-mi drive from Key Largo to Key West is often clogged with traffic on weekends and holidays, it is still a mesmerizing journey into expanses of blue water and blue sky, especially where the road is the only thing separating the ocean from the Gulf. A note about addresses, which are listed by island or mile marker (MM) number: Residents use the abbreviation BS for the Bay Side of the Overseas Highway (U.S. 1) and OS for the Atlantic Ocean side of the highway.

Visitor Information

Florida Keys & Key West Visitors Bureau (⊠ 402 Wall St., Key West 33040, ☎ 800/352–5397). **Greater Key West Chamber of Commerce** (⊠ 402 Wall St., Key West 33040, ☎ 305/294–2587 or 800/527–8539, FAX 305/294–7806). **Islamorada Chamber of Commerce** (⊠ MM 82.5, BS, Box 915, 33036, ☎ 305/664–4503 or 800/322–5397). **Key Largo Chamber of Commerce** (⊠ MM 106, BS, 106000 Overseas Hwy., 33037, ☎ 305/451–1414 or 800/822–1088). **Key West Business Guild** (oriented to gay locals and visitors; ⊠ Box 1208, 33041, ☎ 305/294–4603 or 800/535–7797). **Lower Keys Chamber of Commerce** (⊠ MM 31, OS, Box 430511, Big Pine Key 33043, ☎ 305/872–2411 or 800/872–3722, FAX 305/872–0752). **Marathon Chamber of Commerce &**

Visitor Center (✉ MM 53.5, BS, 12222 Overseas Hwy., 33050, ☎ 305/743–5417 or 800/842–9580).

Arriving and Departing

By Boat

You can travel to Key West via the Intracoastal Waterway through Florida Bay or in Hawk Channel along the Atlantic coast. Marinas abound in the Keys, but be sure to make docking reservations in advance. For more information contact the **Florida Marine Patrol** (✉ MM 49, OS, 2835 Overseas Hwy., Marathon, ☎ 305/289–2320).

By Bus

Greyhound Lines (☎ 800/231–2222) departs Miami International Airport (from Concourse E, Lower Level) for the Keys three times a day. It makes stops at Key Largo, Tavernier Islamorada, Layton, Marathon, Big Pine Key, Ramrod Key, Cudjoe Key, Sugarloaf Shores, and Key West.

By Car

From Miami take U.S. 1 south to Florida City. To avoid Miami traffic, take the Homestead Extension of the Florida Turnpike (toll road) south until it links with U.S. 1; just south of here U.S. 1 becomes the Overseas Highway.

By Plane

Continuous improvements in service now link airports in Miami, Fort Lauderdale/Hollywood, Naples, Orlando, and Tampa directly with Key West International Airport (✉ S. Roosevelt Blvd., ☎ 305/296–5439 or 305/296–7223). Service is provided by **American Eagle** (☎ 800/433–7300), **Cape Air** (☎ 800/352–0714), **Comair** (☎ 800/354–9822), **Gulfstream International Airlines** (☎ 800/992–8532), and **US Airways/US Airways Express** (☎ 800/428–4322). Direct service between Miami and **Marathon** (✉ MM 52, BS, 9000 Overseas Hwy., ☎ 305/743–2155) is provided by American Eagle. US Airways Express connects Marathon with Tampa.

Exploring the Florida Keys

The Keys are divided into the Upper Keys (from Key Largo to Long Key Channel), the Middle Keys (from Long Key Channel to Seven Mile Bridge), and the Lower Keys (from Seven Mile Bridge to Key West). Pause to explore the flora and fauna of the backcountry and the fragile reefs and aquatic life of the surrounding waters as you weave your way south to historically rich Key West.

Upper Keys

The Upper Keys are dominated by **Key Largo,** with its wildlife refuges and nature parks. The 2,005-acre **Key Largo Hammocks State Botanical Site** (✉ 1 mi north of U.S. 1 on Rte. 905, OS, ☎ 305/451–7008) is the largest remaining stand of West Indian tropical hardwood hammock and mangrove wetland in the Keys. **John Pennekamp Coral Reef State Park** (✉ MM 102.5, OS, Box 487, 102601 Overseas Hwy., ☎ 305/451–1202) encompasses 78 square mi of coral reefs, which contain 40 species of coral and more than 650 varieties of fish. Diving and snorkeling here are exceptional. A concessionaire rents canoes and sailboats and offers boat trips to the reef.

The small but earnest **Maritime Museum of the Florida Keys** (✉ MM 102.5, BS, Key Largo, ☎ 305/451–6444) has exhibits depicting the history of shipwrecks and salvage efforts along the Keys, including retrieved treasures, reconstructed wreck sites, and artifacts in various stages of preservation.

Nowhere else in the Keys can you see bird life so close up as at the **Florida Keys Wild Bird Rehabilitation Center** (⊠ MM 93.6, BS, 93600 Overseas Hwy., Tavernier, ☎ 305/852–4486), where at any time the resident population can include ospreys, hawks, pelicans, cormorants, terns, and herons. **Indian Key State Historical Site** (⊠ MM78.5, OS, Islamorada 33036, ☎ 305/664–4815), inhabited by Indians for several thousand years before Europeans arrived, was also a base for early 19th-century shipwreck salvagers until an Indian attack wiped out the settlement in 1840. A virgin hardwood forest still cloaks **Lignumvitae Key State Botanical Site,** punctuated only by the house and gardens built by chemical magnate William Matheson in 1919. For information and reservations contact **Long Key Recreation Area** (⊠ MM 67.5, OS, Box 776, Long Key 33001, ☎ 305/664–4815). Both sites are accessible only by water. Rent a boat at the official state concessionaire, Robbie's Marina (⊠ MM 77.5, BS, 77520 Overseas Hwy., Islamorada, ☎ 305/664–9814).

The Middle Keys

Once you cross **Long Key Viaduct** (Mile Marker 65), one of 42 bridges in the island chain, the Keys become more rustic. The second-longest bridge on the former rail line (known informally as the Overseas Railroad), this 2-mi-long structure has 222 reinforced-concrete arches. The nonprofit **Dolphin Research Center** (⊠ MM 59, BS, ☎ 305/289–0002) offers both a half-day program that teaches dolphin biology and human-dolphin communications and allows you to touch the dolphins out of the water, as well as a 2½-hour instruction-education program that allows you to swim with dolphins.

★ At Marathon are the **Museums of Crane Point Hammock** (Mile Markers 53–47), owned by the Florida Keys Land Trust. Dioramas and displays in the **Museum of Natural History of the Florida Keys** explain the Keys' geology, wildlife, and cultural history. **The Florida Keys Children's Museum** has a 1-mi loop trail, the remnants of a Bahamian village, and the **George Adderly House,** the oldest surviving example of Conch-style architecture outside Key West. From November to Easter, weekly docent-led hammock tours may be available; bring good walking shoes and bug repellent. ⊠ *MM 50, BS, 5550 Overseas Hwy., Marathon,* ☎ *305/743–9100.*

The Lower Keys

The **Seven Mile Bridge,** believed to be the world's longest segmented bridge, is the gateway to the Lower Keys. The delicate Key deer can be viewed at **National Key Deer Refuge** (⊠ Off Watson Blvd., ☎ 305/872–2239), on Big Pine Key (Mile Markers 32–30).

The final key is **Key West,** famous for its semitropical climate, laid-back lifestyle, colorful heritage, and 19th-century architecture. Key West's rich ethnic past comes alive in the **Bahama Village** area (⊠ Thomas and Petronia Sts.), with the peach, yellow, and pink homes of early Bahamian settlers. The **San Carlos Institute** (⊠ 516 Duval St., ☎ 305/294–3887) is a Cuban-American heritage center, with a museum and research library focusing on the history of Key West and 19th- and 20th-century Cuban exiles. History buffs head for **Fort Zachary Taylor State Historic Site** (⊠ Southard St., ☎ 305/292–6713), an important fort during the Civil and Spanish-American wars. It's 88 steps to the top of the 92-ft lighthouse at the **Lighthouse Museum** (⊠ 938 Whitehead St., ☎ 305/294–0012). The adjacent keeper's cottage displays ship models and lighthouse artifacts. Nature lovers will want to visit the **Audubon House and Gardens** (⊠ 205 Whitehead St., ☎ 305/294–2116), with its tropical gardens and large collection of Audubon engravings. For ★ literary types and cat lovers, there is the **Hemingway House** (⊠ 907 Whitehead St., ☎ 305/294–1575), a museum dedicated to the life and work of the author who wrote 70% of his works in Key West, including *For Whom the Bell Tolls* and *The Old Man and the Sea*.

The prettiest spot on the island is **Nancy Forrester's Secret Garden** (⊠ 1 Free School La., ☎ 305/294–0015), where visitors wind their way under the canopy of rare palms and cycads, along trails lined with ferns, bromeliads and bright gingers and heliconias, and past towering native gumbo-limbos strewn with hanging orchids and twining vines. Many brides and grooms have exchanged vows here.

It would be difficult to find anyone who knows more about Key West than Sharon Wells, who conducts **Island City Strolls** (☎ 305/294–8380 or 305/293–0255) walking tours. She was the state historian in Key West for nearly 20 years, owns the historic preservation firm Island City Heritage Trust, and has authored numerous books about Key West, including the *Walking and Biking Guide to Historic Key West,* available free at Key West bookstores. Wells's walking tours cost $10–$15 and last between one and two hours. The Key West Literary Seminar (☎ 305/293–9291) sponsors **Writers' Walk,** a one-hour guided tour of the residences of prominent authors who have lived in Key West (Elizabeth Bishop, Robert Frost, Ernest Hemingway, Wallace Stevens, Tennessee Williams, among others). Tours depart at 10:30 AM on Saturday from the Heritage House Museum (⊠ 410 Caroline St.) and on Sunday from in front of Hemingway House Museum (⊠ 907 Whitehead St.). Tickets are $10 and must be purchased in advance from the Heritage House Museum or Key West Island Bookstore (⊠ 513 Fleming St.).

What to See and Do with Children

Theater of the Sea (⊠ MM 84.5, OS, Islamorada, ☎ 305/664–2431) has dolphin and sea lion shows, a touch tank, a pool where sharks are fed by a trainer, and a "living reef" aquarium. At **Robbie's Marina** (⊠ MM 77.5, BS, Islamorada, ☎ 305/664–9814), where 50 or so tarpon—some as long as 5 ft—gather below the docks waiting to be fed out of the hands of children. At the **Key West Aquarium** (⊠ 1 Whitehead St., ☎ 305/296–2051) kids learn about the marine life found around the Keys in an up-close-and-personal experience with turtles, rays, sharks, parrot fish, eels, and tarpon swimming in glass tanks, coral pools, a pond, and touch tanks.

Dining and Lodging

The Keys have gained a reputation for fine cuisine. Many dishes have a Caribbean accent, mixing tropical fruits, vegetables, and spices with local fish and citrus. Local specialties include conch chowder, Florida lobster, and key lime pie. Accommodations, from historic hotels and guest houses to large resorts and run-of-the-mill motels, are more expensive here than elsewhere in southern Florida. For price ranges *see* Charts 1 (B) and 2 (A) *in* On the Road with Fodor's.

Islamorada

$$ ✕ **Grove Park Cafe.** You can nibble on triangles of freshly baked fo-
★ caccia set in a pool of olive oil and balsamic vinegar as you peruse the menu, which includes specialties like Caribbean conch chowder and crab cakes served either as a salad on mixed greens or as a sandwich on focaccia. The herbs and some of the fruits used in the cooking are grown on the property. ⊠ MM 81.7, OS, 81701 Old Hwy., Upper Matecumbe, ☎ 305/664–0116. AE, D, MC, V. Closed Wed.

$$ ✕ **Manny & Isa's.** What this spot lacks in ambience, it makes up for in always perfect Cuban and Spanish dishes and local seafood selections, like succulent fish fingers served with black beans and rice. There are

several fish, chicken, and pork chop selections. Manny's key lime pie is legendary. ⊠ *MM 81.6, OS, 81610 Old Hwy., Upper Matecumbe,* ☎ *305/664–5019. AE, D, MC, V. Closed Tues. and 4 wks Oct.–Nov.*

$$ ✕ **Squid Row.** This may look like just another cutely named and af-
★ fordable food stop on the way to Key West, but this attitude-free road-
side eatery is devoted to serving the freshest fish you haven't caught
yourself. Seafood wholesalers own it, and they supply the kitchen with
fresh daily specials. ⊠ *MM 81.9, OS,* ☎ *305/664–9865. AE, D, DC,
MC, V.*

$$$$ 🏨 **Cheeca Lodge.** Of the entire Keys hospital industry, this 27-acre re-
★ sort is the most environmentally responsible, for which it has won nu-
merous awards. Renovated guest rooms have a tropical color scheme,
state-of-the-art TVs and VCRs, British colonial–style furniture, and
faintly surreal art prints and romantic waterscapes. Suites have full
kitchens and private screened balconies; fourth-floor rooms in the
main lodge open onto terraces with water views. ⊠ *MM 82, OS, Box
527, Islamorada 33036,* ☎ *305/664–4651 or 800/327–2888,* FAX *305/
664–2893. 203 rooms. 2 restaurants, lounge, 2 pools, saltwater pool,
9-hole golf course, 6 tennis courts, boating, parasailing, fishing, play-
ground. AE, D, DC, MC, V.*

Key Largo

$$ ✕ **Crack'd Conch.** For serious beer connoisseurs there isn't a better lunch
★ or dinner choice. More than 100 brands of beer are served with seafood
sandwiches and entrées like fried alligator and blackened fish. As the
name suggests, conch figures prominently on the menu—in salads, on
sandwiches, or just plain fried. Portions are big. ⊠ *MM 105, OS, 105045
Overseas Hwy.,* ☎ *305/451–0732. AE, D, MC, V. Closed Wed.*

$$ ✕ **The Fish House.** Nets and every imaginable fishy Christmas ornament
★ decorate the dining room at this consistent winner, which is relaxed about
everything except the food. The freshest catch is baked, blackened, broiled,
fried, sautéed, steamed, or stewed in generous portions, served with corn
on the cob, new potatoes, and coleslaw. Key lime pie is homemade. ⊠
MM 102.4, OS, 102401 Overseas Hwy., ☎ *305/451–4665. AE, D, MC,
V. Closed last 2 wks of Sept., 1st wk of Oct.*

$ ✕ **Mrs. Mac's Kitchen.** Popular with locals, this open-air restaurant of-
★ fers nightly dinner specials and a tasty bowl of chili anytime in an in-
formal room where beer cans, bottles, and license plates from around
the world festoon the walls. ⊠ *MM 99.4, BS, 99336 Overseas Hwy.,*
☎ *305/451–3722. No credit cards. Closed Sun.*

$$$$ 🏨 **Sheraton Key Largo Resort.** Tucked away in a hardwood hammock
★ of native plants, this pink-and-turquoise gem recently underwent a
$3 million upgrade. All rooms are spacious and comfortable, with trop-
ical decor; fourth-floor bay-side rooms afford marvelous water views.
Chez Roux, the waterfront restaurant, features a prix-fixe menu of eclec-
tic cuisine with French influences. Lighted nature trails and boardwalks
wind through the woods to a beach. ⊠ *MM 96.9, BS, 97000 Over-
seas Hwy., 33037,* ☎ *305/852–5553, 800/826–1006, or 800/325–
3535;* FAX *305/852–8669. 200 rooms. 2 restaurants, lounge, 2 bar and
grills, 2 pools, hot tub, 2 tennis courts, dock, windsurfing, boating, fish-
ing. AE, D, DC, MC, V.*

$$–$$$$ 🏨 **Kona Kai Resort.** Eleven cottages sit in a garden of fruits and rare
★ and native plants—a setting that alone puts this resort on the short list
of the Keys' best places to stay. Studios and one- and two-bedroom suites
with full kitchens are spacious and light-filled; the decor features beautiful tropical furnishings. Beachfront hammocks and a heated pool
make it easy to relax while owners Joe and Ronnie Harris pamper guests.
An art gallery showcases works by southern Florida artists. ⊠ *MM 97.8,
BS, 97802 Overseas Hwy., 33037,* ☎ *305/852–7200 or 800/365–7829,*

FAX 305/852–4629. *11 units. Pool, hot tub, tennis courts, basketball, boating, volleyball, AE, DC, MC, V.*

$$ 🏨 **Largo Lodge.** A tropical garden surrounds the guest houses at this
★ vintage-1950s resort, where every room is decorated differently and a
flock of resident ibis graze on the grounds. ✉ *MM 101.5, BS, 101740
Overseas Hwy., 33037,* ☎ *305/451–0424 or 800/468–4378. 7 units.
Dock. AE, MC, V.*

Key West

$$$ ✕ **Louie's Backyard.** Key West paintings and pastels adorn this ocean-
★ front institution, where you dine outside under the mahoe tree. The
menu changes regularly but might include roasted rack of Australian
lamb with huckleberry port, whipped sweet potatoes, and fried root
vegetable strips; grouper with Thai peanut sauce; and stir-fried Asian
vegetables. Top off the meal with Louie's lime tart or the irresistible
chocolate terrine Grand Marnier with crème anglaise. ✉ *700 Waddell
Ave.,* ☎ *305/294–1061. AE, DC, MC, V.*

$$$ ✕ **Pier House Restaurant.** Steamships from Havana once docked at the
★ pier jutting into the Gulf of Mexico. Now guests watch pleasure boats
glide by in the harbor, while at night the restaurant shines lights into
the water, attracting schools of brightly colored parrot fish. The menu
has American and Caribbean items like conch with spicy island chili
sauce, vegetable slaw, pickled ginger, and wasabi; Black Angus fillet
of beef prepared with a dark rum and green-peppercorn sauce; and for
dessert, Chocolate Decadence with raspberry coulis. ✉ *1 Duval St.,*
☎ *305/296–4600, ext. 555. AE, D, DC, MC, V. No lunch.*

$ ✕ **El Siboney.** This sprawling, family-style restaurant specializes in
traditional Cuban dishes such as roast pork with black beans and rice.
The atmosphere is relaxed and friendly. ✉ *900 Catherine St.,* ☎ *305/
296–4184. Reservations not accepted. No credit cards. Closed Sun.
and 2 wks in June.*

$$$$ 🏨 **Marquesa Hotel.** This coolly elegant restored 1884 home is Key West's
★ finest lodging. Guests relax among richly landscaped pools and gar-
dens against a backdrop of brick steps rising to the villalike suites on
the property's perimeter. Elegant rooms contain eclectic antique and
reproduction furnishings and botanical print fabrics. The lobby resembles
a Victorian parlor, with antique furniture, Audubon prints, flowers,
and wonderful photos of early Key West. Although the clientele is mostly
straight, the hotel is very gay-friendly. ✉ *600 Fleming St., 33040,* ☎
305/292–1919 or 800/869–4631, FAX *305/294–2121. 27 rooms.
Restaurant, 2 pools. AE, DC, MC, V.*

$$$$ 🏨 **Paradise Inn.** Renovated cigar makers' cottages and authentically
★ reproduced Bahamian-style houses with sundecks and balconies stand
in the midst of a lush tropical garden with a pool and lily pond light-
years away from the bustle of Key West. Inside, French doors allow
light to stream in on the earth-toned fine fabrics and upholstering. Gra-
cious appointments include phones and whirlpools in marble bath-
rooms, plush bath robes, polished oak floors, armoires, room safes,
minibars, and complimentary breakfast pastries from Louie's Back-
yard. One suite was specially designed for travelers with disabilities.
✉ *819 Simonton St., 33040,* ☎ *305/293–8007 or 800/888–9648,*
FAX *305/293–0807. 3 cottages, 15 suites. Pool, hot tub, concierge. AE,
D, DC, MC, V.*

$$$–$$$$ 🏨 **Curry Mansion Inn.** Wicker furniture and pastel colors characterize
this modern guest house, which blends beautifully with the adjoining
turn-of-the-century Curry Mansion (open for self-guided tours). ✉ *511
Caroline St., 33040,* ☎ *305/294–5349 or 800/253–3466,* FAX *305/294–
4093. 28 rooms. Pool. Continental breakfast. AE, D, DC, MC, V.*

$$$–$$$$ ★ 🏨 **La Concha Holiday Inn.** This seven-story Art Deco hotel in the heart of downtown is Key West's tallest building and dates from 1926. The lobby's polished floor of pink, mauve, and green marble and a conversation pit with comfortable chairs are among the details beloved by La Concha's guests. Large rooms are furnished with 1920s-era antiques, lace curtains, and big closets. The restorers kept the old building's original louvered room doors, light globes, and floral trim on the archways. ☒ *430 Duval St., 33040,* ☎ *305/296–2991 or 800/745– 2191,* 𝔽𝔸𝕏 *305/294–3283. 160 rooms. Restaurant, 3 bars, pool, bicycles. AE, D, DC, MC, V.*

$$$–$$$$ 🏨 **Pier House.** Easily accessible to Key West attractions, this hotel complex offers the tranquillity of a tropical island escape within its grounds. The Caribbean Spa section has rooms and suites with hardwood floors and two-poster plantation-style beds. ☒ *1 Duval St., 33040,* ☎ *305/ 296–4600 or 800/327–8340,* 𝔽𝔸𝕏 *305/296–7569. 142 rooms. 3 restaurants, 4 bars, pool, exercise room, beach. AE, D, DC, MC, V.*

Marathon

$ ★ ✕ **7 Mile Grill.** The walls of this open-air diner built in 1954 at the Marathon end of Seven Mile Bridge are lined with beer cans, mounted fish, sponges, and signs describing individual menu items. The prompt, friendly service rivals the great food at breakfast, lunch, and dinner. Favorites include freshly squeezed orange juice, a cauliflower-and-broccoli omelet, conch chowder, fresh fish sandwiches, and foot-long chili dogs. ☒ *MM 47, BS, 1240 Overseas Hwy.,* ☎ *305/743–4481. No credit cards. Closed Wed.–Thurs. and at owner's discretion Aug.–Sept.*

$$–$$$$ 🏨 **Banana Bay Resort & Marina.** This 10-acre waterfront resort is situated among fruit trees, native and tropical plants, and, of course, bananas. As the quintessential resort for active vacationers, it boasts the largest freshwater pool in the Keys and a marina with boat ramp; arrangements can be made for fishing, sailing, and diving. Rooms, decorated in a Caribbean plantation style, have either one king or two double beds and are loaded with amenities. ☒ *MM 49.5, BS, 4590 Overseas Hwy., Marathon 33050,* ☎ *305/743–3500 or 800/226–2621,* 𝔽𝔸𝕏 *305/743–2670. 60 units. Pool, 2 tennis courts, exercise room, beach, dock. Continental breakfast. AE, D, DC, MC, V.*

$$–$$$ 🏨 **Coral Lagoon.** Surrounded by lush landscaping on a short deep-water canal, each pastel-color duplex cottage has a hammock on a private sundeck. Units have king or twin beds and a sofa bed, central air, ceiling fans, video players ($1 tape rental), wall safes, hair dryers, free dockage, barbecues, a library, and complimentary morning coffee. ☒ *MM 53.5, OS, 12399, Marathon 33050,* ☎ *305/289–0121,* 𝔽𝔸𝕏 *305/289– 0195. 18 units. Kitchenettes, pool, dock. AE, D, MC, V.*

Nightlife and the Arts

Key West is the Keys' hub for artistic performances and nightlife. This city alone claims among its current residents 55 full-time writers and 500 painters and craftspeople. The most popular entertainment is the nightly gathering of street vendors, performers, and visitors on **Mallory Square Dock** to celebrate the sunset. The **Tennessee Williams Fine Arts Center** (☒ Florida Keys Community College, 5901 College Rd., ☎ 305/ 296–9081, ext. 5) offers dance, music, plays, and star performers from November to April. **Capt. Tony's Saloon** (☒ 428 Greene St., ☎ 305/ 294–1838) is a landmark bar noted for its connection with Ernest Hemingway. Hemingway liked to gamble in the club room at **Sloppy Joe's** (☒ 201 Duval St., ☎ 305/294–5717), a noisy bar popular with tourists.

Outdoor Activities and Sports

Biking

Cyclists are now able to ride all but a tiny portion of the bike path that runs along the Overseas Highway from Mile Marker 106 south to Mile Marker 73, then picks up again at Mile Marker 70 to Mile Marker 66, then again from Mile Marker 53 to the Seven Mile Bridge. Trails crisscross the Marathon area; most popular is the 2-mi section of the old **Seven Mile Bridge** leading to Pigeon Key. For rentals in Key Largo and Marathon, contact **Equipment Locker Sport & Cycle** (⊠ Tradewinds Plaza, MM 101, OS, 101487 Overseas Hwy., Key Largo, ☎ 305/453–0140; ⊠ MM 53, BS, 11518 Overseas Hwy., Marathon, ☎ 305/289–1670). In Islamorada **Pete's Bike Shop** (⊠ MM 82.9, BS, 82229 Overseas Hwy., Islamorada, ☎ 305/451–1910) rents adult, children's, and tandem bikes. Another good way to explore Key West is on mopeds. For rentals contact **Keys Moped & Scooter** (⊠ 523 Truman Ave., Key West, ☎ 305/294–0399) or **Moped Hospital** (⊠ 601 Truman Ave., Key West, ☎ 305/296–3344).

Diving and Snorkeling

The Keys are a diver's paradise, with miles of living coral reefs populated with 650 species of rainbow-hued tropical fish, as well as four centuries of shipwrecks to explore. Outstanding diving areas include **John Pennekamp Coral Reef State Park** (⊠ MM 102.5, OS, Key Largo, ☎ 305/451–1202) and **Looe Key Reef,** 5 mi off Ramrod Key (⊠ MM 27.5). Also try **American Diving Headquarters** (⊠ MM 105.5, BS, 10550 Overseas Hwy., Key Largo, ☎ 305/451–0037) and **Looe Key Dive Center** (⊠ MM 27.5, OS, Ramrod Key, ☎ 305/872–2215 or 800/942–5397). A new plan is in effect, led by the **Florida Keys National Marine Sanctuary** (⊠ Planning Office, 5550 Overseas Hwy. [main house], Marathon, ☎ 305/743–2437), to manage the natural resources of the Keys for private use (mainly fisheries and tourism), research, and preservation.

Fishing and Boating

Deep-sea fishing on the ocean or Gulf and flat-water fishing in the backcountry shallows are popular. Numerous marinas rent all types of boats and water-sports equipment. Particularly popular are the various glass-bottom-boat tours to the coral reefs. Check with local chambers of commerce for information on charter- and party-boat operators. In the Upper Keys try **Tag 'Em** for light tackle, fly or deep-sea game fishing (⊠ c/o Holiday Isle, MM 84, OS, Islamorada, ☎ 305/852–8797 or 305/664–2321, ext. 642) or **Hubba Hubba** for backcountry fishing (⊠ c/o Bud 'n' Mary's Fishing Marina, MM 79.8, OS, Islamorada, ☎ 305/664–9281.) **Adventure Charters** (⊠ 6810 Front St., Stock Island, ☎ 305/296–0362) charters out of Key West.

Golf

Key Colony Beach Par 3 (⊠ MM 53.5, OS, 8th St., Key Colony Beach near Marathon, ☎ 305/289–1533) is a nine-hole public course. **Key West Resort Golf Club** (⊠ 6450 E. College Rd., Stock Island, ☎ 305/294–5232) is an 18-hole public course.

Beaches

Since the natural shorelines of the Keys are a combination of marshes, rocky outcroppings, and grassy wetlands, most beaches for sunbathing and swimming are man-made from imported sand. The exception is **Bahia Honda State Park** (⊠ MM 37, OS, Bahia Honda Key, ☎ 305/872–2353), which offers a naturally sandy beach, plus a nature trail, campground and waterfront cabins (call for reservations up to 60 days in advance), marina, and dive shop. **Anne's Beach** (⊠ MM 73.5, OS, Islamorada, ☎ 305/295–4385 or 888/227–8136) has a half-mile elevated wooden boardwalk that crosses a wetlands hammock at the edge of the shore. Covered picnic areas along the boardwalk provide a place to rest or enjoy the view while eating. The water is shallow for almost a quarter mile. **Sombrero Beach** (⊠ MM 50, OS, Sombrero Road, Marathon, ☎ 305/295–4385 or 888/227–8136) has areas for swimmers, jet boats, and windsurfers. Behind the narrow, sandy beach is a large, grassy park with grills, picnic kiosks with water taps, showers, rest rooms, playground, volleyball, and soda machine. The park is accessible for travelers with disabilities. Of the several Key West beaches, **Smathers Beach** (⊠ S. Roosevelt Blvd.) has 2 mi of sandy beach and good windsurfing. **Higgs Memorial Beach** (⊠ White St.) is popular for sunbathing. Many hotels and motels also have their own small, shallow-water beach areas. Among those open to the public is **Plantation Yacht Harbor Resort & Marina** (⊠ MM 87, BS, Plantation Key, ☎ 305/852–2381); there's a tiki bar just behind the crescent beach.

Shopping

The Keys are a thriving artists' community, so art is in good supply here. **Kona Kai Resort Gallery** (⊠ MM 97.8, BS, Key Largo, ☎ 305/852–7200) showcases works by South Florida artists, including Everglades photographer Clyde Butcher. **Rain Barrel** (⊠ MM 86.7, BS, 86700 Overseas Hwy., Islamorada, ☎ 305/852–3084) is a 3-acre crafts village with eight resident artists and works by scores of others. Across the street an enormous fabricated lobster by artist Richard Blaes stands in front of **Treasure Village** (⊠ MM 86.7, OS, 86729 Old Hwy., Islamorada, ☎ 305/852–0511), which has a dozen crafts and specialty shops plus the excellent Made to Order eat-in and carryout restaurant. **Redbone Gallery** (⊠ MM 81, OS, 200 Industrial Dr., Islamorada, ☎ 305/664–2002) specializes in art with a fishing and marine theme. Key West's unique specialty shops, such as **Fast Buck Freddie's** (⊠ 500 Duval St., Key West, ☎ 305/294–2007), which sells banana-leaf-shaped furniture, have gained an international reputation. In a town with a gazillion T-shirt shops, **Last Flight Out** (⊠ 706A Duval St., ☎ 305/294–8008) stands out for its selection of classic namesake T's, collectibles, and specialty clothing and gifts that appeal to aviation types and those reaching for the stars.

SOUTHWEST FLORIDA

Swimming, sunbathing, sailing, and shelling draw increasing numbers of visitors to the 200-mi coastal stretch between the Tampa Bay area and the Everglades. Venturing inland from the miles of sun-splashed beaches along the Gulf of Mexico, many visitors discover the culturally rich and ethnically diverse towns, interesting historical sites, and stellar attractions, such as Busch Gardens. Often this something-for-everyone mix is available at more affordable prices than elsewhere in Florida. The region is divided into three areas: Tampa Bay (including Tampa, St. Petersburg, Clearwater, and Tarpon Springs), Sarasota (including Bradenton and Venice), and Fort Myers/Naples.

Visitor Information

Greater Tampa: Chamber of Commerce (⊠ Box 420, 33601, ☎ 813/228–7777). **Lee County:** Visitor and Convention Bureau (⊠ 2180 W. 1st St., Fort Myers 33950, ☎ 941/338–3500 or 800/533–4753). **Naples Area:** Chamber of Commerce (⊠ 3620 N. Tamiami Trail, 33940, ☎ 941/262–6141). **St. Petersburg:** Chamber of Commerce (⊠

100 2nd Ave. N, 33701, ☎ 813/821–4069). **Sanibel-Captiva:** Chamber of Commerce (✉ Causeway Rd., Sanibel 33957, ☎ 941/472–1080). **Sarasota:** Convention and Visitors Bureau (✉ 655 N. Tamiami Trail, 34236, ☎ 941/957–1877 or 800/522–9799). **Tampa/Hillsborough:** Convention and Visitors Association (✉ 111 Madison St., Suite 1010, Tampa 33601-0519, ☎ 800/826–8358).

Arriving and Departing

By Bus

Greyhound Lines (☎ 800/231–2222) provides statewide service, including stops at Tampa, St. Petersburg, Sarasota, and Fort Myers. For local bus service contact **Hillsborough Area Regional Transit** (☎ 813/254–4278) for the Tampa area, **Sarasota County Area Transit** (☎ 813/951–5850) for Sarasota, and **Lee County Transit System** (☎ 813/939–1303) for the Fort Myers area.

By Car

From the Georgia-Florida border, it's a three-hour drive via I–75 south to Tampa, four hours to Sarasota, five to Fort Myers, and six to Naples. U.S. 41 (the Tamiami Trail) also traverses the region, but because it passes through many towns' business districts, traffic can be extremely heavy, particularly from Tampa south. Naples is linked to Fort Lauderdale, on the eastern side of the state, via Alligator Alley (Route 84).

By Plane

Most major U.S. airlines serve at least one of the region's airports. **Tampa International** (☎ 813/870–8700), 6 mi from downtown, is also served by international airlines. **Sarasota-Bradenton Airport** (☎ 813/359–5200) is 5 mi north of downtown Sarasota off U.S. 41. **Southwest Florida Regional Airport** (☎ 813/768–1000) is about 12 mi south of Fort Myers and 25 mi north of Naples.

By Train

Amtrak connects most of the country with Tampa (✉ 601 N. Nebraska Ave., ☎ 813/221–7600 or 800/872–7245).

Exploring Southwest Florida

The Tampa Bay Area

Tampa is the commercial center of southwestern Florida, with a bustling international port and the largest shrimp fleet in the state. Known as the City by the Bay, Tampa pays homage to its coastal setting with the
★ **Florida Aquarium** (✉ 701 Channelside Dr., ☎ 813/273–4000), whose 83-ft-high glass dome is already a landmark. More than 4,300 specimens of fish, other animals, and plants represent 550 species native to Florida. East of downtown is the **Seminole Indian Village** (✉ 5221 Orient Rd., I–4 Exit 5, ☎ 813/620–3077), where alligator wrestling and demonstrations of traditional Seminole crafts are presented. Reserve a day in Tampa for a journey through **Busch Gardens,** a 335-acre African theme park with rides, live shows, and a monorail "safari." ✉ *3000 E. Busch Blvd.,* ☎ *813/987–5082.* ✆ *$36.15.*

★ With cobblestone streets and wrought-iron balconies, Tampa's **Ybor City** (pronounced *Ee*-bor) is one of only three National Historic Landmark districts in Florida. Cubans expanded their cigar-making industry to this city in 1866. The ornately tiled **Columbia Restaurant** and the stores lining 7th Avenue are representative of this enclave's ethnic history and vitality. Today once-empty cigar factories, like the one at **Ybor Square** (✉ 1901 13th St.), house boutiques, shops, restaurants, and nightclubs. To get here, take I–4 west to Exit 1 (22nd Street) and go south five blocks to 7th Avenue.

On the Gulf about 25 mi north of Tampa is colorful **Tarpon Springs.** Famous for its sponge divers, the town reflects the heritage of its predominantly Greek population. At **Weeki Wachee Spring,** "mermaids" present shows in an underwater theater. ✉ *45 mi north of Tampa on U.S. 19 and Rte. 50, Weeki Wachee,* ☎ *904/596–2066 or 800/678–9355.* ⌸ *$27.95.*

You can watch manatees up close at **Homosassa Springs State Wildlife Park** (✉ 1 mi west of U.S. 19 on Fish Bowl Dr., ☎ 904/628–2311), where you can also see reptile and alligator shows, cruise the Homosassa River, and view sea life in a floating observatory.

Head south from Tampa and cross Old Tampa Bay on I–275 to get to the heart of **St. Petersburg;** set on a peninsula with three sides bordered by bays and the Gulf of Mexico, this city has beautiful beaches. With more than 1,500 pieces, the **Salvador Dali Museum** (✉ 1000 3rd St. S, ☎ 813/823–3767) has the world's largest collection of originals by the Spanish surrealist. **Great Explorations!** (✉ 1120 4th St. S, ☎ 813/821–8885) is a hands-on museum with mind-stretching puzzles and games and a 90-ft pitch-black maze you crawl through.

The Sarasota Area

Known for its plentiful, clean beaches and profusion of golf courses, the Sarasota area, south of Tampa Bay via U.S. 41 or U.S. 301, is also a growing cultural center and is the winter home of the Ringling Brothers Barnum & Bailey Circus. At **De Soto National Memorial** (✉ 75th St. NW, Bradenton, ☎ 941/792–0458) costumed guides recount Spanish conquistador Hernando de Soto's 16th-century landing and expedition. Near Bradenton is **Gamble Plantation State Historical Site** (✉ 3708 Patten Ave., Ellenton, ☎ 941/723–4536), the only surviving pre–Civil War plantation house in South Florida.

★ In Sarasota you'll find the **Ringling Museums** (✉ U.S. 41, ☎ 941/359–5700), which include the Venetian-style mansion of circus magnate John Ringling, his art museum with its collection of Rubens paintings, and a circus museum. The **Marie Selby Botanical Gardens** (✉ 811 S. Palm Ave., ☎ 941/366–5731) has world-class orchid displays as well as a small museum of botany and art in a gracious restored mansion on the grounds. For a good beach escape head for the barrier island of **Siesta Key,** across the water from Sarasota. To reach Siesta Key, take Route 41 south from southern Sarasota to either Siesta Drive or Stickney Point Road, which both lead west to the island.

The Fort Myers/Naples Area

The bustle of commercially oriented Fort Myers gives way to the relaxed atmosphere of the Gulf communities in growing Lee County. Beach lovers head for the resort islands of Estero (popular with young singles) and Captiva and Sanibel (both with superb shelling and fine fishing). Most of the beautiful residences here are hidden by Australian pines, but the beaches and tranquil Gulf waters are readily accessible.

Fort Myers is a small inland city, a half hour from the nearest beach. One of the most scenic stretches of highway in southeastern Florida, **McGregor Boulevard** is framed by hundreds of towering royal palms. Fort Myers's premier attraction, **Thomas A. Edison's Winter Home** (✉ 2350 McGregor Blvd., ☎ 941/334–3614), on a 14-acre estate, houses Edison's laboratory and a museum devoted to his inventions. Next door is **Mangoes,** the winter house of the inventor's longtime friend, automaker Henry Ford.

The sophisticated city of **Naples** has excellent beaches and golf courses and an upscale shopping district. In the Naples area you can return to Florida's unspoiled past at the **Corkscrew Swamp Sanctuary** (⊠ Rte. 846 east of I–75, ☎ 941/657–3771), an 11,000-acre tract that the National Audubon Society set aside to protect 500-year-old trees and endangered birds.

What to See and Do with Children

Tampa's **Adventure Island** (⊠ 4545 Bougainvillea Ave., ☎ 813/987–6300) has water slides and man-made waves; it's closed December–February. Kids enjoy the bird and reptile shows at **Sarasota Jungle Gardens** (⊠ 3701 Bayshore Rd., ☎ 941/355–5305); also on site are a petting zoo and a museum displaying seashells and butterflies. **Babcock Wilderness Adventures** (⊠ Rte. 31 east of Fort Myers, ☎ 941/656–6104) has 90-minute tours for viewing wildlife, taking you by swamp buggy through a 90,000-acre swamp-woodland area; reservations are essential. **Naples Teddy Bear Museum** (⊠ 2511 Pine Ridge Rd., ☎ 941/598–2711) houses more than 3,000 bears.

Dining and Lodging

Around **Tampa** the ethnic diversity of the region makes for some adventurous dining, from honey-soaked Greek baklava to Cuban saffron rice casserole. A generous mix of roadside motels, historic hotels, and sprawling resorts can be found here.

Raw bars and seafood restaurants are everywhere in and around **Sarasota**; there are also many Continental restaurants and several family-style places run by members of the Amish community. Tamiami Trail (U.S. 41), which traverses the region, is lined with inexpensive motels, while the islands have more expensive resort complexes and high-rise hotels.

In **Fort Myers** and **Naples,** seafood reigns supreme. A particular treat is a succulent claw of the native stone crab, usually served with drawn butter or a tangy mustard sauce; stone crabs are in season from mid-October through mid-May. Many restaurants offer early-bird dinner menus for seating before 6. It's hard to find restaurants on Sanibel and Captiva islands that aren't expensive; for budget options (both dining and lodging) you'll have better luck in Fort Myers and Naples. For price ranges *see* Charts 1 (B) and 2 (A) *in* On the Road with Fodor's.

Bradenton

$$ ⊞ **Holiday Inn Riverfront.** Suites overlook a courtyard at this Spanish-style motor lodge near the Manatee River. Rooms, with burgundy carpeting and mahogany furnishings, are a bit dark, but a third have river views. ⊠ *100 Riverfront Dr. W, 34205,* ☎ *941/747–3727,* ℻ *941/746–4289. 153 rooms. Restaurant, bar, pool, hot tub, exercise room. AE, DC, MC, V.*

Captiva

$$$$ ⊞ **South Seas Plantation Resort and Yacht Harbor.** This busy 330-acre
★ property has nine types of accommodations, among them harborside villas, Gulf cottages, and private houses. Numerous activities include sailing, shelling, and strolling on the landscaped grounds covered with exotic vegetation. ⊠ *South Seas Plantation Rd., Captiva 33924,* ☎ *941/472–5111 or 800/237–3102,* ℻ *941/472–7541. 620 rooms. 4 restaurants, 2 bars, pool, beauty salon, golf, tennis, docks, windsurfing, boating, waterskiing, fishing, recreation room, children's programs, playground. AE, DC, MC, V.*

Fort Myers and Fort Myers Beach

$$$$ ✕ **Peter's La Cuisine.** Smack in the middle of downtown Fort Myers,
★ two blocks off the river, is this charming restaurant in a restored brick
building. The dining room's extrahigh ceiling gives a spacious feel, and
exposed brick walls, dim lighting, and a refined atmosphere provide
a pleasant background for Continental cuisine with a twist. After dinner wander upstairs for a cordial and some great blues. ⊠ *2224 Bay
St.,* ☎ *941/332–2228. AE, MC, V. No lunch weekends.*

$$ ✕ **Snug Harbor.** This harbor-front restaurant serves absolutely fresh
seafood—courtesy of the restaurant's private fishing fleet—in a casual,
rustic atmosphere. ⊠ *645 San Carlos Blvd., Fort Myers Beach,* ☎ *941/
463–4343. Reservations not accepted. AE, MC, V.*

$ ✕ **Prawnbroker Restaurant and Fish Market.** This popular restaurant
★ has an abundance of seafood seemingly just plucked from Gulf waters
plus some selections for culinary landlubbers. This place is almost al-
ways crowded—and for good reason. ⊠ *13451 McGregor Blvd.,* ☎
941/489–2226. AE, MC, V. No lunch.

$$$ 🛏 **Outrigger Beach Resort.** This informal, family-oriented resort is set
on a wide beach overlooking the Gulf of Mexico. Rooms and efficiencies
are decorated in bright prints. The resort also has a broad deck for sunning, tiki huts to sit under when you want to escape from the heat,
and a beachfront pool. ⊠ *6200 Estero Blvd., Fort Myers Beach 33931,*
☎ *941/463–3131,* ℻ *941/463–6577. 144 units. Pool, shuffleboard,
volleyball, beach, jet skiing, bicycles, laundry. MC, V.*

$$$ 🛏 **Sheraton Harbor Place.** On the Caloosahatchee River in down-
town Fort Myers, this modern pink high-rise has bright rooms with
peach accents and lots of windows with panoramic views of the water
and surrounding city. ⊠ *2500 Edwards Dr., Fort Myers 33901,* ☎ *941/
337–0300,* ℻ *941/337–1530. 437 rooms. Bar, pool, hot tub, tennis
court, exercise room, dock, recreation room. AE, DC, MC, V.*

Naples

$$$ ✕ **Bistro 821.** The decor for this trendy restaurant is spare but so-
phisticated. Entrées include marinated leg of lamb with basil mashed
potatoes, snapper baked in parchment, wild mushroom pasta, vodka
penne, risotto, and a seasonal vegetable plate. ⊠ *821 5th Ave. S,* ☎
941/261–5821. Reservations essential. AE, DC, MC, V. No lunch.

Palmetto

$$ ✕ **Crab Trap.** Try the wild pig or seafood dishes at this rustic spot near
Bradenton. ⊠ *U.S. 19 at Terra Ceia Bridge,* ☎ *941/722–6255. Reser-
vations not accepted. D, MC, V.*

St. Petersburg Beach

$$$$ 🛏 **Don CeSar Beach Resort and Spa.** Still echoing with the ghosts of
★ Scott and Zelda Fitzgerald, this sprawling beachfront "Pink Palace"
has long been a Gulf Coast landmark. Turn-of-the-century elegance and
spaciousness are everywhere, as is superb service. You can indulge in
various treatments and sea scrubs at the beach spa. ⊠ *3400 Gulf
Blvd., 33706,* ☎ *813/360–1881,* ℻ *813/367–7597. 279 rooms. 3
restaurants, 3 bars, 2 pools, 2 spas, tennis court, exercise room, beach,
boating, jet skiing, parasailing, children's programs, meeting rooms.
AE, DC, MC, V.*

Sarasota

$$$ ✕ **Cafe L'Europe.** This art-filled café is on fashionable St. Armand's Cir-
★ cle. The menu may include such dishes as Wiener schnitzel sautéed in
butter and topped with anchovies, olives, and capers or Dover sole served
with fruit. ⊠ *431 St. Armand's Circle,* ☎ *941/388–4415. AE, DC,
MC, V.*

$$$ 🏨 **Hyatt Sarasota.** This contemporary hotel is ideally located, near the city center and the major art and entertainment venues. Some rooms overlook Sarasota Bay. ⊠ *1000 Blvd. of the Arts, 34236,* ☎ *941/953–1234,* FAX *941/952–1987. 297 rooms. Restaurant, bar, pool, sauna, health club, dock. AE, DC, MC, V.*

Siesta Key

$$ ✕ **Ophelia's on the Bay.** Sample mussel soup, eggplant crepes, chicken potpie, seafood linguine, or cioppino, among other things, at this waterfront restaurant. ⊠ *9105 Midnight Pass Rd.,* ☎ *941/349–2212. AE, D, DC, MC, V. No lunch.*

Tampa

$$ ✕ **Bern's Steak House.** This nationally known steak house has more
★   than just steak. Organically grown vegetables from the owner's farm are the specialty here, and scrumptious desserts are served in upstairs rooms equipped with TV and radio. ⊠ *1208 S. Howard Ave.,* ☎ *813/251–2421. AE, DC, MC, V. No lunch.*

$$ ✕ **Columbia.** An institution in Ybor City since 1905, this light and spacious Spanish restaurant serves excellent paella, with some flamenco dancing on the side. ⊠ *2117 E. 7th Ave.,* ☎ *813/248–4961. AE, DC, MC, V.*

$$ 🏨 **Holiday Inn Busch Gardens.** This well-maintained family-oriented motor lodge is just 1 mi west of Busch Gardens (transportation to the park provided). Rooms are bright and spacious; some look out on a central courtyard with garden and pool. ⊠ *2701 E. Fowler Ave., 33612,* ☎ *813/971–4710,* FAX *813/977–0155. 395 rooms. Restaurant, bar, pool, sauna, exercise room. AE, DC, MC, V.*

Tarpon Springs

$$ ✕ **Louis Pappas' Riverside Restaurant.** This waterfront landmark is always crowded with diners savoring the fine Greek fare, including a Greek salad made with feta cheese, onions, and olive oil. ⊠ *10 W. Dodecanese Blvd.,* ☎ *813/937–5101. AE, DC, MC, V.*

Nightlife and the Arts

The region between Tampa and Sarasota hums with cultural activities. Professional theater, dance, and music events are presented at **Tampa Bay Performing Arts Center** (⊠ 1010 W. C. MacInnes Pl., Tampa, ☎ 813/222–1000 or 800/955–1045) and **Ruth Eckerd Hall** (⊠ 1111 McMullen Booth Rd., Clearwater, ☎ 813/791–7400). Broadway touring companies of plays, concerts, dance, ice-skating, and other shows are held at Sarasota's **Van Wezel Performing Arts Hall** (⊠ 777 N. Tamiami Trail, Sarasota, ☎ 941/953–3366). Other major venues in the city are the **Florida West Coast Symphony Center** (⊠ 709 N. Tamiami Trail, ☎ 941/953–4252), the **Sarasota Opera** and the **Sarasota Ballet** (⊠ Opera House, 61 N. Pineapple Ave., ☎ 941/953–7030), and the **Asolo Center for the Performing Arts** (⊠ 5555 N. Tamiami Trail, ☎ 941/351–8000).

The **Naples Philharmonic Center for the Arts** (⊠ 5833 Pelican Bay Blvd., ☎ 941/597–1111) presents plays, concerts, and art exhibits. The **Naples Dinner Theatre** (⊠ 1501 Immokalee Rd., ☎ 941/597–6031) is famous for its professional productions and hearty buffet.

Outdoor Activities and Sports

Biking

Sanibel Island offers the best biking in the region, with extensive paths along the waterways and through wildlife refuges. On Sanibel you can rent bicycles by the hour at **Bike Route** (⊠ 2330 Palm Ridge Rd., ☎ 941/472–1955).

Boating and Sailing

Sailing is popular on the calm bays and Gulf waters. Sailing schools include **O'Leary's Sarasota Sailing School** (✉ U.S. 41, ☎ 941/953–7505) and **Fort Myers Yacht Charters** (✉ Port Sanibel Yacht Club, South Fort Myers, ☎ 941/466–1800). For powerboat rentals contact **Boat House of Sanibel** (✉ Sanibel Marina, ☎ 941/540–8050). **Jensen's Marina** (✉ Captiva, ☎ 941/472–5800) rents little powerboats perfect for fishing and shelling.

Canoeing

Canoeists can explore many waterways here, including those at **Myakka River State Park** (✉ Rte. 72, 15 mi south of Sarasota, ☎ 941/361–6511). **Tarpon Bay Marina** (✉ 900 Tarpon Bay Rd., Sanibel, ☎ 941/472–8900) has canoes and equipment for exploring the waters of the J. N. "Ding" Darling National Wildlife Refuge. With several locations throughout Florida, **Canoe Outpost** offers canoe and camping trips on the **Little Manatee River** (✉ 18001 U.S. 301S, Wimauma, ☎ 941/634–2228) and the **Peace River** (✉ Rte. 7, Arcadia, ☎ 941/494–1215).

Fishing

The Tampa Bay area and Fort Myers are major fishing centers. Speckled trout and kingfish are often caught in the Tampa Bay inlets. Deep-sea fishing enthusiasts can charter boats or join a party boat to catch tarpon, marlin, grouper, redfish, and shark. Charter outfitters include **Florida Deep Sea Fishing** (✉ 1 Corey Ave., St. Petersburg Beach, ☎ 813/360–2082). Fishing is popular in Sanibel. Call **Captain Pat Lovetro** (✉ ☎ Sanibel Marina, 634 N. Yachtman Dr., 941/472–2723) for half-day, six-hour, and full-day trips.

Golf

Championship and other courses abound here; all those listed have 18 holes. **Babe Zaharias Golf Course** (✉ 11412 Forest Hills Dr., Tampa, ☎ 813/932–4401); **Lely Flamingo Island Golf Club** (✉ 8004 Lely Resort Blvd., Naples, ☎ 941/793–2223); the **Bay Beach Club Executive Golf Course** (✉ 7401 Estero Blvd., Fort Myers, ☎ 941/463–2064) offers lessons; **Longboat Key Club** (✉ 301 Gulf of Mexico Dr., Longboat Key, ☎ 941/383–8821); **Pelican's Nest Golf Course** (✉ Bonita Springs, ☎ 941/947–4600); the **Dunes** (✉ 949 Sand Castle Rd., Sanibel, ☎ 941/472–2535) rents golf clubs and offers lessons.

Spectator Sports

Baseball: For information on the 17 major league teams that hold their spring training and exhibition games in southwestern Florida, call the **Florida Sports Foundation** (☎ 904/488–0990).

Dog Racing: Naples/Fort Myers Greyhound Track (✉ 10601 Bonita Beach Rd., ☎ 941/992–2411; year-round). **Sarasota Kennel Club** (✉ 5400 Bradenton Rd., Sarasota, ☎ 813/355–7744; Dec.–June). **Tampa Greyhound Track** (✉ 8300 N. Nebraska Ave., Tampa, ☎ 813/932–4313; July–Dec.).

Football: Tampa Bay Buccaneers (✉ Tampa Stadium, 4201 N. Dale Mabry Hwy., ☎ 813/461–2700 or 800/282–0683; Aug.–Dec.).

Horse Racing: Tampa Bay Downs (✉ Race Track Rd., Oldsmar, ☎ 813/855–4401; Dec.–mid-Apr.) holds Thoroughbred races.

Beaches

The waters of the Gulf of Mexico tend to be cloudy, so snorkeling and diving are best done on the Atlantic side. The southwestern beaches attract people who enjoy sunbathing on quiet stretches of sand, shelling, and watching spectacular sunsets.

In the Bradenton area the popular **Manatee County Beach,** on Anna Maria Island, has picnic facilities, showers, lifeguards, and rest rooms. **Fort Myers Beach,** on Estero Island 18 mi from downtown Fort Myers, attracts families and young singles; hotels, restaurants, and condominiums run its length. The island's shores slope gradually into the usually tranquil and warm Gulf waters. Along Gulf Shore Boulevard in Naples, **Lowdermilk Park** has 1,000 ft of beach, picnic tables, showers, rest rooms, and a pavilion with vending machines.

In the St. Petersburg area the 900-acre **Fort DeSoto Park** encompasses five islands. Its miles of beaches include fishing piers, picnic sites, and a waterskiing and boating area. **Lighthouse Park,** at the southern end of Sanibel Island, attracts a mix of singles, families, and shellers. Beautiful **Siesta Beach,** on Siesta Key near Sarasota, features a concession stand, picnic areas, nature trails, and facilities for soccer, softball, volleyball, and tennis. **Caspersen Beach,** on Beach Drive in southern Venice, is one of the country's largest parks. Beachcombers find lots of shells and sharks' teeth here.

Shopping

Seven blocks of fine shops and restaurants line Tampa's Swan Avenue in **Old Hyde Park Village** (☎ 813/251–3500). In Pinellas Park is **Wagonwheel** (✉ 7801 Park Blvd., ☎ 813/544–5319), a weekend flea market with about 2,000 vendors. For unique gifts, shop for natural sponges on **Dodecanese Boulevard** in Tarpon Springs. If you're looking for Cuban cigars, try **Ybor City** on Tampa's east side.

Art lovers can browse through the art galleries on **Main Street** and **Palm Avenue** in downtown Sarasota. A British telephone booth or an Australian boomerang is available for a price at the unique shops of Harding Circle on fashionable **St. Armand's Key,** west of downtown Sarasota across the Ringling Causeway.

For an eye-popping display of shells, coral, and jewelry, visit the **Shell Factory** (✉ 2787 N. Tamiami Trail, North Fort Myers, ☎ 941/995–2141). For boutiques selling resort wear, designer fashions, and jewelry, try the **Royal Palm Square** area (✉ Colonial Blvd. between McGregor Blvd. and U.S. 41) in Fort Myers. The largest shopping area in Naples is **Olde Naples,** an eight-block area bordered by Broad Avenue on the north and 4th Street South on the east. The **Waterside Shops** (✉ Seagate Dr. and U.S. 41), known by locals as Bell Tower because of its landmark, are anchored by a Saks Fifth Avenue and a Jacobson's department store and house 50 shops and several noteworthy eating spots.

THE GOLD AND TREASURE COASTS

The Gold Coast exudes wealth and opulence, but it's also steeped in natural beauty. Famous for years as spring-break heaven for the college crowd, Fort Lauderdale now attracts families by offering a variety of recreational, sports, cultural, and historical activities. Farther north is the international high-society resort of Palm Beach, with its elegant mansions and world-class shopping. Following downtown Fort Lauderdale's lead, West Palm Beach is trying to renew itself through a combination of governmental efforts and the arts to become the hub of Palm Beach County and the Treasure Coast. Inland about 50 mi is 448,000-acre Lake Okeechobee, noted for catfish, bass, and perch fishing. Heading north from West Palm Beach to Sebastian Inlet, the Treasure Coast offers barrier islands, beaches, and sea-turtle havens to the east and citrus groves and cattle ranches to the west.

Visitor Information

Greater Fort Lauderdale: Convention & Visitors Bureau (✉ 200 E. Las Olas Blvd., Suite 1500, 33301, ☎ 954/765–4466). **Palm Beach County:** Convention & Visitors Bureau (✉ 1555 Palm Beach Lakes Blvd., Suite 204, West Palm Beach 33401, ☎ 561/471–3995). Chamber of Commerce of the Palm Beaches (✉ 401 N. Flagler Dr., West Palm Beach 33401, ☎ 561/833–3711).

Arriving and Departing

By Bus

Greyhound Lines (☎ 800/231–2222) stops in Fort Lauderdale, and **Broward County Mass Transit** (☎ 954/357–8400) serves the surrounding county. **CoTran** buses (☎ 561/233–1111) ply the Greater Palm Beach area.

By Car

Two major north–south routes, I–95 and U.S. 1, connect the region with Miami to the south and Jacksonville to the north. Alligator Alley (I–75) runs east–west from Fort Lauderdale to Naples.

The four-lane route Okeechobee Boulevard carries traffic from west of downtown West Palm Beach, near the Amtrak station in the airport district, directly to the Flagler Memorial Bridge and into Palm Beach. Flagler Drive will be given over to pedestrian use by the end of the decade.

By Plane

Major foreign and domestic carriers serve the **Fort Lauderdale–Hollywood International Airport** (✉ 4 mi south of downtown Fort Lauderdale off U.S. 1, ☎ 954/359–6100) and **Palm Beach International Airport** (✉ Congress Ave. and Belvedere Rd., West Palm Beach, ☎ 561/471–7400).

By Train

Amtrak (☎ 800/872–7245) provides daily service along the northeast coast to Fort Lauderdale, Hollywood, and Deerfield Beach in Broward County and to West Palm Beach.

Exploring the Gold and Treasure Coasts

Fort Lauderdale and Palm Beach dazzle the visitor with their fabulous houses and pricey shops, shimmering beaches, plentiful sports activities, first-class museums, and cultural events. North of Fort Lauderdale are the Treasure Coast's 70 mi of soothing sand, sea, and nature refuges.

Fort Lauderdale's picturesque **Las Olas Boulevard** takes you through the Isles, where expensive homes line canals dotted with yachts. After this the boulevard becomes an upscale shopping street, with Spanish colonial buildings housing boutiques and galleries. The **Museum of Art** (✉ 1 E. Las Olas Blvd., ☎ 954/763–6464) has an extensive early 20th-century European and American art collection; it is closed Monday. Palm-lined **Riverwalk** (✉ Along New River off Broward Blvd.) is a paved promenade that's being extended on both banks of the New River, with historic, scenic, and cultural attractions. Don't miss a visit to the redesigned **Fort Lauderdale beachfront,** along Route A1A. The beach side remains open and uncluttered even though across the road are shops, restaurants, and hotels. For an interesting side trip from Fort Lauderdale, head south a few miles to the **Seminole Native Village** (✉ 4150 N. Rte. 7, Hollywood, ☎ 954/961–5140) to observe Native American lifestyles and arts or to take part in the action at the high-stakes bingo parlor and low-stakes poker tables.

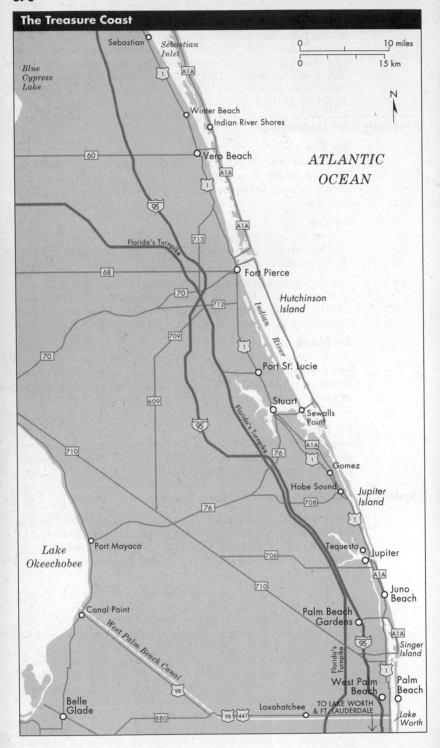

The Treasure Coast

As you travel north from Fort Lauderdale along U.S. 1, pause to admire the 1920s Spanish-style architecture in affluent **Boca Raton.** In the posh island community of **Palm Beach,** you can rub shoulders with the rich and famous as you stroll along the 12-mi-long island's **Worth Avenue,** one of the world's premier shopping streets. To recapture the glitter and flamboyance of Florida's boom years, when railroad magnate Henry M. Flagler first established Palm Beach as a playground for the wealthy, visit his ornate hotel, the **Breakers,** a legendary bastion of wealth and privilege (☞ Dining and Lodging, *below*). Henry Flagler's palatial 73-room Whitehall Mansion, now **Flagler Museum,** has original furnishings and an art collection. ✉ *Cocoanut Whitehall Way,* ☎ *561/ 655–2833. Closed Sun.–Mon.*

After visiting Palm Beach, take a drive past the secluded mansions along **County Road** and around the northern tip of the island. Directly across the Fort Worth inlet from Palm Beach is **West Palm Beach,** on the mainland. The **Norton Gallery of Art** (✉ 1451 S. Olive St., ☎ 561/832– 5194) has a fine collection of French Impressionists; it is closed Sunday–Monday. Southwest of West Palm Beach, at **Lion Country Safari** (✉ Southern Blvd. [Rte. 80], ☎ 561/793–1084), you can drive (with car windows closed) on 8 mi of paved roads through a 500-acre cageless zoo where 1,000 wild animals roam free. Lions, giraffes, zebras, ostriches, and elephants are among the animals in residence.

It's an abrupt shift from the man-made world of Palm Beach into primitive Florida at **Arthur R. Marshall Loxahatchee National Wildlife Refuge,** a wilderness of marshes, wetlands, and bountiful wildlife south of West Palm Beach and west of Boynton Beach. Stroll the nature trails, fish for bass and panfish, or paddle your own canoe through the waterways. *Headquarters:* ✉ *U.S. 441 between Rtes. 804 and 806,* ☎ *561/734–8303.*

Explore the upper Treasure Coast at a leisurely pace by taking U.S. 1 and Route A1A north from West Palm Beach along the Indian River, which separates the barrier islands from the mainland. Of major interest from April to August are the sea turtles that nest on the beaches; check with local chambers of commerce for information on turtle watches or learn about the turtles at **Loggerhead Park Marine Life Center of Juno Beach.** ✉ *1200 U.S. 1,* ☎ *561/627–8280. Closed Sun.–Mon.*

Drive atop the sand dunes at **Jupiter,** on the Intracoastal Waterway at the mouth of the scenic Loxahatchee River. Pause to photograph the impressive 105-ft **Jupiter Lighthouse** (☎ 561/747–8380), one of the oldest lighthouses on the Atlantic coast. At **Jupiter Island's Blowing Rocks Preserve** (☎ 561/575–2297), water sprays burst through holes in the shore's limestone facade at high tide. The preserve is home to large bird communities and a wealth of plants native to beachfront dune, marsh, and hammock. The revival of downtown **Stuart** is transforming this onetime fishing village into a magnet for people who want to live and work in a small-town atmosphere. The affluent community of **Vero Beach** has elegant houses, many dating from the 1920s. I–95 takes you back to Fort Lauderdale.

What to See and Do with Children

The Palm Beach area is not geared to family-oriented activities, but Fort Lauderdale and surrounding Broward County offer several child-pleasing attractions. One of the best is the **Museum of Discovery and Science** (✉ 401 S.W. 2nd St., ☎ 954/467–6637), along Fort Lauderdale's Riverwalk. It has an IMAX theater and interactive exhibits on ecology, health, and outer space.

Dining and Lodging

The Gold and Treasure coasts have a mix of American, European, and Caribbean cuisines, all emphasizing local fish and seafood. Accommodations are expensive in the Palm Beach area, but many inexpensive motels line U.S. 1 and the major exits of I–95 throughout the region. B&B accommodations are popular in Palm Beach County; contact **Open House Bed & Breakfast** (✉ Box 3025, Palm Beach 33480, ☎ 561/842–5190). For price ranges *see* Charts 1 (B) and 2 (A) *in* On the Road with Fodor's.

Boca Raton

$$$–$$$$ ✕ **La Vieille Maison.** Closets transformed into private dining nooks are
★ part of the charm of this 1920s home turned elegant French restaurant serving such dishes as pompano fillet with a pecan-chardonnay sauce. ✉ 770 E. Palmetto Park Rd., ☎ 407/391–6701. AE, D, DC, MC, V.

$ ✕ **Tom's Place.** It's worth the wait in line to relish the mouthwatering ribs or chicken in homemade barbecue sauce and the sweet potato pie in this casual family-run eatery. ✉ 7251 N. Federal Hwy., ☎ 407/997–0920. Reservations not accepted. MC, V. Closed Sept. No lunch Sun.–Mon.

Fort Lauderdale

$$$ ✕ **Down Under.** Under a bridge approach by the Intracoastal Waterway, this elegant dining room serves up Florida farm-raised striped bass with fennel and broth and many grilled meats. ✉ 3000 E. Oakland Park Blvd., ☎ 954/563–4123. AE, D, DC, MC, V.

$$ ✕ **Shirttail Charlie's.** After dining on crab balls or coconut shrimp with piña colada sauce on the outdoor deck or in the upstairs dining room of this 1920s-style restaurant, enjoy a free cruise on the New River. ✉ 400 S.W. 3rd Ave., ☎ 954/463–3474. AE, D, MC, V.

$$$ ▦ **Riverside Hotel.** This 1936 hotel amid the upscale shops on Las Olas Boulevard has an attentive staff, murals by well-known artist Bob Jenny (one of which stretches across 725 square ft of the building's facade), and antique oak furnishings in the guest rooms. ✉ 620 E. Las Olas Blvd., 33301, ☎ 954/467–0671 or 800/325–3280, ℻ 954/462–2148. 110 rooms. 2 restaurants, bar, pool, volleyball, dock. AE, DC, MC, V.

Hutchinson Island

$$$$ ✕▦ **Indian River Plantation.** This luxury resort on 192 island acres
★ evokes a Victorian seaside ambience with its latticework trim, tin roofs, and cool verandas. Feast on steak Diane or fresh snapper at the intimate Inlet Restaurant or try the Sunday champagne brunch at Scalawags. ✉ 555 N.E. Ocean Blvd., 34996, ☎ 561/225–6990 or 800/947–2148, ℻ 561/225–0003. 324 rooms, 150 condominiums. 5 restaurants, bar, 3 pools, outdoor spa, 3 golf courses, 13 tennis courts, boating, beach. AE, DC, MC, V.

Lake Worth

$ ✕ **John G's.** Although short on decor, this beachfront breakfast and lunch eatery is long on crowd-pleasing dishes, such as stuffed sandwiches, eggs prepared in every conceivable way, and seafood creations such as Greek shrimp on linguine with feta cheese. ✉ Off Rte. A1A, Lake Worth Public Beach, ☎ 561/585–9860. Reservations not accepted. No credit cards. No dinner.

Palm Beach

$$ ✕ **Ta-boo.** Open 24 hours, this re-creation of a 1940s bistro offers such fare as gourmet pizza and grilled chicken with arugula in three settings: a courtyard, a parlor with fireplace, and a gazebo. ✉ 221 Worth Ave., ☎ 561/835–3500. AE, MC, V.

$$$$ ✕⚃ **The Breakers.** Dating to 1926 and enlarged in 1969, this opulent
★ Italian Renaissance–style resort sprawls over 140 splendidly manicured
acres. Cupids frolic in the Florentine fountain at the main entrance,
while majestic ceiling vaults and frescoes grace the lobby. A $75 mil-
lion renovation modernized the resort and enhanced its elegance without sacrificing old-world luxury. Many rooms have been enlarged, and
all have been redecorated. You can dine on Continental specialties such
as herb-crusted rack of lamb in the hotel's tapestry-filled Florentine
Dining Room. ⊠ *1 S. County Rd., 33480,* ☎ *561/655–6611 or 800/
833–3141,* ℻ *561/659–8403. 562 rooms. 5 restaurants, 2 lounges,
pool, saunas, 2 golf courses, 20 tennis courts, croquet, health club, shuffleboard, beach, boating, children's programs. AE, D, DC, MC, V.*

$$–$$$ ⚃ **Palm Beach Sea Lord Hotel.** This comfortable off-the-beaten-track
motel in a garden setting has rooms overlooking the pool, the ocean,
or Lake Worth. The reasonably priced café adds to the at-home, comfy
feeling and attracts repeat customers. ⊠ *2315 Ocean Blvd., 33480,* ☎
℻ *561/582–1461. 40 units. Restaurant, pool, beach. AE, D, MC, V.*

Spas

Fort Lauderdale

$$$$ ⚃ **Palm-Aire Spa Resort.** This 750-acre resort has both a luxurious resort hotel and a spa complex that promotes physical fitness and stress
reduction. Large guest rooms have separate dressing rooms and private terraces. ⊠ *2601 Palm-Aire Dr. N, Pompano Beach 33069,* ☎
*954/972–3300 or 800/272–5624. 184 units. Restaurant, pools, hot
tubs, massage, saunas, spa, steam rooms, 3 golf courses, 37 tennis courts,
aerobics, exercise room, racquetball, squash. AE, D, MC, V.*

$$$$ ⚃ **Registry Resort & Spa Fort Lauderdale.** The resort's spacious rooms
have tropical decor and balconies overlooking a lake or a golf course.
Menus follow the nutritional guidelines of the American Heart Association and the American Cancer Society. Fitness programs are available, and the resort offers combination spa-tennis and spa-golf packages.
⊠ *250 Racquet Club Rd., 33326,* ☎ *954/389–3300 or 800/327–8090,*
℻ *954/384–0563. 493 rooms. 4 restaurants, 2 lounges, 5 pools,
beauty salon, spa, 2 golf courses, 24 tennis courts, bowling, horseback
riding, roller-skating rink, shops. AE, D, MC, V.*

Palm Beach

$$$$ ⚃ **Hippocrates Health Institute.** Personalized programs here are su-
pervised, highly structured, and emphasize holistic health and lifestyle
management. Guests stay in a spacious hacienda or at private cottages
on the 20-acre wooded estate. ⊠ *1443 Palmdale Ct., West Palm Beach
33411,* ☎ *561/471–8876, 561/471–8868, or 800/842–2125. 15
rooms. Pool, massage. AE, MC, V.*

$$$$ ⚃ **PGA National Resort & Spa.** At this sybaritic getaway where golf
and tennis pros exercise during tournaments, the spa facilities include
the signature mineral pools with salts from around the world. Choose
from large guest rooms with tropical decor or cottage units with two
bedrooms and a kitchen. ⊠ *400 Ave. of the Champions, Palm Beach
Gardens 33418,* ☎ *561/627–2000 or 800/633–9150,* ℻ *407/622–
0261. 336 rooms, 85 cottages. 3 restaurants, 2 pools, beauty salon,
massage, 5 golf courses, 19 tennis courts, aerobics, exercise room. AE,
DC, MC, V.*

Nightlife and the Arts

Fort Lauderdale and the Palm Beach area offer a full roster of performing
arts events. Major venues include **Broward Center for the Performing
Arts** (⊠ 201 S.W. 5th Ave., Fort Lauderdale, ☎ 954/462–0222) and

Raymond F. Kravis Center for the Performing Arts (⌧ 701 Okeechobee Blvd., ☎ 561/832–7469), the cultural center of Palm Beach. Many of the cultural events in Vero Beach take place at the **Riverside Theatre** (⌧ 3250 Riverside Park Dr., ☎ 561/231–6990). The **Jupiter Dinner Theatre** (⌧ 1001 E. Indiantown Rd., Jupiter, ☎ 561/747–5566) is known for the Broadway and film stars who regularly perform in its productions. Fort Lauderdale has the liveliest nightlife, with comedy clubs, discos, and clubs featuring music for all ages and tastes; popular ones include **Baja Beach Club** (⌧ Coral Ridge Mall, 3200 N. Federal Hwy., ☎ 954/561–2432), with karaoke and performing bartenders, and **O'Hara's Pub & Sidewalk Cafe** (⌧ 722 E. Las Olas Blvd., ☎ 954/524–1764), which has nightly live jazz and blues.

Outdoor Activities and Sports

Biking

The beautiful **Palm Beach Bicycle Trail** runs for 10 mi along the shoreline of Lake Worth. For bike rentals try **Palm Beach Bicycle Trail Shop** (⌧ 223 Sunrise Ave., ☎ 561/659–4583).

Diving

A popular place to dive is the 23-mi-long, 2-mi-wide **Fort Lauderdale Reef,** one of 80 dive sites in Broward County. Palm Beach County offers excellent drift diving and anchor diving off the Atlantic coast. Try **Pro Dive** (⌧ Radisson Bahia Mar Beach Resort, 801 Seabreeze Blvd., Fort Lauderdale, ☎ 954/761–3413 or 800/772–3483) for diving equipment and packages.

Fishing

Anglers can deep-sea or freshwater fish year-round. Pompano, amberjack, and snapper are caught off the numerous piers and bridges, while Lake Okeechobee yields bass and perch. Sailfish are a popular catch on deep-sea charters, offered by such companies as **Radisson Bahia Mar Beach Resort** (⌧ 801 Seabreeze Blvd., ☎ 954/764–2233) and **B-Love Fleet** (⌧ 314 E. Ocean Ave., Lantana, ☎ 561/588–7612).

Golf

Among the 50-plus golf courses in Greater Fort Lauderdale is **Colony West Country Club** (⌧ 6800 N.W. 88th Ave., Tamarac, ☎ 954/726–8430). The **Breakers Hotel Golf Club** (⌧ 1 S. County Rd., ☎ 561/655–6611 or 800/833–3141) has 36 holes. **Palm Beach Par 3** (⌧ 2345 S. Ocean Blvd., 33480, ☎ 561/547–0598) has 18 holes, including four on the Atlantic and three on the inland waterway.

Spectator Sports

Baseball: The Gold and Treasure coasts host spring training for several major league teams. **Baltimore Orioles** (⌧ Fort Lauderdale Stadium, 5301 N.W. 12th Ave., West Palm Beach, ☎ 954/776–1921); **Montreal Expos** (⌧ West Palm Beach Municipal Stadium, 1610 Palm Beach Lakes Blvd., West Palm Beach, ☎ 561/683–6012); **Los Angeles Dodgers** (⌧ Holman Stadium, 4101 26th St., Vero Beach, ☎ 561/569–4900); **New York Mets** (⌧ St. Lucie County Sport Complex, 525 N.W. Peacock Blvd., Port St. Lucie, ☎ 561/871–2115).

Dog Racing: Greyhounds race at **Palm Beach Kennel Club** (⌧ 1111 N. Congress Ave., Palm Beach, ☎ 561/683–2222; year-round) and **Hollywood Greyhound Track** (⌧ 831 N. Federal Hwy., Hallandale, ☎ 954/454–9400; Dec.–Apr.).

Horse Racing: Gulfstream Park Race Track (⌧ 901 S. Federal Hwy., Hallandale, ☎ 954/454–7000; Jan.–mid-Mar.). **Pompano Harness Track** (⌧ 1800 S.W. 3rd St., Pompano Beach, ☎ 954/972–2000; Oct.–Aug.).

Polo: This sport of the wealthy is played at the **Palm Beach Polo and Country Club** (✉ 13420 South Shore Blvd., West Palm Beach, ☎ 561/793–1440), which has games on Sunday, January–April.

Beaches

Crystal-clear warm waters are the main draw of the miles of beaches along the Atlantic coast. Each coastal town has a public beach area; many, like **Pompano Beach,** have fishing piers. The area is popular with snorkelers and divers.

The **beachfront,** along Route A1A between Las Olas Boulevard and Sunrise Boulevard in Fort Lauderdale, is a very popular beach; shops, restaurants, and hotels line the road. In Dania the **John U. Lloyd Beach State Recreation Area** (✉ 6503 N. Ocean Dr., ☎ 954/923–2833), the locals' favorite, is a fine beach with picnicking, fishing, and canoeing facilities and 251 acres of mangroves to explore. **Bathtub Beach,** on Hutchinson Island north of Jupiter, has placid waters and a gentle sea slope, making it ideal for children.

Shopping

Both Palm Beach and Fort Lauderdale have shopping districts that cater to a high-society clientele. In Fort Lauderdale expensive boutiques are clustered along tree-lined **Las Olas Boulevard.** In Palm Beach more than 250 specialty shops and pricey boutiques, with such famous names as Gucci and Cartier, beckon to well-heeled shoppers along **Worth Avenue.** A few miles west of Fort Lauderdale proper is **Sawgrass Mills Mall** (✉ Flamingo Rd. and Sunrise Blvd., Sunrise), which has 270 stores.

ELSEWHERE IN FLORIDA

Everglades and Biscayne National Parks

Arriving and Departing

Miami International Airport (☞ Miami, *above*) is about 35 mi from Homestead–Florida City, gateways to the national parks. Traveling south by car, take U.S. 1 or the Florida Turnpike to the gateway towns.

What to See and Do

★ **Everglades National Park,** the country's largest remaining subtropical wilderness, contains more than 1.4 million acres—half land, half water—that can be explored by boat, by bike, on foot, and partly by car. This slow-moving "river of grass" is a maze of saw-grass marshes, mangrove swamps, salt prairies, and pinelands that shelter a variety of plants and animals, even though increased pollution by pesticide runoff from local farms has reduced the number of birds and brought the Florida panther to near extinction. The new visitor center is superb; the three park entrances are in Homestead, along U.S. 41 (Tamiami Trail), and on the west coast of Florida, in Everglades City. ✉ *Box 279, Homestead 33030; Main Visitor Center, 40001 Rte. 9336, Florida City;* ☎ *305/242–7700.*

Biscayne National Park is the nation's largest marine park and the largest national park in the continental United States with a living coral reef. It covers about 274 square mi, mostly underwater, and has several ecosystems. Shallow Biscayne Bay is home to the manatee; the upper Florida Keys harbor moray eels and brilliantly colored parrot fish in a 150-mi coral reef; bald eagles and other large birds inhabit the mainland mangrove forests. A new visitor center with interactive exhibits, a glass-bottom-boat tour, canoeing, snorkeling, and scuba diving are popular ways to experience the park. ⊠ *9700 S.W. 328th St., Box 1369, Home-stead 33090,* ☎ *305/230–7275.*

The Panhandle: Northwestern Florida

Arriving and Departing

Pensacola Regional Airport (☎ 904/435–1746) serves the region. I–10 and U.S. 90 are the main east–west highways across the top of the state, U.S. 98 runs along the coast, and U.S. 231, 331, and 29 and Route 85 traverse the Panhandle north–south.

What to See and Do

The Panhandle has been dubbed the Emerald Coast for its profusion of pine forests, magnolias, live oaks dripping with Spanish moss, lush bayous and swamps, and white-sand beaches lapped by blue-green waters. Historical and archaeological sites vie for attention with beautiful beaches, golf, hunting, hiking, water sports, and outstanding fishing.

Stroll through the historic districts of **Pensacola** and absorb some of the city's colorful Spanish, French, British, and Civil War past. **Fort Walton Beach** is a family vacation playground famous for its beaches and spectacular sand dunes. **Eglin Air Force Base** (⊠ Rte. 85, ☎ 904/882–3931), in Fort Walton Beach, includes 10 auxiliary fields and a total of 21 runways. Kids especially enjoy the **Indian Temple Mound Museum** (⊠ 139 Miracle Strip Pkwy. [U.S. 98], Fort Walton Beach, ☎ 904/833–9595), where they can learn all about the prehistoric peoples who lived
★ in the region during the past 10,000 years. **Grayton Beach State Recreation Area,** near the recently created "old-fashioned" community of Seaside, has one of the most scenic beaches along the Gulf Coast, if not the country.

Fort Walton Beach's neighbor is the bustling fishing village of **Destin,** popular with anglers, sun worshipers, and gourmets. For simple relaxation head for the snow-white beaches, miles of waterways, and amusement parks of **Panama City Beach,** a prime vacation area and the new in spot for students on spring break. The **Pensacola Visitor Information Center** (⊠ 1401 E. Gregory St., 32501, ☎ 904/434–1234 or 800/874–1234) provides information on the Choctawhatchee Bay region.

Northeastern Florida

Arriving and Departing

Jacksonville International Airport (☎ 904/741–4902) serves the region. I–10 is the major east–west artery through the north, and I–4 from Tampa enters the region near Daytona Beach. The primary north–south routes are I–95 along the east coast and I–75 south from Valdosta, Georgia.

What to See and Do

Variety is the key word for northeastern Florida: You can see live-oak-framed roads and plantations that recall the Old South all along St. Johns River; Thoroughbred horse farms in Ocala; impressive savannas in Gainesville; the Civil War heritage of Tallassee, the state capital; and the cosmopolitan city of Jacksonville. The beaches range from rocky shorelines to the glistening sand beaches of Jacksonville and the famous hard-packed, drivable beach at Daytona. The **Daytona 500** auto race is held annually at Daytona International Speedway (⊠ U.S. 92, ☎ 904/254–2700). Jacksonville is the host of collegiate football's **Gator Bowl** (☎ 904/396–1800).

St. Augustine (⊠ Visitor Information Center, 10 Castillo Dr., 32084, ☎ 904/825–1000), the oldest permanent settlement in the United States, dates to 1565. Explore the 300-year-old Spanish fortress of **Castillo de San Marcos National Monument** (⊠ 1 Castillo Dr., ☎ 904/829–6506), which guards Matanzas Bay. Stroll down St. George Street through the restored Spanish colonial village of **San Agustín Antiguo** and glimpse life in the 1700s. Drink from the spring reputed to be the fountain of youth discovered by Ponce de León in 1513 at the **Fountain of Youth Archaeological Park** (⊠ 155 Magnolia Ave., ☎ 904/829–3168).

Silver Springs, the state's oldest attraction and the world's largest formation of clear artesian springs, offers glass-bottom-boat tours and a jungle cruise. ⊠ *Rte. 40, 1 mi east of Ocala,* ☎ *904/236–2121.* ☜ *$26.95.*

Amelia Island (⊠ Amelia Island–Fernandina Beach Chamber of Commerce, 102 Centre St., Fernandina Beach 32034, ☎ 904/261–3248), just north of Jacksonville, contains the historic town of Fernandina Beach, with its 19th-century mansions. North of Fernandina Beach lies **Fort Clinch State Park** (☎ 904/261–4212), with a brick fort, nature trails, swimming, and living history reenactments.

For more information on the region, contact the **Jacksonville and Its Beaches Convention and Visitors Bureau** (⊠ 6 E. Bay St., Suite 200, 32202, ☎ 904/353–9736) and the **Tallahassee Area Convention and Tourist Bureau** (⊠ 200 E. College Ave., 32302, ☎ 800/628–2866).

GEORGIA

Updated by
Jane F. Garvey

Capital	Atlanta
Population	7,353,000
Motto	Wisdom, Justice, and Moderation
State Bird	Brown thrasher
State Flower	Cherokee rose
Postal Abbreviation	GA

Statewide Visitor Information

Georgia Department of Industry, Trade and Tourism (✉ Box 1776, Atlanta 30301, ☎ 404/656–3590 for visitor information or 800/847–4842). There are 11 **visitor centers** at various border points and 45 locally operated **welcome centers** in Atlanta, Savannah, and throughout the state.

Scenic Drives

Along the coast Jekyll Island's **North Riverview Drive** offers scenery ranging from historic homes in Jekyll Island Historic District to vast expanses of marshland. **Route 157** north from Cloudland Canyon State Park to the Tennessee border at Lookout Mountain has views of northwestern Georgia's Cumberland Mountains. **U.S. 76** east from Dalton to the Chattooga River traverses the North Georgia Mountains and beautiful sections of the Chattahoochee National Forest.

National and State Parks

National Parks

The **Andersonville National Historic Site** (✉ Rte. 1, Box 800, Andersonville 31711, ☎ 912/924–0343), which served as a Confederate prison camp, is the official site of the National Prisoners of War Museum for all POWs from the Civil War through Desert Storm. **Chattahoochee River National Recreation Area** (✉ 1978 Island Ford Pkwy., Dunwoody 30350, ☎ 770/952–4419) offers river swimming, hiking trails, and picnic areas. **Kennesaw Mountain National Battlefield** (✉ 900 Kennesaw Mountain Dr., Kennesaw 30152, ☎ 770/427–4686), a 2,884-acre park outside Atlanta, commemorates one of the Civil War's most decisive battles and offers 16 mi of hiking trails.

State Parks

Cloudland Canyon State Park (✉ Rte. 2, Box 150, Rising Fawn 30738, ☎ 706/657–4050), on the west side of Lookout Mountain in the state's northwest corner, has cabin facilities, camping, and dramatic scenery. **Vogel State Park** (✉ 7485 Vogel State Park Rd., Blairsville 30512, ☎ 706/745–2628), a 221-acre park surrounded by the Chattahoochee National Forest, includes a 17-acre lake with swimming and fishing. The park has cottages and campsites. **Providence Canyon,** known as Georgia's Grand Canyon (✉ Rte. 1, Box 158, Lumpkin 31815, ☎ 912/838–6202), is the result of erosion caused by poor farming practices. It is a day park for picnicking, exploring, or hiking.

ATLANTA

Atlanta is one of the fastest-growing cities in the United States, with a skyline that is constantly changing. Initially founded as a railroad center, the city has blossomed into a major metropolis with more than 3 million people. It is an aviation hub and a regional leader in commerce and industry; perhaps these are some of the reasons it was selected as host of the 1996 Summer Olympic Games. But for all its modernity, the city's winning character is still defined by its southern hospitality and its near-picture-perfect residential neighborhoods.

Visitor Information

Atlanta Chamber of Commerce (⊠ 235 International Blvd., 30303, ☎ 404/880–9000). **Convention and Visitors Bureau information centers** (⊠ Peachtree Center Mall, 233 Peachtree St., 30303, ☎ 404/222–6688 or 800/285–2682; also ⊠ Underground Atlanta, 65 Upper Alabama St.; ⊠ Georgia World Congress Center, 285 International Blvd.; ⊠ Hartsfield International Airport, North Terminal at West Crossover; and ⊠ Lenox Square Mall, 3393 Peachtree Rd.).

Arriving and Departing

By Bus

Greyhound Lines (⊠ 232 Forsyth St., ☎ 404/584–1728 or 800/231–2222) provides transportation to downtown Atlanta, Decatur, Hapeville, and Norcross.

By Car

Atlanta is commonly referred to as the Crossroads of the South, and for good reason. Between South Carolina and Alabama, I–85 runs northeast–southwest through Atlanta and I–20 runs east–west; I–75 runs north–south through the state. I–285 makes a 65-mi loop around the metropolitan area.

By Plane

Hartsfield Atlanta International Airport (☎ 404/530–6600) has scheduled flights by most major domestic and foreign carriers. Traffic to downtown Atlanta, about 13 mi north of the airport via I–75N and I–85N, can be congested during rush hour. Cab fare is about $18 for one person, $20 for two people, and $24 for three or more. Cabs are found near the baggage claim area. The **Metropolitan Atlanta Rapid Transit Authority** (MARTA; ☎ 404/848–4711) rapid-rail subway system is one of the quickest and easiest ways to reach the downtown, Buckhead, Midtown, and the Lenox Square and Perimeter Mall districts; the fare is $1.50. MARTA also goes directly to the airport.

By Train

Amtrak (☎ 404/881–3060 or 800/872–7245) serves Brookwood Station (⊠ 1688 Peachtree St.).

Getting Around Atlanta

Atlanta is a sprawling city, making a car a necessity, but it contains a number of walkable neighborhoods and districts with interesting architecture and attractions.

By Car

Major public parking lots downtown are at the **CNN Center** (⊠ Entrance off Techwood Dr.), the **Georgia World Congress Center** (⊠ Off International Blvd.), **Peachtree Center, Macy's** (⊠ Carnegie Way, 1 block off Peachtree St.), and **Underground Atlanta** (⊠ 65 Upper Alabama St.). Buckhead and Midtown have on-street parking and more lots.

By Public Transportation

MARTA (☎ 404/848–4711) operates buses and a modern rapid-rail subway system. Fare for either is $1.50; exact change or a token is required.

The rapid-rail trains operate from 5:30 AM to 1:17 AM; bus schedules depend on the route.

By Taxi
You can hail a cab fairly easily at hotels in the downtown or Buckhead district. **Buckhead Safety Cab** (☎ 404/233–1152 or 404/233–1153) and **Checker Cab** (☎ 404/351–1111) offer 24-hour service. With advance reservations, **Carey Executive Limousine** (☎ 404/223–2000) also provides 24-hour service.

Orientation Tours

Bus and Van Tours
Atlanta Discovery Tours (☎ 770/667–1414) and **American Sightseeing Atlanta** (☎ 404/233–9140 or 800/572–3050) pick you up at area hotels for customized sightseeing or shopping tours. **Gray Line of Atlanta** (⊠ 2541 Camp Creek Pkwy., College Park 30337, ☎ 404/767–0594, FAX 404/756–1399) offers tours of downtown, Midtown, and Buckhead; some include Stone Mountain and the King Center.

Walking Tours
Atlanta Preservation Center (⊠ Suite 3, 156 7th St., 30303, ☎ 404/876–2041 or 404/876–2040 for tour hot line) has guided tours on selected days, including 10 of historic neighborhoods available from March through November and a tour of the Fox Theatre offered year-round.

Exploring Atlanta

Beginning downtown, you can move north past an eclectic mix of Renaissance Revival towers and contemporary glass-and-steel skyscrapers; through Midtown's genteel, garden-filled neighborhoods punctuated by parks and museums; and into upscale Buckhead, lined with mansions and glitzy shopping centers bursting with designer-name boutiques.

Downtown
Atlanta had its inauspicious beginning as a 19th-century settlement and later became a railway hub; a few sites from the earliest days are preserved downtown. A three-level, six-block entertainment and shopping center called **Underground Atlanta** (⊠ 65 Upper Alabama St., ☎ 404/523–2311) encompasses some of the original city center's storefronts and streets. The **World of Coca-Cola** (⊠ 55 Martin Luther King Dr., ☎ 404/676–5151) gives free samples and has three floors of memorabilia from the century-old soft drink company. Reservations are essential for groups of 20 or more.

At the corner of Marietta Street and Techwood Drive is the **CNN Center** (⊠ 1 CNN Center, ☎ 404/827–2300 or 404/827–2400), headquarters of Cable News Network. There are daily guided tours of its behind-the-scenes workings, including newscasters in action.

Woodruff Park, at the corner of Peachtree Street and Park Place, is named for Robert W. Woodruff, the late Coca-Cola magnate. In warm weather the park is a favorite alfresco lunch spot. Near CNN Center, **Centennial Olympic Park** (⊠ Marietta St. and Techwood Dr.), a legacy of the 1996 Centennial Olympic Games, enhances the streetscape with green space and sculpture. It will become the setting for special events, such as the Arts Festival of Atlanta, formerly held in Piedmont Park. Thrusting into the sky a block north of Woodruff Park are the striking angles of the red-marble tower that is the **Georgia-Pacific Building** (⊠ 133 Peachtree St., at John Wesley Dobbs Ave.). Built on the site of Loew's Grand Theatre, where *Gone With the Wind* premiered in 1939, the

Downtown Atlanta

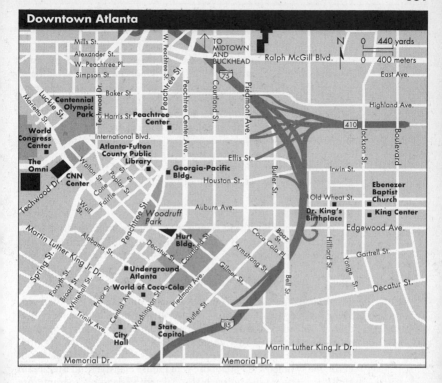

corporate flagship building houses the **High Museum of Art, Folk Art and Photography Galleries** (✉ 30 John Wesley Dobbs Ave., ☎ 404/577–6940), a branch of the High Museum (☞ Midtown, *below*).

★ Walking tours of the **Martin Luther King, Jr., National Historic District** start from the **King Center** (✉ 449 Auburn Ave., ☎ 404/524–1956), established by King's widow, Coretta Scott King. Inside the center are a museum, a library, and a gift shop; in front is King's tomb, where an eternal flame burns.

The Queen Anne–style bungalow that was **Dr. King's birthplace** (✉ 501 Auburn Ave., ☎ 404/331–3920) is open for tours. Three generations of the King family have preached at **Ebenezer Baptist Church** (✉ 407 Auburn Ave., ☎ 404/688–7263).

The **Georgia State Capitol** houses government offices and a museum. Built in 1889, its dome is gilded with gold leaf from ore mined in nearby Dahlonega, the site of the nation's first gold rush. ✉ *206 Washington St.,* ☎ *404/656–2844. Free.*

Peachtree Center (☎ 404/614–5000), a climate-controlled complex filled with shops, restaurants, hotels, and offices, is on the city's main thoroughfare, **Peachtree Street.** In the center's Marriott Marquis Two Tower is the **Atlanta International Museum of Art and Design** (✉ 285 Peachtree Center Ave., ☎ 404/688–2467), which specializes in international art, design, and crafts exhibitions.

Midtown

Midtown, just north of downtown, was the heart of Atlanta's hippie scene during the 1960s and early '70s and now is the city's primary art and theater district and the home of a large segment of Atlanta's gay population, as well as young families, young professionals, artists, and musicians. The area is popular for its bars, restaurants, and specialty shops. Like downtown, it has a distinctive skyline created by the many office towers erected during the past decade.

The Egyptian-style **Fox Theatre** (✉ 660 Peachtree St., ☎ 404/881–2100), the city's oldest movie palace, hosts splashy events ranging from touring companies of Broadway plays to rock concerts; tours are offered year-round (☞ Orientation Tours, *above*). The **Road to Tara Museum** (✉ Georgian Terrace Bldg., 659 Peachtree St., ☎ 404/897–1939) has an impressive collection of *Gone With the Wind* memorabilia. Designed by architect Richard Meier, the **High Museum of Art** (✉ 1280 Peachtree St., ☎ 404/733–4444) showcases a major collection of American contemporary and decorative art as well as sub-Saharan African art. The Victorian mansion **Rhodes Memorial Hall** (✉ 1516 Peachtree St., ☎ 404/881–9980) is the headquarters for the **Georgia Trust for Historic Preservation.**

Buckhead

A large portion of Buckhead, 5 mi north of Midtown on Peachtree Street, is to Atlanta what Beverly Hills is to Los Angeles. This residential and shopping area is home to fine dining, designer boutiques, and expensive homes. To see the manicured lawns and mansions of Atlanta's elite, take a scenic drive along Tuxedo, Valley, and Habersham roads.

The white-columned **Georgia Governor's Mansion** (✉ 391 W. Paces Ferry Rd., ☎ 404/261–1858) is decorated with an impressive collection of Federal-period antiques; the neoclassical mansion is open for tours. The **Atlanta History Center** (✉ 130 W. Paces Ferry Rd., ☎ 404/814–4000)—comprising the **Atlanta History Museum,** the **Tullie Smith Farm,** the symmetrical **Palladian Swan House** mansion, and **McElreath Hall**—is a 32-acre site where historical artifacts and photographs are displayed.

Parks and Gardens

Piedmont Park, in Midtown between 10th Street and the Prado, is the city's premier urban green space, with a children's playground, tennis courts, a swimming pool, and paved paths for biking, running, and roller skating. You can rent bikes and in-line skates from **Skate Escape** (✉ 1086 Piedmont Ave., ☎ 404/892–1292), across the street. The park was designed for the 1895 Cotton States and International Exposition by Frederick Law Olmsted.

Adjoining Piedmont Park is the 30-acre **Atlanta Botanical Garden,** with landscaped gardens and the climate-controlled Fuqua Conservatory, containing tropical, desert, and endangered plants. ✉ *1345 Piedmont Ave., ½ mi north of 14th St., ☎ 404/876–5858. Free Thurs. after 3. Closed Mon.*

Stone Mountain Park (✉ U.S. 78E, ☎ 770/498–5690), 7 mi northeast of the city, features the world's largest sculpture, a memorial to Confederate war heroes Jefferson Davis, Robert E. Lee, and Stonewall Jackson (a cable car takes you 825 ft up the mountain face for a closer look). The 3,200-acre park also contains an antebellum plantation and museums and offers a ride on a railroad, a cruise on a riverboat, and nightly laser shows in summer. Many popular special events here showcase southern history and culture as well as food and entertainment.

What to See and Do with Children

The *Atlanta Journal and Constitution*'s Saturday weekend guide has a "Kids" listing that highlights special happenings. The **Fernbank Science Center** (✉ 156 Heaton Park Dr., ☎ 404/378–4311) has an authentic *Apollo* spacecraft and a planetarium. The **Center for Puppetry Arts** (⊠ 1404 Spring St., ☎ 404/873–3391) displays puppets from around the world, holds puppet-making workshops, and stages original productions. It's closed Sunday. **SciTrek** (⊠ 395 Piedmont Ave., ☎ 404/522–5500), in Midtown, is among the top 10 science museums in the country, with hands-on exhibits and Kidspace, a special area for two- to seven-year-olds. **Zoo Atlanta** (⊠ 800 Cherokee Ave., ☎ 404/624–5600) is in Grant Park, just south of downtown.

★ The unique **Atlanta Cyclorama,** a huge circular painting, depicts the Battle of Atlanta (1864), when the city was burned by General Sherman. ⊠ *Grant Park, 800 Cherokee Ave., ☎ 404/624–1071 for tickets, 404/658–7625 for information.*

Six Flags over Georgia, a large theme park, has dozens of rides (including roller coasters and water rides), musical revues, and concerts by top-name artists. ⊠ *I–20W at 7561 Six Flags Rd., Austell, ☎ 770/739–3400. ☜ $32 adults; $21 children 3–9. Closed Nov.–Feb.*

Dining

Atlanta prides itself on a wide selection of international restaurants. Italian, French, Moroccan, and Thai restaurants all command the attention of Atlanta's dining public, but not to be overlooked are the many offerings reflecting both the traditional and new-style cuisine of the Deep South. For price ranges *see* Chart 1 (A) *in* On the Road with Fodor's.

$$$$ ✕ **City Grill.** The grand setting of this downtown restaurant in the historic Hurt Building includes high ceilings, bucolic murals, and romantic table lamps. The menu is American with a southern flair. ⊠ *50 Hurt Plaza, ☎ 404/524–2489. AE, D, DC, MC, V. Closed Sun. No lunch Sat.*

$$$$ ✕ **The Dining Room, the Ritz-Carlton, Buckhead.** International acclaim praises this restaurant for its imaginative haute cuisine, which incorporates such regional ingredients as Vidalia onions. The menu changes daily. ⊠ *3434 Peachtree Rd., ☎ 404/237–2700. Reservations essential. Jacket and tie. AE, D, DC, MC, V. Closed Sun. No lunch.*

$$$ ✕ **Abruzzi Ristorante.** Some of the city's finest Italian cuisine is attentively served at this elegant restaurant. Pasta is beautifully prepared, especially the *papardelle* with game sauce, as are such regional specialties as quail over polenta. ⊠ *2355 Peachtree Rd., ☎ 404/261–8186. Jacket required. AE, DC, MC, V. Closed Sun. No lunch Sat.*

$$$ ✕ **Bacchanalia.** Having won many accolades since opening in 1993,
★ this restaurant never disappoints. The influence is largely Mediterranean with touches of Asia; the $35 prix-fixe menu is recommended. There is no smoking here. ⊠ *3125 Piedmont Rd., ☎ 404/365–0410. Reservations essential. AE, DC, MC, V. Closed Sun.–Mon. No lunch.*

$$$ ✕ **Ciboulette.** French bistro food and atmosphere have Atlantans lin-
★ ing up for foie gras, hot smoked salmon, duck confit, and roast squab. ⊠ *1529 Piedmont Ave., ☎ 404/874–7600. AE, D, DC, MC, V. Closed Sun. No lunch.*

$$$ ✕ **Pricci.** The stamp of acclaimed designer Patrick Kuleto is apparent in the chic decor of this hot spot. Deceptively simple Italian fare focuses on pasta and seafood. Some specialties (sea bass in parchment paper) are designed for delicious healthy dining. ⊠ *500 Pharr Rd., ☎ 404/237–2941. AE, D, DC, MC, V. No lunch weekends.*

$$–$$$ ✕ **South City Kitchen.** The cuisine at this bright, popular restaurant is
★ the traditional Low Country style of coastal South Carolina; the catfish is superb, and the desserts are delicious. ⊠ *1144 Crescent Ave., ☎ 404/873–7358. AE, DC, MC, V.*

$$ ✕ **Buckhead Diner.** This establishment, adorned with a shimmering
★ metallic exterior, serves hearty American diner fare with an upscale twist,
such as veal meat loaf, as well as dishes like crab spring rolls and as-
paragus. Prepare to wait at busy times. ⊠ *3073 Piedmont Rd.,* ☎ *404/
262–3336. Reservations not accepted. AE, D, DC, MC, V.*

$ ✕ **The Colonnade Restaurant.** For traditional southern cuisine, such
★ as ham steak, turkey and dressing, and southern-style vegetables, in-
siders head for the Colonnade, an Atlanta institution since 1927. ⊠
1879 Cheshire Bridge Rd., ☎ *404/874–5642. Reservations not accepted.
No credit cards.*

$ ✕ **Luna Sí.** Funky meets uptown chic at this delightfully relaxed loft
★ restaurant, where wholesome cuisine in a healthy environment (smok-
ing is strictly prohibited) is the order of every day. Butter and fat are
nowhere to be seen here, and fried dishes are done in virgin olive oil.
The prix-fixe menus are worth it. ⊠ *1931 Peachtree St.,* ☎ *404/355–
5993. AE, DC, MC, V. No lunch weekends.*

Lodging

The city's booming convention business means hotel and motel options
in all price ranges. The downtown, Buckhead, and north I–285 areas
have the greatest concentration of accommodations. For price ranges
see Chart 2 (A) *in* On the Road with Fodor's.

$$$$ ▦ **Atlanta Marriott Marquis.** The lobby of this popular convention hotel
seems to stretch forever to the skylighted roof 50 stories above. Tra-
ditionally furnished guest rooms open onto this central atrium. ⊠ *265
Peachtree Center Ave., 30303,* ☎ *404/521–0000,* FAX *404/586–6299.
1,742 rooms. 5 restaurants, 4 bars, indoor and outdoor pools, health
club, concierge, business services. AE, D, DC, MC, V.*

$$$$ ▦ **JW Marriott.** The Marriott is connected to Lenox Square Mall and
is across from a subway station. The 25-story hotel's subdued style fo-
cuses on intimacy and comfort; irregularly shaped rooms have over-
size baths with a separate shower stall and tub. ⊠ *3300 Lenox Rd.,
30326,* ☎ *404/262–3344,* FAX *404/262–8689. 401 rooms. Restaurant,
2 lounges, indoor pool, health club. AE, D, DC, MC, V.*

$$$$ ▦ **Ritz-Carlton, Buckhead.** An elegant lobby with fine art, a fireplace,
★ and comfortable, authentic antique furniture invites lingering over af-
ternoon tea before returning to rooms containing luxury linens, mar-
ble baths, and reproduction period furnishings. ⊠ *3434 Peachtree Rd.,
30326,* ☎ *404/237–2700,* FAX *404/239–0078. 553 rooms. 3 restau-
rants, lounge, indoor pool, health club. AE, D, DC, MC, V.*

$$$$ ▦ **Swissôtel.** An international clientele frequents this European-style
luxury hotel, featuring a chic, modern glass exterior, sophisticated
Biedermeier-style interiors, and fabulous art on view in the public
spaces. ⊠ *3391 Peachtree Rd., 30326,* ☎ *404/365–0065 or 800/
253–1397, 404/365–8787. 377 rooms. Restaurant, bar, indoor pool,
health club, concierge, business services. AE, D, DC, MC, V.*

$$$ ▦ **Embassy Suites.** This Buckhead high-rise is just blocks from two of
the city's top shopping centers, Phipps Plaza and Lenox Square. Suites
range from basic bedroom and sitting-room combinations to luxurious rooms with wet bars; a few standard rooms are available. All units
have microwaves and refrigerators. ⊠ *3285 Peachtree Rd., 30305,*
☎ *404/261–7733,* FAX *404/261–6857. 328 rooms. Restaurant, lounge,
indoor and outdoor pools, exercise room. AE, D, DC, MC, V.*

$$ ▦ **Buckhead Bed & Breakfast Inn.** Built in 1996, the inn sits on a busy
corner but provides an intimacy and coziness lacking in large hotels.
⊠ *70 Lenox Pointe, 30324,* ☎ *404/261–8284 or 888/224–8797,* FAX
404/237–9224. 19 rooms. Full breakfast. AE, MC, V.

$ 🖭 **Quality Hotel Downtown.** Renovated in 1996, this quiet hotel has rooms have views of downtown; some rooms have balconies. ⊠ *89 Luckie St., 30303,* ☎ *404/524–7991,* 𝔽𝔸𝕏 *404/525–0672. 75 rooms. Restaurant, pool. AE, DC, MC, V.*

Nightlife and the Arts

Arts and nightlife events (and special events throughout the city) are listed in the *Atlanta Journal and Constitution* and *Creative Loafing* newspapers, both available at newsstands, and in *Peachtree, Presenting the Season,* and *KNOW ATLANTA* magazines, available at visitor information centers and in hotels. The **Arts Hotline** (☎ 404/853–3278) also gives daily arts and nightlife information. Ticket brokers include **TicketMaster** (☎ 404/249–6400 or 800/326–4000) and **Ticket-X-Press** (☎ 404/231–5888).

Nightlife

Underground Atlanta (☞ Shopping, *below*) and the **Buckhead, Virginia-Highland,** and **Little Five Points** neighborhoods are Atlanta's nightlife centers. Virginia-Highland's **Atkins Park Bar & Grill** (⊠ 794 N. Highland Ave., ☎ 404/876–7249), one of the city's oldest neighborhood bars, attracts a 30-something crowd. **Blind Willie's** (⊠ 828 N. Highland Ave., ☎ 404/873–2583) offers New Orleans– and Chicago-style blues. **Eddie's Attic** (⊠ 515B N. McDonough St., ☎ 404/377–4976), next to the MARTA station in nearby Decatur, is the best venue for local acoustic acts. For contemporary rock try the **Point** (⊠ 420 Moreland Ave., ☎ 404/659–3522).

The Arts

Most touring **Broadway productions** make their way to Atlanta's **Fox Theatre** (☞ Midtown *in* Exploring Atlanta), **Center Stage** (⊠ 1374 W. Peachtree St., ☎ 404/874–1511), or the Civic Center (⊠ 395 Piedmont Ave., ☎ 404/523–6275). The **Alliance Theater Company** (⊠ 1280 Peachtree St., ☎ 404/733–5000) is one of the city's leading theatrical groups. Woodruff Arts Center's **Symphony Hall** (⊠ 1280 Peachtree St., ☎ 404/733–5000) is the home of the acclaimed **Atlanta Symphony Orchestra.** The **Atlanta Ballet Company** (☎ 404/873–5811) performs at the Fox Theatre. In summer the **Atlanta Opera** (☎ 404/355–3311) usually presents three operas at the Fox Theatre.

Outdoor Activities and Sports

Golf

The only public course near downtown, **Bobby Jones Golf Course** (⊠ 384 Woodward Way, ☎ 404/355–1009) has some of the city's worst fairways and greens; still, the 18-hole, par-71 course is always crowded. The **Alfred Tup Holmes Club** (⊠ 2300 Wilson Dr., ☎ 404/753–6158) is known for numerous doglegs and blind shots. **Browns Mill Golf Course** (⊠ 480 Cleveland Ave., ☎ 404/366–3573) is considered the best operated by the City of Atlanta. **North Fulton Golf Course** (⊠ 216 W. Wieuca Rd., ☎ 404/255–0723) has one of the best layouts in the city. The **Sugar Creek Golf Course** (⊠ 2706 Bouldercrest Rd., ☎ 404/241–7671), in southeast Atlanta, has good Bermuda greens. Outside I–285, in the suburbs, the best public course is the **Southerness Golf Club** (⊠ 4871 Flat Bridge Rd., Stockbridge, ☎ 770/808–6000). Among Stone Mountain Park's (⊠ U.S. 78, ☎ 770/498–5715) courses, **Stonemont,** an 18-hole course, is the best. The formerly private **Lakeside Country Club** (⊠ 3600 Old Fairburn Rd., ☎ 404/344–3620), just outside I–285 in southwestern Atlanta, offers many challenges. **Eagle Watch Golf Club** (⊠ 3055 Eagle Watch Dr., Woodstock, ☎ 770/591–1000), designed by Arnold Palmer, appeals to golfers of all skill levels.

Tennis

Bitsy Grant Tennis Center (✉ 2125 Northside Dr., ☎ 404/351–2774) has 13 clay courts and 10 hard courts. This center in Chastain Park is the area's best public facility.

Piedmont Park (✉ Piedmont Ave. between 10th St. and the Prado, ☎ 404/872–1507) has 12 hard courts with lights. Access the tennis center from Park Drive off Monroe Drive; even though the sign reads DO NOT ENTER, the security guard will show you the parking lot.

Spectator Sports

Tickets for the teams listed below are available through **TicketMaster** (☎ 404/249–7630 or 800/326–4000).

Baseball: Atlanta Braves (✉ Atlanta-Turner Field, I–75/85 Exit 91, Fulton St.; I–20 westbound Exit 24, Capitol Ave.; or eastbound Exit 22, Windsor St./Spring St.; ☎ 404/522–7630).

Basketball: Atlanta Hawks (✉ Omni, 1 CNN Center, Suite 405, ☎ 404/827–3865).

Football: Atlanta Falcons (✉ 1 Georgia Dome Dr., ☎ 404/223–9200).

Hockey: Atlanta Knights (✉ Omni, 1 CNN Center, Suite 405, ☎ 404/525–8900).

Shopping

Antiques Stores

Shops selling antique pine pieces, collectibles, and unique crafts line **Bennett Street** in Buckhead. European furnishings and fine art are offered in more than 25 shops in Buckhead's **2300 Peachtree Road** complex. **Miami Circle,** a street on the northern edge of Buckhead off Piedmont Road, is another mecca for lovers of antiques, with such stores as the **Gables Antiques** (✉ 711 Miami Circle, ☎ 404/231–0734) and **Williams Antiques** (✉ 631 Miami Circle, ☎ 404/264–1142). **Chamblee Antique Row** (✉ 3519 Broad St., Chamblee, ☎ 770/455–0751) has antiques stores and malls. Chamblee, northeast of the city, is a flea market and antiques hunter's delight. There are also stores and flea markets along Peachtree Industrial Boulevard.

Shopping Districts

Atlanta's shopping centers are generally open Monday–Saturday 10–6 and Sunday noon–5; many stay open until 9 or 9:30 several weeknights and most weekends. The primary downtown shopping areas are **Underground Atlanta,** where specialty boutiques, chain stores, and push-carts mix with restaurants and nightclubs; and the stretch of Peachtree between **Macy's** and **Peachtree Center Mall.** North of downtown in Buckhead, **Lenox Square** (✉ 3393 Peachtree St.) and **Phipps Plaza** (✉ 3500 Peachtree Rd.) attract shoppers from throughout the Southeast. Lenox's new second level has expanded its size to more than 250 stores, while Phipps's now has more than 100 stores. **Perimeter Mall** (✉ 400 Ashford-Dunwoody Rd., Dunwoody) serves the Dunwoody area, and **Cumberland Mall** (✉ I–285 at Cobb Pkwy.) and **Galleria** (✉ 1 Galleria Pkwy.) are the most convenient to I–75/I–285.

SAVANNAH

Four hours southeast of Atlanta, and a world away from the bustling, modern metropolis, lies Savannah, wrapped in a mantle of Old World grace. Established in 1733, the city preserves its heritage in a 2½-square-mi historic district, the nation's largest urban landmark. Here 1,000 structures have been restored, and families still live in the 19th-century mansions and town houses. Known as the City of Festivals, Savannah rarely lets a weekend pass without some sort of celebration, from the St. Patrick's Day bash in March to the Riverfront Seafood Festival in April, from the spring azalea and dogwood festivals to the house tours and concerts at Christmas.

Visitor Information

Convention and Visitors Bureau (⊠ 222 W. Oglethorpe Ave., 31401, ☎ 912/944–0456 or 800/444–2427). **Visitors Center** (⊠ 301 Martin Luther King Jr. Blvd., 31499, ☎ 912/944–0455).

Arriving and Departing

By Bus
Greyhound Lines (⊠ 610 W. Oglethorpe Ave., ☎ 800/231–2222).

By Car
I–95, running north–south along the coast, and I–16, leading east from Macon, intersect west of Savannah; I–16 dead-ends in downtown. The Coastal Highway (U.S. 17) runs north–south through town, and U.S. 80 runs east–west.

By Plane
Savannah International Airport, served by major airlines, is 18 mi west of town on I–16. There is no bus service into town, but **McCall's Limousine Service** (☎ 912/966–5364 or 800/673–9365) runs a van between the airport and the city for $15 per person one-way.

By Train
The **Amtrak** station (⊠ 2611 Seaboard Coastline Dr., ☎ 912/234–2611 or 800/872–7245) is 4 mi southwest of downtown.

Getting Around Savannah

Savannah's historic district is best seen on foot so you can better observe the intricate architectural details. It's laid out in a grid pattern, and a number of strategically placed benches allow for frequent rests. If you bring a car, park it in one of the numerous metered and off-street pay lots here.

Exploring Savannah

A good way to start a tour is by picking up information at the **Visitors Center** (☞ Visitor Information, *above*) in the old Central Georgia railway station. For entertainment of every sort, visit the restored **City Market** (⊠ W. St. Julian St. between Ellis and Franklin Squares), a four-block area of shops, art galleries, restaurants, and blues clubs.

Near the riverfront narrow cobblestone streets wind from Bay Street down to Factors Walk and below it, to River Street and the revitalized **River Front** district. A multimillion-dollar face-lift in 1977 transformed this once-musty warehouse district into a nine-block marketplace with boutiques, restaurants, and taverns. The **Ships of the Sea Museum** (⊠ 41 Martin Luther King Jr. Blvd., ☎ 912/232–1511) displays memorabilia ranging from models of the earliest ships and nuclear submarines to nautical folk art.

★ The **Isaiah Davenport House** (⊠ 324 E. State St., ☎ 912/236–8097), one of the city's finest examples of Federal architecture, is furnished with Chippendale, Hepplewhite, and Sheraton antiques. Within the graceful **Telfair Mansion and Art Museum** (⊠ 121 Barnard St., ☎ 912/232–1177), designed by William Jay, is the South's oldest public art museum,

Savannah and the Golden Isles

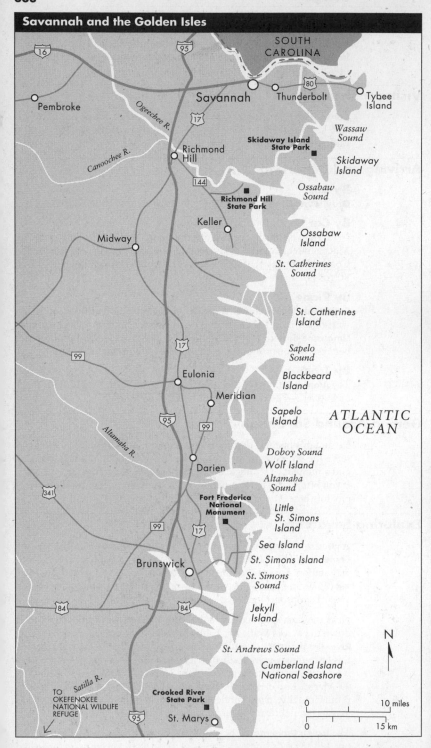

SOUTH CAROLINA

Pembroke

16

95

80

Savannah

Thunderbolt

Tybee Island

Ogeechee R.

17

Wassaw Sound

Skidaway Island State Park

Canoochee R.

Richmond Hill

Skidaway Island

144

Richmond Hill State Park

Ossabaw Sound

Keller

Ossabaw Island

Midway

St. Catherines Sound

17

St. Catherines Island

99

Sapelo Sound

Eulonia

Blackbeard Island

Meridian

95

99

Sapelo Island

ATLANTIC OCEAN

Altamaha R.

Doboy Sound

Wolf Island

Darien

Altamaha Sound

341

Fort Frederica National Monument

Little St. Simons Island

99

17

Sea Island

St. Simons Island

Brunswick

St. Simons Sound

84

84

Jekyll Island

St. Andrews Sound

Cumberland Island National Seashore

N

Satilla R.

TO OKEFENOKEE NATIONAL WILDLIFE REFUGE

Crooked River State Park

95

St. Marys

0   10 miles

0   15 km

displaying American, French, and German Impressionist paintings from the 18th and 19th centuries along with classical sculptures. The **Juliette Gordon Low Birthplace/Girl Scout National Center** (✉ 142 Bull St., ☏ 912/233–4501), in a Regency town house that was the city's first National Historic Landmark, displays memorabilia and family furnishings of the founder of the Girl Scouts of America.

At the corner of Oglethorpe Avenue and McDonough Street, **Colonial Park Cemetery** is the burial ground for some of the city's earliest and most notable residents, such as Button Gwinnett, a signatory of the Declaration of Independence. **Cathedral of St. John the Baptist** (✉ 222 E. Harris St., ☏ 912/233–4709), a late-19th-century structure, contains Austrian stained-glass windows, an Italian marble altar, and German-made stations of the cross. Tours are by appointment only.

★ The **Andrew Low House** (✉ 329 Abercorn St., ☏ 912/233–6854), built in 1848, was the childhood home of Juliette Gordon Low's husband, William. Some of the city's most impressive ironwork decorates the exterior; inside is a fine collection of 19th-century antiques. The **Green-Meldrim House** (✉ 14 W. Macon St., ☏ 912/233–3845) was built in 1852 for cotton merchant Charles Green. Now a parish house for St. John's Episcopal Church, it is furnished with 16th- through 18th-century antiques; one piece is original to the house.

Midnight in the Garden of Good and Evil

In his 1994 bestseller, *Midnight in the Garden of Good and Evil,* John Berendt focuses on the action surrounding the mysterious death of one Savannahian and the ensuing trials. Read the book before you visit the city. *Note: Unless otherwise indicated, the sites mentioned in the book are not open to the public.*

Songwriter Johnny Mercer's great-grandfather began building **Mercer House** (✉ 429 Bull St., on Monterey Sq.) in 1860. The redbrick Italianate mansion became the home of Jim Williams, the book's main character. Here his sometime house partner Danny Hansford was shot and died, and Williams himself died in the house in 1990. Today, Williams's sister lives here quietly. Jim Williams lived and worked in **Armstrong House** (✉ 447 Bull St.) before purchasing the Mercer House. **Lee Adler's home** (✉ 425 Bull St.), residence of one of Williams's biggest adversaries, is half of the double town house facing West Wayne Street.

At **the first of Joe Odom's homes** (✉ 16 E. Jones St.), Odom, a combination tax lawyer, real estate broker, and piano player, hosted a steady stream of visitors. Author Berendt loaded up on a greasy-spoon-style breakfast at **Clary's Café** (✉ 404 Abercorn St., ☏ 912/233–0402). **Hamilton-Turner House** (✉ 330 Abercorn St., ☏ 912/233–4800), a Second Empire–style mansion built in 1873, was acquired by Mandy Nichols, Joe Odom's fiancée. The sturdily elegant towering hulk is now a house museum.

The three Williams murder trials took place at **Chatham County Courthouse** (✉ 133 Montgomery St.) over the course of about eight years.

Club One (✉ 1 Jefferson St. ☏ 912/232–0200), the gay club where the Lady Chablis still bumps and grinds down the catwalk, is a must stop. Call to find out when Chablis sings. Emma Kelly sings at **Hard Hearted Hannah's East** (☞ Nightlife, *below*). She moved here after her club went bankrupt under Joe Odom's direction.

Bonaventure Cemetery (✉ 330 Bonaventure Rd., ☏ 912/651–6843), east of downtown, is the final resting place for both Jim Williams and Danny Hansford. The haunting female tombstone figure from the book's cover has been removed to protect surrounding graves.

Outside Savannah

From Savannah a 30-minute drive east on Victory Drive (U.S. 80/ Tybee Rd.) leads across a bridge to **Tybee Island.** About 5 mi long and 2 mi wide, Tybee has expansive white-sand beaches for shelling, crabbing, and swimming, as well as covered picnic facilities, a marina, and a wide variety of seafood restaurants, motels, and shops. The **Tybee Museum** (☎ 912/786–4077), which faces the **Tybee Lighthouse,** the state's oldest and tallest, traces the island's history from early Native American days. The museum is free.

Parks and Gardens

★ Integral to Savannah's design is its park system: 24 **town squares**— large and small and each with a historic monument or a graceful fountain—dot the historic district. The earliest square is Johnson Square, near City Market; food carts are typically parked along its edges. On West Macon Street is **Forsyth Park,** site of frequent outdoor concerts; at the center of its shady 20 acres, which include a jogging path and the Fragrant Garden for the Blind, is a graceful white fountain.

Dining

In Savannah your can choose from an abundance of restaurants serving regional seafood dishes. Barbecue (done southern-style—smoked meat with sauce applied after it's cooked) is also popular. If you want something fancier, the city has a number of fine Continental restaurants. For price ranges *see* Chart 1 (A) *in* On the Road with Fodor's.

$$$$ ✕ **Elizabeth on 37th.** This restaurant has earned a national reputation
★ for the fine seafood and delicate sauces of owner-chef Elizabeth Terry, the 1995 winner of the James Beard Award for Best Chef in the Southeast. The cuisine is complemented by the renovated mansion's authentic Savannah decor. ⊠ *105 E. 37th St.,* ☎ *912/236–5547. AE, D, DC, MC, V. Closed Sun. No lunch.*

$$$ ✕ **Bistro Savannah.** This establishment, housed in a circa 1878 build-
★ ing, specializes in fresh regional fare that uses both farmed and wild ingredients. Local shrimp and Cajun tasso ham on grits, pecan chicken, and shrimp and crab fritters are among the highlights. ⊠ *309 W. Congress St.,* ☎ *912/233–6266. AE, MC, V. No lunch.*

$ ✕ **Johnny Harris.** What started as a small roadside stand in 1924 is now one of the city's culinary mainstays. The menu includes steaks, fried chicken, seafood, and barbecued meats spiced with the restaurant's famous sauce. There's live piano or guitar music on Friday night and dancing on Saturday night. ⊠ *1651 E. Victory Dr.,* ☎ *912/354–7810. AE, DC, MC, V. Closed Sun.*

$ ✕ **Nita's Place.** Juanita Dixon, queen of her tiny, supremely plain
★ restaurant, welcomes all with her cheerful voice. Hot tables hold the reasons you'll come back: splendid gumbo, hoecakes, sweet potato pie, and fried chicken. ⊠ *140 Abercorn St.,* ☎ *912/238–8233. Reservations not accepted. D, MC, V. Closed Sun. No dinner.*

$ ✕ **Mrs. Wilkes Dining Room.** Come to this unassuming basement
★ restaurant for homey cooking served family style. Patrons line up at breakfast and lunch for such quintessential southern dishes as biscuits, grits, collard greens, mashed potatoes, and fried chicken. ⊠ *107 W. Jones St.,* ☎ *912/232–5997. Reservations not accepted. No credit cards. Closed weekends. No dinner.*

Lodging

For price ranges *see* Chart 2 (B) *in* On the Road with Fodor's.

$$$$ 🏨 **Ballastone Inn & Townhouse.** At this handsome 1838 stucco inn, centrally located on the city's major thoroughfare, 18th- and 19th-century antiques decorate the double parlor. This decor continues in the guest rooms, each with its own color scheme and some with working fireplaces. ⊠ *14 E. Oglethorpe Ave., 31401,* ☎ *912/236–1484 or 800/ 822–4553,* ℻ *912/236–4626. 25 rooms. In-room VCRs, concierge. AE, MC, V.*

$$$$ 🏨 **Kehoe House.** Built by an Irish immigrant who made his fortune in the ironworks industry, this imposing Renaissance Revival mansion was restored in 1993 as a bed-and-breakfast inn. Elegance, sumptuous furnishings and finishes and a superb location on Columbia Square all make for a superior experience. ⊠ *123 Habersham St., 31401,* ☎ *912/ 232–1020 or 800/820–1020,* ℻ *912/231–1587. 15 rooms. In-room VCRs, concierge. AE, D, DC, MC, V.*

$$$–$$$$ 🏨 **DeSoto Hilton.** This popular convention hotel has comfortable guest rooms and an expansive lobby. Corner king rooms provide good views of the heart of the historic district. ⊠ *15 E. Liberty St., 31401,* ☎ *912/ 232–9000 or 800/426–8483,* ℻ *912/231–1633. 251 rooms. 2 restaurants, pool, concierge. AE, D, DC, MC, V.*

$$$ 🏨 **The Gastonian.** The city's most deluxe accommodations are found
★ at this 1868 inn two blocks from Forsyth Park. The two adjacent Regency Italianate mansions have been beautifully restored and maintained by live-in owners. Full breakfasts and tea are served in lushly appointed rooms filled with period antiques. Nine rooms have hot tubs, whirlpools, or Japanese soak tubs. ⊠ *220 E. Gaston St., 31401,* ☎ *912/232–2869 or 800/322–6603,* ℻ *912/234–0710. 13 rooms. Outdoor hot tub, concierge. AE, MC, V.*

$$$ 🏨 **Presidents' Quarters.** Two Victorian town houses, built in 1855 and
★ furnished in reproduction period-style furniture, are each named for an early American president. Guests are greeted with wine and fruit in their rooms. The third floor is no-smoking. ⊠ *225 E. President St., 31401,* ☎ *912/233–1600 or 800/233–1776,* ℻ *912/238–0849. 16 rooms. Outdoor hot tub, concierge. Afternoon tea. AE, D, DC, MC, V.*

Nightlife

Savannah's nightlife is a reflection of the city's laid-back, easygoing personality. Some clubs feature live reggae, hard rock, and other contemporary music, but most stay with traditional blues, jazz, and piano-bar vocalists. **Hard Hearted Hannah's East** (⊠ Pirate's House, 20 E. Broad St., ☎ 912/233–2225) features Emma Kelly, the famed Lady of 6,000 Songs, performing Tuesday through Saturday. For authentic blues and sometimes rock, check out **Crossroads** (⊠ 219 W. St. Julian St., ☎ 912/234–5438), which showcases local and national talent Monday through Saturday. Irish music fills the air Wednesday through Saturday at **Kevin Barry's Irish Pub** (⊠ 117 W. River St., ☎ 912/233–9626), a must-stop on St. Patrick's Day.

Shopping

Savannah's many specialty shops sell such merchandise as English antiques, antiquarian books, and Low Country handmade quilts. Stores in the historic district are housed in ground floors of mansions and town houses or in renovated warehouses along the waterfront. The **River Front** and **City Market** areas have a variety of shops. For discount shopping, find **Savannah Festival Factory Stores** (⊠ 11 Gateway Blvd. S, ☎ 912/ 925–3089), off I–95 at Exit 16.

THE GOLDEN ISLES

An hour south of Savannah lie the Golden Isles, a chain of barrier islands stretching along Georgia's coast to the Florida state line. The three most developed—Jekyll Island, Sea Island, and St. Simons Island—are the only ones accessible by car; they are connected to the mainland near Brunswick by a network of causeways. A ferry from St. Marys connects Cumberland Island National Seashore with the mainland, and a launch transports visitors from St. Simons to Little St. Simons, a private vacation retreat. Spring, when temperatures are mild, is the ideal time for a visit; the superb beaches attract large crowds in summer.

Visitor Information

Cumberland Island National Seashore (⊠ National Park Service, Box 806, St. Marys 31558, ☎ 912/882–4335). **Jekyll Island:** Welcome center (⊠ 901 Jekyll Island Causeway, 31527, ☎ 912/635–3636 or 800/841–6586, FAX 912/634–4004). **Little St. Simons Island** (⊠ Little St. Simons Island Retreat, 31522, ☎ 912/638–7472). **St. Simons Island:** Chamber of Commerce and Visitors Center (⊠ Neptune Park, 530B Beachview Dr., 31522, ☎ 912/638–9014). **Sea Island** (⊠ The Cloister resort, 31561, ☎ 912/638–3611 or 800/732–4752).

Arriving and Departing

By Bus

Greyhound Lines (☎ 800/231–2222) connects Brunswick with surrounding towns and cities, including Savannah and Jacksonville, Florida.

By Boat

To reach Cumberland Island, you must reserve passage on the **Cumberland Queen** ferry, which leaves from St. Marys for the 45-minute journey. For a schedule, reservations, and fare information, contact Cumberland Island National Seashore (☞ Visitor Information, *above*).

By Car

From Brunswick take the **Jekyll Island Causeway** ($2 per car) to Jekyll Island or the **F. J. Torras Causeway** (35¢) to St. Simons. From St. Simons you can reach Sea Island via the **Sea Island Causeway.** Only residents and park service personnel are allowed to drive cars on Cumberland Island.

By Plane

Glynco Jetport, on the mainland 6 mi outside Brunswick, is served by Delta affiliate Atlantic Southeast Airlines (☎ 800/282–3424). International airports are in Savannah, an hour's drive north, and in Jacksonville, Florida, an hour's drive south, but there are no scheduled international flights operating at either airport. Jekyll and St. Simons islands maintain small airstrips for private planes.

Exploring the Golden Isles

St. Simons Island

St. Simons, north of Jekyll and Cumberland islands, offers the contrasting beauties of white-sand beaches and salt marshes. As large as Manhattan and with more than 14,000 residents, it's the Golden Isles' most complete and commercial resort destination: Visitors here are well served with numerous hotels, beachfront cottages, and condominiums, as well as four golf-course developments.

At the island's south end, the **Village** is dotted with T-shirt and souvenir shops, boutiques, restaurants, and a public pier for fishing and crabbing. Overlooking the ocean is **Neptune Park,** with a playground, a miniature golf course, and picnic tables shaded by live oaks. Also in the park is the **St. Simons Lighthouse,** built in 1872; climb to the top for a view of the beachfront or visit the **Museum of Coastal History** (⊠ 101 12th St., ☎ 912/638–4666) in the former light keeper's cottage.

Fort Frederica National Monument, on the island's north end, contains the foundation ruins of a fort and buildings inhabited by English soldiers and civilians in the mid-18th century. Tours begin at the **National Park Service visitor center** (⊠ Off Frederica Rd., ☎ 912/638–3639). Visit the Gothic-style, cruciform **Christ Church** (⊠ Frederica Rd., ☎ 912/638–8683) and read a visual story of its history on three stained-glass windows. The church was rebuilt in 1886 after having been destroyed by Union troops during the Civil War.

Little St. Simons Island

Accessible by private boat, Little St. Simons is a Robinson Crusoe–style getaway just 6 mi long and less than 3 mi wide. Owned and operated by one family since the early 1900s, the island's only development is a rustic but comfortable guest compound (☞ Dining and Lodging, *below*). The island's forests and marshes are inhabited by deer, armadillos, horses, raccoons, alligators, otters, and more than 200 species of birds. There's a 7-mi stretch of beach for swimming and water sports; other activities include horseback riding, nature walks, fishing, and shrimping and crabbing expeditions.

Sea Island

Five-mile-long Sea Island's main attraction is the Cloister, a Spanish Mediterranean–style resort (☞ Dining and Lodging, *below*). This luxurious, low-key property has a beach club with a health spa, formal and casual restaurants, and many outdoor activities. Outside the resort, beautiful mansions line Sea Island Drive.

Jekyll Island

The golf courses and system of bike paths crisscrossing Jekyll can be enjoyed year-round. Jekyll Island was once the favored retreat of the Vanderbilts, Rockefellers, Morgans, and other American aristocrats. Many of these millionaires' mansions are part of the **Jekyll Island Historic District** (⊠ Exit 6 off I–95, ☎ 800/841–6586) and are open for tours. An 11-acre water park, **Summer Waves** (⊠ 210 S. Riverview Dr., ☎ 912/635–2074), ranks as a top summer attraction.

Cumberland Island National Seashore

★ The largest and most remote of the Golden Isles, **Cumberland Island** is a 16 mi × 3 mi sanctuary of marshes, dunes, beaches, forests, lakes, ponds, estuaries, and inlets. You can tour the unspoiled terrain and the ruins of Thomas Carnegie's **Dungeness** estate on your own or join history and nature walks led by park service rangers (☞ Visitor Information, *above*). Bear in mind that you must bring along whatever food, beverages, sunscreen, and insect repellent you may need; the island has no shops or markets.

Dining and Lodging

For price ranges *see* Charts 1 (B) and 2 (A) *in* On the Road with Fodor's.

Cumberland Island

$$$$ ✕☷ **Greyfield Inn.** Built by the Carnegie family, this turn-of-the-century house is the island's only lodging and stands by itself in the prim-

itive landscape; its wide, colonnaded porches beckon invitingly. The inn is furnished with its original Asian and English antiques; burnished hardwood floors are warmed by antique Persian rugs. Rates include all meals, which are delightful: hearty breakfasts, box lunches, and festive dinners. ⊠ *Box 900, Fernandina Beach, FL 32035,* ☎ *904/ 261–6408. 13 rooms. MC, V.*

Jekyll Island

$$$–$$$$ ✕⊡ **Jekyll Island Club Hotel.** This renovated 1886 hotel is a turreted Victorian, complete with wraparound veranda and croquet lawn. Guest rooms are spacious and decorated to reflect the hotel's 19th-century origins. The Grand Dining Room serves gourmet cuisine; meal-plan rates are available. ⊠ *371 Riverview Dr., 31527,* ☎ *912/635–2600 or 800/535–9547,* ℻ *912/635–2818. 134 rooms. 2 restaurants, pool, 9 tennis courts, bicycles. AE, D, DC, MC, V.*

Little St. Simons Island

$$$$ ✕⊡ **Little St. Simons Island Retreat.** Guests stay in spacious, airy rooms
★ with private baths in one of four buildings: a two-bedroom cottage; the 1917 Hunting Lodge, with two antiques-filled guest rooms; or one of two houses with four guest rooms each. The buildings all have screened porches and wraparound decks. Meals, which are included in the rate, are served family style in the main dining room and include platters heaped with fresh fish, home-baked breads, and pies. ⊠ *Box 21078, 31522,* ☎ *912/638–7472,* ℻ *912/634–1811. 15 rooms. Pool, horseback riding, fishing. MC, V.*

St. Simons Island

$ ✕ **Crab Trap.** Count on a crowd in high season at this spot popular for fresh seafood with side orders of hush puppies, coleslaw, corn on the cob, and batter-dipped fries. ⊠ *1209 Ocean Blvd.,* ☎ *912/638– 3552. Reservations not accepted. MC, V.*

$$–$$$ ⊡ **King and Prince Beach and Golf Resort.** This beachfront hotel-and-condominium complex has spacious guest rooms and two- and three-bedroom villas. ⊠ *201 Arnold Rd. (Box 20798), 31522,* ☎ *912/ 638–3631 or 800/342–0212,* ℻ *912/634–1720. 139 rooms, 45 villas. 2 restaurants, lounge, indoor and outdoor pools, indoor and outdoor hot tubs, golf course, 4 tennis courts. AE, D, DC, MC, V.*

$$–$$$ ⊡ **Days Inn St. Simons Island.** This chain motel offers sizable, clean rooms with microwaves and minirefrigerators. ⊠ *1701 Frederica Rd., 31522,* ☎ *912/634–0660,* ℻ *912/638–7115. 101 rooms. Pool, bicycles. Continental breakfast. AE, MC, V.*

Sea Island

★ ✕⊡ **The Cloister.** At this classic resort, contemporary ocean-side villas, condominiums, and rental homes have grown up around a 1920s Spanish Mediterranean–style hotel with large guest rooms. Formal dining, casual grill lunches, and seafood and breakfast buffets are included in rate. A spa offers a fully equipped fitness room, daily aerobics classes, facials, massages, and other beauty treatments. ⊠ *The Cloister, Sea Island 31561,* ☎ *912/638–3611 or 800/732–4752,* ℻ *912/ 638–5823. 262 rooms. 4 restaurants, 2 pools, spa, 54 holes of golf, 12 tennis courts, horseback riding, windsurfing, fishing, bicycles. Full breakfast. No credit cards.*

Campgrounds

Cumberland Island National Seashore (☞ *Visitor Information, above*) maintains two tent campgrounds, one with rest rooms and showers, the other with cold-water spigots only.

Outdoor Activities and Sports

Biking

The flat terrain along the islands' coastlines is ideal for biking. Sea Island, Jekyll Island, and St. Simons have paved bike paths. You can rent bikes from the **Cloister** (☎ 912/638–3611), on Sea Island, or **Barry's Beach Service** (✉ 1300 Ocean Blvd., ☎ 912/638–8053) and **Benjy's Bike Shop** (✉ 130 Retreat Pl., ☎ 912/638–6766), both on St. Simons.

Fishing

The Intracoastal Waterway and the Atlantic Ocean are teeming with trout, barracuda, snapper, amberjack, and other fish. On St. Simons, **Ducky II Charter Boat Service** (✉ 402 Kelsall Ave., ☎ 912/634–0312) organizes deep-sea and river fishing. **Martin Noble** (✉ Rte. 9, ☎ 912/634–1219) handles both offshore and inshore fishing for St. Simons. **St. Simons Transit Company** (✉ 106 Airport Rd., ☎ 912/638–5678) organizes river and deep-sea fishing expeditions. **Taylor Fish Camp** (✉ Lawrence Rd., ☎ 912/638–7690) offers guided fishing trips through the marshes.

Golf

St. Simons Island has four courses: **Hampton Club** (✉ 100 Tabbystone Dr., ☎ 912/634–0255), with 18 holes; **St. Simons Island Club** (✉ 100 Kings Way, ☎ 912/638–5131), with 18 holes; **Sea Island Golf Club** (✉ 100 Retreat Ave., ☎ 912/638–5110), with 36 holes; and **Sea Palms Golf and Tennis Resort** (✉ 5445 Frederica Rd., ☎ 912/638–3351), with 27 holes. Though it has several courses, Jekyll Island is known for two in particular: **Oceanside** (✉ Beachview Dr., ☎ 912/635–2170), with 9 holes, and **Jekyll Island Golf Courses** (✉ Captain Wylly Dr., ☎ 912/635–2368 or 912/635–3464), with three 18-hole courses—Indian Mound, Oleander, and Pine Lake.

Tennis

Jekyll Island Tennis Courts (✉ Captain Wylly Dr., ☎ 912/635–3154) offers 13 clay courts, of which seven are lighted. The center hosts USTA-sanctioned tournaments. **Sea Palms Golf and Tennis Resort** (✉ 5445 Frederica Rd., ☎ 912/638–3351) offers 12 Rubico courts, three of which are lighted.

Beaches

Wide expanses of clean, sandy beaches skirt all the islands. Choose where to spread your beach towel according to how you want to spend your afternoon. St. Simons' **East Beach** attracts large groups and families and offers sailboat rentals. The beaches rimming **Jekyll Island** are usually not too busy during the week but become crowded on weekends. On **Sea Island** you can rent sailboats, sea kayaks, and boogie boards. The dunes and beaches of **Cumberland Island National Seashore** offer peaceful isolation.

ELSEWHERE IN GEORGIA

Okefenokee National Wildlife Refuge

Arriving and Departing

The refuge is near the Georgia-Florida border, 40 minutes northwest of Jacksonville, Florida, and 40 minutes southwest of the Golden Isles. From Atlanta take I–75 south to U.S. 82 into Waycross. From the Golden Isles take U.S. 84W to U.S. 301S.

What to See and Do

★ **Okefenokee National Wildlife Refuge** (⊠ Folkston, ☎ 912/496–3331), covering about 730 square mi, is a vast peat bog once part of the ocean floor and now 100 ft above sea level. Its thick vegetation is inhabited by at least 54 reptile species (including alligators), 49 mammal species, and 234 types of birds.

The **Okefenokee Swamp Park** (⊠ 8 mi south of Waycross, ☎ 912/283–0583) offers guided tours to the refuge. Boardwalks lead to an observation tower; guided boat tours are offered, or you can rent a canoe ($9). There's an eastern entrance at the **Suwanee Canal Recreation Area** (⊠ Near Folkston, ☎ 912/496–7156); the 11-mi waterway was built more than a century ago. Wilderness canoeing and camping in the Okefenokee's interior are by reserved fee permit only. Permits are tough to get, especially in cool weather. Call refuge headquarters (☎ 912/496–3331) *exactly 60 days* in advance of the desired starting date. There's also a western entrance at **Stephen C. Foster State Park** (⊠ Rte. 1, Fargo, ☎ 912/637–5274), an 80-acre park with boat rides through a swamp, a half-mile nature trail, restored homesteads, and a large forest of cypress and black gum trees.

Dining and Lodging

$$ ✕☲ **Pond View Inn.** This comfortable two-story inn on a 300-acre farm overlooks a pond. David and Sara Rollison run the dining room, which is known for Rock Cornish hens, steak, local fish, cornbread, and homemade desserts. Guests may arrange for dinner any day of the week; the restaurant (reservations essential) is closed to the public on Sunday and Monday. This inn is only 12 mi from the Waycross entrance to Okefenokee and 35 mi from the Folkston entrance. ⊠ *4299 Grady St., Blackshear 31516,* ☎ *912/449–3697 or 800/585–8659. 4 rooms. Restaurant. AE, MC, V.*

Andersonville

Arriving and Departing

Take I–75 south from Macon to Route 49 and follow the signs that read THE ANDERSONVILLE TRAIL to Andersonville.

What to See and Do

The tiny town of Andersonville itself grew up around a railway stop. The depot is the **Andersonville Welcome Center** (⊠ 114 Church St., ☎ 912/924–2558). Antiques and memorabilia fill the restored storefront shops that form its center. The first weekend in October is the Andersonville Historic Fair, which fills the town with thousands of visitors. The Memorial Day Weekend fair is not quite as big as the fall event but still worth attending. The theme of both festivals is the Civil War. Both offer opportunities to buy collectibles.

★ **Andersonville National Historic Site** (⊠ Rte. 1., Box 800, Andersonville, 31711, ☎ 912/924–0343), which opened in 1864, was the Civil War's most notorious prisoner-of-war site: 13,000 Union prisoners died here. Today it is the site of a new prisoner-of-war museum, and it serves as a final resting place for U.S. veterans and their spouses. The site's living history event (called Andersonville Revisited) takes place the last weekend in February. People dressed as guards and prisoners reenact the Andersonville experience.

Dining and Lodging

$$$ ✕☲ **Windsor Hotel.** Americus, only 10 mi from Andersonville, has one of America's most intriguing historic hotels. A monument to Victorian architecture, this Romanesque structure dominates downtown and is the symbol of the city. The entrance lobby, rich in Moorish detail, is

breathtaking. In the fine dining room French chef Patrick Quillec blends French cuisine with local ingredients. ⊠ *125 W. Lamar St., Americus 31709,* ☎ FAX *912/924–1555. 54 rooms. Restaurant, bar. AE, MC, V. No dinner Sun.*

Callaway Gardens

Arriving and Departing

Callaway Gardens is on U.S. 27 in Pine Mountain, 70 mi southwest of Atlanta. From Atlanta drive south on I–85, I–185, and U.S. 27.

What to See and Do

★ **Callaway Gardens** is a 2,500-acre, year-round horticultural fantasyland and resort in the foothills of the Appalachian Mountains. More than 60 years ago the Callaway family discovered a rare, bright red azalea in the woods, which inspired them to begin buying worn-out cotton fields and transforming them into impressive gardens.

On the grounds are the **Cecil B. Day Butterfly Center,** the largest glass-enclosed tropical conservatory of living butterflies in North America, and the **John A. Sibley Horticultural Center,** one of the most advanced garden greenhouse complexes in the world. Walking trails and paved paths traverse the world's largest collection of hollies and more than 700 varieties of azaleas and wildflowers. ⊠ *Hwy. 27, Pine Mountain,* ☎ *706/663–2281 or 800/282–8181.*

Historic Sites Along I–75

Arriving and Departing

Take I–75 north to the Tennessee state line and look for the brown state historic markers that indicate a historic site.

What to See and Do

The Civil War halted construction of Godfrey Barnsley's 26-room Italianate house, **Barnsley Gardens** (⊠ Barnsley Gardens Rd. off Hall Station Rd., ☎ 770/773–7480); in 1988 new owners found the estate and its gardens in ruins and began restoring the gardens. The 30 acres of shrubbery, trees, ponds, fountains, and flowers were designed in the style popular during Barnsley's time; the house remains in ruins but is safe to tour. A restaurant and a gift shop specializing in herbs and plants are on the site. Take I–75 north to Exit 128 (Adairsville), turn west, and follow the excellent signs.

New Echota State Historic Site (⊠ Rte. 225, 1 mi east of I–75N [exit 131], near Calhoun, ☎ 706/629–8151) is the location of the 1825–1838 capital of the Cherokee Nation, whose constitution was patterned after that of the United States. Some buildings have been reconstructed. Native Americans frequently hold special events at the site.

The **Chief Vann House** (⊠ 82 Rte. 225, Chatsworth, ☎ 706/695–2598), a two-story brick edifice, was built around 1800 by Moravian artisans hired by Chief James Vann, a leader of the Cherokee Nation. Vann also used slave labor. To get there, take Exit 131 from I–75 to Route 52A going west.

The **Chickamauga and Chattanooga National Military Park** (⊠ U.S. 27 off I–75 [Exit 141], south of Chattanooga, TN, ☎ 706/866–9241), established in 1890, was the nation's first military park. It stands on the site of one of the Civil War's bloodiest battles, with casualties that totaled more than 30,000. Monuments, battlements, and weapons adorn the road that traverses the 8,000-acre park, with markers explaining the action. An excellent visitor center offers reproduction memorabilia, superb books, and a film on the battle.

Dining and Lodging

$–$$ ✕ **J.J.'s.** Locals enjoy the "day-old" ribs for their crispy tenderness, but the standout is the smoked catfish. Collard greens and fruit cobblers are good, too. The posted menu only recites the specials (stew, for example), so ask for details. ⊠ *1517 Dean St., Rome,* ☎ *706/234–7895. Reservations not accepted. No credit cards. Closed Sun.*

$$$ ⊡ **Claremont House.** A beautifully restored 1890s Victorian residence, the inn has huge rooms furnished in period antiques. Breakfast is sumptuous, with eggs Benedict, stuffed French toast, and similar fare. Claremont House is about 30 minutes from Barnsley Gardens, New Echota, and the Chief Vann House. ⊠ *906 E. 2nd Ave., Rome, 30161,* ☎ *706/291–0900 or 800/254–4797. 5 rooms. AE, MC, V.*

NORTH CAROLINA

Updated by
Susan Ladd

Capital	Raleigh
Population	7,323,000
Motto	To Be Rather Than to Seem
State Bird	Cardinal
State Flower	Dogwood
Postal Abbreviation	NC

Statewide Visitor Information

North Carolina Division of Travel and Tourism (✉ 430 N. Salisbury St., Raleigh 27603, ☎ 919/733–4171 or 800/847–4862). **Welcome centers:** I–77S near Charlotte, I–77N near Dobson, I–85S near Kings Mountain, I–85N near Norlina, I–95S near Rowland, I–95N near Roanoke Rapids, I–26 near Columbus, and I–40W near Waynesville.

Scenic Drives

The **Blue Ridge Parkway** (☞ Virginia), with more than 250 mi of mountain views, nature exhibits, historic sites, parks, and hiking trails, extends from the Virginia state line to the Great Smoky Mountains National Park entrance near Cherokee. **U.S. 441** from Cherokee to Gatlinburg, Tennessee, cuts through the middle of the national park for about 35 mi, climbing to a crest of 6,643 ft at Clingmans Dome, a short distance from Newfound Gap. Portions of **U.S. 64** travel through the Hickory Nut Gorge between Lake Lure and Chimney Rock and the Cullasaja Gorge between Lake Toxaway and Franklin, affording spectacular views of mountain peaks and cascading waterfalls. **Route 12**, which connects the Outer Banks, offers great views of the ocean and a landscape dotted with lighthouses and weathered beach cottages.

National and State Parks

The state tourism division's travel guide (☞ Statewide Visitor Information, *above*) includes a complete listing of state and national parks and recreation areas as well as state forests.

National Parks

Cape Hatteras National Seashore (✉ Rte. 1, Box 675, Manteo 27954, ☎ 919/473–2111), a natural habitat for hundreds of species of birds, wild animals, and aquatic life, stretches 75 mi from Nags Head to Ocracoke and encompasses 30,318 acres of marshland and sandy beaches. **Cape Lookout National Seashore** (✉ 131 Charles St., Harkers Island 28531, ☎ 919/728–2250) extends 55 mi from Portsmouth Island to Shackleford Banks and includes 28,400 acres of uninhabited land and marsh, accessible only by boat or ferry. Portsmouth, a deserted village that was inhabited from 1753 until 1971, is being restored, and wild ponies roam the Shackleford Banks. **Great Smoky Mountains National Park** (✉ 107 Park Headquarters Rd., Gatlinburg, TN 37738, ☎ 423/436–1200), with 8.5 million visitors a year, is the most visited national park in the country. Its 507,757 acres straddle the North Carolina–Tennessee border and offer camping, hiking, fishing, historic sites, and nature lore (☞ Tennessee). To enter the park from North Carolina, take U.S. 441 north from Cherokee.

State Parks

On the Intracoastal Waterway south of Wilmington, 1,773-acre **Carolina Beach State Park** (⊠ Box 475, Carolina Beach 28428, ☎ 910/458–7770, 910/458–8206 for marina) offers camping, fishing, swimming, boating, picnicking, and hiking. **Fort Macon** (⊠ Box 127, Atlantic Beach 28512, ☎ 919/726–3775) centers on the fort built in 1834 to guard Beaufort Inlet. **Hanging Rock State Park** (⊠ Box 278, Danbury 27016, ☎ 910/593–8480) offers rock climbing and rappelling, hiking, camping, picnicking, and swimming. **Jockey's Ridge State Park** (⊠ Box 592, Nags Head 27959, ☎ 919/441–7132) offers hang-gliding instruction and flights from a 140-ft sand dune, the tallest in the East. **Kerr Lake State Recreation Area** (⊠ 269 Glass House Rd., Henderson 27536, ☎ 919/438–7791) encompasses 106,860 acres and includes eight designated recreation sites around a huge man-made lake. **Merchant's Millpond** (⊠ Rte. 1, Box 141-A, Gatesville 27938, ☎ 919/357–1191) can be explored by canoe. **Mt. Mitchell** (⊠ Rte. 5, Box 700, Burnsville 28714, ☎ 704/675–4611) offers camping on the highest mountain in the East (6,684 ft).

THE PIEDMONT

The Piedmont is the heartland of North Carolina, a vast area of rolling hills that extends from the coastal plain, which is east of the Triangle area (Raleigh, Durham, and Chapel Hill), to the foothills of the Blue Ridge Mountains, which are west of Charlotte and the Triad area (Greensboro, Winston-Salem, and High Point). Scattered along I–40, I–77, and I–85, the major arteries of the region, are the state's largest towns, cities, and industries. Here also are large rivers and woodlands; historic villages dating to the mid-1700s; crafts, antiques, and outlet shops; world-renowned colleges and universities; and one of the largest concentrations of golf courses in the world.

Visitor Information

Charlotte: Charlotte Visitor Information Center (⊠ 330 S. Tryon St., 28202, ☎ 704/331–2700 or 800/231–4636). **Durham:** Convention & Visitors Bureau (⊠ 101 E. Morgan St., 27701, ☎ 919/687–0288 or 800/446–8604). **Raleigh:** Capital Area Visitor Center (⊠ 301 N. Blount St., 27611, ☎ 919/733–3456); Convention and Visitors Bureau (⊠ 225 Hillsborough St., Suite 400, 27602, ☎ 919/834–5900 or 800/849–8499). **Winston-Salem:** Convention & Visitors Bureau (⊠ 601 N. Cherry St., Suite 100, 27101, ☎ 910/725–2361 or 800/331–7018).

Arriving and Departing

By Bus

Greyhound Lines (☎ 800/231–2222) provides service to Charlotte, Raleigh, Durham, Chapel Hill, Greensboro, and Winston-Salem.

By Car

I–40, U.S. 64, and U.S. 74 run east–west through the Piedmont; I–77 runs north from Charlotte; I–85 runs from Charlotte northeast through Greensboro and the Raleigh area.

By Plane

Major carriers serve **Charlotte-Douglas International Airport** (⊠ Charlotte, ☎ 704/359–4013), **Raleigh-Durham International Airport** (⊠ Raleigh, ☎ 919/840–2123), and **Piedmont Triad International Airport** (⊠ Greensboro, ☎ 910/665–5666). Taxi and limousine services are available at all airports.

By Train
Amtrak (☎ 800/872–7245) provides service to stations in 16 Piedmont cities, including Charlotte, Greensboro, and Raleigh. The *Carolinian* connects the three cities daily.

Exploring the Piedmont

Begin exploring the Piedmont in **Charlotte,** the region's largest city. At **Discovery Place** (✉ 301 N. Tryon St., ☎ 704/372–6261 or 800/935–0553), an award-winning hands-on science museum, you can enjoy a touch tank, aquariums, an indoor rain forest, an Omnimax theater, a planetarium, and special exhibits.

The **Hezekiah Alexander Homesite,** built in 1774, is the city's oldest dwelling. Named for the settler who built it, the site includes a log kitchen; costumed docents give guided tours. ✉ *3500 Shamrock Dr.,* ☎ *704/568–1774. Closed Sun.–Mon.*

Though it has served as a home for art since 1936, the **Mint Museum of Art** was originally built in 1837 as a U.S. mint. In recent years it has hosted internationally acclaimed exhibits. ✉ *2730 Randolph Rd.,* ☎ *704/337–2000. Closed Mon.*

A three-hour drive north from Charlotte on I–85 will bring you to **Durham,** a city once known for its tobacco production, but better known today for Duke University. **Duke University Chapel** (✉ West Campus, ☎ 919/681–1704), an ornate Gothic-style cathedral, is open for tours and free organ concerts.

Raleigh, the state's capital and a 30-minute drive on I–40, is easily explored on foot. The Greek Revival–style **state capitol** (✉ Capitol Square, ☎ 919/733–4994), built in 1840, commands the highest point in Capitol Square. It contrasts visually with the more contemporary legislative building, one block north, where sessions are currently held. The new **North Carolina Museum of History** (✉ 5 E. Edenton St., ☎ 919/715–0200) combines artifacts, audiovisual programs, and interactive exhibits to bring the state's history to life; admission is free. The **Executive Mansion** (✉ 200 N. Blount St., ☎ 919/733–3456), a turn-of-the-century Queen Anne–style structure in brick with gingerbread trim, is the governor's home.

The **North Carolina Museum of Art** exhibits art ranging from ancient Egyptian to contemporary. The Museum Cafe is a favorite place for lunch or Friday-night entertainment. ✉ *2110 Blue Ridge Blvd.,* ☎ *919/839–6262. Free. Closed Mon.*

★ An hour and a half west of Raleigh on I–40 is **Winston-Salem. Old Salem,** a restored 18th-century village, re-creates the life of the Moravians, a Protestant sect that settled in the area in 1766. Also in the village is the **Museum of Early Southern Decorative Arts,** displaying period furnishings. ✉ *600 S. Main St.,* ☎ *910/721–7350.*

What to See and Do with Children

Enjoy thrilling rides at **Paramount's Carowinds** (✉ 15423 Carowinds Blvd., ☎ 704/588–2600 or 800/888–4386), a 91-acre theme amusement park straddling the North Carolina–South Carolina border near Charlotte; adult admission is $28.95. Thirty minutes south of Greensboro on U.S. 220, Asheboro's **North Carolina Zoological Park** (☎ 910/879–7000 or 800/488–0444) is home to more than 1,100 animals and 60,000 exotic and tropical plants. In Chapel Hill, 15 minutes south of Durham on U.S. 15/501, children can stargaze at the University of Carolina's **Morehead Planetarium** (☎ 919/962–1247). In Durham the **North Carolina Museum of Life and Science** (✉ 433 Murray Ave., ☎ 919/220–5429) exhibits an eclectic assortment of life-size dinosaur models, NASA artifacts, hands-on activities, and live animals. Children love the resident snakes and animal exhibits at Durham's **North Carolina Museum of Natural Sciences** (✉ 102 N. Salisbury St., ☎ 919/733–7450), which they can view for free.

Dining and Lodging

The Piedmont has a growing number of upscale restaurants and ethnic eateries, as well as restaurants that specialize in the more traditional barbecue, fresh seafood, fried chicken, and country ham. Lodging is available at economy motels, upscale convention hotels, bed-and-breakfasts, and resorts. Breakfast may be included in the room rate, and children often stay free in their parents' room. Many city hotels offer weekend packages with discounted rates and extra amenities. For price ranges *see* Charts 1 (B) and 2 (B) *in* On the Road with Fodor's.

Chapel Hill

$$$$ ✕🏨 **Fearrington House.** Set on an old farm, this elegant French-style
★ country inn is a member of Relais & Châteaux. Rooms are decorated with chintz and antique reproductions, and the cuisine is a deft blend of regional and French. ✉ *Fearrington Village Center, Pittsboro 27312,* ☎ *919/542–2121,* FAX *919/542–4202. 29 rooms. 2 restaurants, pool, bicycles, shops. AE, MC, V.*

Charlotte

$$$ ✕ **Bravo!** This hotel restaurant is known not only for its authentic Italian cuisine but also for its singing waitstaff. Sunday brunch is available. You might feel more comfortable in a jacket. ✉ *Adams Mark Hotel, 555 S. McDowell St.,* ☎ *704/372–5440. AE, D, MC, V.*

$–$$ ✕ **Pizzarrelli Trattoria.** Wood-burning brick ovens are the key to delicious pizzas at this popular Italian restaurant. The owner is a former opera star who often sings for his patrons. ✉ *9101 Pineville–Matthews Rd., Pineville,* ☎ *704/543–0647. AE, D, MC, V.*

$$$ ✕🏨 **The Dunhill.** Built in 1929, the hotel has reproduction 18th-century furnishings. Its restaurant, Monticello's, gets rave reviews for beautifully presented California cuisine. ✉ *237 N. Tryon St., 28202,* ☎ *704/332–4141 or 800/354–4141,* FAX *704/376–4117. 60 rooms. Restaurant, lounge. AE, D, DC, MC, V.*

$$$ ✕🏨 **Hyatt Charlotte at Southpark.** Rooms ring a four-story atrium lobby at this modern hotel, popular with business travelers. The restaurant serves northern Italian cuisine. ✉ *5501 Carnegie Blvd., 28209-3462,* ☎ *704/554–1234 or 800/233–1234,* FAX *704/554–8319. 262 rooms. Restaurant, lounge, pool, health club. AE, D, DC, MC, V.*

$$$ 🏨 **Morehead Inn.** Though it caters to corporate clients, this Dilworth inn, built in 1917 as a private residence and renovated in the '90s, has all the comforts of a luxurious home. ✉ *1122˚E. Morehead St., 28204,* ☎ *704/376–3357,* FAX *704/335–1110. 12 rooms. Meeting rooms. Continental breakfast. AE, DC, MC, V.*

Durham

$$$ ✕ **Magnolia Grill.** This award-winning bistro is consistently one of the
★ finest, most innovative places to dine in the state. On the daily menu you're likely to find grilled jumbo sea scallops on spicy black beans with blood-orange-and-onion marmalade or grilled hickory-smoked

pork tenderloin in a sun-dried cherry *jus* with fresh horseradish, roasted beets, and a gratin of sweet potatoes and caramelized onions. ⊠ *1002 9th St.,* ☎ *919/286–3609. MC, V. Closed Sun. No lunch.*

$$$$ ⊞ **Washington Duke Hotel & Golf Club.** This luxurious inn on the cam-
★ pus of Duke University overlooks a Robert Trent Jones golf course. Duke family memorabilia are displayed in the public rooms; the bar is called the Bull Durham. ⊠ *3001 Cameron Blvd., 27706,* ☎ *919/ 490–0999 or 800/443–3853,* FAX *919/688–0105. 171 rooms. Restaurant, lounge, pool, golf course, jogging. AE, DC, MC, V.*

Raleigh

$$$ ✕ **Angus Barn, Ltd.** Housed in a huge rustic barn, this Raleigh fixture
★ is known for its steaks, baby back ribs, prime rib, homemade desserts, and 35-page wine list. ⊠ *U.S. 70 W at Airport Rd.,* ☎ *919/781–2444. Reservations not accepted Sat. AE, DC, MC, V.*

$$ ✕ **Neo-China.** In more suburban North Raleigh, the focal points of the plush decor are a series of life-size bas-reliefs of the human form and the charcoal-and-cream color scheme. Seafood lovers will delight in the lobster tail, crab legs, scallops, and jumbo shrimp on a vegetable bed in a smoky white sauce. ⊠ *6602–1 Glenwood Ave.,* ☎ *919/783– 8383. AE, DC, MC, V.*

$$$ ⊞ **Oakwood Inn.** This 1871 B&B in the Oakwood Historic District
★ downtown is furnished with Victorian period pieces. ⊠ *411 N. Bloodworth St., 27604,* ☎ *919/832–9712 or 800/267–9712,* FAX *919/836– 9263. 6 rooms. AE, D, DC, MC, V.*

$$–$$$ ⊞ **Velvet Cloak Inn.** This elegant brick hotel with delicate wrought-iron decorations is a favorite spot for wedding receptions and political gatherings. Guest rooms have European-style decor. Afternoon tea is a tradition. ⊠ *1505 Hillsborough St., 27605,* ☎ *919/828–0333 or 800/334–4372, 800/662–8829 in NC,* FAX *919/828–2656. 176 rooms. Restaurant, lounge, indoor pool. AE, DC, MC, V.*

Winston-Salem

$$ ✕ **Old Salem Tavern Dining Room.** Moravian dishes, such as chicken pie and Wiener schnitzel, are served by waiters in Moravian costume. In summer you can dine outside on the patio or under the arbor. ⊠ *736 S. Main St.,* ☎ *910/748–8585. AE, D, MC, V.*

$$$ ⊞ **Henry F. Shaffner House.** This majestic Queen Anne, built around
★ 1907 with tiger oak paneling and the finest materials, offers luxurious accommodations and lots of personal attention in a wonderfully convenient setting near old Salem and the many downtown attractions. ⊠ *150 S. Marshall St., 27101,* ☎ *910/777–0052 or 800/952–2256,* FAX *910/777–1188. 8 rooms. AE, MC, V.*

Nightlife and the Arts

In Winston-Salem, the **North Carolina School for the Arts** (⊠ 200 Waughton St., ☎ 910/721–1945) stages events and performances. The **Eastern Music Festival** (⊠ 200 N. Davie St., ☎ 910/333–7450) brings six weeks of classical music concerts to Greensboro in summer. High Point's **North Carolina Shakespeare Festival** (⊠ 220 E. Commerce St., ☎ 910/841–6273) mounts several productions with nationally known actors from August through October and *A Christmas Carol* in December. **North Carolina Blumenthal Center for the Performing Arts** (⊠ 130 N. Tryon St., ☎ 704/333–4686), in Charlotte, hosts operas, concerts, plays, and other cultural events. The **North Carolina Symphony Orchestra** (⊠ 2 E. South St., ☎ 919/733–2750) performs in Raleigh's

Memorial Auditorium, also home to the **North Carolina Theatre** (☎ 919/831–6942).

Outdoor Activities and Sports

Golf

The Sandhills area, in the southern part of the Piedmont, has more than three dozen courses, including Pinehurst's famous Number 2. For details contact the **Pinehurst Area Convention and Visitors Bureau** (✉ Box 2270, Southern Pines 28388, ☎ 910/692–3330 or 800/346–5362).

Spectator Sports

Basketball: Charlotte Hornets (✉ Charlotte Coliseum, Tyvola Rd. off Billy Graham Pkwy., ☎ 704/357–0489) is the state's NBA team. The Piedmont is a college basketball fan's dream, with Atlantic Coast Conference rivals **Duke University** (☎ 919/681–2583) in Durham, **North Carolina State** (☎ 919/515–2106) in Raleigh, the **University of North Carolina** in Chapel Hill (☎ 919/962–2296), and **Wake Forest University** (☎ 910/759–5613) in Winston-Salem playing games November through March.

Football: Carolina Panthers (✉ Ericsson Stadium, 800–1 S. Mint St., Charlotte, ☎ 704/358–7800), one of the National Football League's youngest franchises, recently began playing in their new 72,520-seat stadium.

NASCAR Racing: The Coca-Cola 600 and UAW-GM 500 races draw huge crowds to the **Charlotte Motor Speedway** (☎ 704/455–3200), off I–85 near Concord.

Shopping

The Piedmont is a mecca for lovers of **antiques and crafts**; towns such as Waxhaw, Cameron, Pineville, and Matthews are devoted almost entirely to antiques. For directions and information call Charlotte's visitor center (☞ Visitor Information, *above*). One of the country's largest antiques centers is **Metrolina Expo** (✉ 7100 N. Statesville Rd., ☎ 704/596–4643), near Charlotte. **High Point,** 20 minutes southwest of Greensboro, is known as the furniture capital of the world.

In the Seagrove area, between Greensboro and Pinehurst, nearly 60 shops produce and sell handmade **pottery.** Burlington, between Greensboro and Durham, is a hub for **outlet stores.** Charlotte and Raleigh are major retail centers; the latter is home to one of the largest **farmers' markets** in the Southeast.

THE COAST

A chain of barrier islands flanks the bulk of the North Carolina coast. The Outer Banks stretch some 130 mi from the Virginia state line south to Cape Lookout; the southern coast, to the South Carolina line, includes the Cape Fear River region and Wilmington, the state's primary port. To these shores English settlers came more than 400 years ago to establish a colony on Roanoke Island, then mysteriously disappeared. Called the Graveyard of the Atlantic because of the hundreds of ships that met their demise here, the Outer Banks proved a safe hiding place for marauding pirates in the 1700s. For many years the region remained isolated, home only to a few fishermen and their families, but now, linked by bridges and ferries, the islands are a popular vacation spot. Nearby, the Albemarle region comprises charming towns full of early architecture. Hundreds of films have been shot in Wilmington, which has a restored historic district and waterfront. On the surrounding coast visitors can tour old plantation houses and azalea gardens, study sea life, and bask in the sun at nearby beaches.

Visitor Information

Cape Fear Coast: Convention and Visitors Bureau (⊠ 24 N. 3rd St., Wilmington 28401, ☎ 910/341–4030 or 800/222–4757). **Carteret County:** Tourism Development Bureau (⊠ 3409 Arendell St., Morehead City 28557, ☎ 919/726–8148 or 800/786–6962). **Craven County:** Convention and Visitors Bureau (⊠ Box 1413, New Bern 28563, ☎ 919/637–9400 or 800/437–5767). **Dare County:** Tourist Bureau (⊠ Box 399, Manteo 27954, ☎ 919/473–2138). **Historic Albemarle Tour, Inc.** (⊠ Box 1604, Washington 27859, ☎ 919/974–2950). **Ocracoke:** Visitor Center (⊠ Cape Hatteras National Seashore, NC12 Hwy., Ocracoke 27960-0340, ☎ 919/928–4531).

Arriving and Departing

By Boat

There are more than 100 marinas along the Intracoastal Waterway, including **Manteo Waterfront Docks** (☎ 919/473–3320) and the **Park Service Docks** (☎ 919/928–5111) in Ocracoke. Beaufort is a popular stopover. The Wilmington area has public marinas at Carolina Beach State Park (☎ 910/458–8206) and Wrightsville Beach (☎ 910/256–6666). The **North Carolina Coastal Boating Guide,** compiled by the North Carolina Department of Transportation (☎ 919/733–2520), has a comprehensive list of marinas and other facilities for boaters.

By Bus

Greyhound Lines (☎ 800/231–2222) serves Elizabeth City, on the Albemarle Sound; Wilmington; and Norfolk, Virginia.

By Car

Roads link the mainland to the Outer Banks at their northern end: U.S. 158 enters from the north, near Kill Devil Hills, and U.S. 64/264 enters Manteo on Roanoke Island, from the west. These connect with Route 12, the main route in the region, running south from Corolla to Ocracoke Island. Toll ferries (☎ 800/293–3779) connect Ocracoke with Cedar Island, to the south, and with Swan Quarter on the mainland; a free ferry travels between Hatteras Island and Ocracoke Island. From I–95 near Raleigh, U.S. 70 leads to Cedar Island via New Bern and Morehead City, and I–40 serves Wilmington.

By Plane

The closest airports are **Raleigh-Durham International** (☞ Arriving and Departing *in* the Piedmont, *above*); **New Hanover International Airport,** in Wilmington (☎ 910/341–4125); and Virginia's **Norfolk International** (☎ 757/857–3200). Southeast Airlines (☎ 919/473–3222) provides charter service from **Dare County Regional Airport** (⊠ Airport Rd., ☎ 919/473–2600), at the north end of Roanoke Island.

Exploring the Coast

Start your tour of the Outer Banks at Nags Head and Kill Devil Hills, where the Cape Hatteras National Seashore begins (☞ National and State Parks, *above*). You can drive from Nags Head to Ocracoke in a day, but allow plenty of time in summer, when ferries are crowded. During major storms and hurricanes, follow the evacuation signs to safety.

Kill Devil Hills is the site of the first flight in history. The **Wright Brothers National Memorial** (⊠ U.S. 158 Bypass, ☎ 919/441–7430) is a

North Carolina's Outer Banks

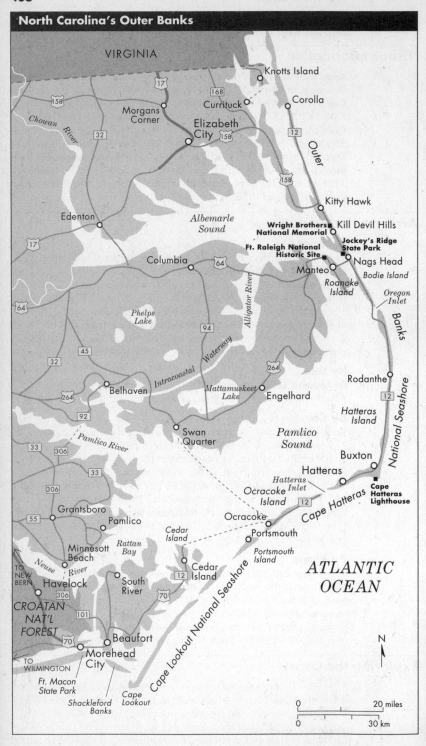

tribute to Wilbur and Orville's feat of December 17, 1903. A replica of the *Flyer* is housed in the visitor center.

Roanoke Island, accessible from U.S. 158 Bypass via U.S. 64/264, is the site of several attractions. From mid-June to September the outdoor drama *Lost Colony* (☎ 919/473–3414 or 800/488–5012) reenacts the story of the first colonists, who settled on Roanoke Island in 1587 and then disappeared. The **Elizabethan Gardens** (✉ U.S. 64, Manteo, ☎ 919/473–3234) are a lush re-creation of a 16th-century English garden. They're closed on weekends in December and January. **Fort Raleigh National Historic Site** (☎ 919/473–5772) is a restoration of the original 1585 earthworks. A re-creation of a 16th century vessel is moored in Shallow Bag Bay at the *Elizabeth II* **State Historic Site** (☎ 919/473–1144), except when on educational voyages in the off-season (call ahead).

Take a day trip to visit **Elizabeth City,** on the Albemarle Sound. The **Museum of the Albemarle** (✉ 1116 U.S. 17S, ☎ 919/335–1453), closed Monday, has displays on local history. **Edenton,** the state capital from 1722 to 1743, lies west of Elizabeth City. In 1774 to protest English taxation, 51 local women staged the Edenton Tea Party. Be sure to see the Jacobean-style **Cupola House and Gardens,** on West Water and Broad Streets, which was built circa 1725. The **Chowan County Courthouse** has been in continuous use since its construction in 1767. Three colonial governors are buried in the graveyard behind **St. Paul's Church.**

Traveling south from Nags Head on Route 12, you'll cross the Herbert C. Bonner Bridge, which arches for 3 mi over Oregon Inlet to **Hatteras Island,** where the blue marlin reigns. The **Cape Hatteras Lighthouse** (☎ 919/995–4474), at 208 ft, is the tallest lighthouse in America and can be climbed in summer. The visitor center has a small museum. Board the free ferry at the south end of Hatteras Island for the half-hour trip to **Ocracoke Island,** cut off from the world for so long that its natives speak with a quasi-Elizabethan accent. The 1823 **Ocracoke Lighthouse** is the state's oldest operating lighthouse.

Beaufort, settled in 1710, is a seaport town with several historic houses and sites. The **Beaufort Historic Site,** in the center of town, comprises several restored buildings dating from 1767 to 1859, including the Carteret County Courthouse and the Apothecary Shop and Doctor's Office. Don't miss the Old Burying Grounds (1731). Here Otway Burns, a privateer in the War of 1812, is buried under his ship's cannon; a nine-year-old girl who died at sea is buried in a rum keg; and an English soldier saluting the king is buried upright in his grave. Tours on an English-style double-decker bus depart from here. ✉ *138 Turner St.,* ☎ *919/728–5225. Closed Sun.*

Beaufort's **North Carolina Maritime Museum** (✉ 315 Front St., ☎ 919/728–7317) documents the state's seafaring and coastal history. The museum includes the **Watercrafts Center,** which offers boatbuilding classes. Its education staff also provides year-round programs, including trips to the marsh and barrier islands.

Morehead City is a fishing and boating center across Bogue Sound from Bogue Banks. **Atlantic Beach** and **Emerald Isle** are popular family beaches.

New Bern, northwest of Morehead City, was the state capital during English rule until immediately after the Revolution. The reconstructed **Tryon Palace at New Bern** (✉ 610 Pollock St., ☎ 919/638–1560), an elegant Georgian building, was the Colonial capitol and the home of

Royal Governor William Tryon in the 1770s. An audiovisual orientation is given, costumed interpreters conduct tours of the house and gardens, and (in summer) actors deliver monologues describing a day in the life of the governor. The stately **John Wright Stanly House** (circa 1783), the **Dixon-Stevenson House** (circa 1826), and **New Bern Academy** (circa 1809) are within the Tryon Palace complex.

U.S. 17S leads to **Wilmington,** which was the state's largest town until 1910, when the demands of the railroad industry outgrew the facilities of the harbor. The **USS *North Carolina* Battleship Memorial** (☎ 910/251–5797), one of Wilmington's major attractions, is permanently docked off U.S. 421. You can take the river taxi from Riverfront Park (in summer only) for a self-guided tour.

Wilmington's restored waterfront and historic district, with its 18th-century churches, can be explored with the aid of a self-guided walking-tour map from the Cape Fear Coast Convention and Visitors Bureau (☞ Visitor Information, *above*). The 1770 **Burgwin-Wright House,** on Market Street, is built on the foundation of a jail. Downtown's Italianate **Zebulon Latimer House** was built in 1852 and can be seen from Third Street.

The **St. John's Museum of Art** houses a permanent collection of prints by Mary Cassatt (⌧ 114 Orange St., ☎ 910/763–0281); it's closed on Monday. Open from Tuesday through Sunday, the **Cape Fear Museum** (⌧ 814 Market St., ☎ 910/341–7413) traces the natural and cultural history of Cape Fear River country.

U.S. 421 leads south from Wilmington to the **Fort Fisher State Historic Site** (⌧ Kure Beach, ☎ 910/458–5538), the largest Confederate earthwork fortification of the Civil War. War relics and artifacts from sunken Confederate blockade runners are on display. The site is closed Monday from November through March. Not far from Kure Beach is one of the **North Carolina Aquariums** (⌧ Fort Fisher, ☎ 910/458–8257), with its freestanding 20,000-gallon shark tank.

On the west side of the Cape Fear River, south of Wilmington on Route 133, a passenger ferry links Southport and **Bald Head Island** (☎ 910/457–5003). On the island you can take a historic tour and see the 109-ft Old Baldy Lighthouse, dating from 1817; have a picnic or lunch at one of the restaurants; play golf; or go fishing and swimming.

What to See and Do with Children

Children may enjoy flying a kite from the tallest sand dune in the East (about 140 ft) in **Jockey's Ridge State Park** (☞ National and State Parks, *above*). Three **North Carolina Aquariums** are open free of charge: on Roanoke Island (☎ 919/473–3493); at Pine Knoll Shores on Bogue Banks (☎ 919/247–4004); and at Fort Fisher (☎ 910/458–8257).

Dining and Lodging

Fresh seafood is in abundant supply, prepared almost any way. Hearty southern cooking, with chicken, ham, and fresh vegetables, is also widespread. Cottages, condominiums, motels, resorts, B&Bs, and country inns abound all along the coast. Most places offer lower rates from September through May. Condos and beach cottages may be rented through local realtors by the week or month. For price ranges *see* Charts 1 (B) and 2 (B) *in* On the Road with Fodor's.

Beaufort

$$ ✕ **Beaufort House Restaurant.** Seafood Alfredo, gumbo, prime rib, and
★ homemade desserts are tops on the menu at this contemporary dock-

side eatery. ⊠ *Boardwalk,* ☎ *919/728–7541. D, MC, V. Closed Jan.–Feb.*

$$$ ★ ▦ **Langdon House.** You'll sleep surrounded by antiques at this B&B built in 1733. Sumptuous southern breakfasts are created by host Jimm Prest. ⊠ *135 Craven St., 28516,* ☎ *919/728–5499. 4 rooms. No credit cards.*

Duck

$$$$ ★ ✕▦ **Sanderling Inn Resort & Conference Center.** For special pampering, come to this remote beachside resort. Though the inn was built in 1985 and offers modern amenities, its stately, mellow look makes it appear older. The restaurant, housed in an old lifesaving station, offers such delicacies as crab cakes, roast Carolina duckling with black-cherry sauce, and fricassee of shrimp. ⊠ *1461 Duck Rd., 27949,* ☎ *919/261–4111 or 800/701–4111,* ℻ *919/261–1638. 88 rooms, 29 efficiencies. Restaurant, lounge, pool, tennis courts, health club. AE, D, MC, V.*

$$$ ▦ **Advice 5¢.** The name may be quirky, but this B&B in the heart of Duck, just a short walk from downtown shops and restaurants, is often booked for its quiet, casual, contemporary atmosphere. Beds in each room are dressed with crisp, colorful linens. All rooms have ceiling fans, shuttered windows, and their own baths stocked with thick cotton towels. ⊠ *111 Scarborough La., 27949,* ☎ *919/255–1050 or 800/238–4235. 5 rooms. MC, V.*

Kill Devil Hills

$$ ✕ **Etheridge Seafood Restaurant.** The fish come straight from the boat to the kitchen at this family-owned restaurant decorated with fishing gear. ⊠ *U.S. 158 Bypass, Milepost 9.5,* ☎ *919/441–2645. MC, V. Closed Nov.–Feb.*

$$–$$$ ▦ **Ramada Inn.** Guest rooms in this convention-style hotel have private balconies with ocean views and are equipped with refrigerators and microwave ovens. The hotel restaurant, Peppercorns, which overlooks the ocean, serves breakfast and dinner; lunch is available on the sundeck next to the pool. ⊠ *1701 South Virginia Dare Tr., off U.S. 158, Milepost 9.5 (Box 2716), 27948,* ☎ *919/441–2151 or 800/635–1824,* ℻ *919/441–1830. 172 rooms. Restaurant, pool, hot tub, meeting rooms. AE, D, DC, MC, V.*

Manteo

$$ ✕ **Weeping Radish Brewery and Restaurant.** This Bavarian-style restaurant and microbrewery is known for its German cuisine and annual Octoberfest weekend held after Labor Day, featuring German and blues bands. Tours of the brewery are given on request. ⊠ *U.S. 64,* ☎ *919/473–1157. D, MC, V.*

$$$ ✕▦ **Tranquil House Inn.** This waterfront B&B is only a few steps from shops and restaurants, and bikes are provided for adventures beyond. The restaurant, named 1587, serves gourmet dinners; it's closed from December through February. ⊠ *Queen Elizabeth Ave. (Box 2045), 27954,* ☎ *919/473–1404 or 800/458–7069,* ℻ *919/473–1526. 25 rooms. Restaurant. Continental breakfast, evening wine and cheese. AE, D, MC, V.*

Morehead City

$$ ★ ✕ **Sanitary Fish Market and Restaurant.** In business for more than a half century, this basic, pine-paneled institution built out over the edge of Bogue Sound continues to please with heaping platters of fresh

seafood—served fried, steamed, or broiled, with hush puppies, coleslaw, and french fries. ⊠ *501 Evans St.,* ☎ *919/247–3111. D, MC, V. Closed Dec.–Jan.*

Nags Head

$$ ✕ **Lance's Seafood Bar & Market.** You can contemplate the fishing and hunting memorabilia while you dine on steamed or raw seafood. Shells are disposed of through the hole in the table. ⊠ *U.S. 158 Bypass, Milepost 14,* ☎ *919/441–7501. AE, MC, V.*

$$–$$$ 🏨 **First Colony Inn.** This historic B&B with ocean views was built in
★ 1932. All rooms are smoke free, and some have four-poster or canopy beds and armoires. The breakfast is known for its hot ham-and-cheese braid and French toast. ⊠ *6720 S. Virginia Dare Trail, 27959,* ☎ *919/441–2343 or 800/368–9390,* FAX *919/441–9234. 26 rooms. Pool. AE, D, MC, V.*

New Bern

$$–$$$ ✕ **Harvey Mansion Restaurant and Lounge.** Swiss owner-chef Beat Zut-
★ tel excels in regional and international award-winning dishes. Original art decorates the walls of her restaurant, in a 1797 house near the confluence of the Trent and Neuse rivers. ⊠ *221 Tryon Palace Dr.,* ☎ *919/638–3205. AE, D, DC, MC, V.*

$$$ 🏨 **Harmony House Inn.** At this historic B&B convenient to all the at-
★ tractions, you can sleep in spacious rooms where Yankee soldiers stayed during the Civil War. Today they are furnished with a mixture of antiques and reproductions. The inn serves a hot breakfast buffet and complimentary white and dessert wines in the evening. ⊠ *215 Pollock St., 28560,* ☎ *919/636–3810 or 800/636–3113,* FAX *919/636–3810. 10 rooms. AE, D, MC, V.*

Ocracoke

$–$$ ✕🏨 **Island Inn and Dining Room.** This well-worn turn-of-the-century inn has third-floor rooms with cathedral ceilings and lovely views. The dining room is known for oyster omelets, crab cakes, and hush puppies. ⊠ *Rte. 12 (Box 9), 27960,* ☎ *919/928–4351,* FAX *919/928–4352. 35 rooms. Pool. D, MC, V.*

Southport

$$$–$$$$ ✕🏨 **Bald Head Island.** Reached by ferry from Southport, this self-contained, carless community complete with grocery store, restaurants, and golf course has bleached-wood villas and shingled cottages that have won architectural design awards. Guests travel the island on foot, bicycles, or in golf carts. Historic day tours (with lunch) are available for $35. ⊠ *Box 3069, Bald Head Island 28461,* ☎ *919/457–5000 or 800/234–1666,* FAX *919/457–9232. 170 homes/condos/villas, 2 B&Bs. 3 restaurants, pool, golf, tennis, hiking, boating, bicycles, fishing. AE, DC, MC, V.*

Wilmington

$$ ✕ **Pilot House.** This Chandler's Wharf restaurant is known for its Sun-
★ day brunch, award-winning cream-based Carolina bisque, and shrimp and grits—a lunch favorite. You can dine indoors on linen tablecloths secured by vases of fresh flowers or on a riverside deck. ⊠ *2 Ann St.,* ☎ *910/343–0200. AE, D, MC, V.*

$$$ 🏨 **Blockade Runner Resort Hotel.** This two-story, 1960s-vintage oceanside complex is widely known for both its food and its service. Guest rooms, which open off the exterior balcony, overlook either the inlet or the ocean. The Ocean Terrace Restaurant serves an especially pop-

ular Saturday seafood buffet and Sunday brunch. ⊠ *275 Waynick Blvd., Wrightsville Beach 28480,* ☎ *910/256–2251 or 800/541–1161,* FAX *910/256–5502. 150 rooms. Restaurant, pool, spa, boating, bicycles, meeting rooms. AE, D, DC, MC, V.*

$$$ 🏨 **Inn at St. Thomas Court.** In the heart of the historic district, this trio
★ of former commercial buildings (including a convent) has been trans-
formed into 34 luxurious suites, each uniquely decorated in turn-of-
the-century style. ⊠ *101 S. 2nd St., 28401,* ☎ *910/343–1800 or 800/
525–0909,* FAX *910/251–1149. AE, D, DC, MC, V.*

Campgrounds

Camping is permitted in designated areas of the **Cape Hatteras** and **Cape Lookout national seashores** from mid-April through mid-October and at most state parks (☞ National and State Parks, *above*). Private campgrounds are scattered all along the coast. For more information contact the state's division of tourism (☞ Statewide Visitor Information, *above*).

Nightlife and the Arts

A favorite haunt on the Wilmington waterfront is the **Ice House Beer Garden** (⊠ 115 S. Water St., ☎ 910/763–2084), an indoor-outdoor bar featuring live rhythm and blues. In Wrightsville Beach at the **Blockade Runner Resort** (⊠ 275 Waynick Blvd., ☎ 910/256–2251), there's a lounge, live jazz, a weekly comedy show, and during summer, weekly dinner theater . Plays and concerts take place in **Thalian Hall Center for the Performing Arts** (⊠ 310 Chestnut St., ☎ 910/343–3664 or 800/523–2820), built in 1855–58 and recently restored.

Outdoor Activities and Sports

Boating

You can travel hundreds of miles over the sounds and inlets of this vast region along the Intracoastal Waterway. For marina and docking information, pick up a copy of the *North Carolina Coastal Boating Guide* or contact the appropriate county chamber of commerce (☞ Visitor Information, *above*).

Fishing

The region teems with bass, billfish, flounder, mullet, spot, trout, and other fish. Fishing is permitted from piers all along the coast and from certain bridges and causeways. Charter boats for deep-sea fishing are available at the **Oregon Inlet Fishing Center** (☎ 919/441–6301), on the Outer Banks, and **Wrightsville Beach Charters** (☎ 910/256–3576), near Wilmington; the *Carolina Princess* (☎ 919/726–5479), in Morehead City, is available for charter. Licenses for freshwater fishing are available by calling the North Carolina Wildlife Commission (☎ 919/715–4091). No license is needed for saltwater fishing.

Golf

Among the public and semiprivate courses in the Greater Wilmington area is the breathtaking **Bald Head Island Golf Course** (☎ 910/457–7310), designed by George Cobb. Ocean Isle, near the South Carolina state line, also has a number of outstanding courses. Contact the Cape Fear Coast Convention and Visitors Bureau (☞ Visitor Information, *above*) or the South Brunswick Islands Chamber of Commerce (⊠ Box 1380, Shallotte 28459, ☎ 910/754–6644).

Scuba Diving

With more than 600 known shipwrecks off the coast of the Outer Banks, diving opportunities are legion. Dive shops include **Nags Head Pro Dive Shop** (⊠ 3941 S. Croatan Hwy., Suite 114, Wilmington, ☎ 919/441–

7594), **Aquatic Safaris** (✉ 5751-4 Oleander Drive, Wilmington, ☎ 910/ 392–4386), and **Olympus Dive Center** (✉ 713 Shepard St., Morehead City, ☎ 919/726–9432).

Surfing and Windsurfing

Kitty Hawk Kites (☞ Shopping, *below*) provides gear and instruction. Rentals are also available at shops in Wilmington, Wrightsville Beach, and Carolina Beach.

Beaches

Cape Hatteras and **Cape Lookout national seashores** offer more than 100 mi of beaches. **Atlantic Beach** and **Emerald Isle,** on Bogue Banks near Morehead City; **Wrightsville, Carolina,** and **Kure beaches,** near Wilmington; and **Ocean Isle,** farther south, are other top spots.

Shopping

You can find **nautical items** at antiques shops and **hand-carved wooden ducks and birds** at local crafts shops in Duck, a few miles north of Nags Head, and in Wanchese, at the south end of Roanoke Island. In Nags Head **Kitty Hawk Kites** (☎ 919/441–4124 or 800/334–4777), the largest kite store on the East Coast, offers every type of kite and windsock known to humanity. New Bern and Wilmington are centers for **antiques**; in Wilmington many shops are at Chandler's Wharf, the Cotton Exchange, and the Water Street Market on the waterfront.

THE MOUNTAINS

The majestic peaks, meadows, and valleys of the Appalachian, Blue Ridge, and Smoky mountains characterize the west end of the state, which is divided into three distinct regions: the southern mountains (home to the Cherokee Reservation); the northern mountains, known as the High Country (Boone, Blowing Rock, Banner Elk); and the central mountains, anchored by Asheville, for decades a retreat for the wealthy and famous. National parks, national forests, handmade crafts centers, and the Blue Ridge Parkway are the area's main attractions, providing prime opportunities for shopping, skiing, hiking, bicycling, camping, fishing, canoeing, or just taking in the breathtaking views.

Visitor Information

Appalachian Trail Conference (✉ 100 Otis St., Asheville 28802, ☎ 704/ 254–3708). **Asheville:** Convention and Visitors Bureau (✉ Box 1010, Asheville 28802, ☎ 704/258–6111 or 800/257–1300). **Blowing Rock:** Chamber of Commerce (✉ Box 406, 28605, ☎ 704/295–7851). **Blue Ridge Parkway:** Superintendent (✉ 400 BB&T Bldg., 1 Pack Sq., Asheville 28801, ☎ 704/298–0398). **Boone:** Chamber of Commerce (✉ 208 W. Howard St., 28607, ☎ 704/262–3516 or 800/852–9506). **NC High Country Host** (✉ 1700 Blowing Rock Rd., Boone 28607, ☎ 704/264–1299 or 800/438–7500). **Smoky Mountain Host of NC** (✉ 4437 Georgia Rd., Franklin 28734, ☎ 704/369–9606 or 800/432– 4678).

Arriving and Departing

By Bus

Greyhound Lines (☎ 800/231–2222) serves Asheville.

By Car

You can reach Asheville from the east or the west via I–40. I–26 begins in Asheville and heads south, connecting with I–240, which circles the city. U.S. 23/19A runs through the city.

The High Country is reached off I–40 via U.S. 321 at Hickory, Route 181 at Morganton, and U.S. 221 at Marion. U.S. 421 is a major east–west artery. The Blue Ridge Parkway bisects the region, traveling over mountain crests in the High Country.

By Plane

Asheville Regional Airport (⊠ Rte. 280, Fletcher, ☎ 704/684–2226) is 15 mi south of Asheville.

Exploring the Mountains

The largest and most cosmopolitan city in the mountains, **Asheville** has been rated America's favorite place to live of cities of its size. The city's downtown is a pedestrian-friendly place, with upscale shopping, art galleries, museums, restaurants, and nightlife.

The 92,000-square-ft **Pack Place Education, Arts & Science Center,** in downtown Asheville, houses the **Asheville Art Museum, Colburn Gem & Mineral Museum, Health Adventure,** and **Diana Wortham Theatre.** The **YMI Cultural Center,** also maintained by Pack Place, is directly across the street. ⊠ *2 Pack Sq.,* ☎ *704/257–4500. Closed Mon. June– Oct. and Mon.–Tues. Nov.–May.*

★ East of Asheville is the astonishing **Biltmore Estate,** built in the 1890s as the home of George Vanderbilt. The 250-room French Renaissance–style château is filled with priceless antiques and art treasures. The grounds, landscaped by Frederick Law Olmsted, include 75 acres of elaborate gardens, 72 acres of vineyards, and a state-of-the-art winery. ⊠ *Exit 50 off I–40E,* ☎ *704/255–1700 or 800/543–2961.* ☑ *$27.95 (prices vary for special events).*

The **North Carolina Arboretum,** 426 acres that were part of the original Biltmore Estate, completes the dream of Frederick Law Olmsted and features southern Appalachian flora in a stunning number of settings, including the Quilt Garden, whose bedding plants are arranged in patterns reminiscent of Appalachian quilts. There is also the formal Stream Garden, capitalizing on the Bent Creek trout stream that runs through the heart of the grounds. ⊠ *Immediately southwest of Asheville adjacent to the Blue Ridge Pkwy.,* ☎ *704/665–2492.*

A 20-minute drive from Asheville is Madison County, home to the picturesque village of Hot Springs, a way station for hikers on the Appalachian Trail, and the **Hot Springs Spa.** These mineral springs maintain a natural 100°F temperature year-round, and since the turn of the century, they have provided relief for visitors suffering a variety of ailments, including rheumatism and arthritis. ⊠ *1 Bridge St.,* ☎ *704/622–7676 or 800/462–0963.*

The **Great Smoky Mountains Railway** is one of the most popular attractions in western North Carolina and just 45 mi west of Asheville. Choose from five different routes (fares vary) and diesel-electric or steam locomotives. Open-sided cars or cabooses are ideal for picture taking as the spectacular scenery glides by. ⊠ *Box 397, Dillsboro 28725,* ☎ *704/586–8811 or 800/872–4681. Closed Jan.–Mar.*

The most scenic route from Asheville to the Boone–Blowing Rock area is via the **Blue Ridge Parkway** (☎ 704/271–4779), a stunningly beautiful 469-mi road that gently winds through mountains and meadows and crosses mountain streams on its way from Waynesboro, Virginia, to Cherokee, North Carolina. The parkway is generally open year-round but often closes during heavy snows and icy conditions. Maps and information are available at visitor centers along the highway.

At Milepost 316.3 on the Blue Ridge Parkway is the **Linville Falls Visitor Center** (⊠ Rte. 1, Box 789, Spruce Pine 28777, ☎ 704/765–1045). From here it's an easy half-mile hike to one of North Carolina's most photographed waterfalls.

Just off the parkway, on U.S. 221 at Milepost 305, is **Grandfather Mountain,** which soars 6,000 ft and is famous for its mile-high swinging bridge. Sweaty-palmed visitors cross the 228-ft bridge, which sways over a 1,000 ft drop into Linville Valley. The **Natural History Museum** has exhibits on native minerals, flora and fauna, and pioneer life. The United Nations has designated Grandfather Mountain a Biosphere Reserve. ☎ 704/733–4337 or 800/468–7325. Closed in inclement weather.

Blowing Rock refers to both a quiet mountain village and the nearby 4,000-ft rock for which it was named. Visitors to this looming outcrop can enjoy views from its **observation tower** (☎ 704/295–7111) and its gardens of mountain laurel and other native plants. The tower is closed in January and February.

Boone, named for frontiersman Daniel Boone, lies at the convergence of three major highways—U.S. 321, U.S. 421, and Rte. 105. *Horn in the West* (⊠ Amphitheater off U.S. 321, ☎ 704/264–2120), a project of the Southern Appalachian Historical Association, is an outdoor drama that traces the story of Daniel Boone. Boone's **Appalachian Cultural Museum** (⊠ University Hall near Greene's Motel, U.S. 321, ☎ 704/262–3117) is dedicated to the history and culture of the region from the geographic origins of the mountains to the beginnings of stock car racing. Also showcased are the many other aspects of mountain life—from antiques to quilts to the development of the tourism industry.

What to See and Do with Children

Blue Ridge Gemstone Mine, midway between Boone and Asheville, is in a region with one of the richest mineral deposits in the country. Dig for your own gems here after purchasing gem buckets, which range in price from $5 to the $100 one, called the Mother Lode. ⊠ Box 327, Little Switzerland 28749, ☎ 704/765–5264. Closed Jan.–Mar.

An old-fashioned family theme park is what you will find at **Tweetsie Railroad,** where rides on a train pulled by an authentic steam locomotive and gold panning are among the offerings. ⊠ Box 388, Blowing Rock 28605, ☎ 704/264–9061 or 800/526–5740. Closed Nov.–late May.

Dining and Lodging

The spirit of the pioneers who settled the mountains has always been present in the area's food and shelter—basic, hardy, and family-oriented. Be sure to make reservations early for visits in the fall, when every nook and cranny is crammed with leaf peepers.

Asheville

$$$ ✕ **Cafe on the Square.** When owners Bill and Shelagh Burns moved to Asheville from San Francisco, they brought California-style cuisine with them. The menu is heavy on fresh seafood and pastas cooked with various salsas, chutneys, and simple marinades. Their signature dishes are hickory-smoked chicken in a marsala-and-shiitake mushroom

cream sauce and peanut butter pie. ⊠ *1 Biltmore Ave.,* ☎ *704/251–5565. AE, D, DC, MC, V.*

$$ ✕ **Mountain Smoke House.** Mountain barbecue and pig-pickin' buffets combined with bluegrass music and clogging add up to a lively experience for those who want more than food when they go out. The aroma will lead you to this dinner-only family-style restaurant, which serves as a showcase for local musicians. ⊠ *20 S. Spruce St.,* ☎ *704/ 253–4871. AE, D, DC, MC, V.*

$$$$ ✕⌑ **Grove Park Inn.** This is Asheville's premier resort, and it's just as ★ beautiful and exciting as it was the day it opened in 1913. The guest list has included Henry Ford, Thomas Edison, Harvey Firestone, and Warren G. Harding. Novelist F. Scott Fitzgerald stayed here while his wife, Zelda, was in a nearby sanitorium. The inn, whose two newer wings are in keeping with the original design, is furnished with oak antiques in the Arts and Crafts style. ⊠ *290 Macon Ave., 28804,* ☎ *704/252– 2711 or 800/438–5800,* ℻ *704/253–7053 for guests or 704/252–6102 for reservations. 510 rooms. 4 restaurants, 2 pools, hot tub, sauna, 18-hole golf course, 12 tennis courts, health club, racquetball, children's programs, meeting rooms, airport shuttle. AE, D, DC, MC, V.*

$$$$ ✕⌑ **Richmond Hill Inn.** Once a private residence, this elegant Victo-★ rian mansion is on the National Register of Historic Places. Rooms in the mansion are furnished with canopy beds, Victorian sofas, and other antiques, while the more modern cottages have contemporary pine poster beds. Gabrielle's, named for the former mistress of the house—wife of the congressman and ambassador Richmond Pearson—is known for innovative cuisine such as grilled medallions of antelope with wild boar sausage. The restaurant is only open to the public for dinner and Sunday brunch; jacket and tie are required. ⊠ *87 Richmond Hill Dr., 28806,* ☎ *704/252–7313 or 800/545–9238,* ℻ *704/252–8726. 27 rooms, 9 cottages. Restaurant, croquet, meeting rooms. AE, MC, V.*

Boone

$$ ✕⌑ **High Country Inn.** A popular honeymoon destination that also draws skiers, golfers, and other groups interested in the discount packages, the inn, made of native stone and surrounded by ponds, offers rooms that range from luxurious to comfortable. Geno's, a popular sports bar, and the Waterwheel, a restaurant specializing in German cuisine, are here. ⊠ *1785 Rte. 105S (Box 1339), 28607,* ☎ *704/264–1000 or 800/ 334–5605,* ℻ *704/262–0073. 120 rooms. Indoor-outdoor pool, hot tub, sauna, exercise room, meeting rooms. AE, D, MC, V.*

Hot Springs

$$ ✕⌑ **Bridge Street Cafe & Inn.** This renovated storefront, circa 1922, is right on the Appalachian Trail and overlooks Spring Creek. Upstairs are brightly decorated rooms and two shared baths filled with antiques. One of the bathrooms has a claw-foot tub. The café downstairs has a hand-built wood-fired oven and grill from which emerge gourmet pizzas. ⊠ *Bridge St. (Box 502), 28743,* ☎ *704/622–0002,* ℻ *704/622– 7282. 4 rooms. Café. AE, D, MC, V. Closed Nov.–mid-Mar.*

Little Switzerland

$$–$$$ ✕⌑ **Switzerland Inn and Chalet Restaurant.** This Swiss-style lodge overlooking the mountains offers lodge rooms, parlor-bedroom suites, and a lovely honeymoon cottage with a fireplace. The prime rib and seafood buffet served each Friday night is a big draw. ⊠ *Milepost 334, off Blue Ridge Pkwy. (Box 399), 28749,* ☎ *704/765–2153 or 800/654–4026,* ℻ *704/765–0049. 66 rooms. Restaurant, pool, lobby lounge, 2 ten-*

nis courts, shuffleboard, shops. Full breakfast. AE, D, MC, V. Closed Nov.–Apr.

Nightlife

In Asheville, next door to the historic Kress Building, is **31 Patton** (☎ 704/285–0949), where you can take salsa dance classes, listen to rock music, or play pool. **Shadrack's** (☎ 704/264–1737), a cavernous establishment in Boone reminiscent of the Grand Ole Opry building, has an all-you-can-eat buffet and a large dance floor, where dancers young and old shake a leg to live country and bluegrass tunes.

Outdoor Activities and Sports

Canoeing and White-Water Rafting

Near Boone and Blowing Rock, the New River, a federally designated Wild and Scenic River (Classes I and II) provides hours of excitement for canoeists, as do the Watauga River, Wilson Creek, and the Toe River. The Toe becomes the Nolichucky River as it goes into Tennessee. As the Nolichucky traverses the deepest, most spectacular canyon east of the Grand Canyon, its rapids offer heart-pounding excitement for the adrenaline deprived. **Carolina Wilderness** (☎ 800/872–7437), **Edge of the World Outfitters** (☎ 704/898–9550 or 800/789–EDGE), and **High Mountain Expeditions** (☎ 704/295–4200 or 800/262–9036) provide trips down the Nolichucky via raft.

Ski Areas

Downhill skiing is available at **Appalachian Ski Mountain,** at Blowing Rock (☎ 704/295–7828); **Hawksnest Golf & Ski Resort** (☎ 704/963–6561 or 800/822–4295), at Seven Devils; **Ski Beech** (☎ 704/387–2011), at Beech Mountain; and **Sugar Mountain** (☎ 704/898–4521), at Banner Elk.

Shopping

The **Folk Art Center** (☎ 704/298–7928), at Milepost 382 on the Blue Ridge Parkway, sells authentic mountain arts and crafts made by the 700 artisans of the Southern Highland Handicraft Guild. **Biltmore Village** on the Biltmore Estate is a cluster of specialty shops, restaurants, and galleries built along cobbled sidewalks. Here there's a decided turn-of-the-century English hamlet feel, and everything—from children's books to music, antiques, one-of-a-kind imports, and wearable art—can be found.

SOUTH CAROLINA

Updated by
Mary Sue
Lawrence

Capital	Columbia
Population	3,699,000
Mottoes	While I Breathe, I Hope; Prepared in Mind and Resources
State Bird	Carolina wren
State Flower	Yellow jessamine
Postal Abbreviation	SC

Statewide Visitor Information

South Carolina Department of Parks, Recreation and Tourism (✉ 1205 Pendleton St., Box 71, Columbia 29202, ☎ 803/734-0235 or 800/ 872-3505). **Welcome centers:** U.S. 17 near Little River; I-95 near Dillon, Santee and Lake Marion, and Hardeeville; I-77 near Fort Mill; I-85 near Blacksburg and Fair Play; I-26 near Landrum; I-20 at North Augusta; and U.S. 301 near Allendale.

Scenic Drives

The **Cherokee Foothills Scenic Highway** (Route 11), passing small towns, peach orchards, and historical sites, traverses 130 mi of Blue Ridge foothills in the northwest corner of the state. The **Ashley River Road** (Route 61), which parallels the river for about 11 mi north of Charleston, leads to famous plantations and gardens. The **Savannah River Scenic Highway** (follow signs from Route 28 near North Augusta to Route 24 near Westminster) follows the Savannah River for 100 mi along the Georgia border, winding past three lakes.

National and State Parks

National Parks

At **Cowpens National Battlefield** (✉ Rte. 11, Box 308, Chesnee 29323, ☎ 864/461-2828) the American patriots defeated the British in 1781; exhibits in the visitor center explain the battle. **Kings Mountain National Military Park** (✉ I-85 near Blacksburg; Box 40, Kings Mountain, NC 28086, ☎ 803/936-7921), where patriot forces whipped the redcoats in 1780, has exhibits depicting the famous battle and a self-guided trail. For white-water enthusiasts, the **Chattooga National Wild and Scenic River** (✉ U.S. Forest Service, 4931 Broad River Rd., Columbia 29210-4021, ☎ 803/561-4000) forms the border between South Carolina and Georgia for 40 mi. **Congaree Swamp National Monument** (✉ Old Bluff Rd., Hopkins 29061, ☎ 803/776-4396) contains the oldest and largest trees east of the Mississippi River.

State Parks

Several of South Carolina's 48 state parks operate like resort communities, with everything from deluxe accommodations to golf. **Hickory Knob State Resort Park** (✉ Rte. 1, Box 199-B, McCormick 29835, ☎ 864/391-2450 or 800/491-1764), on Strom Thurmond Lake, offers fishing, golfing, and skeet shooting. **Devil's Fork State Park** (✉ 161 Holcombe Circle, Salem 29676, ☎ 864/944-2639) has luxurious accommodations overlooking beautiful Lake Jocassee. **Calhoun Falls State Park** (✉ Rte. 81, Calhoun Falls 29628, ☎ 803/447-8267) has a full-service marina, a campground, nature trails, and a picnic area.

The state's **coastal parks**—known for broad beaches, camping facilities, and nature preserves—draw the most visitors and are often booked months in advance. **Huntington Beach State Park** (⊠ Murrells Inlet 29576, ☎ 803/237–4440) has a splendid beach, surf fishing, and a salt-marsh boardwalk, as well as Atalaya, a Moorish-style mansion. **Myrtle Beach State Park** (⊠ U.S. 17, Myrtle Beach 29577, ☎ 803/238–5325) has cabins and year-round nature programs. **Hunting Island State Park** (⊠ St. Helena Island 29920, ☎ 803/838–2011), a secluded domain of beach, has nature trails and varied fishing. For more information contact the **South Carolina Division of State Parks** (⊠ 1205 Pendleton St., Columbia 29201, ☎ 803/734–0159).

CHARLESTON

The port city of Charleston has withstood three centuries of epidemics, earthquakes, fires, and hurricanes to become one of the South's best-preserved and most beloved cities. Residents have lovingly restored old downtown homes and commercial buildings, as well as more than 180 historic churches—so many that Charlestonians call their home the "Holy City." Each spring the city—festooned with dogwood and azaleas—celebrates its heritage with symphony galas, plantation oyster roasts, candlelight tours of historic homes and churches, and the renowned Spoleto Festival USA, a celebration of the arts staged in streets and performance halls throughout the city.

Visitor Information

Visitor Information Center (⊠ Box 975, 375 Meeting St., 29402, ☎ 803/853–8000 or 800/868–8118).

Arriving and Departing

By Boat

Boaters arriving at Charleston Harbor via the Intracoastal Waterway may dock at City Marina (⊠ Lockwood Blvd., ☎ 803/724–7357) or at the Isle of Palms's Wild Dunes Yacht Harbor (☎ 803/886–5100).

By Bus

Greyhound Lines (⊠ 3610 Dorchester Rd., North Charleston, ☎ 800/231–2222).

By Car

I–26 crosses the state from northwest to southeast and ends at Charleston. U.S. 17, a north–south coastal route, passes through the city.

By Plane

Charleston International Airport (☎ 803/767–1100), 12 mi west of downtown Charleston along I–26, is served by Air South, Continental, Delta, United, and US Airways. **Low Country Limousine Service** (☎ 803/767–7111 or 800/222–4771) charges $15 per person (or $10 per person for two or more) to downtown; you need to make advance reservations. Some hotels also provide shuttle service.

By Train

Amtrak (⊠ 4565 Gaynor Ave., North Charleston, ☎ 803/744–8264 or 800/872–7245).

Getting Around Charleston

You can park your car and walk in the city's historic district, but you'll need a car to see attractions in outlying areas. **Charleston Transit** (☎ 803/747–0922) provides bus service within the city and to James Island, Isle of Palms, Sullivans's Island, Mount Pleasant, and North

Charleston. It also operates the trolley-style Downtown Area Shuttle buses, called DASH (☎ 803/747–0922). Fare for either is 75¢, exact change, or $2 for a one-day DASH pass, available at the Visitor Information Center. **Taxi companies** include Yellow Cab (☎ 803/577–6565), Safety Cab (☎ 803/722–4066), and Low Country Limousine (☎ 803/767–7111 or 800/222–4771).

A popular option is a **horse-drawn-carriage tour.** Guides are generally very knowledgeable and often provide snippets of history and humor. Tours conducted by the **Old South Carriage Co.** (☎ 803/723–9712), whose guides wear Confederate uniforms, depart from the corner of Anson and North Market streets. **Carolina Carriage Co.** (☎ 803/723–8687) tours leave from Market Square. **Palmetto Carriage Works** (☎ 803/723–8145) has one-hour tours. **Charleston Carriage Co.** (☎ 803/577–0042), the city's oldest, conducts one-hour tours of the historic district.

Exploring Charleston

You can get a quick orientation to the city by viewing *Forever Charleston,* a 24-minute multimedia presentation shown at the visitor center (☞ Visitor Information, *above*).

★ The **Charleston Museum** (✉ 360 Meeting St., ☎ 803/722–2996), founded in 1773, is across from the visitor center (where there's parking for $1 per hour). The 500,000 items in the collection include Charleston silver, fashions, toys, and snuffboxes, as well as exhibits on natural history, archaeology, and ornithology.

Also part of the museum are two historic homes. The **Joseph Manigault House** (✉ 350 Meeting St.) was designed in 1803 and is noted for its carved-wood mantels and elaborate plasterwork. Furnishings are British, French, and American antiques, including rare tricolor Wedgwood pieces. The **Heyward-Washington House** (✉ 87 Church St.) was the residence of President George Washington during his 1791 visit and the setting for DuBose Heyward's *Porgy.* The mansion is notable for fine period furnishings by local craftspeople and includes a restored 18th-century kitchen. You can purchase a combined ticket for admission to the museum and both houses.

The heart of Charleston is the **Old City Market,** between Meeting and East Bay streets, with restaurants, shops, and produce stands. Here you can buy vegetables, fruits, benne-seed (sesame) wafers, sweet-grass baskets (☞ Shopping, *below*), jewelry, seashells, and other craft items.

Dock Street Theatre (✉ 135 Church St., ☎ 803/720–3968) combines the reconstructed early Georgian playhouse that originally stood on the site with the 1809 Planter's Hotel; call for tour information.

St. Michael's Episcopal Church (☎ 803/723–0603), modeled on London's St. Martin's-in-the-Fields, stands at the corner of Meeting and Broad streets. Completed in 1761, this beautiful structure is Charleston's oldest surviving church. Its steeple clock and bells were imported from England in 1764.

★ **Fort Sumter National Monument** (☎ 803/722–1691), a man-made island in Charleston Harbor, is where the first shot of the Civil War was fired, on April 12, 1861. National Park Service rangers conduct free tours of the restored structure, which includes a historical museum. To get here, take a boat from Patriots Point (☞ What to See and Do with Children, *below*) or the City Marina, on Lockwood Boulevard.

Charleston, South Carolina

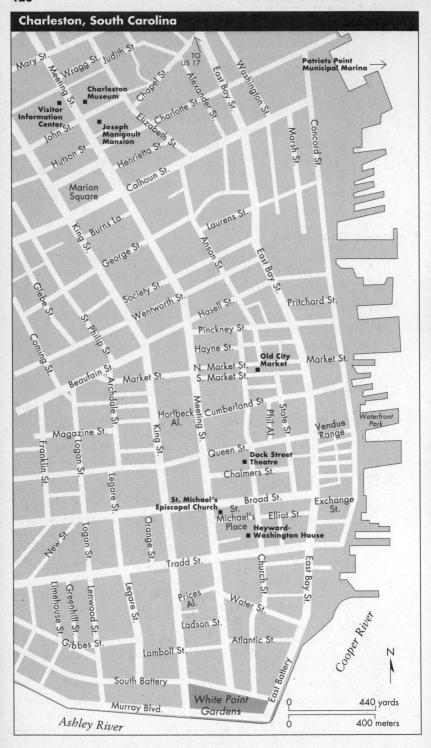

Mary St.
Meeting St.
Wragg St.
Judith St.
Chapel St.
Alexander St.
East Bay St.
Washington St.

TO
US 17

Patriots Point
Municipal Marina

Charleston
Museum

Visitor
Information
Center

John St.

Charlotte St.

Elizabeth St.

Marsh St.

Concord St.

Joseph
Manigault
Mansion

Hutson St.

Henrietta St.

Calhoun St.

Marion
Square

Burns La.

King St.

George St.

Laurens St.

Anson St.

East Bay St.

Glebe St.

St. Philip St.

Society St.

Wentworth St.

Hasell St.

Pritchard St.

Coming St.

Pinckney St.

Hayne St.

N. Market St.

Old City
Market

Market St.

Beaufain St.

Archdale St.

Market St.

S. Market St.

Horlbeck
Al.

Cumberland St.

State St.

Phil Al.

Vendue
Range

Waterfront
Park

Magazine St.

Logan St.

King St.

Meeting St.

Queen St.

Dock Street
Theatre

Franklin St.

Legare St.

Chalmers St.

St. Michael's
Episcopal Church

St.
Michael's
Place

Broad St.

Elliot St.

Exchange
St.

New St.

Logan St.

Orange St.

Heyward-
Washington House

East Bay St.

Tradd St.

Church St.

Legare St.

Lenwood St.

Greenhill St.

Prices
Al.

Water St.

Limehouse St.

Ladson St.

Atlantic St.

Gibbes St.

Lamboll St.

South Battery

East Battery

Cooper River

Murray Blvd.

White Point
Gardens

N

Ashley River

0   440 yards

0   400 meters

Plantations, Parks, and Gardens

Charleston is famous for public parks, magnificent plantations, and secret gardens that lie hidden behind the walls of private homes. **White Point Gardens,** on the point of the narrow Battery Peninsula bounded by the Ashley and Cooper rivers, is a popular gathering spot. The new **Waterfront Park,** along Concord Street on the Cooper River, has a fishing pier, unique interactive fountains, a picnic area, and landscaped gardens.

★ **Drayton Hall** (☏ 803/766–0188), built between 1738 and 1742, is 9 mi northwest of downtown via Ashley River Road (Route 61). The only plantation on the Ashley River to survive the Civil War, it is unfurnished, which serves to highlight the original plaster moldings, opulent hand-carved woodwork, and other ornamental details. This is considered one of the nation's finest examples of Georgian Palladian architecture.

★ **Magnolia Plantation and Gardens** (☏ 803/571–1266), 2 mi beyond Drayton Hall on Route 61, was begun in 1865. Its gardens hold one of the largest collections of azaleas and camellias in North America. Nature lovers can canoe through the 125-acre Waterfowl Refuge, see the 60-acre Audubon Swamp Garden along boardwalks and bridges, explore 500 acres of wildlife trails, and visit the petting zoo.

Middleton Place (☏ 803/556–6020 or 800/782–3608), 4 mi north of Magnolia Plantation on Route 61, is the site of the nation's oldest land-scaped gardens, dating from 1741. Much of the mansion was destroyed during the Civil War, but a restored wing houses impressive collections of silver, furniture, paintings, and historical documents. Children will enjoy the working plantation.

An avenue of oaks leads to **Boone Hall Plantation** (☏ 803/884–4371), 8 mi north of Charleston on U.S. 17 and said to have inspired the painting MGM filmed to represent Tara in *Gone With the Wind.* You can explore the gardens, the first floor of the mansion, and the original slave quarters. Lunch is served in the old cotton gin.

Charles Towne Landing State Park (✉ Hwy. 171, ☏ 803/556–4450), across the Ashley River Bridge, is built on the site of a 1670 settlement. It includes a reconstructed village and fortifications, a replica of a 17th-century sailing vessel, gardens with bike trails and walking paths, and an animal park.

Cypress Gardens (✉ 24 mi north of Charleston via U.S. 52, ☏ 803/553–0515) was created from a swamp that was once the freshwater reserve of a vast rice plantation. You can explore the inky waters by boat or walk along paths lined with moss-draped cypress trees and flowering bushes.

What to See and Do with Children

Patriots Point (✉ U.S. 17, ☏ 803/884–2727), in Mount Pleasant, is the world's largest naval and maritime museum and home to the Medal of Honor Society. Berthed here are the aircraft carrier *Yorktown,* the nuclear ship *Savannah,* the World War II submarine *Clamagore,* the cutter *Ingham,* and the destroyer *Laffey.* It's open daily.

Dining

Best known for Low Country specialties like she-crab soup, sautéed shrimp, red rice, grits, and pecan pie, Charleston is also famous for contemporary cookery blending down-home cooking with haute cuisine. For price ranges *see* Chart 1 (B) *in* On the Road with Fodor's.

$$$ ✕ **Union Hall.** This new hot spot, with a comfortable front bar area and trendy dining room overlooking the kitchen, serves up superb mussels marinara, carpaccio of beef tenderloin, and pasta and risotto dishes, plus desserts such as apple-oatmeal tart. ⊠ *16 N. Market St.,* ☎ *803/853–4777. AE, D, DC, MC, V.*

$$ ✕ **Carolina's.** Always bustling, Carolina's draws Charlestonians and visitors alike. Its black, white, and peach bistro decor includes terracotta tiles and 1920s French posters. Fans return for the "appeteasers" and late-night (until 1 AM) menu offerings, such as black-eyed-pea cakes, pasta with crawfish and *tasso* (spiced ham) in a spicy cream sauce, crab wontons, and pecan brittle basket with fruit and ice cream. ⊠ *10 Exchange St.* ☎ *803/724–3800. AE, MC, V. No lunch.*

$$ ✕ **Magnolias.** Housed in an 1823 warehouse and decorated in a mag-
★ nolia theme, this self-designated "uptown/down South" restaurant is prized for its Low Country fare, including shrimp and sausage over creamy grits with tasso gravy. Many entrées come with collard greens, buttermilk mashed potatoes, or succotash. ⊠ *185 E. Bay St.,* ☎ *803/ 577–7771. AE, MC, V.*

$$ ✕ **Slightly North of Broad.** This whimsical eatery has several seats that overlook the action-packed kitchen. Low Country cuisine is given trendy treatment here: Try the corn fritters with caviar and crème fraîche or the grilled, barbecued tuna. You can order almost every item as either an appetizer or entrée. ⊠ *192 E. Bay St.,* ☎ *803/723–3424. Reservations not accepted. AE, D, DC, MC, V.*

$–$$ ✕ **Gaulart and Maliclet French Cafe.** Chic and upbeat, the café serves
★ ethnic and bistro French food. The menu of soups, salads, and sandwiches is enlivened by such evening specials as seafood Normandy and chicken sesame. ⊠ *98 Broad St.,* ☎ *803/577–9797. AE, DC, MC, V.*

$ ✕ **Mike Calder's Deli & Pub.** Soups, salads, sandwiches, daily home-cooked specials, and 15 different draft beers are offered in what was once a pharmacy in the historic district. ⊠ *288 King St.,* ☎ *803/577– 0123. Reservations not accepted. AE, D, MC, V.*

Lodging

Hotels and inns on the peninsula are generally more expensive than those in outlying areas of the city. Rates tend to increase during festivals, when reservations are essential. From December 1 to March 1 some rates drop by as much as 50%. Nearby world-class accommodations include the Kiawah Island, Wild Dunes, and Seabrook Island resorts. For price ranges *see* Chart 2 (A) *in* On the Road with Fodor's.

$$$$ 🏨 **Charleston Place.** Rooms have period reproductions, French bed
★ linens, and fax machines at this graceful low-rise hotel, now an Orient Express property, near upscale shops in the historic district. The Charleston Grill, with its mahogany-paneled walls and wrought-iron chandeliers, is an elegant backdrop for dining. ⊠ *130 Market St., 29401,* ☎ *803/722–4900 or 800/611–5545,* 𝔽𝔸𝕏 *803/724–7215. 440 rooms. 2 restaurants, 2 lounges, indoor pool, hot tub, sauna, steam room, exercise room, concierge floor. AE, D, DC, MC, V.*

$$$–$$$$ 🏨 **John Rutledge House Inn.** The 1763 main house, built by a signa-
★ tory of the U.S. Constitution, has ornate ironwork on its facade. Two carriage houses (each with four rooms) complete this luxury bed-and-breakfast. Rooms have plaster molding and wood floors and are decorated with antiques and four-poster beds. ⊠ *116 Broad St., 29401,* ☎ *803/723–7999 or 800/476–9741,* 𝔽𝔸𝕏 *803/720–2615. 19 rooms. Continental breakfast, afternoon tea. AE, MC, V.*

$$$–$$$$ 🏨 **Kiawah Island Resort.** Choose from inn rooms and completely equipped one- to five-bedroom villas and private homes in two luxurious resort villages on 10,000 mostly undeveloped acres. Inn rooms

are decorated in pastel beachy shades, and most have an ocean or wooded view. At press time (summer 1997), the inn was slated to be torn down and replaced with a larger hotel in 1999. ⊠ *21 mi south of Charleston via U.S. 17; 12 Kiawah Beach Dr., Kiawah Island 29455,* ☎ *803/768–2121 or 800/654–2924,* FAX *803/768–6099. 150 rooms, 500 villas and homes. 3 restaurants, 5 bars, 4 18-hole golf courses, 26 tennis courts, beach, bicycles, children's programs. AE, D, DC, MC, V.*

$$$–$$$$ ⊞ **Mills House Hotel.** This luxurious property in the historic district is a reconstruction of a 19th-century hotel that once stood on the site. Antique furnishings and period decor lend charm to public areas; guest rooms are small and a bit standard. The elegant Barbadoes Room serves some of the city's best seafood. ⊠ *115 Meeting St., 29401,* ☎ *803/577–2400 or 800/874–9600,* FAX *803/722–2112. 214 rooms. Restaurant, 2 lounges, pool. AE, D, DC, MC, V.*

$$$ ⊞ **Hawthorn Suites Hotel.** This deluxe hotel at the Old City Market has a restored entrance portico from an 1874 bank, a refurbished 1866 firehouse, and three lush gardens. The spacious suites, decorated with 18th-century reproductions and canopy beds, include full kitchens or wet bars. ⊠ *181 Church St., 29401,* ☎ *803/577–2644 or 800/527–1133,* FAX *803/577–2697. 179 rooms. Hot tub, exercise room. Continental breakfast, afternoon refreshments. AE, D, DC, MC, V.*

$$–$$$ ⊞ **Hampton Inn–Historic District.** This downtown property has hard-
★ wood floors and a fireplace in the lobby, spacious guest rooms furnished in period reproductions, and a courtyard garden. ⊠ *345 Meeting St., 29403,* ☎ *803/723–4000 or 800/426–7866,* FAX *803/722–3725. 171 rooms. Pool. AE, D, DC, MC, V.*

$–$$ ⊞ **Days Inn–Historic District.** Spacious, quiet rooms with king-size beds are available at this modest motel. ⊠ *155 Meeting St., 29401,* ☎ *803/722–8411 or 800/325–2525,* FAX *803/723–5361. 124 rooms. Restaurant, pool. AE, D, DC, MC, V.*

$–$$ ⊞ **Heart of Charleston Quality Inn.** Convenient courtyard parking as well as a location across from the convention center and many must-see spots draw loyal repeat visitors. Rooms are modern motel style. ⊠ *125 Calhoun St., 29401,* ☎ *803/722–3391 or 800/845–2504,* FAX *803/577–0361. 126 rooms. Restaurant, pool. AE, D, DC, MC, V.*

Nightlife and the Arts

Nightlife

Lowcountry Legends Music Hall (⊠ 30 Cumberland St., ☎ 803/722–1829 or 800/348–7270) is Charleston's Preservation Hall, serving up music, legends, and folktales unique to the region. Top music clubs include **Windjammer** (⊠ 1000 Ocean Blvd., ☎ 803/886–8596), on the Isle of Palms, an oceanfront spot with live rock music. In the market area try the **Jukebox** (⊠ 4 Vendue Range, ☎ 803/723–3431) for beach music and dancing. **Chef & Clef Restaurant** (⊠ 102 N. Market St., ☎ 803/722–7032) has jazz on the first floor and blues on the third. **Charlie's Little Bar,** above Saracen's Restaurant (⊠ 141 E. Bay St., ☎ 803/723–6242), has live jazz or blues most weekends. **Serenade** (⊠ 37 John St., ☎ 803/973–3333) is a musical revue of jazz and Broadway tunes. Another option is dining and dancing on the luxury yacht *Spirit of Charleston* (☎ 803/722–2628).

The Arts

Spoleto Festival USA (⊠ Box 704, 29402, ☎ 803/722–2764), a world-class annual celebration founded by maestro Gian Carlo Menotti in 1977, showcases opera, dance, theater, symphonic and chamber music, jazz, and the visual arts from late May through early June.

The **Charleston Symphony Orchestra** (☎ 803/723–7528) presents a variety of series at Gaillard Municipal Auditorium (✉ 77 Calhoun St., ☎ 803/577–4500), and chamber and pops series elsewhere.

Beaches

South Carolina's climate allows swimming from April through October. There are public beaches at Beachwalker Park on Kiawah Island; Folly Beach County Park and Folly Beach on Folly Island; the Isle of Palms; and Sullivan's Island. Resorts with private beaches include Fairfield Ocean Ridge on Edisto Island; Kiawah Island Resort (☞ Lodging, *above*); Seabrook Island; and Wild Dunes Resort on the Isle of Palms. For more information contact Charleston's Visitor Information Center (☞ Visitor Information, *above*).

Shopping

The three-block **Old City Market** (☞ Exploring Charleston, *above*) yields colorful produce and varied gifts, including the sweet-grass baskets unique to this area. The craft, originally introduced by West Africans brought here as slaves, is now practiced by only a handful of their descendants. The baskets are priced from $15 to more than $200. (They are also sold at stands along U.S. 17 north of town, near Mount Pleasant; if you have the heart to bargain, you *may* be able to get a better price here than in Charleston.)

Elegant antiques shops line King Street, among them **Geo. C. Birlant & Co.** (✉ 191 King St., ☎ 803/722–3842), with 18th- and 19th-century English selections and the famous Charleston Battery bench. **Livingston and Sons Antiques** (✉ 163 King St., ☎ 803/723–9697; ✉ 2137 Savannah Hwy., ☎ 803/556–6162) offers period furniture, clocks, and other items. **Ben Silver** (✉ 149 King St., ☎ 803/577–4556) has beautiful ties and buttons. Among the town's chic art galleries are the **Birds I View Gallery** (✉ 119-A Church St., ☎ 803/723–1276), with bird paintings and prints by Anne Worsham Richardson. The **Virginia Fouché Bolton Art Gallery** (✉ 127 Meeting St., ☎ 803/577–9351) sells original paintings and limited-edition lithographs of Charleston scenes, and the **Marty Whaley Adams Gallery** (✉ 120 Meeting St., ☎ 803/853–8512) carries original watercolors and monotypes plus prints and posters by this Charleston artist. **Historic Charleston Reproductions** (✉ 105 Broad St., ☎ 803/723–8292) has superb replicas of Charleston furniture and accessories approved by the Historic Charleston Foundation.

THE COAST

The South Carolina coast is a land of extremes, from glitzy to gracious. The Grand Strand, from the state's northeastern border to historic Georgetown, is one of the East Coast's family-vacation megacenters and the state's top tourist area. Here you'll find 60 mi of white-sand beaches, championship golf courses, campgrounds, seafood restaurants, malls and factory outlets, and, at last count, nearly a dozen live-entertainment theaters with everything from country-and-western music to magic acts. The Low Country is the area between Georgetown and the state's southeastern boundary, including Beaufort, as well as the barrier islands of Hilton Head, Edisto, and Fripp. Beaufort is a gracious antebellum town with a compact historic district of lavish 18th- and 19th-century homes. Hilton Head's exclusive resorts and genteel good life make it one of the coast's most popular vacation getaways.

Visitor Information

Beaufort: Chamber of Commerce (✉ 1006 Bay St., Box 910, 29901-0910, ☎ 803/524–3163). **Georgetown:** Chamber of Commerce and Information Center (✉ 102 Broad St., Box 1776, 29442, ☎ 803/546–8436 or 800/777–7705). **Hilton Head Island:** Chamber of Commerce (✉ Box 5647, 29938, ☎ 803/785–3673). **Myrtle Beach:** Area Chamber of Commerce and Information Center (✉ 1200 North Oak St., Box 2115, 29578-2115, ☎ 803/626–7444 or 800/356–3016, ext. 136, for brochures). **Pawleys Island:** Pawleys Island Chamber of Commerce (✉ U.S. 17, Box 569, 29585, ☎ 803/237–1921).

Arriving and Departing

By Boat

The South Carolina coast is accessible by boat via the Intracoastal Waterway. At **Myrtle Beach** you may dock at Hague Marina (☎ 803/293–2141), Harbor Gate (☎ 803/249–8888), and Marlin Quay (☎ 803/651–4444). **Hilton Head** has several marinas, including Shelter Cove Marina (☎ 803/842–7002), Harbour Town Marina (☎ 803/671–2704), and Schilling Boathouse (☎ 803/681–2628).

By Bus

Greyhound Lines (☎ 800/231–2222) serves Myrtle Beach and Beaufort.

By Car

Major interstates connect with U.S. 17, the principal north–south coastal route.

By Plane

The **Myrtle Beach International Airport** (☎ 803/448–1589) is served by US Airways, Air Canada, Air South, American Eagle, Conair, Delta's Atlantic Southeast Airlines, G. P. Express, Jet Xpress, Midway, and Spirit. **Hilton Head Island Airport** (☎ 803/689–5400) is served by US Airways Express. **Savannah International Airport** (☞ Savannah *in* Georgia) is about an hour's drive from Hilton Head.

By Train

Amtrak (☎ 800/872–7245) does not make stops in this area, although several of its stops are within driving distance: Florence is about 70 mi northwest of the Grand Strand; Yemassee, about 22 mi northwest of Beaufort; and Savannah, about 40 mi southwest of Hilton Head.

Exploring the Coast

With its high-rise beachfront hotels, nightlife, and amusement parks, **Myrtle Beach** is the hub of the Grand Strand. Downtown has a festive look, with its T-shirt shops, ice cream parlors, and amusement parks, including the **Myrtle Beach Pavilion and Amusement Park** (✉ 9th Ave. N and Ocean Blvd., ☎ 803/448–6456), **Ripleys Believe It or Not Museum** (✉ 901 N. Ocean Blvd., ☎ 803/448–2331), and the **Myrtle Beach National Wax Museum** (✉ 1000 N. Ocean Blvd., ☎ 803/448–9921). Attractions are open daily from mid-March through early October, but the schedule varies the rest of the year.

★ **Murrells Inlet,** a picturesque fishing village where you'll find fishing charters and some of the most popular seafood restaurants on the Strand, is south of Myrtle Beach via U.S. 17. **Brookgreen Gardens** (☎ 803/237–4218 or 800/849–1931), a few miles south of Murells Inlet off U.S. 17, is set on four former Colonial rice plantations. Begun in 1931, the gardens contain more than 2,000 plant species as well as more than 500 sculptures, including works by Frederic Remington and Daniel Chester French. Several miles down U.S. 17 from Brookgreen Gardens,

Pawleys Island has weathered old summer cottages nestled in groves of oleander and oak. The famed Pawleys Island hammocks have been made by hand here since 1880.

Georgetown, on the shores of Winyah Bay at the end of the Grand Strand, was founded in 1729 and soon became the center of America's Colonial rice empire. Today you can enjoy its quaint waterfront and historic homes and churches. The **Rice Museum** (⊠ Front and Screven Sts., ☎ 803/546–7423) traces the history of rice cultivation through maps, tools, and dioramas. It is housed in a graceful structure topped by an 1842 clock and tower.

Beaufort, about 18 mi east of U.S. 17 on U.S. 21 (about 70 mi southeast of Charleston) is a handsome waterfront town. Established in 1710, it achieved prosperity at the end of the 18th century, when Sea Island cotton became a major cash crop. A few lavish houses built by wealthy landowners and merchants have been converted into bed-and-breakfast inns or museums; others are open for tours part of the year. The **Arsenal/Beaufort Museum,** housed in a Gothic-style arsenal built in 1795 and remodeled in 1852, has exhibits on prehistoric relics, Native American pottery, the Revolutionary and Civil wars, and decorative arts. ⊠ *713 Craven St.,* ☎ *803/525–7077. Closed Wed., Sun.*

Hilton Head Island, a 42-square-mi semitropical barrier island settled by cotton planters in the 1700s, has developed as a resort destination. Oak and pine woods, lagoons, and a temperate climate provide an incomparable environment for tennis, water sports, and golf. Choice stretches of the island are occupied by resorts, many of which have shops, restaurants, marinas, and recreational facilities open to the public.

Hilton Head is blessed with vast nature preserves, including the **Sea Pines Forest Preserve,** a 605-acre wilderness tract within the resort of the same name (☎ 803/842–1449). The preserve's most interesting site is the 3,400-year-old Native American shell ring.

What to See and Do with Children

Called the "miniature golf capital of the world," Myrtle Beach has courses on such themes as dinosaurs, tropical islands, ghosts, and pirates, as well as **Hawaiian Rumble** (⊠ 3210 Rte. 17S, ☎ 803/272–7812), with a volcano that really shakes. **Wild Water** (⊠ 910 Hwy. 17S, Surfside, ☎ 803/238–9453) is one of many area water parks that are fun for kids and adults alike.

Dining and Lodging

Freshwater and ocean fish and shellfish reign supreme throughout the region, from family-style restaurants—where they're served with hush puppies and coleslaw—to elegant resorts and upscale restaurants featuring haute cuisine. You can have your choice of hotels, cottages, villas, or high-rise condominiums. Attractive package plans are available between Labor Day and spring break. For price ranges *see* Charts 1 (B) and 2 (A) *in* On the Road with Fodor's.

Beaufort

$$$$ ✕🔟 **Beaufort Inn.** Guest rooms in this peach-color 1907 Victorian have pine floors, tasteful floral and plaid fabrics, and comfortable chairs. The inn's superb restaurant serves unique Low Country specialties. Dinner highlights include benne-seed shrimp and crab cakes and peanut-encrusted chicken in a ginger-cilantro peanut sauce. ⊠ *809 Port Republic St., 29902,* ☎ *803/521–9000, ℻ 803/521–9500. 15 rooms. Restaurant. Full breakfast, afternoon tea. AE, MC, V.*

$$$$ **★** ⊞ **Rhett House Inn.** This stately 1820 Greek Revival mansion in the center of town is popular among visiting celebrities, who have included Barbra Streisand, Jeff Bridges, and Dennis Quaid. Completely refurbished by the owners, the inn is filled with antiques and original art. ⊠ *1009 Craven St., 29902,* ☎ *803/524–9030,* F̲A̲X̲ *803/524–1310. 10 rooms. Continental breakfast, high tea. AE, MC, V.*

$$$$ ⊞ **Two Suns Inn.** Overlooking the water, this 1917 B&B is run by the gregarious Kay family. Each room has its own theme—from Victorian to Asian—and your hosts offer everything from gourmet breakfasts to sightseeing advice to business facilities. ⊠ *1705 Bay St., 29902,* ☎ F̲A̲X̲ *803/522–1122 or* ☎ *800/532–4244. 5 rooms. AE, MC, V.*

Georgetown

$$$–$$$$ ⊞ **1790 House.** Built in the center of town after the Revolution, at the peak of Georgetown's rice culture, this restored white Georgian house with a wraparound porch contains Colonial antique and reproduction furnishings. ⊠ *630 Highmarket St., 29440,* ☎ *803/546–4821 or 800/ 890–7432. 6 rooms. Bicycles. Full breakfast, evening refreshments. AE, D, MC, V.*

$ ✕ **Kudzu Bakery.** Here you can lunch on flavorful soups, sandwiches with homemade breads, and the best desserts in town. ⊠ *714 Front St.,* ☎ *803/546–1847. MC, V. Closed Wed., Sun. No dinner.*

Hilton Head Island

$$$$ ✕ **Harbourmaster's.** This spacious restaurant with harbor views offers such dishes as chateaubriand and New Zealand rack of lamb with brandy demiglaze. After dining you can linger in Neptune's Lounge. ⊠ *Shelter Cove Marina off U.S. 278,* ☎ *803/785–3030. Reservations essential. Jacket required. AE, DC, MC, V. Closed Sun. and Jan.*

$$$ **★** ✕ **Starfire Contemporary Bistro.** Ultrafresh ingredients are served in a pleasingly unique way at this small, hip eatery. Try the wild mushroom soup with roasted rosemary, salmon with spiced seed crust atop a crunchy cucumber salad, and chocolate sorbet with homemade biscotti. ⊠ *37 New Orleans Rd.,* ☎ *803/785–3434. AE, MC, V. No lunch.*

$$$$ **★** ⊞ **Westin Resort, Hilton Head Island.** Among the island's most luxurious properties, this sprawling horseshoe-shape hotel has a lushly landscaped oceanfront setting. Recently redecorated guest rooms have down pillows, hunting colors, and comfortable wicker and contemporary furniture. Public areas display fine Asian porcelain, screens, and paintings. ⊠ *2 Grass Lawn Ave., 29928,* ☎ *803/681–4000 or 800/228– 3000,* F̲A̲X̲ *803/681–1087. 450 rooms. 3 restaurants, 2 lobby lounges, pool, health club, beach, children's programs. AE, D, DC, MC, V.*

$$$–$$$$ ⊞ **Palmetto Dunes Resort.** This huge complex includes the Hyatt Regency Hilton Head, the island's largest resort hotel. Rooms are spacious, with light-color carpets, a king- or queen-size bed, and works by local artists. Each has a balcony, a coffeemaker, and an iron and ironing board. Golf and tennis are nearby. The complex also includes the Hilton Resort, formerly the Mariner's Inn. These spacious oceanfront rooms have kitchenettes and are colorfully decorated in a Caribbean motif. *Hyatt:* ⊠ *U.S. 278 (Box 6167), 29938,* ☎ *803/ 785–1234 or 800/233–1234,* F̲A̲X̲ *803/842–4695. 506 rooms. 3 restaurants, bar, indoor pool, outdoor pool, spa, health club, beach, boating, concierge floor. AE, D, DC, MC, V. Hilton:* ⊠ *23 Ocean La., 29938,* ☎ *803/842–8000 or 800/845–8001,* F̲A̲X̲ *803/842–4988. 323 rooms. Restaurant, pool, hot tub, sauna, health club, volleyball, boating, fishing, bicycles. AE, D, DC, MC, V.*

Myrtle Beach

$$ ✕ **Sea Captain's House.** This picturesque restaurant with nautical decor and a fireplace has sweeping ocean views. Home-baked breads and desserts accompany Low Country fare. ✉ *3002 N. Ocean Blvd.,* ☎ *803/448–8082. AE, D, MC, V. Closed mid-Dec.–mid-Feb.*

$ ✕ **Latif's Cafe and Bar.** The lunch crowd loves this hot spot, which has pastry cases full of homemade breads, cakes, and cookies. The soups are garden fresh, and there are yummy shrimp and black bean cakes, as well as traditional and Asian chicken salads. ✉ *503 61st Ave. N,* ☎ *803/449–1716. AE, D, DC, MC, V. No dinner Sun.*

$$$–$$$$ ⌂ **The Breakers Resort Hotel.** The Breakers is one of the better values along the Grand Strand. There are 24 types of room configurations—the suites with kitchenettes are ideal for families. All the major attractions are within walking distance. ✉ *2006 N. Ocean Blvd. (Box 485), 29578-0485,* ☎ *803/444–4444 or 800/845–0688,* 📠 *803/626–5001. 390 rooms. Restaurant, bar, 3 outdoor pools, 1 indoor pool, 4 hot tubs, saunas, exercise room, video games. AE, D, DC, MC, V.*

$$$–$$$$ ⌂ **Kingston Plantation.** Set amid 145 acres of ocean-side woodlands, this 20-story glass-sheathed tower is part of the Kingston Plantation complex of shops, restaurants, hotels, and condominiums; it's easily the nicest resort in town. Guest rooms have bleached-wood furnishings and attractive art. ✉ *9800 Lake Dr., 29572,* ☎ *803/449–0006 or 800/876–0010,* 📠 *803/497–1110. 614 suites. 2 restaurants, 2 bars, kitchenettes, sauna, 6 tennis courts, aerobics, health club. AE, D, DC, MC, V.*

North Myrtle Beach

$$–$$$ ✕ **Oak Harbor Inn.** A local favorite since it opened in 1990, this airy restaurant is on a quiet stretch of beach and overlooks picturesque Vereen's Marina. A house specialty is chicken Annie: boneless breast of chicken in puff pastry laced with ham and Swiss and blue cheeses, and garnished with Mornay sauce. ✉ *1407 13th Ave. N,* ☎ *803/249–4737. AE, D, MC, V. No lunch.*

Pawleys Island

$ ✕ **Island Country Store.** This little place, though tucked in an unattractive spot, has terrific crab cakes plus hickory-smoked barbecue, roast chicken, and pizza (and they deliver). ✉ *The Island Shops, U.S. 17,* ☎ *803/237–8465. AE, MC, V.*

$$$–$$$$ ⌂ **Litchfield Beach and Golf Resort.** The inn's contemporary gray-blue wood units on stilts, as well as a diverse range of other rentals from condos to villas, are within the expansive grounds, which include three private golf clubs. The beach is a short walk away. ✉ *U.S. 17, 2 mi north of Pawleys Island; Drawer 320, 29585,* ☎ *803/237–3000 or 800/845–1897,* 📠 *803/237–4282. 96 suites, 254 condominiums, cottages, and villas. Restaurant, 2 pools, spa, 3 18-hole golf courses, 24 tennis courts, health club, racquetball. AE, D, DC, MC, V.*

Nightlife and the Arts

Nightlife

Country-and-western shows are popular along the Grand Strand, which is fast emerging as the eastern focus of country music culture. Music lovers have several shows to choose from, including the 2,250-seat **Alabama Theater** (✉ At Barefoot Landing, 4750 U.S. 17, North Myrtle Beach, ☎ 803/272–1111 or 800/342–2262); **Carolina Opry** (✉ 82nd Ave. N, Myrtle Beach, ☎ 803/238–8888 or 800/843–6779); **Eddie Miles Theater: Salute to Elvis** (✉ 701 Main St., North Myrtle Beach,

☎ 803/238–8888 or 800/843–6779); **Dolly Parton's Dixie Stampede** (✉ 8901B U.S. 17 Business, Myrtle Beach, ☎ 803/497–9700 or 800/433–4401); and **Legends in Concert** (✉ 301 U.S. 17 Business, Surfside Beach, ☎ 803/238–7827 or 800/843–6779). The **House of Blues** (✉ 4640 U.S. 17S, N. Myrtle Beach, ☎ 803/272–3000), adjacent to Barefoot Landing, presents blues, rock, jazz, and country on stages in its restaurant and in its concert hall.

Shagging (the state dance) is popular at **Studebaker's** (✉ U.S. 17 at 21st Ave. N, Myrtle Beach, ☎ 803/626–3855 or 803/448–9747). You can also try the shag at **Duck's** (✉ 229 Main St., North Myrtle Beach, ☎ 803/249–3858). At **Broadway at the Beach** (✉ U.S. 17 Bypass between 21st and 24th Sts., N. Myrtle Beach, ☎ 803/444–3200) you'll find an assortment of bars and nightclubs, including Hard Rock Cafe, Planet Hollywood and the new NASCAR cafe.

Hilton Head's hotels and resorts feature a variety of musical entertainment. **Monkey Business** (✉ Park Plaza, ☎ 803/686–3545) is a new dance nightclub in Hilton Head. In Beaufort, **Bananas** (✉ 910 Bay St., ☎ 803/522–0910) has live bands on weekends. **Plum's** (✉ 904½ Bay St., ☎ 803/525–1946), also in Beaufort, has a late-night bar and live bands during the weekends.

The Arts

Area **festivals** include the Canadian/American Days Festival in March, the Sun Fun Festival in early July, and the Atalaya Arts Festival in fall. At Art in the Park, held in Myrtle Beach's Chapin Park three times each summer, you can buy handmade crafts and original artwork by local artists. Hilton Head's new **Self Family Arts Center** (✉ Shelter Cove Lane, ☎ 803/842–2787) has a theater and art gallery, including a theater program for youth. During the warmer months there are free **outdoor concerts** at Harbour Town and Shelter Cove in Hilton Head.

Outdoor Activities and Sports

Biking

Pedaling is popular along the firmly packed beaches and pathways of **Hilton Head Island.** Rentals are available at most hotels and resorts and at such shops as Harbour Town Bicycles (✉ Heritage Plaza, ☎ 803/785–3546) and South Beach Cycles (✉ Sea Pines Plantation, ☎ 803/671–2453).

Fishing

Fishing is usually good from early spring through December. Licenses, required for fresh- and saltwater fishing from a private boat, can be purchased at local tackle shops. The **Grand Strand** has several piers and jetties, and fishing and sightseeing excursions depart from Murrells Inlet, North Myrtle Beach, Little River, and the Intracoastal Waterway at Route 544. Fishing tournaments are popular. On **Hilton Head** you can fish, pick oysters, dig for clams, or cast for shrimp.

Golf

The Grand Strand has 100 courses, most of them public and many of championship quality. **Myrtle Beach Golf Holiday** (☎ 803/448–5942 or 800/845–4653) offers package plans throughout the year; most area hotels have golf packages, too. Some of **Hilton Head**'s 29 courses are among the world's best; several are open to the public, including Palmetto Dunes (☎ 803/785–1138), Sea Pines (☎ 803/842–8484), Port Royal (☎ 803/689–5600), and Shipyard Golf and Racquet Clubs (☎ 803/785–5353). Sea Pines' Harbour Town Golf Links (☎ 803/671–2448) hosts the annual MCI Classic.

Horseback Riding

On Hilton Head trails wind through woods; horses can be rented at Sea Pines' **Lawton Stables** (☎ 803/671–2586).

Tennis

There are more than 200 courts throughout the **Grand Strand,** including free municipal courts in Myrtle Beach, North Myrtle Beach, and Surfside Beach. **Hilton Head** offers more than 300 courts; four resorts on the island—Sea Pines, Shipyard Plantation, Palmetto Dunes, and Port Royal—are rated among the top 50 tennis destinations in the United States. Each April top women professionals participate in the Family Circle Magazine Cup Tennis Tournament at Sea Pines Racquet Club.

Water Sports

In **Myrtle Beach** surfboards, Hobie Cats, Jet Skis, Windsurfers, and sailboats are for rent at Downwind Sails (⊠ Ocean Blvd. at 29th Ave. S, ☎ 803/448–7245). On **Hilton Head** you can take windsurfing or kayaking lessons and rent equipment from Outside Hilton Head, at either Sea Pines Resort's South Beach Marina (☎ 803/671–2643) or Shelter Cove Plaza (☎ 803/686–6996).

Beaches

Almost all **Grand Strand** beaches are open to the public. The widest expanses are in North Myrtle Beach. The ocean side of **Hilton Head Island** has wide stretches of gently sloping white sand extending the island's 12-mi length. Although resort beaches on Hilton Head are reserved for guests and residents, there are about 35 public-beach entrances, from Folly Field to South Forest Beach near Sea Pines.

Shopping

The Grand Strand is a great place to find bargains. **Waccamaw Pottery and Outlet Park** (⊠ U.S. 501 at the Waterway, Myrtle Beach, ☎ 803/236–1100) is one of the nation's largest outlet centers, with 3 mi of shops. In North Myrtle Beach shoppers head for the **Barefoot Landing** shopping center (⊠ 4898 S. Kings Hwy., ☎ 803/272–8349). The **Hammock Shops at Pawleys Island** (⊠ U.S. 17, ☎ 803/237–8448) sell the famous handmade hammocks; there are about a dozen boutiques and restaurants, too. Hilton Head specialty shops include **Red Piano Art Gallery** (⊠ 220 Cordillo Pkwy., ☎ 803/785–2318) and, for shell and sand-dollar jewelry, the **Bird's Nest** (⊠ Coligny Plaza, off Coligny Circle, ☎ 803/785–3737). On St. Helena Island near Beaufort, the **Red Piano Too Art Gallery** (⊠ 853 Sea Island Parkway, ☎ 803/838–2241) is filled with quirky folk and southern art, beads, and pottery.

ELSEWHERE IN SOUTH CAROLINA

Columbia

Arriving and Departing

I–20 leads northeast from Georgia to Columbia. I–77 runs south to Columbia, where it terminates. I–26 runs north–south through town.

What to See and Do

Columbia, in the middle of the state, was founded in 1786 as the capital city. The capitol, the **State House** (⊠ Main and Gervais Sts., ☎ 803/734–2430), completed in 1855 from local granite, contains marble and mahogany accents and a replica of Houdon's statue of George Washington. The capitol is closed for renovation through 1997 and part of 1998, but areas of the grounds are accessible, and you can see where Sherman shelled the State House, each hit marked by a bronze star.

The **South Carolina State Museum** (✉ 301 Gervais St., ☎ 803/737–4595), set in a refurbished textile mill, interprets state history through exhibits on archaeology, fine arts, and scientific and technological accomplishments. It has a sophisticated gift shop.

★ Two miles from the capitol area is **Riverbanks Zoological Park and Botanical Garden** (✉ I–26 at Greystone Blvd., ☎ 803/779–8717), with more than 450 species of birds and animals cared for in their natural habitats. The park also has a reptile house, an aquarium, and a cage-free aviary with a tropical rain forest.

The **Columbia Metropolitan Convention and Visitors Bureau** (✉ 1012 Gervais St., Box 15, 29202, ☎ 803/254–0479 or 800/264–4884) has brochures and maps; it also presents a short film on area history.

Dining and Lodging

$$–$$$ ✗ **Motor Supply Co. Bistro.** Dine on cuisine from around the world at this restaurant in the heart of town. Fresh seafood and homemade desserts are among the many offerings. On Sunday there's brunch and dinner. ✉ 920 Gervais St., ☎ 803/256–6687. AE, DC, MC, V.

$–$$ ✗ **Maurice Gourmet Barbecue–Piggie Park.** One of the South's best-
★ known barbecue chefs, Maurice Bessinger has a fervent national following for his mustard sauce–based, pit-cooked ham barbecue. He also serves barbecued chicken, ribs, and baked beans. ✉ 1600 Charleston Hwy., ☎ 803/796–0220. D, MC, V.

$$$ ▥ **Adam's Mark.** This upscale downtown hotel is near state offices and the University of South Carolina. The freshly decorated hotel has leather armchairs, suspended lights, and brass accents in public areas. Guest rooms are contemporary, with period reproduction armoires and desks. Finlay's Restaurant, in a spectacular atrium, has American fare. ✉ 1200 Hampton St., 29201, ☎ 803/771–7000 or 800/444–2326, FAX 803/254–2911. 300 rooms. Restaurant, sports bar, indoor pool, hot tub, health club, business services. AE, D, DC, MC, V.

$$$ ▥ **Claussen's Inn.** This small hotel, in a converted bakery warehouse in the attractive Five Points neighborhood, is near nightlife and specialty shops. Undergoing a sprucing-up at press time, it has an airy lobby with a Mexican tile floor; the rooms, some two stories, are arranged around it. There are eight loft suites with downstairs sitting rooms and spiral staircases to sleeping areas furnished with period reproductions and four-poster beds. ✉ 2003 Greene St., 29205, ☎ 803/765–0440 or 800/622–3382, FAX 803/799–7924. 29 rooms. Hot tub, meeting rooms. AE, MC, V.

6 The Mississippi Valley

Arkansas, Kentucky, Louisiana, Mississippi, Tennessee

By Craig
Seligman

Updated by
Honey Naylor

*S*tand on a shore of the Mississippi River, and you're swept with large emotions: Here are the waters that have sweetened the delta and fed the imagination of the South. The five states that constitute the Mississippi Valley all sweat history; each has Civil War battlefields and citizens with long, long memories. You can find the New South here, of course, but the Old South—of Cotton Is King, of Christ Is Coming, of aristocracy and its flip side, poverty—is never far away.

The soil is rich: No sight in the world affects a southerner like the fields of cotton ready for harvest. The region isn't only farmland, though; Tennessee, Kentucky, and Arkansas are blessed with some of the most beautiful mountain scenery in America. The metropolises, from Louisville to Shreveport to Jackson, have their big-city grandeur and decay. Outside them you'll see the regal old plantation houses, but you'll also pass along godforsaken stretches of state road with tumbledown shanties that can look more desolate than any city slum.

Yet the folk culture that sprouted among the poor people of these states took root and spread its branches far out into the world. Nashville calls itself the capital of country music; Memphis will always mean rhythm and blues; New Orleans is the cradle of jazz. And all three cities—all three musics—had a hand in delivering rock and roll. Graceland, the Memphis mansion where Elvis lived and died in tacky majesty, stands now as an unofficial monument to the best American art and the worst American taste.

The region gave the world not only music beloved the world over but also its own revered cuisine. A visitor can find ambrosial ribs in the barbecue palaces of Memphis or at hole-in-the-wall luncheonettes on Arkansas roadsides. Those lucky enough to have tasted fried chicken or fried catfish down here have been known to lose their taste for chicken and catfish anywhere else. Forget low fat. Forget nouvelle. The scent of collard greens stewing in pork fat, of sweet potatoes glistening with sugar and butter, emanates from some deep place as central to the culture as the one that produced the Mississippi blues of Muddy Waters and the long, hypnotic pauses of Faulkner.

Farther downriver the spirit changes. The sauces become more complex; the music turns airier, and so does the mood. The fundamentalism of the Bible Belt loosens into a kind of good-time Catholicism whose motto is *Laissez les bons temps rouler*—Let the good times roll. Cajun festivals, for everything from gumbo to petroleum, are just about always happening—any excuse for a party. The biggest excuse, of course, is Mardi Gras (Fat Tuesday), the day before Lent begins, which is celebrated throughout southern Louisiana and all along the Gulf Coast. By the time the Mississippi gets this close to the Gulf, its width is monumental, but the water is warm, unhurried. And so is New Orleans. It's as though the river chose this city as the place to deposit all the richness it has picked up on its long journey. You come here to slow down, relax, enjoy the good life, and dedicate your days to pleasure.

When to Go

The best times to visit the Mississippi Valley states are **April** and **October,** when temperatures and humidity are comfortable: in Louisiana and Mississippi, the mid-70s; in the mountains of Arkansas, Kentucky, and Tennessee, the 60s, cooling off to the mid-40s at night. In **spring** everything is in glorious bloom, while in the **fall** the trees, especially in the mountains, are bright with turning leaves. You can tour magnificent historic mansions in spring and fall.

If you dislike crowds, avoid New Orleans during Mardi Gras (February or March, depending on when Easter falls) and Louisville during the Kentucky Derby (the first Saturday in May). Visits during these times require flight and hotel reservations long in advance; also, expect hotel prices to jump.

Festivals and Seasonal Events

Winter

JAN.–FEB.➤ The **Dixie National Rodeo/Western Festival/Livestock Show** (☎ 601/961–4000 or 800/354–7695) in **Jackson, Mississippi,** offers rodeos and other events.

FEB. 11➤ **Mardi Gras** (☎ 504/566–5031) in **New Orleans, Louisiana,** caps two or more weeks of madness—street festivals, parades with fantastic floats, marching bands, and eye-popping costumes.

Spring

MAR.–APR.➤ In Mississippi, **spring pilgrimages** to elegant antebellum mansions are held throughout the state, with **Natchez** (☎ 800/647–6724 or 800/647–6742) claiming grande-dame status, followed by **Columbus** (☎ 800/327–2686) and **Vicksburg** (☎ 800/221–3536).

LATE APR.➤ The **Annual Arkansas Folk Festival** (☎ 501/269–8068), in **Mountain View,** salutes the folk culture of the Ozarks with music, dance, crafts, a parade, and a rodeo. The **Festival International de Louisiane** (☎ 318/232–3737), in **Lafayette,** brings together more than 600 local and far-flung performers in music, visual arts, theater, dance, cinema, and cuisine for a dizzying globe-grazing extravaganza.

LATE APR.–EARLY MAY➤ The **New Orleans Jazz & Heritage Festival** (☎ 504/522–4786) draws thousands of musicians, fans, and artisans for a 10-day all-out jam session.

The Mississippi Valley

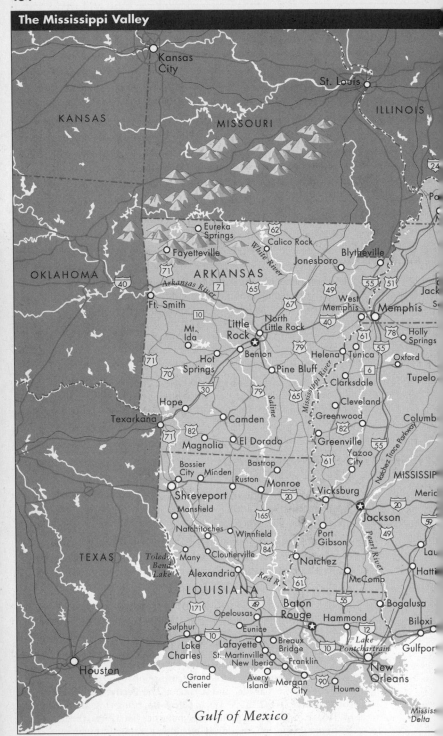

Kansas City

St. Louis

ILLINOIS

KANSAS

MISSOURI

24

OKLAHOMA

Eureka Springs

62 Calico Rock

White River

Fayetteville

Blytheville

71

ARKANSAS

Jonesboro

40

Arkansas River

7

65

49

West Memphis

55 51

Jack

Ft. Smith

10

67

Memphis

78

Mt. Ida

Little Rock

North Little Rock

40

61

Holly Springs

Benton

79

Helena

Tunica

55

Oxford

Hot Springs

70

Pine Bluff

6

Clarksdale

Tupelo

71

30

Saline

79

Mississippi River

Hope

65

Cleveland

Texarkana

Camden

Greenwood

Columb

82

Magnolia

El Dorado

Greenville

55

Bossier City

Minden

Bastrop

61

Yazoo City

MISSISSIP

Ruston

Monroe

Vicksburg

Meric

Shreveport

20

20

Jackson

59

Mansfield

165

49

Natchitoches

Winnfield

Port Gibson

Lau

TEXAS

Toledo Bend Lake

Many

Cloutierville

84

Natchez

Pearl River

Hatti

Alexandria

Red R.

McComb

LOUISIANA

61

171

Opelousas

49

Baton Rouge

Hammond

55

Bogalusa

Sulphur

Eunice

12

Biloxi

10

Lafayette

Breaux Bridge

Lake Pontchartrain

Gulfpor

Lake Charles

St. Martinville

New Iberia

Franklin

10

Grand Chenier

Avery Island

Morgan City

90

Houma

New Orleans

Houston

Gulf of Mexico

Mississ Delta

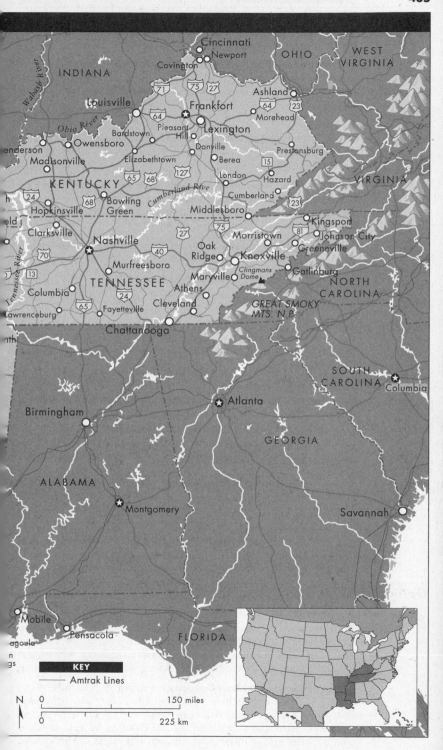

INDIANA

Cincinnati
Newport
Covington
OHIO
WEST VIRGINIA

71
75
27

Louisville
Frankfort
Ashland
64
23

64
Lexington
Morehead

Ohio River
Bardstown
Pleasant Hill
Danville
Prestonsburg

Owensboro
Elizabethtown
Berea
15

enderson
Madisonville
127

KENTUCKY
65
68
London
Hazard
VIRGINIA

h
24
68
Cumberland Rive
Cumberland
23

eld
Hopkinsville
Bowling Green
Middlesboro
Kingsport
81
Johnson City

Clarksville
75
Morristown
Greeneville

Nashville
27
Oak Ridge
Knoxville
Gatlinburg

70
40
Maryville
Clingmans Dome
NORTH CAROLINA

13
Murfreesboro
Athens
GREAT SMOKY MTS. N.P.

Columbia
TENNESSEE
24
Cleveland
SOUTH CAROLINA
Columbia

awrenceburg
65
Fayetteville

nth
Chattanooga

Birmingham
Atlanta

GEORGIA

ALABAMA

Montgomery
Savannah

Mobile
Pensacola
agoula
n
gs
FLORIDA

KEY
— Amtrak Lines

N

0   150 miles
0   225 km

MAY➤ The **Memphis in May International Festival** (☎ 901/525–4611), a monthlong salute to the city, includes music on Beale Street and the **World Championship Barbecue Cooking Contest.**

MAY 3➤ In **Louisville** the **Kentucky Derby,** one of horse racing's premier events, is preceded by a 10-day festival (☎ 502/584– 6383) with parades, riverboat races, and many a mint julep. For racing information, call Churchill Downs (☎ 502/636–4402).

Summer

EARLY JUNE➤ The **Great French Market Tomato Festival** (☎ 504/522–2621), in **New Orleans,** is one of many food festivals held throughout the state this month.

MID-JUNE➤ The **International Country Music Fan Fair** (☎ 615/889–7503), in **Nashville, Tennessee,** lets country music fans mix with their favorite stars in a weeklong celebration featuring live shows, exhibits, autograph sessions, and special concerts.

AUG.➤ **Memphis, Tennessee,** pulls out all the stops for the **Elvis International Tribute Week** (☎ 901/543–5333 or 901/332–3322).

LATE AUG.➤ **Louisville's Kentucky State Fair** (☎ 502/367–5000) draws some half-million people, with rooster-crowing contests, top-name concerts, a horse show, and an amusement park.

Autumn

EARLY SEPT.➤ The **Zydeco Music Festival** (☎ 318/942–2392), in **Plaisance, Louisiana,** is the original festival devoted to the state's indigenous musical genre.

LATE SEPT.➤ The **Festivals Acadiens** (☎ 318/232–3737) attract more than 100,000 annually to see, hear, taste, and experience Cajun life in **Lafayette,** the capital of French Louisiana.

EARLY OCT.➤ The first full weekend of the month, **Allart, Tennessee,** hosts the two-day **Great Pumpkin Festival** (☎ 615/879–9948), with contests, crafts, and gospel singing.

EARLY OCT.➤ Held on the weekend preceding Columbus Day, the **King Biscuit Blues Festival** (☎ 870/338–9144), named after a revered local blues radio-program broadcast since the 1940s, draws national and regional blues and gospel acts to **Helena, Arkansas.**

LATE OCT.➤ The **Canton Flea Market Arts and Crafts Festival** (☎ 601/859–1307 or 800/844–3369), the largest one-day crafts show in the Southeast, takes place on Courthouse Square in **Canton, Mississippi.**

Getting Around the Mississippi Valley

By Boat

In Louisiana ferries cross the Mississippi River in New Orleans, Carville, and St. Francisville. In Tennessee there are ferries across the Cumberland River near Nashville, Cumberland City, and at Dixon Springs; and across the Tennessee River at Dayton, Clifton, Saltillo, and near Decatur.

The **Delta Queen Steamboat Company** (✉ Robin St. Wharf, New Orleans, LA 70130, ☎ 800/543–1949), the nation's only overnight riverboat, offers paddle-wheeler cruises on the Mississippi, Ohio, Tennessee, Arkansas, Atchafalaya, and Cumberland rivers as far east as Chattanooga, as far west as Tulsa, Oklahoma, and as far north as Minneapolis.

By Bus

Greyhound Lines (☎ 800/231–2222) provides service to cities and towns throughout the region.

By Car

I–30 cuts diagonally across southern and central Arkansas. I–40 goes east–west through central Arkansas and central Tennessee. I–24 cuts diagonally across western Kentucky. I–64 runs east–west through Louisville. I–65 is a north–south route through Tennessee and central Kentucky. I–75 runs north–south through eastern Kentucky and Tennessee. I–55 runs from southern Louisiana north through Mississippi and Arkansas. I–49 cuts a diagonal swath north—south between Lafayette and Shreveport. I–10 runs east–west through southern Mississippi and New Orleans. I–20 is the major east–west road through northern Louisiana and Mississippi. There are bridges over the Mississippi River in New Orleans, Destrehan, Lutcher, Donaldsonville, and Baton Rouge, Louisiana, and in Vicksburg, in Natchez, and near Greenville, Mississippi. The river is bridged in Arkansas at Lake Village and Helena; in Tennessee at Memphis and east of Dyerburg; and in Kentucky at Hickman, Columbus, and Cairo.

By Plane

New Orleans International Airport (☎ 504/464–0831), **Cincinnati/Northern Kentucky International Airport** (☎ 606/283–3151), **Nashville International Airport** (☎ 615/275–1600), and **Standiford Field** (⊠ Louisville, ☎ 502/367–4636) are served by most domestic carriers.

By Train

Amtrak (☎ 800/872–7245) serves all states of the Mississippi Valley.

ARKANSAS

By Marcia
Schnedler

Capital	Little Rock
Population	2,510,000
Motto	The People Rule
State Bird	Mockingbird
State Flower	Apple blossom
Postal Abbreviation	AR

Statewide Visitor Information

Arkansas Department of Parks and Tourism (⊠ 1 Capitol Mall, Little Rock 72201, ☎ 501/682–7777 or 800/628–8725). The Arkansas Tourist Information Center has 13 branches on major highways at locations near the borders with other states.

Scenic Drives

Arkansas's billing as the Natural State is appropriate: The state has more than 17 million acres of public and private forests, 600,000 acres of lakes, and 9,700 mi of rivers and streams. Its **Ozark** and **Ouachita mountains** rival New England's for scenic vistas and fall colors, which can be seen along meandering roadways, including seven State and National Forest Scenic byways. **Route 7** between Arkadelphia and Harrison winds over both ranges and through two national forests. The **Talimena Trail** stretches across mountain crests from Mena to Talihina, Oklahoma, passing through **Queen Wilhelmina State Park.** The **St. Francis Scenic Byway**—part of the **Great River Road** that follows the Mississippi River—leads through wild terrain between Marianna and Helena/West Helena.

National and State Parks

Arkansas boasts 340 public and private campgrounds with some 9,800 campsites and has more than 300 trails stretching over 1,622 mi. The *Camper's and Hiker's Guide* and *Arkansas State Parks* booklet, both available from the state tourism department (☞ Statewide Visitor Information, *above*), provide locations, fees, and other useful information. Arkansas also is a mecca for fly-fishing and warm-water angling, as well as for hunting duck, deer, wild turkey and small game. Contact the **Arkansas Game and Fish Commission** (☎ 501/223–6378 or 800/364–4263).

National Parks

★ The **Buffalo National River** (⊠ Box 1173, Harrison 72602-1173, ☎ 870/741–5443), backed by limestone bluffs, became the first federally protected river in 1972. Its 132 mi are noted for canoeing, white-water rafting, hiking, fishing, wilderness areas, and historic sites. The **Ouachita National Forest** (⊠ USFS, Box 1270, Hot Springs 71902, ☎ 501/321–5202), dotted by crystal lakes, is the oldest and largest in the South. The **Ozark National Forest** (⊠ Box 1008, Russellville 72801, ☎ 501/968–2354) encompasses wild hills, hollows, rivers, and streams, as well as Arkansas's highest peak—the 2,753 ft of Mt. Magazine. **Hot Springs National Park** (⊠ Box 1860, Hot Springs 71902, ☎ 501/624–3383) features Bathhouse Row—eight renovated turn-of-the-century spa facilities—plus campgrounds and hiking in nearby Gulpha Gorge. **Felsenthal National Wildlife Refuge** (⊠ Box 1157, Crossett 71635, ☎ 870/364–3167) is a mosaic of wetlands, lakes, and rivers that draw fishers, boaters, and wildlife watchers.

State Parks

Arkansas has 49 state parks, museums, and monuments; 27 have campgrounds, and 12 include lodges and cabins. **Devil's Den** (✉ 11333 W. Ark. 74, West Fork 72774, ☎ 501/761–3325) is set in an Ozark valley that has caves, crevices, bluffs, and Civilian Conservation Corps structures from the 1930s. **Village Creek** (✉ 201 CR 754, Wynne 72396, ☎ 870/238–2440) lies atop Crowley's Ridge, a forested highland, unusual in this area, which slices through the Mississippi Delta. Volunteers participate in seasonal excavations in **Parkin Archaeological State Park** (✉ Box 1110, Parkin 72373-1110, ☎ 870/755–2500) to uncover the remains of a Native American village chronicled by Hernando de Soto's Spanish expedition of 1541. **Petit Jean** (✉ Rte. 3, Box 340, Morrilton 72110, ☎ 501/727–5441), perched on a mountaintop, comprises canyons, waterfalls, a lake, a lodge, and cabins, plus the Museum of Automobiles. **Lake Chicot** (✉ 2542 Ark. 257, Lake Village 71653, ☎ 870/265–5480) sits on a 20-mi-long oxbow lake edged by cypress and noted for fishing and bird-watching.

LITTLE ROCK

Little Rock, on the south bank of the Arkansas River, is the state's geographical, governmental, and financial center, as well as a major convention hub. Spanish and French explorers passed the site in the 16th and 17th centuries, naming it La Petite Roche because of a small outcrop that marked the transition from the flat Mississippi Delta region to the Ouachita Mountain foothills. A simple translation turned the town into Little Rock when it became the territorial capital in 1821; the capital had been at Arkansas Post, the first European settlement in the lower Mississippi River valley. Most visitors come to Arkansas to enjoy the outdoors, and they can find it within an hour of Little Rock's downtown: world-renowned duck hunting in rice-growing regions to the southeast and wild scenic vistas, streams, and trails in forested mountains to the north and west.

Visitor Information

Little Rock Convention & Visitors Bureau (✉ Box 3232, Little Rock 72203, ☎ 501/376–4781 or 800/844–4781).

Arriving and Departing

By Car

I–40 and I–30 lead to Little Rock, as do U.S. 65 and U.S. 67.

By Plane

Most major airlines fly into **Little Rock National Airport** (✉ 501/372–3439), 5 mi east of downtown off I–440. Major Little Rock hotels provide airport shuttles. Cab fare to downtown is about $8. For taxis, call **Black & White/Yellow Cabs** (☎ 501/374–0333) or **Capitol Cab** (☎ 501/568–0462).

Getting Around Little Rock

By Bus

Central Arkansas Transit (☎ 501/375–1163) serves Little Rock and North Little Rock.

By Car

Little Rock is easily negotiated by interstate highways and major streets. Plenty of parking facilities and taxis are available.

Exploring Little Rock

A series of free walking/driving tours lead through several historic areas in and near downtown. The **MacArthur Park Historic District** takes in a few of the remaining antebellum buildings, including the 1843 **Trapnall Hall** (✉ 423 E. Capitol Ave., ☎ 501/372–4791), as well as fine Victorian-era architecture. The birthplace of General Douglas MacArthur, in the eponymous park, is part of an 1838 arsenal being remade into a military history museum. The park also includes the modern **Arkansas Arts Center** (✉ 9th and Commerce Sts., ☎ 501/372–4000), with an outstanding children's theater, a museum school, a gift shop, and a restaurant. The **Decorative Arts Museum** (✉ 7th and Rock Sts., ☎ 501/372–4000) is set in an 1840 mansion.

The area surrounding the **governor's mansion** (✉ 1800 Center St., ☎ 501/376–6884) encompasses elegant post–Civil War and turn-of-the-century churches and homes. The 1881 Italianate **Villa Marre** (✉ 1321 S. Scott St., ☎ 501/374–9979), whose facade was featured in the TV series *Designing Women,* is now a museum.

★ Historic public buildings in the riverfront district include the **Old State House** (✉ 300 W. Markham St., ☎ 501/324–9685), constructed between 1833 and 1842 and now a museum. The **Arkansas Territorial Restoration** (✉ 200 E. 3rd St., ☎ 501/324–9351) shows off restored and furnished frontier buildings. Its museum store sells the work of more than 200 Arkansas crafts artists.

The neoclassic **state capitol** (✉ Capitol Ave. and Woodlane, ☎ 501/682–5080), built between 1899 and 1915 on a hilltop west of downtown, shows off an imposing rotunda, grand marble staircases and columns, stained-glass skylights, murals, and six intricately crafted 4-inch-thick brass doors from Tiffany & Co.

Outside Little Rock

Just 15 mi west of downtown is **Pinnacle Mountain State Park** (✉ 11901 Pinnacle Valley Rd., Roland 72135, ☎ 501/868–5806), whose habitats range from high upland peaks to river bottomlands lined with hardwoods and ancient cypress.

Less than 30 minutes east of downtown on U.S. 165 is the state park–operated **Plantation Agriculture Museum,** whose exhibits interpret the history of cotton agriculture. ✉ *4815 Hwy. 161, Scott,* ☎ *501/961–1409. Closed Mon. except holidays.*

Several miles beyond Scott off U.S. 165 sits **Toltec Mounds Archaeological State Park,** the remains of a large Native American ceremonial and governmental complex inhabited from AD 600 to AD 950. ✉ *490 Toltec Mounds Rd., Scott,* ☎ *501/961–9442. Closed Mon.*

Parks and Gardens

War Memorial Park (✉ North off I–630 at Fair Park Ave. and W. Markham St., ☎ 501/3871–4770), one of the city's oldest and most popular parks, contains a public golf course, tennis courts, a football stadium, and the baseball park of the minor-league Arkansas Travelers. It also has a fitness center, a small amusement park, and a zoo.

Riverfront Park edges both sides of the Arkansas River. On the Little Rock side it lies behind the Old State House and Convention Center, with playgrounds, a history pavilion, and an amphitheater. On the North Little Rock side it has the dock for the **Spirit** (☎ 501/376–4150), a paddlewheel riverboat that has both excursion and dining cruises.

What to See and Do with Children

In historic Union Train Station, the interactive **Children's Museum of Arkansas** lets kids make stationery in the post office, shop at the farmers' market, or contribute to the Kids Gallery of collectibles. ✉ *1400 W. Markham St.,* ☎ *501/374–6655. Closed Mon.*

The **Aerospace Education Center** (✉ 3301 E. Roosevelt Rd., ☎ 501/376–4629) has an **IMAX theater**, a small museum, and a library. The **Arkansas Museum of Science & History** (✉ 500 E. Markham St., ☎ 501/396–7050 or 800/880–6475) explores science and culture with hands-on exhibits. The **Little Rock Zoo** (✉ 1 Jonesboro Dr., ☎ 501/663–4733) has gorillas, giant anteaters, and 175 other species.

Dining and Lodging

Some of the counties outside the city are dry. For price ranges *see* Charts 1 (B) *and* 2 (B) *in* On the Road with Fodor's.

$$–$$$ ✕ **Alouette's.** This prestigious French Continental restaurant provides
★ formal and café-style settings in its richly decorated Venetian Room and somewhat more casual Salons Napoleon and Bastille. Its innovative menu changes biannually. An extensive wine list includes older vintages, and there is a full bar. ✉ *11401 N. Rodney Parham Rd.,* ☎ *501/225–4152. AE, D, DC, MC, V. Closed Sun.*

$$ ✕ **Spaule.** This casually elegant spot has won numerous national and regional awards for its new American cuisine since its 1995 debut. Its menu and wine list change monthly and feature dishes such as cornmeal-crusted fried oysters and roasted veal. Gorgonzola glazes are a specialty. ✉ *5713 Kavanaugh Blvd.,* ☎ *501/664–3663. Reservations not accepted. AE, MC, V. Closed Sun.*

$–$$ ✕ **Trio's.** Intriguing lunch and dinner menus combine Caribbean, Italian, and southwestern elements plus its trademark pasta dishes. ✉ *8201 Cantrell Rd.,* ☎ *501/221–3330. AE, D, DC, MC, V. Closed Sun.*

$ ✕ **Franke's Cafeteria.** This family-owned local institution serves simple, good food for lunch, or for an early dinner at its Rodney Parham and University restaurants. ✉ *11121 N. Rodney Parham Rd.,* ☎ *501/225–4487;* ✉ *300 S. University Ave.,* ☎ *501/663–4461;* ✉ *400 W. Capitol St.,* ☎ *501/372–1919. D, MC, V. Capitol location closed weekends.*

$$$ ▥ **Arkansas Excelsior Hotel.** Atop the Statehouse Convention Center on the banks of the Arkansas River, the Excelsior features concierge as well as standard floors. Amenities include modem hookups in every room. Its three stylish dining spots include the award-winning Josephine's Library Restaurant. Fashionable shops line its arcade. ✉ *3 Statehouse Plaza, 72201,* ☎ *501/375–5000 or 800/527–1745,* ℻ *501/375–4721. 417 rooms. Airport shuttle. AE, D, DC, MC, V.*

$$$ ▥ **Capital Hotel.** A careful restoration of this 1872 National Historic Landmark calls attention to the classic cast-iron facade, the atrium lobby's mosaic floors, lead-glass skylight, handsome columns, and high-ceiling rooms. Its restaurant, Ashley's, offers fine dining, with casual lunches and dinners served in the lounge. ✉ *111 W. Markham St., 72201,* ☎ *501/374–7474 or 800/766–7666,* ℻ *501/370–7091. 102 rooms. AE, D, DC, MC, V.*

$$ ▥ **Embassy Suites.** Scheduled at press time to open in the fall of 1997, this all-suite hotel lies in west Little Rock, the city's fast-growing area, which is 10–15 minutes from downtown. Its two-room suites include sofa beds and kitchenettes. ✉ *11301 Financial Centre Pkwy., 72211,* ☎ *501/312–9000,* ℻ *501/312–9455. 251 suites. Indoor pool, sauna, health club, business services. AE, D, DC, MC, V.*

$$ ⊡ **Holiday Inn–Select.** This award-winning Holiday Inn, in west Little Rock, is convenient to downtown as well as numerous nearby restaurants and businesses. ⊠ *201 S. Shackleford Rd., 72211,* ☎ *501/ 223–3000,* FAX *501/223–2833. 261 rooms. Pool, health club, business center, airport shuttle. AE, D, DC, MC, V.*

Motels

⊡ **Hampton Inn I–30** (⊠ 6100 Mitchell Dr., 72209, ☎ 501/562–6667, FAX 501/568–6832), 122 rooms, pool; $. ⊡ **La Quinta–North** (⊠ 4100 McCain Blvd., North Little Rock 27117, ☎ 501/945–0808, FAX 501/ 945–0393), 122 rooms, pool; $. ⊡ **Motel 6** (⊠ 10524 W. Markham St. [at I–430], 72205, ☎ 501/225–7366, FAX 501/227–7426), 146 rooms, pool; $.

Nightlife and the Arts

The Weekend section in the Friday issue of the *Arkansas Democrat-Gazette* and the weekly *Arkansas Times* list nightlife and arts events, and you can call the recorded "What's Happening" (☎ 501/372–3399).

Nightlife

Juanita's (⊠ 1300 S. Main St., ☎ 501/372–1228) serves up Mexican fare daily along with an eclectic mix of evening entertainment—from rock to jazz, bluegrass, folk, Latin, reggae, and more. **Vino's** (⊠ 923 W. 7th, ☎ 501/375–8466) presents avant-garde Red Octopus theater productions and is home to the Little Rock Folk Club and other concert-giving organizations. It also has a microbrewery and tasty pizzas.

At the **After Thought** (⊠ 2721 Kavanaugh Blvd., ☎ 501/663–1196) the piano bar serves as a background for conversation, though the Monday Jazz Project is for listeners. The **Bobbisox Lounge,** at the Holiday Inn Airport (⊠ I–440 Airport Exit, ☎ 501/490–1000), is a popular spot for DJ dancing.

The Arts

The **Arkansas Repertory Theater** (⊠ 601 Main St., ☎ 501/378–0405) produces popular and avant-garde theater fare. The **Arkansas Symphony Orchestra** (⊠ Various locations, ☎ 501/666–1761) plays classical and Pops music. **Wildwood Park for the Performing Arts** (⊠ 20919 Denny Rd., ☎ 501/821–7275) offers opera, jazz, cabaret, chamber performances, and festivals year-round.

The **Broadway Theater Series** (⊠ Box 131, 72203, ☎ 501/661–1500) brings in national touring companies of Broadway shows, ballet, ice shows, concerts, and lectures. At **Murry's Dinner Playhouse** (⊠ 6323 Asher Ave., ☎ 501/562–3131) a buffet combines with Broadway comedies and musicals or solo performances. The **UALR Fine Arts Galleries & Theatre** (⊠ 2801 S. University, ☎ 501/569–3291) stages concerts and theatrical productions as well as exhibitions. The **Robinson Center** (⊠ Markham St. and Broadway, ☎ 501/376–4781) is the city's major theater for the performing arts.

Shopping

Major department stores are at **Park Plaza** and **University Mall,** on either side of Markham Street at University Avenue in Little Rock, and at **McCain Mall** at Arkansas 67/U.S. 167 and McCain Boulevard in North Little Rock. The **River Market** (⊠ 400 E. Markham St., ☎ 501/375– 2552) features a farmers' market with home-grown produce and the indoor Market Hall, open year-round and providing southern barbecue, ethnic foods, gourmet items, fresh flowers and herbs, a café, and special events. Galleries, specialty shops, and boutiques lie along winding **Kavanaugh Boulevard** and **Rodney Parham Road.**

THE ARKANSAS OZARKS

The forested mountains and hollows, sparkling waters, and calcite caverns of the Arkansas highlands provide a breathtaking backdrop for self-taught folk musicians getting together on a town square, for the display of handicrafts from pioneer days, and for tiny towns barely changed from a century ago. Yet the Ozarks also encompass upscale shopping malls, fine arts centers, and sophisticated restaurants. The region boasts superb fishing and canoeing on its rivers, as well as boating and water sports on its lakes. Networks of trails lace through the mountains, from easygoing, accessible paths to the rugged 178-mi-long Ozark Highlands trail. Dozens of scenic byways lead past exquisite vistas. Civil War battlefields at Pea Ridge and Prairie Grove, ecotours exploring natural and human history, railway excursions, antiques, outdoor theater, great golfing, and lively festivals and fairs round out the appeal of this scenic playground.

Visitor Information

Northwest Arkansas Tourism Association (⊠ Box 5176, Bella Vista 72714, ☎ 888/398–3444). **Ozark Mountains Region** (⊠ Box 137, Yellville 72687, ☎ 800/544–6867) covers the central Ozarks. **Ozark Gateway Tourist Council** (⊠ Box 4049, Batesville 72503, ☎ 870/793–9316 or 800/264–0316) handles the eastern Ozarks.

Arriving and Departing

By Car

To reach northwest Arkansas from Little Rock, take I–40 west, then turn north on U.S. 71. The fastest route to other parts of the Ozarks from Little Rock is U.S. 65 north from I–40 at Conway and then the appropriate highway to your destination. At Harrison, U.S. 62 leads from U.S. 65 to Eureka Springs, Pea Ridge National Military Park, and U.S. 71 at Rogers.

By Plane

American Eagle, US Airways Express, Northwest Airlink, Trans World Express, and **Atlantic Southeast Airlines** have scheduled flights into Fayetteville's Drake Field (☎ 501/521–4750). A Northwest Arkansas regional airport is scheduled to open between July and mid-October 1998 and will be west of Lowell.

Exploring the Arkansas Ozarks

Fayetteville, Springdale, Rogers, and Bentonville—together Arkansas's fastest-growing metropolitan area—feature walking/driving tours of each of their fascinating historic districts. The **Shiloh Museum of Ozark History,** in Springdale (⊠ 118 W. Johnson St., ☎ 501/750–8165), and the **Rogers Historical Museum** (⊠ 322 S. 2nd St., Rogers, ☎ 501/621–1154) lead you through the history and culture of the region. **Headquarters House,** in Fayetteville (⊠ 118 E. Dickson St., ☎ 501/521–2970), served as both Union and Confederate headquarters during the Civil War. Bentonville's **Peel Mansion & Gardens** (⊠ 400 S. Walton Blvd., ☎ 501/273–9664) belonged to a pioneer businessman and U.S. Congressman.

Pea Ridge National Military Park, 10 mi northeast of Rogers on U.S. 62 (☎ 501/451–8122), and **Prairie Grove Battlefield Park,** 10 mi southwest of Fayetteville on Arkansas on the same highway (☎ 501/

846–2990), preserve the sites of decisive Civil War battles. The **University of Arkansas** in Fayetteville, where the hallowed Razorback teams and where President Bill and Hilary Rodham Clinton taught law, features sports museums and a lively arts calendar. Vintage cars on the **Arkansas and Missouri Railroad,** in Springdale (⊠ 306 E. Emma St., ☎ 501/751–8600 or 800/687–8600), make daylong trips through the Ozarks to Van Buren and back.

Eureka Springs, with more than 50 B&Bs and 60 motels and hotels plus cabins and campsites, has greeted visitors since its beginnings as a Victorian-era spa. Now it's just as much a scene for family holidays as romantic weddings and honeymoons and serves as a base for scenic mountain drives, visits to colorful caverns, and outdoor activities. The town puts on a packed schedule of festivals. Visitors find country music shows in town, while opera, classical music, jazz, and other styles are on the summer schedule of **Inspiration Point Fine Arts Colony** (⊠ U.S. 62W, ☎ 501/253–8595).

Victorian homes and shops, including fine arts and crafts galleries that sponsor monthly evening events, line Main and Spring streets as they wind uphill from a narrow valley. The tall, airy **Thorncrown Chapel** (⊠ U.S. 62W, ☎ 501/253–7401) takes advantage of its woodland setting. The 33-acre **Eureka Springs Gardens** sprawl up the hillsides from a spring (⊠ U.S. 62W, ☎ 501/253–9256). The *Belle of the Ozarks* floats along 60 mi of Beaver Lake shoreline (⊠ Starkey Marina off U.S. 62W, ☎ 501/253–6200). Vintage steam locomotives of the **Eureka Springs & North Arkansas Railway** chug into the Ozarks from a historic depot (⊠ 299 N. Main St., ☎ 501/253–9623).

★ The **Ozark Folk Center** (⊠ Box 500, Mountain View 72560, ☎ 870/ 269–3851) is a unique state park devoted to the perpetuation and lively demonstration of traditional Ozark Mountain crafts, acoustic music, and dance. The park has a lodge, gift shop, and the **Iron Skillet Restau-**
★ **rant.** In neighboring **Mountain View** the music continues in informal sessions on the **courthouse square,** surrounded by crafts, antiques, and other shops in old stone buildings.

★ The U.S. Forest Service leads year-round tours of the **Blanchard Springs Caverns** (⊠ Box 1279, Mountain View 72560, ☎ 870/757–2211), 15 mi northwest of Mountain View off Arkansas 14, providing the state's premier underground experience.

At **Ozark Ecotours** (⊠ Box 513, Jasper 72641, ☎ 870/46–5898), local residents/guides take small groups on one-day trips into the rugged Buffalo River landscape to learn about Native American, pioneer, Civil War, and outlaw history and lore in the areas where events actually happened, as well as to explore its bountiful natural history. Some trips require only easygoing hikes; others involve canoeing, caving, and horseback riding.

Dining and Lodging

For price ranges *see* Charts 1 (B) *and* 2 (B) *in* On the Road with Fodor's.

Eureka Springs

$$ ✕ **Cottage Inn.** A highly regarded dining spot, it serves fresh-made Mediterranean cuisine, including rich cream of mushroom soup, and has an extensive wine list. ⊠ *U.S. 62W,* ☎ *501/253–5282. MC, V. Closed Mon.*

$$ ✕ **DeVito's.** Trout is king on the Italian-American menu. ⊠ *5 Center St.,* ☎ *501/253–6807. AE, D, MC, V. Closed Wed.*

$$ ✕ **Ermilio's.** This cozy spot serves creative Italian-American fare. ⊠ *26 White St.*, ☎ *501/253–8806. Reservations not accepted. MC, V. Closed Thurs. No lunch Sun.*

$–$$ ⊡ **Comfort Inn.** This modern Victorian-style motel includes a deluxe Continental breakfast. ⊠ *Rte. 6 (Box 7), 72632,* ☎ *501/253–5241,* ℻ *501/253–6502. 57 rooms. Pool. AE, D, DC, MC, V.*

$$$ ⊡ **Heartstone Inn and Cottages.** Eureka Springs' largest B&B has accommodations graced with antiques in a Victorian home and in cottages. ⊠ *35 Kingshighway, 72632,* ☎ *501/253–8916. 11 rooms, 2 cottages. Refrigerators, kitchenettes, massage. Full breakfast. AE, MC, V. Closed Jan.–Feb.*

Fayetteville

$–$$ ✕ **AQ Chicken House.** Since 1947, it's been open and serving chicken as fresh as it gets. The menu has a full range of other entrées. ⊠ *1925 N. College Ave., Fayetteville,* ☎ *501/443–7555;* ⊠ *U.S. 71B, Springdale,* ☎ *501/751–4633. AE, D, DC, MC, V.*

$$ ✕⊡ **Fayetteville Clarion.** The hotel is near the University of Arkansas and historic districts. ⊠ *1255 S. Shiloh Dr., Fayetteville 72701,* ☎ *501/ 521–1166,* ℻ *501/521–1204. Restaurant, café, bar, indoor pool, hot tub, sauna, exercise room, recreation room, airport shuttle. AE, D, DC, MC, V.*

Johnson

$$$ ✕ **James at the Mill.** One of Arkansas's finest dining spots, this restau-
★ rant serves seasonally changing variations of what chef-owner Miles James has christened Ozark Plateau cuisine, traditional southern dishes updated with a nouvelle American twist, with lots of fresh local produce, game, and dry-aged rib-eye steaks in inventive combinations. The restaurant and its wine list have won numerous awards. ⊠ *3906 Greathouse Springs Rd., Johnson,* ☎ *501/443–1400. AE, D, DC, MC, V. Closed Sun. No lunch Sat.*

$$$ ⊡ **Inn at the Mill.** Part of James at the Mill, this inn in a rural setting is built around a restored 1835 mill and pond. ⊠ *3906 Greathouse Springs Rd., Johnson 72741,* ☎ *501/443–1800,* ℻ *501/521–8091. 48 rooms. Restaurant. Continental breakfast. AE, D, DC, MC, V.*

Lakeview

$$–$$$$ ✕⊡ **Gaston's White River Resort.** This lodge draws serious anglers as
★ well as families with first-class cottages, pool, tennis courts, private airstrip, a marina, and an outstanding restaurant. ⊠ *1 River Rd., Lakeview 72642,* ☎ *870/431–5202,* ℻ *870/431–5216. 74 rooms. Restaurant, bar. MC, V.*

Ponca

$$$ ✕⊡ **Buffalo Outdoor Center.** Log cabins with fully furnished kitchens and fireplaces are at two sites on the Buffalo River. The extensive array of outdoor activities includes hiking trails, canoe and raft floats, kayaking, fishing, guided fishing trips, mountain biking, horseback trail rides, and hot air ballooning. ⊠ *Box 1, Ponca 72670,* ☎ ℻ *870/861– 5514;* ⊠ *Rte. 1, Box 56, St. Joe 72675,* ☎ *870/439–2244,* ℻ *870/ 439–2200. 15 cabins at Ponca, 10 cabins at Silver Hill. D, MC, V.*

Rogers

$$ ✕ **Tale of the Trout.** This country spot has raised its own trout for 50 years and also features steak, quail, and seafood. Shorts, hats, and caps are not allowed. ⊠ *94 New Hope Rd., Rogers,* ☎ *501/636–0508. AE, D, DC, MC, V. Closed Sun.*

Springdale

$$$ 🏨 **Holiday Inn Northwest Arkansas.** Convenient to interstates, this hotel has a five-story atrium and waterfall. ⊠ *1500 S. 48th St., Springdale 72762,* ☎ *501/751–8300,* ℻ *501/751–4640. Restaurant, bar, indoor pool, hot tub, sauna, exercise room, nightclub, meeting rooms. AE, D, DC, MC, V.*

Nightlife and the Arts

Friday's Northwest Arkansas Weekend section in the *Arkansas Democrat-Gazette* lists nightlife and arts events.

The **Walton Arts Center,** in Fayetteville (⊠ 495 Dickson St., ☎ 501/443–9216), presents a wide range of performing and fine arts events. The **Arts Center of the Ozarks,** in Springdale (⊠ 214 S. Main St., ☎ 501/751–5441), has a similarly active schedule. The area's major club and café scene is along Fayetteville's **Dickson Street** between the University of Arkansas campus and Walton Arts Center.

WESTERN ARKANSAS

Western Arkansas reaches from **Fort Smith** and **Van Buren**—which preserve the region's wild and woolly frontier heritage as well as its Victorian era—south through the ancient forests and rivers of the Ouachita Mountains (pronounced *Wash*-i-taw). The quartz-rich mountains cradle **Hot Springs,** nicknamed the Spa City, which was the boyhood home of President Bill Clinton. Five crystal-clear Diamond Lakes also lure vacationers who love water and beautiful scenery. The region's rivers offer white-water trips and scenic canoeing and fishing. The Ouachitas are laced with top-notch trail systems and campsites.

Visitor Information

Fort Smith Convention and Visitors Bureau (⊠ 2 N. B St., 72901, ☎ 501/783–8888 or 800/637–1477). The **Hot Springs Convention & Visitors Bureau** (⊠ Box K, Hot Springs 71902, ☎ 800/772–2489) provides information for the city and surrounding five-county region.

Arriving and Departing

By Car

The easiest way to arrive and get around is by car. From Little Rock, I–30 and U.S. 70 lead to Hot Springs. I–40 reaches Fort Smith and Van Buren.

By Plane

Lone Star/Aspen Mountain Air flies from Dallas–Fort Worth to Hot Springs' municipal airport, and there is a shuttle service between Hot Springs and Little Rock National Airport (☎ 800/643–1505). **American Eagle, ASA,** and **Northwest** fly into Fort Smith Regional Airport.

Exploring Western Arkansas

Native Americans called today's Hot Springs the Valley of the Vapors, whose 47 thermal springs were first encountered by Spanish explorer Hernando de Soto in 1547. In 1832 the U.S. Congress created the first federal reserve around the springs, which in 1921 became a national park. In the 1920s Hot Springs was a gambling town famed for its therapeutic bathhouses. Get a feel for this opulent era on Bathhouse Row at the **Fordyce Bathhouse,** now the Hot Springs National Park Visitor Center (⊠ 369 Central Ave., Box 1860, 71902, ☎ 501/624–3383). Only a handful of spas providing mineral baths remain, including the old-fashioned **Buckstaff** (✉ 509 Central Ave., ☎ 501/623–2308), a 1912 National Historic Landmark, and five hotels and health spas.

Hot Springs offers a host of tourist activities and events, such as a wax museum, country music and comedy shows, and land-and-lake tours on an "Amphibious Duck." The 400-passenger **Belle of Hot Springs** sails Lake Hamilton daily on sightseeing, lunch, and dinner-dance cruises (✉ 5200 Central Ave./Ark. 7S, ☎ 501/525–4438). At the restored headquarters of **Mountain Valley Spring Company,** enjoy free samples of natural spring water (✉ 150 Central Ave., ☎ 501/623–6671). The **Museum of Hot Springs** includes the stories of the city's gambling-era and famous sports heroes (✉ 201 Central Ave., ☎ 501/624–5545). President Bill Clinton's boyhood homes at 1011 Park Avenue and 213 Scully Street, his schools, church, and favorite teenage hangouts are detailed in a brochure and map available at the Hot Springs Visitor Center at Spring and Central avenues.

Dig for crystals or browse among those already cleaned and polished at **Ron Coleman Mining,** 14 mi north of Hot Springs on Arkansas 7 (☎ 501/984–5443).

Fort Smith was established in 1817 on the Indian frontier. The Fort Smith visitor center is in **Miss Laura's** (✉ 2 N. B St., ☎ 501/783–8888 or 800/637–1477), the only former brothel on the National Register of Historic Places. From there a trolley carries visitors to museums, historic homes, and other sights. The **Fort Smith National Historic Site** (✉ 3rd St. and Rogers Ave., ☎ 501/783–3961) includes the remains of two successive frontier forts. The **Old Fort Museum** traces regional history (✉ 320 Rogers Ave., ☎ 501/783–7841). The **Fort Smith Trolley Museum** contains a 1926 streetcar and other early transportation memorabilia (✉ 100 S. 4th St., ☎ 501/783–0205). The **Patent Model Museum** demonstrates American inventiveness (✉ 400 N. 8th St., ☎ 501/782–9014). The **Darby House** was the boyhood home of General William O. Darby, who organized and commanded Darby's Rangers in World War II (✉ 311 N. 8th St., ☎ 501/782–3388).

Van Buren, just north over the Arkansas River, was also settled in the early 1800s as a riverboat stop and prospered as a trade and supply center. Van Buren's century-old **Main Street** runs six blocks from the Old Frisco Depot to the county courthouse. It's an architectural and historic delight, with shops filled with antiques and country crafts, cafés, restaurants, and a theater. From the foot of Main the **Frontier Belle** cruises the Arkansas River (✉ Box 1241, 72956, ☎ 501/471–5441). From April through October the **Arkansas & Missouri Railroad** makes three-hour excursions into the Ozarks from the depot (✉ 306 E. Emma, Springdale, ☎ 501/751–8600 or 800/687–8600).

What to See and Do with Children

The **Mid-America Museum** (✉ 400 Mid-America Blvd., off U.S. 270W, ☎ 501/767–3461 or 800/632–0583) explores science and nature in interactive exhibits. A great view awaits atop the 216-ft **Hot Springs Mountain Tower** (✉ On Hot Springs Mountain Dr. off Fountain St., ☎ 501/623–6035).

Dining and Lodging

For price ranges *see* Charts 1 (B) *and* 2 (B) *in* On the Road with Fodor's.

Hot Springs and the Ozarks

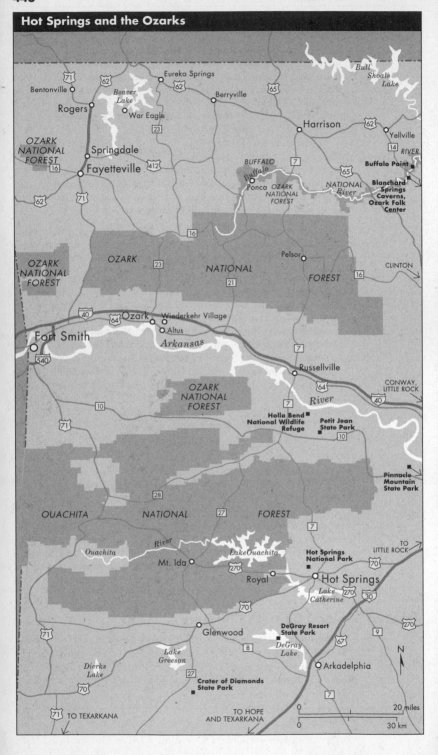

Bull Shoals Lake

Bentonville
71

62
Eureka Springs
62
65
Berryville

Beaver Lake
Rogers
War Eagle
23

Harrison
62
Yellville
14
RIVER

OZARK NATIONAL FOREST
16
Springdale
412
Fayetteville

7

BUFFALO
Buffalo Point

62
71

Buffalo
Ponca
OZARK NATIONAL FOREST
65

Blanchard Springs Caverns, Ozark Folk Center

NATIONAL River

16

OZARK
23
NATIONAL
21

Pelsor
FOREST
16
CLINTON

OZARK NATIONAL FOREST

40
64
Ozark
Wiederkehr Village
Altus

Fort Smith
540
Arkansas
7
Russellville

CONWAY, LITTLE ROCK

64
40

10

OZARK NATIONAL FOREST
7
River

71
Holla Bend National Wildlife Refuge
Petit Jean State Park
10

Pinnacle Mountain State Park

28

OUACHITA
NATIONAL
27
FOREST

7

Ouachita
River
Lake Ouachita
TO LITTLE ROCK

Ouachita
Mt. Ida
Hot Springs National Park
70

270
Royal
Hot Springs
270
30

70
Lake Catherine

71
Glenwood
8
DeGray Resort State Park
DeGray Lake
67
9
270

Lake Greeson
27
Arkadelphia

Dierks Lake

70
Crater of Diamonds State Park

N

71 TO TEXARKANA
TO HOPE AND TEXARKANA

20 miles

0
0
30 km

7

Fort Smith

$$–$$$ ✕ **Folie à Deux.** This fine-dining spot has won awards for its Continental dishes, including steak Nicholas, and its extensive wine list. ✉ *2909 Old Greenwood Rd.,* ☏ *501/648–0041. AE, D, DC, MC, V. Closed Sun.*

$$ ✕ **Emmy's.** Hearty German cuisine is presented in this old-line restaurant. ✉ *602 N. 16th St.,* ☏ *501/783–0012. AE, D, DC, MC, V. Closed Sun.–Mon.*

$ ✕ **Jerry Neel's Barbecue.** This casual eatery has catered for U.S. presidents. ✉ *1823 Phoenix Ave.,* ☏ *501/646–8085. MC, V. Closed Sun.*

$$$ ▥ **Holiday Inn Fort Smith Civic Center.** Many historic sites are within walking distance. ✉ *700 Rogers Ave., 72901,* ☏ *501/783–1000,* ⅁ *501/783–0312. 255 rooms. Restaurant, lounge, room service, indoor pool, sauna, exercise room, nightclub, airport shuttle. AE, D, DC, MC, V.*

$$ ▥ **Hampton Inn.** This motel is convenient to I–540, restaurants, and shopping, with a buffet breakfast included in the rate. ✉ *6201-D Rogers Ave., 72901,* ☏ *501/452–2000,* ⅁ *501/452–6668. 143 rooms. Refrigerators, pool, hot tub, exercise room. AE, D, DC, MC, V.*

Hot Springs

$–$$ ✕ **Yanni's in the Park.** Open daily for breakfast, lunch, and dinner, this cheery spot serves luscious Greek and American cuisine and wines. ✉ *211 Fountain St.,* ☏ *501/338–6655. AE, D, MC, V.*

$ ✕ **McClard's.** This old-fashioned barbecue spot was a favorite of President Bill Clinton as a teenager. ✉ *505 Albert Pike,* ☏ *501/624–9586. No credit cards. Closed Sun.–Mon., Dec. 21–Jan. 21, 1 wk in July.*

$$–$$$ ▥ **Lake Hamilton Resort and Conference Center.** All rooms in this luxurious all-suite resort have balconies and lake views. ✉ *2810 Albert Pike, 71913,* ☏ *501/767–5511 or 800/426–3184,* ⅁ *501/767–8576. 104 suites. Restaurant, bar, indoor and outdoor pools, hot tub, massage, sauna, marina. AE, D, DC, MC, V. Closed Christmas wk.*

$$$ ▥ **Arlington.** This historic spa hotel is a slightly faded grande dame. ✉ *239 Central Ave., 71901,* ☏ *501/623–7771 or 800/643–1502,* ⅁ *501/623–6191. 484 rooms. 3 restaurants, lounge, lobby bar, 2 pools, beauty salon, spa, golf/tennis privileges, exercise room, shops, game room, convention center, meeting rooms. AE, D, MC, V.*

Outdoor Activities and Sports

For information on trails, scenic drives, and campsites, contact **Ouachita National Forest** (✉ USFS Box 1270, Hot Springs 71902, ☏ 501/321–5202). Nearby Arkansas state parks include **DeGray Lake Resort** (✉ Rte. 3, Box 490, Bismarck 72191-8194, ☏ 870/865–2851 or 800/606–2426), with a lodge, golf course, marina, campsites, horseback riding, and activities.

Spectator Sports

Thoroughbred racing: At Hot Spring's **Oaklawn Jockey Club** from late January through late April (✉ 2705 Central Ave., ☏ 800/625–5296).

Shopping

Dozens of artists and gallery owners have transformed Hot Springs' Victorian downtown into a vibrant, cosmopolitan arts district. A **Gallery Walk** takes place the first weekend of each month. The **Hot Springs Mall** and **Hot Springs Factory Outlet Stores** lie about 4 mi south of downtown on Arkansas 7/Central Avenue.

ELSEWHERE IN ARKANSAS

Texarkana

Arriving and Departing

From Little Rock take I–30 to Texarkana, which straddles the Arkansas-Texas border.

What to See and Do

The **Post Office** and **Photographer's Island** (✉ 500 State Line Ave.) are half in Arkansas, half in Texas. Winnings from a poker game made possible the 1885 **Ace of Clubs House** (✉ 5th and Pine Sts., ☎ 903/793–4831), with period furnishings, which was built—not surprisingly—in the shape of the playing card. The **Texarkana Historical Museum** is in the city's oldest brick building (✉ 219 State Line Ave., ☎ 903/793–4831). Opened in 1924, the elaborate **Perot Theater** (✉ 219 Main St., ☎ 903/792–4992) was restored by native son and presidential hopeful H. Ross Perot. Across the street, a mural pays tribute to another native son, ragtime composer Scott Joplin.

Hope

Arriving and Departing

I–30 leads from Little Rock to Hope.

What to See and Do

Hope is Arkansas's watermelon capital, growing some of the largest and tastiest melons in the world. It's also the birthplace of President Bill Clinton, who lived here until he was six. Start in the **Hope Visitor Center,** in the restored 1912 railroad depot (✉ S. Main and Division Sts., ☎ 870/777–3640). Until age four, Clinton lived with his grandparents at 117 South Hervey (at press time it was undergoing restoration, though it may be open to the public by 1998), then at the modest home at 321 East 13th Street. He attended Miss Marie Purkins' School for Little Folks (✉ 601 E. 2nd St.) and Brookwood Elementary School, on Spruce Street.

★ Near Hope is **Old Washington Historic State Park** (✉ Box 98, Washington, ☎ 870/983–2684), established in 1824 on the Southwest Trail and the Confederate state capital after Little Rock's capture. Some 40 buildings remain from the 1820s–1870s. **Crater of Diamonds State Park** (✉ Rte. 1, Box 364, Murfreesboro, ☎ 870/285–3113), near Murfreesboro, is North America's only public diamond mine; you can keep what you find.

Helena

Arriving and Departing

From Little Rock take I–40, turning south on U.S. 49.

What to See and Do

One of the oldest Mississippi River settlements and a Civil War battle site, Helena is home to the **Delta Cultural Center** (✉ 95 Missouri St., ☎ 870/338–8919), which documents the roots of the Delta blues, pioneer days, and the river life described by Mark Twain. Helena shows off numerous antebellum and postwar mansions, several of which are now B&Bs. A Confederate burial ground is in **Maple Hill Cemetery** (✉ 1801 Holly St.), while **Magnolia Cemetery,** founded in the 1850s as a segregated resting place for African-Americans, is found by going north on College Street and then turning right on Wire Road for a quarter of a mile. Each October Helena hosts the **King Biscuit Blues Festival** (☎ 870/338–9144), which has gained international acclaim.

KENTUCKY

Updated by
Susan Reigler

Capital	Frankfort
Population	3,884,000
Motto	United We Stand, Divided We Fall
State Bird	Cardinal
State Flower	Goldenrod
Postal Abbreviation	KY

Statewide Visitor Information

Kentucky Department of Travel Development (✉ 2200 Capital Plaza Tower, Frankfort 40601, ☎ 502/564–4930 or 800/225–8747). **Welcome centers:** I–75S at Florence, I–65N at Franklin, I–64W at Grayson, I–24E at Paducah, I–75N at Williamsburg, and U.S. 68 at Maysville.

Scenic Drives

A loop drive of rugged **Red River Gorge** in the eastern Kentucky mountains starts near Natural Bridge State Park, on **Route 77** near Slade. **Forest Development Road 918** is a 9-mi National Scenic Byway in the Daniel Boone National Forest, near Morehead. The 35-mi stretch of **Little Shepherd Trail** (U.S. 119) between Harlan and Whitesburg is breathtaking in fall. **Old Frankfort Pike** between Lexington and Frankfort passes through classic bluegrass countryside.

National and State Parks

National Parks
Daniel Boone National Forest (✉ U.S. 27, Whitley City; 100 Vaught Rd., Winchester 40391, ☎ 606/745–3100) offers spectacular mountain scenery, especially in the Red River Gorge Geological Area, known for its natural arches, native plants, and 300-ft cliffs. **Land Between the Lakes** (✉ 100 Van Morgan Dr., Golden Pond 42211, ☎ 502/924–2000) is an uninhabited 40-mi-long peninsula between Kentucky and Barkley lakes that is run as a demonstration project in environmental
★ education and resource management. **Mammoth Cave National Park** (✉ Entrances on Rte. 70, 10 mi west of Cave City, and on Rte. 255, 8 mi northwest of Park City; Mammoth Cave 42259, ☎ 502/758–2328) is a 350-mi-long complex of twisting underground passages full of colorful mineral formations.

State Parks
Kentucky's 34 state parks are ideal for hiking or simply taking in the beauty of the countryside; most also offer facilities for picnicking, camping, water sports, and horseback riding. Sixteen have rustic but comfortable lodges and/or cottages; 28 have tent and trailer sites, available April–October; 13 have year-round campgrounds. For information contact **Kentucky Department of Parks** (✉ Capital Plaza Tower, Frankfort 40601, ☎ 800/255–7275).

LOUISVILLE

Louisville (locally pronounced *loo*-uh-vul) was founded in 1778 by a Revolutionary War hero, General George Rogers Clark, and named for King Louis XVI as gratitude for France's help during the war. The city's charter was signed in 1780 by Thomas Jefferson, then the governor of Virginia, of which Kentucky was the westernmost district.

Louisville's culture and history have been greatly influenced by its location inside a bend in the mighty Ohio River and smack in the center of the eastern half of the nation. During the first half of the 19th century the city was a bustling river port. With the railroad's advent, it became a hub of train traffic. Waves of European immigrants settled into colorful neighborhoods that retain much of their character today. Louisville attracts crowds of visitors every May for the nation's premier horse race: the Kentucky Derby.

Visitor Information

Area Chamber of Commerce (✉ 600 W. Main St., 40202, ☎ 502/625–0060). **Convention & Visitors Bureau** (✉ 400 S. 1st St., 40202, ☎ 502/584–2121 or 800/792–5595).

Arriving and Departing

By Bus
Greyhound Lines (✉ 720 W. Muhammad Ali Blvd., ☎ 800/231–2222).

By Car
Louisville is well endowed with interstates. I–64 runs east–west, I–71 northeast, and I–65 north–south. I–264, also known as the Henry Watterson Expressway, rings the city. These converge downtown in a ramp-ridden area known as Spaghetti Junction; confusion here can result in a quick trip to Indiana.

By Plane
Louisville International Airport (☎ 502/367–4636) is 15 minutes south of downtown on I–65. It has a modern, spacious, comfortable terminal and is served by most major carriers. Cab fare from the airport to downtown Louisville runs about $15.

Getting Around Louisville

The downtown area is defined north–south by Broadway and the Ohio River, east–west by Preston and 18th streets. The **Transit Authority of River City** (✉ 1000 W. Broadway, ☎ 502/585–1234) operates local buses ($1 at peak times, 75¢ other times), as well as a free trolley along 4th Avenue between Broadway and the river. A car is needed for explorations beyond downtown.

Exploring Louisville

Downtown
The heart of Louisville is thick with historic sites. **West Main Street** has more examples of 19th-century cast-iron architecture than anyplace else in the country except New York City's SoHo. The **Hart Block** (✉ 728 W. Main St.), a five-story building designed in 1884 at the height of Louisville's Victorian era, has a facade that is a jigsaw puzzle of cast-iron pieces bolted together. Other historic attractions include the tiny **St. Charles Hotel** (✉ 634 W. Main St.), constructed before 1832. The Roman Catholic **Cathedral of the Assumption** (✉ 443 S. 5th St.), a Gothic Revival structure built between 1849 and 1852, was restored between 1985 and 1994. The **Jefferson County Courthouse** (✉ 531 W. Jefferson St.), a Greek Revival landmark designed by Gideon Shyrock, was built in 1835 with the intent of luring the state government to Louisville.

On the contemporary side, the grand **Humana Building** (✉ 500 W. Main St.) of 1985 is the eclectic work of architect Michael Graves. The **American Life and Accident Building** (✉ 3 Riverfront Plaza), designed by Mies van der Rohe and completed in 1973, is known as the Rusty

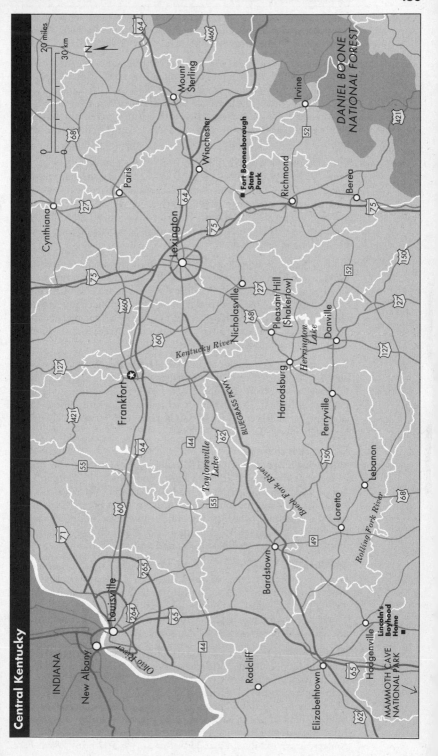

Central Kentucky

DANIEL BOONE NATIONAL FOREST

INDIANA

New Albany

Louisville

Ohio River

Frankfort

Lexington

Cynthiana

Paris

Mount Sterling

Winchester

Fort Boonesborough State Park

Irvine

Richmond

Berea

Nicholasville

Pleasant Hill (Shakertown)

Danville

Kentucky River

Herrington Lake

Harrodsburg

Perryville

Lebanon

Loretto

Rolling Fork River

Beech Fork River

BLUEGRASS PKWY.

Taylorsville Lake

Bardstown

Radcliff

Elizabethtown

Hodgenville

Lincoln's Boyhood Home

MAMMOTH CAVE NATIONAL PARK

20 miles
30 km

Building because of its covering of oxidized Cor-Ten steel. Just off the riverfront Belvedere Promenade, the 1988 **Louisville Falls Fountain** spews water in the form of a 375-ft-tall fleur-de-lis, the city's symbol.

The **Kentucky Center for the Arts** (☞ Nightlife and the Arts, *below*), on Riverfront Plaza, is home to a distinguished collection of 20th-century sculpture by such artists as Louise Nevelson, Alexander Calder, and Jean Dubuffet. The **Louisville Science Center/IMAX Theatre** (⊠ 727 W. Main St., ☎ 502/561–6103), a 19th-century warehouse full of science arcades and demonstrations, includes an Egyptian mummy's tomb, a Foucault pendulum, and lots of hands-on exhibits.

★ Look for the giant baseball bat in front of the **Louisville Slugger Museum** (⊠ 800 W. Main St., ☎ 502/588–7228) and the giant baseball seemingly lodged in a pane of the plate glass factory next door. Visitors can enjoy interactive exhibits such as a "virtual pitch," in which a computerized baseball comes hurtling at you at 90 mph. A tour of the adjoining Hillerich & Bradsby factory, where the famous baseball bats are made, is included.

Hikers, bikers, and in-line skaters will enjoy the scenic 6.9-mi **River-Walk,** stretching from downtown's 4th Street Wharf westward to Chickasaw Park. The path parallels the Ohio shore and offers a variety of vistas, from the locks and dam on the shipping channel to quiet, wooded portions where it's possible to spot deer. Parking is available at 4th Street, 8th Street, 10th Street, 31st Street, and at Lannan, Shawnee Park, and Chickasaw Parks.

While near the river, check out the ***Belle of Louisville*** (☎ 502/574–2355), usually moored at City Wharf at 4th and River streets. Built in 1914, the gingerbread-trim steamboat is the oldest Mississippi-style stern-wheeler still afloat. Should you grow tired, you can hire a horse-drawn carriage from **River City Horse Carriage** (☎ 502/895–7268) or **Louisville Horse Trams** (☎ 502/581–0100).

Other Attractions

Butchertown was settled in the 1830s, largely by Germans who worked in meatpacking plants in the vicinity and lived in "shotgun" and "camelback" houses built in the shadow of the still-in-business (as your nose will tell you) **Bourbon Stock Yards.** In 1814 French immigrants settled in **Portland,** where goods came ashore to be portaged past the falls of the Ohio River. Today barges carry 5 million tons of cargo per month through the **McAlpine Locks and Dam** (⊠ 27th St.).

The **Cherokee Triangle,** a classic Victorian village of grand homes on broad tree-lined streets, was built between 1870 and 1910. A few miles out Bardstown Road from the triangle is **Farmington** (☎ 502/452–9920), a Federal-style mansion built in 1810 from a design by Thomas Jefferson, whose special touches include two octagonal rooms and an adventurously steep hidden staircase.

★ **Old Louisville** is the most elegant of Louisville's neighborhoods. Its architectural styles include Victorian Gothic, Richardsonian Romanesque, Queen Anne, Italianate, Châteauesque, and Beaux Arts. Lead- and stained-glass windows, turrets, and gargoyles are much in evidence. The southern edge of Old Louisville harbors the **University of Louisville** campus. Its **J. B. Speed Art Museum** has masterworks by Rembrandt, Rubens, Picasso, Henry Moore, and many others, as well as frequent contemporary exhibits. ⊠ *2035 S. 3rd St.,* ☎ *502/636–2893. Free. Closed Mon.*

Just south of the university is **Churchill Downs,** world famous as the home of the Kentucky Derby. Since the track's opening in 1875, scores of heroic three-year-old Thoroughbreds have thundered past its famous twin spires into legend. During the regular racing season check out "**Dawn at the Downs**" (☎ 502/636–3351), a program that allows fans to visit the track shortly after daybreak on Saturday, when the horses are out for exercise and the infield grass and flower beds are bejeweled with dew. It's magical. The **Kentucky Derby Museum** (☎ 502/637–1111) documents the careers of the champions. During the annual Kentucky Derby Festival—the two weeks leading up to and including Derby Day (the first Saturday in May)—be prepared to pay more for everything in Louisville, from lodging to transportation. ⊠ *700 Central Ave.,* ☎ *502/636–4400. Closed Dec.–Mar. and July–Sept.*

Just east of Louisville is pastoral **Locust Grove** (☎ 502/897–9845), once the home of Louisville's founder. Three presidents—James Monroe, Andrew Jackson, and Zachary Taylor—slept here.

Outside Louisville

In bourbon country, about 25 mi south of the city, is **Bernheim Forest** (⊠ Rte. 245 just off I–65, ☎ 502/543–2451). This 10,000-acre preserve features 1,800 species of plants, a nature center, a museum, picnic areas, hiking trails, and lakes; in spring it has the state's best show of rhododendrons and azaleas. A few miles southeast on scenic Route 245 is Clermont, site of the **Jim Beam American Outpost Museum** (☎ 502/543–9877), which has a collection of the famous Jim Beam bourbon decanters and a film about making bourbon.

Farther southeast on Route 245 is **Bardstown,** a historic city in a bucolic setting, best known as the site of **My Old Kentucky Home State Park** (⊠ 1 mi east of Bardstown on U.S. 150, ☎ 502/348–3502); it is closed January–February. **Federal Hill,** its Georgian Colonial mansion, was visited by Stephen Foster in 1852, shortly before he wrote "My Old Kentucky Home," sung on Kentucky Derby Day.

Southeast of Bardstown, on Route 52 near Loretto, is **Maker's Mark Distillery** (☎ 502/865–2881), a National Historic Landmark and a working distillery that you can tour for free; it is closed weekends January–February. Southwest of Bardstown is the **Abraham Lincoln Birthplace National Historic Site** (⊠ 3 mi south of Hodgenville on U.S. 31E/Rte. 61, ☎ 502/358–3137), where Lincoln was born February 12, 1809. About 110 acres of the original Thomas Lincoln farm are included in the 116-acre park.

Parks and Gardens

In 1891 Louisville's Board of Parks hired Frederick Law Olmsted, designer of New York's Central Park, to design a system of public lands that would be "free to all forever." Among the results were **Shawnee Park** in the west, a plain of river bottomland; **Cherokee Park** in the east, where Beargrass Creek wanders among woods and meadows; and **Iroquois Park** in the south, a tall, rugged escarpment offering vistas of the city. Sometimes overlooked by visitors and natives alike is little **Tyler Park,** on Baxter Avenue, an Olmsted-designed jewel that is an envelope of solitude in the midst of city bustle.

What to See and Do with Children

The **Louisville Zoo** (⊠ 1100 Trevilian Way, ☎ 502/459–2181) exhibits more than 1,600 animals in naturalistic environments. In summer **Kentucky Kingdom—The Thrill Park** (⊠ Kentucky Fair and Exposition Center, ☎ 502/366–2231) has rides and games, including three roller coasters, a water park, and a playground for young children. **Stage One: The Louisville Children's Theatre** (⊠ 425 W. Market St., ☎ 502/584–

7777 or 800/283–7777) offers professional productions on weekends
from October to May.

Dining

Louisville has eating options to suit any taste or pocketbook: from sophisticated gourmet restaurants with adventurous menus and tuxedoed
waiters to no-frills family-style eateries where a server might put a thumb
through your sandwich. In general, a casual atmosphere prevails; you
won't often encounter dress codes. For price ranges *see* Chart 1 (B) *in*
On the Road with Fodor's.

$$$ ✗ **Cafe Metro.** Art deco ambience and creative Continental cuisine are
hallmarks. All entrées have a set price and range from baked quail stuffed
with veal, currants, and pine nuts to seafood in puff pastry. Decadent
desserts are de rigueur. ⊠ *1700 Bardstown Rd.,* ☎ *502/458–4830.
AE, DC, MC, V. Closed Sun.*

$$$ ✗ **English Grill.** The oak-paneled dining room evokes a 19th-century
★ London gentlemen's club. The menu, a marvelous blend of Continen-
tal and Kentucky specialties, changes with the seasons; recent choices
include breast of duck with terrine of foie gras and corn, grilled loin
of lamb marinated with lemon and mint, and a bourbon *anglaise*
dessert soufflé. ⊠ *4th St. and Broadway in the Brown Hotel,* ☎ *502/
583–1234. AE, D, DC, MC, V.*

$$$ ✗ **Lilly's.** Owner-chef Kathy Cary's innovative "haute Kentucky" fare
★ makes the most of farm-fresh produce and meats. Her seasonal menus
include such dishes as sweetbreads and morels cooked with country
ham and hard-boiled eggs or slow-roasted rabbit with lamb sausage.
The stylish dining room, in green, black, and purple, is as eye catch-
ing as the food is palate pleasing. ⊠ *1147 Bardstown Rd.,* ☎ *502/451–
0447. AE, MC, V. Closed Sun.*

$$$ ✗ **Vincenzo's.** Deep leather chairs, 17th-century paintings, and crisp
★ tablecloths provide the setting for just-so service. For the main course
consider *vitello alla Sinatra* (spinach-stuffed veal scallopini with wine
sauce). The award-winning wine list has many excellent Italian and California vintages. ⊠ *Humana Bldg., 150 S. 5th St.,* ☎ *502/580–1350.
AE, D, DC, MC, V. Closed Sun.*

$$ ✗ **Asiatique.** Euro-Asian preparations are the order of the day in this
casual suburban eatery decorated with modern art. Smoked salmon
quesadilla with goat cheese and Asian-style salsa, lemongrass-scented
beef medallions, and roasted quail on a noodle pancake typify the fare.
Order any of the desserts made with ginger ice cream. ⊠ *106 Sears
Ave.,* ☎ *502/899–3578. AE, DC, MC, V.*

$$ ✗ **Baxter Station Bar and Grill.** Just east of downtown, this former neighborhood bar serves up pub grub with flair. Crab cakes and calamari
are on the menu along with burgers and a fine fried-fish sandwich. There
is an excellent selection of imported and microbrewed beers on tap.
In good weather there's outdoor seating. ⊠ *1201 Payne St.,* ☎ *502/
584–1635. AE, MC, V.*

$$ ✗ **Lynn's Paradise Cafe.** Look for the giant red coffeepot and cup-and-
★ saucer fountain out front. The funky decor owes much to Bakelite and
Formica. Portions at breakfast, lunch, and dinner are enormous; in the
morning have the breakfast burrito, for lunch try the Dagwood-size
sandwiches. Dinner (Wednesday through Saturday only) features fa-
mous meat loaf and a bourbon-teriyaki salmon. ⊠ *984 Barret Ave.,*
☎ *502/583–3447. MC, V. Closed Mon.*

$$ ✗ **Uptown Café.** Just down the road from its sister bistro, the upscale
★ Cafe Metro, the Uptown serves imaginative appetizers (including a lus-
cious shrimp bisque), one of the best Caesar salads anywhere, and entrées like duck ravioli and salmon croquettes, making this a local

favorite for fine food at a moderate price. Ask for a booth in the cozy back room. All wines are available by the glass. ⊠ *1624 Bardstown Rd.,* ☎ *502/458–4212. AE, DC, MC, V.*

$ ✕ **Check's Cafe.** The fare in this Germantown eatery, like the atmosphere and the service, is decidedly down-home. Among menu favorites are chili, fish, and bratwurst sandwiches. ⊠ *1101 E. Burnett Ave.,* ☎ *502/637–9515. No credit cards.*

$ ✕ **El Mundo.** This tiny hole-in-the-wall Mexican cantina serves up some of the most authentic south-of-the-border fare in the city. The chile *rellenos* (stuffed green peppers) and enchiladas are highly recommended. Take advantage of the self-serve hot sauces. ⊠ *2345 Frankfort Ave.,* ☎ *502/899–9930. No credit cards. Closed Sun.*

$ ✕ **Mazzoni's Oyster Cafe.** The deep-fried oysters rolled in cornmeal batter are supposedly a Louisville invention. This very casual diner also serves a rich oyster stew and real pan-fried oyster dinner. ⊠ *2804 Taylorsville Rd.,* ☎ *502/451–4436. No credit cards. Closed Sun.*

Lodging

Like any port city, Louisville has a long tradition of hospitality to visitors. You can choose either a lovingly restored, pricey downtown hotel or a budget room in a place that promises to leave the light on for you. Bed-and-breakfast accommodations can be found through **Kentucky Homes B&B** (⊠ 1219 S. 4th Ave., Louisville 40203, ☎ 502/635–7341). For price ranges *see* Chart 2 (B) *in* On the Road with Fodor's.

$$$ ☷ **Camberly Brown Hotel.** This 16-story historic hotel (built in 1923) has been fully restored, with Old English–style furnishings, artwork, atmosphere, and service. ⊠ *335 W. Broadway, 40202,* ☎ *502/583–1234 or 800/866–7666,* ℻ *502/587–7006. 294 rooms. Restaurant, bar, exercise room. AE, D, DC, MC, V.*

$$$ ☷ **Hyatt Regency Louisville.** Hyatt's familiar plant-filled atrium and glass-and-brass lobby are the focus of this 18-story hotel. The rooms have been done in a back-to-nature theme, with redwood and soft pastels. ⊠ *320 W. Jefferson St., 40202,* ☎ *502/587–3434,* ℻ *502/581–0133. 388 rooms. Restaurant, bar, indoor pool, spa, tennis, children's program, concierge. AE, D, DC, MC, V.*

$$$ ☷ **The Seelbach.** The refurbished guest rooms in this 11-story land-
★ mark (built in 1905), now part of the Doubletree chain, have four-poster beds, armoires, and marble baths with gold fixtures. ⊠ *500 4th Ave., 40202,* ☎ *502/585–3200 or 800/333–3399,* ℻ *502/585–3200, ext. 292. 322 rooms. Restaurant, bar, concierge. AE, D, DC, MC, V.*

$$ ☷ **Executive Inn.** The English Tudor style of this six-story hotel near the airport is carried through from the public areas to the rooms, which may seem snug or gloomy, according to your taste. Some have private patios or balconies. ⊠ *978 Phillips La. (off I–64), 40209,* ☎ *502/367–6161 or 800/626–2706; 800/222–8284 in KY;* ℻ *502/367–6161. 465 rooms. Restaurant, bar, indoor and outdoor pools, exercise room. AE, D, DC, MC, V.*

$$ ☷ **Galt House East.** Overlooking the river, this downtown hotel has
★ an elaborately landscaped, modern 18-story atrium, but the room furnishings are of the grandpa's-overstuffed-chair variety, emphasizing old-fashioned comfort. ⊠ *141 N. 4th Ave., 40202,* ☎ *502/589–3300 or 800/843–4258,* ℻ *502/585–4266. 600 rooms. Restaurant, bar, pool. AE, D, DC, MC, V.*

$$ ☷ **Old Louisville Inn Bed & Breakfast.** The guest rooms in this 1901 brick house have elaborately carved mahogany woodwork and are furnished with antiques. The atmosphere and service have a pleasant taken-back-in-time quality. ⊠ *1359 S. 3rd St., 40208,* ☎ *502/635–1574,* ℻ *502/637–5892. 11 rooms. MC, V.*

$ ⌨ **Breckinridge Inn.** This two-story motor hotel is clean, plain, and comfortable. The predominant style in the guest rooms is art deco. ⊠ *2800 Breckinridge La. (at I–264), 40220,* ☎ *502/456–5050,* FAX *502/451–1577. 123 rooms. Restaurant, bar, indoor pool, sauna, tennis. AE, D, DC, MC, V.*

$ ⌨ **Days Inn Downtown.** This conveniently located eight-story motor
★ hotel has clean, spacious rooms decorated with muted colors in Early American style. ⊠ *101 E. Jefferson St., 40202,* ☎ *502/585–2200,* FAX *502/585–2200, ext. 123. 177 rooms. Restaurant, bar, indoor pool, hot tub. AE, D, DC, MC, V.*

$ ⌨ **Wilson Inn.** Far from downtown and painted a horrid salmon color outside, this five-story motor hotel has a pleasant, tree-filled lobby. Milder pastels and earth tones predominate in the plain, contemporary rooms. ⊠ *9802 Bunsen Pkwy. (I–64 at Hurstbourne La.),* ☎ *502/499–0000 or 800/333–9457,* FAX *502/499–0000, ext. 152. 76 rooms. AE, D, DC, MC, V.*

Nightlife and the Arts

For news of arts and entertainment events, look for *Louisville* magazine on newsstands and for the Friday and Saturday editions of the *Courier-Journal* newspaper.

Nightlife

The **Comedy Caravan Nightclub** (⊠ 1250 Bardstown Rd., in the Mid-City Mall, ☎ 502/459–0022) and the **Legends Comedy Club** (⊠ 9700 Bluegrass Pkwy., in the Hurstbourne Hotel & Conference Center, ☎ 502/459–0022) present circuit comics of the stand-up variety. **Coyote's** (⊠ 116 W. Jefferson St., ☎ 502/589–3866) has live country music, a raucous but friendly clientele, and free instruction in two-step and line dancing. **Country Palace Jamboree** (⊠ 421 N. Main St., Mount Washington, about 20 min south of Louisville, ☎ 502/955–8452) is a fun place for families that like country music and dancing. The **Connection** (⊠ 130 S. Floyd St., ☎ 502/585–5752) is a giant entertainment complex consisting of a restaurant, a bar with a Thursday-night talent show and the best and biggest dance floor in town, and a theater with female impersonator revues on the weekends.

The Arts

Actors Theatre of Louisville (⊠ 316 W. Main St., ☎ 502/585–1210) is a Tony Award–winning repertory theater in a bank building (circa 1837) designated a National Historic Landmark. The **Broadway Series** (⊠ 611 W. Main St., ☎ 502/584–7469) hosts touring productions of Broadway's best. **Shakespeare in the Park** (⊠ Central Park at S. 4th St., ☎ 502/634–8237) transforms Louisville into the bard's town on summer weekends.

The three stages at the **Kentucky Center for the Arts** (⊠ 5 Riverfront Plaza, ☎ 502/562–0100 or 800/283–7777) are alive with entertainment ranging from Broadway to Bach, bagpipes to bluegrass. The **Louisville Orchestra** (⊠ 609 W. Main St., ☎ 502/584–7777 or 800/283–7777) has received international attention for its recordings of contemporary works.

Spectator Sports

Horse racing: The Kentucky Derby at **Churchill Downs** (☞ Exploring Louisville, *above*) is a *very* tough ticket—unless you're willing to join tens of thousands of seatless young revelers in the infield, where you're unlikely to get even a glimpse of a horse.

Shopping

Shopping Districts

The Galleria (✉ 4th Ave. between Liberty St. and Muhammad Ali Blvd., ☎ 502/584–7170), a glass-enclosed mall with 80 stores and 11 fast food restaurants, is a city melting pot and the best place to shop downtown. **Bardstown Road,** southeast of downtown, is a 2-mi strip for strolling and browsing in antiques shops, bookstores, and boutiques. The **Jefferson Mall** (☎ 502/968–4101), 10 mi south of downtown on Outer Loop, is a huge enclosed mall with more than 100 stores.

Department Stores

Lazarus (✉ Jefferson Mall, ☎ 502/966–1800; ✉ Oxmoor Center, ☎ 502/423–3000) had been the city's leading department store for more than a decade when upscale **Jacobson's** (✉ Oxmoor Center, ☎ 502/327–0200) came on the scene in 1994. Both faced additional competition when **Dillard's** opened three stores in the Louisville area in 1995. **Bigg's** "hypermarket" (✉ 12975 Shelbyville Rd., Middletown, ☎ 502/244–4760) is what its name suggests. It has everything from pastries to chain saws at bargain prices.

Specialty Stores

The **Kentucky Art & Craft Gallery** (✉ 609 W. Main St., ☎ 502/589–0102) sells top-quality crafts. **Baer Fabrics** (✉ 515 E. Market St., ☎ 502/583–5521) has been amassing its world-renowned collection of buttons since 1905. **Joe Ley Antiques** (✉ 615 E. Market St., ☎ 502/583–4014) has an outstanding 2-acre litter of hardware, fixtures, and doodads.

LEXINGTON AND THE BLUEGRASS

Lexington, the world capital of racehorse breeding and burley tobacco (a thin-bodied, air-cured variety), was named by patriotic hunters who camped here in 1775 shortly after hearing news of the first battle of the Revolutionary War at Lexington, Massachusetts. A log structure built by a member of that historic hunting party is preserved to this day on the campus of Transylvania University. The Bluegrass is a lush region of rolling hills, meandering streams, and manicured horse farms.

Visitor Information

Frankfort/Franklin County: Tourist and Convention Commission (✉ 100 Capital Ave., Frankfort 40601, ☎ 502/875–8687 or 800/960–7200). **Lexington:** Greater Lexington Convention & Visitors Bureau (✉ Suite 363, 430 W. Vine St., 40507, ☎ 606/233–1221 or 800/845–3959). **Richmond:** Tourism Commission (✉ Box 250, City Hall, 40476, ☎ 606/623–1000).

Arriving and Departing

By Car

The Lexington area and the Bluegrass are well served by I–64 east–west, I–75 north–south, and the state parkway system, a toll network that bisects the state east–west.

By Plane

Lexington Bluegrass Airport (✉ 4000 Versailles Rd., ☎ 606/254–9336), 4 mi west of downtown Lexington, is served by Delta, US Airways, and regional lines.

Exploring Lexington and the Bluegrass

Lexington

Take a tour in a horse-drawn carriage from **Lexington Livery Company** (☎ 606/259–0000); a 30-minute tour is $25. In the **Gratz Park Historic District,** near 2nd Street and Broadway, are two fine houses from 1814: the lavish, privately owned **Gratz House** (⊠ 231 N. Mill St., no phone), built by a rich hemp manufacturer, and the **John Hunt Morgan House** (⊠ 201 N. Mill St., ☎ 606/233–3290), the home first of a swashbuckling Confederate general and then his great-grandson, Thomas Hunt Morgan, who won a Nobel Prize in 1933 for proving the existence of the gene. Check out the statue of General Morgan on the lawn of the **Fayette County Courthouse** (⊠ 215 W. Main St.). When it was unveiled in 1911, it caused quite a stir because it portrays the Rebel raider astride a stallion, though his best-known mount was a mare, Black Bess.

The Greek Revival campus of **Transylvania University** (⊠ 300 N. Broadway, ☎ 606/233–8120), the first college west of the Alleghenies (established in 1780), has left its mark on two U.S. vice presidents, 50 senators, 34 ambassadors, and 36 Kentucky governors. The 1832 **Mary Todd Lincoln House** (⊠ 578 W. Main St., ☎ 606/233–9999) belonged to the parents of Abraham Lincoln's wife and displays Lincoln and Todd family memorabilia. The museum is closed December through mid-March. U.S. Senator Henry Clay, the Great Compromiser, was a green 20-year-old lawyer when he came to Lexington in 1797 and opened his **law office** (⊠ 176–178 N. Mill St., no phone).

Two attractions at the **University of Kentucky** (⊠ Euclid Ave. and S. Limestone St., ☎ 606/257–3595) are an **anthropology museum** (⊠ 201 Lafferty Hall, ☎ 606/257–7112), with exhibits on evolution and Kentucky culture, and an **art museum** (⊠ 121 Singletary Center for the Arts, ☎ 606/257–5716), which has an interesting permanent collection and frequent special exhibits.

A Lexington curiosity is the huge **castle** (⊠ Just west of the city on Versailles Rd.), with eight turrets and 70-ft-tall corner towers. A Fayette County developer began, but never finished, construction in 1969 on what was to be his private residence. The **Headley-Whitney Museum** (⊠ Old Frankfort Pike, ☎ 606/255–6653) houses an eclectic, personal three-building collection of Asian porcelains, masks, paintings, shells, and jeweled bibelots.

The Bluegrass

Kentucky's **Bluegrass** area has more than 400 horse farms, some with Thoroughbred barns as elegant as French villas. Among the famous breeding farms is **Calumet** (⊠ Just west of the city on Versailles Rd./U.S. 60, no phone), which has produced a record eight Kentucky Derby winners. The antebellum mansion at **Manchester Farm** (⊠ Van Meter Rd., no phone) is said to have been the inspiration for Tara in *Gone With the Wind.* **Spendthrift** (⊠ Ironworks Pike, ☎ 606/299–5271) is one of the few farms that routinely welcome visitors. Famous horses from the **C. V. Whitney Farm,** on Paris Pike, have included Regret, the first filly to win the Kentucky Derby, and the appropriately named Upset, the only horse ever to finish ahead of the legendary Man o' War. **Normandy** (⊠ Paris Pike, no phone) has a famous L-shape barn, built in 1927, with a clock tower and roof ornaments in animal shapes. You'll note that the plank fencing used by these farms to separate their paddocks is sometimes painted white, sometimes black. Some farm operators claim the traditional white provides better visibility for the horses and is more attractive. Others note that black requires less frequent repainting—a serious economic factor for farms that must maintain miles of such fences, which cost about $18,000 per mile to install (painting extra).

Southward on scenic U.S. 25 is **Fort Boonesborough State Park** (☎ 606/527–3131 or 800/255–7275), a reconstruction of one of Daniel Boone's early forts, with a museum and demonstrations of pioneer crafts. In Richmond visit **White Hall State Historic Site** (☎ 606/623–9178), home of the abolitionist Cassius Marcellus Clay, a cousin of Henry Clay and an ambassador to Russia. The elegant mansion combines two houses and two styles, Georgian and Italianate.

In Berea, where the Bluegrass meets the mountains, you'll find charming, tuition-free **Berea College** (☎ 606/986–9341), founded in 1855, whose 1,500 students—most from Appalachia—work for their education. On the campus is the **Appalachian Museum** (⊠ Jackson St., ☎ 606/986–9341, ext. 6078), which charts regional history through arts and crafts.

★ The **Shaker Village of Pleasant Hill** (⊠ Hwy. 68, ☎ 606/734–5411), 25 mi southwest of Lexington, has 27 restored buildings of frame, brick, or stone erected between 1805 and 1859 by members of a religious sect noted for industry, architecture, and furniture making. In Harrodsburg, the first permanent settlement in Kentucky, **Old Fort Harrod State Park** (☎ 606/734–3314) has a full-scale reproduction of the old fort, built on its original 1774 site.

About 15 mi south of Lexington the beautiful, deep blue-green **Kentucky River** flows gently but relentlessly through the Bluegrass. The combination of rolling river and rugged rock faces makes for dramatic landscapes. Take Jacks Creek Pike from Lexington through one of the most enchanting parts of Kentucky to **Raven Run Nature Sanctuary** (☎ 606/272–6105), a place of rugged, forested hills and untouched wildlife along the Kentucky River.

In lovely Danville, 30 mi southwest of Lexington, you can visit the **McDowell House and Apothecary Shop** (⊠ 125 S. 2nd St., ☎ 606/236–2804), the residence and shop of Dr. Ephraim McDowell (a noted surgeon of the early 19th century), refurnished with period pieces. West of Danville on U.S. 150 and north on U.S. 68 is **Perryville Battlefield** (☎ 606/332–8631), the site of Kentucky's most important (and bloodiest) Civil War battle, where 4,241 Union soldiers and 1,822 Confederates were killed or wounded.

Frankfort, between Louisville and Lexington on I–64, was chosen as the state capital in 1792 as a compromise between those cities' rival claims and has been caught in the middle ever since. The **state capitol** (☎ 502/564–3449), overlooking the Kentucky River at the south end of Capitol Avenue, is notable for its Ionic columns, high central dome, and lantern cupola; guided tours are given. Outside the capitol is the famous **Floral Clock,** a working outdoor timepiece whose face—made of thousands of plants—is swept by a 530-pound minute hand and a 420-pound hour hand.

In Frankfort Cemetery, on East Main Street, you can visit **Daniel Boone's grave** (he died in Missouri, but his remains were returned to Kentucky in 1845). The restored Georgian-style **Old Governor's Mansion** (⊠ 420 High St., ☎ 502/564–5500), built in 1798, served as the residence of 33 governors until a new mansion was built in 1914. The later **governor's mansion** (☎ 502/564–3449) is styled on the Petit Trianon, Marie Antoinette's villa at Versailles.

What to See and Do with Children

Kentucky Horse Park (✉ 4089 Iron Works Pike, off I–75, Lexington, ☎ 606/233–4303) is not just a Thoroughbred showcase; it offers films, a breeds show, and farm tours, as well as a museum, an art gallery, and campgrounds. The interactive exhibits at the **Lexington Children's Museum** (✉ 401 W. Main St., ☎ 606/258–3256) include an archaeology dig. **Lexington Children's Theatre** (☎ 606/254–4546) offers performances for young audiences.

Dining and Lodging

Although Lexington offers varied dining options, including Continental and ethnic cuisines, most restaurants outside the city are decidedly down-home. Menus tend toward country-fried steak, country ham, and fried chicken. Many of the best places to dine are so out of the way and unimpressive looking that you probably won't discover them on your own. Don't be bashful about asking the locals for guidance. For price ranges *see* Chart 1 (B) *in* On the Road with Fodor's.

Most of the best places to lay one's weary head are restored historic properties, often modestly priced, that are short on amenities but long on charm. State park lodges and cottages are bargains, rustic but comfortable. In many rural areas you'll have to settle for bare-bones accommodations. In Lexington **Dial Accommodations** (✉ 430 W. Vine St., ☎ 606/233–7299) can help with reservations. For price ranges *see* Chart 2 (B) *in* On the Road with Fodor's.

Berea

$$ ✕🏠 **Boone Tavern.** This grand old Colonial-style hotel (1909) is op-
★ erated by Berea College and outfitted with furniture handmade by students. The restaurant (jacket and tie for dinner) is famous for its spoon bread, chicken flakes in bird's nest, and Jefferson Davis pie. ✉ *Main and Prospect Sts. (Box 2345), 40403, ☎ 606/986–9358 or 606/986–9359. 57 rooms. Restaurant. AE, D, DC, MC, V.*

Harrodsburg

$$ ✕🏠 **Beaumont Inn.** Guest rooms at this exemplar of southern hospitality are scattered among four timeworn (but polished) buildings furnished with antiques. The restaurant specializes in corn pudding and cured Kentucky country ham. ✉ *638 Beaumont Dr., 40330, ☎ 606/734–3381. 33 rooms. Restaurant, pool, tennis. AE, D, DC, MC, V. Closed mid-Dec.–mid-Mar.*

$$ ✕🏠 **Inn at Pleasant Hill.** Rooms in 27 restored buildings (circa 1800)—some with four stories and no elevators—are furnished with Shaker reproductions and hand-woven rugs and curtains. The restaurant, Trustees' House at Pleasant Hill, serves hearty family-style meals and specializes in a tangy Shaker lemon pie for which people have been known to drive a hundred miles; reservations are essential. ✉ *3500 Lexington Rd., 40330, ☎ 606/734–5411. 80 rooms. Restaurant. MC, V.*

Lexington

$$ ✕ **A la Lucie.** This chef-owned eatery has a Parisian Left Bank ambience, with a tin roof, terrazzo floors, hot colors, green plants, and eclectic art. French, German, and American dishes appear on the menu, but the specialty is whatever seafood is at its seasonal best. ✉ *150 N. Limestone St., ☎ 606/252–5277. AE, DC, MC, V. Closed Sun.*

$$ ✕ **Alfalfa Restaurant.** In this small, woody, old-fashioned restaurant,
★ the fare is home-cooked organically grown vegetarian and ethnic dishes. The menu, written on a chalkboard, may include ham-and-apple quiche; the house salad is lavish. Each Wednesday a different cui-

sine—Greek, Italian, Indian, etc.—is served. ⊠ *557 S. Limestone St.,* ☎ *606/253–0014. MC, V. No dinner Mon.*

$$ ✕ Atomic Cafe. The Bluegrass region may not seem like the place for Caribbean cuisine, but the conch fritters taste fresh off the boat. Jerk chicken and pork dishes are fiery. And shrimp lovers should check out the coconut-battered variety served here. Decor is suitably tropical, with evocative murals. ⊠ *265 N. Limestone St.,* ☎ *606/254–1969. MC, V. Closed Sun.–Mon.*

$$ ✕ Dudley's Restaurant. Chic but unpretentious, this restaurant in a 100-year-old schoolhouse has a courtyard shaded by huge tulip trees. A favorite on the Continental menu is pasta with chicken, sun-dried tomatoes, and vegetables. ⊠ *380 S. Mill St.,* ☎ *606/252–1010. AE, MC, V.*

$$ ✕ Lexington City Brewery. This microbrewery and brew pub in a new shopping center on the edge of the tobacco warehouse district serves up excellent wood-oven pizzas and German sausage platters to go with the topflight beer. Winner's Gold Ale and Smiley Pete's stout are must-sips. ⊠ *1050 S. Broadway,* ☎ *606/259–2739. AE, MC, V.*

$$ ✕ Merrick Inn. A spacious, comfortable, not-too-formal restaurant occupies a sprawling, white-columned building that was formerly a horse farm (circa 1890), decorated in the Williamsburg style. The extensive menu offers steak, lamb, and a variety of pastas, but the Merrick's specialty is fresh seafood of the season (its signature dish is fried walleye pike). ⊠ *3380 Tates Creek Rd.,* ☎ *606/269–5417. AE, DC, MC, V. Closed Sun.*

$ ✕ Joe Bologna's. This longtime college hangout occupies a church built ★ in 1890; the original stained-glass windows are still in place. You can feast on small or large servings of an assortment of pastas, as well as pizza. ⊠ *120 W. Maxwell St.,* ☎ *606/252–4933. MC, V.*

$$$ ▦ Camberly Club Hotel. In an elegantly refurbished three-story medical building dating from 1887, the guest rooms are furnished with antiques. ⊠ *120 2nd St., 40507,* ☎ *606/231–1777 or 800/227–4362,* FAX *606/233–7593. 52 rooms. Restaurant, bar, concierge. AE, D, DC, MC, V.*

$$$ ▦ Marriott's Griffin Gate Resort. This gleaming, contemporary seven-★ story resort hotel caters to a youngish crowd that likes physical activities and physical comforts. The rooms have private patios or balconies. ⊠ *1800 Newtown Pike, 40511,* ☎ *606/231–5100,* FAX *606/231–5100, ext. 7580. 409 rooms. Restaurant, bar, indoor pool, tennis, health club. AE, D, DC, MC, V.*

$$ ▦ Campbell House Inn. Striving for a B&B ambience, this three-story motel has modern but homey rooms, with traditional furnishings. ⊠ *1375 Harrodsburg Rd., 40504,* ☎ *606/255–4281 or 800/354–9235; 800/432–9254 in KY;* FAX *606/254–4368. 370 rooms. Restaurant, bar, pool, tennis. AE, D, DC, MC, V.*

$$ ▦ Courtyard by Marriott. The trademark of this three-story motel is a sunny, gardenlike central courtyard. The green, brown, and mauve rooms are modern, with light woodwork and oversize desks. ⊠ *775 Newtown Ct., 40511,* ☎ *606/253–4646,* FAX *606/253–9118. 146 rooms. Restaurant, bar, indoor pool, hot tub, exercise room. AE, D, DC, MC, V.*

$ ▦ Wilson Inn. This five-story motor hotel resembles its Louisville counterpart: well away from downtown, contemporary in style with a tree-filled lobby, and colored a garish salmon outside but with pleasant pastels and earth tones inside. ⊠ *2400 Buena Vista Dr., 40505,* ☎ *606/293–6113 or 800/945–7667,* FAX *606/293–6113, ext. 157. 110 rooms. AE, D, DC, MC, V.*

Nightlife and the Arts

Nightlife

After-dark offerings in Lexington are pretty sparse and pretty tame. From Thursday through Sunday you might check out the **Brewery** (⊠ 509 W. Main St., ☎ 606/255–2822), a friendly Texas-roadhouse-style bar where the tunes are classic rock and classic country. Or you can visit **Comedy Off Broadway** (⊠ 3199 Nicholasville Rd., ☎ 606/271–5653), where stand-up comics crack wise.

The Arts

Lexington's performing arts scene is vigorous. For information on performances contact the **Actors' Guild** (☎ 606/233–0663), **Lexington Ballet** (☎ 606/233–3925), **Lexington Philharmonic** (☎ 606/233–4226), and **Opera of Central Kentucky** (☎ 606/231–6994). Concerts, plays, and lectures are also presented at **Transylvania University** and the **University of Kentucky.**

Outdoor Activities and Sports

Kentucky's lakes and streams provide great **fishing** for more than 200 species. You're seldom more than a 30-minute drive away from a public **golf** course. The state parks and national forests are full of **hiking** trails. Eastern Kentucky has several rivers that offer mild to moderate **white-water rafting** opportunities. For information contact the parks department (☞ National and State Parks, *above*), tourism offices (☞ Visitor Information, *above*), or the state **Department of Fish and Wildlife Resources** (⊠ 1 Game Farm Rd., Frankfort 40601, ☎ 502/564–4336).

Spectator Sports

Horse racing: Keeneland Race Course (⊠ 4201 Versailles Rd., Lexington, ☎ 606/254–3412 or 800/456–3412); April and October.

Shopping

In Lexington **Fayette Mall** (⊠ 3473 Nicholasville Rd., ☎ 606/272–3493) has more than 100 stores and a dozen places to eat. For something out of the ordinary, try **Dudley Square** (⊠ 380 S. Mill St., no phone), in a restored 1881 school building; its shops feature antiques, prints, quilts, and the like. **Victorian Square** (⊠ 401 W. Main St., ☎ 606/252–7575) is an entire downtown block of renovated Victorian buildings that now contain tony retail and dining establishments. Lexington also has a plethora of **antiques shops;** the Convention & Visitors Bureau (☞ Visitor Information, *above*) maintains a list.

LOUISIANA

By Honey
Naylor

Capital	Baton Rouge
Population	4,351,000
Motto	Union, Justice, and Confidence
State Bird	Pelican
State Flower	Magnolia
Postal Abbreviation	LA

Statewide Visitor Information

Louisiana Office of Tourism (⊠ Box 94291, Baton Rouge 70804-9291, ☎ 800/334–8626).

Scenic Drives

Gators laze along the exotic **Creole Nature Trail,** a circular drive out of Lake Charles designated a National Scenic Byway. **Routes 56 and 57** also form a circular drive south of Houma, where shrimp boats dock along the bayous from May to December. **Route 82** runs through the coastal marshes and wildlife refuges along the Gulf of Mexico. The **Longleaf Trail Scenic Byway,** south of Natchitoches, is a 17-mi highway through the Kisatchie National Forest linking Routes 117 and 119. **Route 182** runs for much of the way alongside Bayou Teche in southern Louisiana.

National and State Parks

National Parks

The **Jean Lafitte National Historical Park and Preserve** (⊠ 365 Canal St., New Orleans 70130, ☎ 504/589–3882) maintains coastal wetlands south of New Orleans and offers nature trails and canoeing through exotic swampland. The 100,000-acre Kisatchie Ranger District of the **Kisatchie National Forest** (⊠ Box 2128, Natchitoches 71457, ☎ 318/473–7160) has hiking and equestrian trails through hardwood and pine forests.

State Parks

A prehistoric Native American site dating to between 1800 BC and 500 BC, the 400-acre **Poverty Point State Commemorative Area,** in the extreme northeast corner of Louisiana (⊠ Rte. 577, Box 276, Epps 71237, ☎ 318/926–5492), is one of the country's most important excavations, with hiking trails and an interpretive center in addition to the ancient Native American mounds. The 600-acre **Louisiana State Arboretum** (⊠ Rte. 3, Box 494, Ville Platte 70586, ☎ 318/363–6289), lush with trees and plants native to the state, has 2½ mi of nature trails. Fishing, boating, and camping (cabins are available) are all possibilities in the 6,500-acre **Chicot State Park** (⊠ Rte. 3, Box 494, Ville Platte 70586, ☎ 318/363–2403) and at **Bayou Segnette,** near New Orleans (⊠ 7777 Westbank Expressway, Westwego 70094, ☎ 504/436–1107), **Lake Bistineau State Park** (⊠ Box 589, Doyline 71023, ☎ 318/745–3503), **Lake Fausse Point State Park** (⊠ Rte. 5, Box 5648, St. Martinville 70582, ☎ 318/229–4764), **North Toledo Bend State Park** (⊠ Box 56, Zwolle 71486, ☎ 318/645–4715), and **Sam Houston Jones State Park** (⊠ Rte. 4, Box 294, Lake Charles 70601, ☎ 318/855–2665).

NEW ORLEANS

Strategically situated on the Mississippi River, New Orleans is Louisiana's largest and most important city. From its beginnings in 1718 the city has played a vital role in the nation's history. To wrest control of the port city from the French in 1803, President Thomas Jefferson paid Napoléon $15 million and got the entire Louisiana Territory in the bargain. The Big Easy is the home of the splashiest festival in all North America: Mardi Gras, which is held each February or March, depending on when Lent falls. New Orleans is a fun-loving city with an insouciant spirit reminiscent of the Caribbean. As Jelly Roll Morton said, New Orleans is "the place where the birth of jazz originated." And local chefs gave the world exotic Creole cuisine. The French Quarter (also known as the Vieux Carré), with its honky-tonk Bourbon Street, is one of the nation's favorite partying places.

Visitor Information

New Orleans Metropolitan Convention & Visitors Bureau (⊠ 1520 Sugar Bowl Dr., 70112, ☎ 504/566–5031 or 800/672–6124, ℻ 504/566–5046). **New Orleans Welcome Center** (⊠ 529 St. Ann St., in the French Quarter, ☎ 504/568–5661).

Arriving and Departing

By Boat

You can arrive from northern ports in grand 19th-century style aboard one of the authentic overnight steamboats that home-port in New Orleans—the *Delta Queen,* the *Mississippi Queen,* or the *American Queen*—all run by the **Delta Queen Steamboat Company** (⊠ 30 Robin St. Wharf, 70130, ☎ 800/543–1949, ℻ 504/585–0630).

By Bus and Train
Union Passenger Terminal (⊠ 1001 Loyola Ave., ☎ 504/528–1610).

By Car
I–10 is the major east–west artery through the city; I–55, which runs north–south, connects with I–10 west of town. I–59 heads for the northeast. U.S. 61 and U.S. 90 also run through the city.

By Plane
New Orleans International Airport (also known as Moisant Field, ☎ 504/464–0831), 15 mi west of New Orleans, is served by most major domestic and some foreign carriers. Cab fare for the 20- to 30-minute trip to downtown is $21 for one or two passengers, $8 for each additional passenger, plus tip. The 24-hour **Airport Shuttle** (☎ 504/522–3500) drops passengers off at all hotels. Buses operated by **Louisiana Transit** (☎ 504/737–9611) run between the airport and the Central Business District; the fare is $1.10 (exact change in coins).

Getting Around New Orleans

The French Quarter is best savored on leisurely strolls; the Central Business District (CBD) is also easily walkable.

By Car
Driving in New Orleans can be maddening. French Quarter streets are often clogged with traffic, street signs are indecipherable, and tow trucks operate with lightning speed. Leave your car in a secured garage until it's needed for excursions.

By Ferry

A ferry (*Crescent City Connection,* ☎ 504/364–8100) crosses the Mississippi from the Canal Street Wharf to Algiers, leaving the pier every 25 minutes. It's free outgoing and $1 returning.

By Public Transportation

The **Regional Transit Authority,** or RTA (☎ 504/248–3900, TTY 504/248–2838), operates the bus and streetcar system and staffs a 24-hour information line.

Bus and **St. Charles Streetcar** fare is $1 (exact change); the **Riverfront Streetcar** ($1.25 exact change) links attractions along the Mississippi. The **Vieux Carré Shuttle** runs through the French Quarter to the foot of Canal Street. VisiTour passes, good on all RTA buses and streetcars, cost $4 (one day) and $8 (three days).

By Taxi

Cabs cruise the French Quarter and the CBD but not beyond. Reliable companies with 24-hour service are **United Cabs** (☎ 504/522–9771) and **Yellow-Checker Cabs** (☎ 504/943–2411). The fare is $1.70 at the flag drop, 20¢ for each additional ⅕ mi, and 50¢ for each additional passenger.

Orientation Tours

Bus and Van Tours

Two- to three-hour city tours, full- and half-day tours to plantation country, and a hop-on/hop-off trolley tour that stops at 10 attractions are available from **Gray Line** (☎ 504/587–0861 or 800/535–7788). **New Orleans Tours** (☎ 504/592–0560, 504/592–1991, or 800/543–6332) and **Tours by Isabelle** (☎ 504/391–3544) do city tours as well as bayou/swamp outings. Gray Line and New Orleans Tours also offer combination bus-and-paddlewheel tours. **Le 'Ob's Tours** (☎ 504/288–3478) runs a daily city tour that focuses on the heritage of African-Americans, as well as a plantation tour and a black bayou/Cajun tour.

Cruises

Riverboat sightseeing and dinner-jazz cruises are offered by the **New Orleans Steamboat Company** (☎ 504/586–8777) and **New Orleans Paddle Wheels** (☎ 594/524–0814). Bayou tours are offered by **Honey Island Swamp Tours** (☎ 504/641–1769) and **Cypress Swamp Tours** (☎ 504/581–4501).

Walking Tours

Kith & Kin (☎ 800/733–7423), novelist Anne Rice's family company, conducts walking and bus tours of the Garden District and environs. Tours start at 2624 St. Charles Avenue. **Friends of the Cabildo** (☎ 504/523–3939) offers tours of the French Quarter. Rangers of the **Jean Lafitte National Historical Park and Preserve** (☎ 504/589–2636) conduct free tours of the Quarter and the Garden District. **Heritage Tours** (☎ 504/949–9805) offers literary tours of the Quarter. **Save Our Cemeteries** (☎ 504/588–9357) conducts tours of above-ground cemeteries. Free maps for self-guided walking tours are available at the New Orleans Welcome Center (☞ Visitor Information, *above*).

Exploring New Orleans

The French Quarter and the CBD

★ The **French Quarter** is the original colony founded in 1718 by French Creoles. A carefully preserved historic district that's also a residential district, the Quarter is also home to some famous French Creole restaurants and many a jazz club. An eclectic crowd ambles in and out of small two- and three-story frame, old-brick, and pastel-stucco buildings, most of which date from the mid-19th century. Baskets of splashy subtropical plants dangle from the eaves of buildings with filigreed galleries, dollops of gingerbread, and dormer windows. Secluded courtyards are awash in greenery and brilliant blossoms.

The heart of the Quarter is **Jackson Square,** a pretty green park surrounded by a flagstone pedestrian mall and centered by an equestrian statue of Andrew Jackson. Originally known to Creoles as Place d'Armes, the square was renamed in the mid-19th century for the man who defeated the British in the Battle of New Orleans. The mall is alive with sidewalk artists, food vendors, Dixieland bands, tap dancers, and clowns.

St. Louis Cathedral is a quiet reminder of the city's spiritual life. The present church dates from 1794 and was restored in 1849. Tours are conducted daily except during services. **Pirate's Alley** and **Père Antoine's Alley,** two ancient flagstone passageways redolent of bygone days, run alongside St. Louis Cathedral.

Two 18th-century buildings of the **Louisiana State Museum** flank St. Louis Cathedral. As you face the church, the **Cabildo** is on the left, the **Presbytère** on the right. Transfer papers for the Louisiana Purchase of 1803 were signed on the second floor of the Cabildo. New Orleans's rich multicultural history is explored through historic documents and artifacts, among them a death mask of Napoléon—one of only three in the world. The Presbytère, originally built as a home for priests of the church, today houses changing exhibits. ⊠ *751 Chartres St.,* ☎ *504/568–6968. Closed Mon.*

You can see what life was like for upscale 19th-century Creole apartment dwellers in the state museum's **1850s House,** which contains period furnishings, antique dolls, and a quaint kitchen. ⊠ *523 St. Ann St.,* ☎ *504/568–6968. Closed Mon.*

The **Pontalba Buildings,** which line Jackson Square on St. Ann and St. Peter streets, are among the oldest apartment houses in the country. Built between 1849 and 1851, they have some of the city's loveliest ironwork galleries.

The promenade of **Washington Artillery Park,** across Decatur Street from Jackson Square, affords a splendid perspective on the square and ★ Ol' Man River. Northeast of Jackson Square is the **French Market**—a complex of shops, offices, and eating places in a row of renovated buildings that once housed markets during Spanish and French rule. Here **Café du Monde** provides a 24-hour haven for café au lait and beignets (a unique New Orleans concoction: squares of fried dough dusted with powdered sugar).

The **Old U.S. Mint,** which lies downriver of Jackson Square, houses exhibits on jazz and Mardi Gras. This was the first branch of the U.S. Mint, in operation from 1838 until 1861. It's now part of the Louisiana State Museum. ⊠ *400 Esplanade Ave.,* ☎ *504/568–6968. Closed Mon.*

★ The **Old Ursuline Convent,** erected in 1749 by order of Louis XV, is the only building remaining from the original colony. The Sisters of Ursula, who arrived here in 1727, occupied the building from 1749 to 1824. Guided tours of the complex take in the splendid **St. Mary's Church.** ⊠ *1100 Chartres St.,* ☎ *504/529–3040. Closed Mon.*

The **Gallier House** was built about 1857 by famed architect James Gallier Jr. as his family home. This is one of the best-researched house-

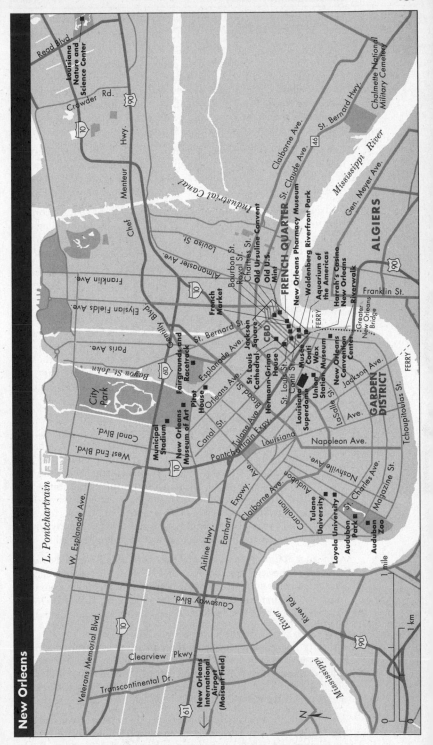

New Orleans

museums in the city and a fine example of how well-heeled Creoles lived. ⊠ *1118–32 Royal St.,* ☎ *504/523–6722. Closed Sun.*

The tattered cottage at 941 Bourbon Street—dating from the late 18th century and typical of houses of the period—is **Lafitte's Blacksmith Shop,** a popular neighborhood bar. According to legend the cottage was once a front for pirate Jean Laffite's smuggling and slave trade. The **LaBranche House** (⊠ 740 Royal St.), dating from about 1840, wraps around the corner of Royal and St. Peter streets. Its filigreed double galleries are the most photographed in the city.

The **New Orleans Pharmacy Museum** is a musty old place where the nation's first licensed pharmacist lived and worked. It's full of ancient and mysterious medicinal things. ⊠ *514 Chartres St.,* ☎ *504/565–8027. Closed Mon.*

★ At the **Hermann-Grima House,** guides take you through the Georgian-style town house, built in 1831, and its picturesque outbuildings. On Thursday in winter you can watch Creole cooking demonstrations—sorry, no tastings! ⊠ *820 St. Louis St.,* ☎ *504/525–5661. Closed Sun.*

Not to be missed are the tableaux in the **Musée Conti Wax Museum,** which wax lifelike on such Louisiana legends as Andrew Jackson, Jean Laffite, and Marie Laveau, the 19th-century voodoo queen. ⊠ *917 Conti St.,* ☎ *504/525–2605.*

Canal Street, the upriver border of the French Quarter, is a main thoroughfare of the CBD as well as the dividing line between Uptown and Downtown. Nerve center of the nation's second-largest port, the CBD has the city's newest high-tech convention hotels, along with ritzy shopping malls, fast-food chains, stores, foreign agencies, and the mammoth Superdome.

Also planned for Canal Street was the city's first land-based casino. Construction of **Harrah's Casino New Orleans,** began—and ended—in 1995. In May 1995 Harrah's opened a temporary facility in the renovated Municipal Auditorium in Armstrong Park. In November 1995 the temporary casino closed its doors, perhaps permanently, and Harrah's ceased construction of the Canal Street casino. The gaming business in New Orleans is on the order of a protracted Keystone Kops routine, and the future of the casinos is a crapshoot. At press time Harrah's was still working out a bankruptcy plan, even as the city and the casino tried hammering out an agreement for a smaller facility.

At the foot of Canal Street, hard by the Mississippi River, is the **Aquarium of the Americas** (☎ 504/565–3033), which offers close encounters with aquatic creatures in 60 displays in four major environments. In 1995 a multimillion-dollar wing was added that includes an IMAX
★ theater. The 16-acre **Woldenberg Riverfront Park,** around the aquarium, affords an excellent view of the river.

The ferry landing is across from the aquarium, adjacent to which is **Riverwalk.** This busy area comprises Spanish Plaza, a broad, open expanse of mosaic tile with a magnificent fountain; the Riverwalk shopping mall; and docks for sightseeing riverboats. Amazingly, a freighter that crashed into Riverwalk in late 1996 left no long-term scars.

After touring the French Quarter and the adjacent CBD, you can head upriver (west) to the Garden District and Uptown. Mid-City, between the Quarter and Lake Pontchartrain, is home to the **Fair Grounds Race Track** (☞ Spectator Sports, *below*). North of town, **Lake Pontchartrain,** popular for boating and fishing, is lined with marinas, picnic grounds, and seafood restaurants.

The Garden District and Uptown

Nestled between St. Charles, Louisiana, and Jackson avenues and Magazine Street, the **Garden District** is aptly named. Shunned by the French Creoles when they arrived in the early 19th century, American settlers built palatial estates upriver and surrounded them with lavish lawns. Many of the elegant Garden District houses were built during New Orleans's Golden Age, from 1830 until the Civil War. Some of these private homes are open to the public during Spring Fiesta tours.

Uptown is the area just upriver of the Garden District. Across from **Audubon Park** (☞ Parks and Gardens, *below*), **Tulane** and **Loyola** universities stand side by side on St. Charles Avenue.

Mid-City

In lush City Park (☞ Parks and Gardens, *below*), the **New Orleans Museum of Art** displays Italian paintings from the 13th to the 18th centuries, 20th-century European and American paintings and sculptures, Chinese jade, and the *Imperial Treasures*, by Peter Carl Fabergé. ⊠ *1 Collins-Diboll Dr., ☎ 504/488–2631. Closed Mon.*

The **Pitot House,** which sits across Bayou St. John from City Park, is a West Indies–style house built in the late 18th century. It is furnished with Louisiana and other American 19th-century antiques. ⊠ *1440 Moss St., ☎ 504/482–0312. Closed Sun.–Tues.*

Parks and Gardens

City Park (⊠ City Park Ave., ☎ 504/482–4888), in Mid-City, is a 1,500-acre urban oasis shaded by majestic live oak trees. Its offerings include golf courses and tennis courts; lagoons for boating, canoeing, and fishing; botanical gardens; and a children's amusement park with a carousel and pony rides.

Smaller but no less lush, the 400-acre **Audubon Park** (⊠ 6500–6800 blocks of St. Charles Ave.) features a 2-mi jogging trail with exercise stations, a riding stable, a swimming pool, tennis courts, a golf course, and a zoo.

The **Audubon Zoo** covers 58 acres of Audubon Park. Wooden walkways afford an up-close look at more than 1,800 animals in natural-habitat settings, including a Louisiana swamp and an African savanna. There's also a petting zoo and elephant and camel rides. ⊠ *6500 Magazine St., ☎ 504/861–2537.*

What to See and Do with Children

The **Louisiana Children's Museum** (⊠ 420 Julia St., ☎ 504/523–1357) features hands-on activities that are both educational and fun. **Le Petit Théâtre du Vieux Carré** (☞ Nightlife and the Arts, *below*) presents children's shows. **Louisiana Nature and Science Center** (⊠ 11000 Lake Forest Blvd., ☎ 504/246–9381) has a planetarium and nature trails through forests and wetlands.

Dining

New Orleans is renowned for Creole and Cajun cuisine. The essence of Creole is in its classic French-style sauces and distinctive seasonings; Cajun cooking, with its hearty ingredients, tends to be more rustic in style. For price ranges *see* Chart 1 (A) *in* On the Road with Fodor's.

$$$$ ✕ **Antoine's.** Established in 1840, Antoine's is the oldest restaurant in the United States under continuous family ownership. An elegant place, it originated oysters Rockefeller, pompano *en papillote*, and puffed-up soufflé potatoes. There is a moderately priced luncheon menu. ⊠ *713 St. Louis St., French Quarter,* ☎ *504/581–4422. Reservations essential on weekends. Jacket required for dinner. AE, DC, MC, V.*

$$$$ ✕ **Arnaud's.** Beveled glass, ceiling fans, and tile floors create an aura
★   of traditional southern dining. The lively Sunday jazz brunch is a classic New Orleans experience. In late 1996 Arnaud's Bar became a cigar bar, and the Richelieu Room opened for late-night live music, supping, and dancing. ⊠ *813 Bienville St., French Quarter,* ☎ *504/523–5433. Reservations essential. Jacket required. AE, DC, MC, V.*

$$$$ ✕ **Commander's Palace.** Housed in a renovated Victorian mansion, this
★   elegant restaurant offers the best sampling in New Orleans of old Creole cooking, prepared with a combination of American and French touches. Entrées include veal chop Tchoupitoulas (hickory grilled with Creole seasoning—peppercorn, honey, and roasted peppers) and trout with roasted pecans. ⊠ *1403 Washington Ave., Garden District,* ☎ *504/899–8221. Reservations essential. Jacket required. AE, DC, MC, V.*

$$$$ ✕ **Grill Room.** At this top-rated spot new American cuisine with strong
★   Continental overtones is served in an opulent setting highlighted by original artwork. As the name suggests, there's a grill, over which much good fish is prepared. ⊠ *Windsor Court Hotel, 300 Gravier St., CBD,* ☎ *504/522–1992. AE, DC, MC, V.*

$$$$ ✕ **K-Paul's Louisiana Kitchen.** National celebrity chef Paul Prudhomme's restaurant is a shrine to New Orleans Cajun cooking. Reservations are accepted for dinner only; the long lines for lunch may be shortened with the restaurant's 1997 expansion. In any case, the food is superb. ⊠ *416 Chartres St., French Quarter,* ☎ *504/524–7394. Closed weekends.*

$$$ ✕ **Nola.** A spin-off of the pricier and plusher Emeril's, Nola serves down-
★   to-earth southern Louisiana dishes in energetic and colorful surroundings. A brick oven churns out sterling breads, roasted Gulf fish, and a belt-busting mixed grill. ⊠ *534 St. Louis St., French Quarter,* ☎ *504/522–6652. Reservations essential. AE, D, DC, MC, V. No lunch Sun.*

$$$ ✕ **Palace Cafe.** A split-level restaurant with the ambience of a Parisian café, the Palace has a spiral staircase, a tile floor, wood paneling, and splashy murals. Specialties are seafood, game, and rotisserie chicken basted in garlic oil. Wait till you see the menu of chocolate desserts. ⊠ *605 Canal St., CBD,* ☎ *504/523–1661. DC, MC, V.*

$$ ✕ **Galatoire's.** Operated by the fourth generation of the family own-
★   ers, Galatoire's is a tradition in New Orleans. Every imaginable Creole dish is served in a large, brightly lighted room with mirrors on all sides. Avoid the long lines by arriving after 1:30 PM. ⊠ *209 Bourbon St., French Quarter,* ☎ *504/525–2021. Reservations not accepted. Jacket and tie after 5 PM and all day Sun. AE, MC, V. Closed Mon.*

$$ ✕ **Napoleon House.** This ancient bar with peeling sepia walls and Napoleonic memorabilia has introduced a more ambitious menu to augment its popular *muffuletta* (an Italian sandwich of meats, cheeses, and olive salad served on an oversize round roll). The taped classical music and mellow ambience make this a popular spot for chilling out. ⊠ *500 Chartres St., French Quarter,* ☎ *504/524–9752. AE, MC, V.*

$ ✕ **Camellia Grill.** This classy lunch counter with linen napkins and a
★   maître d' serves the best omelets in town all day long, as well as great hamburgers, pecan pie, cheesecake, and banana cream pie. Expect long lines on weekends for breakfast. ⊠ *626 S. Carrollton Ave., Uptown,* ☎ *504/866–9573. Reservations not accepted. No credit cards.*

$ ✕ **Praline Connection.** Down-home cooking in the southern Creole style is the forte of these laid-back restaurants. The fried or stewed chicken, smothered pork chops, barbecued ribs, and collard greens are definitively done. ⊠ *542 Frenchmen St., Faubourg Marigny,* ☎ *504/943–*

3934; ⊠ *901 S. Peters St., Warehouse District,* ☎ *504/523–3973. Reservations not accepted. AE, MC, V.*

Lodging

Reserve well in advance of your New Orleans stay, especially during Mardi Gras or other seasonal events. Hotels frequently offer special packages at reduced rates, but never during Mardi Gras, when rates are much higher. For price ranges *see* Chart 2 (A) *in* On the Road with Fodor's.

$$$$ 🏨 **Fairmont Hotel.** The Fairmont, in the CBD, is one of the oldest grand hotels in America. Its lobby is decked out in blue-and-gold Victorian splendor. Special touches in every room include down pillows and terry-cloth robes. ⊠ *University Pl., 70140,* ☎ *504/529–7111 or 800/ 527–4727,* 🖷 *504/529–4764. 806 rooms. 3 restaurants, bars, room service, pool, beauty salon, 2 tennis courts, exercise room, business services, valet parking. AE, D, DC, MC, V.*

$$$$ 🏨 **Windsor Court Hotel.** Consistently rated one of the top luxury ho- ★ tels in the country, this CBD gem features canopy and four-poster beds, wet bars, and high tea served daily in the plush lobby lounge. ⊠ *300 Gravier St., 70130,* ☎ *504/523–6000 or 800/262–2662,* 🖷 *504/ 596–4513. 315 rooms. 2 restaurants, lounge, pool, hot tub, sauna, steam room, health club, laundry service, parking (fee). AE, DC, MC, V.*

$$$ 🏨 **Royal Orleans Hotel (Omni).** An elegant white-marble hotel in the French Quarter, the Royal O is reminiscent of a bygone era. Rooms, though not exceptionally large, are well appointed, with marble baths (telephone in each) and marble-top dressers and tables. ⊠ *621 St. Louis St., 70140,* ☎ *504/529–5333,* 🖷 *504/529–7089. 346 rooms. 2 restaurants, 3 lounges, pool, barbershop, beauty salon, exercise room, business services, parking (fee). AE, D, DC, MC, V.*

$$ 🏨 **Holiday Inn Château Le Moyne.** The atmosphere and decor of this French Quarter inn are mostly Old World, with eight suites in restored Creole cottages that retain the original cedar ceilings and exposed beams. ⊠ *301 Dauphine St., 70112,* ☎ *504/581–1303,* 🖷 *504/523– 5709. 171 rooms. Restaurant, lounge, pool, valet parking. AE, D, DC, MC, V.*

$$ 🏨 **Josephine Guest House.** European antiques fill the rooms of this restored Italianate mansion in the Garden District, built in 1870. The bathrooms are impressive in both size and decor. A complimentary Continental breakfast, served on Wedgwood china from a silver tray, can be brought to your room. ⊠ *1450 Josephine St., 70130,* ☎ *504/524–6361 or 800/ 779–6361,* 🖷 *504/523–6484. 6 rooms. AE, D, DC, MC, V.*

$$ 🏨 **Le Richelieu.** This small, friendly hotel in the French Quarter offers ★ many amenities usually found in luxury high-rises. Some rooms have mirrored walls, walk-in closets, and refrigerators; all have hair dryers. Luxury suites are available. ⊠ *1234 Chartres St., 70116,* ☎ *504/ 529–2492 or 800/535–9653,* 🖷 *504/524–8179. 86 rooms. Restaurant, lounge, pool, free parking. AE, D, DC, MC, V.*

$$ 🏨 **Pontchartrain Hotel.** Maintaining the grand tradition is the hallmark ★ of this quiet, elegant European-style hotel, which has reigned in the Garden District for more than 60 years. Accommodations range from lavish sun-filled suites to small pension-style rooms with shower-baths. ⊠ *2031 St. Charles Ave., 70140,* ☎ *504/524–0581 or 800/777– 6193,* 🖷 *504/529–1165. 104 rooms. 2 restaurants, piano bar, concierge, parking. AE, D, DC, MC, V.*

$ 🏨 **Rue Royal Inn.** This circa-1850 home has balcony rooms overlooking a courtyard and Royal Street; two suites have whirlpool baths. Each room has a coffeemaker and a small refrigerator. ⊠ *1006 Royal*

St., 70116, ☎ *504/524–3900 or 800/776–3901,* FAX *504/558–0566. 17 rooms. AE, D, DC, MC, V.*

$ ☎ **St. Charles Guest House.** Rooms in this simple, family-run guest house in the Garden District vary from large to small; the latter, with shared baths and no air-conditioning, are suitable for backpackers. ✉ *1748 Prytania St.,* 70130, ☎ *504/523–6556,* FAX *504/529–2952. 26 rooms, 22 with bath. Lounge, pool. AE, MC, V.*

Nightlife and the Arts

The Friday edition of the *Times-Picayune* and the weekly *Gambit* (free) carry comprehensive calendars of arts and entertainment events. *New Orleans* magazine (on newsstands) and *This Week in New Orleans* and *Where: New Orleans* (both available free in hotels) also publish calendars of events. Credit card purchases of tickets for events at the Saenger Performing Arts Center and UNO Lakefront Arena can be made through **TicketMaster** (☎ 504/522–5555 or 800/488–5252).

Nightlife

New Orleans is a 24-hour town, meaning there are no legal closing times, and it ain't over till it's over. Bourbon Street in the French Quarter is lined with clubs; many local hangouts are Uptown.

BARS

Pat O'Brien's (✉ 718 St. Peter St., French Quarter, ☎ 504/525–4823) has three lively bars. **Lafitte's Blacksmith Shop** (✉ 941 Bourbon St., French Quarter, ☎ 504/523–0066) and the **Napoleon House** (✉ 500 Chartres St., French Quarter, ☎ 504/524–9752) are longtime favorite hangouts.

CASINOS

With the 1995 closing of **Harrah's Casino New Orleans,** the only casino gambling in the city is on board three riverboats. Some actually cruise, but others, contrary to state law, offer dockside gambling. Bally's **Belle of Orleans** (Lake Pontchartrain) joins the **Boomtown Belle** (Harvey Canal on the West bank) and the **Treasure Chest** (Lake Pontchartrain in Kenner).

JAZZ

Aboard the **Creole Queen** (✉ Poydras St. Wharf, CBD, ☎ 504/529–4567) you'll cruise with jazz and a buffet. Live traditional jazz is also on land at the **Palm Court Jazz Cafe** (✉ 1204 Decatur St., French Quarter, ☎ 504/525–0200), **Pete Fountain's** (✉ 2 Poydras St., CBD, ☎ 504/523–4374), and **Preservation Hall** (✉ 726 St. Peter St., French Quarter, ☎ 504/523–8939).

R&B, CAJUN, ROCK, NEW WAVE

Top-notch local and nationally known musicians perform at **House of Blues** (✉ 225 Decatur St., French Quarter, ☎ 504/529–2583) and **Margaritaville Café** (✉ 1104 Decatur St., French Quarter, ☎ 504/592–2565). An institution, **Professor Longhair's Tipitina's** (✉ 501 Napoleon Ave., Uptown, ☎ 504/897–3943) is a laid-back place with a mixed bag of music. **Jimmy's Music Club** (✉ 8200 Willow St., Uptown, ☎ 504/861–8200) is popular with the college crowd. Industrial-strength rock rolls out of the sound system at the **Hard Rock Café** (✉ 440 N. Peters St., ☎ 504/529–8617). Two-step to a Cajun band at the **Maple Leaf Bar** (✉ 8316 Oak St., Uptown, ☎ 504/866–9359), **Mulate's** (✉ 201 Julia St., Warehouse District, ☎ 504/522–1492), and **Michaul's** (✉ 840 St. Charles Ave., CBD, ☎ 504/522–5517).

The Arts

CONCERTS

Free jazz concerts are held on weekends in **Dutch Alley** (French Market at St. Philip St., ☎ 504/596–3424).

THEATER

The avant-garde and the satirical are among the offerings at **Contemporary Arts Center** (✉ 900 Camp St., ☎ 504/523–1216). **Le Petit Théâtre du Vieux Carré** (✉ 616 St. Peter St., ☎ 504/522–2081) presents more traditional fare as well as children's theater. Touring Broadway shows and top-name talent appear at the **Saenger Performing Arts Center** (✉ 143 N. Rampart St., ☎ 504/524–2490). Nationally known artists perform at **Kiefer UNO Lakefront Arena** (✉ 6801 Franklin Ave., ☎ 504/286–7222).

Outdoor Activities and Sports

Biking

Bikes can be rented at **Bicycle Michael's** (✉ 518 Frenchmen St., ☎ 504/945–9505) and **French Quarter Bicycles** (✉ 518 Dumaine St., ☎ 504/529–3136).

Boating

Canoes, rowboats, and pedal boats can be rented for lazing along **City Park's lagoons** (✉ Dreyfous Dr., ☎ 504/483–9371).

Golf

There are four 18-hole courses at **City Park,** as well as a 100-tee double-decker driving range (✉ 1040 Fillmore Dr., ☎ 504/483–9396), and an 18-hole course at **Audubon Park** (✉ 473 Walnut St., ☎ 504/865–8260.

Tennis

There are 39 courts at **City Park's Wisner Tennis Center** (✉ Dreyfous Dr., ☎ 504/482–4888) and 10 courts in **Audubon Park** (✉ Rear of park off Tchoupitoulas St., ☎ 504/895–1042).

Spectator Sports

Baseball: The **New Orleans Zephyrs** (✉ 6000 Airline Hwy., Metairie, ☎ 504/734–5155), a Class AAA minor-league team of the Houston Astros, now play their home games at Zephyr Stadium in Jefferson Parish.

Football: The **New Orleans Saints** play in the Superdome (✉ 1 Sugar Bowl Dr., ☎ 504/522–2600). The **Sugar Bowl Classic** (☎ 504/525–8573) is played annually in the Dome around New Year's. The **Super Bowl,** hosted by New Orleans in 1997, has been played more times in this city than in any other.

Horse Racing: There is Thoroughbred racing from Thanksgiving Day to April at the **Fair Grounds** (✉ 1751 Gentilly Blvd., ☎ 504/944–5515). At press time tents put up after a December 1993 fire still have yet to be replaced by permanent buildings.

Shopping

Louisiana's **tax-free shopping** program grants shoppers from other countries a sales-tax rebate. Retailers who display the tax-free sign issue vouchers for the 9% sales tax, which can be redeemed on departure. Present the vouchers with your passport and international plane ticket at the tax-rebate office at New Orleans International Airport and receive up to $500 in cash back. If the amount redeemable exceeds $500, a check for the difference will be mailed to you. Store hours are generally Monday through Saturday from 10 to 5:30 or 6, Sunday from noon

to 5. Many stores in the French Quarter and in malls stay open till 9.
Sales are advertised in the daily *Times-Picayune.*

Shopping Districts

Most of the **French Quarter**'s ritzy antiques stores, musty bazaars, art
galleries, and boutiques are housed in quaint 19th-century structures.
The sleek indoor malls of the **CBD** include **Riverwalk** (✉ 1 Poydras St.),
with more than 200 specialty shops and restaurants; **Canal Place** (✉
1 Canal Pl.), with more than 40 tony shops, a food court, and cinemas; and **New Orleans Centre** (✉ 1400 Poydras St.), connected by a
walkway to the Superdome and a hotel. The **Warehouse District** neighborhood of the CBD, especially Julia Street off St. Charles Avenue, is
a major center for art galleries. Upriver from the CBD, **Magazine
Street** has 6 mi of antiques stores and boutiques, many in once-grand
Victorian houses, and **Riverbend** has specialty shops and restaurants,
many cradled in small Creole cottages.

Department Stores

Maison Blanche (✉ 901 Canal St., CBD, ☎ 504/566–1000) is the local
department store, with branches in suburban shopping centers.

Specialty Stores

ANTIQUES

Royal Street in the Quarter is lined with elegant antiques stores; **Magazine Street** has everything from Depression glass to Persian rugs. The
Royal Street Guild and the Magazine Street Merchants' Association
publish pamphlets that are available free at the New Orleans Welcome
Center (☞ Visitor Information, *above*).

FLEA MARKET

Locals as well as tourists turn out for the **French Market Flea Market,**
open daily from 7 to 7.

FOOD

Bayou to Go (✉ New Orleans International Airport, Concourse C,
☎ 504/468–8040) has packaged Louisiana food products. **Old Town
Praline Shop** (✉ 627 Royal St., ☎ 504/525–1413) has the best pra-
lines in town.

JAZZ RECORDS

For hard-to-find vintage items, go to **Record Ron's** (✉ 1129 Decatur
St.; ✉ 407 Decatur St., ☎ 504/524–9444).

MASKS

Handmade Mardi Gras masks are available at **Little Shop of Fantasy**
(✉ 523 Dumaine St., ☎ 504/529–4243) and **Rumors** (✉ 513 Royal
St., ☎ 504/525–0292).

Side Trip to Plantation Country

Arriving and Departing

By car take I–10 or U.S. 61 west from New Orleans and follow the
signs to the various plantations. Plantation Country maps are available at the New Orleans Welcome Center (☞ Visitor Information, *above*).
Many local tour operators include visits to plantations in their itineraries
(☞ Orientation Tours, *above*).

What to See and Do

Plantation Country lies upriver from New Orleans. You can see what
went with the wind and hear tales of Yankee invaders and ghosts in
some of the fine restored antebellum plantations sprinkled around the
Great River Road between New Orleans and Baton Rouge, the state
capital. The drive is marred by industrial plants, but elegant mansions

such as **Nottoway** (✉ 2 mi north of White Castle, ☎ 504/545–2730) and **Houmas House** (✉ Rte. 942, ½ mi off Rte. 44 near Burnside, ☎ 504/473–7841) make the trip worthwhile.

CAJUN COUNTRY

Cajun Country, or Acadiana, comprises 22 parishes (counties) of southern Louisiana to the west of New Orleans. This is the cradle of the Cajun craze that swept the nation in the 1980s.

Cajuns are descendants of 17th-century French settlers who established a colony they called l'Acadie (*Cajun* is a corruption of *Acadian*) in the present-day Canadian provinces of Nova Scotia and New Brunswick. After the British expelled the Acadians in the mid-18th century (their exile is described in Longfellow's epic poem *Evangeline*), they eventually found a home in southern Louisiana. They have been here since 1762, sharing their unique cuisine and culture with the nation and imbuing the region with a distinctive flavor summed up in the Cajun phrase "Laissez les bons temps rouler!" ("Let the good times roll!")

Visitor Information

Southwest Louisiana Convention & Visitors Bureau (✉ 1211 N. Lakeshore Dr., Lake Charles 70601, ☎ 318/436–9588 or 800/456–7952, FAX 318/494–7952). **Lafayette: Convention & Visitors Bureau** (✉ 1400 N.W. Evangeline Thruway, Box 52066, Lafayette 70505, ☎ 318/232–3808, 800/346–1958, or 800/543–5340 in Canada; FAX 318/232–0161).

Arriving and Departing

By Bus
Greyhound (☎ 800/231–2222) has frequent daily service to Lafayette, Lake Charles, and environs.

By Car
The fastest route from New Orleans through Cajun Country is west on I–10. U.S. 90 is a slower but more scenic drive. If you have time, take the back roads for exploring this area. A ferry across the Mississippi costs $1 per car; most bridges are free.

By Plane
Lafayette Regional Airport (☎ 318/232–2808) is served by American Eagle, Atlantic Southeast (Delta), Continental, and Northwest Airlink. Lake Charles Regional Airport (☎ 318/477–6051) is served by American Eagle and Continental.

By Train
Amtrak (☎ 800/872–7245) serves Franklin, Schriever, Lafayette, New Iberia, and Thibodaux.

Exploring Cajun Country

U.S. 90 dips down south of New Orleans into Terrebonne Parish, a major center for shrimp and oyster fisheries (the blessing of the shrimp fleets in Chauvin and Dulac is a colorful April event). A slew of swamp tours are based here, including **Annie Miller's Terrebonne Swamp & Marsh Tours** (☎ 504/879–3934). **Hammond's Cajun Air Tours** (☎ 504/876–0584) takes passengers up for a gull's-eye view of the alligators and other critters that inhabit the coastal wetlands.

Morgan City, on the Atchafalaya River, struck it rich when the first producing offshore oil well was completed on November 14, 1947, and the Kerr-McGee Rig No. 16 ushered in the black-gold rush. In 1917 the original *Tarzan of the Apes* was filmed in Morgan City; at the town **Information Center** (✉ 725 Myrtle St., ☎ 504/384–3343) you can see a video of the film.

Route 182 west of Morgan City branches off U.S. 90 and ambles northwest toward Lafayette. For much of the way the road travels along ★ **Bayou Teche,** the largest of the state's many bayous. (*Teche* is an Indian word meaning "snake." According to an ancient legend, the death throes of a giant snake carved the bayou.) The road runs by rice paddies and canebrakes, and on the bayous you can see Cajun pirogues (canoelike boats) and cypress cabins built on stilts.

Franklin is an official Main Street U.S.A. town (a title bestowed by the National Trust for Historic Preservation). The street, lined with old-fashioned street lamps, rolls out beneath an arcade of live oaks. Six antebellum homes are open for tours in and around town. One of them, Oak Lawn Manor, is the home of Louisiana governor Mike Foster. Franklin is nestled on Route 182, along a bend in Bayou Teche, and there is a splendid view of it from Parc sur le Teche.

New Iberia is northwest of Franklin. Called the "Queen City of the Teche," it was founded in 1779 by Spanish settlers who named it for their homeland. **Shadows-on-the-Teche** (✉ 317 E. Main St., ☎ 318/369–6446), one of the South's best-known plantation homes, was built in 1834 for sugar planter David Weeks. The big brick house is virtually enveloped in moss-draped live oak trees.

★ Red-hot Tabasco sauce is a 19th-century Louisiana creation; on **Avery Island** at McIlhenny's **Tabasco Company** (✉ Rte. 329, ☎ 318/369–6243), southwest of New Iberia, you can tour the factory where it's still being manufactured by descendants of its creator. Here also are the 200-acre **Jungle Garden,** lush with tropical plants, and **Bird City,** a sanctuary with flurries of snow-white egrets.

★ Like Avery Island, **Rip Van Winkle Gardens,** formerly known as Live Oak Gardens (✉ 284 Rip Van Winkle Rd., off Rte. 14, ☎ 318/365–3332), is actually a salt dome, capped by lush vegetation. The 19th-century American actor Joseph Jefferson, who toured the country portraying Rip Van Winkle, built a winter home here. His three-story house is surrounded by lovely formal and informal gardens.

Route 31 is a pretty country road that hugs the banks of the Teche between New Iberia and St. Martinville to the north. The little town of **St. Martinville** is awash with legends. Now a sleepy village, it was known in the 18th century as Petit Paris, a refuge for aristocrats fleeing the French Revolution. It was also a major debarkation point for exiled Acadians. Longfellow's poem was based on the true story of two young lovers who were separated for years during the Acadian exile. The **Evangeline Oak** (✉ Evangeline Blvd. at Bayou Teche) is said to be the place where the ill-starred lovers met again—albeit briefly. On the town square is **St. Martin de Tours,** mother church of the Acadians, and the **Petit Paris Museum,** which has a Mardi Gras collection. Be sure to visit the small cemetery behind the church, where a bronze statue depicts the real-life Evangeline.

The hamlet of **Breaux Bridge,** just north of St. Martinville, calls itself the "crawfish capital of the world." The **Crawfish Festival,** held each May, draws more than 100,000 people. The town's other claim to fame is the Cajun food and music spot **Mulate's** (☞ Dining and Lodging, *below*).

Lafayette, 15 minutes west of Breaux Bridge, proudly proclaims itself the capital of French Louisiana. In this part of the state some 40% of the residents speak Cajun French, a 17th-century dialect. As most Cajuns also speak standard French as well as English, this is a superb place to test your language skills. **Cajun Mardi Gras** rivals its sister celebration in New Orleans. Lafayette is a good base for exploring the region.

The **Lafayette Natural History Museum** (⊠ 637 Girard Park Dr., ☎ 318/291–5544), within luxuriant **Girard Park,** offers workshops, movies, concerts, laser-light shows, and a planetarium. It's also the venue for the annual **Louisiana Native and Contemporary Crafts Festival,** held each September.

The **Acadiana Park Nature Station** (⊠ E. Alexandre St., ☎ 318/291–6181) is a three-story cypress-pole structure with an interpretive center, discovery boxes for children, a nature trail, and guided tours (for

★ a fee). The **Acadian Cultural Center** (⊠ 501 Fisher Rd., ☎ 318/232–0789 or 318/232–0961), a unit of the **Jean Lafitte National Historical Park and Preserve,** traces the history of the Acadians through numerous audiovisual exhibits, including an excellent introductory film dramatizing the Acadian exile. The **Children's Museum of Acadiana,** opened in 1996, has hands-on exhibits (⊠ 201 E. Congress St., ☎ 318/232–8500).

Small towns dot the flatlands west of Lafayette; residents are called Prairie Cajuns. **Eunice,** a tiny speck of a town, is home to *Rendez-Vous des Cajuns* (☞ Nightlife and the Arts, *below*) and the **Prairie Acadian Cultural Center** (⊠ Corner of S. 3rd St. and Park Ave., ☎ 318/457–8499). In a former railroad depot, the **Eunice Museum** (⊠ 220 S. C. C. Duson Dr., ☎ 318/457–6540) contains displays on Cajun culture, including its music and Mardi Gras. Eunice and the surrounding villages of Mamou, Church Point, and Iota are the major stomping grounds for the annual **Courir de Mardi Gras,** which features a band of masked and costumed horseback riders on a mad dash through the countryside.

North of Lafayette, **Grand Coteau** is a religious and educational center, and the entire peaceful little village is on the National Register of Historic Places. Of particular note in Grand Coteau is the **Church of St. Charles Borromeo,** a simple wooden structure with an ornate high-baroque-style interior. A splendid antebellum mansion, **Chretien Point Plantation** (⊠ 665 Chretien Point Rd., 12 mi north of Lafayette, ☎ 318/662–5876) is now a bed-and-breakfast. The staircase in Tara, Scarlett O'Hara's home in *Gone With the Wind,* was modeled on the one in this house.

Opelousas, the third-oldest town in the state, is a short drive from Grand Coteau on I–49. Founded by the French in 1720, the town was named for the Appalousa Indians, who lived here centuries before the French and Spanish arrived. For a brief period during the Civil War, Opelousas served as the state capital. At the intersection of I–49 and U.S. 190, the **Opelousas Tourist Information Center** (☎ 318/948–6263) houses memorabilia of Jim Bowie, the Alamo hero who spent his boyhood here. The **Opelousas Museum and Interpretive Center** (⊠ 329 N. Main St., ☎ 318/948–2589) traces the history of this region.

Tucked away in the far southwest corner of the state, **Lake Charles** is a straight shot (71 mi) from Lafayette on I–10. Called Charlie's Lake in the 1760s, the city has more than 50 mi of rivers, lakes, canals, and bayous. The **Imperial Calcasieu Museum** (⊠ 204 W. Sallier St., ☎ 318/439–3797) has an extensive collection on Lake Charles and Imperial Calcasieu Parish, including an old-fashioned pharmacy, an

Audubon collection, a Gay '90s barbershop, and a fine arts gallery. The **Children's Museum** (⊠ 925 Enterprise Blvd., ☎ 318/433–9420) has innovative hands-on exhibits, including a miniature courtroom and grocery store, a brass-rubbing center, and interactive computer games.

The **Creole Nature Trail** (☞ Scenic Drives, *above*) begins on Route 27 in Sulphur and continues on Route 82. Beautiful in spring, this drive goes to the **Sabine Wildlife Refuge,** where a paved trail meanders into the wilds. There is an interpretive center and a tower at the end of the trail, which gives you an excellent view of the wilderness. (Take along insect repellent!)

You can make a detour off the Creole Nature Trail and continue east on Route 82 (Hug-the-Coast Highway), which whips along the windswept coastal marshes to the **Rockefeller Wildlife Refuge,** in **Grand Chenier.** At this 84,000-acre preserve, thousands of ducks, geese, gators, wading birds, and otters while away the winter months.

Dining and Lodging

With the state's wealth of waterways, it is no surprise that Louisiana tables are laden with seafood in every imaginable and innovative variety. In southern Louisiana sea creatures are prepared with a Cajun flair. Sleeping accommodations run from homey B&Bs to chain motels to luxury hotels to elegant antebellum mansions open for overnighters. For price ranges *see* Charts 1 (B) and 2 (B) *in* On the Road with Fodor's.

Breaux Bridge

$$ ✕ **Mulate's.** This renowned roadhouse with tables covered in check-
★ ered plastic features Cajun seafood and dancing to live Cajun music noon and night. ⊠ *325 W. Mills Ave.,* ☎ *318/332–4648 or 800/422–2586, 800/634–9880 in LA. AE, MC, V.*

Carencro

$–$$ ✕ **Prudhomme's Cajun Café.** In a suburb of Lafayette, celebrity chef
★ Paul Prudhomme's sister Enola has a country-kitchen café with outstanding Cajun fare. ⊠ *4676 N.E. Evangeline Thruway,* ☎ *318/896–7964. AE, MC, V. Closed Mon.*

Lafayette

$$ ✕ **Prejean's.** Housed in a cypress cottage, this local favorite has a cozy
★ oyster bar, red-checked cloths, and live music nightly. Huge platters of traditional and new Cajun seafood are the specialties. ⊠ *3480 U.S. 167N, next to Evangeline Downs,* ☎ *318/896–3247. AE, DC, MC, V.*

$$$ 🏨 **Holiday Inn Central–Holidome.** Built around an atrium that's banked with greenery, this modern motel has rooms done in contemporary decor and 17 acres within which you can find almost everything you'd ever need for a long life. ⊠ *Box 91807, 70509,* ☎ *318/233–6815 or 800/942–4868,* FAX *318/225–1954. 250 rooms. Restaurant, lounge, picnic area, pool, sauna, 2 tennis courts, jogging, recreation rooms, playground, airport shuttle. AE, D, DC, MC, V.*

$–$$ 🏨 **Best Western Hotel Acadiana.** Near Bayou Vermilion, this is a plush
★ hotel whose rooms have thick carpeting, marble-top dressers, and wet bars. Even-numbered rooms face the pool. The hotel also has rooms for people with disabilities. ⊠ *1801 W. Pinhook Rd., 70508,* ☎ *318/233–8120 or 800/826–8386, 800/874–4664 in LA,* FAX *318/234–9667. 304 rooms. Restaurant, lounge, pool, free parking. AE, D, DC, MC, V.*

Lake Charles

$$$ ✕ **Café Margaux.** You might feel more comfortable in a jacket and tie
★   at this restaurant, where candlelight, tuxedoed waiters, and a 5,000-
bottle mahogany wine cellar provide the setting for specialties that in-
clude rack of lamb *en croûte* and fillet of flounder with lump crabmeat
and brown meunière sauce. ✉ *765 Bayou Pines,* ☎ *318/433–2902.*
Reservations essential. AE, MC, V. Closed Sun.

$$ 🏨 **Holiday Inn, Lake Charles.** Perched between the lake and the interstate, this hotel has traditional furnishings in rooms done in soothing
earth tones. Hotel guests can stroll the Casino Walk to board the *Players Riverboat Casino* (☞ Nightlife and the Arts, *below*), which docks
next door. There are rooms for nonsmokers and for people with disabilities.
✉ *505 N. Lakeshore Dr., 70601;* ☎ *318/433–7121 or 800/367–1814,*
800/433–8809 in LA; 📠 *318/436–8459. 270 rooms. Restaurant, coffee shop, pool, laundry, free parking. AE, D, DC, MC, V.*

$–$$ 🏨 **Chateau Charles Hotel & Conference Center.** Set on 25 acres, the hotel
includes two-bedroom suites with wet bars, microwaves, and minire-
frigerators, as well as rooms for nonsmokers and for guests with disabilities. ✉ *Box 1269, 70602,* ☎ *318/882–6130 or 800/935–6130,*
📠 *318/882–6601. 248 rooms. Restaurant, lounge, laundry. AE, D,
DC, MC, V.*

Napoleonville

$$$ 🏨 **Madewood.** Expect gracious southern hospitality in this antiques-
★   filled Greek Revival plantation mansion, which is both elegant and cozy.
There are rooms in the main mansion and suites in a restored outbuilding.
✉ *4250 Rte. 308, 70390,* ☎ *504/369–7151 or 800/375–7151. 8 rooms.
Breakfast and dinner. AE, D, MC, V.*

New Iberia

$$$ ✕🏨 **leRosier.** Across the street from Shadows-on-the-Teche, leRosier
is a four-room B&B whose shining star is the restaurant, presided over
by chef Hallman Woods III. Among other accomplishments, Hall has
prepared a five-course crawfish degustation for the James Beard Foundation. Expect fresh ingredients and succulent seafood in his small white-
cloth dining room. ✉ *314 E. Main St.,* ☎ *318/367–5306. Reservations
essential for dinner. AE, MC, V.*

Opelousas

$ ✕ **Palace Café.** This down-home coffee shop on the town square, op-
erated by the same family since 1927, serves steak, fried chicken, sandwiches, burgers, and seafood. Locals flock here for the homemade
baklava. ✉ *167 W. Landry St.,* ☎ *318/942–2142. MC, V.*

St. Martinville

$$ ✕🏨 **La Place d'Evangeline.** Rooms are spacious at this B&B on the
banks of the Bayou Teche. The restaurant serves hearty portions of
seafood and Cajun dishes; the homemade bread is superb. ✉ *220
Evangeline Blvd., 70582,* ☎ *318/394–4010. 5 rooms. AE, MC, V.*

Nightlife and the Arts

Nightlife

CAJUN MUSIC

Mulate's in Breaux Bridge and **Prejean's** in Lafayette (☞ Dining and
Lodging, *above*) and **Randol's** (✉ 2320 Kaliste Saloom Rd., Lafayette,
☎ 318/981–7080) regularly feature Cajun music and dancing. **Belizaire's**
(✉ 2307 N. Parkerson Ave., Crowley, ☎ 318/788–2501) is a great
place for Cajun food and dancing. **Slim's Y-Ki-Ki** (✉ Rte. 167, Wash-
ington Rd., Opelousas, ☎ 318/942–9980), a black Cajun club, is one
of the best Cajun dance venues in the state. **Fred's Lounge** (✉ 420 6th

St., Mamou, ☎ 318/468–5411) is a bar with live Saturday-morning radio broadcasts (8–1) and plenty of dancing. ***Rendez-Vous des Cajuns*** (✉ Liberty Theatre, Park Ave. at 2nd St., Eunice, ☎ 318/457–6577) is a live Saturday-night radio show, mostly in French, that's been described as a combination of the *Grand Ole Opry,* the *Louisiana Hayride,* and the *Prairie Home Companion.*

GAMBLING

In Lake Charles gamblers find action on the two riverboats at **Players Island Hotel-Casino-Entertainment Complex** (☎ 800/977–7529) and on the **Isle of Capri** riverboat casino (☎ 800/843–4753), where there is a slew of slots and gaming tables.

The Arts

CONCERTS

Major concert attractions are booked into Lafayette's **Cajundome** (✉ 444 Cajundome Blvd., ☎ 318/265–2100), **Heymann Performing Arts & Convention Center** (✉ 1373 S. College Rd., ☎ 318/268–5540), and the **Lake Charles Civic Center** (✉ 900 Lakeshore Dr., Lake Charles, ☎ 318/491–1256).

THEATER

The **Lake Charles Little Theater** (✉ 813 Enterprise Blvd., Lake Charles, ☎ 318/433–7988) puts on plays and musicals. The **Théâtre 'Cadien** (✉ Lafayette, ☎ 318/893–5655 or 318/262–5810) performs plays in French at various venues. **Lafayette Community Theater** (✉ 529 Jefferson St., ☎ 318/235–1532) offers contemporary plays with a Cajun flair.

Outdoor Activities and Sports

Biking

These flatlands and lush parks make for easy riding. Bikes can be rented at **Pack & Paddle** (✉ 601 E. Pinhook Rd., Lafayette, ☎ 318/232–5854).

Canoeing

Paddling is almost a breeze on the easygoing Whisky Chitto Creek. Canoes can be rented at **Arrowhead Canoe Rentals** (✉ 9 mi west of Oberlin on Rte. 26, ☎ 318/639–2086 or 800/637–2086).

Fishing

Trips to fish, sightsee, bird-watch, or hunt can be arranged at **Cajun Fishing Tours** (✉ 1925 E. Main St., New Iberia, ☎ 318/364–7141). **Sportsman's Paradise** (☎ 504/594–2414) is a charter-fishing facility 20 mi south of Houma. **Salt, Inc. Charter Fishing Service** (☎ 504/594–6626 or 504/594–7581), on Route 56 south of Houma at Coco Marina, offers fishing trips in the bays and barrier islands of lower Terrebonne Parish as well as into the Gulf of Mexico. **Hackberry Rod & Gun** (☎ 318/762–3391), in Cameron (in the far southwest corner of the state), is a charter saltwater-fishing service.

Golf

City Park Golf Course (✉ Mudd Ave. and 8th St., Lafayette, ☎ 318/268–5557), **Pine Shadows Golf Center** (✉ 750 Goodman Rd., Lake Charles, ☎ 318/433–8681), and **Vieux Chêne Golf Course** (✉ Youngsville Hwy., Broussard, ☎ 318/837–1159) all have 18 holes.

Hiking and Nature Trails

The Old Stagecoach Road in Lake Charles's **Sam Houston Jones State Park** is a favorite for hikers who want to explore the park and the various tributaries of the Calcasieu River; the **Louisiana State Arboretum** in Ville Platte is a 600-acre facility with 4 mi of nature trails (for both, ☞ National and State Parks, *above*). There are 7 mi of hiking trails in the **Port Hudson State Commemorative Area,** near Baton Rouge (⊠ 756 W. Plains–Port Hudson Rd. [Hwy. 61], Zachary, ☎ 504/654–3775). Near Natchitoches backpackers and hikers explore the 8,700-acre **Kisatchie Hills Wilderness** with its Backbone Trail, part of the Kisatchie National Forest (☞ National and State Parks, *above*).

Horseback Riding
Trail rides, pony rides, and even hayrides are offered on weekends at **Broken Arrow Stables** (⊠ 3505 Broken Arrow Rd., off Rte. 3013, New Iberia, ☎ 318/369–7669).

Spectator Sports
Home games of the 1995-franchised **Ice Gators,** of the East Coast Hockey League, as well as NBA exhibition and collegiate basketball, professional soccer exhibition games, wrestling, and other sports events take place at the **Cajundome** (⊠ 444 Cajundome Blvd., Lafayette, ☎ 318/265–2100).

Thoroughbred racing: April through Labor Day at **Evangeline Downs** (⊠ I–10 at I–49, Lafayette, ☎ 318/896–7266).

Shopping
For Cajun food to go, try the **Cajun Country Store** (⊠ 401 E. Cypress St., Lafayette, ☎ 318/233–7977) and **B. F. Trappey's & Sons** (⊠ 900 E. Main St., New Iberia, ☎ 318/365–8281).

Antiques seeking is a favorite pastime here. In Lafayette you can root around **Ruins & Relics** (⊠ 802 Jefferson, at Taft St., ☎ 318/233–9163) and **Solomon's Splendor Antique Mall** (⊠ 731 Rue de Belier, ☎ 318/984–5776).

ELSEWHERE IN LOUISIANA

Natchitoches and North-Central Louisiana

Arriving and Departing
I–49 cuts diagonally from southeast to northwest, connecting Lafayette with Shreveport. Route 1 runs diagonally from the northwest corner all the way to Grand Isle on the Gulf of Mexico.

What to See and Do
Nestled in the piney hills of north-central Louisiana, **Natchitoches** (pronounced *nak*-a-tish) is the oldest permanent European settlement of the Louisiana Purchase, four years older than New Orleans. The town has a quaint 33-block Historic Landmark District, with brick-paved streets and buildings garbed in lacy ironwork. In the center of the downtown area is pretty Cane River Lake, edged with live oak trees and rolling green lawns. Natchitoches appeared in the film version of *Steel Magnolias.* You can take trolley tours of town and cruises on the water. Popular events include the **Christmas Festival of Lights,** which draws about 150,000 people annually, and the **October Pilgrimage,** when several historic houses are open for tours.

Route 494 follows the Cane River Lake southward from Natchitoches, bordered by arching trees and dotted with handsome plantation houses. Famed primitive artist Clementine Hunter lived and worked at **Melrose Plantation** (⊠ Rte. 119, Melrose, ☎ 318/379–0055), where nine quaint buildings can be toured. Twenty miles south of Natchitoches, ★ the **Kate Chopin House** (⊠ Rte. 495, Cloutierville, ☎ 318/379–2233) was home in the 19th century to Kate Chopin, author of *The Awakening.* It now houses the **Bayou Folk Museum.**

To the west of Natchitoches, 15 mi south of Many, lies **Hodges Gardens** (⊠ U.S. 171, ☎ 318/586–3523), 4,700 acres of rolling pine forests with streams, waterfalls, and multilevel formal botanical gardens, where flowers and shrubs bloom year-round. Just to the west is the huge **Toledo Bend Lake,** a camping, boating, and bass-fishing delight, which lies along the Texas border.

The **Natchitoches Parish Tourist Commission** (⊠ 781 Front St., Box 411, 71458, ☎ 318/352–8072) has information on the entire area, including walking- and driving-tour maps.

Dining and Lodging

NATCHITOCHES

$$ ✕ **The Landing.** This popular white-cloth bistro offers pasta, chicken, veal, and seafood dishes; the spicy country-fried steak is a specialty. ⊠ *530 Front St.,* ☎ *318/352–1579. AE, MC, V.*

$ ✕ **Lasyone's Meat Pie Kitchen.** Natchitoches meat pies are known throughout the state, and this casual little spot does them better than anybody. ⊠ *622 2nd St.,* ☎ *318/352–3353. No credit cards.*

$$ 🏨 **Holiday Inn.** Comfortable and predictable rooms can be found in this link in the long chain. ⊠ *Hwy. 1 South Bypass, 71457,* ☎ *318/ 357–8281 or 800/465–4329. 145 rooms. Restaurant, lobby lounge, pool. AE, D, DC, MC, V.*

$ 🏨 **Fleur-de-lis.** The hosts of the town's oldest B&B will make you feel right at home. ⊠ *336 2nd St., 71457,* ☎ *318/352–6621 or 800/489– 6621. 5 rooms. AE, MC, V.*

Shreveport and Northern Louisiana

Arriving and Departing

Shreveport Regional Airport is served by American Eagle, Continental Express, Delta, Northwest, TWA, and US Airways. I–20 and U.S. 80 run east–west through the northern part of the state; Route 1 cuts diagonally from the northwest corner to the Gulf of Mexico; I–49 connects Shreveport with southern Louisiana. Other north–south routes are U.S. 171, 71, 165, and 167.

What to See and Do

While southern Louisiana dances to Cajun tunes and dines on Creole and Cajun fare, most of northern Louisiana has more in common with Mississippi, Georgia, and other southern states; Shreveport's ties are largely to neighboring Texas. North of Alexandria the flat marshlands and gray earth give way to stands of pine trees and bluffs of rich, red clay. It is not for naught that Louisiana is known as Sportsman's Paradise. Both the northern and southern regions of the state are laced with rivers and lakes, with ample places for camping, fishing, and hunting.

Shreveport and Bossier City, joined by the Red River, constitute the largest metropolitan area in northern Louisiana. A cultural center, **Shreveport** has a symphony orchestra, resident opera and ballet companies, and excellent community-theater productions. The prestigious
★ **R. W. Norton Art Gallery** (⊠ 4747 Creswell Ave., ☎ 318/865–4201) has superb European and American art, including the area's largest permanent collection of works by Frederic Remington and Charles M. Russell. The **Louisiana State Exhibit Museum** (⊠ Fairgrounds, ☎ 318/ 632–2020) has extensive displays and dioramas depicting the state's history, including a large collection of Native American artifacts from Poverty Point and other important excavations in Louisiana. The **Ark-La-Tex Antique and Classic Vehicle Museum** (⊠ 601 Spring St., ☎ 318/ 222–0227) traces automotive history in both classic and vintage mod-

els. The **Sci-Port Discovery Center** (✉ 528 Commerce St., ☎ 318/424–3466) is a hands-on interactive science museum, with exhibits for all ages as well as national traveling exhibitions. The **American Rose Center** (✉ Jefferson-Paige Rd., ☎ 318/938–5402), headquarters of the American Rose Society, is a 118-acre piney-woods park with more than 20,000 rosebushes in more than 60 individual gardens. The place lights up like a Christmas tree during the Christmas in Roseland show, which runs from the day after Thanksgiving through New Year's Eve.

In **Bossier City** the **Eighth Air Force Museum** (✉ Barksdale Air Force Base, ☎ 318/456–3067) has World War II aircraft, dioramas, uniforms, and barracks of the Second Bomb Wing and the Eighth Air Force, which are headquartered at Barksdale Air Force Base. Four **riverboat casinos** now float on the water here: *Harrah's Casino, Shreveport* (✉ Shreveport, ☎ 800/427–7247), *Isle of Capri Casino & Hotel* (✉ Bossier City, ☎ 318/678–7777 or 800/843–4753), the *Horseshoe Riverboat Casino & Hotel* (✉ Bossier City, ☎ 800/895–0711), and *Casino Magic* (✉ I–20 Exit 19B, ☎ 318/746–0711). **Louisiana Downs** (✉ I–20 in Bossier City, ☎ 318/747–7223), one of the South's largest racetracks, has Thoroughbred racing from April through October.

South of Shreveport, the **Mansfield Battle Park** (✉ Rte. 2, 4 mi south of Mansfield, ☎ 318/872–1474) is the site of the last major Confederate victory of the Civil War. More than 30,000 men were involved in the bitter battle. The site contains monuments and an interpretive center with audiovisual displays.

The **Shreveport-Bossier Convention & Tourist Bureau** (✉ 629 Spring St., Shreveport 71166, ☎ 318/222–9391 or 800/551–8682, 🖷 318/222–0056) has free maps and information on the region. There are four visitor centers (✉ Southpark Mall, Jewella Rd., Shreveport 71166; ✉ 100 John Wesley Blvd., Bossier City 71111; ✉ Pierre Bossier Mall, Airline Dr., Bossier City 71111; ✉ Mall St. Vincent, St. Vincent & Southern Aves., Shreveport; ☎ 318/227–9880).

Dining and Lodging

SHREVEPORT

$$$ ✗ **Monsieur Patout.** An enchanting jewel box of a restaurant, this small, *très intime* restaurant serves classic French cuisine. ✉ *855 Pierremont Rd., ☎ 318/868–9822. Reservations essential. AE, D, DC, MC, V.*

$$ ✗ **Superior Bar & Grill.** Even with a reservation you may have to hang out in the bar to wait for a table, but the fine mesquite-grilled steaks and Mexican food are worth the wait. ✉ *6123 Line Ave., ☎ 318/869–3243. AE, D, MC, V.*

$$ 🏨 **Sheraton Pierremont Hotel.** In this luxury property near the convention center, every guest room has a wet bar, a refrigerator, three phones, and a modem line. It is in compliance with ADA regulations, and no-smoking rooms are available. ✉ *1419 E. 70th St., 71105, ☎ 318/797–9900 or 800/321–4182, 🖷 318/798–2923. 270 rooms. Restaurant, lounge, pool, health club.*

$$ 🏨 **Holiday Inn/Downtown Riverfront.** Renovated in 1996, the Holiday Inn is just two blocks from Harrah's riverboat casino. It has remote-control TVs and VCRs; movie rentals are available. ✉ *102 Lake St., 71101, ☎ 318/222–7717 or 800/284–8209. 185 rooms. Restaurant, lobby lounge, health club, airport shuttle.*

MISSISSIPPI

Updated by
Charlotte
Durham

Capital	Jackson
Population	2,716,000
Motto	By Virtue and Arms
State Bird	Mockingbird
State Flower	Magnolia
Postal Abbreviation	MS

Statewide Visitor Information

Mississippi Division of Tourism Development (⊠ Box 22825, Jackson 39205, ☎ 601/359–3297 or 800/927–6378).

Scenic Drives

The **Natchez Trace Parkway** cuts a 313-mi swath across Mississippi from northeast of Tupelo to Natchez in the southwest, passing through Jackson at the center of the state. **U.S. 90** runs along the Mississippi Sound from Alabama to Louisiana, offering views of Gulf Coast beaches, ancient live oaks, and historic homes. Along the Mississippi River, **U.S. 61**—also known as Blues Alley and the birthplace of that musical form—runs through flat Delta cotton land to the hills of Vicksburg, then through Natchez to Louisiana.

National and State Parks

National Parks
Gulf Islands National Seashore (⊠ 3500 Park Rd., Ocean Springs 39564, ☎ 601/875–9057) includes Ship, Horn, and Petit Bois islands and has nature trails and expeditions into the marsh. Vicksburg's **National Military Park** (⊠ Visitor Center, 3201 Clay St. [U.S. 80], I–20 Exit 4B, Vicksburg 39180, ☎ 601/636–0583) is second only to Gettysburg in interest and beauty.

State Parks
Just north of Port Gibson **Grand Gulf Military Monument** (⊠ Rte. 2 off U.S. 61, Box 392, Port Gibson 39150, ☎ 601/437–5911) marks an area destroyed by federal gunners during the Civil War and includes an observation tower, waterwheel, and display of bloodstained Civil War uniforms. **J. P. Coleman State Park** (⊠ 13 mi north of Iuka off U.S. 25; Rte. 5, Box 504, Iuka 38852, ☎ 601/423–6515) includes scenic Pickwick Lake, which has cabins, camping, hiking, and swimming. **Tishomingo State Park** (⊠ 15 mi south of Iuka and 3 mi north of Dennis off U.S. 25; Rte. 1, Box 880, Tishomingo 38873, ☎ 601/438–6914), which vies with J. P. Coleman for the title of most spectacular Mississippi park, lies in the Appalachian foothills, making its terrain unique in Mississippi. Bring your own provisions to enjoy hiking and water sports.

THE NATCHEZ TRACE

The Natchez Trace Parkway is a long, thin park running for more than 300 mi from Nashville to Natchez, crossing early paths worn by the Choctaw and Chickasaw, flatboatmen, outlaws, itinerant preachers, post riders, soldiers, and settlers. The parkway extends almost 450 mi, with other sections in Alabama and Tennessee. Meticulously manicured by the National Park Service, it is unmarred by billboards, and commercial vehicles are forbidden to use it.

Visitor Information

Natchez–Adams County: Convention & Visitors Bureau (✉ 422 Main St., Natchez 39120, ☎ 601/446–6345 or 800/647–6724). **Natchez Trace Parkway:** Visitor Center (✉ 2680 Natchez Trace Pkwy., Tupelo 38801, ☎ 601/680–4025 or 800/305–7417). **Jackson:** Metro Jackson Convention and Visitors Bureau (✉ Box 1450, 39215, ☎ 601/960–1891 or 800/354–7695).

Arriving and Departing

By Car

The Natchez Trace is interrupted at Jackson; I–55 and I–20, which run through the city, connect the two segments. Natchez, at the southwestern end of the Natchez Trace Parkway, is also served by U.S. 61.

By Plane

Jackson's **International Airport** (☎ 601/939–5631), east of the city off I–20, 10 minutes from downtown, is served by American, Continental Express, Delta, Northwest Airlink, US Airways Express, TWA, and ValuJet.

By Train

Amtrak (☎ 800/872–7245) stops in Jackson on its way south from Memphis to New Orleans.

Exploring the Natchez Trace

The Mississippi segment of the Natchez Trace begins near Tupelo, in the northeast corner of the state in a hilly area of dense forests and sparkling streams. Enjoy this natural beauty at **J. P. Coleman State Park** or **Tishomingo State Park** (☞ National and State Parks, *above*).

Tupelo

Tupelo (named after the gum tree), the largest city in northern Mississippi, sits in scenic hill country. It's the site of the 1864 Civil War battle of the same name.

At Milepost 266 in Tupelo is the **Natchez Trace Parkway Visitor Center** (☞ Visitor Information, *above*), offering exhibits and the *Official Map and Guide,* with detailed mile-by-mile information on places from Nashville to Natchez.

The city is now famous as **Elvis Presley's birthplace** (✉ 306 Elvis Presley Dr., ☎ 601/841–1245); the singer was born in a tiny, two-room shotgun house on January 8, 1935. The surrounding **Elvis Presley Park** includes a museum, a gift shop, and the **Elvis Presley Memorial Chapel.**

From Tupelo to Jackson

The three-hour trip from Tupelo to Jackson can easily take an entire day if you stop to read the brown wooden markers describing historic sites, explore nature trails, and admire the neat fields, trees, and wildflower meadows along the way. At Ridgeland the **Mississippi Crafts Center** (✉ Trace Milepost 102.4, ☎ 601/856–7546) sells high-quality crafts in a dogtrot log cabin created by members of the Craftsman's Guild of Mississippi. Rest rooms and picnic tables are available.

Jackson

Jackson, the state capital, has an interesting downtown, with many small museums and most of the city's notable architecture. The **Jim Buck Ross Mississippi Agriculture and Forestry Museum** (✉ 1150 Lakeland Dr., ☎ 601/354–6113) includes 10 old Mississippi farm buildings, as well

The Natchez Trace

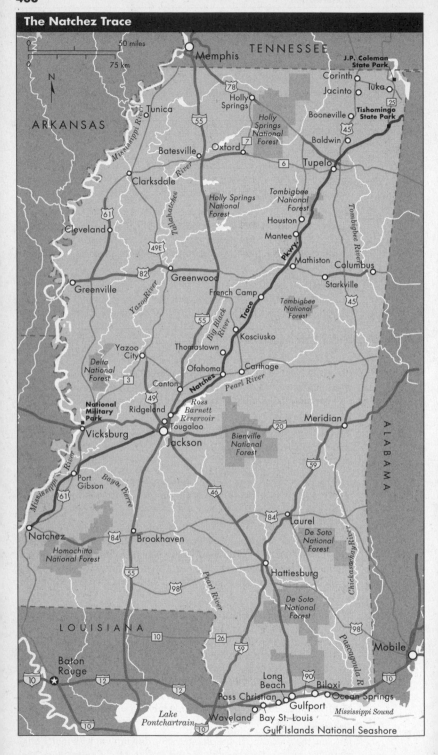

0   50 miles
0   75 km

N

TENNESSEE

Memphis

J.P. Coleman
State Park

Corinth
Jacinto   Iuka

Booneville   **Tishomingo
State Park**

78

Holly
Springs

*Holly
Springs
National
Forest*

Baldwin

ARKANSAS

55

Tunica

Oxford

7

6

Tupelo

25

45

Batesville

Tallahatchie River

Mississippi River

Clarksdale

61

*Holly Springs
National
Forest*

*Tombigbee
National
Forest*

Houston

Cleveland

Mantee

Pkwy.

Tombigbee River

49E

82

Greenwood

Mathiston

Columbus

Greenville

Starkville

45

Yazoo River

French Camp

Trace

*Tombigbee
National
Forest*

55

Big Black River

Kosciusko

Yazoo
City

Thomastown

*Delta
National
Forest*

Ofahoma

Carthage

3

Canton

Natchez

Pearl River

**National
Military
Park**

Ridgeland

*Ross
Barnett
Reservoir*

Tougaloo

Meridian

49

Vicksburg

Jackson

*Bienville
National
Forest*

20

ALABAMA

59

61

Port
Gibson

Bayou Pierre

46

Mississippi River

84

Laurel

*De Soto
National
Forest*

Chickasawhay River

Natchez

*Homochitto
National Forest*

84

Brookhaven

55

98

Hattiesburg

*De Soto
National
Forest*

Pearl River

LOUISIANA

10

26

59

98

Mobile

Baton
Rouge

10

12

Pascagoula R.

10

Long
Beach

90

Biloxi

12

Pass Christian

Ocean
Springs

*Lake
Pontchartrain*

Waveland   Bay St. Louis

Gulfport

Mississippi Sound

10

Gulf Islands National Seashore

as a working farm and a 1920s crossroads town. The general store sells snacks and souvenirs; just outside the gates a shop sells Mississippi crafts, and a down-home restaurant serves blue-plate lunches (veggies, crisp fried catfish).

The **Mississippi Museum of Art** has changing exhibits and a permanent collection of more than 40,000 works, including 19th- and 20th-century American, southern, and Mississippi art. Its high-tech, hands-on Impressions Gallery (free) combines art and education. ⊠ *201 E. Pascagoula St.,* ☎ *601/960–1515. Closed Sun.–Mon.*

The **Governor's Mansion** has been the official home of the state's first family since its completion in 1841. It was also General W. T. Sherman's headquarters during his occupation of Jackson in 1863. The mansion is beautifully furnished with antiques. ⊠ *300 E. Capitol St.,* ☎ *601/359–3175. Closed Sat.–Mon.*

The **New Capitol** (⊠ 400 High St., ☎ 601/359–3114), dating from 1903, sits in Beaux Arts splendor, its dome topped by a gold-plated copper eagle with a 15-ft wingspan. Elaborate interior architectural details include two stained-glass skylights and a painted ceiling.

The **Manship House** (1857) is a restored Gothic Revival home built by the mayor who surrendered the city to General Sherman during the Civil War. ⊠ *420 E. Fortification St. (enter parking area from Congress St.),* ☎ *601/961–4724. Closed Sun.–Mon.*

Port Gibson

Port Gibson, about 60 mi southwest of Jackson, is the oldest surviving town along the Trace. Along **Church Street** many houses and churches have been restored; here, too, is the much-photographed **First Presbyterian Church** (1859), its spire topped by a 10-ft hand pointing heavenward. Information on the town's historic sites is available from the **Port Gibson Chamber of Commerce** (⊠ South end of Church St., ☎ 601/437–4351).

Grand Gulf Military Monument (⊠ Rte. 2 off U.S. 61, ☎ 601/437–5911), just north of Port Gibson, was built on the site of the town of Grand Gulf, once the most thriving river port between New Orleans and St. Louis. Grand Gulf was partially destroyed in the 1850s when capricious currents caused the Mississippi to change its course and flood much of the town. Already in decline, Grand Gulf was completely destroyed by Union gunners during the Civil War. Children especially love the steep trail, the observation tower, the waterwheel, and the blood-stained Civil War uniforms on display.

Natchez

Because Natchez had little military significance, it survived the Civil War almost untouched. Today it is famous for the opulent plantation homes and stylish town houses built between 1819 and 1860, when cotton plantations and the bustling river port poured riches into the city. A number of these houses are open year-round, but others are open only during Natchez Pilgrimage weeks, when crowds flock to see them. The pilgrimages—started in 1932 by the women of Natchez as a way to raise money for preservation—are held twice a year: three weeks in October and four weeks in March and April. Tickets are available at **Pilgrimage Tour Headquarters** (⊠ 220 State St., 39121, ☎ 601/446–6631 or 800/647–6742), where all tours originate. **Carriage tours** of downtown Natchez begin at Pilgrimage Tour Headquarters.

★ **Rosalie** (⊠ 100 Orleans St., ☎ 601/445–4555), built in 1823, established the ideal form of the southern mansion, with its white columns, hipped roof, and red bricks. Furnishings purchased for the house in

1858 include a famous Belter parlor set. A trip down south is not complete without a visit to the grand and gracious **Stanton Hall** (✉ 400 High St., ☎ 601/442–6282), one of the most photographed houses in the country. Built around 1857 for cotton broker Frederick Stanton, the palatial former residence is now run as a house-museum by the Pilgrimage Garden Club. **Longwood** (✉ 140 Lower Woodville Rd., ☎ 601/442–5193) is the largest octagonal house in the United States. Construction began in 1860, but the outbreak of the Civil War prevented its completion; unfinished and mysterious, it is guaranteed to interest both adults and children.

What to See and Do with Children

Jackson's **Zoological Park** (✉ 2918 W. Capitol St., ☎ 601/352–2580) has animals, including many endangered species, in natural settings.

Dining and Lodging

For price ranges *see* Charts 1 (B) and 2 (B) *in* On the Road with Fodor's.

Jackson

$$$ ✕ **Nick's.** Large and elegant, this restaurant serves nouvelle versions of regional dishes. Lunch specialties are grilled catfish and pork medallions; for dinner try eggplant stuffed with deviled crab or blackfish. ✉ *1501 Lakeland Dr.,* ☎ *601/981–8017. Jacket and tie. AE, MC, V.*

$$ ✕ **The Mayflower.** A perfect 1930s period piece with black-and-white tile floors, booths, and Formica counters, this café specializes in Greek salads, fresh fish sautéed in lemon butter, and people-watching until all hours. ✉ *123 W. Capitol St.,* ☎ *601/355–4122. MC, V.*

$$ ✕ **The Palette.** In a light-filled gallery in the Mississippi Arts Center is one of the state's finest lunch spots. Try the Wine Country Pie, eight layers of meats, cheeses, and vegetables under a flaky crust. ✉ *201 E. Pascagoula St.,* ☎ *601/960–2003. MC, V. Closed Mon. No dinner.*

$$ ✕ **Ralph & Kacoo's.** Here you'll dine on authentic hot-and-spicy Cajun food while listening to recorded music from southern Louisiana. The crawfish étouffée is superb. ✉ *100 Dyess Rd., just off I–55 and County Line Rd.,* ☎ *601/957–0702. AE, MC, V.*

$$$$ 🏨 **Millsaps-Buie House.** This 1888 Queen Anne Victorian, restored as a bed-and-breakfast in 1987, is listed on the National Register of Historic Places. Guest rooms are individually decorated with antiques, and the staff is attentive. ✉ *628 N. State St., 39202,* ☎ *601/352–0221 or 800/784–0221,* 🕿 *601/352–0221. 11 rooms. AE, DC, MC, V.*

$$$ 🏨 **Edison Walthall Hotel.** The cornerstone and huge brass mailbox are about all that remain of the original 1920s Walthall Hotel, but the marble floors and paneled library/writing room almost fool you into thinking this is a restoration. The rooms have standard hotel decor, with some wicker furniture. ✉ *225 E. Capitol St., 39201,* ☎ *601/948–6161 or 800/932–6161,* 🕿 *601/948–0088. 208 rooms. Restaurant, bar, pool, hot tub. AE, DC, MC, V.*

$$$ 🏨 **Renaissance Playa Hotel.** This high-rise convention hotel in the north end of town is sleekly contemporary, but the rooms are decorated in traditional style. ✉ *1001 County Line Rd., 39211,* ☎ *601/957–2800 or 800/228–9898,* 🕿 *601/957–3191. 300 rooms. Restaurant, bar, airport shuttle. AE, DC, MC, V.*

Natchez

$$ ✕ **Cock of the Walk.** The famous original of a regional franchise, this restaurant, in an old train depot overlooking the Mississippi River, spe-

cializes in fried catfish fillets, fried dill pickles, hush puppies, mustard greens, and coleslaw. ⊠ *200 N. Broadway, on the Bluff,* ☎ *601/446–8920. AE, D, DC, MC, V.*

$$ ✕ **Natchez Landing.** The view of the Mississippi River from the porch tables is enthralling, especially when the *Delta Queen* and the *Mississippi Queen* steamboats dock. Specialties of the house include barbecue (pork ribs, chicken, and beef) and catfish, fried or grilled. ⊠ *35 Silver St., Under-the-Hill,* ☎ *601/442–6639. AE, MC, V.*

$$ ✕ **Pearl Street Pasta.** The fresh pasta dishes at this intimate restaurant, including pasta primavera and breast of chicken with *tasso* (spiced ham), onions, and mushrooms over angel-hair pasta, suggest a taste of Italy in the Mississippi heartland. ⊠ *105 S. Pearl St.,* ☎ *601/442–9284. AE, MC, V.*

$$$ 🏠 **Dunleith.** At stately, colonnaded Dunleith a wing for overnight guests has rooms with antiques, fireplaces, and wonderful views of the landscaped grounds. Guests receive a complimentary tour of the house. ⊠ *84 Homochitto St., 39120,* ☎ *601/446–8500 or 800/433–2445. 12 rooms. AE, MC, V.*

$$$ 🏠 **Monmouth.** This plantation mansion (circa 1818) was owned by Mississippi governor John A. Quitman from 1826 until his death in 1858. Guest rooms—in the main house, in servants' quarters, and in garden cottages—are furnished with tester beds and antiques. ⊠ *36 Melrose Ave., 39120,* ☎ *601/442–5852 or 800/828–4531,* ℻ *601/446–7762. 25 rooms. AE, MC, V.*

$$$ 🏠 **Natchez Eola.** This 1920s hotel has an elegant formal lobby and small guest rooms with reproduction antique furniture. Many rooms have views of the river. ⊠ *110 N. Pearl St., 39120,* ☎ *601/445–6000 or 800/888–9140,* ℻ *601/446–5310. 122 rooms. Restaurant. AE, DC, MC, V.*

$$ 🏠 **Ramada Hilltop Motel.** Recently remodeled, this comfortable motel sits on a bluff overlooking the Mississippi River to the north and Louisiana to the west. ⊠ *130 John R. Junkin Dr., 39120,* ☎ *601/446–6311 or 800/272–6232,* ℻ *601/446–6321. Restaurant, lounge, pool. AE, DC, MC, V.*

Tupelo

$$ ✕ **Harvey's.** A local favorite, Harvey's serves consistently good chow. Specialties are prime rib and pasta. ⊠ *424 S. Gloster St.,* ☎ *601/842–6763. AE, MC, V. Closed Sun.*

$$ ✕ **Jefferson Place.** This rambling late-Victorian house is lively inside, with red-check tablecloths and bric-a-brac. It's popular with the college crowd and specializes in short orders and steaks. ⊠ *823 Jefferson St.,* ☎ *601/844–8696. AE, MC, V. Closed Sun.*

$ ✕ **Vanelli's.** Family pictures and scenes of Greece decorate this comfortably nondescript restaurant. Specialties (all homemade) include pizza with a choice of 10 toppings, lasagna, moussaka, and Greek salad. ⊠ *1302 N. Gloster St.,* ☎ *601/844–4410. AE, D, DC, MC, V.*

$$ 🏠 **Ramada Inn.** This modern hotel caters to business travelers and conventions as well as families. Breakfast and lunch buffets are served. ⊠ *854 N. Gloster St., 38801,* ☎ ℻ *601/844–4111. 240 rooms. Restaurant, pool. AE, DC, MC, V.*

$ 🏠 **Trace Inn.** This old, rustic inn on 15 acres near the Natchez Trace offers neat rooms and friendly service. ⊠ *3400 W. Main St., 38801,* ☎ *601/842–5555,* ℻ *601/844–3105. 134 rooms. Restaurant, pool, playground. AE, D, MC, V.*

Nightlife

Jackson

For live entertainment on weekends try **Hal and Mal's** (✉ 200 S. Commerce St., ☎ 601/948–0888). At the **Dock** (✉ Main Harbor Marina at Ross Barnett Reservoir, ☎ 601/856–7765), the mood is set by people who step off their boats to dine, drink, and listen to rock or rhythm and blues. **Rodeos** (✉ 6107 Ridgewood Rd., ☎ 601/957–9300) is a spot where patrons line up outside to line-dance inside.

Natchez

After dark head for **Under-the-Hill,** a busy strip of restaurants, gift shops, and bars on the river. Gambling is offered at the permanently docked riverboat casino the **Lady Luck** (☎ 601/445–0605), and there's live music on weekends at **Under-the-Hill Saloon** (✉ 25 Silver St., ☎ 601/446–8023).

Shopping

Everyday Gourmet (✉ 2905 Old Canton Rd., Jackson, ☎ 601/362–0723; ✉ 1625 E. Country Line Rd., Jackson, ☎ 601/977–9258) stocks state products including pecan pie, muscadine jelly, jams, cookbooks, fine ceramic tableware, and bread and biscuit mixes.

OXFORD AND HOLLY SPRINGS

Holly Springs and Oxford, in northern Mississippi, are sophisticated versions of the Mississippi small town. In these courthouse towns incorporated in 1837, you'll find historic architecture, arts and crafts, literary associations, and those unhurried pleasures of southern life that remain constant from generation to generation: entertaining conversation, good food, and nostalgic walks at twilight. Oxford and Lafayette counties were immortalized as "Jefferson County" and "Yoknapatawpha County" in the novels of Oxford native William Faulkner.

Visitor Information

Holly Springs: Chamber of Commerce (✉ 154 S. Memphis St., 38365, ☎ 601/252–2943). **Oxford:** Chamber of Commerce (✉ 115 Courthouse Sq., 38655, ☎ 601/234–4651).

Arriving and Departing

By Bus

Greyhound Lines has a station in Holly Springs (✉ 490 Craft St., ☎ 800/231–2222).

By Car

Oxford is accessible from I–55; it is 23 mi east of Batesville on Route 6. **Holly Springs,** near the Tennessee state line, is reached via U.S. 78 and Routes 4, 7, and 311.

By Train

Amtrak (☎ 800/872–7245) stops in Batesville.

Exploring Oxford and Holly Springs

Oxford

Even if you're not a Faulkner fan, this is a great place to experience small-town living. You won't be bored; the kinds of characters who fascinated Faulkner still live here, and the University of Mississippi keeps

In case you want to see the world.

At American Express, we're here to make your journey a smooth one. So we have over 1,700 travel service locations in over 120 countries ready to help. What else would you expect from the world's largest travel agency?

do more

Travel

In case you want to be welcomed there.

We're here to see that you're always welcomed at establishments everywhere. That's why millions of people carry the American Express® Card – for peace of mind, confidence, and security, around the world or just around the corner.

do more

Cards

In case you're running low.

We're here to help with more than 118,000 Express Cash locations around the world. In order to enroll, just call American Express before you start your vacation.

do more

Express Cash

things lively. Oxford's **Courthouse Square** is a National Historic Landmark. At its center is the white-sandstone **Lafayette** (pronounced Luh-*fay*-it) **County Courthouse,** rebuilt in 1873 after Union troops burned it; the courtroom on the second floor is original. There's an information center at the nearby city hall.

University Avenue, from South Lamar Boulevard to the university, is one of the state's most beautiful sights when the trees flame orange and gold in the fall or when the dogwoods blossom in spring. The **University of Mississippi,** the state's beloved Olę Miss, opened in 1848. Its tree-shaded campus centers on the **Grove,** surrounded by historic buildings. Facing it is the beautifully restored antebellum **Barnard Observatory** (☎ 601/232–5993), which houses the **Center for the Study of Southern Culture,** with exhibits on southern music, folklore, and literature and the world's largest blues archive (40,000 records). The **Mississippi Room** (☎ 601/232–7408), in the John Davis Williams Library, contains a permanent exhibit on Faulkner, including the Nobel Prize for literature he won in 1949, as well as first editions of works by other Mississippi authors. The room is closed on weekends.

★ **Rowan Oak** (circa 1848) was William Faulkner's home from 1930 until his death in 1962. The two-story white-frame house with square columns is now a National Historic Landmark owned by the university. The writer's typewriter, desk, and other personal items still evoke his presence. ⊠ *Old Taylor Rd.,* ☎ *601/234–3284. Closed Mon.*

Faulkner's funeral was held at Rowan Oak, and he was buried in the family plot in **St. Peter's Cemetery** (⊠ Jefferson and N. 16th Sts.). Another Faulkner pilgrimage site is **College Hill Presbyterian Church** (⊠ 8 mi northwest of Oxford on College Hill Rd., ☎ 601/234–5020), where he and Estelle Oldham Franklin were married June 20, 1929.

Holly Springs

Holly Springs, 29 mi north of Oxford on Route 7, contains more than 200 structures (61 of which are antebellum homes) listed on the National Register of Historic Places. These include the 1858 **Montrose** (⊠ 307 E. Salem Ave., ☎ 601/252–2943), open by appointment only, and the privately owned Salem Avenue mansions **Oakleigh, Cedarhurst,** and **Airliewood.**

Dining and Lodging

For price ranges *see* Charts 1 (B) and 2 (B) *in* On the Road with Fodor's.

Holly Springs

$ ✕ **Phillips Grocery.** Constructed in 1882 as a saloon for railroad workers, it's decorated today with antiques and crafts and serves big, old-fashioned hamburgers. ⊠ *541-A Van Dorn Ave.,* ☎ *601/252–4671. No credit cards. Closed Sun.*

$ ✕ **City Cafe.** Breakfast and lunch specials pack them in at this meat-and-three eatery serving homemade soups, roast beef, and fried chicken livers. ⊠ *135E Van Dorn Ave.,* ☎ *601/252–9895. No credit cards.*

$$ ▥ **Heritage Inn.** Rooms are comfortable if nondescript, with either a king-size bed or two doubles, and the lunch buffet has home-style southern cooking. The motel is on U.S. 78 where it meets Routes 7 and 4. ⊠ *U.S. 78 (Box 476), 38635,* ☎ FAX *601/252–1120. 48 rooms. Restaurant, pool. AE, DC, MC, V.*

Oxford

$$ ✗ **Downtown Grill.** The Grill could be a club in Oxford, England, but the balcony overlooking the square is pure Oxford, Mississippi. Specialties include seafood gumbo and Cajun-style spicy catfish Lafitte. ⊠ *110 Courthouse Sq.,* ☏ *601/234–2659. AE, D, MC, V.*

$ ✗ **Smitty's.** Look for home-style cooking here: red-eye gravy and grits, biscuits with blackberry preserves, fried catfish, chicken and dumplings, corn bread, and black-eyed peas. The atmosphere is down-home. ⊠ *208 S. Lamar Blvd.,* ☏ *601/234–9111. No credit cards.*

$$$ 🏨 **Holiday Inn.** These functional rooms are typical of the genre. The restaurant, however, prepares a surprisingly good breakfast. ⊠ *400 N. Lamar Blvd., 38655,* ☏ *601/234–3031,* ℻ *601/234–2834. 100 rooms. Restaurant, pool. AE, DC, MC, V.*

$$$ 🏨 **Oliver-Britt House.** In a restored house built about 1900, this conveniently located B&B has pleasant rooms and is run in a casual fashion. ⊠ *512 Van Buren Ave., 38655,* ☏ *601/234–8043. 5 rooms. Dining room. AE, MC, V.*

Nightlife

In Oxford the **Gin** (⊠ E. Harrison St. and S. 14th St., ☏ 601/234–0024) offers live dance music. The **Hoka** (⊠ 304 S. 14th St., ☏ 601/234–3057) is an Oxford warehouse turned movie theater and restaurant.

Shopping

At Oxford's well-stocked **Square Books** (⊠ 160 Courthouse Sq., ☏ 601/236–2262), you can chat with the knowledgeable staff about local writers and savor cappuccino or dessert.

ELSEWHERE IN MISSISSIPPI

The Delta

Arriving and Departing
U.S. 61 runs from Memphis through the Delta to Vicksburg, Natchez, and Baton Rouge, Louisiana.

What to See and Do
Between Memphis and Vicksburg (☞ Vicksburg, *below*) is the **Delta,** a vast agricultural plain created by the Mississippi River. Drive through the Delta, with side trips to **Tunica**'s gambling halls or down Route 1 (the Great River Road) or Route 8 for good views of the Mississippi.

Clarksdale, a pleasant spot for lunch, has a renovated Carnegie Library that houses a music museum. The exhibits and programs of the **Delta Blues Museum** trace the history of the blues and its influence on other music. ⊠ 114 Delta Ave., ☏ 601/627–6820. *Free. Closed Sun.*

The historic port city of **Greenville** has produced an extraordinary number of writers, including William Alexander Percy, Ellen Douglas, Hodding Carter, and Shelby Foote. It's also noted as the home of Doe's (☞ Dining and Lodging, *below*).

The **Mississippi Welcome Center** (⊠ 4210 Washington St., Vicksburg 39180, ☏ 601/638–4269) has good regional information. The **Greenville/Washington County Convention and Visitors Bureau** (⊠ 410 Washington Ave., Greenville 38701, ☏ 601/334–2711 or 800/467–3582) provides information on the region and details the Delta boyhood of Jim Henson, creator of Kermit the Frog.

Dining

CLARKSDALE

$ ✕ **Rest Haven.** The Delta's large Lebanese community influences the food, making Middle Eastern food regional fare here. Among the favorites are *kibbe* (seasoned lean ground steak with cracked wheat), spinach and meat pies, and cabbage rolls. Daily plate-lunch specials include chicken and dumplings. ⊠ *419 State St. (U.S. 61),* ☎ *601/624–8601. No credit cards. Closed Sun.*

CLEVELAND

$$$$ ✕ **KC's Restaurant.** The eclectic, sophisticated menu at this funky but fabulous restaurant changes every two weeks, but it always has French, Italian, Asian, and southwestern influences. Count on seeing wild game, fresh fish, free-range meats, and organic vegetables. ⊠ *U.S. 61N at 1st St.,* ☎ *601/843–5301. AE, MC, V. No lunch Sat., no dinner Sun.*

GREENVILLE

$$$ ✕ **Doe's.** This tumbledown building is visually as uninspiring as any restaurant you'll find. But when you see that huge steak hanging off your plate, you'll know why this place is famous. Hot tamales (a popular takeout item) are a specialty. ⊠ *502 Nelson St.,* ☎ *601/334–3315. MC, V. No lunch.*

Ocean Springs

Arriving and Departing

U.S. 90 runs through the heart of Ocean Springs.

What to See and Do

On the Mississippi Gulf Coast, this oak-shaded town originated in 1699 as a French fort. It is now known as the former home of artist Walter Anderson. The **Walter Anderson Museum of Art** (⊠ 510 Washington Ave., ☎ 601/872–3164) displays Anderson's work, including his cottage studio with intricately painted walls. The artist (1903–65) revealed his ecstatic communion with nature in thousands of drawings and watercolors, most kept secret until his death.

★ Ocean Springs is the headquarters of the **Gulf Islands National Seashore** (☞ National Parks, *above*). On the mainland there are nature trails and ranger programs. Out in the Gulf, pristine Ship, Horn, and Petit Bois islands, for which the park is named, have beaches as white and soft as sugar—some of the country's best. Excursion boats to Ship, rimmed by about 7 mi of this remarkable sand, leave from Biloxi in summer and from Gulfport from May through October. Charter operators regularly take wilderness lovers to Horn and Petit Bois, both nationally designated wilderness areas, where camping is permitted. The **Ocean Springs Chamber of Commerce** (⊠ Box 187, 39566, ☎ 601/875–4424) has information on this area.

Dining and Lodging

BILOXI

$$ 🏨 **Broadwater Beach Resort Village.** This sprawling property comes complete with a casino and a marina. Accommodations vary depending on which of the two resort hotels you choose, and rates vary according to room size and location. ⊠ *2110 Beach Blvd., 39533,* ☎ *601/388–2211 or 800/647–3964,* FAX *601/385–1801. 550 rooms. 4 restaurants, 4 pools, 2 18-hole golf courses, 10 tennis courts, exercise room, basketball, volleyball, boating, casino, playground. AE, D, DC, MC, V.*

$$ 🏨 **Treasure Bay.** Formerly the Royal D'Iberville, the hotel has spacious rooms now bright with chintz, along with a casino. Furniture is hotel-

functional; the large public areas are comfortably contemporary. ⊠ *1980 W. Beach Blvd., 39530,* ☎ *601/385–6000. 268 rooms. Restaurant, bar, 2 pools, casino, meeting rooms. AE, D, DC, MC, V.*

GULFPORT

$$ ✕ **Vrazel's.** Dining nooks with windows facing the beach add charm to this eatery. Special attractions include the red snapper, Gulf trout, flounder, and shrimp prepared every which way. ⊠ *3206 W. Beach Blvd. (U.S. 90),* ☎ *601/863–2229. AE, D, DC, MC, V. Closed Sun. No lunch Sat.*

OCEAN SPRINGS

$$ ✕ **Germaine's.** Formerly Trilby's, this little house surrounded by live oaks has served many a great meal to its faithful clientele. The atmosphere is reminiscent of New Orleans, with unadorned wooden floors, fireplaces, and attentive service. Specialties include mushrooms *le marin,* crabmeat au gratin, trout *desoto,* veal Angela, and chicken chardonnay. ⊠ *1203 Bienville Blvd., U.S. 90E,* ☎ *601/875–4426. AE, DC, MC, V. Closed Mon. No dinner Sun.*

$$ ✕ **Jocelyn's Restaurant.** The coast seafood served in this old frame house
★ is as good as it gets. Crab, trout, flounder, and, when available, snapper are subtly seasoned and presented with garnishes as bright and original as modern art. ⊠ *U.S. 90E, opposite Sunburst Bank,* ☎ *601/ 875–1925. Reservations not accepted. No credit cards.*

Vicksburg

Arriving and Departing
I–20 runs east–west and U.S. 61 north–south through Vicksburg.

What to See and Do
During the Civil War the Confederacy and the Union vied for control of this strategic location on the Mississippi Delta across the river from Louisiana. Tours of grand antebellum homes and 24-hour riverfront gambling are other draws. Vicksburg's **National Military Park** (☞ National Parks, *above*) is second only to Gettysburg in interest and beauty. After a 47-day siege the city surrendered to Ulysses S. Grant on July 4, 1863, giving the Union control of the river and sounding the death knell for the Confederacy. Battle positions are marked, and monuments line the 16-mi drive through the park.

The **Vicksburg Convention and Visitors Bureau** (⊠ Box 110, Vicksburg 39181, ☎ 601/636–9421 or 800/221–3536) has abundant information.

Dining and Lodging
$ ✕ **Walnut Hills.** If you're yearning for authentic regional cooking, this restaurant is a must. Don't miss the outstanding fried chicken, served with such vegetables as fresh snap beans or purple-hull peas. For dessert try the blackberry cobbler. ⊠ *1214 Adams St., at Clay St.,* ☎ *601/638–4910. AE, DC, MC, V. Closed Sat. No dinner Sun.*

$$$$ ▦ **Cedar Grove.** This 1840s mansion and its grounds cover an entire
★ city block. The entire house is furnished with period antiques. Hear nearby river traffic from the quiet, gaslighted grounds or survey the watery scene from the rooftop garden. A house tour and hearty southern breakfast are included. ⊠ *2200 Oak St., 39180,* ☎ *601/636–1000 or 800/862–1300,* 𝔽𝔸𝕏 *601/634–6126. 35 rooms. Restaurant, piano bar, pool, tennis court, croquet, bicycles. AE, D, DC, MC, V.*

$$$ ▦ **Duff Green Mansion.** This 1856 mansion was used as a hospital during the Civil War. Each guest room is decorated with antiques, including
★ half-tester beds. A large southern breakfast and a tour of the home are included. ⊠ *1114 1st East St., 39180,* ☎ *601/636–6968 or 800/992– 0037. 7 rooms. Pool. AE, MC, V.*

TENNESSEE

Updated by
Charlotte
Durham

Capital	Nashville
Population	5,320,000
Motto	Agriculture and Commerce
State Bird	Mockingbird
State Flower	Iris
Postal Abbreviation	TN

Statewide Visitor Information

Tennessee Department of Tourist Development (⊠ Box 23170, Nashville 37202, ☎ 615/741–2158).

Scenic Drives

U.S. 421 from Bristol to Trade passes through the Cherokee National Forest and crosses the Appalachian Trail. **Route 73** south from Townsend leads through a high valley ringed by the Great Smoky Mountains to the pioneer village of Cades Cove in Great Smoky Mountains National Park. **Route 25** from Gallatin to Springfield travels through an area of Thoroughbred farms and antebellum houses. Between Monteagle and Chattanooga **I–24** winds through the Cumberland Mountains.

National and State Parks

National Parks

Great Smoky Mountains National Park (⊠ Gatlinburg 37738, ☎ 423/ 423–1200) encompasses tall peaks and lush valleys, with camping and fishing sites and more than 900 mi of horse and hiking trails.

State Parks

The State Parks Division of the **Tennessee Department of Environment and Conservation** (⊠ 401 Church St., L&C Tower, 7th floor, Nashville 37243, ☎ 615/532–0103 or 800/421–6683) provides information on Tennessee's 50-plus state parks. The 16,000-acre **Fall Creek Falls State Resort Park** (⊠ Rte. 3, Pikeville 37367, ☎ 423/881–5241 or 423/881– 3297) has the highest waterfall east of the Rockies. Thick stands of cypress trees make **Reelfoot Lake State Resort Park** (⊠ Rte. 1, Box 296, Tiptonville 38079, ☎ 901/253–7756), in northwestern Tennessee, a favorite wintering ground for the American bald eagle. **Roan Mountain State Resort Park** (⊠ Rte. 1, Box 236, Roan Mountain 37687, ☎ 423/772–3303), in northeastern Tennessee, has a 600-acre natural rhododendron garden that blooms in late June.

MEMPHIS

On the bluffs overlooking the Mississippi River, Memphis is Tennessee's largest city and the commercial and cultural center of the western part of the state. It is a blend of southern tradition and modern efficiency, where aging cotton warehouses stand near sleek new office buildings and old-fashioned paddle wheelers steam upriver past the city's newest landmark, the gleaming stainless-steel Pyramid Arena. Memphis is perhaps best known for its music and for the two extraordinary men who introduced that music to the world: W. C. Handy, the Father of the Blues, and Elvis Presley, the King of Rock and Roll.

Visitor Information

Convention & Visitors Bureau (⊠ 47 Union Ave., 38103, ☎ 901/543–5300). **Visitors Information Center** (⊠ 340 Beale St., 38103, ☎ 901/576–8171).

Arriving and Departing

By Boat

Memphis is one stop on the paddle-wheeler cruises of the **Delta Queen Steamboat Co.** (⊠ Robin Street Wharf, New Orleans, LA 70130, ☎ 800/543–1949). The *Delta Queen* (a National Historic Landmark), the *Mississippi Queen,* and the *American Queen* travel between St. Louis and New Orleans.

By Bus

Greyhound Lines (⊠ 203 Union Ave., ☎ 800/231–2222).

By Car

Memphis is reached via the north–south I–55 or the east–west I–40. I–240 loops around the city.

By Plane

Memphis International Airport (☎ 901/922–8000), 9 mi south of downtown, is served by most major airlines and is a hub for Northwest Airlines. Driving time to downtown is about 15 minutes on I–240. Cab fare runs about $17 plus tip. **Yellow Cab** (☎ 901/577–7700) operates a limousine service between the airport and downtown for a flat rate of $75.

By Train

Amtrak (⊠ 545 S. Main St., ☎ 800/872–7245).

Getting Around Memphis

Memphis's streets are well marked, and there's plenty of parking, so the city is easily explored by car. The **Memphis Area Transit Authority** (☎ 901/274–6282) operates buses ($1.10) throughout downtown and the suburbs (additional fare for zones outside the city limits); a trolley (50¢) runs between the north and south ends of downtown.

Exploring Memphis

Downtown

Memphis begins at the Mississippi River, which is celebrated in a 52-acre river park (☎ 901/576–6595) on **Mud Island.** A footbridge and monorail at 125 Front Street get you to the island, where a five-block **River Walk** replicates the Mississippi's every twist, turn, and sandbar from Cairo, Illinois, to New Orleans. Also in the park are the **Mississippi River Museum,** the famed World War II B-17 bomber *Memphis Belle,* an amphitheater, shops, and a pool.

The 32-story, 22,000-seat stainless-steel **Pyramid Arena** (⊠ 1 Auction Ave., ☎ 901/526–5177), opposite the north end of Mud Island, opened in 1991. Tours are available. **Magevney House,** built in the 1830s by a pioneer schoolteacher, is Memphis's oldest dwelling. It's a 20-minute walk from the Pyramid Arena. ⊠ *198 Adams Ave.,* ☎ *901/526–4464. Closed Mon.*

The beautifully restored **Peabody Hotel** stands at the corner of Union Avenue and 2nd Street. **Beale Street,** south of the Peabody Hotel, is where W. C. Handy played the blues in the early decades of the 20th century and where clubs and restaurants are thriving again. The **W. C. Handy Memphis Home and Museum** recalls the influential blues mu-

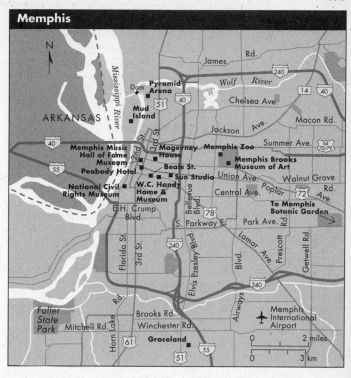

Memphis

sician through a variety of memorabilia. ⊠ *352 Beale St.,* ☎ *901/522–8300. Closed Labor Day–Apr.*

Exhibits in the **Memphis Music Hall of Fame Museum**—rare photographs, film footage, audiotapes, and memorabilia—trace the development of blues, country, and rock and roll, as well as the city's role in it all. ⊠ *97 S. 2nd St.,* ☎ *901/525–4007.*

The motel where Dr. Martin Luther King Jr. was assassinated in 1968 has been transformed into the **National Civil Rights Museum,** which documents the movement through exhibits and audiovisual displays. ⊠ *406 Mulberry St.,* ☎ *901/521–9699. Free Mon. 3–5. Closed Tues.*

In Overton Park the popular 70-acre **Memphis Zoo** (⊠ *2000 Galloway Ave.,* ☎ *901/725–3400*) has the new 9-acre Cat Country. The **Memphis Brooks Museum of Art,** in Overton Park, houses a collection of fine and decorative arts from antiquity to the present. ⊠ *2080 Poplar Ave.,* ☎ *901/722–3500. Free, except for special exhibits. Closed Mon.*

★ **Graceland,** the estate once owned by Elvis Presley, is 12 mi southeast of downtown. A guided tour of the Colonial-style mansion, automobile museum, and burial site reveals the spoils of stardom. ⊠ *3717 Elvis Presley Blvd.,* ☎ *901/332–3322 or 800/238–2000. Reservations essential, especially in summer. Closed Tues. Nov.–Feb.*

Sun Studio (⊠ *706 Union Ave.,* ☎ *901/521–0664*), the birthplace of rock and roll, is where Elvis Presley, Jerry Lee Lewis, B. B. King, and Roy Orbison launched their careers. Tours are given daily; the studio is seven blocks east of downtown.

Parks and Gardens

Overton Park, a few miles east of downtown on Poplar Avenue, offers picnic areas, sports fields, hiking and biking trails, a nine-hole golf course, and a cluster of major cultural attractions (☞ Other Attractions, *above*). In East Memphis the 96-acre **Memphis Botanic Garden** (⊠ 750 Cherry Rd., ☎ 901/685–1566) is planted with scores of different species, from camellias to cacti.

What to See and Do with Children

At the **Children's Museum of Memphis** (⊠ 2525 Central Ave., ☎ 901/458–2678) youngsters can touch, climb, and explore their way through a child-size city. The **Memphis Pink Palace Museum and Planetarium** (⊠ 3050 Central Ave., ☎ 901/320–6320) has a mix of natural history and cultural history exhibits plus planetarium laser shows and an IMAX theater. **Chucalissa Archaeological Museum** (⊠ 1987 Indian Village Dr., ☎ 901/785–3160) is a reconstruction of a Native American village that existed on the banks of the Mississippi from AD 1000 to AD 1500. Skilled Choctaw craftspeople fashion jewelry, weapons, and pottery outside the **C. H. Nash Museum,** which houses historic versions of the same articles.

Dining

Although Memphis restaurants have a pleasing array of cuisines, the local passion remains barbecue; the city has 70-odd barbecue restaurants. For price ranges *see* Chart 1 (B) *in* On the Road with Fodor's.

$$$$ ✕ **Chez Philippe.** Chef José Gutierrez serves imaginative and sophis-
★ ticated dishes in ornate surroundings. Nightly creations may include lamb with goat cheese and garlic or halibut with fried leeks and sundried cherry sauce. ⊠ *The Peabody, 149 Union Ave.,* ☎ *901/529–4188. Jacket required. AE, DC, MC, V. Closed Sun. No lunch.*

$$$$ ✕ **Raji.** Chef Raji Jallepalli blends nouvelle styles and Indian seasonings in subtle dishes such as grilled scallops and lobster in lentil pastry with a ginger-flavor beurre blanc. The dining rooms in a former residence are elegant. ⊠ *712 W. Brookhaven Circle,* ☎ *901/685–8723. Reservations essential. AE, MC, V. Closed Sun.–Mon. No lunch.*

$$$ ✕ **La Tourelle.** This turn-of-the-century bungalow in Overton Square has the romantic ambience of a French country inn. Five-course prix-fixe meals with an emphasis on fresh seafood supplement the à la carte menu. You might feel more comfortable in a jacket and tie. ⊠ *2146 Monroe Ave.,* ☎ *901/726–5771. MC, V.*

$$ ✕ **Cafe Max.** The atmosphere is lively at this bistro in East Memphis, where selections include pasta, seafood, and grilled meats. ⊠ *6161 Poplar Ave.,* ☎ *901/767–3633. AE, D, MC, V. No lunch.*

$$ ✕ **Landry's Seafood House.** A converted riverfront warehouse, this place packs 'em in for such seafood dishes as fried shrimp and stuffed flounder. ⊠ *263 Wagner Pl.,* ☎ *901/526–1966. AE, DC, MC, V.*

$$ ✕ **Paulette's.** This Overton Square classic has served delicious crepes
★ and salads and excellent grilled chicken, salmon, and swordfish in the atmosphere of a European inn. Save room for the hot chocolate crepes. ⊠ *2110 Madison Ave.,* ☎ *901/726–5128. AE, D, DC, MC, V.*

$ ✕ **Cafe Olé.** This popular midtown hangout offers a healthier version of Mexican cuisine (no animal fats are used), including spinach enchiladas and chili *rellenos* (cheese-stuffed fried green chilis). ⊠ *959 S. Cooper St.,* ☎ *901/274–1504. AE, D, DC, MC, V.*

$ ✕ **Charlie Vergos' Rendezvous.** Tourists and locals alike flock to this downtown basement restaurant to savor Vergos's "dry" barbecued pork ribs and other barbecue specialties. ⊠ *52 S. 2nd St.,* ☎ *901/523–2746. AE, DC, MC, V. Closed Sun.–Mon. No lunch Tues.–Thurs.*

$ ✕ **Corky's.** There's always a line at this no-frills East Memphis bar-
★ becue restaurant. Once you taste the ribs (or sandwiches, or beef or pork platters), you'll understand why. ⊠ *5259 Poplar Ave.,* ☎ *901/ 685–9744. AE, D, DC, MC, V.*

$ ✕ **The Cupboard.** Owner Charles Cavallo knows fresh produce, and his cooks turn out masterful "meat-and-three" plates. Lucky is the soul who visits when both macaroni and cheese and fried green tomatoes are offered. ⊠ *1495 Union Ave.,* ☎ *901/276–8015. MC, V.*

Lodging

Memphis hotels are especially busy during the monthlong Memphis-in-May International Festival and in mid-August, during Elvis Tribute Week; book well ahead at these times. For bed-and-breakfasts contact the **Bed & Breakfast Reservation Service** (⊠ Box 41621, Memphis 38174, ☎ 901/726–5920 or 800/336–2087, ℻ 901/725–0194). For price ranges *see* Chart 2 (B) *in* On the Road with Fodor's.

$$$ ▣ **Adam's Mark Memphis.** Set in the flourishing eastern suburbs near I–240, this 27-story glass tower has views of the sprawling metropolis and its outskirts. ⊠ *939 Ridge Lake Blvd., 38120,* ☎ *901/684–6664 or 800/444–2326,* ℻ *901/762–7411. 380 rooms. Restaurant, coffee shop, lounge, pool, health club. AE, D, DC, MC, V.*

$$$ ▣ **French Quarter Suites.** This pleasant Overton Square hotel is reminiscent of a New Orleans–style inn. All suites have oversize whirlpool tubs, and some have balconies. ⊠ *2144 Madison Ave., 38104,* ☎ *901/ 728–4000 or 800/843–0353,* ℻ *901/278–1262. 105 suites. Restaurant, bar, pool, health club. AE, D, DC, MC, V.*

$$$ ▣ **Peabody Hotel.** Even if you're not staying here, it's worth a stop to
★ see this 12-story downtown landmark, built in 1925. The lobby preserves its original stained-glass skylights and the travertine-marble fountain that is home to the hotel's resident ducks. The rooms are decorated in a variety of period styles. ⊠ *149 Union Ave., 38103,* ☎ *901/ 529–4000 or 800/732–2639,* ℻ *901/529–3600. 454 rooms. 3 restaurants, bar, lounge, indoor pool, health club. AE, DC, MC, V.*

$$ ▣ **Country Suites by Carlson.** This three-story hotel in East Memphis provides many of the comforts of home, such as kitchenettes. The decor includes teal carpeting and Aztec-pattern draperies. ⊠ *4300 American Way, 38118,* ☎ *901/366–9333 or 800/456–4000,* ℻ *901/366–7835. 121 suites. Pool, hot tub, health club. AE, D, DC, MC, V.*

$$ ▣ **Holiday Inn East.** Close to I–240 and the bustling Poplar/Ridgeway
★ office complex, this sleek 10-story hotel is popular with business travelers. ⊠ *5795 Poplar Ave., 38119,* ☎ *901/682–7881 or 800/465–4329,* ℻ *901/682–7881, ext. 7760. 246 rooms. Restaurant, lounge, pool, health club. AE, D, DC, MC, V.*

$$ ▣ **Radisson Hotel.** Across the street from the Peabody, this downtown hotel has its own lobby fountain and waterfall. Glass-walled elevators whisk guests to rooms around a 10-story atrium. ⊠ *185 Union Ave., 38103,* ☎ *901/528–1800 or 800/333–3333,* ℻ *901/526–3226. 283 rooms. Restaurant, lounge, pool, hot tub, sauna. AE, D, DC, MC, V.*

$ ▣ **Howard Johnson Lodge East.** All units have private patios or balconies; many have refrigerators and microwave ovens, and four have kitchens. ⊠ *1541 Sycamore View, 38134,* ☎ *901/388–1300 or 800/ 446–4656,* ℻ *901/388–1300, ext. 247. 96 rooms. Pool, coin laundry. Continental breakfast. AE, D, DC, MC, V.*

$ ▣ **Executive Inn.** This four-story motor lodge near Graceland has spacious, well-appointed rooms with tasteful touches of country decor. ⊠ *3222 Airways Blvd., 38116,* ☎ *901/332–3800 or 800/221–2222,* ℻

901/345–2448. 118 rooms. Pool, exercise room, coin laundry. DC, MC, V.

$ ▥ **La Quinta Inn–Medical Center.** Convenient to midtown, this two-story inn has spacious, well-maintained rooms. ⊠ *42 S. Camilla St., 38104,* ☎ *901/526–1050 or 800/531–5900,* ⒻⒶⓍ *901/525–3219. 130 rooms. Pool. AE, D, DC, MC, V.*

Nightlife and the Arts

Call the Memphis **events hot line** (☎ 901/681–1111) for information about performances in the city.

Nightlife

To hear the blues as they were meant to be played, head for the clubs on Beale Street. Among the most popular clubs is **B. B. King's Blues Club** (⊠ 147 Beale St., ☎ 901/524–5464), where B. B. himself occasionally performs. **Blues Hall/Rum Boogie Cafe** (⊠ 182 Beale St., ☎ 901/528–0150) is also a good spot for the blues.

The Arts

The **Orpheum Theatre** (⊠ 203 S. Main St., ☎ 901/525–3000) hosts touring Broadway shows, as well as performances by the Memphis Opera (☎ 901/678–2706) and the Memphis Concert Ballet (☎ 901/763–0139). The **Memphis Symphony Orchestra** (⊠ 3100 Walnut Grove Rd., No. 402, ☎ 901/324–3627) performs at various locations from September through May.

Spectator Sports

Baseball: An **AAA team** was scheduled, at press time, to play at Tim McCarver Stadium (⊠ 800 Home Run La., ☎ 901/272–1687) until a new stadium is built.

Football: Conference USA's top college team plays in the **St. Jude Liberty Bowl** (☎ 901/274–4600) between Christmas and New Year's at Liberty Bowl Memorial Stadium (⊠ 335 S. Hollywood) at the Mid-South Fairgrounds complex.

Golf: Southwind Tournament Players Club (⊠ 3325 Club, at Southwind, ☎ 901/748–0534) hosts the **St. Jude Federal Express Golf Tournament** each summer, drawing the tour's top pros.

Tennis: The **International Indoor Tennis Tournament** (☎ 901/765–4400) is played in February at the Racquet Club (⊠ 5111 Sanderlin Ave., East Memphis).

Shopping

The **Mid-America Mall** (☎ 901/362–9315), on Main Street between Beale and Poplar, is one of the nation's longest pedestrian malls. It was overhauled and turned into a trolley mall in 1993. **Oak Court Mall** (⊠ 4465 Poplar Ave., ☎ 901/682–8928), in the busy Poplar/Perkins area of East Memphis, has 70 specialty stores and two department stores. **Overton Square** (⊠ 24 S. Cooper St., ☎ 901/272–1495)—a three-block midtown shopping, restaurant, and entertainment complex in vintage buildings and newer structures—has upscale boutiques and specialty shops. **Wolfchase Galleria** (⊠ 2760 N. Germantown Pkwy., at Rte. 64, about 18 mi east of downtown Memphis, ☎ 901/381–2769), the county's newest and largest mall, opened in 1997. **Belz Factory Outlet Mall** (⊠ 3536 Canada Rd., Exit 20 off I–40, 20 mi east of downtown Memphis, Lakeland, ☎ 901/386–3180) includes 50 stores from Linens 'n Things to Van Heusen.

NASHVILLE

Hailed as Music City, U.S.A. (country music, that is), and the birthplace of the Nashville Sound, Tennessee's capital city is also a leading center of higher education, appropriately known as the Athens of the South. The city has spawned such dissimilar institutions as the Grand Ole Opry and Vanderbilt University and has prospered from them both, becoming one of the mid-South's most vibrant communities.

Visitor Information

Nashville Convention & Visitors Bureau (⊠ 161 4th Ave. N, 37219, ☎ 615/259–4700). **Visitor information center** (⊠ I–65 and James Robertson Pkwy., Exit 85, ☎ 615/259–4747).

Arriving and Departing

By Bus
Greyhound Lines (⊠ 200 8th Ave. S, ☎ 800/231–2222).

By Car
I–65 leads into Nashville from the north and south; I–24, from the northwest and southeast; I–40, from the east and west.

By Plane
Nashville International Airport (☎ 615/275–1675), about 8 mi east of downtown, is served by major airlines. To reach downtown by car, take I–40 west. Cab fare runs about $16–$18 plus tip. **Downtown Airport Express** (☎ 615/275–1180) has service to downtown hotels for $8–$10.

Getting Around Nashville

The central city is bisected by the Cumberland River; numbered avenues are west of and parallel to it, and numbered streets east of and parallel to it.

By Bus
Metropolitan Transit Authority (MTA) buses (☎ 615/862–5950) serve the county; fare is $1.35 in exact change.

By Trolley
Nashville Trolley Company (☎ 615/862–5969) trolleys cover downtown and Music Row in summer months; the fare is 90¢.

Exploring Nashville

Downtown
Downtown attractions can be covered rather easily on foot. Overlooking the river is **Fort Nashborough** (⊠ 170 1st Ave. N), a replica of the crude log fort built in 1779 by Nashville's first settlers. In the **District,** the historic 2nd Avenue area south of Church Street, 19th-century buildings have been handsomely restored to house restaurants, clubs, boutiques, offices, and residences.

The **Downtown Presbyterian Church** (⊠ 5th Ave. and Church St., ☎ 615/254–7584), an Egyptian Revival tabernacle (circa 1851), was designed by noted Philadelphia architect William Strickland. **Ryman Auditorium and Museum** (⊠ 116 5th Ave. N, ☎ 615/254–1445, 615/889–6611 for tickets), the home of the Grand Ole Opry from 1943 to 1974, is a shrine for die-hard fans. The Ryman was recently renovated and once again hosts performances.

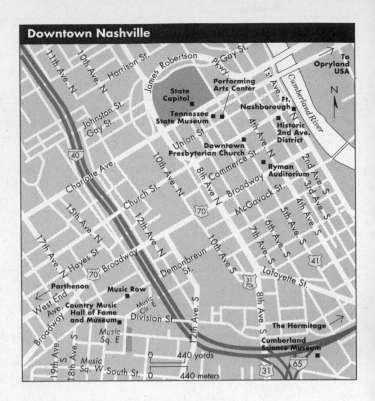

Downtown Nashville

The James K. Polk Office Building is home to the **Tennessee State Museum,** where more than 6,000 artifacts trace the history of life in Tennessee. ⊠ *505 Deaderick St.,* ☎ *615/741–2692. Closed Mon.*

In a park along Charlotte Avenue is the Greek Revival **state capitol** (☎ 615/741–2692), designed by William Strickland, who is interred here along with the 11th U.S. president, James Polk, and his wife.

Other Attractions

Music Row (⊠ Demonbreun St. exit off I–40) is the heart of Nashville's recording industry and the center of numerous country music attractions. A ticket to the **Country Music Hall of Fame and Museum** (⊠ 4 Music Sq. E, ☎ 615/255–5333) includes admission to the legendary **RCA Studio B,** a few blocks away, where Elvis, Dolly Parton, and other greats once recorded.

★ **Opryland USA,** an attraction-filled musical theme park, has 22 rides and more than a dozen live-music shows. ⊠ *2802 Opryland Dr. (via Briley Pkwy.),* ☎ *615/889–6611.* ⊡ *$28.99. Closed weekdays Oct.– early May.*

Since 1974 Opryland has been the home of the **Grand Ole Opry.** Each weekend top stars perform at the nation's oldest continuous radio show, which is broadcast from the world's largest broadcast studio (it seats 4,424); advance ticket purchase is advised. ⊠ *2804 Opryland Dr.,* ☎ *615/889–3060.*

The **Hermitage,** 12 mi east of downtown (Exit 221 off I–40), was built by Andrew Jackson, the seventh U.S. president, for his wife, Rachel. Their life and times are reflected with great care in the mansion, visitor center, and grounds. Both Jackson and his wife are entombed here. ⊠ *4580 Rachel's La., Hermitage,* ☎ *615/889–2941.*

Two miles west of downtown in Centennial Park—built for the 1897 Tennessee Centennial Exposition—stands the **Parthenon,** an exact copy of the Athenian original and now used as an art gallery. *Athena Parthenos* is a 42-ft copy of a statue in the original Parthenon. ⊠ *West End and 25th Aves.,* ☎ *615/862–8431. Closed Mon.*

Parks and Gardens

The 14,200-acre **J. Percy Priest Lake** (⊠ 11 mi east of downtown off I–40, ☎ 615/889–1975) is surrounded by parks where you can swim, fish, camp, hunt, hike, bike, picnic, paddle, or ride horseback. Thirty
★ acres of gardens at the **Cheekwood–Tennessee Botanical Gardens and Museum of Art** (⊠ 1200 Forrest Park Dr., ☎ 615/353–2140) show-case annuals, perennials, and area wildflowers.

What to See and Do with Children

At the **Cumberland Science Museum** (⊠ 800 Ridley Blvd., ☎ 615/862–5160), children are invited to touch, smell, climb, and explore. The toy collection at the **Nashville Toy Museum** (⊠ 2613 McGavock Pike, ☎ 615/883–8870) spans more than 150 years. The 50-acre **Nashville Zoo** (⊠ 1710 Ridge Rd. Circle, Joelton, ☎ 615/370–3333) includes an African savanna and a reptile house.

Dining

If you expect Nashville dining to be all cornbread, turnip greens, and grits, you're in for a surprise. Here you will find some of Tennessee's most sophisticated restaurants alongside the popular "meat-and-threes" (diners serving meat with three vegetable side dishes). For price ranges *see* Chart 1 (B) *in* On the Road with Fodor's.

$$$ ✕ **Mario's.** Country music stars, visiting celebrities, and local society
★ come here to see and be seen—and to savor the memorable pasta, seafood, and veal dishes created by chef Sandro Bozzatto. ⊠ *2005 Broad-way,* ☎ *615/327–3232. Reservations essential. Jacket and tie. AE, D, DC, MC, V. Closed Sun. No lunch.*

$$$ ✕ **The Merchants.** An outdoor patio is an extra feature at this opulent three-level restaurant. Specialties include fresh seafood, grilled meats, and key lime pie. ⊠ *401 Broadway,* ☎ *615/254–1892. AE, DC, MC, V. No lunch weekends.*

$$$ ✕ **Wild Boar.** This restaurant serves excellent Continental cuisine, with game, trout, duck, and beef on the menu; it also has an outstanding wine cellar. ⊠ *2014 Broadway,* ☎ *615/329–1313. AE, D, DC, MC, V. No lunch weekends.*

$$ ✕ **F. Scott's.** This elegant café and wine bar has one of the largest wine
★ selections in town. Try the grilled chicken on black beans with roasted-pepper sauce, mango salsa, and smoked-tomato relish. ⊠ *2210 Crest-moor,* ☎ *615/269–5861. AE, D, DC, MC, V.*

$$ ✕ **Mère Bulles.** This intimate District restaurant has river-view dining, a Continental menu, and an extensive wine list. Live entertainment—often jazz or folk music—is served up nightly. ⊠ *152 2nd Ave. N,* ☎ *615/256–1946. AE, D, MC, V.*

$$ ✕ **106 Club.** A black baby-grand piano, a shiny black-enamel bar, and patrons sporting jacket and tie set the tone in this intimate art-deco-style dining room in suburban Belle Meade. The cuisine is a mix of California nouvelle and international favorites. ⊠ *106 Harding Pl.,* ☎ *615/356–1300. AE, D, DC, MC, V. No lunch.*

$ ╳ **Elliston Place Soda Shop.** The burgers are tasty and the ice cream sodas are frothy at this old-fashioned soda shop, where the 1950s atmosphere has been preserved. The chocolate shake is Nashville's best. ⊠ *2111 Elliston Pl.,* ☎ *615/327–1090. No credit cards. Closed Sun.*

$ ╳ **Hermitage House Smorgasbord.** No need to be shy about helping yourself to the bountiful spread of salads, meats, vegetables, and desserts here. Don't miss the apple fritters. ⊠ *4144 Lebanon Rd., Hermitage,* ☎ *615/883–9525. MC, V.*

$ ╳ **Loveless Cafe.** The appeal here is true down-home southern cooking: featherlight homemade biscuits and preserves, country ham and redeye gravy, and fried chicken. ⊠ *8400 Rte. 100,* ☎ *615/646–9700. No credit cards. Closed Mon.*

$ ╳ **Old Spaghetti Factory.** This District spot offers a wide range of pasta dishes in a lively atmosphere that's great for families. ⊠ *160 2nd Ave. N,* ☎ *615/254–9010. D, MC, V.*

$ ╳ **Sylvan Park Restaurant.** The original location is a beacon for meat-and-three fans; purists say the three spin-off eateries aren't quite as good. ⊠ *4502 Murphy Rd.,* ☎ *615/292–9275. No credit cards.*

Lodging

For information on B&Bs in the area, contact **Bed & Breakfast About Tennessee** (⊠ Box 110227, Nashville 37222, ☎ 615/331–5244 or 800/458–2421) or **Bed & Breakfast Adventures** (⊠ Box 150586, Nashville 37215, ☎ 615/383–6611). For price ranges *see* Chart 2 (B) *in* On the Road with Fodor's.

$$$ 🏨 **Loews Vanderbilt Plaza.** This beautiful hotel near Vanderbilt University has a well-deserved reputation for attentive service. ⊠ *2100 West End Ave.,* 37203, ☎ *615/320–1700 or 800/235–6397, ℻ 615/320–5019. 351 rooms. 2 restaurants, 2 lounges. AE, D, MC, V.*

$$$ 🏨 **Opryland Hotel.** This massive plantation-style hotel adjacent to
★ Opryland has a 2-acre glass-walled conservatory filled with 10,000 tropical plants and a skylighted indoor area replete with water cascades and a half-acre lake. ⊠ *2800 Opryland Dr.,* 37214, ☎ *615/889–1000, ℻ 615/871–7741. 2,041 rooms. 5 restaurants, coffee shop, 3 pools, exercise room, golf course, tennis court. AE, D, MC, V.*

$$$ 🏨 **Stouffer Renaissance Nashville Hotel.** This ultracontemporary highrise adjoins the Nashville Convention Center and the Church Street Centre Mall. The spacious rooms have period reproduction furnishings. ⊠ *611 Commerce St.,* 37203, ☎ *615/255–8400 or 800/468–3571, ℻ 615/255–8163. 673 rooms. Restaurant, coffee shop, deli, pool, spa, health club. AE, D, DC, MC, V.*

$$ 🏨 **Courtyard by Marriott–Airport.** This handsome low-rise motor inn
★ offers some amenities found in higher-price hotels: spacious rooms, king-size beds, and oversize desks. ⊠ *2508 Elm Hill Pike,* 37214, ☎ *615/883–9500 or 800/321–2211, ℻ 615/883–0172. 145 rooms. Restaurant, pool, hot tub, sauna, exercise room. AE, D, DC, MC, V.*

$$ 🏨 **Hampton Inn Vanderbilt.** The rooms at this contemporary inn near Vanderbilt University are colorful and spacious. There's a hospitality suite for social or business use. ⊠ *1919 West End Ave.,* 37203, ☎ *615/329–1144 or 800/426–7866, ℻ 615/320–7112. 171 rooms. Pool. AE, D, DC, MC, V.*

$$ 🏨 **Holiday Inn–Briley Parkway.** The Holidome Indoor Recreation Center at this chain property has a pool, sauna, hot tub, game room, and more. The guest rooms are spacious and well lighted. ⊠ *2200 Elm Hill Pike (at Briley Pkwy.),* 37210, ☎ *615/883–9770 or 800/465–4329, ℻ 615/391–4521. 385 rooms. Restaurant, bar, pool, exercise room. AE, DC, MC, V.*

$$ ⊞ **Ramada Inn Across from Opryland.** This contemporary, low-rise motor inn is closer to the theme park than any other hotel except the Opryland. ⊠ *2401 Music Valley Dr., 37214,* ☎ *615/889–0800 or 800/ 272–6232,* ℻ *615/883–1230. 297 rooms. Restaurant, indoor pool, hot tub. AE, D, DC, MC, V.*

$ ⊞ **Comfort Inn Hermitage.** Near the Hermitage, this inn offers comfortable accommodations, some with water beds or whirlpool baths. ⊠ *5768 Old Hickory Blvd., 37076,* ☎ *615/889–5060,* ℻ *615/871– 4137. 106 rooms. Pool. AE, D, DC, MC, V.*

$ ⊞ **La Quinta Inn–Metro Center.** Guest rooms are spacious and well lighted, with a large working area and an oversize bed. ⊠ *2001 Metrocenter Blvd., 37228,* ☎ *615/259–2130 or 800/531–5900,* ℻ *615/242– 2650. 121 rooms. Pool. AE, DC, MC, V.*

$ ⊞ **Wilson Inn.** Three miles from Opryland, this five-story hotel is clean and convenient. Many rooms have kitchens. ⊠ *600 Ermac Dr., 37214 (Elm Hill Pike exit from Briley Pkwy.),* ☎ *615/889–4466 or 800/333– 9457,* ℻ *615/889–0484. 110 rooms. Pool. AE, D, MC, V.*

Nightlife and the Arts

Nightlife

For country music try the famous **Bluebird Cafe** (⊠ 4104 Hillsboro Rd., Green Hills, ☎ 615/383–1461), where singers try out their latest material. The **Stock Yard Bull Pen Lounge** (⊠ 901 2nd Ave. N, ☎ 615/255– 6464) is a restaurant-lounge with nightly live country entertainment and dancing. There's a variety of live music downtown at **Mère Bulles** (☞ Dining, *above*). **Exit/In** (⊠ 2208 Elliston Pl., ☎ 615/321–4400) showcases blues and rock. **Blue Sky Court** (⊠ 412 4th Ave. S, ☎ 615/256– 4562), convenient to downtown and Vanderbilt University, focuses on rock and blues. In the **District** (☞ Exploring Nashville, *above*), check out the Wildflower Saloon (⊠ 120 2nd Ave. N, ☎ 615/251–1000) and local versions of Planet Hollywood (⊠ 322 Broadway, ☎ 615/313– 7827) and the Hard Rock Cafe (⊠ 100 Broadway, ☎ 615/742–9900).

The Arts

The **Tennessee Performing Arts Center** (⊠ 505 Deaderick St., ☎ 615/ 737–4849) holds performances by the Nashville Ballet (☎ 615/244– 7233), Nashville Opera (☎ 615/292–5710), Nashville Symphony Orchestra (☎ 615/329–3033), and Tennessee Repertory Theatre (☎ 615/244–4878). The center's Andrew Jackson Hall also hosts touring Broadway shows. Call **TicketMaster** (☎ 615/737–4849) for tickets and information about arts events.

Shopping

Downtown, the trilevel **Church Street Centre** (⊠ 7th Ave. and Church St., ☎ 615/254–4260) includes the Castner-Knott department store. The huge **Bellevue Center** mall, in southwest Nashville (⊠ Bellevue exit from I-40, ☎ 615/646–8690), has more than 120 stores. Antiques lovers may want to browse through the shops along **8th Avenue South.** For the latest look in country-and-western wear, two-step over to the **District** (☞ Exploring Nashville, *above*).

EAST TENNESSEE

From the Great Smoky Mountains to the rippling waters of the Holston, French Broad, Nolichucky, and Tennessee rivers, East Tennessee offers a cornucopia of scenic grandeur and recreational opportunities. Mountain folkways may persist in certain smaller communities, but cities such as Knoxville and Chattanooga are modern and quite diverse.

Visitor Information

Chattanooga: Area Convention and Visitors Bureau (✉ 1001 Market St., 37402, ☎ 615/756–8687 or 800/322–3344). **Knoxville:** Area Convention and Visitors Bureau (✉ 500 Henley St., 37902, ☎ 615/523–7263 or 800/727–8045).

Arriving and Departing

By Bus

Greyhound (☎ 800/231–2222) has stops in Chattanooga and in Knoxville.

By Car

I–75 runs north–south from Kentucky through Knoxville, then to Chattanooga. I–81 heads southwest from the Virginia border at Bristol, ending at I–40 northeast of Knoxville. I–40 enters from North Carolina and continues west to Knoxville, Nashville, and Memphis.

By Plane

Knoxville Airport (☎ 615/970–2773), served by American Eagle, ComAir, Delta, Northwest, Trans World Express, United, and US Airways, is about 12 mi from town. The **Chattanooga Airport** (☎ 615/855–2200), served by American Eagle, ASA, ComAir, Delta, Northwest Airlink, and US Airways, is about 8 mi from town.

Exploring East Tennessee

Founded in 1786, **Knoxville** became the first state capital when Tennessee was admitted to the Union in 1796. Today it is home to the main campus of the **University of Tennessee,** as well as the headquarters of the **Tennessee Valley Authority** (TVA), with its vast complex of hydroelectric dams and recreational lakes.

Among the historic sites in Knoxville is the 1792 **Governor William Blount Mansion,** where the governor and his associates planned the admission of Tennessee as the 16th state in the Union. ✉ *200 W. Hill Ave.,* ☎ *423/525–2375. Closed Mon.*

The **Armstrong-Lockett House,** an 1834 farm mansion, is now a showcase of American and English furniture and English silver. ✉ *2728 Kingston Pike,* ☎ *423/637–3163. Closed Mon. and Jan.–Feb.*

Housed in the 1874 U.S. Customs House, the **East Tennessee Historical Center** displays books, documents, and artifacts relating to the history of the state. ✉ *800 Market St.,* ☎ *423/544–5744. Closed Mon.*

The **Knoxville Museum of Art,** opened in 1992, has four exhibition galleries with contemporary prints, drawings, and paintings. ✉ *410 10th St., in World's Fair Park,* ☎ *423/525–6101. Closed Mon.*

The **Knoxville Zoological Gardens** (✉ Rutledge Pike S, Exit 392 off I–40, ☎ 423/637–5331) is famous for its reptile complex and for its breeding of large cats and African elephants.

Gatlinburg, the busy, tourist-oriented northern gateway to **Great Smoky Mountains National Park,** is southeast of Knoxville via U.S. 441/321. Set in the narrow valley of the Little Pigeon River (actually a turbulent mountain stream), Gatlinburg has an abundance of family attractions, including the **Gatlinburg Sky Lift** (☎ 423/436–4307) to the top of Crockett Mountain. The **Ober Gatlinburg Tramway** (☎ 423/436–5423) goes to a mountaintop amusement park, ski center, and shopping mall/crafts market. The tramway is closed March 3–14.

Pigeon Forge, about 6 mi north of Gatlinburg on U.S. 441, has factory outlet malls and family attractions. One Pigeon Forge highlight is **Dollywood,** Dolly Parton's popular theme park, with rides, live music, and a re-created mountain village. ⊠ *700 Dollywood La.,* ☎ *423/428–9488 or 800/365–5996.* 🎟 *$26.99. Closed Jan.–late Apr.*

Newfound Gap, south from Gatlinburg on scenic U.S. 441, provides a haunting view of the Tennessee–North Carolina border. From here a 7-mi spur road leads to **Clingmans Dome**—at 6,643 ft, the highest point in Tennessee.

Chattanooga, a city of Civil War battlefields, museums of all kinds (art, antiques, history, even knives and tow trucks), and a famous choo-choo, is southwest of Knoxville off I–75. Begin your meandering here with a stop at the **Chattanooga Visitors Center** (⊠ 2 Broad St., ☎ 423/266–7111). Dominating Chattanooga's skyline is 2,215-ft **Lookout Mountain,** 6 mi away, with panoramic views of seven states and the world's steepest **Incline Railway** (⊠ 827 E. Brow Rd., ☎ 423/821–4224). From Lookout Mountain Scenic Highway, tours depart every 15 minutes to the 145-ft **Ruby Falls** (⊠ 1550 Scenic Hwy., ☎ 423/821–2544), 1,120 ft underground and reached by elevator.

★ The **Tennessee Aquarium** (⊠ 1 Broad St., ☎ 423/265–0695), opened in 1992, is the world's largest freshwater aquarium, with 350 species of fish, mammals, birds, reptiles, and amphibians. Surrounding the aquarium is **Ross's Landing Park and Plaza,** commemorating Chattanooga's Civil War history as well as its role as a major railroad town.

Oak Ridge, about 100 mi northeast of Chattanooga (take U.S. 27 to I–40E or I–75 to I–40W), is where atomic energy was secretly developed during World War II. The **American Museum of Science and Energy** (⊠ 300 S. Tulane Ave., ☎ 423/576–3200) focuses on the uses of nuclear, solar, and geothermal energy.

What to See and Do with Children

The **Gatlinburg/Pigeon Forge area** is home to many amusement parks and offbeat museums, such as the **Guinness World Records Museum** (☎ 423/436–9100). In Knoxville youngsters like the hands-on displays and audiovisual exhibits at the **East Tennessee Discovery Center and Akima Planetarium** (⊠ 516 N. Beaman St., ☎ 423/594–1480). The **Creative Discovery Children's Museum** (⊠ 4th and Chestnut Sts., ☎ 423/757–0510), in Chattanooga, has exhibits in four areas: invention, art, music, and science.

Dining and Lodging

Expect hearty food in the mountains: barbecued ribs, thick pork chops, and country ham with red-eye gravy. For reservations in hotels, motels, chalets, and condominiums in Gatlinburg, contact **Smoky Mountain Accommodations Reservation Service** (⊠ 526 E. Parkway, Suite 1, Gatlinburg 37738, ☎ 423/436–9700 or 800/231–2230). For B&B reservations contact **Tennessee Bed & Breakfast Innkeepers' Association** (⊠ Box 120428, Nashville 37212, ☎ 423/321–5482 or 800/820–8144). For price ranges *see* Charts 1 (B) and 2 (B) *in* On the Road with Fodor's.

Chattanooga

$$$ ✕ **The Loft.** Locals and visitors alike flock to this cozy, candlelit restaurant for its clublike ambience, extensive wine list, and hearty specialties. The varied entrées include broiled or blackened amberjack, king crab legs, seafood fettuccine, and steak—all served with soup, salad,

home-baked bread, fresh vegetables, and a baked potato or wild rice pilaf. ✉ *328 Cherokee Blvd.*, ☎ *615/266–3601. AE, D, DC, MC, V.*

$$$ ✕ **Perry's Seafood.** One of Tennessee's best restaurants, Perry's specializes in grilled and sautéed fish. ✉ *850 Market St.*, ☎ *423/267–0007. AE, D, DC, MC, V.*

$$$ ✕ **212 Market.** Creative American cuisine is served at this hip spot di-
★   rectly across from the Tennessee Aquarium. The fish entrées are especially good, the homemade breads scrumptious, and the wine list impressive. ✉ *212 Market St.*, ☎ *423/265–1212. AE, MC, V.*

$$ ✕ **Big River Grille Brewing & Works.** This restored trolley warehouse is now handsomely appointed, with high ceilings, exposed brick walls, and hardwood floors. You can watch the inner workings of the microbrewery through a soaring glass wall by the bar. The sandwiches and salads are large; to wash them down, try the sampler of six brews. ✉ *222 Broad St.*, ☎ *423/267–2739. AE, D, DC, MC, V.*

$ ✕ **Town & Country.** Even though this meat-and-three fixture across the bridge from the Tennessee Aquarium seats more than 425, expect to wait a bit for the mouthwatering southern cuisine. Good food and low prices have kept the crowds happy for more than 40 years. ✉ *110 N. Market St.*, ☎ *423/267–8544. AE, D, DC, MC, V.*

$$$$ ☷ **Bluff View Inn.** Chattanooga's best B&B, this 1928 Colonial Revival mansion hugs a bluff high above the Tennessee River and is part of the Bluff View Art District, which comprises five houses, three restaurants, and a sculpture garden. Tastefully decorated bedrooms have whirlpool baths and fireplaces. ✉ *412 E. 2nd St., 37403*, ☎ *423/265–5033*, ℻ *423/757–0124. 9 rooms. 3 restaurants. Full breakfast. DC, MC, V.*

$$ ☷ **Chattanooga Choo-Choo Holiday Inn.** The hotel adjoins the 1905 Southern Railway Terminal, now a 30-acre complex with restaurants, shops, exhibits, gardens, and an operating trolley. Rooms are luxuriously appointed, especially the 48 restored Victorian-era parlor cars. ✉ *1400 Market St., 37402*, ☎ *423/266–5000 or 800/872–2529*, ℻ *423/265–4635. 360 rooms. 5 restaurants, 2 pools, 2 hot tubs, 3 tennis courts, shops. AE, DC, MC, V.*

$$ ☷ **Chattanooga Marriott.** The city's largest hotel is convenient to town attractions. ✉ *2 Carter Plaza, 37402*, ☎ *423/756–0002 or 800/841–1674*, ℻ *423/266–2254. 343 rooms. 2 restaurants, indoor and outdoor pools, health club, recreation room. AE, DC, MC, V.*

$$ ☷ **Radisson Read House.** The Georgian-style Read House, on the Na-
★   tional Register of Historic Places, dates from the 1920s and has been impeccably restored to its original grandeur. Guest rooms in the main hotel continue the Georgian motif; rooms in the annex are more contemporary. ✉ *827 Broad St., 37402*, ☎ *423/266–4121 or 800/333–3333*, ℻ *423/267–6447. 238 rooms. 2 restaurants, pool, hot tub, sauna. AE, D, DC, MC, V.*

Gatlinburg

$$ ✕ **Burning Bush Restaurant.** Reproduction furnishings evoke a Colonial atmosphere, but the menu leans toward Continental. Specialties include broiled Tennessee quail. ✉ *1151 Parkway*, ☎ *423/436–4669. AE, D, MC, V.*

$$ ✕ **Smoky Mountain Trout House.** Trout is prepared eight ways, or you can have prime rib, country ham, or fried chicken. This restaurant is a truly rustic mountain cottage. ✉ *410 N. Parkway*, ☎ *423/436–5416. AE, DC, MC, V. Closed Dec.–Mar.*

$$$ ☷ **Buckhorn Inn.** This country inn about 6 mi outside town has wel-
★   comed guests to its rustic rooms and cottages since 1938. The moun-

tain views are spectacular. ⊠ *2140 Tudor Mountain Rd., 37738,* ☎ *423/436–4668. 6 rooms, 4 1-bedroom cottages, 2 2-bedroom guest houses. Full breakfast, dinner. MC, V.*

$$ 🏨 **Holiday Inn Resort Complex.** Near the Convention Center and the
★ Ober Gatlinburg aerial tramway, this hotel offers the Holidome Indoor Recreation Center, with a pool and other attractions. ⊠ *520 Airport Rd., 37738,* ☎ *423/436–9201 or 800/435–9201,* 🆁🅰🆇 *423/436–7974. 402 rooms. 2 restaurants, 3 pools, hot tub, 2 saunas, exercise room, nightclub. AE, D, DC, MC, V.*

Knoxville

$$$ ✕ **Regas Restaurant.** This cozy Knoxville classic, with fireplaces and
★ original art, has been around for 70 years. The specialty, prime rib, is sliced to order and served with horseradish sauce. ⊠ *318 Gay St.,* ☎ *423/637–9805. AE, D, DC, MC, V. No lunch Sat., no dinner Sun.*

$$ ✕ **Copper Cellar/Cumberland Grill.** A favorite of the college crowd and young professionals, the original downstairs Copper Cellar has an intimate atmosphere. Upstairs, the Cumberland Grill serves salads and sandwiches. Both serve outstanding desserts. ⊠ *1807 Cumberland Ave.,* ☎ *423/673–3411. AE, DC, MC, V.*

$$$ 🏨 **Hyatt Regency Knoxville.** This handsome, contemporary adaptation
★ of an Aztec pyramid sits atop a hill overlooking the city and nearby mountains. The nine-story atrium lobby blends modern furnishings with artwork in Central American motifs. ⊠ *500 Hill Ave. SE, 37901,* ☎ *423/637–1234 or 800/233–1234,* 🆁🅰🆇 *423/522–5911. 387 rooms. Restaurant, coffee shop, sports bar, pool, exercise room, playground. AE, D, DC, MC, V.*

$ 🏨 **Luxbury Hotel.** Midway between downtown Knoxville and Oak Ridge, this affordable hotel has oversize rooms with spacious work areas. ⊠ *420 Peters Rd. N, 37922,* ☎ *423/539–0058 or 800/252–7748,* 🆁🅰🆇 *423/539–4887. 98 rooms. Pool. AE, D, DC, MC, V.*

Nightlife and the Arts

Chattanooga

The **Tivoli Theater** (⊠ 399 McCaulley Ave., ☎ 423/757–5050) presents concerts and operas. The **Market Street Performance Hall** (⊠ 221 Market St., ☎ 423/267–2498) has nightly entertainment in a renovated trolley-car barn. The **Chattanooga Little Theatre** (⊠ 400 River St., ☎ 423/267–8534) stages productions year-round. For jazz try **Birdland** (⊠ 2510 E. Main, ☎ 423/697–7484). For rock or blues head to **Sandbar** (⊠ 1011 Riverside Dr., ☎ 423/622–4432).

Gatlinburg

Sweet Fanny Adams Theatre and Music Hall (⊠ 461 Parkway, ☎ 423/436–4038) stages original musical comedies and Gay '90s revues, and hotel lounges offer DJs and live entertainment.

Knoxville

The **Bijou Theater** (⊠ 803 S. Gay St., ☎ 423/522–0832) offers seasonal ballet, concerts, and plays. **Carousel Theatre,** on the University of Tennessee campus (☎ 423/974–5161), is theater-in-the-round with student and professional actors. **Old City,** on the north side of downtown, has a variety of lively restaurants, clubs, and shops. Try **Manhattan's** (⊠ 101 S. Central St., ☎ 423/525–4463), in Old City, for blues. For authentic Tex-Mex music and food there's **Amigo's** (⊠ 116 S. Central St., ☎ 423/546–9505), in Old City. **Patrick Sullivan's** (⊠ 100 N. Central St., ☎ 423/694–9696) has saloon-style food and live rock and roll on weekends.

Outdoor Activities and Sports

Fishing

East Tennessee's lakes offer seasonal angling for striped bass, walleye, white bass, and muskie. **Gatlinburg**'s streams and rivers are stocked with trout from April to November. There are boat-launch ramps at **Norris Dam State Resort Park** (☎ 423/426–7461), north of Knoxville, and **Booker T. Washington State Park** (☎ 423/894–4955), near Chattanooga.

Golf

East Tennessee courses open to the public include **Brainerd Golf Course** (☎ 423/855–2692), in Chattanooga, **Whittle Springs Municipal Golf Course** (☎ 423/525–1022), in Knoxville, and **Bent Creek Mountain Inn and Country Club** (☎ 423/436–2875), in Gatlinburg.

Hiking

A scenic portion of the **Appalachian Trail** runs along high ridges in the Great Smoky Mountains National Park (✉ Gatlinburg, ☎ 423/436–1200). The trail can be reached at Newfound Gap, off U.S. 441.

Horseback Riding

McCarter's Riding Stables (✉ U.S. 441 south of Gatlinburg, ☎ 423/436–5354) is open mid-March–October.

Rafting and Canoeing

East Tennessee has five white-water rivers: Ocoee, Hiwassee, French Broad, Tellico, and Nolichucky. The rafting season runs from April to early November; for canoe rentals and guided raft trips contact **Outdoor Adventure Rafting** (✉ Ocoee, ☎ 800/627–7636), **Wildwater, Ltd.** (✉ Ducktown, ☎ 800/451–9972), and **Rafting in the Smokies** (✉ Gatlinburg, ☎ 423/436–5008).

Ski Area

Ober Gatlinburg Ski Resort (✉ 1001 Parkway, ☎ 423/436–5423) has three lifts and 10 downhill slopes.

Shopping

At the **Great Smoky Arts and Craft Community** (✉ Glades and Buckhorn Rds. off U.S. 321, 3 mi east of Gatlinburg, ☎ 423/436–3301), a collection of 70 shops and crafts studios along 8 mi of rambling country road, you will find wood carvings, cornhusk dolls, dulcimers, handmade quilts, and other Appalachian folk crafts. Chattanooga's **Warehouse Row** (✉ 12th and Market Sts., ☎ 423/267–1111) contains factory outlets for such top designers as Ellen Tracy, Ralph Lauren, and Perry Ellis.

7 The Midwest and Great Lakes

Illinois, Indiana, Michigan, Minnesota, Ohio, Wisconsin

By Holly Hughes

Updated by Richard Bak

T*he midwest is America, that prototypical vision of neat farmland, affluent suburbs, and compact, skyscrapered downtowns strung together along purposefully straight silver highways. Sauk Centre, Minnesota, was the setting for Sinclair Lewis's Main Street; Muncie, Indiana, was the subject of the sociological study called* Middletown, USA. *It is no accident that stand-up comedians use midwestern town names— Peoria, Sheboygan, Kokomo, Kalamazoo—to mean "the heart of the country." Transplanted midwesterners spend the rest of their lives longing for broad, clear horizons; thick, shady stands of beech and maple trees; and hazy summer afternoons when kids sell lemonade from sidewalk stands. People seem genuinely friendlier and more down-to-earth here.*

Six states—Ohio, Indiana, Michigan, Illinois, Wisconsin, and Minnesota—occupy what was originally the Northwest Territory, a vast tract of forest and meadow awarded to the United States in the 1783 Treaty of Paris. Unlike the stark Great Plains to the west, this is gently rolling landscape, punctuated by rivers, woods, and trees. It is defined by great geological features: to the east, the Appalachian Mountains; to the north, the Great Lakes; to the south, the Ohio River; to the west, the majestic Mississippi River.

Smarting from years of being labeled "the sticks," midwestern cities are always trying to prove themselves, cheerfully rehabilitating their downtowns, rooting for their major league ball teams, and building

The Midwest and Great Lakes

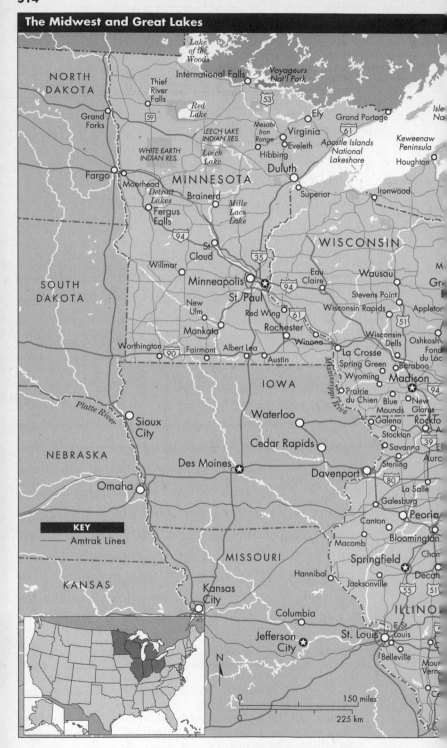

NORTH DAKOTA

Grand Forks

Thief River Falls

International Falls

Lake of the Woods

Voyageurs Nat'l Park

Grand Portage

Isle Na

Red Lake

Ely

Virginia

Grand Portage

Keweenaw Peninsula

Mesabi Iron Range

Eveleth

Apostle Islands National Lakeshore

Houghton

LEECH LAKE INDIAN RES.

WHITE EARTH INDIAN RES.

Hibbing

Duluth

Fargo

Moorhead

Detroit Lakes

MINNESOTA

Superior

Ironwood

Leech Lake

Brainerd

Mille Lacs Lake

Fergus Falls

WISCONSIN

St. Cloud

Willmar

Minneapolis

Eau Claire

Wausau

Gr

M

SOUTH DAKOTA

New Ulm

St. Paul

Red Wing

Stevens Point

Mankato

Rochester

Wisconsin Rapids

Appleton

Worthington

Fairmont

Albert Lea

Winona

La Crosse

Wisconsin Dells

Oshkosh

Fond du Lac

Austin

IOWA

Spring Green

Wyoming

Baraboo

Madison

Prairie du Chien

Blue Mounds

New Glarus

Rockfo

Platte River

Sioux City

Waterloo

Galena

Stockton

A

NEBRASKA

Cedar Rapids

Savanna

Sterling

39

Aurc

Des Moines

Davenport

Omaha

La Salle

Galesburg

Peoria

Canton

KANSAS

MISSOURI

Macomb

Bloomington

Springfield

Chan

Hannibal

Jacksonville

Decat

Kansas City

Columbia

ILLINO

Jefferson City

St. Louis

E. St. Louis

Belleville

Moun Vern

Ce

KEY
Amtrak Lines

N

0   150 miles

0   225 km

gleaming convention centers and festival malls. Ohio has no fewer than five important cities (Cleveland, Cincinnati, Columbus, Dayton, and Toledo). Minnesota's major population center comprises two cities, Minneapolis and St. Paul, which means that there are twice as many parks and museums as you'd expect. Indiana's capital, Indianapolis, is a beautifully laid-out city that's also the amateur-sports capital of the country. Michigan has the home of America's auto industry, Detroit, which still offers attractions despite economic problems. Milwaukee, Wisconsin, poised on the western shore of Lake Michigan, is a rich melting pot of immigrant cultures, as is vibrant and powerful Chicago, Illinois, the region's one great metropolis.

But it's never more than an hour's drive from these cities to northern lake resorts, historic villages along sleepy back roads, utopian colonies, and pleasant university towns. Big swatches of forest and lakeshore are protected as parkland, and gorgeous scenic drives edge the Great Lakes and the dramatic bluffs of the Mississippi and Ohio river valleys.

When to Go

Summer is the most popular time to visit the Midwest and the Great Lakes. Generally, the farther north you go, the fewer people you'll find. Prices in most places peak in July and August. Daily temperatures average in the 80s in Illinois, Indiana, and Ohio, though July and August heat waves can push them high into the 90s. In Michigan, Wisconsin, and Minnesota, temperatures run 10° cooler. These three states have the best **fall** foliage, though you can see good color in all six. Depending on the weather, the leaves usually begin to turn in mid-September and reach their most colorful by mid-October. In **winter** Michigan has the only significant downhill skiing in the region, but cross-country is extremely popular in Wisconsin and Minnesota. The Midwest usually gets at least one subzero cold snap every year. For the rest of winter expect temperatures in the 20s and 30s and about 10° colder in northern Michigan, Wisconsin, and Minnesota. Sudden snowstorms can make winter driving unpredictable and treacherous. **Spring** is damp and clammy, with erratic weather and temperatures ranging from the 30s to the 60s.

Festivals and Seasonal Events

Winter

JAN.➤ **International Falls, Minnesota,** hosts **Ice Box Days** (☎ 218/283–9400), a weeklong festival of snow-sculpture and ice-fishing contests, and the Freeze Your Gizzard Blizzard Run.

The six-day **Plymouth International Ice Sculpture Spectacular** (☎ 313/459–9696), in **Plymouth, Michigan,** features 150 carvers from around the world, nightly light shows, and a life-size ice carousel.

The best snowmobile racers in the country come to **Eagle River, Wisconsin,** to compete on a half-mile banked ice track at the **World's Championship Snowmobile Derby** (☎ 715/479–4424).

LATE JAN.–EARLY FEB.➤ The 12-day **St. Paul, Minnesota, Winter Carnival** (☎ 612/297–6953) celebrates winter with a sleigh and cutter parade, an ice palace, car races on the ice, and ice sculptures by artists from around the world.

Spring

MARCH➤ During **Eagle Watch Weekend** (☎ 507/452–2272 or 800/657–4972) the spring migration of bald eagles can be viewed along the Mississippi River in the vicinity of **Winona, Minnesota.**

MAY➤ The monthlong **Indianapolis 500 Festival** (☎ 317/636–4556 or 317/241–2500) culminates in the most famous car race in the United States.

The **Holland Tulip Festival** (☎ 616/396–4221), in **Michigan,** showcases flowers and Dutch traditions.

Summer

EARLY JUNE➤ The **Detroit Grand Prix** (☎ 313/393–7749), held on scenic **Belle Isle,** in **Detroit,** is the cornerstone of a three-day downtown event featuring parties and several support races.

LATE JUNE–EARLY JULY➤ **Milwaukee, Wisconsin,** holds **Summerfest** (☎ 414/273–2680 or 800/837–3378), a lakefront festival with rock, jazz, and popular music.

JULY➤ The **Minneapolis Aquatennial** (☎ 612/331–8371) celebrates the lakes of **Minnesota** with sailing regattas, waterskiing competitions, and other water-related events.

The two-day **Chicago-to-Mackinac Boat Race** (☎ 312/861–7777) is one of the most challenging sailboat races in the country.

Some 350,000 people flock to **Traverse City, Michigan,** during the **National Cherry Festival** (☎ 800/872–8377) to sample the best of the local orchards.

The **Great Circus Parade** (☎ 414/273–7222) through the streets of **Milwaukee** is highlighted by scores of antique circus wagons from Baraboo's famous Circus World Museum.

LATE JULY➤ The **Pro Football Hall of Fame Game** (☎ 330/456–8207) and induction ceremonies, in **Canton, Ohio,** kick off the football season.

The **Cincinnati Riverfront Stadium Festival** (☎ 513/871–3900) is the largest festival in the country devoted to rhythm and blues.

LATE JULY–EARLY AUG.➤ The **Experimental Aircraft Association Fly-In** (☎ 414/426–4800), in **Oshkosh, Wisconsin,** gathers close to a million people and 30,000 aircraft from around the world.

AUG.➤ The **Wisconsin State Fair** (☎ 414/266–7000) attracts crowds to **Milwaukee** for livestock and crop shows, midway attractions, and stage shows.

The **Illinois State Fair** (☎ 217/782–6661), in **Springfield,** has livestock shows, car and horse races, food, and entertainment.

LATE AUG.➤ The **Michigan State Fair** (☎ 313/369–8250), in **Detroit,** is the nation's oldest state fair, with an animal birthing center and top musical acts performing inside the band shell.

For the 137th consecutive year, the citizens of **Young America, Minnesota,** recall their German roots with **Stiftungsfest** (☎ 612/467–3365), which features a parade, an arts fair, and ethnic food and music.

Autumn

EARLY SEPT.➤ On Labor Day weekend, the **Detroit Montreux Jazz Festival** (☎ 313/259–5400) attracts more than 700,000 jazz fans.

OCT.➤ On the last Sunday of the month, the **Chicago Marathon** (☎ 312/951–0660) draws runners from all over the world.

Getting Around the Midwest and Great Lakes

By Bus
The major intercity carrier is **Greyhound Lines** (☎ 800/231–2222). **Indian Trails** (☎ 800/248–3849) operates between Chicago and many cities in Michigan. In southern Wisconsin **Van Galder Bus Lines** (☎ 608/257–5593 or 800/747–0094) runs from Madison and Milwaukee to Chicago's O'Hare Airport and downtown Amtrak station.

By Boat
From mid-May to October passenger and automobile **ferry** service operates between Ludington, Michigan, and Manitowoc, Wisconsin (☎ 616/845–5555).

By Car
I–80 and I–90 converge near Cleveland and run along the northern borders of Ohio and Indiana until they split at Chicago. I–80 then cuts across Illinois into Iowa, while I–90 curves up through Wisconsin and goes across southern Minnesota. Other major arteries are I–70, crossing the southern parts of Ohio, Indiana, and Illinois; I–94, which goes from Detroit across Michigan, hugs Lake Michigan through Indiana and Illinois, then crosses Wisconsin and Minnesota; and I–75, which stretches from Sault Sainte Marie, Michigan, to Cincinnati, Ohio. State routes and county roads provide a closer look at rural areas and are in good repair throughout the region.

By Plane
The region is served by all major airlines: American, Delta, Northwest, United, and US Airways. The largest airports are **Cleveland Hopkins International Airport** (☎ 216/265–6000), in Ohio; **Detroit Metropolitan Wayne County Airport** (☎ 313/942–3550), in Michigan; **General Mitchell Field** (☎ 414/747–5300), in Milwaukee, Wisconsin; **Indianapolis International Airport** (☎ 317/248–9594), in Indiana; **Minneapolis/St. Paul International Airport** (☎ 612/726–5555), in Minnesota; and **O'Hare International Airport** (☎ 312/686–2200), in Chicago, Illinois.

By Train
Amtrak (☎ 800/872–7245) is the primary passenger railroad serving the entire region. All routes go through Chicago. Among cities with commuter train service between the central city and the suburbs are Chicago (☎ 312/836–7000), Cleveland (☎ 216/621–9500), and Indianapolis (☎ 317/267–3000).

ILLINOIS

By Elizabeth
Gardner

Updated by
Eve Becker

Capital
Population
Motto
State Bird
State Flower
Postal Abbreviation

Springfield
11,846,500
State Sovereignty—National Union
Cardinal
Wood violet
IL

Statewide Visitor Information

Illinois Bureau of Tourism (✉ James R. Thompson Center, 100 W. Randolph St., Suite 3-400, Chicago 60601, ☎ 800/223–0121).

Scenic Drives

The Illinois part of the **Lake Michigan Circle Tour** follows the shoreline along Lake Shore Drive through Chicago and passes through the elegant suburbs of the North Shore: Evanston, Winnetka, Glencoe, Highland Park, and Lake Forest. **Great River Road** follows the Mississippi River, stretching the length of Illinois (more than 500 mi) from East Dubuque to Cairo (pronounced *kay*-ro).

National and State Parks

National Park
Shawnee National Forest (✉ 901 S. Commercial St., Harrisburg 62946, ☎ 618/253–7114) blankets the southern tip of Illinois with 250,000 acres of wilderness; it is here that glaciers stopped flattening the state during the last Ice Age.

State Parks
Illinois has more than 260 state parks, conservation areas, fish and wildlife areas, and recreation areas. For a magazine on state parks, contact the **Illinois Department of Natural Resources** (✉ 524 S. 2nd St., Springfield 62701-1787, ☎ 217/782–7454). **Illinois Beach State Park** (✉ Lake Front, Zion 60099, ☎ 847/662–4811), on Lake Michigan near the Wisconsin border, has sandy beaches along 6½ mi of shoreline. **Rend Lake/Wayne Fitzgerrell State Park** (✉ 11094 Ranger Rd., Whittington 62897, ☎ 618/629–2320) has the state's second-largest inland lake, where you can fish, sail, and swim. **Starved Rock State Park** (✉ Box 509, Utica 61373, ☎ 815/667–4726), on the Illinois River between LaSalle and Ottawa, has 18 canyons formed during the melting of the glaciers.

CHICAGO

From the elegance of Michigan Avenue's shops to the stunning sweep of the lakefront skyline, Chicago has much to offer. The Loop, the city's central business district, is a living museum of skyscraper architecture, while many outlying neighborhoods retain the grace and homey quality of pre–World War II America. Chicago's arts community is world class, and strong ethnic communities embrace immigrants from countries as disparate as Croatia and Cambodia, all of whom leave their cultural stamp on the city.

Visitor Information

Chicago Office of Tourism: Visitor Information Center (✉ Chicago Cultural Center, 77 E. Randolph St., 60602, ☎ 312/744–2400 or 800/

226–6632) and walk-in centers (✉ Water Tower, 806 N. Michigan Ave.; Navy Pier's Illinois Marketplace, 600 E. Grand Ave.). **Mayor's Office of Special Events:** General Information and Activities (✉ 121 N. La Salle St., Room 703, 60602, ☎ 312/744–3315 or 312/744–3370 for recordings).

Arriving and Departing

By Bus
Greyhound Lines (✉ 630 W. Harrison St., ☎ 800/231–2222).

By Car
From the east the Indiana Toll Road (I–80/90) leads to the Chicago Skyway (also a toll road), which runs into the Dan Ryan Expressway (I–90/94); take the Dan Ryan west to any downtown exit. From the south you can take I–57 to the Dan Ryan. From the west follow I–80 to I–55, which is the major artery from the southwest and leads into Lake Shore Drive. From the north I–94 and I–90 eastbound merge about 10 mi north of downtown to form the John F. Kennedy Expressway (I–90/94).

By Plane
Every national airline, most international airlines, and a number of regional carriers fly into **O'Hare International Airport,** some 20 mi northwest of downtown Chicago. One of the world's busiest airports, it is a hub for United and American airlines. The **Chicago Transit Authority** (☎ 312/836–7000) subway station is in the underground concourse between terminals; for $1.50, trains will take you into the Loop. **Airport Express** (☎ 312/454–7799 or 800/654–7871) provides express coach service from the airport to major downtown and Near North hotels for a fare of $14.75 one-way. Metered taxicab service is available at O'Hare; expect to pay $25–$30 (plus tip) to Near North and downtown locations.

Most major carriers also use **Midway Airport,** on the city's southwest side. The **Chicago Transit Authority**'s Orange Line runs from Midway to the Loop, where you can transfer to other lines. Or for $10.75 you can take an **Airport Express** bus from Midway to hotels in the Loop and Near North.

By Train
Amtrak serves Chicago's Union Station (✉ 225 S. Canal St., at Jackson St., ☎ 800/872–7245).

Getting Around Chicago

The best way to see Chicago is on foot, supplemented by public transportation or taxi. Streets are laid out in a grid, the center of which is the intersection of Madison Street, which runs east–west, and State Street, which runs north–south.

By Car
Leave your car behind if you're seeing the Loop, the Near North Side, or Lincoln Park. You'll need a car to go to the suburbs or outlying city neighborhoods. Downtown abounds with parking lots charging from $7 to $15 a day.

By Public Transportation
The **Chicago Transit Authority** and the **RTA** (☎ 312/836–7000 for both) will provide information on how to get around on city rapid-transit and bus lines, suburban bus lines, and commuter trains; the base fare is $1.50.

By Taxi

Taxis are metered, with fares beginning at $1.60; each additional mile or minute of waiting time costs $1.40. Taxi drivers expect a 15% tip. Major companies are **American United Cab** (☎ 773/248–7600), **Checker Taxi Association** (☎ 312/243–2537), and **Yellow Cab** (☎ 312/829–4222).

Orientation Tours

The **Chicago Architecture Foundation** (✉ 224 S. Michigan Ave., ☎ 312/922–3432) offers downtown walking tours; bus tours; a river cruise; neighborhood tours; and tours of two Prairie Avenue house museums, the Glessner House and the Henry B. Clarke House. **Chicago Motor Coach Co.** (☎ 312/666–1000) offers narrated tours of Chicago landmarks in double-decker buses. Tours depart from the Sears Tower (✉ Franklin and Jackson Sts.), the bridge at Michigan and Wacker streets, and the Water Tower (✉ Pearson and Michigan Sts.), among other locations. **Wendella Sightseeing Boats** (✉ Lower Michigan Ave. at the Wrigley Bldg., ☎ 312/337–1446) and **Mercury Chicago Skyline Cruise-line** (✉ Lower Wacker Dr., ☎ 312/332–1353) offer guided tours of the Chicago River and Lake Michigan. Cruises run May through September.

Exploring Chicago

Outside downtown and the Loop, Chicago is a city of neighborhoods whose rich ethnic diversity gives the city its special air.

The Loop

Walking through Chicago's central business district (defined by and named for the loop of the elevated train that circles it) is like taking a course in the history of American commercial architecture. From the Monadnock Building, the tallest load-bearing masonry structure in the world, to the Sears Tower, technically the tallest building of any kind in the world, Chicago's skyscrapers have unique personalities. Keep an eye out for sculptures by Picasso, Calder, Miró, and other artists that adorn the plazas of many buildings.

The **Chicago Cultural Center** (✉ 78 E. Washington St., at Michigan Ave., ☎ 312/346–3278) used to be the city's main library; now it's used primarily for exhibits, lectures, and performances, all free. Two splendid Tiffany-glass domes are among its treasures.

The terra-cotta **Reliance Building** (✉ State and Washington Sts.), designed by John Root and Charles Atwood in 1894, has the distinctive Chicago window, an innovation in early skyscrapers—two small panes of glass, which open to catch the Lake Michigan breezes, flank a large center panel. The **Richard J. Daley Center** (✉ Dearborn and Washington Sts.), named for the late mayor, father of the current mayor Richard Daley, is headquarters for the Cook County court system; in the plaza is a 52-ft Cor-Ten steel sculpture by Picasso.

Spacious halls, high ceilings, and plenty of marble define the handsome neoclassical **Chicago City Hall/Cook County Building,** designed by Holabird and Roche in 1911. If you're lucky, you may catch the city council in session—usually a good show, with plenty of hot air. Helmut Jahn's 1985 **James R. Thompson Center** (✉ Clark and Randolph Sts.), which houses state offices, has a jarring futuristic design that provides a striking contrast to the city's classically styled civic structures.

A softly curving building emphasizing the bend in the Chicago River, **333 West Wacker Drive** was constructed in an irregular shape dictated

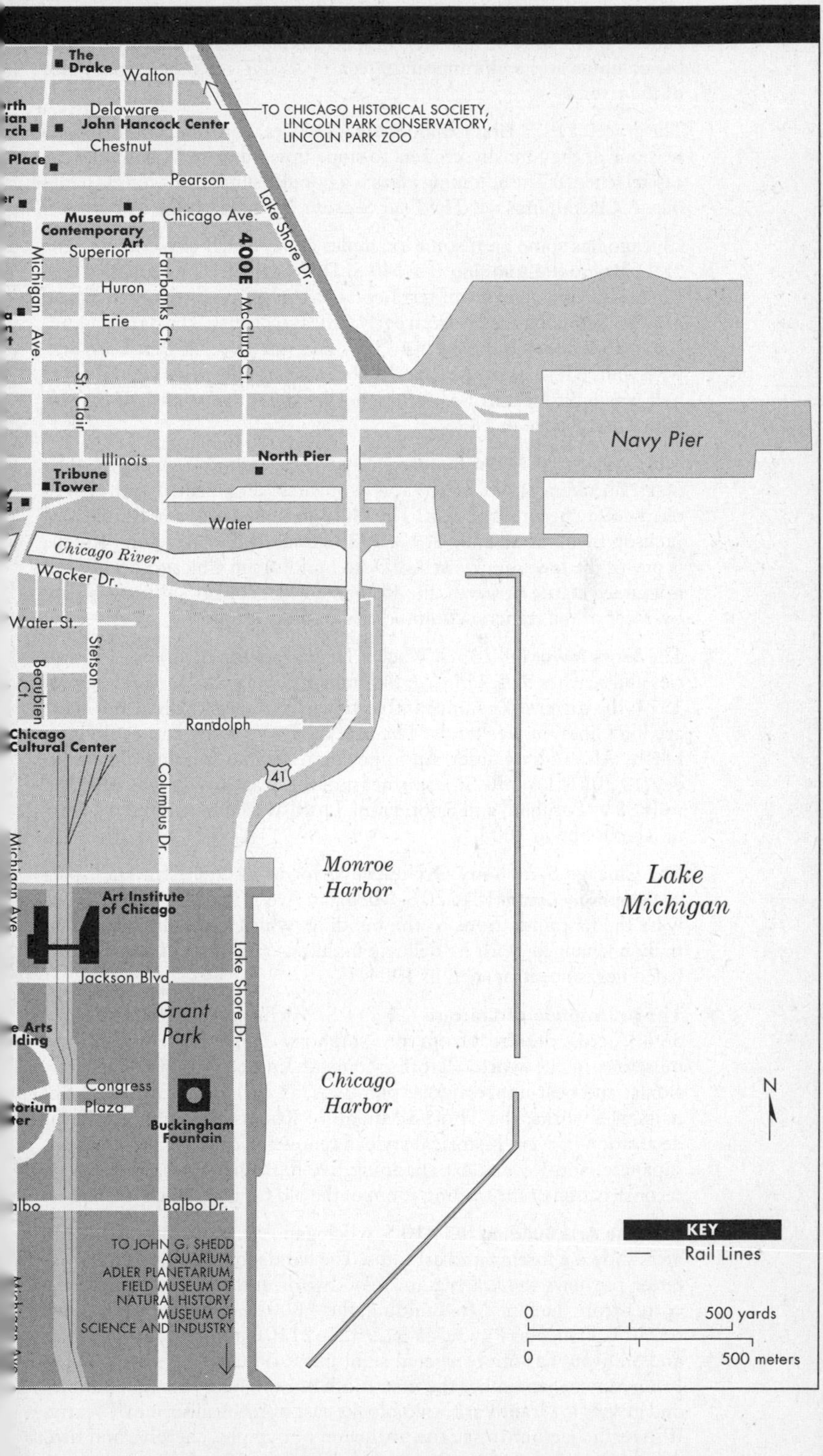
The Drake
Walton
Delaware
John Hancock Center
Chestnut
Place
Pearson
Museum of Contemporary Art
Chicago Ave.
Superior
Huron
Erie
Michigan Ave.
Fairbanks Ct.
400E
McClurg Ct.
Lake Shore Dr.
TO CHICAGO HISTORICAL SOCIETY, LINCOLN PARK CONSERVATORY, LINCOLN PARK ZOO
St. Clair
Illinois
North Pier
Tribune Tower
Navy Pier
Water
Chicago River
Wacker Dr.
Water St.
Stetson
Beaubien Ct.
Randolph
Chicago Cultural Center
41
Columbus Dr.
Michigan Ave.
Monroe Harbor
Lake Michigan
Art Institute of Chicago
Jackson Blvd.
Grant Park
Lake Shore Dr.
Congress
Plaza
Chicago Harbor
N
Buckingham Fountain
Balbo Dr.
TO JOHN G. SHEDD AQUARIUM, ADLER PLANETARIUM, FIELD MUSEUM OF NATURAL HISTORY, MUSEUM OF SCIENCE AND INDUSTRY
KEY
Rail Lines
0
500 yards
0
500 meters

by the triangular parcel on which it sits. The building, designed by Kohn, Pedersen, Fox in 1983 and set in a spacious plaza, has forest green marble columns and a shimmering green-glass skin resembling the color of the river.

The graceful 1973 **First National Bank** (⊠ Dearborn and Madison Sts.) was one of the first skyscrapers to slope upward from its base like the capital letter *A*. The adjoining plaza is a popular summer lunchtime hangout. A Chagall mosaic, *The Four Seasons,* is at the northeast corner.

Chicago has some handsome examples of very early skyscrapers. The 1894 **Marquette Building** (⊠ 140 S. Dearborn St.), by Holabird and Roche, features an exterior terra-cotta bas-relief and interior reliefs and mosaics depicting scenes from early Chicago history. The darkly handsome **Monadnock Building** (⊠ 53 W. Jackson Blvd., at Dearborn St.), with walls 6 ft thick at the base, has been beautifully restored; the north half was built by Burnham and Root in 1891, the south half by Holabird and Roche in 1893.

The Gothic-style **Fisher Building** (⊠ 343 S. Dearborn St.), designed by D. H. Burnham & Co. in 1895, is exquisitely ornamented with carved terra-cotta cherubs and fish. The **Chicago Board of Trade** (⊠ 141 W. Jackson Blvd., at La Salle St.), a 1930 design by Holabird and Roche, is one of the few important Art Deco buildings in Chicago. At the top is a gilded statue of Ceres, the Roman goddess of agriculture—an apt overseer of the frenetic commodities trading within.

★ The **Sears Tower** (⊠ 233 S. Wacker Dr., at Jackson Blvd.) has 110 stories and reaches to 1,454 ft. A Skidmore, Owings & Merrill design of 1974, the tower offers unbeatable views from the sky deck, but there are long lines on weekends. The Wacker Drive lobby has a jolly mobile by Alexander Calder. An imposing red-stone building, the **Rookery** (⊠ 209 S. La Salle St.), northeast of the Sears Tower, was designed in 1888 by Burnham and Root; Frank Lloyd Wright remodeled the magnificent lobby in 1905.

The **Chicago Symphony Orchestra** performs in Orchestra Hall, part of **Symphony Center** (⊠ 220 S. Michigan Ave.). The 1997 renovations were the first alterations to the building, which had remained essentially unchanged, with its delicate moldings and dramatically layered balconies, since it opened in 1904.

★ The **Art Institute of Chicago** (⊠ 111 S. Michigan Ave., ☎ 312/443–3600), across the street from the Symphony Center, is one of the finest museums in the world. It offers outstanding collections of impressionist and post-impressionist paintings, as well as medieval and Renaissance works; the Thorne Miniature Rooms, illustrating interior decoration in every historical style; a renowned collection of Chinese, Japanese, and Korean art spanning five millennia; and a meticulous reconstruction of the trading room of the old Chicago Stock Exchange.

The **Fine Arts Building** (⊠ 410 S. Michigan Ave.) contains movie theaters showing foreign and art films. The handsome detailing on the exterior previews the marble and woodwork in the lobby. Around the corner from the Fine Arts Building, the 4,000-seat **Auditorium Theatre** (⊠ 50 E. Congress Pkwy., ☎ 312/922–2110), built in 1889 by Adler and Sullivan, has unobstructed sight lines and near-perfect acoustics. From May to September the mammoth **Buckingham Fountain** bubbles and gushes in **Grant Park,** two blocks east of the Auditorium Theatre. It's worth a detour to see the profusion of nymphs, cherubs, and fish. A light show takes place 9–11 PM from May to September.

The **Harold Washington Library Center** (✉ 400 S. State St., ☎ 312/747–4999), a postmodern homage to classical-style public buildings, was completed in 1991. Said to be the largest municipal library in the nation, it includes a performing arts auditorium, winter garden, and nearly 71 mi of shelves.

At the **John G. Shedd Aquarium** (✉ 1200 S. Lake Shore Dr., ☎ 312/939–2438), the dazzling oceanarium, with four beluga whales and several Pacific dolphins, is the big draw. But don't miss the sharks, tarpon, turtles, and myriad smaller fish and other aquatic forms in the coral reef exhibit. The **Adler Planetarium** (✉ 1300 S. Lake Shore Dr., ☎ 312/322–0300) is a museum with astronomy exhibits and a popular program of sky shows. The **Field Museum of Natural History** (✉ S. Lake Shore Dr. at E. Roosevelt Rd., ☎ 312/922–9410) is one of the country's great natural history museums. The breadth of its collections and experiential exhibits is enormous. Don't miss the eerie exhibit on ancient Egypt; the fascinating Life over Time display, which traces the evolution of life on Earth from amoebas to dinosaurs to early humans; and the multimedia Africa exhibit.

Magnificent Mile

The Magnificent Mile stretches along Michigan Avenue from the Chicago River to Oak Street. Here you'll find such high-price shops as Gucci, Tiffany & Co., and Chanel; venerable hotels such as the Drake and the Inter-Continental; and two fascinating art museums.

Fronting the Chicago River is the ornate **Wrigley Building** (✉ 410 N. Michigan Ave.), headquarters of the chewing gum empire. The base of the **Tribune Tower** (✉ 435 N. Michigan Ave.), a 1930s Gothic-style skyscraper just north of the Chicago River, incorporates pieces of other buildings and monuments from around the world, including Westminster Abbey, the Parthenon, and the pyramids.

For a waterfront detour and a great view of the skyline, make a stop at **Navy Pier** (✉ 600 E. Grand Ave., ☎ 312/595–7437 for special events information), a former shipping pier that now has shops; restaurants and bars; **Skyline Stage,** an outdoor pavilion for music, dance, and drama performances; a huge Ferris wheel providing skyline vistas; an **IMAX theater** (☎ 312/595—-0090); the **Chicago Children's Museum** (☞ What to See and Do with Children, *below*); and a number of vessels offering cruises on Lake Michigan. **North Pier** (✉ 435 E. Illinois St., ☎ 312/836–4326), one block south and two blocks west of Navy Pier, is a huge old warehouse converted into a waterfront mall, with boutiques, gift shops, restaurants, and an arcade with virtual reality games.

In its massive, modular new home, the **Museum of Contemporary Art** (✉ 220 E. Chicago Ave., ☎ 312/280–2660), closed Monday, houses exhibitions of 20th-century works and includes a terraced outdoor sculpture garden. The **Terra Museum of American Art** (✉ 666 N. Michigan Ave., ☎ 312/664–3939), a small museum that opened in the late 1980s with industrialist Daniel Terra's superb private collection, includes works by almost every major American painter, including Whistler, Sargent, the Wyeths, and Cassatt; it is closed Monday.

One of the few buildings to survive the Chicago fire of 1871, the **Water Tower** (✉ Michigan Ave. at Pearson St.) sits like a giant sand castle at the heart of the Magnificent Mile and now houses a visitor center where you can pick up maps and brochures.

The gray-marble high-rise called **Water Tower Place** (✉ 835 N. Michigan Ave., ☎ 312/440–3165) has restaurants, a cinema, two department stores, and a variety of chain stores and boutiques. The **observatory** on the 94th floor of the 100-story **John Hancock Center** (⊠ 875 N. Michigan Ave., ☎ 312/751–3681) offers amazing views of the city. Have a drink in the bar on the 96th floor and save yourself the observatory fee. A change of pace from the North Michigan Avenue shops, the **Fourth Presbyterian Church** (⊠ 126 E. Chestnut St.) is a small, Gothic-style jewel with a courtyard offering refuge from the surrounding bustle. During the week, the sanctuary offers occasional organ recitals and concerts.

Lincoln Park

Lincoln Park is the area that stretches from North Avenue to Diversey Parkway and from the lakefront on the east to about Racine Avenue on the west. The adjoining lakefront park is also called Lincoln Park (causing visitors occasional confusion), though it stretches several miles farther north than the neighborhood.

The **Chicago Historical Society** (⊠ 1601 N. Clark St., ☎ 312/642–4600) is a stately brick building with a sparkling, modern glass addition on the Clark Street side. Permanent exhibits include the costumes alcove and the Chicago history galleries, where you can view Lincoln's deathbed and the Bible of abolitionist John Brown. Children enjoy climbing aboard the Pioneer locomotive, Chicago's first train and the largest artifact in the museum's collection.

The 35-acre **Lincoln Park Zoo** (⊠ 2200 N. Cannon Dr., ☎ 312/742–2000), the nation's oldest, is free and home to all the requisite zoo denizens, including koalas, reptiles, great apes, and lowland gorillas. In Lincoln Park's **South Pond,** just south of the Lincoln Park Zoo, you can rent paddleboats May–October. The **Lincoln Park Conservatory** (⊠ 2400 N. Stockton Dr., ☎ 312/742–7736), which borders the Lincoln Park Zoo, has a palm house, a fernery, a cactus house, special exhibits, and large outdoor gardens; all are free.

★ You'll find elegant town houses and small apartment buildings from the late 1800s and early 1900s in the **Lincoln Park neighborhood,** the heart of which are Fullerton Avenue, Lincoln Avenue, and Halsted Street. The area declined after World War II as residents moved to the suburbs, but it was rediscovered in the 1970s; it's not uncommon now to see million-dollar prices on some of the restored houses. The **Biograph Theater** (⊠ 2433 N. Lincoln Ave., ☎ 773/348–4123), where the gangster John Dillinger met his end at the hands of the FBI, is on the National Register of Historic Places and still shows first-run movies.

Other Attractions

River North—a former warehouse neighborhood west of Michigan Avenue, bounded roughly by Clark Street, Chicago Avenue, Orleans Street, and the Chicago River—bloomed during the mid-1980s gentrification craze and now offers a number of art galleries. The Visitor Welcome Center in the Water Tower (⊠ Michigan Ave. at Pearson St.) carries the *Chicago Gallery News,* which lists addresses, hours, and current exhibits.

The **Museum of Science and Industry** (⊠ E. 57th St. and S. Lake Shore Dr., ☎ 773/684–1414), on the lake in Hyde Park about 7 mi south of the Loop, is a treasure trove of gadgetry, applied science, and hands-on exhibits. There's a genuine German U-boat, a reproduction coal mine, Colleen Moore's Fairy Castle (a dollhouse to end all dollhouses), actual spacecraft from early NASA missions, and a giant-screen Omnimax theater.

Parks and Gardens

Most of Chicago's more than 20 mi of shoreline is parkland or beach reserved for public use. A 19-mile path stretches along the lakefront, snaking through **Lincoln Park** (☞ Exploring Chicago, *above*), **Grant Park** (just east of the Loop), and **Jackson Park** (just south of the Museum of Science and Industry, with a wooded island and a Japanese garden) and winding past half a dozen harbors, two golf courses, Navy Pier, Buckingham Fountain, the lakefront museums, McCormick Place, and all the city's popular beaches. Bikes are the best way to cover maximum territory; they can be rented in summer at the concession as you enter at the Lincoln Park entrance at Fullerton Avenue and Cannon Drive. Bicycle thieves sometimes lurk in the comparatively deserted stretch south of McCormick Place; it's safe enough on weekends, but don't risk it alone during the week or at night.

There are hundreds of parks in neighborhoods throughout the city and suburbs. Charging no admission, the **Garfield Park Conservatory** (⌧ 300 N. Central Park Blvd., ☏ 312/746–5100) maintains 5 acres of plants and flowers under glass and holds four shows a year. The **Chicago Botanic Garden** (⌧ 1000 Lake Cook Rd., Glencoe, ☏ 847/835–8208), north of the city, covers 385 acres and has 15 separate gardens and three greenhouses. The **Morton Arboretum** (⌧ Rte. 53 north of I–88, Lisle, ☏ 630/719–2465), in the western suburbs, has 1,700 acres of woody plants, woodlands, and outdoor gardens.

What to See and Do with Children

At the **Lincoln Park Zoo** (☞ Exploring Chicago, *above*), youngsters especially enjoy the **Children's Zoo** and the **Farm-in-the-Zoo** (farm animals plus a learning center with films and demonstrations). At **Brookfield Zoo** (⌧ 1st Ave. and 31st St., Brookfield, ☏ 708/485–0263), one of the nation's best, the animals inhabit naturalistic settings that give visitors the feeling of being in the wild. On Navy Pier the **Chicago Children's Museum** (⌧ 700 E. Grand Ave., ☏ 312/527–1000) has plenty of fascinating and educational hands-on exhibits. It is closed Monday from Labor Day to Memorial Day. **Kohl Children's Museum** (⌧ 165 Green Bay Rd., Wilmette, ☏ 847/256–6056) offers kids activity-filled touch-and-feel exhibits. It is closed Monday from fall through spring.

Dining

Chicago has everything: from traditional aged steaks, ribs, and the ubiquitous Vienna hot dog to the loftier offerings of many excellent French and Italian restaurants to the more unusual fare of Middle Eastern, Thai, and Vietnamese establishments. Most eating places listed below are in the Near North, River North, and Loop areas, within walking distance of the major hotel districts. A few are a bit farther out, in the city's residential neighborhoods and ethnic enclaves.

For clusters of ethnic restaurants too numerous to mention here, try Greektown, at Halsted and Madison streets; Chinatown, at Wentworth Avenue and 23rd Street; Little Italy, on Taylor Street between Racine and Ashland avenues; Argyle Street between Broadway and Sheridan Road (for Chinese and Vietnamese); Devon Avenue between Leavitt Street and Sacramento Avenue (Indian), and Clark Street from Belmont Avenue to Addison Street (Thai, Japanese, Chinese, Korean, Jamaican, Ethiopian, and Mexican).

Restaurant listings appear in the monthly *Chicago* magazine and in the Friday editions of the *Chicago Tribune* and the *Chicago Sun-Times*

(Weekend section). For price ranges *see* Chart 1 (A) *in* On the Road with Fodor's.

$$$$ ✕ Ambria. Set in an art nouveau building in Lincoln Park, Ambria serves contemporary French food and light cuisine. The seasonal menu emphasizes natural juices and vegetable reductions to accompany the entrées. ⊠ *2300 N. Lincoln Park W,* ☎ *773/472–5959. Reservations required. Jacket required. AE, D, DC, MC, V. Closed Sun. No lunch.*

$$$$ ✕ Charlie Trotter's. This top-of-the-line Lincoln Park town house ac-
★ commodates 28 tables. Owner and chef Charlie Trotter prepares stellar new American cuisine, incorporating flavors from around the globe into classic French dishes. The prix-fixe degustation menus include 7–10 courses. ⊠ *816 W. Armitage Ave.,* ☎ *773/248–6228. Reservations required. Jacket and tie. AE, D, DC, MC, V. Closed Sun.–Mon. No lunch.*

$$$$ ✕ Everest. On the 40th floor of a postmodern skyscraper in the heart
★ of the financial district, this restaurant serves dishes squarely in the classic French tradition but with appeal to contemporary tastes. ⊠ *440 S. La Salle St.,* ☎ *312/663–8920. Reservations required. Jacket and tie. AE, D, DC, MC, V. Closed Sun.–Mon. No lunch.*

$$$$ ✕ Le Français. Only serious eaters should make the pilgrimage to this
★ classic haute French outpost in the northwestern suburbs. Dinner takes the entire evening, and the tab can easily top $100 per person. The menu changes nightly to reflect the best ingredients available—and the whim of the chef. Try the 10-course degustation menu, a comparative bargain, available for $75 weeknights. ⊠ *269 S. Milwaukee Ave., Wheeling,* ☎ *847/541–7470. Reservations required. Jacket required. AE, D, DC, MC, V. Closed Sun. No lunch Mon. and Sat.*

$$$$ ✕ Spiaggia. In elegant pink-and-teal quarters overlooking the lake, Spiaggia offers the most opulent Italian dining in town, with elaborate stuffed pastas, veal chops in a vodka-cream sauce, and other richly inventive dishes. Save room for dessert. ⊠ *980 N. Michigan Ave.,* ☎ *312/ 280–2750. Reservations required. Jacket required. AE, D, DC, MC, V. No lunch Sun.*

$$$$ ✕ Trio. The elaborate contemporary cuisine at this acclaimed restau-
★ rant has Asian, French, and Italian influences. The decor is tastefully restrained, but the presentation is often whimsical: Food may be served on such unique objects as painters' palettes and mirrors. An eight-course degustation menu, priced at $75, offers the chef's choice of specialties. ⊠ *1625 Hinman, Evanston,* ☎ *847/733–8746. Reservations required. Jacket required. AE, D, DC, MC, V. No lunch. Closed Mon.*

$$$ ✕ Arun's. Long considered the city's best—and most expensive—Thai restaurant, Arun's is known for its congenial staff, its elegant dining room showcasing Thai art, and, last but not least, superbly presented dishes made with the freshest ingredients. ⊠ *4156 N. Kedzie Ave.,* ☎ *773/539–1909. AE, D, DC, MC, V. Closed Mon. No lunch.*

$$$ ✕ Le Titi de Paris. It's worth the trip to the suburb of Arlington Heights on Chicago's northwest side for chef Pierre Pollin's classic French dishes in a refined, floral setting. ⊠ *1015 W. Dundee Rd., Arlington Heights,* ☎ *847/506–0222. Reservations required. AE, D, DC, MC, V. Closed Sun.–Mon. No lunch Sat.*

$$$ ✕ Morton's of Chicago. Chicago's best steak house offers beautiful, hefty steaks cooked to perfection. Excellent service, a classy ambience, and a very good wine list add to the appeal. Vegetarians and budget watchers should look elsewhere. ⊠ *1050 N. State St.,* ☎ *312/266–4820. AE, D, DC, MC, V. No lunch.*

$$$ ✕ Printer's Row. Named after its recently chic loft neighborhood in
★ the South Loop, this warm and attractive restaurant offers inventive and satisfying American cuisine. The house special is venison, and you'll

always find a different preparation on the menu. ⊠ *550 S. Dearborn St.,* ☎ *312/461–0780. Reservations required on weekends. AE, D, DC, MC, V. Closed Sun. No lunch Sat.*

$$–$$$ ✕ **Frontera Grill/Topolobampo.** In Frontera Grill's cozy, colorful store-
★ front, genuine regional Mexican cooking goes way beyond burritos and chips: from charbroiled catfish (with pickled red onions and jicama salad) to garlicky skewered tenderloin (with *poblano* peppers, red onion, and bacon). Topolobampo, next door, shares the owners and the kitchen; it offers a more stately atmosphere and affords the chef an opportu-nity to experiment with more expensive ingredients. ⊠ *445 N. Clark St.,* ☎ *312/661–1434. Reservations required at Topolobampo. AE, D, DC, MC, V. Closed Sun.–Mon. No lunch Sat. at Topolobampo.*

$$ ✕ **The Berghoff.** This Loop institution has oak paneling, a bustling am-bience, two huge dining rooms, and a splendid bar with Berghoff beer on tap. Expect a wait of 15 minutes or so at midday. American favorites augment the menu of German classics (Wiener schnitzel, sauerbraten). ⊠ *17 W. Adams St.,* ☎ *312/427–3170. AE, MC, V. Closed Sun.*

$$ ✕ **Cafe Ba-Ba-Reeba!** Chicago's best-known purveyor of tapas (var-ied small portions of edibles, which originated as accompaniments to drinks in Spanish bars), this large, open restaurant and its prominent bar are usually crowded with upscale young folk. The wide selection of cold and warm tapas ranges from stuffed cannelloni to veal with mushrooms. ⊠ *2024 N. Halsted St.,* ☎ *773/935–5000. Reservations not accepted. AE, D, DC, MC, V. No lunch Mon.*

$$ ✕ **Klay Oven.** The understated but pleasing decor and outstanding cui-sine make this Chicago's best Indian restaurant. Clay tandoor ovens bake mouthwatering tandoori chicken, mahi-mahi, and tiger prawns; a variety of chutneys adds zip to every bite. Try the luncheon buffet. ⊠ *414 N. Orleans St.,* ☎ *312/527–3999. AE, DC, MC, V.*

$$ ✕ **Le Bouchon.** Chef-owner Jean-Claude Poilevey offers bistro fare with a reasonable price tag at this intimate 40-seat French restaurant in Bucktown. The onion tart is a signature appetizer. Typical entrées include ragout of duck and sautéed rabbit with shallots and mustard. ⊠ *1958 N. Damen Ave.,* ☎ *773/862–6600. AE, D, DC, MC, V. Closed Sun. No lunch.*

$$ ✕ **New Rosebud Cafe.** Specializing in good, old-fashioned southern Ital-
★ ian cuisine, Rosebud serves a superior red sauce, and the roasted pep-pers, homemade sausage, and exquisitely prepared pastas are not to be missed. The wait for a table can stretch to an hour or more despite confirmed reservations. ⊠ *1500 W. Taylor St.,* ☎ *312/942–1117. AE, D, DC, MC, V. No lunch weekends.*

$$ ✕ **Tuttaposto.** This upscale taverna specializes in Mediterranean cui-sine prepared with such healthful ingredients as legumes and whole grains. Wood-burning ovens cook seafood and meat entrées to perfection, and a small selection of regional wines complements meals nicely. ⊠ *646 N. Franklin St.,* ☎ *312/943–6262. AE, D, DC, MC, V. No lunch weekends.*

$$ ✕ **Yoshi's Cafe.** Unassuming on the outside but casually elegant on the inside, Chef Yoshi Katsumura's restaurant specializes in Asian-influ-enced French bistro cuisine. Dishes are gorgeously presented; try the fresh seafood, such as tuna tartare with homemade guacamole. ⊠ *3257 N. Halsted St.,* ☎ *773/248–6160. AE, DC, MC, V. Closed Mon. No lunch.*

$ ✕ **Ann Sather.** These three light and airy restaurants—all on the North Side—emphasize home-style food and service. Specialties include omelets, Swedish pancakes, homemade cinnamon rolls, potato sausage, chicken croquettes, and sandwiches. ⊠ *929 W. Belmont Ave.,* ☎ *773/ 348–2378;* ⊠ *5207 N. Clark St.,* ☎ *773/271–6677, no dinner;* ⊠ *2665 N. Clark St.,* ☎ *773/327–9522, no dinner. AE, DC, MC, V.*

$ ✕ **Big Bowl.** This trendy Asian café specializes in noodle dishes, pot stickers, and big bowls of soup. The newer Cedar Street location is more lively than the original on Erie. ⊠ *159½ W. Erie St.,* ☎ *312/787–8297;* ⊠ *6 E. Cedar St.,* ☎ *312/640–8888. AE, D, DC, MC, V.*

$ ✕ **Pizzeria Uno/Pizzeria Due.** This is where Chicago deep-dish pizza ★ got its start. Uno has been remodeled to resemble its franchised cousins in other cities, but its pizzas retain their light crust and distinctive tang. There's usually a shorter wait for a table at Pizzeria Due (same ownership and menu, different decor and longer hours), a block away. ⊠ *Uno: 29 E. Ohio St.,* ☎ *312/321–1000;* ⊠ *Due: 619 N. Wabash Ave.,* ☎ *312/943–2400. AE, D, DC, MC, V.*

$ ✕ **Reza's.** This loftlike space with polished wood floors, exposed brick walls, and a relaxed ambience serves large portions of excellent tangy chicken kebabs, lentil soup, and other Mediterranean and Persian fare. The Ontario Street restaurant in the River North area may be more convenient, but it doesn't match the Clark Street branch in decor or cuisine. ⊠ *5255 N. Clark St.,* ☎ *773/561–1898;* ⊠ *432 W. Ontario St.,* ☎ *312/664–4500. AE, MC, V.*

$ ✕ **Three Happiness.** The specialty of this cavernous, kitchen table–style Chinatown joint is its dim sum (Chinese-style brunch), served every day from 10 AM to 2 PM; the crowd begins to form at 9:30 on weekends. Go with a group to mix and match the little dishes of steamed and fried dumplings, rice cakes, custard squares, and other appetizers. ⊠ *2130 S. Wentworth Ave.,* ☎ *312/791–1228. Reservations not accepted weekends. AE, D, DC, MC, V.*

Lodging

Chicago is the country's biggest convention town, and accommodations can be tight when major events are scheduled. Most hotels offer weekend specials when no big shows are on. Virtually every hotel chain has at least one property in Chicago, and some have several. Hotels are concentrated in the Loop and the Near North Side. **Bed and Breakfast Chicago** (⊠ Box 14088, 60614, ☎ 312/951–0085) handles more than 50 B&Bs in the downtown area. For price ranges *see* Chart 2 (A) *in* On the Road with Fodor's.

$$$$ 🏨 **The Drake.** The grandest of Chicago's traditional hotels was built ★ in 1920 in the style of an Italian Renaissance palace; today it continues to attract illustrious guests such as Princess Di. The spacious rooms are furnished with dark wood and floral upholstery with a 19th-century flavor; many have splendid lake views. ⊠ *140 E. Walton Pl., 60611,* ☎ *312/787–2200 or 800/553–7253,* FAX *312/787–1431. 535 rooms. 3 restaurants, exercise room, concierge. AE, D, DC, MC, V.*

$$$$ 🏨 **The Fairmont.** This 37-story neoclassical structure of Spanish pink granite is next to the Illinois Center complex (where guests have access to a huge athletic facility) and offers fine views of the lake and Grant Park. The sizable rooms are decorated in soft hues and have every modern convenience, including in-room faxes and modem lines. ⊠ *200 N. Columbus Dr., 60601,* ☎ *312/565–8000,* FAX *312/856–1032. 692 rooms. 3 restaurants, in-room modem lines, laundry service and dry cleaning, concierge, business services. AE, D, DC, MC, V.*

$$$$ 🏨 **Four Seasons.** Occupying 17 floors in a major building, this luxuri- ★ ous hostelry offers spectacular lake and city views. Suggesting the decor of an English manor house, the smallish rooms have Italian marble, handcrafted woodwork, custom-woven rugs, and tasteful prints. ⊠ *120 E. Delaware Pl., 60611,* ☎ *312/280–8800,* FAX *312/280–1748. 344 rooms. Restaurant, café, pool, health club, concierge. AE, D, DC, MC, V.*

$$$$ 🏨 **Hotel Inter-Continental Chicago.** A grand architectural gem, the ★ Inter-Continental has a dramatic lobby, ornately painted ceilings, mar-

ble steps, and a second-floor terra-cotta fountain. The Italianate junior-Olympic-size pool helped earn the hotel national landmark status in 1993. Its North Tower is less inspiring. ⊠ *505 N. Michigan Ave., 60611,* ☎ *312/944–4100 or 800/628–2112,* 𝔽𝔸𝕏 *312/944–3050. 844 rooms. 2 restaurants, pool, health club, concierge, business services. AE, D, DC, MC, V.*

\$\$\$\$ ⊞ **Sutton Place Hotel.** This ultramodern hotel has a sleek, art deco lobby and similarly stylish guest rooms; penthouse rooms and some public areas have original photographs by Robert Mapplethorpe. Features such as VCRs and CD players in every room give the place a high-tech ambience. ⊠ *21 E. Bellevue Pl., 60611,* ☎ *312/266–2100 or 800/606– 8188,* 𝔽𝔸𝕏 *312/266–2141. 246 rooms. Restaurant, exercise room, concierge. AE, D, DC, MC, V.*

\$\$\$ ⊞ **Chicago Hilton and Towers.** Built in 1927, this huge grand hotel in the South Loop has a lavishly restored lobby filled with gilt and crystal. The large ballroom is worthy of Marie Antoinette; guest rooms offer amenities and comfort. ⊠ *720 S. Michigan Ave., 60605,* ☎ *312/922– 4400,* 𝔽𝔸𝕏 *312/922–5240. 1,543 rooms. 4 restaurants, pool, health club, concierge, business services. AE, D, DC, MC, V.*

\$\$\$ ⊞ **Claridge Hotel.** Nestled among Victorian houses on a tree-lined Near North street, this 1930s building is tastefully decorated. It's intimate rather than bustling, and the decor is simple. ⊠ *1244 N. Dearborn Pkwy., 60610,* ☎ *312/787–4980 or 800/245–1258,* 𝔽𝔸𝕏 *312/266–0978. 173 rooms. Restaurant, bar, concierge. AE, D, DC, MC, V.*

\$\$\$ ⊞ **Palmer House Hilton.** Built in 1871 by the Chicago merchant Potter Palmer, this hotel has public areas that reflect the opulence of that era, including a frescoed rococo lobby. Its modern guest rooms are more ordinary. ⊠ *17 E. Monroe St., 60603,* ☎ *312/726–7500,* 𝔽𝔸𝕏 *312/263– 2556. 1,639 rooms. 4 restaurants, pool, exercise room, concierge. AE, D, DC, MC, V.*

\$\$\$ ⊞ **The Raphael.** On a quiet, pretty street just off the Magnificent Mile,
★ this hotel has Old World charm. The lobby has two-story cathedral windows, the modern guest rooms are tastefully decorated, and the staff is attentive. ⊠ *201 E. Delaware Pl., 60611,* ☎ *312/943–5000 or 800/ 821–5343,* 𝔽𝔸𝕏 *312/943–9483. 172 rooms. Restaurant, lounge, dry cleaning. AE, D, DC, MC, V.*

\$\$ ⊞ **City Suites Hotel.** Ten minutes north of the Loop in the Lakeview neighborhood, this small, reasonably priced European-style hotel has a fireplace in the lobby and cozy guest rooms with chic black-and-white tile baths. The location is unbeatable. ⊠ *933 W. Belmont Ave., 60657,* ☎ *773/404–3400 or 800/248–9108,* 𝔽𝔸𝕏 *773/404–3405. 45 rooms. Parking (fee). AE, D, DC, MC, V.*

\$\$ ⊞ **Lenox House.** Conveniently located near North Michigan Avenue, this Lenox's one-room "suites" each have a Murphy bed, a sofa bed, and a wet-bar kitchen, all done in generic '80s style. Junior and courtyard suites have two rooms. ⊠ *616 N. Rush St., 60611,* ☎ *312/337– 1000 or 800/445–3669,* 𝔽𝔸𝕏 *312/337–7217. 324 suites. 2 restaurants, bar, concierge. AE, D, DC, MC, V.*

\$ ⊞ **Chicago International Hostel.** Near Loyola University in the Rogers Park neighborhood, this hostel's dormitory-style accommodations, with five or six to a room, cost \$13 a night, including linens. A kitchen is available. ⊠ *6318 N. Winthrop Ave., 60660,* ☎ *773/262–1011. 100 beds, 6 private rooms. Coin laundry. No credit cards.*

Motels

⊞ **Best Western River North** (⊠ 125 W. Ohio St., 60610, ☎ 312/467– 0800 or 800/727–0800, 𝔽𝔸𝕏 312/467–1665), 148 rooms, restaurant, pool, health club, free parking; *\$\$.* ⊞ **Comfort Inn of Lincoln Park** (⊠ 601 W. Diversey Pkwy., 60614, ☎ 312/348–2810, 𝔽𝔸𝕏 312/348–1912),

74 rooms; *$$*. ▣ **Hojo Inn** (⊠ 720 N. La Salle St., 60610, ☎ 312/664–8100, ꜰᴀx 312/664–2365), 71 rooms, restaurant, free parking; *$*. ▣ **Ohio House** (⊠ 600 N. La Salle St., 60610, ☎ 312/943–6000, ꜰᴀx 312/943–6063), 50 rooms, coffee shop, free parking; *$*.

Nightlife and the Arts

For listings of arts and entertainment events, check the monthly *Chicago* magazine (on newsstands) or the Friday editions of the *Chicago Tribune* or the *Chicago Sun-Times*. Two free weeklies, the *Reader* (available Thursday) and *New City* (available Wednesday), which can be found at bookstores, restaurants, and bars, are the best sources for what's happening in clubs and small theaters and for showings of noncommercial films.

Nightlife

Chicago comes alive at night with something for everyone, from loud and loose to sophisticated and sedate. Shows usually begin at 9 PM; cover charges generally range from $3 to $10, depending on the day of the week. Most bars are open until 2 AM, and some larger dance clubs even serve until 4 AM.

BLUES CLUBS

In the years following World War II, Chicago-style blues grew into its own musical form. After fading in the '60s, Chicago blues is coming back, although more strongly on the trendy North Side than on the South Side, where it all began. **Kingston Mines** (⊠ 2548 N. Halsted St., ☎ 773/477–4646) is the 30-year king of Chicago blues clubs, with bands on two stages weekends. The intimate **B.L.U.E.S.** (⊠ 2519 N. Halsted St., ☎ 773/528–1012) pulses with music in a rather small space. The elaborate **House of Blues** (⊠ 329 N. Dearborn Ave., ☎ 312/527—2583), a recent import to Chicago's blues scene, features top-notch groups playing in an ornate, theaterlike setting with unconventional art adorning the walls. **Buddy Guy's Legends** (⊠ 754 S. Wabash Ave., ☎ 312/427–0333), owned by the famous blues man, sits in a spacious former storefront. The **New Checkerboard Lounge** (⊠ 423 E. 43rd St., ☎ 773/624–3240) is in a rough neighborhood but has a long pedigree.

COMEDY CLUBS

Many comedy clubs have a drink minimum instead of or in addition to a cover charge. The granddaddy of all comedy clubs is **Second City** (⊠ 1616 N. Wells St., ☎ 312/337–3992), which usually has two different revues playing at once. The best stand-up comedy in town is found at **Zanies** (⊠ 1548 N. Wells St., ☎ 312/337–4027). **Improv Olympic** (⊠ 3541 N. Clark St., ☎ 773/880–0199) presents improv troupes as well as staged shows.

FOLK CLUBS

No Exit Cafe/Gallery (⊠ 6970 N. Glenwood Ave., ☎ 773/743–3355), a coffeehouse right out of the 1960s, offers folk, jazz, and poetry readings. **Old Town School of Folk Music** (⊠ 909 W. Armitage Ave., ☎ 773/525–7793) mixes local talent and outstanding nationally known performers.

JAZZ CLUBS

Jazz Showcase (⊠ 59 W. Grand Ave., ☎ 312/670–2473) books nationally known groups in its classy River North home. The **Gold Star Sardine Bar** (⊠ 680 N. Lake Shore Dr., ☎ 312/664–4215), a tiny spot in a splendid renovated building, hosts top names that attract a trendy clientele. **Pops for Champagne** (⊠ 2934 N. Sheffield Ave., ☎ 773/472–1000) features jazz combos and a popular champagne bar. The **Green Mill** (⊠ 4802 N. Broadway, ☎ 773/878–5552), a Chicago institution off the beaten track, books solid, sizzling local acts in an ornate '40s space.

ROCK CLUBS

Metro (✉ 3730 N. Clark St., ☎ 773/549–0203) presents progressive nationally known and local artists. Downstairs from Metro, **Smart Bar** throbs with punk and funk tunes. The **Cubby Bear** (✉ 1059 W. Addison St., ☎ 773/327–1662), across from Wrigley Field, offers a variety of rock, fusion, and country-tinged acts. In the hip Wicker Park neighborhood, the **Double Door** (✉ 1572 N. Milwaukee Ave., ☎ 773/489–3160) books top and up-and-coming local artists. **Lounge Ax** (✉ 2438 N. Lincoln Ave., ☎ 773/525–6620) offers alternative rock bands nightly. The **Wild Hare** (✉ 3530 N. Clark St., ☎ 773/327–4273) is the city's premier reggae club.

FOR SINGLES

Chicago's legendary Rush Street singles scene is actually on **Division Street** between Clark and State; here you'll find such bars as **Mother's** (✉ 26 W. Division St., ☎ 312/642–7251), featured in the movie . . . *About Last Night.* **Butch McGuire's** (✉ 20 W. Division St., ☎ 312/337–9080) is jammed with out-of-towners on the make. **North Pier** (✉ 435 E. Illinois St.) has several popular singles spots, including the **Baja Beach Club** (☎ 312/222–1993) and **Dick's Last Resort** (☎ 312/836–7870). There's a cluster of bar life in the neighborhood around **Halsted and Armitage streets** in Lincoln Park.

ECLECTIC

The hip and arty Wicker Park/Bucktown area has many bars and nightclubs, especially near the intersection of Milwaukee, Damen, and North avenues. Enter **Red Dog** (✉ 1958 W. North Ave., ☎ 773/278–1009), a funky dance club, through the unmarked door in the alley. **Mad Bar** (✉ 1640 N. Damen Ave., ☎ 312/227–2277), a see-and-be-seen Bucktown bar, showcases live music periodically.

GAY BARS

The area around Halsted Street approximately between Wellington Avenue and Addison Street has the city's highest concentration of gay bars, including the yuppified **Roscoe's Tavern & Cafe** (✉ 3356 N. Halsted St., ☎ 773/281–3355). **Fusion** (✉ 3631 N. Halsted St., ☎ 773/975–6622), open Friday and Saturday only, is a pulsating disco above a Brazilian restaurant. A country-western bar, **Charlie's** (✉ 3726 N. Broadway, ☎ 773/871–8887), plays achy-breaky tunes.

The Arts

Chicago is a splendid city for the arts, with more than 50 theater groups, world-class orchestra and opera companies, dozens of smaller musical ensembles, and several movie theaters that go way beyond commercial Hollywood offerings.

THEATER

Half-price theater tickets are available for many productions on the day of performance at **Hot Tix** booths (✉ 108 N. State St. and Chicago Place, 700 N. Michigan Ave., 6th floor, ☎ 312/977–1755 for both). Chicago is home to many commercial theaters. With excellent acoustics, the **Auditorium Theatre** (✉ 50 E. Congress Pkwy., ☎ 312/922–2110) offers popular Broadway musicals, such as those by Andrew Lloyd Webber. In Lincoln Park the **Royal George Theatre Center** (✉ 1641 N. Halsted St., ☎ 312/988–9000) has a cabaret theater with bar, and a smaller gallery theater. The grand, renovated **Shubert Theatre** (✉ 22 W. Monroe St., ☎ 312/977–1700), built in 1906, is home to touring Broadway plays, musicals, and dance companies. Small, offbeat companies—of varying professionalism—often find their way to the three stages of the **Theatre Building** (✉ 1225 W. Belmont Ave., ☎ 773/327–5252).

Several local ensembles have made the big jump into national prominence, most notably the successful **Steppenwolf** (✉ 1650 N. Halsted St., ☎ 312/335–1650). **Victory Gardens** (✉ 2257 N. Lincoln Ave., ☎ 773/871–3000) showcases local playwrights on its four stages. The city's oldest repertory theater, the **Goodman Theatre** (✉ 200 S. Columbus Dr., ☎ 312/443–3800) offers polished presentations of both contemporary works and classics.

MUSIC

The **Chicago Symphony Orchestra** performs from September to May at the newly renovated Orchestra Hall (✉ 220 S. Michigan Ave., ☎ 312/294–3000 or 800/223–7114) under the direction of Daniel Barenboim. In summer the Chicago Symphony moves outdoors to take part in the **Ravinia Festival** (☎ 312/728–4642), in suburban Highland Park.

OPERA

From September to March the **Lyric Opera of Chicago** (✉ 20 N. Wacker Dr., ☎ 312/332–2244) performs grand opera with international stars; tickets are difficult to come by. The **Chicago Opera Theater** (✉ Merle Reskin Theatre, 60 E. Balbo Ave., ☎ 773/292–7578) specializes in English-language productions of smaller-scale works.

DANCE

Ballet Chicago (☎ 312/251–8838) is the city's oldest resident classical ballet company. The **Joffrey Ballet of Chicago** (☎ 312/739–0120) moved to the city from New York three years ago. **Hubbard Street Dance Chicago** (☎ 312/663–0853) is popular for its contemporary, jazzy vitality.

FILM

In addition to the usual commercial theaters, Chicago has several venues for the avant-garde, vintage, or merely offbeat. **Facets Multimedia** (✉ 1517 W. Fullerton Ave., ☎ 773/281–4114) presents rare and exotic film. The **Film Center of the Art Institute** (✉ Columbus Dr. at Jackson Blvd., ☎ 312/443–3737) sometimes offers lectures in conjunction with its films. The **Fine Arts Theatre** (✉ 418 S. Michigan Ave., ☎ 312/939–3700) shows first-run avant-garde and foreign flicks. The ornate **Music Box Theatre** (✉ 3733 N. Southport Ave., ☎ 773/871–6604), a 1920s movie palace, shows many independent films. **Chicago Filmmakers** (✉ 1543 W. Division St., ☎ 773/384–5533) offers experimental and documentary fare.

Spectator Sports

Baseball: Chicago Cubs (✉ Wrigley Field, 1060 W. Addison St., ☎ 773/404–2827); **Chicago White Sox** (✉ Comiskey Park, 333 W. 35th St., ☎ 312/674–1000 or 312/559–1212 for tickets).

Basketball: Chicago Bulls (✉ United Center, 1901 W. Madison St., ☎ 312/455–4000).

Football: Chicago Bears (✉ Soldier Field, 425 E. McFetridge Dr., ☎ 847/295–6600).

Hockey: Chicago Blackhawks (✉ United Center, 1901 W. Madison St., ☎ 312/455–7000 or 312/559–1212 for tickets).

Horse racing: Arlington International Racecourse (✉ Wilke Rd. at Euclid Ave., Arlington Heights, ☎ 847/255–4300) offers daytime Thoroughbred racing May–October; **Hawthorne Race Course** (✉ 3501 S.

Laramie Ave., Cicero, ☎ 708/780–3700) has both harness racing January–February and Thoroughbred racing September–December; **Sportsman's Park** (⊠ 3301 S. Laramie Ave., Cicero, ☎ 773/242–1121) offers Thoroughbred racing February–May and harness racing May–October; and **Maywood Park** (⊠ North and 5th Aves., Maywood, ☎ 708/343–4800) has harness racing February–May and October–December.

Shopping

Shopping Districts

The **Loop** and the **Magnificent Mile** (☞ Exploring Chicago, *above*, for both) are filled with major department and upscale specialty stores. **Oak Street** between Michigan Avenue and State Street has such top-of-the-line stores as Barney's New York (⊠ 25 E. Oak St., ☎ 312/587–1700) and Giorgio Armani (⊠ 113 E. Oak St., ☎ 312/751–2244). Three vertical (multiple-story) malls combine department stores and specialty shops: **Water Tower Place** (☞ Exploring Chicago, *above*); the **900 North Michigan Avenue** complex (☎ 312/915–3916); and **Chicago Place** (⊠ 700 N. Michigan Ave., ☎ 312/642–4811). The **Lincoln Park neighborhood** has several worthwhile shopping strips. Clark Street between Armitage, 2000 north, and Diversey, 2800 north, avenues is home to a number of clothing boutiques and specialty stores. From Diversey north to School Street 3300 north are several large antiques stores, more boutiques, and some bookstores.

Department Stores

Marshall Field's & Co. (⊠ 111 N. State St., at Randolph St., ☎ 312/781–1000), the city's biggest department store, takes up an entire city block. With 500 departments, it's the second-largest retail store in the country. **Carson Pirie Scott & Co.** (⊠ 1 S. State St., ☎ 312/641–7000) doesn't have the grandeur or style of its North Michigan Avenue competitors, but it does have spectacular ornamental ironwork around the main entrance. To keep up with the latest fashion trends, visit **Bloomingdale's** (⊠ 900 N. Michigan Ave., ☎ 312/440–4460). For couture clothing don't miss the tony **Neiman Marcus** (⊠ 737 N. Michigan Ave., ☎ 312/642–5900). **Saks Fifth Avenue** (⊠ Chicago Place, 700 N. Michigan Ave., ☎ 312/944–6500) is a must for those in search of high style.

Specialty Stores

MUSIC

Jazz Record Mart (⊠ 444 N. Wabash Ave., ☎ 312/222–1467) stocks a major collection of records, compact discs, and tapes, including many rare, historic jazz and blues recordings and obscure imports. **Tower Records and Video** (⊠ 2301 N. Clark St., ☎ 773/477–5994) provides one-stop shopping for every musical taste under the sun.

Side Trip to Oak Park

Arriving and Departing

Take I–290 west to Harlem Avenue and exit from the left lane. Turn right at the top of the ramp, head north on Harlem Avenue to Chicago Avenue, turn right, and proceed to Lake Street.

What to See and Do

Founded in the 1850s, just west of the Chicago border, Oak Park is one of Chicago's oldest suburbs and a living museum of Prairie School residential architecture. The **Frank Lloyd Wright Home and Studio** (⊠ 951 Chicago Ave., corner of Forest Ave., ☎ 708/848–1976) was built in 1889 and restored after a long period of neglect by a group of citizens working with the National Trust for Historic Preservation. The poured-concrete **Unity Temple** (✉ 875 Lake St., ☎ 708/383–8873), which Frank Lloyd Wright designed in 1905, was the architect's first public building. Learn about Ernest Hemingway's first 20 years at the **Ernest Hemingway Museum** (✉ 200 N. Oak Park Ave., ☎ 708/848–2222), closed Monday through Thursday. The **Ernest Hemingway Birthplace** (✉ 339 N. Oak Park Ave., ☎ 708/848–2222), closed Monday, Tuesday, and Thursday, is the Victorian home where the Nobel Prize–winning author was born in 1899. The **Oak Park Visitors Center** (✉ 158 N. Forest Ave., ☎ 708/848–1500 or 888/625–7275) sells tour tickets and provides further information on the area.

Side Trip to Baha'i House of Worship

Arriving and Departing
Take Lake Shore Drive north until it ends at Hollywood, then turn right onto Sheridan Road and follow it about 10 mi.

What to See and Do
Baha'i House of Worship (✉ 100 Linden Ave., Wilmette, ☎ 847/853–2300) is a lovely nine-sided building whose wealth of architectural styles and icons from the world's religions symbolizes unity. The symmetry and harmony of the building are paralleled in the formal gardens that surround it.

Side Trip to Woodstock

Arriving and Departing
Take I–90 west and exit on Route 47 going north. Make a left on Calhoun Street and then a right on Dean Street.

What to See and Do
Woodstock, 65 mi north of Chicago, is a Victorian oasis set in rolling countryside. The city square, lined with antiques stores and restaurants, is home to summer band concerts and ice cream socials. Most of *Groundhog Day,* starring Bill Murray, was filmed here. The **Woodstock Opera House** (✉ 121 Van Buren St., ☎ 815/338–5300), constructed in 1890, was restored to its original ornate style in 1977. Orson Welles and Paul Newman cut their teeth here, and the facility still houses musical and theatrical productions. The **Old Court House Arts Center** (✉ 101 N. Johnson St., ☎ 815/338–4525), built in 1857, contains gallery space that showcases area artists' works. In the basement is the former jail, now the **Tavern on the Square** restaurant (☎ 815/334–9540); diners can eat Tuesday through Sunday in the old cell blocks. The center is closed Monday through Wednesday. The **Chester Gould–Dick Tracy Museum** (☎ 815/338–8281), in the Old Court House Arts Center (☞ *above*), displays the artwork of Chester Gould, the creator of the Dick Tracy comic strip, who lived and worked in Woodstock. It, too, is closed Monday through Wednesday. The **Woodstock Chamber of Commerce** (✉ 136 Cass St., 60018, ☎ 815/338–2436) has more information on the area.

GALENA AND NORTHWESTERN ILLINOIS

The tiny town of Galena (population: 3,600) has beautifully preserved pre–Civil War architecture, with houses in Federal, Italianate, and Gothic Revival styles; a large concentration of antiques shops; and (rare in the Midwest) hilly terrain. There's good biking, cross-country skiing, fishing, hunting, and camping in the region.

Lead mining took off here in the 1820s, and Galena had a near-monopoly on the shipping of ore down the Mississippi until the railroad came through in 1854. A depression later that decade and then the Civil War disrupted the lead trade and sent the city into an economic decline from which it never recovered. As a result, Galena today looks much as it did in the 1850s. Galena's other claim to fame is its location as a home of Ulysses S. Grant, commander of the Union Army in the Civil War and later the 18th president of the United States.

The region surrounding Galena is dotted with tiny towns that have been similarly bypassed by the 20th century. Among their offbeat charms are an antique-tractor museum (in Stockton) and the world's largest mallard hatchery (in Hanover). Stockton is also a time capsule of turn-of-the-century architecture, and much of Mount Carroll is registered as a National Historic District.

Visitor Information

Galena/Jo Daviess County: Chamber of Commerce (⊠ 101 Bouthillier St., Galena 61036, ☎ 815/777–0203 or 800/747–9377).

Arriving and Departing

By Car

From Chicago take I–90 86 mi to Rockford, then Route 20 West 81 mi to Galena. From Iowa pick up Route 20 at Dubuque and continue 16 mi east across the Mississippi.

Exploring Galena and Northwestern Illinois

In Galena the **Ulysses S. Grant Home** (⊠ 500 Bouthillier St., ☎ 815/777–0248), built in 1860 in the Italianate bracketed style, was presented to Grant in 1865 by Galena residents in honor of his service to the Union. The family lived there until Grant's victory in the 1868 presidential election. In 1904 Grant's children gave the house to the city of Galena. Now a state historic site, the house has been meticulously restored to its 1868 appearance.

The heart of the **Belvedere Mansion and Gardens** (⊠ 1008 Park Ave., ☎ 815/777–0747) is the 1857 Italianate mansion built for a steamboat magnate. It has been lavishly furnished by the current owners in a fashion that some locals consider gaudy; accoutrements include the famous green drapes from the movie *Gone with the Wind* and furnishings from Liberace's estate. The mansion is closed November through March.

The **Galena/Jo Daviess County Historical Society & Museum** (⊠ 211 S. Bench St., ☎ 815/777–9129) provides interesting background on the area. A large Civil War exhibit shows the effect of the war on Galena's development. Display cases house period dolls, toys, clothing, and household artifacts.

Galena's oldest house is the 1826 **Dowling House** (⊠ 220 Diagonal St., ☎ 815/777–1250). The **Toy Soldier Collection** (⊠ 245 N. Main St., ☎ 815/777–0383) contains two floors of antique toy soldiers and military miniatures. **Galena Trolley Tours** (⊠ 314 S. Main St., ☎ 815/777–1248) offers tours of the town.

A huge swath of rolling countryside east of town, the **Galena Territory** started as a vacation-home development in the early 1980s but has taken on a life of its own as a recreation area. Hunting, fishing, and golf are popular. Watch out for deer on the back roads; they're everywhere.

Mallards outnumber people 200 to 1 in **Hanover,** southeast of Galena, off Route 20 on Route 84. The **Whistling Wings Hatchery** (⊠ 113 Washington St., ☎ 815/591–3512) has some 200,000 mallards and offers tours by appointment. **Savanna,** on Route 84 along the Mississippi, has a number of large, well-preserved 19th-century houses. In **Mount Carroll,** east of Savanna on Route 52, rolling hills and gracious 19th-century frame and masonry buildings recall a small New England town, complete with town square. The **Campbell Center for Historic Preservation** (⊠ 203 E. Seminary St., ☎ 815/244–1173) has workshops on architectural and fine arts preservation.

Stockton, about 30 mi east of Galena on Route 20, is Illinois's highest town, at 1,000 ft; the business district preserves many of the lacy, cupola-topped structures beloved by the Victorians. At **Arlo's Tractor Collection/Museum** (⊠ 7871 S. Ridge Rd., ☎ 815/947–2593) there are 60 restored antique tractors, all in working order. The museum is closed November through April; tours are by appointment only.

Dining and Lodging

Galena-area restaurant fare runs to hearty steaks, burgers, and ribs. Several bakeries along Galena's Main Street offer tempting cookies and pastries. A stay in one of the area's 40-odd B&Bs is almost de rigueur; some are right in town, whereas others are in the Galena Territory or other rustic outlying areas. The chamber of commerce (☞ Visitor Information, *above*) has a complete list of B&Bs and other types of lodging; it also keeps track of vacancies. For price ranges *see* Charts 1 (B) and 2 (A) *in* On the Road with Fodor's.

East Dubuque

$$ ✕ **Timmerman's Supper Club,** a swanky restaurant across the parking lot from Timmerman's Lodge and under separate ownership, has spectacular views, rib-eye steaks, and DJs on weekends. ⊠ *7777 Timmerman Dr.,* ☎ *815/747–3316. AE, D, MC, V.*

$–$$ 🖼 **Timmerman's Lodge.** Perched on a bluff above the Mississippi River, this modern complex is popular with riverboat gamblers in neighboring Dubuque, Iowa. Most of the rooms are 1980s Holiday Inn style, but a few have antique furnishings and decor. ⊠ *7777 Timmerman Dr., 61025,* ☎ *815/747–3181 or 800/336–3181,* ℻ *815/747–6556. 74 rooms. Restaurant, sports bar, pool, sauna. AE, D, MC, V.*

Galena

$$–$$$ ✕ **El Dorado.** This Galena gem offers outstanding, unusual prepara-
★   tions, using many organically grown ingredients and free-range meats. A Southwest motif prevails in the lofted space with exposed brick walls. Wild game specials include a mixed grill of locally raised venison, Texas antelope, and wild boar sausage. ⊠ *219 N. Main St.,* ☎ *815/ 777–1224. Reservations required. DC, MC, V. Closed Tues., and Wed. Sept.–May. No lunch.*

$$ ✕ **Cafe Italia.** Featured in the movie *Field of Dreams,* this cozy Italian restaurant done in wood and tile serves reliable versions of minestrone, lasagna, veal parmigiana, and other standards. ⊠ *301 N. Main St.,* ☎ *815/777–0033. AE, D, DC, MC, V.*

$$–$$$ ✕🖼 **Chestnut Mountain Resort.** Perched on a bank of the Mississippi, 8 mi southeast of downtown Galena, the main building has a Swiss chalet look. The bedrooms, decorated in woods and florals, overlook the ski slopes. The dining room, with a spectacular view of the river, offers adequate steak-and-burger fare. ⊠ *8700 W. Chestnut Rd., 61036,* ☎ *815/777–1320 or 800/397–1320,* ℻ *815/777–1068. 119 rooms. Restaurant, bar, indoor pool, tennis courts, mountain bikes, downhill skiing. AE, D, DC, MC, V.*

$$–$$$ ✕🏨 **DeSoto House Hotel.** Opened in 1855, the DeSoto House served as presidential campaign headquarters for Ulysses S. Grant, and Lincoln really did sleep here. The spacious rooms are furnished in a style reminiscent of the 1860s. The stately Generals' Restaurant serves straightforward steaks, chops, and seafood; the Courtyard Restaurant is open for breakfast and lunch. ✉ *230 S. Main St., 61036,* ☎ *815/ 777–0090 or 800/343–6562,* FAX *815/777–9529. 55 rooms. 2 restaurants, pub. AE, D, DC, MC, V.*

Galena Territory

$$$$ ✕🏨 **Eagle Ridge Inn and Resort.** This rustic yet elegant establishment calls itself the "inn resort for golf," but golf is just the beginning of this plush complex on 6,800 acres. Guest rooms are spacious, with sleeping and sitting areas done in dark woods and floral fabrics; all have views of lake or woodland. The formal Woodlands restaurant offers excellent American cuisine. ✉ *444 Eagle Ridge Dr., Galena 61036,* ☎ *815/777–2444 or 800/892–2269,* FAX *815/777–4502. 80 rooms; 320 condominiums, town houses, and homes. Restaurant, indoor pool, 4 golf courses, exercise room, horseback riding, boating, cross-country skiing, children's programs. AE, D, DC, MC, V.*

Motels

🏨 **Best Western Quiet House Suites** (✉ Rte. 20E, Galena 61036, ☎ 815/777–2577, FAX 815/777–0584), 42 suites, pool, exercise room; *$$$.* 🏨 **Palace Motel** (✉ 11383 Rte. 20W, Galena 61036, ☎ 815/777–2043, FAX 815/777–8113), 64 rooms; *$$.* 🏨 **Grant Hills Motel** (✉ Rte. 20E, Galena 61036, ☎ 815/777–2116), 35 rooms, pool, playground; *$$.*

Nightlife

The **Depot Theater** (✉ 314 S. Main St., ☎ 815/777–1248), at the Galena Trolley Depot, presents cabaret-style theater in a candlelighted space. Shows tend to be historical in nature, such as Jim Post's *Mark Twain and the Laughing River.*

20 West (✉ 334 Spring St., ☎ 815/777–4259), a jazz bar and coffeehouse, has live entertainment in a room full of overstuffed sofas, armchairs, and board games.

Outdoor Activities and Sports

Biking
Hilly back roads around Galena offer challenging bicycling. The **Old Stagecoach Trail** runs parallel to Route 20, winding from Lena through Apple River and Warren to Galena. **Chestnut Mountain Resort** (☞ Dining and Lodging, *above*) rents mountain bikes, or try Dubuque, Iowa. The chamber of commerce (☞ Visitor Information, *above*) has maps.

Fishing
Licenses can be purchased at marinas, bait shops, hardware stores, and other outlets, or contact the **Illinois Bureau of Tourism** (☞ Statewide Visitor Information, *above*) or the **Illinois Department of Natural Resources** (✉ 2612 Locust St., Sterling 61081, ☎ 815/625–2968).

Golf
Apple Canyon Lake Golf Course (✉ 14A40 Canyon Club Dr., Apple Canyon Lake, ☎ 815/492–2477), nine holes. **Eagle Ridge Inn and Resort,** in Galena Territory (☞ Dining and Lodging, *above*), one 9-hole, two 18-hole, and a championship 18-hole course. **Lacoma Golf Course** (✉ 8080 Timmerman Dr., East Dubuque, ☎ 815/747–3874), two 9-hole and one 18-hole course.

Hiking and Backpacking

Mississippi Palisades State Park (✉ 16327A Rte. 84N, Savanna, ☎ 815/273–2731), about 30 mi south of Galena, has hiking trails with river views and nature preserves with accessible lookouts. More cliffs and canyons, in addition to five hiking trails, can be found at **Apple River Canyon State Park** (✉ 8763 E. Canyon Rd., north of Rte. 20 near Stockton, ☎ 815/745–3302).

Horseback Riding

Shenandoah Riding Center (✉ Galena Territory, 200 N. Brodrecht Rd., off Rte. 20E, Galena, ☎ 815/777–2373) has lessons, trails, and hay and sleigh rides.

Ski Areas

Cross-Country

Eagle Ridge Inn and Resort (☞ Dining and Lodging, *above*) maintains more than 35 mi of groomed trails. **Lacoma Golf Course** (☞ Golf *in* Outdoor Activities and Sports, *above*) opens its 260-acre course to skiers, but you have to break your own trails. **Mississippi Palisades State Park** (☞ Hiking and Backpacking *in* Outdoor Activities and Sports, *above*) also has marked trails.

Downhill

It's not the Alps, or even the Catskills, but if you want downhill skiing in Illinois, try **Chestnut Mountain Resort** (☞ Dining and Lodging, *above*), with 19 runs that overlook the Mississippi.

Shopping

Galena's Main Street is lined with more than 20 antiques stores and art galleries, plus a variety of boutiques, crafts shops, restaurants, and bakeries. There are more good antiquing and many artists' studios in **Stockton, Warren,** and **Elizabeth.**

ELSEWHERE IN ILLINOIS

Springfield

Arriving and Departing

Loop I–55 runs north–south through the city. I–72 comes from Champaign and Decatur to the east. The Amtrak route from Chicago to St. Louis stops in Springfield.

What to See and Do

Illinois's capital, Springfield has perhaps the highest concentration anywhere of sites dedicated to Abraham Lincoln, among them the **Lincoln Home National Historic Site** (✉ 426 S. 7th St., ☎ 217/492–4150), the only home Lincoln ever owned, now at the center of a restored four-block historic area. Springfield's Oak Ridge Cemetery is home to the free **Lincoln Tomb State Historic Site** (✉ 1500 N. Monument Ave., ☎ 217/782–2717), the final resting place for Lincoln, Mary Todd, and three of their four sons. On Tuesday nights during the summer, catch the Civil War Retreat Ceremony held at the tomb. The **Illinois Vietnam Veterans Memorial** (☎ 217/782–2717), dedicated in 1988, is also at Oak Ridge Cemetery.

The **Lincoln-Herndon Law Offices** (✉ 6th and Adams Sts., ☎ 217/785–7960) provide glimpses into Lincoln's life and career before he became president. The **Old State Capitol** (✉ 5th and Adams Sts., ☎ 217/785–7960), where Lincoln delivered his "House Divided" speech and where he lay in state before burial, has been restored to the way it looked during Lincoln's legislative years. **Lincoln's New Salem State Historic Site** (✉ Rte. 97 near Petersburg, ☎ 217/632–4000), which lies about 20 mi northwest of Springfield, is a reconstructed village where Lincoln spent his early adulthood; in summer volunteers in period dress re-create village life.

Aside from Lincolniana, Springfield also boasts the **Dana-Thomas House** (✉ 301 E. Lawrence Ave., ☎ 217/782–6776), built by Frank Lloyd Wright from 1902 to 1904 for a local socialite and now a state historic site. Elaborately restored in the late 1980s, it's among the most perfectly preserved examples of early Wright architecture, art glass, and furniture. It's open Wednesday through Sunday.

The **Springfield Convention and Visitors Bureau** (✉ 109 N. 7th St., 62701, ☎ 217/789–2360 or 800/545–7300) has information on area attractions.

Dining and Lodging

$$$ ✕ **Gumbo Ya Ya's.** This creole and Cajun restaurant offers live entertainment along with thick, spicy gumbo, hearty jambalaya, shrimp étouffée, and blackened steak and seafood. The view from the 30th floor is the best in town. ✉ *Springfield Hilton, 700 E. Adams St.,* ☎ *217/789–1530. AE, D, DC, MC, V. No dinner Sun.*

$$ ✕ **Cafe Brio.** Mexican cuisine with Caribbean and Mediterranean influences makes for such unusual dishes as chiles *rellenos* stuffed with chicken and plantains, or tacos filled with shrimp and *chipotle* chiles. Margaritas are made with fresh lime juice. ✉ *524 E. Monroe St.,* ☎ *217/544–0574. AE, MC, V. No dinner Sun.*

$$$ ✕🏨 **Springfield Hilton.** The 30-story hotel has good city views and spacious rooms, decorated in grays and maroons. In the heart of downtown, it's within walking distance of Lincoln historical sites. ✉ *700 E. Adams St., 62701,* ☎ *217/789–1530,* FAX *217/789–0709. 367 rooms. Restaurant, café, pub, indoor pool, health club. AE, D, DC, MC, V.*

$$ ✕🏨 **Mansion View Inn & Suites.** Across the street from the historic Governor's Mansion, the hotel is tastefully decorated, with warm public areas. The smallish rooms with motel-like outdoor entrances have cherry-wood furniture and rich fabrics; some have Jacuzzis. ✉ *529 S. 4th St., 62701,* ☎ *217/544–7411 or 800/252–1083,* FAX *217/544–6211. 93 rooms. Restaurant, free parking. AE, D, DC, MC, V.*

Riverboat Gambling

In recent years casino-style riverboat gambling has become one of the most popular attractions outside Chicago. Replicas of 19th-century riverboats stretch along the Mississippi River from northern Illinois to the southern part of the state. There are no betting limits in Illinois, and no one under 21 is allowed in gaming areas.

Aurora

ARRIVING AND DEPARTING

Aurora is about 40 mi west of Chicago. From Chicago take I–290 west to Route 88 and that west again to Route 31. Proceed south to Galena Boulevard and turn left.

WHAT TO SEE AND DO

Hollywood Casino–Aurora (✉ 1 New York St. Bridge, ☎ 708/801–7000) has two four-tiered casino boats on the Fox River. As suggested by its name, the casino is decorated with Hollywood memorabilia from movies such as *Batman* and *Forrest Gump*. The pavilion houses two full-service restaurants, a buffet, and a sandwich shop. The **Paramount Arts Centre** (✉ 23 E. Galena Blvd., ☎ 708/896–6666), one block south of the Hollywood Casino pavilion, has hosted the likes of Frank Sinatra, Willie Nelson, and Liza Minnelli.

Joliet

ARRIVING AND DEPARTING
Joliet is about 45 mi southeast of downtown Chicago, off I–55S.

WHAT TO SEE AND DO
Several casino riverboats are docked on the Des Plaines River in Joliet. The two triple-deck boats of **Harrah's Casino** (✉ 151 N. Joliet St., ☎ 800/427–7247) float in the heart of downtown. The pavilion includes a steak house, buffet, coffee shop, and snack area and offers weekend entertainment. The **Empress River Casino** (✉ Off Rte. 6 on Empress Dr., ☎ 708/345–6789) consists of two boats, one with two gaming levels, the other with three levels; both have the full assortment of games of chance. The casino is in the southwest corner of Joliet, 50 mi from downtown Chicago.

INDIANA

By Peggy
Ammerman
Bowman

Capital	Indianapolis
Population	5,840,500
Motto	The Crossroads of America
State Bird	Cardinal
State Flower	Peony
Postal Abbreviation	IN

Statewide Visitor Information

Indiana Department of Commerce, Division of Tourism (✉ 1 N. Capitol Ave., Suite 700, Indianapolis 46204, ☎ 317/232–8860 or 800/289–6646).

Scenic Drives

Charming 19th-century river towns front the **Ohio River Scenic Route** from Madison to Aurora on Routes 56 and 156. Trace Indiana's early frontier history along the **Chief White Eyes Trail** from Madison to Dillsboro on Route 62. The 50-mi **Lincoln Heritage Trail–George Rogers Clark Trail,** on Routes 462, 62, and 162 from Corydon to Gentryville, takes a gentle ride across southern hill country. From Newburgh to Sulphur the **Hoosier Heritage Trail Scenic Route** follows the Ohio River's squiggly course, then cuts north through state forests on Route 66. Indiana's 40-mi portion of the 1,100-mi **Lake Michigan Circle Tour** around the second largest of the Great Lakes follows I–90 and I–94 from Illinois to Michigan.

National and State Parks

National Parks

A columned, circular stone building at **George Rogers Clark National Historical Park** (✉ 401 S. 2nd St., Vincennes 47591, ☎ 812/882–1776) pays tribute to Clark's campaign to wrest Fort Sackville from the

★ British during the Revolutionary War. At **Indiana Dunes National Lakeshore** (✉ 1100 N. Mineral Springs Rd., Porter 46304, ☎ 219/926–7561) dune grasses, arctic bearberries, and prickly pear cacti mingle along more than 20 mi of Lake Michigan shoreline and inland marshes. Walk in the footsteps of young Abraham Lincoln at the **Lincoln Boyhood National Memorial** (✉ Box 1816, Lincoln City 47552, ☎ 812/937–4541). Ridge-topped trails at the 188,000-acre **Hoosier National Forest** (✉ 811 Constitution Ave., Bedford 47421, ☎ 812/275–5987) afford glimpses of quiet lakes and pass through dense woodlands in the state's south-central corridor, which stretches to the banks of the Ohio River.

State Parks

Indiana's 21 state parks are operated by the **Department of Natural Resources** (✉ 402 W. Washington St., Indianapolis 46204, ☎ 317/232–4124 or 800/622–4931 in IN) and are open daily year-round. **Falls of the Ohio** (✉ 201 W. Riverside Dr., Clarksville 47129, ☎ 812/280–9970) showcases 220 acres of the world's largest naturally exposed Devonian fossil beds. At **Spring Mill** (✉ Rte. 60, Box 376, Mitchell 47446, ☎ 812/849–4129) tour a reconstructed 1800s pioneer village and gristmill on its original site, hike an 80-acre tract of virgin hardwood forest, then explore two caves on foot or by boat. Just 15 mi apart, **Turkey Run** (✉ Rte. 1, Box 164, Marshall 47859, ☎ 317/597–2635) and **Shades**

(✉ Rte. 1, Box 72, Waveland 47989, ☎ 317/435–2810) both skirt Sugar Creek and are criss-crossed by steep, glacially scoured sandstone ravines blanketed in moss and ferns. A bird's-eye view of **Chain O' Lakes** (✉ 2355 E. 75 St., Albion 46701, ☎ 219/636–2654) glimpses eight kettle lakes resembling dark blue ink squirts linked by narrow channels. There are more than 212 acres of water, along with 7 mi of shoreline and woodlands.

INDIANAPOLIS

In the 1980s Indianapolis was nicknamed Cinderella by *Newsweek* and *Travel Holiday* because of its surprising health at a time when many other midwestern cities were suffering from unemployment and declining population. The road to prosperity began in 1970, when Indianapolis merged with surrounding Marion County to create a consolidated governmental organization. Called Unigov, this city-county dynamo effected its improvements through a strategic partnership of public- and private-sector interests. Helping to fuel the city's newfound vitality, an internationally recognized collection of topflight sports facilities gave Indianapolis the moniker Amateur Sports Capital of the World. At the same time a dazzling assortment of museums, performance halls, and stretches of spruced-up green space filled in the center of the downtown grid. In 1995 the framework was finally completed with the unveiling of Circle Centre, a swanky, villagelike enclosed complex of shops and entertainment attractions set behind historic storefront facades.

Visitor Information

City Center (✉ 201 S. Capitol Ave., 46225, ☎ 317/237–5200 or 800/468–4639). **Convention & Visitors Association** (✉ 1 RCA Dome, Suite 110, 46225, ☎ 317/639–4282 or 800/556–4639).

Arriving and Departing

By Bus

Greyhound Bus Terminal (✉ 127 N. Illinois St., ☎ 317/267–3071 or 800/231–2222).

By Car

With more segments of interstate highway (I–65, I–69, I–70, I–74, and I–465) intersecting here than anywhere else in the country, Indianapolis is indisputably a driving city. Car rentals are available at major hotels and at the airport.

By Plane

The **Indianapolis International Airport** (☎ 317/487–7243) is served by major and commuter airlines. The trip from the airport to downtown or to the west side of town is about 20–25 minutes. To the other sides of town it's a 30- to 45-minute drive. By taxi or limo, the cost is $8–$20 to downtown, $22–$26 elsewhere. **Indy Connection** (☎ 317/241–2522) offers a special rate of $8 per passenger.

By Train

Indianapolis Union Station (✉ 350 S. Illinois St., ☎ 317/263–0550 or 800/872–7245) has Amtrak service.

Getting Around Indianapolis

It's easy to get around, and the center is comfortable for walking. Address numbering is logical, based on a rectangular coordinate system, with each block roughly equal to 100. The intersection of Washington and Meridian streets, just south of Monument Circle, is the zero point for numbering in all directions. **Metro buses** (☎ 317/632–1900 or 317/635–3344) run from 4:45 AM to 11:45 PM on heavily traveled routes, with shorter schedules in the suburbs. Fares (75¢, $1 during rush hour) are payable upon boarding. **Metro Taxi** (☎ 317/634–1111) and **Yellow Cab** (☎ 317/487–7777) are radio dispatched; call ahead to be sure of getting a cab, unless you're at the airport or downtown. The fare is $1.25 for the first ⅓ mile and 36¢ for each additional ⅕ mile.

Exploring Indianapolis

Attractions extend into a wider metropolitan area than the original square-mile downtown area. Many of the museums, arts and entertainment venues, and shopping areas, all generally within a 45-minute drive, are scattered around, both downtown and beyond in the contiguous counties.

Downtown

Monument Circle is Indianapolis's centerpiece. Avenues radiate from it across the grid of streets, as in Washington, D.C. (Indianapolis architect Alexander Ralston was a protégé of Pierre L'Enfant). At the center is the **Soldiers' and Sailors' Monument,** a 284-ft spire crowned by the 30-ft bronze statue *Victory,* better known as *Miss Indiana.* A newly renovated observation area offers a panoramic view. Overlooking the monument is the **Hilbert Circle Theatre,** a vintage 1916 movie palace that is now the home of the Indianapolis Symphony Orchestra (☎ 317/262–1100), with tours by appointment. Also on the circle is the city's oldest church, **Christ Church Cathedral** (☎ 317/636–4577), an 1857 English Gothic country–style masterpiece, with a spire, steep gables, bell tower, and arched Tiffany windows; tours are also available here by appointment.

Assemble a meal of ethnic and deli fare at the vintage-1886 **City Market** and savor it amid the sounds of lunchtime entertainment most Fridays on the outdoor terrace. ⊠ *222 E. Market St.,* ☎ *317/634–9266. Closed Sun.*

The **Indiana State Museum,** in the Old City Hall, showcases the state's history and culture. ⊠ *202 N. Alabama St.,* ☎ *317/232–1637.*

The circa-1929 Gothic Tudor–style Masonic **Scottish Rite Cathedral** contains a 54-bell carillon and a 7,000-pipe organ. ⊠ *650 N. Meridian St.,* ☎ *317/262–3100. Closed weekends.*

The massive limestone-and-marble **Indiana World War Memorial** pays tribute to fallen Hoosier veterans of World War I, World War II, the Korean War, and the Vietnam War. ⊠ *431 N. Meridian,* ☎ *317/232–7615.*

Housed in a contemporary adobe building, the **Eiteljorg Museum** of American Indians and Western Art displays works by Frederic Remington and Georgia O'Keeffe, among others. ⊠ *500 W. Washington St.,* ☎ *317/636–9378. Closed Mon. Sept.–May.*

One of only nine in the nation, **IMAX 3D Theater** (☎ 317/262–8080) is the newest attraction at White River State Park, which runs along a downtown waterway.

The **Indiana Convention Center & RCA Dome,** reaching 19 stories and one of just six major air-supported domed stadiums in the world, is the home of the NFL's Indianapolis Colts and the newly updated National Track & Field Hall of Fame ⊠ *1 N. Capitol Ave.,* ☎ *317/262–3452.*

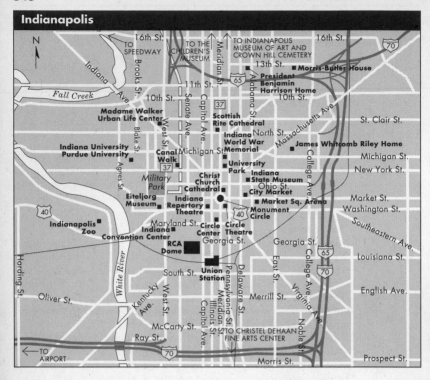

The Romanesque Union Station is a restored 1888 landmark with magnificent stained glass in a vaulted, skylighted ceiling. ⊠ *39 Jackson Pl.,* ☎ *317/267–0701.*

Ornate Victorian furnishings, political mementos, and period ball gowns of the nation's 23rd president and first lady fill the 1875 **President Benjamin Harrison Home.** ⊠ *1230 N. Delaware St.,* ☎ *317/631–1898.*

The **Morris-Butler House**, a beautifully restored 1865 Second Empire–style gem, is filled with fancy furnishings, dazzling chandeliers, and rich woodwork. ⊠ *1204 N. Park Ave.,* ☎ *317/636–5409. Closed Mon. and 1st 2 wks of Jan.*

In the historic **Lockerbie Square** neighborhood, the **James Whitcomb Riley Museum Home,** acclaimed as one of nation's finest examples of Victoriana, remains almost as the noted poet left it. ⊠ *528 Lockerbie St.,* ☎ *317/631–5885. Closed Mon. and 1st 2 wks of Jan.*

Midtown/Crosstown

Presenting "Jazz on the Avenue" Friday nights and once frequented by jazz legends Ella Fitzgerald and Wes Montgomery, the 1927 **Madame Walker Urban Life Center** was named for the country's first black female self-made millionaire. ⊠ *617 Indiana Ave.,* ☎ *317/236–2099. Tours by appointment.*

Playscape, the world's largest water clock, a planetarium, IWERKS CineDome Theater, a new science center, and nine other major galleries make up the **Children's Museum of Indianapolis.** Be sure to take a spin on a turn-of-the-century carousel and explore a limestone cave. ⊠ *3000 N. Meridian St.,* ☎ *317/924–5431.*

The **Indianapolis Museum of Art,** a five-pavilion complex and botanical gardens on 152 acres of manicured lawns, houses works by J. M. W.

Turner, the old masters, and the neoimpressionists, along with major Asian, African, and decorative arts collections. ⊠ *1200 W. 38th St.,* ☎ *317/923–1331. Closed Mon.*

At century-old **Crown Hill Cemetery,** the nation's third largest, notorious criminal John Dillinger cozies up to President Benjamin Harrison and a host of American authors. ⊠ *3402 Boulevard Pl.,* ☎ *317/925–8231.*

South Side

The stunning **Christel DeHaan Fine Arts Center** at the University of Indianapolis contains exhibition space and a 500-seat concert hall renowned for its acoustics. ⊠ *1400 E. Hanna Ave.,* ☎ *317/788–3566.*

West Side

The **Indianapolis Motor Speedway Hall of Fame Museum** displays 30 Indy 500–winning cars, as well as classic and antique autos. ⊠ *4790 W. 16th St.,* ☎ *317/484–6747.*

At the **Indiana Medical History Museum** a turn-of-the-century pathology laboratory exhibits 15,000 medical treatment and health-care artifacts. ⊠ *3045 W. Vermont St.,* ☎ *317/635–7329.*

Parks and Gardens

Jog, bike, hike, golf, or participate in water sports at the rustic 4,200-acre **Eagle Creek Park and Nature Preserve** (⊠ 7840 W. 56th St., ☎ 317/293–4828). An exceptionally well-planned network of woodland trails and riverfront boardwalks traverses hilly terrain at **Holliday Park** (⊠ 6349 Springmill Rd., ☎ 317/327–7180). The downtown **Canal Walk,** a 10½-block vestige of the historic 400-mi canal system linking the Great Lakes and the Ohio River, is an urban haven, with benches, fountains, and wide walkways lining both sides of the canal.

What to See and Do with Children

The **Children's** and **Speedway museums** and **Holliday Park** (☞ Parks and Gardens, *above*), with its jumbo-size playground, are essential destinations for families; so is the **Indianapolis Zoo** (⊠ 1200 W. Washington St., ☎ 317/630–2001), with its 3,000 animals and whale and dolphin pavilion. Stop by **Hook's American Drug Store Museum** (⊠ 1180 E. 38th St., ☎ 317/924–5886) at the Indiana State Fairgrounds and sip a frothy old-fashioned ice cream soda.

Dining

For price ranges *see* Chart 1 (A) *in* On the Road with Fodor's.

$$$$ ✕ **Benvenuti.** This elegant downtown restaurant specializes in contemporary northern Italian cuisine. Homemade lobster ravioli, grilled veal chops, and legendary cream of roasted bell pepper soup are specialties. ⊠ *36 S. Pennsylvania St.,* ☎ *317/633–4915. AE, D, DC, MC, V. Reservations essential.*

$$$$ ✕ **Peter's Restaurant & Bar.** Its creatively prepared regional cuisine changes with the seasons but may include pomegranate-glazed Indiana duckling accompanied by sweet potato custard and mustard greens. Chilean sea bass is seared and basted with a spicy orange-chili marinade. ⊠ *8505 Keystone Crossing,* ☎ *317/465–1165. AE, D, MC, V.*

$$$ ✕ **Snax/Something Different.** Served amid industrial-chic decor, tapas at Snax are just enough to whet an appetite for dinner, which is served next door at Something Different. Menus change monthly and feature inventive cuisine such as grilled halibut with wilted spinach, fried lily root, and lemon-caper cream. ⊠ *2411 E. 65th St.,* ☎ *317/257–7973.*

$ ✕ **Charlie & Barney's Bar & Grill.** This chain of upbeat eateries is known for its chili, which comes in five variations, including sirloin steak chili and chili pie. ✉ *1130 W. 86th St.,* ☎ *317/844–2399;* ✉ *723 Broad Ripple Ave.,* ☎ *317/253–5263;* ✉ *225 E. Ohio St.,* ☎ *317/637–5851;* ✉ *Merchants Plaza, 101 W. Washington St.,* ☎ *317/636–3101. AE, D, DC, MC, V.*

$ ✕ **Shapiro's Delicatessen & Cafeteria.** The strawberry cheesecake and corned beef sandwiches piled high on rye are signature items at this nationally known deli, an Indianapolis institution since 1904. ✉ *808 S. Meridian St.,* ☎ *317/631–4041;* ✉ *2370 W. 86th St.,* ☎ *317/872–7255. Reservations not accepted. No credit cards.*

Lodging

For price ranges *see* Chart 2 (A) *in* On the Road with Fodor's.

$$$ 🏨 **Canterbury Hotel.** At this 60-year-old hostelry, cozy and luxuriously
★   renovated guest rooms are equipped with armoires, queen-size four-poster beds, and elegant baths. A covered skywalk leads to Circle Centre. ✉ *123 S. Illinois St., 46225,* ☎ *317/634–3000 or 800/538–8186,* FAX *317/685–2519. 99 rooms. Restaurant, bar. AE, D, DC, MC, V.*

$$$ 🏨 **Omni Severin Hotel.** Across from historic Union Station, this hotel has crystal chandeliers, a marble staircase, and cast-iron balustrades recalling the hotel's 1913 origins. Guest rooms are a blend of traditional and Mediterranean styles. ✉ *40 W. Jackson Pl., 46225,* ☎ *317/634–6664 or 800/843–6664,* FAX *317/687–3619. 423 rooms. Restaurant, bar, indoor pool. AE, D, DC, MC, V.*

$$ 🏨 **University Place Conference Center & Hotel.** Rooms in this hotel on the shared campus of Indiana and Purdue universities are handsomely appointed, with desks, easy chairs, and 18th-century reproduction furnishings. ✉ *850 W. Michigan St., 46202,* ☎ *317/269–9000 or 800/627–2700,* FAX *317/231–5168. 276 rooms. 2 restaurants, bar. AE, D, DC, MC, V.*

$$ 🏨 **Radisson Plaza & Suite Hotel Indianapolis.** This upscale high-rise hotel is conveniently located in the middle of the north-side Keystone at the Crossing shopping and entertainment complex (☞ Shopping, *below*), a 40-minute drive from downtown or the airport. A covered skywalk connects to 100 shops and restaurants. ✉ *8787 Keystone Crossing 46240,* ☎ *317/846–2700 or 800/333–3333,* FAX *317/574–6780. 552 rooms. Restaurant, lounge. AE, D, DC, MC, V.*

$ 🏨 **Holiday Inn Southeast.** This six-story high-rise on the beltway is popular for business and social functions. ✉ *5120 Victory Dr., 46203,* ☎ *317/783–7751,* FAX *317/787–1545. 140 rooms. Restaurant, lounge. AE, D, DC, MC, V.*

Nightlife and the Arts

Nightlife

Pub crawling is best in out-of-the-way neighborhoods such as **Broad Ripple Village** (☞ Shopping, *below*). Cruise the off-beat **Massachusetts Avenue Art District** scene for interesting art galleries, unusual shops, and neighborhood eateries and taverns. Christmas lights and checkered flags are year-round decor at the **Chatterbox Tavern** (✉ 435 Massachusetts Ave., ☎ 317/636–0584), where a varied clientele stops by for late-night jazz. On Level 4 of **Circle Centre,** there are nightclubs, nine cinemas, and virtual reality and arcade games.

The Arts

NUVO Newsweekly, Indianapolis Monthly magazine, Friday's edition of the *Indianapolis News,* and the Sunday edition of the *Indianapolis Star* list arts and events. Tickets for plays and concerts can be obtained through **Court Side Tickets** (⊠ 6100 N. Keystone Ave., ☎ 317/254–9500 or 800/627–1334), **TicketMaster** (⊠ 2 W. Washington St., ☎ 317/239–5151), **Tickets Up Front & Travel** (⊠ 1099 N. Meridian St., ☎ 317/633–6400), or **Premium Tickets & Tours** (⊠ 2113 Broad Ripple Ave., ☎ 317/251–0163 or 800/768–0898).

MUSIC

Indianapolis Symphony Orchestra (⊠ 45 Monument Circle, ☎ 317/639–4300) performs at the Hilbert Circle Theatre from September through May and outdoors at Conner Prairie in summer (☞ Hamilton County *in* Side Trips from Indianapolis, *below*).

Forty-five minutes northeast of Indianapolis, **Deer Creek Music Center** (⊠ 12880 E. 146th St., Noblesville, ☎ 317/776–3337 or 317/841–8900) brings top-name pop, jazz, and rock performers to an outdoor facility.

The **Indianapolis Opera** (⊠ 250 E. 38th St., ☎ 317/283–3531) stages productions from its grand opera repertoire along with new works each season.

THEATER

Indiana's only resident professional theater, the **Indiana Repertory Theatre** (⊠ 140 W. Washington St., ☎ 317/635–5252) presents major works in a restored 1917 movie palace downtown.

Beef & Boards Dinner Theatre (⊠ 9301 N. Michigan Rd., ☎ 317/872–9664) stages Broadway shows along with a sumptuous dinner buffet on the northwest side.

Original musical revues are presented at **American Cabaret Theatre** (⊠ 401 E. Michigan, ☎ 317/631–0334).

Spectator Sports

Baseball: Indianapolis Indians (⊠ Victory Field, 501 W. Maryland St., ☎ 317/269–3545).

Basketball: Indiana Pacers (⊠ Market Square Arena, 300 E. Market St., ☎ 317/263–2100).

Football: Indianapolis Colts (⊠ RCA Dome, 100 S. Capitol Ave., Box 535000, ☎ 317/297–7000).

Ice hockey: Indianapolis Ice (⊠ 222 E. Ohio St., Suite 810, ☎ 317/266–1234).

Soccer: Indianapolis Twisters (⊠ 222 E. Ohio St., Suite 800, ☎ 317/231–2870).

Shopping

Downtown, the **Nordstrom** (☎ 317/636–2121) and **Parisian** (☎ 317/971–6200) department stores headline the roster of more than 120 shops at **Circle Centre** (⊠ 49 W. Maryland St., ☎ 317/681–8000). On the north side of town, the **Fashion Mall,** at Keystone at the Crossing (⊠ 9000 Keystone Crossing, ☎ 317/574–4000), is anchored by the upscale **Jacobson's** (☎ 317/574–0088) and **Parisian** (☎ 317/581–8200) department stores. About 20 minutes north of downtown, **Broad Ripple Village** (⊠ 62nd St. at Broad Ripple and College Aves., ☎ 317/251–2782) has art galleries, gift shops, and boutiques.

Side Trips from Indianapolis

Bloomington, Brown County, and Columbus

About an hour's drive south of the capital city on Route 46, the flat expanse of farmland dominating the upper two-thirds of the state gives way to hilly terrain. In **Bloomington,** home of Indiana University, ethnic restaurants, boutiques, galleries, and shops surround the courthouse square and fill the block-long Fountain Square Mall (☎ 812/336–3681), distinguished by its historic storefront facades. For information contact the **Bloomington/Monroe County Convention and Visitors Bureau** (✉ 2855 N. Walnut St., 47404, ☎ 812/334–8900 or 800/800–0037).

Columbus is a forward-thinking city and an architectural mecca dotted with more than 50 contemporary-style structures by world-renowned architects. Contact the **Columbus Area Visitors Center** (✉ Box 1589, 5th and Franklin Sts., 47202, ☎ 812/378–2622 or 800/468–6564) for information.

In picturesque Brown County, the quaint village of **Nashville** was a gathering place for artists in the early 1900s. Today, country-cooking eateries and shops nestle in alongside artists' studios and galleries throughout town. Contact the **Nashville/Brown County Convention and Visitors Bureau** (✉ Box 840, 47448, ☎ 812/988–7303 or 800/753–3255).

Centerville and Richmond

Beginning in the 1820s, historic **Centerville** and **Richmond,** on the Ohio state line, saw as many as 200 wagons pass daily on the National Road, a western immigration trail (now U.S. Highway 40). Today this stretch of road, dubbed Antique Alley, is an antiques lover's paradise, with more than 550 dealers. The **Richmond–Wayne County Convention and Tourism Bureau** (✉ 5701 National Rd. E, 47374, ☎ 317/935–8687 or 800/828–8414) has information on the area. Three forks of the Whitewater River converge in a gorge with scenic vistas, trails, and the stunning **Thistlethwaite Falls** (✉ Richmond Parks & Recreation, ☎ 317/983–7275).

Hamilton County

Towns in this county northeast of downtown were once simply bedroom communities for Indianapolis. But restoration of the stately, mansard-roofed county courthouse in Noblesville coincided with a renaissance of museums, shops, and restaurants. Relive the past at **Conner Prairie** (☎ 317/776–6000), an extensive, re-created 1830s pioneer village complex in Fishers. Contact the **Hamilton County Convention & Visitors Bureau** (✉ 11601 Municipal Dr., Fishers 46038, ☎ 317/598–4444 or 800/776–8687) for information.

Parke County

Dubbed the Covered-Bridge Capital of the World, Parke County has some 30 bridges scattered about within an hour's drive west of Indianapolis (take Route 136). Every October Rockville and nearby towns take part in the weeklong **covered-bridge festival,** with crafts fairs, quilts and antiques shows, and barbecue beef and bean soup dinners. During the **maple syrup festival** in early spring, sugar shacks open their doors for a peek inside. The **Parke County Convention and Visitors Bureau** (✉ Box 165, Rockville 47872, ☎ 317/569–5226) provides details about the area.

Zionsville

Brick streets and Stick-style, early 19th-century wood cottages create a fairy-tale setting. Though just a 30-minute drive from downtown's domed stadiums and shiny new high-rises, Zionsville seems to be perfectly preserved. The state's only officially recognized hunt club is here, along with quaint shops and restaurants. Contact the **Zionsville Visitors Center** (✉ 135 S. Elm St., ☎ 317/873–3836).

SOUTHERN INDIANA

Dense stands of oak, hickory, and maple crown the rolling terrain that dominates southern Indiana. Tucked among the hills and valleys are 19th-century riverfront towns, caves that beg to be explored, and vast stretches of clear blue water.

Visitor Information

Southern Indiana: Clark/Floyd/Harrison Counties Convention and Visitors Bureau (⌷ 540 Marriott Dr., Jeffersonville 47129, ☎ 812/282–6654 or 800/552–3842). **Lincoln Hills Area:** Lincoln Hills/Patoka Lake Association (⌷ Courthouse Annex, Cannelton 47520, ☎ 812/547–7028). **Madison Area:** Visitors Council (⌷ 301 E. Main St., Madison 47250, ☎ 812/265–2956). **Vincennes Area:** Chamber of Commerce (⌷ Box 553, Vincennes 47591, ☎ 812/882–6440). **Evansville and New Harmony:** Evansville Convention and Visitors Bureau (⌷ 623 Walnut St., Evansville 47708, ☎ 812/425–5402 or 800/433–3025).

Arriving and Departing

By Bus

Service between Indianapolis and Vincennes is available on **Greyhound Lines** (☎ 800/231–2222) and **I-V Coaches** (☎ 317/634–3198). **White Star** (☎ 812/265–2662) travels between Madison and Indianapolis.

By Car

The major road through this region is I–64. From Indianapolis take I–70 and U.S. 41 to Vincennes, I–65 and Route 7 to Madison, and I–65 to New Albany. From Louisville, Kentucky, take I–65; from Cincinnati, Ohio, take I–74.

Exploring Southern Indiana

Three-hundred-year-old **Vincennes** brims with history. **Grouseland** (⌷ 3 W. Scott St., ☎ 812/882–2096) was the home of Indiana Territory governor William Henry Harrison. The log-and-mud **Old French House** (⌷ 509 N. 1st St., ☎ 812/885–4173) dates to 1806. In the southwesternmost corner of Indiana, quaint **New Harmony** was the site of two 19th-century utopian communities; contact Historic New Harmony, Inc. (⌷ Box 579, New Harmony 47631, ☎ 812/682–4482) for information.

In the historic Riverside District of **Evansville,** columned mansions such as the **John Augustus Reitz Home** (⌷ 224 S.E. 1st St., ☎ 812/423–3749) overlook the Ohio River. The **Evansville Museum of Arts and Science** (⌷ 411 S.E. Riverside Dr., ☎ 812/425–2406) has American and European art from 1700 to the present, a planetarium, and a reconstructed turn-of-the-century village.

In **Corydon,** Indiana's first capital, browse through 10,000 square ft of antiques in two downtown malls. Corydon's Federal-style **capitol** (⌷ Chestnut and Capitol Sts., ☎ 812/738–4890) is where the state's first constitution was drafted. The **Corydon Scenic Railroad** (⌷ Walnut and Water Sts., ☎ 812/738–8000) makes a 90-minute trip through the countryside. Tour a pioneer village and caverns with waterfalls at **Squire Boone Caverns & Village** (⌷ Box 411, Corydon 47112, ☎ 812/732–4381).

Dubbed the Williamsburg of the Midwest, **Madison** is an antebellum-era town whose entire main street and 100 additional blocks are listed on the National Register of Historic Places. See the gleaming white Greek Revival **James F. D. Lanier Mansion** (⌷ 511 W. 1st St.,

☎ 812/265–3526), whose portico overlooks the Ohio River. Contact the **Madison Area Convention and Visitors Bureau** (✉ 301 E. Main St., ☎ 800/559–2956).

What to See and Do with Children

Holiday World Theme Park and Splashin' Safari Water Park, in Santa Claus (✉ Intersection of Rtes. 162 and 245, ☎ 812/937–4401 or 800/467–2682), has gift shops, museums, musical shows, water rides, and Santa himself. Bengal tigers, elephants, macaws, monkeys, and other exotic creatures inhabit the **Mesker Park Zoo** (✉ 2421 Bement Ave., Evansville, ☎ 812/428–0715).

Dining and Lodging

Southern Indiana is well supplied with roadside motels and hotels, but for the ultimate lodging experience, try one of the many local bed-and-breakfasts in the area. Contact the **Indiana Bed and Breakfast Association** (✉ Box 1127, Goshen 46526). For price ranges see Charts 1 (B) and 2 (B) in On the Road with Fodor's.

Santa Claus

$$$ ✕▥ **Santa's Lodge.** This two-story hostelry resembles a huge barn, with century-old hand-hewn barn timbers supporting the spacious lobby. Christmas decorations, antiques, and touches of cedar and oak deck the halls. ✉ *Box 193, Santa Claus 47579,* ☎ *812/937–1902 or 800/640–7895,* ☏ *812/937–1902. 46 rooms. Restaurant, pool. AE, MC, V.*

Corydon

$$ ▥ **Kintner House Inn.** Once the headquarters of Confederate general John Hunt Morgan, the inn dates to the mid-1800s. ✉ *101 S. Capitol St., at Chestnut St., 47112,* ☎ *812/738–2020. 14 rooms. MC, V.*

New Harmony

$$ ✕▥ **New Harmony Inn.** Set on spacious grounds overlooking a small lake, this inn has a fine restaurant that draws diners from the tristate area. ✉ *506 North St. (Box 581), 47631,* ☎ *812/682–4491 or 800/782–8605,* ☏ *812/682–4491, ext. 329. 99 rooms. 2 restaurants, indoor pool, 2 tennis courts, health club. AE, D, MC, V.*

Outdoor Activities and Sports

Biking

Four routes on the **Hoosier Bikeway System** (✉ Dept. of Natural Resources, 402 W. Washington St., Room W271, Indianapolis 46204, ☎ 317/232–4200) run through this area.

Fishing

At **Patoka Lake** (✉ R.R. 1, Birdseye, ☎ 812/685–2464) and **Markland Dam,** on the Ohio River off Route 156, each season brings record catches of bass, carp, and catfish.

NORTHERN INDIANA

Stretches of shifting dunes and inviting beaches along Lake Michigan give way to a neat grid of lush farmland dotted with Amish communities in northeastern Indiana. The state's second-largest city, Fort Wayne, has lake country to the west and charming Amish towns like Grabill to the northwest and east.

Visitor Information

Amish Land: Elkhart Convention and Visitors Bureau (✉ 219 Caravan Dr., Elkhart 46514, ☏ 219/262–8161 or 800/262–8161). **Fort Wayne:** Convention and Visitors Bureau (✉ 1021 S. Calhoun St., 46802, ☏ 219/424–3700 or 800/767–7752). **Lake Country:** Kosciusko County Convention and Visitors Bureau (✉ 313 S. Buffalo St., Warsaw 46580, ☏ 219/269–6090 or 800/800–6090). **North Coast:** Lake County Convention and Visitors Bureau (✉ 5800 Broadway, Suite S, Merrillville 46410, ☏ 219/980–1617 or 800/255–5253); Porter County Convention and Visitors Bureau (✉ 528 Indian Oak Mall, Chesterton 46304, ☏ 219/926–2255 or 800/283–8687). **South Bend/Mishawaka:** Convention and Visitors Bureau (✉ 401 E. Colfax Ave., South Bend 46634, ☏ 219/234–0079 or 800/392–0051).

Arriving and Departing

By Bus

United Limo, in Osceola (☏ 219/674–6993), provides daily service to and from Chicago. Other service is available on **Greyhound Lines** (✉ 4671 Terminal Dr., South Bend, ☏ 800/231–2222).

By Car

Major east–west roads are I–80/90 and U.S. 12 and 20. Traversing the region north–south are I–65, I–69, and U.S. 31 and 41.

By Plane

The **Michiana Regional Transportation Center** (✉ 4477 Terminal Dr., ☏ 219/233–2185) is served by national and regional carriers.

By Train

South Shore Line (✉ 2702 W. Washington St., South Bend, ☏ 219/233–3111 or 800/356–2079). **Amtrak** (☏ 800/872–7245).

Exploring Northern Indiana

Among the many outdoor areas are the **Indiana Dunes National Lakeshore** (☞ National and State Parks, *above*) and **Gibson Woods Nature Preserve** (✉ Gibson Woods County Park, 6201 Parish Ave., Hammond, ☏ 219/844–3188), a fine specimen of dune and swale topography.

Fans flock to **South Bend** each year to see the **University of Notre Dame**'s Fighting Irish. Be sure to stop by the landmark Golden Dome (☏ 219/239–7367). On the university campus, the **Snite Museum of Art** (☏ 219/631–5466) contains works by Rembrandt, Chagall, and Picasso. Downtown South Bend's **East Race Waterway** (☏ 219/235–9328) attracts kayakers, tubers, and rafters.

The 75-mi corridor from South Bend southeast to Fort Wayne goes through Indiana's **Amish Country. Amish Acres** (✉ Rte. 19, 1600 W. Market St., Nappanee, ☏ 219/773–4188 or 800/800–4942) is a working farm with a restaurant and an inn. The **Borkholder Dutch Village** (✉ County Rd. 101, Nappanee, ☏ 219/773–2828) has more than 350 arts, crafts, and antiques booths. More than 1,000 vendors crowd the open-air **Shipshewana Auction & Flea Market** (✉ Box 185, Rte. 5S, Shipshewana 46565, ☏ 219/768–4129) every Tuesday and Wednesday from May through October. The **Old Bag Factory** (✉ 1100 Chicago Ave., Goshen 46526, ☏ 219/534–2302), a massive redbrick structure dating to 1895, houses 18 shops, including a custom hardwood-furniture maker and a potter. Just outside Fort Wayne, **Grabill** seems caught in a time warp, with Amish buggies hitched up all around town. West of Fort Wayne, hundreds of **kettle lakes,** as well as Lake

Wawasee and Lake Maxinkuckee, attract summer vacationers (☞ Visitor Information, *above*).

What to See and Do with Children

Costumed interpreters recount daily life on a re-created pioneer-era farm at **Buckley Homestead County Park** (⊠ 3606 Belshaw Rd., Lowell, ☎ 219/696–0769). More than 222 species of jungle life, large and small, reside at the lakeside **Washington Park Zoological Gardens** (⊠ Lakefront, Michigan City, ☎ 219/873–1510).

Dining and Lodging

For inn bookings contact the **Indiana Bed and Breakfast Association** (⊠ Box 1127, Goshen 46526). For price ranges *see* Charts 1 (B) and 2 (B) *in* On the Road with Fodor's.

Amish Country

$$$ 🏨 **Checkerberry Inn.** Set on 100 acres, this elegant hostelry has the state's only professional croquet course, a walking lane, and woodlands. ⊠ *62644 County Rd. 37, Goshen 46526,* ☎ *219/642–4445,* ℻ *219/642–4445. 14 rooms. Restaurant, pool, tennis, croquet. MC, V.*

$$ 🏨 **Essenhaus Country Inn.** A three-story softly lighted atrium with a potbelly stove is the centerpiece of this simple but modern inn. ⊠ *240 U.S. 20, Middlebury 46540,* ☎ *219/825–9471,* ℻ *219/825–9471. 31 rooms. Restaurant, lounge. MC, V.*

Indiana's North Coast

$$$ ✕ **Miller Bakery Cafe.** This cozy bakery turned eatery has received rave reviews for its inventive fare. Start dinner with cornbread custard, a savory bread pudding with cilantro pesto, or try the wild mushroom ragout. Then move on to New Zealand rack of lamb with coarse whole-grain mustard sauce, or sautéed veal medallions with caramelized mushrooms. ⊠ *555 S. Lake St., Gary,* ☎ *219/938–2229. MC, V. Closed Sun.*

$$$ 🏨 **Hutchinson Mansion Inn.** This 1876 mansion spanning almost one city block is filled with stained-glass windows and marble fireplaces. ⊠ *220 W. 10th St., Michigan City 46360,* ☎ *219/879–1700. 9 rooms. Library, recreation room.*

South Bend/Mishawaka

$$ 🏨 **Varsity Clubs of America.** Resembling a jumbo redbrick, white-pillared fraternity house, this all-suite hotel has a collection of Notre Dame memorabilia. ⊠ *3800 N. Main St., Mishawaka 46545,* ☎ *219277–0500 or 800/946–4822. 60 suites. Lounge, exercise room. AE, DC, MC, V.*

MICHIGAN

By Don
Davenport

Updated by
Richard Bak

Capital	Lansing
Population	9,594,000
Motto	If You Seek a Pleasant Peninsula, Look About You
State Bird	Robin
State Flower	Apple blossom
Postal Abbreviation	MI

Statewide Visitor Information

Michigan Department of Commerce Travel Bureau (✉ Box 30226, Lansing 48909, ☎ 800/543–2937). **Information centers:** I–94 at New Buffalo and Port Huron; I–69 at Coldwater; U.S. 23 at Dundee; U.S. 2 at Ironwood and Iron Mountain; U.S. 41 at Marquette and Menominee; I–75 at St. Ignace, Sault Sainte Marie, and Monroe; U.S. 27 in a rest area 1 mi north of Clare; and Route 108 in Mackinaw City.

Scenic Drives

Route BR–15 between Pentwater and Montague follows the Lake Michigan shoreline for about 25 mi. **Route M–23** between Tawas City and Mackinaw City follows the Lake Huron shoreline for more than 160 mi. In the Upper Peninsula **Route M–28** follows the Lake Superior shoreline between Marquette and Munising.

National and State Parks

National Parks
Isle Royale National Park (✉ Houghton 49940, ☎ 906/482–3310), 48 mi off the Michigan coast in Lake Superior, is a wilderness park and can be reached by ferry from Houghton or Copper Harbor or by ★ seaplane from Houghton. **Pictured Rocks National Lakeshore** (✉ Box 40, Munising 49862, ☎ 906/387–2607), in the Upper Peninsula, extends 40 mi along Lake Superior between Munising and Grand Marais. **Sleeping Bear Dunes National Lakeshore** (✉ 9922 Front St., Box 277, Empire 49630, ☎ 616/326–5134) encompasses 33 mi of lower Michigan's Lake Michigan shore and includes the Manitou Islands. The 71,000-acre preserve has the highest sand dunes outside the Sahara.

State Parks
Michigan has 94 state parks, including 23 in the Upper Peninsula, many with spectacular waterfalls. Most parks allow camping. A motor-vehicle permit, available at each park entrance, is required for admission. The *Michigan Travel Guide,* available from the Michigan Department of Commerce Travel Bureau (☞ Statewide Visitor Information, *above*), details park facilities.

Brimley State Park (✉ Rte. 2, Box 202, Brimley 49715, ☎ 906/248–3422), overlooking Lake Superior's Whitefish Bay, is one of 14 parks where you can rent a tent already set up and equipped with two cots and two sleeping pads. **Porcupine Mountains State Park** (✉ Rte. M–107, Ontonagon 49953, ☎ 906/885–5275), on the rugged western edge of the Upper Peninsula, is one of 13 parks with cabins to rent. At **J. W. Wells State Park** (✉ Rte. M–35, Cedar River 49813, ☎ 906/863–9747), some cabins are mere yards from the softly lapping Lake Michigan shoreline.

DETROIT

Founded seven decades before the American Revolution, Detroit is a busy industrial city that produces roughly a quarter of the nation's autos, trucks, and tractors. The riverfront harbor is one of the busiest ports on the Great Lakes. Downtown, a constant flow of traffic moves in and out of the Detroit–Windsor Tunnel and across the Ambassador Bridge, both of which connect Detroit with Windsor, Ontario, in Canada, directly across the Detroit River.

Nearly half of Michigan's total population lives within the metropolitan area. More than 150 ethnic groups are represented, including almost 900,000 African-Americans and more than 400,000 people of Polish descent, and the city's Arab population is among the largest in North America. This wealth of cultural diversity is reflected in language, music, food, art, and entertainment.

Visitor Information

Detroit Visitor Information Center (⊠ 2 E. Jefferson Ave., 48226; in Hart Plaza just west of the Renaissance Center, ☎ 313/567–1170).

Arriving and Departing

By Bus
Greyhound Lines (⊠ 1000 W. Lafayette St., ☎ 800/231–2222).

By Car
I–75 enters Detroit from the north and south, U.S. 10 from the north. Approaching from the west and northeast is I–94; from the west, I–96 and I–696. From the east Canadian Route 401 becomes Route 3 when entering Detroit from Windsor via the Ambassador Bridge and Route 3B when entering via the Detroit–Windsor Tunnel.

By Plane
Detroit Metropolitan Wayne County Airport (☎ 313/942–3550) in Romulus, about 26 mi west of downtown Detroit, is served by most major airlines, with nearly 1,000 arrivals and departures daily.

Commuter Transportation Company (☎ 313/941–3252) operates buses from the metropolitan airport to major downtown hotels from 6:45 AM to midnight; the fare is $13 one-way, $24 round-trip. Taxis to and from the airport take about 45 minutes; the fare is about $33 one-way.

By Train
Amtrak (⊠ 16121 Michigan Ave., Dearborn, ☎ 800/872–7245).

Getting Around Detroit

By Car
Detroit is the Motor City; everyone drives. Most downtown streets are one-way; a detailed map is a necessity. The main streets into downtown are Woodward Avenue (north–south) and Jefferson Avenue (east–west). Rush hours should be avoided.

By Public Transportation
The **Department of Transportation** (☎ 313/933–1300) operates bus service throughout Detroit; the fare is $1. **Suburban Mobility Authority Regional Transportation** (☎ 313/962–5515) provides suburban bus service. The **People Mover** (☎ 313/224–2160) is an elevated, automated monorail that makes a 14-minute, 3-mi circuit of 13 downtown stations. Trains run about every three minutes; the fare is 50¢ (tokens are sold at each station).

Pick up the phone.
Pick up the miles.

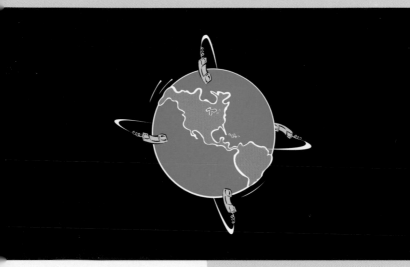

1-800-FLY-FREE

Is this a great time, or what? :-)

Now when you sign up with MCI you can receive up to 8,000 bonus frequent flyer miles on one of seven major airlines.

Then earn another 5 miles for every dollar you spend on a variety of MCI services, including MCI Card® calls from virtually anywhere in the world.*

You're going to use these services anyway. Why not rack up the miles while you're doing it?

Urban planning.

CITYPACKS

The ultimate guide to the city—a complete pocket guide plus a full-size color map.

www.fodors.com

By Taxi

The taxi fare is $1.40 at the flag drop, plus $1.40 per mile. Taxis can be ordered by phone or hired at stands at most major hotels. The two largest companies are **Checker Cab** (☎ 313/963–7000) and **City Cab** (☎ 313/833–7060).

Exploring Detroit

Starting from the Renaissance Center, on the banks of the river downtown, you can move outward to east Detroit, then on to the near northwest side, the cultural heart of Detroit.

Downtown

Detroit's most prominent landmark, the big, brassy **Renaissance Center,** known as the Ren Cen, dominates the city's skyline with six office towers and the spectacular 73-story Westin Hotel, one of the tallest hotels in the world. This gleaming waterfront complex is a city within a city, with more than 90 retail stores, services, and restaurants. There's a People Mover stop right at the center.

Old Mariners' Church (⊠ 170 E. Jefferson Ave., ☎ 313/259–2206) was made famous in Gordon Lightfoot's song "The Wreck of the *Edmund Fitzgerald*." The 75-acre **Civic Center,** next to Old Mariners' Church, is a riverfront mecca for entertainment, festivals, and sports. At the heart of the Civic Center is **Philip A. Hart Plaza,** designed by Isamu Noguchi. In warm weather lunchtime crowds come here to enjoy the open spaces, the sculpture, and the computer-controlled **Dodge Fountain.**

Randolph Rogers, who created the bronze doors of the U.S. Capitol, also designed **Cadillac Square,** site of many presidential speeches and the 1872 **Civil War Soldiers' and Sailors' Monument.** The blinking red light atop the 47-story **Penobscot Building** (⊠ 645 Griswold, ☎ 313/961–8800), the state's tallest office tower, has been part of the Detroit skyline since 1928. A statue of Steven T. Mason, the first governor, stands over his grave in **Capitol Park,** site of Michigan's first capitol.

Grand Circus Park was envisioned as a full circus, as architectural circles were referred to then, when Detroit was rebuilt after a disastrous fire in 1805; only half was completed. A fountain in the west park honors Thomas A. Edison.

Greektown, one of Detroit's most popular entertainment districts, is centered on Monroe Avenue. It percolates day and night with markets, bars, coffeehouses, shops, boutiques, and restaurants serving authentic Greek fare with an American flair.

Second Baptist Church (⊠ 441 Monroe, ☎ 313/961–0920), organized in 1836, is Detroit's oldest black congregation. It was here that African-Americans gathered to celebrate the Emancipation Proclamation. **Old St. Mary's Catholic Church** (⊠ 646 Monroe Ave., ☎ 313/961–8711), built in 1885, began as a parish of German and Irish immigrants in 1833.

Bricktown is a refurbished industrial corner of downtown filled with dining spots and bars. Characterized by a multitude of brick facades, it's a good place for a leisurely lunch, a shopping spree, or cocktails.

The opulent **Fox Theatre** (⊠ 2211 Woodward Ave., ☎ 313/983–6611), which opened in 1928 as America's largest movie palace, today is an Art Deco showcase for big-name musical acts and large-screen movies.

East Detroit

In the 1880s the section east of the Renaissance Center, between the river and Jefferson Avenue, blossomed with lumberyards, shipyards, and railroads. Known as **Rivertown,** the area is seeing new life today—

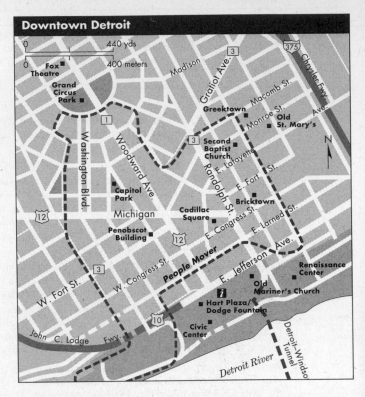

Downtown Detroit

with parks, shops, restaurants, and nightspots set in rejuvenated warehouses and carriage houses. **Stroh River Place,** opened in 1988, has attracted businesses, restaurants, and shops to a 21-acre site that stood empty for years.

Rivertown is the home of **Pewabic Pottery** (✉ 10125 E. Jefferson Ave., ☎ 313/822–0954), founded in 1907, which produced the brilliantly glazed ceramic Pewabic tiles found in buildings throughout the nation. The pottery houses a ceramics museum, a workshop, and a learning center.

Farmers and city slickers alike have gathered in the historic open-air **Eastern Market** (✉ 2934 Russell St., ☎ 313/833–1560) since 1892 to barter and bargain over fresh produce, meats, fish, and plants. Public shopping hours are Saturday 10–6; sales are in bulk only.

Near Northwest Detroit

Two and a half miles from downtown via Woodward Avenue is the **University Cultural Center,** a world of art, history, and science clustered throughout some 40 city blocks.

The **Children's Museum** (✉ 67 E. Kirby St., ☎ 313/494–1210) has exhibits on everything from dolls and toys to birds to life in other cultures. A planetarium shows the night sky in Detroit and in faraway lands. The **Detroit Historical Museum** (✉ 5401 Woodward Ave., ☎ 313/833–1805) features Collectors in Toyland, part of an ongoing exhibit of the Lawrence Scripps Wilkinson toy collection. Streets of Old Detroit is a walk through the city's history from 1701.

The **Detroit Institute of Arts,** with more than 100 galleries, displays 5,000 years of world-famous art treasures, including works by van Gogh, Rembrandt, and Renoir. Diego Rivera's *Detroit Industry,* four immense frescoes, is a must-see. ✉ *5200 Woodward Ave.,* ☎ *313/833–7900. Closed Mon.–Tues.*

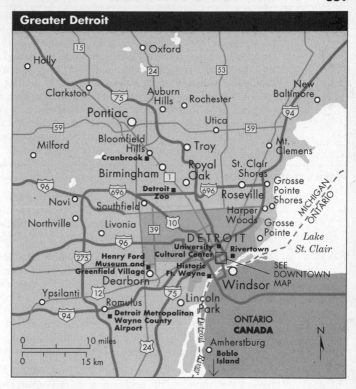

Greater Detroit

Home to 1.3 million books, the Cultural Center branch of the **Detroit Public Library** is the system's largest. Its Burton Historical Collection is the state's most comprehensive on city, state, and Great Lakes lore. ✉ *5201 Woodward Ave.,* ☎ *313/833–1000 or 313/833–1722 for recorded information. Closed Sun.–Mon.*

The **International Institute of Metropolitan Detroit** (✉ 111 E. Kirby St., ☎ 313/871–8600) is a museum, a working social agency for the foreign born, and a lunchtime café. Its Gallery of Nations displays the arts and crafts of 43 countries. The newly expanded and relocated **Museum of African-American History** (✉ 315 E. Warren Ave., ☎ 313/833–9800), the largest museum of its kind in the country, tells the story of the black experience in America through exhibits and audiovisual presentations.

Other Attractions

More than 1,200 animals from 300 species live uncaged in natural habitats at the **Detroit Zoological Park** (✉ 8450 W. Ten Mile Rd., Royal Oak, ☎ 810/398–0903). Highlights include the world's largest "penguinarium" and a walk-through aviary with tropical birds and plants.

Dearborn's **Henry Ford Museum and Greenfield Village,** America's largest indoor-outdoor museum, details the country's evolution from a rural to an industrial society, with exhibits covering communications, transportation, domestic life, agriculture, and industry. Greenfield Village preserves 80 famous historic structures, including the bicycle shop where the Wright brothers built their first airplane, Thomas Edison's laboratory, an Illinois courthouse where Abraham Lincoln practiced law, and the Dearborn farm where Ford himself was born. An ongoing exhibit, the Automobile in American Life, is a lavish collection of chrome and neon that traces the country's love affair with cars. ✉ *20900 Oakwood Blvd.,* ☎ *313/271–1620. Village buildings closed Jan.–Mar.*

Cranbrook, in Bloomfield Hills, is a cultural and educational center with a graduate art academy and college preparatory schools. **Historic Cranbrook House** (⊠ 380 Lone Pine Rd., ☎ 810/645–3149), a mansion built for newspaper publisher George Booth, has lead-glass windows, art objects, and formal gardens with fountains and sculpture. The **Cranbrook Academy of Art Museum** (⊠ 500 Lone Pine Rd., ☎ 810/645–3312) has major exhibitions of contemporary art and a permanent collection that includes works by Eliel and Eero Saarinen and Charles Eames. **Cranbrook Institute of Science** (⊠ 550 Lone Pine Rd., ☎ 810/645–3210) has intriguing hands-on physics experiments, geology displays, and dinosaur excavation exhibits.

Parks and Gardens

Belle Isle (☎ 313/267–7115), a 1,000-acre island park in the Detroit River 3 mi southeast of the city center, is reached by way of East Jefferson Avenue and East Grand Boulevard. It offers woods, walking trails, sports facilities, a nine-hole golf course, and a ½-mi-long beach.

Among Belle Isle's other attractions is the **Whitcomb Conservatory** (☎ 313/267–7134), with one of the largest orchid collections in the country. **Belle Isle Aquarium,** (☎ 313/267–7159), the nation's oldest freshwater aquarium, exhibits more than 200 species of fish, reptiles, and amphibians. The **Belle Isle Nature Center** (☎ 313/267–7157) has changing exhibits and presentations on local natural history. The **Belle Isle Zoo** (☎ 313/267–7160), closed November through April, has an elevated walkway offering views of animals roaming in natural settings.

Also on Belle Isle, the **Dossin Great Lakes Museum** has displays about Great Lakes shipping, the prohibition era in Detroit, and an ongoing exhibition—the Storm of 1913—recalling the Great Lakes' worst-ever storm. Visitors can listen to ship-to-shore radio messages and view the river and city through a periscope. ⊠ *100 Strand Dr.,* ☎ *313/267–6440. Closed Mon.–Tues.*

What to See and Do with Children

Many of Detroit's attractions will interest children, including the **People Mover** (☞ Getting Around Detroit, *above*); the **Children's Museum, Detroit Historical Museum,** and **Detroit Institute of Arts** (☞ Near Northwest Detroit *in* Exploring Detroit, *above*); **Cranbrook Institute of Science, Detroit Zoological Park,** and **Henry Ford Museum and Greenfield Village** (☞ Other Attractions *in* Exploring Detroit, *above*); and **Belle Isle Aquarium, Nature Center,** and **Zoo** (☞ Parks and Gardens, *above*).

Dining

Each wave of immigrants to Detroit has made its culinary mark: You'll find soul food restaurants in the inner city, a vibrant Mexican community on the west side, and Greek restaurants in Greektown. Detroiters often dine across the river in Windsor, Ontario, which offers its own rich mix of ethnic restaurants (a favorable rate of exchange makes the Canadian restaurants excellent values). For price ranges *see* Chart 1 (A) *in* On the Road with Fodor's.

$$$$ ✕ **Van Dyke Place.** The evening ritual at this restored turn-of-the-cen-
★   tury mansion starts with dinner in main-floor dining rooms, followed by dessert and coffee in the upstairs drawing rooms. The French-inspired menu includes such dishes as rack of lamb with chick-pea crust. ⊠ *649 Van Dyke Ave.,* ☎ *313/821–2620. Jacket and tie. AE, MC, V. Closed Sun.–Mon.*

$$$$ ✗ **The Whitney.** One of Detroit's most opulent restaurants was once the
★ mansion of lumber baron David Whitney. Chef Paul Grosz oversees a
large menu of creative American dishes, snappy pastas, and ultrafresh
seafood. ✉ *4421 Woodward Ave.,* ☎ *313/832–5700. Reservations essential. Jacket and tie. AE, D, MC, V. No lunch Mon.–Sat.; Sun. brunch.*

$$$ ✗ **Caucus Club.** This venerable Detroit institution is a period piece from
the era when elegant restaurants had boardroom decor, with lots of oil
paintings and wood. The menu is of similar vintage: corned beef hash,
steaks, chops, Dover sole, and its famous baby-back ribs. ✉ *150 W. Congress St.,* ☎ *313/965–4970. AE, D, DC, MC, V. Closed weekends.*

$$$ ✗ **Rattlesnake Club.** Superchef Jimmy Schmidt's menu offers innovative treatments of pickerel, salmon, and veal, as well as the club's signature rack of lamb. The decor is contemporary, in marble and rosewood,
with terrific views of the Detroit River and Windsor skyline. ✉ *300 River
Pl.,* ☎ *313/567–4400. AE, D, DC, MC, V. Closed Sun.*

$$$ ✗ **The Summit.** This revolving restaurant on the 71st floor of the
Westin Hotel has a superb view of Detroit. The menu includes charbroiled steaks and swordfish à la Louisiana. ✉ *Renaissance Center,*
☎ *313/568–8600. Jacket and tie. AE, D, DC, MC, V.*

$$ ✗ **Blue Nile.** Silverware is optional when you dine Ethiopian style; richly
★ seasoned meats and vegetables are served on communal trays covered
with *injera,* a pancakelike flat bread, chunks of which are torn off and
used as scoops for the other foods. ✉ *Trappers Alley, 508 Monroe Ave.,*
☎ *313/964–6699. AE, D, DC, MC, V.*

$$ ✗ **Fishbone's Rhythm Kitchen Cafe.** This authentic New Orleans–style
★ restaurant in the heart of Greektown is loud, brash, funky, and fun. Seasonal offerings on the spicy Creole menu include gator, gumbo, crawfish, and gulf oysters on the half shell. The best year-round bet is the whiskey
ribs. ✉ *400 Monroe Ave.,* ☎ *313/965–4600. AE, D, DC, MC, V.*

$$ ✗ **Lelli's Inn.** When Detroiters think Italian, Lelli's comes to mind. The
★ exceptional veal, minestrone, red sauce, and homemade ice creams offset the less-than-intimate atmosphere of the cavernous 650-seat dining room. ✉ *7618 Woodward Ave.,* ☎ *313/871–1590. Jacket and tie.
AE, DC, MC, V. No dinner Mon.*

$ ✗ **Elwood Bar & Grill.** One of the city's best-preserved examples of Art
Deco is right across the street from the Fox Theatre, making this a popular spot for concert goers. The vast, well-tended bar, swing-era music,
and lively crowd make up for the rather basic American menu. However, you won't go wrong ordering one of the soups or peppery potato
chips—all homemade. ✉ *2100 Woodward Ave.,* ☎ *313/961–7485.
AE, MC, V. No dinner Mon.*

$ ✗ **Pegasus Taverna.** Popular with the throngs who visit Greektown,
the Pegasus menu includes such staples as moussaka, roast leg of lamb,
and stuffed grape leaves. The Greektown experience isn't complete without an order of *saganaki* (flaming *kasseri* cheese ignited tableside) and
a little retsina or ouzo to drink. ✉ *558 Monroe Ave.,* ☎ *313/964–
6800. AE, D, DC, MC, V.*

$ ✗ **Traffic Jam & Snug.** This charmingly funky hangout near the Wayne
State campus is friendly and fun. The wide-ranging menu includes an
exotic selection of breads, cheeses, ice creams, sausages, and even hamburgers. ✉ *511 W. Canfield St.,* ☎ *313/831–9470. Reservations not accepted. D, DC, MC, V. No dinner Sun. and Mon.; no lunch weekends.*

$ ✗ **Under the Eagle.** As is typical of Detroit's modestly priced Polish
cafés, the Eagle's food is first-rate, with generous portions of stick-to-your-ribs roast duckling and kielbasa. For the adventuresome there's
czarnina (duck-blood soup). ✉ *9000 Joseph Campau St.,* ☎ *313/
875–5905. No credit cards. Closed Wed.*

$ ✗ **Wah Court.** Across the river in Windsor, Ontario, just steps from
★ the Ambassador Bridge, this no-frills Cantonese restaurant is known

for its abundant menu of nearly 200 items. Dim sum, the traditional Chinese tea snacks, is served daily, with the biggest selection on Sunday. ✉ *2037 Wyandotte Ave. W, Windsor,* ☎ *519/254–1388. Reservations not accepted. MC, V.*

Lodging

If you opt not to stay in Detroit, accommodations in suburban Troy, with its high concentration of corporate businesses headquarters, and Dearborn, where the Ford Motor Company has its headquarters, are quickly and easily reached by freeways and expressways. Most hotels, motels, and inns offer reduced-price weekend packages. For price ranges *see* Chart 2 (A) *in* On the Road with Fodor's.

$$$$ 🏨 **Crowne Plaza Hotel Pontchartrain.** The Pontch, as it is familiarly known, is tastefully decorated in neutral shades accented by green-and-rose fabrics. The light, airy rooms all have wonderful views of the city and the river; do not, however, accept a room at the back of the hotel—which is across the street from a fire station—unless you are a heavy sleeper. ✉ *2 Washington Blvd., 48226,* ☎ *313/965–0200 or 800/537–6624,* 📠 *313/965–9464. 416 rooms. Restaurant, lounge, pool, health club, concierge. AE, DC, MC, V.*

$$$$ 🏨 **Hyatt Regency Dearborn.** Opposite Ford's world headquarters, this large hotel is only five minutes from the Henry Ford Museum and Greenfield Village. ✉ *Fairlane Town Center, Dearborn 48126,* ☎ *313/593–1234,* 📠 *313/593–3366. 771 rooms. 2 restaurants, coffee shop, 2 lounges, indoor pool, sauna, parking (fee). AE, D, DC, MC, V.*

$$$$ 🏨 **Omni International.** One of Detroit's most modern hotels, the Omni
★ is connected by skywalk to the Renaissance Center and by People Mover to much of the rest of downtown. Rooms are bright and large, with luxurious furniture. ✉ *333 E. Jefferson Ave., 48226,* ☎ *313/222–7700,* 📠 *313/222–6509. 254 rooms. Restaurant, lounge, indoor pool, sauna, 2 tennis courts, health club, racquetball, concierge, parking (fee). AE, D, DC, MC, V.*

$$$$ 🏨 **Ritz-Carlton, Dearborn.** Since opening in 1989, the Ritz has ac-
★ quired a reputation for impeccable taste and service. Its mahogany-paneled walls, overstuffed settees, and antique art suggest a clubby, British elegance. Reinforcing that image is a traditional afternoon high tea and hors d'oeuvres served in the lobby lounge. ✉ *300 Town Center Dr., Dearborn 48126,* ☎ *313/441–2000 or 800/241–3333,* 📠 *313/441–2051. 308 rooms. Restaurant, grill, bar, indoor pool, sauna, exercise room, parking (fee). AE, D, DC, MC, V.*

$$$$ 🏨 **Westin Hotel.** At 73 stories, this hotel is best summed up as megabig
★ costing megabucks. The rooms are neither large nor special, but each commands a waterfront view of the city and of neighboring Windsor, Ontario. The lobby is sumptuously decorated in granite, marble, brass, and earth tones. ✉ *Renaissance Center, Jefferson Ave. at Randolph St., 48243,* ☎ *313/568–8000 or 800/228–3000,* 📠 *313/568–8146. 1,400 rooms. Restaurant, lounge, indoor pool, health club, jogging, parking (fee). AE, D, DC, MC, V.*

$$$ 🏨 **Dearborn Inn and Marriott Hotel.** Across from the Henry Ford Museum and Greenfield Village, this property includes five replicas of the historic Colonial homes associated with such famous Americans as Patrick Henry, Edgar Allan Poe, and Walt Whitman. ✉ *20301 Oakwood Blvd., Dearborn 48124,* ☎ *313/271–2700 or 800/228–9290,* 📠 *313/271–7464. 220 rooms. 2 restaurants, lounge, pool, 2 tennis courts, exercise room. AE, D, DC, MC, V.*

$$–$$$ 🏨 **Guest Quarters.** This suite hotel is a feast for the eyes, with an eight-story atrium full of trees, flowers, ivy, a small fountain, and a mini-waterfall. All the decor, from carpeting to upholstery to café tablecloths, combines to create an outdoorsy ambience. ✉ *850 Tower Dr., Troy 48098,* ☎ *810/879–7500 or 800/424–2900,* 𝔽𝔸𝕏 *810/879–9139. 251 suites. Café, lounge, indoor pool, sauna, health club. Full breakfast. AE, D, DC, MC, V.*

$$–$$$ 🖭 **Mayflower Bed and Breakfast Hotel.** The rooms have a homey atmosphere, with lots of prints and pastels; some have whirlpool baths. Shopping, golf, and cross-country skiing are nearby. ✉ *827 W. Ann Arbor Trail, Plymouth 48170,* ☎ *313/453–1620,* 𝔽𝔸𝕏 *313/453–0193. 73 rooms. 2 restaurants, lounge. Full breakfast. AE, D, DC, MC, V.*

$$–$$$ 🖭 **Somerset Inn.** In the heart of Troy's corporate district, 25 mi north of Detroit, this is a favorite with the business set. Guest rooms are rather small and standard, but the entry level is lovely, with marble floors, greenery, and several small sitting rooms tucked around the perimeter. ✉ *2601 W. Big Beaver Rd., Troy 48084,* ☎ *810/643–7800 or 800/ 228–8769,* 𝔽𝔸𝕏 *810/643–2296. 250 rooms. Restaurant, bar, 2 pools, health club. AE, D, DC, MC, V.*

$$ 🖭 **Drury Inn.** Decorated mostly in earth tones, the spacious rooms have brick and stucco walls and neat, clean, and modern furnishings, including fabric-covered tub chairs. ✉ *575 W. Big Beaver Rd., Troy 48084,* ☎ *810/528–3330 or 800/325–8300,* 𝔽𝔸𝕏 *810/528–3330, ext. 479. 150 rooms. Pool. Full breakfast. AE, D, DC, MC, V.*

$$ 🖭 **Shorecrest Motor Inn.** This pleasant, no-frills two-story hotel is conveniently located two blocks east of the Renaissance Center and within walking distance of downtown attractions. ✉ *1316 E. Jefferson Ave., 48207,* ☎ *313/568–3000 or 800/992–9616,* 𝔽𝔸𝕏 *313/568–3002. 54 rooms. Restaurant. AE, D, DC, MC, V.*

Nightlife and the Arts

Nightlife

Much of Detroit's nightlife is centered downtown. In Greektown tourists crowd the **Bouzouki Lounge** (✉ 432 E. Lafayette St., ☎ 313/964–5744) to see and hear traditional Greek music, folksingers, and belly dancers. **Baker's Keyboard Lounge** (✉ 20510 Livernois Ave., ☎ 313/864– 1200), a dimly lighted, smoke-filled jazz club, is a Detroit institution.

In Rivertown the **Soup Kitchen Saloon** (✉ 1585 Franklin St., ☎ 313/ 259–2643) is the home of the Detroit blues. The **Rhinoceros Restaurant** (✉ 265 Riopelle St., ☎ 313/259–2208) and **Woodbridge Tavern** (✉ 289 St. Aubin, ☎ 313/259–0578) are former speakeasies where downtown professionals loosen their ties and stomp their feet. Poetry readings, art exhibitions, and no-nonsense live acts give **Alvin's** (✉ 5756 Cass St., ☎ 313/832–2355) a bohemian appeal, especially among students at nearby Wayne State University.

The Arts

Metro Times, a free weekly tabloid available throughout the metropolitan area, has a comprehensive calendar of events. Also check the arts sections of the *Detroit News* and *Detroit Free Press.*

The **Detroit Repertory Theater** (✉ 13103 Woodrow Wilson Ave., ☎ 313/ 868–1347) is one of the city's oldest resident theater companies. Touring Broadway shows and nationally known entertainers appear at the **Fisher Theater** (✉ 3011 W. Grand Blvd., ☎ 313/872–1000) and the **Masonic Temple** (✉ 500 Temple St., ☎ 313/832–2232). **Detroit Symphony Orchestra Hall** (✉ 3177 Woodward Ave., ☎ 313/833–3700) is home to the **Chamber Music Society of Detroit** and the **Detroit Symphony.**

Spectator Sports

Baseball: Detroit Tigers (✉ Tiger Stadium, 2121 Trumbull Ave., at Michigan Ave., ☎ 313/962–4000).

Basketball: Detroit Pistons (⊠ The Palace of Auburn Hills, 2 Championship Dr., Auburn Hills, 30 mi north of Detroit, ☎ 810/377–0100).

Football: Detroit Lions (⊠ Pontiac Silverdome, Pontiac, 30 mi north of Detroit, ☎ 810/335–4151).

Hockey: Detroit Red Wings (⊠ Joe Louis Arena, downtown on the riverfront, ☎ 313/567–6000).

Shopping

The once fashionable downtown shopping district along Woodward Avenue is now largely a collection of eclectic boutiques. In the Renaissance Center is the **World of Shops,** with some 80 retail outlets. The shops of the **Millender Center,** which can be reached by all-weather walkways from the Ren Cen or the City-County Building, include a bakery, a bank, beauty and barber shops, bookstores, and jewelers.

The **Eastern Market** (☞ East Detroit *in* Exploring Detroit, *above*) is open to the public Saturday 10–6, and stores around it are open daily. The **New Center One Mall** (in the University Cultural Center) has weatherproof skywalks connecting its more than 50 stores, galleries, and restaurants to the Fisher Building, the General Motors Building, and the Hotel St. Regis. The **Somerset Collection,** in suburban Troy, has well-known upscale chains, such as **Neiman Marcus.** Across the street from the Somerset Collection is the newly opened **Somerset North,** a megamall whose anchor stores include **Nordstrom.**

Crowley's, whose major store is at New Center One Mall (☎ 313/874–5100), is well known for fashions for men, women, and children. The leader in fashion and home furnishings is **J. L. Hudson's,** whose flagship is at Fairlane Town Mall, in Dearborn (☎ 313/436–7600).

ELSEWHERE IN MICHIGAN

Ann Arbor

Arriving and Departing
Ann Arbor, 50 mi west of downtown Detroit, is intersected by U.S. 23 and I–94.

What to See and Do
Leafy, liberal, and young (thanks to the student population of the University of Michigan), Ann Arbor is consistently rated among the country's most desirable communities. The downtown shopping district, which extends along **Main Street,** is known for its specialty stores run by knowledgeable, independent owners. The State Street area, closer to campus, has one of the finest concentrations of book and music stores in the country. Among them is the original **Borders Books and Music** (⊠ 612 E. Liberty, ☎ 313/668–7100), started in 1971 by two University of Michigan graduates. On campus are three exceptional museums. The natural history exhibits at the **University of Michigan Exhibit Museum** (⊠ 1109 Geddes Ave., ☎ 313/764–0478) range from miniature dioramas to towering dinosaur skeletons. The **Kelsey Museum of Archaeology** (⊠ 434 S. State St., ☎ 313/764–9304) houses ancient Greek, Egyptian, Roman, and Near Eastern artifacts. The **University of Michigan Museum of Art** (⊠ S. State St. at S. University St., ☎ 313/764–0395) has a permanent collection of 13,000 pieces, including works by Rodin, Picasso, and Monet. Try your hands at the 250 working-science exhibits at the **Ann Arbor Hands-On Museum** (⊠ Huron St. at N. 5th St.), housed inside an 1882 firehouse downtown.

Mackinac Island

Arriving and Departing

By car, take I–75 north from Detroit to Mackinaw City. Island ferries depart from Mackinaw City and St. Ignace, at the northern end of the Mackinac Bridge.

What to See and Do

No autos are allowed on **Mackinac Island** (island, town, and straits are all pronounced *Mack*-i-naw), but the quaint Victorian village begs to be explored on foot. A small park at the eastern end of the village, along the boardwalk, offers terrific views of the Mackinac Bridge and ships passing through the straits. Farther afield, 8 mi of paved roads circle the island; bicycles rent by the hour or day at concessions near the ferry docks on Huron Street. **Mackinac Island Carriage Tours** (✉ Main St., ☎ 906/847–3573) offers horse-drawn tours covering historic points of interest, including Fort Mackinac, Arch Rock, Skull Cave, Surrey Hill, and the Grand Hotel.

Old Fort Mackinac (☎ 906/847–3328), perched on a bluff above the harbor, was a British stronghold during the American Revolution and the War of 1812. Fourteen original buildings are preserved as a museum; costumed guides offer tours and reenactments. **Marquette Park,** directly below the fort along Main Street, commemorates the work of French missionary Jacques Marquette with a bark chapel patterned after those built on the island in the 1600s. The venerable **Grand Hotel** (☎ 906/847–3331), now more than a century old, charges visitors $6 just to look, but the Victorian opulence of the public rooms and the view from the world's longest porch are worth it. **Mackinac Island Chamber of Commerce** (✉ Box 451, Mackinac Island 49757, ☎ 906/847–3783) provides information on island attractions.

Keweenaw Peninsula

Arriving and Departing

The Keweenaw, in the northwestern section of the Upper Peninsula, is reached by U.S. 41.

What to See and Do

Curving into Lake Superior like a crooked finger, the Keweenaw (*Key*-wa-naw) was the site of extensive copper mining from the 1840s to the 1960s. In **Hancock,** the **Arcadian Copper Mine** (☎ 906/482–7502) has a ¼-mi guided tour of workings no longer in operation. **Houghton** is home to Michigan Technical University, whose **E. A. Seaman Mineralogical Museum** (☎ 906/487–2572) has displays of minerals native to the Upper Peninsula.

North on U.S. 41, the Victorian stone architecture in **Calumet** gives just a hint of the wealth in the copper towns during the boom days. Restoration is under way at the circa-1900 **Calumet Theater** (☎ 906/337–2610), where stars such as Lillian Russell, Sarah Bernhardt, and Douglas Fairbanks Sr. performed. At **Coppertown, U.S.A.** (☎ 906/337–4354), a visitor center tells the story of the mines, towns, and people of the Keweenaw. North of Coppertown, in the old mining town of Delaware, **Delaware Copper Mine Tours** (☎ 906/289–4688) provides guided walking tours through the first level of a 145-year-old mine.

At the tip of the Keweenaw Peninsula, **Copper Harbor,** Michigan's northernmost community, is an always uncrowded biking and camping destination. **Fort Wilkins State Park** (☎ 906/289–4215) contains the restored buildings of an Army post established in 1844 and abandoned in 1870. The complex also has copper-mine shafts, hiking trails, and campgrounds. **Brockway Mountain Drive** climbs 900 ft above Copper Harbor to provide magnificent views of the peninsula and Lake Superior. **Keweenaw Tourism Council** (✉ 326 Shelden Ave., Houghton 49931, ☎ 906/482–2388 or 800/338–7982) provides information on peninsula attractions.

Lake Michigan Shore

Arriving and Departing

U.S. 31 edges Lake Michigan from St. Joseph to Mackinaw City.

What to See and Do

The Lake Michigan shoreline, which extends from the southwestern corner of the state up to the Mackinac Bridge, is one of Michigan's greatest natural resources. Its placid waters, cool breezes, and sugary beaches (including some of the largest sand dunes in the world) have attracted generations of tourists, including such regulars as Al Capone, Ernest Hemingway, and L. Frank Baum (who wrote many of his books about Oz over the course of several summer vacations here).

Resort towns, some of which triple in population between Memorial Day and Labor Day, dot the shoreline. **St. Joseph** is a picturesque community whose turn-of-the-century downtown and two 1,000-ft-long piers make it ideal for walkers. The artists' colony of **Saugatuck** has many fine restaurants and shops, an active gay and lesbian community, and enough B&Bs to qualify it as bed-and-breakfast capital of the state. **Saugatuck Dune Rides** (☎ 616/857–2253) offers freewheeling dune-buggy rides along Lake Michigan. In **Douglas,** the S.S. *Keewatin* (☎ 616/857–2151), one of the Great Lakes' last passenger steamboats, is permanently docked as a maritime museum.

Near Douglas is **Holland,** home of the famous **Tulip Time Festival** (☎ 616/396–4221), held for 10 days each May. The **De Klomp Wooden Shoe and Delftware Factory** (✉ 12755 Quincy St., ☎ 616/399–1900) is the only place outside the Netherlands where earthenware is hand-painted and fired using Delft blue glaze.

North of Holland is the eastern shore's largest city, **Muskegon.** This industrial town offers the **Muskegon Winter Sports Complex** (☎ 616/744–9629), with the Midwest's only luge run. The **Frauenthal Center for the Performing Arts** (✉ 417 W. Western St., ☎ 616/722–4538) is a gaudy Art Deco theater that is home to traveling Broadway-quality plays, silent-film showings, the West Shore Symphony Orchestra, and the Miss Michigan Pageant. Eight miles north of Muskegon is **Michigan's Adventure Amusement Park** (✉ Russell Rd. exit off U.S. 31, ☎ 616/766–3377), with more than 20 thrill rides, 10 water slides, a wave pool, shows, games, food, and the only two roller coasters in Michigan.

A two-hour drive north of Muskegon is **Traverse City,** the state's premier sports-vacation spot. Much to the chagrin of longtime residents, the area south of Grand Traverse Bay was "discovered" by sportsmen—and developers—about 25 years ago. Unfortunately, the roads have not kept pace with the boom in sailors, golfers, and skiers. The two-lane highways can resemble parking lots, particularly during the popular **National Cherry Festival** (☎ 616/947–1120), which draws an estimated 400,000 people each summer. For a pleasant diversion follow Route 37 around the **Old Mission Peninsula,** filled with the cherry orchards and vineyards that are the area's main industry next to tourism. Spring, when crowds are small and the orchards are in bloom, is a good time to visit.

Some of the finest views of Lake Michigan are found on the **Leelanau Peninsula,** the finger that juts into Little Traverse Bay. Follow Route 119 between **Harbor Springs,** a resort village overlooking Little Traverse Bay, and **Cross Village,** where the **Chief Andrew J. Blackbird Museum** (☏ 616/526–7731) houses a collection of Ottawa and Ojibwa Native American artifacts. The **West Michigan Tourist Association** (✉ 136 E. Fulton St., Grand Rapids 49503, ☏ 616/456–8557) provides information on lakeside attractions.

MINNESOTA

By Don
Davenport and
Karin Winegar

Updated by
Aaron Cieslicki

Capital	St. Paul
Population	4,657,800
Motto	Star of the North
State Bird	Common loon
State Flower	Pink lady's slipper
Postal Abbreviation	MN

Statewide Visitor Information

Minnesota Office of Tourism (✉ 100 Metro Sq., 121 7th Pl. E, St. Paul 55101, ☎ 612/296–5029 or 800/657–3700). There are 12 visitor centers around the state.

Scenic Drives

U.S. 61, along the Mississippi River between Red Wing and Winona, is often compared with the Rhine Valley in beauty; between Duluth and the Canadian border (☞ Duluth and the North Shore, *below*), it hugs the edge of Lake Superior for 160 mi, providing spectacular views of the lake and its rocky shoreline. **Route 59,** between Fergus Falls and Detroit Lakes, traverses some of central Minnesota's prime lake country.

National and State Parks

National Parks

Voyageurs National Park (☞ The Iron Range and Boundary Waters, *below*), in far northern Minnesota, has 30 major lakes and is part of the watery highway that makes up the state's northern border with Canada.

Pipestone National Monument, in southwestern Minnesota, protects the red stone quarry mined for centuries by Native Americans for material to carve their ceremonial pipes. The quarry is still in use, and traditional stone craft is still practiced at the **cultural center** in the Monument Headquarters (✉ Hwy. 75, Pipestone 56164, ☎ 507/825–5464).

State Parks

Minnesota has 68 state parks, 62 of which offer camping facilities. For information contact the **Department of Natural Resources** (✉ DNR Information Center, 500 Lafayette Rd., Box 40, St. Paul 55155-4040, ☎ 612/296–6157).

Fort Snelling State Park, just south of downtown St. Paul (✉ Rte. 5 and Post Rd., St. Paul, ☎ 612/725–2389), preserves the historic fort built at the junction of the Mississippi and Minnesota rivers in 1819. **Itasca State Park** (✉ HC05, Box 4, Lake Itasca 56460, ☎ 218/266–2114) is Minnesota's oldest state park, established in 1891 to protect the headwaters of the Mississippi River, which rises from Lake Itasca. **Soudan Underground Mine State Park** (✉ 1379 Stuntz Bay Rd., Soudan 55782, ☎ 218/753–2245) offers hiking trails and tours of the Soudan Mine, Minnesota's oldest and largest iron mine, which operated until 1962. **Gooseberry Falls State Park** (✉ 1300 Hwy. 61, Two Harbors 55616, ☎ 218/834–3855) and **Temperance River State Park** (✉ Hwy. 61, Box 33, Schroeder 55613, ☎ 218/663–7476), with roaring waterfalls and scenic vistas, are typical of parks found along Lake Superior's shore.

MINNEAPOLIS AND ST. PAUL

Drawing comparisons between Minneapolis and St. Paul is much like comparing two favorite aunts—a difficult task. St. Paul has a slightly reserved air about it; Minneapolis is brasher, noisier, and busier. Both cities have tall, gleaming glass skylines; St. Paul's is designed to blend with the city's Art Deco and Victorian architecture, while Minneapolis's is more eclectic. St. Paul has preserved much of its architectural heritage, while most of downtown Minneapolis is new. Both cities straddle the Mississippi River, and riverboat traffic calls at the Twin Cities from as far away as New Orleans.

There are 2.3 million people in the Greater Minneapolis/St. Paul metropolitan area, but Minneapolis wins the population race with 368,000. The strong Scandinavian strain in the cities' ancestry has not prevented them from constructing miles-long skyway systems. Residents can drive downtown, park, walk to work, go to lunch, shop, see a show, and return to their cars without once setting foot outdoors—a blessing in the blustery Minnesota winters.

Visitor Information

Minneapolis: Convention and Visitors Association (⊠ 4000 Multifoods Tower, 33 S. 6th St., 55402, ☎ 612/661–4700 or 800/445–7412). **St. Paul:** Convention and Visitors Bureau (⊠ 55 E. 5th St., Suite 102, 55101, ☎ 612/297–6985 or 800/627–6101).

Arriving and Departing

By Bus

Greyhound Lines has stations in St. Paul (⊠ 25 W. 7th St., ☎ 612/222–0509 or 800/231–2222) and in Minneapolis (⊠ 29 N. 9th St., ☎ 612/371–3323 or 800/231–2222).

By Car

The major north–south route through the area is I–35, which divides into I–35W bisecting Minneapolis and I–35E through St. Paul. I–94 goes east–west through both cities. A beltway circles the Twin Cities, with I–494 looping through the southern suburbs and I–694 cutting through the north.

By Plane

Minneapolis/St. Paul International Airport (☎ 612/726–5555) lies between the cities on I–494, 8 mi south of downtown St. Paul and 10 mi south of downtown Minneapolis. It is served by most major domestic airlines and several foreign carriers. From the airport to either city, **Metropolitan Transit Commission** (☎ 612/349–7000) buses cost $1 ($1.25 during rush hour); taxis take about 30 minutes and charge $17–$20 to downtown Minneapolis and $14–$16 to St. Paul.

By Train

St. Paul's **Amtrak** station (⊠ 730 Transfer Rd., ☎ 800/872–7245) serves both cities.

Getting Around Minneapolis and St. Paul

Both cities are laid out on a grid, with streets running north–south and east–west. However, many downtown streets parallel the Mississippi River and run on a diagonal, and not all streets cross the river. Both downtowns have extensive skyway systems. Many St. Paul attractions can be reached on foot, but most of those in Minneapolis require wheels. Express fare on **Metropolitan Transit Commission** (☎ 612/

349–7000) buses between Minneapolis and St. Paul during rush hour is $1.75. Within each city's central business district the fare is 50¢. Outside the downtown area the fare is $1, $1.25 during peak hours (6–9 AM and 3:30–6:30 PM).

Taxi fare is about $3.50 for the first 1¼ mi and approximately $1.50 for each additional mile. The largest taxi firms in St. Paul are **Yellow** (☎ 612/222–4433) and **City Wide** (☎ 612/489–1111); in Minneapolis, **Blue and White** (☎ 612/333–3333) and **Yellow** (☎ 612/824–4444). **Town Taxi** (☎ 612/331–8294) serves both cities and all suburbs.

Exploring Minneapolis and St. Paul

Minneapolis

Downtown Minneapolis is easily walkable in any season. The climate-controlled skyway system connects hundreds of shops and restaurants. In general, skyways remain open during the business hours of the buildings they connect.

The Mississippi River's **Falls of St. Anthony,** discovered by Father Louis Hennepin three centuries ago, drop 16 ft at the eastern edge of downtown. Harnessed by dams and diminished in grandeur, the historic falls are today bypassed by the **Upper St. Anthony Lock** (⊠ Foot of Portland Ave.), which allows river traffic to reach industrial sections of Minneapolis. An observation deck provides views of lock operations.

The **Stone Arch Bridge,** a railroad bridge over the Mississippi River near the Upper St. Anthony Lock, was built in the late 19th century by railroad baron James J. Hill; it was recently restored and reopened to foot and bicycle traffic. Guided walking tours of the **St. Anthony Falls Historic District** are offered weekends April 15–September 30 (☎ 612/627–5433).

The **University of Minnesota,** with an enrollment of close to 50,000, is one of the largest campuses in the country. **Dinkytown,** on the east bank, is an area of campus bars, nightspots, university shops, record emporiums, and bookstores. **Seven Corners,** on the west bank, is home to the **West Bank Theater District,** with popular theaters and after-hours hangouts.

The University of Minnesota's **James Ford Bell Museum of Natural History** (⊠ University Ave. SE at 17th Ave., ☎ 612/624–7083) has dioramas of Minnesota wildlife, an art gallery of wildlife paintings, and a touch-and-see room for kids. The newest and most talked about building on campus is the **Weisman Art Museum** (⊠ 333 E. River Rd., ☎ 612/625–9494), a wild-looking metallic structure designed by famed avant-garde architect Frank Gehry. Inside are student and faculty works as well as a permanent collection of 1900–1950 American art.

Downtown Minneapolis, much of it built in the past 25 years, towers skyward several blocks west of the university. Two of the downtown's more recent additions are the 57-story **Norwest Center** (⊠ 77 S. 7th St.), designed by Cesar Pelli, and its smaller companion, **Gaviidae Common** (⊠ 651 Nicollet Mall), the latest downtown shopping mecca. The mirrored, 51-story **IDS Building** (⊠ 80 S. 8th St.) contains Crystal Court, a focal point of the skyway system, with shops, restaurants, and offices. The 42-story **Piper Jaffray Tower** (⊠ 222 S. 9th St.), sheathed in aqua glass, and the 17-story **Lutheran Brotherhood Building** (⊠ 625 4th Ave. SE), in copper-color glass, are sparkling members of the skyline. At the **Foshay Tower** (⊠ 821 Marquette Ave., ☎ 612/341–2522)—Minneapolis's first skyscraper, constructed in 1929—a 31st-floor observation deck provides spectacular views of the city.

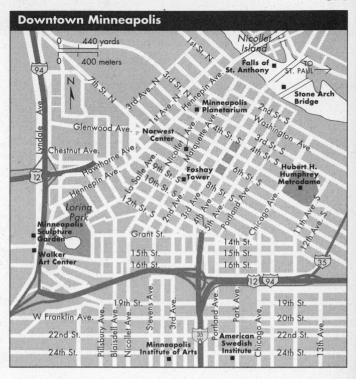

Downtown Minneapolis

Nicollet Mall, a mile-long pedestrian mall, runs from 2nd Street to Grant Avenue, with an extensive system of skyways connecting many shops and a public library. Inside the library, the **Minneapolis Planetarium** (⊠ 300 Nicollet Mall, ☎ 612/372–6644) offers sky shows that tour the night sky and investigate the latest discoveries in space science.

Another downtown landmark, the inflated **Hubert H. Humphrey Metrodome** (⊠ 900 S. 5th St., ☎ 612/332–0386), is home to the Minnesota Twins baseball team and the Minnesota Vikings and University of Minnesota football teams. Behind-the-scenes tours of locker rooms, the playing field, and the press box are available.

The **Minneapolis Institute of Arts,** 1 mi south of downtown and west of I–35W, displays more than 80,000 works of art from every age and culture, including works by the French Impressionists, rare Chinese jade, and a photography collection ranging from 1863 to the present. ⊠ 2400 3rd Ave. S, ☎ 612/870–3131. Closed Mon.

The **American Swedish Institute** is set in a 33-room Romanesque château filled with decorative woodwork. The museum, five blocks east of the Minneapolis Institute of Arts, houses collections of art, pioneer items, Swedish glass, ceramics, and furniture relating to the area's Swedish heritage. ⊠ 2600 Park Ave., ☎ 612/871–4907.

★ The **Walker Art Center** houses an outstanding collection of 20th-century American and European sculpture, prints, and photography, as well as traveling exhibits. Adjacent to the museum is the **Minneapolis Sculpture Garden,** the nation's largest outdoor urban sculpture garden. The **Irene Hixon Whitney Footbridge,** designed by sculptor Siah Armajani, connects the arts complex to Loring Park, across I–94. ⊠ 725 Vineland Pl., adjoining the Guthrie Theater, ☎ 612/375–7600. Closed Mon.

Greater Minneapolis

St. Paul

Like its twin, downtown St. Paul is easily explored on foot thanks to its all-weather, climate-controlled skyway system. The Mississippi River makes a huge loop and runs east–west through the city.

The **Minnesota Museum of American Art,** on the second floor of the historic Landmark Center, has a permanent collection strong in Asian and 19th- and 20th-century American art, along with changing exhibits of contemporary sculpture, paintings, and photography. ⊠ *75 W. 5th St.,* ☎ *612/292–4355. Donation requested. Closed Mon.*

City Hall and the **Ramsey County Courthouse** (⊠ 15 W. Kellogg Blvd., ☎ 612/266–8500) look out across the Mississippi River from a 20-story building of a design known as American Perpendicular. Here, Memorial Hall (4th Street entrance) features Swedish sculptor Carl Milles's towering **Vision of Peace** statue, the largest carved-onyx figure in the world, standing 36 ft high and weighing 60 tons.

Rice Park, at the corner of West 5th and Washington streets, is St. Paul's oldest urban park, dating from 1849. It's a favorite with downtowners. Facing Rice Park on the north is the **Landmark Center** (⊠ 75 W. 5th St., ☎ 612/292–3225), which is the restored Old Federal Courts Building, constructed in 1902. This towering Romanesque Revival structure has a six-story indoor courtyard, stained-glass skylights, and a marble-tile foyer. Of particular interest are a branch of the **Minnesota Museum of American Art;** and the **Schubert Club Musical Instrument Museum** (☎ 612/292–3268), with an outstanding collection of keyboard instruments dating from the 1700s.

On the south side of Rice Park is the block-long Italian Renaissance Revival **St. Paul Public Library.** On the west side of Rice Park is the **Ord-**

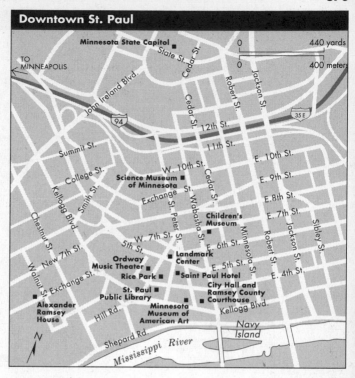

Downtown St. Paul

Minnesota State Capitol
TO MINNEAPOLIS
State St.
St. Peter St.
Robert St.
Jackson St.
0   440 yards
0   400 meters
John Ireland Blvd.
94
35 E
Cedar St.
Summit St.
12th St.
11th St.
College St.
Smith St.
W. 10th St.
Cedar St.
E. 10th St.
E. 9th St.
Science Museum of Minnesota
Exchange St.
Wabasha St.
E. 8th St.
E. 7th St.
Kellogg Blvd.
Chestnut St.
St. Peter St.
Children's Museum
New 7th St.
5th St.
W. 7th St.
E. 6th St.
Robert St.
Jackson St.
Sibley St.
Ordway Music Theater
Landmark Center
E. 5th St.
Walnut St.
Exchange St.
Rice Park
Saint Paul Hotel
E. 4th St.
Alexander Ramsey House
St. Paul Public Library
City Hall and Ramsey County Courthouse
Hill Rd.
Minnesota Museum of American Art
Kellogg Blvd.
Shepard Rd.
Navy Island
Mississippi River

way Music Theater (☞ Nightlife and the Arts, *below*), a state-of-the-art
auditorium with faceted-glass walls set in a facade of brick and copper.

West of Rice Park is the **Alexander Ramsey House,** home to the first
governor of the Minnesota Territory. Built in 1872, the restored French
Second Empire mansion has 15 rooms containing marble fireplaces,
period furnishings, and rich collections of china and silver. ⊠ *265 S.
Exchange St.,* ☎ *612/296–8760. Closed Jan.–Apr.*

The **Science Museum of Minnesota** has exhibits on archaeology, technology, and biology; the **Physical Sciences and Technology Gallery** offers many exciting hands-on exhibits. In the **McKnight Omnitheater**
70mm films are projected overhead on a massive tilted screen. ⊠ *30
E. 10th St.,* ☎ *612/221–9488. Closed Mon. Labor Day–Dec. 19.*

Constructed of more than 25 varieties of marble, sandstone, and granite, the **Minnesota State Capitol** (⊠ University Ave. between Aurora
and Cedar Sts., ☎ 612/296–2881) is just northwest of downtown St.
Paul. Its 223-ft-high marble dome is the world's largest.

The Cathedral of St. Paul (⊠ 239 Selby Ave., ☎ 612/228–1766), a classic Renaissance-style domed church echoing St. Peter's in Rome, lies
a half mile southwest of the capitol. Inside are beautiful stained-glass
windows, statues, paintings, and other works of art, as well as a small
historical museum on the lower level.

★ **Summit Avenue,** which runs 4½ mi from the cathedral to the Mississippi River, has the nation's longest stretch of intact residential Victorian architecture. F. Scott Fitzgerald was living at 599 Summit in 1918
when he wrote *This Side of Paradise.* The **James J. Hill House** (⊠ 240
Summit Ave., ☎ 612/297–2555), once home of the transportation pioneer and builder of the Great Northern Railroad, is a Richardsonian
Romanesque mansion, with carved woodwork, tiled fireplaces, and a

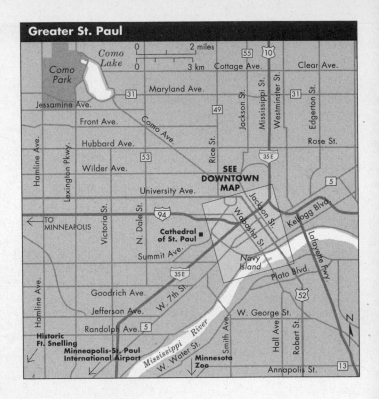

skylighted art gallery hosting changing exhibits. The **governor's mansion** (⊠ 1006 Summit Ave., ☎ 612/297–2161) is open for tours Thursday, May through October. **Mt. Zion Temple** (⊠ 1300 Summit Ave., ☎ 612/698–3881) is the home of the oldest (1856) Jewish congregation in Minnesota.

Other Attractions

In Minneapolis's Apple Valley suburb, the **Minnesota Zoo** houses some 1,700 animals in natural settings along six year-round trails. There's also a monorail, the Zoo Lab, a seasonal children's zoo, bird and animal shows, and daily films and slide shows. ⊠ *13000 Zoo Blvd., Apple Valley,* ☎ *612/431–9200.*

At the confluence of the Mississippi and Minnesota rivers is **Historic Fort Snelling.** The northernmost outpost in the old Northwest Territories, it remained an active military post until after World War II. Seventeen buildings have been restored, and costumed guides portray 1820s fort life with demonstrations of blacksmithing, carpentry, and military ceremonies. The History Center has exhibits and short films on the fort. ⊠ *Rtes. 5 and 55, near the International Airport south of St. Paul,* ☎ *612/725–2389. Fort closed Nov.–Apr.; History Center closed weekends Nov.–Apr.*

Parks and Gardens

Minneapolis

Minnehaha Park, on the Mississippi near the airport, contains Minnehaha Falls, which was made famous by Longfellow's *Song of Hiawatha.* Above the waterfall is a statue of Hiawatha and Minnehaha. Minnehaha Parkway, which follows Minnehaha Creek, offers 15 mi of jogging, biking, and roller-skating trails running west to Lake Harriet, one of the many lakes in Minneapolis.

Wirth Park (⊠ I–394 and Theodore Wirth Pkwy., just west of downtown) has not only bicycling and walking paths through wooded areas but also the **Eloise Butler Wildflower Garden**—a little Eden of local forest and prairie flora. Wirth also has a moderately challenging 18-hole public golf course—which doubles as a popular cross-country skiing spot in winter.

St. Paul

Como Park (⊠ N. Lexington Ave. at Como Ave.) has picnic areas, walking trails, playgrounds, and tennis and swimming facilities. **Como Park Zoo** (☎ 612/478–8200) is home to large cats, land and water birds, primates, and aquatic animals. The adjacent **Como Park Conservatory**, in a domed greenhouse, has sunken gardens, a fern room, biblical plantings, and seasonal flower shows.

What to See and Do with Children

Kids can operate a thunderstorm and investigate the animal world, among other things, in six interactive displays at the **Children's Museum,** in downtown St. Paul (⊠ 7th St. and Wabasha, ☎ 612/225-6000), which is closed Monday. The **Children's Theater Company** (⊠ 2400 3rd Ave. S, Minneapolis, ☎ 612/874–0400) puts on a season of adventurous plays for all ages. Also great for kids are **Upper St. Anthony Lock,** the **Minneapolis Planetarium,** and **Foshay Tower** (☞ Minneapolis, *above*); the **Science Museum of Minnesota** and the **Minnesota State Capitol** (☞ St. Paul, *above*); the **Minnesota Zoo** and **Historic Fort Snelling** (☞ Other Attractions, *above*); and St. Paul's **Como Park Zoo** (☞ Parks and Gardens, *above*).

Dining

Despite the diverse gastronomic traditions introduced to the Twin Cities by the new immigrant population, the majority of Minnesotans of Scandinavian and German descent still demand things be "toned down a bit" and are somewhat wary of any seasonings more exotic than salt and pepper. No matter what the cuisine, Minnesotans rarely dress up when they eat out. At all but the most stellar restaurants the unofficial dress code is urban casual-but-tidy attire. For price ranges *see* Chart 1 (B) *in* On the Road with Fodor's.

Minneapolis

$$ ✕ **Café Un Deux Trois.** This elegant marble-filled bistro with a 1920s feel takes up much of the main floor of the Foshay Tower, Minneapolis's first skyscraper. Food is simply and well prepared; specials include steak au poivre, roasted Long Island duckling, and sautéed calves' liver. ⊠ 114 S. 9th St., ☎ 612/673–0686. AE, DC, MC, V.

$$$ ✕ **D'Amico Cucina.** From the faux *marbre* plates and gleaming white linens to the marble floors and leather chairs, this is haute cuisine with a modern Italian accent. Artistic presentations from the kitchen, including fresh pastas, are on a menu that changes with the seasons. ⊠ Butler Sq., 100 N. 6th St., ☎ 612/338–2401. AE, D, DC, MC, V.

$$$ ✕ **Goodfellow's.** The emphasis at this plush restaurant is on regional American cuisine. The menu changes every three to four months, offering regional game such as venison, pheasant, and trout in season, as well as excellent presentations of lamb, veal, and pork dishes. ⊠ City Center, 40 W. 7th St., ☎ 612/332–4800. AE, D, MC, V. Closed Sun.

$$$ ✕ **Kincaid's Steak, Chop and Fish House.** Kincaid's imposing decor of marble, brass, glass, and wood combines with eclectic cuisine to create an up-to-date steak house. The kitchen does competent interpretations of Continental and all-American entrées, from filet mignon to

mesquite-grilled salmon to grilled rosemary lamb and roasted chicken Dijon. ⊠ *8400 Normandale Lake Blvd., Bloomington,* ☎ *612/921–2255. AE, D, DC, MC, V.*

$$$ ✕ **Whitney Grille.** In the lavish Whitney Hotel, the Grille has a flower-filled garden plaza and a hushed main dining room decorated in rich woods and muted floral fabrics. The regional American specialties change seasonally, and have included pheasant stuffed with lobster, spinach, and shiitake mushrooms and grilled beef tenderloin in cabernet sauce. ⊠ *150 Portland Ave.,* ☎ *612/372–6405. AE, D, DC, MC, V.*

$$ ✕ **Chez Bananas.** Inflatable toys set the tone for Caribbean food served in a warehouse storefront. Offerings include red coconut curry chicken with black beans and rice and a beef tenderloin fillet. ⊠ *129 N. 4th St.,* ☎ *612/340–0032. AE, DC, MC, V.*

$$ ✕ **Loring Cafe.** The Loring offers a terrific view of handsome Loring Park, bohemian-chic decor, and a menu that changes nightly, including pasta, vegetarian, and meat dishes. For an appetizer, don't miss the artichoke ramekin. ⊠ *1624 Harmon Pl.,* ☎ *612/332–1617. AE, MC, V.*

$ ✕ **Black Forest Inn.** This student and artist hangout is famous for its huge selection of bottled and tap beers; its hearty German cuisine, especially Wiener schnitzel with potato pancakes and applesauce; and its lovely courtyard. ⊠ *1 E. 26th St.,* ☎ *612/872–0812. AE, D, DC, MC, V.*

$ ✕ **Bryant-Lake Bowl.** This 1930s-era eight-lane bowling alley now contains one of the Twin Cities' hippest restaurants. Impressive wine and beer lists complement such specials as soft-shell tacos and fresh ravioli with four cheeses—and after your meal you can still bowl a few frames or catch a performance in the attached 75-seat theater. The place is also known for its inexpensive breakfasts. ⊠ *810 W. Lake St.,* ☎ *612/825–3737. AE, D, DC, MC, V.*

St. Paul

$$ ✕ **Dakota Bar and Grill.** The Twin Cities' best jazz club also serves an inventive menu of midwestern fare, including smoked pheasant fritters and salmon-walleye croquettes. Like the music, the atmosphere is contemporary and cool in color and mood. Sunday brunch is served. ⊠ *Bandana Sq., 1021 E. Bandana Blvd.,* ☎ *612/642–1442. AE, D, DC, MC, V. No lunch.*

$ ✕ **Khyber Pass Cafe.** In a corner storefront in a sleepy neighborhood, this small restaurant with decor that includes antique dresses, beadwork, rugs, and photos has barely a dozen tables. The small menu of sometimes-spicy Afghan cuisine includes such dishes as chicken broiled on a skewer and served with coriander chutney. ⊠ *1399 St. Clair Ave.,* ☎ *612/698–5403. No credit cards. Closed Sun.–Mon.*

$$ ✕ **Saint Paul Grill.** The Saint Paul Hotel's stylish bistro sports contemporary decor and affords a lovely view of Rice Park. The menu is American: dry-aged steaks, a variety of fish dishes, pastas, chicken pot-pie, homemade roast beef hash, and weekly specials. ⊠ *350 Market St.,* ☎ *612/224–7455. AE, D, DC, MC, V.*

$ ✕ **Cafe Latte.** This furiously successful and almost-always-jammed cafeteria offers an eclectic selection of soups, salads, breads, and stews. The chicken chili and Caesar salad are specialties, as are the several varieties of chocolate cake. ⊠ *850 Grand Ave.,* ☎ *612/224–5687. AE, DC, MC, V.*

$ ✕ **Mickey's Diner.** This streamlined quintessential 1930s diner, with lots of chrome and vinyl, a lunch counter, and a few tiny booths, is listed on the National Register of Historic Places. The stick-to-the-ribs fare and great breakfasts make it a local institution. ⊠ *36 W. 7th St., at St. Peter St.,* ☎ *612/222–5633. D, MC, V.*

Lodging

There is no shortage of lodging in the Twin Cities. Accommodations are available in the downtowns, along I–494 in the suburbs and industrial parks of Bloomington and Richfield (known as the Strip), and near the Minneapolis/St. Paul International Airport. A number of hotels are attached to shopping centers as well, the better to ignore Minnesota's fierce winters and summer heat. For price ranges *see* Chart 2 (A) *in* On the Road with Fodor's.

Minneapolis

$$$ 🏨 **Hyatt Regency Hotel.** A wide, sweeping lobby with a fountain and potted trees is the focal point of this hotel, within easy walking distance of downtown. Bedrooms are decorated in contemporary jade, peach, and gray fabrics and carpeting. ✉ *1300 Nicollet Mall, 55403,* ☎ *612/370–1234,* FAX *612/370 1463. 554 rooms. Restaurant, coffee shop, sports bar, sauna. AE, D, DC, MC, V.*

$$$ 🏨 **Marriott City Center Hotel.** At this sleek 31-story hotel within the City Center shopping mall, rooms have a contemporary look in peach and jade. Members of the waitstaff in the restaurants are also professional singers and perform during meals. ✉ *30 S. 7th St., 55402,* ☎ *612/349–4000,* FAX *612/332–7165. 626 rooms. 2 restaurants, lounge, sauna, health club, valet parking. AE, D, DC, MC, V.*

$$–$$$ 🏨 **Whitney Hotel.** An 1880s flour mill converted into a small, elegant,
★ genteel hotel, the Whitney provides suite accommodations; about half overlook the Mississippi. The lobby is decorated in rich woods, brass, and marble. ✉ *150 Portland Ave., 55401,* ☎ *612/339–9300 or 800/ 248–1879,* FAX *612/339–1333. 134 rooms. 2 restaurants, lounge, valet parking. AE, D, DC, MC, V.*

$$ 🏨 **Holiday Inn Metrodome.** A 10-minute bus ride from downtown, this showy hotel is in the heart of the theater and entertainment district and is close to both the Metrodome and the University of Minnesota. ✉ *1500 Washington Ave. S, 55454,* ☎ *612/333–4646 or 800/448– 3663,* FAX *612/333–7910. 287 rooms. Restaurant, lounge, indoor pool, sauna. AE, D, DC, MC, V.*

$$ 🏨 **Nicollet Island Inn.** This charming 1893 limestone inn is on Nicollet Island in the middle of the Mississippi River, with downtown Minneapolis on one shore and the Riverplace and St. Anthony Main restaurant-office complexes on the other. The comfortable rooms are decorated with Early American reproduction furniture; some have river views. ✉ *95 Merriam St., 55401,* ☎ *612/331–1800,* FAX *612/331– 6528. 24 rooms. Restaurant, bar, lounge. AE, D, DC, MC, V.*

$$ 🏨 **Regal Minneapolis Hotel.** The desk staff is cheery enough, but the decor in the public areas is a bit somber. Rooms in the 12-story hotel have contemporary furniture and provide sweeping views of downtown. ✉ *1313 Nicollet Mall, 55403,* ☎ *612/332–0371 or 800/522–8856,* FAX *612/359–2160. 330 rooms. Restaurant, lounge, indoor pool, sauna, exercise room. AE, DC, MC, V.*

St. Paul

$$$ 🏨 **Embassy Suites–St. Paul.** This hotel is decorated in neo–New Orleans Garden District style, with terra-cotta, brickwork, tropical plants, and a courtyard fountain. It is close to I–35E and within walking distance of major downtown businesses. ✉ *175 E. 10th St., 55101,* ☎ *612/224–5400,* FAX *612/224–0957. 210 suites. Restaurant, pool, sauna, airport shuttle. AE, D, DC, MC, V.*

$$$ 🏨 **Saint Paul Hotel.** Built in 1910, this stately stone hotel overlooks Rice Park, the center of genteel St. Paul. Renovated in 1990, the rooms have an eclectic traditional decor. ✉ *350 Market St., 55102,* ☎ *612/*

292–9292 or 800/292–9292, FAX 612/228–9506. 285 rooms. 2 restaurants, bar. AE, D, DC, MC, V.

$$ 🏨 **Best Western Kelly Inn.** A popular spot for state legislators whose home districts are far away, this hotel within walking distance of the state capitol has essentially remained the same clean, efficient inn for 30 years. ✉ 161 St. Anthony St., 55103, ☎ 612/227–8711, FAX 612/227–1698. 126 rooms. Restaurant, lounge, pool, wading pool, sauna. AE, DC, MC, V.

$$ 🏨 **Holiday Inn Express.** In what was once a paint shop for the Pacific Northern Railroad, this hotel is connected by skyway to the Bandana Square shopping center. Rooms are decorated with contemporary furnishings. ✉ 1010 W. Bandana Blvd., 55108, ☎ 612/647–1637. 115 rooms. Indoor pool, wading pool, hot tub, sauna. AE, D, DC, MC, V.

$$ 🏨 **Radisson Hotel Saint Paul.** This 22-story riverside tower has a lobby with Asian touches and rooms (most with a river view) decorated in traditional American style. ✉ 11 E. Kellogg Blvd., 55101, ☎ 612/292–1900, FAX 612/224–8999. 494 rooms. Restaurant, indoor pool, exercise room. AE, D, DC, MC, V.

$$ 🏨 **Sheraton Midway–St. Paul.** This contemporary four-story hotel is in the busy district centered on Snelling and University avenues. Hallways decorated in shades of pink lead into bright, comfortable rooms (some no-smoking) with contemporary oak woodwork. ✉ 400 Hamline Ave. N, 55104, ☎ 612/642–1234 or 800/535–2339, FAX 612/642–1126. 211 rooms. Restaurant, lounge, indoor pool, exercise room. AE, D, DC, MC, V.

Nightlife and the Arts

Nightlife

With closings at 1 AM, "the wee small hours" does not apply to the Twin Cities. Most nightspots are trendy and upscale and attract a youngish crowd. The Twin Cities also has nightspots that serve a sizable gay and lesbian community.

MINNEAPOLIS

The intimate **Fine Line Music Café** (✉ 318 1st Ave. N, ☎ 612/338–8100) showcases locally and nationally known jazz and rock musicians. In a former bus station, **First Avenue** (✉ 29 N. 7th St., ☎ 612/332–1775) attracts top rock groups and is a great place for dancing; the club was featured in the movie *Purple Rain*. Blues, rock, and alternative bands take the stage six nights a week at the **Cabooze** (✉ 917 Cedar Ave. S, ☎ 612/338–6425). The best gay bar in downtown Minneapolis is the **Gay Nineties** (✉ 408 S. Hennepin Ave., ☎ 612/333–7755).

ST. PAUL

Gallivan's (✉ 354 Wabasha St., ☎ 612/227–6688) is a downtown classic, with a cozy fireplace and live music. The **Heartthrob Cafe** (✉ World Trade Center, 30 E. 7th St., ☎ 612/224–2783) has a vintage '50s atmosphere combined with '90s music. The **Dakota Bar and Grill** (✉ Bandana Sq., 1021 E. Bandana Blvd., ☎ 612/642–1442) is one of the best jazz bars in the Midwest and features some of the Twin Cities' finest performers. The **Artist's Quarter** (✉ 366 Jackson St., ☎ 612/292–1359), decorated in a dark jazz-minimalist style, showcases local and national jazz performers. For blues check out the **Blue Saloon** (✉ 601 Western Ave. N, ☎ 612/228–9959). One of Central St. Paul's most popular gay bars is **Rumours** (✉ 490 N. Robert St., ☎ 612/224–0703).

The Arts

The calendar section of the monthly *Mpls.–St. Paul* magazine has extensive listings of events, as does the free monthly *Twin Cities Directory*. Check out the *St. Paul Pioneer Press*, the Minneapolis-based *Star*

Tribune, and the free newsweeklies *City Pages* and *Twin Cities Reader* for events. **Ticketmaster** (☎ 612/989–5151) sells tickets for sporting events, concerts, theater, attractions, and special events.

The West Bank Theater District has the highest concentration of theaters in Minneapolis, including the **University of Minnesota Theater** (⊠ 330 21st Ave. S, ☎ 612/625–4001). The award-winning **Guthrie Theater** (⊠ 725 Vineland Pl., ☎ 612/377–2224) has a repertory company known for its balance of classics and avant-garde productions. The acclaimed **Minnesota Orchestra** performs in Orchestra Hall (⊠ 1111 Nicollet Mall, ☎ 612/371–5656). Broadway touring companies and concert tours perform at the **State Theater** (⊠ 805 Hennepin Ave., ☎ 612/339–7007) and the **Orpheum** (⊠ 910 Hennepin Ave., ☎ 612/339–7007), once an RKO Orpheum Theater and now restored to its 1920s grandeur.

The **Great American History Theater** (⊠ 30 E. 10th St., ☎ 612/292–4323) presents plays about Minnesota and midwestern history. The **Penumbra Theater Company** (⊠ 270 Kent St., ☎ 612/224–3180) is Minnesota's only black professional theater company. The **Ordway Music Theater** (⊠ 345 Washington St., ☎ 612/224–4222) is home to the St. Paul Chamber Orchestra and the Minnesota Opera.

Outdoor Activities and Sports

Beaches

With 22 lakes, Minneapolis has scores of beaches. **Thomas Beach,** at the south end of Lake Calhoun, is one of the most popular. Further information is available from the Minneapolis Parks and Recreation Board (☎ 612/661–4875).

Spectator Sports

Baseball: Minnesota Twins (⊠ Hubert H. Humphrey Metrodome, 501 Chicago Ave. S, Minneapolis, ☎ 612/375–1116).

Basketball: Minnesota Timberwolves (⊠ Target Center, 600 1st Ave. N, Minneapolis, ☎ 612/337–3865).

Football: Minnesota Vikings (⊠ Hubert H. Humphrey Metrodome, 501 Chicago Ave. S, Minneapolis, ☎ 612/333–8828).

Shopping

The Twin Cities offers everything from tiny specialty shops to enclosed shopping malls with large department stores. The skyway systems in each city connect hundreds of stores and shops.

Minneapolis

Among the many shops along **Nicollet Mall** (☞ Exploring Minneapolis and St. Paul, *above*) are Dayton's (⊠ 700 Nicollet Mall), the city's largest department store, and Gaviidae Common (⊠ 651 Nicollet Mall), with three levels of upscale shops, including branches of Saks Fifth Avenue and Neiman Marcus. **The Conservatory** (⊠ 800 Nicollet Mall) has a number of fine boutiques and restaurants. **City Center** (⊠ 7th St. and Hennepin Ave.) has 60 shops and 19 restaurants. **Riverplace** and **St. Anthony Main,** on the east bank of the Mississippi, have restaurants and movie theaters housed in historic structures. A few miles south is **Uptown,** a smaller shopping center on Calhoun Square (⊠ Lake and Hennepin Aves.), which has more than 40 shops and several restaurants.

St. Paul

The World Trade Center (⊠ 30 E. 7th St.), downtown, has more than 100 specialty shops and restaurants, including Dayton's. **Bandana Square** (⊠ 1021 Bandana Blvd. E), in the former Great Northern Railroad repair yard in northwestern St. Paul, has a variety of specialty stores. **Victoria Crossing** (⊠ 850 Grand Ave.) is a collection of small shops and specialty stores that anchors the dozens of other shops spanning Grand Avenue from Dale Street to Prior Avenue.

Bloomington

Bloomington, south of Minneapolis, is Minnesota's third-largest city and home to the **Mall of America** (⊠ Cedar Ave. and Killebrew Dr., ☎ 612/883–8800), the world's largest enclosed mall. Appropriately nicknamed the Megamall, it has more than 400 stores and shops, including Macy's, Bloomingdale's, Sears, and Nordstrom. Beneath its central dome is Camp Snoopy, a large amusement park.

ELSEWHERE IN MINNESOTA

Southeastern Minnesota

Arriving and Departing

From the Twin Cities follow U.S. 61 southeast along the Mississippi River.

What to See and Do

This picturesque corner of the state has high, wooded bluffs that provide vast panoramas of the Mississippi River. The river towns and villages are noted for their charming 19th-century architecture. **Red Wing** is famous for boots and pottery bearing its name. Levee Park, Bay Point Park, and Covill Park offer views of the Mississippi, which widens into Lake Pepin here. The historic **St. James Hotel** (⊠ 406 Main St., ☎ 612/388–2846) has been restored to its 1875 Victorian elegance and has boutiques, shops, and an art gallery; the public spaces recall the heyday of riverboats. Contact the **Red Wing Chamber of Commerce** (⊠ 420 Levee St., Box 133, 55066, ☎ 612/388–4719 or 800/498–3444) for further information.

Frontenac State Park (☎ 612/345–3401), 10 mi south of Red Wing on U.S. 61, has a fur-trading post, scenic overlooks, and Native American burial grounds.

Winona is an early lumbering town settled by New Englanders and Germans. Here **Garvin Heights Scenic Lookout** (⊠ Huff St. past U.S. 14 and U.S. 61) offers picnic facilities, hiking trails, and scenic views from atop a 575-ft bluff. The **Julius C. Wilkie Steamboat Center** (⊠ Foot of Main St. in Levee Park, ☎ 507/454–1254) is a steamboat replica that contains a museum with exhibits on steamboating and river life. Exhibits of the local Polish heritage found at the **Polish Cultural Institute** (⊠ 102 N. Liberty St., ☎ 507/454–3431) include family heirlooms and many religious artifacts. For more information contact the **Winona Chamber and Convention Bureau** (⊠ 67 Main St., Box 870, 55987, ☎ 507/452–2272 or 800/657–4972).

The famous **Mayo Clinic** (⊠ 200 1st St., ☎ 507/284–2511), which offers tours of its facilities, is in Rochester, west of Winona on U.S. 14. **Mayowood,** the former residence of Dr. Charles H. Mayo, one of the brothers who founded the clinic, has 55 rooms furnished with French, Spanish, English, and American antiques; tickets for tours are purchased at the **Olmsted County History Center** (⊠ 1195 County Rd. 22 SW,

☎ 507/282–9447). The **Rochester Art Center** (✉ 320 E. Center St., ☎ 507/282–8629) features exhibitions of major works by regional and national artists. The **Rochester Convention and Visitors Bureau** (✉ 150 S. Broadway, Suite A, 55904, ☎ 507/288–4331 or 800/634–8277) provides information on city attractions.

Duluth and the North Shore

Arriving and Departing
From the Twin Cities head north on I–35.

What to See and Do
Set at the edge of the north-woods wilderness and the western end of Lake Superior is **Duluth**, a city of gracious old homes with one of the largest ports on the Great Lakes. **Skyline Parkway**, a 16-mi scenic boulevard above the city, offers views of Lake Superior and the harbor. Narrated boat tours of Duluth-Superior Harbor, which has 50 mi of dock line, are offered by **Vista Fleet Excursions** (✉ 5th Ave. W and the waterfront, ☎ 218/722–6218). The **Aerial Lift Bridge** (✉ Canal Dr.), an unusual elevator bridge 386 ft long, spans the canal entrance to the harbor. Not far from the harbor, the **Depot** (✉ 506 W. Michigan St., ☎ 218/727–8025), an 1892 landmark train station, houses the **Lake Superior Museum of Transportation**, with an extensive collection of locomotives and rolling stock. **Lake Superior Zoological Gardens** (✉ 72nd Ave. W and Grand Ave., ☎ 218/723–3747) has a children's zoo and animals from all over the world. The **Duluth Convention and Visitors Bureau** (✉ 100 Lake Place Dr., 55802, ☎ 218/722–4011 or 800/438–5884) provides information on the city.

Lake Superior's rugged **North Shore** is best viewed from U.S. 61 north of Duluth. **Gooseberry Falls State Park** (✉ 1300 Hwy. 61, Two Harbors 55616, ☎ 218/834–3855) and **Temperance River State Park** (✉ Hwy. 61, Box 33, Schroeder 55613, ☎ 218/663–7476), with roaring waterfalls and scenic vistas, are typical of parks found along Lake Superior's shore.

The Iron Range and Boundary Waters

Arriving and Departing
From Duluth take U.S. 53 north.

What to See and Do
The discovery of iron ore in the north woods brought an influx of immigrants who wove a rich and varied cultural heritage. Known as the Range because it encompasses the huge Mesabi and Vermilion iron ranges, the region is ringed by deep forests and many lakes.

Eveleth, which produces taconite, a form of processed iron ore, is home to the **United States Hockey Hall of Fame** (✉ 801 Hat Trick Ave., ☎ 218/744–5167), where pictures, films, and artifacts tell the story of hockey in America. In Virginia, 2 mi north of Eveleth, rimmed with open-pit mines and reserves of iron ore, the **Mine View in the Sky observation platform,** at the southern edge of town, overlooks part of the vast Rochleau Mine works. The **Virginia Historical Society Heritage Museum** (✉ 800 Olcott Park, 9th Ave. N, ☎ 218/741–1136) has exhibits on iron mining and other local history.

West of Virginia on U.S. 169 is **Hibbing,** the largest town in the Mesabi Range and the place where the Greyhound bus system began. The **Greyhound Origin Center** (✉ Hibbing Memorial Center Bldg., 5th Ave. and 23rd St., ☎ 612/263–5814) has displays and artifacts on the history of the company. Tours of the **Hull-Rust Mahoning Mine,** the world's largest open-pit iron ore mine, may be arranged during the summer at the Hibbing Area Chamber of Commerce (✉ 211 E. Howard St., Box 727, 55746, ☎ 218/262–3895). Programs on astronomy and space exploration are offered at the **Paulucci Space Theater** (✉ U.S. 169 and 23rd St., ☎ 218/262–6720).

★ Ely, east of Virginia on U.S. 169, lies in the heart of the Superior National Forest. It is the gateway to the western portion of the **Boundary Waters Canoe Area,** a federally protected area of more than 1,000 pristine lakes surrounded by dense forests. Area outfitters rent canoes and camping equipment and provide assistance in planning canoe trips. For information on outfitters and canoe trips, contact the **Ely Chamber of Commerce** (✉ 1600 Sheridan St., 55731, ☎ 218/365–6123 or 800/777–7281). The **Vermilion Interpretive Center** (✉ 1900 E. Camp St., ☎ 218/365–3226), closed in winter, has exhibits on the Vermilion iron range, the fur trade, and Native Americans.

International Falls, at the northern terminus of U.S. 53 on the Canadian border, is known as the "icebox of the nation" because of its severe winters. The town lies at the western edge of **Voyageurs National Park** (☞ National and State Parks, *above*), where the **Rainy Lake Visitor Center** (✉ 11 mi east of International Falls on Rte. 11, ☎ 218/286–5258) offers a slide show, exhibits, maps, and information, as well as guided boat tours of the lake and other points in the park. In town is the **Koochiching County Historical Museum** (✉ 214 6th Ave., Box 1147, ☎ 218/283–4316), with exhibits on early settlement, gold mining, and Native Americans. The **International Falls Chamber of Commerce** (✉ 301 2nd Ave., 56649, ☎ 218/283–9400 or 800/325–5766) offers brochures and information on area outfitters, camping, and attractions.

OHIO

Updated By
Jeff Hagan

Capital	Columbus
Population	11,173,000
Motto	With God, All Things Are Possible
State Bird	Cardinal
State Flower	Scarlet carnation
Postal Abbreviation	OH

Statewide Visitor Information

Ohio Division of Travel and Tourism (⊠ Box 1001, Columbus 43266, ☎ 800/282–5393). **Ohio Historical Society** (⊠ 1982 Velma Ave., Columbus 43211, ☎ 614/297–2300).

Scenic Drives

The **Lake Erie Circle Tour** consists of nearly 200 mi of state routes and U.S. highways along the Lake Erie shoreline from Toledo to Conneaut (☞ Northwest Ohio and the Lake Erie Islands, *below*). **Route 7,** which runs parallel to the Ohio River along the state's southeastern border, cuts through the French-settled village of Gallipolis; the site of Ohio's only significant Civil War battle, near Pomeroy; and Marietta, the historic first city of the Northwest Territory.

National and State Parks

National Parks

National monuments include the **Hopewell Culture National Historic Park** (☞ Columbus, *below*) and **Perry's Victory and International Peace Memorial,** in Put-in-Bay (☞ Northwest Ohio and the Lake Erie Islands, *below*). **William Howard Taft's boyhood home** (⊠ 2038 Auburn Ave., Cincinnati, ☎ 513/684–3262) is a national historic site. The **Cuyahoga Valley National Recreation Area** (⊠ 15610 Vaughn Rd., Brecksville 44141, ☎ 216/526–5256) occupies 22 mi of forested valley between Cleveland and Akron along the Cuyahoga River.

State Parks

Of the 72 state parks, eight have Ohio State Park Resorts (☎ 800/282–7275), which offer 16 locations for cabin rentals, swimming, boating, golf, and tennis, as well as lodging, dining, and meeting facilities. For more information contact the **Ohio Department of Natural Resources.** ⊠ *Ohio State Parks Information Center, Fountain Sq., Bldg. C–1, Columbus 43224,* ☎ *614/265–7000.*

COLUMBUS

Ohio's largest city and the state capital, Columbus is known for its entrepreneurial spirit and economic vitality. The state's largest university, Ohio State, is here, as are the headquarters of a number of Fortune 500 companies, many of whose executives claim they would not leave the city—even if they were promoted.

Visitor Information

Greater Columbus Convention and Visitors Bureau (⊠ 10 W. Broad St., Suite 1300, 43215, ☎ 614/221–6623 or 800/354–2657).

Arriving and Departing

By Bus
Greyhound Lines (⊠ E. Town St. at 3rd St., ☎ 800/231–2222) serves Columbus.

By Car
Columbus is in the center of the state, at the intersection of I–70 and I–71.

By Plane
Port Columbus International Airport, 10 mi east of downtown Columbus, is served by major airlines and by **ComAir** (☎ 800/354–9822), **Midwest Express,** and **Skyway** (☎ 614/238–7750). A cab from the airport to downtown costs about $16; the airport shuttle costs $6.50.

Getting Around Columbus
Downtown is fairly compact and easily walkable. Some government buildings are connected to each other and to nearby buildings through underground walkways. The **Central Ohio Transit Authority** (☎ 614/228–1776), or COTA, operates buses within Columbus.

Exploring Columbus

At the heart of downtown is the domeless Greek Revival **state capitol** (⊠ Corner of High and Broad Sts., ☎ 614/752–9777), distinguished by its skylights, stained glass, and period details. A seven-year renovation completed in 1996 reduced the number of offices in order to approximate the building's original spaciousness; a sunny, airy atrium now connects the two buildings. The lively **Riffe Gallery** (⊠ 77 S. High St., ☎ 614/644–9624), in the Vern Riffe Center for Government and the Arts, has works by Ohio artists. **COSI** (pronounced co-*sigh*), the **Center of Science and Industry** (⊠ 280 E. Broad St., Columbus, ☎ 614/228–2674), has colorful hands-on exhibits including a planetarium and an animal lab with basketball-playing rats.

The **Short North** (☎ 614/421–1030), a strip of trendy shops, clubs, vintage clothing and antiques stores, restaurants, and art galleries north of downtown, holds the Gallery Hop the first Saturday of every
★ month. The **Wexner Center for the Arts** (⊠ N. High St. at 15th Ave., ☎ 614/292–0330 or 614/292–3535), on the Ohio State University campus, houses contemporary art in a dramatic building designed by Peter Eisenmann.

★ **German Village** (☎ 614/221–8888), a neighborhood of tightly packed brick homes built by immigrants in the 19th century, lies just south of downtown. In the **Brewery District** (☎ 614/621–2222), next to German Village, old breweries have been turned into restaurants and bars.

South of Columbus, in Chillicothe, is the **Hopewell Culture National Historical Park** (⊠ On Rte. 23 north of Rte. 23, ☎ 614/774–1125). Here burial and ceremonial earth mounds rise from the ground in mysterious formations, the handiwork of Native Americans, mostly the Hopewell people.

What to See and Do with Children

COSI (☞ Exploring Columbus, *above*) has colorful hands-on exhibits and traveling shows that kids and adults love. World-renowned zookeeper "Jungle" Jack Hanna presides over three generations of gorillas and other creatures of the wild at the **Columbus Zoo** (⊠ 9990 Riverside Dr., ☎ 614/645–3550), about 18 mi northwest of downtown off I–270.

Dining

Restaurants in Columbus range from yuppie chic to down-home. Fine restaurants can be found in the Short North, tucked away in German Village, and in suburban neighborhoods. For price ranges *see* Chart 1 (B) *in* On the Road with Fodor's.

$$$ ✕ **Lindey's.** This German Village favorite has enough out-of-the-way rooms to get lost in—and a menu to match, including a Sunday jazz brunch with a gumbo du jour. ⊠ *169 E. Beck St.,* ☎ *614/228–4343. AE, D, DC, MC, V.*

$$ ✕ **Rigsby's Cuisine Volatile.** As the name suggests, this café is purposely unpredictable: Each day brings a new selection of American twists on Mediterranean cuisine—all part of a menu devised by Kent Rigsby, who studied at the San Francisco Culinary Academy. The kitchen freezer is only used for ice cream; everything else is as fresh as it gets. ⊠ *698 N. High St.,* ☎ *614/461–7888. AE, D, DC, MC, V. Closed Sun.*

$$ ✕ **Spagio.** This copper-, glass-, and oak-clad spot in the heart of up-and-coming Grandview still buzzes, despite the added competition in the neighborhood. The name is a combination of two words: *spa,* for the healthy fare available here, and *gio,* for geography, because its far-reaching menu evokes the flavors of the world. ⊠ *1295 Grandview Ave.,* ☎ *614/486–1114. Reservations not accepted. AE, DC, MC, V. Closed Sun.*

$ ✕ **Katzinger's Deli.** An enormous menu and a serve-yourself pickle barrel make this New York–style deli in German Village a favorite. ⊠ *475 S. 3rd St.,* ☎ *614/228–3354. MC, V.*

$ ✕ **Schmidt's Sausage Haus.** Homemade sausage hangs from the ceiling in this old-fashioned place reminiscent of a butcher shop. ⊠ *240 E. Kossuth St.,* ☎ *614/444–6808. AE, D, DC, MC, V.*

Lodging

Downtown Columbus and nearby German Village offer a wide range of accommodations, from elegant to merely efficient. For price ranges *see* Chart 2 (B) *in* On the Road with Fodor's.

$$$ ⌘ **Westin Hotel, Columbus.** Even after a $8 million renovation com-
★ pleted in early 1997, this venerable 1897 hotel has maintained much of its Victorian charm, from the rich marble-and-wood lobby to the well-appointed rooms. ⊠ *310 S. High St., 43215,* ☎ *614/228–3800,* ℻ *614/228–7666. 196 rooms. Restaurant, lounge, parking (fee). AE, D, DC, MC, V.*

$$$ ⌘ **Hyatt Regency, Columbus.** Adjacent to the convention center, this ultramodern high-rise hotel caters mainly to businesspeople. (The Hyatt on Capitol Square is more for the political crowd.) ⊠ *350 N. High St., 43215,* ☎ *614/463–1234,* ℻ *614/280–3034. 632 rooms. Restaurant, lounge, pool, exercise room, parking (fee). AE, D, DC, MC, V.*

$$ ⌘ **Courtyard by Marriott.** Refurbished in 1994, this contemporary hotel is comfortable and convenient to everything. ⊠ *35 W. Spring St., 43215,* ☎ *614/228–3200,* ℻ *614/228–6752. 149 rooms. Restaurant, lounge. AE, D, DC, MC, V.*

$ ⌘ **German Village Inn.** Friendly service and low rates are the advantages of this no-frills German Village hotel close to downtown. ⊠ *920 S. High St., 43206,* ☎ *614/443–6506,* ℻ *614/443–5663. 46 rooms. AE, D, DC, MC, V.*

Nightlife and the Arts

Three free weekly newspapers—the *Columbus Guardian,* the *Other Paper,* and *Columbus Alive!*—have complete listings of goings-on in the city.

Nightlife

Columbus's hot spots are near the Ohio State University campus (expect crowds on nights the OSU Buckeyes football team plays) and in the Short North. Almost every bar in town broadcasts the locally beloved Ohio State University Buckeyes' football games. Live music is available on weekends at the **Short North Tavern** (⊠ 674 N. High St., ☎ 614/221–2432). You can catch the latest music videos on the large screen of the **Union Station Video Cafe** (⊠ 630 N. High St., ☎ 614/228–3740). **Stache's** (⊠ 2404 N. High St., ☎ 614/263–5318), north of the campus, showcases breakthrough rock artists, some traditional blues acts, and timeless eclectic music.

The Arts

The Columbus Association for the Performing Arts (☎ 614/469–0939) operates the **Capitol Theatre,** in the Riffe Center (⊠ 77 S. High St., ☎ 614/460–7214), and the **Ohio Theater** (⊠ 55 E. State St., ☎ 614/469–1045 or 614/469–0939 for tickets), home to the **Columbus Symphony Orchestra** (☎ 614/228–8600) and the **BalletMet** (☎ 614/229–4860 or 614/229–4848 for tickets). **Opera/Columbus** and touring Broadway shows take the stage at the **Palace Theatre** (⊠ 34 W. Broad St., ☎ 614/469–9850 or 614/431–3600 for tickets).

Shopping

Columbus is the world headquarters of Leslie Wexner's empire of clothing stores, which include the Limited, Express, Structure, Henri Bendel, Victoria's Secret, and Abercrombie & Fitch, all of which are represented downtown in **Columbus City Center** (⊠ 111 S. 3rd St., ☎ 614/221–4900). You can't miss **Lazarus** (⊠ 141 S. High St., ☎ 614/463–2121), the granddaddy of Columbus department stores; its old-fashioned water tower sticks up out of the skyline like a Tootsie Roll Pop. **Ohio Factory Shops** (⊠ 8000 Factory Shops Blvd., Jeffersonville, ☎ 614/948–9090 or 800/746–7644), 35 minutes south of Columbus, has more than 80 outlets. The **Wexner Center for the Arts** (☞ Exploring Columbus, *above*) has a gift shop with intriguing items, some handcrafted.

CINCINNATI

Cincinnati is a well-regulated city with a proud history, an active riverfront, and a bustling downtown. A river's width from the South, in many respects it resembles a southern city: Its summers are hot and humid, a result of being in a basin along the Ohio River, and its politics are known to be on the conservative side.

Visitor Information

Greater Cincinnati Convention and Visitors Bureau (⊠ 300 W. 6th St., at Plum St., 45202, ☎ 513/621–6994 or 800/246–2987).

Arriving and Departing

By Bus
Greyhound Lines (⊠ 1005 Gilbert Ave., ☎ 800/231–2222).

By Car
I–71, I–75, and I–74 all converge on downtown Cincinnati.

By Plane
Cincinnati/Northern Kentucky International Airport is 12 mi south of downtown, off I–275, in Kentucky. It is served by major airlines and

by **ComAir** (☎ 800/354–9822). **Jetport Express** (☎ 606/767–3702) makes regular trips from the airport to downtown hotels ($10 one-way, $15 round-trip). Taxis downtown cost about $25 plus tip.

By Train

Amtrak (✉ Union Terminal, 1301 Western Ave., ☎ 800/872–7245).

Getting Around

Downtown Cincinnati is eminently walkable. Skywalks connect hotels, convention centers, stores, and garages. **Metro** (☎ 513/621–4455) runs buses out of Government Square (✉ 5th St. between Walnut and Main Sts.); there is also a downtown loop bus (Bus 79).

Exploring Cincinnati

Fountain Square (✉ 5th and Vine Sts.) is the center of downtown Cincinnati. The city is laid out along the river, with numbered streets running east–west (2nd Street is Pete Rose Way); north–south streets have names. Vine Street divides the city into east and west.

If you have only an hour in Cincinnati, spend it at **Carew Tower** (✉ 5th and Race Sts.) looking at the gorgeous Rookwood pottery in the arcade. The Art Deco interior of the **Omni Netherland Plaza Hotel** shouldn't be missed; its marble-and-rosewood interior, filled with mirrors and murals, is so richly detailed that the hotel provides an architectural walking tour.

You can cross the Ohio River from Cincinnati into Covington, Kentucky, on the **Roebling Suspension Bridge,** built by John A. Roebling, who would later design the Brooklyn Bridge. **Covington Landing,** a floating entertainment complex in the form of a side-wheeler and a wharf, is west of Roebling Bridge. Beyond the Covington wharf is **BB Riverboats** (☎ 606/261–8500), running river tours year-round. **Covington** itself, east of Roebling Bridge, is a neighborhood of fine antebellum mansions, with wonderful views from Riverside Drive.

On the Ohio side of the Ohio River, the narrow streets and funky houses of **Mount Adams,** the first hill east of downtown, are reminiscent of San Francisco. The yard of the **Immaculata Church** (✉ Pavillion and Guido Sts., ☎ 513/721–6544) provides a sterling view of the city.

Eden Park, on Mt. Adams, is the site of the **Krohn Conservatory** (☎ 513/421–4086), a greenhouse and garden center with more than 5,000 species of plants. Also in Eden Park is the **Cincinnati Art Museum** (☎ 513/721–5204), which has an outstanding collection of Near Eastern and ancient art. The **Contemporary Arts Center** (✉ 115 E. 5th St., ☎ 513/345–8400 or 513/721–0390) presents some of today's most cutting-edge artists. The **Taft Museum** (✉ 316 Pike St., ☎ 513/241–0343) is famous for its Chinese porcelains.

You could spend a full day in the magnificently restored **Museum Center at Union Terminal,** which looks like a huge Art Deco cabinet radio. This historic former train station houses the **Museum of Natural History** (☞ What to See and Do with Children, *below*), the **Cincinnati Historical Society,** and the **Robert D. Lindner Family OmniMax Theater** (TicketMaster, ☎ 513/749–4949). ✉ *1301 Western Ave. (off I–75 at Ezzard Charles Dr.),* ☎ *513/287–7000 or 800/733–2077.*

Parks and Gardens

Bicentennial Commons, an outdoor recreation center at Sawyer Point on the Ohio River, uses monuments to tell the story of Cincinnati's ori-

588

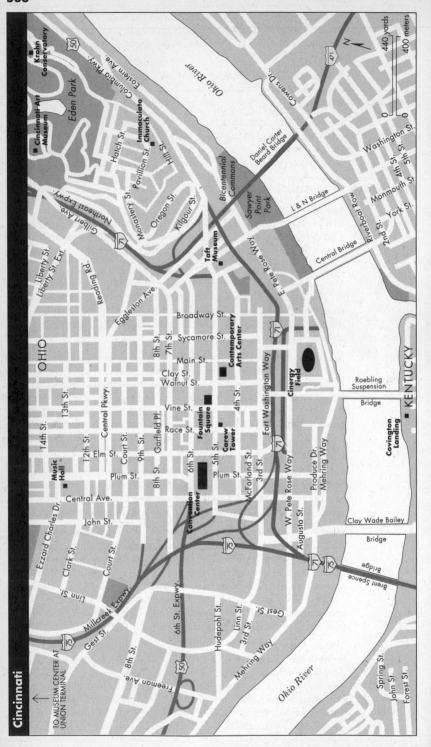

Cincinnati

gins as a river town. Look for the famous flying pigs, a playful reminder of the city's prominence as a meatpacking center.

What to See and Do with Children

The **Museum of Natural History,** in the Museum Center at Union Terminal (☞ Exploring Cincinnati, *above*), has the Children's Discovery Center, a cave with real bats (behind glass), and an Ice Age diorama where you can go behind the glass. The **Cincinnati Zoo and Botanical Garden** (✉ 3400 Vine St., ☎ 513/281–4700), famous for its white Bengal tigers, is the second-oldest zoo in the country. Follow the pawprint signs off I–75 Exit 6 or I–71 Exit 7.

Paramount's **Kings Island Theme Park,** 24 mi north of Cincinnati in Kings Mills, has eight theme areas, including a water park and the world's longest wooden roller coaster. ✉ *I–71 Exit 24,* ☎ *800/288–0808.* ☞ *$30.95. Closed Labor Day–mid-Apr. and weekdays mid-Apr.–Memorial Day.*

Dining

Famous for its chili, Cincinnati has more good restaurants than the most ravenous traveler could sample in any one visit, including high-rise revolving restaurants, riverboat restaurants, and rathskellers. For price ranges *see* Chart 1 (B) *in* On the Road with Fodor's.

$$$ ★ ✕ **The Celestial.** Request a table with a view at this spot on top of Mt. Adams serving French and American cuisine. ✉ *1071 Celestial St.,* ☎ *513/241–4455. Jacket required. AE, DC, MC, V. Closed Sun.*

$$$ ★ ✕ **The Maisonette.** Since 1964 this has been ranked among the foremost restaurants in the United States. The food is fresh and French, the atmosphere plush and formal. ✉ *114 E. 6th St.,* ☎ *513/721–2260. Reservations essential. Jacket required. AE, D, DC, MC, V. Closed Sun.*

$$ ✕ **Lenhardt's.** This informal restaurant dishes up schnitzel, Viennese and Hungarian goulash, sauerbraten, and potato pancakes. Be sure to try the homemade apple strudel. ✉ *151 W. McMillan St.,* ☎ *513/281–3600. AE, D, MC, V. Closed Sun.–Mon., 1st 2 wks in Aug., 2 wks at Christmas.*

$$ ✕ **Montgomery Inn at the Boathouse.** The barbecued ribs are famous, and you can't get any closer to the river without swimming in it. ✉ *925 Eastern Ave.,* ☎ *513/721–7427. AE, D, DC, MC, V. No lunch weekends.*

$ ✕ **Rookwood Pottery.** Families consume giant hamburgers and other American fare in wood-and-brick dining rooms that contain what were once the kilns of the famous Mt. Adams pottery. ✉ *1077 Celestial St.,* ☎ *513/721–5456. AE, DC, MC, V.*

Lodging

Downtown Cincinnati has several choice hotels. Many offer weekend packages including tickets to Reds or Bengals games. Staying in the suburbs is less expensive. For price ranges *see* Chart 2 (B) *in* On the Road with Fodor's.

$$$ ★ ✕🏨 **Cincinnatian Hotel.** Stars are drawn to this sedate French Second Empire–style hotel with an unusual contemporary interior. Reservations are essential at the Palace (☎ 513/381–6006), where the chef delights diners with his regional American cuisine—and his crème brûlée. ✉ *601 Vine St., 45202,* ☎ *513/381–3000 or 800/942–9000, 800/332–2020 in OH,* FAX *513/651–0256. 147 rooms. 2 restaurants, lounge, health club, concierge, parking (fee). AE, D, DC, MC, V.*

$$$ ⊞ **Omni Netherland Plaza.** Downtown's grand Art Deco hotel is in
★ the Carew Tower (☞ Exploring Cincinnati, *above*). The two-story lobby
is impressive, with bas-relief sculptures and dramatic fountains and light
fixtures; guest rooms have 10-ft ceilings and soft pastel colors. The restau-
rant, Orchids, serves American cuisine in the exquisite Palm Court. ⊠
35 W. 5th St., 45202, ☎ *513/421–9100,* FAX *513/421–4291. 621
rooms. 2 restaurants, lounge, pool, health club, concierge, parking (fee).
AE, D, DC, MC, V.*

$$ ⊞ **Amos Shinkle Town House B&B.** The master bedroom in this antebellum mansion, once home to the man who hired John A. Roebling
to build a suspension bridge across the Ohio River, has a whirlpool
and a crystal chandelier in the bathroom. ⊠ *215 Garrard St., Covington, KY 41011,* ☎ *606/431–2118. 7 rooms. Parking. AE, D, DC,
MC, V.*

$$ ⊞ **Best Western Mariemont Inn.** Staying at this inn 10 mi east of down-
town is like staying at Henry VIII's hunting lodge. Everything is in the
Tudor style—even the cash machine. ⊠ *6880 Wooster Pike (U.S. 50),
Mariemont 45227,* ☎ *513/271–2100,* FAX *513/271–1057. 60 rooms.
Restaurant, pub, free parking. AE, D, DC, MC, V.*

Nightlife and the Arts

Nightlife
At Covington Landing, **Howl at the Moon Saloon** (⊠ Foot of Madison
Ave., Covington KY, 41011, ☎ 606/491–7733) features dueling piano
players and sing-alongs. In Mt. Adams, **Longworth's** (⊠ 1108 St. Gre-
gory St., ☎ 513/579–0900) has a DJ, a garden, and live music on the
weekends. The **Incline** (⊠ 1071 Celestial St., ☎ 513/241–4455), a so-
phisticated bar at the Celestial Restaurant, spotlights vocalists.

The Arts
The **Music Hall** (⊠ 1241 Elm St., ☎ 513/721–8222), built in the 18th
century in a style since dubbed "sauerbraten Gothic," is home to the **Cincin-
nati Symphony Orchestra** as well as the **Cincinnati Pops Orchestra** (☎
513/381–3300), which performs from September through May at the
Music Hall and June and July at Riverbend; the **Cincinnati Opera** (☎
513/241–2742), with performances in June and July; and the **Cincinnati
Ballet** (☎ 513/621–5219), with performances from October through May.

Spectator Sports
Baseball: Cincinnati Reds (⊠ 100 Cinergy Field, ☎ 513/421–4510).

Football: Cincinnati Bengals (⊠ 1 Bengals Dr., ☎ 513/621–3550).

Shopping
Upscale shopping is available in **Tower Place** (⊠ 4th and Race Sts.),
an atrium shopping mall. Skywalks connect Tower Place with **McAlpin's**
and **Saks Fifth Avenue** (via Carew Tower). Over the Roebling Bridge
in Covington, Kentucky, **Mainstrasse Village** has gift and antiques
shops and vintage clothing boutiques.

NORTHWEST OHIO AND
THE LAKE ERIE ISLANDS

Between Toledo and Cleveland lie a stretch of the Lake Erie shore and
a group of islands that constitute the Riviera and Madeira of Ohio.
Families rent cottages at Catawba Point or Put-in-Bay (the port village
on South Bass Island) and swim, fish, and boat, topping the week off
with a trip to Cedar Point Amusement Park in Sandusky.

Visitor Information

Erie County: Visitors Bureau (✉ 231 W. Washington Row, Sandusky 44870, ☎ 419/625–2984 or 800/255–3743) covers Cedar Point, Kelleys Island, and Sandusky. **Ottawa County:** Visitors Bureau (✉ 109 Madison St., Port Clinton 43452, ☎ 419/734–4386 or 800/441–1271) covers Catawba, Lakeside, Marblehead, Port Clinton, Oak Harbor, and Put-in-Bay. **Greater Toledo:** Convention and Visitors Bureau (✉ SeaGate Convention Center, 401 Jefferson Ave., 2nd floor, 43604, ☎ 419/321–6404 or 800/243–4667). **Kelleys Island:** Chamber of Commerce (✉ Box 783F, 43438, ☎ 419/746–2360). **Put-in-Bay:** Chamber of Commerce (✉ Box 250-BN, 43456, ☎ 419/285–2832).

Arriving and Departing

By Boat

Ferries serve the Lake Erie islands from May through October. **Put-in-Bay Jet Express** (☎ 800/245–1538), from Port Clinton to Put-in-Bay, takes passengers and bicycles only and offers late-night service. Starting in March, **Miller Boat Line** (☎ 419/285–2421) takes passengers and cars (reservations required) from Catawba to Lime Kiln Dock (on the opposite side of South Bass Island from Put-in-Bay) and to Middle Bass Island. **Neumann Boat Line** (☎ 419/798–5800) takes passengers from Marblehead to Kelleys Island.

By Bus

Greyhound Lines has national service from Toledo (✉ 811 Jefferson Ave., ☎ 800/231–2222). **Toledo Area Regional Transit Authority** (TARTA; ☎ 419/243–7433) covers Toledo and its suburbs.

By Car

The Ohio Turnpike (I–80/90) runs between 5 and 10 mi south of the Lake Erie shoreline. For Toledo take Exit 4 (I–75) or Exit 5 (U.S. 280); for Port Clinton, Exit 6 (Route 53); for Sandusky, Exit 7 (U.S. 250). Toledo is on I–75. Route 2 hugs the lake between Toledo and Sandusky; Route 269 loops out to Marblehead.

By Plane

Toledo Express Airport is served by six airlines. For **Cleveland Hopkins Airport** *see* Arriving and Departing *in* Cleveland, *below.* **Griffing Island Airlines** (☎ 419/734–3149), out of **Port Clinton Airport** (✉ 3255 E. State Rd.), and **Griffing Flying Service** (☎ 419/626–5161), out of **Griffing–Sandusky Airport** (✉ 3115 Cleveland Rd., east of Sandusky), fly to the Lake Erie islands.

By Train

Amtrak (☎ 800/872–7245) stops in Toledo and Sandusky.

Exploring Northwest Ohio and the Lake Erie Islands

Though not a tourist town, **Toledo** has its attractions. The Toledo Mud Hens, a Detroit Tigers farm team, play in **Ned Skeldon Stadium,** at Lucas County Recreation Center (✉ 2901 Key St., off U.S. 24, Maumee, ☎ 419/893–9481). The **Toledo Museum of Art** (✉ 2445 Monroe St., at Scottwood Ave., off I–75, ☎ 419/255–8000) offers a small fine collection of European and American paintings, ancient Greek and Egyptian statues, and an important assortment of glass.

Vacationland begins at **Port Clinton,** a center for fishing excursions, which lies at the northern base of the Marblehead Peninsula, some 30 mi east of Toledo on Route 2 (☞ Outdoor Activities and Sports, *below*). Port Clinton is also the base for a ferry to South Bass Island's **Put-in-Bay** (☞ Arriving and Departing, *above*), a port village consisting of a marina, a grassy lakefront park dotted with small cannons, and a strip of shops, bars, and restaurants, with a vintage wooden merry-go-round. Now a town of wild parties, Put-in-Bay was the site of Commodore Oliver Hazard Perry's naval victory over the British in the War of 1812. From the top of **Perry's Victory and International Peace Memorial,** a single massive Doric column east of downtown, you can see all the way to Canada. From May through September you can make a popular day excursion by hopping on a ferry to **Middle Bass Island** and sampling the wares of the **Lonz Winery** (☎ 419/285–5411), which looks like a European monastery.

Back on the mainland, at the eastern tip of the peninsula, is **Marble-head,** site of the oldest continuously working lighthouse on Lake Erie. From Marblehead it's a short ferry ride to **Kelleys Island,** which has two remarkable geologic features: Glacial grooves (waves in the rock) carved during the Ice Age can be seen on the north shore, and the south shore has prehistoric Native American pictographs.

Sandusky, a small port city with lush gardens enlivening its town square, makes a good touring base. It's near the highways and ferries and offers thousands of motel rooms as well as a few romantic Victorian hideaways.

What to See and Do with Children

Cedar Point Amusement Park is in the *Guinness Book of Records* because it has the most roller coasters in the world (12, and counting), among them the fastest one and the highest wooden one. It also has Snake River Falls, the tallest, deepest, and fastest water ride in the world; a water park; and a mile-long sandy beach. ⊠ *Off U.S. 250N,* ☎ *419/627–2350.* ⊠ *$29.95. Closed Oct.–May, weekdays in Sept.*

Outdoor Activities and Sports

Beaches and Water Sports

The best Lake Erie beach is at **East Harbor State Park,** off Route 163 on Marblehead Peninsula. **Cedar Point Amusement Park** also offers good swimming (☞ What to See and Do with Children, *above*). You can rent boats of all sorts and take sailing lessons from **Adventure Plus Yacht Charters and Sailing** at the Sandusky Harbor Marina (☎ 419/625–5000).

Fishing

The western Lake Erie Basin is known as the "walleye capital of the world." Toledo even has the **Walleye Hot Line** (☎ 419/893–9740), which operates March through May. Smallmouth bass and Lake Erie perch are also plentiful. Nonresident fishing licenses are sold at bait shops, or contact the **Division of Wildlife** (☎ 419/625–8062). There's ice fishing if the lake freezes.

The breakwater in Port Clinton and the pier at Catawba Point are both good fishing spots. Per-head fishing boats leave from Fisherman's Wharf in Port Clinton (☎ 419/734–6388) and from Battery Park Marina in Sandusky (☎ 419/625–5000), among other places.

Dining and Lodging

The chambers of commerce in Put-in-Bay and on Kelleys Island (☞ Visitor Information, *above*) give advice on lodging, which should be arranged well in advance. For price ranges *see* Charts 1 (B) and 2 (B) *in* On the Road with Fodor's.

Catawba Point

$$ ✕ **Mon Ami.** This well-established winery and restaurant has a chalet-
★ style dining room with 4-ft-thick stone walls and a patio surrounded
by wooden casks. Pasta and fresh fish are the specialties. ⊠ *3845 E.
Wine Cellar Rd., off N.E. Catawba Rd. (Rte. 53),* ☎ *419/797–4445
or 800/777–4266. AE, MC, V.*

Grand Rapids

$$ ☷ **Mill House.** This country-Victorian house on the Maumee River 40
minutes from downtown Toledo was built in 1900 as a working grist-
mill. A recent renovation has brought a mix of antiques and hand-painted
furniture to the four French Country–style guest rooms, one of which
has its own private entrance and whirlpool tub. ⊠ *24070 Front St.,
43522,* ☎ *419/832–6455. 4 rooms. AE, MC, V.*

Marblehead

$$ ☷ **Old Stone House Bed & Breakfast.** Brenda Anderson, the new owner
of this Federal-style mansion, redecorated in 1996. ⊠ *133 Clemons
St., 43440,* ☎ *419/798–5922. 13 rooms. Free parking. D, MC, V.*

Port Clinton

$$ ✕ **Garden at the Lighthouse.** Up a garden path is a Victorian house
originally built for the lighthouse keeper. Fresh fish and chicken dishes
are served there by candlelight. ⊠ *226 E. Perry St.,* ☎ *419/732–
2151. AE, D, DC, MC, V. Closed Sun. Sept.–May.*

$$ ✕☷ **Island House Hotel.** This 110-year-old redbrick hotel with tall win-
dows has a dining room serving fresh fish. ⊠ *102 Madison St., 43452,*
☎ *419/734–2166 or 800/233–7307. 39 rooms. Restaurant, 2 lounges,
free parking. AE, D, DC, MC, V.*

$$ ☷ **Beach Cliff Lodge.** Families who fish can bunk down in this unpretentious place, close to the ferry and the state park, with freezers and
fish-cleaning services. ⊠ *4189 N.W. Catawba Rd., 43452,* ☎ *419/797–
4553. 8 rooms, 19 cottages. Free parking. No credit cards.*

Put-in-Bay

$$ ✕ **Crescent Tavern.** If you can eat only one meal in Put-in-Bay, this restau-
rant inside a gracious Victorian house is the place. The seafood, steak,
and pasta are all satisfying. ⊠ *Delaware Ave.,* ☎ *419/285–4211. D,
MC, V.*

$ ✕ **Frosty's.** With a bar and a pool table on one side, pizza and Formica
tables on the other, this noisy place caters to rowdies and families alike.
⊠ *Delaware Ave.,* ☎ *419/285–4741. D, MC, V.*

$$ ☷ **Park Hotel.** This white-frame hotel, dating from the 1870s, has etched
glass and a gracious Victorian lobby, but it's also smack in the middle
of the island revelry. Bring earplugs. ⊠ *Box 60, 43456,* ☎ *419/285–
3581. 26 rooms. MC, V.*

Sandusky

$$$ ☷ **Hotel Breakers.** Built in 1905 to resemble a French château, with a
five-story rotunda, stained glass, and vintage wicker furniture, this is *the*
place to stay on the beach at Cedar Point, especially if you can get a tur-
ret room. ⊠ *Box 5006, 44871,* ☎ *419/627–2106. 400 rooms. 4 restau-
rants, lounge, pool, beach, shuffleboard. D, MC, V. Closed Oct.–Apr.*

$$ ☷ **Radisson Harbour Inn.** This big hotel, successfully disguised as a ram-
bling, weathered beach house, was recently purchased by Cedar Point
Amusement Park, so changes may be in the works. ⊠ *2001 Cleveland
Rd., at Cedar Point Causeway, 44870,* ☎ *419/627–2500. 237 rooms.
Restaurant, 2 lounges, pool, exercise room, fishing, free parking. AE,
D, DC, MC, V.*

$$ ⊞ **Wagner's 1844 Inn.** There are canopy beds and globe lamps in the three guest rooms at this inn a block from downtown. Other features available for common use are a pool table, TV, and travel library. Continental breakfast is included in the room rate. ⊠ *230 E. Washington St., 44870,* ☎ *419/626–1726. 3 rooms. D, MC, V.*

Toledo

$ ✕ **Tony Packo's Cafe.** Before Max Klinger ever mentioned it on *M*A*S*H,* this place was famous for its Tiffany lamps and Hungarian hot dogs. Don't miss the autographed hot dog buns. ⊠ *1902 Front St.,* ☎ *419/691–6054. AE, D, MC, V.*

$$ ⊞ **Crowne Plaza.** This is the only downtown hotel right on the Maumee River. Walkways connect it with office buildings and the convention center. Built in 1984, it was remodeled in 1995. ⊠ *2 SeaGate/Summit St., 43604,* ☎ *419/241–1411,* FAX *419/241–8161. 241 rooms. Restaurant, lounge, exercise room, concierge, free parking. AE, D, DC, MC, V.*

Motels

The majority of area motels are in and around Sandusky, on the roads to Cedar Point. Price categories shown reflect high-season rates (June–August). ⊞ **Best Western Resort Inn** (⊠ 1530 Cleveland Rd., Sandusky 44870, ☎ 419/625–9234), 106 rooms, restaurant, pool; *$$$.* ⊞ **Comfort Inn** (⊠ 11020 U.S. 250, Milan Rd., Milan 44846, ☎ 419/ 499–4681), 103 rooms, pool; *$$.*

Campground

Bass Island Resort and Camping has tent and RV sites, hot showers, a beach, bike rentals, boat rentals, and charter-fishing packages. ⊠ *Box 69, Middle Bass Island 43446,* ☎ *419/285–6121. Closed Oct.–Mar.*

CLEVELAND

Since the early 1990s Cleveland's image has improved dramatically. The lake and the river have been cleaned up, new buildings have altered the skyline, and the Flats—the industrial area along the Cuyahoga River—is booming with restaurants and nightclubs. Earlier in the decade the city and the county built Gateway, the collective name for a new arena and baseball stadium just south of downtown. The city's bicentennial celebration in 1996 brought even more changes, including a new science museum that took its place beside the celebrated Rock and Roll Hall of Fame and Museum, which opened in 1995—welcome additions to a city already boasting a world-class orchestra and a stunning art museum.

Visitor Information

Cleveland Convention and Visitors Bureau, Visitor Information Center (⊠ 3100 Terminal Tower, 50 Public Sq., ☎ 216/621–4110 or 800/ 321–1001).

Arriving and Departing

By Bus

Greyhound Lines (⊠ E. 15th St. and Chester Ave., ☎ 800/231–2222).

By Car

I–90 runs east–west through downtown Cleveland. I–71 and I–77 come up from the south. Driving from the east on the Ohio Turnpike (I–80), take Exit 10 to I–71N.

By Plane

Cleveland Hopkins International Airport, 10 mi southwest of downtown, is served by major airlines and several commuter lines. From here the **Rapid Transit Authority** rail system (☎ 216/621–9500) takes 20 minutes to Public Square and costs $1.50. A taxi takes twice as long and costs about $20.

By Train

Amtrak (✉ 200 Memorial Shoreway NE, ☎ 800/872–7245).

Getting Around

The RTA rapid-transit system (☎ 216/621–9500), though not extensive, efficiently bridges east and west, with Tower City as its hub. RTA buses travel from Public Square on five downtown loop routes. A light rail system, the **Waterfront Line,** links Tower City with the Flats entertainment district, the Rock and Roll Hall of Fame and Museum and the Great Lakes Science Center (both at North Coast Harbor), and municipal parking lots.

Exploring Cleveland

Begin your tour of Cleveland at **Terminal Tower,** the city's central landmark. **Tower City Center,** an office and shopping complex, includes the shops of the Avenue (☞ Shopping, *below*). Pick up a copy of "Walks," a brochure outlining some popular Cleveland walking tours, at the **visitor center** just inside the entrance to Tower City Center. The **Old Arcade** runs between Superior and Euclid avenues, a short block east of Public Square. Built in 1890, this is still downtown's most beautiful building. Like a nave without a cathedral, it rises five stories, with brass railings, ironwork, a bridge, and a skylight.

South of Public Square on Ontario Street you'll find **Gund Arena** (✉ 1 Center Court, ☎ 216/420–2000), a sports venue that hosts basketball, hockey, indoor football, concerts, and other events. Next to the arena is **Jacobs Field** (✉ 2401 Ontario St., ☎ 216/420–4200), a trapezoid-shaped baseball park that looks brand-new and old-fashioned at the same time.

★ To see the lake, take East 9th Street to North Coast Harbor, formerly the East 9th Street Pier. The **Rock and Roll Hall of Fame and Museum** (✉ 1 Key Plaza, ☎ 216/781–7625 or 800/282–5393 for a brochure) has 55 high- and low-tech exhibits—from touch-screen computer kiosks exploring performer influences to the actual analog Sun recording studio, where Elvis Presley, Carl Perkins, and Roy Orbison made their first records. Stage costumes that once belonged to Chuck Berry and Iggy Popp, handwritten lyrics by Jimi Hendrix, Janis Joplin's Porsche, and a number of thought-provoking films are among the museum's holdings. **The Great Lakes Science Center** (✉ 601 Erieside, ☎ 216/694–2000) focuses on the environment and technology, particularly in relation to the Great Lakes. The 165,000-square-ft museum opened in 1996 and includes dozens of hands-on exhibits and a 324-seat Omnimax Theater. From June through September, the ***Goodtime III*** (☎ 216/861–5110) gives sightseeing tours on the Cuyahoga River. At sunset both the lake and the skyline glow.

University Circle, reached by rapid transit or a 15-minute drive from downtown, has more than 50 cultural institutions. The centerpiece of University Circle is the **Cleveland Museum of Art** (✉ 11150 E. Blvd., ☎ 216/421–7340), a white-marble temple set among spring-flowering trees and reflected in a lagoon. The free museum is world renowned for its medieval European collection, Egyptian art, and European and

Cleveland

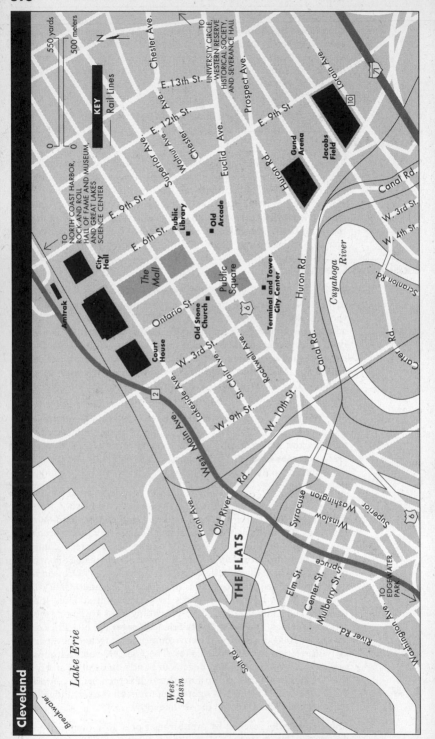

KEY

Rail Lines ▬▬▬

0 _____ 550 yards
0 _____ 500 meters

N

Lake Erie

Breakwater

West Basin

Salt Rd.

Front Ave.

Old River Rd.

THE FLATS

Elm St.
Center St.
Mulberry St.
Spruce St.

River Rd.

Syracuse
Winslow
Washington
Superior

Washington Ave.

TO EDGEWATER PARK

9

West Main Ave.
Lakeside Ave.

Amtrak

2

Court House

City Hall

The Mall

Ontario St.

Old Stone Church

W. 3rd St.

W. 9th St.

W. 10th St.

St. Clair Ave.

Rockwell Ave.

E. 6th St.

E. 9th St.

Superior Ave.

Walnut Ave.

E. 12th St.

E. 13th St.

Chester Ave.

Chester

Euclid Ave.

Prospect Ave.

E. 9th St.

Public Library

Old Arcade

Public Square

Terminal and Tower City Center

6

Huron Rd.

Huron Rd.

Canal Rd.

Canal Rd.

Cuyahoga River

Scranton Rd.

Carter Rd.

W. 3rd St.
W. 4th St.

Canal Rd.

Gund Arena

Jacobs Field

Lorain Ave.

10

7

TO NORTH COAST HARBOR, ROCK AND ROLL HALL OF FAME AND MUSEUM, AND GREAT LAKES SCIENCE CENTER

TO UNIVERSITY CIRCLE, WESTERN RESERVE HISTORICAL SOCIETY, AND SEVERANCE HALL

American paintings; it is closed Monday. The **Western Reserve Historical Society** (✉ 10825 East Blvd., ☎ 216/721–5722) has an extensive Napoleonic collection and in the Crawford Auto-Aviation Museum, just about every old car you'd want to see. It too is closed Monday.

Severance Hall, home of the Cleveland Orchestra (☞ Nightlife and the Arts, *below*), has the city's most beautiful Art Deco interior.

Parks and Gardens

At **Edgewater Park,** just west of downtown, there is a spot where you can swim while enjoying a startlingly close-up view of downtown. The park also includes a fishing pier, a bait shop, a fitness course, playgrounds, and picnic facilities. The stiff wind off the lake attracts a coterie of kite flyers, windsurfers, and the occasional hang glider. Drive through the **Cleveland Cultural Gardens** (✉ Martin Luther King Blvd. in University Circle, north of Chester Ave. and south of I–90, ☎ 216/664–2517) to see gardens representing more than 20 nationalities. The **Rockefeller Park Greenhouse** (✉ 750 E. 88th St., ☎ 216/664–3103), the oldest civic horticultural center in the country, houses seasonal flower and plant exhibits indoors; outdoors you'll find a Japanese garden, a formal English garden, and a talking garden for people with vision impairments.

What to See and Do with Children

The **Children's Museum** (✉ 10730 Euclid Ave., ☎ 216/791–5437), the **Health Museum** (✉ 8911 Euclid Ave., ☎ 216/231–5010), the **Great Lakes Science Center** (✉ 601 Erieside Ave., ☎ 216/694–2000), the **Museum of Natural History** (✉ 1 Wade Oval Dr., ☎ 216/231–4600), and the **Cleveland Metroparks Zoo** (✉ Brookside Park Dr. off W. 25th St., ☎ 216/661–6500) are guaranteed kid pleasers. Narrated tours on **Lolly the Trolley** (☎ 216/771–4484) leave from Burke Lakefront Airport. **Cedar Point Amusement Park** is an hour away, in Sandusky (☞ Northwest Ohio and the Lake Erie Islands, *above*). **Geauga Lake** (✉ Off Rte. 43, Aurora, ☎ 800/843–9283 or 216/562–7131 in OH) is an amusement park about 20 mi southeast of Cleveland; it's closed October–April. Just down the road from Geauga Lake is **Sea World** (☎ 216/995–2121; 216/562–8101 or 800/637–4268 for recording), which is closed September through May.

Dining

Ethnic food is a specialty in Cleveland, whether it's a Polish hot dog smothered with Cleveland's famous Stadium Mustard, an open-pit barbecued spare rib, or a spicy burrito. There are restaurant rows in the Flats, the Warehouse District, the area around Gund Arena and Jacobs Field, Little Italy, and on Coventry Road in Cleveland Heights. For price ranges *see* Chart 1 (B) *in* On the Road with Fodor's.

$$$ ✗ **The Palazzo.** The two granddaughters of the original owner prepare and serve northern Italian cuisine in this romantic hideaway. Whether turning out updated versions of her recipes or new dishes inspired by annual trips back to Italy, they do their grandma proud. ✉ *10031 Detroit Ave.,* ☎ *216/651–3900. AE, MC, V. Closed Sun.–Wed.*

$$$ ✗ **Sammy's.** Fresh fish, a raw bar, venison, and linguine are some of the specialties of this restaurant in a converted warehouse with terrific Cuyahoga views. ✉ *1400 W. 10th St.,* ☎ *216/523–5560. Reservations required. AE, D, DC, MC, V. Closed Sun.*

$$ ✗ **La Dolce Vita.** Strolling mariachi musicians on the weekends and live opera on Monday nights give this place a festive mood; daily specials

of veal, seafood, risotto, and eggplant add to the pleasure. Though the restaurant is a bit fancier than most of its homey neighbors in Little Italy, it is not at all stuffy. ✉ *12112 Mayfield Rd.,* ☎ *216/721–8155. Reservations required Mon. AE, D, MC, V.*

$$ ✕ **Keka.** The rustic Spanish cuisine here includes an adventurous tapas menu and family-style meals. Inexpensive tapa standouts include a plateful of roasted redskin potatoes with cumin and mustard seeds, served with garlic mayonnaise. Simple Spanish wine is authentically served in plain glasses; only the very good stuff is poured into stemware. ✉ *2523 Market St.,* ☎ *216/241–5352. AE, MC, V. Closed Mon.*

$$ ✕ **Luchita's.** This basic Mexican restaurant is jammed on the weekends—and for good reason: great authentic Mexican fare in generous portions, along with friendly service. What more do you need? Oh, yeah, the margaritas are good, too. ✉ *3456 W. 117th St.,* ☎ *216/252–1169. AE, MC, V. Closed Mon.*

$ ✕ **Nate's Deli and Restaurant.** This breakfast and lunch spot on the near West Side serves traditional deli fare as well as Middle Eastern specialties. The rich and creamy hummus may be the best in town. ✉ *1923 W. 25th St.,* ☎ *216/696–7529. No credit cards. Closed Sun.*

$ ✕ **Tommy's.** An institution on hippie-tinged Coventry Road, Tommy's serves hefty salads and sandwiches, many of them vegetarian, and embarrassingly large but delicious milk shakes made with Cleveland's own Pierre's ice cream. ✉ *1824 Coventry Rd., Cleveland Heights,* ☎ *216/ 321–7757. MC, V.*

Lodging

Cleveland has taken great strides in correcting the shortage of hotels downtown. Since 1990 the Ritz-Carlton, the Cleveland Marriott, and the Wyndham Hotel have opened, and a half-dozen other hotels are on the drawing board. Downtown hotels offer weekend packages, whereas suburban ones have lower weekday rates. For price ranges *see* Chart 2 (A) *in* On the Road with Fodor's.

$$$$ 🏨 **Cleveland Marriott Key Center.** Attached to Key Tower, the tallest building in Cleveland, this hotel faces the historic Mall and abuts Public Square. Plush accommodations are complemented by fantastic views of Lake Erie and the lights and bridges of the Flats. ✉ *127 Public Sq., 44114,* ☎ *216/696–9200,* FAX *216/696–0966. 401 rooms. Restaurant, lounge, exercise room, concierge, parking (fee). AE, D, DC, MC, V.*

$$$$ 🏨 **Embassy Suites Hotel.** This downtown former apartment complex debuted in 1990 as Cleveland's first all-suite hotel. Decor is modern but warmly elegant, with decidedly private club–style furnishings. ✉ *1701 E. 12th St., 44114,* ☎ *216/523–8000,* FAX *216/523–1698. 268 suites. Restaurant, health club. AE, D, DC, MC, V.*

$$$$ 🏨 **Ritz-Carlton.** The city's only four-star hotel is filled with antiques
★   and original 18th-century artwork. The Riverview Room restaurant offers excellent views of the Flats. ✉ *1515 W. 3rd St., 44113,* ☎ *216/ 623–1300,* FAX *216/623–0515. 208 rooms. Restaurant, lounge, pool, exercise room, concierge, parking (fee). AE, D, DC, MC, V.*

$$$$ 🏨 **Renaissance Cleveland Hotel.** The city's original grand hotel has a lobby with an ornate Carrara marble fountain. The rooms, done in burgundy and pale green, have period furniture and good views. ✉ *24 Public Sq., 44113,* ☎ *216/696–5600,* FAX *216/696–0432. 491 rooms. 2 restaurants, 2 bars, pool, health club, concierge. AE, D, DC, MC, V.*

$$$ 🏨 **Baricelli Inn.** Every room is different in this turn-of-the-century brownstone mansion, now a B&B, convenient to University Circle. Contemporary European and American dinners are served in the dining room (closed Sunday). ✉ *2203 Cornell Rd., 44106,* ☎ *216/791–*

6500, FAX *216/791–9131. 7 rooms. Restaurant, free parking. AE, DC, MC, V.*

$$$ 🏨 **Mario's International Spa and Hotel.** This rustic barn-board lodge, furnished with antiques and Victorian draperies, started out as a hair salon. The restaurant has spa dining, Roman pizza, and six-course northern Italian dinners. ⊠ *35 E. Garfield Rd. (Rtes. 82 and 306), Aurora 44202,* ☎ *216/562–9171,* FAX *216/562–2386. 14 rooms. Restaurant, spa, free parking. AE, D, DC MC, V.*

$$$ 🏨 **Omni International Hotel.** Although it's on the grounds of the renowned Cleveland Clinic (and there are special rates for clinic patients), there's nothing clinical about this luxurious international hotel. The Classics Restaurant (no lunch Saturday and closed Sunday) has French and Continental cuisine. ⊠ *2065 E. 96th St. (at Carnegie Ave.), 44106,* ☎ *216/791–1900,* FAX *216/231–3329. 274 rooms. 3 restaurants, bar, exercise room, laundry service, concierge, free parking. AE, D, DC, MC, V.*

$$$ 🏨 **Sheraton Cleveland City Center Hotel.** This hotel is geared to business travelers, with upgraded communications systems and additional phones and work space in all rooms. ⊠ *777 St. Clair Ave., 44114,* ☎ *216/771–7600 or 800/321–1090 in OH,* FAX *216/566–0736. 475 rooms. Restaurant, health club, meeting rooms. AE, D, DC, MC, V.*

$$ 🏨 **Holiday Inn–Lakeside.** Across from Burke Lakefront Airport and convenient to the train station, the Rock and Roll Hall of Fame and Museum, and the Great Lakes Science Center, this hotel has lake views and a country-club feel. ⊠ *1111 Lakeside, 44114,* ☎ *216/241–5100,* FAX *216/241–5437. 370 rooms. Restaurant, bar, pool, exercise room, parking (fee). AE, D, DC, MC, V.*

$$ 🏨 **Ramada Inn–Southeast.** This seven-story suburban hotel, with a restful lobby done in blue and gray, is convenient to Sea World and Geauga Lake. ⊠ *24801 Rockside Rd. (at I–271), Bedford Heights 44146,* ☎ FAX *216/439–2500. 130 rooms. Restaurant, pub, pool, free parking. AE, D, DC, MC, V.*

$ 🏨 **Brooklyn YMCA.** Bare-bones single rooms for men are available on a first-come, first-served basis. ⊠ *3881 Pearl Rd., 44109,* ☎ *216/749–2355. 69 rooms. Pool, exercise room, laundry, free parking. D, MC, V.*

Motels

Motels are concentrated around the Berea–Middleburg Heights exit off I–71 (near the airport), the Rockside Road/Brecksville exit off I–77, and the Chagrin Boulevard/Beachwood exit off I–271. Closer to Aurora, the rates are higher in summer. 🏨 **Aurora Woodlands Best Western Inn** (⊠ 800 N. Aurora Rd., Aurora 44202, ☎ 216/562–9151), 140 rooms, restaurant, pool, exercise room; *$$$.* 🏨 **Radisson Inn Beachwood** (⊠ 26300 Chagrin Blvd., Beachwood 44122, ☎ 216/831–5150 or 800/221–2222), 196 rooms, 6 suites, restaurant, lounge, pool, exercise room; *$$.* 🏨 **La Siesta Motel** (⊠ 8300 Pearl Rd., Strongsville 44136, ☎ 216/234–4488), 38 rooms; *$.* 🏨 **Quality Inn Airport** (⊠ 16161 Brook Park Rd., Cleveland 44142, ☎ 216/267–5100 or 800/228–5151, FAX 216/267–2428), 153 rooms, bar, 2 pools; *$.*

Nightlife and the Arts

Nightlife

Nightlife is concentrated on both banks of the Flats—where the crowd is young and into everything from darts to karaoke, from oldies rock to punk rock—as well as in the more mature Warehouse District. The **Powerhouse,** a beautifully restored building that was originally a power station for Cleveland's trolley cars, entertains at the south end of the Flats with its Improv Comedy Club (☎ 216/696–4677) and other shops and restaurants. Trendy **Whiskey** (⊠ 1575 Merwin Ave., ☎ 216/

522–1575), open Saturday night only, offers dramatic views of the river, provided you don't drink too much of the nightclub's namesake specialty. For a look at the Flats the way it used to be, try the **Harbor Inn** (✉ 1219 Main Ave., ☎ 216/241–3232). **Wilbert's** (✉ 1360 W. 9th St., ☎ 216/771–2583), between the Warehouse District and the Flats, specializes in roots rock 'n roll. At **Liquid Café & Bar** (✉ 1212 West 6th St., ☎ 216/479–7717), a board game–strewn pub in the Warehouse District, patrons sit in comfy chairs and impress the opposite sex with seven-letter Scrabble words—or by sinking their opponent's battleship.

The Arts

Playhouse Square Center (✉ 1501 Euclid Ave., at E. 17th St., ☎ 216/771–8403) is home to the **Cleveland Ballet, Cleveland Opera,** and the **Great Lakes Theater Festival.** The **Cleveland Play House** (✉ 8500 Euclid Ave., ☎ 216/795–7000) and **Karamu House** (✉ 2355 E. 89th St., ☎ 216/795–7070) are near University Circle. **Severance Hall** (✉ 11001 Euclid Ave., ☎ 216/231–1111) is home to the **Cleveland Orchestra,** except during summer, when the orchestra moves to a pastoral outdoor shed, **Blossom Music Center** (☎ 216/566–8184 or 888/225–6776), between Cleveland and Akron. Tickets to many events are sold through **TicketMaster** (☎ 216/241–5555) and **Advantix** (☎ 216/241–6000).

Spectator Sports

Baseball: Cleveland Indians (✉ Jacobs Field, 2401 Ontario St., at Carnegie Ave., ☎ 216/420–4200).

Basketball: Cavaliers (✉ Gund Arena, Ontario St. at Huron Rd., ☎ 216/420–2000).

Shopping

Cleveland has two glitzy downtown malls, the **Galleria** (✉ 1301 E. 9th St., ☎ 216/861–4343) and the **Avenue** (✉ Tower City Center, ☎ 216/241–8550), with views of the river. The **West Side Market** (✉ Corner of W. 25th St. and Lorain Rd.), the world's largest indoor/outdoor farmers' market, sells freshly baked breads, fruit picked that morning, and perhaps the sharpest cheddar cheese you've ever eaten.

ELSEWHERE IN OHIO

Neil Armstrong Air and Space Museum

Arriving and Departing

The museum is off I–75, halfway between Cincinnati and Toledo (about an hour from either), in Wapakoneta, Neil Armstrong's hometown.

What to See and Do

Ohio is a leading producer of astronauts. The **Neil Armstrong Air and Space Museum** helps you feel what it's like to go into space. ✉ *I–75 Exit 111,* ☎ *419/738–8811. Closed Dec.–Feb.*

Dayton

Arriving and Departing

Dayton is 54 mi north of Cincinnati on I–75, just below the interchange with I–70. **Dayton International Airport** is served by several major carriers and commuter lines.

What to See and Do

Aviation is central to the history of Dayton. The **Dayton/Montgomery County Convention and Visitors Bureau** (✉ 1 Chamber Plaza, Suite A, 5th and Main Sts., 45402, ☎ 937/226–8211 or 800/221–8235, 800/221–8234 in OH) publishes a helpful visitors' guide and operates an information center at the United States Air Force Museum (☞ *below*).

The **Dayton Aviation Heritage National Historical Park** (☎ 937/225–7705) includes the field where Dayton natives Orville and Wilbur Wright first practiced flying, the **Wright Brothers Bicycle Shop** (✉ 22 S. Williams St.), the **Wright Memorial**, and the home of a Wright Brothers associate, noted African-American poet Paul Laurence Dunbar.

The **United States Air Force Museum** (✉ Wright-Patterson Air Force Base, Springfield Pike, ☎ 937/255–3284), an internationally known attraction, explains the story of flight, from Icarus to the Space Age. The **IMAX theater** shows flight-related films several times daily (☎ 937/253–4629). Also here are museum shops, a café, and picnic tables. Take I–75 to the Route 4/Harshman Road Exit.

The **National Afro-American Museum and Cultural Center,** south of Dayton, is one of the largest African-American museums in the United States. Among the many exhibits exploring history and art is the permanent From Victory to Freedom, which examines black politics from the '40s through the '60s. ✉ *1350 Brush Row Rd., Wilberforce 45384 (Rte. 72 to Rte. 42, Brush Rd. Exit),* ☎ *937/376–4944. Closed Mon.*

Akron

Arriving and Departing

Akron is about 25 mi south of Cleveland, off I–77.

What to See and Do

The **Akron/Summit Convention and Visitors Bureau** (☎ 330/374–7560 or 800/245–4254) has information on attractions and events around the Rubber City, where you just might catch the Goodyear blimp landing across from Goodyear Park. **Inventure Place and National Inventors Hall of Fame** not only honors famous inventors and inventions in a striking museum in downtown Akron, it also hopes to inspire the next generation of inventors. This hands-on museum means it; there's even a room where you can take computers apart—and not put them back together. ✉ *221 S. Broadway, at University Ave.,* ☎ *330/762–4463 or 800/968–4332.*

Canton

Arriving and Departing

Canton is about 50 mi south of Cleveland, off I–77.

What to See and Do

The **Canton/Stark County Convention & Visitors Bureau** (✉ 229 Wells Ave. NW, Canton 44703, ☎ 330/452–0243 or 800/533–4302) maintains an information center along the approach road to the Hall of Fame. The **Pro Football Hall of Fame,** its dome shaped like a football in kickoff position, is a mecca to football fans. Two enshrinement halls are the serious purpose, but displays include a chronology of the game, mementos of the great players, and video replays showing great moments in football. ✉ *2121 George Halas Dr. NW (Fulton Rd. Exit off I–77 and U.S. 62),* ☎ *330/456–8207.*

WISCONSIN

By Don
Davenport

Updated by
Joanne
Kempinger
Demski

Capital	Madison
Population	5,160,000
Motto	Forward
State Bird	Robin
State Flower	Wood violet
Postal Abbreviation	WI

Statewide Visitor Information

Wisconsin Department of Tourism (✉ Box 7606, Madison 53707, ☎ 608/266–2161 or 800/432–8747).

Information centers: I–90N at Rest Area 22, near Beloit; I–94E at Rest Area 25, near Hudson; I–94N at Rest Area 26, near Kenosha; I–90E at Rest Area 31, near La Crosse; Route 12N at Rest Area 24, near Genoa City; Prairie du Chien, at the Route 18 bridge; 123 W. Washington Ave., Madison; Highways 2 and 53 in Superior; Highways 151 and 61 near Dickeyville; Highways 51 and 2 in Hurley; and at 342 N. Michigan Ave., in Chicago, Illinois.

Scenic Drives

As part of the **Great River Road,** Route 35 follows the Mississippi River between Prairie du Chien and Prescott, offering many vistas. Route 107, between Merrill and Tomahawk, travels along the 400-mi-long **Wisconsin River valley.** In northeastern Wisconsin Routes 57 and 42 circle the **Door County Peninsula,** providing 250 mi of spectacular Lake Michigan scenery.

National and State Parks

National Park
Apostle Islands National Lakeshore (☞ Elsewhere in Wisconsin, *below*).

State Parks
Wisconsin's state park system includes 48 parks and recreation areas, nine forests, and numerous trails. Camping is allowed in 36 state parks and seven state forests. The **Wisconsin Department of Natural Resources** (✉ Bureau of Parks and Recreation, Box 7921, Madison 53707, ☎ 608/266–2181) provides information.

Devil's Lake State Park (✉ S5975 Park Rd., Baraboo 53913, ☎ 608/356–8301) is one of the state's most popular, with hiking, camping, and 500-ft-high bluffs overlooking Devil's Lake. **Pattison State Park** (✉ 6294 S. State Rd. 35, Superior 54880, ☎ 715/399–8073) is distinctive for the 165-ft Big Manitou Falls, Wisconsin's highest waterfall and the fourth highest east of the Rocky Mountains. **Peninsula State Park** (✉ Hwy. 42, Fish Creek 54212, ☎ 414/868–3258) covers nearly 4,000 acres on the shores of Green Bay. Offering golf, hiking, bicycling, and lakeshore camping, it is one of the state's most heavily used parks. **Wyalusing State Park** (✉ 13342 County Rte. C, Bagley 53801, ☎ 608/996–2261) stands at the confluence of the Wisconsin and Mississippi rivers, providing sweeping vistas of the river valleys.

MILWAUKEE

On the shores of Lake Michigan, Wisconsin's largest city is an international seaport and the state's primary commercial and manufacturing center. A small-town atmosphere prevails in Milwaukee, which is not so much a city as a large collection of neighborhoods. Modern steel-and-glass high-rises occupy much of the downtown area, but its early heritage persists in the restored and well-kept 19th-century buildings that share the city skyline. First settled by Potawatomi and later by French fur traders in the late 18th century, the city boomed in the 1840s with the arrival of German brewers, whose influence is still present.

Milwaukee has also become known as a city of festivals. The **Summerfest** is the largest festival held each year, but there are also many ethnic and music festivals each summer on the lakefront. **Winterfest** is held during the cold months. Another annual highlight is the **Great Circus Parade,** a July spectacle that features scores of antique circus wagons from the famed Circus World Museum, in Baraboo.

Visitor Information

Greater Milwaukee: Convention and Visitors Bureau (✉ 510 W. Kilbourn Ave., 53203, ☎ 414/273–7222 or 800/231–0903).

Arriving and Departing

By Bus
Greyhound Lines (✉ 606 N. 7th St., ☎ 800/231–2222).

By Car
From the north, I–43 provides controlled access into downtown Milwaukee. I–94 leads to downtown from Chicago and other points south and west of the city. If you are traveling to sites in the wider metropolitan area, from I–94 you can connect to I–894, which bypasses central Milwaukee.

By Plane
General Mitchell International Airport (✉ 5300 S. Howell Ave., ☎ 414/747–5300), 6 mi south of downtown via I–94, is served by several domestic and international carriers. **Milwaukee County Transit System** (☎ 414/344–6711) operates buses to and from the airport; fare is $1.35, and exact change is required. Taxis between the airport and downtown take about 20 minutes; fare runs from $16 to $18.

By Train
Amtrak (✉ 433 W. St. Paul Ave., ☎ 800/872–7245).

Getting Around Milwaukee

Lake Michigan is the city's eastern boundary; Wisconsin Avenue is the main east–west thoroughfare. The Milwaukee River divides the downtown area east and west. The East–West Expressway (I–94/I–794) is the dividing line between north and south. Streets are numbered in ascending order from the Milwaukee River west well into the suburbs. Many downtown attractions are near the Milwaukee River and can be reached on foot. **Milwaukee County Transit System** (☞ Arriving and Departing by Plane, *above*) provides bus service. **Taxis** can be ordered by phone. The fare is $3 for the first mile and $1.50 for each additional mile. The largest firms are **Yellow Cab** (☎ 414/271–1800) and **City Veterans** (☎ 414/291–8080).

Exploring Milwaukee

Downtown

Milwaukee's central business district is 1 mi long and only a few blocks wide and is divided by the Milwaukee River. On the east side the **Iron Block Building** (⊠ N. Water St. and E. Wisconsin Ave.) is one of the few remaining ironclad buildings in the United States. Its metal facade was brought in by ship from an eastern foundry and installed during the Civil War. In the 1860s Milwaukee exported more wheat than any other port in the world; the mass exportation gave impetus to the building of the **Grain Exchange Room** in the Mackie Building (⊠ 225 E. Michigan St.). The 10,000-square-ft trading room has three-story-high columns and painted ceiling panels that depict Wisconsin wildflowers.

★ The **Milwaukee Art Museum,** in the lakefront War Memorial Center, houses notable collections of paintings, drawings, sculpture, photography, and decorative arts. Its permanent collection is strong in European and American art of the 19th and 20th centuries. ⊠ *750 N. Lincoln Memorial Dr.,* ☎ *414/224–3200. Closed Mon.*

En route from the lakefront to the river, stop a moment at **Cathedral Square.** This quiet park (⊠ E. Kilbourn Ave. and Jefferson St.) was built on the site of Milwaukee's first courthouse. Across the street from Cathedral Square, **St. John's Cathedral,** dedicated in 1853, was the first Roman Catholic cathedral built in Wisconsin.

The **Milwaukee County Historical Center,** a museum housed in a former bank building, displays early firefighting equipment, military artifacts, toys, and women's fashions. It also contains a research library with naturalization records and genealogical resources. ⊠ *910 N. Old World 3rd St.,* ☎ *414/273–8288. Free.*

The banks of the Milwaukee River are busy in summer, especially at noon, when downtown workers lunch in the nearby parks and public areas, such as **Père Marquette Park,** on the river (⊠ Old World 3rd St. and W. Kilbourn Ave.).

There are also river **cruises** of Milwaukee's harbor and lakefront during warm weather. **Iroquois Harbor Cruises** (⊠ Clybourn St. Bridge on the west bank, ☎ 414/332–4194) offers harbor cruises aboard a 149-passenger vessel. **Celebration Excursions Inc.** (⊠ 502 N. Harbor Dr., on the east bank, ☎ 414/278–1113) and **Edelweiss Cruise Dining** (⊠ 1110 N. Old World 3rd St., on the west bank, ☎ 414/272–3625) run lunch, brunch, cocktail, and dinner cruises.

As you cross the river to the west side, notice that the east-side streets are not directly opposite the west-side streets and that the bridges across the river are built at an angle. This layout dates from the 1840s, when the area east of the river was called Juneautown and the region to the west was known as Kilbourntown. The rival communities had a fierce argument over which would pay for the bridges that connected them; so intense was the antagonism that citizens venturing into rival territory carried white flags. The Great Bridge War, as it was called, was finally settled by the state legislature in 1845, but the streets on either side of the river were never aligned.

★ Considered among the best natural history museums in the country, the **Milwaukee Public Museum** is known for its collection of more than 6 million specimens and artifacts. Its award-winning walk-through exhibits include the "Streets of Old Milwaukee," depicting the city in the 1890s; a two-story rain forest; and the "Third Planet" (complete with full-size dinosaurs), where visitors walk into the interior of the Earth

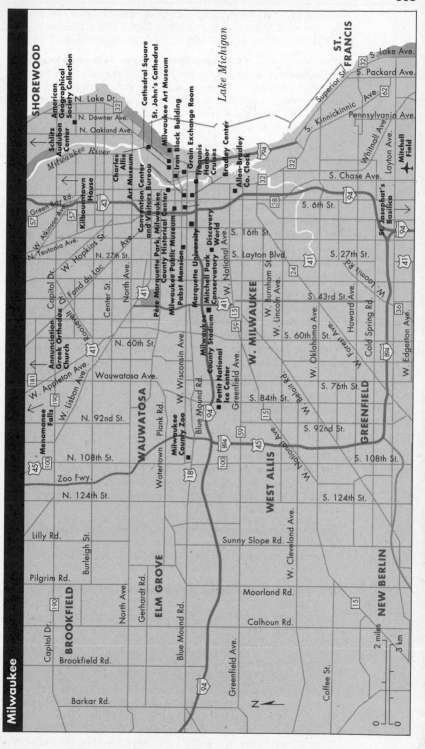

Milwaukee

SHOREWOOD

American Geographical Society Collection
N. Lake Dr.
N. Downer Ave.
N. Oakland Ave.
Schlitz Audubon Center

Cathedral Square
St. John's Cathedral
Milwaukee Art Museum
Iron Block Building
Grain Exchange Room
Iroquois Harbor Cruises
Bradley Center
Allen-Bradley Co. Clock

Lake Michigan

ST. FRANCIS
S. Lake Ave.
S. Packard Ave.
Superior St.
S. Kinnickinnic Ave.
Pennsylvania Ave.
Whitnall Ave.
Layton Ave.
Mitchell Field

Milwaukee River

Charles Allis Art Museum
Kilbourntown House
Green Bay Rd.
W. Atkinson Ave.
Convention Center and Visitors Bureau
Pete Marquette Park, Milwaukee County Historical Center
Milwaukee Public Museum
Pabst Mansion

S. Chase Ave.
St. Josephat's Basilica

N. Teutonia Ave.
W. Hopkins St.
N. 27th St.
Capitol Dr.
Fond du Lac Ave.
North Ave.
Center St.
Roosevelt Dr.

Marquette University
Mitchell Park Conservatory
Discovery World
W. National Ave.

S. 6th St.
S. 16th St.
S. Layton Blvd.
S. 27th St.
W. Loomis Rd.

Annunciation Greek Orthodox Church
N. Appleton Ave.
N. Lisbon Ave.
W. Appleton Ave.
W. Lisbon Ave.
Menomonee Falls
N. 92nd St.

Milwaukee County Stadium
Pettit National Ice Center
Greenfield Ave.

W. MILWAUKEE
S. Burnham St.
S. Lincoln Ave.
W. Oklahoma Ave.
S. 43rd St.
S. 60th St.
Howard Ave.
Forest Home Ave.
Cold Spring Rd.
W. Edgerton Ave.

WAUWATOSA
Wauwatosa Ave.
Plank Rd.
Watertown Plank Rd.
Milwaukee County Zoo
Blue Mound Rd.
W. Wisconsin Ave.

GREENFIELD
S. 76th St.
S. 84th Ave.
S. 92nd St.

N. 108th St.
N. 124th St.
Zoo Fwy.

WEST ALLIS
W. National Ave.
Beloit Rd.
S. 108th St.
S. 124th St.

Lilly Rd.
Burleigh St.
Pilgrim Rd.
Capitol Dr.
BROOKFIELD
Brookfield Rd.
North Ave.
Gerhardt Rd.
ELM GROVE
Blue Mound Rd.
Barkar Rd.

Sunny Slope Rd.
W. Cleveland Ave.
Moorland Rd.
Calhoun Rd.
Greenfield Ave.
Coffee St.

NEW BERLIN

2 miles
3 km
0

to learn about its history. In cooperation with Discovery World, the museum recently opened the **Humphrey IMAX Dome Theater,** the first of its kind in Wisconsin. ⊠ *800 W. Wells St.,* ☎ *414/278–2702.*

Discovery World, as the **James Lovell Museum of Science, Economics, and Technology** in the Milwaukee Public Museum is called, has more than 140 interactive exhibits on magnets, motors, electricity, health, and computers. It also puts on the "Great Electric Show" and the "Light Wave–Laser Beam Show" on some weekdays and on weekends. ⊠ *712 W. Wells St.* ☎ *414/765–9966.*

St. Joan of Arc Chapel (☎ 414/288–6873), a small, stone 15th-century chapel, was moved from its original site near Lyon, France, in 1964 and reconstructed on the central mall of the Marquette University campus. One of the stones was reputedly kissed by Joan before she was sent to her death and is discernibly colder than the others.

The **Patrick and Beatrice Haggerty Museum of Art** houses Marquette University's collection of more than 6,000 works of art, including Renaissance, Baroque, and modern paintings, sculpture, prints, photography, and decorative arts; it also offers changing exhibitions. ⊠ *13th and Clybourn Sts.,* ☎ *414/288–7290.*

★ The **Pabst Mansion,** completed in 1892 for the beer baron Captain Frederick Pabst, is one of Milwaukee's treasured landmarks. The 37-room Flemish Renaissance–style mansion has a tan pressed-brick exterior with carved-stone and terra-cotta ornamentation. Inside are woodwork, ironwork, marble, tile, and stained glass. ⊠ *2000 W. Wisconsin Ave.,* ☎ *414/931–0808.*

★ Milwaukee's unique **Mitchell Park Conservatory** consists of three 85-ft-high glass domes housing tropical, arid, and seasonal plants and flowers; its lilies and poinsettias are spectacular at Easter and Christmas. There are picnic facilities on the grounds. ⊠ *524 S. Layton Blvd.,* ☎ *414/649–9800.*

Other Attractions
The **Allen-Bradley Co. Clock** is a Milwaukee landmark and, according to the *Guinness Book of Records,* "the largest four-faced clock in the world." Great Lakes ships often use the clock as a navigational reference point. ⊠ *1201 S. 2nd St.*

★ The **Milwaukee County Zoo** has more than 3,000 wild animals and birds, including endangered species. Educational programs, a petting zoo, narrated tram tours, miniature-train rides, and cross-country skiing trails are additional draws. ⊠ *10001 W. Bluemound Rd.,* ☎ *414/771–3040.*

The **American Geographical Society Collection,** in the Golda Meir Library on the University of Wisconsin–Milwaukee campus, has an exceptional assemblage of maps, old globes, atlases, and charts, plus about 200,000 books and journals. ⊠ *2311 E. Hartford Ave.,* ☎ *414/229–6282.* ▣ *Free. Closed weekends.*

The **University of Wisconsin** (☎ 414/229–5070) has three worthwhile art venues. The **Art Museum** (⊠ 3253 N. Downer Ave., holds a permanent collection of Greek and Russian icons and 20th-century European paintings and prints. The **Fine Arts Gallery** (⊠ 2400 E. Kenwood Blvd.) displays the works of students and faculty members. Changing exhibits are held at the **Art History Gallery** (⊠ 3203 N. Downer Ave.). All three venues are free, and all are closed Monday; the museum is closed Tuesday as well.

The **Charles Allis Art Museum** occupies an elegant Tudor-style house built in 1911 for the first president of the Allis-Chalmers Manufacturing

Company. The home has stained-glass windows by Louis Comfort Tiffany and a stunning worldwide collection of paintings and objets d'art, including works by major 19th- and 20th-century French and American painters. ⊠ *1801 N. Prospect Ave.,* ☎ *414/278–8295. Closed Mon.–Tues.*

The **Lowell Damon House,** completed in 1847, is a classic example of colonial-style architecture. ⊠ *Wauwatosa Ave. and Rogers St.,* ☎ *414/273–8288. Closed Mon.–Tues. and Thurs.–Sat.*

Forests, ponds, marshland, and nature trails attract nature lovers to the **Schlitz Audubon Center,** a 225-acre wildlife area with an environmental research and education center. ⊠ *1111 E. Brown Deer Rd.,* ☎ *414/352–2880. Closed Mon.*

The **Annunciation Greek Orthodox Church** was Frank Lloyd Wright's last major work; the famed Wisconsin architect called it his "little jewel." Since it opened in 1961, the blue-domed Byzantine-style church has drawn visitors from all over the world. It can only be seen on Tuesday and Friday by prearranged group tour. ⊠ *9400 W. Congress St.,* ☎ *414/461–9400.*

Built by immigrant parishioners and local craftsmen at the turn of the century, **St. Josephat's Basilica** has a copper dome modeled after the one atop St. Peter's in Rome. Inside is a remarkable collection of relics. ⊠ *601 W. Lincoln Ave.,* ☎ *414/645–5623.*

The **Pettit National Ice Center** has an Olympic-size skating rink, two hockey rinks, and plenty of space for jogging. Visitors can spend time on the ice or watch local Olympic speed skaters practice. ⊠ *500 S. 84th St.,* ☎ *414/266–0100.*

In the Vicinity

★ The entire downtown district of **Cedarburg,** most of it built of Niagara limestone by 19th-century pioneers, is on the National Register of Historic Places. **Cedar Creek Settlement** (⊠ N70 W6340 Bridge Rd., ☎ 800/827–8020) is a collection of crafts and antiques shops in the historic Wittenberg Woolen Mill, which was built in 1864 and operated until 1969. Wisconsin's last remaining **covered bridge** (⊠ Off Hwy. 143) crosses Cedar Creek 3 mi north of town. The 120-ft white-pine bridge was built in 1876 and retired in 1962. A small park beside the bridge invites picnicking.

★ **Old World Wisconsin,** the State Historical Society's living history museum near Eagle, celebrates the state's ethnic heritage in architecture, with more than 65 historic buildings on 576 acres in the Southern Kettle Moraine State Forest. The restored farm and village buildings gathered from across the state depict 19th- and 20th-century rural Wisconsin. All were originally built and inhabited by European immigrants; they are grouped in German, Norwegian, Danish, and Finnish farmsteads. Costumed interpreters representing each ethnic group relate the story of immigration to Wisconsin and perform chores, such as making soap, that were intrinsic to rural life a century ago. ⊠ *S103 W37890 Hwy. 67,* ☎ *414/594–6300,* FAX *414/594–6342. Closed Nov.–Apr.*

Kohler is a planned, landscaped village surrounding the factories of the plumbing-fixtures manufacturer Kohler Company. The **Kohler Design Center** (⊠ 101 Upper Rd., ☎ 414/457–3699) houses the company's ceramic art collection, archives, and artifacts from an earlier factory and village, plus a showroom of decorator bathrooms, all free and open to the public. Guided tours of **Waelderhaus** (⊠ W. Riverside Dr., ☎ 414/452–4079), a reproduction of founder John M. Kohler's ancestral home in Austria, are offered daily, for free. The **Woodlake Kohler**

Complex, in nearby Sheboygan, comprises more than 25 shops, galleries, and restaurants. The **American Club** (⊠ Highland Dr., ☎ 414/457–8000 or 800/344–2838), built as a company-owned hotel for workers, is now a posh resort hotel on the National Register of Historic Places. The compound has two 18-hole golf courses, an indoor sports complex, a 500-acre wilderness preserve, and several restaurants.

Parks and Gardens

★ The 660-acre **Whitnall Park** (⊠ 5879 S. 92nd St., in suburban Hales Corners), one of the largest municipal parks in the nation, has an 18-hole golf course, a variety of recreational facilities, picnic areas, and nature and cross-country skiing trails. Within the park is the internationally famous **Alfred L. Boerner Botanical Gardens** (☎ 414/425–1130), with trees, shrubs, and flowers in formal and informal gardens. The park's **Wehr Nature Center** (☎ 414/425–8550) has wildlife exhibits, woodlands and wetlands, a lake, nature trails, and wild gardens.

What to See and Do with Children

At the **Milwaukee Public Museum** (☞ Downtown *in* Exploring Milwaukee, *above*), the **Wizard Wing** has hands-on natural history and human history exhibits. Kids love the Milwaukee Public Central Library's **Discovery World** (☞ Downtown *in* Exploring Milwaukee, *above*). The **Milwaukee County Zoo** (☞ Other Attractions *in* Exploring Milwaukee, *above*) is sure to have strong appeal for the younger set. **Wm. K. Walthers, Inc.** (⊠ 5601 W. Florist Ave., ☎ 414/527–0770), maker of model railroad equipment since 1932, is the world's largest distributor of trains and accessories; more than 84,000 items are housed in a single warehouse.

Dining

Milwaukee's culinary style has been shaped to a great extent by the Germans who first settled here—though other culinary influences are much in evidence as well. Many of Milwaukee's fine restaurants are noted for their decadent desserts. For price ranges see Chart 1 (A) in On the Road with Fodor's.

$$$ ✕ **English Room.** In the Pfister Hotel, Milwaukee's premier hotel
★ restaurant is adorned with original 19th-century paintings. Recommended dishes are rack of lamb, seared crab cakes, and lobster-and-shrimp bisque. Service is formal. ⊠ *424 E. Wisconsin Ave., ☎ 414/390–3832. AE, D, DC, MC, V. No lunch weekends.*

$$$ ✕ **Mike and Anna's.** At this small, trendy restaurant in a working-class neighborhood on the south side, the changing menu might include herb-crushed salmon with white-wine-and-butter sauce. Ask for directions when making reservations. ⊠ *2000 S. 8th St., ☎ 414/643–0072. AE, MC, V. Closed Mon. No lunch.*

$$ ✕ **Boder's on the River.** Tie-back curtains, fireplaces, and antiques give this suburban restaurant a cheerful country look. Roast duckling and baked whitefish are a few of the Wisconsin specialties. Come for Sunday brunch or the Friday-night fish buffet. ⊠ *11919 N. River Rd. 43W, Mequon, ☎ 414/242–0335. AE, D, DC, MC, V. Closed Mon.*

$$ ✕ **Chip and Py's.** In the northern suburbs, this stylish restaurant has light gray dual-level dining rooms, a huge fireplace, and contemporary art. There's an eclectic menu and live jazz on weekends and Wednesday evenings. ⊠ *1340 W. Town Square Rd., Mequon, ☎ 414/241–9589. AE, D, DC, MC, V. Closed Mon. No lunch Sun.*

$$ ✕ **Giovanni's.** This bright Sicilian eatery serves large portions of rich Italian food. Veal steak Giovanni is excellent, and pasta is a sure bet.

⊠ *1683 N. Van Buren St.,* ☎ *414/291–5600. AE, D, DC, MC, V. No lunch weekends.*

$$ ✕ **Grenadier's.** Imaginative dishes combine classical European style with
★ Asian or Indian flavors; offerings include tenderloin of veal with raspberry sauce and angel-hair pasta. The handsome, darkly furnished piano bar also has tables. ⊠ *747 N. Broadway St.,* ☎ *414/276–0747,* FAX *414/276–1424. Jacket required. AE, D, DC, MC, V. Closed Sun. No lunch Sat.*

$$ ✕ **Harold's.** Velvet-back booths, low lighting, etched glass, and rich greenery set a romantic, if slightly generic, mood at this restaurant in the Grand Milwaukee Hotel. Oysters Rockefeller and rack of lamb Provençal are typical of the traditional fare. ⊠ *4747 S. Howell Ave.,* ☎ *414/481–8000. AE, D, DC, MC, V. Closed Sun. Memorial Day– Labor Day. No lunch weekends.*

$$ ✕ **Jake's.** There are two locations for this longtime Milwaukee favorite that earned its reputation with perfectly prepared steaks and heaps of french-fried onion rings. The best menu choices include escargot, roast duckling, and Bailey's chocolate-chip cheesecake. ⊠ *6030 W. North Ave., Wauwatosa,* ☎ *414/771–0550;* ⊠ *21445 W. Capitol Dr., Brookfield,* ☎ *414/781–7995. AE, DC, MC, V. No lunch.*

$$ ✕ **Karl Ratzsch's Old World Restaurant.** In the authentic German
★ atmosphere of this family-owned restaurant, dirndl-skirted waitresses serve schnitzel, roast duckling, and sauerbraten while diners listen to piano music. The main dining room is decorated with murals, chandeliers made from antlers, and antique beer steins. ⊠ *320 E. Mason St.,* ☎ *414/276–2720. AE, D, DC, MC, V. No lunch.*

$$ ✕ **Sanford.** Named for its chef, Sanford D'Amato, this elegant restau-
★ rant is in a remodeled grocery store. Entrées are contemporary American and have won national acclaim for D'Amato. ⊠ *1547 N. Jackson St.,* ☎ *414/276–9608. AE, D, DC, MC, V. Closed Sun. No lunch.*

$$ ✕ **Steven Wade's Cafe.** Unusual dishes distinguish Steven Wade's: Try
★ Norwegian salmon fillet poached with vanilla sauce or Wisconsin ostrich. Once a suburban paint-and-wallpaper store, the café has a cozy Victorian style with a fireplace and a tiny five-seat bar. ⊠ *17001 W. Greenfield Ave., New Berlin,* ☎ *414/784–0774. AE, D, DC, MC, V. Closed Sun. No lunch Sat. and Mon.*

$ ✕ **De Marinis.** The 108th Street site of this popular Italian-American restaurant has excellent pasta dishes and a mean shrimp Italiano. The Conway and Main Street locations—with more relaxed atmospheres and less extensive menus—shine with their pesto-and-artichoke-packed Garden Pizza. ⊠ *1427 S. 108th St., West Allis,* ☎ *414/257–3765;* ⊠ *N88 W15229 Main St., Menomonee Falls,* ☎ *414/253–1568;* ⊠ *1211 E. Conway St.,* ☎ *414/481–2348. AE, D, MC, V.*

$ ✕ **Elsa's on the Park.** Across from Cathedral Square Park, this chic but casual place attracts talkative young professionals for big, juicy hamburgers and pork chop sandwiches. Frequently changing artistic displays are backed by copper and stainless steel accents. ⊠ *833 N. Jefferson St.,* ☎ *414/765–0615. AE, MC, V. No lunch weekends.*

$ ✕ **Sky Room Pub & Restaurant.** You can watch small aircraft take off or land at Timmerman Field from the windows of this friendly, well-run restaurant. Specials change daily, but consistent favorites are the prime rib, large steaks, and massive Greek salads. The Friday-night beer-battered cod fry and clam chowder specials are also worth a try. ⊠ *9305 W. Appleton Ave.,* ☎ *414/461–5850. MC, V. Closed Sun.*

$ ✕ **Three Brothers.** Set in an 1887 tavern, one of Milwaukee's revered ethnic restaurants serves chicken *paprikash* (a stewed chicken dish with paprika), roast lamb, Serbian salad, and homemade desserts at old-style kitchen tables. It's about 10 minutes from downtown, on the near south side. ⊠ *2414 S. St. Clair St.,* ☎ *414/481–7530. No credit cards. Closed Mon. No lunch.*

$ ✕ **Watts Tea Shop.** This genteel spot for breakfast, lunch, or tea with scones is above George Watts & Sons, Milwaukee's premier store for china, crystal, and silver. Indulge in fresh-squeezed juice and a custard-filled sunshine cake. ⊠ *761 N. Jefferson St.,* ☎ *414/276–6352. AE, D, MC, V. Closed Sun. No dinner.*

Lodging

In summer accommodations should be booked well ahead, especially for weekends. For price ranges *see* Chart 2 (A) *in* On the Road with Fodor's.

$$$$ 🏨 **Pfister Hotel.** Many of the rooms in Milwaukee's grand old hotel,
★ built in 1893, have been combined to create suites with enlarged bathrooms. Rooms in the tower, built in 1975, are bright and contemporary with a Victorian accent in keeping with the original hotel. A collection of 19th-century art hangs in the elegant Victorian lobby. ⊠ *424 E. Wisconsin Ave., 53202,* ☎ *414/273–8222 or 800/558–8222; 800/472–4403 in WI;* FAX *414/273–0747. 307 rooms. 3 restaurants, lounge, indoor pool, nightclub. AE, D, DC, MC, V.*

$$$ 🏨 **Embassy Suites–Milwaukee West.** The sweeping atrium lobby, with
★ fountains, potted plants, and glass elevators, is the focal point of this hotel in the western suburbs. The two-bedroom suites are decorated in pastels and earth tones, with contemporary furnishings. ⊠ *1200 S. Moorland Rd., Brookfield 53005,* ☎ *414/782–2900 or 800/444–6404,* FAX *414/796–9159. 203 suites. Restaurant, lounge, indoor pool, sauna, hot tub, exercise room. AE, D, DC, MC, V.*

$$$ 🏨 **Grand Milwaukee Hotel.** Across from the airport, the Grand is the largest hotel in the state. The bright rooms are decorated in earth tones; the marble-walled lobby is illuminated with chandeliers; and a swimming pool cools the central courtyard. ⊠ *4747 S. Howell Ave., 53207,* ☎ *414/481–8000 or 800/558–3862,* FAX *414/481–8065. 510 rooms. 2 restaurants, lounge, 2 pools, 7 tennis courts, health club, racquetball, cinema, nightclub. AE, D, DC, MC, V.*

$$$ 🏨 **Hyatt Regency.** This centrally located high-rise hotel has an 18-story open atrium and a revolving restaurant on top. The rooms are airy, with plush contemporary furnishings. ⊠ *333 W. Kilbourn Ave., 53203,* ☎ *414/276–1234 or 800/233–1234,* FAX *414/276–6338. 483 rooms. 3 restaurants, 3 lounges, exercise center. AE, D, DC, MC, V.*

$$$ 🏨 **Wyndham Milwaukee Center.** In the center of the city's growing the-
★ ater district by the river, this hotel has an opulent lobby tiled with Italian marble. Guest rooms are contemporary, with mahogany furnishings. The hotel has an excellent Sunday brunch as well as a pasta bar. ⊠ *139 E. Kilbourn Ave., 53202,* ☎ *414/276–8686 or 800/996–3426,* FAX *414/276–8007. 221 rooms. Restaurant, lounge, hot tub, sauna, 2 steam baths, health club. AE, D, DC, MC, V.*

$$ 🏨 **Astor Hotel.** Close to Lake Michigan, the Astor has the air of an old grand hotel. Most of the rooms have been remodeled and furnished with antiques and period reproductions, but they retain old bathroom fixtures. ⊠ *924 E. Juneau Ave., 53202,* ☎ *414/271–4220 or 800/558–0200, 800/242–0355 in WI,* FAX *414/271–6370. 97 rooms. Restaurant, lounge, free parking. AE, D, DC, MC, V.*

Motels

🏨 **Best Western Midway Hotel–Airport** (⊠ *5105 S. Howell Ave., 53207,* ☎ *414/769–2100 or 800/528–1234,* FAX *414/769–0064*), 139 rooms, restaurant, lounge, indoor pool, sauna, hot tub, recreation area; *$$.* 🏨 **Holiday Inn–South** (⊠ *6331 S. 13th St., 53221,* ☎ *414/*

764–1500 or 800/465–4329, ꜰᴀx 414/764–6531), 159 rooms, restaurant, lounge, pool, sauna, recreation room, playground; *$$*. 🏨 **Holiday Inn Express** (✉ 11111 W. North Ave., Wauwatosa 53226, ☎ 414/778–0333 or 800/465–4329, ꜰᴀx 414/778–0331), 122 rooms; *$$*.

Nightlife and the Arts

Milwaukee Magazine (on newsstands) lists arts and entertainment events. Also check the daily entertainment sections of the *Milwaukee Journal Sentinel*.

Nightlife

You'll find clubs, bars, and a slew of friendly saloons. The **Safe House** (✉ 779 N. Front St., ☎ 414/271–2007), with a James Bond spy-hideout decor, is a favorite hangout for young people and out-of-towners. **Major Goolsby's** (✉ 340 W. Kilbourn Ave., ☎ 414/271–3414) is regarded as one of the country's top-10 sports bars. Jazz fans go to the **Estate** (✉ 2423 N. Murray Ave., ☎ 414/964–9923), a cozy club with progressive jazz.

The Arts

Milwaukee's theater district is in a two-block downtown area bounded by the Milwaukee River, East Wells Street, North Water Street, and East State Street. Most tickets are sold at box offices.

The **Riverside Theater** (✉ 116 W. Wisconsin Ave., ☎ 414/224–3000) hosts touring theater companies, Broadway shows, and other entertainment. The **Pabst Theater** (✉ 144 E. Wells St., ☎ 414/286–3663) presents a wide variety of live entertainment. The Milwaukee Center (✉ 108 E. Wells St., ☎ 414/224–9490) is home to the **Milwaukee Repertory Theater.** The **Marcus Center for the Performing Arts** (✉ 929 N. Water St., ☎ 414/273–7206) comprises the **Milwaukee Symphony Orchestra, Milwaukee Ballet Company, Florentine Opera Company,** and **First Stage Milwaukee.**

Spectator Sports

Baseball: Milwaukee Brewers (✉ Milwaukee County Stadium, 201 S. 46th St., ☎ 414/933–9000).

Basketball: Milwaukee Bucks (✉ Bradley Center, 1001 N. 4th St., ☎ 414/227–0500).

Hockey: Milwaukee Admirals (✉ Bradley Center, 1001 N. 4th St., ☎ 414/227–0550).

Beaches

Lake Michigan is the place to swim, but be prepared: Mid-summer water temperatures linger in the 50s and 60s. Among the most popular of the narrow sandy beaches are **Bradford Beach** (✉ 2400 N. Lincoln Memorial Dr.), **Doctors Beach** (✉ 1870 E. Fox La., Fox Point), **Grant Beach** (✉ 100 Hawthorne Ave., South Milwaukee), and **McKinley Beach** (✉ 1750 N. Lincoln Memorial Dr.). The **Milwaukee County Aquatic Department** (☎ 414/961–6165) has information.

Shopping

Using the downtown skywalk system, it's possible to browse in hundreds of stores over several blocks without once setting foot outside. Downtown Milwaukee's major shopping area is on Wisconsin Avenue west of the Milwaukee River. The major downtown retail center, the **Grand Avenue Mall** (✉ 275 W. Wisconsin Ave.), spans four city blocks and contains more than 160 specialty shops and 17 eateries. **Historic Third Ward,** a turn-of-the-century wholesale and manufacturing district listed on the National Register of Historic Places, borders the harbor, the river, and downtown. Two Milwaukee landmarks, **Usinger's Sausage** and **Mader's Restaurant,** are near the Historic Third Ward, on Old World 3rd Street. **Jefferson Street,** stretching four blocks from Wisconsin to Kilbourn, offers upscale stores and shops. **George Watts and Son, Inc.** (⊠ 761 N. Jefferson St., ☎ 414/291–5120) has more than a thousand patterns of china, silver, and crystal.

In the metropolitan area, **Mayfair Mall** (⊠ 2500 N. Mayfair Rd., Wauwatosa, near the Milwaukee County Zoo), has more than 160 shops that surround a multistory atrium complete with swaying bamboo. Some 145 stores at **Northridge Shopping Center** (⊠ 7700 W. Brown Deer Rd.) include a Younkers department store, Boston Store, Sears, and JCPenney. Wisconsin's largest shopping center, **Southridge Mall** (⊠ 5300 S. 76th St., Greendale) has more than 145 specialty stores and five major department stores. **Brookfield Square** (⊠ 95 N. Moorland Rd., Brookfield) is a sprawling suburban complex with about 100 stores. **Bayshore** (⊠ 5900 N. Port Washington Rd., Glendale) has about 70 stores, including Sears and the Boston Store.

About 40 minutes south of downtown Milwaukee, on I–94E, you'll find two large discount shopping malls. The **Factory Outlet Centre,** just off Highway 50, has more than 100 stores with brand-name merchandise. Two miles south of the Factory Outlet Centre, off Highway 165, is **Lakeside Market Place** with more than 75 designer outlet stores.

ELSEWHERE IN WISCONSIN

Madison and Southern Wisconsin

Arriving and Departing
Take I–94 west from Milwaukee to Madison.

What to See and Do
Madison, named after President James Madison, is the state capital and home to the University of Wisconsin. The center of the city lies on an eight-block-wide isthmus between lakes Mendota and Monona. The Roman Renaissance–style **Wisconsin State Capitol** (☎ 608/266–0382), built between 1906 and 1917, dominates the downtown skyline; there are tours daily. A farmers' market is held on Capitol Square each Saturday from May through October. The **State Historical Society Museum** (⊠ 30 N. Carroll St., Capitol Sq., ☎ 608/264–6555) has permanent and changing exhibits on Wisconsin history, from prehistoric Native American cultures to contemporary social issues.

Capitol Square is connected to the university's campus by State Street, a mile-long tree-lined shopping district of imports shops, ethnic restaurants, and artisans' studios. The **Madison Art Center,** in the lobby of the **Civic Center** (⊠ 211 State St., ☎ 608/257–0158), has a large permanent collection and frequent temporary exhibitions.

The **University of Wisconsin,** which opened in 1849 with 20 students, now has an enrollment of about 40,000. The university's **Elvehjem Museum of Art** (⊠ 800 University Ave., ☎ 608/263–2246) is one of the state's best, with a permanent collection of paintings, sculpture, and decorative arts dating from 2300 BC to the present. Away from downtown, the **University Arboretum** (⊠ 1207 Seminole Hwy., ☎ 608/263–7888) has more than 1,200 acres of natural plant and animal communities, such as prairie and forest landscapes, and horticultural collections of upper Midwest specimens.

The free **Henry Vilas Zoo** (✉ 702 S. Randall Ave., ☎ 608/266–4732) has exhibits of nearly 200 animal species plus a petting zoo. On Madison's south side, **Olbrich Botanical Gardens** (✉ 3330 Atwood Ave., ☎ 608/246–4550) has 14 acres of outdoor rose, herb, and rock gardens and a glass-pyramid conservatory with tropical plants and flowers. The **Greater Madison Convention and Visitors Bureau** (✉ 615 E. Washington Ave., 53703, ☎ 608/255–2537 or 800/373–6376) offers information on Madison attractions.

Blue Mounds is at the eastern edge of Wisconsin's lead-mining region. **Blue Mound State Park** (✉ 2 mi northwest of Blue Mounds, ☎ 608/437–5711) offers glorious vistas from towers on one of the hill's summits. **Cave of the Mounds** (✉ Cave of the Mounds Rd., ☎ 608/437–3038) is small, but filled with diverse and colorful mineral formations. It's closed weekdays from mid-November to mid-March.

Nestled in a picturesque valley near Blue Mounds is **Little Norway,** a restored 1856 Norwegian homestead with its original log buildings and an outstanding collection of Norwegian antiques and pioneer arts and crafts. ✉ *3576 Hwy. JG North, Blue Mounds,* ☎ *608/437–8211. Closed Nov.–Apr.*

Founded in 1845 by Swiss settlers from the canton of Glarus, the village of **New Glarus** retains its Swiss character in language, food, architecture, and festivities. The **Swiss Historical Village** (✉ 612 7th Ave., ☎ 608/527–2317) contains original buildings from early New Glarus as well as reconstructions and has displays that trace Swiss immigration to America.

Frank Lloyd Wright chose the farming community of **Spring Green,** on the Wisconsin River, for his home Taliesin and for his architectural school. Wright's influence is evident in a number of buildings in the village; notice the use of geometric shapes, low flat-roofed profiles, cantilevered projections, and steeplelike spires. Tours of **Taliesin** buildings, designed and built by Wright, include his home and office for nearly 50 years, the 1903 Hillside Home School, galleries, a drafting studio, and a theater. ✉ *3 mi south of Spring Green on Hwy. 23,* ☎ *608/588–7900. Closed Dec.–Apr.*

The extraordinary multilevel, stone **House on the Rock** stands atop a 60-ft chimney of rock overlooking the Wyoming Valley. Begun by artist Alex Jordan in the early 1940s and opened to the public in 1961, the complex now includes re-creations of historic village streets, complete with shops, and extensive collections of dolls, cannons, musical machines, and the world's largest carousel. ✉ *5754 Hwy. 23,* ☎ *608/935–3639. Closed Jan.–mid-Mar.*

The renowned **American Players Theater** presents Shakespeare and other classics in a beautiful, wooded outdoor amphitheater near the Wisconsin River. ✉ *County Rte. C and Golf Course Rd., Box 819, Spring Green,* ☎ *608/588–7401. Closed Mon. and mid-Oct.–mid-June.*

On the western edge of the state, **Prairie du Chien** dates from 1673, when explorers Marquette and Joliet reached the confluence of the Wisconsin and Mississippi rivers 6 mi to the south. It became a flourishing fur market in the late 17th century, and today it is a bustling river community where the steamers *Delta Queen* and *Mississippi Queen* call in summer. The **Villa Louis Mansion** (✉ 521 Villa Louis Rd., ☎ 608/326–2721) was built in 1870 by the family of the fur trader Hercules Dousman, who was Wisconsin's first millionaire. Open to the public from May through October, it contains one of the finest collections of Victorian decorative arts in the country. The **Astor Fur Warehouse,** on the villa grounds, has exhibits on the fur trade of the upper Mississippi. Near the fur warehouse is **Wyalusing State Park** (☞ National and State Parks, *above*).

Wisconsin Dells and Baraboo

Arriving and Departing

Take I–90 west from Milwaukee to Madison, then I–90/94 northwest to the Dells. Baraboo is off U.S. 12 to the south of I–90/94.

What to See and Do

One of the state's foremost natural attractions is the **Wisconsin Dells,** nearly 15 mi of soaring, eroded rock formations created over thousands of years as the Wisconsin River cut into soft limestone. The two small communities encompassed by the Dells—Wisconsin Dells and Lake Delton, with a combined population of fewer than 4,000—draw nearly 3 million visitors annually to frolic in the water parks, play miniature golf, and enjoy the rides, shows, and other planned attractions that today nearly overshadow the area's scenic wonders.

During the summer and fall tourist seasons you can view the river and its spectacular rock formations on cruise boats or aboard World War II amphibious vehicles that travel on both land and water. A variety of water parks offers a thrilling range of slides, wave pools, and innertube and raft rides, along with a host of other diversions. The notorious Confederate spy Belle Boyd, who died here while on a speaking tour in 1910, is buried in **Spring Grove Cemetery.**

When you need a break from the nonstop action, **Mirror Lake State Park** (✉ Just south of the Dells off U.S. 12, ☎ 608/254–2333) offers camping, hiking, scenery, and 20 mi of cross-country ski trails. **Rocky Arbor State Park** (✉ 1 mi north off U.S. 12, ☎ 608/254-8001 in summer, 608/254–2333 off-season) is another good choice for downtime, with camping, hiking, and great scenery. For more information contact the **Wisconsin Dells Visitor and Convention Bureau** (✉ 701 Superior St., Wisconsin Dells 53965, ☎ 608/254–4636 or 800/223–3557).

South of Wisconsin Dells is **Baraboo,** former site of an early 19th-century fur-trading post run by a Frenchman named Baribault. It is best known as the place where the five Ringling brothers began their circus careers in 1882 and as the winter headquarters of their Ringling Brothers Circus from 1884 to 1918. The **Circus World Museum** (✉ 426 Water St., ☎ 608/356–8341), a State Historical Society site, preserves the history of the more than 100 circuses that began in Wisconsin. Along with an outstanding collection of antique circus wagons, the museum presents big-top performances featuring circus stars of today in summer and fall. The **Baraboo Chamber of Commerce** (✉ 124 2nd St., 53913, ☎ 608/356–8333 or 800/227–2266) supplies information on the town.

Door County

Arriving and Departing

Take I–43 north from Milwaukee to Green Bay, then Route 57 north.

What to See and Do

Jutting out from the Wisconsin mainland like the thumb on a mitten, 70-mi-long **Door County Peninsula** is bordered by the waters of Lake Michigan and Green Bay. It was named for the Porte des Morts (Door of Death), a treacherous strait separating the peninsula from nearby offshore islands. Scores of ships have come to grief in Door County waters, but today large Great Lakes freighters often slip through the Door to seek shelter in the lee of the islands during Lake Michigan's autumn storms. Soil conditions and climate make the peninsula ideal for cherry and apple production, and its orchards produce more than 20 million pounds of fruit each year. The peninsula is carpeted in blossoms when the trees bloom in late May.

A visit to the peninsula can include stops at a half dozen quaint lakeshore towns, each filled with charming restaurants, shops, and inns. First-time visitors often make a circle tour via Routes 57 and 42. The Lake Michigan side of the peninsula is somewhat less settled and the landscape rougher. The peninsula's rugged beauty attracts large numbers of artists, whose works are shown in studios, galleries, and shops in all the villages.

Sturgeon Bay, the peninsula's chief community and a busy shipbuilding port, sits on a partially man-made ship canal connecting the waters of Lake Michigan and Green Bay. Here the recently relocated **Door County Maritime Museum** (⊠ At foot of bridge leading into town, ☎ 414/743–5958) has displays on local shipbuilding and commercial fishing. It's closed November through April.

Beside Route 57, along the peninsula's Lake Michigan side, you can see the rocky shoreline and sea caves at **Cave Point County Park,** near Valmy. Just north of **Jacksonport** you'll cross the 45th parallel, halfway between the equator and the north pole.

Northport, at the tip of the Door County Peninsula, is the port of departure for the daily car ferries to **Washington Island,** 6 mi offshore; passenger ferries leave from nearby Gills Rock. The island's 600 inhabitants celebrate their heritage with an annual **Scandinavian festival,** in August. From the end of May to mid-October narrated tram tours aboard the Washington Island *Cherry Train* (☎ 414/847–2039) or the *VikingTour Train* (☎ 414/854–2972) leave from the ferry dock. The island has nearly 100 mi of roads and is popular with cyclists. You may take your own bicycle on the ferry or rent one on the island. To really get away from it all, take the ferry from Washington Island to remote **Rock Island State Park,** a wilderness area permitting only hiking and backpack camping.

Back on the mainland, on the **Green Bay** side of the peninsula, the villages evoke New England in atmosphere and charm and provide exceptional views of Green Bay, where sunsets can be breathtaking. **Fish Creek** is home to the **Peninsula Players Theater** (☎ 847/864–6104), called America's oldest professional resident summer theater. Here, too, is beautiful **Peninsula State Park,** which offers hiking and bicycling.

Complete your visit to Door County by sampling the region's famed **fish boil,** which originated more than 100 years ago. It's a simple but delicious meal that has reached legendary status in the region. A huge caldron of water is brought to a boil over a wood fire. A basket of red potatoes is cooked in the caldron, followed by a basket of fresh local whitefish steaks. At the moment the fish is cooked to perfection, kerosene is dumped on the fire, and the flames shoot high in the air, causing the caldron to boil over, expelling most of the fish oils and fat. The steaming whitefish is then served with melted butter, potatoes, coleslaw, and another favorite, Door County cherry pie. The **Door County Chamber of Commerce** (⊠ Box 406, Sturgeon Bay 54235-0406, ☎ 414/743–4456 or 800/527–3529) provides information on county attractions.

Dining and Lodging

You'll find a plethora of appealing restaurants and accommodations here, including many bed-and-breakfast inns housed in Victorian Painted Ladies. For price ranges *see* Charts 1 (A) and 2 (A) *in* On the Road with Fodor's.

$ ✕ **Al Johnsons Swedish Restaurant and Butik.** Breakfast is the specialty at this restaurant with a grass roof on which goats graze in summer. Specialties include Swedish limpa bread and waffles topped with fresh fruit and whipped cream. ⊠ *702 N. Bay Shore Dr., Sister Bay,* ☎ *414/854–2626. AE, DC, MC, V.*

$ ✕ **Sister Bay Café.** This quaint café on Sister Bay's main street serves Scandinavian-American specials such as Norwegian farmer's stew, heart-shaped waffles topped with pecan-apple compote, and *risegrot*— a hot, creamy rice pudding–like dish that's a breakfast favorite. ⊠ *611 Bay Shore Dr., Sister Bay,* ☎ *414/854–2429. DC, MC, V. Closed some weekends off-season.*

$ ✕ **The Cookery.** Door County products—mostly cherries—are used in many of the dishes on this restaurant's breakfast, lunch and dinner menus. Its pantry offers goodies to go. Don't miss the cherry muffins and cherry-chocolate-chip cookies. ⊠ *Main St. and Hwy. 42, Fish Creek,* ☎ *414/868–3634. Closed weekdays off-season.*

$$$ 🏨 **Baileys Harbor Yacht Club Resort.** A 1,000-acre wildlife sanctuary
★ and nature preserve near the waterfront provide the backdrop for the rooms, suites, villas, and cottages of this resort. Some suites have gas fireplaces and large whirlpool baths. ⊠ *8150 Ridges Rd., Baileys Harbor 54202,* ☎ *414/839–2336, FAX 414/839–2093. 83 rooms. Indoor and outdoor pools, tennis, boating, fishing, bicycles, cross-country skiing. AE, D, MC, V.*

$$$ 🏨 **Landmark Resort and Conference Center.** The largest resort in Door County, the Landmark is in a wooded area overlooking a golf course and rolling farmland. Rooms are traditionally styled, and many have spectacular views. ⊠ *7643 Hillside Rd., Egg Harbor 54207,* ☎ *414/868–3205, FAX 414/868–2569. 293 rooms. Restaurant, 1 indoor and 3 outdoor pools, steam rooms, exercise room, tennis, basketball, horseshoes, shuffleboard, volleyball. AE, D, DC, MC, V.*

$$ 🏨 **High Point Inn.** This new, modern facility overlooks the town of Ephraim. Clean and comfortable one-, two-, and three-bedroom condominium suits are available. ⊠ *10386 Water St., Ephraim 54211,* ☎ *414/854–9773, FAX 414/854–9738. 42 rooms. Indoor and outdoor pools, exercise room. D, MC, V.*

$$ 🏨 **White Lace Inn.** True to its name, the rooms at this inn have plenty of white lace, as well as antique furnishings, fireplaces, and whirlpools. Gardens surround the four houses, which are connected by a gazebo. There's also a cozy lobby with Victorian furniture and original hardwood floors, walls, and ceilings. ⊠ *16 N. 5th Ave., Sturgeon Bay 54235,* ☎ *414/743–1105. 19 rooms. AE, D, MC, V.*

$$ ✕🏨 **Inn at Cedar Crossing.** On the first floor of this inn in Sturgeon
★ Bay's historic district sample some of the area's best cuisine, then retire upstairs to a room with a four-poster bed, fireplace, whirlpool, and sitting area. ⊠ *336 Louisiana St., Sturgeon Bay 54235,* ☎ *414/743–4200, FAX 414/743–4422. 9 rooms. D, MC, V.*

$$ ✕🏨 **White Gull Inn.** Since 1896 the White Gull has been offering in-
★ timate lodging and excellent food. Cottages and rooms are rustic and old-fashioned, with hardwood floors, canopy beds, braided rugs, and porches. A variety of lamb, beef, and seafood dishes with unusual sauces is served in the candlelighted, antiques-filled restaurant. Reservations

are a must, even in winter. ⊠ *4225 Main St., Fish Creek 54212,* ☎ *414/868–3517,* 𝐅𝐀𝐗 *414/868–2367. 10 rooms, 4 cottages. Restaurant. AE, D, DC, MC, V.*

Bayfield and the Apostle Islands

Arriving and Departing

Take I–94 west from Milwaukee to Portage, U.S. 51 north to Hurley, U.S. 2 west to Ashland, and then Route 13 north to Bayfield.

What to See and Do

Known as the gateway to the Apostle Islands National Lakeshore, the commercial fishing village of **Bayfield,** population 700, also has some worthwhile attractions of its own. At the **Cooperage Museum** (⊠ 1 Washington Ave., ☎ 715/779–3400), Wisconsin's only working barrel factory and museum, you can watch local coopers ply their trade from spring through fall. At **Lake Superior Big Top Chautauqua** (⊠ 3 mi south of Bayfield off Hwy. 13, ☎ 715/373–5552), concerts, plays, lectures, and original historical musicals are performed under canvas in the spirit of old-time summer tent shows. The **Bayfield Chamber of Commerce** (⊠ Box 138, 54814, ☎ 715/779–3335 or 800/447–4094) provides information on area attractions.

★ Accessible from Bayfield, the **Apostle Islands National Lakeshore** comprises 21 of Lake Superior's 22 Apostle Islands and a segment of mainland near Bayfield. Named by French missionaries who mistakenly thought the islands numbered 12, the Apostles encompass 42,000 acres spread over 600 square mi of Lake Superior. Primitive camping and hiking are allowed on most of the islands. Sailing is a favorite pastime here, as is charter boat fishing for lake trout or whitefish. **Lakeshore headquarters** (⊠ Washington Ave. and 4th St., Box 4, Bayfield 54814, ☎ 715/779–3397) offers publications, exhibits, and a movie about the Apostle Islands. In summer the **Little Sand Bay Visitor Center** (⊠ 13 mi north of Bayfield on Rte. 13, ☎ 715/779–3459) has exhibits and daily guided tours of a former commercial fishing operation. **Stockton Island,** the largest island in the national lakeshore, has a visitor center (☎ 715/779–3397) with natural and cultural history exhibits and a park naturalist on duty. The island is closed Labor Day to Memorial Day. Guided tours of the **Raspberry Island Lighthouse** buildings and gardens are offered, as are guided tours of historic **Manitou Island Fish Camp,** on Manitou Island (closed Labor Day to Memorial Day).

The car- and passenger-carrying **Madeline Island Ferry** (⊠ Washington Ave., Bayfield, ☎ 715/747–2051) connects Bayfield to **Madeline Island.** Here the village of **LaPointe** was established in the early 17th century as a French trading post. The **Madeline Island Historical Museum** (⊠ Ferry Dock, La Pointe, ☎ 715/747–2415), on the site of a former fur-trading post, houses exhibits on island history. Narrated island tours are given by **Madeline Island Bus Tours** (⊠ Ferry Dock, La Pointe, ☎ 715/747–2051) from mid-June through Labor Day. **Big Bay State Park** (☎ 715/747–6425) has camping, a long sandy beach, picnic areas, and hiking and nature trails; sea kayaking and biking are especially popular here. The **Madeline Island Chamber of Commerce** (⊠ Box 274, La Pointe 54850, ☎ 715/747–2801, 𝐅𝐀𝐗 715/747–2800) provides information on area attractions.

8 The Great Plains

Iowa, Kansas, Missouri, Nebraska, North Dakota, Oklahoma, South Dakota

By Suzanne De Galan

Updated by Diana Lambdin Meyer

T*he name Great Plains evokes an image of flat farmland stretching to the horizon, unbroken save for the occasional cluster of buildings marking a town or farmstead. Those who go there, however, know this limitless terrain destroys as many preconceived images as it confirms. The seemingly uniform landscape actually encompasses geography as diverse as the towering buttes that loom over the horizons of western South Dakota and the fertile river valleys that crisscross the eastern boundaries of Missouri and Kansas.*

The cultural legacy of the Great Plains owes as much to such artists as Louis Sullivan and Grant Wood as to the cowboy and Native American artifacts that stud the region. And although European settlement came later here, St. Louis existed more than a decade before the signing of the Declaration of Independence; and Coronado had already explored Kansas two centuries before that.

The area that now comprises the states of Iowa, Missouri, Oklahoma, Kansas, Nebraska, and North and South Dakota saw its greatest European settlement in the 19th century. Railroad companies lured thousands of immigrants with large, inexpensive parcels of land; towns sprang up along rail lines and pioneer trails; and Native Americans were inexorably forced into smaller and smaller territories. The sod-breaking plow and hardy winter wheat helped transform the long- and short-grass prairies of the high plains into America's breadbasket. In the remaining grasslands cattle fed where bison once reigned.

Life on the Great Plains in the 19th century was harsh and sometimes violent, yet it's a life that today's residents love to re-create. Countless historical theme parks and Old West towns dot the region, along with abundant archaeological and Civil War battle sites, U.S. Army forts, pioneer trail markers, and museums of Native American and pioneer lore. Great Plains folk think nothing of journeying 100 mi to see a building covered with thousands of bushels of corn (the Corn Palace in Mitchell, South Dakota) or wrecked cars arranged to resemble the monoliths of Stonehenge. This tendency achieves its ultimate expression in Mt. Rushmore, where the 60-ft faces of four U.S. presidents have been carved into a wall of South Dakota granite.

But alongside these landmarks and oddities lies another Great Plains. To know it, you must drive its hundreds of miles of roads bisecting fields of grain or leave the highway for one of its small towns, just to walk the Main Street and see the serene, mellow old houses. Here, somewhere between myth and reality, the true spirit of this region is revealed.

When to Go

The traditional tourist season for most of the Great Plains is **summer,** despite the soaring temperatures and high humidity common throughout the region. In fact, many tourist attractions, particularly in North and South Dakota, are open only during June, July, and August. Northern states, such as the Dakotas and Nebraska, are generally cooler, with average temperatures in the 80s rather than the 90s, but you should be prepared for anything in this variable region. **Winter** weather is equally extreme, especially in Nebraska and the Dakotas, where subzero temperatures and snowy conditions are not uncommon. South Dakota offers excellent cross-country skiing and snowmobiling, but again, make sure hotels and restaurants are open. **Spring** and **fall** can be excellent times to visit, with moderate temperatures (anywhere from 40°F to 70°F) and crowds at a minimum. Fall in the Ozarks or in such places as the eastern border of Iowa has the added attraction of colorful foliage, usually in mid- to late October.

Festivals and Seasonal Events

MAY➤ At the **Oklahoma Cattlemen's Association Range Round-up** (☎ 405/282–3004) in **Guthrie** cowhands compete in saddle bronco riding, wild cow roping, and other contests.

JUNE➤ The **Oklahoma Mozart International Festival** (☎ 918/336–9900) in **Bartlesville** holds concerts, barbecues, and powwows celebrating the composer and local culture.

Nebraskaland Days (☎ 308/532–7939) is a Western hootenanny in **North Platte** that's highlighted by the Buffalo Bill Rodeo.

The **Red Earth Native American Cultural Festival** (☎ 405/427–5228), in **Oklahoma City,** attracts hundreds of Native American dancers from the United States and Canada for competitions and performances.

JULY➤ The **Kansas City Blues & Jazz Festival** (☎ 800/530–5266) features performances by nationally known blues and jazz artists on three stages.

On Independence Day weekend, **National Tom Sawyer Days** (☎ 573/221–2477) features Americana-oriented activities such as fence-painting in Mark Twain's hometown of **Hannibal, Missouri.**

JULY➤ The **Black Hills and Northern Plains Indian Powwow and Exposition** (☎ 605/394–4115) is the best known of many powwows held annually across **South Dakota.**

JULY–AUG.➤ In Kansas, the **Dodge City Roundup Rodeo** (☎ 316/225–2244) is a five-day rodeo during the city's Dodge City Days festival.

The Great Plains

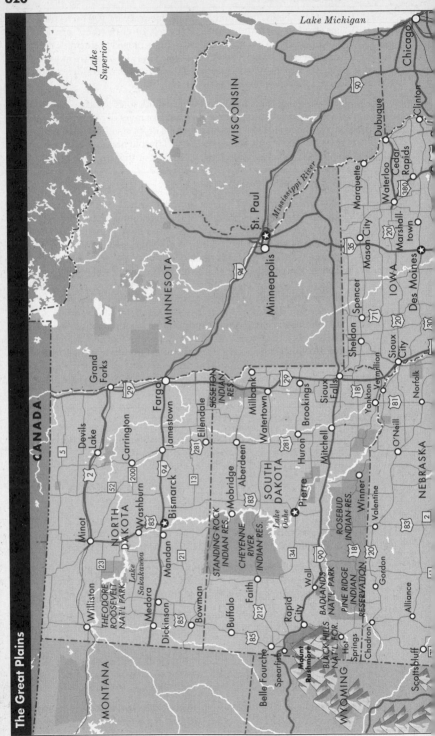

Lake Michigan

Chicago

Lake Superior

WISCONSIN

Mississippi River

St. Paul

Minneapolis

Dubuque

Marquette

Clinton

Cedar Rapids

Waterloo

Marshalltown

Mason City

MINNESOTA

94

35

IOWA

Sheldon

Spencer

Des Moines

Sioux City

CANADA

Grand Forks

Fargo

Jamestown

SISSETON INDIAN RES.

Ellendale

Millbank

Watertown

Brookings

Sioux Falls

Vermillion

Yankton

NEBRASKA

Norfolk

Devils Lake

Carrington

5

2

29

281

Aberdeen

Huron

Mitchell

O'Neill

52

200

Washburn

Bismarck

13

Mobridge

STANDING ROCK INDIAN RES.

SOUTH DAKOTA

Pierre

Winner

Valentine

Minot

NORTH DAKOTA

83

Mandan

21

CHEYENNE RIVER INDIAN RES.

Lake Oahe

ROSEBUD INDIAN RES.

18

20

Gordon

83

23

Williston

THEODORE ROOSEVELT NAT'L PARK

Lake Sakakawea

Dickinson

85

Bowman

Medora

Buffalo

Faith

212

34

Wall

BADLANDS NAT'L PARK

PINE RIDGE INDIAN RESERVATION

Alliance

90

Rapid City

Belle Fourche

Spearfish

Mount Rushmore

BLACK HILLS NAT'L FOR.

Hot Springs

Chadron

Scottsbluff

WYOMING

MONTANA

380

20

71

29

90

18

81

2

85

212

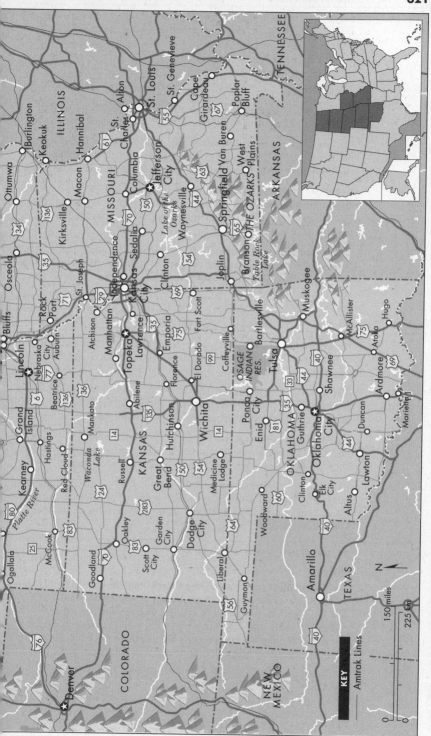

AUG.➤ The **Iowa State Fair** (☎ 515/262–3111), in **Des Moines,** is a short course in farm machinery, animals, crops, and crafts; less bucolically minded visitors can enjoy carnival rides and musical entertainment.

Days of '76 (☎ 605/578–1876), in **Deadwood, South Dakota,** celebrates the town's wild and woolly gold rush days with a parade, a rodeo, and other activities.

South Dakota's **Sturgis Motorcycle Classic** (☎ 605/347–6570) draws more than 175,000 bike buffs from around the country each year.

Pioneer Days at Bonanzaville USA (☎ 701/282–2822) transforms the pioneer village of **West Fargo, North Dakota,** into a living museum for two days, with costumed shopkeepers, tradespeople, and townspeople.

EARLY SEPT.➤ **Santa-Cali-Gon Days** (☎ 816/252–4745), in **Independence, Missouri,** celebrates the opening of the West through the Santa Fe, California, and Oregon trails, all of which originated in this gateway town.

The **United Tribes International Powwow** (☎ 701/255–3285) brings Native Americans from around the country to **Bismarck, North Dakota,** to exhibit art, hold dance competitions, and celebrate cultural ties.

OCT.➤ **Octoberfest** (☎ 573/486–2744) in **Hermann, Missouri,** draws thousands of people each weekend to celebrate this Missouri River town's German and wine-making heritage.

Norsk Hostfest (☎ 701/852–2368), in **Minot, North Dakota,** brings in crowds from throughout the region to sample Scandinavian foods, dancing, and costumes.

The **Covered Bridge Festival** (☎ 515/462–1185) in **Winterset, Iowa,** includes tours of Madison County's six restored covered bridges as well as visits to sights made famous by the eponymous movie.

NOV.➤ The **American Royal** (☎ 816/221–5242 or 800/767–7700) is an annual celebration of **Kansas City**'s heritage, featuring rodeos, horse shows, livestock shows, and a no-holds-barred barbecue.

EARLY DEC.➤ **Christmas on the River** (☎ 816/741–2000), in **Parkville, Missouri,** rings in the holiday season with a 1,000-voice children's choir, Santa's arrival by riverboat, and performances of Dickens's *A Christmas Carol.*

Getting Around the Great Plains

By Bus
The major intercity carrier is **Greyhound Lines** (☎ 800/231–2222). In addition, **Jefferson Lines** (☎ 612/332–8745) serves some cities in Kansas, Missouri, Iowa, and Oklahoma. **Jackrabbit Lines** (☎ 605/348–3300) serves all of South Dakota and a few destinations in neighboring states. Many Greyhound stops in this region are small towns that have no ticket booth; call to check whether you must purchase your ticket in advance.

By Car
Three interstates converge at Oklahoma City: I–40, running east–west through Oklahoma; I–44, which proceeds northeast from Oklahoma City to Tulsa, Oklahoma, and through Missouri to St. Louis; and I–35, one of two major north–south arteries in the Great Plains. From Oklahoma City I–35 proceeds north through Wichita and Kansas City, Kansas, and Des Moines, Iowa. Another north–south route is I–29, which begins in Kansas City and runs along the eastern borders of Nebraska, South Dakota, and North Dakota, passing through

Omaha, Sioux Falls, Fargo, and Grand Forks. Major east–west arteries are I–94 in North Dakota, which passes through Medora, the Bismarck-Mandan area, and Fargo; I–90 in South Dakota, running from Rapid City to Sioux Falls; I–80 through Nebraska and Iowa, which links North Platte, Lincoln, and Omaha with Des Moines and Iowa City; and I–70, which bisects Missouri and Kansas and links St. Louis with Kansas City and points west. Roads are generally in good condition throughout the region. However, these main arteries are often closed for short periods because of winter blizzard conditions.

By Plane

Major domestic carriers serve the region, including American, Continental, Delta, Northwest, United, and US Airways. The largest airports are in Missouri, **Lambert–St. Louis International Airport** (☎ 314/426–8000) and **Kansas City International Airport** (☎ 816/243–5237); in Iowa, **Des Moines International Airport** (☎ 515/256–5050); in Oklahoma, **Will Rogers World Airport** (☎ 405/681–5311) and **Tulsa International Airport** (☎ 918/838–5000); and in South Dakota, **Sioux Falls Regional Airport** (☎ 605/336–0762).

By Train

Amtrak (☎ 800/872–7245) provides some service through the Great Plains but not necessarily to the major cities, and South Dakota and Oklahoma are not served at all.

IOWA

By Marcia
Andrews

Updated by
Diana Lambdin
Meyer

Capital	Des Moines
Population	2,851,800
Motto	Our Liberties We Prize and Our Rights We Will Maintain
State Bird	Eastern goldfinch
State Flower	Wild rose
Postal Abbreviation	IA

Statewide Visitor Information

The **Division of Tourism** (✉ Iowa Dept. of Economic Development, 200 E. Grand Ave., Des Moines 50309, ☎ 515/242–4705 or 800/345–4692) has 18 welcome centers along I–35 and I–80 and in towns throughout the state. For regional visitor information call or write **Eastern Iowa Tourism Association** (✉ 116 E. 4th St., Box 485, Vinton 52349, ☎ 319/472–5135 or 800/891–3482), **Central Iowa Tourism Region** (✉ Box 454, Webster City 50595, ☎ 515/832–4808 or 800/285–5842), and **Western Iowa Tourism Region** (✉ 502 Coolbaugh St., Red Oak 51566, ☎ 712/623–4232).

Scenic Drives

Perhaps Iowa's most beautiful scenic drive is the series of roads that take you south along the high bluffs and verdant banks of the Mississippi River on the state's eastern border (☞ Dubuque and the Great River Road, *below*). In southeast Iowa **Route 5** from Des Moines to Lake Rathbun, near Centerville, makes a nice detour for those heading south on I–35; to return to the interstate, take **Route 2W** from Centerville for about 50 mi.

National and State Parks

National Parks
Effigy Mounds National Monument (☞ Exploring Dubuque and the Great River Road, *below*) has scenic hiking trails along prehistoric burial mounds. Iowa has four federal reservoir areas around large man-made lakes: **Coralville Lake** (✉ 2850 Prairie du Chien Rd. NE, Iowa City 52240, ☎ 319/338–3543), **Rathbun Lake** (✉ Rte. 3, Centerville 52544, ☎ 515/647–2464), **Lake Red Rock** (✉ R.R. 3, Box 149A, Knoxville 50138-9522, ☎ 515/828–7522), and **Saylorville Lake** (✉ 5600 N.W. 78th Ave., Johnston 50131, ☎ 515/276–4656).

The **Walnut Creek National Wildlife Refuge** (☎ 515/994–2415), 20 mi east of Des Moines on I–80, has 8,600 acres of reconstructed tallgrass prairie, 5 mi of hiking trails accessible to travelers with disabilities, a prairie education center, and an elk and bison viewing area.

State Parks
Iowa's 76 state parks include 5,700 campsites, many with shower facilities and electrical hookups. Some well-developed parks with modern campsites, cabins, lodge rentals, and boat rentals are **Clear Lake** (☎ 515/357–4212), near Mason City; **George Wyth Memorial** (☎ 319/232–5505), near Waterloo; **Lacey-Keosauqua** (☎ 319/293–3502), near Keosauqua; and **Lake of Three Fires** (☎ 712/523–2700), near Bedford. Virgin prairie areas, part of the state park system but lacking facilities, include **Cayler Prairie**, near the Great Lakes area in northwestern Iowa; **Hayden Prairie**, near the Minnesota border in the northeastern

corner of the state; **Kalsow Prairie,** about 90 mi northwest of Des Moines; and **Sheeder Prairie,** about 50 mi west of Des Moines. Contact the **Department of Natural Resources** (☎ 515/281–5145) for more information.

DES MOINES

Viewed from an airplane or a car topping a hill, the capital of Iowa is a cluster of office towers that seem to pop out of a green corduroy landscape. Downtown straddles the vee of two rivers—the Raccoon and the Des Moines; the '80s-built skyline faces granite government buildings and a classic gold-domed capitol across four bridges. Major businesses in this relatively hassle-free city of more than 400,000 residents include insurance, finance, publishing, and agribusiness. Although hardly a glittering metropolis—the city annually plays host to a horde of farmers and agriculture buffs at the Iowa State Fair—neither is Des Moines a village. The U.S. presidential race starts here with the Iowa Caucuses, and every cultural wave breaks on Des Moines's shores—eventually.

Visitor Information

Des Moines visitor centers are in the **airport** lobby (☎ 515/287–4396) and in the **skywalk** above the corner of 6th and Locust streets downtown (☎ 515/286–4960).

Arriving and Departing

By Bus
Greyhound Lines (☎ 800/231–2222) and **Jefferson** (☎ 515/283–0074) share a terminal at Keosauqua Way and 12th Street.

By Car
I–80, the major east–west thoroughfare through the state, and I–35, Iowa's main north–south route, intersect northwest of Des Moines and link with I–235, which runs across the northern part of town.

By Plane
Des Moines International Airport (☎ 515/256–5100), about 3 mi south of downtown, has scheduled service by major domestic airlines. The drive into town takes about 10 minutes in normal traffic. Cab fare, including tip, is less than $10. Hotel shuttles serve the route, and major car rental companies are in the airport.

Getting Around Des Moines

Streets both in the city and in suburban Urbandale and West Des Moines are laid out in a grid, which makes getting around fairly easy. However, a car is essential, as attractions are scattered about the city and suburbs. Downtown is compact enough to explore in comfortable shoes.

Exploring Des Moines

Downtown
Start a walking tour of downtown Des Moines at the **capitol complex** (⌂ E. 9th St. and Grand Ave., ☎ 515/281–5591 or 800/451–2625), on the east bank of the Des Moines River. There you can see the elaborate murals in the rotunda of the capitol and climb into the dome, covered in 22-karat gold leaf. Near the capitol, the **Botanical Center** (⌂ 909 E. River Dr., ☎ 515/242–2934) has flower exhibits and a three-story, dome-topped jungle. The **State Historical Building of Iowa** (⌂ 600 E. Locust St., ☎ 515/281–5111), one block west of the capitol, shakes off any dusty-old-stuff image with its postmodern design, ab-

stract sculpture of neon and glass, and striking fountain display. The building houses the state archives, library, and museum.

Just west of downtown in Greenwood-Ashworth Park, the **Des Moines Art Center** (⊠ 4700 Grand Ave., ☎ 515/277–4405) houses a permanent collection of contemporary art. Also in Greenwood-Ashworth Park is the **Science Center of Iowa** (⊠ 4500 Grand Ave., ☎ 515/274–4138), whose interactive programs include laser shows, a planetarium, and a space shuttle simulator appropriate for all ages.

Some of the city's most interesting historic buildings can be found on the west side of the Des Moines River (follow Locust Street from the east side). Self-guided walking tours are detailed in brochures from Downtown Des Moines, Inc. (⊠ Suite 100B, 601 Locust St., ☎ 515/245–3880). The **Sherman Hill Historic District** has impressive Victorian houses. The **Court Avenue District** contains a number of restored 19th-century warehouses and other commercial buildings, many of which now house shops, restaurants, and entertainment venues.

Outside the City

Living History Farms, a 600-acre open-air museum a few miles northwest of Des Moines, is well worth a half-day's exploration. The farms are a trip back in time through the sights, sounds, and smells of an 18th-century Native American village, two working farms of 1850 and 1900, and an 1875 town. ⊠ 2600 N.W. 111th St., Urbandale 50322, ☎ 515/278–2400. Closed Nov.–Apr.; call for special events in winter.

Dining

Des Moines's staple fare is Italian, followed closely by Chinese food, although lately there has been a trend toward more exotic cuisines, such as Thai, Indian, and Middle Eastern. Downtown, sample Court Avenue's lineup of pubs and Italian, Tex-Mex, and Cajun places. For price ranges *see* Chart 1 (B) *in* On the Road with Fodor's.

$$$ ✕ **Anna's.** In the Savery Hotel downtown, Anna's features large chan-
★   deliers, an elevated bar, and a wall of wine bottles. The menu includes prime rib and lighter versions of Continental dishes. ⊠ *401 Locust St.,* ☎ *515/244–2151. AE, D, MC, V. No lunch.*

$$$ ✕ **8th Street Seafood Bar and Grill.** Lighted by skylights and flanked by a busy bar, the raised dining area seats a stylish crowd. Seafood is the draw, cooked simply and well. ⊠ *1261 8th St., West Des Moines,* ☎ *515/223–8808. AE, DC, MC, V. No lunch.*

$$ ✕ **Cafe Su.** Dim sum appetizers are the specialty at this chic restaurant in the Valley Junction shopping area in West Des Moines. Contemporary decor complements the traditional Chinese cuisine. ⊠ *225 5th St.,* ☎ *515/274–5102. AE, D, DC, MC, V. Closed Sun. and Mon.*

$$ ✕ **The Greenbrier.** In the northern suburb of Johnston, this restaurant offers a large menu mixing elegant and basic fare with such choices as Iowa pork chops, rack of lamb, and fish. Frosted glass and dark wood accent the three dining rooms and bar. ⊠ *5810 Merle Hay Rd., Johnston,* ☎ *515/253–0124. No reservations. AE, D, MC, V. Closed Sun.*

$$ ✕ **Jesse's Embers.** Just west of downtown, Jesse's is prized for grilled prime steaks cooked over an open pit in the main dining room. The room is small, plain, and crowded with neighborhood people waiting in the bar, but service is swift. ⊠ *3301 Ingersoll Ave.,* ☎ *515/255–6011. AE, MC, V. Closed Sun.*

$ ✕ **Des Moines Art Center Restaurant.** For an elegant interlude with light fare, this solarium with sculpture and a pool is unique. For lunch there are soups, salads, sandwiches, and desserts. ⊠ *4700 Grand Ave.,* ☎

515/277–4405. MC, V. Closed Sun.–Mon. No dinner, except Thurs. by reservation.

$ ✕ **Drake Diner.** The sharp New Age look of chrome and neon adds
★ fun to a traditional soup, salad, and sandwich menu. Students from nearby Drake University mix with older patrons. ⊠ 1111 25th St., ☎ 515/277–1111. AE, D, DC, MC, V.

$ ✕ **El Patio.** Just west of downtown, this converted bungalow filled with southwestern artifacts seats diners in colorful rooms and on a covered patio. More Tex than Mex, the food is still a cut above the fare found at chains. ⊠ 611 37th St., ☎ 515/274–2303. AE, MC, V. No lunch.

$ ✕ **India Cafe.** Classic aromatic dishes range from zingy lamb vindaloo
★ to mild tandoori chicken. The restaurant's peach-color walls are hung with Indian paintings, and seating is at booths and tables with armchairs. ⊠ Parkwood Plaza, 86th and Douglas Sts., Urbandale, ☎ 515/278–2929. AE, MC, V.

Lodging

You'll find little in the way of historic or lavish hotels in Des Moines; most establishments cater to business travelers and offer modern amenities and convenient locations. Downtown renovations or newer suburban hotels dominate, with low-cost motels clustered near interstate exits and the occasional suburban bed-and-breakfast (Iowa Bed and Breakfast Innkeepers' Association, ⊠ 9001 Hickman Rd., Suite 2B, Des Moines 50322, ☎ 800/888–4667) for variety. For price ranges see Chart 2 (B) in On the Road with Fodor's.

$$$ ✕🏨 **Des Moines Marriott.** The downtown location on the skywalk is a plus. Rooms are plush contemporary, with unobstructed views of the city from the higher floors. The restaurant here, Quenelle's, serves rich Continental fare. ⊠ 700 Grand Ave., 50309, ☎ 515/245–5500, FAX 515/245–5567. 415 rooms. 2 restaurants, lounge, pool, health club. AE, D, MC, V.

$$$ 🏨 **Embassy Suites Hotel on the River.** Across the bridge from the Court
★ Avenue District, this hotel has seven balconies ringing an atrium with a waterfall. Beyond this, the hotel lacks flash, which it makes up for with complimentary breakfast and lots of attentive service. ⊠ 101 E. Locust St., 50309, ☎ 515/244–1700, FAX 515/244–2537. 234 suites. Restaurant, 2 lounges, pool, health club, convention center. AE, MC, V.

$$ 🏨 **Drake Inn.** Next to Drake University, this attractive low-rise hotel has
★ airy rooms. ⊠ 1140 24th St., 50311, ☎ 515/255–4000 or 800/252–7838, FAX 515/255–1192. 52 rooms. 2 meeting rooms. AE, D, MC, V.

$$ 🏨 **Holiday Inn Downtown.** Just north of downtown, the hotel has fresh but ordinary rooms and a few suites with whirlpool baths. ⊠ 1050 6th Ave., 50314, ☎ 515/283–0151, FAX 515/283–0151. 245 rooms. Restaurant, lounge, pool. AE, D, MC, V.

$$ 🏨 **Valley West Inn.** Next to West Des Moines's big mall, the three-story inn has simply furnished rooms decorated in rosy fabrics and blond woods. ⊠ 3535 Westown Pkwy., West Des Moines 50265, ☎ 515/225–2524 or 800/833–6755, FAX 515/225–9058. 136 rooms. Restaurant, lounge, pool, hot tub, meeting rooms. AE, D, MC, V.

$ 🏨 **Airport Comfort Inn.** Two blocks from the airport, the hotel offers free 24-hour airport shuttle service. The three-story building has plain rooms, and big beds, and complimentary breakfast served in the lobby. ⊠ 5231 Fleur Dr., 50321, ☎ 515/287–3434. 55 rooms. Pool, airport shuttle. AE, MC, V.

$ 🏨 **Heartland Inn.** On the northeastern edge of Des Moines, next to an
★ amusement complex, this three-story rustic building offers complimentary Continental breakfast in the lobby. ⊠ 5000 N.E. 56th St., Al-

toona 50009, ☎ *515/967–2400 or 800/334–3277,* ⓕⓐⓧ *515/967– 0150. 87 rooms. Pool, spa. AE, D, DC MC, V.*

The Arts

Just west of downtown in Greenwood-Ashworth Park, the **Des Moines Art Center** (⊠ 4700 Grand, ☎ 515/277–4405) hosts poetry readings, lectures, and film presentations. It also houses a permanent collection of contemporary art (☞ Exploring Des Moines, *above*).

Spectator Sports

Track and Field: The Drake Relays (⊠ Drake University, Forest and 27th St., ☎ 515/271–3791) in late April draw track and field athletes from 744 colleges, universities, and high schools, as well as some big-name Olympians and professional athletes.

Shopping

Valley Junction (☎ 515/222–3642), six square blocks 5 mi west of downtown Des Moines, has a mix of antiques stores and contemporary shops selling country furnishings, collectibles, and Iowa souvenirs.

EAST-CENTRAL IOWA

This region east of Des Moines is a mix of historic towns, trim farmsteads, and forested river valleys. Cedar Rapids is the largest town in the area; Iowa City, about 25 mi south, is the home of the University of Iowa. The area is perhaps best known to tourists for the Amana colonies, a cluster of seven villages west of Iowa City that were founded in the 19th century as a utopian religious community.

Visitor Information

Amana Colonies: Welcome Center (⊠ U.S. 151 and Rte. 220; Box 303, Amana 52203, ☎ 319/622–6262 or 800/245–5465), with information and a lodging reservation service. **Cedar Rapids area:** Convention and Visitors Bureau (⊠ 119 1st Ave. SE, 52401, ☎ 319/622–3828 or 800/735–5557). **Iowa City/Coralville:** Visitors Bureau (⊠ 408 1st Ave., Coralville 52241, ☎ 319/337–6592).

Arriving and Departing

By Car
I–80, the state's major east–west thoroughfare, runs from Des Moines east to Iowa City. From Iowa City I–380 passes Lake MacBride on the way north to Cedar Rapids. From Cedar Rapids U.S. 151 meanders southwest for about 25 mi through a rural farmscape to Middle Amana, the start of the cluster of Amana colonies.

By Plane
The **Cedar Rapids/Iowa City Municipal Airport** (☎ 319/362–8336), 7 mi south of Cedar Rapids and just off I–380, is served by American Eagle, Delta Connection, US Airways, TWA, Northwest/Northwest Airlink, and United.

Exploring East-Central Iowa

★ Your tour of east-central Iowa should begin at the **Amana Colonies,** as the seven villages of Amana are known (☞ Visitor Information, *above*): Amana itself (site of the welcome center), West Amana, South Amana, High Amana, East Amana, Middle Amana, and Homestead.

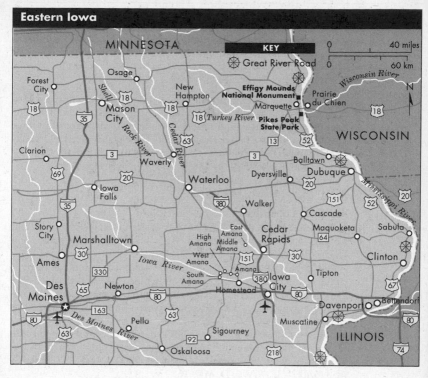

Eastern Iowa

Although descendants of the German/Swiss immigrants who founded the community voted to end its communal way of life in 1932, little has changed visibly.

A 25-mi circuit of the Amana Colonies takes in nearly 500 restored buildings, including barns and kitchens now housing museums, and a schoolhouse, together designated a National Historic Landmark. Crafts hunters favor the shopping opportunities here, where members of the Amana community still manufacture prized woolen goods, furniture, wine, cheese, baskets, and more. Shoppers may find bargains at the original **Amana Appliance Store** (⊠ 4423 220th Trail, ☎ 319/622–7656), founded after residents voted to abandon their communal life. The **Museum of Amana History** (⊠ 4310 220th Trail, ☎ 319/622–3567) is filled with historical artifacts and documents relating to the settlement of the area.

Cedar Rapids is on U.S. 151 in east-central Iowa, just north of the Amana Colonies. In the 19th and early 20th centuries, waves of Czechoslovakian immigrants settled in this manufacturing town. A sampling of Czech heritage is on view at the **Czech Village, Museum and Immigrant Home** (⊠ 10–119 16th Ave. SW, ☎ 319/362–8500). Cedar Rapids also boasts the world's largest permanent collection of paintings by renowned native son Grant Wood, at its **Museum of Art** (⊠ 410 3rd Ave. SE, ☎ 319/366–7503).

Iowa City, in east-central Iowa, served as the seat of state government until the capital was moved to Des Moines in the mid-19th century. The golden dome of the **Old Capitol** (⊠ 24 Old Capital Dr., ☎ 319/335–0548) is now the focal point of the beautiful but hilly campus of the **University of Iowa** on the banks of the Iowa River.

West Branch, a community of 2,000 with more than two dozen buildings listed on the National Register of Historic Places, is just west of

Iowa City on I–80. At the **Herbert Hoover Presidential Library and Birth-place** (⊠ Parkside Dr. and Main St., ☎ 319/643–5301), you can see the cottage where the future president was born to Quaker parents in 1874; it contains period furnishings, many of them original.

Dining and Lodging

Amana kitchens are bountiful in rich German meals, often served family style. Try the locally made rhubarb wine. Hotels in Cedar Rapids tend to cater to business travelers, but the Amanas, like many Iowa towns, are home to a burgeoning number of B&Bs (Iowa Bed and Breakfast Innkeepers' Association, ⊠ 9001 Hickman Rd., Suite 2B, Des Moines 50322, ☎ 800/888–4667). Iowa City has a fair number of decent chain hotels and motels. For price ranges *see* Charts 1 (B) and 2 (B) *in* On the Road with Fodor's.

Amana Colonies

$$ ✕ **Ox Yoke Inn.** Traditional German-American food is served in an Old Country–inspired setting, including walls lined with beer steins. ⊠ *Main St., Amana,* ☎ *319/622–3441. AE, D, MC, V.*

 $ ✕ **Bill Zuber's Restaurant.** The comfortable surroundings haven't changed much since the 1950s. Neither has the menu, which is a primer on German cuisine: lots of baked or fried meat, plus salad, vegetables, and dessert, all for a reasonable price. ⊠ *Main St., Homestead,* ☎ *319/622–3911. AE, D, MC, V.*

 $ ✕ **Brick Haus Restaurant.** In the middle of prime Amana shopping, the
★   restaurant features long tables covered in checkered cloths and large portions of Wiener schnitzel *mit* spaetzle. ⊠ *728 47th Ave., Amana,* ☎ *319/622–3278. AE, D, MC, V.*

$$ ▦ **Amana Holiday Inn.** For the most part this is standard Holiday Inn material, but it's enlivened by such rustic touches as a pool and sauna in a barnlike setting. ⊠ *Exit 225 off I–80; Box 187, Little Amana 52203,* ☎ *319/668–1175 or 800/633–9244,* FAX *319/668–2853. 156 rooms. Restaurant, lounge. AE, D, MC, V.*

$$ ▦ **Rawson's Bed & Breakfast.** Once a kitchen workers' dormitory when
★   Homestead still practiced communal living, this unique establishment has two large, distinctive rooms, with exposed beams and brick walls, and one suite. All three have period furnishings and fabrics and lavish baths. ⊠ *Box 118, Homestead 52235,* ☎ *319/622–6035. 3 rooms. D, MC, V.*

 $ ▦ **Die Heimat Country Inn.** This two-story B&B has small rooms decorated with locally made, traditional furnishings and deluxe rooms with canopy beds. ⊠ *Box 160, Homestead 52236,* ☎ *319/622–3937. 19 rooms. Picnic area, meeting rooms. D, MC, V.*

Cedar Rapids

$$$ ▦ **Collins Plaza.** In this seven-balcony hotel north of downtown, rooms are large, with traditional furnishings and pastel colors. ⊠ *1200 Collins Rd. NE, 52402,* ☎ *319/393–6600 or 800/541–1067,* FAX *319/393–2308. 221 rooms. 2 restaurants, lounge, pool, spa, airport shuttle. AE, DC, D, MC, V.*

Iowa City

$$ ✕ **Givanni's.** Neon lights enhance the exposed-brick walls at this popular Italian/American/vegetarian restaurant in the downtown pedestrian mall. ⊠ *109 E. College St.,* ☎ *319/338–5967. AE, D, DC, MC, V.*

Motel

▦ **Heartland Inn** (⊠ 3315 Southgate Ct. SW, Cedar Rapids 52304, ☎ 319/362–9012 or 800/334–3277, FAX 319/362–9694), 87 rooms, pool, spa; $.

Walcott

✕ **Iowa-80 Kitchen.** With a native stone fireplace, beamed ceiling, and spacious dining room, this is one of the most elegantly furnished truck stops in the country. A 48-ft salad bar, an in-house bakery, laundry facilities, and a warehouse store answer all a traveler's needs. ✉ 755 W. Iowa 80 Rd., 52773, ☎ 319/284–6965. D, MC, V.

Shopping

The commercial hub of Amana shopping is the eight-block center of Amana, just east of the visitor center. The **Woolen Mill Salesroom** (✉ 800 48th Ave., ☎ 319/622–3432) sells all manner of woolens, from clothing for men, women, and kids to blankets; you can take a self-guided tour of the mill. On weekdays at the **Furniture and Clock Shop** (✉ 724 48th Ave., ☎ 319/622–3291), you can watch craftspeople making the products sold here. The **Old Fashioned High Amana Store** (☎ 319/622–3797), 2 mi west of the visitor center, is fragrant, creaky, and full of old-time-type gifts. A block from the Old Fashioned High Amana Store, the **Amana Arts Guild Center** (✉ Box 114, ☎ 319/622–3678) sells high-quality quilts and crafts. **Little Amana,** at I–80 and U.S. 151, is more of a quick-stop outlet for woolens, gifts, and souvenirs than a typical Amana village. The **Tanger Factory Outlet Center** (✉ Exit 220 off I–80, Williamsburg, ☎ 800/552–1151) has 70 stores mainly selling women's designer clothing at discounted prices.

DUBUQUE AND THE GREAT RIVER ROAD

The mighty Mississippi River forms the eastern border of Iowa, and the top third of this border, from the Minnesota line to Dubuque, combines the oldest settlements, highest bluffs, and closest river access of the entire stretch. The **Great River Road** is a network of federal, state, and county roads that wind along this magnificent stretch of riverbank.

Visitor Information

Tourist Information Center (✉ Port of Dubuque Welcome Center, 3rd St. and Ice Harbor, Dubuque 52001, ☎ 319/556–4372 or 800/798–8844).

Arriving and Departing

By Bus

Greyhound Lines (☎ 800/231–2222) links Dubuque to most major cities; its local bus station is in the lower level of the Julien Inn (✉ 200 Main St.). **Prairie Trailways** (☎ 800/877–2457) provides direct, daily service between Dubuque and the Chicago area Amtrak stations.

By Car

Link up with Iowa's **Great River Road** from the north on U.S. 18 at Prairie du Chien, Wisconsin, or pick up the scenic route anywhere along Iowa's eastern border. For its entire length the Great River Road is marked with a 12-spoke pilot's wheel symbol.

Exploring Dubuque and the Great River Road

Just 11 mi south of the Michigan border, the **Municipal Park,** in Lansing, Michigan, provides spectacular views of the Mississippi River. The **Effigy Mounds National Monument** (☎ 319/873–3491), north of McGregor along the Great River Road, has hiking trails that run alongside eerie, animal-shaped prehistoric Native American burial mounds. One-, four-, and six-hour walks lead to cliff-top views of the upper Mississippi River valley.

Pikes Peak State Park (☎ 319/873–2341), 3 mi south of McGregor, affords a view of the Wisconsin River as it links up with the Mississippi. The stretch of road approaching **Balltown,** 7 mi north of Dubuque, reveals green hills rolling down to the river.

Dubuque is full of river merchants' homes, some of them lavish Victorian houses turned B&Bs, snuggled against the limestone cliffs that back this small harbor town. Here you can get out of your car and explore **Cable Car Square** (☎ 319/583–5000), at 4th and Bluff streets, site of two dozen shops and restaurants. Ride **Fenelon Place Elevator** (☎ 319/582–6496) to the top of a 200-ft bluff for a sweeping view of the city.

What to See and Do with Children

Dyersville, 25 mi west of Dubuque on U.S. 20, found fame as a setting for the 1988 movie *Field of Dreams.* The field, about 3 mi north of town, has been preserved as a tourist attraction (✉ 28963 Lansing Rd., ☎ 319/875–8404). Call ahead for the scheduled appearances of ghost players (the field is closed November–March). Dyersville itself has several interesting museums, including the **National Farm Toy Museum** (✉ 1110 16th Ave. SE, ☎ 319/875–2727).

Dining and Lodging

Ethnic and family-style restaurants line Dubuque's 4th Street at Cable Car Square. As with the rest of the state, B&Bs are abundant here (Iowa Bed and Breakfast Innkeepers' Association, ✉ 9001 Hickman Rd., Suite 2B, Des Moines 50322, ☎ 800/888–4667). For price ranges *see* Charts 1 (B) and 2 (B) *in* On the Road with Fodor's.

Balltown

$ ✕ **Breitbach's Country Dining.** This funky, rambling piece of folk ar-
★   chitecture has a good home-style kitchen. ✉ *563 Balltown Rd.,* ☎ *319/ 552–2220. No credit cards.*

Dubuque

$$–$$$ ✕ **Ryan House.** A restored Victorian house provides a lavish period setting for updated light Continental cuisine. ✉ *1375 Locust St.,* ☎ *319/556–5000. AE, D, MC, V.*

$$ ✕ **Yen Ching.** This café offers predictable Chinese food, with a few spicy Hunan dishes for variety. ✉ *926 Main St.,* ☎ *319/556–2574. AE, MC, V. Closed Sun.*

$$$ 🏠 **Hancock House.** This meticulously restored Victorian perched halfway
★   up a bluff has four-poster beds, lace-covered windows, ornate fireplaces, and a rare Tiffany lamp collection. ✉ *1105 Grove Terr., 52001,* ☎ *319/557–8989,* 🗎 *319/583–0813. 9 rooms. Hot tubs. D, MC, V.*

$$ 🏠 **Redstone Inn.** Discovering this establishment is like finding a British manor on the prairie. Bedrooms are grand and baths lavish. ✉ *504 Bluff St., 52001,* ☎ *319/582–1894,* 🗎 *319/582–1893. 15 rooms. Lounge. AE, D, MC, V.*

ELSEWHERE IN IOWA

Iowa's Great Lakes

Arriving and Departing

Take I–80 west from Des Moines and U.S. 71 north to Spirit Lake or take I–35 north from Des Moines to U.S. 18, which leads west to the Great Lakes area.

What to See and Do

The Iowa Great Lakes lie in the northwest corner of the state. The region has six lakes (including West Okoboji—one of only three true bluewater lakes in the world) and a dozen vacation resorts. Climb aboard the **Queen II** excursion boat (✉ Arnolds Park, ☎ 712/332–5159) for a tour of West Okoboji. The **Iowa Great Lakes Chamber of Commerce** (✉ Box 9, Arnolds Park 51331, ☎ 712/332–2107) has more information on the area.

Lodging

$$$$ ⊞ **Village East Resort.** Overlooking Brooks Golf Course and East Lake Okoboji, this resort offers indoor and outdoor pools, tennis, and racquetball. Additional draws are a pro shop and weight room. ✉ *Box 499, Okoboji 51355-0499, ☎ 712/332–2161 or 800/727–4561. 101 rooms. AE, D, DC, MC, V.*

$$$ ⊞ **Beaches Resort.** On the quiet north end of West Lake Okoboji, newly painted cottages offer simple but comfortable furnishings at this family-oriented resort. ✉ *15109 215th Ave., Spirit Lake 51360, ☎ 712/ 336–2230. 6 cottages, 5 apartments, 1 house. Restaurant, boating, recreation room. MC, V.*

Riverboat Gambling on the Mississippi River

Arriving and Departing

From Des Moines take I–80 east to Davenport and follow signs to the riverfront.

What to See and Do

Davenport, the largest of the Quad Cities (the other three are Bettendorf in Iowa and Rock Island and Moline in Illinois), introduced casino riverboat gambling to the nation. In downtown Davenport, with plenty of hotels, restaurants, and antiques shops within walking distance, the **President Riverboat Casino** (✉ 130 West River Dr., ☎ 800/ 262–8711), listed as a National Historic Landmark, is as big as a football field, with five decks decorated in Victorian splendor.

The Covered Bridges Region

Arriving and Departing

Take I–35 south from Des Moines to U.S. 92, which leads west into Madison County.

What to See and Do

Made famous by Robert James Waller's novel *The Bridges of Madison County* and the eponymous 1995 hit movie, **Madison County,** 50 mi southwest of Des Moines, is home to six covered bridges that date to the 1880s. Bus tours (☎ 515/462–1185) of the bridges take place all day, or you can take a self-guided one. Tours are also available at Francesca's Farmhouse and other buildings used as sites for the movie. The Covered Bridge Festival is held here each October. In Winterset, the **birthplace of John Wayne** (✉ 224 S. 2nd St., ☎ 515/462–1044) is furnished with family memorabilia and authentic turn-of-the-century pieces; you can watch Wayne's films in the gift shop.

Lodging

$$ ⊞ **Hutchings-Wintrode Bed and Breakfast.** This 1886 brick home, just four blocks from the courthouse, is newly refurbished with antiques and period decor. ✉ *503 E. Jefferson St., Winterset 50273, ☎ 515/ 462–3095. 3 rooms. MC, V.*

$$ ⊞ **Ringgenberg Haus.** This tastefully furnished early 20th-century home has a two-room suite and a second guest room, which share a

bath. ⊠ *214 N. 8th St., Winterset 50273,* ☎ *515/462–9931. 2 rooms. No credit cards.*

$$ ⊞ **A Step-Away Bed and Breakfast.** This 1880s store turned B&B and art gallery is just a step away from the attractive courthouse square in Winterset. Each of the two rooms has a private bath and cable TV. ⊠ *104 W. Court St., Winterset 50273,* ☎ *515/462–5956. 2 rooms. D, MC V.*

KANSAS

By Janet
Majure

Updated by
Diana Lambdin
Meyer

Capital	Topeka
Population	2,572,200
Motto	To the Stars Through Difficulties
State Bird	Western meadowlark
State Flower	Wild native sunflower
Postal Abbreviation	KS

Statewide Visitor Information

Kansas Department of Commerce, Travel & Tourism Division (⊠ 700 S.W. Harrison St., Suite 1300, Topeka 66603, ☎ 913/296–2009 or 800/252–6727).There are **visitor information centers** on I–70W in Kansas City (☎ 913/299–2253), on I–70E in Goodland (☎ 913/899–6695), on I–35N at South Haven (☎ 316/892–5283), and in Topeka (☎ 913/296–3966).

Scenic Drives

Route 177 south from I–70 to historic Council Grove provides lovely views—especially in late afternoon or early morning—of the undulating Flint Hills.

National and State Parks

National Parks

Federal sites include the **Fort Larned National Historic Site** (☞ The Santa Fe Trail Region, *below*); the **Fort Scott National Historic Site** (⊠ Old Fort Blvd., Fort Scott 66701, ☎ 316/223–0310 or 800/245–3678), which centers on a fort built in 1842 to keep the peace in Native American territory; and the **Cimarron National Grassland** (⊠ Box 300, 242 E. Hwy. 56, Elkhart 67950, ☎ 316/697–4621), less than a mile from central Elkhart, which offers a self-guided auto tour of key Santa Fe Trail sites.

State Parks

Kansas has 24 state parks, most associated with recreational lakes, run by the **Department of Wildlife and Parks** (⊠ 512 S.E. 25th Ave., Pratt 67124, ☎ 316/672–5911). Two of the best are **Scott County State Park** (⊠ R.R. 1, Box 50, Scott City 67871, ☎ 316/872–2061), containing archaeological evidence of the northernmost Native American pueblo and the first white settlement in Kansas, and **Milford State Park** (⊠ 8811 State Park Rd., Milford 66514, ☎ 913/238–3014), with a 37,000-acre reservoir, a nature center, and a fish hatchery.

EAST-CENTRAL KANSAS

Heading west from Kansas City across east-central Kansas, you'll follow in the footsteps of pioneers who traveled the Oregon, Santa Fe, Smoky Hill, and Chisholm trails. Native American history, Civil War sites, and the Old West loom large along this 150-mi stretch of prairie.

Visitor Information

Abilene: Convention & Visitors Bureau (⊠ 201 N.W. 2nd St., 67410, ☎ 913/263–2231 or 800/569–5915). **Atchison:** Visitor Center (⊠ 200 S. 10th St., 66002, ☎ 913/367–2427 or 800/234–1854). **Kansas City, Kansas:** Convention & Visitors Bureau (⊠ 727 Minnesota Ave.,

66110, ☎ 913/321–5800 or 800/264–1563); **Overland Park Convention & Visitors Bureau** (✉ 10975 Benson Dr., Suite 360, 66210, ☎ 913/491–0123 or 800/262–7275). **Lawrence:** Convention & Visitors Bureau (✉ 734 Vermont St., 66044, ☎ 913/865–4411 or 800/318–8995). **Topeka:** Convention & Visitors Bureau (✉ 1275 S.W. Topeka Blvd., 66612, ☎ 913/234–1030 or 800/235–1030).

Arriving and Departing

By Bus
Greyhound Lines (☎ 800/231–2222) connects Kansas City, Lawrence, Topeka, and Abilene en route to Denver. **Jefferson Lines** (☎ 800/735–7433) serves Kansas City, Overland Park, and Lawrence.

By Car
I–70W enters Kansas from Kansas City, Missouri; I–70E, from Colorado. Most attractions are just off the interstate. Note: Kansas weather is extremely variable. Listen to the radio for forecasts, as ice storms, heavy snowfalls, flash floods, and high winds can make driving treacherous. Road conditions are also posted at toll booths along I–70.

By Plane
The biggest airport serving east-central Kansas is **Kansas City International Airport** (☞ Missouri). US Airways Express serves Topeka's **Forbes Field** (☎ 913/862–6515).

By Train
Amtrak (☎ 800/872–7245) serves Lawrence, Topeka, and Kansas City.

Exploring East-Central Kansas

Along I–70 you'll encounter an array of historic sites. **Kansas City,** which straddles the border between Kansas and Missouri, was a major provisioning point for frontier travelers in the 19th century.

The **Mahaffie Farmstead & Stagecoach Stop** once served the Santa Fe Trail, one of the routes established in the 19th century for trade and later for westward expansion. There are guided tours of the stone house, one of three buildings here listed on the National Register of Historic Places. ✉ *1100 Kansas City Rd., Olathe 66061, ☎ 913/782–6972. Closed Jan. and weekends Feb.–Apr.*

In Fairway, a Kansas City suburb, the **Shawnee Indian Mission** (✉ 3403 W. 53rd St., ☎ 913/262–0867) was begun in 1839 as a school to teach English and trade skills to Native Americans. Two of its three buildings can be toured. In Overland Park, another suburb, college-sports history is recounted through photographs, videos, and sound tracks at the **National Collegiate Athletic Association Visitors Center** (✉ 6201 College Blvd., ☎ 913/339–0000).

About 40 mi west of Kansas City on I–70 is **Lawrence.** After being raided and burned during the Civil War because of the antislavery stance of its citizens, the town was rebuilt by William Quantrill and a band of Confederate sympathizers; many structures dating from this time remain. Stroll along Massachusetts Street through the lovely downtown area, where turn-of-the-century buildings and retail shops retain a small-town flavor.

A few blocks away from Massachusetts Street is the scenic main campus of the 29,000-student **University of Kansas.** Lining Jayhawk Boulevard is an assortment of university buildings, including the Romanesque structure of native limestone that houses one of the school's four museums: the **University of Kansas Natural History Museum** (✉ Dyche Hall, ☎ 913/864–4540), which displays fossils, mounted animals, and rotating exhibits. Also in Lawrence is **Haskell Indian Nations University** (✉ 23rd and Barker Sts., ☎ 913/749–8448), which has provided higher education for Native Americans since 1884.

Fifty miles northwest of Kansas City on Route 7 and overlooking the Missouri River is **Atchison,** the birthplace of famed aviator Amelia Earhart. Her birthplace is now a private museum owned by the Ninety-Nines, an international group of women pilots. ✉ *223 N. Terrace St., 66002,* ☎ *913/367–4217. Closed Oct.–Apr.*

About 70 mi west of Kansas City on I–70 is **Topeka,** with its outstanding classical state **capitol** (✉ 10th and Harrison Sts., ☎ 913/296–3966), begun in 1866 and completed nearly 40 years later. Lobby murals include a striking depiction of abolitionist John Brown by John Steuart Curry. The ornate senate chambers, with bronze columns and variegated-marble accents, are magnificent. West of downtown Topeka, the **Kansas Museum of History** (✉ 6425 S.W. 6th St., ☎ 913/272–8681), perversely situated in a modernist box of a building, explains Kansas's history from the Native American era to the present. Just outside Topeka, the **Combat Air Museum** (✉ Hangars 602 and 604, Forbes Field, ☎ 913/862–3303) has two hangars full of military aircraft dating from World War I. **Historic Ward-Meade Park** (✉ 124 N. Fillmore St., ☎ 913/295–3888) is as lovely as it is historic, with a restored mansion, a cabin, a train depot, a one-room schoolhouse, and botanical gardens.

The United States' newest national park, the treeless 11,000-acre **Flint Hills National Prairie,** was signed into law in 1996. Extending from Nebraska to Oklahoma, the park contains the last large vestiges of the bluestem, or tallgrass, prairie that once covered much of the Great Plains. Wagon tours and visits to the area are coordinated through the **Z Bar/Spring Hill Ranch** (✉ Rte. 1, Strong City 66869, ☎ 316/273–8494). The historic **Grand Central Hotel** in Cottonwood Falls (☎ 316/273–6763) has been welcoming guests since 1884.

The small town of **Abilene,** about 85 mi west of Topeka, is famous for cattle drives and for Dwight D. Eisenhower. The **Eisenhower Center** complex includes the late president's **boyhood home**—the 19th-century clapboard looks out of place among the surrounding limestone buildings—as well as the **Eisenhower Museum,** the **Eisenhower Presidential Library,** and the **Place of Meditation,** a chapel where the president, his wife, Mamie, and their son, Doud Dwight, are interred. The museum displays memorabilia of Eisenhower's life, from his youth in Abilene and his success as a general during World War II through his popular presidency. ✉ *S. Buckeye and 4th Sts.,* ☎ *913/263–4751.*

Also in Abilene is the **Dickinson County Historical Museum** (✉ 412 S. Campbell St., ☎ 913/263–2681), offering exhibits on the life of the Plains Indians. The **Greyhound Hall of Fame** (✉ 407 S. Buckeye St., ☎ 913/263–3000) documents the history of this illustrious canine breed.

What to See and Do with Children

Children will enjoy the dinosaur bones and live snakes at Lawrence's **University of Kansas Natural History Museum** and Discovery Place at Topeka's **Kansas Museum of History,** with hands-on exhibits about 19th-century clothes, tools, and household items (for both, ☞ Exploring East-Central Kansas, *above*). **Gage Park** in Topeka (✉ 635 Gage Blvd., ☎ 913/295–3838) has a carousel and is home to the **Topeka Zoo** (☎ 913/272–5821).

Dining and Lodging

Typical Kansas roadhouse fare is chicken-fried steak and fried chicken. In addition, good barbecue and Mexican food can be found in the area's cities and towns. Accommodations range from business-class hotels in the Kansas City suburb of Overland Park to the basic roadside motels that predominate in the western part of the region to bed-and-breakfasts (Kansas Bed & Breakfast Association, ✉ Rte. 1, Box 93, WaKeeney 67672). For price ranges *see* Charts 1 (B) and 2 (B) *in* On the Road with Fodor's.

Abilene

$$ ✕ **Kirby House.** The traditional midwestern fare served here is nothing special, but the quietly elegant setting, in a restored Victorian mansion, makes up for it. ✉ *205 N.E. 3rd St.,* ☎ *913/263–7336. AE, D, MC, V.*

$ ✕ **Mr. K's Farmhouse.** Once a favorite of Dwight and Mamie Eisenhower, the "house on the hill" serves fried chicken and homemade desserts. ✉ *407 S. Van Buren,* ☎ *913/263–7995. D, MC, V. Closed Mon.*

Kansas City

$$$ ✕ **Tatsu's French Restaurant.** French cuisine with an Asian flair is
★ found in the unexpected setting of a suburban shopping strip. ✉ *4603 W. 90th St., Prairie Village,* ☎ *913/383–9801. AE, MC, V. Closed Sun. No lunch Sat.*

$$ ✕ **Dick Clark's American Bandstand Grill.** Rock 'n' roll history comes alive in this diner owned by America's perpetual teenager. Vintage posters, gold albums, and artists' contracts on the walls complement a variety of dishes of various regional cuisines. Clark and other music celebrities often stop in. ✉ *10975 Metcalf Ave., Overland Park,* ☎ *913/451–1600. AE, D, MC, V.*

$$ ✕ **Hayward's Pit Bar-B-Que.** Locals flock to this hillside restaurant for
★ piles of succulent smoked beef, ribs, chicken, pork, and sausage. The combination plate lets you try three of them. ✉ *11051 Antioch Rd., Overland Park,* ☎ *913/451–8080. AE, MC, V.*

$$$ ▦ **Doubletree Hotel.** Adjacent to two major highways, a business park, and a scenic public jogging trail, this 18-story hotel is convenient to shopping, restaurants, and a bowling alley. The public spaces have an Asian motif, complete with botanical prints, cloisonné vases, and folding screens; guest rooms are decorated in shades of taupe and teal. ✉ *10100 College Blvd., Overland Park 66210,* ☎ *913/451–6100,* FAX *913/451–3873. 357 rooms. Restaurant, lounge, indoor pool, hot tub, sauna, health club, racquetball. AE, D, DC, MC, V.*

$$$ ▦ **Overland Park Marriott Hotel.** This upscale hotel in a suburban busi-
★ ness area has a marble-floor lobby and traditionally furnished rooms. The concierge level has slightly larger rooms and a lobby lounge serving food and drinks. ✉ *10800 Metcalf Ave., Overland Park 66210,* ☎ *913/451–8000,* FAX *913/451–5914. 390 rooms. 2 restaurants, lobby lounge, pool, health club. AE, D, DC, MC, V.*

Lawrence

$$ ✕ **Free State Brewing Co.** Kansas's first brew pub since 1886 serves
★ dishes like fish-and-chips and a Burgundy beef sandwich (shredded beef brisket on a baguette, smothered with gravy) to complement the selection of beers made here. Brewery tours are offered on Saturday. ✉ *636 Massachusetts St.,* ☎ *913/843–4555. Reservations not accepted. AE, D, MC, V.*

$$ ▦ Eldridge Hotel. Listed on the National Register of Historic Places,
★   this downtown hotel offers attractive suites that include a parlor and
wet bar; rooms on the top (fifth) floor afford good views. The down-
town location means some traffic noise but great convenience. ⊠ *701
Massachusetts St., 66044,* ☎ *913/749–5011 or 800/527–0909,* 𝖥𝖠𝖷 *913/
749–4512. 48 suites. Restaurant, bar, hot tub, exercise room. AE, D,
MC, V.*

Topeka

$$$ ✕▦ Heritage House. This turn-of-the-century clapboard home, once
the site of the Menninger Clinic, has B&B rooms ranging from dra-
matic to cozy. The intimate restaurant serves a frequently changing
Continental menu for lunch and dinner; jacket and tie are required.
⊠ *3535 S.W. 6th St., 66606,* ☎ *913/233–3800,* 𝖥𝖠𝖷 *913/233–9793.
10 rooms. Restaurant. AE, D, DC, MC, V.*

$$ ▦ Club House Inn. In western Topeka near the Kansas Museum of His-
tory, this modern white-stucco B&B inn has spacious rooms, many over-
looking a landscaped courtyard, and suites with kitchenettes. ⊠ *924
S.W. Henderson St., 66615,* ☎ *913/273–8888,* 𝖥𝖠𝖷 *913/273–5809. 121
rooms. Pool, hot tub. AE, D, DC, MC, V.*

Motels

I–70 is lined with chain hotels (☞ Lodging *in* Chapter 1: The Gold
Guide). ▦ **Best Western Inn** (⊠ 2210 N. Buckeye St., Abilene 67410,
☎ 913/263–2050, 𝖥𝖠𝖷 913/263–7230), 62 rooms, restaurant, lounge,
indoor pool, hot tub; $.

Campgrounds

Four Seasons RV Acres (⊠ 6 mi east of Abilene off I–70; 2502 Mink
Rd., Abilene 67410, ☎ 913/598–2221 or 800/658–4667). **KOA Camp-
grounds of Lawrence** (⊠ 1473 Hwy. 40, Lawrence 66044, ☎ 913/842–
3877). **KOA Campground** (⊠ Rte. 1, Grantville 66429, ☎ 913/
246–3419). Camping is also available in state parks at reservoirs.

Nightlife

The **New Theatre** (⊠ 9229 Foster St., ☎ 913/649–7469), an Equity
theater and restaurant, stages first-run and recent musicals and come-
dies.

Outdoor Activities and Sports

Fishing

Most of east-central Kansas follows the Kansas River, called the Kaw
River locally, where a series of large-scale flood-control reservoirs af-
ford good fishing for walleye, bass, and crappie. Good sites include
Clinton State Park (⊠ 798 N. 1415 Rd., Lawrence 66049); **Perry State
Park** (⊠ R.R. 1, Box 464A, Ozawkie 66070), near Topeka; **Tuttle
Creek State Park** (⊠ 5020-B Tuttle Creek Blvd., Manhattan 66502);
and **Milford State Park** (☞ National and State Parks, *above*). Licenses
are required and can be purchased at county clerks' offices, state parks
offices, and some retail outlets. The **Kansas Department of Fish and
Game** (☎ 316/672–5911) has further information.

Hiking

Kansas's reservoirs are bordered by state parks with marked nature
trails. The **Konza Prairie** (⊠ 5 mi off I–70 at Exit 307, McDowell Creek
Rd., ☎ 913/532–6620), an 8,600-acre section of tallgrass prairie set
aside for research and preservation, has a self-guided nature trail.

Spectator Sports

Basketball: Jayhawks (⊠ Memorial Stadium, 11th and Mississippi Sts., ☎ 913/864–3141 or 800/344–2957).

Horse and dog racing: Woodlands (⊠ 99th St. and Leavenworth Rd., Kansas City, ☎ 913/299–9797) offers greyhound racing year-round and horse racing in late summer.

Shopping

Lawrence Riverfront Factory Outlets (⊠ 1 Riverfront Plaza, ☎ 913/842–5511), at the north end of downtown, has nearly 50 stores. The mall's north-side picture windows are an excellent vantage point for the nearly 20 bald eagles whose home is in the cottonwood trees on the banks of the Kansas River, which rushes past the front of the mall. The **Tanger Center** (⊠ 1035 N. 3rd St., ☎ 913/842–6290), about a mile north of downtown, has 25 factory outlet stores from major-name manufacturers of clothing, shoes, and other goods.

THE SANTA FE TRAIL REGION

Although the Santa Fe Trail spans the entire state, the towns in western Kansas are most closely associated with its lore and history. This is the Kansas we know from film and myth: remote, flat, treeless, littered with tumbleweeds, windy, but imbued with a romance identified with such names as Wyatt Earp and Dodge City. Towns sprang up here first along the trail, then near the railroad lines that followed. Today agriculture is the mainstay. Tourism is growing, but don't expect resorts.

Visitor Information

Dodge City: Convention & Visitors Bureau (⊠ Box 1474, 4th and Spruce Sts., 67801, ☎ 316/225–8186). **Hutchinson:** Convention & Visitors Bureau (⊠ 117 N. Walnut St., 67501, ☎ 316/662–3391). **Larned:** Chamber of Commerce (⊠ 502 Broadway, 67550, ☎ 316/285–6916 or 800/747–6919).

Arriving and Departing

By Bus

Greyhound Lines (☎ 800/231–2222) connects with **TNM&O Coaches** (☎ 316/276–3731) to provide service to Dodge City from Wichita. The **Hutchinson Shuttle Service** (☎ 316/662–5205) connects with Great Bend, Newton, Wichita, and other cities in central Kansas.

By Car

From Kansas City or Topeka take I–70 west and I–135 south, then Route 61 to Hutchinson. Eastbound travelers enter Dodge City via U.S. 50 or U.S. 56.

By Plane

Dodge City Regional Airport (☎ 316/227–8679), about 2 mi east of downtown, is served by US Airways Express.

By Train

Amtrak (☎ 800/872–7245) serves Hutchinson, Newton, Garden City, and Dodge City.

Exploring the Santa Fe Trail Region

Hutchinson is home to the state fairgrounds and some of the world's largest grain elevators, but what really makes this small town worth a visit is the **Kansas Cosmosphere & Space Center.** Housing more than $100 million worth of space exhibits, the center's museum has the largest collection outside the Smithsonian Institution. Various displays—including interactive exhibits—explain the history of space exploration and solutions to the many challenges of human flight. Recently acquired exhibits include the *Apollo 13 Odyssey* command module and the world's largest display of Soviet space artifacts. The center also has a planetarium and an Omnimax theater. ⊠ *1100 N. Plum St.,* ☎ *316/ 662–2305 or 800/397–0330.*

Travel west out of Hutchison on 4th Street (which becomes County Road 636) for about 30 mi, and you will see signs to the **Quivira National Wildlife Refuge** (⊠ Rte. 3, Box 48A, Stafford 67578, ☎ 316/ 486–2393). More than 250 bird species have been spotted on its 21,000 acres, including regular migrations of bald eagles, pelicans, and whooping cranes.

Drive north through the Quivira refuge, then turn west on County Road 484, which becomes Route 19, to **Larned,** a well-preserved Old West town. Two miles west of Larned on Route 156, the **Santa Fe Trail Center** (☎ 316/285–2054) details the history of the trail and displays artifacts from early 20th-century prairie life. About 6 mi west of Larned on Route 156 is **Fort Larned National Historic Site** (⊠ R.R. 3, ☎ 316/ 285–6911), a meticulous restoration of an 1868 prairie fort that protected travelers on the Santa Fe Trail and, later, railroad workers. Buffalo Soldiers (post–Civil War regiments of black soldiers) were stationed here. The site includes a museum, restored barracks, and a history/nature trail; a video paints a distinctly unromantic picture of the fort's history and mission.

Turn south on the first road west of Fort Larned, which intersects with U.S. 56. Follow this southwest to **Dodge City,** which capitalizes on its 19th-century reputation as the "wickedest little city in America." Founded 5 mi west of Fort Dodge in anticipation of the arrival of the Santa Fe Railroad, the town thrived on the drinking and gambling of buffalo hunters and cowboys. It was here that lawmen Bat Masterson and Wyatt Earp earned their fame.

Dodge City's **Boot Hill Museum** (⊠ Front St., 316/227–8188) includes exhibits on Native American history, the Santa Fe Trail, and the town's early life; Front Street, a reconstruction of houses, saloons, and other businesses that existed before the original town burned in 1885; and a Boot Hill cemetery re-creation (the remains of those buried here were moved years ago). In summer gunfights, medicine shows, and stagecoach rides are staged daily.

Follow U.S. 50 west for 9 mi to the **Santa Fe Trail tracks,** a 140-acre preserve where, more than 125 years later, ruts from wagons on the trail are still visible in the sandy prairie earth.

Dining and Lodging

Motels hold sway in this part of the state, and you'll find few fancy restaurants, though many offer fresh and flavorful food. If you're traveling in summer, make reservations early for lodging; for restaurants, reservations on weekends are advised. Note: The term *red beer* on menus means beer mixed with tomato juice (it's good—really!). Kansas's liquor laws vary from county to county; in dry counties alcohol is served only in private clubs, to which many hotels offer courtesy memberships (ask when you call to reserve). For price ranges *see* Charts 1 (B) and 2 (B) *in* On the Road with Fodor's.

The Santa Fe Trail Region

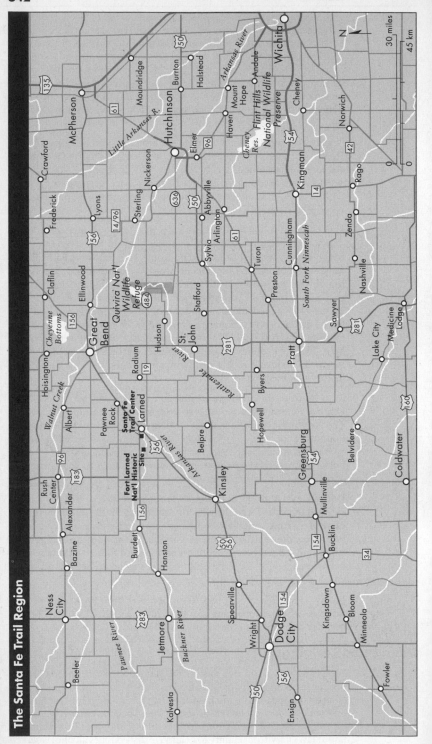

Dodge City

$$ ✗ Big Art's. Those in search of basic American sandwiches, steaks, and shakes will be satisfied here. ✉ *1005 W. Wyatt Earp Blvd.,* ☎ *316/ 227–2424. AE, MC, V.*

$$ ✗ El Charro. Mexican dishes such as "enchilada delights," topped with cheese, lettuce, tomato, and sour cream, make this a favorite. ✉ *1209 W. Wyatt Earp Blvd.,* ☎ *316/225–0371. MC, V. Closed Sun.*

$$ ✗ Saigon Market. Fresh ingredients for Vietnamese dishes are cooked
★ to order and colorfully presented in the restaurant half of this market, which is housed in a funky strip mall. ✉ *1202 E. Wyatt Earp Blvd.,* ☎ *316/225–9099. Reservations not accepted. No credit cards. Closed Mon.*

$$ ⊞ Best Western Silver Spur Lodge. You'll find clean, pleasant, undistinguished rooms at this sprawling complex just five minutes from Front Street. ✉ *1510 W. Wyatt Earp Blvd., 67801,* ☎ *316/227–2125,* FAX *316/227–2030. 121 rooms. 2 restaurants, lounge, pool. AE, D, DC, MC, V.*

Hutchinson

$ ✗ Anchor Inn. Two large brick-walled rooms in older downtown build-
★ ings are the setting for Mexican dishes that use the restaurant's distinctive homemade flour tortillas. Portions are bounteous. ✉ *126–128 S. Main St.,* ☎ *316/669–0311. Reservations not accepted weekend evenings. MC, V. Closed Sun. May–Sept.*

$ ✗ Roy's Hickory Pit BBQ. This tiny restaurant seating 36 serves barbecued pork spare ribs, beef brisket, sausage, ham, and turkey. There's nothing else on the menu besides beans, salad, and bread—but who needs more? ✉ *1018 W. 5th St.,* ☎ *316/663–7421. Reservations not accepted. No credit cards. Closed Sun.–Mon.*

$$ ⊞ Ramada Inn Hutchinson. Rooms in the "minidome" section of this
★ busy convention hotel look onto a quiet, landscaped courtyard. "Maindome" rooms open onto a recreation area with a putting green and a swimming pool. ✉ *1400 N. Lorraine St., 67501,* ☎ *316/669 9311 or 800/362–5018,* FAX *316/669–9830. 220 rooms. Restaurant, lounge, indoor pool, 2 tennis courts, exercise room. AE, D, DC, MC, V.*

Larned

$ ✗ Harvest Inn. Chicken, steaks, and seafood are on the menu at this family restaurant; food is also served in the accompanying bar, the Grain Club. ✉ *718 Ft. Larned Ave.,* ☎ *316/285–3870. Reservations not accepted. D, MC, V.*

Motels

EconoLodge and Super 8 (☞ Lodging *in* Chapter 1: The Gold Guide) are in Dodge City. ⊞ **Best Western Townsman Inn** (✉ 123 E. 14th St., Larned 67550, ☎ 316/285–3114, FAX 316/285–7139), 44 rooms, pool; *$.* ⊞ **Quality Inn City Center** (✉ 15 W. 4th St., Hutchinson 67501, ☎ 316/663–1211, FAX 316/663–6636), 98 rooms, restaurant, lounge, pool; *$.* ⊞ **Scotsman Inn** (✉ 322 E. 4th St., Hutchinson 67501, ☎ 316/669–8281), FAX 316/669–8282), 48 rooms; *$.*

Campgrounds

Gunsmoke Campground (✉ R.R. 2, W. Hwy. 50, Dodge City 67801, ☎ 316/227–8247). **Melody Acres RV Park** (✉ 1009 E. Blanchard St., Hutchinson 67501, ☎ 316/665–5048). **Watersports Campground** (✉ 500 E. Cherry St., Dodge City 67801, ☎ 316/225–9003 or 316/225–8044).

Nightlife

In Dodge City, the **Boot Hill Museum Repertory Co.** (☞ Exploring the Santa Fe Trail Region, *above*) puts on the 19th-century–style Long Branch Variety Show. Also in Dodge City, the **Longhorn Saloon** (⊠ 706 N. 2nd St., ☎ 316/225–3546) has a restaurant as well as a 1,350-square-ft wooden dance floor for western stomping.

Outdoor Activities and Sports

Hiking

At **Dillon Nature Center,** in Hutchinson (⊠ 3002 E. 30th St., ☎ 316/663–7411), a 2-mi-long National Recreation Trail takes in woods, prairie, and wetlands.

Spectator Sports

Rodeo: The Professional Rodeo Cowboys Association's biggest Kansas rodeo is the **Dodge City Roundup Rodeo** (☎ 316/225–2244), held for five days each summer during the Dodge City Days festival.

ELSEWHERE IN KANSAS

Wichita

Arriving and Departing

Wichita lies about 190 mi southwest of Kansas City on the Kansas Turnpike (I–35). Most visitors arrive by car or fly into **Wichita Mid-Continent Airport** (☎ 316/946–4700), served by most major domestic carriers.

What to See and Do

Originally a frontier town, **Wichita** is known today as one of the air capitals of the world—Beech, Cessna, and Learjet are based here, and Boeing has a major installation. The city is also home to such corporate giants as Coleman, which manufactures camping equipment, and Pizza Hut.

The **Indian Center Museum** (⊠ 650 N. Seneca St., ☎ 316/262–5221) features artifacts from numerous tribes, including the Crow and the Sioux. The **Old Cowtown Museum** (⊠ 1871 Sim Park Dr., ☎ 316/264–0671) is a re-created 19th-century town. At **Botanica, the Wichita Gardens** (⊠ 701 N. Amiden, ☎ 316/264–0448), more than 9 acres of perennials and woody plants are displayed among dozens of fountains and pools. The **Wichita Greyhound Park** (⊠ 10 mi from downtown Wichita on I–135, ☎ 316/755–4000 or 800/872–2894) offers live horse- and greyhound racing, as well as simulcast races from around the country. The **Convention and Visitors Bureau** (⊠ 100 S. Main St., Suite 100, 67202, ☎ 316/265–2800 or 800/288–9424) has information on individual sites.

Fort Scott

Arriving and Departing

Fort Scott is an easy 100-mi drive south of Kansas City on Route 69. Designated a National Military Highway, the route is sparsely populated but dotted with several historical markers describing the Indian and Civil War battles that took place in the region.

What to See and Do

The violence and bloodshed in this area during the period leading up to the Civil War are considered by many historians to have had a greater impact on the start of the war than the shots fired at Fort Sumter. Today

★ nine of the original buildings at the **Fort Scott National Historic Site** (⊠

Old Fort Blvd., ☎ 316/223–0310) are fully restored, and daily reenactments demonstrate life in this frontier post. Fort Scott offers numerous summer and fall festivals and activities.

The **Fort Scott Visitor Center** (✉ 231 E. Wall St., Fort Scott 66701, ☎ 800/245–3678) has an hourly trolley tour (no tours December–March) that highlights the area's Victorian-era homes and shopping center, the Old Congregational Church, the Fort Scott National Historic Site, and one of the 12 national military cemeteries.

MISSOURI

By Lori Dodge
Rose

Updated by
Diana Lambdin
Meyer

Capital   Jefferson City
Population   5,359,000
Motto   Let the Welfare of the People
                         Be the Supreme Law
State Bird   Eastern bluebird
State Flower   Hawthorn
Postal Abbreviation MO

Statewide Visitor Information

The **Missouri Division of Tourism** (✉ Truman State Office Bldg., Box 1055, Jefferson City 65102, ☎ 573/751–4133, 800/877–1234 in MO) operates six visitor centers to serve travelers as they enter Missouri on major interstates.

Scenic Drives

Route 21 from St. Louis to Doniphan in extreme southern Missouri passes through national forests and rugged hill country. Scenic routes in the Ozark Mountains of southwestern Missouri include **Route 76, Route 248,** and **U.S. 65** south of Springfield.

National and State Parks

National Parks

The **Ozark National Scenic Riverways** (✉ National Park Service, Box 490, Van Buren 63965, ☎ 573/323–4236) includes the Current and Jacks Fork rivers, two south-central Missouri rivers that were the first to be federally protected. Both offer good canoeing. The **Mark Twain National Forest** (✉ 401 Fairgrounds Rd., Rolla 65401, ☎ 573/364–4621) is in southern Missouri.

State Parks

Lake of the Ozarks State Park (☞ Exploring the Ozarks, *below*) is the largest state park in Missouri. The popular **Missouri River State Trail,** known to locals as the Katy Trail, is a walking-and-cycling path, much of it along the Missouri River between Sedalia and St. Charles. Other significant parks include **Elephant Rocks** (✉ Belleview 63623, ☎ 573/364–4621), **Johnson's Shut-Ins** (✉ Middle Brook 63656, ☎ 573/546–2450), **Mastodon State Park** (✉ Imperial 63052, ☎ 314/464–2976), and **Onondaga Cave State Park** (✉ Leasburg 65535, ☎ 573/245–6576). For more information contact the **Missouri Department of Natural Resources** (Division of State Parks, ✉ Box 176, Jefferson City 65101, ☎ 573/751–2479 or 800/334–6946).

ST. LOUIS

Founded by the French in 1764 as a fur-trading settlement on the west bank of the Mississippi River, St. Louis today is best known for the soaring silver arch so impressive to travelers entering the city from the east. In its early days the city thrived as a river port, then as a rail hub, and today it's the world headquarters for such diverse corporations as Anheuser-Busch and the Boeing Corporation. The building of the Gateway Arch more than 25 years ago did more than commemorate the city's role in westward expansion—it helped spark the rebirth of a downtown that had been abandoned in the rush for the suburbs.

Visitor Information

Convention and Visitors Commission (✉ 10 S. Broadway, Suite 1000, 63102, ☎ 314/421–1023 or 800/888–3861) is open weekdays from 8:30 to 5. **Visitor centers** are at the airport and downtown (✉ 308 Washington Ave., ☎ 314/241–1764). The **Missouri Tourist Information Center** (☎ 314/869–7100) is just west of the Missouri-Illinois border, on I–270 at the Riverview exit.

Arriving and Departing

By Bus

Greyhound Lines (✉ 1450 N. 13th St., ☎ 800/231–2222).

By Car

From I–70, I–55, and I–44 follow the exits for downtown St. Louis. From U.S. 40 (I–64) from the west, exit at Broadway.

By Plane

Lambert–St. Louis International Airport (☎ 314/426–8000), 10 mi northwest of downtown on I–70, has scheduled flights by most major domestic and foreign carriers. It's about 20 minutes by car from the airport to downtown St. Louis; taxis cost about $20. Transportation is also provided to downtown stops by the **Bi-State** bus (☎ 314/231–2345) and to downtown hotels by **Airport Express** shuttle vans (☎ 314/429–4950).

By Train

Amtrak (✉ 550 S. 16th St., ☎ 314/331–3300 or 800/872–7245).

Getting Around St. Louis

Downtown sights can be explored on foot; elsewhere you'll need a car. **MetroLink** (☎ 314/231–2345), the city's light rail system, stops near major attractions downtown. Rides are free between Laclede's Landing and Union Station weekdays from 10 to 3.

Exploring St. Louis

Downtown

A ride to the top of the 630-ft **Gateway Arch** is a must. The centerpiece of the 91-acre **Jefferson National Expansion Memorial Park,** the arch was built in 1966 to commemorate the city where thousands of 19th-century pioneers stopped for provisions before traveling west. A tram takes visitors up through one of the arch's legs to an observation room where you get a terrific view of the city and the Mississippi. Below it is the underground visitor center and the **Museum of Westward Expansion.** ✉ *On the riverfront at Market St.,* ☎ *314/425–4465.*

Just down the steps from the Gateway arch is the Mississippi riverfront and its cobblestone levee, where permanently moored **riverboats** house a handful of mostly fast food restaurants. The *Tom Sawyer* and *Becky Thatcher* (☎ 314/621–4040), replicas of 19th-century steamboats, offer one-hour sightseeing trips and two-hour dinner cruises. Nearby is the **President Casino on the** *Admiral,* (☎ 314/622—1111), a noncruising riverboat that offers casino gambling in a Las Vegas–style environment. Northwest of the Gateway arch is **Laclede's Landing,** nine square blocks of cobblestone streets and restored 19th-century warehouses, now filled with shops, galleries, restaurants, and nightspots.

On the western edge of the arch grounds is St. Louis's oldest church, the **Basilica of St. Louis, the King** (✉ 209 Walnut St., no phone), a simple Greek Revival structure, built 150 years ago and now a favorite

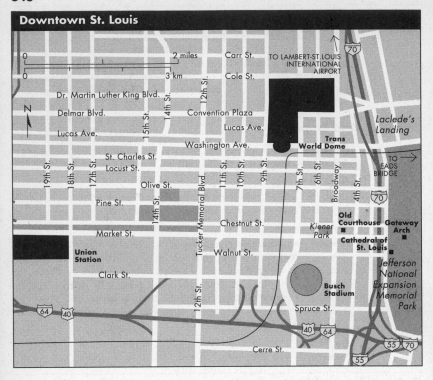

Downtown St. Louis

setting for weddings. West of the arch on Market Street, the **Old Courthouse** (⊠ 11 N. 4th St., ☎ 314/425–4465) houses displays and photographs of early St. Louis.

South of the courthouse is **Busch Stadium,** home of the St. Louis Cardinals (☞ Spectator Sports, *below*). Just across the street is the **National Bowling Hall of Fame** (☎ 314/231–6340), where you can bowl in a 1930s alley and learn more about the history of the sport. On the northeast side of the stadium is the **St. Louis Cardinals Hall of Fame,** displaying sports memorabilia and audio and video highlights of the city's baseball history. ⊠ *Off I-40 (exit at 9th St.),* ☎ *314/421–3263. Closed weekends Jan.–Mar.*

Other Attractions

St. Louis is home to the world's largest brewer, **Anheuser-Busch,** maker of Budweiser beer. Tours at the company's world headquarters, in south St. Louis, include the stables where the famous Clydesdale horses are kept. ⊠ *12th and Lynch Sts.,* ☎ *314/577–2626. Closed Sun.*

On the western edge of town is **Forest Park** (⊠ North of U.S. 40 between Kingshighway and Skinker Blvds.), whose grounds include a variety of attractions. The **St. Louis Zoo** (☎ 314/781–0900) has a high-tech education center. The **St. Louis Art Museum** (☎ 314/721–0072) has outstanding pre-Columbian and German expressionist collections. The **St. Louis Science Center** (⊠ 5050 Oakland Ave., ☎ 314/289–4444) contains more than 600 hands-on exhibits on ecology, space, and humanity.

A mind-boggling collection of mosaics covers the walls, ceilings, and three domes of the **Cathedral of St. Louis** (⊠ Lindell Blvd. and Newstead Ave., ☎ 314/533–2824), also known as the New Cathedral.

The **Missouri Botanical Garden** (⊠ 4344 Shaw Ave., ☎ 314/577–5100), known locally as Shaw's Garden for founder Henry Shaw, is a 15-minute drive southwest of downtown. Highlights include an impressive Japanese garden and a tropical rain forest housed in a geodesic dome.

St. Louisans love **Ted Drewes'** frozen custard (⊠ 6726 Chippewa St., ☎ 314/481–2652) so much they'll stand in lines that spill into the street, but don't worry—the lines move fast. You'll label yourself a tourist if you have to ask what a concrete is (it's frozen custard so thick it won't budge even when you flip the cup upside down).

What to See and Do with Children

Six Flags over Mid-America–St. Louis (⊠ I–44 and Allenton Rd., Eureka, ☎ 314/938–4800), about 30 mi southwest of St. Louis, has amusement rides and shows. **Grant's Farm** (⊠ 10501 Gravois, ☎ 314/843–1700), closed from November through March, is a favorite of St. Louis children for its petting zoo, animal preserve, and train ride to visit the Clydesdales; reservations are essential. **The Magic House** (⊠ 516 Kirkwood Blvd., ☎ 314/822–8900) is a restored Victorian house with interactive learning experiences.

Dining

St. Louis's Hill neighborhood has an Italian restaurant on nearly every corner; other ethnic restaurants are found throughout the city. Even the abundant steak houses carry an Italian dish or two. The Central West End and Laclede's Landing have a number of restaurants, as does Clayton, the St. Louis County seat, about 7 mi west of downtown. For price ranges *see* Chart 1 (B) *in* On the Road with Fodor's.

$$$$ ✕ **Tony's.** St. Louis's only five-star restaurant since the 1950s, Tony's has been run by the Bommarito family for three generations. Superb Italian dishes and prime steaks make it a favorite. ⊠ *410 Market St.,* ☎ *314/231–7007. Jacket and tie. Reservations essential. AE, D, DC, MC, V. No lunch. Closed Sun.*

$$$ ✕ **Cardwell's.** At this sophisticated Clayton establishment, diners can eat in the airy café with marble-top tables and French doors or in the more formal, elegant dining room. The frequently changing menu may include salmon with a sesame-seed crust or perhaps even wild boar. ⊠ *8100 Maryland St.,* ☎ *314/726–5055. AE, MC, V. Closed Sun.*

$$$ ✕ **Sidney Street Cafe.** Tables for two in the atrium and a candlelighted dining room lend romance to this former storefront in the Benton Park neighborhood. The eclectic cuisine includes raspberry or tequila-lime chicken. ⊠ *2000 Sidney St.,* ☎ *314/771–5777. AE, D, DC, MC, V. Closed Sun.–Mon.*

$$ ✕ **Blue Water Grill.** Grilled seafood with a southwestern flair is the specialty at this small, festive restaurant near the Hill. On Monday night diners can mix and match "Flying Saucers," an assortment of miniature entrées. ⊠ *2607 Hampton Ave.,* ☎ *314/645–0707. AE, MC, V. Closed Sun.*

$$ ✕ **Cunetto's House of Pasta.** There's usually a wait at this popular restau-
★ rant on the Hill, but relaxing in the cocktail lounge is part of the experience. Once seated, you'll find plenty of veal and beef dishes from which to choose, as well as more than 30 different pastas. ⊠ *5453 Magnolia Ave.,* ☎ *314/781–1135. Reservations not accepted for dinner. AE, DC, MC, V. Closed Sun.*

$ ✕ **Blueberry Hill.** At this St. Louis original, in the hip University City
★ neighborhood, you can order a burger and a Rock 'n Roll beer, plunk a quarter into the famous 2,000-tune jukebox, and let the good times

roll. ⊠ *6504 Delmar Blvd.,* ☎ *314/727–0880. Reservations not accepted. AE, D, DC, MC, V.*

$ ✕ **Big Sky Café.** Owned and operated by the same family as the Blue
★ Water Grill (☞ *above*), this casual café is popular with the business
lunch crowd in Webster Groves. Try the pungent garlic mashed potatoes. ⊠ *45 S. Old Orchard,* ☎ *314/962–5757. AE, MC, V.*

$ ✕ **Rigazzi's.** Generous, inexpensive servings of pasta keep locals coming back to this no-frills pasta house on the Hill. ⊠ *4945 Daggett St.,*
☎ *314/772–4900. AE, MC, V. Closed Sun.*

Lodging

Most of St. Louis's big hotels are downtown or in Clayton, about 7
mi west. For bed-and-breakfasts in town, call or write **Bed and Breakfasts of St. Louis, River Country of Missouri and Illinois** (⊠ 1900
Wyoming St., St. Louis 63118, ☎ 314/771–1993). For price ranges
see Chart 2 (A) *in* On the Road with Fodor's.

$$$ ⊡ **Hotel Majestic.** This small European-style hotel downtown is often
the choice of visiting celebrities. The building, more than 80 years old,
was renovated in 1987 and filled with reproduction antiques. ⊠ *1019
Pine St., 63101,* ☎ *314/436–2355 or 800/451–2355,* ⅋⅍ *314/436–0223.
94 rooms. Restaurant, lounge, valet parking. AE, D, DC, MC, V.*

$$$ ⊡ **Hyatt Regency St. Louis at Union Station.** Most of the rooms are in
a contemporary garden setting beneath the arched trusses of Union Station's original train shed. The Regency Club offers deluxe rooms and
suites. ⊠ *1 St. Louis Union Station, 63103,* ☎ *314/231–1234,* ⅋⅍ *314/
436–6827. 536 rooms. 2 restaurants, 2 lounges, pool, health club, valet
parking. AE, D, DC, MC, V.*

$$$ ⊡ **Ritz-Carlton, St. Louis.** This luxury hotel in Clayton is filled with chandeliers and museum-quality oil paintings. Some rooms on the top
floors have views of the downtown St. Louis skyline. ⊠ *100 Carondelet Plaza, Clayton 63105,* ☎ *314/863–6300,* ⅋⅍ *314/863–3525. 301
rooms. 2 restaurants, 2 lounges, indoor pool, health club. AE, D, DC,
MC, V.*

$$ ⊡ **Drury Inn–Union Station.** Lead-glass windows and marble columns
★ give historic charm to this former YMCA. Among its assets are its complimentary breakfasts and its excellent location next door to Union Station. ⊠ *201 S. 20th St., 63103,* ☎ *314/231–3900,* ⅋⅍ *314/231–3900.
176 rooms. Restaurant, indoor pool. AE, D, DC, MC, V.*

Motels

⊡ **Budgetel Inn West Port** (⊠ 12330 Dorsett Rd., 63043, ☎ 314/878–
1212, ⅋⅍ 314/878–3409), 145 rooms, breakfast room; *$.* ⊡ **Fairfield
Inn by Marriott** (⊠ 9079 Dunn Rd., 63042, ☎ 314/731–7700, ⅋⅍ 314/
731–7700, ext. 709), 135 rooms, pool; *$.* ⊡ **Red Roof Inn** (⊠ 5823
Wilson St., ☎ 314/645–0101, ⅋⅍ 314/645–0101, ext. 444), 110
rooms; *$.*

Nightlife and the Arts

Nightlife

Much of St. Louis's nightlife can be found in the jazz and blues clubs
in the redeveloped areas of **Laclede's Landing,** on the riverfront, and
in **Soulard,** on the southern edge of downtown. For gambling head to
the **President Riverboat Casino** (⊠ 800 N. 1st St., ☎ 314/622–3000
or 800/772–3647), **Casino St. Charles** (⊠ S. 5th St., ☎ 314/949–7777),
or upriver to the *Alton Belle* **Riverboat Casino** (⊠ 219 Piasa St., Alton,
IL, ☎ 618/474–7500 or 800/336–7568). To find out who's playing
where, consult the *St. Louis Post-Dispatch*'s Thursday calendar section or the free weekly paper the *Riverfront Times.*

The Arts

The **Fabulous Fox Theatre** (⊠ 527 N. Grand Blvd., ☎ 314/534–1678) hosts major shows and concerts. The **Riverport Amphitheatre** (⊠ 14141 Riverport Dr., ☎ 314/298–9944) stages big-name concerts. The **St. Louis Symphony Orchestra** presents programs at **Powell Symphony Hall** (⊠ 718 N. Grand Blvd., ☎ 314/534–1700). For tickets to major events call **Dialtix** (☎ 314/291–7600).

Spectator Sports

Baseball: St. Louis Cardinals (⊠ Busch Stadium, 250 Stadium Plaza, ☎ 314/421–3060).

Football: St. Louis Rams (⊠ Trans World Dome, 801 Convention Plaza, ☎ 800/847–7267).

Ice hockey: St. Louis Blues (⊠ Kiel Center, 1401 Clark Ave., ☎ 314/291–7600).

Incline roller hockey: St. Louis Vipers (⊠ 1819 Clarkson Blvd., ☎ 314/530–1967).

Soccer: St. Louis Ambush (⊠ 7547 Ravensridge, ☎ 314/962–4625).

Shopping

For browsing in boutiques and specialty shops, try **Union Station** (⊠ 18th and Market Sts.), an impressive former train station, and **Laclede's Landing** (☞ Exploring St. Louis, *above*). The **Central West End,** along Euclid Avenue east of Forest Park, is an area of hip boutiques and restaurants. The city's most sophisticated shoppers head for **Plaza Frontenac** (⊠ Clayton Rd. and Lindbergh Blvd., ☎ 314/432–0604), home to nearly 50 upscale stores. Antiques and crafts lovers should visit historic downtown **St. Charles** (⊠ I–70 and First Capital Dr.), seven cobblestoned blocks of shops and restaurants on the banks of the Missouri River.

KANSAS CITY

With upwards of 200 fountains, more than any city except Rome, and more boulevard miles (155) than Paris, Kansas City is attractive and cosmopolitan. This spread-out metropolitan area, which straddles the Missouri-Kansas line, has a rich history as a frontier river port and trade center, where wagon trains were outfitted before heading west on the Santa Fe and Oregon trails. Through the years it has been home to the nation's second-largest stockyards, to saxophone player Charlie "Bird" Parker and his Kansas City–style bebop, and to some of the best barbecue in the world.

Visitor Information

Greater Kansas City: The Convention and Visitors Bureau (⊠ 1100 Main St., Suite 2550, 64105, ☎ 816/221–5242 or 800/767–7700) is in City Center Square in downtown Kansas City. Its visitor information (☎ 816/691–3800) offers a weekly recording of activities. The **Missouri Information Center** (⊠ I–70 and Blue Ridge Cutoff; 4010 Blue Ridge Cutoff, 64133, ☎ 816/889–3330) overlooks the Truman Sports Complex.

Arriving and Departing

By Bus

Greyhound Lines (⊠ 11th St. and Troost Ave., ☎ 800/231–2222).

By Car

From I–70 or I–35 exit at Broadway for downtown. From the airport, I–29 from the north merges with I–35 north of the city.

By Plane

Kansas City International Airport (☎ 816/243–5237), 20 minutes northwest of downtown on I–29, is served by major domestic airlines. Taxi service is zoned; the maximum fare from the airport to downtown Kansas City is $26. For $11 **KCI Shuttle** buses (☎ 816/243–5950) will take you to major downtown hotels.

By Train

Amtrak (✉ 2200 Main St., ☎ 816/421–3622 or 800/872–7245).

Getting Around Kansas City

Attractions are scattered throughout the metropolitan region, making cars important for visitors. However, **Kansas City Trolley**'s replica trolleys (☎ 816/221–3399) travel between downtown, Crown Center, Westport, and the Country Club Plaza; the drivers are usually entertaining and well versed in local history.

Exploring Kansas City

Plaza, Midtown, Downtown

Kansas City's **Country Club Plaza** (✉ 47th and Main Sts., ☎ 816/753–0100) is known for its more than 180 fine shops and restaurants, its Spanish-style architecture, and its annual display of holiday lights from Thanksgiving to January, when hundreds of thousands of gaily colored bulbs outline the plaza's buildings. Here you'll also find many of the city's fountains and statues. Several blocks east of the plaza is

★ the **Nelson-Atkins Museum of Art** (✉ 4525 Oak St., ☎ 816/561–4000), known principally for its outstanding Asian art collection and the Henry Moore Sculpture Garden on the south grounds.

The **Kemper Museum of Contemporary Art and Design** (☎ 816/753–5784) is the latest addition to the Kansas City art scene. Next to the **Kansas City Art Institute** (✉ 4420 Warwick, ☎ 816/561–4852), the Kemper has more than 700 works of art encompassing a broad range of media.

Before there was a Kansas City, there was a **Westport** (✉ North of the Plaza at Broadway and Westport Rd., ☎ 816/756–2789), built along the Santa Fe Trail as an outfitting center for wagon trains heading west. Today this area is filled with renovated and new buildings housing trendy shops, restaurants, and nightspots.

On the crest of a hill at the northern edge of Penn Valley Park, north
★ of Westport, is the **Liberty Memorial** (✉ 100 W. 26th St., ☎ 816/221–1918), dedicated to those who served in World War I. Extensive structural renovation has temporarily closed the tower's 217-ft observation deck and the museum. However, museum items are on display in the **Town Pavillion** (✉ 12th and Main Sts.).

Just across Main Street from the Liberty Memorial is **Crown Center** (✉ Grand Ave. and Pershing Rd., ☎ 816/274–8444), an 85-acre shopping mall and entertainment, office, and hotel complex. In summer free Friday night concerts are held on the terrace; a covered outdoor ice-skating rink is open in winter. Kansas City–based Hallmark Cards, the largest maker of greeting cards in the world, built Crown Center and has its headquarters here. Monday through Saturday you can stop by the **Hallmark Visitors Center** (☎ 816/274–3613), which features a display about the history of the greeting card industry and a bow-making machine (you get to keep the bow).

Downtown and Midtown Kansas City

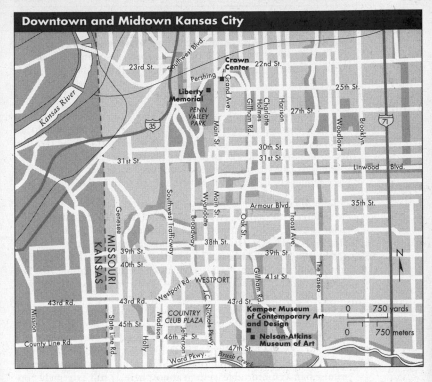

Downtown the **Treasures of the Steamboat *Arabia*** museum (⊠ 4th and Grand Sts., ☎ 816/471–4030) houses goods—from French perfume to buttons to coffeepots—all salvaged from the *Arabia*'s muddy grave 132 years after it sank in the Missouri River in 1856.

Other Attractions

Just east of Kansas City is **Independence,** once the home of President Harry S. Truman. Truman's life and career are the focus at the **Harry S. Truman Library and Museum** (⊠ U.S. 24 and Delaware St., ☎ 816/833–1225). The **Truman Home** (⊠ 219 N. Delaware St., ☎ 816/254–9929; ⊠ 223 Main St., for ticket center), which is closed Sunday, was the summer White House for Harry and Bess Truman during his presidency.

Fleming Park (⊠ 22807 Woods Chapel Rd., ☎ 816/795–8200), in Blue Springs south of Independence, contains the 970-acre Lake Jacomo. Also in Fleming Park is **Missouri Town 1855** (☎ 816/524–8770), a reproduction 1800s town created from more than 30 transplanted period houses, barns, stores, and outbuildings. The staff and volunteers dress in period clothing at this living-history museum.

Just north of downtown Kansas City is the historic riverboat community of **Weston** (☎ 816/640–2909). All buildings in the five-block downtown shopping area are listed on the National Register of Historic Places. Weston is the birthplace of Buffalo Bill Cody and home to one of the nation's oldest distilleries, **McCormick Distilling Co.** (⊠ 1 McCormick La., ☎ 816/640–2276), closed December–February.

What to See and Do with Children

★ **Worlds of Fun/Oceans of Fun** (⊠ I–435 and Worlds of Fun Dr., ☎ 816/454–4545) are two adjoining theme parks, with shows, rides, and attractions for people of all ages. **Kaleidoscope,** part of the Hallmark complex at Crown Center (✉ 25th and McGee, ☎ 816/274–8300), is a hands-on creative arts center for children. The **Kansas City Zoo** (✉ I–435 and 63rd St., ☎ 816/871–5701) has been renovated to include a 5,000-acre African plains exhibit as well as an IMAX theater (☎ 816/871–5858).

Dining

Kansas City is best known for its steaks and barbecue, although locals argue over which places serve the best. Both Country Club Plaza and Westport have a variety of good eating places, from elegant restaurants to sidewalk cafés to neighborhood joints dispensing barroom grub. For price ranges *see* Chart 1 (B) *in* On the Road with Fodor's.

$$$ ✕ **Cafe Allegro.** Among the favorite entrées at this trendy restaurant are salmon with Chinese mustard glaze and tuna tartare. The brick interior is hung with paintings by local artists. ✉ *1815 W. 39th St.,* ☎ *816/561–3663. AE, DC, MC, V. No lunch weekends.*

$$$ ✕ **Plaza III–The Steakhouse.** This handsome, nationally known restau-
★   rant at Country Club Plaza serves excellent steaks, prime rib, and seafood; its steak soup is legendary. ✉ *4749 Pennsylvania Ave.,* ☎ *816/753–0000. AE, D, DC, MC, V. No lunch Sun.*

$$$ ✕ **Savoy Grill.** Locals often choose this historic, turn-of-the-century beauty when celebrating a special occasion. Maine lobster and a T-bone steak from the restaurant's own herd are good choices here. ✉ *219 W. 9th St.,* ☎ *816/842–3890. AE, D, DC, MC, V. No lunch Sun.*

$$ ✕ **Golden Ox.** It's a little out of the way, but this steak house, serving prime rib in a comfortable western atmosphere, is still extremely popular. ✉ *1600 Gennessee St.,* ☎ *816/842–2866. AE, D, DC, MC, V. No lunch Sun.*

$$ ✕ **West Side Cafe.** This has become one of Kansas City's hottest
★   spots—in more ways than one. The spicy tandoori chicken highlights a menu of Indian, Greek, and North African food. Seating is limited, so arrive early or be ready for a wait. ✉ *723 Southwest Blvd.,* ☎ *816/472–0010. AE, D, MC, V. No dinner Sun.–Tues.*

$ ✕ **Arthur Bryant's.** Although there are reportedly more than 70 bar-
★   becue joints in Kansas City, Bryant's—low on decor but high on taste—tops the list for many Kansas Citians, who don't mind standing in line to order from the counter. ✉ *1727 Brooklyn Ave.,* ☎ *816/231–1123. AE, MC, V.*

$$ ✕ **Stroud's.** This sprawling building on Kansas City's north side was
★   once the first stagecoach stop for travelers on their way to St. Joseph. After feasting on fried chicken and homemade pies, take a stroll around the grounds, complete with ponds, geese, and swans. ✉ *5410 N.E. Oak Ridge Dr.,* ☎ *816/454–9600. AE, DC, MC, V.*

Lodging

Kansas City offers a core of major hotels within walking distance of Country Club Plaza and Westport or in the Crown Center complex. For a listing of B&Bs contact **Bed and Breakfast Kansas City** (✉ Box 14781, Lenexa 66285, ☎ 913/888–3636). For price ranges *see* Chart 2 (B) *in* On the Road with Fodor's.

$$$ ▥ **The Raphael.** Built in 1927 as an apartment house, the Raphael today
★   enjoys its status as the only intimate, European-style hotel in the city. Despite its small size, many rooms are large and have excellent views of the plaza. ✉ *325 Ward Pkwy., 64112,* ☎ *816/756–3800 or 800/821–5343,* ℻ *816/756–3800. 123 rooms. Restaurant, lounge, valet parking. AE, D, DC, MC, V.*

$$$ ⊞ **Ritz-Carlton.** This luxury hotel, filled with crystal chandeliers, im-
★ ported marble, and fine art, was completely renovated in 1990. Some
of the luxuriously appointed rooms have balconies and views of the
plaza. ⊠ *401 Ward Pkwy., 64112,* ☎ *816/756–1500,* FAX *816/756–*
1635. 366 rooms. 2 restaurants, 2 bars, pool, health club, valet park-
ing. AE, D, DC, MC, V.

$$$ ⊞ **Westin Crown Center.** Part of the Crown Center complex, the Westin
has a bustling lobby complete with a five-story waterfall and a natu-
ral limestone cliff. All rooms have views; the best ones face Crown Center Square to the east. ⊠ *1 Pershing Rd., 64108,* ☎ *816/474–4400,*
FAX *816/391–4438. 774 rooms. 3 restaurants, pool, putting green, ten-*
nis courts, health club. AE, D, DC, MC, V.

$$ ⊞ **Drury Inn–Stadium.** Across from the sports complex, this chain hotel
offers clean, comfortable rooms; for a few dollars more you can have
a minisuite, with a king-size bed, a recliner, and a microwave. ⊠ *3830*
Blue Ridge Cutoff, 64133, ☎ *816/923–3000,* FAX *816/923–3000. 133*
rooms. Pool. AE, D, DC, MC, V.

$$ ⊞ **Quarterage Hotel.** The larger rooms at this intimate brick hotel in
Westport have either a queen-size bed or two doubles; the smaller, less
expensive ones have a double and a balcony. ⊠ *560 Westport Rd.,*
64111, ☎ *816/931–0001 or 800/942–4233,* FAX *816/931–8891. 123*
rooms. Sauna, health club. AE, D, DC, MC, V.

$$ ⊞ **Ramada Hotel KCI.** One of many hotels near the international air-
port, the newly remodeled Ramada offers 24-hour courtesy trans-
portation to the airport and local restaurants. ⊠ *7300 N.W. Tiffany*
Springs Rd., 64153, ☎ *816/741–9500,* FAX *816/741–0655. 249 rooms.*
Restaurant, pool, health club, volleyball. AE, D, MC, V.

Nightlife and the Arts

Nightlife

Much of Kansas City's nightlife can be found in the Westport and Plaza
areas. The **Grand Emporium** (⊠ 3832 Main St., ☎ 816/531–1504) is
the place in town for blues. The city is justly proud of its jazz heritage,
and live performances are featured at several establishments; for in-
formation call the **Jazz Hotline** (☎ 816/763–1052).

Standford's Comedy House (⊠ 504 Westport Rd. ☎ 816/6753–7454)
features local and national comedians.

Riverboat gambling is popular along the banks of this Missouri River
town. Three noncruising boats in the Kansas City area are the **Argosy**
(⊠ Hwy. 9 and I–635, Riverside, ☎ 816/741–7568), **Harrah's Casino**
(⊠ Armour Rd., North Kansas City, ☎ 816/471–3364), and **Sam's**
Town (⊠ E. 18th St., North Kansas City, ☎ 816/764–4757).

The Arts

The **Folly Theater** (⊠ 12th and Central Sts., ☎ 816/842–5500) and
the larger **Midland Center for the Performing Arts** (⊠ 1228 Main St.,
☎ 816/471–8600) have shows and concerts. The **Lyric Opera of**
Kansas City and the **Kansas City Symphony** perform at the **Lyric The-**
atre (⊠ 11th and Central Sts., ☎ 816/471–7344). For information
on upcoming events check the Friday and Sunday editions of the
Kansas City Star. Call **TicketMaster** (☎ 816/931–3330) for tickets to
main events.

Spectator Sports

Baseball: Kansas City Royals (⊠ Kauffman Stadium, Truman Sports
Complex, I–70 and Blue Ridge Cutoff, ☎ 816/921–8000).

Football: Kansas City Chiefs (⊠ Arrowhead Stadium, Truman Sports Complex, ☎ 816/924–9400).

Indoor soccer: Kansas City Attack (⊠ Kemper Arena, 1800 Gennessee, ☎ 816/474–2255).

Outdoor soccer: Kansas City Wizards (⊠ 706 Broadway, Suite 100, 64105, ☎ 816/472–4625).

Shopping

Kansas City's finest shopping is at **Country Club Plaza,** and a number of specialty shops and boutiques are concentrated in **Westport** and at **Crown Center** (for all, ☞ Exploring Kansas City, *above*).

THE OZARKS

The Ozark hill region of southern Missouri is famed for its wooded mountaintops; clear, spring-fed streams; and its water playgrounds of Lake of the Ozarks and Table Rock Lake. Branson, the nation's second country music capital after Nashville, attracts 5 million visitors a year to its star-studded theaters.

Visitor Information

Greater Lake of the Ozarks: Convention and Visitors Bureau (⊠ Box 827, Osage Beach 65065, ☎ 573/348–1599 or 800/386–5253). **Table Rock Lake/Kimberling City Area:** Chamber of Commerce (⊠ Box 495, Kimberling City 65686, ☎ 417/739–2564). **Branson:** Branson Lakes Area Chamber of Commerce (⊠ Box 220, 65616, ☎ 417/334–4136). **Springfield:** Convention and Visitors Bureau and Tourist Information Center (⊠ 3315 E. Battlefield Rd., 65804-4048, ☎ 417/881–5300 or 800/678–8766).

Arriving and Departing

By Car
Many of the towns and attractions in this wide-ranging region can be reached from I–44, which cuts diagonally across the state from St. Louis to Springfield (about 210 mi). Branson lies about 40 mi south of Springfield on U.S. 65. The Lake of the Ozarks is centrally located between St. Louis and Kansas City.

Exploring the Ozarks

Central Missouri's **Lake of the Ozarks,** formed by the damming of the Osage River in 1931, is the state's largest lake, with 1,300 mi of shoreline sprawling over 58,000 acres. In summer crowds of vacationing families descend on the numerous resorts, motels, and tourist attractions; better times to visit may be spring, when the dogwoods are abloom, and fall, when the wooded hills come alive with color.

Lake of the Ozarks State Park (⊠ U.S. 54, ☎ 573/348–2694), just south of Osage Beach, encompasses 90 mi of shoreline and offers hiking trails, other recreational activities, and tours of **Ozark Caverns** (☎ 314/346–2500).

You're deep in the country's Bible Belt when you reach **Springfield** (off I–44), home to two Bible colleges and a theological seminary and near several sights and cultural events with religious themes. For many people the first stop in Springfield has little to do with religion. The enormous **Bass Pro Shops Outdoor World** (⊠ 1935 S. Campbell Ave., ☎

417/887–1915), dubbed the "Sportsman's Disney World," has cascading waterfalls, a wildlife trophy collection, a boat showroom, sporting goods shops—and about 6 million visitors a year.

The visitor center at **Wilson's Creek National Battlefield** (⊠ Rte. ZZ and Farm Rd. 182, ☎ 417/732–2662), southwest of Springfield, documents the first major Civil War battle fought west of the Mississippi. In Mansfield, roughly 40 mi east of Springfield on U.S. 60, is the **Laura Ingalls Wilder Home** (⊠ Rte. A, ☎ 417/924–3626), a National Historic Landmark, where the much-loved children's author wrote her *Little House* books. Museum displays include Laura's handwritten manuscripts (written with pencil on school tablets) and Pa's fiddle. About ★ 70 mi west of Springfield is the **George Washington Carver National Monument** (⊠ Off Rte. V, ☎ 417/325–4151), honoring the birthplace of the famous black botanist and agronomist. Just north of the Carver Monument is the **Precious Moments Chapel,** in Carthage, where more than 1 million fans of porcelain dolls visit the chapel and creator Sam Butcher's home each year (⊠ 1421 Chapel Rd., ☎ 800/543–7975).

About 40 miles south of Springfield on U.S. 65 is **Lake Taneycomo,** the first of Missouri's man-made lakes. Along its riverlike length small resorts are concentrated in towns such as Forsyth and Rockaway Beach. Lake Taneycomo's larger, more developed neighbor, **Table Rock State Park** (⊠ Branson, ☎ 417/334–4704), has boating, picnicking, and plenty of motels, resorts, and commercial campgrounds. **Kimberling City** is the main resort town serving Lake Taneycomo and Table Rock.

With more than 60,000 seats in such star-studded venues as the Roy Clark Celebrity Theatre and the Cristy Lane Theatre (for both, ☞ Nightlife and the Arts, *below*), **Branson** is a country music mecca to rival Nashville. Most of the town's recent growth has occurred along Route 76, already crowded with miniature golf courses, bumper car concessions, souvenir and hillbilly crafts shops, motels, and resorts.

A few miles west of Branson is the **Shepherd of the Hills Homestead and Outdoor Theatre,** a working pioneer homestead, with a gristmill, a sawmill, and smith and wheelwright shops. The *Shepherd of the Hills* inspirational drama is performed here outdoors. ⊠ *Rte. 76,* ☎ *417/ 334–4191. Closed Jan.–Apr.*

What to See and Do with Children

★ Boating, swimming, and roadside attractions such as miniature golf and water parks beckon to kids of all ages. **Silver Dollar City** (⊠ Rte. 76, ☎ 417/338–8100), just west of Branson, features Ozark artisans demonstrating traditional crafts, along with rides and music shows. **White Water** (⊠ Rte. 76, Branson, ☎ 417/334–7488) is the place for water-soaked rides and activities.

Shopping

Osage Village (⊠ U.S. 54, Osage Beach, ☎ 573/348–2065) is a major factory-outlet mall with about 115 stores.

Outdoor Activities and Sports

Canoeing

The Ozarks have some of the finest streams in the country, such as the **Current** and **Jacks Fork rivers,** two waterways protected as the **Ozark National Scenic Riverways** (☞ National and State Parks, *above*). For a list of outfitters contact the Missouri Division of Tourism (☞ Visitor Information, *above*).

Fishing

Bull Shoals Lake, Lake Taneycomo, and **Table Rock Lake** all offer excellent fishing for bass, catfish, trout, and other fish. Other good spots include **Lake of the Ozarks** and **Truman Lake.** Contact the **Missouri Department of Conservation** (⊠ Box 180, Jefferson City 65102, ☎ 573/751–4115) for information on permits, costs, and seasons.

Hiking and Backpacking

The partially completed **Ozark Trail** passes through national and state forest and parkland as well as private property. For information and maps contact the **Missouri Department of Natural Resources** (⊠ Division of State Parks, 101 Adams St., Jefferson City 65101, ☎ 573/751–2479 or 800/334–6946) or individual state parks (☞ National and State Parks, *above*).

Dining and Lodging

To find out about B&Bs in the area, contact the **Ozark Mountain Country Bed and Breakfast** reservation service (⊠ Box 295, Branson 65616, ☎ 417/334–4720 or 800/695–1546). For price ranges *see* Charts 1 (B) and 2 (B) *in* On the Road with Fodor's.

Branson Area

$$ ✕ **Candlestick Inn.** Fresh local trout is a specialty at this restaurant over-
★ looking Lake Taneycomo. The two elegant dining rooms have floor-to-ceiling glass. ⊠ *Rte. 76E, Branson,* ☎ *417/334–3633. AE, D, DC, MC, V. No lunch. Closed 1st 2 wks of Jan.*

$$ ✕ **Outback Steak and Oyster Bar.** This rustic, Australian-style oysters-and-steak place has a veranda overlooking its own swamp, where a fake crocodile rests on a log. Servers greet you with "G'day!" ⊠ *1914 Rte. 76W, Branson,* ☎ *417/334–6306. AE, D, MC, V.*

$$ ▦ **Holiday Inn Branson.** Although this modern hotel is not on Lake Taneycomo, you can view the lake from some rooms. Service is friendly, and the location is convenient to area attractions. ⊠ *1420 Rte. 76W (Box 340), Branson 65616,* ☎ *417/334–5101,* ℻ *417/334–0789. 220 rooms. Restaurant, lounge, pool. AE, D, DC, MC, V.*

$$ ▦ **Kimberling Inn Resort and Conference Center.** This small resort motel on Table Rock Lake is within walking distance of the Kimberling City Shopping Village, where there are crafts shops, restaurants, and bowling. ⊠ *Box 159B, Kimberling City 65686,* ☎ *417/739–4311 or 800/833–5551. 120 rooms. 3 restaurants, lounge, 3 outdoor and indoor pools, miniature golf, tennis court, boating. AE, D, DC, MC, V.*

Lake of the Ozarks

$$ ✕ **Blue Heron.** This seasonal restaurant serving steak and seafood is popular with lake visitors, who enjoy cocktails poolside before moving to the dining room overlooking the lake. ⊠ *Bus. Rte. 54 and Rte. HH, Osage Beach,* ☎ *573/365–4646. Reservations not accepted. AE, D, MC, V. No lunch. Closed Sun.–Mon. and Dec.–Feb.*

$$ ✕ **Shooters 21.** This large, popular lakeside bar and restaurant has both casual and fine dining. Bar fare includes such favorites as spicy chicken wings, potato skins, and burgers. ⊠ *54–56 Lake Rd., Osage Beach, Mile Marker 21,* ☎ *573/348–2100. AE, D, MC, V.*

$$$ ✕▦ **Lodge of the Four Seasons.** Golf is the primary draw here. There's
★ also fine dining in the Toledo Room. Come in winter, when rates drop dramatically. ⊠ *Box 215, Lake Ozark 65049,* ☎ *573/365–3000 or 800/843–5253,* ℻ *573/865–8525. 311 rooms. 3 restaurants, 2 lounges,*

indoor pool, 3 outdoor pools, 45 holes of golf, 17 tennis courts, lake. AE, D, DC, MC, V.

$$$ ✕⊞ **Marriott's Tan-Tar-A Resort and Golf Club.** One of the top choices
★ in the region for vacations and business meetings, the resort offers nu-
merous recreational opportunities and fine dining at its Windrose
Restaurant. ⊠ *Rte. KK, Osage Beach 65065,* ☎ *573/348–3131 or 800/
826–8272,* ℻ *573/348–3206. 938 rooms. 5 restaurants, 3 lounges,
2 indoor pools, 2 outdoor pools, 1 indoor-outdoor pool, 27-hole and
9-hole golf courses, 6 tennis courts, health club. AE, D, DC, MC, V.*

$$ ⊞ **Holiday Inn Resort and Conference Center.** The hotel does not have
lake access, but for a slightly higher rate you can have a view of it. ⊠
Bus. Rte. 54 (Box 1930), Lake Ozark 65049, ☎ *573/365–2334 or
800/532–3575,* ℻ *314/365–6887. 217 rooms. Restaurant, lounge, indoor pool, 2 outdoor pools, miniature golf, exercise room. AE, D, DC,
MC, V.*

Springfield

$$$ ✕ **Hemingway's Blue Water Cafe.** In the Bass Pro Shops Outdoor
World (☞ Exploring the Ozarks, *above*), this restaurant offers seafood,
steak, pasta, and poultry in a tropical atmosphere. ⊠ *1935 S. Camp-
bell Ave.,* ☎ *417/887–3388. AE, D, MC, V.*

$$ ⊞ **Radisson Inn and Conference Center.** The rooms at this hotel in the
southern end of town are clean and comfortable; the lobby is more or-
nate, with a deep-green-and-burgundy color scheme and marble-top
desks. ⊠ *3333 S. Glenstone Ave., 65804,* ☎ *417/883–6550,* ℻ *417/
883–5720. 200 rooms. Restaurant, lounge, indoor and outdoor pools.
AE, D, DC, MC, V.*

$$ ⊞ **University Plaza Holiday Inn.** Boasting the largest conference cen-
ter in Missouri, this hotel has guest rooms arranged around a nine-
story atrium. ⊠ *333 John Q. Hammons Pkwy., 65806,* ☎ *417/
864–7333,* ℻ *417/831–5893, ext. 7177. 271 rooms. 2 restaurants,
2 lounges, indoor and outdoor pools, 2 tennis courts, exercise room.
AE, D, DC, MC, V.*

Motels

⊞ **EconoLodge** (⊠ 2808 N. Kansas Expressway, Springfield 65803, ☎
417/869–5600), 83 rooms; *$.* ⊞ **Red Roof Inn** (⊠ 2655 N. Glenstone
Ave., Springfield 65803, ☎ 417/831–2100), 112 rooms; *$.*

Campgrounds

Missouri Association of RV Parks and Campgrounds (⊠ 3020 S. Na-
tional, No. D149, Springfield 63102-2121, ☎ 573/564–7993). In the
Lake of the Ozarks area: **Deer Valley Park and Campground** (⊠ Sun-
rise Beach, ☎ 314/374–5277), closed mid-October–mid-April; **Lake
of the Ozarks State Park** (☞ Exploring the Ozarks, *above*); **Majestic
Oaks Park** (⊠ Lake Ozark, ☎ 314/365–1890), closed November–
March. In the Branson area: **Blue Mountain Campground** (⊠ Branson,
800/779–2114); **Port of Kimberling Marina and Campground** (⊠ Kim-
berling City, ☎ 417/739–5377); **Silver Dollar City Campground** (⊠ Bran-
son, ☎ 417/338–8189 or 800/477–5164), closed November–March.

Nightlife and the Arts

Among the music shows in the Lake of the Ozarks region is the **Kin-
Fokes Country Music Show** (⊠ Camdenton, ☎ 573/346–6797). Music
theaters in Branson include **Andy Williams Moon River Theater** (☎ 417/
334–4500), **Baldknobbers Hillbilly Jamboree Show** (☎ 417/334–
4528), **Christy Lane Theater** (☎ 417/335–5111), **Grand Palace** (☎ 417/

336–4636), **Jim Stafford Theater** (☎ 417/335–8080), **Mel Tillis Theater** (☎ 417/335–6635), **Mickey Gilley's Family Theater** (☎ 417/334–3210), **Presley's Mountain Music Jubilee** (☎ 417/334–4874), **Roy Clark Celebrity Theater** (☎ 417/334–0076), and the **Shoji Tabuchi Show** (☎ 417/334–7469). Contact the Branson Lakes Area Chamber of Commerce (☞ Visitor Information, *above*) for a complete listing.

ELSEWHERE IN MISSOURI

Hannibal

Getting There
Hannibal is about two hours north of St. Louis on U.S. 61.

What to See and Do
Hannibal is Mark Twain country. His boyhood home is preserved at
★ the **Mark Twain Home and Museum** (⊠ 208 Hill St., ☎ 573/221–9010). The **Mark Twain Cave** (⊠ Rte. 79, ☎ 573/221–1656) is where Tom Sawyer and Becky Thatcher got lost in Twain's classic *Adventures of Tom Sawyer.* Contact the **Hannibal Visitors and Convention Bureau** (⊠ 320 Broadway, Box 624, 63401, ☎ 573/221–2477).

Ste. Genevieve

Getting There
Ste. Genevieve is about one hour south of St. Louis on I–55.

What to See and Do
Numerous historic homes in this small river town, the oldest permanent settlement in Missouri, include examples of 18th-century French creole architecture, characterized by vertical log construction. The **Great River Road Interpretive Center** (⊠ 66 S. Main St., 63670, ☎ 573/883–7097) houses the visitor center.

St. Joseph

Getting There
St. Joseph is about one hour north of Kansas City on I–29.

What to See and Do
During the short experiment called the Pony Express, riders set out on the 2,000-mi trip to Sacramento, California, from what is now St. Joseph's **Pony Express National Memorial** (⊠ 914 Penn St., ☎ 816/279–5059). The **Jesse James Home** (⊠ 12th and Penn Sts., ☎ 816/232–8206) is where a reward money–seeking member of James's own gang shot and killed the notorious outlaw. The bullet hole in the wall is still visible. The **St. Joseph Convention and Visitors Bureau** (⊠ Box 445, 109 S. 4th St., 64502, ☎ 816/233–6688 or 800/785–0360) has information.

NEBRASKA

Updated by
Diana Lambdin
Meyer

Capital	Lincoln
Population	1,652,000
Motto	Equality Before the Law
State Bird	Western meadowlark
State Flower	Goldenrod
Postal Abbreviation	NE

Statewide Visitor Information

The **Nebraska Department of Economic Development, Division of Travel and Tourism** (⊠ Box 94666, Lincoln 68509, ☎ 402/471–3791 or 800/228–4307) staffs 24 rest and information areas along I–80.

Scenic Drives

Route 2, from Grand Island west to Crawford, is a long, lonesome road through the Sandhills, traversing 332 mi of delicate wildflowers, tranquil rivers, and placid cattle. The 130-mi drive north on **U.S. 83** from North Platte to Valentine offers a fine view of the Sandhills' native shortgrass prairie. **U.S. 26** from Ogallala to Scottsbluff is a 128-mi historic segment of the Oregon Trail, passing such natural landmarks as Ash Hollow; Courthouse, Jail, and Chimney rocks; and Scotts Bluff National Monument.

National and State Parks

National Parks
Homestead National Monument, near Beatrice (⊠ Rte. 3, Box 47, 68310, ☎ 402/223–3514), commemorates the post-1862 homestead movement and the pioneers who braved the rigors of the prairie frontier. **Nebraska National Forest,** at Halsey (⊠ Box 38, 69142, ☎ 308/533–2257), is the largest planted forest in the country.

State Parks
The **Nebraska Game and Parks Commission** (⊠ Box 30370, Lincoln 68503, ☎ 402/471–0641) manages and provides information on all eight state parks. Among them are **Fort Robinson State Park** (☞ Exploring Northwest Nebraska, *below*); **Eugene T. Mahoney State Park** and **Platte River State Park** (☞ Exploring Southeast Nebraska, *below*); and **Indian Cave State Park,** in the state's southeast corner (⊠ 2 mi north and 5 mi east of Shubert; Box 30, 68437, ☎ 402/883–2575). A day pass or an annual one may be purchased at any state park and is good for admission to all of them.

SOUTHEAST NEBRASKA

This is a land of city sophistication and country charm. Visitors can tour museums and historic buildings, shop in restored warehouses, and ride riverboats.

Visitor Information

Lincoln: Convention and Visitors Bureau (⊠ 1221 N St., 68508, ☎ 402/434–5335 or 800/423–8212). **Nebraska City:** Convention and Visitors Bureau (⊠ 806 1st Ave., 68410, ☎ 402/873–6654). **Omaha:** Greater Omaha Convention and Visitors Bureau (⊠ 6800 Mercy Rd., Suite 202, 68106, ☎ 402/444–4660 or 800/332–1819).

Arriving and Departing

By Bus
Omaha and Lincoln are served by **Greyhound Lines** (☎ 800/231–2222).
Local bus service is provided in Lincoln by **StarTran** (☎ 402/476–1234)
and in Omaha by **Metro Area Transit** (☎ 402/341–0800).

By Car
I–80 links Des Moines with Omaha (I–480 serves downtown Omaha)
and Lincoln. U.S. 75S from Omaha leads to Nebraska City. From Lincoln Route 2 goes to Nebraska City. To get to Beatrice, take U.S. 77
south from Lincoln.

By Plane
Eppley Airfield, about 3 mi from downtown Omaha, is served by most
domestic carriers, as well as by **GP Express** (☎ 800/525–0280) and
United Express (☎ 800/554–5111). Cab fare from the airport to
downtown is about $8. **Lincoln Municipal Airport,** about 3 mi from down-
town Lincoln, is served by several major airlines. Taxis to downtown
cost about $10. **Eppley Express** (☎ 308/234–6066 or 800/888–9793)
runs an airport van from Lincoln Municipal Airport to Eppley Airfield
($17 fare).

By Train
Amtrak's (☎ 800/872–7245) *Desert Wind, Pioneer,* and *California
Zephyr* stop in Lincoln and Omaha.

Exploring Southeast Nebraska

Nebraska's multistory state capitol dominates the Lincoln skyline; the
river city of Omaha is the region's center of commerce and industry.
Minutes away from both downtowns are expansive prairies, state
parks, and attractions that chronicle the opening of the West to settlement.

Omaha is a quintessentially friendly midwestern city offering an impressive number of amenities found in larger metropolitan areas, including a refurbished 12-block market area by the river. The **Henry Doorly
Zoo** (⊠ 3701 S. 10th St., ☎ 402/733–8401) has the world's largest
indoor rain forest—the Lied Jungle—and a saltwater aquarium. "Ride
the rails" at the **Western Heritage Museum** (⊠ 801 S. 10th St., ☎ 402/
444–5071), where you're invited to climb aboard at Nebraska's largest
restored art deco railroad station. Formerly Omaha's Union Station,
the museum highlights the history of the Omaha and Union Pacific railroads through interactive exhibits. Lifelike sculptures of soldiers, sales-
men, and other rail travelers of the 1930s and '40s sit in restored train
cars and "talk" about the politics, music, and society of the time.

Father Flanagan's **Boys Town** (⊠ 138th St. and W. Dodge Rd., 68010,
☎ 402/498–1140) lies just outside Omaha, about 2 mi west of I–680.
It remains the only official village in the nation created just for children. Founded in 1917 and made famous by the 1938 movie with Spencer
Tracy and Mickey Rooney, the town includes schools, churches, and
farmland.

In Fremont, about 50 mi northwest of Bellevue, you can board the historic **Fremont and Elkhorn Valley Railroad** (⊠ 1835 N. Somers Ave.,
☎ 402/727–0615) for a tour through the lush Elkhorn River valley.
Hop the **Fremont Dinner Train** (⊠ 650 N. H St., ☎ 800/942–7245)
for a dining experience reminiscent of rail travel in the 1940s. It offers dinner and mystery trips during its scenic 30-mi run.

About 60 mi south of Fremont on I–80W halfway between Lincoln and Omaha are the **Eugene T. Mahoney State Park** (✉ Near Ashland, ☎ 402/944–2523) and the **Platte River State Park** (✉ Rte. 50, then 2 mi west on Spur 13E near Louisville, ☎ 402/234–2217). You'll find campsites at Mahoney and cabins at Platte River. Both offer riding, swimming, hiking, and spectacular vistas of the Platte River valley. Platte River also features buffalo stew cookouts.

The **Strategic Air Command Museum** recently relocated from Bellevue the Mahoney State Park area. The museum provides a glimpse of aviation wonders and includes a children's interactive gallery. Stroll beneath the wings of aircraft that changed the course of history, see missiles huge and small, view rare film footage, and browse through an extensive collection of military artifacts.

Lincoln, home of the University of Nebraska and the state government, rises to meet you as you drive along I–80W. Scan the city's skyline from atop the **Nebraska capitol** (✉ 1445 K St., ☎ 402/471–0448), with its 400-ft spire that towers over the surrounding plains. Free tours of the capitol are offered daily from 9 to 4.

A five-minute drive north from the capitol will take you to the **University of Nebraska,** at 14th and U streets. There you'll find the **State Museum of Natural History** (☎ 402/472–2642), nicknamed Elephant Hall due to its huge collection of extinct animals that once roamed the Great Plains. Also on the university's campus is the **Ralph Mueller Planetarium** (☎ 402/472–2641), which offers laser shows. At **Nine-Mile Prairie** (✉ 1 mi west of N.W. 48th St. and Fletcher Ave.) you can park your car and get out to hike the natural prairies.

From Lincoln you can take Route 2 southeast to U.S. 75, then U.S. 136 southeast to Brownville. At the **Brownville State Recreation Area,** the *Spirit of Brownville* riverboat (☎ 402/825–6001) offers sightseeing, dining, and dancing cruises on the mighty Missouri River. Just south of Brownville Bridge is the **Captain Meriwether Lewis and Missouri River History Museum** (☎ 402/825–3341), featuring a restored side-wheeler dredge once used on the river.

U.S. 75N brings you to **Nebraska City,** a tidy town rimmed with historic sites and apple orchards, including the **Arbor Day Farm** (✉ 100 Arbor Ave., ☎ 402/873–8710), where you can buy apple cider and visit the gift shop year-round. Apples are available in season, and lip-smacking desserts are served in the Pie Garden from May through October.

Hop the **Nebraska City Trolley** (☎ 402/873–3000) at stops throughout town. It links historic sites to 11 downtown factory outlets clustered around 8th and 1st Corso streets and to the **VF Factory Outlet Mall** (✉ 1001 Rte. 2, ☎ 402/873–7727), which sells merchandise ranging from toy trucks to sweaters. The trolley stops at **John Brown's Cave** (✉ 1908 4th Corso St., ☎ 402/727–5630), a museum, a historic village, and a stop on the Underground Railroad.

★ While in Nebraska City peek into the past with a visit to the **Arbor Lodge State Historical Park and Arboretum** (✉ 2nd and Centennial Aves., ☎ 402/873–7222). On the grounds are the 52-room mansion and carriage house of J. Sterling Morton, the 19th-century politician and lover of trees who inaugurated the first Arbor Day, now observed nationwide as a day for planting trees. The mansion was later inhabited by his son, Morton Salt baron Joy Morton.

Dining and Lodging

Dining choices in this varied region range from international cuisine to quiche to pizza. Lodging runs from full-service hotels to comfortable B&Bs (Nebraska Association of Bed and Breakfast, ⌧ Rte. 2, Box 17, Elgin 68636, ☎ 402/843–2287). For price ranges *see* Charts 1 (B) and 2 (B) *in* On the Road with Fodor's.

Brownville

$$$ ✕🏠 **Thompson House Bed and Breakfast.** This Victorian three-story house has a game room and parlor. Rooms are decorated with antiques, including kerosene lamps. ⌧ *Box 162, 68321,* ☎ *402/825–6551. 5 rooms. MC, V.*

Lincoln

$$ ✕ **Billy's.** A fascinating collection of political memorabilia and antiques
★ captures the elegance of a bygone era in this upscale restaurant. The menu includes all the classics: steak Diane, charbroiled chicken, and the like. ⌧ *1301 H St.,* ☎ *402/474–0084. AE, D, DC, MC, V.*

$$ ✕ **Misty's Restaurant.** Adorned with Cornhusker football paraphernalia, this is, by locals' accounts, the prime-rib palace of the Plains. ⌧ *6235 Havelock Ave.,* ☎ *402/466–8424. AE, D, MC, V.*

$ ✕ **Rock 'n' Roll Runza.** Waitresses on roller skates serve Runzas—a hamburger-cabbage sandwich—at this '50s-style restaurant. ⌧ *210 N. 14th St.,* ☎ *402/474–2030. D, MC, V.*

$ ✕ **Valentino's Restaurant.** Besides pizza with original or home-style crust,
★ the restaurant also serves Italian specials and dessert pizzas with such toppings as cherry and cream cheese. ⌧ *3457 Holdrege St.,* ☎ *402/ 467–3611. AE, D, MC, V.*

$$$ 🏠 **The Cornhusker.** The lobby of this elegant hotel has a grand curving staircase, hand-painted murals, and an Italian-marble floor. East- and south-wing rooms have good views of downtown Lincoln. ⌧ *333 S. 13th St., 68508,* ☎ *402/474–7474,* 🖷 *402/474–1847. 290 rooms. 2 restaurants, indoor pool, exercise room, meeting rooms. AE, D, DC, MC, V.*

$$ 🏠 **Rogers House Bed and Breakfast.** Built in 1914, this ivy-covered
★ brick mansion was converted into a B&B by the current owners in 1984. The antiques-filled public areas, with oak floors, include a living room with fireplace and a sunroom where guests eat breakfast. ⌧ *2145 B St., 68502,* ☎ *402/476–6961,* 🖷 *402/476–6473. 12 rooms. AE, D, MC, V.*

Nebraska City

$ ✕ **Teresa's Family Restaurant.** Booths line the walls of this casual, fam-
★ ily-style place, where old-fashioned food, such as homemade lemon pie and meat loaf, is offered at yesterday's prices. ⌧ *812 Central Ave.,* ☎ *402/873–9100. MC, V.*

$ ✕ **Ulbrick's.** This converted gas station and café is nothing fancy, but
★ the made-from-scratch family-style dinners of fried chicken, creamed corn and cabbage, and homemade egg noodles are exceptional. ⌧ *1513 S. 11th St.,* ☎ *402/873–5458. No credit cards.*

$ 🏠 **Whispering Pines.** Nestled among pines on 6½ quiet acres, this 112-year-old two-story brick house has been completely refurbished as a B&B and filled with antiques. ⌧ *21st St. and 6th Ave., 68410,* ☎ *402/ 873–5850. 5 rooms. Hot tub. D, MC, V.*

Omaha

$$ ✕ **Bohemian Cafe.** Gaily painted Czech plates hang on the walls of this family-style restaurant, where you can try such Czechoslovakian favorites as goulash. ✉ *1406 S. 13th St.,* ☎ *402/342–9838. D, MC, V.*

$$ ✕ **Johnny's Café.** Since 1922 this has been *the* place to eat near the famous Omaha Stockyards. Mouthwatering steaks are the specialty, but seafood and midwestern dishes other than steak are offered as well. ✉ *4702 S. 27th St.,* ☎ *402/731–4774. AE, D, DC, MC, V.*

$$ ✕ **Mr. C's.** Christmas lights surround you at this Italian steak house, ★ where the lasagna and manicotti are as good as the sirloin. ✉ *5319 N. 30th St.,* ☎ *402/451–1998. AE, DC, MC, V.*

$ ✕ **Austins.** Throw your peanut shells on the floor at this casual eatery where the atmosphere is western and the food pure country. Chicken-fried steak, prime rib, and barbecued ribs are the specialties. ✉ *12020 Anne St.,* ☎ *402/896–5373. Reservations not accepted. AE, MC, V.*

$ ✕ **Garden Café.** Home-style cooking with everything made from scratch is what this café in the historic Old Market is known for. Noteworthy are the potato casseroles, soups, salads, and desserts. ✉ *12th and Harvey Sts.,* ☎ *402/422–1574. AE, DC, MC, V.*

$ ✕ **Neon Goose.** Dine under a chandelier or on the fresh-air veranda at this lively restaurant with piano bar. Good menu choices are unusual quiches, melt-in-your-mouth omelets, and fresh seafood. ✉ *1012 S. 10th St.,* ☎ *402/341–2063. AE, DC, MC, V.*

$$$ 🏨 **Marriott Hotel.** Built in the 1980s, this six-story hotel in suburban Omaha offers comfort but little flash. There's a gift shop here, and you can take advantage of nearby shopping at the upscale Regency Fashion Court area. ✉ *10220 Regency Circle, 68114,* ☎ *402/399–9000,* 🗏 *402/399–0223. 301 rooms. 2 restaurants, pool, exercise equipment. AE, D, DC, MC, V.*

$$$ 🏨 **Red Lion Hotel.** This 19-story hotel has a luxurious chandeliered lobby ★ and spacious rooms in mauve and mint green. It's in the heart of downtown, close to the Old Market and Creighton University. ✉ *1616 Dodge St., 68102,* ☎ *402/346–7600,* 🗏 *402/346–5722. 413 rooms. Restaurant, pool, sauna. AE, D, DC, MC, V.*

Motels

🏨 **Oak Creek Inn** (✉ 2808 S. 72nd St., Omaha 68124, ☎ 402/397–7137), 102 rooms, pool, hot tub, sauna, spa/exercise room; *$$.* 🏨 **Harvester Motel** (✉ 1511 Center Park Rd., Lincoln 68512, ☎ 402/423–3131), 80 rooms, lounge, pool; *$.*

Campgrounds

Indian Cave State Park (☞ National and State Parks, *above*) and **Eugene T. Mahoney State Park** (☞ Exploring Southeast Nebraska, *above*) offer excellent tent and RV camping.

Outdoor Activities and Sports

Fishing

The 13 Salt Valley lakes surrounding Lincoln, especially **Branched Oak** (✉ N.W. 140th St. and W. Raymond Rd.) and **Pawnee** (✉ N.W. 98th and W. Adams Sts.), offer a variety of fish, including largemouth bass, northern pike, walleye, and channel catfish. For more information about fishing in Nebraska, contact the **Game and Parks Commission** (☎ 402/471–0641).

Spectator Sports

Football: University of Nebraska Cornhuskers (✉ 117 S. Stadium St., ☎ 402/472–3111).

Shopping

Nebraska Furniture Mart (⊠ 700 S. 72nd St., Omaha, ☎ 402/397–6100 or 800/359–1200) is reputed to be the largest furniture store west of the Mississippi. Omaha's **Old Market** (⊠ Between 10th and 13th Sts., ☎ 402/346–4445) is a collection of boutiques, galleries, and restaurants in the oldest part of town. Lincoln's charming, restored warehouse shopping district, **Historic Haymarket** (⊠ Between 7th and 9th Sts. and between O and S Sts., ☎ 402/435–7496), has quaint antiques stores, novelty gift shops, and some fine restaurants.

NORTHWEST NEBRASKA

Here the Great Plains end and the Old West begins—a rugged, beautiful land, with dramatic buttes and bluffs, Ponderosa pines, craggy ridges, and canyons.

Visitor Information

Alliance: Box Butte Visitors Committee (⊠ Alliance Chamber of Commerce, Box 571, 69301, ☎ 308/762–1520). **Chadron:** Chamber of Commerce (⊠ Box 646, 69337, ☎ 308/432–4401). **Scottsbluff:** Scotts Bluff County Convention and Visitors Bureau (⊠ Box 1350, 69361, ☎ 308/632–2133 or 800/788–9475). **Valentine:** Visitor Center (⊠ Box 201, 69201, ☎ 402/376–2969 or 800/658–4024).

Arriving and Departing

By Car
From Omaha and Lincoln take I–80 west about 275 mi to U.S. 26, which closely follows the Oregon and Mormon trails as it takes you to Scottsbluff. To bypass Kearney and North Platte, take I–80 to Grand Island, then scenic Route 2 to the north, which runs parallel to I–80 through Nebraska's Sandhills.

Exploring Northwest Nebraska

You can retrace the route of the wagon trains by exiting I–80 near Ogallala and heading west on U.S. 26. Four miles south of Bridgeport on Route 88, you can see **Courthouse** and **Jail rocks,** sandstone outcroppings that pioneers used as landmarks on the trail west. One mile south of the junction of U.S. 26 and Route 92 and 4 mi south of Bayard, the **Chimney Rock National Historic Site** (☎ 308/586–2581) is an impressive outcropping that pioneers described as "towering to the heavens." The visitor center, open year-round, offers displays and a 15-minute film. Oregon Trail wagon traces are still visible at the **Scotts Bluff National Monument** (⊠ 3 mi west of Gering on Rte. 92, ☎ 308/436–4340), an enormous bluff that rises out of the rocky plains. Once described as the "Lighthouse of the Plains," it now has a museum at its base.

About 35 mi north of Mitchell on Route 29, the **Agate Fossil Beds National Monument** has fossil deposits dating back 20 million years. A museum (☎ 308/668–2211) preserves and displays fossils and Native American artifacts, including personal items that belonged to Chief Red Cloud and to Captain James H. Cook, the frontiersman, cattle driver, and Army scout who discovered the fossils on his land.

North on Route 29 to Harrison, then east on U.S. 20 is **Fort Robinson State Park** (☎ 308/665–2900), where activities include trail rides, historic tours, cookouts, swimming, trout fishing, hiking, and stagecoach rides. From late May to late August visitors can also enjoy summer theater productions. Tent sites and electrical hookups are available.

Western Nebraska

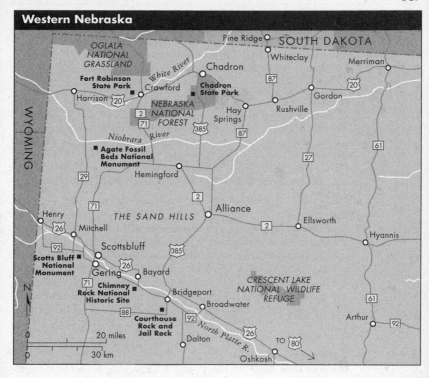

Dining and Lodging

Travelers to the region chow down at casual, out-of-the-way restaurants, wagon train–style cookouts, and ranches. Inexpensive cattle ranches and B&Bs (Nebraska Association of Bed and Breakfast, ⊠ Rte. 2, Box 17, Elgin 68636, ☎ 402/843–2287) provide charming alternatives to chain motels. For price ranges *see* Charts 1 (B) and 2 (B) *in* On the Road with Fodor's.

Bayard

$$$ ✕⌂ **Oregon Trail Wagon Train.** Enjoy sleeping under the stars and eat-
★ ing cookouts of fire-grilled rib eyes, stew, spoon bread, and vinegar pudding on covered-wagon tours through some of Nebraska's remaining short-grass prairies. One- to six-day treks are available. ⊠ *Rte. 2 (Box 502), 69334,* ☎ *308/586–1850,* ℻ *308/586–1848. Reservations essential. MC, V.*

Crawford

$ ⌂ **Fort Robinson State Park Lodge.** Dating to the 1800s, this historic fort in Fort Robinson State Park includes a two-story lodge with large verandas and tall columns. Built in 1909 as an enlisted men's barracks, the lodge now has 23 modern rooms with private baths but no telephones or TVs. Cabins with 2 to 12 bedrooms are also available, and the 1874 officers' quarters can sleep groups up to 60 people. ⊠ *3 mi west of Crawford; Box 392, Crawford 69339,* ☎ *308/665–2900,* ℻ *308/665–2906. MC, V.*

Oshkosh

$ ✕ **S & S Cafe.** This café serves hearty fish dishes, thick steaks, and juicy burgers. The atmosphere is completely unpretentious—there's even a bullet hole in the wall. ⊠ *Hwy. 26,* ☎ *308/772–3811. MC, V.*

Scottsbluff

$ ✕ **Grampy's Pancake House.** This large family-style restaurant is divided into three dining rooms with booths and tables, where tasty breakfast offerings include omelets, blintzes, and strawberry pancakes. Lunch and dinner are also served here. ⊠ *1802 E. 20th Pl.,* ☎ *308/ 632–6906. D, MC, V.*

Motels

▣ **Scottsbluff Inn** (⊠ 1901 21st Ave., Scottsbluff 69361, ☎ 308/635– 3111 or 800/597–3111 for reservations only, FAX 308/6357646), 138 rooms, restaurant, lounge, pool, sauna, exercise room; *$$.* ▣ **Landmark Inn** (⊠ 246 Main St., Bayard 69334, ☎ 308/586–1375 or 800/ 658–4424), 10 rooms, *$.* ▣ **Town Line Motel** (⊠ Box 423, 3591 Hwy. 20, Crawford 69339, ☎ 308/665–1450 or 800/903–1450), 24 rooms, kitchenettes; *$.*

Ranches

$$ ▣ **Meadow View Ranch Bed and Breakfast Bunkhouse.** Guests stay in the converted bunkhouse of this 5,000-acre working ranch 18 mi from the South Dakota border. Accommodations include a kitchenette, a living room, and two bedrooms. Complimentary breakfast is served in the ranch kitchen, and picnic lunches are packed on request. Activities include horseback riding, fishing, hiking in the nearby Sandhills, wagon rides, and cattle drives. ⊠ *HC 91, Box 29, Gordon 69343,* ☎ *308/282–0679. Bunkhouse sleeps 7. No credit cards. Closed Nov.–Apr.*

Campgrounds

Chadron State Park (☞ Hiking and Backpacking *in* Outdoor Activities and Sports, *below*) and **Fort Robinson State Park** (☞ Exploring Northwest Nebraska, *above*) offer tent and RV camping.

Outdoor Activities and Sports

Hiking and Backpacking

Fort Robinson State Park (☞ Exploring Northwest Nebraska, *above*) and **Chadron State Park** (⊠ 8 mi south of Chadron on U.S. 385, ☎ 308/ 432–6167) offer an abundance of trails.

ELSEWHERE IN NEBRASKA

Lake McConaughy and Ogallala

Arriving and Departing

From Lincoln and Omaha take I–80 west to Ogallala.

What to See and Do

★ **Lake McConaughy State Recreation Area** and the **Kingsley Dam** (⊠ 9 mi north of Ogallala on Rte. 61, ☎ 308/284–3542) annually attract thousands of visitors, who come to camp, fish, go boating, and enjoy the natural white-sand beaches here. In Ogallala **Front Street** (☎ 308/ 284–6000) depicts an 1880s Main Street, complete with wooden boardwalk, jail, barbershop, and cowboy museum. The restaurant proudly serves Nebraska steaks and puts on nightly western shows Memorial Day through Labor Day. The **Mansion on the Hill** (⊠ W. 10th and Spruce, ☎ 308/284–4066) is a museum with exhibits on 19th-century cattle drives. Ogallala is also home to the infamous **Boot Hill Cemetery** (⊠ W. 10th and Parkhill Dr.).

Red Cloud

Arriving and Departing

From Lincoln and Omaha take I–80 west to Grand Island, then U.S. 34 south to U.S. 281, and then U.S. 281 south.

What to See and Do

Red Cloud was the home of Pulitzer Prize–winning author Willa Cather. The **Willa Cather Historical Center** (⊠ 326 N. Webster St., ☎ 402/746–2653) is dedicated to the author, who loved the Plains—610 acres of which are preserved as the **Cather Memorial Prairie** (⊠ 5 mi south of Red Cloud).

On the National Register of Historic Places is the **Starke Round Barn,** 4 mi east of Red Cloud on Highway 136. Built in 1902, this three-story barn is held together by balanced tension and stress rather than nails or pegs.

The Great Platte River Road

Arriving and Departing

From Omaha and Lincoln take I–80 west.

What to See and Do

Westward-bound pioneers on the Mormon and Oregon trails once hugged the shores of the Platte River, a verdant natural pathway. Today I–80 follows the same route, cutting through the state's heartland and affording glimpses of this pioneer past. **Sculpture gardens** dot the landscape along the highway for 500 mi across the Nebraska plains. At nine rest areas large stone-and-metal artworks constitute what some critics have called a "museum without walls."

The **Stuhr Museum of the Prairie Pioneer,** in Grand Island, houses Native American and Old West artifacts and features the 60-building Railroad Town, which includes the birthplace of actor Henry Fonda, antique farm machinery, a restored 19th-century farmhouse, and people in period costumes. ⊠ *Junction of U.S. 34 and U.S. 281,* ☎ *308/385–5316. Railroad Town closed mid-Oct.–Apr.*

From early March to mid-April visitors flock to an area near Grand Island and Kearney to witness the migration of thousands of Sandhill cranes as they pause here before resuming their flight north. The **Platte River Whooping Crane Habitat Maintenance Trust** (☎ 308/384–4633) and the **Lillian Rowe Audubon Sanctuary** (☎ 308/468–5282) offer tours. The **Crane Meadows Nature Center** (⊠ ½ mi south of I–80 at the Alda exit, ☎ 308/382–1820) also has a visitor center.

Fort Kearny State Historical Park (⊠ 4 mi south of I–80 on Rte. 44 and then 4 mi east on L–50A, ☎ 308/234–9513) has a re-created stockade and interpretive exhibits detailing the role of the outpost on the frontier.

★ **Harold Warp's Pioneer Village** (⊠ Junction of U.S. 6, U.S. 34, and Rte. 10 in Minden, ☎ 308/832–1181) has an extensive collection of pioneer memorabilia; horse-drawn covered-wagon rides; and crafts demonstrations. **Gothenburg's** downtown Ehmen Park contains an original Pony Express station (☎ 308/537–2680). The Old West comes alive in **North Platte,** where Buffalo Bill Cody and his famous Wild West show began. You can tour his ranch house, enjoy trail rides, or chow down on buffalo stew in the **Buffalo Bill Ranch State Historical Park** (☎ 308/535–8035), 6 mi northwest of I–80. In Hastings, which lies near the junction of U.S. 34 and Highway 281, you'll find the **Hastings Museum** (⊠ 1330 N. Burlington Ave., ☎ 402/461–2399), which has exhibits on natural history and the history of the frontier; related films are shown in its IMAX theater.

The Dancing Leaf Earth Lodge Cultural Learning Center (⊠ Box 121, Stockville, ☎ 308/367–4233) offers modern travelers the opportunity to experience primitive Native American life. Earth lodges, a natural trail, spiritual bonding points, and archaeological sites are among the attractions.

Lodging

$ 🏠 **Home Comfort B&B.** On 15 acres of Nebraska farmland, this comfortable bed-and-breakfast is within walking distance of Harold Warp's Pioneer Village. ⊠ *1523 N. Brown, Minden 68959*, ☎ *308/832–0533. No credit cards.*

Sandhills/Valentine Region

Arriving and Departing

From Lincoln and Omaha take I–80 west to Grand Island. Go north on U.S. 281 to Route 22; then follow it west 9 mi and go north on Route 11. At Burwell follow Route 91 west, U.S. 183 north, and U.S. 20 west to Valentine.

What to See and Do

Fort Hartsuff State Historical Park is a restored 1870s infantry post with guides in period uniforms and costumes. ⊠ *3 mi north of Elyria off Rte. 11,* ☎ *308/346–4715. Vehicle admission charged. Closed Nov.–Apr.*

For a view of the Great Plains as it once was, you can take a drive through hundreds of miles of mixed-grass prairie, where outdoor attractions beckon. The **Niobrara River** draws canoeists from throughout the state. Outfitters include Dryland Aquatics (⊠ Box 33C, Sparks 69220, ☎ 402/376–3119), A&C Canoe Rentals (⊠ 518 N. Ray St., Valentine 69201, ☎ 402/376–2839), Brewers Canoers (⊠ 433 E. U.S. 20, Valentine 69201, ☎ 402/376–2046), Graham Canoe Outfitters (⊠ HC 13, Box 16A, Valentine 69201, ☎ 402/376–3708), and Little Outlaw Canoe & Tube Rentals (⊠ Box 15, Valentine 69201, ☎ 402/376–1822). Native wildlife is abundant at the **Valentine National Wildlife Refuge** (⊠ HC 14, Box 67, Valentine 69201, ☎ 402/376–1889), south of Valentine on U.S. 83. Its 70,000 acres of prairie and wetlands shelter ducks, geese, hawks, eagles, deer, coyotes, beavers, and other species. There are trails for driving or hiking through this open country; information kiosks are at entrances to the refuge.

The **Fort Niobrara National Wildlife Refuge** (⊠ HC 14, Box 67, Valentine 69201, ☎ 402/376–3789), 5 mi east of Valentine on Route 12, rewards you with a forested terrain and large species, such as bison, elk, and longhorn cattle. A visitor center and picnic facilities are available.

NORTH DAKOTA

By Kevin
Bonham

Updated by
Sue Berg

Capital	Bismarck
Population	644,000
Motto	Liberty and Union, Now and Forever, One and Inseparable
State Bird	Western meadowlark
State Flower	Wild prairie rose
Postal Abbreviation	ND

Statewide Visitor Information

North Dakota Tourism Department (✉ Liberty Memorial Bldg., 604 E. Blvd., Bismarck 58505, ☎ 701/328–2525 or 800/435–5663). **Welcome centers:** along I–94E, 1 mi west of **Beach;** off I–94 at the **Oriska Rest Area,** 12 mi east of Valley City; off I–29N at the **Lake Agassiz Rest Area,** 8 mi south of Hankinson interchange; along I–29S, 1 mi north of the **Pembina** interchange; one block west of the junction of U.S. 2 and U.S. 85 in **Williston;** at the junction of U.S. 12 and U.S. 85 in **Bowman;** at the 45th Street interchange off I–94W in **Fargo;** and on U.S. 2, 10 mi east of Grand Forks at **Fisher's Landing.**

Scenic Drives

The **Pembina Gorge** in northeastern North Dakota is a beautiful forested valley created by glaciers and the winding Pembina River; from I–29 at the Joliette exit near the northern boundary of the state, drive west on Route 5, then north on Route 32 to Walhalla. **Theodore Roosevelt National Park's South Unit loop road** begins near park headquarters in Medora and winds 36 mi through an eerie world of lonesome pinnacles and spires, steep gorges, and ravaged buttes. The 26-mi **North Unit Road** begins at the park entrance along U.S. 85, 15 mi south of Watford City; the high ground above the Little Missouri River has dramatic overlooks, and a lower area near the visitor center features a series of slump rocks, huge sections of bluff that gradually slid intact to the valley floor.

National and State Parks

National Park
Theodore Roosevelt National Park (☞ Exploring the Badlands, *below*).

State Parks
North Dakota's state parks are open year-round. Among the most scenic are **Cross Ranch State Park,** 40 mi north of Mandan, off Highway 25 (✉ HC 2, Box 152, Sanger 58567, ☎ 701/794–3731); **Fort Abraham Lincoln State Park** (☞ Exploring the Missouri River Corridor, *below*); two parks on U.S. 2 and Highway 19 that are part of **Devils Lake State Parks** (✉ Rte. 1, Box 165, Devils Lake 58301, ☎ 701/766–4015); **Lake Sakakawea State Park,** 1 mi north of Pick City, off Garrison Lake (✉ Box 732, Riverdale 58565, ☎ 701/487–3315); and **Icelandic State Park,** on Route 5, 5 mi west of Cavalier (✉ 13571 Hwy. 5, Cavalier 58220, ☎ 701/265–4561). All parks listed offer camping facilities.

For camping reservations at any of the state parks during the summer season, contact the **North Dakota Parks and Recreation Department** (✉ 1835 E. Bismarck Expressway, Bismarck 58554, ☎ 701/328–5357 or 800/807–4723).

MISSOURI RIVER CORRIDOR

The Missouri River is both a geographic and a symbolic barrier between the two North Dakotas—the east and the west. The state capital of Bismarck, on the east bank of the river, is a busy political hub, while at sprawling Lake Sakakawea, a short drive to the northwest, urban life seems a world away.

Visitor Information

Bismarck-Mandan: Convention and Visitors Bureau (⊠ Box 2274, 107 W. Main, Bismarck 58501, ☎ 701/222–4308 or 800/767–3555). **Minot:** Convention and Visitors Bureau (⊠ Dakota Square Mall, 58701, ☎ 701/857–8206 or 800/264–2626).

Arriving and Departing

By Bus
Greyhound Lines (☎ 800/231–2222) and **Minot-Bismarck Bus Service** (☎ 701/223–6576) serve Bismarck and Minot (☎ 701/852–2477).

By Car
I–94, the state's major east–west thoroughfare, runs through the Bismarck-Mandan area. U.S. 83 runs north–south from Bismarck to Minot, the state's second- and fourth-largest cities, respectively. U.S. 2 runs east–west along the top half of the state, including Minot.

By Plane
Bismarck Municipal Airport (☎ 701/222–6502) and **Minot International Airport** (☎ 701/857–4724) are served by Northwest and United Express. Both are about 5 mi from downtown; cab fare is about $5.

By Train
Amtrak (☎ 800/872–7245) stops in Minot and Williston.

Exploring the Missouri River Corridor

As with the rest of North Dakota, most of the attractions described here are open in the summer only (often Memorial Day–Labor Day); be sure to call ahead before you visit. The 19-story **state capitol** (⊠ 600 E. Boulevard Ave., 58505, ☎ 701/328–2480), in north Bismarck, is visible for miles across the Dakota prairie; tours of the limestone-and-marble Art Deco structure, built in the 1930s, are offered weekdays year-round and also on weekends Memorial Day–Labor Day. The **North Dakota Heritage Center** (⊠ 612 E. Boulevard Ave., ☎ 701/328–2666) is the state's largest museum and archive. Exhibits include Native American and pioneer artifacts and natural history displays. The facility is across the street from the capitol. The **Former Governors' Mansion State Historic Site** (⊠ 4th St. and Ave. B, ☎ 701/328–2666) is an elegant Victorian structure containing political memorabilia and period furnishings. The **Lewis and Clark Riverboat,** departing from the Port of Bismarck (⊠ N. River Rd., ☎ 701/255–4233), offers summer cruises on the Missouri River, plying the same route taken by the traders, trappers, and settlers of the last century.

Custer buffs often visit **Fort Abraham Lincoln State Park** (⊠ Hwy. 1806, Mandan, ☎ 701/663–9571). You can also reach the park from Bismarck by crossing the river on I–94 to Mandan, then either traveling 4 mi south on Route 1806 or taking the 9-mi **Fort Lincoln Trolley** (☎ 701/663–9018) from south Mandan. Among the reconstructed buildings at the fort are the barracks (where you can stay overnight for $15) and the **Custer House,** a replica of the 1870s house where General George

Armstrong Custer lived with his wife, Libby, before his fateful expedition to the Little Big Horn. Nearby is the reconstructed **On-A-Slant Indian Village**, once home to the Mandan tribe.

From Bismarck take U.S. 83 north to Washburn, then Route 200A west to the **Knife River Indian Villages National Historic Site** (⊠ ¼ mi north of Stanton, ☎ 701/745–3309). The area preserves depressions formed by the Hidatsa and Mandan tribes' earth lodges, circular earth-and-timber structures. Pottery shards and other artifacts are displayed at the museum and interpretive center. There's also a full-size furnished replica of an earth lodge.

Twenty miles north of Stanton is the 600-square-mi **Lake Sakakawea,** affording countless recreational opportunities, including swimming and boating. State parks and small resort communities are sprinkled along its shores. Free tours of the **Garrison Dam power plant** are conducted by the U.S. Army Corps of Engineers (☎ 701/654–7441). For more information on the lake, contact the tourism department (☞ Statewide Visitor Information, *above*).

Dining and Lodging

For a listing of area bed-and-breakfasts, contact the tourism department (☞ Statewide Visitor Information, *above*). For price ranges *see* Charts 1 (B) and 2 (B) *in* On the Road with Fodor's.

Bismarck

$$ ✕ **Caspar's East 40.** The walls of this intimate spot are covered from
★ floor to ceiling with an eclectic collection of antiques, including the skates of the restaurant's namesake, European chef Caspar Borggreve. Borggreve's family continues to run the ever-popular establishment. Dine on prime rib or Greek specialties. ⊠ *1401 E. Interchange Ave.,* ☎ *701/ 258–7222. AE, MC, V.*

$$ ✕ **Peacock Alley Bar and Grill.** In what was once the historic Patter-
★ son Hotel, this restaurant enjoys local fame as the scene of countless political deals, captured in period photographs. The menu features seafood specials such as Cajun firecracker shrimp and regional dishes such as pheasant in white-wine sauce. ⊠ *422 E. Main St.,* ☎ *701/255– 7917. AE, DC, MC, V.*

$ ✕ **Fiesta Villa.** This family-run Mexican restaurant is suitably housed in a mission-style building. Beef or chicken fajitas are a good choice here, and they go well with the excellent margaritas. ⊠ *4th and Main Sts.,* ☎ *701/222–8075. AE, D, MC, V.*

$$ ▥ **Radisson Inn.** Rooms here are spacious and comfortable, with overstuffed chairs and soothing color schemes. The hotel is across from Bismarck's largest shopping mall, Kirkwood Plaza. ⊠ *800 S. 3rd St., 58504,* ☎ *701/258–7700,* ℻ *701/224–8212. 306 rooms. Restaurant, bar, indoor pool, sauna, health club. AE, D, DC, MC, V.*

Mandan

$$ ✕ **Captain's Table Restaurant.** As the name suggests, the decor follows a maritime theme. Menu selections hail from around the world; the specialty is a peppery South American–style steak whose recipe is a closely guarded secret. ⊠ *Best Western Seven Seas Inn* (☞ *below*), *I-94, Exit 152,* ☎ *701/663–3773. AE, D, DC, MC, V.*

$ ✕ **Mandan Drug.** For a fun lunch (the place is open 9–6), follow a sand-
★ wich or homemade soup with an old-fashioned cherry soda or a brown cow—that's a root beer float with chocolate ice cream. The homemade candy is hard to resist. ⊠ *316 Main St.,* ☎ *701/663–5900. MC, V. Closed Sun.*

$$ \quad ☷ \quad **Best Western Seven Seas Inn and Conference Center.** Nautical decor fills the public areas, from scrimshaw displays to 200-year-old anchors to carpeting made to resemble ship's planking. Rooms continue the theme with maritime art. ⊠ *I–94, Exit 152; 2611 Old Red Trail, 58554,* ☎ *701/663–7401 or 800/597–7327,* 𝔽𝔸𝕏 *701/663–0025. 103 rooms. Restaurant, bar, pool, casino. AE, D, DC, MC, V.*

Minot

$$ \quad ☷ \quad **Best Western International Inn.** Larger-than-average rooms have con-
★ temporary furnishings at this five-story hotel on a hill above downtown Minot. ⊠ *1505 N. Broadway, 58703,* ☎ *701/852–3161 or 800/735–4493,* 𝔽𝔸𝕏 *701/838–5538. 270 rooms. Restaurant, bar, pool, casino. AE, D, DC, MC, V.*

Motel

☷ **Expressway Inn** (⊠ 200 E. Bismarck Expressway, Bismarck 58504, ☎ 𝔽𝔸𝕏 701/222–2900 or ☎ 800/456–6388), 163 rooms, pool, indoor hot tub, recreation room; *$$*.

Campgrounds

There are campgrounds at **Fort Abraham Lincoln State Park** (☞ Exploring the Missouri River Corridor, *above*) and **Lake Sakakawea State Park** (☞ National and State Parks, *above*).

Nightlife

Gambling

Prairie Knights Casino, on Standing Rock Reservation, 44 mi south of Mandan on Route 1806, is the fanciest of the five reservation casinos in North Dakota, with murals by Native American artists and first-class food. The games (slots, blackjack, poker), two bars, and two restaurants are open 24 hours a day. The Lodge at Prairie Knights is an adjacent hotel with a gift shop that sells Native American items. ⊠ *HC 1, Box 26A, Fort Yates 58538,* ☎ *701/854–7777 or 800/425–8277,* 𝔽𝔸𝕏 *701/ 854–3795.*

Outdoor Activities and Sports

Biking

The 246-mi **Lewis and Clark Bike Tour** follows the Missouri River along Routes 1804, 200, and 22, from the South Dakota border to the Montana border. Contact the tourism department (☞ Statewide Visitor Information, *above*) for details. **Dakota Cyclery** (⊠ 1606 E. Main Ave., Bismarck, ☎ 701/222–1218) rents bicycles and can provide information about area biking.

Fishing

Walleye and northern pike are the big catches on Lake Sakakawea. The **North Dakota Game and Fish Department** (⊠ 100 N. Bismarck Expressway, Bismarck 58501, ☎ 701/328–6300) provides a list of area fishing guides. The *North Dakota Hunting and Fishing Guide* outlines seasons and regulations and is available through the tourism department (☞ Statewide Visitor Information, *above*).

Hiking

The 17-mi **Roughrider Trail,** along Missouri River bottomland, is a treasure. For details contact the Parks and Recreation Department (☞ National and State Parks, *above*).

Shopping

Kirkwood Mall, between South 3rd and South 7th streets in Bismarck, has five major department stores and 100 specialty shops, including locally owned Maxwell's, a cozy bookstore with a special section for regional reading materials.

Across the river in Mandan, the **Five Nations Arts** (✉ 401 W. Main, ☏ 701/663–4663) sells handmade Native American star quilts, beadwork, sculptures, and more.

THE BADLANDS

★ Theodore Roosevelt, who ranched in western North Dakota in the late 1800s, once said, "I would never have been president if it had not been for my experiences in North Dakota." He was referring to the **Badlands,** where a national park that bears his name is now the heart of this wide-open country, largely unchanged since the president's time.

Visitor Information

Medora: Theodore Roosevelt Medora Foundation (✉ c/o Rough Riders, 1 Main St., Box 198, 58645, ☏ 800/633–6721 or 701/623–4444). **Williston:** Convention and Visitors Bureau (✉ 10 Main St., 58801, ☏ 701/774–9041). **Dickinson:** Convention and Visitors Bureau (✉ 24 2nd St. W, 58601, ☏ 800/279–7391).

Arriving and Departing

By Bus
Greyhound Lines (☏ 800/231–2222) stops in Dickinson and Medora.

By Car
I–94 crosses the Badlands, with an exit at Medora for the South Unit of Theodore Roosevelt National Park. U.S. 85 links the park's North and South units.

By Plane
Bismarck Municipal Airport (☞ Missouri River Corridor, *above*) is the nearest large airport. The commuter airline United Express serves **Williston Airport** (☏ 701/774–8594) and **Dickinson Airport** (☏ 701/225–5856).

Exploring the Badlands

Theodore Roosevelt National Park (✉ Box 7, Medora 58645, ☏ 701/623–4466) is divided into three units, separated by about 50 mi of Badlands and the **Little Missouri National Grasslands.** Scenic loops through the **South Unit** (☞ Scenic Drives, *above*) are marked with low speed limits to protect the bison, wild horses, mule deer, pronghorn antelope, and bighorn sheep that roam here. You can get a panoramic view of the Badlands from the park's **Painted Canyon Overlook and Visitors Center** (☏ 701/623–4466), on I–94, 7 mi east of Medora, a good place to start a tour. The center provides picnic tables from which to enjoy the sweeping vista.

If you're up for an hour-long horseback ride in the **South Unit** of the park, contact **Peaceful Valley Ranch** (☏ 701/623–4496), 7 mi north of the park entrance. They'll take you on some of the park's 80 mi of marked horse trails. The visitor center will provide you with maps if you prefer to hike.

The **North Unit,** off U.S. 85 south of Watford City, offers the same scenic driving and hiking opportunities but in a less crowded setting. This is a good place to spot the wildlife you may have missed in the South Unit.

Western North Dakota

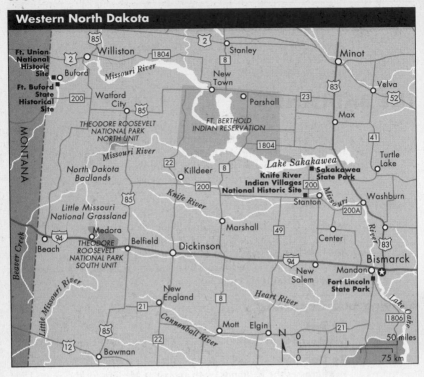

Outside the park, historic **Medora** is a walkable small town with a number of tiny shops, museums, and other attractions. The **Château de Mores** (✉ ½ mi southwest of Medora on Hwy. 10, ☎ 701/623–4355), an elegant 26-room mansion on a bluff overlooking the town, was built in the mid-1880s by the Marquis de Mores, a French nobleman who ran a short-lived cattle and meat-packing enterprise from here. You can see a collection of antique dolls in the **Medora Doll House.** The **Museum of the Badlands** displays Native American artifacts, wildlife exhibits, and wax figures depicting frontier days. The **Schafer Heritage Center** is an art gallery with an exhibit about Harold Schafer, who since the early 1960s has been investing his Mr. Bubble fortune in rebuilding Medora. The Theodore Roosevelt Medora Foundation (☞ Visitor Information, *above*) oversees these three sights, which are open June through August only; call ahead for more information.

Dickinson, an oil-boom-and-bust community on I–94, is now renowned for its dinosaur deposits. You can see 10 full-scale dinosaurs and other fossil, mineral, and animal collections at the **Dakota Dinosaur Museum** (✉ 200 Museum Dr., off I–94, Exit 61, ☎ 701/225–3466).

Fort Buford State Historic Site (☎ 701/572–9034), 22 mi southwest of Williston via Route 1804, is built around the 1866 fort that once imprisoned famous Native American leaders, including Sioux leader Sitting Bull and Nez Percé chief Joseph. It is closed mid-September through mid-May. Two miles west of Fort Buford on Route 1804 is the **Fort Union Trading Post** (☎ 701/572–9083). This national historic site is a reconstructed fur trading post of John Jacob Astor's American Fur Company. Fort Union dominated the fur trade along the upper Missouri River from 1828 to 1867 and hosted such notable visitors as Prince Maximilian of Germany and John James Audubon.

Dining and Lodging

For price ranges *see* Charts 1 (B) and 2 (B) *in* On the Road with Fodor's.

Medora

$$ ✕ **Rough Rider Hotel Dining Room.** Housed in a two-story wood-
★ frame building, this rustic restaurant features barbecued buffalo ribs,
along with prime rib and other beef specialties. ⊠ *Main St.,* ☎ *701/
623–4444. AE, MC, V. Operates as a B&B Oct.–Apr.*

$ ✕ **Chuckwagon Cafeteria.** This large wood-paneled cafeteria with west-
ern decor often hosts patio cookouts. Main courses include prime rib
and ham, and a large array of side dishes, soups, and salads is offered.
⊠ *Main St.,* ☎ *701/623–4444. MC, V. Closed mid-Sept.–mid-May.*

$ ✕ **Trapper's Kettle Restaurant.** Be prepared for reminders of the fur
trade at this restaurant's two locations—traps, furs, stuffed and mounted
animals, and a canoe, which holds the salad bar. Go for chili topped
with melted cheese. ⊠ *I–94 and U.S. 85, Belfield,* ☎ *701/575–8585;*
⊠ *3901 2nd Ave. W, Williston,* ☎ *701/774–2831. MC, V.*

Williston

$$ ✕ **El Rancho Restaurant.** The Old West atmosphere here was replaced
★ by the earthy colors and art of the Southwest, but beef—especially prime
rib—remains the specialty. Seafood and chicken are also on the menu.
⊠ *1623 2nd Ave. W,* ☎ *701/572–6321. AE, D, DC, MC, V.*

Motels

▥ **Badlands Motel** (⊠ Box 198, Medora 58645, ☎ 701/623–4422),
116 rooms, pool; closed Oct.–Apr.; $. ▥ **Medora Motel** (⊠ E. River
Rd., Medora 58645, ☎ 701/623–4422), 190 rooms, pool; closed Oct.–
Apr.; $. ▥ **El Rancho Motor Hotel** (⊠ 1623 2nd Ave. W, Williston
58801, ☎ FAX 701/572–6321 or 800/433–8529), 92 rooms, restaurant,
bar, coffee shop; $. ▥ **Hospitality Inn** (⊠ I–94 and Rte. 22, Dickinson
58601, ☎ 701/227–1853 or 800/422–0949, FAX 701/225–0090), 149
rooms, restaurant, pool, hot tub, sauna, recreation room; $.

Campgrounds

Cottonwood Campground (⊠ 5 mi inside Theodore Roosevelt National
Park, ☎ 701/623–4466). **Medora Campground** (⊠ Medora, ☎ 701/
623–4435). **Red Trail Campground** (⊠ Box 367, Medora, ☎ 701/623–
4317 or 800/621–4317).

Nightlife

The *Medora Musical* (☎ 701/623–4444), in the outdoor **Burning Hills
Amphitheater,** is a theater tribute to western Americana, featuring
everything from singing to history to fireworks.

Outdoor Activities and Sports

Biking

The roads in the north and south units of Theodore Roosevelt National
Park are challenging and scenic.

Hiking and Backpacking

All units of Theodore Roosevelt National Park offer spectacular hiking and backpacking opportunities. The Little Missouri National
Grasslands, which stretches between the main park units, is also a popular spot (☞ Exploring the Badlands, *above*).

Shopping

Specialty shops lining Medora's Main Street include **Chateau Nuts** (☎ 701/623–4825), which stocks every nut imaginable in quantities large enough to make a squirrel's heart race.

ELSEWHERE IN NORTH DAKOTA

The Lakes Region

Arriving and Departing

U.S. 2 is the principal east–west route through the region, connecting with I–29 at Grand Forks. U.S. 281 runs north–south through the region, with secondary roads leading to lakes and area attractions. Devils Lake is served by **United Express. Amtrak** stops in Devils Lake and Rugby.

What to See and Do

Jamestown, at U.S. 281 and I–94, marks the southern end of this region, with the world's largest buffalo sculpture and a live bison herd, both clearly visible from I–94.

Devils Lake, the heart of the lakes region, is surrounded by hundreds of smaller lakes and prairie potholes filled with marsh water. A major breeding ground for North America's migratory waterfowl, the area offers fine birding. Devils Lake itself has excellent jumbo perch and walleye fishing and uncrowded beaches. For more information on fishing in the area, contact the **Game and Fish Department** (⊠ 100 N. Bismarck Expressway, Bismarck 58501, ☎ 701/328–6300). On the Devils Lake Sioux Indian Reservation is the **Fort Totten State Historic Site** (⊠ Rte. 57, ☎ 701/766–4441), the best-preserved military fort west of the Mississippi River. Built in 1867, it later served as one of the nation's largest government-run schools for Native Americans. It is closed mid-September through mid-May.

At **Rugby,** west of Devils Lake on U.S. 2, is the geographical center of North America. Marked by a stone monument, the landmark includes a spacious **Geographical Center Historical Museum** (☎ 701/776–6414) containing thousands of objects, such as 19th-century farming equipment and antique cars. It is closed mid-September through mid-May.

★ The **International Peace Garden** (☎ 701/263–4390), 13 mi north of Dunseith on U.S. 281, is a 2,300-acre garden straddling the border between Canada and the United States and planted as a symbol of peace between the two nations. In addition to the 100,000 flowers planted annually, the garden includes an 18-ft floral clock, the Peace Tower, and the Peace Chapel. For more information on the Lakes Region, contact **Devils Lake Tourism & Promotion** (⊠ Box 879, Devils Lake 58301, ☎ 701/662–4903 or 800/233–8048).

Dining and Lodging

For price ranges *see* Charts 1 (B)and 2 (B) *in* On the Road with Fodor's.

$$ ✕ **Birchwood Steakhouse and Northern Lights Lounge.** Delicious prime rib is a staple at this lakeside restaurant bordering Canada. ⊠ *North of Rte. 43, Lake Metígoshe,* ☎ *701/263–4283. MC, V.*

$ ✕ **Mr. & Mrs. J's.** The "Pig-out Omelette" is the specialty; a huge salad bar complements traditional foods. ⊠ *U.S. 2E, Devils Lake,* ☎ *701/662–8815. D, MC, V.*

MOTEL

🏨 **Dakota Motor Inn** (⊠ Hwy. 2E, Devils Lake 58301, ☎ 701/662-4001 or 800/280–4001), 80 rooms; *$.*

CAMPGROUND

Grahams Island State Park (⊠ Rte. 1, Box 165, Devils Lake 58301, ☎ 701/766–4015) is 15 mi southwest of Devils Lake, off Route 19.

The Red River Valley

Arriving and Departing

I–94 links Fargo with Minneapolis–St. Paul to the east and with Billings, Montana, to the west. I–29 connects Fargo with Grand Forks, 75 mi north, and with Sioux Falls, South Dakota, to the south. **Hector International Airport** (☎ 701/241–1501), in Fargo, and **Grand Forks International Airport** (☎ 701/795–6981) are served by Northwest, Mesaba, and United Express. **Amtrak** (☎ 800/872–7245) also serves both cities. **Greyhound Lines** (☎ 800/231–2222) provides service to Fargo and Grand Forks.

What to See and Do

The **Red River of the North** forms the eastern boundary of North Dakota with Minnesota. The fertile valley formed by the river was the destination of northern European immigrants in the late 19th century and still contains more than a third of the state's population. The region is an enormous shopping hub, drawing bargain hunters from Minnesota, Canada, and the rest of North Dakota. Awesomely devastating floods rolled through the Red River Valley in April 1997. Despite delays by Congress to pass a flood-relief bill, the region has moved quickly to recover from the floods, but you may still encounter lingering effects, especially in Grand Forks, the hardest-hit city.

In the southeast corner of the state, off I–29, is **Wahpeton.** You can ride on the restored 1926 **Prairie Rose Carousel** (10 mi east of I–29); rides cost $1. Nearby is the **Ehnstrom Nature Center and Chahinkapa Park Zoo** (☎ 701/642–8709), with such native species as eagles, bison, and elk. Ten miles west of I–29 is Mooreton's **Bagg Bonanza Farm** (☎ 701/224–8989), a national historic site that re-creates the *Bonanza*-like farm life of the late 1800s and early 1900s. Nine of the 21 buildings have been restored. It is closed Monday. Head north 50 mi on I–29 to **Fargo,** the state's largest city. **Bonanzaville USA** (⊠ Exit 65, I–29, West Fargo, ☎ 701/282–2822) is a pioneer village and museum with 40 original and re-created buildings that show life in 1880s Dakota Territory. **Roger Maris Baseball Museum** (⊠ West Acres Shopping Center, I–29 and 13th Ave. S, ☎ 701/282–2222) honors baseball's all-time best single-season home-run hitter. Hands-on learning is the theme at the **Children's Museum at Yunker Farm** (⊠ 1201 28th Ave. N, 58102, ☎ 701/232–6102).

Seventy-five miles north of Fargo on I–29 is **Grand Forks,** the state's cultural and technological center. Grand Forks is home to the **North Dakota Museum of Art** (⊠ Centennial Dr., ☎ 701/777–4195) and the **Center for Aerospace Sciences** (⊠ 4125 University Ave., ☎ 701/777–2791), both at the **University of North Dakota.** Seventy miles north of Grand Forks via I–29, the **Pembina State Museum** (⊠ 375 Hwy. 59, ☎ 701/825–6840) has exhibits on North Dakota history and an observation tower. Just west, in **Icelandic State Park** (☞ National and State Parks, *above*), the **Pioneer Heritage Interpretive Center** (☎ 701/265–4561) uses artifacts and exhibits to showcase the ethnic diversity of the region.

For further information on the area, contact the **Fargo/Moorhead Convention and Visitors Bureau** (⊠ 2001 44th St. SW, Fargo 58103, ☎ 701/282–3653 or 800/235–7654), **Grand Forks Convention and Visitors Bureau** (⊠ 4251 Gateway Dr., 58203, ☎ 701/746–0444 or 800/866–4566), or **Wahpeton Visitors Center** (⊠ 120 N. 4th St., 58075, ☎ 701/642–8559 or 800/892–6673).

Dining and Lodging

For price ranges *see* Charts 1 (B) and 2 (B) *in* On the Road with Fodor's.

\$\$ ✕ **Old Broadway Food and Brewing Co.** Featuring Gay '90s decor under 18-ft ceilings, with a plethora of antiques, the restaurant and microbrewery are in the circa 1900 Stern's clothing store. Ribs, smoked on the premises, are popular. ⊠ *22 N. Broadway, Fargo,* ☎ *701/237–6161. AE, D, DC, MC, V.*

\$\$ ✕ **Sanders 1907.** Tiny, elegant, and intimate, Sanders has lots of mir-
★   rors, exceptional local artwork, and exuberant rosemaling on its booths. Fabulous pâté; wonderful salads and breads; such entrées as prime rib cooked with garlic, basil, rosemary, and olive oil; and desserts like pecan torte and "chocolate decadence" make this a delightful gastronomic experience. ⊠ *312 Kittson Ave., Grand Forks,* ☎ *701/746–8970. AE, DC, MC, V.*

MOTELS

🏨 **Best Western Doublewood Inn and Conference Center** (⊠ 3333 13th Ave. S, Fargo 58103, ☎ 701/235–3333 or 800/433–3235), 173 rooms, restaurant, lounge, indoor pool, casino; *\$\$\$*. 🏨 **Road King Inn** (⊠ 3300 30th Ave. S, Grand Forks 58201, ☎ 701/746–1391 or 800/950–0691), 85 rooms, indoor pool, hot tub; *\$\$*.

OKLAHOMA

By Matt
Schofield

Updated by
Barbara
Palmer

Capital	Oklahoma City
Population	3,301,000
Motto	Labor Conquers All Things
State Bird	Scissor-tailed flycatcher
State Flower	Mistletoe
Postal Abbreviation	OK

Statewide Visitor Information

Oklahoma Tourism and Recreation Department (⊠ 15 N. Robinson Ave., Oklahoma City 73102, ☎ 405/521–2409 or 800/652–6552). **State Historical Society** (⊠ 2100 N. Lincoln Blvd., Oklahoma City 73105, ☎ 405/521–2491).

Scenic Drives

Route 49 traverses the prairies and granite peaks of the Wichita Mountains Wildlife Refuge (☞ Exploring Southwestern Oklahoma, *below*). **Route 10,** which follows the Spring, Neosho, and Illinois rivers from Wyandotte through Grove to Gore, is a winding drive through the Cherokee Nation. **Route 1** through the northern section of the Ouachita National Forest (☞ National and State Parks, *below*), from Talihina east about 50 mi to the state border, makes a beautiful drive in autumn, when the forest foliage is most colorful.

National and State Parks

National Park

The **Ouachita National Forest** (⊠ HC 64, Box 3467, Heavener 74937, ☎ 918/653–2991), in southeastern Oklahoma, is a scenic region of small mountain ranges.

State Parks

Oklahoma has 52 state parks, and all but two offer camping. Some of the best are **Alabaster Caverns State Park** (⊠ Rte. 1, Box 32, Freedom 73842, ☎ 405/621–3381), **Beavers Bend Resort Park** (☞ Exploring Southeastern Oklahoma, *below*), **Roman Nose Resort Park** (⊠ Rte. 1, Watonga 73772, ☎ 405/623–4215); **Quartz Mountain State Park** (☞ Exploring Southwestern Oklahoma, *below*), and **Red Rock Canyon State Park** (⊠ Box 502, Hinton 73047, ☎ 405/542–6344).

CENTRAL OKLAHOMA

Oklahoma's image as a western state was largely forged in central Oklahoma, where pickup trucks, cowboy boots, and oil wells are still the ultimate status symbols. The Chisholm Trail, the most famous of the cattle trails that moved Texas cattle north through Indian Territory after the end of the Civil War, came through here 130 years ago, and the country's largest live cattle auction still gets under way in Oklahoma City's Stockyards City every Monday morning. Many towns in central Oklahoma, including Guthrie, Oklahoma City, and Norman, share a common heritage: They were born in one day, following the April 22, 1889, land run, which opened a parcel of land in central Oklahoma to non-Indian settlement. Would-be homesteaders lined up on the borders and literally raced for claims.

Visitor Information

The *Daily Oklahoman*'s Friday weekend section and the *Gazette* (a free weekly distributed in Oklahoma City and Norman restaurants and hotels) list events. **Guthrie:** Convention and Visitors Bureau (⊠ 212 W. Oklahoma St., Box 995, 73044, ☎ 405/282–1947 or 800/299–1889). **Oklahoma City:** Convention and Visitors Bureau (⊠ 189 W. Sheridan St., 73102, ☎ 405/297–8912 or 800/225–5652). **Norman:** Convention and Visitors Bureau (⊠ 200 S. Jones, 73069, ☎ 405/366–8095 or 800/767–7260).

Arriving and Departing

By Bus
Greyhound Lines (⊠ 427 W. Sheridan St., Oklahoma City, ☎ 800/231–2222).

By Car
Interstate 35 takes travelers north and south through central Oklahoma; I–40 crosses east and west. Interstate 44, which runs diagonally from the northeast to the southwest, intersects both I–35 and I–40 in Oklahoma City.

By Plane
The **Will Rogers World Airport** (☎ 405/681–5311), in southwestern Oklahoma City, is served by major domestic airlines.

Getting Around Central Oklahoma

A car is a necessity here since public transportation is limited.

Exploring Central Oklahoma

Oklahoma City, the state's capital, dominates central Oklahoma, but **Guthrie,** 20 mi north on I–35, is a fitting place to begin a tour; the town was the state capital from territorial days until 1910. After a bitter political fight, the capital was moved to Oklahoma City, and Guthrie was forgotten. Two decades ago the town's architectural treasures were rediscovered—more than 400 city blocks of turn-the-century commercial and residential properties remained, with most of their stained-glass windows and stamped-tin ceilings intact. The downtown district, the largest urban area listed on the National Register of Historic Places, is filled with gift shops, antiques malls, and restaurants. **First Capital Trolley** (☎ 405/282–6000) makes regular tours of downtown Guthrie, beginning from the corner of Second Street and Harrison Avenue. A handful of museums and architectural sites offer historical perspective: The **State Capital Publishing Museum** (⊠ 301 W. Harrison Ave., ☎ 405/282–4123) has exhibits about territorial life as well as vintage printing presses. On weekdays you can tour the elaborate rooms in the **Scottish Rite Temple,** one of the world's largest Masonic lodges. The rooms were designed to illustrate the evolution of Western thought (⊠ 900 E. Oklahoma Ave., ☎ 405/282–1281.)

Oklahoma City, 20 mi south of Guthrie, is making a slow recovery from the 1995 bombing of the Murrah Federal Building, which destroyed or damaged scores of buildings downtown. The chain-link fence blocking off the site has become part of the city's landscape, as visitors tuck notes, flowers, T-shirts, and other remembrances into its wires. Bricktown, a restaurant-and-entertainment district, is bustling, but other attractions are outside the downtown area.

A walk through the **Crystal Bridge Tropical Conservatory,** a glass botanical tube at the **Myriad Botanical Gardens** (⊠ 301 W. Reno Ave.,

☎ 405/297–3995), takes visitors through habitats ranging from desert to rain forest, complete with a 35-ft waterfall.

Most Oklahoma City attractions are found east and north of downtown, including the limestone-and-granite **Oklahoma State Capitol** (⊠ N.E. 23rd St. and Lincoln Blvd., ☎ 405/521–3356), where those oil wells you see on the grounds aren't just for show; although the earliest well dried up in 1986, the remainder actually do pump oil.

A 100,000-square-ft expansion at the **National Cowboy Hall of Fame and Western Heritage Center,** (⊠ 1700 N.E. 63rd St., ☎ 405/478–2250), north of the capitol off I–44, has allowed for much more of the hall's vast collections of paintings, sculpture, and artifacts to be exhibited. The new Children's Corral gives hands-on experience with bedrolls, saddles, lariats, and the like.

Machine-made mists and a waterfall at the **Oklahoma City Zoological Park** (⊠ 2101 N.E. 50th St., ☎ 405/424–3344) help create a natural habitat for western lowland gorillas, orangutans, and chimpanzees. The new 4.2-acre Cat Forest is home to a pride of lions, snow leopards, and other wild cats.

Thoroughbred and quarter-horse pari-mutuel races are scheduled at **Remington Park** (⊠ 1 Remington Pl., ☎ 405/424–9000 or 800/456–9000) in fall, spring, and summer. It's closed Tuesday; call ahead for race dates and reservations.

Four roller coasters, faux saloons and livery stables, and staged gunfights entertain visitors at **Frontier City Theme Park,** a 70-acre western-style amusement park. Seven musical and entertainment revues play daily from Memorial Day to Labor Day. ⊠ *11501 N.E. Expressway,* ☎ *405/478–2412. Closed weekdays Sept.–May.*

Dining and Lodging

In Oklahoma City, the Bricktown neighborhood, a renovated warehouse section downtown, is a favorite dining spot for locals. Western Avenue north of 50th Street is known as Restaurant Row; the trendiest new places debut there. For price ranges *see* Chart 1 (B) *in* On the Road with Fodor's.

Oklahoma City hotels offer few surprises. The more expensive ones have restaurants, clubs, and lounges, but rooms generally differ little from those in moderately priced establishments. If you don't plan to spend a lot of time at the hotel, you may be better off stopping at one of the chain motels along the highways. For price ranges *see* Chart 2 (B) *in* On the Road with Fodor's.

Ames

$$$ ☷ **Island Guest Ranch.** At this 2,800-acre working ranch 90 mi north
★ of Oklahoma City, guests help herd cattle, ride horses, fish, hike, and attend staged powwows and team roping and penning in the ranch's own rodeo arena. Rooms, each with private bath, are in two rustic bunkhouses; hearty meals are served in the main log lodge. Rates include all meals and activities; reservations should be made at least several weeks in advance. The owners will meet you at the airport on request. ⊠ *Ames 73718,* ☎ *405/753–4574 or 800/928–4574,* ℻ *405/753–4574. 10 rooms. MC, V. Closed Oct.–Mar.*

Guthrie

$$ ✕ **Granny Had One.** Though this is both an antiques store and tearoom, the menu is the main draw: It offers everything from peanut-butter-and-jelly sandwiches to smoked salmon to steak, with homemade soups and bread a specialty. ⊠ *113 W. Harrison St.,* ☎ *405/282–4482. AE, D, DC, MC, V.*

$$ ✕ **Blue Belle Saloon and Restaurant.** Cowboy movie star Tom Mix tended bar in this corner tavern before he went to Hollywood. Today the bar has an extensive sandwich and salad menu, along with steaks, pork chops, crab legs, and, for dessert, cobbler. ⊠ *224 W. Harrison,* ☎ *405/282–6660. AE, DC, MC, V.*

Oklahoma City

$$$ ✕ **Coach House.** The dark-wood-paneled walls of this small, cozy
★   restaurant are covered with images of the hunt, a theme reflected in the menu, which features pheasant, quail, and venison. Other specialties include scallops with roasted corn cakes, and, for dessert, individual chocolate cakes. ⊠ *6437 Avondale Dr.,* ☎ *405/842–1000. AE, MC, V.*

$$ ✕ **Bricktown Brewery.** Even the shrimp are steamed in beer in this airy brew pub, where blowups of historical photographs are displayed against exposed brick. Land Run Lager and Copperhead Ale complement the chicken pot pie, fish-and-chips, and bratwurst. ⊠ *1 Oklahoma Ave.,* ☎ *405/232–2739. AE, DC, MC, V.*

$$ ✕ **Cattlemen's Steakhouse.** Beef is the star attraction at this classic steak
★   house, where diners are surrounded by western murals and paraphernalia such as cattle-branding irons. Spur-wearing cowboys frequent the restaurant, which is in the heart of Stockyards City. ⊠ *1309 S. Agnew Ave.,* ☎ *405/236–0416. AE, D, DC, MC, V.*

$$$ 🏨 **Clarion Hotel and Conference Center.** The furnishings from Jimmy and Tammy Faye Bakker's bankrupt Christian theme park and hotel have found a home here: Expect turndown service, lighted makeup mirrors, and lots of maroons, mauves, and pinks. The hotel is conveniently close to museums and the capitol. ⊠ *4345 N. Lincoln Blvd., 73105,* ☎ *405/528–2741 or 800/741–2741,* 𝐅𝐀𝐗 *405/525–8185. 68 rooms. Restaurant, lounge, pool, tennis courts. AE, D, DC, MC, V.*

$$$ 🏨 **Medallion Hotel.** Rooms at this 15-story glass-and-stone building in the heart of downtown are furnished in soothing neutrals. ⊠ *1 N. Broadway, 73102,* ☎ *405/235–2780,* 𝐅𝐀𝐗 *405/272–0369. 399 rooms. Restaurant, lounge, pool. AE, D, DC, MC, V.*

$ 🏨 **Comfort Inn.** This motel shares its restaurant and lounge with the more luxurious Clarion Hotel, but rooms here can be as much as a third cheaper. ⊠ *4445 N. Lincoln Blvd., 73105,* ☎ *405/528–6511,* 𝐅𝐀𝐗 *405/ 525–8185. 240 rooms. Restaurant, lounge, pool. AE, D, DC, MC, V.*

$$ 🏨 **Montford Inn Bed and Breakfast.** Native American collectibles and
★   football memorabilia (the University of Oklahoma is nearby) mix elegantly with antiques in this supremely comfortable inn. Rooms are equipped with fireplaces, jetted tubs, writing desks, king-size beds, televisions tucked inside armoires, and coffeepots. A two-bedroom cottage is similarly appointed and equipped with a kitchenette. ⊠ *322 W. Tonhawa, Norman 73069,* ☎ *405/321–2200 or 800/321–8969,* 𝐅𝐀𝐗 *405/321–8347. 10 rooms. AE, D, MC, V.*

Motels

🏨 **Motel 6** has several locations. Among the best: **Airport** (⊠ 820 S. Meridian, 73108, ☎ 405/946–6662, 𝐅𝐀𝐗 405/946–4058), 128 rooms, pool; **North** (⊠ 11900 N.E. Expressway, 73131, ☎ 405/478–8666, 𝐅𝐀𝐗 405/478–7442), 101 rooms, pool. Both are inexpensive (*$*).

Shopping

The **Choctaw Indian Trading Post** (⊠ 1520 N. Portland St., ☎ 405/ 947–2490) is a good source for Native American artifacts, art, and crafts. The **Route 66** gallery and gift shop (⊠ 50 Penn Pl., 5000 N.

Pennsylvania Ave., ☎ 405/848–6166) sells jewelry and sculpture by regional artists, plus T-shirts, caps, and calendars commemorating the old highway's neon glory days.

NORTHEASTERN OKLAHOMA

The Ozark Mountains lap over from Arkansas into northeastern Oklahoma to form the Grand Lake O' the Cherokees region. The infamous Cherokee Trail of Tears—along which thousands of Cherokee traveled in the 1830s when they were forcibly resettled from their Georgia homes—ended here. And with a dozen more Native American tribes headquartered here, powwows and tribal museums are plentiful. Today tribal governments are vital once again, and Native American art, language, and customs are actively being preserved.

Visitor Information

Tahlequah: Chamber of Commerce (✉ 123 E. Delaware St., 74464, ☎ 918/456–3742). **Tulsa:** Visitor Information Center and Chamber of Commerce (✉ 616 S. Boston St., 74119, ☎ 918/585–1201).

Arriving and Departing

By Plane

Tulsa International Airport (☎ 918/838–5000), 10 mi northeast of downtown Tulsa, is served by major domestic airlines. Average cab fare to the downtown area is about $12. Major hotels have shuttle bus service.

By Car

In Tulsa I–44 and I–244 form a downtown loop. The Keystone, Cherokee, and Broken Arrow expressways also lead downtown. From Tulsa U.S. 75 leads north to the Bartlesville area. I–44 is the main route northeast from Tulsa and connects with many smaller, more scenic highways. A 400-mi segment of the old Route 66 travels through Oklahoma; the 100-mi leg that connects with I–35 north of Oklahoma City and I–44 just west of Tulsa is the easiest to follow. Watch for old gas stations, shady city parks, and tiny grocery stores in towns such as Chandler and Sapulpa. Route 66 parallels I–44 northeast of Tulsa, where classic landmarks include **Arrowood Trading Post** (✉ 2700 N. Old Highway 66, Catoosa, ☎ 918/266–3663). The **Buffalo Ranch** (✉ 1 mi north of Afton on Rte. 66, ☎ 918/257–4544) is classic Route 66 kitsch, with a bison herd out back and a huge selection of souvenirs.

By Bus

Greyhound Lines (✉ 317 S. Detroit St., ☎ 800/231–2222) serves Tulsa.

Exploring Northeastern Oklahoma

The oil money that built **Tulsa** in the 1920s left a legacy of Art Deco architecture second in size only to that of Miami, Florida; stop by the chamber of commerce (☞ Visitor Information, *above*) for a walking-tour map that includes more than a dozen downtown buildings. About 3 mi from the downtown area is the **Gilcrease Museum** (✉ 1400 Gilcrease Museum Rd., ☎ 918/596–2700). Its collection, dedicated to western art and Americana, includes paintings by such artists as Frederic Remington and James McNeill Whistler, as well as a wide-ranging selection of Native American art and artifacts. A few miles southeast of downtown is the **Philbrook Museum of Art** (✉ 2727 S. Rockford Rd., ☎ 918/749–7941), where a wide-ranging collection is housed inside the Italianate villa of former oil baron Waite Phillips.

686

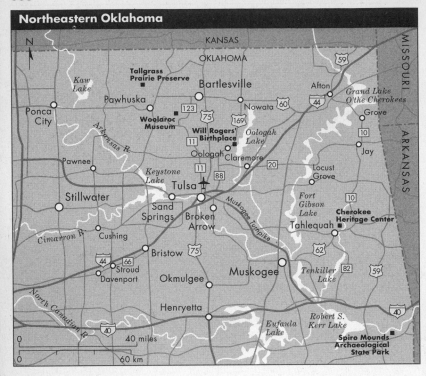

Northeastern Oklahoma

Northwest of Tulsa and 8 mi north of Pawhuska on the Tallgrass Prairie Drive is the **Tallgrass Prairie Reserve** (☎ 918/287–4803), a 52,000-acre swath of unbroken tallgrass prairie that is home to a bison herd, a cowboy bunkhouse, and hiking trails.

From Pawhuska take Route 60 east to Route 123 through the **Prairie Wild Horse Refuge** (☎ 918/336–1564), home to 1,200 horses, which travelers can spot on either side of the highway.

★ Also on Route 123 is **Woolaroc,** perhaps the top attraction in the state. It includes a drive-through wildlife preserve, where bison and 40 other species roam (visitors must remain in their vehicles). The preserve surrounds a museum packed with western lore: gun and rifle exhibits; Native American artifacts; western art, including works by Remington and Russell; and such memorabilia as Theodore Roosevelt's saddle. The historic Woolaroc Lodge, formerly used by oilman Frank Phillips, is filled with every animal trophy imaginable. ⊠ *Box 1647, Bartlesville 74005,* ☎ *918/336–0307. Closed Mon. Sept.–May.*

Southeast of Woolaroc by way of Nowata lies the Dog Iron Ranch and **Will Rogers Birthplace** (⊠ 2 mi east of Oologah, ☎ 918/275–4201). The great humorist's childhood home, built in 1875, is a two-story log-and-clapboard structure containing period furnishings; you'll also find Longhorn cattle and barnyard animals on the grounds of the working ranch. On Route 88 in Claremore is the sandstone **Will Rogers Memorial** (☎ 800/324–9455), where Rogers and members of his family are buried; it also has memorabilia, a theater that shows Rogers's movies and newsreels, and a hands-on children's museum.

Take I–44 and U.S. 59 to **Grove** and the **Grand Lake O' the Cherokees.** Numerous recreational options here include a dinner cruise or sightseeing tour aboard the *Cherokee Queen* riverboat (☎ 918/786–4272).

About 50 mi south of Grove on Route 10 is **Tahlequah,** home to the Cherokee Nation. The **Cherokee Heritage Center,** 3 mi south of Tahlequah off U.S. 62, offers daily evening performances of the drama *Trail of Tears;* the **Cherokee National Museum/Adams Corner** here includes a re-creation of the 16th-century Cherokee village Tsa-La-Gi. ⊠ *Willis Rd.,* ☎ *918/456–6007. Closed Sun. June–Aug., weekends Sept.–May.*

Southwest of Tahlequah on U.S. 62 is **Okmulgee,** whose sandstone **Creek Council House** (⊠ 106 W. 6th St., ☎ 918/756–2324), on a shady square, has been meticulously restored. The two-story structure was the center of Creek political life from 1878 until the turn of the century, when tribal governments were liquidated. It's now a museum, a library, and a center for the preservation of the Creek language.

Dining and Lodging

Tulsa probably has the best dining in the state, and you'll look hard to find any restaurants that qualify as expensive. Outside the city there are always the fast food chains; a better option may be to pack a picnic lunch. Tulsa also offers a fair number of comfortable though unexciting hotels. For price ranges *see* Charts 1 (B) and 2 (B) *in* On the Road with Fodor's.

$ ★ ✕ **Nelson's Buffeteria.** This lively, old-fashioned lunchroom shows off 1940s decor and the best chicken-fried steak in town. Food is served cafeteria style. ⊠ *514 S. Boston St.,* ☎ *918/584–9969. No credit cards. Closed weekends. No dinner.*

$$$ ✕▦ **Adam's Mark Hotel.** Next door to the Performing Arts Center, this plush hotel is connected to a shopping mall with an indoor ice-skating rink. Each room has a stocked minibar and tiny balcony. The staff is considered the best in Tulsa. Bravo Ristorante, in the hotel's dining room, offers traditional Italian cuisine served by a wait staff of both professional and student vocalists who deliver arias with your meal. ⊠ *100 E. 2nd St., 74103,* ☎ *918/582–9000 or 800/444–2326,* ℻ *918/560–2261. 468 rooms. Restaurant, 2 lounges, indoor and outdoor pools, exercise room. AE, D, DC, MC, V.*

$$$ ✕▦ **Doubletree Inn Downtown.** Visitors are welcomed with chocolate chip cookies in this modern high-rise. The Grille draws a crowd with its innovative southwestern cuisine. A skywalk connects the hotel to the Tulsa Convention Center. ⊠ *616 W. 7th St., 74127,* ☎ *918/587–8000,* ℻ *918/587–1642. 449 rooms. 2 restaurants, bar, indoor pool, spa. AE, D, DC, MC, V.*

Motels

▦ **Best Western Trade Winds Central Motor Hotel** (⊠ 3141 E. Skelly Dr., 74135, ☎ 918/749–5561, ℻ 918/749–6312), 167 rooms, lounge, exercise room, pool; *$$.* ▦ **Motel 6** (⊠ 1011 S. Garnett Rd., 74128, ☎ 918/234–6200, ℻ 918/234–9421), 153 rooms, pool; (⊠ 5828 W. Skelly Dr., 74107, ☎ 918/445–0223, ℻ 918/445–2750), 155 rooms, pool; *$.*

Campgrounds

Lake Tenkiller State Park (⊠ HCR 68, Box 1095, Vian 74962, ☎ 918/489–5643) has secluded cabins and campgrounds overlooking a limestone-lined lake. The cabins and shelters at **Osage Hills State Park** (⊠ Red Eagle Rte., Box 84, Pawhuska 74056, ☎ 918/336–4141) were built in the '30s by the Civilian Conservation Corps on rolling hills covered with blackjack oak. **Sequoyah State Park** (⊠ Rte. 1, Box 198–3, Hulbert 74441, ☎ 918/772–2046) offers camping with a swimming beach, marina, and heated pool; 54 cabins; and a 101-room lodge (☎ 918/772–2545).

The Arts

Tulsa's downtown **Performing Arts Center** (✉ 110 E. 2nd St., ☎ 918/596–7122) is a hub for the city's active cultural scene. The **Tulsa Ballet Theatre** (✉ 4512 S. Peoria Ave., ☎ 918/749–6006) is a nationally acclaimed company that performs from September through April. The **Tulsa Philharmonic** (✉ 2901 S. Harvard Ave., ☎ 918/747–7445), whose season runs September–May, and the **Tulsa Opera** (✉ 1610 S. Boulder, ☎ 918/582–4035), running November–April, hold most of their performances at the Performing Arts Center downtown.

Outdoor Activities and Sports

Fishing

Tulsa World's sports section has up-to-date fishing information, or check with the **Department of Wildlife and Conservation** (☎ 405/521–2221). Fishing licenses can be purchased in most tackle shops.

Hiking and Backpacking

Every park in the area has hiking trails. For general information call the **Tourism and Recreation Department** (☞ Statewide Visitor Information, *above*).

Shopping

Cherry Street, a six-block stretch between Utica and Peoria avenues along 15th Street in Tulsa, is home to antiques stores, bars, bakeries, and sandwich shops.

SOUTHWESTERN OKLAHOMA

The frontier doesn't seem far away in this rugged, sparsely populated region; oceans of grass are broken by blue granite mountains, and almost every small town has a saddle shop. During the 19th century this was the domain of the buffalo and the Kiowa and Comanche tribes; travelers may still spot Native American tepees and brush arbors in rural areas during the summer.

Visitor Information

Lawton: Chamber of Commerce (✉ Box 1376, 73502, ☎ 405/355–3541).

Arriving and Departing

By Bus

Greyhound Lines (✉ 15 N.E. 20th St., ☎ 800/231–2222) serves Lawton.

By Car

As with the rest of the state, you'll need a car to tour this region. Most of the area falls between I–44 and I–40 southwest of Oklahoma City; U.S. and state highways on our tour connect with these interstates.

By Plane

The **Will Rogers World Airport** (☞ Central Oklahoma, *above*) gives the best access to the region.

Exploring Southwestern Oklahoma

At the foot of the Wichita Mountains, **Lawton** makes a good base for exploring the region. The **Museum of the Great Plains** (✉ 601 Ferris

Ave., ☏ 405/581–3460) has a reproduction trading post and an outdoor fort recalling the pre–Louisiana Purchase days when the Red River was the international border with Spain.

A short drive north of Lawton on I–44 brings you to the **Fort Sill Military Reservation** (✉ Key Gate off Sheridan Rd., ☏ 405/442–8111 or 405/351–5123), built in 1869 for the Native Americans of the southern plains. Seven original buildings contain exhibits on the fort's history. Geronimo's Guardhouse is named for the famous Chiricahua Apache warrior, who died at the fort in 1909 as a prisoner of war. The Fort Sill Apache Tribe dances the Apache fire dance here in September.

Just north of Lawton I–44 crosses U.S. 49, which runs along the northern border of Fort Sill and westward to the **Wichita Mountains Wildlife Refuge,** one of the most beautiful areas in the state. Here the wildlife is thick and the scenery—boulder-topped mountains overlooking clear, still lakes—often breathtaking. The refuge is home to bison, Longhorn cattle, and other species. The best rock climbing and mountain biking in the state are to be found here; hiking trails are abundant and camping is allowed, but backcountry camping and biking are by permit only. ✉ Rte. 1, Indiahoma, ☏ 405/429–3222. Guided tours by reservation.

From the western end of the Wichita Mountains Wildlife Refuge, U.S. 54 and 62 lead southwest to Altus. From here travel north on U.S. 283/Route 44 to **Quartz Mountain State Park** (✉ Lone Wolf, ☏ 405/563–2238). A state-run lodge is being rebuilt following a fire, but the scenery alone is worth the trip—bare rock outcroppings reflected in pristine Altus Lake and abundant wildflowers in spring. You can also explore caves, visit the park's nature center, or take advantage of the guided tours and special programs offered throughout the year.

Dining and Lodging

This is not an area where either cuisine or accommodations shines. When possible, pack lunches for park picnic; at night you'll probably have to content yourself with chain restaurants. Unless you plan to camp, your hotel will probably be little more than a convenient base for exploring a fascinating region. For price ranges see Charts 1 (B) and 2 (B) in On the Road with Fodor's.

Altus

$$ 🏨 **Best Western.** Popular with business travelers, this hotel offers a number of rooms with refrigerators and two phones. ✉ 2804 N. Main St., 73521, ☏ 405/482–9300, ⨳ 405/482–2245. 104 rooms. Lounge, refrigerators, indoor pool. AE, D, DC, MC, V.

Lawton

$ ✕ **Woody's BBQ.** Enjoy pork ribs or beef brisket in one of two rustic
★ dining rooms featuring ceiling fans and wood trim. Side dishes include okra, fried mushrooms, and "wood chips" (fried potatoes with melted cheese and bacon). ✉ 1107 W. Lee Blvd., ☏ 405/355–4950. MC, V.

$$ 🏨 **Howard Johnson Lodge and Convention Center.** The public areas of this low-rise stucco hotel just off I–44 have eclectic decor ranging from Victorian-style frosted glass to a rustic chandelier of antlers. Whirlpool suites have high-tech glass and chrome. ✉ 1125 E. Gore St., 73501, ☏ 405/353–0200, ⨳ 405/353–6801. 144 rooms. Restaurant, indoor pool, tennis courts. AE, D, DC, MC, V.

Meers

$ ✕ **Meers Store.** All that's left of a boomtown that grew up during a brief gold rush in 1901 are this eatery and a federal seismographic station by the cash register. The restaurant's claim to fame is not gold but the Meersburger—a 7-inch burger made of 100% Longhorn beef. ⊠ *Rte. 115, 4 mi east of the Wichita Mountains Wildlife Refuge,* ☎ *405/ 429–8051. No credit cards.*

Motels
🏨 **Hospitality Inn** (⊠ 202 E. Lee St., Lawton 73501, ☎ 405/355–9765, FAX 405/355–2360), 130 rooms, pool, laundry; *$.* 🏨 **Ramada Inn** (⊠ 601 N. 2nd St., Lawton 73507, ☎ 405/355–7155, FAX 405/353– 6162), 98 rooms, restaurant, lounge, pool; *$.*

Campgrounds
Quartz Mountain State Park (☞ Exploring Southwestern Oklahoma, *above*) has camping facilities. For camping information on other state parks in the area, contact the state tourism department (☞ Statewide Visitor Information, *above*).

Outdoor Activities and Sports

Fishing
The best bets are Altus Lake or any of the lakes at the Wichita Mountains Wildlife Refuge (☞ Exploring Southwestern Oklahoma, *above*). The sports section in the *Daily Oklahoman* has fishing reports for the lakes in the area, or contact the **Department of Wildlife and Conservation** (☎ 405/521–3855).

Hiking and Backpacking
Check specific parks (☞ National and State Parks, *above*) or contact the **Tourism and Recreation Department** (☞ Statewide Visitor Information, *above*).

SOUTHEASTERN OKLAHOMA

Home to the Choctaw Tribe since the 1830s, the green and hilly southeastern corner of the state seems a world apart from the rest of Oklahoma. Here are pine and hardwood forests, populated by plentiful game and traversed by fast-running mountain streams. Outdoor enthusiasts will most appreciate this part of the state, where food, lodging, and entertainment tend toward the rustic.

Visitor Information

Kiamichi Country: Regional Tourism Association (⊠ Box 638, Wilburton, 74578, ☎ 918/465–2367 or 800/722–8180).

Arriving and Departing

By Bus
Greyhound Lines offers bus service to Wilburton and Idabel (☎ 800/ 231–2222).

By Car
Much of southeastern Oklahoma is accessible only by two-lane roads. From I–40E near Sallisaw U.S. 259 takes travelers south. From I–35S take U.S. 70 west.

By Plane
The **Will Rogers World Airport** (☎ 405/681–5311) in southwest Oklahoma City offers the best access to the northern Ouachita National Forest area. Extreme southeastern Oklahoma is closer to Dallas and the **Dallas–Fort Worth International Airport** (☎ 214/574–6720).

Getting Around Southeastern Oklahoma

This sprawling, mountainous region requires a car. Highways are generally well marked, but navigating along winding mountain roads can require patience and a little extra time.

Exploring Southeastern Oklahoma

Spectacular views can be seen from the **Talimena Scenic Byway,** marked SH−1 and running east−west through the heart of the Ouachita National Forest. The highway extends west into the Sans Bois Mountain area and intersects with southbound U.S. 259, which takes travelers into the Kiamichi Mountains.

U.S. 59, south from I−40E, takes visitors to the **Overstreet-Kerr Living History Farm** (✉ Rte. 2, Box 693, Keota, 74941, ☎ 918/966−3396), where century-old strains of livestock and crops are being preserved. A three-story farmhouse, the former home of a prosperous farmer and his Choctaw wife, is also open for tours.

U.S. 59 intersects with SH−9, the road to Spiro and **Spiro Mounds Archaeological State Park** (✉ Rte. 2, Box 339AA, 74959, ☎ 918/962−2062). Once the headquarters of a confederation of 60 tribes, the park—which is closed Monday and Tuesday—contains remains of 11 earthen mounds used as dwellings by the Spiro, an ancient people who lived here from about AD 600 to 1450. A 1½-mi trail runs alongside the mounds, and a visitor center contains artifacts.

Southwest of Spiro is Wilburton and **Robbers Cave State Park** (✉ Box 9, 74578, ☎ 918/465−2562), where a cave hidden in 100-ft sandstone bluffs is said to have been a hideout for such notorious outlaws as the Daltons and the James Gang. Steps have been carved into the rock, and guided tours, complete with colorful tales, are conducted by a park naturalist.

No development has been allowed in the 26,445-acre **Winding Stair National Recreation Area** (✉ HC 64, Box 3467, Heavener 74937, ☎ 918/653−2991), but there are plenty of picnic areas and easy trails within a short distance of the Talimena Scenic Byway. The scenic byway intersects with U.S. 259, which takes travelers south to **Beavers Bend Resort Park** (✉ Box 10, Broken Bow 74728, ☎ 405/494−6300). Built on the Mountain Fork River at the edge of the Ouachita National Forest, the park is so secluded that wild turkeys have been spotted strolling on the resort's golf fairways. The history and culture of the forest from prehistoric times to the present are interpreted at the park's **Forest Heritage Center** (☎ 405/494−6497).

Dining and Lodging

Lodging is decidedly rustic in southeast Oklahoma, and room service is virtually nonexistent. Many restaurants close by 9 PM. For price ranges *see* Chart 1 (B) *in* On the Road with Fodor's.

Hochatown

$ ✕ **Stevens Gap Restaurant.** Here you can sample regional specialties like catfish fillets served with hush puppies and baked sweet potatoes or southern-fried chicken, fried okra, and brown beans. You can also get breakfast (biscuits, gravy, and the works) all day long. ✉ *U.S. 259 and Stevens Gap Rd.,* ☎ *405/494−6350. No credit cards.*

$$$ 🏨 **Lakeview Lodge.** Every room at this state-operated lodge has a bal-
★ cony view of Broken Bow Lake and the pristine wilderness. A full break-
fast is served in the lodge's Great Room, where a fire roars in a native
stone fireplace when weather warrants. ⊠ *U.S. 259 (Box 10), Broken
Bow 74728,* ☎ *405/494–6179,* ℻ *405/494–6179. 40 rooms. Break-
fast room, golf course. AE, D, DC, MC, V.*

Krebs

$$ ✕ **Pete's Place.** Pete Prichard started selling sandwiches and illicit
★ "Choc" beer—named for the Choctaws who lived in the area—out of
his house in 1925; now his grandchildren operate a sprawling restaurant with a (legal) microbrewery and 15 private dining rooms clustered
around three main dining areas. ⊠ *120 S.W. 8th St.,* ☎ *918/423–2042.
No lunch Mon.–Sat.; no dinner Sun. AE, D, DC, MC, V.*

Octavia

$$$ 🏨 **Eagle Creek Guest Cottages.** Seven cottages are spread out over 40
acres on the backside of a mountain; some are on the banks of Big Eagle
Creek or on a private lake. Some of the pine-and-calico cabins have
native stone fireplaces, whirlpools, and big back porches. All have full
kitchens, VCRs, microwave ovens, televisions, and great views. ⊠
U.S. 259 (HC 15, Box 250), Smithville 74957, ☎ *405/254–7597. 7
cottages. VCRs, kitchens. AE, D, DC, MC, V.*

Wilburton

$$ 🏨 **Belle Starr View Lodge.** Overlooking a valley in Robbers Cave State
Park, the lodge has comfortable rooms with color TVs but no phones.
Breakfast requires a bit of a hike to the park restaurant. ⊠ *Rte. 2 (Box
9), Wilburton* ☎ *918/465–2562,* ℻ *918/465–5763. 20 rooms. AE,
D, DC, MC, V.*

Outdoor Activities and Sports

Boating and Fishing

Mountain Fork River is stocked with rainbow trout; there are brown trout
in the Lower Mountain Fork. The required trout-fishing stamp is ob-
tainable at park offices and bait shops. The Mountain Fork River is also
popular with canoeists. **Beavers Bend River Floats** (⊠ Rte. 4, 11–7, Broken Bow, ☎ 405/494–6070) rents canoes and provides transportation.
WW Trading Post and Canoes (⊠ R.R. 1, Box 532, ☎ 405/584–6856)
rents fly-fishing equipment and supplies, along with canoes.

Hiking and Backpacking

The **Ouachita Trail,** a 46-mi hiking and horse trail through the Ouachita National Forest, was pieced together from bison paths, military
roads, and centuries-old footpaths. Backcountry camping is allowed
all along the trail; numerous campgrounds have also been established.
For maps and information contact the Choctaw Ranger District (⊠
HC 64, Box 3467, Heavener 74937, ☎ 918/653–2991).

SOUTH DAKOTA

By Doug
Cunningham

Updated by
Tom Griffith

Capital	Pierre
Population	732,000
Motto	Great Faces, Great Places
State Bird	Chinese ring-necked pheasant
State Flower	Pasqueflower
Postal Abbreviation	SD

Statewide Visitor Information

South Dakota Department of Tourism (⊠ 711 E. Wells Ave., Pierre 57501, ☎ 800/732–5682) makes available state highway maps and the annual *South Dakota Vacation Guide* free of charge. Call the **Department of Transportation** for maps of summer road construction (☎ 605/773–3571) and winter road-condition reports (☎ 605/773–3536).

Scenic Drives

The beautiful **Needles Highway** (Route 87) offers views of spectacular needle-sharp granite spires. **Iron Mountain Road** (U.S. 16A) has views of Mt. Rushmore over pigtail bridges and through tunnels. Both highways run through Custer State Park (☞ National and State Parks, *below*). U.S. 14A follows scenic **Spearfish Canyon.**

National and State Parks

National Parks

For **Badlands National Park** and **Black Hills National Forest,** *see* The West, *below.* **Jewel Cave National Monument,** 53 mi southwest of Rapid City on U.S. 16 (⊠ R.R. 1, Box 60AA, Custer 57730, ☎ 605/673–2288), gets its name from the calcite crystals lining the walls of one of the world's longest caves. Scenic, historic, and spelunking tours are offered June–August. **Wind Cave National Park,** 50 mi south of Rapid City on U.S. 385 (⊠ R.R. 1, Box 190, Hot Springs 57747, ☎ 605/745–4600), is 28,000 acres of prairie and forest above one of the world's longest caves with perhaps the world's best collection of box work—a honeycomb-like calcite formation. Five different guided tours are offered daily June–August.

State Parks

South Dakota's state park system encompasses 13 parks. The crown
★ jewel is **Custer State Park** (⊠ HC 83, Box 70, Custer 57730, ☎ 605/255–4464 or 800/710–2267 for campground reservations), which has 73,000 spectacular acres of grasslands and pine-covered hills that are home to bison, deer, bighorn sheep, prairie dogs, and pronghorn.

THE BLACK HILLS, DEADWOOD, AND THE BADLANDS

Unlike the agricultural eastern half of the state, this is a land of prairies, pine forests, and desolate, rocky landscapes. It's also where most of the state's tourists go—to visit such places as Deadwood, the 19th-century mining town turned gambling mecca, and Mt. Rushmore, where the stern grandeur of those giant carvings of four presidents on its face remains after more than 50 years.

Affordable Adventures (⊠ Box 546, Rapid City 57709, ☎ 605/342–7691, FAX 605/341–4614) specializes in individual and group tours to many of western South Dakota's most scenic and historical locations, including Rapid City, Mt. Rushmore, Custer State Park, Crazy Horse Memorial, Badlands National Park, Wounded Knee, and Pine Ridge.

Visitor Information

Black Hills, Badlands and Lakes Association (⊠ 900 Jackson Blvd., Rapid City 57702, ☎ 605/341–1462, FAX 605/341–4614). **Deadwood Visitors Bureau** (⊠ 3 Siever St., 57732, ☎ 605/578–1102 or 888/433–2396). **Rapid City:** Chamber of Commerce and Convention & Visitors Bureau (⊠ Civic Center, Box 747, 444 N. Mt. Rushmore Rd., 57709, ☎ 605/343–1744 or 800/487–3223, FAX 605/348–9217). **Wall:** USDA Forest Service Buffalo Gap National Grasslands Visitor Center (⊠ Box 425, 57790, ☎ 605/279–2125) has 24 exhibits informing travelers on local history, flora and fauna, and activities in the national grasslands, including rockhounding.

Arriving and Departing

By Bus
Gray Line of the Black Hills (⊠ Box 1106, Rapid City 57709, ☎ 605/342–4461) offers bus tours of the region, including trips to Mt. Rushmore and Black Hills National Forest. **Jack Rabbit Lines** (⊠ 301 N. Dakota, Sioux Falls 57102, ☎ 800/444–6287) serves Wall, Rapid City, Mitchell, and Pierre, the capital.

By Car
Unless you are traveling with a package tour, a car is essential here. Make rental reservations early; Rapid City has a large number of business travelers, and rental agencies are often booked. I–90 bisects the state slightly south of its center; it leads to Wall and Rapid City. From Rapid City U.S. 14 leads to towns and attractions in the northern part of the Black Hills, while U.S. 16 winds through its southern half. Route 44 is an alternate route between the Black Hills and the Badlands. The Black Hills have seven tunnels with limited clearance; they are marked on state maps and in the state's tourism booklet.

By Plane
Rapid City Regional Airport (☎ 605/393–9924), 10 mi southeast of downtown via Route 44, is served by Northwest Airlines, Skywest (a Delta connection), and United Express.

Exploring the Black Hills, Deadwood, and the Badlands

The Black Hills
As with the rest of the state, many of the region's attractions are open only in the summer; be sure to call ahead before you visit. To the locals **Rapid City** is West River, meaning west of the Missouri. South Dakota's second-largest city, this cross between western town and progressive community is a good base from which to explore the Black Hills. Cowboy boots are common here, and business leaders often travel by pickup truck or four-wheel-drive vehicle. Yet the city supports a convention center and a modern, acoustically advanced performance hall and has more than its share of bookstores downtown, along with a modern shopping mall on the outskirts.

The **Journey** (⊠ 222 New York St., near the Rushmore Plaza Civic Center, ☎ 605/394–6923), a new museum that opened in May 1997, combines the collections of the **Sioux Indian Museum**, the **Minnilusa Pioneer Museum**, the **Museum of Geology**, the **State Archaeological**

Research Center, and a private collection of American Indian artifacts into a sweeping pageant of the history and evolution of the Black Hills. In Box Elder, just outside Rapid City, is the **South Dakota Air & Space Museum** (⌧ 2890 Davis Dr., ¾ mi north of I–90 Exit 66, ☎ 605/385–5188). Outside the Ellsworth Air Force Base (base tours offered in summer), it displays a model of a Stealth bomber that's 60% actual size, General Dwight D. Eisenhower's Mitchell B-25 bomber, and numerous other planes, as well as a once-operational missile silo.

The vast **Black Hills National Forest** (⌧ R.R. 2, Box 200, Custer 57730, ☎ 605/673–2251) covers 1.3 million acres on the state's western

★ edge. Its most famous attraction is Keystone's **Mt. Rushmore National Memorial** (⌧ 21 mi southwest of Rapid City on U.S. 16, ☎ 605/574–2523), the granite cliff where the faces of Presidents Washington, Jefferson, Lincoln, and Theodore Roosevelt are carved. Sculptor Gutzon Borglum labored at this monumental task for more than 14 years; it was finally finished by his son, Lincoln, in 1941. The memorial is spectacular in the morning light and at night, when a special lighting ceremony (June–mid-September) dramatically illuminates the carving.

Also in Keystone, the **Rushmore-Borglum Story** museum (⌧ 342 Winter St., ☎ 605/666–4448) contains newsreel footage of the original blasting of the rock face, as well as exhibits and drawings about the project and its artist.

Nineteen miles southwest of Keystone on U.S.16/385, another monu-

★ mental likeness is emerging; when finished, the **Crazy Horse Memorial** (☎ 605/673–4681) will depict the Lakota warrior who defeated General Custer at Little Bighorn. The site includes a visitor center and the **Indian Museum of North America.** Expect frequent blasting at this work-in-progress, which will be the world's largest sculpture when completed.

Southeast of the Crazy Horse Monument is **Wind Cave National Park** (☞ National and State Parks, *above*). In Lakota tradition it was from Wind Cave that the first Lakota people were tricked by *Iktomi* (spider person) into leaving their ancestral home.

Sturgis, 29 mi northwest of Rapid City via I–90, is a sleepy town of about 5,600 whose population swells to 200,000–215,000 during the first full week of August. Since 1938 the **Black Hills Motor Classic** (☎ 605/347–6570) has drawn enthusiasts from around the world; during this event many businesses turn their buildings over to sellers of leather goods, rally T-shirts, and other biker-related paraphernalia.

In Spearfish, about 45 mi northwest of Rapid City via I–90, the **Black Hills Passion Play** (☎ 605/642–2646) has since 1939 been recounting the last seven days in the life of Jesus Christ.

The films *Dances with Wolves* (which won the 1990 Academy Award for best picture) and *Thunderheart* have generated new interest—and new businesses—in the Black Hills. **Ft. Hays Film Set** (⌧ Moon Meadows Rd. and Hwy. 16, Rapid City, ☎ 605/394–9653) displays photos and shows a video taken during the making of *Dances with Wolves.* A chuck wagon dinner show is also available.

Deadwood

Following the legalization of gambling in 1989, **Deadwood**'s town planners rushed to revitalize and refurbish this once-infamous gold-mining boomtown—41 mi northwest of Rapid City—for the projected onslaught of visitors. Streets have been repaved with bricks, and Main Street utility lines have been buried in order to keep all traces of the 20th century out of view of visitors. Gaming halls and casinos now

The Black Hills

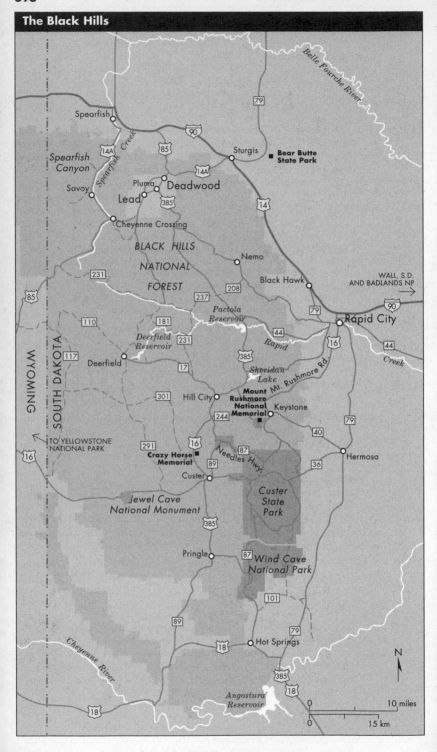

make up almost every storefront downtown; the refurbished old hotels have their own gambling rooms. If a place with gambling can be
wholesome, this is it (the maximum bet is $5), but it wasn't always so.
This is the Old West town where Wild Bill Hickok was shot during a
poker game and where Poker Alice Tubbs was famous for smoking big
cigars.

Mt. Moriah Cemetery, above Deadwood, is the final resting place for
Hickok, Calamity Jane, and other notorious Deadwood residents.
From there one has a panoramic view of Deadwood. The **Adams
Memorial Museum** (✉ 54 Sherman St., ☎ 605/578–1714) has three
floors of displays, including the first locomotive used in the Black
Hills, photographs of the town's early days, and the largest gold nugget
ever discovered in the Hills.

Lead (pronounced Leed), 50 mi north of Rapid City via I–90 and Alternate Route 14A, is a mining community born in the Black Hills gold
rush frenzy of the late 19th century. **Homestake Visitor Center** (✉ 160
W. Main St., ☎ 605/584–3110) offers surface tours of the oldest operating underground gold mine in the western hemisphere and an area
for viewing the mine's massive open cut. Free ore samples are available. The town itself contains a number of historic houses, many once
home to immigrant miners. **Black Hills Mining Museum** (✉ 323 W. Main,
☎ 605/584–1605) shows the history of mining through life-size models, video presentations, and guided tours through a simulated mine.

The Badlands

Badlands National Park (✉ Box 6, Interior 57750, ☎ 605/433–5361),
80 mi east of Rapid City off I–90, can seem like another planet. Millions of years of erosion have left these 244,000 acres with desolate
gorges, buttes, and ridges colored in rust, pink, and gold. Scenic overlooks are marked. The **Ben Reifel Visitor Center,** 2 mi north of Interior via Route 377 or from I–90 off Exit 131 or 110, offers information
and maps.

South of the park, on the Pine Ridge Indian Reservation, is the **Wounded
Knee Massacre Monument,** a commemoration on the site where more
than 300 Sioux, mostly women and children, were killed when soldiers
opened fire after a brief skirmish in 1890.

If you're traveling on I–90, you'll see the signs every few miles for **Wall
Drug** (☎ 605/279–2175), the pharmacy turned tourist mecca that enticed depression-era travelers with offers of free ice water. The store
has nearly every tourist trinket imaginable plus a restaurant seating more
than 500, the Hole-in-the-Wall Bookstore—which has an excellent selection of western literature—a chapel, a selection of knives and boots,
and western art. **Wall** itself, a sleepy community on the edge of the Badlands, has several motels and restaurants.

What to See and Do with Children

★ The fossilized remains of ancient mammoths at the **mammoth site** (✉
1 block north of the U.S. 18 Bypass, Hot Springs, ☎ 605/745–6017)
should prove fascinating to children and adults alike. The site, discovered
in 1974, is believed to contain up to 100 mammoths (51 have been
unearthed so far) in the sinkhole where they came to drink some
26,000 years ago. A visitor center is built over the area; excavation is
in progress. **Flintstones, Bedrock City** (✉ Intersection of U.S. 16 and
385, Custer, ☎ 605/673–4079) is a full-scale tribute to the enduring
cartoon characters, complete with a curio shop, a train ride, a drive-
in restaurant serving brontoburgers, and camping.

Bear Country U.S.A. (⊠ 8 mi south of Rapid City on U.S. 16, ☎ 605/343–2290) is a drive-through wildlife park featuring black bears, wolves, and most other North American wildlife, as well as a walk-through wildlife center with bear cubs, wolf pups, and other offspring. In Rapid City **Storybook Island** (⊠ Near intersection of Jackson Blvd. and Sheridan Lake Rd., ☎ 605/342–6357) lets children romp through scenes from fairy tales and nursery rhymes. **Reptile Gardens** (⊠ 6 mi south on U.S. 16, ☎ 605/342–5873) features the Bewitched Village, where a variety of animal shows are staged. Children may ride miniature horses and see giant tortoises outside in the floral gardens.

Dining and Lodging

During the summer reservations are helpful and often required to ensure lodging; calling two or three days ahead is usually adequate. For price ranges *see* Charts 1 (B) and 2 (B) *in* On the Road with Fodor's.

Deadwood

$$ ✕ **Jake's.** This fine-dining restaurant takes up the fourth floor of the Midnight Star Casino, a renovated former clothing store owned by actor Kevin Costner. (The rest of the building contains a bar and grill and a gaming hall.) Entrées are prepared by a world-class chef. ⊠ *677 Main St.,* ☎ *605/578–1555. AE, D, DC, MC, V.*

$ ✕ **Deadwood Social Club.** On the second floor of historic Saloon No. ★ 10, this warm restaurant wraps you in wood and old-time photos of Deadwood's past. Its menu stretches from free-range chicken and angel-hair pasta with exquisite sauces to melt-in-your-mouth rib eyes. Downstairs is the saloon, billed as "the only museum in the world with a bar." ⊠ *657 Main St.,* ☎ *605/578–3346. MC, V.*

$$–$$$ 🏨 **Bullock Hotel.** This 1895 hotel has been meticulously restored to its ★ ornate Victorian origins. The first floor, containing the gaming hall, has high ceilings and brass-and-crystal chandeliers. Guest rooms are furnished with Victorian reproductions and have large windows. The hotel has also opened the nearby Branch House, which offers four suites and four rooms decorated in mission-style furnishings. ⊠ *633 Main St., 57732,* ☎ *605/578–1745 or 888/428–5562,* FAX *605/578–1382. 36 rooms. Restaurant, lounge, beauty salon, massage, spa, exercise room. AE, D, MC, V.*

$$–$$$ 🏨 **The Mineral Palace Hotel & Gaming.** This is a contemporary hotel and restaurant with three gaming halls, a cappuccino bar, and a gift shop. Rooms are large and comfortable, and its royal suite hosts a Jacuzzi tub, round king-size bed, and remote-control fireplace. ⊠ *607 Main St., 57732,* ☎ *605/578–2036 or 800/847–2522,* FAX *605/578–2037. 63 rooms. Restaurant, lounge. AE, D, DC, MC, V.*

Interior

$ ✕🏨 **Cedar Pass Lodge.** In Badlands National Park, the lodge's wood-★ frame cabins with knotty pine interiors have a 1950s look. Each one- and two-bedroom cabin has a private bath. The restaurant specializes in Indian tacos (fried bread covered with traditional taco fixings). It also serves up hearty meat-and-potatoes fare. In 1997 the lodge began offering tours to the nearby Pine Ridge Reservation. ⊠ *1 Cedar St. (Box 5), Interior 57750,* ☎ *605/433–5460,* FAX *605/433–5560. 24 cabins. Restaurant. AE, D, DC, MC, V. Closed Nov.–mid-Mar.*

Rapid City

$$ ✕ **Circle B Ranch.** Chuck wagon suppers include barbecued beef, biscuits, and all the trimmings. The ranch also offers western shows and wagon rides. ⊠ *16 mi west of Rapid City on U.S. 385, 1 mi north of Rte. 44,* ☎ *605/348–7358. D, MC, V. Closed Sept.–May. No lunch.*

$$ ✕ **Firehouse Brewing Co.** This former firehouse serves up hearty fare such as marinated buffalo steak, rancher's (beef) pie, and rosemary chicken. A wide variety of beers, from light to stout, are brewed on the premises. ⊠ *610 Main St., Rapid City,* ☎ *605/348–1915. AE, D, DC, MC, V.*

$$ ✕ **Fireside Inn Restaurant & Lounge.** Seating in one of the two dining rooms here is around a huge slate fireplace. The large menu includes prime rib, seafood, and Italian dishes. ⊠ *6½ mi west of Rapid City on Rte. 44,* ☎ *605/342–3900. Reservations not accepted. MC, V.*

$$ ✕ **Flying T Chuckwagon.** At this converted barn, ranch-style meals of barbecued beef, potatoes, and baked beans are served on tin plates. Afterward, diners settle back to watch a western show featuring music and cowboy comedy. ⊠ *6 mi south of Rapid City on U.S. 16,* ☎ *605/342–1905. Reservations essential. No credit cards. Closed mid-Sept.–late May. No lunch.*

$$ ✕ **Landmark Restaurant and Lounge.** This hotel restaurant is popular for its lunch buffet and for specialties that include prime rib, beef Wellington, freshwater fish, and wild game. ⊠ *Alex Johnson Hotel, 523 6th St., Rapid City,* ☎ *605/342–1210. AE, D, DC, MC, V.*

$$ ✕ **American Pie Bistro.** Here you get an unusual combination of city sophistication and home-cooked meals, including fancied-up meat-and-potato dishes such as apricot roast chicken and rack of lamb, as well as tomato-basil shrimp. ⊠ *710 St. Joseph St., Rapid City,* ☎ *605/343–3773. AE, MC, V.*

$$–$$$ ▨ **Alex Johnson Hotel.** Western elegance pervades this nine-story hotel
★ in a historic landmark. The lobby has leather wing chairs, a soaring beamed ceiling, and a torch chandelier made of Lakota war lances. The rooms are furnished with replicas of the original furniture when the hotel opened in 1928. The hotel was officially dedicated to the Lakota Indians, so Native American patterns and artwork predominate. ⊠ *523 6th St., Rapid City 57701,* ☎ *605/342–1210 or 800/888–2539. 144 rooms. Restaurant, lounge, pub. AE, D, DC, MC, V.*

$$–$$$ ▨ **Holiday Inn Rushmore Plaza.** Opened in 1990, this eight-story hotel has a lobby with an atrium, glass elevators, and a 60-ft waterfall. Rooms have mauve and gray tones. ⊠ *505 N. 5th St., Rapid City 57701,* ☎ *605/348–4000,* ℻ *605/348–9777. 205 rooms, 46 suites. Restaurant, lounge, pool, sauna, exercise room. AE, D, DC, MC, V.*

Sturgis

$ ✕ **World Famous Roadkill Cafe.** Started by two bike-rally enthusiasts, the café promises on its Day-Glo menu to bring food "from your grill to ours!" including the "Chicken That Didn't Quite Cross the Road," "Smidgen of Pigeon," and the daily special "Guess That Mess!" These clever menu titles hide the fact that the café actually offers standard fare, from breakfast to tuna melt and buffalo and beef burgers, as well as a car-filling collection of roadkill cookbooks and novelty items. ⊠ *1333 Main St., Sturgis,* ☎ *605/347–4502. Reservations not accepted. MC, V.*

Wall

$–$$ ✕ **Cactus Family Restaurant and Lounge.** This full-menu restaurant in downtown Wall specializes in delicious hot cakes and pies. A giant roast beef buffet is offered in summer. ⊠ *519 Main St., Wall,* ☎ *605/279–2561. D, MC, V.*

$ ✕ **Elkton House Restaurant.** This comfortable restaurant with sunroom
★ and wood paneling has fast service and a terrific hot roast beef sandwich, served on white bread with gravy and mashed potatoes. ⊠ *South Blvd., Wall,* ☎ *605/279–2152. D, MC, V.*

Motel

🏨 **Badlands Budget Host Motel** (✉ HC 54, Box 115, Interior 57750, ☎ 605/433–5335 or 800/388–4643), 15 rooms, pool, playground, convenience store; closed mid-Sept.–May; $.

Campgrounds

For information on state campgrounds contact the **Department of Game, Fish, and Parks** (✉ 523 E. Capitol Ave., Pierre 57501, ☎ 605/773–3485 or 800/710–2267 for camping reservations).

Around Deadwood: Custer Crossing Campground and Store (✉ HCR 73, Box 1527, Deadwood 57732, ☎ 605/584–1009), 15 mi south of town; **Deadwood Gulch Resort** (✉ Hwy. 85S, Box 643, Deadwood 57732, ☎ 605/578–1294 or 800/695–1876) on the southern edge of town; **Deadwood KOA** (✉ Box 451, Deadwood 57732, ☎ 605/578–3830), 1 mi west of town; and **Wild Bill's Campground** (✉ HCR 73, Box 1101, Deadwood 57732, ☎ 605/578–2800), on U.S. 385.

Around the Badlands: Circle 10 Campground (✉ Rte. 1, Box 51½, Philip 57567, ☎ 605/433–5451).

Outdoor Activities and Sports

Fishing

Some of the best fishing in the state lies east of the Badlands in the large lakes along the Missouri River, but mountain streams throughout the Black Hills offer good trout fishing. Custer State Park has trout fishing in several lakes. For more information contact the state Department of Tourism's **fishing division** (☎ 800/445–3474).

Hiking

The **Centennial Trail,** 111 mi long, runs through the Black Hills National Forest, from the Plains Indians' sacred site at Bear Butte in the north to Wind Cave National Park, passing from grasslands into the hills in the high country. For more information contact the state Department of Tourism (☞ Statewide Visitor Information, *above*).

Snowmobiling

With 310 mi of marked and groomed trails, the Black Hills is a premier spot in the country for snowmobiling. A map of the trail network is available from the Department of Tourism (☞ Statewide Visitor Information, *above*). For trail conditions, updated three times weekly, call 800/445–3474.

Ski Areas

The Black Hills' winter-sports magazine, *Romancing the Snow,* has information on cross-country and downhill skiing and is available from the Black Hills, Badlands, and Lakes Association (☞ Visitor Information, *above*). For ski reports call 800/445–3474.

Cross-Country Skiing

The Black Hills offer skiing on 600 mi of abandoned logging roads, railroad beds, and fire trails, as well as several trail networks, including the **Big Hill** (16 mi of trails on the rim of Spearfish Canyon). Information is available from **Ski Cross Country** (✉ 701 3rd St., Spearfish 57783, ☎ 605/642–3851), a ski equipment sales and rental shop.

Downhill Skiing

Deer Mountain Ski Area (✉ Box 622, Deadwood 57732, ☎ 605/584–3230) has 25 trails, a 700-ft vertical drop, and one triple chair- and two Poma lifts. Lessons, rentals, and cross-country trails are available. **Terry Peak Ski Area** (✉ Box 774, Lead 57754, ☎ 605/584–2165 or

800/456–0524 for ski conditions) offers a 1,052-ft vertical drop, five chairlifts, and state-of-the-art snowmaking. A rental shop, lessons, and a lodge are available.

Shopping

Rapid City stores carry western souvenirs, crafts, and clothing. Nearly every gift shop carries the locally famous "Black Hills Gold," a combination of metals that produce distinctive green and red tints; you can watch jewelry being made at **Landstrom's Original Black Hills Gold Creations** (⊠ 405 Canal St., Rapid City, ☎ 800/770–5000). **Prairie Edge Trading Co. & Galleries** (⊠ 606 Main St., Rapid City, ☎ 605/342–3086) displays fine art and crafts of the Plains Indians, as well as works by various other Great Plains artists, in a restored 1886 three-story building. A turn-of-the-century-style trading company in the same building has books, regional crafts, and a world-class collection of Italian glass beads. **Prince & Pauper Bookshop** (⊠ 612 St. Joseph St., Rapid City, ☎ 605/342–7964 or 800/354–0988) has a large selection of books by regional and Native American authors, as well as rare and out-of-print local-history books. **Alex Johnson's Mercantile** (⊠ 608 St. Joseph St., Rapid City, ☎ 605/343–2383) sells books, wood carvings, jewelry, and unique gifts.

Rushmore Mall (⊠ Just off I–90 outside Rapid City, ☎ 605/348–3378) contains such specialty shops as **Leather Unlimited** (for coats and jackets) as well as department and western stores. Among the latter is **RCC-Western Stores** (☎ 605/341–6633), which has one of the largest selections of boots in the area and can outfit you from head to toe in the latest western fashions.

For Native American art, jewelry, baskets, and other goods, check out the gift shop of the **Indian Museum of North America** (☞ The Black Hills *in* Exploring the Black Hills, Deadlands, and the Badlands, *above*).

ELSEWHERE IN SOUTH DAKOTA

Sioux Falls

Arriving and Departing

Sioux Falls is in the southeastern corner of the state, at the intersection of I–90 and I–29. **Sioux Falls Regional Airport** (☎ 605/336–0762) is served by Northwest, TWA, and United airlines.

What to See and Do

Sioux Falls, the state's largest city, is an ideal starting point for most attractions in the eastern part of the state. The city is a commercial hub; restaurants, hotels, and shops are numerous. The **Great Plains Zoo and Delbridge Museum of Natural History** (⊠ 805 S. Kiwanis Ave., ☎ 605/339–7059) contains, besides its live-animal displays, one of the world's largest collections of mounted animals. The **Old Courthouse Museum** (⊠ 200 W. 6th St., ☎ 605/335–4210) is a massive Romanesque structure made of a native red stone called Sioux quartzite. It houses exhibits on the history of the area, including Native American artifacts. The **Pettigrew Home and Museum** (⊠ 131 N. Duluth Ave., ☎ 605/339–7097) was built in 1889 and was later the home of South Dakota's first full-term senator, Richard F. Pettigrew. The Queen Anne–style home contains period furnishings and Native American and natural history exhibits.

Dining

$$ ✕ **Minerva's.** Wooden floors, a salad bar, and a strong wine list complement a menu that focuses on pasta, fresh seafood, and aged steak. ✉ *301 S. Phillips,* ☎ *605/334–0386. AE, D, DC, MC, V. Closed Sun.*

$ ✕ **Champps Sports Cafe.** A lively atmosphere and great pub fare—pastas, sandwiches, hamburgers, fries, onion rings—make this a fun, reliable spot. ✉ *2101 W. 41st St., in Western Mall,* ☎ *605/331–4386. AE, D, DC, MC, V.*

Mitchell

Arriving and Departing

Mitchell is 70 mi west of Sioux Falls on I–90.

What to See and Do

The city of Mitchell trumpets the "world's only" **Corn Palace** (✉ 604 N. Main St., ☎ 605/996–7311 or 800/257–2676). This fanciful structure, built in 1892, is topped by gaily painted Moorish domes, with a facade covered with multicolored corn, grain, and grasses in various designs and murals. Inside is an exhibition hall built to showcase the state's agricultural production. The exterior designs are changed annually. Across the street from the Corn Palace is the **Enchanted World Doll Museum** (✉ 615 N. Main St., ☎ 605/996–9896), with 4,000 antique and modern dolls displayed in 400 scenes. For further information contact the **Mitchell Department of Tourism** (✉ Box 776, 57301, ☎ 605/996–7311 or 800/257–2676, ℻ 605/996–8273).

Dining

$ ✕ **Chef Louie's Steakhouse.** Steaks, barbecued ribs, and seafood are served in a casual setting. Pheasant is a seasonal specialty in the summer and fall. ✉ *601 E. Havens,* ☎ *605/996–7565. AE, D, DC, MC, V. Closed Sun.*

DeSmet

Arriving and Departing

From Sioux Falls follow I–29 north for 49 mi, then U.S. 14 west for about 37 mi.

What to See and Do

Fans of the *Little House* children's books may want to visit the town where author Laura Ingalls Wilder lived for 15 years. The Ingalls family moved to DeSmet in 1879 and lived first in a shanty, next in a farmhouse, and then in town in a home that Pa Ingalls built in 1887. The first and last are open to the public and contain period furnishings and memorabilia. The community also hosts the annual **Laura Ingalls Wilder Pageant** (✉ Laura Ingalls Wilder Memorial Society, Box 344, DeSmet 57231, ☎ 605/854–3383 or 605/854–3181), held late June– early July.

Pierre

Arriving and Departing

Pierre (pronounced "Peer") is on U.S. 83, about 225 mi west of Sioux Falls.

What to See and Do

The **state capitol** (✉ 500 E. Capitol Ave., ☎ 605/773–3765), a magnificent Greek Revival building completed in 1910, has a rich interior decorated with mosaic floors, stained-glass skylights, allegorical murals, and an impressive columned staircase. The state historical society has a museum and archives at the **Cultural Heritage Center** (✉ 900

Governors Dr., ☎ 605/773–3458). Exhibits focus on the history of the state with emphasis on the city of Pierre, which evolved from a French trading post in the early 1800s. The first of three phases for a permanent exhibit (South Dakota Experience) was completed in 1992. It offers a taste of the state from 1743, the year European trappers first arrived, through the beginning of the 20th century. The second phase, completed in the fall of 1994, focuses on the life of the Plains Indians prior to 1743. The third phase, not scheduled for completion until 2000, will cover 20th-century events. For information from the tourist office, *see* Visitor Information, *above*.

Dining

$ ✕ **Cattlemen's Club.** The sawdust floors provide an authentic Wild West ambience, and the view overlooking Lake Sharp is incomparable. Locals come for the terrific steaks. ✉ *East of town on Hwy. 34,* ☎ *605/ 224–9774. D, MC, V. Closed Sun.*

9 The Southwest

Arizona, Nevada, New Mexico, Texas, Utah

By Edie Jarolim

Updated by
Stacy Clark

A region that seems to demand superlatives, the Southwest is the ruggedly beautiful, wide-open land out of which America's myths continue to emerge. Cowboys and Indians, Old World conquistadors and new religions, rising and falling fortunes in gold, copper, and oil—all feed into the vision of an untamed territory with limitless horizons.

Of course, Phoenix, Dallas, and Salt Lake City are sophisticated metropolises, and Santa Fe is becoming a rival Los Angeles in wealth and number of art galleries per square foot. Las Vegas is sui generis, an unbridled, peculiarly American phenomenon. Foodies all over the country sing the praises of the delicately spiced southwestern cuisine, an outgrowth of Asian immigration into the area, now duplicated in cosmopolitan restaurants nationwide. Nor is there a region that has better Mexican food, whether you like it Tex-Mex, Sonoran, or New Mexican style. Southwestern furnishings—an eclectic blend that might include mission chests, Navajo blankets, Mexican tinwork mirrors, *ristras* (strings of red chili peppers), and even bleached cow skulls à la Georgia O'Keeffe—have become so popular in upscale homes that they're a bit of a cliché.

But other, more ancient cultures vie here with contemporary ones. The country's largest Indian reservation, that of the Navajo Nation, occupies millions of acres and traverses state boundaries, and dozens of other tribes—among them Hopi, Zuni, and Apache—live in the region as well. It is their vanishing presence and, above all, the area's natural phenomena—spectacular canyons, a vast salt lake, eerily towering rock formations, and clear, lambent light—that continue to capture the imagination of visitors and residents alike. The southwestern landscape is a glorious lesson in geologic upheaval to be learned at such sites as Arches National Park in Utah, Carlsbad Caverns in New Mexico, and the Grand Canyon in Arizona.

Clearly anything is possible in such an unrestrained place. The heyday of the western movie may be over, but when 1990s screen heroines Thelma and Louise light out for freedom, they find it in the Southwest, still the most natural setting for outlandish deeds and grand gestures.

When to Go

In the semiarid climate of most of the Southwest, **spring** is the season of choice, with cool, fresh, clear weather. In March and April, when temperatures average in the 70s, short-lived wildflowers produce carpets of extravagant color in many parts of the region, including some deserts as well as in temperate areas like East Texas. **Summer** is dry and often very hot, sometimes unpleasantly so, across the Southwest; but water sports abound, and dramatic mountain chains offer another cool respite. Summer thunderstorms are typical in most areas. After spring, **fall**—from September to November, in general—is the preferred time to visit, with temperatures falling back into the 70s and 80s, and gorgeous foliage to be seen in many areas. Skiers flock to slopes across the Southwest in **winter.** In general, temperatures vary greatly even within the same state and season because of the great variety of microclimates in the Southwest's mountains, deserts, plains, and forests.

Festivals and Seasonal Events

MID-JAN.➤ Utah's **Sundance Film Festival** (☎ 801/328–3456), with screenings and workshops in the ski resort town of **Park City** and in **Salt Lake City,** is one of the premier events for independent filmmakers worldwide and offers the chance to rub shoulders, or ski poles, with movie stars like the festival's founder, Robert Redford.

LATE JAN.➤ The **Cowboy Poetry Gathering** (☎ 702/738–7508), in **Elko, Nevada,** has become famous both for the authentic characters it draws from around the Southwest and for the gentle quality of the verse these rough-hewn men and women produce.

EARLY FEB.➤ Arizona's **Tubac Festival** (☎ 602/398–2704) is the state's oldest arts-and-crafts show, a nine-day extravaganza that includes exhibitions, strolling performers, and food galore.

MID.-FEB.➤ **Washington's Birthday Celebration** (☎ 210/722–0589), in **Laredo, Texas,** and in **Nuevo Laredo,** its sister city across the border, is a binational celebration of parades and fiestas honoring the first successful New World revolutionary.

FEB.–MAR.➤ Twenty thousand animals are shown at **Houston**'s **Livestock Show & Rodeo** (☎ 713/791–9000), a truly Texas-size event held under the curved roof of the Astrodome. Rodeos and country music abound.

EARLY MAR.➤ High-quality artwork is the norm at the **Heard Museum Guild Indian Fair and Market** (☎ 602/252–8840), a juried invitational for Native American artists held in **Phoenix, Arizona.**

LATE APR.➤ Native Americans celebrate **American Indian Week** (☎ 505/843–7270) in **Albuquerque, New Mexico,** with dance, arts and crafts, and a trade show at the Indian Pueblo Cultural Center.

LATE APR.➤ Texas's **Fiesta San Antonio** (☎ 210/227–5191), more than a century old, commemorates the Battle of San Jacinto with a festival of music, food, sports, art shows, and the River Parade.

MAY 5➤ **Cinco de Mayo,** a fiesta celebrating Mexican history and heritage, is held in many cities and towns across the Southwest.

The Southwest

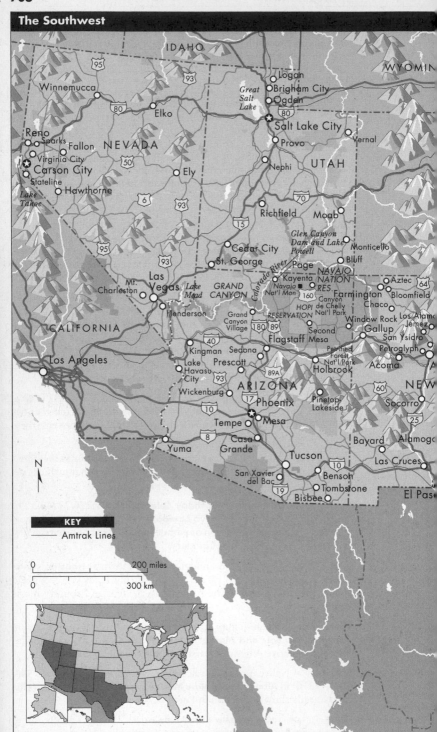

KEY
— Amtrak Lines

0 _____ 200 miles
0 _____ 300 km

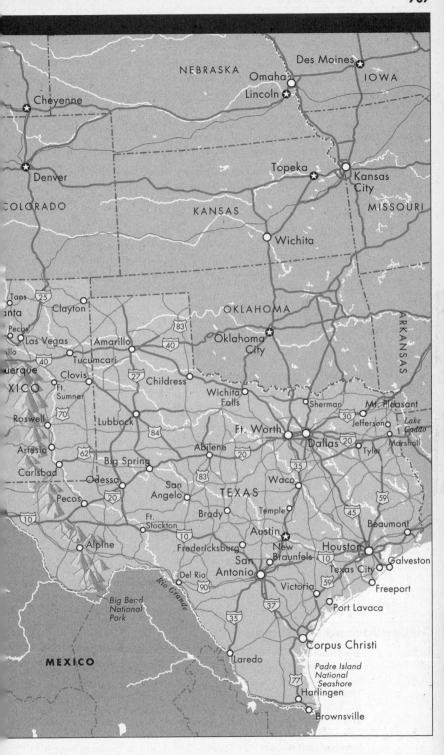

LATE JUNE➤ New Mexico's craftspeople are world famous, and some of the best display and sell their work at the **New Mexico Arts & Crafts Fair** (☏ 505/884–9043) in **Albuquerque.**

EARLY JULY➤ The **National Basque Festival** (☏ 702/738–7547), in **Elko, Nevada,** celebrates the heritage of the Basque people (recruited to the area from northern Spain because of their remarkable shepherding abilities) in the American West.

MID-JULY➤ The popular **Mormon Miracle Pageant** (☏ 435/835–2212) is a musical drama of American and Mormon history set against the backdrop of the temple in **Manti, Utah.**

LATE JULY➤ The **Fiesta de Santiago y Santa Ana** (☏ 505/758–3873 or 800/732–8267), a colorful street party and fair, which began as a trade fair nearly 300 years ago, is the major annual event in **Taos, New Mexico.**

LATE JULY–EARLY AUG.➤ The **Festival of the American West** (☏ 435/750–1143 or 800/225–3378), hosted for more than 20 years by Utah State University, is now held on a newly built site at Jensen Living Historical Farm, near **Logan.** It includes "The Great West Fair" and a multimedia pageant, "The West: America's Odyssey."

LATE AUG.➤ The **Nevada State Fair** (☏ 702/688–5767), in **Reno,** offers a week of rides, farm animal competitions, livestock shows, fast food, and all the other accouterments of a real state fair.

MID-SEPT.➤ On the first weekend after Labor Day, Zozobra, or "Old Man Gloom," is burned to open the annual **Fiestas de Santa Fe** (☏ 505/984–6760 or 800/777–2489), in **New Mexico.** During the celebration, Santa Fe Plaza is filled with music, dancing, and food vendors.

LATE SEPT.–LATE OCT.➤ The **State Fair of Texas** (☏ 214/421–8716), the nation's largest state fair, holds its three-week annual run at **Dallas**'s State Fair Park, declared a National Historic Landmark in 1986 for its Art Deco architecture.

MID-OCT.➤ The **Albuquerque International Balloon Fiesta** (☏ 505/821–1000), in which more than 600 colorful hot-air balloons rise in spectacular unison with the dawn, is probably **New Mexico**'s best-known event.

EARLY NOV.➤ The outdoor **Fine Folk Festival** (☏ 602/890–2613), with 250 performers, draws some 150,000 people to **Mesa, Arizona,** every year.

EARLY DEC.➤ The ghost town of **Madrid, New Mexico,** is reawakened with street lights and an arts-and-crafts festival during its **Christmas Open-House Celebration** (☏ 505/473–0743).

Getting Around the Southwest

By Plane

America West, American, Delta, and Southwest all provide extensive service to and among the southwestern states; Continental, TWA, and United offer more limited service. The region's major airports include, in Texas, **Dallas–Fort Worth International Airport** (☏ 214/574–8888) and **Houston Intercontinental Airport** (☏ 713/230–3100); in Nevada, **Reno Tahoe International Airport** (☏ 702/328–6400) and **McCarran International Airport** (☏ 702/261–5743), in Las Vegas; in New Mexico, **Albuquerque International Airport** (☏ 505/842–4366); in Arizona, **Sky Harbor International Airport** (☏ 602/273–3300), in Phoenix; and in Utah, **Salt Lake International Airport** (☏ 801/575–2400).

By Car

The Southwest is traversed by two of the country's major east–west highways: I–80, the northern route, which passes through Salt Lake City, Utah, and Reno, Nevada; and I–40, which enters Texas at the Oklahoma border, heading to Los Angeles by way of Amarillo, Texas; Albuquerque, New Mexico; and Flagstaff, Arizona. Other east–west arteries include I–10, which links New Orleans and Los Angeles via Houston, San Antonio and El Paso, Texas, and Tucson and Phoenix, Arizona; and I–20, which connects Dallas and El Paso. The major north–south routes of the region are I–15, which heads south from Salt Lake City to Las Vegas; I–25, from Denver to El Paso by way of Albuquerque; and I–35, from Oklahoma to the Mexican border by way of Dallas and Fort Worth.

By Train

Amtrak (☎ 800/872–7245) serves all the states of the region, with one major line between New Orleans and Los Angeles, and another passing through southeastern Colorado to Albuquerque and Flagstaff.

By Bus

Greyhound Lines (☎ 800/231–2222) provides service to towns and cities throughout the region.

ARIZONA

By Edie Jarolim

Capital	Phoenix
Population	4,428,000
Motto	God Enriches
State Bird	Cactus wren
State Flower	Saguaro cactus
Postal Abbreviation:	AZ

Statewide Visitor Information

Arizona Office of Tourism (⌧ 2702 N. 3rd St., Suite 4015, Phoenix 85004, ☎ 602/230–7733 or 800/842–8257, ⅢX 602/240–5475).

Scenic Drives

The drive from the South Rim to the North Rim of the Grand Canyon follows U.S. 89 through the **Arizona Strip,** a starkly beautiful, largely uninhabited part of the state. Almost all the Grand Canyon drives are breathtaking, especially West Rim Drive on the South Rim and the dirt road to Point Sublime on the North Rim. Fall foliage is spectacular on U.S. 89A from Flagstaff to Sedona via **Oak Creek Canyon.** From Tucson, I–10 east of Benson passes through the startling rock formations of **Texas Canyon.**

National and State Parks

National Parks

Among the state's national parks are **Grand Canyon National Park** (☞ Grand Canyon National Park, *below*), **Petrified Forest National Park** (☞ Northeast Arizona, *below*), and **Saguaro National Park** (☞ Tucson and Southern Arizona, *below*); **Canyon de Chelly** (☞ Northeast Arizona, *below*) is a national monument. For Native American ruins in scenic settings, visit **Walnut Canyon National Monument** and **Wupatki National Monument** (☞ Flagstaff, *below*), in the Flagstaff area, **Tuzigoot National Monument,** south of Sedona, and **Navajo National Monument** (☞ Northeast Arizona, *below*). Little-visited spots of unusual beauty include **Sunset Crater Volcano National Monument** (☞ Flagstaff, *below*), west of Flagstaff, and **Chiricahua National Monument,** in the southeastern part of the state.

State Parks

Arizona's 24 state parks run a wide spectrum, from the relatively tiny 54-acre **Slide Rock,** near Sedona, to 13,000-acre **Lake Havasu,** notable for hosting London Bridge. Boating and water-sports enthusiasts congregate at **Alamo Lake State Park,** north of Wickenburg, and **Roper Lake State Park** near Safford. Desert rats will like **Catalina State Park,** near Tucson, and the **Boyce Thompson Southwestern Arboretum,** an hour east of Phoenix. Head to **Red Rock State Park,** just outside Sedona, and **Tonto Natural Bridge State Park,** close to Payson, for dramatic scenery. For a taste of the state's lively frontier history, visit **Riordon Mansion Historical State Park,** in Flagstaff; **Jerome State Historic Park,** in north-central Arizona; **Tombstone Courthouse State Historic Park** and **Tubac Presidio Historic Park,** in the southeast; and **Yuma Territorial Prison State Historic Park,** in the southwest. The **Arizona State Parks Department** (⌧ 1300 W. Washington St., Phoenix 85007, ☎ 602/542–4174) provides information on all the above parks.

GRAND CANYON NATIONAL PARK

Not even the finest photographs pack a fraction of the impact of a personal experience of the Grand Canyon. This awesome, vastly silent ancient erosion of the surface of our planet is 277 mi long, 17 mi across at its widest spot, and more than 1 mi deep at its lowest point. Its twisted and contorted layers of rock reveal a fascinating geological profile of the earth. All around you, otherworldly stone monuments change colors with the hours.

Visitor Information

Before you go, write to **Grand Canyon National Park** (⊠ Box 129, Grand Canyon 86023, ☎ 520/638–7888) for a complimentary *Trip Planner.* Accommodations: **Amfac Parks and Resorts** (⊠ 14001 E. Iliff, Suite 600, Aurora, CO 80014, ☎ 303/297–2757, 520/638–2631 for same-day reservations). North and South Rim camping: **Destinet** (⊠ Box 85705, San Diego, CA 92186-5705, ☎ 800/365–2267). A free newspaper, the *Guide,* which contains a detailed area map, is available at both rims.

Arriving and Departing

By Bus
Greyhound Lines (☎ 800/231–2222) stops at Flagstaff and Williams. **Nava-Hopi Tours** (☎ 800/892–8687 or 520/774–5003 in Flagstaff) offers bus service to the canyon's South Rim from Flagstaff and Williams.

By Car
From the east, west, or south, the best access to the Grand Canyon is from Flagstaff, either northwest on U.S. 180 (81 mi) to Grand Canyon Village on the South Rim or for a scenic route, north on U.S. 89 to Route 64W; from Utah, take U.S. 89S. To visit the North Rim, some 210 mi from Flagstaff, follow U.S. 89 north to Bitter Springs, and then take U.S. 89A to the junction of Route 67. From the west on I–40, the most direct route to the South Rim is via Route 64 to U.S. 180. Summer traffic approaching the South Rim is very congested around Grand Canyon Village. Visitors facilities at the more remote North Rim open May 15. From October 15 through December 1 or until heavy snows close the road, the park remains open for day use only.

The quickest route from Los Angeles is U.S. 93, which intersects with I–40 in Kingman, Arizona.

By Plane
McCarran International Airport (☎ 702/261–5743), in Las Vegas, Nevada, is the primary hub for flights to **Grand Canyon National Park Airport** (☎ 520/638–2446). Carriers include **Air Nevada** (☎ 800/634–6377), **Air Vegas** (☎ 702/736–3599), and **Scenic Airlines** (☎ 800/535–4448). You can make connections from **Sky Harbor International Airport** (☎ 520/273–3300), in Phoenix, with two commuter lines, **Sky Cab** (☎ 800/999–1778) and **West Wind** (☎ 602/991–5557). The **Tusayan Grand Canyon Shuttle** (☎ 520/638–0871) operates between Grand Canyon airport and the nearby towns of Tusayan and Grand Canyon Village. The **Fred Harvey Transportation Company** (☎ 520/638–2822 or 520/638–2631) provides taxi service.

By Train
The town closest to the Grand Canyon served directly by **Amtrak** (☎ 520/774–8679 or 800/872–7245) is Flagstaff. From Williams you can take the historic **Grand Canyon Railway** (☎ 800/843–8724) to the South Rim.

Exploring Grand Canyon National Park

Access to both the South Rim and North Rim areas of the Grand Canyon is carefully managed by the National Park Service. Unfortunately, large crowds converge on the South Rim every summer, and there is talk of limiting auto access to the area. Still, the most trafficked spots are popular for good reason. However, a walk into the canyon itself opens up a totally new and extraordinary perspective.

South Rim

From **Mather Point,** at the outskirts of Grand Canyon Village, you'll get the first glimpse of the canyon from one of the most impressive and accessible vistas on the rim.

Scenic overlooks on the 25-mi-long East Rim Drive include **Yaki Point,** where the much-traveled Kaibab Trail starts the canyon descent to the inner gorge; **Grandview Point,** which supports large stands of ponderosa and piñon pine, oak, and juniper; and **Moran Point,** a favorite spot for photographers. At the **Tusayan Ruins and Museum** (☎ 520/638–2305), 3 mi east of Moran Point, partially intact rock dwellings offer evidence of early habitation in the gorge. **Lipan Point** is the widest spot in the canyon. The highest points along the tour are **Desert View** and the **Watchtower,** site of a lookout tower with a panoramic view of the Grand Canyon (☎ 520/638–2736) and a trading post with Native American art (☞ Shopping, *below*).

Back in Grand Canyon Village, the paved Village Rim Trail (about a mile round-trip) starts at **Hopi House,** one of the canyon's first curio stores (☞ Shopping, *below*). Stops along the way include the historic **El Tovar Hotel,** the jewel in the crown of the country's national park system (☞ Dining and Lodging, *below*); **Lookout Studio,** a combination lookout point, museum, and gift shop; **Bright Angel Trailhead,** the starting point for the best-known trail to the bottom of the canyon; and **Bright Angel Lodge,** with a fireplace made of regional rocks arranged in layers that match those of the canyon.

On West Rim Drive you can get an unobstructed view from **Trailview Overlook** of the distant San Francisco Peaks, Arizona's highest mountains. At **Maricopa Point** you'll see the towering headframe of an early Grand Canyon mining operation. The **Abyss** reveals a sheer canyon drop of 3,000 ft. Pima Point provides a bird's-eye view of the Tonto Plateau and the Tonto Trail, which winds for more than 90 mi through the canyon. **Hermits Rest,** the westernmost viewpoint, and **Hermit Trail** (☞ Outdoor Activities and Sports, *below*), which descends from it, were named for Louis Boucher, a 19th-century prospector who had a roughly built home down in the canyon. The West Rim Drive is closed to auto traffic in summer; from early May through September free shuttle buses leave daily from Grand Canyon Village for Hermits Rest.

North Rim

The relative solitude of the North Rim, set in deep forest near the 9,000-ft crest of Kaibab Plateau in the isolated Arizona Strip, is well worth the extra miles on the road. From central Arizona, the only route into this area is more than 200 mi of lonely road to the northwest of Flagstaff. From late fall through early spring the North Rim and its facilities are closed because heavy snows cut off highway access to the area.

The trail to **Bright Angel Point,** one of the most awe-inspiring overlooks on either rim, starts on the grounds of the Grand Canyon Lodge (☞ Dining and Lodging, *below*), a massive stone structure built in 1928 by the Union Pacific Railroad. At 8,803 ft, **Point Imperial** is the canyon's

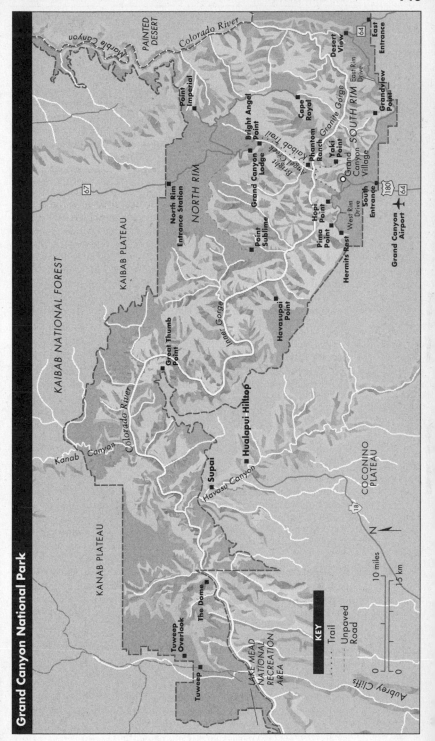

Grand Canyon National Park

PAINTED DESERT

Marble Canyon

Colorado River

Point Imperial

NORTH RIM

North Rim Entrance Station

67

KAIBAB PLATEAU

KAIBAB NATIONAL FOREST

Bright Angel Point

Grand Canyon Lodge

Point Sublime

Great Thumb Point

Inner Gorge

Colorado River

Kanab Canyon

KANAB PLATEAU

Supai

Havasu Canyon

Hualapui Hilltop

Havasupai Point

COCONINO PLATEAU

18

The Dome

Tuweep Overlook

Tuweep

LAKE MEAD NATIONAL RECREATION AREA

Aubrey Cliffs

Cape Royal

Colorado River

Bright Angel/Kaibab Trail

Phantom Ranch

Angel Creek

Granite Gorge

Desert View

East Rim Drive

64

East Entrance

Grandview Point

SOUTH RIM

Yaki Point

Grand Canyon Village

180

64

South Entrance

West Rim Drive

Hopi Point

Pima Point

Hermits Rest

Grand Canyon Airport

N

10 miles

5 km

KEY

····· Trail

--- Unpaved Road

0

0

highest viewpoint. **Cape Royal,** the southernmost viewpoint on the North Rim, is a popular outlook.

What to See and Do with Children

Inquire at the visitor center or the Tusayan Museum about the Junior Ranger program publication, which lists activities geared toward children ages 4–14. Gentle horses can be rented at the **Moqui Lodge** (⊠ Tusayan, ☎ 520/638–2424). Short mule rides suitable for young children leave from the Grand Canyon Lodge for the easier trails along the North Rim; make reservations with **Canyon Trail Rides** (☎ 801/ 679–8665).

Dining and Lodging

It's difficult to find rooms in the South Rim area in summer. The North Rim is less crowded but has limited lodging facilities. Make reservations as soon as your itinerary is set, even as much as six months in advance. If you can't find accommodations in the immediate South Rim area, try the nearby communities of Williams, only an hour away by car, or Flagstaff. Camping inside the park is permitted only in designated areas. For information on park camping and reservations, contact Destinet (☞ Visitor Information, *above*). The Arizona Office of Tourism (☞ Statewide Visitor Information, *above*) offers a campground directory. For price ranges *see* Charts 1 (B) and 2 (B) *in* On the Road with Fodor's.

South Rim

$$$ ✕⛺ **El Tovar Hotel.** Reminiscent of a grand European hunting lodge, El Tovar has maintained a tradition of excellent service and luxury since 1905. The hotel's fine restaurant, set in a room of hand-hewn logs and beamed ceilings, serves Continental dishes such as veal française. ⊠ *Amfac Parks and Resorts, 14001 E. Iliff Ave., Suite 600, Aurora, CO 80014,* ☎ *303/297–2757,* ℻ *303/297–3175 for reservations or 520/ 638–2631. 80 rooms. Restaurant, bar. AE, D, DC, MC, V.*

$$–$$$ ✕⛺ **Bright Angel Lodge.** Built in 1935, this log-and-stone structure a few yards from the canyon rim has rooms in the main lodge or in quaint cabins (some with fireplaces) scattered among the pines. The informal steak house overlooks the abyss. ⊠ *Amfac Parks and Resorts, 14001 E. Iliff Ave., Suite 600, Aurora, CO 80014,* ☎ *303/297–2757,* ℻ *303/ 297–3175 for reservations or 520/638–2631. 30 rooms, 11 with bath; 47 cabins. Restaurant, bar, coffee shop. AE, D, DC, MC, V.*

$$–$$$ ⛺ **Grand Canyon National Park Lodges.** The five Fred Harvey Company lodges on the South Rim—Maswik Lodge, Yavapai Lodge, Moqui Lodge, Kachina Lodge, and Thunderbird Lodge—are all comfortable, if not luxurious. The setting, rather than the amenities, is the draw here. Moqui is on U.S. 180, just outside the park, while the others are in Grand Canyon Village. ⊠ *Amfac Parks and Resorts, 14001 E. Iliff Ave., Suite 600, Aurora, CO 80014,* ☎ *303/297–2757,* ℻ *303/297–3175. 1,000 rooms. Restaurants. AE, D, DC, MC, V.*

CAMPGROUNDS

In Grand Canyon Village, **Mather Campground** (☞ Destinet *in* Visitor Information, *above*) has RV and tent sites. **Trailer Village** (⊠ Amfac Parks and Resorts, 14001 E. Iliff Ave., Suite 600, Aurora, CO 80014, ☎ 303/297–2757) has RV sites. Commercial and Forest Service campgrounds outside the park include **Flintstone Bedrock City** (⊠ Grand Canyon Hwy., HCR 34, Box A, Williams 86046, ☎ 520/635–2600), with tent and RV sites; **Grand Canyon Camper Village** (⊠ Tusayan; Box 490, Grand Canyon 86023, ☎ 520/638–2887), with RV and tent sites; and **Ten X Campground** (⊠ Kaibab National Forest, Tusayan Ranger District, Box 3088, Grand Canyon 86023, ☎ 520/638–2443), with larger sites for families (closed in winter).

Bottom of the Canyon

$ ✕⚏ **Phantom Ranch.** Dormitory accommodations for hikers and cabins for hikers and mule riders nestle in a grove of cottonwood trees at the bottom of the canyon. The restaurant has a limited menu, with meals served family style. Arrangements—and payment—for both food and lodging should be made 9–11 months in advance. ⊠ *Amfac Parks and Resorts, 14001 E. Iliff Ave., Suite 600, Aurora, CO 80014, ☎ 303/ 297–2757, Ⅸ 303/297–3175 for reservations or 520/638–2631. 4 dorms with shared bath, 11 cabins with outside shower. Dining room. AE, D, DC, MC, V.*

CAMPGROUNDS

For information about the campgrounds at **Indian Gardens,** about halfway down the canyon, and **Bright Angel,** near the bottom, contact the Backcountry Reservations Office (☞ Hiking *in* Outdoor Activities and Sports, *below*).

North Rim

$$ ✕⚏ **Grand Canyon Lodge.** This historic stone structure, built in 1928, ★ has comfortable though not luxurious rooms. The lounge area, with hardwood floors and high beamed ceilings, has a spectacular view of the canyon through massive plate-glass windows. Surprisingly sophisticated fare is served in the huge dining room. ⊠ *Amfac Parks and Resorts, 14001 E. Iliff, Suite 600, Aurora, CO 80014, ☎ 303/297– 2757, ⅨX 303/297–3175 for reservations or 520/638–2611. 44 rooms, 157 cabins. Bar, dining room, cafeteria. AE, D, DC, MC, V.*

CAMPGROUNDS

North Rim Campground (☞ Destinet *in* Visitor Information, *above*), inside the park, has RV and tent sites. Forest Service facilities outside the park include **Demotte Campground** (⊠ Kaibab National Forest, North Kaibab Ranger District, Box 248, Fredonia 86022, ☎ 520/643– 7395), also with tent and RV sites.

Outdoor Activities and Sports

Hiking

Park rangers or visitor center personnel have detailed area maps of the many canyon trails. Overnight hikes require a permit; write **Backcountry Reservations Office** (⊠ Box 129, Grand Canyon 86023, no phone). It's wise to make a reservation in advance. If you arrive without one, go to the Backcountry Reservations Office, either near the entrance to Maswik Lodge, on the South Rim, or at the North Rim's ranger station. Plan on five days if you want to hike the gorge from rim to rim.

One of the most scenic hiking paths from the South Rim to the bottom of the canyon (8 mi), the well-maintained **Bright Angel Trail** has a steep (4,460-ft) ascent and should be attempted only by persons in good physical condition. The 9-mi **Hermit Trail,** which has some inspiring views of Hermit Gorge and the Redwall and Supai formations, is recommended for experienced long-distance hikers. The steep **South Kaibab Trail** begins near Yaki Point, on East Rim Drive near Grand Canyon Village. **North Kaibab Trail,** the only maintained trail into the canyon from the North Rim, connects at the bottom of the canyon with the South Kaibab Trail.

Mule Trips

Mule trips down the precipitous trails to the inner gorge are nearly as well known as the canyon itself. Inquire via **Amfac** (⊠ 14001 E. Iliff,

Suite 600, Aurora, CO 80014, ☎ 303/297–2757) about prices and restrictions for riders. Be sure to book months in advance.

Rafting

Reservations for white-water rafting trips, which last from 3 to 18 days, must often be made more than six months ahead of time. For a complete list of park-service-approved concessionaires, contact the **River Permits Office** (⊠ Grand Canyon National Park, Box 129, Grand Canyon 86023, ☎ 520/638–7888). **Fred Harvey Transportation Company** (☎ 520/638–2822) specializes in smooth-water rafting day trips.

Shopping

Native American items sold at most of the lodges and at major gift shops are authentic. The **Desert View Trading Post** (⊠ East Rim Dr., ☎ 520/638–2360) sells a mix of Southwest souvenirs and Native American crafts. The **El Tovar Hotel Gift Shop** (⊠ Near the rim in Grand Canyon Village, ☎ 520/638–2631) features silver jewelry. **Hopi House** (⊠ East of El Tovar Hotel, ☎ 520/638–2631) has a wide variety of Native American artifacts, some of museum quality.

NORTHEAST ARIZONA

Most of northeast Arizona, a vast and lonely land of shifting red dunes and soaring buttes, belongs to the Navajo and Hopi peoples. Throughout the area, excellent Native American arts and crafts may be found in shops, galleries, and trading posts. Visitors are also welcome to observe certain ancient cultural traditions, such as Hopi ceremonial dances; however, the privacy, customs, and laws of the tribes should be respected. Within the stunning landscapes of Navajo National Monument and Canyon de Chelly, both on the Navajo reservation, the mysterious ruins of ancestral tribes who wandered here thousands of years ago can be haunting. Just below the southeastern boundary of the Navajo reservation, straddling I–40, Petrified Forest National Park is an intriguing geologic open book of the Earth's distant past. Above the far northwest corner of the Navajo reservation on U.S. 80 lies Glen Canyon Dam. Behind it more than 120 mi of Lake Powell's emerald waters are held in precipitous canyons of erosion-carved stone.

Visitor Information

Glen Canyon National Recreation Area (⊠ Box 1507, Page 86040, ☎ 520/608–6200). **Hopi Tribe Office of Public Relations** (⊠ Box 123, Kykotsmovi 86039, ☎ 520/734–2441). **Navajo Tourism Department** (⊠ Box 663, Window Rock 86515, ☎ 520/871–7371). **Page/Lake Powell:** Chamber of Commerce (⊠ 106 S. Lake Powell Blvd., Box 727, Page 86040, ☎ 520/645–2741 or 888/261–7243).

Arriving and Departing

By Bus

Greyhound Lines (☎ 800/231–2222) goes to Phoenix and Flagstaff. Travel by the **Navajo Transit System** (☎ 520/729–4002), which has fixed routes throughout the reservation, is inexpensive but slow.

By Car

From the east or west I–40 passes through Flagstaff, a good entry point to the region. From the north or northwest U.S. 89 brings you to Page. From the northeast U.S. 64 leads west from Farmington, New Mexico. A tour of Navajo and Hopi country involves driving long distances among widely scattered communities, so a detailed road map is essential.

Especially recommended is the map of the northeast put out by the Navajo Tourism Department (☞ Visitor Information, *above*). In this sparsely populated area, service stations are rare, so be sure to take care of necessary maintenance before your trip. Never drive into dips or low-lying road areas during a heavy rainstorm; flash floods are very sudden and extremely dangerous.

By Plane

No major airlines fly directly to this area. You'll need to make flight connections in Phoenix (☞ Arriving and Departing *in* Metropolitan Phoenix, *below*) to travel on to either **Flagstaff Pullium Airport** (☎ 520/556–1234) or to **Page Municipal Airport** (☎ 520/645–2494), near Lake Powell.

By Train

Amtrak (☎ 520/774–8679 or 800/872–7245) stops in Flagstaff, a good jumping-off point for a car trip into the area.

Exploring Northeast Arizona

Some 115 mi east of Flagstaff off I–40, **Petrified Forest National Park** is strewn with fossilized tree trunks whose wood cells were replaced over the centuries by brightly hued mineral deposits. The park's 94,000 acres include portions of the **Painted Desert**, a colorful but essentially barren and waterless series of windswept plains, hills, and mesas. Also look for fascinating Native American petroglyphs. ⊠ Box 2217, Petrified Forest, AZ 86028, ☎ 520/524–6228.

Window Rock, northeast of Petrified Forest, is the capital of the Navajo Nation and the business and social center for families from the surrounding rural areas. Visit the **Navajo Nation Museum** (⊠ Rte. 264 next to Navajo Nation Inn, ☎ 520/871–6673), which is devoted to Navajo art, culture, and history; it's closed weekends in winter. The adjoining Navajo Arts and Crafts Enterprise (☞ Shopping, *below*) displays local work.

Northwest of Window Rock and occupying nearly 84,000 acres, **Canyon de Chelly** (pronounced duh-*shay*) is one of the Southwest's most extraordinary national monuments. Gigantic stone formations rise hundreds of feet above small streams, hogans, tilled fields, peach orchards, and grazing lands, and thousand-year-old pictographs made by the ancestors of the Pueblo people cover some of its sheer cliff walls. Paved rim drives offer marvelous views. There are also horseback and Jeep tours of the canyon. ⊠ Box 588, Chinle 86503, ☎ 520/674–5500 or 520/674–5501.

At the approximate center of the Navajo reservation lies the 4,000-square-mi **Hopi reservation,** a series of stone-and-adobe villages built on high mesas. On First Mesa is the town of **Walpi,** built on solid rock and surrounded by steep cliffs. Its 30 residents defy modernity and live without electricity and running water. In Second Mesa's oldest and largest village, **Shungopavi,** the famous Hopi snake dances—no longer open to the public—are held in August of even-number years. Also on Second Mesa is the **Hopi Cultural Center** (☎ 520/734–6650) with a pueblo-style museum, shops, and a good restaurant and motel (☞ Dining and Lodging, *below*). The center is closed weekends. **Kykotsmovi,** at the eastern base of Third Mesa, is known for its greenery and peach orchards. It is the site of the Hopi Tribal headquarters. Atop Third Mesa, **Oraibi,** established around AD 1150, is widely believed to be the oldest continuously inhabited community in the United States.

Monument Valley, on the Utah border north of Kayenta, will look familiar if you've seen westerns. This sprawling expanse of soaring red buttes, eroded mesas, deep canyons, and naturally sculpted rock formations was populated by the ancestors of the Pueblo people and has been home to generations of Navajo. Within this vast area lies the 30,000-acre **Monument Valley Navajo Tribal Park** and its 17-mi self-guided tour. ⊠ *Visitor center, 3½ mi off U.S. 163, 24 mi north of Kayenta,* ☏ *801/727–3353.*

At **Navajo National Monument,** southwest of Monument Valley off U.S. 160, two unoccupied 13th-century cliff pueblos, **Keet Seel** and **Betatakin,** stand under the overhang of soaring orange and ocher cliffs. The largest Native American ruins in Arizona, these pueblos, too, were built by the ancestors of the Pueblo people, whose reasons for abandoning them prior to AD 1300 are still disputed by scholars. ⊠ *HC 71 (Box 3), Tonalea 86044,* ☏ *520/672–2366.*

For information on the construction of **Glen Canyon Dam and Lake Powell,** 136 mi north of Flagstaff on U.S. 89, stop at the **Carl Hayden Visitor Center** (⊠ Glen Canyon Dam, ☏ 520/608–6404). The best way to see eerie, man-made Lake Powell as it twists through rugged canyon country is by boat (☞ Outdoor Activities and Sports, *below*). Take a half-day excursion to **Rainbow Bridge National Monument,** a 290-ft red-sandstone arch that straddles one of the lake's coves.

Dining and Lodging

Northeast Arizona is vast, and few communities have places to eat; Page, Window Rock, Fort Defiance, Ganado, Chinle, Holbrook, Hopi Second Mesa, Keams Canyon, Tuba City, Kayenta, Goulding's Trading Post/Monument Valley, and Cameron all have restaurants and fast-food service. No alcoholic beverages are sold on the Navajo and Hopi reservations, and possession or consumption of alcohol is against the law in these areas.

Similarly, half the battle in this big land is knowing in which of the scattered communities lodging can be found. Towns noted above also offer accommodations. In summer it is especially wise to make reservations. For price ranges *see* Charts 1 (B) and 2 (B) *in* On the Road with Fodor's.

Cameron

$$ ✕☳ **Cameron Trading Post and Motel.** A good place to stop if you're driving from the Hopi mesas to the Grand Canyon, this motel has southwestern-style rooms. Hearty fare—including traditional fry bread, Navajo tacos, and Navajo stew—is served in the wood-beamed dining room. A market, curio shop, art gallery, and RV park are also on site. ⊠ *54 mi north of Flagstaff on U.S. 89 (Box 339), 86020,* ☏ *520/ 679–2231 or 800/338–7385,* ℻ *520/679–2350. 62 units. Restaurant, café. AE, DC, MC, V.*

Chinle/Canyon de Chelly

$$$ ✕☳ **Holiday Inn Canyon de Chelly.** Opened on the site of a former trading post, this Navajo-staffed complex has pastel-tone contemporary-style rooms. Restaurant service can be erratic, but the food more than compensates. ⊠ *BIA Rte. 7 (Box 1889), Chinle 86503,* ☏ *520/674–5000,* ℻ *520/674–8264. 108 rooms. Restaurant, pool. AE, D, DC, MC, V.*

$$$ ✕☳ **Thunderbird Lodge.** At the mouth of Canyon de Chelly, this establishment with manicured lawns and cottonwood trees has stone-and-adobe units with Navajo decor. In the cafeteria, an inexpensive American menu is prepared by an all-Navajo staff. ⊠ *½ mi south of canyon visitor center (Box 548), Chinle 86503,* ☏ *520/674–5841 or 800/679–2473. 72 rooms. Cafeteria. AE, D, DC, MC, V.*

Cottonwood Campground (⊠ Near visitor center, Canyon de Chelly National Monument, Box 588, Chinle 86503, ☎ 520/674–5500) has group sites and free individual sites.

Hopi Reservation–Second Mesa

$$ ✕⊞ **Hopi Cultural Center Motel.** High atop Second Mesa, this pueblo-
★ style lodging has immaculate rooms with white walls and Native American decor. A comfortable, inexpensive restaurant serves traditional Native American dishes, including Hopi blue-corn pancakes and *nok qui vi* (lamb stew). ⊠ *Rte. 264 (Box 67), 86043,* ☎ *520/734–2401,* FAX *520/734–6651. 33 units. Restaurant. AE, D, DC, MC, V.*

Kayenta

$$$ ⊞ **Holiday Inn.** Typical of the chain except for the southwestern decor, this accommodation near Monument Valley has comfortable rooms. It also has one of the few swimming pools in the area. ⊠ *South of junction of U.S. 160 and 163 (Box 307), 86033,* ☎ *520/697–3221,* FAX *520/ 697–3349. 160 rooms. Restaurant, pool. AE, D, DC, MC, V.*

$$ ⊞ **Wetherill Inn Motel.** This clean and cheerful two-story motel without frills was named for frontier explorer John Wetherill. There is a café nearby. ⊠ *U.S. 163 (Box 175), 86033,* ☎ *520/697–3231. 54 rooms. AE, D, DC, MC, V.*

Keams Canyon

$ ✕ **Keams Canyon Restaurant.** At this typical rural roadside spot, you'll find American dishes and a few Native American items, including Navajo tacos. ⊠ *Keams Canyon Shopping Center (off Rte. 264),* ☎ *520/738–2296. MC, V.*

Lake Powell/Page

$$$$ ✕⊞ **Wahweap Lodge.** On a promontory above Lake Powell, the lodge
★ serves as the center for area recreational activities. Many guest rooms, furnished in oak and with southwestern colors, have lake views. The semicircular Rainbow Room gives a panoramic view of the lake; specialties on the seasonally changing southwestern standard American menu might include coho salmon with Dijon mustard cream sauce. River-rafting excursions, houseboat rentals, and other outdoorsy pursuits are available. ⊠ *U.S. 89, 5 mi north of Page (Box 1597), Page 86040,* ☎ *520/645–2433 or 800/528–6154. 350 rooms. Restaurant, bar, boating, waterskiing, fishing. AE, D, DC, MC, V.*

$$ ✕⊞ **Weston's Empire House.** This classic 1950s-style motel is on Page's main street, 7 mi north of Lake Powell. The smoky bar is the real western thing. ⊠ *107 S. Lake Powell Blvd. (Box 1747), 86040,* ☎ *520/ 645–2406 or 800/551–9005,* FAX *520/645–2647. 69 rooms. Restaurant, bar, pool. MC, V.*

Monument Valley, Utah

$$$$ ✕⊞ **Goulding's Lodge.** This comfortable motel, which often serves as the headquarters for film location crews, has cozy rooms with southwestern-design bedspreads, Native American art, and spectacular views of Monument Valley. The motel's Stagecoach Restaurant serves good standard fare and some Native American dishes. ⊠ *2 mi west of U.S. 163, just north of UT border (Box 360001), Monument Valley, UT 84536,* ☎ *801/727–3231 or 800/874–0902. 62 rooms. Restaurant, indoor pool. AE, D, DC, MC, V.*

Mitten View Campground (⊠ Monument Valley Navajo Tribal Park, near visitor center, ☎ 801/727–3287) has some sites available year-round. **Good Sam Campground** (⊠ Off U.S. 163 near Goulding's

Trading Post, ☎ 801/727–3232, ext. 425) operates mid-March–October.

Navajo National Monument

CAMPGROUNDS

Navajo National Monument (☞ Exploring Northeast Arizona, *above*) has two small free campgrounds, one only open May–October; RVs longer than 25 ft are discouraged.

Window Rock

$$ ✕🖭 **Navajo Nation Inn.** Native American government officials frequent this motel in the Navajo Nation's tribal capital. Spanish colonial furniture and Navajo art decorate the rooms. An inexpensive restaurant serves American and Navajo fare, including fry bread, tacos, and mutton stew. ⊠ *North side of Rte. 264 (Box 2340), 86515,* ☎ *520/871–4108 or 800/662–6189,* 🖷 *520/871–5466. 56 units. Restaurant. AE, DC, MC, V.*

Outdoor Activities and Sports

Boating

Rental boats and water-sports equipment, as well as excursion boats, are available at **Wahweap Marina** (⊠ U.S. 89, 5 mi north of Page, ☎ 520/645–2433 or 800/528–6154).

Hiking

There's excellent hiking in **Canyon de Chelly.** Guides are required for all but the White House Ruin Trail; contact the visitor center. In addition to casual hikes along the rim areas, **Navajo National Monument** offers guided hikes (☎ 520/672–2367) to Betatakin (early May–mid-Oct.); a permit is needed for the unsupervised longer hike to Keet Seel (Memorial Day–Labor Day).

Horseback Riding

Edward Black (☎ 800/551–4039 or 801/739–4285) gives long and short trail rides from his stable in the Monument Valley area. Also, year-round rides are offered at **Bigman's** (☎ 520/677–3219).

Shopping

You may find exactly what you want at a good price from a roadside vendor, but the following have dependable selections of Native American wares. **Cameron Trading Post** (⊠ 54 mi north of Flagstaff on U.S. 89, ☎ 520/679–2231 or 800/338–7385) sells Navajo, Hopi, Zuni, and New Mexico Pueblo jewelry, rugs, baskets, and pottery. **Navajo Arts and Crafts Enterprise** (⊠ Off Rte. 264, next to Navajo Nation Inn, ☎ 520/871–4108 or 800/662–6189), in Window Rock, stocks fine authentic Navajo products. **Hubbell Trading Post** (⊠ Rte. 264, 1 mi west of Ganado, ☎ 520/755–3254) is famous for its "Ganado red" Navajo rugs and has a good collection of crafts.

FLAGSTAFF

Flagstaff, set against a lovely backdrop of pine forests and the snow-capped San Francisco Peaks, is the largest city in north-central Arizona. A popular base for exploring the Grand Canyon and Navajo-Hopi country, the city is burgeoning with motels and restaurants.

Visitor Information

The **Flagstaff Visitors Center** (⊠ 1 E. Rte. 66, 86001, ☎ 520/774–9541 or 800/842–7293) has information on the area.

Arriving and Departing

Flagstaff is 138 mi north of Phoenix and 80 mi south of the Grand Canyon, at the junction of I–40 and I–17.

Exploring Flagstaff

The **Historic Railroad District,** where many interesting shops and buildings are concentrated, is near the Santa Fe railroad station. To view an architectural masterpiece built by two lumber-baron brothers, visit the **Riordan Mansion State Park** (⊠ 1300 Riordan Ranch St., ☎ 520/779–4395). The **Lowell Observatory** (⊠ 1400 W. Mars Hill, ☎ 520/774–2096) offers educational displays on astronomy and allows visitors to peer through its 24-inch telescope on some evenings (schedules vary seasonally). Set in a striking native-stone building, the **Museum of Northern Arizona** (⊠ 3101 N. Fort Valley Rd., ☎ 520/774–5213) traces the natural and cultural history of the Colorado Plateau.

Arizona Snowbowl & Flagstaff Nordic Center (☎ 520/779–1951) offers fine downhill and cross-country skiing in winter and excellent views and good hiking trails in summer; you'll see the exit 5 mi north of town on U.S. 180. In a lovely pine forest about 10 mi southeast of Flagstaff, off I–40, is **Walnut Canyon National Monument** (⊠ Walnut Canyon Rd., ☎ 520/526–3367), the site of 14th-century cliff dwellings. The 2,000-square-mi San Francisco Volcanic Field, about 20 mi north of Flagstaff on U.S. 89, is home to **Sunset Crater Volcano National Monument** (☎ 520/556–7042). You can take a 20-mi loop road from Sunset Crater to **Wupatki National Monument** (☎ 520/556–7040), rich in Native American history.

Dining and Lodging

For price ranges *see* Charts 1 (B) and 2 (B) *in* On the Road with Fodor's.

$$$ ✕ **Cottage Place.** Unexpectedly elegant in a town known for hearty food and drive-through service, this restaurant in a 50-year-old cottage serves Continental cuisine in a series of intimate dining rooms. Try the artichoke chicken breast or chateaubriand for two carved table-side. ⊠ 126 W. Cottage Ave., ☎ 520/774–8431. AE, MC, V. Closed Mon. No lunch.

$$ ✕ **Pasto.** This downtown Italian restaurant is popular with a young crowd for its good and plentiful food at reasonable prices. Such southern Italian standards as lasagna appear on the menu along with more innovative fare like artichoke orzo. ⊠ 19 E. Aspen St., ☎ 520/779–1937. MC, V. No lunch.

$$$$ ▦ **Inn at Four Ten.** This quiet but convenient downtown bed-and-breakfast, in a beautifully restored 1907 building, has spacious two-room suites. A full gourmet breakfast is served. ⊠ 410 N. Leroux St., 86001, ☎ 520/774–0088 or 800/774–2008. 8 suites. Kitchenette. AE, MC, V.

$$$$ ▦ **Little America of Flagstaff.** Rooms in this popular hotel on wooded grounds are surprisingly ornate, with brass chandeliers and French provincial–style furnishings. It's one of the few places in town that offer room service, and a courtesy van gives complimentary rides to the airport and bus and train stations. ⊠ 2515 E. Butler Ave. (Box 3900), 86004, ☎ 520/779–2741 or 800/352–4386, ℻ 520/779–7983. 248 rooms. Restaurant, bar, coffee shop, pool, exercise room. AE, D, DC, MC, V.

Nightlife and the Arts

Nightlife

There's usually a country-and-western band at the **Museum Club** (✉ 3404 E. Rte. 66, ☎ 520/526–9434), a lively cowboy honky-tonk. **Main Street Bar and Grill** (✉ 14 S. San Francisco St., ☎ 520/774–1519) features bluegrass, jazz, or rock. **Charly's** (✉ 23 N. Leroux St., ☎ 520/779–1919) attracts a loyal local following to its late-night jazz and blues bands. **Monsoon's** (✉ 22 E. Rte. 66, ☎ 520/774–7929) books an eclectic array of live music, from alternative to world beat.

The Arts

Between the **Flagstaff Symphony Orchestra** (✉ Ardrey Auditorium, on campus of Northern Arizona University, corner of Riordan Rd. and Knowles Dr., ☎ 520/774–5107), **Theatrikos Community Theater** (✉ 11 W. Cherry Ave., ☎ 520/774–1662), and Northern Arizona University's **School of Performing Arts** (☎ 520/523–5661), you're bound to find something cultural. In August the **Flagstaff Festival of the Arts** (☎ 520/774–7750 or 800/266–7740) fills the air with music.

The **Coconino Center for the Arts** (✉ 2300 N. Fort Valley Rd., ☎ 520/779–6921) hosts a Festival of Native American Arts each July and August. The center also sponsors the Trappings of the American West from mid-May to early June, which focuses on cowboy art. From May through September the **Museum of Northern Arizona** (☞ Exploring, *above*) features a Celebration of Native American Art.

SEDONA AND ENVIRONS

Sedona is perhaps the most attractive stopover en route north from Phoenix to the Grand Canyon. Startling formations of deep red rocks, like Capitol Butte or Bell Rock, gently caress what is almost always a clear blue sky—made to seem even bluer by the dark green of forests. Filmmakers in the 1940s and '50s saw this as a quintessential Wild West landscape and shot more than 80 films in the area. Now an upscale art colony, Sedona is also a center of interest to New Age enthusiasts, who believe the area contains important vortices (energy centers).

Visitor Information

For information on the area contact **Sedona–Oak Creek Canyon Chamber of Commerce** (✉ U.S. 89A and Forest Rd., Box 478, Sedona 86339, ☎ 520/282–7722 or 800/288–7336).

Arriving and Departing

By Car

Sedona is 125 mi north of downtown Phoenix and 27 mi south of Flagstaff, at the south end of Oak Creek Canyon on U.S. 89A.

By Plane

There are no commercial flights into Sedona.

Exploring Sedona and Environs

In Sedona itself shopping is the main activity: **Tlaquepaque Mall** (✉ Rte. 179, ☎ 520/282–4838) has the largest concentration of upscale shops. The **Chapel of the Holy Cross** (✉ Chapel Rd., ☎ 520/282–4069) is worth a visit for its striking architecture and stunning vistas.

Scenic hiking spots close to town include **Long Canyon, Devil's Kitchen,** and **Boynton Canyon,** and there are almost limitless other opportunities for hikes and walks; stop at the **Sedona Ranger District** office (✉

250 Brewer Rd., ☎ 520/282–4119) Monday–Saturday for more information. Enjoy the area's rock formations at **Red Rock State Park** (☎ 520/282–6907), 5 mi southwest of Sedona. Visit **Slide Rock State Park** (☎ 520/282–3034), 8 mi north of Sedona in beautiful Oak Creek Canyon, for a picnic and a plunge into a natural swimming hole.

Perched on Cleopatra Hill, **Jerome** is about 37 mi southwest of Sedona on U.S. 89A. This town was once known as the Billion Dollar Copper Camp, but after the last mines closed in 1953, the booming population of 15,000 dwindled to 50 determined souls, earning Jerome the "ghost town" designation it still holds, though the population has risen to almost 450 folks. Today, with many artsy boutiques, Jerome is a shopper's haven. Also worth a visit is Jerome State Historic Park and the Mine Museum.

Dining and Lodging

For price ranges *see* Charts 1 (A) and 2 (A) *in* On the Road with Fodor's.

$$$ ✕ **Pietro's.** Good northern Italian cuisine is served by a friendly, attentive staff in a lively (often noisy) room. Creative pastas might include fettuccine with duck, cabbage, and figs; the veal *piccata* is excellent. ✉ *2445 W. Hwy. 89A,* ☎ *520/282–2525. AE, D, DC, MC, V. No lunch.*

$$ ✕ **Heartline Café.** This plant-filled café west of Sedona serves tasty south-
★ western-style food, such as grilled salmon marinated in tequila and lime. A sampler for two allows you and your companion to try all of the luscious desserts on the menu. ✉ *1610 W. U.S. 89A,* ☎ *520/282–0785. AE, D, DC, MC, V. No lunch Sun.*

$$$$ ▥ **Enchantment Resort.** All rooms of this Boynton Canyon resort are
★ in pueblo-style casitas and have dazzling views of the surrounding forest and canyons. Many offer fireplaces, some have kitchenettes, and two have private pools. The sports facilities here are excellent. ✉ *525 Boynton Canyon Rd., 86336,* ☎ *520/282–2900 or 800/826–4180,* ℻ *520/282–9249. 162 rooms. Restaurant, bar, 4 pools, spa, 12 tennis courts, putting green, health club, hiking. AE, D, MC, V.*

$$ ▥ **Sky Ranch Lodge.** An excellent value in an expensive town, the lodge has simply furnished rooms with southwestern touches, such as Mexican tiles surrounding the dressers. Some rooms have fireplaces and kitchenettes; others, balconies with views of Sedona's red-rock canyons. ✉ *Airport Rd. (Box 2579), 86339,* ☎ *520/282–6400,* ℻ *520/282–7682. 92 rooms, 2 cottages. Pool, hot tub. MC, V.*

PRESCOTT

In a forested bowl among the Mingus Mountains, Prescott was Arizona's first territorial capital and remains the Southwest's richest store of late-19th-century New England–style architecture. Because of its temperate climate, in summer the town draws escapees from the Phoenix heat—as well as retirees year-round. The town's two institutions of higher learning, Yavapai and Prescott colleges, ensure a younger scene, too. Many visitors come to buy reasonably priced antiques and collectibles on the stretch of Cortez Street east of Courthouse Plaza.

Visitor Information

Prescott Chamber of Commerce (✉ 117 W. Goodwin St., 86303, ☎ 520/445–2000 or 800/266–7534).

Arriving and Departing

By Bus
Greyhound Lines (✉ 820 E. Sheldon St., ☎ 520/445–5470 or 800/ 231–2222).

By Car
Prescott is 34 mi southwest of Jerome via U.S. 89A. From Phoenix take I–17 north for 60 mi to Cordes Junction, and then drive northwest on Hwy. 69 for 36 mi into town.

By Plane
There are daily flights from Phoenix into **Prescott Municipal Airport** (☎ 520/445–78600), 10 mi north of town.

Exploring Prescott

Courthouse Plaza, bounded by Gurley and Goodwin streets to the north and south and Cortez and Montezuma streets to the west and east, is the heart of the city. **Whiskey Row,** named for a string of brawling pioneer taverns, runs along Montequma Street, flanking the plaza's west side; it was once host to 20 saloons and houses of pleasure (it's more subdued these days). However, the historic bars are still a fun stop.

Two blocks west of Courthouse Plaza, the **Sharlot Hall Museum** (✉ 415 W. Gurley St., ☎ 520/445–3122), devoted to the area's history, includes the log cabin that housed the territorial governor and three restored late-19th-century houses.

The **Phippen Museum of Western Art** (✉ 4701 Hwy. 89 N, ☎ 520/ 778–1385), about 5 mi north of downtown, hosts work by many prominent artists of the West, along with the painting and bronze sculpture of George Phippen.

Dining and Lodging

For price ranges *see* Charts 1 (B) and 2 (B) *in* On the Road with Fodor's.

$$ ✕ **Nolaz.** Come here for spicy New Orleans–style fare—jambalaya, Creole shrimp, blackened salmon—and a friendly down-home atmosphere to match. ✉ *216 W. Gurley St.,* ☎ *520/445–3765. AE, MC, V. Closed Sun. No lunch Sat.*

$–$$ ✕ **Prescott Brewing Company.** In addition to the pub fare you'd expect, including fish-and-chips, you'll also find a surprising range of vegetarian selections. Four good beers are brewed on the premises. ✉ *130 W. Gurley St.,* ☎ *520/771–2795. AE, D, DC, MC, V.*

$$$$ 🏨 **Prescott Resort Conference Center and Casino.** Many guests at this upscale property don't notice the great views of the mountain ranges surrounding Prescott; they're too busy at the hotel casino. Attractive southwestern-style rooms all have wet bars and coffeemakers. ✉ *1500 Hwy. 69, Prescott 86201,* ☎ *520/776–1666 or 800/967–4637,* 🆕 *520/ 776–8544. 161 rooms. Restaurant, piano bar, refrigerators, indoor-outdoor pool, sauna, tennis courts, exercise room, racquetball, casino. AE, D, DC, MC, V.*

$$$–$$$$ 🏨 **Hassayampa Inn.** Built in 1927 for early automobile travelers, the
★ Hassayampa Inn oozes character. Rooms are individually decorated, a number with original furnishings like oak headboards inset with tiles. A cocktail in the elegant lounge and a full breakfast, both complimentary, are included in the reasonable rates. ✉ *122 Gurley St., Prescott 86301,* ☎ *520/778–9434 or 800/322–1927 in AZ. 68 rooms. Restaurant, bar. AE, D, DC, MC, V.*

METROPOLITAN PHOENIX

One of America's newest, fastest-growing major urban centers, metropolitan Phoenix lies at the northern tip of the Sonoran Desert, in the Valley of the Sun, named for its 330-plus days of sunshine each year. Now-chic Scottsdale began in 1901 as less than a dozen adobe houses and 30-odd tents put up by seekers of healthful desert air. Glendale and Peoria on the west side and Tempe, Mesa, Gilbert, and Chandler on the east constitute the nation's third-largest Silicon Valley. Excellent hiking, golf, shopping, and dining and some of the best luxury resorts in the country make Phoenix desirable as a vacation spot as well as a business destination.

Visitor Information

Phoenix Chamber of Commerce (⊠ Bank One Plaza, 201 N. Central Ave., Suite 2700, Phoenix 85073, ☎ 602/254–5521). **Phoenix and Valley of the Sun Convention and Visitors Bureau** (⊠ Arizona Center, 400 E. Van Buren St., Suite 600, Phoenix 85004).

Arriving and Departing

By Bus
Greyhound Lines (⊠ 2115 W. Buckeye Rd., ☎ 602/389–4207 or 800/231–2222).

By Car
From the west you'll probably come to Phoenix on I–10. I–40 enters Arizona in the northwest; U.S. 93 continues to Phoenix. From the east I–10 brings you from El Paso into Tucson, then north to Phoenix. The northeastern route, I–40 from Albuquerque, leads to Flagstaff, where I–17 goes south to Phoenix.

By Plane
Sky Harbor International Airport (☎ 602/273–3300), 3 mi east of downtown Phoenix, is home base for America West and a hub for Southwest. It is also served by other major airlines. By car, Tempe is 10 minutes from the airport; Scottsdale about 20 minutes; Glendale and Mesa, 25 minutes; and Sun City, 30–45 minutes. **Valley Metro** (☎ 602/253–5000) buses connect with downtown Phoenix or Tempe for $1.25. A **taxi** trip into downtown Phoenix costs from $6.50 to $12 plus tip. **Supershuttle** (☎ 800/258–3826) can run 25% less than a taxi for longer trips.

By Train
Amtrak (⊠ 401 W. Harrison St., ☎ 602/253–0121 or 800/872–7245).

Getting Around Metropolitan Phoenix

If you plan to see anything beyond Phoenix, Scottsdale, or Tempe's pedestrian-friendly downtowns, you will need a car.

Exploring Metropolitan Phoenix

★ The **Heard Museum** has an exceptional collection of fine art, basketry, pottery, and kachina dolls that makes it the foremost showcase of southwestern Native American art and artifacts. Interactive exhibits, a multimedia show, and live demonstrations by artisans add to the experience. ⊠ *22 E. Monte Vista Rd.,* ☎ *602/252–8848 or 602/252–8840.*

A piece of the city as it was at the turn of the century still stands in parklike **Heritage Square** (⊠ 7th and Monroe Sts., ☎ 602/262–5071), at the east end of downtown. Western painting is the focus of the galleries at the **Phoenix Art Museum** (⊠ 1625 N. Central Ave., ☎ 602/257–1222). The **Desert Botanical Garden** (⊠ 1201 N. Galvin Pkwy., ☎ 602/941–1217), with the world's largest collection of desert plants in a natural setting, is an urban oasis.

Scottsdale, a nearby suburb, has a downtown rich in historic sites, nationally known art galleries, and lots of clever boutiques. Historic **Old Town,** with its rustic storefronts and wooden sidewalks, has the look of the Old West. Tour **Taliesen West** (⊠ Cactus Rd. and Frank Lloyd Wright Blvd., ☎ 602/860–8810) for a look at the western studio, school, and home of master architect Frank Lloyd Wright.

Casa Grande Ruins National Monument, an hour's drive south of Phoenix, includes the 35-ft-tall Casa Grande (Big House), built around 1350. It was constructed by the Hohokam Indians, who farmed this area from more than 1,500 years ago until they vanished around 1450. A small museum features other artifacts. ⊠ *1 mi north of Coolidge on Rte. 87,* ☎ *520/723–3172.*

What to See and Do with Children

Lively hands-on exhibits at the **Arizona Science Center** make learning fun. Discover the science of making gigantic soap bubbles or the technology of satellite weather systems. ⊠ *147 E. Adams St.,* ☎ *602/256–9388.*

At the **Hall of Flame,** retired firefighters lead tours through more than 100 restored fire engines and tell harrowing tales of the "world's most dangerous profession." Kids can climb on a 1916 engine, operate alarm systems, and learn lessons of fire safety from the pros. ⊠ *6101 E. Van Buren St.,* ☎ *602/275–3473.*

Chock-full of amusing oddities, the **Mystery Castle** was constructed out of native stone, railroad refuse, kitchen appliances, and anything else its builder could get his hands on. ⊠ *800 E. Mineral Rd.,* ☎ *602/268–1581.*

Five designated trails wind through the 125-acre **Phoenix Zoo,** which manages to replicate habitats of both an African savanna and a tropical rain forest. Ruby, an Asian elephant, puts her brush to canvas to rival the best of abstract expressionists. Children can help groom goats and sheep at the zoo's big red barn. ⊠ *455 N. Galvin Pkwy.,* ☎ *602/273–7771.*

Dining

Steak houses, from cowboy to fancy, abound in the area, as do excellent Mexican restaurants. Lighter, spicier, and generally more upscale fare may be found in Phoenix at the numerous restaurants serving southwestern-international cuisine. For price ranges *see* Chart 1 (A) *in* On the Road with Fodor's.

$$$–$$$$
★
✕ **Christopher's.** You have two choices here: monogrammed-linen-and-silver fine dining or the less expensive, upbeat bistro next door. Both spots have menus worthy of the Champs-Elysées; creative fish, chicken, and more exotic game dishes are all flawlessly prepared and majestically presented. ⊠ *2398 E. Camelback Rd.,* ☎ *602/957–3214. Reservations essential. Jacket required. AE, D, DC, MC, V.*

$$$–$$$$
★
✕ **Roxsand.** An industrial-chic double-tier room is the setting for outstanding "fusion" cuisine, with Greek, Asian, Continental, and Caribbean influences (among others). Be on the lookout for sizzling sea-scallop salad and the sea bass with a horseradish crust. ⊠ *Biltmore Fashion Park, 2594 E. Camelback Rd.,* ☎ *602/381–0444. AE, DC, MC, V.*

$$$–$$$$
✕ **Windows on the Green.** The innovative haute southwestern cuisine here rivals views of the lush fairway at the Phoenician resort. Tortilla soup with wood-smoked chicken and avocado is a memorable starter,

and the tender "Campfire-style" fillet of salmon a worthy follow-up. ⊠ *6000 E. Camelback Rd.,* ☎ *602/423–2530. AE, D, DC, MC, V. Closed Mon. Oct.–May.*

$$$ ✕ **Tarbell's.** Ingredients like goat cheese in the salad, molasses-lime glaze on the grilled salmon, and fennel sausage on the pizza highlight this heralded newcomer's creative American bill of fare. The huge paintings and the by-the-glass wine list are equally impressive. ⊠ *3213 E. Camelback Rd.,* ☎ *602/955–8100. AE, D, DC, MC, V. No lunch.*

$$$ ✕ **Marquesa.** In two soft-hued, intimate rooms at the Scottsdale Princess, traditional Catalan dishes follow authentic tapas appetizers. Paella with lobster, chicken, pork, shellfish, and *chistora* (Spanish sausage) looks almost as wonderful as it tastes. ⊠ *7575 E. Princess Dr., Scottsdale,* ☎ *602/585–4848. AE, D, DC, MC, V. No lunch Mon.–Sat.*

$$ ✕ **Greekfest.** In a tasteful Athens-style taverna, featherlight appetizer-
★ size spinach pies, sweet and succulent lamb, and fresh stuffed grape leaves make a memorable meal. ⊠ *1940 E. Camelback Rd.,* ☎ *602/ 265–2990. Reservations essential. AE, D, DC, MC, V. No lunch Sun.*

$$ ✕ **Mint Thai.** At this tiny, graceful place southeast of Mesa, you'll find the valley's most varied Thai menu. The *rama* beef in peanut sauce, prepared with delicacy and power, is amazing. ⊠ *1111 N. Gilbert Rd., Gilbert,* ☎ *602/497–5366. AE, MC, V. No lunch Sun. in summer.*

$$ ✕ **Richardson's.** This neighborhood haunt can be noisy and crowded, but the chile rellenos, enchiladas, and other first-rate Mexican-style New Mexican standbys pack 'em in until midnight. Try the Santa Fe chicken, spiced with jalapeño hollandaise sauce. ⊠ *1582 E. Bethany Home Rd.,* ☎ *602/265–5886. AE, DC, MC, V.*

$$ ✕ **Rustler's Rooste.** Decorated in a playful miner-cowpoke style, this western restaurant has great views of Phoenix, as well as excellent steaks, juicy barbecued ribs and chicken, and homemade ice cream. ⊠ *7777 S. Pointe Pkwy.,* ☎ *602/431–6474. AE, D, DC, MC, V. No lunch.*

$–$$ ✕ **Sam's Cafe.** A meal at this casual grill begins with warm, chewy breadsticks with mild red-chili cream cheese and ends with complimentary white-chocolate tamales. In between, the menu offers an eclectic variety of Southwest interpretations—from delicious Sedona spring rolls to lasagna and barbecued salmon. ⊠ *Arizona Center, 455 N. 3rd St.,* ☎ *602/252–3545;* ⊠ *Biltmore Fashion Park, 2566 E. Camelback Rd.,* ☎ *602/954–7100. AE, D, DC, MC, V.*

$ ✕ **Los Dos Molinos.** Down-home New Mexico–style cooking graces
★ colorful tile tables in this bustling adobe cantina, once the garage of Tom Mix, a star of silent-film westerns. Chimichangas and shrimp Veracruz are among the spicy delights; ask the friendly servers to help you gauge the heat. Caution: The homemade, fresh green- and red-chili salsas can rip your lips off. ⊠ *8646 S. Central Ave., Phoenix,* ☎ *602/ 243–9113. Reservations not accepted. AE, D, MC, V. Closed Mon.*

Lodging

Famous for its world-class resorts, metropolitan Phoenix has a considerable array of lodging options, from luxury and executive hotels to no-frills roadside motels. For price ranges *see* Chart 2 (A) *in* On the Road with Fodor's.

$$$$ ▥ **The Boulders.** The desert setting of the valley's most serene luxury
★ resort among hill-size granite boulders is gorgeous. The rooms have wood-beam ceilings, kiva fireplaces that burn real logs, and huge bath-dressing areas. The Boulders is in Carefree, 12 mi north of Scottsdale. ⊠ *34631 N. Tom Darlington Dr., Carefree 85377,* ☎ *602/488–90009 or 800/553–1717,* 𝔽𝔸𝕏 *602/488–4118. 194 casitas. 4 restaurants, 2 pools, spa, 2 18-hole golf courses, 6 tennis courts, health club, hiking, horseback riding. AE, D, DC, MC, V.*

$$$$ 🏨 **The Phoenician.** It's not exactly typical Southwest, with its crystal chandeliers and marble floors, but this swanky resort isn't stuffy, either. The Centre for Well-Being is among the best spas in the state. Rooms are spacious; ask for one facing south to enjoy views of the resort's pools and the city. ✉ *6000 E. Camelback Rd., Scottsdale 85251,* ☎ *602/941–8200 or 800/888–8234,* 🖷 *602/947–4311. 645 rooms. 4 restaurants, 2 bars, 9 pools, spa, 18-hole golf course, 12 tennis courts, concierge, business services, valet parking. AE, D, DC, MC, V.*

$$$$ 🏨 **Pointe Hilton on South Mountain.** The Southwest's largest resort, it's also the most convenient—close to the airport, downtown Phoenix, and the eastern valley. The sports facilities are super. ✉ *7777 S. Pointe Pkwy., Phoenix 85044,* ☎ *602/438–9000 or 800/876–4683,* 🖷 *602/431–6535. 638 suites. 4 restaurants, 3 pools, saunas, 18-hole golf course, 10 tennis courts, health club, hiking, horseback riding, shops. AE, D, DC, MC, V.*

$$$$ 🏨 **Ritz-Carlton.** This neo-Federal mid-rise facing the Biltmore Fashion Park hides a luxury hotel that pampers travelers. Daily afternoon tea is a highlight. ✉ *2401 E. Camelback Rd., Phoenix 85016,* ☎ *602/468–0700,* 🖷 *602/468–0793. 295 rooms. 2 restaurants, 2 bars, pool, 2 saunas, tennis court, exercise room, concierge, 2 concierge floors, valet parking. AE, D, DC, MC, V.*

$$$–$$$$ 🏨 **Hilton Suites.** A more luxurious version of the frequent-traveler suites concept, this property, 2 mi north of downtown, is likely to become a classic. The design is modern, colorful, and bold. ✉ *10 E. Thomas Rd., Phoenix 85012,* ☎ *602/222–1111,* 🖷 *602/265–4841. 226 suites. Restaurant, bar, pool, sauna, exercise room, gift shop. AE, D, DC, MC, V.*

$$$ 🏨 **Best Western Executive Park.** One of downtown's hidden jewels,
★   this small facility is simply but elegantly decorated. Prints by southwestern masters line the walls. ✉ *1100 N. Central Ave., Phoenix 85004,* ☎ *602/252–2100,* 🖷 *602/340–1989. 107 rooms. Restaurant, bar, pool, sauna, health club. AE, D, DC, MC, V.*

$$$ 🏨 **Camelback Courtyard by Marriott.** This four-story hostelry delivers compact elegance in its public areas and no-frills comfort in its rooms and suites. ✉ *2101 E. Camelback Rd., Phoenix 85016,* ☎ *602/955–5200,* 🖷 *602/955–1101. 166 rooms. Restaurant, bar, pool, spa, exercise room. AE, D, DC, MC, V.*

$$ 🏨 **San Carlos Hotel.** Built in 1927, this downtown landmark retains lots of historic touches, including pedestal sinks in the rooms and Austrian crystal chandeliers in the lobby. The 3-inch concrete walls in the rooms ensure quiet. ✉ *202 N. Central Ave., Phoenix 85004,* ☎ *602/253–4121 or 800/528–5446,* 🖷 *602/253–6668. 126 rooms. Restaurant, deli, pub, pool, exercise room. AE, D, DC, MC, V.*

$ 🏨 **Ambassador Inn.** Close to the airport and shopping and recreational facilities, this cheerful hotel is set around an enclosed courtyard with a fountain. ✉ *4727 E. Thomas Rd., Phoenix 85018,* ☎ *602/840–7500 or 800/624–6759,* 🖷 *602/840–5078. 200 rooms. Restaurant, bar, pool, exercise room, airport shuttle. AE, D, DC, MC, V.*

$ 🏨 **Motel 6 Scottsdale.** Though amenities aren't a priority here, the best bargain in Scottsdale lodging is steps away from Scottsdale Fashion Square and close to the specialty shops of 5th Avenue. ✉ *6848 E. Camelback Rd., Scottsdale 85251,* ☎ *602/946–2280,* 🖷 *602/949–7583. 122 rooms. Pool, spa. AE, D, DC, MC, V.*

Nightlife and the Arts

Cultural and entertainment events are listed in the free weekly *New Times* newspaper, distributed Wednesday. The Friday "Weekend" and

Sunday "Arts" sections of the *Arizona Republic* also detail the current goings-on.

Nightlife

Nightclubs, restaurants, and upscale bars abound in downtown's **Arizona Center** and farther north, on Camelback Road, in the **Biltmore Fashion Park.** Scottsdale's Main Street comes alive for **Art Walk,** held Thursday evening 7–9. **Mill Avenue,** near the ASU campus, is the center of action in Tempe.

The Arts

Downtown Phoenix's **Symphony Hall** (✉ 225 E. Adams St., ☎ 800/ AT–CIVIC) and **Herberger Theater Center** (✉ 222 E. Monroe St., ☎ 602/254–7399) are home to many performing arts groups.

Outdoor Activities and Sports

Golf

The Valley of the Sun is a mecca for year-round golf, having more than 100 courses, from par-3 to PGA-championship links. For a detailed listing contact the **Arizona Golf Association** (7226 N. 16th St., Suite 200, Phoenix 85020, ☎ 602/944–3035 or 800/458–8484 in AZ).

Hiking

Phoenix has some of the best-trod hiking trails in the world, and the area favorite is in **Squaw Peak Park** (✉ 2701 Squaw Peak Dr., north of Lincoln Dr., east of South Peak Pkwy., ☎ 602/262–7901). The 1¼-mi trail to the top is steep; plan for an hour each direction. **Camelback Mountain** (✉ E. McDonald Dr. and Tatum Blvd., ☎ 602/256–3220), the city's most prominent landmark, presents a challenging climb that will take anywhere from one to three hours. The mountains of **South Mountain Park** (✉ 10919 S. Central Ave., south of Baseline Rd., ☎ 602/495–0222) contain more than 40 mi of multiuse trails. Rangers can help you plan hikes to see some of the 200 Native American petroglyph sites in the park.

Spectator Sports

Baseball: Arizona Diamondbacks (✉ Bank One Ballpark, 201 E. Jefferson, ☎ 602/514–8500). Seven major-league baseball teams train in the Phoenix area during March. Contact the **Cactus League Baseball Association** at the Mesa Convention and Visitor's Bureau (✉ 120 N. Center St., Mesa 85201, ☎ 602/827–4700 or 800/283–6372) for information.

Basketball: Phoenix Suns (✉ America West Arena, 1 Phoenix Suns Plaza, 201 E. Jefferson St., ☎ 602/379–7900).

Football: Arizona Cardinals (✉ Sun Devil Stadium, 5th St. and College Ave., Tempe, ☎ 602/379–0102).

Golf: The **Phoenix Open** (✉ 17020 N. Hayden Rd., Scottsdale, ☎ 602/ 870–4431) is held each January at the Tournament Players Club of Scottsdale.

Rodeo: Parada del Sol (☎ 602/990–3179) festivities begin in January; the rodeo is held the first week in February. **Rodeo of Rodeos** (✉ 4133 N. 7th St., Phoenix, ☎ 602/263–8671), one of the Southwest's oldest and best, is held every March.

Shopping

The valley is a shopper's delight, with everything from glitzy malls in Phoenix and Mesa to charming boutiques and galleries on downtown Scottsdale's 5th Avenue.

Arizona Center (✉ 400 E. Van Buren St., Phoenix, ☎ 602/271–4000) is a modern, open-air center with two tiers of shops and restaurants. The vast sunken garden and fountains make this mall a downtown oasis. Anchored by Saks Fifth Avenue and Macy's, the upscale **Biltmore Fashion Park** (✉ 24th St. and Camelback Rd., Phoenix, ☎ 602/955–8400) has posh shops as well as some of the city's most popular restaurants and cafés.

Scottsdale's **5th Avenue,** between Goldwater Boulevard and Scottsdale Road, is home to creative shops and galleries featuring clothing, furniture, and Native American jewelry and crafts. Anchored by Neiman Marcus, Robinson's May, and Dillard's department stores, retractable skylights open to reveal sunny skies above at the swank **Scottsdale Fashion Square** (✉ Scottsdale and Camelback Rds., Scottsdale, ☎ 602/990–7800.) The ritzy **Borgata** (✉ 6166 N. Scottsdale Rd., ☎ 620/998–1822) has more than 50 boutiques in an Italian village–style complex.

On the west side, **Metrocenter** (✉ I–17 and Peoria Ave., Phoenix, ☎ 602/997–2641) is the largest mall in the Southwest. Thirty miles east of Phoenix, **Superstition Springs Center** (✉ Hwy. 60 and Superstition Springs Rd., Mesa, ☎ 602/832–0212) has the usual complement of shops and eateries, a botanical garden, and a 15-ft Gila monster slide for the kids. The town of Casa Grande, some 45 minutes to the south via I–10, is home to two huge outlet malls, **Factory Stores of America** (✉ Exit 194, ☎ 800/746–7872) and **Tanger Factory Outlet Center** (✉ Exit 198, ☎ 800/482–6437).

TUCSON

Tucson, Arizona's second-largest city, has a small-town atmosphere enriched by its deep Hispanic and Old West roots. Because of its large university and myriad resorts, the city has many cultural and recreational options.

Visitor Information

Convention and Visitors Bureau (✉ 130 S. Scott Ave., 85701, ☎ 520/624–1817 or 800/638–8350).

Arriving and Departing

By Bus
Greyhound Lines (✉ 2 S. 4th Ave., ☎ 520/792–3475 or 800/231–2222). **Arizona Shuttle Service** (☎ 520/795–6771) runs express buses from Phoenix's Sky Harbor Airport to Tucson.

By Car
From Phoenix, 111 mi to the northwest, or from the east, take I–10 to Tucson. From the south take I–19.

By Plane
Tucson International Airport (☎ 520/573–8000), 8½ mi south of downtown, is served by 12 carriers, some of which serve Mexico as well as domestic destinations.

By Train
Amtrak (✉ 400 E. Toole Ave., ☎ 520/623–4442 or 800/872–7245).

Exploring Tucson

With more than 320 days of sunshine a year, Tucson is a mecca for outdoor activities, including historical tours. The city covers more than 500 square mi in a valley ringed by mountains, so a car is neces-

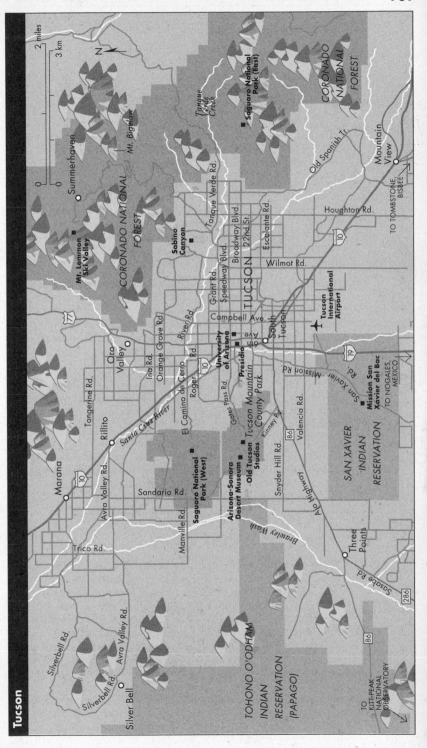

sary. The downtown area, just east of I–10 off the Broadway-Congress exit, is easy to navigate on foot.

In the El Presidio neighborhood, the **Tucson Museum of Art and Historic Block** (⊠ 140 N. Main Ave., ☎ 520/624–2333) takes visitors back 200 years to the time when the city was a fortress and Arizona was still part of New Spain.

The city divides the **Saguaro National Park** (☎ 520/733–5158 for west, 520/733–5153 for east) into two sections; the one west of town is the most heavily visited. Both are forested by the huge saguaro cactus, a native of the Sonoran Desert that is known for its towering height (often 50 ft) and for arms that reach out in strange configurations.

Among the museums on the **University of Arizona** campus (⊠ At the corner of Park Ave. and Union Blvd.) that give insight into the area's past, present, and future are the **Center for Creative Photography** (☎ 520/621–7968), the **Arizona Historical Society's Museum** (☎ 520/628–5774), the **Arizona State Museum** (☎ 520/621–6302), and the **Grace H. Flandrau Science Center and Planetarium** (☎ 520/621–4515). Entrance to all of these museums is free.

Just southwest of Tucson, the 1692 **Mission San Xavier del Bac** (⊠ I–19 Exit 92, San Xavier Rd., ☎ 520/294–2624) is the oldest Catholic church in the United States still serving the community for which it was built: the Tohonó O'odham Indian tribe. Inside, this beautiful Spanish-Moorish-style structure contains a wealth of painted statues, carvings, and frescoes.

What to See and Do with Children

★ Near Saguaro National Park West, the **Arizona–Sonora Desert Museum** (⊠ 2021 N. Kinney Rd., ☎ 520/883–2702) is one of the state's most popular tourist attractions. In this desert microcosm, birds and animals busy themselves in a natural habitat ingeniously planned to allow the visitor to look on without disturbing them.

Reopened in 1997 after a fire shut it down for nearly two years, **Old Tucson Studios** (⊠ 201 S. Kinney Rd., in Tucson Mountain Park, ☎ 520/883–0100) is a western theme park where more than 250 westerns have been shot over the past 50 years.

Dining

For price ranges *see* Chart 1 (A) *in* On the Road with Fodor's.

$$$ ✕ **Janos.** This historic Presidio district restaurant serves up delightfully
★ innovative southwestern cuisine, such as pan-seared salmon with a smoky maple-syrup glaze. Come here for a special, big-splurge evening. ⊠ *150 N. Main Ave.,* ☎ *520/884–9426. Reservations essential. AE, DC, MC, V. Closed Sun. Nov.–mid-May; Sun.–Mon. mid-May–Nov. No lunch.*

$$$ ✕ **Ventana Room.** A triumph of understated elegance, this dining room serves contemporary Continental cuisine. Specials might include grilled loin of venison with pecans. ⊠ *Loews Ventana Resort, 7000 N. Resort Dr.,* ☎ *520/299–2020. Reservations essential. AE, D, DC, MC, V. No lunch.*

$$ ✕ **Bocatta.** Decked out in florals and Victoriana, this romantic restaurant augments its northern Italian menu—penne with chicken, artichokes, and pine nuts, say—with southern French touches. For dessert, the profiteroles are superb. ⊠ *5605 E. River Rd.,* ☎ *520/577–9309. AE, DC, MC, V. No lunch.*

$$ ✕ **Café Terra Cotta.** Everything about this restaurant says Southwest, from the decor to the food. Contemporary specialties include prawns

stuffed with herbed goat cheese and pork tenderloin with black beans. ⊠ *4310 N. Campbell Ave.,* ☎ *520/577–8100. AE, D, DC, MC, V.*

$$ ✕ **Kingfisher.** This chic restaurant has a loyal following for its excellent American regional cuisine, its bourbon selection, and its late (for Tucson) dining hours—until midnight. ⊠ *2564 E. Grant Rd.,* ☎ *520/ 323–7739. AE, D, DC, MC, V. No lunch weekends.*

$–$$ ✕ **Café Poca Cosa.** Arguably Tucson's best restaurant, this café serves
★ consistently innovative Mexican fare in a marvelously colorful, lively setting. The chalkboard menu changes daily; ingredients are always fresh and tasty. ⊠ *Park Inn, 88 E. Broadway,* ☎ *520/622–6400. Reservations essential. MC, V. Closed Sun.*

$–$$ ✕ **Pinnacle Peak Steakhouse.** Tourists love this cowboy steak house— it's fun, it's Tucson, and the food ain't half bad either. ⊠ *6541 E. Tanque Verde Rd.,* ☎ *520/296–0911. Reservations not accepted. AE, D, DC, MC, V. No lunch.*

Lodging

For price ranges *see* Chart 2 (A) *in* On the Road with Fodor's.

$$$$ ☷ **Arizona Inn.** Although this landmark 1930s-era inn is close to the
★ university and downtown, it is secluded on 14 acres of lushly landscaped grounds. All rooms have patios and lovely period furnishings. ⊠ *2200 E. Elm St., 85719,* ☎ *520/325–1541 or 800/933–1093,* ℻ *520/881– 5830. 83 rooms. 2 restaurants, bar, tea shop, pool, 2 tennis courts, croquet, Ping-Pong, library. AE, MC, V.*

$$$$ ☷ **Canyon Ranch.** At this well-known health spa surrounded by spec-
★ tacular desert scenery, guests are pampered while shaping up in the rigorous program. The food is unobtrusively healthful, and rooms are luxuriously furnished in muted southwestern tones. Minimum stay is four nights. ⊠ *8600 E. Rockcliff Rd., 85715,* ☎ *520/749–9000 or 800/742–9000,* ℻ *520/749–1646. 153 rooms. Restaurant, 4 pools, spa, 8 tennis courts, basketball, health club, racquetball, squash. AE, D, MC, V.*

$$$$ ☷ **Miraval.** This hotel, which opened some 20 mi north of Tucson in 1995, is giving Canyon Ranch a run for its money with its even more secluded desert setting, beautiful southwestern rooms, and myriad health-oriented programs, many incorporating Eastern ideas. Meals, including tasty all-you-can-eat buffets (calories and fat content noted, of course), and tips are all part of a set fee. ⊠ *5000 East Via Estancia Miraval, Catalina 85739,* ☎ *520/825–4000 or 800/825–4000,* ℻ *520/ 792–5870. 106 rooms. 2 restaurants, bar, 3 pools, spa, 2 tennis courts, exercise room, croquet, biking, horseback riding. AE, D, DC, MC, V.*

$$$$ ☷ **Sheraton Tucson El Conquistador.** This friendly golf and tennis re-
★ sort is nestled in the foothills of the Santa Catalinas. Both private casitas and the main hotel building offer appealing rooms in light woods and pastels. Biosphere 2, famous for its New Age experiments in survival, is just up the road. ⊠ *10000 N. Oracle Rd., 85737,* ☎ *520/544– 5000 or 800/325–7832,* ℻ *520/544–1224. 428 rooms. 4 restaurants, piano bar, 4 pools, hot tub, sauna, 45-hole golf course, 31 tennis courts, 2 exercise rooms, horseback riding, racquetball, volleyball. AE, D, DC, MC, V.*

$$$$ ☷ **Tanque Verde Ranch.** One of the country's oldest guest ranches covers more than 600 acres in the beautiful Rincon Mountains. The rooms are furnished in tasteful southwestern style; most have patios and fireplaces. Rates include meals. ⊠ *14301 E. Speedway Blvd., 85748,* ☎ *520/296–6275 or 800/234–3833,* ℻ *520/721–9426. 74 rooms. Restaurant, indoor and outdoor pools, spa, 5 tennis courts, exercise room, horseback riding. AE, D, MC, V.*

$$$$ ⌂ **Westin La Paloma.** This sprawling pink resort offers lots of options for family relaxation, with top-notch golf, fitness, and beauty centers, the only swim-up bar in Tucson, and Arizona's longest resort water slide. ⌧ *3800 E. Sunrise Dr., 85718,* ☎ *520/742–6000,* FAX *520/577–5878. 487 rooms. 5 restaurants, 2 bars, 3 pools, beauty salon, 3 hot tubs, 27-hole golf course, 12 tennis courts, aerobics, croquet, exercise room, jogging, racquetball, volleyball. AE, D, DC, MC, V.*

$$$$ ⌂ **White Stallion Ranch.** Many scenes from the television show *High Chaparral* were shot on this family-run ranch, set on 3,000 desert mountain acres. Rates include excellent, hearty meals. Rooms are plain but comfortable. ⌧ *9251 W. Twin Peaks Rd., 85743,* ☎ *520/297–0252 or 888/977–2624,* FAX *520/744–2786. 32 rooms. Bar, pool, hot tub, tennis, horseback riding, volleyball. No credit cards. Closed May–Sept.*

$$ ⌂ **Casa Tierra.** For a real desert experience, come to this B&B on 5
★ acres near Saguaro National Park. Rooms in the beamed-ceiling adobe house are arranged around a garden courtyard. ⌧ *11155 W. Calle Pima, 85743,* ☎ FAX *520/578–3058. 3 rooms. Kitchenettes, hot tub. No credit cards. Closed June–mid-Sept.*

$$ ⌂ **Peppertrees.** Just off the University of Arizona campus, this pleasant bed-and-breakfast has lodgings in a beautiful Victorian house and two bungalow-style houses next door. Some units have full kitchens and washer/dryers—ideal for families. ⌧ *724 E. University Blvd., 85719,* ☎ FAX *520/622–7167 or 800/348–5763. 8 rooms. D, MC, V.*

$$ ⌂ **Windmill Inn.** This all-suites property in a chic shopping plaza of-
★ fers well-designed, modern rooms, each with a microwave, two TVs, and three phones. Complimentary coffee, muffins, and a newspaper are delivered to your door. ⌧ *4250 N. Campbell Ave., 85718,* ☎ *520/577–0007 or 800/547–4747,* FAX *520/577–0045. 122 suites. Pool, laundry service. AE, D, DC, MC, V.*

$ ⌂ **Best Western Ghost Ranch Lodge.** The logo of this hotel was designed
★ by Georgia O'Keeffe, a friend of the original owner who opened this place in 1941. The Spanish tile–roof units are spread out over 8 acres near the center of town. ⌧ *801 W. Miracle Mile, 85705,* ☎ *520/791–7565 or 800/456–7565,* FAX *520/791–3898. 83 units. Restaurant, bar, pool, hot tub. AE, D, DC, MC, V.*

$ ⌂ **Hotel Congress.** This downtown hotel, built in 1919 in Art Deco style, attracts a hip young crowd that enjoys the convenient location, popular (and loud on weekends) Club Congress, and low room rates. ⌧ *311 E. Congress St., 85701,* ☎ *520/622–8848 or 800/722–8848,* FAX *520/792–6366. 40 rooms. Restaurant, bar, beauty salon, nightclub. AE, MC, V.*

Campgrounds

The public campground closest to Tucson is at **Catalina State Park** (⌧ 11570 N. Oracle Rd., ☎ 520/628–5798). Recreational vehicles can park in any number of facilities around town; the Convention and Visitors Bureau (☞ Visitor Information, *above*) can provide information about specific locations.

Nightlife and the Arts

Nightlife

Cactus Moon (⌧ 5470 E. Broadway, ☎ 520/748–0049), **Maverick** (⌧ 4702 E. 22nd St., ☎ 520/748–0456), and the **Stampede** (⌧ 4385 W. Ina Rd., ☎ 520/744–7744) are lively country-and-western nightclubs.

The Arts

The **Tucson Symphony Orchestra** (☎ 520/882–8585) and the **Arizona Opera Company** (☎ 520/293–4336) perform in the Tucson Convention Center's Music Hall (⌧ 260 S. Church St., ☎ 520/791–4226).

The **Arizona Theatre Company** (☎ 520/884–8210) is at Tucson's Temple of Music and Art (✉ 330 S. Scott Ave., ☎ 520/622–2823) from September through May.

Outdoor Activities and Sports

Golf

Tucson has five **municipal golf courses** (✉ Tucson Parks and Recreation Dept., ☎ 520/791–4336), as well as many excellent resort courses, such as those at the **Lodge at Ventana Canyon** (✉ 6200 N. Club House La., off Kold Rd., ☎ 520/577–4061), **OmniTucson National Golf Resort and Spa** (✉ 2727 W. Club Dr., ☎ 520/297–2271), **Westin La Paloma** and **Sheraton Tucson El Conquistador** (for the last two, *see* Lodging, *above*). For information about other courses in the area, send $5 for the *Tucson and Southern Arizona Golf Guide* (✉ Madden Publishing, Box 42915, Tucson 85733, ☎ 520/322–0895).

Hiking

For great hiking opportunities around Tucson, head for **Tucson Mountain Park, Mt. Lemmon, Sabino Canyon,** or **Kitt Peak.** A little-visited treasure, **Chiricahua National Monument,** about two hours east of Tucson off I–10, south of Bowie, has spectacular rugged rock vistas. Directly south of Tucson, the Huachuca Mountains, home of **Ramsey Canyon,** are a bird-watcher's paradise. The Santa Ritas, just south of Tucson, host another bird lover's haven, **Madera Canyon.** The local chapter of the **Sierra Club** (☎ 520/620–6401) welcomes out-of-town visitors on its weekend hikes.

Horseback Riding

Tucson stables include **Desert-High Country Stables** (✉ 6501 W. Ina Rd., ☎ 520/744–3789) and **Pusch Ridge Stables** (✉ 13700 N. Oracle Rd., ☎ 520/825–1664).

Shopping

In Tucson, **Old Town Artisans** (✉ 186 N. Meyer Ave., ☎ 520/622–0351) and the **Kaibab Shops** (✉ 2841–43 N. Campbell Ave., ☎ 520/795–6905) both carry a broad selection of fine southwestern crafts and clothing. Hard-core bargain hunters usually head for **Nogales,** the Mexican border town 63 mi south of Tucson on I–19. For work by regional artists, try the **Tubac** artists' community, 45 mi south of Tucson, just off I–19 at Exit 34.

SOUTHERN ARIZONA

Southeastern Arizona is a relatively undiscovered treasure of mountains, deserts, canyons, and dusty little cowboy towns. Of particular interest are Bisbee and Tombstone, which give visitors a taste of Arizona as it was in its Wild West heyday.

Visitor Information

Bisbee: Chamber of Commerce (✉ 7 Main St., Box BA, 85603, ☎ 520/432–5421). **Tombstone:** Office of Tourism (✉ Box 917, 85638, ☎ 520/457–3421 or 800/457–3423).

Arriving and Departing

By Car

East of Tucson, U.S. 80 cuts south from I–10 to Tombstone and Bisbee.

Exploring Southern Arizona

Tombstone

Born on the site of a wildly successful silver mine, this town 67 mi southeast of Tucson on U.S. 80 was headquarters of many of the West's rowdies in the late 1800s. The famous shoot-out at the OK Corral and other gunfights are replayed on Sunday on the town's main drag, **Allen Street.** As you enter Tombstone from the northwest, you'll pass **Boot Hill Graveyard,** where the victims of the OK Corral shoot-out are buried. The **Tombstone Courthouse State Historic Park** (⊠ Toughnut and 3rd Sts., ☎ 520/457–3311) offers an excellent introduction to the town's past.

Bisbee

Once a mining boomtown, Bisbee, set on a mountainside 24 mi south of Tombstone, is now an artists' colony. Arizona's largest pit mine yielded some 94 million tons of copper ore before mining activity halted in the early 1970s; at the **Lavender Pit Mine** you can still see the huge crater left by the process. The **Mining and Historical Museum** (⊠ 5 Copper Queen Plaza, ☎ 520/432–7071) is filled with old photos and artifacts from the town's heyday. Behind the museum is the venerable **Copper Queen Hotel** (☞ Dining and Lodging, *below*), home away from home to such guests as "Black Jack" Pershing, John Wayne, and Teddy Roosevelt. The **Copper Queen mine tour** (⊠ 478 N. Dart Rd., ☎ 520/432–2071), led by retired miners, is an entertaining way to learn about the town's history.

Dining and Lodging

For price ranges *see* Charts 1 (B) and 2 (B) *in* On the Road with Fodor's.

Bisbee

$$ ✕ **Café Roka.** One of the best bargains in southern Arizona, this chic
★ northern Italian restaurant in a historic building offers delicious pasta dinners (including soup and salad) at very reasonable prices. ⊠ *35 Main St.,* ☎ *520/432–5153. MC, V. Closed Sun.–Tues. No lunch.*

$$ ✕ **Stenzel's.** Set in a white-clapboard cottage, Stenzel's is touted for its seafood specialties, ribs, and fettuccine Alfredo. There's a decent wine list. ⊠ *207 Tombstone Canyon,* ☎ *520/432–7611. MC, V. Closed Wed. No lunch weekends.*

$$–$$$ ▦ **Copper Queen Hotel.** This turn-of-the-century hotel in the heart of
★ downtown has thin walls but a lot of Victorian charm. The boom-days memorabilia throughout is fascinating. ⊠ *11 Howell Ave., Drawer CQ, 85603,* ☎ *520/432–2216 or 800/247–5829,* FAX *520/432–4298. 45 rooms. Dining room, bar, pool. AE, D, DC, MC, V.*

$$ ▦ **Clawson House.** Terrific views of town from the sunporch, a light-filled kitchen, and generous but healthy breakfasts are among the reasons to seek out this B&B on Old Bisbee's Castle Rock. ⊠ *116 Clawson Ave. (Box 454), 85603,* ☎ *520/432–5237 or 800/467–5237. 3 rooms, 2 share bath. AE, D, MC, V.*

Tombstone

$ ✕ **Nellie Cashman's.** Come to this homey spot, named for the Tombstone pioneer who opened it in 1882, for juicy pork chops, chicken-fried steak, or for a country breakfast complete with biscuits and gravy. ⊠ *5th and Toughnut Sts.,* ☎ *520/457–2212. AE, D, MC, V.*

$$ ▦ **Best Western Look-Out Lodge.** This motel off U.S. 80 on the way into town has a lot of character. Rooms have views of the Dragoon

Mountains and desert valley. ✉ *U.S. 80W (Box 787), 85638,* ☎ *520/457–2223 or 800/652–6772,* 🖷 *520/457–3870. 40 rooms. Pool. AE, D, DC, MC, V.*

$ 🛏 **Tombstone Boarding House.** Two meticulously restored 1880s adobes sit side by side in a quiet residential neighborhood; guests of this friendly B&B sleep in one house and go next door to have a hearty country breakfast in the other. ✉ *108 N. 4th St. (Box 906), 85638,* ☎ *520/457–3716,* 🖷 *520/457–3038. 8 rooms. No credit cards.*

NEVADA

Updated by
Deke
Castleman

Capital	Carson City
Population	1,603,000
Motto	Battle Born
State Bird	Mountain bluebird
State Flower	Sagebrush
Postal Abbreviation	NV

Statewide Visitor Information

Nevada Commission on Tourism (✉ Capitol Complex, Carson City 89710, ☎ 702/687–4322 or 800/638–2328).

Scenic Drives

The **"Loneliest Road in America"** is U.S. 50, which cuts across the central part of the state from Carson City to Ely. **U.S. 93** north from Las Vegas runs more than 500 mi through long desert valleys and passes 13,061-ft **Wheeler Peak,** the second-highest point in the state. For a good look at the Southwest's desert, particularly in the spring, take **U.S. 93/95** southeast from Las Vegas, turning east onto Route 147 in Henderson, which takes you through Lake Mead National Recreation Area to Valley of Fire State Park (☞ Las Vegas, *below*).

National and State Parks

National Park
Great Basin National Park (✉ Off U.S. 93 at the Nevada-Utah border; Baker 89311, ☎ 702/234–7331) is 77,092 acres of dramatic mountains, lush meadows, alpine lakes, limestone caves, and a stand of bristlecone pines (the oldest living trees in the world), with many areas for camping, hiking, and picnicking.

State Parks
For information on Nevada's 23 state parks, contact the state tourism office (☞ Statewide Visitor Information, *above*). **Washoe Lake State Recreation Area** (✉ Off U.S. 395; 4855 E. Lake Blvd., Carson City 89704, ☎ 702/687–4319), with views of the majestic Sierra Nevada, is popular for fishing and horseback riding.

LAS VEGAS

Las Vegas is known around the world as a fantasy land for adults. It was named Las Vegas, meaning "the meadows," by a Spanish scouting party who found a spring here in the 1820s. Mormons settled the valley briefly in 1855, but until the turn of the century it was little more than a handful of ranches and homesteads. The San Pedro, Los Angeles, and Salt Lake Railroad founded the town of Las Vegas in 1905 as a watering stop for its steam trains. The construction of Hoover Dam in the 1930s brought a large wave of settlers seeking jobs.

The Las Vegas that we know today began shortly after World War II when mobster Benjamin "Bugsy" Siegel decided to build a gambling resort in the desert (gambling had been legalized in the state in 1931). Bugsy built his Flamingo with money borrowed from fellow mobsters, who rubbed him out when the casino flopped. The resort eventually recovered and casino-hotels on the Las Vegas Strip caught on. Now the city is home to 9 of the 10 largest hotels in the world.

Visitor Information

Las Vegas Chamber of Commerce (✉ 711 E. Desert Inn Rd., 89109, ☎ 702/735–1616). **Las Vegas Convention and Visitors Authority** (✉ 3150 Paradise Rd., 89109, ☎ 702/892–0711).

Arriving and Departing

By Bus
Greyhound Lines (✉ 200 S. Main St., ☎ 800/231–2222).

By Car
Major highways leading into Las Vegas are I–15 from Los Angeles and Salt Lake City, U.S. 95 from Reno, and U.S. 93 from Arizona.

By Plane
McCarran International Airport (☎ 702/261–5743), about 2 mi from the southern end of the Strip, is served by major airlines. Taxi fare from the airport to Strip hotels is about $9–$12; to the downtown hotels, about $15–$18; but the best and least-expensive way to reach your hotel ($4–$6 per person) is by **Bell Trans Limousine** (☎ 702/739–7990), which you will find near the taxis.

By Train
Amtrak serves downtown's Union Station (✉ 1 N. Main St., ☎ 702/386–6896 or 800/872–7245).

Getting Around Las Vegas

Taxis, easily found in front of every hotel, are the best way to get around the city. The **Strip bus** (Citizens Area Transit, or CAT, ☎ 702/228–7433) costs $1.50 and links the Strip and the downtown with stops near major hotels. If you want to drive out of town or explore the desert, you can rent a car, but be sure to gas up before you go; you won't find many stations out there.

Exploring Las Vegas

Las Vegas is a relatively small city and is easy to explore on foot, but beware: During the extremely hot months of June, July, and August, walking outside for an extended length of time is not recommended.

The downtown casino center may be only four blocks long, but it is the most brightly lighted four blocks in the world. The $70 million **Fremont Street Experience** was completed in December 1995: It's a four-block pedestrian mall covered by an arched 100-ft-high awning that's lighted by 2 *million* lightbulbs. A kaleidoscopic light-and-sound show is presented here on the hour after dark until midnight. A focal point of downtown is **Jackie Gaughan's Plaza Hotel and Casino** (✉ 1 N. Main St., ☎ 702/386–2110), built on the site of the old Union Pacific train station—the only train station in the world that is actually inside a casino.

Among the downtown hotel-casinos, the **Golden Nugget** (✉ 129 E. Fremont St., ☎ 702/385–7111) has a particularly attractive lobby, where you can see an enormous, 61-pound gold nugget. **Binion's Horseshoe** (✉ 128 E. Fremont St., ☎ 702/382–1600) is an old-fashioned gambling joint that has a display of $1 million in cash. The **Four Queens Hotel** (✉ 202 E. Fremont St., ☎ 702/385–4011) is the home of the biggest slot machine in the world: 18 ft long and 7 ft high, with room for six players.

The **Stratosphere Tower** (✉ 2000 Las Vegas Blvd. S, ☎ 702/380–7777) opened in April 1996. At 1,149 ft, it's the tallest building west of the Mississippi. High-speed elevators whisk you to a 12-story pod with a

Las Vegas

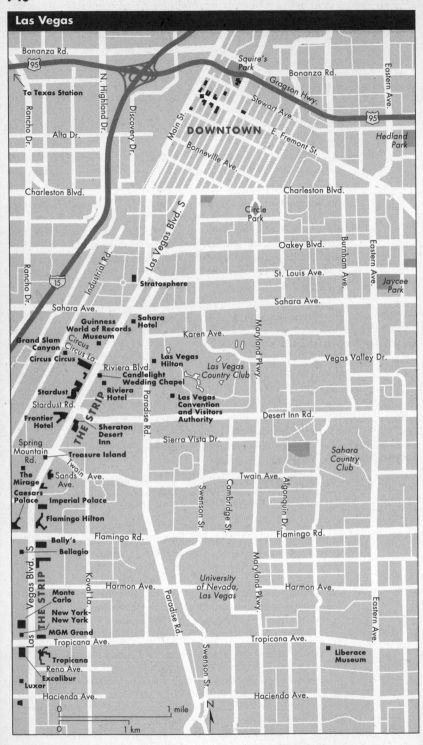

Bonanza Rd.

To Texas Station

Rancho Dr.

N. Highland Dr.

Discovery Dr.

Squire's Park

Bonanza Rd.

Gragson Hwy.

Stewart Ave.

E. Fremont St.

Eastern Ave.

Alta Dr.

Main St.

DOWNTOWN

Bonneville Ave.

Hedland Park

Charleston Blvd.

Charleston Blvd.

Circle Park

Oakey Blvd.

Burnham Ave.

Eastern Ave.

Industrial Rd.

Las Vegas Blvd. S.

St. Louis Ave.

Jaycee Park

Rancho Dr.

Sahara Ave.

Sahara Ave.

Stratosphere

Sahara Ave.

Sahara Hotel

Karen Ave.

Maryland Pkwy.

Guinness World of Records Museum

Grand Slam Canyon

Circus Circus La.

Las Vegas Hilton

Vegas Valley Dr.

Circus Circus

Riviera Blvd.

Candlelight Wedding Chapel

Las Vegas Country Club

Stardust

Riviera Hotel

Paradise Rd.

Las Vegas Convention and Visitors Authority

Stardust Rd.

THE STRIP

Desert Inn Rd.

Frontier Hotel

Sheraton Desert Inn

Sierra Vista Dr.

Sahara Country Club

Spring Mountain Rd.

Treasure Island

Twain Ave.

The Mirage

Sands Ave.

Twain Ave.

Swenson St.

Cambridge St.

Algonquin Dr.

Caesars Palace

Imperial Palace

Flamingo Hilton

Flamingo Rd.

Flamingo Rd.

Bally's

Las Vegas Blvd. S.

Bellagio

Harmon Ave.

Koval La.

University of Nevada, Las Vegas

Maryland Pkwy.

Harmon Ave.

Eastern Ave.

Monte Carlo

THE STRIP

New York-New York

MGM Grand

Tropicana Ave.

Paradise Rd.

Tropicana Ave.

Tropicana

Reno Ave.

Swenson St.

Liberace Museum

Excalibur

Luxor

Hacienda Ave.

Hacienda Ave.

0   1 mile

0   1 km

N

revolving restaurant, bar, wedding chapels, meeting rooms, and—get this—a roller coaster running around outside 900 ft above ground and the Big Shot thrill ride, which thrusts up and free-falls down the needle. Only in Las Vegas.

The **Strip** is a 3½-mi stretch of Las Vegas Boulevard South. It begins at the **Sahara Hotel** (✉ 2535 Las Vegas Blvd. S, ☎ 702/737–2111), which was built in 1952 and has a clock on top of its tallest tower. The **Guinness World of Records Museum** (✉ 2780 Las Vegas Blvd. S, ☎ 702/792–3766) honors such record holders as the tallest man in the world and has videos of some records being set. Next door to Guinness is **Circus Circus** (✉ 2880 Las Vegas Blvd. S, ☎ 702/734–0410), the first Las Vegas hotel to cater to families with children. It has a midway with carnival games, free circus acts, and a 5-acre indoor amusement park called **Grand Slam Canyon** (☎ 702/794–3939) with the world's largest indoor roller coaster. The **Candlelight Wedding Chapel** (✉ 2855 Las Vegas Blvd. S, ☎ 702/735–4179) is the busiest chapel in town.

The **Riviera Hotel** (✉ 2901 Las Vegas Blvd. S, ☎ 702/734–5110) is noted for its four showrooms. The reclusive billionaire Howard Hughes lived in the penthouse of the **Sheraton Desert Inn** (✉ 3145 Las Vegas Blvd. S, ☎ 702/733–4444), one of the smallest and most upscale hotel-casinos on the Strip. Hughes owned the **Frontier Hotel** (✉ 3120 Las Vegas Blvd. S, ☎ 702/794–8200); today it caters to a young crowd, with good, cheap food and low table minimums. At the $670 million palace known as the **Mirage** (✉ 3400 Las Vegas Blvd. S, ☎ 702/791–7111), a volcano erupts in a front yard landscaped with a towering waterfall, lagoons, and tropical plants; inside is a glassed-in tigers' den. Adjacent to (and owned by) the Mirage, the **Treasure Island** resort (✉ 3300 Las Vegas Blvd. S, ☎ 702/894–7111) is loosely based on Robert Louis Stevenson's novel—pirates and sailors engage in ship-to-ship cannon battles in Buccaneer Bay out front.

The **Imperial Palace Hotel and Casino** (✉ 3535 Las Vegas Blvd. S, ☎ 702/731–3311) is the home of the Imperial Palace Auto Collection, which displays more than 300 antique and classic cars, many once owned by the famous and the infamous, such as Adolf Hitler and Al Capone. The **Flamingo Hilton** (✉ 3555 Las Vegas Blvd. S, ☎ 702/733–3111), with the most lush and luxurious pool areas in the city, was the first luxury resort on the Strip, established by Bugsy Siegel in 1946.

The high stakes at the opulent **Caesars Palace** (✉ 3570 Las Vegas Blvd. S, ☎ 702/731–7110) attract serious gamblers. **Bally's** (✉ 3645 Las Vegas Blvd. S, ☎ 702/739–4111) is colossal. Across the Strip from Bally's, the Mirage company is building **Bellagio,** a $1.2 billion megaresort due to open in 1998. Among other stunning features, the 122-acre site will include a 12-acre lake complete with a $30 million musical water-jet ballet.

The emerald green **MGM Grand** (✉ 3799 Las Vegas Blvd. S, ☎ 702/891–1111) houses the largest casino in the world—so large it's divided into four casinos, each delineated by different carpeting. The sprawling grounds of the **Tropicana** (✉ 3801 Las Vegas Blvd. S, ☎ 702/739–2222) are landscaped especially attractively—some of the plantings are more than 40 years old. The blue-and-pink castlelike **Excalibur** (✉ 3850 Las Vegas Blvd. S, ☎ 702/597–7777), built on a medieval theme, is the city's third-largest hotel. **New York–New York** (✉ 3790 Las Vegas Blvd. S, ☎ 702/740–6969), one of the newer megaresorts on the Strip, opened in January 1997. It has 2,200 rooms, a replica of the New York City skyline, and a roller coaster. Next door to New York–New York is the **Monte Carlo** (⊠ 3770 Las Vegas Blvd. S, ☎ 702/730–7777) megaresort; it opened in June 1996 and has 3,000 rooms and a 19th-century Victorian theme. **Luxor** (⊠ 3900 Las Vegas Blvd. S, ☎ 702/ 262–4000) is a 30-story Egyptian-style pyramid, with some of the most high-tech arcade and entertainment options in town. The **Liberace Museum** (⊠ 1775 E. Tropicana Ave., ☎ 702/798–5595), 2 mi east of the Strip, occupies three buildings: one for the entertainer's pianos and cars, one for his costumes, and the third for general memorabilia.

Outside Vegas

The awe-inspiring **Hoover Dam** (⊠ Rte. 93, east of Boulder City, ☎ 702/293–8321), about 35 mi east of Las Vegas, was constructed in the 1930s to tame the destructive waters of the Colorado River and produce electricity. Tours into the 727-ft-high, 660-ft-thick dam are given daily except Christmas.

Construction of the Hoover Dam created **Lake Mead** (⊠ Alan Bible Visitor Center, U.S. 93 and Lakeshore Dr., ☎ 702/293–8906), the largest man-made lake in the western hemisphere, with more than 500 mi of shoreline. It is popular for boating, fishing, and swimming. For water tours of the lake and Hoover Dam, contact **Lake Mead Cruises** (☎ 702/ 293–6180).

Dramatic **Valley of Fire State Park** (⊠ Rte. 169, Overton, ☎ 702/397– 2088), 55 mi northeast of Lake Mead, contains distinctive polychrome sandstone formations and mysterious Anasazi petroglyphs.

Red Rock Canyon (⊠ Rte. 159, ☎ 702/363–1921), though closer to Las Vegas (only 20 mi west) than Valley of Fire, is slightly less spectacular. Still, the sheer sandstone cliffs and twisting ravines are an internationally known mecca for rock climbers. A 13-mi loop drive begins at the canyon visitor center.

For a respite from the noise and excitement of Las Vegas and the heat of the desert, travel 35 mi northwest of the city on U.S. 95 and Route 157 to **Mt. Charleston,** with its forest, canyons, and 12,000-ft peak. The skiing in winter (Lee Canyon) and hiking, camping, and picnicking the rest of the year are excellent.

Though it isn't exactly in the vicinity (it's a five-hour drive; two hours by small plane and one hour by jet), Las Vegas does consider itself a gateway to the awesome, vastly silent **Grand Canyon National Park** (⊠ Box 129, Grand Canyon, AZ 86023, ☎ 520/638–7888; ☞ Arizona). One of the world's greatest wonders, the canyon is stunning in depth and size, and its layers of rock reveal a fascinating geological profile of Earth. **South Rim Travel** (☎ 520/638–2748 or 800/682–4393), through its sister company, TriStar Vacations, has the only jet service from Las Vegas to the Grand Canyon; it is a full-service travel agency that can also arrange rooms, cars, and Colorado River trips. For longer flights in smaller planes at lower elevations, try **Air Nevada** (☎ 702/736–8900).

Casino Gambling

Most major hotels in Las Vegas (as well as in Reno and Lake Tahoe) are centered on large casinos. The three largest casinos in Las Vegas are at MGM Grand, Riviera, and Excalibur (☞ *below*). The games played in the casinos are slots, blackjack, baccarat, craps, roulette, keno, video poker, Let It Ride, Caribbean Stud, wheel of fortune, and track and sports betting. Most larger casinos offer free gaming lessons, usually during the slower morning hours. Slot machines are by far the favorite game; thanks to progressive computer-linked slot jackpots, such as Megabucks and Quartermania, wins have gone into the millions.

With more than 60 major hotel-casinos competing for visitors and their dollars, most try to separate themselves from the pack with some distinguishing characteristic. Those with the most imaginative themes or attractive particulars are listed below.

Binion's Horseshoe Hotel and Casino (⊠ 128 E. Fremont St., ☎ 702/382–1600) is home of the World Series of Poker, the world's highest-paying gambling tournament, and attracts some of the world's largest wagers.

Caesars Palace (⊠ 3570 Las Vegas Blvd. S, ☎ 702/731–7110), a sprawling ersatz temple for serious gamblers with money to burn, lays on the ancient-Rome theme, complete with toga-clad cocktail waitresses and Cleopatra's Barge lounge.

Circus Circus (⊠ 2880 Las Vegas Blvd. S, ☎ 702/734–0410) casino is under a pink-and-white big top and takes on the hurly-burly atmosphere of a three-ring circus. For such a huge hotel, it has surprisingly low minimums, and its slot club is the only one in town that gives a cash rebate for blackjack play.

Excalibur (⊠ 3850 Las Vegas Blvd. S, ☎ 702/597–7777) recalls the days of King Arthur. The casino is cavernous and cacophonous—with 2,630 slot machines, what else could it be?

Flamingo Hilton (⊠ 3555 Las Vegas Blvd. S, ☎ 702/733–3111) bears no resemblance to the "classy little joint" built by Bugsy Siegel in 1946. The splendiferous pink-flamingo theme is rampant in the huge casino, which is typical of a center-Strip megaresort: sprawling, raucous, and all the $5 minimum tables jammed with players. Video poker payouts are good, and the Flamingo is known for offering its slot club members free rooms throughout the year.

Golden Nugget Hotel and Casino (⊠ 129 E. Fremont St., ☎ 702/385–7111) is more Hollywood than Vegas, with white marble, gold leaf, gold-plated elevators, and palm trees.

Jackie Gaughan's Plaza Hotel and Casino (⊠ 1 N. Main St., ☎ 702/386–2110) is the only casino in the world with its own train station; Amtrak stops here twice daily. The casino is low-roller heaven, with penny slots, full-pay nickel video poker, 25¢ craps, and $2 blackjack galore.

Las Vegas Hilton (⊠ 3000 W. Paradise Rd., ☎ 702/732–5111) has the largest sports book in the world, with 46 video screens.

Luxor (⊠ 3900 Las Vegas Blvd. S, ☎ 702/262–4000) re-creates ancient Egypt with its 29-million-cubic-ft pyramid. The casino is roomy, regal, and round.

MGM Grand Hotel and Theme Park (⊠ 3805 Las Vegas Blvd. S, ☎ 702/891–1111) is the world's second-largest casino, with 3,500 slot machines, more than 100 gaming tables, and a Hollywood entertainment theme.

The Mirage (⊠ 3400 Las Vegas Blvd. S, ☎ 702/791–7111) transports you to the South Seas, with thatch-roof gaming areas and tropical plants and flowers flanking an indoor stream and pond. The high-roller slot area has machines that take $500 tokens.

Sheraton Desert Inn (⊠ 3145 Las Vegas Blvd. S, ☎ 702/733–4444) is small, relaxed, and elegant, appealing to the most exclusive clientele in town.

Tropicana (⊠ 3801 Las Vegas Blvd. S, ☎ 702/739–2222) is lush and tropical, with a stunning pool area complete with swim-up blackjack in summer.

Getting Married in Las Vegas

Nevada is one of the easiest—and least- expensive—states in which to get married. There is no blood test or waiting period; all you need is a license ($35) from the Marriage License Bureau (⊠ 200 S. 3rd St., ☎ 702/455–4415), and you're ready to go. In Las Vegas there are about 25 chapels along the Strip, not including the hotel chapels at Bally's, Circus Circus, Excalibur, Imperial Palace, and Riviera (☞ Exploring Las Vegas, *above*). Services start at around $50.

What to See and Do with Children

Wet n' Wild (⊠ 2600 Las Vegas Blvd. S, ☎ 702/737–3819) is a 26-acre amusement park with every water ride imaginable. **Lied Discovery Children's Museum** (⊠ 833 Las Vegas Blvd. N, ☎ 702/382–5473) has hands-on science exhibits. **Southern Nevada Zoological Park** (⊠ 1775 N. Rancho Dr., ☎ 702/648–5955) is a small but enjoyable zoo. Other good bets for children include the view from the top of the **Stratosphere**; the **Circus Circus** midway; **Excalibur**'s Medieval Village, a shopping and dining complex, and Fantasy Faire, a kid's game area; the **Guinness World of Records Museum**; the amusement park at the **MGM Grand**; and the **Imperial Palace Auto Collection** (☞ Exploring Las Vegas, *above*).

Dining

Foods from some 40 countries are represented in Las Vegas restaurants. Dining options range from elegant gourmet meals at the best hotels to all-you-can-eat buffets, for which the city is justly famous. Most hotels have buffets at breakfast ($3–$4), lunch ($5–$7), and dinner ($6–$9). The cheapest buffet is at Circus Circus; the two best are at the Rio and Texas Station. The best Sunday champagne brunch (the Sterling) is also at Bally's. For price ranges *see* Chart 1 (A) *in* On the Road with Fodor's.

$$$$ ✕ **Chin's.** An upscale Chinese restaurant with a bright, contemporary decor, Chin's offers such specialties as strawberry chicken and pepper orange roughy. ⊠ *Fashion Show Mall, 3200 Las Vegas Blvd. S,* ☎ *702/733–8899. AE, D, DC, MC, V.*

$$$$ ✕ **Palace Court.** The flagship restaurant of Caesars Palace is under a
★   beautiful dome in a round room with greenery and floor-to-ceiling picture windows. The fare is classic French; chateaubriand is a specialty. ⊠ *3570 Las Vegas Blvd. S,* ☎ *702/731–7547. Jacket and tie. AE, D, DC, MC, V.*

$$$ ✕ **Le Montrachet.** This quiet place away from the chatter of the slot
★   machines, with elaborate table settings and pastoral scenes on the walls, is the pride of the Las Vegas Hilton. The menu changes with the season, but the rack of lamb is always good. ⊠ *3000 W. Paradise Rd.,* ☎ *702/732–5801. Jacket and tie. AE, D, DC, MC, V.*

$$$ ✕ **Pamplemousse.** The loving creation of Georges LaForges, a former Las Vegas maître d', this restaurant looks like a little French country inn. There is no menu; the waiter recites the daily specials and their method of preparation. ⊠ *400 E. Sahara Ave.,* ☎ *702/733–2066. Jacket required. AE, D, DC, MC, V.*

$$ ✕ **Alpine Village.** You can't miss this place: It looks like a Swiss chalet, inside and out. The fare is German-Swiss; the sauerbraten is something special. Below the main restaurant is a lively rathskeller with oompah music. ⊠ *3003 Paradise Rd.,* ☎ *702/734–6888. AE, D, DC, MC, V.*

$$ ✕ **Battista's Hole in the Wall.** Battista Locatelli, a former opera singer, prides himself on the quality of his mostly northern Italian food, as well as on the cleanliness of his kitchen. Decorated with wine bottles, garlic, and celebrity photos, the restaurant offers lots of specials, with all the free wine you can drink. ⊠ *4041 Audrie St.,* ☎ *702/732–1424. AE, D, DC, MC, V. No lunch.*

$$ ✕ **Bertolini's.** This sidewalk café inside the Forum Shops at Caesars
★ can be noisy, but the northern Italian fare is first rate. Order individual pizzas, soups, salads, and luscious gelato and sorbet. ⊠ *3570 Las Vegas Blvd. S,* ☎ *702/735–4663. AE, MC, V.*

$$ ✕ **The Steak House.** In the center of a dark, quiet room with wood paneling and antique brass, reminiscent of 1890s San Francisco, steaks aged to perfection are cooked over an open-hearth charcoal grill. ⊠ *Circus Circus, 2880 Las Vegas Blvd. S,* ☎ *702/794–3767. AE, D, DC, MC, V. No lunch.*

$$ ✕ **The Tillerman.** Seafood flown in fresh from the West Coast daily is
★ served in a garden setting under a skylight. The yellowfin tuna is especially reliable. ⊠ *2245 E. Flamingo Rd.,* ☎ *702/731–4036. Reservations not accepted. AE, D, DC, MC, V.*

$ ✕ **Roberta's.** This is Las Vegas's most venerable "bargain gourmet" room, at the historic El Cortez downtown. You won't believe the prices, especially for a 16-ounce prime rib or a pound of king crab legs. ⊠ *El Cortez, 600 E. Fremont St.,* ☎ *702/386–0692. AE, MC, V. No lunch.*

$ ✕ **Viva Mercado's.** Don't let the shopping center location fool you: This is one of the most popular Mexican restaurants in town—and for good reason. The room is cozy, and the food is creative, especially the house specials. ⊠ *6182 W. Flamingo Rd.,* ☎ *702/871–8826. Reservations not accepted. AE, MC, V.*

Lodging

Las Vegas lodging ranges from virtual palaces to simple motels. The hotels tend to be a better bet for value; for instance, Circus Circus—one of the largest resort hotels in the world—has among the lowest-priced rooms in town. The largest and most lavish hotels are on the Strip; downtown hotels are generally less expensive. For price ranges *see* Chart 2 (A) *in* On the Road with Fodor's.

$$$$ 🏨 **Caesars Palace.** This hotel caters to an upscale clientele, with world-
★ class service, lavish restaurants, and superstar entertainers like Diana Ross and David Copperfield. Its casino is full of fancy people making sizable wagers. Most guest rooms are opulent, even by Las Vegas standards, and many have Roman-style tubs. ⊠ *3570 Las Vegas Blvd. S, 89109,* ☎ *702/731–7110 or 800/634–6661,* 𝔽𝔸𝕏 *702/731–6636. 1,518 rooms. 9 restaurants, lounge, 2 pools, spa, 4 tennis courts, shops, cinema, casino, showroom. AE, D, DC, MC, V.*

$$$$ 🏨 **The Mirage.** This extravagent hotel, opened in 1989, launched the
★ current building boom in Las Vegas—nine years and counting. It's the centerpiece of the Strip, the standard by which all other new megaresorts are measured. With its lush tropical landscaping, minimal reliance on neon, efficient use of recycled water, rain-forest dome, and tiger and dolphin habitats, the Mirage symbolizes the new Las Vegas. ⊠ *3400 Las Vegas Blvd. S, 89109,* ☎ *702/791–7111 or 800/627–6667,* 𝔽𝔸𝕏 *702/791–7446. 3,049 rooms. 9 restaurants, lounge, pool, 4 tennis courts, exercise room, casino, showroom. AE, D, DC, MC, V.*

$$$$ 🏨 **Sheraton Desert Inn.** Surrounded by a private golf course and offering town houses as well as televised gambling lessons, this hotel is one of the town's more restrained. The elegant rooms have a southwestern ambience. ⊠ *3145 Las Vegas Blvd. S, 89109,* ☎ *702/733–4444 or 800/634–6906,* 𝔽𝔸𝕏 *702/733–4774. 821 rooms. 5 restaurants, lounge, spa, 10 tennis courts, golf course, health club, casino, showroom. AE, D, DC, MC, V.*

$$$ ☒ **Golden Nugget.** The largest and classiest joint in the Glitter Gulch, the Nugget runs the gamut from traditional downtown bargains (dollar blackjack and draft beer) to Strip-style fanciness (a segregated baccarat pit for high rollers). The lobby is decorated with marble and etched glass; guest rooms reflect the same elegance. ☒ *129 E. Fremont St., 89101,* ☎ *702/385–7111 or 800/634–3454,* ℻ *702/386–8362. 1,909 rooms. 5 restaurants, lounge, pool, health club, casino, showroom. AE, D, DC, MC, V.*

$$ ☒ **Bally's.** This is the only hotel in the city with two full-size showrooms: one for headliners and one for the long-running production show *Jubilee!* Many of the attractive guest rooms are suites, and some have round beds under mirrored ceilings. A $25 million elevated monorail links the MGM Grand and Bally's. ☒ *3645 Las Vegas Blvd. S, 89109,* ☎ *702/739–4111 or 800/634–3434,* ℻ *702/739–4405. 2,832 rooms. 9 restaurants, lounge, pool, 10 tennis courts, health club, shops, casino, 2 showrooms. AE, D, DC, MC, V.*

$$ ☒ **Excalibur.** This pink-and-blue turreted castle is the third-largest resort hotel in Las Vegas. Excalibur tries hard to fulfill the promise of its Renaissance theme, with King Arthur's jousting tournament, a medieval midway, and strolling minstrels, mimes, and musicians. This and its inexpensive food make it appeal mostly to families. ☒ *3850 Las Vegas Blvd. S,* ☎ *702/597–7777 or 800/937–7777,* ℻ *702/597–7009. 4,032 rooms. 7 restaurants, lounge, pool, shops, casino, showroom. AE, D, DC, MC, V.*

$$ ☒ **Flamingo Hilton.** The first luxury hotel in Las Vegas, once surrounded only by desert, the Flamingo has 3,500 rooms, a time-share tower, a lush 15-acre pool area, and very reasonable rates. Bugsy would be proud. ☒ *3555 Las Vegas Blvd. S, 89109,* ☎ *702/733–3111 or 800/732–2111,* ℻ *702/733–3528. 3,530 rooms. 8 restaurants, lounge, 4 pools, spa, 4 tennis courts, casino, showroom. AE, D, DC, MC, V.*

$$ ☒ **Harrah's Las Vegas.** In 1997 Harrah's replaced its signature riverboat facade with a more tasteful though nondescript design, as part of a $150 million expansion and renovation. However, it's still the flagship of Harrah's extensive national gambling fleet. The rooms are modest by Strip standards, decorated with muted tones and dark-wood furniture. ☒ *3475 Las Vegas Blvd. S, 89109,* ☎ *702/369–5000 or 800/634–6765,* ℻ *702/369–5008. 1,725 rooms. 5 restaurants, lounge, pool, exercise room, casino, comedy club, showroom. AE, D, DC, MC, V.*

$$ ☒ **Las Vegas Hilton.** This megasize hotel seems even larger because it sits next to the low-rise Convention Center; with 29 floors and three wings, it's one of the most recognizable hotels in town. The rooms are large, and those on the higher floors have great views. A *Star Trek* theme park opened in spring 1997. ☒ *3000 Paradise Rd., 89109,* ☎ *702/732–5111 or 800/732–7117,* ℻ *702/794–3611. 3,174 rooms. 11 restaurants, lounge, pool, spa, putting green, 6 tennis courts, casino, showroom. AE, D, DC, MC, V.*

$$ ☒ **Luxor.** This bronze-color pyramid-shape building recalls ancient Egypt with a sphinx out front and a replica of King Tut's tomb inside. "Inclinators" rise to the top floor at a 39-degree angle. ☒ *3900 Las Vegas Blvd. S, 89119,* ☎ *702/262–4000 or 800/288–1000,* ℻ *702/262–4454. 2,535 rooms. 7 restaurants, lounge, casino, shops, showroom. AE, D, DC, MC, V.*

$$ ☒ **MGM Grand.** This movie-theme megaresort is the largest in the world. Four emerald green hotel towers bring to mind the *Wizard of Oz*; a 33-acre theme park re-creates Hollywood back lots with rides and performances. ☒ *3799 Las Vegas Blvd. S, 89119,* ☎ *702/891–1111 or 800/929–1111,* ℻ *702/891–1030. 5,005 rooms. 9 restau-*

rants, lounge, pool, tennis courts, health club, casino, comedy club, recreation room, 2 showrooms, nursery. AE, D, DC, MC, V.

$$ ⬚ **Rio Suite.** These four red-and-blue towers contain only suites. Ask
★ for a unit on one of the top floors and on the east side, facing the Strip. In February 1997, the fourth expansion in six years added a 41-story tower that contains the most festive casino in town—singers, dancers, and jugglers all in Mardi Gras costumes and a Masquerade Show that features parade floats inching along a 950-ft track suspended from the high ceiling. ✉ *3700 W. Flamingo Rd. (at Valley View), 89109,* ☎ *702/ 252–7777 or 800/888–1808,* FAX *702/253–6090. 2,220 suites. 12 restaurants, lounge, pool, health club, showroom, casino. AE, D, DC, MC, V.*

$$ ⬚ **Riviera.** One of the city's most famous and venerable hotels, the Riviera has one of the largest casinos in the world. The location is convenient to the upper Strip and to the convention center. ✉ *2901 Las Vegas Blvd. S, 89109,* ☎ *702/734–5110 or 800/634–6753,* FAX *702/ 794–9663. 2,220 rooms. 5 restaurants, food court, pool, 2 tennis courts, health club, casino, comedy club, 3 showrooms. AE, D, DC, MC, V.*

$$ ⬚ **Treasure Island.** The hotel's theme is loosely based on Robert Louis Stevenson's novel, and the landscaping and decor are ersatz South Seas. There's a re-created 18th-century pirate village and a monorail to the Mirage. ✉ *3300 Las Vegas Blvd. S, 89109,* ☎ *702/894–7111 or 800/ 944–7444,* FAX *702/894–7446. 2,912 rooms. 5 restaurants, lounge, pool, health club, shops, casino, showroom. AE, D, DC, MC, V.*

$$ ⬚ **Tropicana.** Two high-rise towers loom above beautiful grounds, complete with waterfalls and swans. Room decor is tropical, with bamboo and pastels. ✉ *3801 Las Vegas Blvd. S, 89109,* ☎ *702/739– 2222 or 800/634–4000,* FAX *702/739–2469. 1,912 rooms. 6 restaurants, lounge, 3 pools, 4 tennis courts, health club, racquetball, casino, showroom. AE, D, DC, MC, V.*

$ ⬚ **Circus Circus.** Catering primarily to families with children, the hotel has painted circus tents in the hallways and a generally chaotic atmosphere. The brightly decorated rooms (red carpets and chairs; red-, pink-, and blue-striped wallpaper) are small but clean. ✉ *2880 Las Vegas Blvd. S, 89109,* ☎ *702/734–0410 or 800/634–3450,* FAX *702/ 734–2268. 2,793 rooms. 5 restaurants, casino, 3 pools, camping, chapel. AE, D, DC, MC, V.*

$ ⬚ **Jackie Gaughan's Plaza.** This casino-hotel was built on the original site of the Union Pacific train station and now houses an Amtrak station. Rooms are decorated in light mauve tones; those facing east have a great view of downtown. ✉ *1 Main St., 89101,* ☎ *702/386– 2110 or 800/634–6575,* FAX *702/382–8281. 1,037 rooms. 3 restaurants, lounge, pool, casino, showroom. AE, D, DC, MC, V.*

$ ⬚ **Sahara.** Like many of its neighbors, the Sahara began as a small motor hotel and built itself up by adding towers. It's finally expanding its casino, though it will still serve as a business hotel for the convention center down the street. Tower rooms are large, and those that face south overlook the Strip. ✉ *2535 Las Vegas Blvd. S, 89109,* ☎ *702/737–2111 or 800/634–6666,* FAX *702/791–2027. 2,100 rooms. 5 restaurants, lounge, 2 pools, health club, casino, showroom. AE, D, DC, MC, V.*

$ ⬚ **Sam's Town.** This friendly hotel outside town has an Old West theme that feels authentic because the place is so close to the desert. Some rooms have views of the desert and mountains; the inside-facing rooms overlook an 18-story courtyard complete with trees, creeks, and a waterfall. ✉ *5111 Boulder Hwy., 89122,* ☎ *702/456–7777 or 800/634–6371,* FAX *702/454–8014. 650 rooms. 5 restaurants, lounge, pool, bowling, camping, casino. AE, D, DC, MC, V.*

$ ⊡ **Stardust.** From its first incarnation as a motor hotel to its more re-
cent 32-story tower, the Stardust has been one of the best-known hotels on the Strip. The tower rooms are almost always a bargain. ⊠ *3000
Las Vegas Blvd. S, 89109,* ☏ *702/732–6111 or 800/634–6757,* ℻
*702/732–6296. 2,500 rooms. 6 restaurants, lounge, pool, 2 tennis courts,
health club, casino, showroom. AE, D, DC, MC, V.*

Motels
⊡ **Days Inn–Town Hall** (⊠ 4155 Koval La., 89109, ☏ 702/731–2111
or 800/634–6541, ℻ 702/731–1113), 360 rooms, coffee shop, pool;
$. ⊡ **Motel 6** (⊠ 195 E. Tropicana Ave., 89109, ☏ 702/798–0728,
℻ 702/798–5657), 877 rooms, 2 pools; *$.* ⊡ **Westward Ho** (⊠ 2900
Las Vegas Blvd. S, 89109, ☏ 702/731–2900 or 800/634–6651, ℻ 702/
731–6154), 1,000 rooms, restaurant, 7 pools; *$.*

Nightlife and the Arts

Nightlife
Perhaps no other city in America—or even in the world—has more to
do at night than Las Vegas.

SHOWROOMS
Hotel showrooms seat from several hundred to 2,000. Most are luxurious and intimate, with few, if any, bad seats. The old-style seating
system involves arriving early and tipping the maître d' or captain. The
new trend is reserved seating, which eliminates the waiting and the has-
sle. When a show is expected to sell out, hotel guests are given ticket
preference.

There are four main types of entertainment offered in showrooms: head-
liner shows, such as David Copperfield, Tom Jones, and Liza Minnelli;
big production shows, such as "Jubilee!" Bally's *Jubilee!* or the Tropicana's *Folies Bergères,* which include elaborate song-and-dance numbers, smaller specialty acts, and topless showgirls; small production
shows, with song and dance on a smaller scale, such as *Forever Plaid*
at the Flamingo Hilton; and the lounge shows, offered all over town,
where pop bands play dance music and the only admission is the purchase of a drink or two.

The major hotels' entertainment offerings are as follows: **Bally's,** headliners and large production show; **Caesars Palace,** headliners; **Excalibur,** large production show; **Flamingo Hilton,** large and small production
shows; **Harrah's Las Vegas,** small production show; **Imperial Palace,**
small production show; **Las Vegas Hilton,** Andrew Lloyd Weber's
Starlight Express; **MGM Grand,** headliners and large production shows;
Mirage, Siegfried & Roy; **Rio,** small production show; **Riviera,** large
and small production shows; **Stardust,** large production show; **Sheraton Desert Inn,** headliners; **Treasure Island,** Cirque du Soleil; **Tropicana,** large production show. *See* Exploring Las Vegas *and* Lodging,
both above, for addresses and phone numbers.

COMEDY CLUBS
MGM Grand has **Catch a Rising Star.** Harrah's has the **Improv.** The
Tropicana has the **Comedy Stop.** The Riviera has the **Comedy Club.**

The Arts
Most arts events in Las Vegas are associated with the **University of
Nevada, Las Vegas** (☏ 702/895–3011). For additional information
call the **Allied Arts Council** (☏ 702/731–5419).

Outdoor Activities and Sports

Spectator Sports

Boxing: Caesars Palace and **MGM Grand** present championship bouts.

Golf: PGA Las Vegas Invitational (✉ Sheraton Desert Inn, ☎ 702/382–6616); October.

Rodeo: National Finals Rodeo (✉ Thomas Mack Center, University of Nevada, ☎ 702/731–2115).

Shopping

Las Vegas's best shopping is on the Strip at the **Fashion Show Mall** (✉ 3200 Las Vegas Blvd. S, ☎ 702/369–8382), a collection of 150 shops and department stores, including Saks Fifth Avenue and Neiman Marcus. **Forum Shops at Caesars** (✉ 3570 Las Vegas Blvd. S, ☎ 702/893–4800), a complex of 70 specialty stores adjacent to Caesars Palace, dazzles shoppers with a replicated Roman street, complete with columns, piazzas, fountains, and a simulated-sky ceiling. You'll find Gucci, Ann Taylor, the Museum Company, and the Warner Bros. Studio Store alongside several popular restaurants. **Boulevard Mall** (✉ 3528 S. Maryland Pkwy., ☎ 702/735–8268), about 3 mi from the Strip, is the largest shopping mall in Nevada. **Meadows Mall** (✉ 4300 Meadows La., ☎ 702/878–4849) is on the northwest side of town and has a big merry-go-round for kids. **Gamblers General Store** (✉ 800 S. Main St., ☎ 702/382–9903) carries all manner of gambling paraphernalia.

RENO

Reno, once the gambling and divorce capital of the country, is smaller, less crowded, friendlier, and prettier than Las Vegas. The growth of Reno, which was established in 1859 as a trading station at a bridge over the Truckee River, kept pace with that of the silver mines of nearby Virginia City (starting in 1860), the railroad (which gave Reno its name in 1868), and gambling (legalized in 1931). Today Reno is getting a boost from the National Bowling Stadium—the only one of its kind in the country—as well as the new 1,700-room Silver Legacy downtown.

Visitor Information

Reno-Sparks Convention and Visitors Authority (✉ 4590 S. Virginia St., Reno 89502, ☎ 702/827–7600 or 800/367–7366).

Arriving and Departing

By Bus

Greyhound Lines (✉ 155 Stevenson St., ☎ 702/322–2970 or 800/231–2222).

By Car

The major highways leading to Reno are I–80 (east–west) and U.S. 395 (north–south).

By Plane

Reno-Tahoe International Airport (☎ 702/328–6400), served by national and regional airlines, is on the east side of the city and minutes from downtown.

By Train

Amtrak (✉ 135 E. Commercial Row, ☎ 702/329–8638 or 800/872–7245).

Getting Around Reno

Reno is such a small city that the best way to get around is on foot or by taxi. Taxis are easily hired at the airport and in front of the major hotels; the main taxi firms are **Reno-Sparks Cab Co.** (☎ 702/333–3333), **Whittlesea Checker** (☎ 702/322–2222), and **Yellow** (☎ 702/355–5555). Rental car agencies are at the airport. **Reno Citifare** (☎ 702/348–7433) provides local bus service. Many large hotels have courtesy buses on call.

Exploring Reno

One advantage Reno has over Las Vegas is weather: Its summer temperatures are much more agreeable and therefore much more pleasant for strolling. The city's focal point is the famous Reno Arch, a sign over the upper end of Virginia Street proclaiming it "The Biggest Little City in the World."

As in Las Vegas, gambling is a favorite pastime. Although not as garish as their Vegas counterparts, Reno's casinos still offer plenty of glitter and glitz. With the exception of the Reno Hilton, Peppermill, Atlantis, and John Ascuaga's Nugget, they are crowded into five square blocks downtown. The **Reno Tahoe Gaming Academy** (✉ 300 E. 1st St., ☎ 702/329–5665) conducts a behind-the-scenes tour of the Club Cal-Neva. Some of the better casinos are listed below.

Circus Circus (✉ 500 N. Sierra St., ☎ 702/329–0711 or 800/648–5010), marked by a neon clown sucking a lollipop, is the best stop for families with children. Complete with clowns, games, fun-house mirrors, and circus acts, the midway on the mezzanine above the casino floor is open from 10 AM to midnight.

Club Cal-Neva (✉ 38 E. 2nd St., ☎ 702/323–1046) is the best place in town to gamble, with low limits and optimal rules.

Fitzgeralds (✉ 255 N. Virginia St., ☎ 702/785–3300) celebrates the luck of the Irish with a large green casino and a leprechaun mascot. On the second floor in the Lucky Forest you can kiss Blarney stones.

Flamingo Hilton (✉ 255 N. Sierra St., ☎ 702/322–1111 or 800/648–4882) reproduces its Vegas counterpart, complete with a gigantic, neon pink-feathered flamingo. There's a small gambling museum on the second floor.

Harrah's (✉ 219 N. Center St., ☎ 702/786–3232 or 800/648–3773) debuted in 1937 as the Tango Club and now occupies two city blocks, with a sprawling casino, race and sports book, and arcade. A 29-story Hampton Inn annex opened in 1996. There are low minimums and friendly patrons and workers.

Nevada Club (✉ 224 N. Virginia St., ☎ 702/329–1721) takes you back to the 1940s. Many of its slots are old-fashioned one-armed bandits; line up three cherries, and you might win a classic hot rod. There's a World War II–era diner on the second floor, along with penny slots.

Four casinos lie outside the downtown area. **Reno Hilton** (✉ 2500 E. 2nd St., ☎ 702/789–2000 or 800/648–5080), with 100,000 square ft, is the largest casino in Reno. **Peppermill** (✉ 2707 S. Virginia St., ☎ 702/826–2121 or 800/648–6992) is the gaudiest, glitziest, and noisiest. **Atlantis** (✉ 3800 S. Virginia St., ☎ 702/825–4700 or 800/723–6500) has the best buffet in Reno. And **John Ascuaga's Nugget** (✉ 1100 Nugget Ave., Sparks, ☎ 702/356–3300 or 800/648–1177) is the classiest.

Besides the hotel-casinos, Reno has a number of cultural attractions. On the University of Nevada campus, the sleekly designed **Fleischmann Planetarium** (⊠ 1600 N. Virginia St., ☎ 702/784–4811) has films and astronomy presentations. The **Nevada Historical Society** (⊠ 1650 N. Virginia St., ☎ 702/688–1190) has mining exhibits and Native American artifacts. The **Nevada Museum of Art** (⊠ 160 W. Liberty St., ☎ 702/329–3333), the state's largest art museum, has changing exhibits. More than 220 antique and classic automobiles, including an Elvis Presley Cadillac, are on display at the **National Automobile Museum** (⊠ Mill and Lake Sts., ☎ 702/333–9300).

Downtown River Walk (⊠ S. Virginia St. and the river, ☎ 702/334–2077) is a festive scene year-round and often the location for special events featuring street performers, musicians, dancers, food, art displays, and games. **Victorian Square** (⊠ Victorian Ave. between Rock and Pyramid) is fringed by restored turn-of-the-century houses and Victorian-dressed casinos and storefronts; a bandstand-gazebo is the focal point for the many festivals held here.

Outside Reno

Only 25 mi from Reno (U.S. 395 south to Rte. 341), **Virginia City** was once the largest population center in Nevada, with more than 20,000 residents, 110 saloons, and one church. The Comstock Lode, one of the largest gold and silver deposits ever discovered, was responsible for Virginia City's boom (1860–80). Today it's one of the liveliest and most authentically maintained historic mining towns in the West. Little has changed in Virginia City in more than 100 years. You can still belly up to the grand mahogany bar and hear honky-tonk piano music at the **Bucket of Blood** (☎ 702/847–0322) saloon on C Street. The lavish interiors of **Mackay Mansion** (⊠ 129 D St., ☎ 702/847–0173) and the **Castle** (⊠ B St. just south of Taylor, no phone) offer a glimpse into the past, with such adornments as Oriental rugs, Italian marble, and Brussels lace, as well as table settings made from the silver mined beneath these houses. **Virginia & Truckee Railroad** (⊠ Washington and F Sts., ☎ 702/847–0380) takes visitors on historic steam-powered locomotives through the Comstock mining region. Virginia City's most famous resident was Mark Twain, who lived here from 1861 to 1864 while working as a reporter for the *Territorial Enterprise;* the **Mark Twain Museum** (⊠ 47 S. C St., ☎ 702/847–0525) occupies the newspaper's pressroom and exhibits 19th-century printing equipment. For information contact the **Virginia City Chamber of Commerce** (⊠ C St. across from the post office; Box 464, 89440, ☎ 702/847–0311).

South of Virginia City is **Carson City,** the state capital. The **Nevada State Museum** (⊠ 600 N. Carson St., ☎ 702/687–4811), once a U.S. mint, is packed with exhibits on Nevada natural history, the early mining days, antique gaming devices, and willow baskets woven by Washoe artists. The **Nevada State Railroad Museum** (⊠ 2180 S. Carson St., ☎ 702/687–6953) has an extensive historical collection of passenger and freight cars and two restored Virginia & Truckee trains. The **Carson City Chamber of Commerce** (⊠ 1900 S. Carson St., ☎ 702/882–1565) has information on the town's attractions.

Genoa, the oldest settlement in Nevada, is a quaint Victorian town about 20 mi south of Carson City, just west of U.S. 395. **Mormon Station State Historic Park** (⊠ Foothill Rd. and Genoa La., ☎ 702/687–4379) contains an early log cabin and Mormon artifacts. **Walley's Hot Springs Resort** (⊠ 2001 Foothill Rd., ☎ 702/782–8155) has hot mineral pools dating from 1862.

What to See and Do with Children

Of particular interest to children in Reno are the **Fleischmann Planetarium** and the **National Automobile Museum** (☞ Exploring Reno, *above*). **Wilbur D. May Great Basin Adventure** (✉ 1502 Washington St., ☎ 702/785–4153), in Rancho San Rafael Park, has a mining exhibit that traces the evolution of the Great Basin; also available here are a petting zoo, flume ride, and a touch-and-feel discovery room. In Sparks, **Wild Island** (✉ 250 Wild Island Ct., ☎ 702/331–9453) is a family theme park that includes a water park, a 36-hole mini–golf course, and a state-of-the-art video arcade.

Dining

Reno dining options range from plush gourmet restaurants and extensive hotel buffets to interesting little eateries scattered around the city. As in Las Vegas, the least-expensive dining options are the hotel-casino breakfast, lunch, and dinner buffets. The best buffets are at the **Atlantis, John Ascuaga's Nugget** (☞ Exploring Reno, *above*), and the **Eldorado** (☞ Lodging, *below*). For price ranges *see* Chart 1 (B) *in* On the Road with Fodor's.

$$$ ✕ **Harrah's Steak House.** The hotel-casino's dark and romantic restaurant has been serving prime beef and fresh seafood since 1967. ✉ 219 N. Center St., ☎ 702/786–3232. AE, D, DC, MC, V.

$$$ ✕ **Pimparel's La Table Francaise.** This off-the-beaten-track restaurant, in a converted house, specializes in award-winning French provincial cuisine. It's a favorite of locals celebrating a special occasion. ✉ 3065 W. 4th St., ☎ 702/323–3200. AE, D, DC, MC, V. No lunch.

$$$ ✕ **19th Hole.** This restaurant on the Lakeridge Golf Course has a great view of the city and nearby mountains and serves American and Continental food. ✉ 1200 Razorback Rd., ☎ 702/825–1250. D, MC, V.

$$ ✕ **Café de Thai.** The soups, salads, stir-fry dishes, and satay are all divine, concocted by a Thai chef trained at the Culinary Institute of America. ✉ 3314 S. McCarran, ☎ 702/829–8424. MC, V.

$$ ✕ **John A's Oyster Bar.** This nautically themed restaurant and bar serves the best steamers, pan roasts, cioppino, chowder, shrimp Louie, and cocktails this side of Fisherman's Wharf. ✉ 1100 Nugget Ave., Sparks, ☎ 702/356–3300. AE, D, DC, MC, V.

$$ ✕ **La Strada.** This excellent northern Italian restaurant is upstairs from the Eldorado Casino. The pastas and sauces are homemade, and the gourmet pizzas are made in a wood-fired oven. ✉ 345 N. Virginia St., ☎ 702/786–5700. AE, D, DC, MC, V. No lunch.

$ ✕ **Bertha Miranda's Mexican Restaurant.** Begun as a hole-in-the-wall, it has grown into a highly successful establishment. The food is made fresh by Bertha's family. Be sure to try the salsa. ✉ 336 Mill St., ☎ 702/786–9697. MC, V.

$ ✕ **Blue Heron.** This is one of the few natural foods restaurants you'll find in this meat-and-potatoes state. Get your grains, veggies, tofu, tempeh dishes, and even macrobiotic meals here. ✉ 1091 S. Virginia St., ☎ 702/786–4110. DC, MC, V.

$ ✕ **Louis' Basque Corner.** Basque shepherds once populated northern Nevada, and this is a great place to sample authentic Basque food, which is served family style at large tables covered with red cloths in a wood-paneled dining room. Dishes include oxtail, lamb, and tongue. ✉ 301 E. 4th St., ☎ 702/323–7203. AE, DC, MC, V.

$ ✕ **Nugget Diner.** This is a classic Americana diner; seating is on stools at front and back counters. The Awful Awful Burger is renowned, as is the prime rib. ✉ Nugget Casino, 233 N. Virginia St., ☎ 702/323–0716. MC, V.

Lodging

Most of Reno's hotels are downtown. For price ranges *see* Chart 2 (B) *in* On the Road with Fodor's.

$$$ 🏨 **Flamingo Hilton.** This sister hotel of the Las Vegas and Laughlin Flamingos sports a million-dollar sign and a 21-story tower. The guest rooms facing west have a nice view of the mountains. ✉ *255 N. Sierra St., 89501,* ☎ *702/322–1111 or 800/648–4822,* FAX *702/322–1111. 604 rooms. 4 restaurants, lounge, casino, showroom. AE, D, DC, MC, V.*

$$$ 🏨 **Harrah's.** This is one of the most luxurious hotels in downtown Reno. Large, conservatively decorated guest rooms overlook downtown and the entire mountain-ringed valley. ✉ *219 N. Center St., 89501,* ☎ *702/786–3232 or 800/648–3773,* FAX *702/788–2815. 565 rooms. 6 restaurants, pool, health club, casino, showroom. AE, MC, V.*

$$$ 🏨 **Reno Hilton.** Formerly Bally's, this 27-story hotel near the airport is Nevada's largest hotel north of Las Vegas. Almost everything here is the area's largest: from the buffet to the collection of race and sports books—not to mention the showroom, convention facilities, bowling alley, and arcade. There's a wedding chapel on the premises. ✉ *2500 E. 2nd St., 89595,* ☎ *702/789–2000 or 800/648–5080,* FAX *702/789–2418. 2,001 rooms. 5 restaurants, lounge, pool, tennis courts, health club, bowling, golf, casino, showroom. AE, D, DC, MC, V.*

$$$ 🏨 **Silver Legacy.** Opened in summer 1995, this two-tower Las Vegas–style megaresort centers on a 120-ft-tall mining machine that coins dollar tokens. Skywalks connect to Circus Circus and Eldorado. ✉ *407 N. Virginia St., 89501,* ☎ *702/329–4777 or 800/687–8733. 1,700 rooms. 5 restaurants, lounge, casino. AE, D, DC, MC, V.*

$$ 🏨 **Eldorado.** Known for its fine food and attention to detail, the Eldorado completed an all-suites tower in 1996. Rooms overlook the mountains. ✉ *345 N. Virginia St., 89501,* ☎ *702/786–5700 or 800/648–5966,* FAX *702/322–7124. 836 rooms. 8 restaurants, lounge, pool, casino. AE, D, DC, MC, V.*

$$ 🏨 **John Ascuaga's Nugget.** This casino-hotel in neighboring Sparks offers some of the largest and most luxurious rooms around—as well as a resident elephant named Bertha. A new 1,000-room tower was completed in early 1997. ✉ *1100 Nugget Ave., Sparks 89431,* ☎ *702/356–3300 or 800/648–1177,* FAX *702/356–3434. 1,983 rooms. 7 restaurants, lounge, indoor pool, casino, showroom. AE, D, DC, MC, V.*

$ 🏨 **Circus Circus.** This smaller version of the giant Las Vegas hotel has the same atmosphere. The rooms, though small and garish, are good value—when you can get one. ✉ *500 N. Sierra St., 89503,* ☎ *702/329–0711 or 800/648–5010,* FAX *702/329–0599. 1,625 rooms. 3 restaurants, lounge, casino. AE, DC, MC, V.*

$ 🏨 **Comstock.** The lobby and casino have an Old West theme; neon fireworks explode across the exterior tower walls (actual neon lights simulate fireworks—it's quite spectacular). Rooms are small, with Victorian-style decor and city or mountain views. ✉ *200 W. 2nd St., 89501,* ☎ *702/329–1880 or 800/648–4866,* FAX *702/348–0539. 310 rooms. 3 restaurants, lounge, pool, health club, casino. MC, V.*

$ 🏨 **Peppermill.** Three miles from downtown, this is the home of Reno's most colorful casino, but its rooms are plush and sedate. An expansion completed in 1996 added a 440-room tower and additional casino space. ✉ *2707 S. Virginia St., 89502,* ☎ *702/826–2121 or 800/648–6992,* FAX *702/826–5205. 631 rooms. 4 restaurants, lounge, pool, health club, casino. AE, D, DC, MC, V.*

Nightlife and the Arts

Nightlife

As in Las Vegas, Reno area nightlife breaks down into four categories: headliners, big production shows, small production shows, and lounge acts. Offerings at the major Reno hotels follow; for addresses and phone numbers, *see* Lodging, *above*. **Circus Circus** has continual circus acts. **Flamingo Hilton** has small production shows. **Harrah's Reno** has headliners and small production shows. **John Ascuaga's Nugget** has headliners (mostly country and western). **Reno Hilton** has headliners and large production shows.

The Arts

Most of the arts in Reno—such as the **Nevada Festival Ballet** (☎ 702/785–7915), the **Nevada Opera Association** (☎ 702/786–4046), the **Reno Philharmonic** (☎ 702/323–6393), and the **Performing Arts Series** (☎ 702/348–9413)—center on the **University of Nevada, Reno** (☎ 702/784–1110).

Shopping

The **Park Lane Mall** (⊠ 310 E. Plumb La., ☎ 702/825–9452) is the cozier of Reno's two indoor shopping centers; check out the Made in Nevada store. The **Meadowood Mall** (⊠ Virginia St. at McCarran Blvd., ☎ 702/827–8450) is the newer and more spacious and upscale mall. **AAA Slots of Fun** (⊠ 11 E. Plaza, ☎ 702/324–7711) has a large selection of new and used slot and video poker machines for sale.

LAKE TAHOE

Southwest of Reno, Lake Tahoe's vast expanse of crystal-blue water surrounded by rugged peaks is a playground for residents and visitors alike. Half in Nevada and half in California, it is the largest alpine lake in North America, 22 mi long and 12 mi wide. The region offers outstanding skiing in winter; boating, fishing, and mountain sports in summer; and casino entertainment year-round.

Visitor Information

Tahoe-Douglas Chamber of Commerce (⊠ U.S. 50 at the Round Hill Shopping Center, Box 7139, Stateline 89449, ☎ 702/588–4591). **Incline Village/Crystal Bay Visitors and Convention Bureau** (⊠ 969 Tahoe Blvd., Incline Village 89451-9508, ☎ 702/832–1606 or 800/468–2463).

Arriving and Departing

By Car

From Reno take U.S. 395S through Carson City to U.S. 50, which leads to South Lake Tahoe; U.S. 395S to Route 431 leads to North Lake Tahoe.

By Plane

The closest major airport to Lake Tahoe is **Reno-Tahoe International Airport** (☞ Reno, *above*). **Mountain Air Express** (☎ 800/788–4247) flies from Long Beach, California, and Oakland, California, to the **Lake Tahoe Airport** (☎ 916/542–6180), near Stateline.

Exploring Lake Tahoe

A scenic drive circling Lake Tahoe (Routes 28 and 89) offers stunning lake, forest, and mountain vistas. You also can explore the lake aboard the **MS Dixie II** (⊠ Zephyr Cove, ☎ 702/588–3508). **Crystal Bay**, the northernmost community on the Nevada shore, has a small-town, outdoorsy feel, along with several casinos.

Affluent **Incline Village,** 2 mi east of Crystal Bay, has lakeshore residences, weekend condos, and inviting shopping areas. South of Incline Village, the **Ponderosa Ranch** (⊠ Rte. 28, ☎ 702/831–0691) is a Hollywood-style western "town" based on the TV series *Bonanza*. It's closed November through April.

At the south end of the lake are the neon signs of **Stateline,** where four towering and two low-rise casinos cluster in two blocks (☞ Dining and Lodging, *below*). Across the border in California is **South Lake Tahoe,** the most populous town on the lake. Ski Run Boulevard takes you southeast to the **Heavenly Ski Area** (☎ 702/586–7000), where the tram lifts you to fantastic skiing in winter and unbeatable views over the water year-round.

What to See and Do with Children

Aside from water sports on the lake, **Ponderosa Ranch** (☞ Exploring Lake Tahoe, *above*) is the chief attraction for children.

Dining and Lodging

For price ranges *see* Charts 1 (B) and 2 (B) *in* On the Road with Fodor's.

Incline Village

$$$ ✕ **Azzara's.** This typical trattoria serves a dozen different pasta dishes, along with pizza, chicken, lamb, veal, and shrimp, with understated elegance and excellent food. ⊠ *930 Tahoe Blvd.,* ☎ *702/831–0346. No lunch. AE, MC, V.*

$$ ✕ **Lone Eagle Grille.** This restaurant in the Hyatt Regency Hotel has a fantastic view of the lake. Specialties include duck, fish, and steak; there's a salad and dessert buffet. ⊠ *Country Club Dr. at Lakeshore,* ☎ *702/831–1111. AE, D, DC, MC, V.*

Stateline

$$$ ✕ **Empress Court.** Plush velvet booths and etched-glass partitions provide the setting for traditional Chinese cuisine. Try the grilled-squab salad. ⊠ *Caesars Tahoe, U.S. 50,* ☎ *702/588–3515. AE, DC, MC, V. No lunch.*

$$ ✕ **Sage Room Steak House.** A historic landmark in Lake Tahoe, this romantic restaurant is a descendant of the Wagon Wheel Saloon and Gambling Hall, the beginning of what was to become Harvey's Resort. Sautéed prawns Mediterranean are excellent. ⊠ *Harvey's Resort Hotel/Casino, U.S. 50,* ☎ *702/588–2411. AE, D, DC, MC, V.*

$$ ✕ **The Summit.** This 16th-floor restaurant affords a wonderful view. The creative menu includes artfully presented salads, seafood entrées, and decadent desserts. ⊠ *Harrah's Casino/Hotel Lake Tahoe, U.S. 50,* ☎ *702/588–6611. AE, D, DC, MC, V.*

$ ✕ **El Vaquero.** Wrought iron, a fountain, and tiles give this restaurant an authentic Old Mexico feel. The traditional Mexican fare includes enchiladas and chimichangas. At the Taco Cart you can make your own. ⊠ *Harvey's Resort Hotel/Casino, U.S. 50,* ☎ *702/588–2411. AE, D, DC, MC, V.*

$ ✕ **The Forest.** On the 18th floor of Harrah's, this buffet has the best view of any buffet in Nevada. The interior simulates a forest. ⊠ *Harrah's Casino/Hotel Lake Tahoe, U.S. 50,* ☎ *702/588–6611. Reservations not accepted. AE, DC, MC, V.*

$$$ ▦ **Caesars Tahoe.** Once you negotiate the lobby stairs and casino areas, you find hallways with faux Corinthian columns and plush rooms in fantasyland color schemes, such as hot pink with mint green. The indoor pool has a waterfall and a swim tunnel. ⊠ *U.S. 50 (Box 5800), 89449,* ☎ *702/588–3515 or 800/648–3353,* ℻ *702/586–2050. 440 rooms. 5 restaurants, lounge, pool, tennis courts, health club, casino, showroom. AE, D, DC, MC, V.*

$$$ ▦ **Harrah's Casino/Hotel Lake Tahoe.** The rooms are large and com-
★   fortable, and all have two full bathrooms, each complete with telephone and TV. Most rooms also have excellent views of the lake and the mountains. ⊠ *U.S. 50 (Box 8), 89449,* ☎ *702/588–6606 or 800/648–3773,* ℻ *702/586–6607. 533 rooms. 7 restaurants, indoor pool, health club, casino, showroom. AE, DC, MC, V.*

$$$ ▦ **Hyatt Regency Lake Tahoe.** Rooms are large and attractive, with warm color schemes and lake views. Amenities include a private beach, water sports, Camp Hyatt for kids, and a forest-theme casino. ⊠ *Country Club Dr. at Lakeshore, Incline Village 89450,* ☎ *702/832–1234 or 800/233–1234,* ℻ *702/831–7508. 460 rooms. 3 restaurants, lounge, pool, health club, beach, casino. AE, DC, MC, V.*

$$ ▦ **Harvey's Resort Hotel/Casino.** This family-owned hotel is Lake Tahoe's largest resort. The rooms are decorated with soft colors and comfortably furnished in American traditional style. Most have a view of the lake and the mountains. ⊠ *U.S. 50 (Box 128), 89449,* ☎ *702/588–2411 or 800/648–3361,* ℻ *702/588–6643. 740 rooms. 8 restaurants, lounge, spa, tennis courts, casino. AE, D, DC, MC, V.*

Nightlife

Lake Tahoe nightlife centers on the top-name entertainment and production shows at the casino-hotels. **Caesars Tahoe** and **Harrah's** (☞ Dining and Lodging, *above*) both present headliners.

Outdoor Activities and Sports

Fishing

The lake is renowned for mighty Macinkaw and rainbow trout. Nonresident fishing permits are available at most sporting goods stores. For more information call the **Department of Wildlife** (☎ 702/688–1500).

Golf

Edgewood at Tahoe (⊠ Stateline, ☎ 702/588–3566) has 18 holes. **Glenbrook Golf Course** (⊠ Glenbrook, ☎ 702/749–5201) has nine holes. **Incline Village Championship Golf Course** (⊠ 955 Fairway Blvd., ☎ 702/832–1144) has 18 holes. **Incline Village Executive Course** (⊠ 690 Wilson Way, ☎ 702/832–1150) has 18 holes.

Hiking

More than 250 mi of hiking trails traverse the area, many through high mountain passes and along streams and meadows with sweeping views. Contact the **U.S. Forest Service** (☎ 916/573–2600) for information.

Ski Areas

Lake Tahoe has more than 15 world-class alpine (downhill) resorts and nearly a dozen Nordic (cross-country) skiing centers—all within an hour of one another. Elevations range from 6,000 to 10,000 ft, with vertical drops up to nearly 4,000 ft. More than 150 lifts operate during the season, which usually lasts from November through May.

Cross-Country

Diamond Peak (⊠ 1210 Ski Way, Incline Village 89450, ☎ 702/832–1177) has 22 mi of groomed high-elevation track with skating lanes.

Downhill

Diamond Peak (☞ *above*) has seven lifts, 29 runs, and a 1,840-ft vertical drop. **Heavenly Ski Area** (✉ Box 2180, Stateline 89449, ☎ 702/586–7000 or 800/243–2836), straddling the Nevada-California border, has 25 lifts, 71 trails (including the longest run in Tahoe), and a 3,600-ft drop. **Mt. Rose** (✉ 22222 Mt. Rose Hwy., Reno 89511, ☎ 702/849–0704) has the highest base elevation in the area, with unequaled powder skiing, five lifts, 41 runs, and a 1,440-ft drop.

NEW MEXICO

Updated by
C. Coggan
and M. Haddrill

Capital	Santa Fe
Population	1,713,400
Motto	It Grows as It Goes
State Bird	Roadrunner
State Flower	Yucca
Postal Abbreviation	NM

Statewide Visitor Information

Visitor information to New Mexico can be obtained from the **New Mexico Department of Tourism** (✉ Lamy Bldg., 491 Old Santa Fe Trail, Santa Fe 87503, ☎ 505/827–7400 or 800/733–6396, ℻ 505/827–7402). For outdoor activity information, contact the **USDA Forest Service, Southwestern Region** (✉ Public Affairs Office, 517 Gold Ave. SW, Albuquerque 87102, ☎ 505/842–3292). For visiting New Mexico's Native American reservations, contact the **Indian Pueblo Cultural Center** (✉ 2401 12th St. NW, Albuquerque 87102, ☎ 505/843–7270).

Scenic Drives

The old **High Road** is not the most direct route from Santa Fe to Taos, but it takes you through rolling hillsides studded with orchards and tiny picturesque villages set against a rugged mountain backdrop. No visit to northern New Mexico is complete without the 100-mi trip along the **Enchanted Circle,** a breathtaking panorama of deep canyons, passes, alpine valleys, and towering mountains of the verdant Carson National Forest. **Route 66,** America's most nostalgic highway, includes a colorful stretch that now constitutes Albuquerque's Central Avenue. A scenic route between Albuquerque and Santa Fe, the **Turquoise Trail** (Route 14) snakes up through a portion of Cibola National Forest and a number of mining semi–ghost towns.

National and State Parks

National Park
Carlsbad Caverns National Park (☞ Elsewhere in New Mexico, *below*) is a spectacular system of caves and rock formations.

State Parks
New Mexico's 33 state parks range from the high mountain lakes and pine forests of the north to the Chihuahuan Desert lowlands in the south. Pristine and unspoiled, they offer every conceivable outdoor recreational facility. For maps and brochures contact the **State Parks and Recreation Division** (✉ Energy, Minerals, and Natural Resources Dept., 2040 S. Pacheco St., Box 1147, Santa Fe 87504-1147, ☎ 505/827–7173 or 888/667–2757, ℻ 505/827–1376).

Native American Reservations

Two general classifications of Native Americans live in New Mexico: the Pueblos, who established an agricultural civilization here many centuries ago, and the descendants of the nomadic tribes who came into the area much later—the Navajo, Mescalero Apache, and Jicarilla Apache. The settlements of various **Pueblo** tribes are described in the Albuquerque and Santa Fe sections.

The Jicarilla Apache live on a 750,000-acre reservation in north-central New Mexico. The tribe has a well-defined tourist program promoting big-game hunting, fishing, and camping on a 15,000-acre game preserve; for details contact the **Jicarilla Apache Tribe** (⊠ Box 507, Dulce 87528, ☎ 505/759–3242, ℻ 505/759–3005).

A reservation of a half-million acres of timbered mountains and green valleys in southeastern New Mexico is home to the Mescalero Apache. The tribe owns and operates one of the most elegant luxury resorts in the state, Inn of the Mountain Gods, as well as Ski Apache, 16 mi from Ruidoso. Contact the **Mescalero Apache Tribe** (⊠ Tribal Office, Hwy. 70, Box 227, Mescalero 88340, ☎ 505/671–4494).

The Navajo Reservation, home to the largest Native American group in the United States, covers 17.6 million acres in New Mexico, Arizona, and Utah. There are a few towns on the reservation, but for the most part it is a vast area of stark pinnacles, colorful rock formations, high desert, and mountains. The tribe encourages tourism; write or call the **Navajo Nation Tourism Office** (⊠ Box 663, Window Rock, AZ 86515, ☎ 520/871–6436 or 520/871–7371, ℻ 520/871–7381).

ALBUQUERQUE

A large city—its population is nearing the half-million mark—Albuquerque spreads out in all directions with no apparent ground rules. The city seems as free-spirited as the hot-air balloons that take part in the annual October International Balloon Fiesta. As in the rest of New Mexico, Albuquerque's Native American, Spanish, and Anglo cultures are well blended.

Albuquerque began as an important trade and transportation station on the Camino Real–Chihuahua Trail, which wound down into Mexico and remains a travel crossroads today. The original four-block core, known as Old Town, is the city's tourist hub, with unique shops, galleries, museums, and restaurants.

Visitor Information

Convention and Visitors Bureau (⊠ Box 26866, 87125; 20 First Plaza NW, ☎ 505/842–9918 or 800/284–2282).

Arriving and Departing

By Plane
Albuquerque International Airport (☎ 505/842–4366) is 5 mi south of downtown; the trip takes 10–15 minutes. Taxis charge $10–$12 plus tip. **Sun Tran** buses (☎ 505/843–9200) in Albuquerque, which cost 75¢, pick up on the baggage claim level about every 20 minutes.

By Car
I–25 enters Albuquerque from points north and south; I–40, from points east and west.

By Train
Amtrak (☎ 800/872–7245) serves the Albuquerque station (⊠ 214 1st St. SW, ☎ 505/842–9650).

By Bus
Albuquerque is served by **Greyhound Lines** and **TNMO Coaches Transportation Center** (⊠ 300 2nd St. SW, ☎ 505/243–4435 or 800/231–2222).

Exploring Albuquerque

Albuquerque sprawls in all directions, so it's best to see the city by car. Historic and colorful Route 66 is Albuquerque's Central Avenue, unifying as nothing else can the diverse areas of the city: Old Town, to the west, cradled at the bend of the Rio Grande; the downtown business and government centers; the University of New Mexico, to the east; and Nob Hill, a lively strip of restaurants, boutiques, galleries, and shops, farther east. The railroad tracks, running north and south, and east–west Central Avenue divide the city into quadrants: southwest (SW), northwest (NW), southeast (SE), northeast (NE).

The city began in 1706 in what is now Old Town, and tree-shaded **Old Town Plaza** remains the heart of Albuquerque's heritage. The **San Felipe de Neri Church** (✉ 2005 North Plaza NW, ☎ 505/243–4628), facing the plaza, has been enlarged and expanded several times over the years, but its massive adobe walls and other original sections remain intact. Most of the old adobe houses surrounding the plaza have been converted into charming shops, galleries, and restaurants.

The striking glass-and-sandstone **New Mexico Museum of Natural History and Science** presents a simulated active volcano and frigid Ice Age cave, dinosaurs, and an Evolator (short for Evolution Elevator)—a six-minute high-tech ride through 35 million years of New Mexico's geologic history. ✉ *1801 Mountain Rd. NW,* ☎ *505/841–2802.*

The **Indian Pueblo Cultural Center** holds one of the largest collections of Native American arts and crafts in the Southwest, a valuable resource for the study of the region's first inhabitants. The spectacular two-story center is owned and operated by the 19 Pueblo tribes of New Mexico, each with an alcove devoted to its arts and crafts. Free performances of ceremonial dances are given on most weekends and on special holidays. ✉ *2401 12th St. NW,* ☎ *505/843–7270.*

Sandia Peak Aerial Tramway, among the world's longest aerial tramways, makes an awesome 2¾-mi climb from the edge of the city to a point near 10,678-ft Sandia Crest for an overview of Albuquerque—and half of New Mexico. At sunset the sky is a kaleidoscope of colors over the desert. ✉ *10 Tramway Loop NE,* ☎ *505/856–7325. Closed 2 wks in fall and spring for servicing; call ahead.*

On the city's western fringe lies **Petroglyph National Monument,** which contains more than 15,000 ancient rock drawings inscribed as early as AD 1300 in the volcanic rocks and cliffs. ✉ *4735 Unser Blvd. NW, 87120,* ☎ *505/839–4429.*

Outside Albuquerque

Coronado State Monument and Park, a prehistoric Native American pueblo once known as Kuaua, sits on a bluff overlooking the Rio Grande near Bernalillo, 20 mi north of Albuquerque; it is believed to have been the headquarters of Coronado's army of 1,200, who came seeking the legendary Seven Cities of Gold in 1540. ✉ *Off I–25 on Rte. 44 (Box 853), Bernalillo 87004,* ☎ *505/867–5589.*

Fort Sumner State Monument is about 170 mi southeast of Albuquerque, near the Billy the Kid Museum and the cemetery, just off Billy the Kid Road, where he is buried. Artifacts and photographs relating to the fort and to the Bosque Redondo Reservation nearby are on display. Nine thousand Navajo and Mescalero Apache were forcibly relocated to the reservation from 1863 to 1868, brought there by Kit Carson after the infamous "Long Walk" from their original homelands in the Four Corners Area. ✉ *Off I–40 and U.S. 84 (Box 356), Fort Sumner 88119,* ☎ *505/355–2573.*

Bosque Del Apache National Wildlife Refuge (✉ Off I–25, Socorro, ☎ 505/835–1828) is known to bird-watchers around the world as a place to see more than 329 species, including migratory birds. In the winter you'll find more than 30,000 cranes, eagles, and snow geese; spring and fall, look for migrant warblers, flycatchers, and shorebirds; in summer nesting songbirds, waders, and ducks make this their home. The reserve is 90 mi south of Albuquerque off I–25.

Pueblos near Albuquerque

The Native American pueblos near Albuquerque have varying policies on taking photographs, tape recording, or sketching. Permission to visit is sometimes required, and in some cases admission is charged. Call ahead for regulations.

Made up of a series of terraced adobe structures, dominated by the massive mission church of San Estevan del Rey, **Acoma Pueblo** (✉ Box 309, Acoma 87034, ☎ 505/470–4966 or 800/747–0181), also known as Sky City, sits atop a 367-ft mesa that rises abruptly from the valley floor 64 mi west of Albuquerque. Most of its population now live on the valley floor but retain traditional residences without electricity or running water on the mesa. Sky City may be visited only on paid, guided tours. Pueblo artists sell their prized thin-walled pottery.

Santo Domingo Pueblo (✉ Box 99, Santo Domingo 87052, ☎ 505/465–2214), off I–25 at the Santo Domingo exit between Albuquerque and Santa Fe, operates a Tribal Cultural Center, where its outstanding *heishi* (shell) jewelry is sold. The August 4 Corn Dance is one of the most colorful and dramatic of all the Pueblo ceremonial dances.

The sun symbol appearing on New Mexico's flag was adopted from the **Zia Pueblo** (✉ 135 Capital Square Dr., Zia Pueblo 87053, ☎ 505/867–3304), which has been at its present site (40 mi northwest of Albuquerque) since the early 1300s. Skillful Zia potters make polychrome wares, and painters produce highly prized watercolors.

Jemez Pueblo (✉ Box 100, Jemez 87024, ☎ 505/834–7359), 51 mi northwest of Albuquerque, is the state's sole Towa-speaking pueblo. It is noted for its polychrome pottery and fine yucca-frond baskets. The beautiful **San Jose de los Jemez Mission,** a stone structure built in 1622, is at the Jemez State Monument (✉ Box 143, Jemez Springs 87025, ☎ 505/829–3530), 13 mi north of Jemez Pueblo.

What to See and Do with Children

Spend an afternoon at the **Albuquerque Biological Park** (✉ 903 10th St. SW, ☎ 505/764–6200). This unique environmental museum includes the Albuquerque Aquarium, Rio Grande Zoo, and Rio Grande Botanic Garden. The Eel Cave and Shark Tank are real kid pleasers, and the Zoo is home to more than 1,000 animals, including elephants, bison, koalas, and Mexican wolves. Wander through the beautiful gardens, which showcase plants from the Southwest and other climates. **Cliff's Amusement Park** (✉ 4800 Osuna Rd. NE, ☎ 505/881–9373)—closed from mid-October through March—has 24 thrill rides, games, an arcade room, and private picnic areas. At the **Albuquerque Children's Museum** (✉ 800 Rio Grande Blvd. NW, ☎ 505/842–5525), arts and cultural exhibits, a computer lab, and the Make-It-Take-It art room keep youngsters entertained for hours. Don't miss the Bubble Room, where kids can enclose themselves in a giant bubble. **Explora!** (✉ 40 First Plaza Galeria, ☎ 505/842–6188) is a hands-on science center where changing exhibits allow kids to conduct their own experiments such as using wind to make sand dunes and minitornadoes.

Dining

Many of Albuquerque's best restaurants specialize in northern New Mexico cooking, but French, Continental, Mediterranean, Italian, and standard American fare is also available. For price ranges *see* Chart 1 (B) *in* On the Road with Fodor's.

$$$$ ✕ **High Finance Restaurant and Tavern.** In the center of Cibola National Park, this restaurant is accessible via the Sandia Peak Tram, by taking a 3-mi hike, or on a ski trip through the Sandia Ski Area. On the edge of Sandia Peak more than 10,000 ft above sea level, it's a great place to experience a New Mexico sunset; every seat in the house has a view that spans 11,000 square mi. Feast on sesame-fried calamari followed by steak, seafood, or pasta. ⊠ *40 Tramway Rd. NE,* ☎ *505/ 243–9742. Reservations essential. AE, D, DC, MC, V. Closed when tram is being serviced; call ahead.*

$$ ✕ **Artichoke Café.** In a turn-of-the-century brick building just east of ★ downtown, the café offers American, Italian, and some French dishes, as well as delicious broiled salmon, veal, and lamb. Its large, modern dining room, decorated with the work of local artists, spills onto a small courtyard. ⊠ *424 Central Ave. SE,* ☎ *505/243–0200. AE, D, DC, MC, V. Closed Sun. No lunch Sat.*

$$ ✕ **Maria Teresa.** A restored 1840s adobe in Old Town furnished in handsome English antiques is the setting for this appealing restaurant. Aged beef, seafood, chicken, and New Mexican specialties, such as *carne adovada* (cubed pork marinated and baked in red chili), are served. ⊠ *618 Rio Grande Blvd. NW,* ☎ *505/242–3900. AE, DC, MC, V.*

$$ ✕ **Monte Vista Fire Station.** Now a national historic landmark, this spacious, airy restaurant was once a working firehouse. The American menu includes a wide variety of seafood, beef, and pasta dishes; highlights are red-chili ravioli and crab cakes. ⊠ *3201 Central Ave. NE,* ☎ *505/ 255–2424. AE, D, DC, MC, V. No lunch weekends.*

$$ ✕ **Scalo Northern Italian Grill.** The trendy Nob Hill set gathers at this ★ informal eatery for thin-crust pizza and excellent pastas. There's an open kitchen and a full-service bar. ⊠ *3500 Central Ave. SE, in the Nob Hill Business Center,* ☎ *505/255–8781. AE, D, MC, V. No lunch Sun.*

$–$$ ✕ **Rio Bravo Brewpub.** In this loud, lively place, Continental cuisine is dished up alongside novel New Mexican fare such as wild-mushroom enchiladas. Wash it down with one of five beers brewed on site. ⊠ *515 Central Ave. NW,* ☎ *505/242–6800. AE, MC, V. Closed Sun.*

Lodging

For price ranges *see* Chart 2 (B) *in* On the Road with Fodor's.

$$$ 🏨 **Albuquerque Marriott.** This luxury uptown property near the city's largest malls is geared to vacationers as well as executive travelers. Furnishings are contemporary with a Southwest flavor. ⊠ *2101 Louisiana Blvd. NE, 87110,* ☎ *505/881–6800 or 800/334–2086,* 🖷 *505/888– 2982. 411 rooms. 2 restaurants, lobby lounge, indoor-outdoor pool, health club. AE, D, DC, MC, V.*

$$$ 🏨 **Hyatt Regency Albuquerque.** Adjacent to the convention center in the heart of downtown are the two soaring desert-color towers of this totally modern luxury hotel. The spacious rooms are finished in contemporary southwestern style, with a mauve, burgundy, and tan color scheme. ⊠ *330 Tijeras Ave. NW, 87102,* ☎ *505/842–1234,* 🖷 *505/ 766–6710. 395 rooms. Restaurant, 2 lobby lounges, pool, health club. AE, D, DC, MC, V.*

$$–$$$ ★ **⊞ Casas de Sueños.** Long a gathering spot for artists and now a bed-and-breakfast on a 2-acre compound adjacent to Old Town, Houses of Dreams offers attractive *casitas* with decor that runs from Asian to European to southwestern. Treat yourself to one of the suites, each of which has a fireplace and a hot tub on a private patio. ⊠ *310 Rio Grande Blvd. SW, 87104,* ☎ *505/247–4560 or 800/242–8987,* FAX *505/842–8493. 19 casitas. Library, free parking. AE, D, DC, MC, V.*

$$–$$$ **⊞ La Posada de Albuquerque.** The first property opened by New Mexico native Conrad Hilton, this historic hotel in the center of town has been oozing charm and character since 1939. Native American war-dance murals ornament the wall behind the reception desk. Rooms vary in size from small to spacious and are decorated with Southwest and Native American themes; many have fireplaces. ⊠ *125 2nd St. NW, 87102,* ☎ *505/242–9090 or 800/777–5732,* FAX *505/242–8664. 114 rooms. Restaurant, bar, shop. AE, D, DC, MC, V.*

$$–$$$ **⊞ William E. Mauger Estate.** In this elegant 1897 Queen Anne residence downtown, all eight guest rooms are decorated Victorian style. Full breakfasts are served outside on the porch. ⊠ *701 Roma Ave. NW, 87102,* ☎ *505/242–8755. 8 rooms. AE, DC, MC, V.*

$$ **⊞ Radisson Inn.** Arched balconies, desert colors, a courtyard pool, and indoor and outdoor dining add to the Spanish/southwestern flavor of this two-story motor hotel near the airport. Rooms are reliably comfortable. ⊠ *1901 University Blvd. SE, 87106,* ☎ *505/247–0512,* FAX *505/843–7148. 148 rooms. Restaurant, lounge, pool, spa, airport shuttle. AE, D, DC, MC, V.*

Campgrounds

Fifteen minutes south of Albuquerque on I–25, the **Isleta Lakes and Recreation Area** (⊠ Box 383, Isleta 87022, ☎ 505/877–0370) has complete campground facilities with tent sites and RV hookups. Tent sites and RV facilities are found in Albuquerque at the **Albuquerque KOA Central** (⊠ 12400 Skyline Rd. NE, 87123, ☎ 505/296–2729). Just north of town is the **Albuquerque North KOA** (⊠ 555 S. Hill Rd., Box 758, Bernalillo 87004, ☎ 505/867–5227).

Nightlife and the Arts

To find out what's on in town, check the *Albuquerque Journal* on Friday and Sunday or the *Albuquerque Tribune* on Thursday.

Nightlife

El Rey Theater (⊠ 624 Central Ave. SW, ☎ 505/243–7546) presents blues, rock, alternative, jazz, metal, and country bands in a renovated 1941 theater. **Dingo Bar** (⊠ 313 Gold Ave. SW, ☎ 505/243–0663) is a small downtown nightclub drawing big crowds with its mix of jazz, blues, punk, pop, and world-beat dance offerings.

The Arts

The **New Mexico Symphony Orchestra** (⊠ 3301 Menaul Blvd. NE, Suite 4, ☎ 505/881–8999) is among the state's largest performing arts organizations.

Outdoor Activities and Sports

Contact the **Albuquerque Cultural and Recreational Services Department** (⊠ 400 Marquette NW, Box 1293, 87103, ☎ 505/768–3550) for information on its network of parks and recreational programs, including golf courses, paved tracks for biking and jogging, pools, tennis courts, playing fields, playgrounds, and even a shooting range.

Hot-Air Ballooning

The **Albuquerque International Balloon Fiesta** (⊠ 8309 Washington Pl. NE, ☎ 505/821–1000) attracts more than 650 hot-air balloons each October to the world's largest gathering of balloonists. An estimated 1.5 million people attend the nine-day aerial extravaganza to watch as the balloons float over Albuquerque's backyards.

You can also hire a pilot and balloon for your own ride. **Braden's Balloons** (⊠ 3900 2nd St. NW, ☎ 505/281–2714) is a reliable firm. **World Balloon Corporation** (⊠ 4800 Eubank NE, ☎ 505/293–6800) can safely take you up and away.

Shopping

Albuquerque residents mainly shop at malls and outlet stores. **Winrock Center** (⊠ Louisiana Blvd. exit off I–40, ☎ 505/883–6132) is one of the area's main malls. **Coronado Center** (⊠ Louisiana and Menaul Blvds., ☎ 505/881–2700) is New Mexico's largest mall. **Nob Hill,** a seven-block strip of shops stretching along Central Avenue from Girard to Washington streets, is the city's newest and trendiest shopping district. Neon-lighted boutiques, restaurants, galleries, and performing arts spaces encourage strolling and people-watching.

Meander down tiny lanes and through small plazas in **Old Town** Albuquerque, where you can browse in dozens of one-of-a-kind shops, including **V. Whipple's Old Mexico Shop** (⊠ 400 E. San Felipe NW, ☎ 505/243–6070).

SANTA FE

With its crisp, clear air and bright, sunny weather, New Mexico's capital couldn't be more welcoming. Perched on a 7,000-ft plateau at the base of the Sangre de Cristo Mountains, Santa Fe is surrounded by the remnants of a 2,000-year-old Pueblo civilization and filled with evidence of the Spanish, who founded the city as early as 1607. The rows of chic art galleries (Santa Fe claims to be the country's third most important arts center, after New York and Los Angeles), smart restaurants, and shops selling southwestern furnishings and apparel combine to make it uniquely appealing. Its population, an estimated 60,000, swells to nearly double that during the peak summer season and to a lesser degree in the winter, with the arrival of skiers lured by the challenging slopes of the Santa Fe Ski Area and nearby Taos Ski Valley.

Visitor Information

Chamber of Commerce (⊠ 510 N. Guadalupe St., Suite L, De Vargas Center N, 87504, ☎ 505/983–7317). **Convention and Visitors Bureau** (⊠ 201 W. Marcy St., Box 909, 87504, ☎ 505/984–6760 or 800/777–2489, FAX 505/984–6679).

Arriving and Departing

By Plane

Albuquerque International Airport (☎ 505/842–4366) serves both cities. Shuttle bus service is available from Greyhound (☎ 800/231–2222) and Shuttlejack (☎ 505/982–4311). For charter flights between Albuquerque and Santa Fe, contact the Albuquerque airport or the **Santa Fe Municipal Airport** (☎ 505/473–7243).

By Bus

Santa Fe can be reached via **Texas New Mexico & Oklahoma Greyhound** (⊠ 858 St. Michael's Dr., ☎ 505/471–0008 or 800/231–2222).

Bradbury Science Museum (⊠ 15th St. at Central Ave., ☎ 505/667–4444). The area also abounds with interesting archaeological sites, including **Bandelier National Monument** (⊠ HCR1, Box 1, Suite 15, Los Alamos 87544, ☎ 505/672–3861), which has the remains of one of the largest Anasazi centers.

A kind of Williamsburg of the Southwest, **El Rancho de las Golondrinas,** 15 mi south of Santa Fe off I–25, is a reconstruction of a small, traditional New Mexico farming village, complete with grinding mills, a blacksmith shop, animals, working fields, homes, and a *morada* (meeting place) of the Penitente order. ⊠ *La Cienega,* ☎ *505/471–2261. Closed Nov.–Mar.*

About 25 mi southeast of Santa Fe, **Pecos National Historical Park** is the site of a once-flourishing Native American pueblo. An early trading center, Pecos was the largest and easternmost pueblo reached by the Spanish conquistadors in 1541. Franciscan priests built a mission church here in the 1620s, but the pueblo was abandoned in 1838 because of disease and raiding nomadic tribes. ⊠ *Box 418, Pecos 87552,* ☎ *505/757–6032.*

Pueblos near Santa Fe

The Native American pueblos near Santa Fe vary in their craft specialties and in the recreational facilities they offer tourists. Most have ceremonial dances on feast days that are open to the public. Call ahead for regulations on picture-taking and admission policies.

Pojoaque Pueblo (⊠ Rte. 11, Box 71, Santa Fe 87501, ☎ 505/455–2278) features the **Poeh Museum,** a cultural center focusing on the Tewa-speaking Native Americans. The pueblo also operates an official **state tourist center** on U.S. 285, which offers an extensive selection of northern New Mexican arts and crafts.

San Ildefonso Pueblo (⊠ Rte. 5, Box 315-A, Santa Fe 87501, ☎ 505/455–2273), just off the road to Los Alamos, was the home of the most famous of all pueblo potters, Maria Martinez, whose exquisite polished black-on-black pottery is revered among collectors. The pueblo still boasts a number of highly acclaimed potters, as well as other artists and craftspeople.

San Juan Pueblo (⊠ Box 1099, San Juan 87566, ☎ 505/852–4400) is headquarters of the Eight Northern Indian Pueblos Council. In its beautiful arts center, the **Oke Oweenge Crafts Cooperative,** the pueblo's distinctive redware and micaceous clay pottery can be purchased. Two handsome kivas, a New England–style church, and the **Tewa Indian Restaurant** are other attractions.

Santa Clara Pueblo (⊠ Box 580, Española 87532, ☎ 505/753–7326) is home of the beautiful 740-room **Puye Cliff Dwellings,** a national landmark. It is also famous for its shiny red-and-black engraved pottery and for its many well-known painters and sculptors. Tours are offered on weekdays.

What to See and Do with Children

Children will love the colorful works at the **Museum of International Folk Art** (☞ Exploring Santa Fe, *above*). The **Santa Fe Children's Museum** (⊠ 1050 Old Pecos Trail, ☎ 505/989–8359) has hands-on exhibits on the arts and sciences that are both fun and educational; its climbing wall is popular with older kids.

Dining

For price ranges *see* Chart 1 (A) *in* On the Road with Fodor's.

$$–$$$$ ✕ **Coyote Cafe.** Owner-chef Mark Miller offers a 22-ounce rib-eye steak
★ called the Cowboy, served with barbecued black beans and red-chili-
dusted onion rings, and other northern New Mexico specials. In sum-
mer the restaurant opens its less-expensive Rooftop Cantina. ⊠ *132
W. Water St.,* ☎ *505/983–1615. AE, D, DC, MC, V.*

$$$ ✕ **The Compound.** This restaurant shimmers with Old World elegance.
★ The American-Continental menu includes chicken in champagne, roast
loin of lamb, Russian caviar, and New Zealand raspberries. ⊠ *653
Canyon Rd.,* ☎ *505/982–4353. Reservations essential. Jacket and tie.
AE. Closed Jan.–Feb. and Sun.–Mon. No lunch.*

$$$ ✕ **Pink Adobe.** One of the best-known restaurants in town, the Pink
Adobe serves Continental, New Orleans Creole, and local New Mex-
ican favorites in a three-century-old adobe. ⊠ *406 Old Santa Fe Trail,*
☎ *505/983–7712. AE, D, DC, MC, V.*

$$–$$$ ✕ **Café Escalera.** Fresh local ingredients dominate the daily-changing
menu, and the wine list is perfectly suited to the food. The sleek, min-
imalist decor and an extensive bar menu make this a popular choice
for locals. ⊠ *130 Lincoln Ave.,* ☎ *505/989–8188. AE, MC, V.*

$–$$$ ✕ **Café Pasqual's.** Only a block southwest of the Plaza, this cheerful,
★ informal place serves regional specialties and possibly the best south-
western-style breakfast in town. Expect a line outside. ⊠ *210 Don Gas-
par Ave.,* ☎ *505/983–9340. AE, MC, V.*

$$ ✕ **El Nido.** A favorite of Santa Fe Opera fans and performers, this in-
★ stitution has been serving in its cozy, firelighted rooms since the 1920s.
The menu features seafood—including excellent broiled salmon and
other daily specials—as well as choice aged beef, prime rib, and New
Mexican specialties. ⊠ *U.S. 285, 6 mi north of Santa Fe to Tesuque
exit, then 1½ mi farther to restaurant,* ☎ *505/988–4340. AE, MC, V.
Closed Mon.*

$$ ✕ **La Tertulia.** This lovely restaurant in a converted 19th-century convent is almost as well known for its splendid Spanish colonial art col-
lection as for its fine New Mexican cuisine and extraordinary house
sangria. ⊠ *416 Agua Fria St.,* ☎ *505/988–2769. AE, D, MC, V.
Closed Mon.*

$$ ✕ **Ore House on the Plaza.** Here seafood and steaks are artfully pre-
pared, and margaritas come in more than 80 variations. You can eat
on the balcony overlooking the Plaza. ⊠ *50 Lincoln Ave.,* ☎ *505/983–
8687. AE, MC, V.*

$–$$ ✕ **Plaza Café.** The red-leather banquettes, black Formica tables, tile
floors, vintage Santa Fe photos, and coffered tin ceiling haven't changed
since 1918. Standard American fare is served along with an interesting mix of southwestern and Greek specialties. ⊠ *54 Lincoln Ave.,* ☎
505/982–1664. Reservations not accepted. D, MC, V.

$ ✕ **Guadalupe Café.** A local favorite, this informal café features New
Mexican dishes, including sizable *sopaipillas* (fluffy fried bread). The
seasonal raspberry pancakes are one of many breakfast favorites that
keep the place crowded every morning. ⊠ *422 Old Santa Fe Trail,* ☎
505/982–9762. Reservations not accepted. D, MC, V.

$ ✕ **The Shed.** The Shed is housed in a rambling adobe hacienda dating
from 1692 and decorated throughout with festive folk art. Try the red-
chili enchiladas or *posole* (hominy stew). ⊠ *113½ E. Palace Ave.,* ☎
*505/982–9030. Reservations not accepted for lunch. No credit cards.
Closed Sun.*

Lodging

Hotel rates, which fluctuate considerably from place to place, are generally lower from November through April (excluding the Thanksgiving and Christmas holidays), after which they soar. Bed-and-breakfasts often offer less expensive, charming accommodations (**Bed & Breakfast of New Mexico,** ⊠ Box 2805, Santa Fe 87504, ☎ 505/982–3332). For price ranges *see* Chart 2 (A) *in* On the Road with Fodor's.

$$$$ 🖫 **Eldorado Hotel.** One of the city's most luxurious hotels, in the heart of downtown, the Eldorado has rooms furnished in southwestern style. Many have balconies with mountain views. The Old House restaurant is outstanding. There's live music in the lounge nightly. ⊠ *309 W. San Francisco St., 87501,* ☎ *505/988–4455 or 800/955–4455,* FAX *505/995–4455. 219 rooms, 19 casitas. 2 restaurants, piano bar, pool, hot tub, sauna. AF, D, DC, MC, V.*

$$$$ 🖫 **Inn of the Anasazi.** One of Santa Fe's finer hotels, the inn offers rooms
★ with beamed ceilings, kiva fireplaces, and handcrafted furnishings. The amazing restaurant features innovative takes on local and regional cuisine and a large selection of wines. ⊠ *113 Washington Ave., 87501,* ☎ *505/988–3030 or 800/688–8100,* FAX *505/988–3277. 59 rooms. Restaurant. AE, D, DC, MC, V.*

$$$–$$$$ 🖫 **Inn of the Governors.** This unpretentious inn, one of the nicest in town, is two blocks from the Plaza. Rooms have a Mexican theme, with bright colors, hand-painted folk art, southwestern fabrics, and handmade furnishings. ⊠ *234 Don Gaspar Ave. (at Alameda St.), 87501,* ☎ *505/982–4333 or 800/234–4534,* FAX *505/989–9149. 100 rooms. Restaurant, piano bar, pool. AE, DC, MC, V.*

$$$–$$$$ 🖫 **La Fonda.** As the oldest hotel in Santa Fe, this may be the only one
★ that can boast having had both Kit Carson and John F. Kennedy as guests. Each room is unique, with hand-carved and -painted Spanish colonial–style furniture and motifs painted by local artists. ⊠ *100 E. San Francisco St., 87501,* ☎ *505/982–5511 or 800/523–5002,* FAX *505/988–2952. 153 rooms. Restaurant, bar, lounge, pool, spa. AE, D, DC, MC, V.*

$$$–$$$$ 🖫 **La Posada de Santa Fe.** This Victorian-era inn near the Plaza is on 6 acres of beautifully landscaped gardens and expansive green lawns. Most rooms have fireplaces, beamed ceilings, and Native American rugs; the five in the main building are drenched in Victorian decor. ⊠ *330 E. Palace Ave., 87501,* ☎ *505/986–0000 or 800/727–5276,* FAX *505/982–6850. 119 rooms, 20 casitas. Restaurant, bar, pool. AE, DC, MC, V.*

$$–$$$$ 🖫 **Bishop's Lodge.** Three miles north of downtown Santa Fe, in the rolling foothills of the Sangre de Cristo Mountains, this incredible 1,000-acre resort was the retreat of Jean Baptiste Lamy, the first archbishop of Santa Fe. Rooms are in 11 one- and three-story lodges. The restaurant is one of the area's best. ⊠ *Bishop's Lodge Rd., Santa Fe 87504,* ☎ *505/983–6377 or 800/732–2240,* FAX *505/989–8739. 88 rooms. Restaurant, bar, pool, tennis, hiking, horseback riding, children's programs. AE, D, MC, V.*

$$–$$$$ 🖫 **Rancho Encantado.** This elegantly casual 168-acre resort offers a full
★ range of activities in the piñon-covered hills above the distant Rio Grande Valley. Guest rooms have fine Spanish and western antiques; some have fireplaces and/or private patios. Call for directions to Tesuque. ⊠ *1 State Rd. 592, Tesuque; Mailing address: Rte. 4 (Box 57C), Santa Fe 87501,* ☎ *505/982–3537 or 800/722–9339,* FAX *505/983–8269. 29 rooms, 29 villas. Restaurant, 2 pools, spa, tennis, hiking, horseback riding, jogging. AE, D, DC, MC, V.*

$$–$$$ 🖫 **Territorial Inn.** This elegantly remodeled 100-year-old Victorian home is just two blocks from the Plaza. Some rooms have their own

fireplaces. A hot tub is enclosed in a gazebo in the back garden. ✉ *215 Washington Ave., 87501,* ☎ *505/989–7737,* 🖷 *505/986–9212. 10 rooms. AE, DC, MC, V.*

$$–$$$ 🏨 **Hotel Santa Fe.** The largest off-reservation Native American–owned hotel in the country, this comfortable hotel has rooms decorated in traditional southwestern style. Its gift shop sells works by Picurís and other Pueblo Indian artists at prices lower than those of most nearby retail stores; guests get an additional 25% discount. ✉ *1501 Paseo de Peralta, 87505,* ☎ *505/982–1200 or 800/825–9876,* 🖷 *505/984–2211. 131 rooms. Bar, café. AE, D, DC, MC, V.*

Campgrounds

La Bajada Welcome Center (✉ La Bajada Hill, 13 mi southwest of Santa Fe on I–25, ☎ 505/471–5242) provides information on private campgrounds near Santa Fe. **Babbitt's Los Campos RV Park** (✉ 3574 Cerrillos Rd., 87505, ☎ 505/473–1949) is the only full-service RV park within the city limits. The **Santa Fe National Forest** (✉ 1220 S. St. Francis Dr., Box 1689, 87504, ☎ 505/988–6940), right in Santa Fe's backyard, has public sites open from May through October. Operated by the Tesuque Pueblo Indians, **Tesuque Pueblo RV Campground** (✉ U.S. 285/Rte. 5, Box 360-H, 87501, ☎ 505/455–2661), just outside Santa Fe, has RV hookups and tent sites.

Nightlife and the Arts

Check the entertainment listings in Santa Fe's daily newspaper, the *New Mexican,* or the weekly *Santa Fe Reporter,* published on Wednesday, for special performances and events.

Nightlife

The lounges, hotels, and nightspots of Santa Fe offer a wide variety of entertainment options. **Evangelo's,** downtown (✉ 200 W. San Francisco St., ☎ 505/982–9014), has Hawaii à la New Mexico decor, 200 imported beers, and pool tables in a funky basement; bands play upstairs on weekends. **El Farol** (✉ 808 Canyon Rd., ☎ 505/983–9912) features live blues, jazz, and folk music in a rustic centuries-old adobe. **Rodeo Nites** (✉ 2911 Cerrillos Rd., ☎ 505/473–4138) attracts a country-and-western crowd.

The Arts

Artistically and visually the city's crown jewel, the famed **Santa Fe Opera** (✉ U.S. 285, ☎ 505/982–3855) is housed every summer in a modern open-air amphitheater carved into a hillside 7 mi north of the city. The **Santa Fe Symphony** (☎ 505/983–1414) performs from September through May at Sweeney Center (✉ 201 W. Marcy St.). The **Santa Fe Pro Musica** plays at the Lensic Theater (✉ 211 W. San Francisco St., ☎ 505/988–4640) from September through May. The **Santa Fe Chamber Music Festival** (☎ 505/983–2075) brings internationally known musicians to the St. Francis Auditorium at the Museum of Fine Arts (✉ 107 W. Palace Ave.) from July to August.

Outdoor Activities and Sports

Horseback Riding

Bishop's Lodge (✉ Bishop's Lodge Rd., ☎ 505/983–6377) rents horses to guests and nonguests from April through November. **Santa Fe Detours** (✉ 100 E. San Francisco St., ☎ 505/983–6565 or 800/338–6877) offers excursions.

Hot-Air Ballooning

Santa Fe Detours (✉ 100 E. San Francisco St., ☎ 505/983–6565 or 800/338–6877) arranges excursions.

River Rafting
New Wave Rafting Company (✉ 103 E. Water St., Suite F, ☎ 505/984–1444 or 800/984–1444). **Los Rios River Runners** (✉ Box 2734, Taos, ☎ 505/776–8854 or 800/544–1181, FAX 505/776–1842). **Santa Fe Rafting Company and Outfitters** (✉ 1000 Cerrillos Rd., ☎ 505/988–4914 or 800/467–7238). **Kokopelli Rafting Adventures** (✉ 541 Cordova Rd., ☎ 505/983–3734 or 800/879–9035).

Ski Areas

Ski New Mexico (✉ 1210 Luisa St., Suite 8, Santa Fe 87505, ☎ 505/982–5300) provides information on skiing in the Santa Fe area. **Santa Fe Central Reservations** (✉ 320 Artist Rd., Suite 10, Santa Fe 87501, ☎ 505/983–8200 or 800/776–7669) is another source on skiing near Santa Fe.

Cross-Country
Santa Fe National Forest (✉ 1220 S. St. Francis Dr., Box 1689, 87504, ☎ 505/988–6940) has hundreds of miles of trails of varying difficulty, some leading to natural hot springs.

Downhill
The small but excellent **Santa Fe Ski Area** (✉ 1210 Luisa St., Suite 10, Santa Fe 87505, ☎ 505/982–4429 or 505/983–9155) has a 1,650-ft vertical drop, 38 trails, and seven lifts.

TAOS

At the base of the rugged Sangre de Cristo Mountains about 60 mi northeast of Santa Fe, Taos is a small, old frontier town steeped in the history of New Mexico. Stately elms and cottonwood trees, narrow streets, and a profusion of adobe all cast a lingering spell on the memory—and the charming old **Plaza,** surrounded by art galleries and boutiques, adds to the allure. Georgia O'Keeffe, Ansel Adams, and D. H. Lawrence are among Taos's former residents; so are such Wild West figures as Kit Carson and New Mexico's first governor, Charles Bent. Taos is a popular ski resort in winter and a great hiking and mountain-biking venue in the summer.

Visitor Information

Taos County Chamber of Commerce (✉ 1139 Paseo del Pueblo Sur, Drawer 1, Taos 87571, ☎ 505/758–3873 or 800/732–8267).

Arriving and Departing

By Bus
Texas, New Mexico & Oklahoma Coaches, a subsidiary of Greyhound/Trailways, runs buses once a day from Albuquerque to the Taos Bus Station (✉ Corner of Paseo del Pueblo Sur and Paseo del Cañon, ☎ 505/758–1144).

By Car
The main route from Santa Fe to Taos is U.S. 68. From points north, take NM 522; from points east or west, take I–64.

By Plane
The **Taos Municipal Airport** (✉ U.S. 64, ☎ 505/758–4995), 12 mi west of the city, services only private planes and air charters. For air-charter information, call 505/758–4995. **Pride of Taos** (☎ 505/758–8340) runs daily shuttle service to the Albuquerque Airport ($35 one-way, $65 round-trip) and between Taos and Santa Fe ($25 one-way, $50

round-trip); reserve in advance. **Faust's Transportation** (⊠ In nearby El Prado, ☎ 505/758–3410 or 505/758–7359) offers radio-dispatched taxis between the Taos airport and town ($12) and between the Albuquerque airport and Taos ($35 one-way, $65 round-trip).

By Train
Amtrak (☎ 800/872–7245) provides service into Lamy Station (⊠ County Rd. 41, Lamy 87500) a half hour outside Santa Fe, the closest train station to Taos. **Faust's Transportation** (⊠ In nearby El Prado, ☎ 505/758–3410 or 505/758–7359) offers radio-dispatched taxis to the train station.

Getting Around

Taos radiates around its famous central Plaza and is easily maneuvered on foot. The main street through town is Paseo del Pueblo Norte, coming down from Colorado; the route becomes Paseo del Pueblo Sur and heads out toward Santa Fe. **Faust's Transportation** (☎ 505/758–3410 or 505/758–7359), in nearby El Prado, has a fleet of radio-dispatched cabs.

Orientation Tours

Pride of Taos Tours (⊠ Box 1192, Taos 87571, ☎ 505/758–8340) provides 70-minute narrated trolley tours of Taos highlights. The departure point for tours, shuttles, and pickups is next to the Taos County Chamber of Commerce (☞ Visitor Information, *above*) and the Plaza.

Exploring Taos

The **Taos Pueblo**—2 mi north of the Plaza, at the base of the 12,282-ft Taos Mountain—is the home of the Taos Tiwa-speaking Indians, whose apartment-house-style pueblo dwelling is one of the oldest continuously inhabited communities in the United States. Life here predates Marco Polo's 13th-century travels in China and the arrival of the Spanish in America in 1540. Unlike many nomadic Native American tribes forced to relocate to government-designated reservations, the Taos Pueblos have resided at the base of the Taos Mountain for centuries; this continuity has made possible the link between pre-Columbian inhabitants who originally lived in the Taos Valley and their descendants who reside there now.

Four miles south of town is the farming and ranching community **Ranchos de Taos,** which has the beautiful **San Francisco de Asís Church.** Its massive, buttressed adobe walls and graceful towers are a prime example of early Mission architecture. The earthy, clean lines of the exterior walls and supporting bulwarks—casting shapes and shadows—have inspired generations of painters and photographers, including Georgia O'Keeffe and Ansel Adams. ⊠ *Ranchos de Taos,* ☎ *505/758–2754.*

Dining and Lodging

For price ranges *see* Chart 2 (B) *in* On the Road with Fodor's.

$$$$ ✕ **Villa Fontana.** The warm coral walls, intimate dining rooms, and
★ crisp linen tablecloths give this first-class restaurant the rich charm of an Italian country inn. Chef Carlo Gislimberti prepares northern Italian classics such as polenta with chicken livers and venison casserole with blueberries. ⊠ *5 mi north of Taos along Rte. 68N,* ☎ *505/758–5800. AE, D, MC, V. Closed Sun.*

$$$ ✕ **Doc Martin's.** Patrick Lambert brings snap and imagination to this pleasant, casual restaurant in the historic Taos Inn (☞ *below*). Warm duck salad and seared salmon in roasted-garlic cream sauce are among the tasty, well-presented dishes on the menu. Don't skip the superb desserts: Aztec chocolate mousse with roasted-banana sauce or coconut-milk crème brûlée. ✉ *125 Paseo del Pueblo Norte,* ☎ *505/758–1977. AE, D, MC, V.*

$$ ✕ **Jacquelina's.** Named after the owners' six-year-old daughter, this popular, cozy restaurant specializes in southwestern cuisine. Sample crab cakes with black-bean sauce or grilled salmon with tomatillo salsa. The Sunday brunch is superb. ✉ *1541 Paseo del Pueblo Sur,* ☎ *505/751–0399. D, MC, DC. Closed Mon. No lunch Sat.*

$ ✕ **Casa Fresen Bakery.** A jewel in the tiny village of Arroyo Seco on ★ the way to the Taos Ski Valley (☞ Ski Areas, *below*), this café, bakery, and gourmet market has the most delicious deli food in the area. Its freshly baked breads alone are reason enough to stop in. ✉ *8 mi northwest of Taos on Rte. 150,* ☎ *505/776–2969.*

$$–$$$$ 🏨 **Taos Inn.** Only steps from the Plaza, this sprawling hotel with rustic southwestern charm is a prized local landmark—parts of the structure date from the 1600s. Rooms have a southwestern motif, with Native American–style wood-burning fireplaces and furniture built by local artists. ✉ *125 Paseo del Pueblo Norte, 87571,* ☎ *505/758–2233 or 800/826–7466,* 🖷 *505/758–5776. 36 rooms. Restaurant, bar, lounge, library. AE, DC, MC, V.*

$$–$$$ 🏨 **Casa Europa.** Pastures and mountains surround this spacious 17th-century pueblo-style adobe B&B outside town. The delightful rooms have kiva fireplaces and marble bathrooms; there's also a five-room suite with a hot tub. Owners Rudi and Marcia Zwicker serve gourmet breakfasts every morning and European-style homemade pastries every afternoon—except during ski season, when they serve fireside hors d'oeuvres in the evenings instead. ✉ *840 Upper Ranchitos Rd., HC 68 Box 3F, 87571,* ☎ *505/758–9798 or 888/758–9798. 7 rooms. Lounge, hot tub, sauna. MC, V.*

$$–$$$ 🏨 **Mabel Dodge Luhan House.** This Pueblo Indian–style structure on ★ spectacular grounds was the home of heiress and Taos socialite Mabel Dodge Luhan. The nine guest rooms in the main house have an Italian influence and are furnished with turn-of-the-century pieces; rooms in the newer guest house are decorated with regionally hand-carved furniture. There's also a two-bedroom gatehouse cottage. ✉ *242 Morada La., 87571,* ☎ *505/758–9456 or 800/846–2235,* 🖷 *505/737–0365. 18 rooms, 13 with bath, 1 cottage. AE, MC, V.*

$–$$$ 🏨 **Austing Haus.** This soaring timber-frame building offers stunning ★ views of the Taos Ski Valley from its glass-paneled front. Rooms are tastefully and beautifully decorated, some with four-poster beds. The entire facility is spotlessly clean. The restaurant, with its huge etched-glass windows, offers good food in European-style alpine grandeur. ✉ *Taos Ski Valley Rd. (Rte. 150), Box 8, Taos 87525,* ☎ *505/776–2649 or 800/748–2932,* 🖷 *505/776–8751. 52 rooms, 4 chalets. Restaurant, 3 hot tubs. D, MC, V.*

$$ 🏨 **San Geronimo Lodge.** The lodge was originally constructed in 1925 by an Oklahoma socialite wanting to accommodate her friends. Hand-crafted furniture decorates the rooms; most have kiva fireplaces. A country breakfast is served every morning. ✉ *1101 Witt Rd., Taos 87571,* ☎ *505/751–3776 or 800/894–4119. 18 rooms. Lounge, pool, hot tub, massage. MC, V.*

$$ 🏨 **Touchstone Bed & Breakfast.** Nestled against the Taos Pueblo land, this elegant B&B enjoys magnificent views of the mountains. Each luxury suite is distinctively and comfortably furnished with an eclectic collection of antiques, kiva fireplaces, and whirlpool baths. The owner, Bren Price, is an artist, and her work is displayed throughout the inn. ⊠ *110 Mabel Dodge La., 87571,* ☎ *800/758–0192. 8 suites. MC, V.*

Campgrounds
Carson National Forest Service (⊠ Box 558, Taos 87571, ☎ 505/758–6200) provides information about the many camping sites in the forest. **Taos RV Park** (⊠ Hwy. 68, Box 729TCVG, Ranchos de Taos 87557, ☎ 505/758–1667 or 800/323–6009), with 29 spaces, is open year-round.

Ski Areas

In winter, within a 90-mi radius, Taos offers plenty of ski resorts with beginning, intermediate, and advanced slopes, as well as snowmobile and cross-country skiing trails. All these ski resorts offer excellent lodging accommodations and safe, modern child-care programs at reasonable prices.

Cross-Country
Carson National Forest (⊠ Box 558, Taos 87571, ☎ 505/758–6200) has 440 mi of trails. **Enchanted Forest Cross-Country Ski Area** (⊠ Box 219, Red River 87558, ☎ 505/754–2374), near Taos, has 18 mi of trails.

Downhill
Angel Fire Resort (⊠ Drawer B, Angel Fire 87710, ☎ 505/377–6401 or 800/633–7463) has a 2,180-ft drop, 59 trails, and 6 lifts. **Red River Ski Area** (⊠ Box 900, Red River 87558, ☎ 505/754–2223, FAX 505/754–6184) has a 600-ft drop, 44 trails, and 7 lifts. **Sipapu Lodge and Ski Area** (⊠ Box 29, Vadito 87579, ☎ 505/587–2240) offers a 865-ft drop, 19 trails, and 3 lifts. **Taos Ski Valley** (⊠ Box 90, Taos Ski Valley 87525, ☎ 505/776–2291, FAX 505/776–8596) has a whopping 2,612-ft drop, 72 trails, and 11 lifts.

ELSEWHERE IN NEW MEXICO

Carlsbad Caverns National Park

Arriving and Departing
The park is in the southeastern part of the state, 320 mi from Albuquerque via I–25, U.S. 380, and U.S. 285, and 167 mi west of El Paso, Texas, via U.S. 180. **Mesa Airlines** (☎ 800/637–2247 or 505/885–0245 in Carlsbad) offers air-shuttle service between the Albuquerque airport and **Cavern City Air Terminal** in Carlsbad.

What to See and Do
★ **Carlsbad Caverns National Park** (⊠ 3225 National Parks Hwy., Carlsbad 88220, ☎ 505/785–2232) contains one of the world's largest and most spectacular cave systems: 83 caves, with huge subterranean chambers, fantastic rock formations, and delicate mineral sculptures. Only two caves are open to the public for regular tours, with some off-trail viewing options available during special trips. At **Carlsbad Cavern** the descent to the 750-ft level is made by foot or elevator; either way, you can see the Big Room, large enough to hold 14 football fields. Reservations are essential a day in advance for the much-less-accessible **Slaughter Canyon Cave** (☎ 505/785–2232), 25 mi from the main cavern. The last few miles of the road are gravel, and you must plan on a half-mile trek up a 500-ft rise to reach the cave's entrance.

The park is the area's main lure, but the town of **Carlsbad** is an interesting place to see as well. For information contact the Chamber of Commerce (⊠ 302 S. Canal St., 88220, ☎ 505/887–6516). The **Living Desert State Park** (⊠ 1504 Miehls Dr., Carlsbad 88220, ☎ 505/887–5516) is also worth a visit while you're in the area.

Dining and Lodging

For price ranges *see* Charts 1 (B) and 2 (B) *in* On the Road with Fodor's.

$–$$ ✕ **Cortez Cafe.** Ownership of this café, established in 1937, recently changed hands—but the same Southwest fare still makes it a favorite. The Gregory and Azzinaro families offer traditional Mexican dishes such as tostadas *compuestas* and sour cream enchiladas. Chili dishes are easy on the taste buds—they're not too fiery. ⊠ *506 S. Canal St.,* ☎ *505/885–4747. No credit cards.*

$–$$ ✕ **Lucy's.** Have a margarita and one of the tingling-hot chili dishes at this oasis of great Mexican food. Specialties include chicken fajita burritos smothered with chef Adam's special *queso* (cheese) as well as low-fat dishes. ⊠ *701 S. Canal St.* ☎ *505/887–7714. MC, V.*

$$ 🏨 **Holiday Inn Carlsbad Downtown.** Ideal for families, the hotel has a playground, laundry room, and exercise equipment. There is no extra charge for children under 19 who stay in the room with their parents. Soft southwestern colors—beige, rose, and blue—enliven the spacious rooms. Continental cuisine is served in the gourmet restaurant, Ventanas (Windows). ⊠ *601 S. Canal St., Carlsbad 88220,* ☎ *505/885–8500 or 800/742–9586,* 𝔽𝔸𝕏 *505/887–5999. 100 rooms. 2 restaurants, bar, pool, hot tub, sauna, exercise room, playground, laundry service. AE, D, DC, MC, V.*

$ 🏨 **Best Western Motel Stevens.** Prices here are a bargain for the classy accommodations and reliable service. Local scenes of cavern formations and Carlsbad's historic courthouse are etched in mirrored-glass murals and carved into wooden doors. Rooms are decorated in desert colors with mirrored vanities and prints of Western scenes; some have kitchenettes. If you like country-and-western music, there are shows nightly in the Silver Spur bar. The Flume restaurant has a very good prime rib special. ⊠ *1829 S. Canal St., Carlsbad 88220,* ☎ *505/887–2851 or 800/870–2851,* 𝔽𝔸𝕏 *505/887–6338. 202 rooms. Restaurant, lounge, kitchenettes, pool. AE, D, DC, MC, V.*

TEXAS

By Betsy
Tschurr

Capital	Austin
Population	19,128,000
Motto	Friendship
State Bird	Mockingbird
State Flower	Bluebonnet
Postal Abbreviation	TX

Statewide Visitor Information

Texas Department of Tourism (⊠ Box 12728, Austin 78711, ☎ 800/888–8839).

Scenic Drives

In far southwest Texas, **Route 170** from Lajitas through Presidio and into the Chinati Mountains is one of the most spectacular drives in the state, plunging over mountains and through canyons along the Rio Grande (thus its name: El Camino del Rio, or River Road). **U.S. 83** from Leakey to Uvalde is a roller coaster of a ride through the lush western edges of Hill Country, in central Texas. In the northern panhandle, **I–27** from Lubbock to Amarillo carries travelers through the buffalo grass and sheer cliffs of the Llano Estacado (Staked Plain, so named because its lack of trees forced pioneers to tie their horses to stakes). From Center, a small town near the Louisiana border, south into the Sabine National Forest, **Route 87** takes you over several dramatic lakes and through one of the huge pine forests for which east Texas is famous.

National and State Parks

National Parks

Big Bend National Park (⊠ U.S. 385 from Marathon; Superintendent, Big Bend National Park 79834, ☎ 915/477–2251) is the state's premier natural attraction. This overwhelming landscape, laid bare by millions of years of erosion, includes spectacular canyons, a junglelike floodplain, the sprawling Chihuahuan Desert, and the cool woodlands of the Chisos Mountains. Spread out over 801,163 acres, Big Bend teems with animal life, from relatively rare black bears and mountain lions to coyotes, javelinas, gray foxes, beavers, deer, and jackrabbits. More than 430 bird species have been identified here, including such favorites as the roadrunner and such rarities as the Colima warbler. The park is crosshatched with hundreds of miles of trails, dirt roads, and paved roads and offers wild backcountry camping (with permits). For the more timid, there are ranger-led walks, campgrounds, a trailer park, and other amenities. The park's only hotel is the Chisos Lodge (☎ 915/477–2291). River outfitters offer rafting trips through remote canyons of the Rio Grande (☎ 915/424–3219; 800/545–4240 to reserve spots for longer trips).

Davy Crockett National Forest (⊠ Ratcliff Lake; 1240 E. Loop 304, Crockett 75835, ☎ 409/544–2046)—a 161,500-acre park in the "piney woods" of east Texas, about 20 mi east of the historic town of Crockett on Route 7—offers camping, canoeing on the Neches River, a dramatic 19-mi hiking trail, and picnicking facilities and concessions around Ratcliff Lake.

Aransas National Wildlife Refuge (⊠ Rte. 2040, Tivoli, ☎ 512/286–3559), on a peninsula jutting 12 mi into the Gulf of Mexico near Rockport, is the principal wintering ground of the endangered whooping crane. The best time to spot it and some 300 other species of birds is between November and March.

State Parks

You can call a central reservations number (☎ 512/389–8900) to book any campsite in the Texas state park system. **Caddo Lake State Park** (⊠ Rte. 43, ☎ 903/679–3351), on the southern shore of the lake near Karnack, offers camping, overnighting in cabins, fishing, swimming, and boating.

Named after the local term for "high plains," **Caprock Canyons State Park** (⊠ Rte. 1065, Quitaque, ☎ 806/455–1492), in the panhandle, is marked by canyons, striking geologic formations, and an abundance of wildlife, including African aoudad (a kind of sheep), mule deer, and golden eagles.

Enchanted Rock State Park (⊠ Rte. 965, Llano, ☎ 915/247–3903), near Fredericksburg in the Hill Country, is so named because of the noises emitted by the underground heating and cooling of its massive, 500-ft-high dome of solid granite. The rock is the reputed site of ancient human sacrifices.

Fishing is king at **Inks Lake State Park** (⊠ Rte. 29 and Park Rd. 4, Barnet, ☎ 512/793–2223), northwest of Austin at the edge of the Hill Country. Surrounding the lake's crystal-clear waters are extensive amenities, including facilities for camping, trailers, boats, and golf.

★ **Palo Duro Canyon State Park** (⊠ Rte. 217 and Park Rd. 5, ☎ 806/488–2227), set on the high plains east of the panhandle town of Canyon and long a favorite spot for Texan tourists, is a place of rock spires and precipitous cliffs. The site of the last great battle with the Comanche, the park today offers an outdoor amphitheater backed by a 600-ft cliff, where the historical drama *Texas*, written by a local playwright, is presented each year from late June through August (☎ 806/655–2181).

HOUSTON AND GALVESTON

Houston fell on hard times after the oil boom went bust in the 1980s, and the resulting contrast between the downtown's glass-and-steel magnificence with its boarded-up buildings may be the city's oddest feature; however, Houston's economy has been on the rebound since the early 1990s. Another peculiar juxtaposition is the result of a total lack of zoning—unique among major American cities—that has yielded such contrasts as the shacks of the poverty-stricken Fourth Ward overshadowed by glittering skyscrapers. Local lawmakers are working to curtail these zoning irregularities.

The nation's fourth-largest city is nevertheless an international business hub and the energy capital of the United States, evidenced by the Texas-size conventions that periodically fill its major hotels to bursting point. Its port still thrives, and its highways, although plentiful, can be nightmarish with roaring traffic. Large and varied foreign communities and a plenitude of fine ethnic restaurants and world-class cultural institutions lend Houston a distinct cosmopolitan flavor that Dallasites will claim but cannot capture.

Galveston, 50 mi southeast, is Houston's touristy stepchild. An island in the Gulf of Mexico, connected by causeway and bridge to the mainland, it is an odd mix of Victorian architecture and Coney Island–like beach developments. Although virtually all its architecture dates from after 1900, when an unheralded hurricane and consequent tidal waves swept over this 32-mi-long sandbar, Galveston has managed to recapture a historic feel long lost to its northern neighbor. Once a faded has-been, the city is now enjoying a tourist-fueled renaissance evident in energetic renovation efforts. It is artsy, even precious, and well stocked with hotels and restaurants catering to visitors.

Visitor Information

Galveston Island: Convention & Visitors Bureau (⊠ 2106 Seawall Blvd., 77550, in the Moody Center, ☎ 409/763–4311 or 800/351–4237; 800/351–4236 in TX), Strand Visitors Center (⊠ 2016 Strand, ☎ 409/765–7834). **Greater Houston:** Convention & Visitors Bureau (⊠ 801 Congress Ave., 77002, ☎ 713/227–3100 or 800/365–7575).

Arriving and Departing

By Car
Houston is ringed by the I–610 beltway. A tighter loop, comprising several expressways, circles the downtown and provides remarkable views of the city, especially at dawn and dusk. Radiating out from these rings like spokes of a wheel are I–10, heading east to Louisiana and west to San Antonio; U.S. 59, northeast to Longview or southwest to Victoria; and I–45, southeast to Galveston (about an hour away) or north to Dallas. Traffic on all these highways can be extremely heavy during rush hours.

By Bus
Greyhound Lines (⊠ 2121 Main St., Houston, ☎ 800/231–2222). **Texas Bus Lines** (⊠ 714 25th St., Galveston, ☎ 409/765–7731).

By Plane
Houston's two major airports are served by about 22 airlines between them. (Be sure to check which airport you will be using, as many airlines serve both.) **Southwest Airlines** (☎ 713/237–1221 or 800/435–9792) offers particularly extensive, frequent, and inexpensive service among nine Texas cities. The airport more convenient to downtown is **W. P. Hobby Airport** (☎ 713/643–4597), 9 mi to the southeast. During rush hour, the trip into the city will take about 45 minutes; taxi fare runs about $20. **Houston Intercontinental Airport** (HIA; ☎ 713/230–3100), 15 mi north of downtown but closer to the Galleria area, is the city's international airport. The trip downtown during peak hours takes up to an hour; cab fare will run you up to $30. **Shuttles** (☎ 713/523–8888) to several Houston locations serve both Hobby ($10) and HIA ($15); **city express bus service** (☎ 713/635–4000) to HIA costs $1.20. **Galveston Limousine Service** (☎ 713/286–5466 in Houston, 409/740–5466 in Galveston, 800/640–4826 elsewhere in TX) offers hourly service to island locations from both Houston airports for $15–$21.

By Train
In Houston, **Amtrak** (☎ 713/224–1577 or 800/872–7245) trains run out of the old **Southern Pacific Station** (⊠ 902 Washington Ave.).

Galveston's **Center for Transportation and Commerce** (⊠ 2500 Strand, ☎ 409/765–5700) serves as the terminal for the **Texas Limited** (☎ 713/522–0574 or 800/374–7475), a rail line that connects to Houston's **Eureka Station** (⊠ 567 T. C. Jester St.). Available for group charters only, the train has seven restored cars from the 1920s to the 1940s.

Getting Around Houston and Galveston

Both Houston and Galveston almost demand cars. Attractions are spread out, and public transportation is sketchy. Houston's city bus system, **Metro** (☎ 713/635–4000), is difficult for visitors to learn. Similarly, Galveston offers island bus service, but of far more interest is the **Treasure Island Tour Train** (✉ 2106 Seawall Blvd., ☎ 409/765–9564), which departs regularly from just outside the Convention & Visitors Bureau (☞ Visitor Information, *above*) for tours of local sights.

Exploring Houston and Galveston

Houston

Houston can be divided neatly into three major areas. One is its very modern downtown (including the theater district), which spurred one architecture critic to declare the city "America's future." Another is the area a couple of miles south of downtown, where some of the Southwest's leading museums are found along with Rice University and the internationally renowned Texas Medical Center. Finally, there is the ritzy shopping area west of downtown, centered on the Galleria.

DOWNTOWN

You may want to start by taking in the entire urban panorama from the observation deck of I. M. Pei's **Texas Commerce Tower** (✉ 600 Travis St.), at 75 stories the city's tallest building and the world's highest composite tube tower. **Texas Street,** visible from the Commerce Tower, is 100 ft wide, precisely the width needed to accommodate 14 Texas longhorns tip to tip in the days when cattle were driven to market along this route. In **Tranquility Park,** between Walker and Rusk streets east of Smith Street, you can get another perspective on the architecture that distinguishes the city. This cool, human-scale oasis of fountains and diagonal walkways among the skyscrapers was built to commemorate the first words of man on the moon: "Houston, Tranquility Base here. The Eagle has landed."

The major buildings of the theater district are a few steps away from Tranquility Park. The **Jesse H. Jones Hall for the Performing Arts** (✉ 615 Louisiana St., ☎ 713/227–1910), home to the Houston Symphony Orchestra and the Society for the Performing Arts, is a huge hall that appears almost encased by a second, colonnaded building; its teak auditorium is more attractive than the exterior. The **Alley Theatre** (✉ 615 Texas Ave., ☎ 713/228–9341 or 800/259–2553), a fortresslike but innovative low-lying structure, is the venue of the city's only resident professional theater company. The **Gus S. Wortham Theater Center** (✉ 550 Prairie Ave., ☎ 713/523–6300), where the Houston Grand Opera and the Houston Ballet perform in two side-by-side theaters, was completed in 1987. **City hall** (✉ 901 Bagby St.), just northwest of Tranquility Park, is an unremarkable building whose chief interest lies in its allegorical interior murals.

The **Smith–Louisiana corridor,** a daunting canyon formed by towers of glass and steel, runs south from Tranquility Park on the west side of downtown. Most of these buildings were erected before oil prices plunged in 1983. A walk down these streets may be the truest measure of the city's modernism, intensified by the **outdoor sculptures** of Joan Miró, Claes Oldenburg, Louise Nevelson, and Jean Dubuffet. (Dubuffet's *Monument au Fantôme,* on Louisiana Street between Lamar and Dallas streets, is a particular delight to children.) The downtown area may leave you with an eerie sense of emptiness, but there's a good reason for that beyond the universal depopulation of America's urban centers: More than 70 of the major business and government buildings downtown are connected by a 6¾-mi labyrinth of **underground tunnels,** used by those in the know as a welcome escape from the humidity for which Houston is justly infamous.

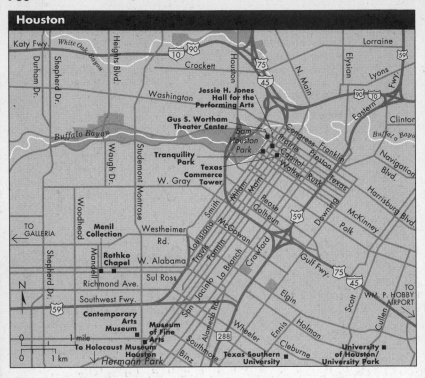

Houston

The lobby of the **Hyatt Regency Houston** is a must-see, particularly if you have children (⊠ 1200 Louisiana St.). Garish and decorated with potted plants and brass aplenty, the lobby's atrium soars 30 stories, circled by balconies and topped by a revolving restaurant cocktail lounge. A ride up in the glass-enclosed cabs of the powerful elevators is dramatic, a sure winner with kids, and a trifle frightening.

THE MUSEUM DISTRICT

The verdant campus of **Rice University,** Texas's finest institution of higher learning, is 4 mi south of downtown on Main Street. Several world-class museums are across the street from the Rice campus.

The **Museum of Fine Arts**'s enormous collection is remarkable for its completeness. Housed in a complicated series of wings and galleries—many designed by Ludwig Mies van der Rohe—the museum now also owns the **Bayou Bend Collection** of American decorative arts, housed across town in the River Oaks mansion neighborhood (⊠ 1 Westcott St., ☎ 713/639–7758); tours are by reservation only. Highlights of the museum's vast offerings include the Straus collection of Renaissance and 18th-century works, the notable Samuel Kress collection of Italian and Spanish Renaissance paintings, and some impressionist works. ⊠ *1001 Bissonnet (north of Rice University), between Montrose and Main Sts.,* ☎ *713/639–7300. Free Thurs. Closed Mon.*

Housed in a stark, cylindrical edifice, the **Holocaust Museum Houston** is an education center as well as a memorial. The main exhibit, "Bearing Witness: A Community Remembers," can be viewed individually or by guided tour. The 30-minute film *Voices* provides a moving oral history. ⊠ *5401 Caroline St.,* ☎ *713/942–8000. Closed Mon.*

The **Contemporary Arts Museum,** housed in an aluminum-sheathed trapezoid, was expanded in 1997 to include larger public areas and more gallery space. The home of avant-garde art in Houston, the museum regularly hosts traveling exhibits. ⊠ *5216 Montrose St.,* ☎ *713/526–0773. Closed Mon.*

The **Menil Collection** is the city's biggest cultural surprise. Opened in 1987 in a spacious building designed by the Italian architect Renzo Piano, the museum's airy galleries contain treasures as diverse as tribal African sculpture and Andy Warhol's paintings of Campbell's soup cans. Also here are works by Léger, Picasso, Braque, and other major modern artists. ⊠ *1515 Sul Ross St.,* ☎ *713/525–9400. Closed Mon.–Tues.*

The moody **Rothko Chapel** (⊠ 3900 Yupon St., at Sul Ross St., ☎ 713/524–9839), just down the street from the Menil Collection, is an octagonal sanctuary hung with 14 paintings by Mark Rothko. At first they look like simple black panels; only when you come close can you see the subtle coloring. Outside the ecumenical chapel is Barnett Newman's sculpture *Broken Obelisk,* symbolizing the life and assassination of Martin Luther King, Jr.

THE GALLERIA AREA

The **Galleria,** one of the world's swankiest shopping malls, is on the west side of Houston, near the intersection of Westheimer Road and I–610. Here four major department stores and 300 shops groan with an abundance of fashionable apparel and other pricey goods; hundreds more stores and sumptuous restaurants line the surrounding streets. Foreign shoppers are known to travel to Houston just to spend money at the Galleria. Several deluxe hotels are also in the area, and River Oaks, a neighborhood of multimillion-dollar mansions, is nearby.

Galveston

History is the main draw in Galveston, once the largest city in Texas. Its wealthy classes built the houses now being restored to their former glory in a frenzy of tourist-driven rehabilitation. These homes as well as some beautifully restored iron-front commercial buildings are concentrated on the northern, or bay, side of the island—especially along a street known as the Strand—and on Broadway, a boulevard that runs east–west through Galveston's midsection. Also hugging the north rim of the island, from 9th to 51st streets, is the harbor, port to about 100 small fishing boats and shrimp trawlers and to the *Elissa,* the tall ship that is Galveston's pride and joy. The southern, or ocean, side of the island is lined with beaches (☞ Beaches, *below*), hotels, parks, and restaurants.

THE STRAND AND BROADWAY

The **Strand,** especially the five blocks from 20th to 25th streets, is the heart of historic Galveston (it's now on the National Register of Historic Places)—and the nucleus of its newfound prosperity. When Galveston was still a powerful port city—before the Houston Ship Channel was dug, diverting most boat traffic inland—this stretch, formerly the site of stores, offices, and warehouses, was known as the Wall Street of the South.

As you stroll up the Strand, you'll pass dozens of trendy shops and the few four- and five-story iron-front buildings not as yet restored, where workers are scurrying about to bring in still more shops, restaurants, and bars. The **Center for Transportation and Commerce** (which also houses the **Railroad Museum,** ⊠ 2500 Strand, ☎ 409/765–5700) is an Art Deco building that was once the Santa Fe Railroad terminal. The **Tremont House,** a block from the Center for Transportation and Commerce, is a onetime dry-goods warehouse converted into a hotel; full of Victorian elegance, it's considered the best hotel on the island.

Broadway is a major thoroughfare just a 20-minute walk or a five-minute drive to the south of the Tremont House. The street is home to the "Broadway Beauties," three of the finest examples of historic restoration in Texas. The Victorian **Bishop's Palace** (⊠ 1402 Broadway, ☎ 409/762–2475) was built in 1886 for Colonel Walter Gresham. The 11 rare stone and wood mantels in the limestone-and-granite castle amply attest to the colonel's fondness for fireplaces. The building's most outstanding feature, however, is the wooden main staircase, a work of art that took 61 craftsmen seven years to carve.

Ashton Villa (⊠ 2328 Broadway, ☎ 409/762–3933), a formal Italianate villa, was built in 1859 of brick—appropriately so, as owner James Moreau Brown started out as a humble mason. A freethinking man, Brown had to install curtains to shield daintier guests from the naked Cupids painted on one wall. The **Moody Mansion** (⊠ 2618 Broadway, ☎ 409/762–7668), built in 1894, is brick, with interiors of exotic woods and gilded trim. Taped voices replicate "typical" period conversations as based on historical documents.

THE ELISSA

In 1961 a marine archaeologist and naval historian named Peter Throckmorton spotted a rotting iron hulk in the shipyards outside Athens, Greece, and realized the 150-ft wreck was what remained of a beautiful square-rigger constructed in 1877. Today, after almost 20 years of work, the Scottish-built *Elissa*—the oldest ship on the Lloyd's Register—has been restored by the Galveston Historical Foundation and hundreds of volunteers. The ship, which in the last century carried cargoes to Galveston Harbor, may be toured above and below decks and is the centerpiece of the **Texas Seaport Museum.** ⊠ *Pier 21,* ☎ *409/763–1877.*

Parks and Gardens

Houston

Hermann Park, with its 545 acres of luxuriant trees, lawns, duck-filled reflecting pools, picnic areas, and an 18-hole golf course, is the city's playground and is only a short drive south of downtown on Main Street. Sitting on the northern perimeter of the Texas Medical Center, the park is also home to the **Houston Zoo** and the **Museum of Natural Science** (☞ What to See and Do with Children, *below*), the **Garden Center,** and the **Miller Outdoor Theater.**

Memorial Park, several miles west of downtown between the 610 Loop and South Shepherd Drive, is 1,500 acres of mostly virgin woodland, a wonderful spot for walkers, joggers, and bikers.

The small downtown **Sam Houston Park,** bounded by Bagby, McKinney, and Dallas streets, preserves a few of the city's 19th-century buildings. Tickets for daily guided tours are available at the Heritage Society (☎ 713/655–1912), on the Bagby side.

Galveston

Stewart Beach Park (⊠ Seawall Blvd. at Broadway, ☎ 409/765–5023) offers a complete bathhouse, an amusement park, bumper boats, a miniature golf course, and even bungee jumping.

Galveston Island State Park, toward the western, unpopulated end of the island (⊠ 3 Mile Rd., ☎ 409/737–1222), is a 2,000-acre natural habitat ideal for birding and walking.

What to See and Do with Children

Houston

In Hermann Park, the Zoological Gardens, commonly known as the **Houston Zoo** (⊠ 1513 N. MacGregor St., ☎ 713/525–3300), includes a petting zoo, an aquarium, and other attractions. The excellent **Museum of Natural Science** (⊠ 1 Hermann Circle Dr., ☎ 713/639–4600), also on park grounds, includes the **Baker Planetarium** and **Wortham IMAX Theatre,** with a six-story-high projection screen.

★ **Six Flags Houston** (⊠ 8400 Kirby Dr., at I–610, ☎ 713/799–1234), combining the former **Astroworld** and **Waterworld,** is one of the country's major amusement complexes and a perennial favorite. Other attractions for children include the **Houston Fire Museum** (⊠ 2403 Milam St., ☎ 713/524–2526), the **Houston Police Museum** (⊠ 17000 Aldine Westfield Rd., ☎ 713/230–2300), and the wacky **Orange Show** (⊠ 2402 Munger St., ☎ 713/926–6368), an irreverent and bizarre labyrinth built over a period of 26 years by a Houston eccentric as a tribute to the humble orange—a Houston must-see.

Adults as well as children may enjoy **Space Center Houston,** 25 mi south of the city. Tram tours take you through NASA's adjacent **Johnson Space Center,** where several rockets are displayed. An IMAX theater was added in 1996. When it's not in use, you can visit **Mission Control** as well. ⊠ *I–45 to the Alvin exit, then 3 mi east on NASA Rd. 1,* ☎ *713/244–2105. Closed Mon.*

Galveston

The island's main draws for children, inevitably, are its 32 mi of beaches and the beachside rides at **Stewart Beach Park** (☞ Parks and Gardens, *above*). Another choice is the **Lone Star Flight Museum** (⊠ Scholes Field Municipal Airport, ☎ 409/740–7722). Children as well as adults will enjoy the collection of classic automobiles at **David Taylor Classics** (⊠ 1918 Ship's Mechanic St., ☎ 409/765–6590).

Dining

For price ranges *see* Chart 1 (B) *in* On the Road with Fodor's.

Houston

$$$ ╳ **Anthony's.** Houston restaurateur Tony Vallone's trendy Westheimer Boulevard version of his high-end restaurant, Tony's, features an expanded Continental menu. Try the veal Gragnon, prepared with shallots, artichokes, and marsala. ⊠ *4007 Westheimer Blvd.,* ☎ *713/961–0552. Jacket and tie. AE, DC, MC, V. Closed Sun.*

$$$ ╳ **Brennan's.** Creole dining with a Texas influence makes this Houston favorite especially popular for Sunday brunch. Spicy venison dishes and turtle soup are standouts. The pleasant surroundings include a lovely patio called the Vieux Carré. ⊠ *3300 Smith,* ☎ *713/522–9711. AE, DC, MC, V.*

$$–$$$ ╳ **Ousie's.** Here you'll find American cuisine with a southern and Asian inflection. Enjoy old favorites like Ousie's Spud (smoked salmon, caviar, and sour cream on a baked potato) or new creations such as sautéed sesame salmon with Chinese vegetables over linguine. Garden and veranda seating enhances a fabulous Sunday brunch. ⊠ *3939 San Felipe,* ☎ *713/528–2264. AE, D, DC, MC, V. Closed Mon.*

$$ ╳ **Spanish Flower.** A bit of a trek north of downtown, this is *the* Mexican restaurant in Houston. A cheerful place of ceramic tiles, potted plants, and outdoor dining, it's open 24 hours a day (except on Tuesday night). ⊠ *4701 N. Main St.,* ☎ *713/869–1706. AE, D, DC, MC, V.*

$ ╳ **This Is It.** The move up the street to larger quarters has not tainted Houston's first stop for genuine soul food. In the Fifth Ward just west of downtown, this eatery offers a buffet of oxtails, pork hocks, chitterlings, black-eyed peas, and the like. This can be a tough neighborhood, so you may want to stick to lunch. ⊠ *207 W. Gray St.,* ☎ *713/659–1508. No credit cards.*

Galveston

$$ ✕ **Gaido's.** Founded in 1911, this restaurant still serves some of the best seafood in town. Try the famous grilled red snapper, lump crabmeat, or oysters as you gaze out picture windows at the gulf. ⊠ *39th and Seawall Blvd.,* ☎ *409/762–9625. AE, MC, V.*

$–$$ ✕ **Benno's on the Beach.** There's a Coney Island feel to this little red, white, and blue joint, cited by some as the best place in Galveston for deep-fried seafood. ⊠ *1200 Seawall Blvd.,* ☎ *409/762–4621. AE, MC, V.*

$$ ✕ **Fisherman's Wharf.** You can tell by the mix—including cops, businesspeople, and high school students—that this waterfront institution is a great deal for fresh seafood. ⊠ *3901 Ave. O,* ☎ *409/765–5708. AE, DC, MC, V.*

Lodging

For price ranges *see* Chart 2 (A) *in* On the Road with Fodor's.

Houston

$$$ 🏨 **Hyatt Regency Houston.** Every room opens onto a balcony overlooking the dramatic atrium. Convenient to all downtown locations, this is a business traveler's choice. ⊠ *1200 Louisiana St., 77002,* ☎ *713/654–1234,* ℻ *713/951–0934. 907 rooms. 4 restaurants, 2 bars, pool, exercise room, parking (fee). AE, D, DC, MC, V.*

$$$$ 🏨 **Luxury Collection.** At press time, the new name of this former Ritz-Carlton had not been decided. Rooms have lovely views over beautifully manicured grounds. ⊠ *1919 Briar Oaks La., 77027,* ☎ *713/840–7600,* ℻ *713/840–0616. 232 rooms. 2 restaurants, bar, tea shop, pool, health club, parking (fee). AE, D, DC, MC, V.*

$$$ 🏨 **The Wyndham Warwick.** With lovely views of Rice University and Hermann Park, the recently renovated Wyndham Warwick is convenient to the museums. ⊠ *5701 Main St., 77005,* ☎ *713/526–1991,* ℻ *713/639–4545. 310 rooms. 2 restaurants, bar, health club. AE, D, DC, MC, V.*

$$–$$$ 🏨 **The Houstonian.** Spread over 18 acres in a heavily wooded area near Memorial Park, just west of downtown, the Houstonian offers luxurious rooms at reasonable prices—and fitness facilities galore. ⊠ *111 N. Post Oak La., 77024,* ☎ *713/680–2626,* ℻ *713/686–3701. 290 rooms. 4 restaurants, 2 bars, 3 pools, tennis courts, basketball, health club, indoor track, racquetball. AE, D, DC, MC, V.*

$–$$ 🏨 **Sara's Bed & Breakfast & Inn.** A pretty example of the Queen Anne–style architecture common in the Houston Heights neighborhood, this turn-of-the-century B&B, about 4 mi northwest of downtown, has a family atmosphere. ⊠ *941 Heights Blvd., 77008,* ☎ *713/868–1130 or 800/593–1130. 13 rooms. AE, DC, MC, V.*

Galveston

$$$–$$$$ 🏨 **San Luis Hotel and Condominiums.** Balconied rooms overlook the gulf at this spiffy if isolated high-rise resort complex, with hotel rooms in one wing and more expensive condominiums in another. ⊠ *5222 Seawall Blvd., 77551,* ☎ *409/744–1500 or 800/445–0090; 800/392–5937 in TX;* ℻ *409/744–8452. 282 hotel rooms, 120 condominiums. 2 restaurants, bar, pool, tennis courts, health club. AE, D, DC, MC, V.*

$$$–$$$$ 🏨 **Tremont House.** Right off the Strand in the heart of old Galveston, this hotel recalls the grandeur of Victorian days. Rooms have soaring ceilings and 11-ft windows, and the four-story atrium lobby boasts a hand-carved 1888 mahogany bar. ⊠ *2300 Ship's Mechanic Row, 77550,* ☎ *409/763–0300 or 800/874–2300,* ℻ *409/763–1539. 117 rooms. Restaurant, bar. AE, DC, MC, V.*

$–$$ 🖪 **Commodore.** Right on the beach, this functional hotel has a large pool and ocean views from many room balconies. ⊠ *3618 Seawall Blvd., 77552,* ☎ *409/763–2375 or 800/231–9921,* ℻ *409/763–2379. 92 rooms. Restaurant, bar, pool. AE, D, DC, MC, V.*

Nightlife and the Arts

Nightlife

Possibly the most interesting bar in Houston is a brick-fronted hole-in-the-wall, **La Carafe** (⊠ 813 Congress Ave., ☎ 713/229–9399), in the city's oldest commercial building. A top venue for pop performers—from the Neville Brothers to fiddler Vassar Clements—is **Fitzgerald's** (⊠ 2706 White Oaks Dr., ☎ 713/862–7580).

The Arts

HOUSTON

Houston's performing arts scene is a busy one, as reflected in its many venues (☞ Downtown *in* Exploring Houston and Galveston, *above*). Ticket information on the city's **symphony orchestra, opera, ballet,** and **Society for the Performing Arts** may be obtained by calling 713/227–5134. Dramas are regularly presented at the **Alley Theatre** (☞ Downtown *in* Exploring Houston and Galveston, *above*). Complete listings of events are carried in the *Houston Chronicle,* the *Houston Post,* and *Key* magazine.

GALVESTON

The recently restored **Grand 1894 Opera House** (⊠ 2020 Post Office St., ☎ 409/765–1894 or 800/821–1894), where performances of various kinds are held from time to time, is worth visiting for the architecture alone. Sarah Bernhardt and Anna Pavlova once each played this storied stage. The **Strand Street Theater** (⊠ 2317 Ship's Mechanic Row, ☎ 409/763–4591) is another venue for occasional dramas.

Spectator Sports

Baseball: Houston Astros (⊠ Astrodome, 8400 Kirby Dr., at Loop 610 and Fannin St., ☎ 713/799–9500).

Basketball: Houston Rockets (⊠ The Summit, 10 Greenway Plaza, ☎ 713/627–3865).

Hockey: Houston Aeros (⊠ The Summit, 10 Greenway Plaza, ☎ 713/627–2376).

Soccer: Houston Hotshots (⊠ The Summit, 10 Greenway Plaza, ☎ 713/468–5100).

Beaches

Galveston's ocean beaches are all open to the public. The eastern end of the island, especially around Stewart Beach Park, is rife with amenities of all kinds, including rentals of surfboards, sailboats, chairs, and umbrellas. To the west are quieter, less crowded beaches.

Shopping

Houston

The city's premier shopping area is the **Galleria** (⊠ Post Oak Blvd. and Westheimer Rd., ☎ 713/622–0663), famed for high-quality stores like

Neiman Marcus, Marshall Field, and Tiffany & Co. **Westheimer Road,** east of the Galleria, offers an array of galleries and artsy shops. Probably the most expensive merchandise found in a Houston mall is at the **River Oaks Shopping Center** (⊠ Shepherd Dr. and Gray St.). Good boots and other western gear are available at **Stelzig's Western Wear** (⊠ 3123 Post Oak Blvd.). The **Village** (⊠ University Blvd. and Kirby Dr.), next to Rice University, was Houston's first mall, developed in 1938, and today includes both boutiques and perennials such as the Gap. The **Parks Shops in Houston Center** (⊠ 1200 McKinney St.), with 70 stores, is a recently built downtown mall that provides a convenient entrance to the city's tunnel system (another is at the downtown Hyatt Regency), which is lined with retail shops. Tunnel maps are free at most banks.

Galveston

The historic stretch of the Strand is the best place to shop in Galveston. The **Old Strand Emporium** (⊠ 2112 Strand, ☎ 409/763–9445) is a charming deli and gourmet grocery. Antiques, collectibles, and peanut products are found at the **Old Peanut Butter Warehouse** (⊠ 100 20th St., ☎ 409/762–8358).

SAN ANTONIO AND THE HILL COUNTRY

The Alamo—symbol either of Texan heroism or Anglo arrogance—is by no means the only reason to visit **San Antonio.** A mélange of easily mingling ethnic groups, it is in many ways Texas's most beautiful and atmospheric city. Northwest of San Antonio is the **Hill Country,** an anomaly in generally flat Texas, rich with pretty landscapes, early American history, and echoes of the linen-to-silk story of Lyndon Baines Johnson, the nation's 36th president.

Visitor Information

Hill Country: Tourism Association (⊠ 1700 Sidney Baker St., Kerrville 78028, ☎ 210/895–5505). **Bandera:** Convention & Visitors Bureau (⊠ 1808 Hwy. 16 S; Box 171, 78003, ☎ 210/796–3045 or 800/364–3833). **Fredericksburg:** Convention & Visitors Bureau (⊠ 106 N. Adams St., 78624, ☎ 210/997–6523). **Kerrville:** Convention & Visitors Bureau (⊠ 1700 Sidney Baker St., 78028, ☎ 210/792–3535 or 800/221–7958). **San Antonio:** Alamo Visitor Center (⊠ 216 E. Crockett St.; Box 845, 78293, ☎ 210/225–8587); Convention & Visitors Bureau (⊠ 317 Alamo Plaza, 78205, ☎ 210/270–8700 or 800/447–3372; also has booths at the airport).

Arriving and Departing

By Plane

More than a dozen airlines serve **San Antonio International Airport** (☎ 210/821–3411), about a 15-minute drive north of downtown. Inexpensive shuttle services (☎ 210/366–3183) operate 24 hours a day. **Southwest Airlines** (☎ 210/617–1221 or 800/435–9792) provides regional service.

By Car

Good highways serve most directions, including I–35 from Dallas and I–10 from Houston. I–410 rings the city, and several highways take you downtown.

By Train

Amtrak serves San Antonio's station (⊠ 1174 E. Commerce St., ☎ 210/223–3226 or 800/872–7245), with daily trains north to Fort Worth, Dallas, east Texas, and Chicago and east to New Orleans and beyond; and Sunday, Tuesday, and Thursday trains west to Los Angeles.

By Bus

Buses run out of San Antonio's **Greyhound station** (⊠ 500 N. St. Mary's St., ☎ 800/231–2222) to all major cities as well as to most local towns.

Exploring San Antonio and the Hill Country

Much of San Antonio can be explored on foot, although some of its attractions will require transportation. For the Hill Country, a car is a must; you can visit several towns in a day, catching some of the landscapes in between as you drive.

San Antonio

At the heart of San Antonio, the **Alamo** (⊠ Alamo Plaza, ☎ 210/225–1391) stands as a repository of Texas history, a monument to the 189 volunteers who died there in 1836 during a 13-day siege by the Mexican dictator and general Santa Anna. They fought not for Texas's independence but for adherence to the liberal 1824 constitution of Mexico, of which Texas was then a part. When the Alamo was finally breached on March 6, at dreadful cost to the Mexican army, the slaughter that followed would be remembered in history as the major turning point of the Texas revolution. Santa Anna claimed victory, but as a liberal aide wrote privately, "One more such 'glorious victory' and we are finished." Indeed, three weeks later, Santa Anna was captured and the revolution completed, as Sam Houston led his sharpshooting volunteers—crying, "Remember the Alamo! Remember Goliad!"—to victory at San Jacinto. Today the historic chapel and barracks contain the guns and other paraphernalia used by William Travis, Davy Crockett, James Bowie, and other Texas heroes. Outside in the peaceful courtyard, a history wall elucidates the history of the Alamo and of the Mission San Antonio de Valero, as this mission—San Antonio's first—was originally called.

On Alamo Plaza is the 1859 **Menger Hotel,** San Antonio's most historic lodging. Its longevity attests to Texas's age-old appreciation of good beer and revelry: As legend has it, William Menger built the hotel to accommodate the many carousers who frequented his brewery, which stood on the same site. Step inside the hotel to see its moody, mahogany bar, a precise replica of the pub in London's House of Lords; Teddy Roosevelt supposedly recruited his Rough Riders, cowboys fresh from the Chisholm Trail drank to excess and fought, and cattlemen closed deals with a handshake over three fingers of rye.

The **Texas Star Trail,** which begins and ends at the Alamo, is a 2½-mi walking tour designated by blue disks in the sidewalks. Information on the trail, which takes you past 80 historic sites and landmarks, is available at the Alamo Visitor Center at Alamo Plaza.

★ **River Walk,** or Paseo del Rio, is the city's leading tourist attraction. Built a full story below street level, it comprises about 3 mi of scenic stone pathways lining both banks of the San Antonio River as it flows through downtown. In some places the walk is peaceful and quiet; in others it is a mad conglomeration of restaurants, bars, hotels, and strolling mariachi bands, all of which can also be seen from river taxis and charter boats. Near La Mansion del Rio hotel (☞ Dining and Lodging, *below*), at the Navarro Street Bridge, is the huge retail-and-entertainment complex known as **South Bank.** Each January parts of the river are drained to clear the bottom of debris, and locals revel in the River Walk Mud Festival and Mud Parade. During the annual Fiesta

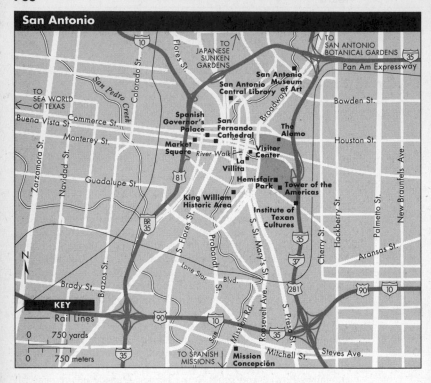

San Antonio

River Parade (April) and Holiday River Parade (November), colorfully festooned floats create a spectacle.

HemisFair Park, onetime the site of a World's Fair and currently home to the 750-ft **Tower of the Americas** (✉ 222 S. Alamo, ☎ 210/207–8615), is southeast of River Walk. An observation deck and a rotating restaurant atop the tower offer bird's-eye views of the city. The University of Texas's **Institute of Texan Cultures** (✉ HemisFair Plaza, ☎ 210/458–2300), just beyond the Tower of the Americas, is an interactive museum focusing on the 30 ethnic groups who made Texas what it is today. Here you can walk through a re-created sharecropper's house; observe and listen to an animated, recorded conversation that might have taken place between a Spanish governor and a Comanche chief in the 1790s; or learn how and when your ancestors settled in Texas.

Leading German merchants settled the **King William Historic Area** in the late 19th century. The elegant Victorian mansions, set in a quiet, leafy neighborhood, are a pleasure to behold; Madison, Guenther, and King William streets are particularly pretty for a stroll or drive. Stop in for a guided tour of the 1876 Victorian **Steves Homestead** (✉ 509 King William St., ☎ 210/225–5924) or the 1860 **Guenther House** (✉ 205 E. Guenther St., ☎ 210/227–1061), home of the family that founded the adjacent Pioneer Flour Mills. At the latter you'll find a small museum of mill memorabilia, a gift shop, and a cheerful restaurant serving fine German pastries and full breakfasts and lunches.

Except for the Alamo, all of San Antonio's historic missions constitute **San Antonio Missions National Park.** Established along the San Antonio River in the 18th century, the missions stand as reminders of Spain's most successful attempt to extend its New World dominion northward from Mexico. All of the missions are active parish churches, and all are beautiful, in their way. Start your tour at the **Missión San José**

(✉ 6539 San José Dr., ☎ 210/932–1001), the "Queen of Missions," where a visitor center illuminates the history of the missions; here you can pick up a map of the **Mission Trail** that connects San José with the others. San José has had its outer wall, Native American dwellings, granary, water mill, and workshops restored. **Misión Concepción** (✉ 807 Mission Rd., ☎ 210/534–1540) is known for its frescoes; **San Juan,** (✉ 9102 Graf, ☎ 210/532–3914) with its Romanesque arches, has a serene chapel; and **Espada** (✉ 10040 Espada Rd., ☎ 210/627–2021), the southernmost mission, includes an Arab-inspired aqueduct that was part of the missions' famous *acequia* water management system.

The **Lone Star Brewery** (✉ 600 Lone Star Blvd., ☎ 210/270–9467)—the self-proclaimed "Home of the National Beer of Texas"—offers an interesting tour. The grounds also contain the **old Buckhorn Bar,** once San Antonio's leading saloon; a cottage used by the writer O. Henry; and the **Buckhorn Hall of Horns, Fins, and Feathers** (☎ 210/270–9467), said to contain the world's largest collection of animal horns. The **San Fernando Cathedral** (✉ Commerce and Flores Sts., ☎ 210/227–1297), in town just west of the river, is where Santa Anna raised his no-quarter flag—an ominous message of no mercy—to intimidate the Alamo defenders. The seat of a bishopric, it was visited by Pope John Paul II in 1987. The beautiful 18th-century **Spanish Governor's Palace** (✉ 105 Plaza de Armas, ☎ 210/224–0601), seat of Spanish power in Texas, is an ideal picnic site.

San Antonio's arts scene is marked by a strong southwestern flavor. The **San Antonio Museum of Art** (✉ 200 W. Jones Ave., ☎ 210/829–7262) houses choice collections of pre-Columbian, Native American, and Spanish colonial art, as well as the brand-new Nelson A. Rockefeller Center for Latin American Art, the nation's largest such facility, with more than 2,500 folk art objects donated from the Rockefeller collection. The **Southwest Craft Center** (✉ 300 Augusta St., ☎ 210/224–1848) is filled with local crafts, many made by artists-in-residence, but may be most remarkable for its building, once an Ursuline school for girls—a fine example of San Antonio's adaptive use of historic structures.

You can't miss the 240,000-square-ft **San Antonio Central Library** (✉ 600 Soledad St., ☎ 210/207–2500): Its burnt-orange color, locally known as enchilada-red, and its modern design by the Mexican architect Ricardo Legoretta have been a source of contention among traditionalists. Inside, the library is fully computerized, providing access to videos, CDs, and laser discs, including a comprehensive Spanish-language interface.

On the outskirts of the city, the **McNay Art Museum** (✉ 6000 N. New Braunfels Ave., Box 6069, ☎ 210/824–5368), in a private mansion with handsome tile floors and a splendid, Moorish-style courtyard, has an impressive collection of post-impressionist and modern paintings and sculpture, along with a theater arts library. Not far from the McNay Art Museum are the **San Antonio Botanical Gardens** (✉ 555 Funston Place, ☎ 210/821–5115), 33 acres containing formal gardens, wildflower-spangled meadows, native Texas vegetation, and a garden that emphasizes textures and scents, specially designed for people who are blind.

The Hill Country
A drive through the Hill Country from San Antonio makes a pleasant excursion. Starting toward the northwest, it's less than an hour's trip on I–10 to the Kerrville area. However, you may want to take the far prettier Route 16, a hilly road that leads to **Bandera** (population: 877), one of the nation's oldest Polish communities (dating from 1855)

790

The Hill Country

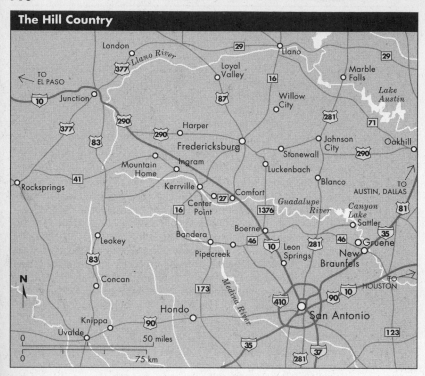

and site of an 1854 Mormon colony. **Boerne** (population: 5,200), on I–10, was founded by Germans and named after a German writer. One of its fine early buildings is the **Kuhlmann-King House,** which can be toured by appointment with the local historical society (⊠ 402 E. Blanco St., ☎ 210/249–2030 or 210/249–8000). **Cascade Caverns** (⊠ Exit 543 off I–10, ☎ 210/755–8080) has a 90-ft underground waterfall and visitor facilities, including RV camping and a pool.

Kerrville, a town of little obvious interest, is said to have the best climate in the nation. This has led to a proliferation of hotels, children's summer camps, guest ranches, and religious centers. **Kerrville State Park** (☎ 210/257–5392), 500 acres along the cypress-edged Guadalupe River, is a good place to spot the white-tail deer that abound in the area. **Fredericksburg,** probably the Hill Country's prettiest town and the heart of its predominantly German-American population, is just 24 mi north of Kerrville, on Route 16. Its main street (bilingually signposted as HAUPT-STRASSE) is a sort of German version of a classic western movie scene— but lined with chic stores, antiques shops, small German eateries, and "Sunday Houses," built by German farmers as hostelries to use on the nights before church. One of Fredericksburg's famous sons was Chester W. Nimitz, commander in chief of the U.S. Pacific fleet in World War II. The restored Nimitz Steamboat Hotel now forms part of the **Admiral Nimitz Museum** (⊠ 340 E. Main St., ☎ 210/997–4379), which displays restored hotel rooms, exhibits on the war in the Pacific, and the Garden of Peace, donated by the Japanese government.

Luckenbach—made famous by the Waylon Jennings and Willie Nelson duet "Let's Go to Luckenbach, Texas"—is actually only a speck (population: 25) on the map. A little east of Fredericksburg on Route 1376, Luckenbach was founded in 1850 and remains largely unchanged, with one unpainted general store and tavern, a rural dance hall, and a blacksmith's shop. Although the rustic little complex is open daily except Wednesday, you may want to stop by on Sunday afternoon, when informal groups of fiddlers, guitarists, and banjo pickers gather under the live oaks.

Anyone who has read a biography of Lyndon B. Johnson will want to visit **Johnson City** (north of San Antonio on Route 281) to see the place where the gawky, huge-eared child who would one day lead America through some of its most troubled moments grew up. Although his was not a Horatio Alger story, Johnson certainly came from an unremarkable town—a dusty, poor place, of which the desire to leave was no doubt one reason for the burning ambition that marked his rise. His small, white-frame boyhood home is about the nicest place in town. A short walk takes you to **Johnson Settlement,** the ranch complex once owned by LBJ's family, and an 1856 dogtrot cabin similar to those the early Johnsons lived in. Free bus tours of these sites and of Johnson's birthplace, one-room school, and grave depart several times a day from the **LBJ State Historical Park** (☎ 210/644–2252 or 210/644–2478), just east of Stonewall on U.S. 290. Exhibits also highlight the history of the Hill Country.

Blanco (just south of Johnson City on Route 281), the onetime county seat, is ornamented by a fine bit of classic Texas: the Second Empire–style **Old Blanco County Courthouse.**

The **myrrh-weeping icon of New Sarov,** at Christ of the Hills Eastern Orthodox Monastery (☎ 210/833–5363), is about 6 mi northwest of Blanco (turn west by the laundromat on to Park Road 23, left on Route 102, then right on Route 103). The icon, a representation of the Virgin Mary, is said to have wept for five months beginning May 7, 1985, and still to weep on occasion. The monks and nuns who inhabit the place claim thousands of miracles, including cures of deadly diseases, through the anointing with tears that is offered to all visitors.

The drive back to San Antonio on U.S. 281 is pretty, but if you have time, go by way of **San Marcos** on Route 32. This road, which skips along parts of a ridge called the **Devil's Backbone,** provides a classic Hill Country drive, replete with deer sightings and appealing landscapes.

What to See and Do with Children

San Antonio

In the heart of San Antonio are several attractions that will keep children occupied for hours. The **Cowboy Museum and Gallery** (⊠ 209 Alamo Plaza, ☎ 210/229–1257), a zippy little museum with goodies like a Sioux necklace made of human finger bones, faces the Alamo. In the Rivercenter mall, the **Alamo IMAX Theatre** (⊠ 849 E. Commerce St., ☎ 210/225–4629 or 800/354–4629) shows the 45-minute film *Alamo . . . The Price of Freedom* on a giant screen five times a day. The **San Antonio Zoo** (⊠ 3903 N. St. Mary's St., ☎ 210/734–7183) has the nation's third-largest animal collection, most in outdoor habitats. Other child-pleasing possibilities are the **Buckhorn Hall of Horns, Fins, and Feathers** and the **Institute of Texan Cultures** (for both, ☞ Exploring San Antonio and the Hill Country, *above*).

At the **Witte Museum** (⊠ 3801 Broadway, Brackenridge Park, ☎ 210/357–1900), a new four-level "science treehouse" is filled with interactive exhibits that let kids lift themselves with pulleys and ropes, play music with laser beams, and launch tennis balls 30 ft in the air. Farther outside of town is the $140 million **Sea World of Texas** (⊠ Ellison Dr. and Westover Hills Blvd., ☎ 210/523–3000 or 800/527–4757;

800/722–2762 in TX); the world's largest marine-life park has an in-
verted roller coaster as well as marine animal shows. **Six Flags Fiesta
Texas** (⊠ I–10 W and Loop 1604, ☎ 210/697–5050), a 200-acre park
set in a limestone quarry surrounded by 100-ft cliffs, is split into four
thematic areas—Hispanic, German, western, and 1950s.

The Hill Country

The **Cascade Caverns** (☞ Exploring San Antonio and the Hill Country, *above*) are near Boerne. The remarkable **Natural Bridge Caverns**
(⊠ Follow signs from Rte. 1863 between San Antonio and New Braunfels, ☎ 210/651–6101) are a mile-long series of multicolored subterranean rooms and corridors. On Route 306, 2 mi southwest of Sattler,
is **Dinosaur Flats,** with "thunder lizard" tracks dating to 100 million
years ago.

Dining and Lodging

The Bandera and Kerrville visitor centers (☞ Visitor Information, *below*)
have information on guest ranches. The Hill Country is chock-full of bed-
and-breakfasts, particularly in tourist towns like Fredericksburg. Ask for
listings at local convention and visitor centers or try the reservation services **Be My Guest** (⊠ 402 W. Main St., Fredericksburg 78624, ☎ 210/
997–7227 or 210/997–8555) and **Gastehaus Schmidt** (⊠ 231 W. Main
St., Fredericksburg 78624, ☎ 210/997–5612). For price ranges *see*
Charts 1 (B) and 2 (A) *in* On the Road with Fodor's.

San Antonio

$$$$ ✕ **Polo's.** Inside the elegant Fairmount Hotel is the equally classic
Polo's. A blend of southwestern nouvelle and Asian cuisine—fare that
has made the cover of *Texas Monthly* magazine—the menu includes
delights like black pasta stuffed with lobster and crab. ⊠ *401 S. Alamo
St.,* ☎ *210/224–8800. AE, DC, MC, V. Closed Sun.*

$$$ ✕ **Biga.** Chef Bruce Auden's inventive Southwest and American offerings
★   are served inside a gracious century-old manse. The wine and beer se-
lection is outstanding. ⊠ *206 E. Locust,* ☎ *210/225–0722. AE, DC,
MC, V. Closed Sun.*

$$ ✕ **Boudro's.** Among the better River Walk options, this cavelike southwestern original serves seafood, steak, and extras such as guacamole
prepared tableside. The wine list is commendable. ⊠ *421 E. Commerce
St.,* ☎ *210/226–8484. AE, D, DC, MC, V.*

$$ ✕ **Liberty Bar.** Built in 1890 and leaning conspicuously at its foun-
dation (attributed to a 1921 flood), the former Liberty Schooner Sa-
loon offers affordable, original new American fare and a wide variety
of beer and wine. ⊠ *328 E. Josephine St.,* ☎ *210/227–1187. AE, D,
DC, MC, V.*

$$ ✕ **Zuni Grill.** With a bright industrial-warehouse brick interior along
the River Walk, this predominantly southwestern restaurant is known
for its fajitas and its Zuni Burger (served with white cheddar). Try a
cactus margarita, made with cactus juice and aged tequila. ⊠ *511 River
Walk,* ☎ *210/227–0864. AE, D, DC, MC, V.*

$–$$ ✕ **County Line Barbecue.** Texas is famous for its barbecued ribs,
smoked brisket, and related fare. In San Antonio there's only one contender. ⊠ *On Rte. 1604, ½ mi west of U.S. 281,* ☎ *210/496–0011.
AE, D, DC, MC, V.*

$ ✕ **Mi Tierra.** At Market Square directly across from the entrance to El
Mercado, this huge, cheerful, and famous restaurant boasts good Tex-
Mex food, wandering mariachis, and a Mexican bakery, all available
24 hours a day. ⊠ *218 Produce Row,* ☎ *210/225–1262. AE, D, DC,
MC, V.*

$$$$ 🏨 **Fairmount.** This historic luxury hotel made the *Guinness Book of Records* when its 3.2-million-pound brick bulk was moved six blocks—and across a bridge—in 1985 to its present location. It's marked by a superrefined atmosphere of canopy beds, overstuffed chairs, and marble baths. ⊠ *401 S. Alamo St., 78205,* ☎ *210/224–8800 or 800/642–3363,* ℻ *210/224–2767. 37 rooms. Restaurant, bar. AE, D, DC, MC, V.*

$$$$ 🏨 **Havana Riverwalk Inn.** The hottest new hotel in town occupies a once-dilapidated Mediterannean Revival structure built in 1914. Every room is an experience: You'll find carved teak and wicker chairs from India, beds fashioned from the grillwork of old buildings, and vintage chairs from French hotels and bistros. Don't miss Club Cohiba, the riverside martini bar. ⊠ *1015 Navarro, 78205,* ☎ *210/222–2008,* ℻ *210/222–2717. 27 rooms. Restaurant, bar.*

$$$$ 🏨 **Hyatt Regency Hill Country Resort.** On the west side of the city near Sea World, this sophisticated Texas country resort occupies a vast stretch of former ranch land. On the grounds is a 4-acre water park with a man-made river where you can go tubing. ⊠ *9800 Hyatt Dr., 78251,* ☎ *210/647–1234 or 800/233–1234,* ℻ *210/681–9681. 500 rooms. 2 restaurants, bar, 2 pools, 18-hole golf course, 3 tennis courts, basketball, health club, volleyball. AE, D, DC, MC, V.*

$$$–$$$$ 🏨 **La Mansion del Rio.** A Spanish motif marks this large hotel on a quiet portion of River Walk. Inside and out it's replete with Mediterranean tiles, archways, and soft wood tones. Rooms are very modern. ⊠ *112 College St., 78205,* ☎ *210/225–2581 or 800/292–7300,* ℻ *210/226–1365. 322 rooms. 2 restaurants, bar, pool. AE, D, DC, MC, V.*

$$$ 🏨 **The Camberly Gunter.** Since 1909 this downtown hotel has been a favorite of cattlemen and business travelers. The marble lobby has a beautiful coffered ceiling supported by massive columns. Rooms have antique reproduction furniture and modern conveniences such as large desks with dataports and two-line phones with voice mail. ⊠ *205 E. Houston St., 78205,* ☎ *210/227–3241,* ℻ *210/227–9305. 312 rooms. Restaurant, bar, café, deli, pool, outdoor hot tub, exercise room, barber shop.*

$$$ 🏨 **Menger Hotel.** Since its 1859 opening, the Menger has lodged,
★ among others, Robert E. Lee, Ulysses S. Grant, Teddy Roosevelt, Oscar Wilde, Sarah Bernhardt, even Roy Rogers and Dale Evans—all of whom must have appreciated the charming, three-story Victorian lobby, sunny dining room, flowered courtyard, and four-poster beds (in the oldest part of the hotel only). ⊠ *204 Alamo Plaza, 78205,* ☎ *210/223–4361 or 800/345–9285,* ℻ *210/228–0022. 320 rooms. Restaurant, bar, pool, health club. AE, D, DC, MC, V.*

$ 🏨 **Bullis House.** The rooms in this historic mansion are spacious and well restored—and a good deal in a town where lodging is surprisingly expensive. A modern youth hostel, next door in a separate building, is also part of Bullis House. ⊠ *621 Pierce St., 78208,* ☎ *210/223–9426. 7 rooms; hostel, 40 beds. Pool. Continental breakfast. AE, D, MC, V.*

The Hill Country

$–$$ ✕ **Friedhelm's.** This Bavarian restaurant is known as the best in town, no small feat in an area of strong Germanic influence full of such eateries. Try the Bavarian schnitzel, a breaded cutlet topped with Emmentaler cheese and jalapeño sauce. ⊠ *905 W. Main St., Fredericksburg,* ☎ *210/997–6300. AE, D, MC, V. Closed Mon.*

$$ 🏨 **Holiday Inn Y.O. Ranch.** This sprawling ranch-theme hotel is named after a well-known 50,000-acre dude ranch to which regular excursions are arranged. The large rooms—sporting cattle horns and the like—carry

out the western theme. ⊠ *2033 Sidney Baker St., Kerrville 78028,* ☎
210/257–4440, 800/531–2800 in TX, FAX *210/896–8189. 200 rooms.*
Restaurant, bar, pool, hot tub, tennis. AE, D, DC, MC, V.

Nightlife and the Arts

Nightlife
Around the 3000 block of San Antonio's **North St. Mary's Street**,
you'll find a colorful assortment of bars and restaurants in converted
commercial buildings, many featuring live entertainment. **River Walk**
favorites include **Durty Nellie's Pub** (⊠ Hilton Palacio del Rio, 200 S.
Alamo St., ☎ 210/222–1400), where sing-alongs are popular. World-
class Jim Cullum's Jazz Band plays superb Dixieland at the **Landing**
(⊠ Hyatt Regency Hotel, 123 Losoya St., ☎ 210/223–7266). Don't
miss the **Menger Hotel bar** (☞ Dining and Lodging, *above*).

The Arts
At San Antonio's **Mexican Cultural Institute** (⊠ 600 HemisFair Plaza,
☎ 210/227–0123), Mexican culture is depicted in film, dance, art, and
other media. A 1929 movie/vaudeville theater has been restored to its
baroque splendor as the **Majestic Performing Arts Center** (⊠ 224 E.
Houston St., ☎ 210/226–5700), a venue for touring Broadway shows
and home to the San Antonio Symphony Orchestra. **Kerrville** annually hosts one of the country's largest folk music festivals, usually held
the last weekend in May and the first two weekends in June.

Outdoor Activities and Sports

Water Sports
Rafting, tubing, and canoeing are popular on the **Guadalupe River** between Canyon Lake, north of San Antonio, and New Braunfels. Try
Jerry's Rentals (⊠ River Rd. north of New Braunfels, ☎ 210/625–
2036), **Rockin' R River Rides** (☎ 210/629–9999), or **Gruene River Co.**
(☎ 210/625–2800), on the river in New Braunfels. With its surrounding steep evergreen hills, **Canyon Lake** is one of the most scenic
lakes in Texas and has two yacht clubs, two marinas, a water-skiing
club, and excellent fishing (an 86-pound flathead catfish is just one local
record).

Spectator Sports

Basketball: San Antonio Spurs (⊠ Alamodome, 100 Montana St., ☎
210/554–7787 or 800/688–7787).

Horse Racing: Retama Park (⊠ I–35, exit 174A, San Antonio, ☎ 210/
651–7000); June–November, Wednesday–Sunday; simulcasts daily,
year-round.

Shopping

San Antonio
With its rich ethnic heritage, this city is a wonderful place to buy Mexican imports, most of them inexpensive and many of high quality. **El
Mercado** is the Mexican market building that is part of **Market Square**
(⊠ 514 W. Commerce St., ☎ 210/227–3662). The building contains
about 35 shops, including stores selling blankets, Mexican dresses, men's
guayabera shirts, and strings of brightly painted papier-mâché vegetables.
The lively **Farmer's Market** is another area of Market Square worth
visiting. **La Villita** (⊠ 418 Villita St.), a restored village a few blocks
south of downtown, is now a conglomeration of crafts shops and
small restaurants, some in adobe buildings dating from the 1820s. It's

noteworthy for its Latin American importers and demonstrations by its resident glassblower. **Rivercenter** (⊠ 849 E. Commerce St., ☎ 210/225–0000) is a fairly standard, if very ritzy, shopping mall right on the river. **Paris Hatters** (⊠ 119 Broadway, ☎ 210/223–3453) is a truly atmospheric place to buy western hats.

The Hill Country

Although the area generally is no shopping mecca, **Fredericksburg**'s main street is lined with antiques shops, imaginative stores, fragrant German bakeries, and western saloons.

AUSTIN

Created as the capital of the then-new Republic of Texas in 1839, **Austin** is a liberal enclave in a generally conservative state and a heavily treed, hilly town in a land commonly known for its monotonous flatness. For many years a quiet university town, within the past two decades Austin has grown rapidly, developing into another Silicon Valley, home to many semiconductor and computer companies. The growth of high-tech industry, combined with the state government and the university, has made for a vital and culturally diverse community; indeed, Austin now has the country's second-fastest-growing job market (the first is Las Vegas).

With numerous clubs and music venues, Austin is a mecca for musicians. Billing itself as the "live music capital of the world," the city has been on the national music map since 1984 when *Austin City Limits,* a showcase for bands that taped at the University of Texas campus, began airing nationwide. Austin then cemented its music reputation by putting on the annual music industry conference called South by Southwest, which draws bands and record company executives from around the world every March. Because of its natural beauty and the economic incentives provided to film there, Austin has hosted numerous TV and film crews; for example, scenes from the 1996 films *Courage Under Fire* and *Michael* were shot in and around the city.

Visitor Information

Austin Convention and Visitors Bureau (⊠ 201 E. 2nd St., 78701, ☎ 512/478–0098). **Chamber of Commerce** (⊠ 111 Congress Ave., 78701, ☎ 512/478–9383).

Arriving and Departing

Between Dallas–Fort Worth and San Antonio on I–35, Austin is accessible from Houston via U.S. 290. **Robert Mueller Municipal Airport** (☎ 512/472–3321) handles local flights. **Bergstrom,** a new airport still under construction at press time, is scheduled to open in 1999. **Amtrak** (⊠ 250 N. Lamar Blvd., 78703, ☎ 512/476–5684 or 800/872–7245) serves the city with three trains weekly west to Los Angeles and the same number north to Chicago. **Greyhound Lines** has a station in Austin (⊠ 916 E. Koenig La., 78751, ☎ 512/454–9686 or 800/231–2222).

Exploring Austin

Austin's downtown is dominated by its impressive **capitol,** constructed in 1888 of Texas pink granite. Tours of this recently renovated edifice and of the adjacent **governor's mansion** (☎ 512/463–5518) start from the **Capitol Complex Visitors Center** (⊠ 112 E. 11th St., 78701, ☎ 512/305–8400 or 512/463–0063 for tour information).

The sprawling **University of Texas** campus flanks the capitol's north end. The campus is home to the **Lyndon Baines Johnson Presidential**

Library and Museum (⊠ 2313 Red River Rd., ☏ 512/916–5136). Also of interest on the UT campus is the **Archer M. Huntingdon Art Gallery** (⊠ 23rd and San Jacinto Sts., ☏ 512/471–7324). Austin's **Lyric Opera** (☏ 512/472–5927), the **Austin Symphony** (☏ 512/476–6064), and **Ballet Austin** (☏ 512/476–2163) all perform at the Performing Arts Center and Bass Concert Hall, adjacent to the Huntingdon Art Gallery. **Guadalupe Street,** which borders the west side of the UT campus, is lined with trendy boutiques and restaurants.

Austin is an outdoor enthusiast's and nature lover's town; many people and companies have moved here to enjoy a quality of life enhanced by pristine waterways and extensive greenbelts for hiking, biking, and running. **Zilker Park,** the city's largest public park, connects to **Town Lake's hike and bike trail. Barton Springs** (☏ 512/476–9044), a huge natural-spring pool, is Zilker Park's main attraction. Built in the early 1900s when the city dammed Barton Creek, the pool is more than ¼ mi long and a constant 68°F. It is considered one of the nation's premier swimming holes, and Austinites cherish it as the jewel of their city. Little ones love swimming in the pool and also enjoy riding on the **miniature Amtrak train** that circles the park's perimeter. ⊠ *2100 Barton Springs Rd.,* ☏ *512/499–6700. No train late Nov.–Mar.*

The **Zilker Botanical Gardens** (⊠ 2220 Barton Springs Rd., ☏ 512/477–8672), across from Zilker Park, offers more than 26 acres of horticultural delights, including butterfly trails and Xeriscape gardens with native plants that thrive in an arid southwestern climate. The **Austin Nature and Science Center** (⊠ 301 Nature Center Dr., ☏ 512/327–8180), adjacent to the botanical gardens, has 80 acres of trails, interactive exhibits teaching about the environment, and animal exhibits.

A bit farther afield, the **Wild Basin Wilderness Preserve** has 227 acres of walking trails with beautiful contrasting views of the hill country and downtown Austin. ⊠ *805 N. Capitol of Texas Hwy., 78746,* ☏ *512/327–7622. Guided tours on weekends.*

The **National Wildflower Research Center,** in a 43-acre complex sponsored by Lady Bird Johnson, is well worth a visit. Extensive plantings of wildflowers provide for blooms in every season. ⊠ *4801 LaCrosse Ave., 78739,* ☏ *512/292–4100. Closed Mon.*

With the stately capitol seated at its north end, **Congress Avenue**—specifically, the bridge at its southern downtown end—is also home to a colony of hundreds of thousands of Mexican bats. Attracted to the small space between the arches of the bridge and the road above, the nocturnal critters swarm into town every evening at dusk, creating a creepy but memorable cocktail-hour spectacle for hundreds of spectators. The grassy expanse on the bridge's northeastern end is a good vantage point.

Dining

Austin's restaurant selection is one of the most varied and sophisticated in Texas. For price ranges *see* Chart 1 (B) *in* On the Road with Fodor's.

$$$ ✕ **Hudson's on the Bend.** A bit outside town, overlooking a bend in beautiful Lake Austin, Hudson's offers an exotic southwestern menu complete with such novelties as grilled tenderloin of ostrich with porcini sauce. ⊠ *3509 Ranch Rd. 620,* ☏ *512/266–1369. Reservations essential. AE, DC, MC, V. No lunch.*

$$–$$$ ✕ **Castle Hill Café.** You'll find irresistible tortilla soup, imaginative salads, and eclectic, eye-pleasing entrées inside this warmly appointed restaurant. It's consistently voted among Austin's finest. ⊠ *1101 W. 5th St.,* ☏ *512/476–0728.*

$$-$$$ ✗ **Bitter End.** A sleek, slightly industrial interior sets the scene for the see-and-be-seen crowd at this worthwhile brew pub. Duck liver pâté, wood-fired pizzas, and an ever-updated Italian-tinged menu are all enhanced by outstanding home-brewed ales. ⊠ *311 Colorado St.,* ☎ *512/478–2337.*

$ ✗ **Güeros.** The ceiling is high, the floorboards worn, and the windows long and tall in this former feed store, now a favorite Tex-Mex restaurant. After President Clinton ordered the Numero Dos during a visit to Austin in 1996, the dish was renamed El Presidente. ⊠ *1412 S. Congress Ave.,* ☎ *512/447–7688. AE, D, DC, MC, V.*

$ ✗ **Cisco's.** This hole-in-the-wall diner in rough-and-tumble East Austin draws all sorts—the famous, the hard-boiled, and the hungover. The house specialty is *migas,* a spicy Mexican dish of scrambled eggs with tomatoes, onions, cheddar cheese, and tortillas. ⊠ *1511 E. 6th St.,* ☎ *512/472–4720. AE, D, DC, MC, V.*

$ ✗ **Threadgill's.** Southern-style food and a friendly atmosphere make Threadgill's a local favorite. Try the chicken-fried steak and homemade cobbler and stay for the evening's musical entertainment. ⊠ *6416 N. Lamar Blvd.,* ☎ *512/451–5440;* ⊠ *301 W. Riverside,* ☎ *512/472–9304. MC, V.*

Lodging

$$$$ 🏨 **Four Seasons.** Built along the banks of Town Lake in downtown Austin, this luxury hotel offers beautiful views of sunsets over the water and the loveliest lakeside Sunday brunch in town. It is also a prime location in summer for watching the bat exodus from under the Congress Avenue Bridge (☞ Exploring Austin, *above*). ⊠ *98 San Jacinto Blvd., 78701,* ☎ *512/478–4500 or 800/332–3442,* ℻ *512/478–3117. 292 rooms. Restaurant, lobby lounge, pool, spa, business services, meeting rooms. AE, DC, MC, V.*

$$$ 🏨 **Driskill Hotel.** Fronting Austin's main downtown street, Congress Avenue, this historic Renaissance Revival edifice was built in 1886. Step inside to see its elegant lobby, complete with vaulted ceilings. ⊠ *604 Brazos St., 78701,* ☎ *512/474–5911 or 800/252–9367,* ℻ *512/474–2188. 177 rooms. Restaurant, piano bar, lobby lounge. AE, D, DC, MC, V.*

$$–$$$ 🏨 **Doubletree Guest Suites.** Conveniently located between downtown and the university, this all-suite hotel is only a block away from the capitol, and many rooms afford views of that stately granite structure. ⊠ *30 W. 15th St., 78701,* ☎ *512/478–7000 or 800/424–2900,* ℻ *512/478–5103. 189 suites. Restaurant, bar, pool, sauna, exercise room. AE, D, DC, MC, V.*

$ 🏨 **The Woodburn House.** Designated a city landmark, this stately Victorian mansion was built in 1909. It sits just north of the university, in Hyde Park, which is a National Register Historic District. Large verandas and period antiques add to its appeal. ⊠ *4401 Ave. D, 78751,* ☎ *512/458–4335,* ℻ *512/458–4319. 4 rooms. AE, MC, V.*

Nightlife

The self-proclaimed "live music capital of the world," Austin is a mecca for musicians from all over the country, as well as home to a thriving local scene. Numerous traveling and homegrown bands play nightly in the city's many music venues, most of which are clustered around downtown's **Sixth Street,** between Red River Drive and Congress Avenue. To find out who's playing where, pick up a free *Austin Chronicle* or Thursday's *Austin American Statesman.* Two of Austin's most distinctive clubs are a little farther afield, however. **Antone's** (⊠ 2915 Guadalupe St., 78705, ☎ 512/474–5314, ℻ 512/474–8397) has been serving up the blues for more than three decades and even produces records on its own label. If country-western and line dancing are your thing, do the two-step at the **Broken Spoke** (⊠ 3201 S. Lamar Blvd., 78704, ☎ 512/442–6189). Rustic, quirky, and no bigger than your parents' basement, the smoky, no-frills **Continental Club** (⊠ 1315 S. Congress Ave., ☎ 512/441–2444) offers country-tinged rock. Nationally known touring bands often play at the **Backyard** (⊠ 13101 Bee Cave Rd., ☎ 512/263–9707), a lovely outdoor spot a bit west of town in the Hill Country. **Liberty Lunch** (⊠ 405 W. 2nd St., ☎ 512/477–0461) is another local musical institution. A restored downtown movie palace, the **Paramount** (⊠ 713 Congress Ave., ☎ 512/472–5470) is home to both musical acts and touring theater companies. Local theater thrives at the **Zachary Scott Theatre** (⊠ 1510 Toomey Rd., ☎ 512/476–0541), named for an Austin native son who was successful in 1930s Hollywood.

DALLAS AND FORT WORTH

These twin cities, separated by 30 mi of suburbs, may be the oddest couple in a state of odd couples. **Dallas** is glitzy and ritzy, a swelling, modernistic business metropolis whose inhabitants go to bed early and to church on Sunday. **Fort Worth,** sneered at as "Cowtown" by its neighbors, lives in the shadow of its wild history as a rip-roaring cowboy town, a place of gunfights and cattle drives—even though its cultural establishment is superior to Dallas's and it has seen a downtown rebirth in recent years. In Fort Worth that fellow in the faded jeans and cowboy hat could well be the president of the bank. In Dallas people tend to be a bit more formal.

Visitor Information

Dallas: Convention & Visitors Bureau (⊠ 1201 Elm St., Suite 2000, 75270, ☎ 214/746–6677, 214/746–6679 for recorded schedule of events, or 800/232–5527); information booths at the municipal airport, Love Field, at Union Station, and at the West End Market Place. **Fort Worth:** Convention & Visitors Bureau (⊠ 415 Throckmorton St., 76102, ☎ 817/336–8791 or 800/433–5747); information booths at the Sid Richardson Collection of Western Art, at the Fort Worth Museum of Science and History, and in the Stockyards.

Arriving and Departing

By Bus

Greyhound Lines (☎ 800/231–2222) has stations in Dallas (⊠ 205 S. Lamar St.) and Fort Worth (⊠ 901 Commerce St.).

By Car

The **Metroplex,** as the Greater Dallas–Fort Worth area is known, is well served by interstates. The main approaches include I–35 from Oklahoma to the north and Waco to the south; I–30 from Arkansas; I–20 from Louisiana or New Mexico; and I–45 from Houston. The twin cities are linked by I–20, which is the southern route, and I–30, generally the more useful road. Dallas is circled by the I–635 ring road, known as the LBJ Freeway, while Fort Worth is looped by I–820.

By Plane

A rare successful collaboration between the rival cities is the **Dallas–Fort Worth International Airport** (☎ 214/574–8888), 17 mi from the business districts of each town. The world's second-busiest airport, it is surprisingly easy to use, though encumbered by slow transportation between terminals. It costs $30 or more to get to downtown Dallas by taxi, usually about $25 to downtown Fort Worth. Cheaper van service is offered by the 24-hour **Supershuttle** (☎ 817/329–2000). The **Airporter Bus Service** (☎ 817/334–0092) serves a downtown Fort Worth terminal and some hotels. Ritzier service comes from **Lone Star Limousine** (☎ 214/238–8884).

Love Field (✉ Cedar Springs at Mockingbird La., Dallas, ☎ 214/670–6073), a $10–$15 taxi ride from downtown Dallas, is the hub of **Southwest Airlines** (☎ 214/263–1717 or 800/435–9792), offering extensive service within Texas to many cities in the four contiguous states and, with stops, to destinations as far away as Chicago.

By Train
Amtrak (☎ 800/872–7245) serves both cities with thrice-weekly trains to east Texas and Chicago and others heading south to San Antonio. Dallas's terminal is **Union Station** (✉ 400 Houston St., ☎ 214/653–1101); in Fort Worth it's the old **Santa Fe Depot** (✉ 1501 Jones St., ☎ 817/332–2931), built in 1900.

Getting Around Dallas and Fort Worth

As much as anywhere in Texas, a car is necessary to see Dallas and Fort Worth, and getting around by car is relatively easy. Both cities have bus systems, but service is sketchy and sometimes just plain bad.

Exploring Dallas and Fort Worth

Dallas
Many thousands visit Dallas, mainly because of the city's unhappy legacy as the assassination site of President John F. Kennedy, which occurred downtown. Also downtown is one of the most remarkable flowerings of skyscraping architecture anywhere—that same skyline familiar to the world from the television show *Dallas*—accompanied by the offerings of a revitalized **West End,** where restaurants and shops fill a former warehouse district. Near the West End are several major cultural
★ institutions, and only a little farther away is **Deep Ellum,** the lively center of the city's alternative scene. A short car trip from downtown you will find historic areas that give a sense of the old Dallas. And to the north, where the city's establishment has long been entrenched, there's shopping galore.

DOWNTOWN
On November 22, 1963, shots rang out on Dealey Plaza, at the west end of downtown, as the presidential motorcade rounded the corner from Houston Street onto the Elm Street approach to the Triple Underpass. Eventually the Warren Commission would conclude—to the continuing disbelief of many Americans—that President Kennedy was gunned down by Lee Harvey Oswald, acting alone and firing from the sixth floor of the **Texas School Book Depository.** Today, the building's first-rate exhibit—called the **Sixth Floor**—provides both riveting details of the assassination and an evenhanded account of the conspiracy theories that continue to emerge. The spot from which Oswald is said to have fired is precisely re-created. At the end of the exhibit is a log that contains brief, moving messages written by visitors. ✉ *411 Elm St.,* ☎ *214/653–6666.*

The **grassy knoll,** from which many believe a second gunman fired, is just to the right of the Book Depository, on the Elm Street side. **Dealey Plaza,** where visitors inevitably congregate to look up at the so-called sniper's perch, is directly across the street. The stark **cenotaph,** designed like an empty house by architect Philip Johnson as a personal tribute to his friend Kennedy, is a short walk from Dealey Plaza, at Main and Market streets.

Downtown Dallas

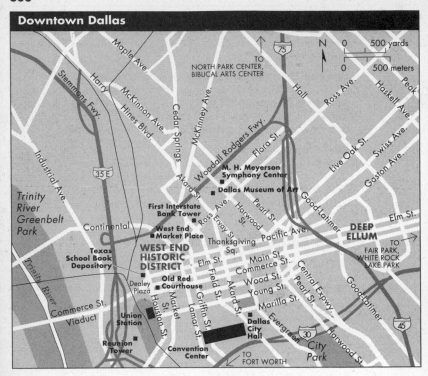

The **West End Historic District** is an area of brick warehouses built between 1900 and 1930 and brought back to life in 1976. Now filled with restaurants, shops, and pedestrian activity, it is one of the city's biggest draws for visitors both day and night. Within the historic district is **West End Market Place** (⊠ 603 Munger Ave., ☎ 214/748–4801), once a candy-and-cracker factory and now a lively, five-story shopping-and-eating center built around an atrium.

The **Old Red Courthouse** (⊠ Main and Houston Sts.) faces Philip Johnson's cenotaph. This 1892 Romanesque building of red sandstone is one of the city's oldest surviving structures and a familiar landmark. The **John Neely Bryan Cabin,** a reconstructed 1841 log cabin and trading post that was the city's first building, is adjacent to the courthouse on the Dallas County Historical Plaza.

The most remarkable thing about the center of downtown, which forms most of the famous Dallas skyline, is that it's so new—almost all its major skyscrapers were completed in the 1980s. Internationally renowned architect I. M. Pei has had a strong influence here. His **First Interstate Bank Tower** (⊠ 1445 Ross Ave.), with its huge green-glass triangular shapes, was built in 1986 and is arguably the city's most spectacular skyscraper. **Dallas city hall** (⊠ 1500 Marilla St.) is another striking Pei creation. Next to the city hall, in **Pioneer Plaza,** stands Robert Summer's interpretation of life on the old Shawnee Trail—70 longhorn steer and three cowboys—said to be the largest bronze sculpture in the world. The installation was completed in 1995.

The **First Republic Bank Plaza** (⊠ 901 Main St.) is visible for miles, thanks to its 70 stepped stories outlined in green lights. Lending a peculiar, science-fiction twist to the skyline is **Reunion Tower** (⊠ 300 Reunion Blvd.), where the Hyatt Regency's restaurant and bar are known for spectacular views of the city. **Thanks-Giving Square** (⊠ Pacific

Ave. and Ervay St.) is a small triangular plaza designed by Philip Johnson. With its spiraling chapel and quiet gardens, it is a peaceful spot, ideal for picnics and rest stops.

Housed in a series of low, white limestone galleries built off a central barrel vault, the **Dallas Museum of Art** (⊠ 1717 N. Harwood St., ☎ 214/922–1200) is in the Arts District, on the north edge of downtown. Its most recent wing, the **Museum of the Americas,** focuses on American art before the arrival of Europeans. In the main museum make a point of seeing Claes Oldenburg's *Stake Hitch,* a huge stake and rope sculpture, along with a remarkable pre-Columbian collection. The **Morton H. Meyerson Symphony Center** (⊠ 2301 Flora St., ☎ 214/670–3600) is a place of sweeping, dramatic curves, ever-changing vanishing points, and surprising views. This 1989 building, another Pei creation, is far more interesting inside than out. **De Musica,** a solid iron sculpture by the great Basque sculptor Eduardo Chillida, rests in front of the Symphony Center.

OTHER ATTRACTIONS

Deep Ellum, a 20-minute walk east from downtown, was born as the city's first black neighborhood. Today it is the throbbing center of Dallas's avant-garde, a place of trend-setting art galleries, bars, clubs, and restaurants. The area centers on Commerce, Main, and Elm streets; its name is a phonetic rendering of *deep elm,* pronounced with a southern drawl.

Fair Park (⊠ 1300 Robert B. Cullum Blvd., ☎ 214/890–2911), just southeast of Deep Ellum, is a 277-acre collection of artfully arranged art moderne buildings. Most of the grounds date from the 1936 Texas Centennial Exhibition, although the park has hosted the Texas State Fair since 1886. Murals and sculptures line the park's central esplanade. In the **Hall of State** (⊠ 3939 Grand Ave., ☎ 214/421–4500) more murals tell the story of Texas in heroic terms. Fair Park also contains six major exhibit spaces: the **African-American Museum** (☎ 214/565–9026); the **Age of Steam Railroad Museum** (☎ 214/428–0101); the **Dallas Aquarium** (☎ 214/670–8443); the **Dallas Horticultural Center** (☎ 214/428–7476); the **Museum of Natural History** (⊠ 3535 E. Grand Ave., ☎ 214/421–3466); and the **Science Place** (☎ 214/428–5555).

In East Dallas **Swiss Avenue** has the city's best representations of two distinct periods. On lower Swiss Avenue (2900 block), nearer to downtown, the **Wilson Block Historic District** is an unaltered block of turn-of-the-century frame houses restored as offices for nonprofit groups. The **Swiss Avenue Historic District** (particularly the 5000–5500 blocks) has a large number of set-back Prairie-style and other mansions.

McKinney Avenue, just north of downtown, is lined with bustling bars and trendy restaurants. A restored **trolley** (☎ 214/855–5267) runs up McKinney from outside the Dallas Museum of Art (at St. Paul and Ross streets). In the **Biblical Arts Center,** (⊠ 7500 Park La., ☎ 214/691–4661), a bit north of McKinney Avenue, you'll find a replica of Christ's tomb at Calvary. In this Dallas oddity, sound and light bring a 124- by 20-ft biblical mural to life. Famous shopping malls like **NorthPark Center** and the **Galleria** (☞ Shopping, *below*) are also in the north end of town.

Fort Worth

Downtown Fort Worth is where you'll find the city's financial core, most of its historic buildings, and Sundance Square, the restored turn-of-the-century neighborhood that is one of the city's main attractions. The Stockyards and adjacent western-theme stores, restaurants, and hotels are a few miles north of downtown, clustered around Main Street and Exchange Avenue. The cultural district, west of downtown out Lancaster Avenue, is home to four well-known museums, a fading coliseum complex, and several parks.

DOWNTOWN

Fort Worth's underrated downtown gracefully manages something few American cities can match: an attractive marriage of modern glass-and-steel towers and human-scale century-old Victorian buildings. The billionaire Bass brothers of Fort Worth are to be thanked for what may be the most eye-pleasing juxtaposition of scale: Rather than tear down several blocks of brick buildings to accommodate the twin towers of their giant City Center development, they created **Sundance Square** (bounded by Houston, Commerce, Second, and Third streets) by restoring the area as a center of tall-windowed restaurants, shops, nightclubs, and offices. Sundance Square's name recalls the Sundance Kid (Harry Longbaugh), who with Butch Cassidy (Robert Leroy Parker) hid out around 1898 in the nearby neighborhood, south and east of the present square, known as Hell's Half-Acre. This was a violent quarter of dank saloons, drunken cowboys, and dirty brothels. The **Sid Richardson Collection of Western Art** (⊠ 309 Main St., ☎ 817/332–6554) conjures up parts of this dark world in the idealized oils of Frederic Remington and Charles Russell.

In Sundance Square, the **Fire Station Museum** (⊠ 215 Commerce St.) houses an exhibit on 150 years of city history. The 1907 building fronts on the street where cattle headed for the Chisholm Trail used to pass.

The wedge-shape **Flatiron Building** (⊠ 1000 Houston St.), also downtown, is topped by gargoyles and panthers. Built in 1907 as medical offices, it was patterned on similar Renaissance Revival structures in New York and Philadelphia. Near the Flatiron Building, the former **Hotel Texas,** now the Radisson Plaza (⊠ 815 N. Main St., ☎ 817/870–2100), is a downtown landmark, the place where President Kennedy slept the night before he was assassinated.

The **Tarrant County Courthouse** (⊠ 100 E. Weatherford St.), on the northern edge of downtown, is an 1895 Beaux Arts building of native red granite. The **Paddock Viaduct,** reached via Main Street, takes traffic over the bluff where early pioneers kept watch for Comanche then leads directly to the Stockyards, several miles north. On the way to the viaduct there's a grim reminder of one of the darker aspects of American history: the former **Ku Klux Klan Building** (⊠ 1012 N. Main St.), now the Ellis Pecan Company.

THE STOCKYARDS

The **Fort Worth Stockyards Historic District** recalls the prosperity brought to the city in 1902 when two major Chicago meatpackers, Armour and Swift, set up plants here to ship meat across the country in refrigerator cars. In the **Livestock Exchange Building** (⊠ 131 E. Exchange Ave.), where cattle agents kept their offices, you'll find the **Stockyards Museum** (☎ 817/625–5082). Across the street from the Livestock Exchange Building, the **Stockyard Station** (⊠ 130 E. Exchange Ave., ☎ 817/625–9715) is a fast-growing marketplace of shops and restaurants, all housed in former sheep pens. **Cowtown Coliseum** (⊠ 121 E. Exchange Ave., ☎ 817/625–1025) is the site of Saturday night rodeos. **Exchange Avenue** is lined with restaurants, clubs, western-wear stores, and famous spots like the **White Elephant Saloon** and the **Stockyards Hotel.** The **Tarantula Excursion Train** (⊠ 2318 8th Ave., ☎ 817/625–7245) offers tours from its south-of-downtown base to the Stockyards; the round-trip fare is $10. Information on the area is available at the **Stockyards Visitors Center** (⊠ 130 E. Exchange Ave., ☎ 817/624–4741).

THE CULTURAL DISTRICT

★ Architect Louis Kahn's last and finest building was the **Kimbell Art Museum,** six long concrete vaults with skylights running the length of each. Mirrored light filters dreamily through these into large, airy galleries. The envy of the curating world for its large acquisitions budget, the Kimbell has wonderful collections of both early 20th-century European art and old masters. Two of its many extraordinary paintings are Munch's *Girls on a Jetty* and Goya's *The Matador Pedro Romero,* depicting the great bullfighter who killed 5,600 of the animals. ⊠ *3333 Camp Bowie Blvd.,* ☎ *817/332–8451. Closed Mon.*

The **Amon Carter Museum** (⊠ 3501 Camp Bowie Blvd., ☎ 817/738–1933), along with the city's two other major museums, is a short walk from the Kimbell. Designed by Philip Johnson, the Amon Carter has a collection of American art centered on Remingtons and Russells. The **Modern Art Museum of Fort Worth** (⊠ 1309 Montgomery St., ☎ 817/738–9215) focuses on such painters as Picasso, Rauschenberg, and Warhol. Biology, geology, computer science, and astronomy are the order of the day at the **Fort Worth Museum of Science and History** (⊠ 1501 Montgomery St., ☎ 817/732–1631).

The **Will Rogers Center** (⊠ 3301 W. Lancaster Ave., ☎ 817/871–8150), near Fort Worth's museums, is a partially restored coliseum-and-stock-pen complex named after the humorist and Fort Worth booster, who described the city as "where the West begins" (and Dallas as "where the East peters out"). The center, which includes an equestrian arena completed in 1995, is used for horse shows and other farm shows, the most famous of which is the annual Southwestern Exposition and Livestock Show, held in late January or early February.

Parks and Gardens

Dallas

Fair Park (☞ Exploring Dallas and Fort Worth, *above*), with its many museums and formal gardens, is one of the city's most visited parks; in October it hosts the three-week State Fair of Texas. At **White Rock Lake Park** (⊠ 8300 Garland Rd., ☎ 214/670–8283), a beautiful and popular 9⅓-mi jogging and bicycling path circles the sailboat-dotted lake. Bikes and skates can be rented along the Garland Road side of the lake. White Rock Lake Park is also home to the **Dallas Arboretum** (⊠ 8525 Garland Rd., ☎ 214/327–8263), 66 acres of gardens and lawns. **Old City Park,** just south of downtown (⊠ 1717 Gano St., ☎ 214/421–5141), is an outdoor museum consisting of more than 33 historic buildings, including log cabins, antebellum mansions, and a Victorian bandstand, all set against the Dallas skyline.

Fort Worth

★ **Water Gardens Park** (⊠ 15th and Commerce Sts.) is a series of man-made waterfalls, walkways, and green areas that provide a cool respite from downtown pavement. At night this Philip Johnson creation is illuminated. Just south of the cultural district, the **Fort Worth Botanic Garden** (⊠ 3220 Botanic Garden Dr., at University Dr., ☎ 817/871–7686) lies on one edge of Trinity Park; its biggest draw is the tranquil Japanese Garden.

What to See and Do with Children

Midway between Dallas and Fort Worth two major theme parks on I–30 beckon children of all ages: **Six Flags over Texas** (⊠ Ballpark Way exit off I–30, ☎ 817/530–6000), with parachute drops, the world's largest wooden roller coaster, and other rides; and **Wet 'N Wild** (⊠ Exit at Rte. 360N, ☎ 817/265–3356)—closed from October through April—with water rides like the 300-ft Kamikaze. The **Mesquite Rodeo,** northeast of Dallas (⊠ 1818 Rodeo Dr., Mesquite, ☎ 214/285–8777), is the biggest rodeo around.

Dallas

The many museums of **Fair Park** (☞ Exploring Dallas and Fort Worth, *above*) are the premier attractions for kids. Older children are as fascinated as their parents by the **Sixth Floor** (☞ Exploring Dallas and Forth Worth, *above*), with its interactive exhibits on the Kennedy assassination. The highlight of the **Dallas Zoo** (⊠ 621 E. Clarendon St., ☎ 214/670–5656) is the Wilds of Africa exhibit, featuring a monorail and lowland gorillas in a natural habitat. Consider a pilgrimage to the **graves of Bonnie Parker** (⊠ Crown Hill Cemetery, 9700 Webbs Chapel Rd.) **and Clyde Barrow** (⊠ Western Heights Cemetery; follow signs on Fort Worth Ave. near Winnetka St.).

Fort Worth

The **Stockyards** is surely the favorite spot for kids. Also popular is the **Fort Worth Museum of Science and History** and its Omni Theater's giant-screen presentations (☞ Exploring Dallas and Fort Worth, *above*).

Dining

For price ranges *see* Chart 1 (A) *in* On the Road with Fodor's.

Dallas

$$$$ ✕ **French Room.** Wonderfully detailed nouvelle touches—such as veal presented to look like a delicately wrought hummingbird—match the world-class service and exquisite baroque style of the dining room of this famous restaurant, in the Adolphus Hotel. ⊠ *1321 Commerce St.,* ☎ *214/742–8200. Reservations essential. Jacket and tie. AE, D, DC, MC, V. No lunch. Closed Sun.–Mon.*

$$$ ✕ **Jennivine.** An intimate yet bustling feel reminiscent of an English pub makes this upscale Continental restaurant a local favorite. Try the excellent rack of lamb. ⊠ *3605 McKinney Ave.,* ☎ *214/528–6010. Reservations essential. AE, D, DC, MC, V. Closed Sun.*

$$ ✕ **Calle Doce.** Authentic *cocina veracruzana*—superb cuisine from the
★ Gulf of Mexico city of Veracruz—attracts power brokers and others who seek the very best. Try *huachinango* (red snapper smothered in sweet red peppers and onions) or seviche (shellfish marinated in lime). ⊠ *415 W. 12th St.,* ☎ *214/941–4304. AE, D, DC, MC, V.*

$ ✕ **Hoffbrau.** They have steak, but it's the best hamburgers in town that make the western-theme Hoffbrau famous. ⊠ *3205 Knox St.,* ☎ *214/ 559–2680. AE, D, DC, MC, V.*

$ ✕ **Mia's.** Film and stage celebrities mix with the "unwashed masses" in this crowded, upbeat Tex-Mex restaurant. You'll have to stand while you wait for seating, but it's worth it. ⊠ *4322 Lemmon Ave.,* ☎ *214/526–1020. MC, V. Closed Sun.*

Fort Worth

$$$ ✕ **Saint-Emilion.** In a brick chalet set back from the street, you'll find country French cuisine—roast duck, for example—matched by a list of 120 French and California wines. ⊠ *3617 W. 7th St.,* ☎ *817/737– 2781. AE, D, DC, MC, V. No lunch Sun.*

$$ ✕ **Joe T. Garcia's.** The city's best-known Tex-Mex restaurant—where margaritas can help soak up the huge portions—is adjacent to its own bakery, also the site where breakfast and lunch are served. Joe T.'s is a convenient stop on the way from downtown to the Stockyards. ⊠ *2201 N. Commerce St.,* ☎ *817/626–4356. No credit cards.*

$–$$ ✕ **Benito's.** In the hospital district just south of downtown, this popular Tex-Mex spot open until 3 AM is known for its tamales and rare seasonal Mexican beers such as Noche Buena. ✉ *1450 W. Magnolia Ave.,* ☎ *817/332–8633. AE, MC, V.*

$ ✕ **Bailey's Barbeque.** Although almost no one gets to sit down in this tiny hole-in-the-wall, it's been crowded since 1931 with judges, lawyers, and other courthouse folk. ✉ *826 Taylor St.,* ☎ *817/335–7469. No credit cards. No dinner. Closed weekends.*

Lodging

For price ranges *see* Chart 2 (A) *in* On the Road with Fodor's.

Dallas

$$$$ 🏨 **Adolphus.** Beer baron Adolphus Busch created this Beaux Arts building, Dallas's finest old hotel, in 1912, sparing nothing in the way of rich ornamentation inside and out. Widely admired by students of architecture, it was lavishly restored in 1981 at a cost of $60 million. ✉ *1321 Commerce St., 75202,* ☎ *214/742–8200 or 800/221–9083,* 🖷 *214/651–3588. 438 rooms. 3 restaurants, 4 bars. AE, D, DC, MC, V.*

$$$ 🏨 **Stoneleigh.** Just north of downtown, this elegant, old brick hotel has long been favored by celebrities—including Oliver Stone while filming his movie on the Kennedy assassination. It is convenient to many restaurants and home to the Dallas Press Club. ✉ *2927 Maple Ave., 75201,* ☎ *214/871–7111 or 800/255–9299,* 🖷 *214/871–9379. 153 rooms. Restaurant, bar, pool. AE, D, DC, MC, V.*

$–$$ 🏨 **La Quinta–North Central.** Although this is standard motor inn fare, it has been freshly renovated, and the location, on Central Expressway a short drive north of downtown, is excellent. ✉ *4440 N. Central Expressway, 75206,* ☎ *214/821–4220,* 🖷 *214/821–7685. 101 rooms. Pool. AE, D, DC, MC, V.*

Fort Worth

$$$ 🏨 **Worthington.** Built in 1981 of white concrete, this 12-story ultramodern hotel stretches along two city blocks, forming a dramatic glassed-in bridge (where lunch, brunch, and tea are served) over Houston Street. There's a spacious austerity to its rooms and lobby. ✉ *200 Main St., 76102,* ☎ *817/870–1000 or 800/433–5677,* 🖷 *817/338–9176. 504 rooms. 3 restaurants, bar, pool, hot tubs, 2 tennis courts, exercise room. AE, D, DC, MC, V.*

$$$ 🏨 **Hyatt Regency.** A typical Hyatt, with its soaring atrium and glass-and-brass look, this downtown hotel is best known for panoramic views from the restaurant atop its 50-story tower. ✉ *300 Reunion Blvd., 75207,* ☎ *214/651–1234 or 800/233–1234,* 🖷 *214/782–8126. 967 rooms. 3 restaurants, 2 bars, pool, hot tub, sauna, 2 tennis courts, health club, jogging track. AE, D, DC, MC, V.*

$$ 🏨 **Miss Molly's.** Once a prim little inn, then a raucous bordello, this place above the Star Café, just outside the Stockyards, has been reincarnated as an attractive B&B. ✉ *109½ W. Exchange Ave., 76106,* ☎ *817/626–1522 or 800/996–6559,* 🖷 *817/625–2723. 7 rooms. AE, D, DC, MC, V.*

$$ 🏨 **Stockyards.** A storybook place that's seen more than its share of cowboys, rustlers, gangsters, and oil barons, the hotel has been used in many a movie. In the Booger Red Saloon, the barstools are saddles. ✉ *109 E. Exchange Ave., 76106,* ☎ *817/625–6427 or 800/423–8471,* 🖷 *817/624–2571. 46 rooms. Restaurant, bar. AE, D, DC, MC, V.*

Nightlife and the Arts

Nightlife

DALLAS

Much of Dallas bar life swirls around lower and upper **Greenville Avenue,** north of downtown. On lower Greenville, **Flip's** (⊠ 1520 Greenville Ave., ☎ 214/824–9944) has a pleasant outdoor terrace, while **Poor David's Pub** (⊠ 1924 Greenville Ave., ☎ 214/821–9891) is one of Dallas's better-known venues. On upper Greenville stop at the **San Francisco Rose** (⊠ 3024 Greenville Ave., ☎ 214/826–2020) for a quiet drink and a bite to eat inside or outdoors. For country music and dancing try **Cowboy's** (⊠ 7331 Gaston Ave., ☎ 214/321–0115). Journalists hang out at what could easily pass for a real Chicago newspaper bar, **Louie's** (⊠ 1839 N. Henderson St., ☎ 214/826–0505).

A younger, more avant-garde scene is found in Deep Ellum, where **Club Dada** (⊠ 2720 Elm St., ☎ 214/744–3232) is one of several trend-setting music spots. **Adair's** (⊠ 2624 Commerce St., ☎ 214/939–9900) is more of a neighborhood bar, complete with pool tables. **Crescent City Cafe** (⊠ 2615 Commerce St., ☎ 214/745–1900) offers Creole cuisine.

FORT WORTH

The area around the Stockyards in particular is crammed with saloons of distinctly western flavor. The best may be the **White Elephant Saloon** (⊠ 106 E. Exchange Ave., ☎ 817/624–8241), whose owner brought keno to Fort Worth. The most famous saloon is **Billy Bob's Texas** (⊠ 2520 Rodeo Plaza, ☎ 817/624–1887), built in an old cattle-pen building and offering big country music names regularly. Downtown, the **Caravan of Dreams** (⊠ 312 Houston St., ☎ 817/877–3000) is a world-class music venue that specializes in jazz and blues greats and also pulls in top eclectic performers like Lyle Lovett. Its rooftop cactus garden and famous jazz, dance, and theater murals have to be seen to be believed.

The Arts

DALLAS

The top performing arts attraction in Dallas is whatever's at the **Morton H. Meyerson Symphony Center** (☞ Exploring Dallas and Fort Worth, *above*), home to the **Dallas Symphony Orchestra** (☎ 214/871–4000). The **Dallas Theater Center** is a resident company that performs at the **Kalita Humphreys Theater** (⊠ 3636 Turtle Creek Blvd., ☎ 214/526–8210), the only theater ever designed by Frank Lloyd Wright. The **Majestic Theatre** (⊠ 1925 Elm St., ☎ 214/880–0137), a beautifully restored 1920s vaudeville house and movie palace, hosts various groups, including the **Dallas Opera** (☎ 214/443–1043). In Fair Park the **Starplex** (⊠ 1818 1st Ave., ☎ 214/421–1111) hosts most of the big-name bands that come to town. The **Dallas Black Dance Theater** (⊠ 2627 Flora St., ☎ 214/871–2376) is famous in the area.

FORT WORTH

The **Casa Mañana Theater** (⊠ 3101 W. Lancaster Ave., ☎ 817/332–9319), a theater-in-the-round under one of Buckminster Fuller's first geodesic domes, plays host to the city's summer series of musicals. Other local theaters include the **Fort Worth Theater** (⊠ 3505 W. Lancaster Ave., ☎ 817/738–6509) and **Stage West** (⊠ 3055 S. University Dr., ☎ 817/784–9378).

Shopping

Dallas

Ever since 1873, when Dallas ensured its future by successfully finagling to become the site of the intersection of two intercontinental rail lines (by sneaking in an amendment to the railroads' enabling law), the city has been the great southwestern mecca of American commerce. The **Galleria** (✉ LBJ Fwy. and Dallas North Tollway, ☎ 214/702–7100), with nearly 200 retailers, is one of Dallas's best-known upscale malls. **NorthPark Center** (✉ Central Expressway and Northwest Hwy., ☎ 214/ 363–7441), developed as the nation's first indoor mall by art collector Ray Nasher, offers a variety of upscale shops and department stores—and rotating exhibits of world-class art on its walls. In downtown Dallas the original **Neiman Marcus** (✉ 1618 Main St., ☎ 214/ 741–9103) is a huge draw.

The **West End Market Place** (✉ 603 Munger Ave., ☎ 214/748–4801) contains more than 50 specialty shops and a variety of eateries. If you're in the mood for the fresh fruit and vegetables for which the Rio Grande Valley is famous, stop by the **Dallas Farmer's Market** (✉ 1010 S. Pearl St., ☎ 214/939–2808), on the southeastern edge of downtown. There are some fine clothing stores on trendy **McKinney Avenue,** and the elegant **Crescent** (✉ 500 Crescent Ct., off McKinney Ave.) offers *very* ritzy shops. **Mariposa** (✉ 2817 Routh St., ☎ 214/871–9103), on a street of fine restaurants and shops, is the best place for Mexican masks, clothing, jewelry, and rugs.

Fort Worth

Both Fort Worth's attitude and its economy have always pointed west, and that's reflected in the shopping you'll find here. Most visitors head right to the **Stockyards,** where there are several good western-wear outlets. Check out **Fincher's** (✉ 115 E. Exchange Ave., ☎ 817/624–7302), a western store since 1902 in a building that began life as a bank; you can still walk into the old vaults. A great place for boots is **M. L. Leddy's Boot and Saddlery** (✉ 2455 N. Main St., ☎ 817/624–3149).

Downtown's **Sundance Square** is a perennial draw, with several small stores. **Tandy Center** (✉ 100 Throckmorton St., ☎ 817/390–3720), a large and modern indoor mall, is attached to Sundance Square and is a better choice for shopping. For fine small items try the **major museums' gift shops. Barber's Book Store** (✉ 215 W. 8th St., ☎ 817/335–5469), specializing in Texana and rare and fine books, is the oldest bookstore in Texas.

Spectator Sports

Baseball: Texas Rangers (✉ The Ballpark at Arlington, 1000 Ballpark Way, Arlington, off I–30, ☎ 817/273–5100).

Basketball: Dallas Mavericks (✉ Reunion Arena, 777 Sports St., ☎ 214/748–1808).

Football: Dallas Cowboys (✉ Texas Stadium, 2401 E. Airport Fwy., Irving, ☎ 214/579–5000).

Hockey: Dallas Stars (✉ Reunion Arena, 777 Sports St., ☎ 214/467–8277).

ELSEWHERE IN TEXAS

East Texas

Arriving and Departing

Between Dallas and Shreveport, Louisiana, lies east Texas, whose main east–west artery is I–20. Marshall, the heart of the region, is about a three-hour drive from Dallas or a half hour from the Louisiana line. **Amtrak** trains serve Marshall every other day.

What to See and Do

Heading into east Texas from the Dallas–Fort Worth area, you'll pass two great boundaries: a natural line, marking the start of a piney, hilly region totally unlike the Great Plains; and a man-made one, the beginning of what was the slaveholding part of the United States. In every way, east Texas—a region once dependent on cotton—feels more southern than western. After Texas seceded from the union in 1861, **Marshall** became the seat of civil authority west of the Mississippi and the wartime capital of Missouri; five Confederate generals are buried in its cemetery. Marshall is full of historic homes, some of which—like the **Starr Family Home** (⊠ 407 W. Travis St., ☎ 903/935–3044)—can be toured; others are small hostelries. One of Marshall's charms is beautiful **Stagecoach Road** (take Poplar Street, which heads east from U.S. 59, and follow markers); in places you can see the results of the stages cutting some 20 ft into the ground on this undisturbed section of the old main road to Shreveport. Off U.S. 59 signs lead to **Marshall Pottery** (☎ 903/938–9201), a huge working pottery factory.

Jefferson, a 20-minute drive north of Marshall, is one of Texas's most historic towns, a charming place on Big Cypress Bayou that once served hundreds of steamboats coming up from New Orleans. When his offer to run track through the town was rebuffed, railroad baron Jay Gould is said to have angrily scrawled in the hotel register of the Excelsior House the prophetic words "The End of Jefferson." Today the superb **Excelsior House** (⊠ 211 W. Austin St., ☎ 903/665–2513), built in the 1850s, is a tribute to the restorer's art (reservations are required months in advance). **Gould's private railroad car** is across the street from the Excelsior House.

Caddo Lake, overhung with Spanish moss and edged with bald cypresses, is a fishing mecca straddling the Texas-Louisiana border. At various times it has been home to the beleaguered Caddo Indians, to bootleggers hiding out in its dense shore growth, to the great singer of spirituals Leadbelly (reared at Swanson's Landing), to thriving steamboat traffic from New Orleans, and to all manner of legend. **Caddo Lake State Park** (☞ National and State Parks, *above*) is on the south shore.

Dining and Lodging

For price ranges *see* Charts 1 (B) and 2 (B) *in* On the Road with Fodor's.

$$ ✕ **Black Swan.** The specialty here is southern cooking with a touch of Creole, served either inside this beautiful historic home or outdoors on a second-floor balcony overlooking the main street. ⊠ *210 W. Austin St., Jefferson,* ☎ *903/665–8929. MC, V. Closed Tues.–Wed.*

$$ ⊞ **Caddo Cottage.** This is the ideal place for a family looking for a quiet time along one of the most beautiful parts of Caddo Lake. The two-story lake house sleeps four. ⊠ *Taylor Island, Uncertain 75661,* ☎ *903/ 789–3988. No credit cards.*

$$ ⊞ **Pride House.** Ornate woodwork and the original stained glass distinguish this old Victorian mansion, one of Jefferson's finest B&Bs. ⊠ *409 E. Broadway, Jefferson 75657,* ☎ *903/665–2675. 10 rooms. MC, V.*

El Paso

Arriving and Departing

At Texas's far southwestern corner, El Paso is an 11-hour drive from San Antonio; about 12 from Dallas–Fort Worth; 6 from Santa Fe, New

Mexico; and 5 from Phoenix, Arizona. **El Paso International Airport** (the major local carrier is Southwest Airlines, ☎ 800/435–9792) and **Amtrak** (✉ Union Station, 700 San Francisco St., ☎ 800/872–7245) serve the city.

What to See and Do

Dramatically situated a few miles between the southern end of the Rockies and the northern terminus of Mexico's Sierra Madre range, **El Paso** (established by the Spanish in 1598) was a major stopping point on the way west during the California gold rush. Outside the city, in El
★ Paso's lower valley, are several important historic sites. **Mission Ysleta** (✉ Old Pueblo Rd., Zaragosa exit off I–10 east of El Paso, ☎ 915/859–9848), circa 1681, is the oldest Spanish mission in the Southwest. Adjacent to the Mission Ysleta is the **Tigua Indian Reservation** (✉ 119 S. Old Pueblo Rd., ☎ 915/859–3916)—closed Monday and Tuesday— home of the oldest ethnic group in Texas and offering Tigua pottery, jewelry, art, and replicas of ancient Native American homes. **Soccoro Mission** (✉ 328 S. Nevares, ☎ 915/859–7718), to the south of the Tigua Indian Reservation, is famed for its fine vigas—the carved ceiling beams that mark local architecture. **San Elizario Presidio** (✉ 1556 San Elizario Rd., ☎ 915/851–2333), a fort built to protect the missions, is also near the Soccoro Mission.

Across the Rio Grande from El Paso is the Mexican city of **Juarez,** which offers often sensational shopping; try the **El Paso–Juarez International Trolley** (✉ Santa Fe and San Francisco Sts., ☎ 915/544–0061). **Scenic Drive** (which you can find by going north on Mesa Street and then right on Rim Road) offers panoramic views of El Paso. **Transmountain Road,** off I–10 west of downtown, takes you through Smuggler's Gap, a dramatic cut across the Franklin Mountains. For information on Juarez and El Paso contact the **El Paso Convention & Visitors Bureau** (✉ 1 Civic Center Plaza, 79901, ☎ 915/534–0696 or 800/351–6024).

Dining and Lodging

For price ranges *see* Charts 1 (B) and 2 (B) *in* On the Road with Fodor's.

$$ ✕ **Tigua Indian Reservation.** In a cheerful feather-and-pottery-be-decked dining room adjacent to the reservation gift shop, this Mexican-flavored restaurant offers delightful Tigua twists. ✉ *122 Old Pueblo Rd.,* ☎ *915/859–3916. AE, D, MC, V. Closed Mon.–Tues.*

$$$ ⌂ **Camino Royal Paso del Norte.** This elegant, brick downtown hotel is listed on the National Register of Historic Places. The jewel of the lobby is the dark-wood circular Dome Bar, which sits under a superb 1912 Tiffany skylight. Guest rooms are functional and large. ✉ *101 S. El Paso St., 79901,* ☎ *915/534–3000 or 800/722–6466,* ᶠᴬˣ *915/ 534–3024. 359 rooms. 2 restaurants, bar, pool, sauna, exercise room, nightclub. AE, D, DC, MC, V.*

South Padre Island

Arriving and Departing

South Padre Island, with Texas's most beautiful beaches, is in the southeastern corner of the state, near the Mexican border town of Matamoros. The island is reached by a bridge across the Intracoastal Waterway from Port Isabel, which, in turn, is accessible from Routes 48 and 100.

What to See and Do

At the southern tip of one of the largest barrier islands in the world—
113-mi-long Padre Island—the resort town and white-sand beaches of
South Padre Island (population: 1,677) attract college students at spring
break but delight nature seekers, beach and sun lovers, and fishermen
★ the rest of the year. North of South Padre Island, the 80½-mi **Padre Island National Seashore** (⊠ 9405 South Padre Island Dr., Corpus Christi
78418, ☎ 512/949–8173) is entirely natural, unchanged from the days
when scavenging Karankawa Indians roamed among its sand dunes, sea
oats, and morning glories. For further information contact the **South
Padre Island Convention & Visitors Bureau** (⊠ 600 Padre Island Blvd.;
Box 3500, 78597, ☎ 210/761–6433 or 800/343–2368).

UTAH

By Stacey
Clark

Capital	Salt Lake City
Population	2,000,000
Motto	Industry
State Bird	California gull
State Flower	Sego lily
Postal Abbreviation	UT

Statewide Visitor Information

Utah Travel Council (⊠ Council Hall, Capitol Hill, Salt Lake City 84114, ☎ 801/538–1030 or 800/200–1160). Nine **regional visitor information centers** supply brochures and travel advice (call the Utah Travel Council for locations), and **welcome centers** are near all major entrances to the state. The **Salt Lake Organizing Committee of the 2002 Olympic Winter Games** (⊠ 257 E. 200 South St., Suite 600, Salt Lake City 84111, ☎ 801/322–2002) can provide information on venues for the games, which will be hosted by Salt Lake City.

Scenic Drives

From Logan **U.S. 89** runs north through a limestone canyon with steep, striated walls, cresting above Bear Lake on the Utah–Idaho border. In northeastern Utah **U.S. 191** jogs north out of Vernal and past geologic formations that are up to a billion years old before meeting **Route 44,** which yields an elongated view of Flaming Gorge National Recreation Area. **Route 12,** in southwestern Utah, turns east from U.S. 89, skirting through Bryce Canyon National Park and Grand Staircase-Escalante National Monument, and then north over aspen-covered Boulder Mountain to Capitol Reef National Park. The *Utah Scenic Byways and Backways* guide is available at visitor and welcome centers.

National and State Parks

National Parks

Utah's five national parks are **Bryce Canyon,** filled with unusual geologic formations; **Capitol Reef,** distinguished by colorfully striped rock walls and ancient petroglyphs; **Zion,** with towering cliffs; **Canyonlands,** with drives through three geologically distinct districts; and **Arches,** known for its sandstone formations (for all, ☞ Exploring Southeastern Utah, *below*).

Utah's seven national monuments include the excavations at **Dinosaur National Monument** (☞ Elsewhere in Utah, *below*); the limestone caverns of **Timpanogos Cave** (⊠ Rte. 3, American Fork 84003, ☎ 801/756–5238 in summer, 801/756–5239 in winter); and the giant, stream-formed spans of **Natural Bridges National Monument** (☞ Elsewhere in Utah, *below*). You can fish or boat at **Glen Canyon National Recreation Area** (☞ Exploring Southeastern Utah, *below*) and **Flaming Gorge National Recreation Area** (☞ Elsewhere in Utah, *below*). **Grand Staircase–Escalante National Monument** achieved monument status in 1996. Though amenities and services remain few, it has stunning river canyons and geologic formations (⊠ 176 E. D. L. Sargent Dr., Cedar City 84720, ☎ 435/586–2401).

State Parks

The **Division of State Parks** (⊠ 1594 W. North Temple St., Salt Lake City 84114, ☎ 801/538–7220) publishes a directory of Utah's 45 state parks. **Goblin Valley State Park** (✉ Box 637, Green River 84525, ☎ 435/564–3633), off I–70 on Route 24 in eastern Utah, has acres of wind-eroded sandstone "goblins" around a desert campground. **This Is the Place State Park** (✉ 2601 Sunnyside Ave., Salt Lake City 84108, ☎ 801/584–8391), on the eastern bench of the Salt Lake Valley, details the trek of Mormon pioneers and re-creates an 1850s township, complete with cooking, crafts-making, and blacksmithing demonstrations.

SALT LAKE CITY

On July 24, 1847, Mormon leader Brigham Young looked out over the Salt Lake Valley and announced to the ragged party behind him, "This is the right place." So began the religious settlement that would become Salt Lake City. The Church of Jesus Christ of Latter-Day Saints, as the Mormon Church is officially known, continues to shape the city, which has evolved into a winter-sports destination, a center for biomedical research, and the gateway to the natural wonders of southern Utah.

Visitor Information

Convention and Visitors Bureau (✉ Salt Palace Convention Center, 180 S. West Temple St., 84101, ☎ 801/521–2868).

Arriving and Departing

By Bus
Greyhound Lines (✉ 160 W. South Temple St., ☎ 800/231–2222).

By Car
I–15 runs north–south through Salt Lake, I–80 east–west. I–215 circles the valley.

By Plane
Salt Lake International Airport (☎ 801/575–2400) is 7 mi north of downtown. Major hotels provide shuttles, and **Utah Transit Authority** (☎ 801/287–4636) buses link the airport to regular city routes. Taxi fare to downtown averages $10–$15 including tip.

By Train
Amtrak (☎ 800/872–7245) serves the city's **Rio Grande Depot** (✉ 320 S. Rio Grande St., ☎ 801/532–3472).

Getting Around Salt Lake City

Salt Lake City streets are laid out geometrically and numbered in increments of 100 in each direction, with Temple Square as their root. Parking is inexpensive, and streets and highways are less crowded than those in comparable urban areas. **Utah Transit Authority** (☎ 801/287–4636) buses and trolleys serve the valley; the fare is $1, with a free-fare zone in downtown shopping areas.

Exploring Salt Lake City

City attractions fan out from Temple Square. To the north is the Capitol Hill District, to the south are shopping and arts locations, to the west is the Great Salt Lake, and to the east lie the ski resorts of the Wasatch Mountains.

Historic **Temple Square** (✉ North Visitors' Center, 50 W. North Temple St., ☎ 801/240–2534) is the 10-acre center of sites important to Mormonism. Two visitor centers house exhibits and art with religious themes. The **Mormon Tabernacle Choir** performs on Thursday and Sat-

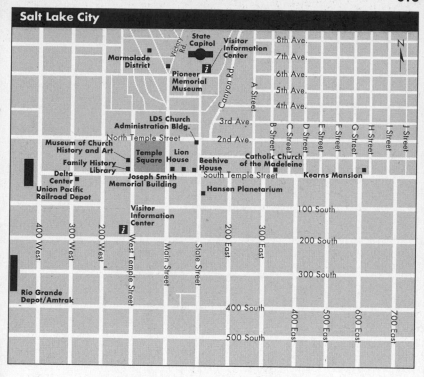

urday in the squat, domed Salt Lake Tabernacle. The six-spired granite **Salt Lake Temple** is open only to church members, but the public may enter (free of charge) the other buildings and monuments on the beautifully landscaped grounds.

East of Temple Square and across Main Street, the **Joseph Smith Memorial Building** (☎ 801/240–1266) is a Mormon community center where visitors can learn how to do computerized genealogical research and can watch an hour-long film on early Mormon history and the emigration of Mormons to the Salt Lake Valley in the mid-19th century. The center also has two restaurants.

On West Temple Street directly west of Temple Square is the **Museum of Church History and Art** (☎ 801/240–3310), displaying Mormon artifacts, paintings, fabric art, and sculptures. Also on West Temple Street, the **Family History Library** (☎ 801/240–2331) provides free public access to the Mormons' huge collection of genealogical records.

On the corner of South Temple and State streets, one block east of Temple Square, is the 1854 **Beehive House** (☎ 801/240–2671), the home of Brigham Young while he served as territorial governor. The **Lion House** (☎ 801/363–5466) received the overflow of Young's large family; it is now a social center and restaurant.

On a hill at the north end of State Street sits the Renaissance Revival–style **state capitol** (✉ 300 N. State St., ☎ 801/538–1563 or 801/538–3000), completed in 1915. Depression-era murals in the rotunda depict events from Utah's past.

The **Pioneer Memorial Museum,** directly west of the state capitol grounds, holds thousands of artifacts, including tools and carriages from the late 1800s and a doll and toy collection. ✉ *300 N. Main St.,* ☎ *801/538–1050. Closed Sun.*

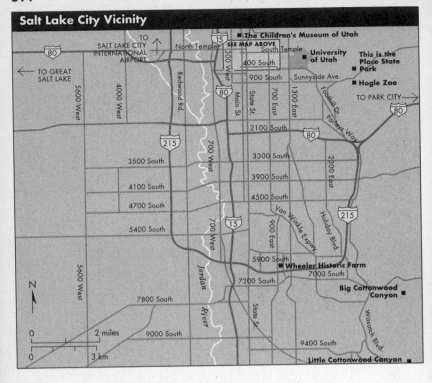

Salt Lake City Vicinity

The **Marmalade District**—the streets bisecting the western slope of Capitol Hill—contains many pioneer houses. Other well-preserved historic houses are on South Temple Street east of Temple Square. Among them is the **Kearns Mansion** (✉ 603 E. South Temple St., ☎ 801/538–1005), the governor's residence; tours are offered. Also on South Temple Street is the early 20th-century **Catholic Church of the Madeleine** (✉ 331 E. South Temple St., ☎ 801/328–8941).

Outside Salt Lake City

About 17 mi west of downtown Salt Lake City via I–80 is the **Great Salt Lake.** Water flows into it, but there is no outlet other than evaporation. This traps minerals and salts, causing the lake to be the most saline body of water on earth except for the Dead Sea. There are two beaches here, each with showers. The south and west shores and neighboring wetlands are prime nesting grounds for many species of migratory, shore, and wading birds. A sunset dinner cruise departs from **Antelope Island State Park** (☎ 801/733–2941).

Rising to more than 11,000 ft east of the Salt Lake Valley, the **Wasatch Mountains** provide an impressive backdrop and recreational escape for city dwellers. Southeast of Salt Lake City are two scenic canyons, Big Cottonwood on Route 190 and Little Cottonwood on Route 210. Resorts here offer hiking, biking, arts festivals and concerts in summer, and skiing in winter (☞ Ski Areas, *below*).

Over the ridge line but merely 29 mi east of Salt Lake City via I–80 is **Park City,** Utah's premier ski destination. Park City's three ski areas will host several events during the 2002 Olympic Winter Games. Park City's historic Main Street has a museum, galleries, shops, and restaurants in restored buildings; several bed-and-breakfasts; three golf courses; and an outlet mall.

Parks and Gardens

Red Butte Gardens (☎ 801/581–5322), east of Salt Lake City's University of Utah campus, has 150 acres of trees, shrubs, herbs, wildflowers, and stream-fed pools tucked into a private canyon in the Wasatch foothills. A concert series is held each summer.

What to See and Do with Children

West of downtown Salt Lake City, the **Children's Museum of Utah** (✉ 840 N. 300 West, ☎ 801/328–3383) lets kids explore the cockpit of a 727 jet plane, the cab of a tractor trailer, strange light effects, and an archaeological dig. Also west of the city, **Raging Waters** (✉ 1200 W. 1700 South, ☎ 801/977–8300) contains 11 pools and 19 rip-roaring slides. The **Utah Museum of Natural History** (✉ University of Utah, 200 S. 1340 East, ☎ 801/581–4303) has Native American artifacts, dinosaur skeletons, and many hands-on science adventures. In the city's eastern foothills, **Hogle Zoo** (✉ 2600 Sunnyside Ave., ☎ 801/582–1631) has more than 1,300 animals. Bring walking shoes and a hat—exhibits are spread out, and shade is at a premium.

Dining

Although liquor laws have some peculiarities, mixed drinks, wine, and beer are available at most restaurants; when in doubt, call ahead. For price ranges *see* Chart 1 (B) *in* On the Road with Fodor's.

$$$$ ✕ **Glitretind.** Dishes such as New England lobster with saffron sauce ★ and Caspian caviar make this restaurant worth the splurge. ✉ *Stein Eriksen Lodge, Deer Valley,* ☎ *435/649–3700. AE, DC, MC, V.*

$$$ ✕ **Santa Fe Restaurant.** Fresh herbs and unusual sauces highlight the ★ southwestern inventions at this restaurant 15 minutes east of downtown in a streamside lodge with mountain views. ✉ *2100 Emigration Canyon Rd.,* ☎ *801/582–5888. MC, V.*

$$ ✕ **Baci Trattoria.** The combination of northern and southern Italian food ★ served in surroundings of marble and stained glass makes Baci a feast for the eyes and the taste buds. ✉ *134 W. Pierpont Ave.,* ☎ *801/328–1500. AE, D, DC, MC, V. Closed Sun.*

$$ ✕ **Lamb's Restaurant.** The decor at Lamb's, which opened in 1919, retains a turn-of-the-century feel. The menu includes beef, chicken, and seafood dishes, plus sandwiches. ✉ *169 S. Main St.,* ☎ *801/364–7166. AE, D, DC, MC, V. Closed Sun.*

$$ ✕ **Market Street Grill.** The stylish black-and-white decor is catchy, but creative preparations of seafood, steaks, and chicken steal the show. ✉ *48 Market St.,* ☎ *801/322–4668. AE, D, DC, MC, V.*

$–$$ ✕ **Creekside Restaurant.** The seasonal colors of the Wasatch Mountains and views of ski runs add to the allure of this Mediterranean-style restaurant. Pizzas with grilled vegetables, caramelized onions, and Gorgonzola cheese, as well as other more conventional toppings, are baked in wood-burning ovens. Pasta, grilled chicken, and steak round out the menu. ✉ *Solitude Resort, 12000 Big Cottonwood Canyon,* ☎ *801/536–5787. AE, D, MC, V.*

$ ✕ **Desert Edge Pub.** This tavern brews 15 beers and ales. The food ranges ★ from sandwiches and sizzling black-bean enchiladas to pasta-salad specials such as penne with shrimp and artichoke hearts. ✉ *600 S. 700 East,* ☎ *801/521–8917. AE, D, MC, V.*

Lodging

Contact the **Utah Hotel and Lodging Association** (✉ 9 Exchange Pl., Suite 812, Salt Lake City 84111, ☎ 801/359–0104 or 800/733–8824) for further suggestions and a statewide reservation service. Prices vary widely with the seasons. The ski resorts listed below are no more than 30 mi away from Salt Lake City. For price ranges *see* Chart 2 (A) *in* On the Road with Fodor's.

$$$-$$$$ **✕ Cliff Lodge at Snowbird Resort.** The large guest rooms at this an-
★ gular gray building have wide glass walls providing spectacular views winter and summer. The redwood-and-brass lobby is sumptuous. ⊠ *Snowbird Resort 84092,* ☎ *801/521–6040 or 800/453–3000,* 𝖥𝖠𝖷 *801/742–3204. 532 rooms. 3 restaurants, 2 lounges, 2 pools, spa, laundry service, coin laundry. AE, D, DC, MC, V.*

$$-$$$ **✕ Anton Boxrud Bed and Breakfast.** Antiques and unusual furnishings from all over the world fill the rooms of this Victorian manor near the governor's mansion and 15 minutes from the city center. The complimentary evening snacks and beverages offered near the parlor's bay window are as delicious as the bountiful breakfasts. ⊠ *57 S. 600 East, 84102,* ☎ *801/363–8035 or 800/524–5511,* 𝖥𝖠𝖷 *801/596–1316. 7 rooms. Hot tub. AE, D, MC, V.*

$$-$$$ **✕ Shadow Ridge Resort.** Accommodations here range from a single hotel room to a two-bedroom condominium suite. All rooms are attractively furnished, and the staff is friendly and experienced. ⊠ *50 Shadow Ridge St. (Box 1820), Park City 84060,* ☎ *435/649–4300 or 800/451–3031,* 𝖥𝖠𝖷 *435/649–5951. 150 rooms. Restaurant, lounge, pool, hot tub, sauna, coin laundry. AE, D, DC, MC, V.*

$$ **✕ Little America.** The sunny tower rooms in this 17-story building are decorated with gentle colors and generously upholstered furniture. The lobby and mezzanine have enormous brick fireplaces. ⊠ *500 S. Main St., 84102,* ☎ *801/363–6781 or 800/453–9450,* 𝖥𝖠𝖷 *801/596–5911. 850 rooms. 2 restaurants, lounge, pool, exercise room, coin laundry, airport shuttle. AE, D, DC, MC, V.*

$$ **✕ Peery Hotel.** Most of the guest rooms in this four-story 1910 hotel
★ are furnished with eclectic antique reproductions and fanciful linens. The plush lobby encourages loitering. ⊠ *110 W. 300 South, 84102,* ☎ *801/521–4300 or 800/331–0073,* 𝖥𝖠𝖷 *801/575–5014. 77 rooms. Restaurant, pool, sauna, exercise room, coin laundry, airport shuttle. AE, D, DC, MC, V.*

$ **✕ Airport Inn.** This motel near the freeway and airport is a good value. The rooms are generically furnished but are reasonably quiet considering the location. ⊠ *2333 W. North Temple St., 84116,* ☎ *801/539–0438 or 800/835–9755,* 𝖥𝖠𝖷 *801/539–8852. 100 rooms. Restaurant, lounge, pool, hot tub, airport shuttle. AE, D, DC, MC, V.*

$ **✕ Skyline Inn.** On the edge of a quiet neighborhood and near restau-
★ rants and shopping, this well-maintained tan-stucco motel has a friendly staff. ⊠ *2475 E. 1700 South, 84108,* ☎ *801/582–5350,* 𝖥𝖠𝖷 *801/582–5350. 24 rooms. Pool, hot tub. AE, D, DC, MC, V.*

Nightlife and the Arts

A calendar of events is available at the **Salt Lake Convention and Visitors Bureau** (☞ Visitor Information, *above*). The free *This Week in Salt Lake* magazine is widely available at stores and visitor centers. The *Salt Lake Tribune* carries daily arts-and-entertainment listings.

Nightlife

Many nightspots are private clubs, meaning that membership is required (temporary memberships cost about $5). Weekends are wild at the **Dead Goat Saloon** (⊠ 165 S. West Temple St., ☎ 801/328–4628), a subterranean hangout with live music and a busy dance floor. The mood at **Club DV8** (⊠ 115 S. West Temple St., ☎ 801/539–8400) is pure punk. A good place to spot Utah Jazz basketball players is **Port O' Call** (⊠

78 W. 400 South, ☎ 801/521–0589), a sports bar with 14 satellite dishes and 26 TVs. The art deco–style **Zephyr Club** (✉ 301 S. West Temple St., ☎ 801/355–2582) has live blues, rock, reggae, and dancing. The **Bay** (✉ 404 S. West Temple St., ☎ 801/363–2623) is a smoke- and alcohol-free club with three dance floors.

The Arts

Salt Lake's best performing arts bets are **Ballet West** (✉ 50 W. 200 South, ☎ 801/355–2787), **Pioneer Theater Company** (✉ 300 S. 1340 East, ☎ 801/581–6961), **Salt Lake Acting Company** (✉ 168 W. 500 North, ☎ 801/363–7522), **Utah Opera Company** (✉ 50 W. 200 South, ☎ 801/355–2787), and **Utah Symphony** (✉ Abravanel Hall, 123 W. South Temple St., ☎ 801/533–6683). Concerts are presented at the **Delta Center** (✉ 300 W. South Temple St., ☎ 801/325–7328).

Spectator Sports

Basketball: Utah Jazz (✉ Delta Center, 300 W. South Temple St., ☎ 801/355–3865).

Ski Areas

Cross-Country

Solitude Nordic Center (✉ Rte. 190, ☎ 801/536–5774 or 800/748–4754) and **White Pine Touring** (✉ Park City, ☎ 435/649–8701) offer cross-country skiing tours, rentals, lessons, and advice.

Downhill

Alta (✉ Rte. 210, ☎ 801/742–3333), 39 runs, 8 lifts, 2,100-ft vertical drop. **Brighton** (✉ Rte. 190, ☎ 801/532–4731 or 800/873–5512), 64 runs, 7 lifts, 1,745-ft drop. **Deer Valley** (✉ Rte. 224, ☎ 435/649–1000 or 800/424–3337), 67 runs, 13 lifts, 2,200-ft drop. **Park City Ski Area** (✉ Rte. 224 off I–80, ☎ 435/649–8111 or 800/222–7275), 89 runs, 13 lifts, gondola, 3,100-ft drop. **Solitude** (✉ Rte. 190, ☎ 801/534–1400 or 800/748–4754), 63 runs and bowls, 7 lifts, 2,047-ft drop, 12 mi of groomed cross-country track. **Snowbird** (✉ Rte. 210, ☎ 801/742–2222 or 800/453–3000), 66 runs, 8 lifts and a high-speed tram, 3,240-ft drop.

Shopping

Directly south of Temple Square, **Crossroads Plaza** (✉ 50 S. Main St., ☎ 801/531–1799) has four floors of stores, theaters, and restaurants. East across Main Street, **ZCMI Center** (✉ 36 S. State St., ☎ 801/321–8745) contains 80 stores and restaurants. Just a few blocks south and east, **Trolley Square** (✉ 600 S. 700 East, ☎ 801/521–9877) once housed electric trolleys; today it has the city's most varied shopping, as well as restaurants and movie theaters. East of I–15 in the south end of the city, the **Factory Stores of America Mall** (✉ 12101 S. Factory Outlet Dr., ☎ 801/572–6440) has discount outlets with everything from cookware and coats to Doc Martens.

SOUTHWESTERN UTAH

Southwestern Utah is a panoply of natural wonders; heading the list are Zion, Capitol Reef, and Bryce Canyon national parks, where clear air and high elevations create spectacular 100-mi vistas. The picturesque towns of St. George, Cedar City, Springdale, and Torrey have historic sites. The weather is mild here year-round.

Visitor Information

Color Country Travel Bureau (⊠ 906 N. 14th St. W, Box 1550, St. George 84771, ☎ 435/628–4171 or 800/233–8824). **Capitol Reef Country** (⊠ Rte. 24, Box 7, Teasdale 84773, ☎ 800/858–7951).

Arriving and Departing

By Bus
Greyhound Lines (☎ 800/231–2222) stops in St. George and Cedar City.

By Car
I–15 and U.S. 89 pass north–south through the region.

By Plane
St. George and **Cedar City airports** are served by Skywest Airlines (☎ 800/453–9417).

Exploring Southwestern Utah

At **Bryce Canyon National Park** millions of years of geologic mayhem have created gigantic bowls filled with strange pinnacles and quilted drapes of stone. An 18-mi scenic drive that skirts the western rim has views of the amphitheaters. ⊠ *Rte. 12, Bryce Canyon 84717, ☎ 435/ 834–5322. Some roads closed Nov.–Mar.*

Once called "Land of the Sleeping Rainbow" because of its colorfully striped cliffs, **Capitol Reef National Park** is dominated by a 100-mi-long stone uplift called the Waterpocket Fold. At the base of this soaring "reef" are still-flourishing riverside orchards planted by early settlers. Hikes lead to petroglyphs and hidden formations. The park also has an impressive backcountry scenic route. ⊠ *Rte. 24 (HC 70, Box 15), Torrey 84775, ☎ 435/425–3791.*

Cedar City is the setting for the state's premier theatrical event: the **Utah Shakespearean Festival** (☎ 435/586–7878 or 800/752–9849), with feasts, bawdy Elizabethan skits, and performances from late June to September in an open-air replica of the Globe Theatre.

The Virgin River carved the towering cliffs of Zion Canyon and still flows along its floor. Spring-fed hanging gardens sprout lush greens along the walls. The roads, tram tours, and horseback and hiking trails of **Zion National Park** (⊠ Rte. 9, Box 1099, Springdale 84767, ☎ 435/ 772–3256) facilitate exploration of the beauties of this vividly hued canyon and its tributaries. It can be very crowded in summer.

To the southwest of Zion National Park, in St. George, you can tour the historic district and **Brigham Young's winter home** (⊠ 89 W. 100 North, ☎ 435/673–5181). In Santa Clara the 130-year-old **house of missionary Jacob Hamblin** (⊠ 3386 Santa Clara Dr., ☎ 435/673–2161) has cotton plants and a vineyard. Both sites are operated by the Mormon Church.

Dining and Lodging

Accommodations Referral Service (☎ 800/259–3343) provides area-wide lodging recommendations. For price ranges *see* Charts 1 (B) and 2 (B) *in* On the Road with Fodor's.

Bryce Canyon

$$–$$$ ✕🏨 **Bryce Lodge.** The lobby and dining room of this rustic 1920s wood-and-sandstone lodge have high ceilings with exposed beams and massive stone fireplaces. The sturdily furnished guest rooms are geared to informal travelers. ⊠ *Bryce Canyon National Park (Box 400), Cedar City 84720,* ☎ *435/834–5361,* ℻ *435/834–3493. 114 rooms. Restaurant. AE, D, DC, MC, V. Closed Nov.–Apr.*

$$ ✕⊞ **Ruby's Inn.** Five two-story buildings contain simply decorated guest rooms; the rough-hewn public areas are in a more rustic-looking structure. The restaurant serves basic American fare, with creative specials. ⊠ *Rte. 63 (Box 1), 84717,* ☎ *435/834–5341 or 800/468–8660,* ℻ *435/834–5265. 369 rooms. Restaurant, pool, hot tub, coin laundry. AE, D, DC, MC, V.*

Cedar City

$$ ✕ **Milt's Stage Stop.** Terrific food and an inviting atmosphere charac-
★ terize this dinner spot in beautiful Cedar Canyon where the specialties include 12-ounce rib-eye steak, prime rib, and fresh seafood. The mountain views are splendid year-round. ⊠ *5 mi east of town on Rte. 14,* ☎ *435/586–9344. AE, D, DC, MC, V.*

St. George

$$ ✕ **Basila's Cafe.** Greek and Italian specialties fill the menu here, along with artfully arranged salads. The surrounding red rock makes outdoor dining particularly captivating at sunset. ⊠ *2 W. St. George Blvd.,* ☎ *435/673–7671. MC, V. Closed Sun.–Mon.*

$$ ✕ **Pancho and Lefty's.** The Mexican cuisine ranges from authentic tamales wrapped in corn husks to avocado-laced taco salads, all further enlivened by the spirited decor and tart margaritas. ⊠ *1050 S. Bluff St.,* ☎ *435/628–4772. AE, MC, V.*

$$ ⊞ **Ramada Inn.** On St. George's major thoroughfare and close to restaurants, shopping, and the historic district, this is one of the city's most convenient and best-appointed properties. ⊠ *1440 E. St. George Blvd., 84770,* ☎ *435/628–2828 or 800/713–9435. 136 rooms. Pool, hot tub, business services, meeting rooms. AE, D, MC, V.*

Springdale

$$ ✕ **Bit and Spur Restaurant and Saloon.** This low-slung eatery serves
★ healthful southwestern-style Mexican food. Works by local artists fill the pine-paneled interior, and the patio is redolent of scents from the herb garden. ⊠ *1212 Zion Park Blvd.,* ☎ *435/772–3498. MC, V.*

$ ✕ **Electric Jim's Parkside Burgers.** Virtually on the boundary of Zion National Park, this casual restaurant with indoor and outdoor tables serves burgers and sandwiches with toppings that turn these old standards into standouts. ⊠ *198 Zion Park Blvd.,* ☎ *435/772–3838. MC, V. Closed Dec.–Jan.*

$$ ⊞ **Cliffrose Lodge and Gardens.** Acres of lawn, trees, and gardens surround this hotel on the banks of the Virgin River, ¼ mi from Zion. Rooms are decorated in desert hues. ⊠ *281 Zion Park Blvd., 84767,* ☎ *435/ 772–3234 or 800/243–8824,* ℻ *435/772–3900. 36 rooms. Pool. AE, D, MC, V.*

$$ ⊞ **Snow Family Guest Ranch.** Just minutes from Zion National Park,
★ this bed-and-breakfast is a western-theme oasis filled with welcome touches, such as window seats with excellent views, inviting common areas—both indoors and out—and breakfasts worth lingering over. ⊠ *533 E. Hwy. 9 (Box 790190), Virgin 84779,* ☎ *435/635–2500 or 800/ 308–7669. 9 rooms. Pool, hot tub. AE, MC, V.*

Torrey

$$ ✕ **Café Diablo.** Ruddy tile floors and crisp white walls make this a pleasant setting for innovative Southwest cuisine—hearty *chipotle*-fried ribs, local trout crusted with pumpkin seeds, jicama salad with egg-

plant sopaipillas, and the like. ⊠ *599 W. Main St.,* ☎ *435/425–3070. MC, V. Closed Nov.–Apr.*

$$$ 🏨 **SkyRidge Bed and Breakfast.** This colorful three-story inn has com-
★   fortable guest rooms with unusual furniture and exceptional views of
the desert and mountains surrounding Capitol Reef National Park. Meals
here are excellent. ⊠ *950 E. Hwy. 24 (Box 750220),* ☎ *435/425–3222,*
FAX *435/425–3222. 6 rooms. Hot tub. MC, V.*

Campgrounds
You can choose from among 100 campgrounds in this region, both pub-
lic and private; for more information contact the **Utah Travel Council**
(☞ Statewide Visitor Information, *above*).

Outdoor Activities and Sports

Biking
A spin along Route 9 through Zion, Route 18 through Snow Canyon,
or the Bryce Canyon Scenic Loop yields classic southwestern scenery.
Route 24 through Capitol Reef accesses historic sites and off-road rid-
ing. **Bicycle Utah** (☎ 800/200–1160) provides a free directory of bik-
ing routes.

Golf
St. George attracts golfers year-round to more than 10 public courses,
including **Dixie Red Hills** (⊠ 1000 N. 700 West, ☎ 435/634–5852),
with nine holes; **Entrada at Snow Canyon** (⊠ 2511 W. Entrada Trail,
☎ 435/674–7500), with 18 holes; and **South Gate** (⊠ 1975 Tonaquint
Dr., ☎ 435/628–0000), with 18 holes. The **Washington County Travel
Council** (☎ 435/634–5747 or 800/869–6635) has more golfing in-
formation.

Hiking and Backpacking
Bryce Canyon, Capitol Reef, and Zion national parks have many trails
of varying difficulty. Zion's paved **Gateway to the Narrows Trail** fol-
lows the Virgin River. Bryce's moderately difficult **Navajo Loop Trail**
yields views of towering Thor's Hammer. Capitol Reef's **Hickman
Bridge Trail** is a short nature trail through a sheltered canyon to the
base of a natural bridge.

SOUTHEASTERN UTAH

For years the canyon country of southeastern Utah has captured the
imagination of filmmakers, serving as the site of such western and ad-
venture films as *Stagecoach, Indiana Jones and the Last Crusade,* and
Thelma and Louise. Rugged Arches and Canyonlands national parks
invite exploration via scenic drives, four-wheeling, hiking, rock climb-
ing, river running, and cycling.

Visitor Information

Grand County: Travel Council (⊠ Main and Center Sts., Box 550, Moab
84532, ☎ 435/259–8825 or 800/635–6622). **San Juan County:** Travel
Council (⊠ 117 S. Main St., Box 490, Monticello 84535, ☎ 435/587–
3235 or 800/574–4386).

Arriving and Departing

By Car
I–70 runs east–west through the region; U.S. 191 slices north–south.

By Plane
Alpine Air (☎ 801/575–2839) flies weekdays from Salt Lake City to **Canyonlands Field,** in Moab.

Exploring Southeastern Utah

The town of **Green River,** at the junction of I–70 and U.S. 6/191, is named for the river running through it and is the major "put-in" for raft trips on the Green River to its confluence with the Colorado.

A sweeping view of the Canyonlands' multicolor upside-down geography is found at **Dead Horse Point State Park** (✉ Rte. 313, ☎ 435/ 259–2614), named for a band of wild horses once stranded on this isolated peninsula.

Arches National Park, just northwest of Moab, contains sandstone formations carved by wind and water. Trails and two scenic roads lead through towering pillars and arches. ✉ Box 907, Moab 84532, ☎ 435/ 259–8161.

Moab, below I–70 on U.S. 191, has become a mecca for mountain bikers, with bike shops, T-shirt stores, restaurants, and motels on virtually every corner. Just south of Moab, Utah's only commercial winery, **Arches Vineyard** (✉ 420 S. Kane Creek Blvd., ☎ 435/259–5397), gives tours and has a tasting room.

The landscape of **Canyonlands National Park,** southwest of Moab, is divided into three geologically distinct districts, each with its own visitor center. Scenic loops, trails, and four-wheel-drive roads lead to views of massive canyons or uplifts crowded with stone spires and other bizarre features. ✉ Rte. 313, Moab 84532, ☎ 435/259–7164.

The city of **Monticello** is 53 mi south of Moab on U.S. 191 but at 7,000 ft elevation compared to Moab's 4,000 has much cooler temperatures. South and west of Monticello, just north of Route 95, a 9-mi scenic drive takes in views of three river-carved bridges at **Natural Bridges National Monument** (✉ Rte. 275, ☎ 435/692–1234).

Southwest of Monticello—take U.S. 191 south and U.S. 95 west or U.S. 95 and Route 276 west—at **Lake Powell,** part of the **Glen Canyon National Recreation Area** (☎ 520/608–6404), is a stark meeting of water and stone, with nearly 2,000 mi of meandering shoreline resulting from the construction of Glen Canyon Dam on the Colorado River. Side canyons and coves hold Indian ruins, rock art, and natural wonders such as the **Rainbow Bridge National Monument.** Spring and fall are the best times to visit—summer temperatures are often over 100°F.

The town of **Bluff,** 48 mi south of Monticello on U.S. 191, rests on the bank of the San Juan River at the border of the vast Navajo Nation. Houses built in the 1880s of sandstone and red adobe are clustered at the town's center.

East of Bluff, **Hovenweep National Monument** (✉ Rte. 262, ☎ 970/ 749–0510) has several tower structures built by Pueblo Indians about 800 years ago.

Dining and Lodging

The cuisine in southeastern Utah tends toward fast food and hearty meals made from local produce. For price ranges *see* Charts 1 (B) and 2 (B) *in* On the Road with Fodor's.

Bluff

$ ✕ **Sunbonnet Cafe.** This small café serves basic American food, but the specialty is the Navajo taco: fry bread heaped with beans, chilies, lettuce, cheese, and tomatoes. ⊠ *Rte. 163,* ☎ *435/672–2201. MC, V.*

$ ▥ **Recapture Lodge.** This locally owned property is unassuming, clean, and comfortable. The evening slide shows are popular. ⊠ *U.S. 191 (Box 309), 84512,* ☎ *435/672–2281,* ℻ *435/672–2284. 36 rooms. Pool, hot tub. AE, D, MC, V.*

Green River

$ ✕ **Ray's Tavern.** Huge hamburgers topped with slabs of tomato and onion and served on a heap of steak fries are the draw here. The crowd is a mix of river runners, tourists, and locals looking for lunch and a game of pool. ⊠ *25 S. Broadway,* ☎ *435/564–3511. No credit cards.*

Moab

$ ✕ **Rio Colorado.** The Rio has standard decor, but its varied menu includes Mexican entrées, steak, pasta, chicken, and salads. All are delicious. ⊠ *2 S. 100 West,* ☎ *435/259–6666. MC, V.*

$$$–$$$$ ▥ **Pack Creek Ranch.** This guest ranch on a forested mountain loop has rustic log cabins and activities ranging from horseback riding—followed by a massage—to cross-country skiing and weekend entertainment. The ranch house sleeps 12. Meals, included in the rates, are substantial and well prepared. ⊠ *La Sal Mt. Loop Rd. (Box 1270), Moab 84532,* ☎ *435/259–5505,* ℻ *435/259–8879. 9 cabins, 1 ranch house. Dining room, kitchenettes, pool, hot tub, sauna. AE, D, MC, V.*

$$ ▥ **Sunflower Hill Bed and Breakfast.** Country touches mark the decor
★   of this stucco-and-weathered-wood dwelling. The breakfast spread might include yogurt and homemade bread or huge fruit muffins. ⊠ *185 N. 3rd East, 84532,* ☎ *435/259–2974. 11 rooms. Kitchenette. MC, V.*

Monticello

$$ ▥ **Grist Mill Inn.** This bed and breakfast, housed in a three-story flour
★   mill built in 1933, has several suites, a next-door cottage, and a cozy antique caboose with a sitting room, kitchen, and snug bedroom. The common areas—a library, dining room, lobby, and parlor—are welcoming, and their decor includes various pieces of mill equipment still in place. ⊠ *64 S. 300 East,* ☎ *435/587–2597 or 800/645–3762. 10 rooms. Hot tub. AE, D, MC, V.*

Campgrounds

Campground directories are provided by the **Grand County Travel Council** and the **San Juan County Travel Council** (☞ Visitor Information, *above*).

Outdoor Activities and Sports

Biking

Southeastern Utah has hundreds of charted mountain-biking trails, including the **Moab Slickrock Trail,** 4 mi east of Moab, a 10-mi rollercoaster route marked only by dashes of paint on raw rock. Bikes are ideal for exploring the landscape and roads of **Hovenweep National Monument** (☞ Exploring Southeastern Utah, *above*). The **Abajo Mountain Loop,** west of Monticello, winds through cool pine and aspen forests. For area-wide rentals and advice, try **Kaibab Tours** (⊠ 391 S. Main St., Moab, ☎ 435/259-7423 or 800/451–1133, ℻ 435/259–6135).

Hiking and Backpacking

Call the travel council of Grand County or San Juan (☞ Visitor Information, *above*) for advice on trails. Remember to bring water along on any hike in this region.

Rafting

Outfitters operate float trips and white-water treks on the Colorado River through black-granite-walled Westwater Canyon and the rapids of Cataract Canyon and also on the Green River through Desolation and Gray canyons, both of which shelter Anasazi Indian ruins. Float trips on the San Juan River wind through petroglyph-etched cliffs. **Raft Utah** (☎ 801/566–2662) publishes a free directory.

ELSEWHERE IN UTAH

Northeastern Utah

Arriving and Departing

U.S. 40 runs east–west through the region. U.S. 191 runs north–south.

What to See and Do

The excavations at **Dinosaur National Monument** (✉ Quarry Visitor Center, Box 128, Jensen 84035, ☎ 435/789–2115) showcase the largest collection of Jurassic-period fossils ever unearthed. Some 2,000 dinosaur bones—discoveries began in 1909—lie exposed in a sandstone face inside the visitor center, 20 mi east of Vernal.

Flaming Gorge National Recreation Area (✉ Box 279, Manila 84046, ☎ 435/784–3445) is north of Dinosaur National Monument via U.S. 191. Behind 500-ft-high Flaming Gorge Dam, Flaming Gorge Lake stretches north for 90 mi between twisting red-rock canyon walls. The lake is popular for boating, camping, and trophy trout fishing.

Dining and Lodging

$$ 🏨 **Best Western Antlers Motel.** This property has the usual amenities and a helpful staff. ✉ 423 W. Main St., Vernal 84078, ☎ 435/789–1202. 43 rooms. Restaurant, pool, hot tub. AE, D, DC, MC, V.

$$ 🏨 **Flaming Gorge Lodge.** With a good restaurant, boat rentals, and guided fishing service, this is the best lodging choice near Flaming Gorge. ✉ Greendale, U.S. 191, Dutch John 84023, ☎ 435/889–3773, FAX 435/889–3788. 45 rooms. Restaurant. AE, D, MC, V.

$$ 🏨 **Weston Lamplighter Inn.** Close to stores, theaters, and restaurants, this motel has nicely furnished rooms and a popular restaurant. ✉ 120 E. Main St., Vernal 84078, ☎ 435/789–0312, FAX 435/781–1480. 100 rooms. Restaurant, pool. AE, D, MC, V.

10 The Rockies

Colorado, Idaho, Montana, Wyoming

By Carolyn
Price

Updated
by Jane
McConnell.

*C*all the Idaho information line, and you'll be asked to press "5" on your touch-tone phone if you would like to report a wolf sighting. Check in with the state's tourist promotion offices, and more than likely you'll be talking to a state-employed prison inmate earning $1 an hour for his or her trouble.

Wolves and outlaws haven't left the Rocky Mountain states of Idaho, Montana, Wyoming, and Colorado, and they evoke the unpredictable charms and crimes of nature and human action that thrived in the Old West: the click of cowboy spurs and the rustling of leather chaps, the broken treaties and betrayals to Native Americans, the energy and innocence of wide-open spaces, boomtowns, and the search for gold.

But most enduring of all are the mountains—a 4,000-mi-long chain that stretches from Alaska to northern New Mexico. Begun about 70 million years ago, when sandstone, shale, granite, marble, and volcanic rock surged and split and gave under the plow of glacial ice, the Rockies emerged to run intermittently along what is now the Idaho-Montana boundary down to a central section sloping through western Wyoming's Yellowstone and Grand Teton national parks and into northern Colorado.

This mountain backdrop still inspires the kind of fear and wonder it once did from mountain folk and Native Americans. What you'll see from atop these summits is a landscape of breathtaking beauty and variety. The westernmost state, Idaho, has terrain encompassing everything from fruit orchards to the tallest sand dunes in the United States. Montana claims 25 million acres of public land, most of it aloft in the northern Rockies. Its Glacier National Park is home to the ptarmigan, wolf, mountain goat, and moose. Wyoming, the ninth-largest and least populated state in the Union, is studded with thermal pools, bubbling hot springs, and, within a square-mile area in Yellowstone National Park, a quarter of the earth's geysers. In Colorado, the ski capital of the United States, high-country lakes, meadows frosted with blue columbine, and treeless alpine tundra assemble in one sweeping vista, while Denver—the Mile-High City—and the university town of Boulder attract visitors and settlers from all corners of the globe.

When to Go

Many visitors think the Rockies have only two seasons: skiing and hiking. But for those willing to risk sometimes capricious weather, fall and spring are the Rockies' best-kept secrets. **Spring** is a good time for fishing, rafting the runoff, or birding and viewing wildlife. **Fall** may be the prettiest season of all, with golden splashes of aspen on the mountainsides, more wildlife at lower elevations, and excellent fishing during spawning. You will also pay less during these shoulder seasons, and you may have a corner of Yellowstone all to yourself. Driving in the **winter** is chancy, and although the interstates are kept open even in fearsome weather, highway passes like the Going-to-the-Sun Highway in Glacier National Park can be blocked from late October to June. High altitude (over 7,000 ft above sea level) and high latitude (the nearer you get to Canada) result in longer winters. Winter visitors should prepare for the possibility of temperatures below zero—but the climate is dry, so the cold is less cruel. Wilderness snowbanks can linger through June, so backcountry hikers generally crowd in from July through Labor Day. **Summer** temperatures rarely rise into the 90s, but the thinner atmosphere at high altitudes makes it necessary for visitors to shield themselves from ultraviolet rays.

Festivals and Seasonal Events

Winter

JAN.➤ **National Western Stock Show and Rodeo** (☎ 303/295–1660), in **Denver,** is the biggest in the world, attracting all the stars of the rodeo circuit for two weeks.

During **Ullr Fest** (☎ 970/453–6018), the town of **Breckenridge, Colorado,** declares itself an independent kingdom and pays homage to the Norse God of snow in a two-week wild revel.

Spring

LATE MAY➤ Memorial Day brings the annual **Bolder Boulder** run (☎ 303/444–7223) to **Boulder, Colorado,** where a top international field and 40,000 ordinary citizens race through the closed streets of town.

Summer

LATE JUNE➤ In Colorado, the **Telluride Bluegrass & Country Music Festival** (✉ 800/624–2422) has become so popular the organizers have had to limit the number of spectators to 10,000.

LATE JULY➤ Wyoming's **Cheyenne Frontier Days** (☎ 800/227–6336 or 800/543–2339 in WY), the rodeo daddy of 'em all, includes evening shows featuring the biggest names in country music, as well as parades and very popular pancake breakfasts.

JUNE–AUG.➤ **Colorado Shakespeare Festival** (☎ 303/492–0554), in **Boulder,** presents three full-scale traditional and nontraditional Shakespeare productions and one non-Shakespearean play Tuesday–Sunday nights. The actors are recruited from around the country.

At the **Aspen Music Festival and School** (☎ 970/925–3254) students from around the world perform with faculty, and world-class soloists and conductors are also featured.

Grand Teton Music Festival (☎ 307/733–1128), the most important classical music concert series in the northern Rockies, attracts musicians from the nation's finest orchestras.

The Rockies

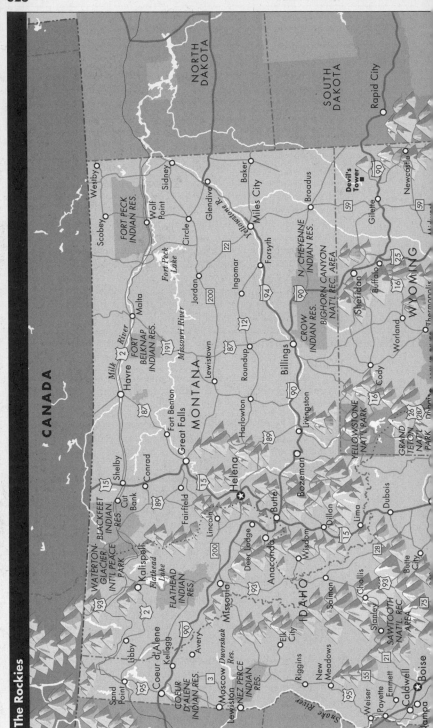

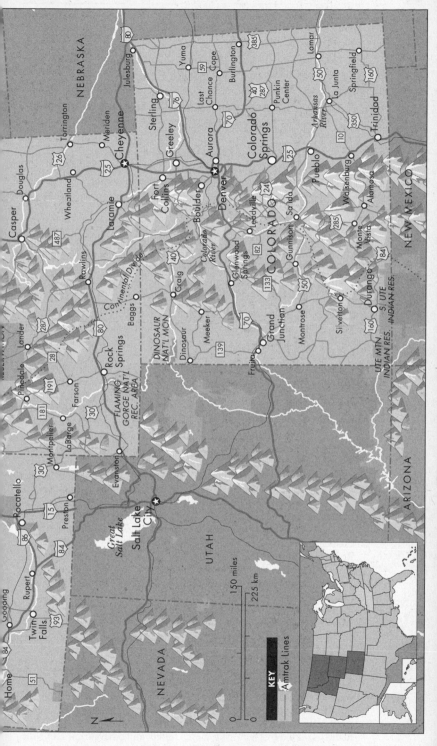

Aug.➤ At the **Cowboy Poetry Gathering** (☎ 406/538–5436) in **Lewiston, Montana,** U.S. and Canadian performers share verses about a man and a horse following a cow.

In **Vail, Colorado,** the **International Festival of Dance** (☎ 970/949–1999) is set amid wildflowers in the outdoor Ford Ampitheater.

Autumn

Early Oct.➤ In **Denver,** the **Great American Beer Festival** (☎ 303/447–0816) is the country's largest beer fest, offering samples of more than 1,000 brews.

Oct.–late Dec.➤ Join the **Eagle Watch** (☎ 406/475–3128) to see hundreds of bald eagles gather annually in Canyon Ferry State Park, near **Helena, Montana,** during freshwater salmon spawning.

Getting Around

By Bus

Greyhound Lines (☎ 800/231–2222) has extensive service throughout Colorado and connects major cities throughout the region, including Cheyenne, Boise, Pocatello, and Missoula. Various smaller bus lines connect with Greyhound to provide service to smaller communities as well as to the parks.

By Car

Major interstates crisscross the region, winding their way through accessible mountain passes. The busiest but least scenic east–west thoroughfare is I–80, which crosses southern Wyoming, passing through Cheyenne and Laramie in the southeast corner. To reach Yellowstone National Park, you must either make the long drive north from Rock Springs or come south from I–90, which crosses southern Montana. In Colorado I–70 runs east–west, passing through Denver and Grand Junction in the west, south of Rocky Mountain National Park. I–15 runs north from Salt Lake City into Idaho and connects with I–84, which heads west to Boise and on to Portland. I–90 passes through Sheridan in northeastern Wyoming before crossing Montana and northern Idaho; it comes within 100 mi of Glacier National Park, which can be reached by going north from Missoula on U.S. 93 and east on U.S. 2. I–15 goes along the east side of the park; you can reach Glacier by driving west on U.S. 89. I–25 comes up from New Mexico and passes through Colorado Springs and Denver in Colorado and Cheyenne and Casper in Wyoming and then joins I–90 in Montana. Throughout the Rockies drivers should be extremely cautious about winter travel, when whiteouts and ice are not uncommon. Because major airports are few and far between, the most popular mode of travel is by car or camper, and by far the busiest driving season is summer. Major attractions such as Glacier and Yellowstone National Park are well away from the interstates, requiring visitors to drive dozens or even hundreds of miles on scenic two-lane highways to the entrances.

By Plane

The **Denver International Airport** is the primary airline hub in the Rockies. Several domestic airlines fly from Denver and Salt Lake into **Jackson Hole Airport** (☎ 307/733–4767), in Wyoming, with additional service during the ski season, including direct flights from Chicago by American Airlines. The **Boise Air Terminal** (☎ 208/383–3110), in Idaho, is served by Delta, Sky West, United, and other airlines. In Montana the **Missoula Airport** (☎ 406/728–4381) and **Glacier Park International Airport** (☎ 406/257–5994), in Kalispell, are served by major domestic airlines. **Salt Lake City Airport** (☎ 801/575–2400) also provides an access point to Wyoming and Idaho.

By Train

Amtrak (☎ 800/872–7245) connects the Rockies to both coasts and all major American cities; trains run through Boise, Salt Lake City, and Denver, with other stops in between. Routes have switched back and forth between Colorado and southern Wyoming in recent years. Amtrak trains also run through northern Montana, with stops in Essex and Whitefish, along the border of Glacier National Park. Connecting motor coach services are provided in the summer from Pocatello, Idaho, to Yellowstone National Park.

COLORADO

By Sandra
Widener

Updated by
Jane
McConnell

Capital   Denver
Population   3,823,000
Motto   Nothing Without Providence
State Bird   Lark bunting
State Flower   Columbine
Postal Abbreviation CO

Statewide Visitor Information

Colorado Travel and Tourism Authority (⊠ 1625 Broadway, Suite 1700, Denver 80202, ☎ 800/433–2656).

Scenic Drives

Colorado has 17 designated scenic routes, which are marked by signs that have blue columbines. The 232-mi **San Juan Skyway** traverses historic ranching and mining towns such as Durango, Silverton, Ouray, Telluride, and Cortez. The **Peak-to-Peak Highway** follows Routes 119, 72, and 7 through gold-mining towns to Rocky Mountain National Park.

National and State Parks

National Parks
Great Sand Dunes National Monument (⊠ 35 mi northeast of Alamosa off Rte. 150; Mosca 81146, ☎ 719/378–2312), with sand dunes almost 700 ft high, has a year-round campground and a nature trail. **Mesa Verde National Park** (⊠ U.S. 160, 8 mi east of Cortez; Mesa Verde National Park 81330, ☎ 970/529–4465) has well-preserved cliff dwellings of the ancient Anasazi Indians. **Rocky Mountain National Park** (⊠ Hwy. 36, Estes Park 80517, ☎ 970/586–1206) presents a picture-book vision of craggy mountains, abundant wildlife, and deep-blue mountain lakes in more than 250,000 acres, with camping, hiking, lodging, and scenic drives.

State Parks
The state's 40 parks provide opportunities to hike, fish, sail, and take in idyllic views. Contact the **Colorado Division of Parks** (⊠ Dept. of Natural Resources, 1313 Sherman St., Denver 80203, ☎ 303/866–3437) for information.

DENVER

In Denver winter weather reports frequently begin with skiing conditions. After the lifts shut down for the summer, weekends are often occupied with trips to the mountains to hike, camp, and fish. The sharp-edged skyscrapers, clean streets, and dozens of well-used parks evoke the image of a young, progressive city, but much of what made Denver what it is lies in its western past. Areas like LoDo, a historic part of lower downtown, buzz with jazz clubs, restaurants, and art galleries housed in century-old buildings.

Visitor Information

Denver Metro Convention and Visitors Bureau (⊠ 225 W. Colfax Ave., 80202, ☎ 303/892–1112).

Arriving and Departing

By Bus
Greyhound Lines (✉ 1055 19th St., ☎ 800/231–2222).

By Car
I–70 (east–west) and I–25 (north–south) intersect near downtown.

By Plane
Denver International Airport (☎ 303/342–2000), 23 mi from downtown Denver, is served by most major carriers. Cab fare downtown should average about $40; **RTD,** the local bus service (☞ Getting Around Denver, *below*), can also get you there. The **Airporter** (☎ 303/333–5833) provides express bus service from the airport to locations in Denver and surrounding areas; a trip to downtown Denver costs $20–$25. Reservations are essential.

By Train
Amtrak (☎ 800/872–7245) serves **Union Station** (✉ 17th St. at Wynkoop St.).

Getting Around Denver

By Car
Driving in Denver is not difficult, and finding a spot in a parking lot is usually easy. Traffic on I–25 and I–70 can be congested during rush hours.

By Public Transportation
A free shuttle bus operates frequently down the length of the 16th Street Mall. The region's public **bus** service, **RTD** (☎ 303/299–6000 or 303/299–6700), has routes throughout Denver and to outlying towns, such as Boulder, Longmont, and Nederland. RTD's **light-rail system** serves the downtown and southwestern regions. Buy bus and rail tokens ($1) at grocery stores or on the bus; rail tokens are also available from machines in the train stations.

By Taxi
Yellow Cab (☎ 303/777–7777) and **Metro Taxi** (☎ 303/333–3333) are two 24-hour taxi services.

Orientation Tours

Gray Line (☎ 303/289–2841) conducts a 2½-hour city tour, a mountain-parks tour, and a mountain-casino tour.

Exploring Denver

At the **Civic Center** is a three-block park, lawns, gardens, and Greek amphitheater. The backdrop for the Civic Center is the **state capitol** (✉ 1475 Sherman St., ☎ 303/866–2604). As a reminder of the state's mining heritage, the dome of the 1886 building is periodically recovered with hammered gold leaf. The balcony affords a panoramic view of the Rockies. The capitol is closed weekends. Just off the Civic Center is the **Colorado History Museum** (✉ 1300 Broadway, ☎ 303/866–3682), with Colorado and western memorabilia and dioramas, plus ★ special exhibits. The **Denver Art Museum** (✉ 100 W. 14th Ave., ☎ 303/640–2793) has an excellent collection of Native American art, as well as superlative holdings in pre-Columbian and Spanish colonial art. The museum is closed Monday. Connected to the art museum by an underground walkway is the new **Denver Public Library** (✉ 10 W. 14th Ave., ☎ 303/640–6200). This Michael Graves–designed building

Denver

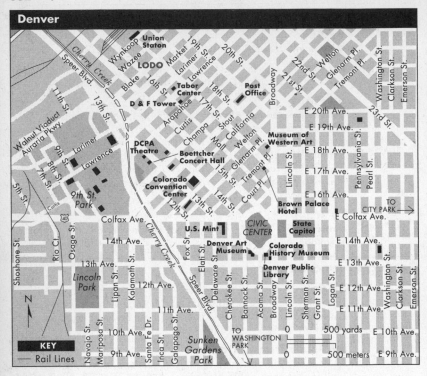

houses a world-renowned collection of books, photographs, and newspapers that chronicle the American West.

Near the Civic Center is the **Denver Mint** (officially known as the United States Mint), where more than 10 billion coins are stamped yearly. Tours are offered. ⊠ *W. Colfax Ave. and Cherokee St.,* ☏ *303/844–3582. Closed weekends.*

Free shuttle buses are the only vehicles allowed on the **16th Street Mall,** which has shade trees, outdoor cafés, historic buildings, and shopping. Just off 17th Street is the **Museum of Western Art** (⊠ 1727 Tremont Pl., ☏ 303/296–1880). Once a frontier-era bordello, it now showcases the work of artists who helped define the western myth: Frederic Remington, Albert Bierstadt, and Charles Russell. Be sure to peek inside

★ the **Brown Palace** (⊠ 321 17th St., ☏ 303/297–3111), built in 1892 and still proud of her antique charms.

The 330-ft **D&F Tower** (⊠ 16th St. at Arapahoe St.) emulates the campanile of St. Mark's Cathedral in Venice. At Curtis and 14th streets is the **Denver Center for the Performing Arts,** a space-age complex of theaters and a symphony hall.

Denver's most charming shopping area is historic **Larimer Square** (⊠ Larimer and 15th Sts.), which showcases some of the city's oldest retail buildings and finest specialty shops. Farther into **LoDo,** north of Larimer Square between Speer Boulevard and Larimer Street, lies an equally historic but quirkier area filled with art galleries, nightclubs, brew pubs, and restaurants.

East of downtown, the **Molly Brown House Museum** (⊠ 1340 Pennsylvania St., ☏ 303/832–4092), a Victorian confection, celebrates the life and times of the scandalous Ms. Brown, whose story was made into the film *The Unsinkable Molly Brown.*

Northeast of downtown, the popular **Denver Zoo** (⊠ E. 23rd St. between York St. and Colorado Blvd., ☎ 303/331–4110), in City Park, has a nursery for baby animals and the Primate Panorama, where visitors can view 29 primate species in simulated natural habitats.

★ Also in City Park is the **Denver Museum of Natural History** (⊠ 2001 Colorado Blvd., ☎ 303/322–7009), with traditional collections and hands-on exhibits, plus a planetarium and an IMAX theater. In the Prehistoric Journey exhibit visitors walk through the seven stages of the earth's development.

Parks and Gardens

Denver has one of the largest city park systems (☎ 303/698–4900 for park headquarters office) in the country, with more than 20,000 acres. **City Park** has lakes, tennis, golf, museums, and the Denver Zoo (☞ Exploring Denver, *above*). Flower gardens and lakes abound in **Washington Park,** which is east of Downing Street between Virginia and Louisiana avenues; this is where young Denver goes to run, rollerblade, bike, play volleyball and tennis, and hang out.

★ On the east side of the city are the **Denver Botanic Gardens** (⊠ 1005 York St., ☎ 303/331–4000). The conservatory houses a rain forest; outside are a Japanese garden, an alpine rock garden with a brilliant display of wildflowers in spring, and other horticulture displays. **Platte River Greenway** is a 20-mi biking, jogging, and rollerblading path that follows Cherry Creek and the Platte River, much of it through downtown Denver.

What to See and Do with Children

At the **Denver Children's Museum** (⊠ 2121 Crescent Dr., ☎ 303/433–7444) interactive exhibits include a working TV station and an outdoor ski hill.

Dining

Beef, buffalo, and burritos have an honored spot in Denver's culinary history, but more sophisticated fare—from Vietnamese to casual French—can be found, too. Cruise LoDo or 17th Avenue east for inventive kitchens, and check out Federal Street for cheap ethnic eats. For price ranges *see* Chart 1 (A) *in* On the Road with Fodor's.

$$$$ ✕ **Cliff Young's.** The maroon chairs, dark banquettes, crisp white
★ napery, and dancing to piano and violin music make this elegant Art Deco restaurant seem frozen in the 1950s. The menu relies on American fare such as free-range veal and Colorado rack of lamb. ⊠ 700 E. 17th Ave., ☎ 303/831–8900. *Jacket required. Reservations essential. AE, D, DC, MC, V. No lunch.*

$$$ ✕ **Buckhorn Exchange.** The neighborhood has deteriorated, but this Denver landmark with handsome men's-club decor still packs 'em in to eat elk, buffalo, and beef and gawk at the deer and other trophies mounted on the walls. ⊠ 1000 Osage St., ☎ 303/534–9505. *AE, D, DC, MC, V. No lunch weekends.*

$$$ ✕ **Strings.** This airy spot with an open kitchen is a preferred hangout
★ for Denver's movers and shakers, as well as visiting celebs, whose autographs are mounted. The food is casual-contemporary; one specialty is spaghetti with caviar and asparagus in champagne cream sauce. ⊠ 1700 Humboldt St., ☎ 303/831–7310. *Reservations essential. AE, D, DC, MC, V. No lunch Sun.*

$$$ ✕ **Zenith American Grill.** Creative variations on the southwestern
★ theme here include smoked sweet-corn soup with barbecued shrimp
and roasted loin of ostrich with blue-corn tamales. The attractive
space has a cool, high-tech look. ⊠ *1750 Lawrence St.,* ☎ *303/820–
2800. Reservations essential. AE, D, DC, MC, V. No lunch weekends.*

$$–$$$ ✕ **La Coupole.** Brass railings, black-leather banquettes and exposed-
brick walls team up with a heavenly coq au vin, bouillabaisse, and *tarte
Tatin* (apple upside-down tart) to transport happy diners to the Left
Bank. ⊠ *2191 Arapahoe St.,* ☎ *303/297–2288. AE, D, DC, MC, V.
Closed Mon.*

$$–$$$ ✕ **Rattlesnake Grill.** This hot spot, created by renowned restaurateur
★ Jimmy Schmidt, has soft track lighting and huge picture windows
overlooking the Cherry Creek Mall. The American menu has creative
southwestern and Italian touches. ⊠ *3000 1st Ave.,* ☎ *303/377–
8000. Reservations essential. AE, MC, V.*

$$ ✕ **Barolo Grill.** This restaurant looks like a chichi farmhouse—dried
flowers in brass urns, straw baskets, and hand-painted porcelain.
Choose from wild boar stewed with apricots; risotto croquettes fla-
vored with minced shrimp; or smoked-salmon pizza. ⊠ *3030 E. 6th
Ave.,* ☎ *303/393–1040. Reservations essential. AE, MC, V. Closed
Sun.–Mon. No lunch.*

$$ ✕ **Denver Chophouse & Brewery.** The best of the many LoDo brew
pubs and restaurants surrounding the ballpark is housed in the old Union
Pacific Railroad warehouse. The food is basic American fare and
plenty of it: steak, seafood, and chicken served with hot cornbread and
honey-butter and "bottomless" salad tossed at the table. ⊠ *1735 19th
St.,* ☎ *303/296–0800. AE, DC, MC, V.*

$ ✕ **Bluebonnet Café and Lounge.** The café's location in a fairly seedy
neighborhood southeast of downtown doesn't stop the crowds from
lining up early. The western decor, the Naugahyde, and the jukebox
set an upbeat mood for killer margaritas and fine burritos. ⊠ *457 S.
Broadway,* ☎ *303/778–0147. Reservations not accepted. MC, V.*

$ ✕ **The Fort.** This adobe structure, complete with flickering *luminarias*
★ and a piñon bonfire in the courtyard, is a perfect replica of Bent's Fort,
a Colorado fur trade center. Buffalo meat and game are the special-
ties; the elk with huckleberry sauce and mesquite-grilled guinea hen
are especially good. Costumed characters from the fur trade wander
the restaurant, playing the mandolin and telling tall tales. ⊠ *U.S. 285
and Hwy. 8,* ☎ *303/697–4771. AE, D, DC, MC, V.*

$ ✕ **T-WA Inn.** This South Asian hole-in-the-wall serves great food, in-
cluding delicate Vietnamese spring rolls and daily specials. ⊠ *555 S.
Federal Blvd.,* ☎ *303/922–4584. AE, MC, V.*

$ ✕ **Wynkoop Brewing Company.** The beer is brewed on the premises,
★ and the pub fare is hearty. Try the shepherd's pie or grilled marlin sand-
wich; then check out the pool hall and cabaret for a full night's en-
tertainment. ⊠ *1634 18th St.,* ☎ *303/297–2700. Reservations not
accepted. AE, D, DC, MC, V.*

Lodging

Denver's lodging choices range from the stately Brown Palace to the
YMCA, with bed-and-breakfasts and other options in between. **Bed
& Breakfast Innkeepers of Colorado** (⊠ Box 38416, Dept. S-95, Col-
orado Springs, 80937-8416, ☎ 800/265–7696) handles B&Bs through-
out the state. **Hostelling International–Rocky Mountain Council** (⊠
Box 2370, Boulder 80306, ☎ 303/442–1166) provides information
about hostels in 10 Colorado locations. For price ranges *see* Chart 2
(A) *in* On the Road with Fodor's.

$$$$ ⊞ **Brown Palace Hotel.** This downtown grande-dame hotel has housed
★ everyone from President Eisenhower to the Beatles. The eight-story lobby
is topped by a glorious stained-glass ceiling. Rooms are decorated in
Victorian style. ⊠ *321 17th St., 80202,* ☎ *303/297–3111 or 800/321–
2599,* 𝔽𝔸𝕏 *303/293–9204. 230 rooms. 4 restaurants, 2 bars, concierge,
parking (fee). AE, D, DC, MC, V.*

$$$–$$$$ ⊞ **Westin Tabor Center.** Oversize rooms at this high-rise overlooking
the 16th Street Mall are done in gray and taupe and have paisley du-
vets. The gourmet restaurant Augusta boasts smashing views and an
equally sensational $50 prix-fixe dinner. ⊠ *1672 Lawrence St., 80202,*
☎ *303/572–9100,* 𝔽𝔸𝕏 *303/572–7288. 420 rooms. 2 restaurants,
lounge, pool, health club, racquetball, shops. AE, D, DC, MC, V.*

$$$ ⊞ **Loews Giorgio.** The 12-story steel-and-black glass facade conceals
★ the unexpected and delightful Italian baroque motif within. Rooms are
spacious and elegant, with Continental touches. It's halfway between
downtown and the Denver Tech Center, which is a residential and shopping outpost. ⊠ *4150 E. Mississippi Ave.,* ☎ *303/782–9300 or 800/
345–9172,* 𝔽𝔸𝕏 *303/758–6542. 219 rooms. Restaurant, bar, airport shuttle. AE, D, DC, MC, V.*

$$$ ⊞ **Oxford.** The city's most charming small hotel was a Denver fixture
★ in the Victorian era. Guest rooms are exquisitely furnished with an-
tiques and reproductions. ⊠ *1600 17th St., 80202,* ☎ *303/628–5400
or 800/228–5838,* 𝔽𝔸𝕏 *303/628–5413. 81 rooms. Restaurant, 2 bars,
health club, parking (fee). AE, D, DC, MC, V.*

$$–$$$ ⊞ **Adam's Mark.** In the mid-1990s the I. M. Pei–designed Radisson
and the old May D&F Department Store across the street from it were
converted into a large, convention-oriented property. The location, at
one end of the 16th Street Mall, is ideal. ⊠ *1550 Court Place, 80202,*
☎ *303/893–3333 or 800/444–2326,* 𝔽𝔸𝕏 *303/623–0303. 1,125 rooms.
3 restaurants, 3 bars, pool, beauty salon, sauna, steam room, exercise
room, laundry service and dry cleaning, concierge, business center, con-
vention center. AE, D, DC, MC, V.*

$$–$$$ ⊞ **Castle Marne.** This B&B with balconies, a four-story turret, and in-
tricate stone- and woodwork is east of downtown near several fine restau-
rants. Rooms are decorated with antiques and art. ⊠ *1572 Race St.,
80206,* ☎ *303/331–0621 or 800/926–2763,* 𝔽𝔸𝕏 *303/331–0623. 9
rooms. Recreation room, free parking. AE, MC, V.*

$$ ⊞ **Queen Anne Inn.** North of downtown in a reclaimed historic area,
★ this B&B (composed of two adjacent Victorian houses) makes a ro-
mantic getaway, with fresh flowers and antiques. An afternoon Col-
orado-wine tasting is free. ⊠ *2147 Tremont Pl., 80205,* ☎ *303/
296–6666 or 800/432–4667,* 𝔽𝔸𝕏 *303/296–2151. 14 rooms. Full
breakfast. AE, D, DC, MC, V.*

$ ⊞ **Comfort Inn/Downtown.** The advantages to this hotel are its rea-
sonable rates and its location, right across from—and connected to—
the Brown Palace in the heart of downtown. Rooms higher up have
panoramic views. ⊠ *401 17th St., 80202,* ☎ *303/296–0400 or 800/
221–2222,* 𝔽𝔸𝕏 *303/297–0774. 229 rooms. Restaurant, bar, parking
(fee). AE, D, DC, MC, V.*

$ ⊞ **Holiday Chalet.** This turn-of-the-century house turned hotel is in the
heart of Capitol Hill, immediately east of downtown. It's full of charm,
with stained-glass windows and homey touches, and each room has a
full kitchen. ⊠ *1820 E. Colfax St., 80218,* ☎ *303/321–9975 or 800/
626–4497,* 𝔽𝔸𝕏 *303/377–6556. 10 rooms. Continental breakfast. AE,
D, DC, MC, V.*

Nightlife and the Arts

Friday's *Denver Post* and *Rocky Mountain News* list entertainment events, as does the weekly *Westword*. **TicketMan** (☎ 303/430–1111) sells tickets to major events. The **Ticket Bus** (✉ 16th St. Mall at Curtis St.) is open from 10 to 6 weekdays and sells half-price tickets the day of performance.

Nightlife

Downtown and **LoDo** host most of Denver's nightlife. Downtown offers more mainstream entertainment, while LoDo is home to rock clubs and small theaters. Remember that Denver's altitude makes you react more quickly to alcohol.

COMEDY

Comedy Works (✉ 1226 15th St., ☎ 303/595–3637) features local and nationally known stand-up comics.

COUNTRY AND WESTERN

The **Grizzly Rose** (✉ I–25 Exit 215, ☎ 303/295–1330), with its miles of dance floor, hosts national bands.

JAZZ

El Chapultepec (✉ 20th St. at Market St., ☎ 303/295–9126) is a smoky dive where visiting jazz musicians often jam after hours.

ROCK

Herman's Hideaway (✉ 1578 S. Broadway, ☎ 303/777–5840) is a favorite for both hot local bands and national acts; there's some blues and reggae, too. **Rock Island** (✉ Wazee and 15th Sts., ☎ 303/572–7625) caters to the young, restless, and hip. The **Mercury Café** (✉ 2199 California St., ☎ 303/294–9281) triples as a health-food restaurant, fringe theater, and rock club specializing in progressive and newer-wave music. The **I-Beam** (✉ 1427 Larmier St., ☎ 303/534–2326) is LoDo's only dance club, with a mix of DJs and live music and the occasional disco night.

The Arts

The modern **Denver Center for the Performing Arts** (✉ 14th and Curtis Sts., ☎ 303/893–3272) houses most of the city's large concert halls and theaters.

DANCE

The **Colorado Ballet** (☎ 303/837–8888), in the performing arts center, specializes in the classics.

MUSIC

The **Colorado Symphony Orchestra** (✉ 13th and Curtis Sts., ☎ 303/986–8742) performs at Boettcher Concert Hall.

THEATER

The **Denver Center Theater Company** (☎ 303/893–4100) presents fine repertory theater. **Robert Garner Attractions** (☎ 303/893–4100) brings Broadway-caliber plays to the city.

Spectator Sports

Baseball: Colorado Rockies (✉ Coors Stadium, 22nd and Wazee Sts., downtown, ☎ 303/762–5437).

Basketball: Denver Nuggets (✉ McNichols Sports Arena, just west of downtown across I–25, ☎ 303/893–3865).

Football: Denver Broncos (✉ Mile High Stadium, 1900 Eliot St., ☎ 303/433–7466).

Hockey: **Colorado Avalanche** (⊠ McNichols Arena, just west of downtown across I–25, ☎ 303/893–6700).

Shopping

Shopping Districts
The Cherry Creek shopping district, 2 mi from downtown, is Denver's best. On one side of 1st Avenue at Milwaukee Street is the **Cherry Creek Shopping Mall,** a granite-and-glass behemoth containing national retailers. On the other side is **Cherry Creek North,** with art galleries and specialty shops. On the **16th Street Mall** are Tabor Center and other large downtown retailers. **South Broadway** between 1st Avenue and Evans Street has blocks of antiques stores; prices are sometimes lower than elsewhere. **LoDo** has the trendiest galleries.

Books
Tattered Cover (⊠ 1st Ave. at Milwaukee St., ☎ 303/322–7727) has four floors of books (more than 400,000 titles), afternoon lectures and musical presentations, and a knowledgeable staff.

Sporting Goods
Gart Brothers Sports Castle (⊠ 1000 Broadway, ☎ 303/861–1122) is a multistory shrine to the Colorado outdoors.

Western Wear
Denver Buffalo Company Trading Post (⊠ 1109 Lincoln St., ☎ 303/832–0884) has top-of-the-line western clothing and souvenirs. **Miller Stockman** (⊠ 16th St. Mall, at California St., ☎ 303/825–5339) is an old-line Denver retailer.

Side Trip to Boulder

Arriving and Departing
From Denver take I–25 north to the Boulder Turnpike (Highway 36). Denver's RTD buses make the 27-mi commute regularly.

What to See and Do
The home of the University of Colorado, **Boulder** is a quintessential college town, but it's also the headquarters of a hard-core group of professional athletes who live to bike and run. The atmosphere is peaceful, new age, and cultural, with a gorgeous backdrop of mountains. One of the city's main attractions is the **Pearl Street Mall,** a see-and-be-seen pedestrian street with benches, grassy spots, great shopping, and outdoor cafés. Weekdays 11–2, the **Celestial Seasonings Plant** (⊠ 4600 Sleepytime Dr., ☎ 303/581–1223) conducts free tours; you'll see raw tea ingredients (the Mint Room is off-limits because of its potent scent), then watch them being blended. Boulder celebrates classical music each summer at its **Colorado Music Festival** (⊠ Chautauqua Park, ☎ 303/449–1397).

Side Trip to Central City and Blackhawk

Arriving and Departing
From I–70 take Highway 58 to Golden, then Highway 6 up Clear Creek Canyon, and finally Highway 119 northwest 1 mi past Blackhawk to Central City. The town is 35 mi from Denver.

What to See and Do
The abandoned mines on the scenic road that leads to these historic towns testify to the silver- and gold-mining heritage of the area. Now that low-stakes gambling has arrived, the jingle of slot machines is constant. The narrow, winding streets are edged with brick storefronts from

the last century. The **Central City Opera House** (☎ 303/292–6700), a small Victorian jewel, stages opera in summer.

Side Trip to Georgetown

Arriving and Departing
Take I–70 west to the Georgetown exit, 46 mi from Denver.

What to See and Do
With its multitude of gingerbread Victorian houses on quiet streets, Georgetown provides a tantalizing glimpse of Colorado's heady mining past. This National Historic District has restaurants, small shops, and the **Georgetown Loop Railroad** (☎ 303/569–2403), a 3-mi narrow-gauge line that travels into the mountains and back.

Side Trip to Golden

Arriving and Departing
From I–70 take Highway 58 to Golden, 12 mi west of Denver.

What to See and Do
Coors (⊠ 13th and Ford Sts., ☎ 303/277–2337) operates the world's largest brewery; daily tours cover the basics of brewing beer and end with a trip to the tasting rooms. The drive up Lookout Mountain to the **Buffalo Bill Grave and Museum** (⊠ Rte. 5 off I–70 Exit 256, or 19th Ave. out of Golden, ☎ 303/526–0747) affords a panoramic view of Denver. Contrary to popular belief, Bill Cody never expressed a burning desire to be buried here: The *Denver Post* bought the corpse from Bill's sister and bribed her to concoct a teary story about his dying wish. Apparently, rival towns were so outraged that the National Guard had to be called in to protect the grave from robbers.

COLORADO SPRINGS AND ENVIRONS

At the center of the state, 65 mi south of Denver, is Colorado Springs, Colorado's second-largest city. In addition to its natural wonders such as Pike's Peak, the region has such man-made attractions as the Air Force Academy and the Broadmoor resort.

Visitor Information

Colorado Springs: Convention and Visitors Bureau (⊠ 104 S. Cascade Ave., 80903, ☎ 719/635–7506 or 800/368–4748).

Arriving and Departing

By Bus
Greyhound Lines (⊠ 120 S. Weber St., ☎ 800/231–2222) serves national routes and **Springs Transit Management** (⊠ 127 E. Kiowa St., ☎ 719/475–9733) local ones.

By Car
From Denver take I–25 south.

By Plane
Colorado Springs Airport (⊠ 7770 Drennan Rd., ☎ 719/550–1900), 20 mi from the city, is served by domestic airlines.

Exploring Colorado Springs and Environs

A mix of attractions surrounding **Colorado Springs** complements the city's Victorian houses and wide-tree-lined streets. The **U.S. Olympic Center** (⊠ 1 Olympic Plaza, ☎ 719/578–4500) conducts tours of the

Central Colorado

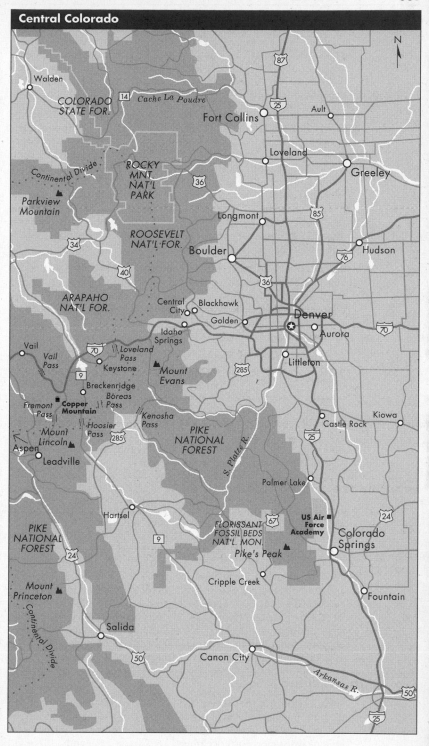

sprawling complex where hundreds of athletes train. The **Broadmoor** (⌧ 1 Lake Ave.) is a rambling ensemble of pink-stucco Italian Renaissance−style hotel buildings combined with gardens and a picture-perfect lake skimmed by black swans. The **Carriage House Museum** (⌧ Lake Circle, ☎ 719/634−7711, ext. 5353), on the Broadmoor's grounds, displays an old stagecoach, vintage cars, and carriages used at presidential inaugurals.

Two routes—a cog railway (⌧ 515 Ruxton Ave., Manitou Springs, ☎ 719/685−5401) and a toll road (10 mi west on Highway 24, left at marked exit at Cascade)—lead to breathtaking views atop **Pike's Peak,** the summit Zebulon Pike claimed could never be scaled. The railway is $23 round-trip; the toll road, $6. The **Air Force Academy** (⌧ 10 mi north on I−25, Exits 156B and 150B, ☎ 719/333−2025) has a futuristic **Cadet Chapel,** with 17 spires, each rising 150 ft. The academy gives guided tours in summer. The **Garden of the Gods** (⌧ Off Ridge Rd., north of U.S. 24, ☎ 719/578−6939) has picnic spots and trails through 1,350 acres of weird, windswept red-rock formations and unusual plant life.

Cripple Creek—24 mi west from Colorado Springs to Divide, then 20 mi south on Highway 67—was once known for vast deposits of gold and has gone upscale with the legalization of low-stakes gambling. The **Cripple Creek and Victor Narrow Gauge Railroad** (☎ 719/689−2640), on the north end of town, runs a 4-mi route (April−October) past old mines and older mountains.

Southwest of Colorado Springs on U.S. 50 is **Cañon City,** gateway to one of the Rockies' most powerful sights. The 1,053-ft-deep **Royal Gorge** (☎ 719/275−7507), often called the Grand Canyon of Colorado, was carved by the Arkansas River more than 3 million years ago. It's spanned by the world's highest **suspension bridge.** Other activities include riding the aerial tram (2,200 ft long and 1,178 ft above the canyon floor) and traveling aboard the **Scenic Railway,** the world's steepest incline rail. A theater presents a 25-minute multimedia show and outdoor musical entertainment in the summer.

What to See and Do with Children

The **Cheyenne Mountain Zoo** (⌧ 4250 Cheyenne Mountain Zoo Rd., ☎ 719/633−9925), set on a mountainside, is a haven for more than 100 endangered species and other animals. Films such as *True Grit* and *Cat Ballou* were shot in **Buckskin Joe Park and Railway** (⌧ Off Hwy. 50, Cañon City, ☎ 719/275−5149), which vividly evokes the Old West. Children love the horse-drawn trolley rides, the horseback rides, and gold-panning. Adults enjoy the live entertainment in the Crystal Palace and Saloon. At the **North Pole and Santa's Workshop** (⌧ Hwy. 24W, Exit 141, ☎ 719/684−9432), kids can feed deer, ride a Ferris wheel and a carousel, try their luck in an arcade, visit Santa at the height of summer, and stuff themselves in the Candy Kitchen, the Sugar Plum Terrace, or an old-fashioned ice cream parlor.

Dining and Lodging

Steak and other basic western foods, along with Mexican dishes, are the most popular options hereabouts. The Colorado Springs Convention and Visitors Bureau (☞ Visitor Information, *above*) provides lodging assistance. For price ranges *see* Charts 1 (B) and 2 (B) *in* On the Road with Fodor's.

Colorado Springs

$$–$$$ × **Corbett's.** The halogen lamps and modern art here are matched by
★ an equally contemporary menu that's light and health conscious. One
good appetizer is house-smoked trout in tangy horseradish sauce set
off by sweet pears and chèvre. ⊠ *817 W. Colorado Ave.,* ☎ *719/471–
0004. Reservations essential. AE, D, DC, MC, V. Closed Sun. No lunch
weekends and fall–spring.*

$–$$ × **El Tesoro.** This historic building doubles as a restaurant and art gallery;
★ exposed brick walls, colorful rugs, and *ristras* (strings) of chili complement the northern New Mexican food, a savory blend of Native American, Spanish, and Anglo influences. The *posole* (hominy with pork and
red chili), green chili, and originals like mango quesadillas are heavenly. ⊠ *10 N. Sierra Madre St.,* ☎ *719/471–0106. D, MC, V. Closed
Sun. No lunch Sat., no dinner Mon.*

$$$–$$$$ ×🏨 **The Broadmoor.** This resort is a Colorado legend. The 1918 build-
★ ings hold plush, traditional rooms; the restaurants serve everything from
formal French to Sunday brunch. The European spa provides such treat-
ments as the Broadmoor Falls water massage, which uses 17 jets of
water. The Carriage House Museum displays antique vehicles. ⊠ *1 Lake
Ave., 80901,* ☎ *719/634–7711 or 800/634–7711,* 🖷 *719/577–5779.
700 rooms. 9 restaurants, 3 bars, 3 pools, beauty salon, spa, 3 golf
courses, 12 tennis courts, health club, horseback riding, squash, boat-
ing, mountain bikes, shops, cinema, children's programs, car rental.
AE, D, DC, MC, V.*

$$ 🏨 **Hearthstone Inn.** Rooms at this B&B are decorated with antiques
★ and stylish country prints. Breakfast might include corn pancakes with
maple syrup and fruit compote. ⊠ *506 N. Cascade Ave., 80903,* ☎ *719/
473–4413 or 800/521–1885. 23 rooms. AE, MC, V.*

Manitou Springs

$$$ × **Briarhurst Manor.** An 1878 stone mansion provides the setting for
chef Sigi Krauss's offerings. Dishes such as chateaubriand are pre-
pared with Colorado ingredients and a European touch. ⊠ *404 Man-
itou Ave.,* ☎ *719/685–1864. AE, D, DC, MC, V. Closed Sun. and 1st
2 wks of Jan. No lunch.*

Motels

🏨 **Le Baron Hotel** (⊠ 314 W. Bijou, Colorado Springs 80905, ☎ 719/
471–8680 or 800/477–8610, 🖷 719/471–0894), 206 rooms, restau-
rant, lounge, pool, exercise room; *$$.* 🏨 **Palmer House/Best Western**
(⊠ I–25 near Exit 145, 3010 North Chestnut St., Colorado Springs
80907, ☎ 719/636–5201 or 800/223–9127, 🖷 719/636–3108), 150
rooms, restaurant, lounge, pool; *$$.*

Outdoor Activities and Sports

Biking

Pike National Forest (⊠ Ranger District Office, 601 S. Weber St., Col-
orado Springs 80903, ☎ 719/636–1602) has mountain-bike trails.

Fishing

Lovers of trout-stream fishing flock to the **South Platte** (⊠ Rte. 67, 28
mi north of Woodland Park). **Elevenmile Reservoir** (⊠ Hwy. 24W to
town of Lake George) has rainbow trout, kokanee salmon, and pike.

Golf

The **Broadmoor** (⊠ 1 Lake Ave., ☎ 719/634–7711) has three 18-hole
courses.

Hiking and Backpacking
Check the **Convention and Visitors Bureau** (☞ Visitor Information, *above*). Some of the best trails are in **Pike National Forest** (☞ Biking, *above*).

Horseback Riding
Academy Riding Stables (✉ 4 El Paso Blvd., ☎ 719/633–5667) rents horses for guided tours through Garden of the Gods park (☞ Exploring Colorado Springs and Environs, *above*). Reservations are essential.

NORTHWESTERN COLORADO

As you climb west from Denver, the mountains rear up, pine forests line the road, and the legendary Colorado of powder skiing, alpine scenery, and the great outdoors begins. As once-primitive mining towns have attracted skiers and scenery buffs, sophisticated dining and lodging have followed.

Visitor Information

Aspen Chamber Resort Association (✉ 328 E. Hyman Ave., 81611, ☎ 970/925–5656; ✉ 425 Rio Grande Pl., 81611, ☎ 970/925–1940). **Glenwood Springs Chamber Resort Association** (✉ 1102 Grand Ave., 80601, ☎ 970/945–6589 or 800/221–0098). **Steamboat Springs Chamber Resort Association** (✉ 1201 Lincoln Ave., ☎ 970/879–0880 or 800/922–2722). **Summit County Chamber of Commerce** (✉ Main St., Frisco 80443, ☎ 800/530–3099). **Vail Valley Tourism and Convention Bureau** (✉ 100 E. Meadow Dr., 81658, ☎ 970/476–1000).

Arriving and Departing

By Bus
Greyhound Lines (☎ 800/231–2222).

By Car
I–70 is the main route to the Summit County resorts, Vail, and Glenwood Springs. From Glenwood Springs, Highway 82 heads to Aspen. Highway 36 leads to Rocky Mountain National Park and Estes Park; Highway 40 heads to Steamboat Springs.

By Plane
Aspen Airport (☎ 970/920–5385) is 7 mi east of town; most flights connect from Denver. **Steamboat Springs Airport** (☎ 970/879–1204) is 3 mi northwest of town. Vail Valley is served by the **Eagle County Airport** (☎ 970/524–9490), 35 mi west of Vail. All are served by regional and national airlines, but Vail has scheduled service only during ski season.

By Train
Amtrak (☎ 800/872–7245) stops in Glenwood Springs, Granby, and Winter Park.

Exploring Northwestern Colorado

Estes Park is the northern gateway to **Rocky Mountain National Park** (☞ National and State Parks, *above*), where **Trail Ridge Road** (closed in winter) provides a spectacular ride on one of the highest auto routes in the world. On the west side of Estes Park is **Grand Lake,** the largest natural lake in Colorado, with the world's highest yacht club. The turn-of-the-century town of the same name is also a snowmobiling mecca in winter.

The closest resort skiing from Denver is off I–70 at **Winter Park,** a family-oriented establishment particularly good for intermediate skiers. It is popular with Denverites, who often travel there via the Ski Train (☎ 303/296–4754) on weekends. The mountains of **Summit County,** 70 mi from Denver off I–70, attract climbers, hikers, and skiers. **Copper Mountain,** the first Club Med in North America, has terrain for most abilities, with an emphasis on intermediate and advanced skiers. **Keystone Resort** encompasses the peaks of **Keystone,** for beginning and intermediate skiers, and **A-Basin,** the **Outback,** and **North Peak,** for serious skiers. **Breckenridge** is an old mining town transformed into a resort. For a change from resort atmosphere and prices, head to **Lake Dillon,** a large reservoir popular with boaters. Up U.S. 40 from I–70, **Steamboat Springs** has great, uncrowded skiing for all abilities and a real western feel.

West of Summit County is **Vail,** celebrated home of the largest ski mountain in North America. Constructed from the ground up to look like a European ski village, the town is huge, varied in its attractions, and pricey. It tends to be more conservative and family oriented than Aspen. **Beaver Creek** was created for those seeking an even more exclusive atmosphere than Vail's; everything here lives up to its billing, from the billeting to the bill of fare. The ski area is geared to intermediate and advanced skiers.

At the turnoff for Aspen on I–70 is **Glenwood Springs,** where the main attraction besides the scenery is the **Yampah Hot Springs** (✉ Pine St., ☎ 970/945–0667), the world's largest outdoor mineral hot springs.

You know all about **Aspen:** the glitz, the rich, the actors and moguls who jam this tiny town during the ski season. It's expensive—and worth it if your passions are people-watching and great skiing. Many prefer the other seasons, though, for the beauty of the setting or the summer **Aspen Music Festival** (☎ 970/925–3254).

Within Aspen's orbit are several **ski areas,** each geared to a different level of ability. Skiers can get a multiday ticket to all four mountains: **Buttermilk,** serving primarily beginners and low-intermediate skiers; **Aspen Highlands,** for intermediate skiers, with some of the highest vertical drops and best views; **Snowmass,** a perfect intermediate hill; and for experts, **Aspen Mountain,** which hosts international competitions.

What to See and Do with Children

Most ski resorts have special programs and activities for children, especially **Winter Park, Keystone, Beaver Creek,** and **Vail.** In summer **Breckenridge** and **Winter Park** open alpine slides.

Dining and Lodging

The celebrity atmosphere of towns like Aspen and Vail attracts celebrity chefs, and hot restaurants come and go as quickly as they do in New York. If you don't want to spend the money to eat with the stars, consider heading to nearby towns, where the atmosphere—and the prices—is more down-home western. The ski resorts make getting accommodations as easy as possible. Calling the following numbers can hook you up with many different kinds lodgings: Aspen (☎ 800/262–7736), Beaver Creek (☎ 800/622–3131), Breckenridge (☎ 800/221–1091), Copper Mountain (☎ 800/458–8386), Keystone (☎ 800/222–0188), Steamboat Springs (☎ 800/922–2722), Vail (☎ 800/525–3875), and Winter Park (☎ 800/729–5813). Condos are the most common and, because they have kitchens, can help cut down on food expenses. For price ranges *see* Charts 1 (A) and 2 (A) *in* On the Road with Fodor's.

Aspen

$$$$ ✕ **Renaissance.** In this abstract rendition of a sultan's tent, owner-chef Charles Dale transforms ordinary ingredients into culinary gold. Opt for his tasting menu—six courses matched with the appropriate glass of wine. Upstairs, the R Bistro presents a sampling of the kitchen's splendors at down-to-earth prices. ✉ *304 E. Hopkins St., Aspen,* ☎ *970/925–2402. Reservations essential. AE, D, DC, MC, V. No lunch.*

$$$–$$$$ ✕ **Syzygy.** Upstairs and unmarked, this restaurant has a sleek mod-
★ ern design and sophisticated food that blends international flavors. ✉ *520 E. Hyman,* ☎ *970/925–3700. Reservations essential. AE, D, DC, MC, V. No lunch.*

$$–$$$ ✕ **Ajax Tavern.** This is a bright, bustling restaurant with mahogany paneling, leather banquettes, and an open kitchen. Nick Morfogen's healthful dishes take advantage of the region's bountiful produce whenever possible and are reasonably priced. ✉ *685 E. Durant Ave.,* ☎ *970/920–9333. Reservations essential. AE, D, DC, MC, V.*

$$$–$$$$ 🏨 **Hotel Jerome.** One of the state's truly grand hotels since 1889 has
★ sumptuous public areas. Rooms and suites are decorated with period furnishings such as carved cherry armoires; many bathrooms have Jacuzzis and separate showers. ✉ *330 E. Main St., 81611, E. Main St., 81611,* ☎ *970/920–1000 or 800/331–7213,* ℻ *970/925–2784. 93 rooms. 2 restaurants, 2 bars, pool, hot tub, airport shuttle. AE, DC, MC, V.*

$$ 🏨 **Snowflake Inn.** The wide-ranging accommodations here are all quite comfortable. The wood-beam lobby, with its stone fireplace, is a convivial gathering place for the complimentary Continental breakfast and afternoon tea. ✉ *221 E. Hyman Ave., 81611,* ☎ *970/925–3221 or 800/247–2069,* ℻ *970/925–8740. 38 units. Pool, outdoor hot tub, sauna. AE, MC, V.*

Beaver Creek

$$$$ 🏨 **Hyatt Regency Beaver Creek.** An antler chandelier, stone fireplaces,
★ and upholstered comfort characterize the public rooms here. Guests exiting the hotel step into their warmed and waiting ski boots and skis. Watch for much lower rates off-season. ✉ *Box 1595, Avon 81620,* ☎ *970/949–1234 or 800/233–1234,* ℻ *970/949–4164. 321 rooms. 3 restaurants, deli, 2 lounges, pool, 8 hot tubs, spa, 5 tennis courts, health club, children's programs. AE, D, DC, MC, V.*

Breckenridge

$$–$$$ 🏨 **B&Bs on North Main St.** From the front parlor with its crackling hearth
★ fire to the dollhouselike accommodations, the Williams House is a dream bed-and-breakfast. A new addition—Barn Above the River—contains five rooms with western decor in a timber-frame barn. ✉ *303 N. Main St.,* ☎ *970/453–2975 or 800/795–2975. 11 rooms, 1 cottage. AE.*

Glenwood Springs

$–$$ 🏨 **Hotel Colorado.** Teddy Roosevelt stayed at this grande dame of northwestern Colorado to take advantage of the adjacent hot springs. The public rooms have been returned to their former glory. Bedrooms are huge and sparsely furnished. ✉ *526 Pine St., 81601,* ☎ *970/945–6511 or 800/544–3998,* ℻ *970/945–7030. 128 rooms. 2 restaurants, bar, beauty salon, exercise room. AE, D, DC, MC, V.*

Grand Lake

$ 🏨 **Grand Lake Lodge.** Set majestically above Grand Lake and bordering Rocky Mountain National Park, the lodge is actually a collection of rustic cabins. Some have wood-burning stoves for heat, others share baths, but all have a comfortable, well-worn atmosphere. ✉ *Box 269, 80447,* ☎ *303/627–3967 in summer or 970/759–5848. 56 cabins. Restaurant, bar, pool, hot tub, hiking, horseback riding. AE, D, MC, V. Closed mid-Sept.–May.*

Keystone

$$–$$$ ✕🏨 **Ski Tip Lodge.** The public room's picture windows overlook a for-
★ est, contributing to the tranquil atmosphere here. The B&B reflects its 1880s origins in its room furnishings, and the American regional cuisine is exceptional. The lodge is a half mile from the slopes. ✉ *Box 38, 80435,* ☎ *970/468–4202 or 800/222–0188. 13 rooms. Restaurant, bar. AE, D, DC, MC, V.*

Steamboat Springs

$$–$$$ ✕ **Antares.** This restaurant is in a splendid Victorian building with field-
★ stone walls, pressed-tin ceilings, and stained glass. The exciting cuisine is inspired by America's rich ethnic stew. You might feast on mussels in a citrus-chili-chardonnay broth, pompano with a pineapple and Pommery mustard fondue, or Maine lobster over chili-pepper linguine. ✉ *57½ 8th St.,* ☎ *970/879–9939. Reservations essential. AE, MC, V. No lunch.*

$–$$ ✕ **La Montaña.** Among the standouts at this Mexican-Southwest es-
★ tablishment are red-chili pasta in a shrimp, garlic, and cilantro sauce; interwoven strands of mesquite-grilled elk, lamb, and chorizo sausage; and elk loin crusted with pecans and bourbon cream sauce. ✉ *Après Ski Way and Village Dr.,* ☎ *970/879–5800. AE, D, MC, V. No lunch.*

$$–$$$ 🏨 **Sky Valley Lodge.** This homey property is a few miles from down-
★ town amid glorious scenery. Warm English country–style rooms are decorated in restful mountain colors. ✉ *31490 E. Hwy. 40, 80477,* ☎ *970/879–7749 or 800/538–7519,* 🖷 *970/879–7752. 24 rooms. Hot tub. Continental breakfast. AE, D, DC, MC, V.*

Vail

$$$ ✕ **Sweet Basil.** A meal here will wake up your taste buds. The menu
★ includes such preparations as a salmon paillard with bok choy, sesame puree, and tomato-cilantro sauce. ✉ *193 E. Gore Creek Dr.,* ☎ *970/ 476–0125. Reservations essential. AE, MC, V.*

$$–$$$ ✕ **Terra Bistro.** Situated in the Vail Athletic Club, where a warm fire-
★ place contrasts with black-iron chairs and black-and-white photographs, this soaring space has an innovative, seasonally changing menu that caters to both meat-and-potatoes diners and vegans. Everything is crisply textured and pungently seasoned. Organic produce and free-range meat and poultry are used whenever possible. ✉ *352 E. Meadow Dr.,* ☎ *970/476–6836. Reservations essential. AE, D, MC, V.*

$$$–$$$$ 🏨 **Sonnenalp.** This centrally located Bavarian-style hotel contains
★ small but luxurious rooms with an authentically German Alpine feeling. Accommodations are in two buildings: the pretty Swiss Chalet and the more contemporary Bavaria Haus. The European spas in both buildings provide almost any kind of après-ski treatment. ✉ *20 Vail Rd., 81657,* ☎ *970/476–5656 or 800/654–8312,* 🖷 *970/476–1639. 186 rooms. 4 restaurants, 3 bars, 3 pools, 2 spas. AE, DC, MC, V.*

Winter Park

$$ ✕🏨 **Gasthaus Eichler.** This is Winter Park's most romantic dining
★ spot, with Bavarian decor, antler chandeliers, and stained-glass windows. Veal and grilled items are served, as well as German classics such as sauerbraten. The Eichler also has 15 cozy Old World rooms, with down comforters, lace curtains, armoires, cable TVs, and whirlpool

tubs. ⊠ *Winter Park Dr., 80482,* ☎ *970/726–5133 or 800/543– 3899. 15 rooms. Hot tubs. AE, D, MC, V.*

Ranches

$$$–$$$$
★ 🏠 **C Lazy U Ranch.** Near Rocky Mountain National Park, this rambling southwestern-style wooden lodge has fireplaces and Navajo rugs in its rooms and cabins. The fare ranges from old-fashioned ranch food (steak and barbecue) to lighter, health-conscious dishes, such as mountain trout stuffed with artichokes. ⊠ *Box 379, Granby 80446,* ☎ *970/ 887–3344,* 𝔽𝔸𝕏 *970/887–3917. 19 rooms, 20 cabins. Bar, dining room, pool, sauna, 2 tennis courts, exercise room, racquetball, volleyball, horseback riding, skating, cross-country skiing, sleigh rides. Closed Apr.– June, Oct.–Dec. 21. No credit cards.*

$$$–$$$$
★ 🏠 **Home Ranch.** This luxurious western lodge in the Steamboat Springs area is a member of the prestigious Relais & Chateaux group. Each log cabin has a wood-burning stove and a hot tub. A shuttle to the slopes is available. ⊠ *Box 822, Clark 80428,* ☎ *970/879–1780,* 𝔽𝔸𝕏 *970/879– 1795. 8 cabins, 6 lodge rooms. Dining room, pool, sauna, hiking, horseback riding, fishing, cross-country skiing. AE, MC, V.*

Campgrounds

You can reserve camping spaces at many of the national-forest campgrounds by phone (☎ 800/280–2267). **Tiger Run Resort** (⊠ 3 mi north of Breckenridge on Hwy. 9, Box 815, 80424, ☎ 970/453–9690) is a retreat for RVs, with tennis courts, a pool, and a recreation room. **Winding River Resort Village** (⊠ Box 629, Grand Lake 80447, ☎ 970/627– 3215) is a combination campground and low-cost dude ranch in a beautiful forest.

Outdoor Activities and Sports

Boating

Sailing regattas are common at Grand Lake. Rent fishing boats and motorboats at **Beacon Landing Marina** (⊠ Grand County Rd. 64, 6 mi south of Grand Lake off Hwy. 34, ☎ 970/627–3671). **Lake Dillon Marina** (⊠ Dillon, ☎ 970/468–5100) rents sailboats and motorboats.

Fishing

Grand Lake and the connected reservoirs Shadow Mountain Lake and Lake Granby are known for their trout fishing. Dillon Reservoir is stocked with salmon and trout. The Lower Blue River, below Dillon Reservoir, is a Gold Medal catch-and-release area, as is the Fryingpan River near Aspen.

Golf

Sheraton Steamboat Golf Club (⊠ 2200 Village Inn Ct., ☎ 970/879– 2220) was designed by Robert Trent Jones Jr. Jack Nicklaus designed the course at the **Breckenridge Golf Club** (⊠ 200 Clubhouse Dr., ☎ 970/453–9104), where reservations are essential. The difficult **Eagle/Vail Golf Course** (⊠ 0431 Eagle Dr., Avon, ☎ 970/949–5267) has reduced fees in fall and spring.

Hiking and Backpacking

To find out about area hiking and backpacking trails, contact the **Holy Cross Ranger District Office** (⊠ 24747 Hwy. 24, Minturn, near Vail, ☎ 970/827–5715), the **Aspen Ranger District Office** (⊠ 806 W. Hallam St., ☎ 970/925–3445), or the **Dillon Ranger District Office** (⊠ Blue River Pkwy., Silverthorne, ☎ 970/468–5400).

Rafting

The Colorado River lures white-water enthusiasts, as does the Arkansas River near Buena Vista. Contact rafting firms through the **Colorado River Outfitters Association** (☎ 303/369–4632), in Denver.

Ski Areas

For **snow conditions** at Colorado resorts, call 303/825–7669.

Cross-Country

Aspen/Snowmass Nordic Trail System (☎ 970/925–1940) contains 48 mi of trails through the Roaring Fork Valley. **Breckenridge Nordic Ski Center** (☎ 970/453–6855) maintains 19 mi of trails. **Copper Mountain/Trak Cross-Country Center** (☎ 303/986–2882) has 16 mi of groomed track and skate lanes. **Devil's Thumb Ranch** (✉ Devil's Thumb, 10 mi north of Winter Park, ☎ 970/726–5632) is a full-service resort with 65 mi of groomed trails. **Frisco Nordic Center** (✉ 112 N. Summit Blvd., ☎ 970/668–0866) has nearly 25 mi of one-way loops. **Keystone Nordic Center at Ski Tip Lodge** (☎ 970/468–4275) provides 11 mi of prepared trails and 35 mi of backcountry skiing through Arapahoe National Forest. **Steamboat Ski Touring Center** (☎ 970/879–8180) has trails on the golf course. **Vail Cross-Country Ski Centers** (☎ 970/479–4391) has information on Vail Valley trails.

Downhill

Aspen Highlands (✉ 1600 Maroon Creek Rd., Aspen 81611, ☎ 970/925–1220) has 619 acres of runs, 8 lifts, and a 3,635-ft vertical drop. **Aspen Mountain** (✉ Box 1248, Aspen 81612, ☎ 970/925–1220) has 631 acres of runs, a gondola, 7 lifts, and a 3,267-ft drop. **Beaver Creek** (✉ Box 7, Vail 81658, ☎ 970/949–5750) has 1,529 acres of runs, 14 lifts, and a 4,040-ft drop. **Breckenridge** (✉ Box 1058, Breckenridge 80424, ☎ 303/453–5000) has 2,031 acres of runs, 18 lifts, and a 3,398-ft drop. **Copper Mountain** (✉ Box 3533, Copper Mountain 80443, ☎ 970/968–2882) has 2,433 acres of runs, 21 lifts, and a 2,601-ft drop. **Keystone** (✉ Box 38, Keystone 80435, ☎ 970/468–2316) has 1,739 acres of runs, 19 lifts, and a 2,900-ft drop. **Snowmass** (✉ Box 5566, Snowmass Village 80446, ☎ 970/923–2010) has 2,655 acres of runs, 17 lifts, and a 4,206-ft drop. **Steamboat** (✉ 2305 Mt. Werner Circle, Steamboat Springs 80487, ☎ 970/879–6111) has 2,500 acres of runs, a gondola, 20 lifts, and a 3,685-ft drop. **Buttermilk** (✉ Box 1248, Aspen 81612, ☎ 970/925–1220) has 410 acres of runs, 7 lifts, and a 2,030-ft drop. **Vail** (✉ Box 7, Vail 81658, ☎ 970/476–5677) has 4,112 acres of runs, a gondola, 26 lifts, and a 3,330-ft drop. **Winter Park** (✉ Box 36, Winter Park 80482, ☎ 970/726–5514) has 1,414 acres of runs, 20 lifts, and a 3,060-ft drop.

Shopping

The town of **Silverthorne** has an outlet shopping complex (✉ I–70 at Silverthorne, ☎ 970/468–9440) with nearly 80 stores.

SOUTHWESTERN COLORADO

Ski areas and red-rock deserts, cowboy hangouts and haunts of ancient cultures mark this region. The feeling is down-home—you may see a cowboy in the distance riding off after stray livestock or walk into a bar where ranchers discussing stock prices sit next to climbers enthusing over an ascent route.

Visitor Information

Southwest Colorado Travel Region (✉ Box 2102, Montrose 81402, ☎ 800/933–4340). **Durango:** Chamber of Commerce (✉ 111 S. Camino del Rio, Box 2587, 81302, ☎ 970/247–0312 or 800/525–8855). **Telluride:** Chamber of Commerce (✉ 666 W. Colorado Ave., Box 653, 81435, ☎ 970/728–3041 or 800/525–3455).

Arriving and Departing

By Bus

Greyhound Lines (☎ 800/231–2222) serves Durango and mountain towns such as Purgatory, Silverton, Ouray, Ridgeway, and Montrose.

By Car

Highway 141 from Grand Junction to Highway 145 leads to Telluride; Highway 550 is the route from Durango to Silverton and Ouray.

By Plane

Durango–La Plata County Airport (☎ 970/247–8143) is 14 mi east of Durango, and **Montrose Regional Airport** (☎ 970/249–3203) is 1 mi from Montrose. **Gunnison County Airport** (☎ 970/641–2304) is 23 mi south of Crested Butte. **Telluride Regional Airport** (☎ 970/728–5313) is 2 mi from Telluride.

Exploring Southwestern Colorado

Telluride is another old mining town turned ski resort but with a difference: Its relative isolation in a box canyon makes it more laid-back than many other Colorado resorts, and its beauty is legendary. The resort provides terrain for skiers of all abilities. The summer brings nationally known **festivals** of film (☎ 970/728–4401), bluegrass (☎ 800/624–2422), and jazz (☎ 970/728–7009). South of Telluride is a complete change of scene: **Mesa Verde** (☞ National and State Parks, *above*), where the forests give way to red-rock cliff dwellings. The structures were fashioned more than 700 years ago by the Anasazi, believed to be the ancestors of the Pueblos.

East of Mesa Verde is **Durango,** which has dramatic views of the San Juan Mountains and still cherishes its frontier traditions. A trip on the **Durango and Silverton Narrow Gauge Railroad** (✉ 479 Main Ave., ☎ 970/247–2733) is worth the trouble of making reservations well in advance. On the eight-hour round-trip on tracks laid between the two towns in 1881, you'll see unspoiled scenery, dramatic gorge crossings, and rails dug into the mountainside. **Silverton** is a smaller, more untouched frontier mining town.

Ouray, about 25 mi up the twisty, breathtaking Million-Dollar Highway, is a sleepy western town surrounded by the San Juan Mountains. Dive into the **Ouray Hot Springs Pool** (☎ 970/325–4638) or, for a more rustic dip, **Orvis Hot Springs** (☎ 970/626–5324). North of Ouray is **Crested Butte,** an old Victorian mining town tucked away in another gorgeous setting; the town serves as base for the excellent Crested Butte ski area 2 mi away, best suited for high-intermediate and expert skiers.

Dining and Lodging

For price ranges *see* Charts 1 (B) and 2 (B) *in* On the Road with Fodor's.

Crested Butte

$$$–$$$$ ✕ **Soupçon.** Mac Bailey, the impish owner-chef of Soupçon ("soup's
★   on," get it?) prepares innovative variations on classic bistro cuisine.

The duck and fish are sublime, as are the two intimate dining rooms, which are inside a log cabin. ✉ *Just off 2nd St. behind the Forest Queen,* ☎ *970/349–5448. Reservations essential. AE, MC, V. No lunch.*

$ ✕ **Slogar.** Set in a lovingly renovated Victorian tavern awash in lace
★   and stained glass, this restaurant turns out some of the plumpest, juiciest fried chicken west of the Mississippi. ✉ *2nd and Whiterock Sts.,* ☎ *970/349–5765. MC, V. No lunch.*

$$–$$$ ✕🏨 **Grande Butte Hotel.** This ski-in/ski-out property delivers everything the luxury hotels do but at down-to-earth prices. Each huge room has a wet bar, a whirlpool tub, and a private balcony. Towering plants, regional paintings and sculptures, and oversize, overstuffed armchairs and sofas fill the public spaces. Giovanni's, the hotel's gourmet restaurant, is excellent. ✉ *Box 5006, Mt. Crested Butte, 81225,* ☎ *970/349–7561 or 800/642–4422,* 🖷 *970/349–4466. 262 rooms. 2 restaurants, lobby lounge, indoor pool, outdoor hot tub, sauna, recreation room, coin laundry, meeting rooms. AE, D, DC, MC, V.*

Durango

$$ ✕ **Ariano's.** Pasta made fresh daily and a sure touch with meats make this northern Italian restaurant one of Durango's most popular. Veal scallopini sautéed with fresh sage and garlic is among the best dishes. ✉ *150 E. 6th St.,* ☎ *970/247–8146. Reservations not accepted. AE, D, DC, MC, V.*

$$ ✕ **Red Snapper.** If you're in the mood for fresh, creatively prepared seafood, head for this congenial place furnished with more than 200 gallons' worth of aquariums. Steak and prime rib are also available—this is a meat-and-potatoes town. ✉ *144 E. 9th St.,* ☎ *970/259–3417. AE, MC, V. No lunch.*

$$$ 🏨 **Strater Hotel.** Author Louis L'Amour made this restored century-
★   old hotel his home during frequent visits to Durango. The meticulously decorated accommodations match the Victorian charm of the public parlors. ✉ *699 Main Ave., 81301,* ☎ *970/247–4431 or 800/247–4431,* 🖷 *970/259–2208. 93 rooms. Restaurant, 2 bars, hot tub. AE, D, DC, MC, V.*

Ouray

$$ ✕🏨 **St. Elmo Hotel.** Originally a miners' hotel, this B&B is welcoming and intimate, with Victorian antiques. The Bon Ton Restaurant downstairs serves northern Italian food. ✉ *426 Main St., 81427,* ☎ *970/325–4951. 9 rooms. Restaurant, bar, hot tub, sauna. AE, D, MC, V.*

Telluride

$$$ ✕ **Campagna.** You'll feel as if you're in a Tuscan farmhouse here, from the oak and terra-cotta floors and vintage photos of the Italian countryside to the assured, classically simple food. Wild mushrooms (porcini or portobello) and wild boar chops are among the enticing possibilities. Finish off your meal with tiramisu and a fiery grappa. ✉ *435 W. Pacific Ave.,* ☎ *970/728–6190. Reservations essential. MC, V. No lunch.*

$$$ ✕ **La Marmotte.** At this rustic restaurant decorated like a French coun-
★   try cottage, the Gallic owners and chefs change the menu constantly, serving such dishes as duck confit or lamb with red-bell-pepper sauce and white beans. ✉ *150 W. San Juan Ave.,* ☎ *970/728–6232. Reservations essential. AE, MC, V. No lunch.*

$$$$ 🏨 **The Peaks at Telluride Resort and Spa.** The pastel-color prisonlike
★   exterior can be excused at this ski-in/ski-out luxury resort, thanks to its revitalizing spa facilities. The setting is glorious, dominated by Mt. Wilson (the peak on the Coors beer can). The rooms are sizable and

have balconies. ⊠ *136 Country Club Dr., 81435,* ☎ *970/728–6800 or 800/223–6725,* FAX *970/728–6567. 177 rooms. 2 restaurants, bar, indoor-outdoor pool, beauty salon, hot tubs, sauna, spa, 5 tennis courts, exercise room, racquetball, squash, water slide. AE, DC, MC, V.*

$$–$$$ 🏨 **San Sophia Inn.** If you eschew Victorian frills, this is the inn for you.
★ Rooms, although smallish, are luxurious, done in handsome desert shades and with pine armoires. ⊠ *330 W. Pacific St., 81435,* ☎ *970/728–3001 or 800/537–4781. 16 rooms. Hot tub. AE, MC, V.*

$$ 🏨 **New Sheridan Hotel.** William Jennings Bryan delivered his rousing "Cross of Gold" speech here in 1896, garnering a presidential nomination in the process. Decor favors exposed brick walls, old tintypes, brass beds, red-velour love seats, and wicker rocking chairs. Turndown service and complimentary breakfast and afternoon tea complete the experience of fin-de-siècle gracious living. The Victorian bar is a local institution. ⊠ *231 W. Colorado Ave., 81435,* ☎ *970/728–4351. 32 rooms. 2 restaurants, bar, 2 hot tubs, exercise room, meeting room. AE, MC, V.*

Ranch

$$$ 🏨 **Skyline Ranch.** Burlap walls, pine furniture, and down comforters
★ deck the rooms in the slab-wood buildings of this rustic western ranch, which has prime horseback riding and fly-fishing. In winter guests cross-country ski or head for downhill skiing at Telluride. The cuisine is French-American, with a menu that changes daily. ⊠ *Off Hwy. 145, 8 mi south of Telluride; Box 67, Telluride 81435,* ☎ *970/728–3757,* FAX *970/728–6728. 10 lodge rooms, 6 cabins. Restaurant, hot tub, sauna, airport shuttle. AE, MC, V.*

Campgrounds

Ranger district offices (☞ Hiking and Backpacking *in* Outdoor Activities and Sports, *below*) have information on campgrounds in the state and national forests. Near Durango is a **KOA** campground (⊠ East on Hwy. 160, ☎ 970/247–0783), which is closed mid-October–April.

Outdoor Activities and Sports

Biking

Crested Butte is mountain-biking mecca; Durango is home to many world-class road cyclists because of the great riding terrain. Bike-rental locations abound in both towns.

Fishing

The Dolores River, in the San Juan National Forest (☞ Hiking and Back-packing, *below*), and the Animas River, near Durango, are good for trout. The Vallecito Reservoir, also near Durango, has pike, trout, and salmon. At **Ridgway State Park** (☎ 970/626–5822), 10 mi north of Ouray, you can catch rainbow trout.

Golf

Some of the best 18-hole courses in the area are **Hillcrest Golf Course** (⊠ 2300 Rim Dr., Durango, ☎ 970/247–1499), **Tamarron** (⊠ 40292 Rte. 550, north of Durango, ☎ 970/259–2000), **Telluride Golf Club** (⊠ Telluride Mountain Village, ☎ 970/728–3856), and **Skyland Country Club** (⊠ 385 Country Club Dr., outside Crested Butte, ☎ 970/349–6127).

Hiking and Backpacking

The 500-mi **Colorado Trail,** from Durango to Denver, is a major route. The **San Juan National Forest District Office** (⊠ 701 Camino del Rio, Room 101, Durango, ☎ 970/247–4874) has information on trails in the area.

Rafting

Rafting is popular on the San Miguel, Dolores, Gunnison, and Animas rivers. Arrange trips through the **Colorado River Outfitters Association** (⊠ Box 440021, Aurora 80044, ☎ 303/369–4632).

Ski Areas

For **snow conditions** at Colorado resorts, call 303/825–7669.

Cross-Country

Trails abound; check with local tourist offices for details. **Purgatory Ski Touring Center** (⊠ Purgatory Ski Area, 1 Skier Pl., Durango 81301, ☎ 970/247–9000) manages 26 mi of trails; **Telluride Nordic Center** (⊠ Box 1784, Telluride 81435, ☎ 970/728–7570) has 48 mi of trails and a free shuttle from the alpine ski area.

Downhill

Crested Butte (⊠ Off Rte. 135, Box A, 81225, ☎ 970/349–2222) has 1,162 acres of runs, 13 lifts, and a 2,775-ft vertical drop. **Purgatory** (⊠ Hwy. 550, ☎ 970/247–9000) has 729 acres of runs, 9 lifts, and a 2,029-ft drop. **Telluride** (⊠ Rte. 145, Box 11155, 81435, ☎ 970/728–3856) has 1,050 acres of runs, 12 lifts, and a 3,522-ft drop.

Shopping

Western Goods

Toh-Atin Gallery (⊠ 145 W. 9th St., Durango, ☎ 970/247–8277) and the related **Toh-Ahtin's Art on Main** (⊠ 865 Main Ave., ☎ 970/247–4540), around the corner, are perhaps the foremost western, Native American, and southwestern fine-art and crafts galleries in Colorado. **North Moon** (⊠ 133 W. Colorado Ave., Telluride, ☎ 970/728–4145) carries painted lodgepole-pine furnishings, contemporary Native American ceramics that depart from tribal traditions, metallic sculptures, and petroglyph-inspired jewelry.

ELSEWHERE IN COLORADO

South Central Colorado

Arriving and Departing

Buena Vista is 90 mi west of Colorado Springs on U.S. 24; the only way to get there is by car. Pueblo is a half hour south of Colorado Springs on I–25 south; Trinidad is just over an hour farther. **Pueblo Memorial Airport** (☎ 719/948–3355) welcomes flights from United Express.

What to See and Do

Hiking, biking, and climbing are king in **Buena Vista,** where the Collegiate Peaks Wilderness Area attracts alumni climbers with its 14,000-ft giants. On the Arkansas River, Buena Vista also bills itself as "the white-water-rafting capital of the world." Contact **Dvorak Kayak & Rafting Expeditions** (⊠ Nathrop, ☎ 800/824–3795) for trip information. Head to the **Mt. Princeton Hot Springs** (⊠ 5 mi west of Nathrop, CR 162, ☎ 719/395–2447) for a restorative soak. The **Buena Vista Heritage Museum** (⊠ E. Main St., ☎ 719/395–8458) contains artifacts from the life and times of the regional pioneers.

Pueblo, a multiethnic working-class steel town in the shadow of Colorado Springs, nonetheless has some glorious historical neighborhoods, such as the **Union Avenue Historic District.** Walking-tour brochures are available at the Chamber of Commerce (⊠ 302 N. Santa Fe Ave., 81003, ☎ 719/542–1704). The **Rosemount Victorian Museum** (⊠ 419 W. 14th St., ☎ 719/545–5290) is an opulent mansion whose rooms are virtually intact. The **Sangre de Cristo Arts Center** (⊠ 210 N. Santa Fe Ave., ☎ 719/543–0130) celebrates regional arts and crafts.

U.S. 50 roughly follows the faded tracks of the **Santa Fe Trail** from the Kansas border through La Junta, where U.S. 350 picks up the scent, traveling southwest to **Trinidad.** If you detour onto the quiet county roads, you can still discern the faint outline of the trail. Here, amid the magpies and prairie dogs, it takes little imagination to conjure visions of the pioneers struggling to travel just 10 mi a day by oxcart over vast stretches of territory. Just east of La Junta, **Bent's Fort** (⊠ 35110 Hwy. 194 E, ☎ 719/384–2596), now a living museum, was the most important stop along the route.

Trinidad has several superb museums, the most significant of which is the **Baca House/Bloom House/Santa Fe Trail Museum Complex** (⊠ 300 E. Main St., ☎ 719/846–7217), two 19th-century mansions that document the effect of the Santa Fe Trail on the community.

Lodging

$$ 🏨 **Abriendo Inn.** This 1906 home is listed on the National Register of
★ Historic Places. ⊠ *300 W. Abriendo Ave., Pueblo 81004,* ☎ *719/544–2703,* 🖷 *719/542–1806. 10 rooms. AE, DC, MC, V.*

$ 🏨 **River Run Inn.** On the Arkansas River, this cozy Victorian home has breathtaking mountain prospects. For those who can't get a room, there's a coed dorm on the property. ⊠ *8495 CR 60, Salida 81201,* ☎ *719/539–3818 or 800/385–6925. 6 rooms; 8 dorm beds. MC, V.*

The San Luis Valley

Arriving and Departing

Alamosa is 150 mi east of Durango on U.S. 160 or 115 mi from Pueblo on U.S. 160E to I–25N. Great Sand Dunes National Monument is on Route 150 north of U.S. 160; San Luis is on Route 159 south of U.S. 160. The **Durango–La Plata Airport** (☎ 970/247–8143) receives daily flights from American, America West, Reno Air, and United Express.

What to See and Do

Nestled between the San Juan Mountains and the Sangre de Cristo range and watered by the mighty Rio Grande and its tributaries, the 8,000-square-mi **San Luis Valley** is the world's largest alpine valley. Its **Alamosa National Vista Wildlife Refuge** (⊠ 9383 El Rancho La., ☎ 719/589–4021) is an important sanctuary for the nearly extinct whooping crane and its cousin, the sandhill. The range of terrain is equally impressive, from the stark moonscape of the Wheeler Geologic Area to the tawny, undulating **Great Sand Dunes National Monument** (⊠ 35 mi from Alamosa, east on U.S. 160 and north on Rte. 150). Created by windswept grains from the Rio Grande floor, the sand dunes—which rise up to 700 ft and stretch for 55 square mi—are an improbable, unforgettable sight, as curvaceous as Rubens's nudes.

San Luis, founded in 1851, is the oldest incorporated town in Colorado. Its Hispanic heritage is celebrated in the **San Luis Museum and Cultural Center** (⊠ 401 Church Pl., ☎ 719/672–3611). Murals depicting famous stories and legends of the area adorn tree-lined streets.

IDAHO

By Peggy
Ammerman

Capital	Boise
Population	1,189,300
Motto	It Is Perpetual
State Bird	Mountain bluebird
State Flower	Syringa
Postal Abbreviation	ID

Statewide Visitor Information

Idaho Travel Council (⊠ Dept. of Commerce, 700 W. State St., Box 83720, Boise 83720-0093, ☎ 208/334–2470 or 800/635–7820).

Scenic Drives

Fourteen historic or scenic byways and segments of 10 historic trails are shown on the Official Idaho Highway Map, available from the Idaho Travel Council (☞ Statewide Visitor Information, *above*). The 35-mi **Lewis and Clark Back Country Byway** loops southeast of the town of Salmon off Route 28 and traces the passage of explorers Meriwether Lewis and George Rogers Clark through the Continental Divide, at the crest of the Beaverhead and Bitterroot Mountains near the Montana state line. The **Lake Coeur d'Alene Scenic Byway** cuts southwest on Route 3 through thick pine forests for 25 mi and then heads north on Route 97, shadowing the crooked eastern lakeshore for 35 mi.

National and State Parks

National Parks

With 40% of its acreage in trees, Idaho is the most heavily forested of the Rocky Mountain states. For information on all of Idaho's forests, contact the **Boise National Forest** (⊠ 1750 Front St., Boise 83702, ☎ 208/354–4100). The Snake River Canyon plunges 1 mi at **Hells Canyon National Recreation Area** (⊠ Box 832, Riggins 83549, ☎ 208/628–3916), making it the deepest river gorge in the nation. Idaho has 3,000 mi of white-water river action, the most in the nation. Legend has it that the Main Salmon River was nicknamed the River of No Return by Lewis and Clark boatmen after they witnessed the waters churn "with great violence from one rock to another . . . foaming and roaring . . . so as to render the passage of anything impossible." Reconsidering, the expedition party backtracked to Montana and pursued an alternate route via the Lolo Pass over the Continental Divide. Today the Main Salmon and its Middle Fork, an acclaimed stretch of white water, are surrounded by the 2-million-acre **Frank Church–River of No Return Wilderness Area** (⊠ Rte. 2, Grangeville 83530, ☎ 208/983–1950). Selected as a training site for U.S. astronauts because of its striking lunarlike appearance, the **Craters of the Moon National Monument** (⊠ Box 29, Arco 83213, ☎ 208/527–3257) covers 83 square mi, with spatter cones, lava caves, and other eerie volcanic-formed features. Part of the **Sawtooth National Recreation Area** (⊠ Star Rte., Ketchum 83340, ☎ 208/726–7672), the jagged Sawtooth Mountains (often called America's Alps), with 42 peaks reaching at least 10,000 ft, join the Boulder and White Cloud ranges and march across 1,180 square mi, beginning just north of Ketchum on Route 75. Other **National Park Service** properties include **Nez Percé National Historical Park** (⊠ Hwy. 95, Spalding 83551, ☎ 208/843–2261); **Hagerman Fossil Beds National Monument** (⊠ Box 570, Hagerman 83332, ☎ 208/837–4793);

and **City of Rocks National Reserve** (✉ Box 169, Almo 83312, ☎ 208/824–5519). Other federal land in Idaho is under the jurisdiction of the **Bureau of Land Management Idaho State Office** (✉ 3380 Americana Terr., Boise 83706, ☎ 208/384–3000).

State Parks

The **Idaho Department of Parks & Recreation** (✉ Box 83720, Boise 83720, ☎ 208/334–4199) maintains 24 state parks. **Heyburn State Park** (✉ Rte. 1, Box 139, Plummer 83851, ☎ 208/686–1308), at the southern tip of Lake Coeur d'Alene on Route 5, encompasses nearly 8,000 acres of land and water and is known for its migratory herons, eagles, and osprey as well as an annual fall harvest of wild rice. Rising 470 ft, North America's tallest single-structured sand dunes are the centerpiece of **Bruneau Dunes State Park** (✉ HC 85, Box 41, Mountain Home 83647, ☎ 208/366–7919), just a stone's throw from the Snake River and roughly 60 mi southeast of Boise on Route 78. Both fly fishers and a third of the Rocky Mountain trumpeter swan population flock to Henry's Fork of the Snake River, which winds through **Harriman State Park** (✉ HC 66, Box 500, Island Park 83429, ☎ 208/558–7368), on U.S. 20, 33 mi southwest of West Yellowstone, Montana.

Outdoor Activities and Sports

The **Idaho Travel Council** (☞ Statewide Visitor Information, *above*) has information about private campgrounds. For camping on federal and state lands, phone the national and state parks listed above. For information about hiking, backpacking, and rafting, contact the regional travel associations and local chambers of commerce (☞ Visitor Information, *below*) or **Idaho Outfitters and Guides Association** (✉ Box 95, Boise 83701, ☎ 208/342–1919).

The fishing season generally runs from the Saturday before Memorial Day through November. The **Idaho Department of Fish & Game** (✉ 600 S. Walnut Ave., Boise 83707, ☎ 208/334–3700) provides information and licenses. The department also publishes a wildlife **Viewing Guide** that lists the best and most easily accessible viewing sites in the state.

SOUTHERN IDAHO

Idaho's longest river, the Snake, carves a steely blue course of nearly 1,000 mi through southern Idaho, linking together a diverse mix of terrain. Vast stretches of fertile farmland give way to desert plateaus blanketed in jet-black lava. Sweeps of sugary sand dunes anchor both the southwestern and eastern portions of the state. In between, waterfalls and springs spill into deep, rugged canyons. Pine-and-sage-clad mountains along the upper fringe of the Snake River plain hint of the taller Northern Rockies peaks that rise within the state's borders.

Visitor Information

Southwest Idaho Travel Association (✉ Box 2106, 168 N. 9th St., Suite 200, Boise 83702, ☎ 208/344–7777 or 800/635–5240). **South Central Idaho Travel Association** (✉ 858 Blue Lakes Blvd., Twin Falls 83301, ☎ 208/733–3974 or 800/255–8946). **Southeastern Idaho Travel Association** (✉ Box 498, Lava Hot Springs 83246, ☎ 208/776–5500 or 800/423–8597). **Yellowstone/Teton Territory Travel Committee** (✉ 505 Lindsay Blvd., Idaho Falls 83402, ☎ 208/523–1010 or 800/634–3246).

Arriving and Departing

By Bus
Greyhound Lines (✉ 1212 W. Bannock St., Boise, ☎ 800/231–2222) serves Boise, Twin Falls, Pocatello, and Idaho Falls. **Sun Valley Stages** (✉ Boise Municipal Airport, ☎ 800/821–9064) provides daily round-trip service between the airport, Sun Valley, and Twin Falls.

By Car
Boise is reached by I–84 from the south and the north.

By Plane
Boise Municipal Airport (☎ 208/383–3110), 3 mi from downtown, is served by national and regional airlines. The **Boise Urban Stages** (☎ 208/336–1010) shuttle bus to town costs $1; taxis cost $7–$10.

By Train
Amtrak (✉ 1701 Eastover Terr., Boise, ☎ 800/872–7245).

Orientation Tours

The **Boise Tour Train** (✉ Capitol Blvd., ☎ 208/342–4796 or 800/999–5993), which runs from May through October from downtown's Julia Davis Park, provides a one-hour introduction to the city.

Exploring Southern Idaho

Boise
The name Boise, French for "wooded," is traced to French-Canadian trappers, who found a tree-laced greenway on the Boise River, a sight for sore eyes after trekking across the area's semiarid plain. Boise and surrounding Ada County now form a modern center of government and business. A mean temperature of 51°F and annual rainfall averaging just under 12 inches create a hospitable setting for the headquarters of seven major corporations and a countywide population of 250,000.

An Old West saloon and relics from Idaho's early history as an Oregon Trail outpost fill the **Idaho State Historical Museum** (✉ 610 N. Julia Davis Dr., ☎ 208/334–2120). The **Boise Art Museum** (✉ 670 S. Julia Davis Dr., ☎ 208/345–8330) displays works based on historical and contemporary themes.

Lady Bluebeard and Diamondfield Jack were among the more notorious felons who did time at the **Old Idaho Territorial Penitentiary** (✉ 2445 Old Penitentiary Rd., ☎ 208/368–6080). In operation from 1870 until 1973, today it welcomes visitors for shorter stays. You can also tour a garden of Idaho native plants, a garden for children, and other theme gardens (open April–October, Tuesday–Sunday) within the penitentiary confines at the **Idaho Botanical Garden** (✉ 2355 Penitentiary Rd., ☎ 208/343–8649).

The **Discovery Center of Idaho** (✉ 131 W. Myrtle St., ☎ 208/343–9895), a hands-on science learning center that's open Tuesday–Sunday, has more than 100 displays. The **Morrison-Knudsen Nature Center** (✉ 600 S. Walnut Ave., ☎ 208/334–2225), open Tuesday–Sunday, has ecosystem exhibits of wetlands, plains, high-desert terrain, and mountain streams.

Eight miles south of downtown Boise (follow South Cole Road from I–84's Exit 50 and follow signs), the **World Center for Birds of Prey** (✉ 5666 Flying Hawk La., ☎ 208/362–8687), open Tuesday–Sunday, has live falcons, California condors, and other birds of prey. Guided 1½ tours throughout the day leave from the visitor center. Thirty miles southwest of Nampa (from I–84's Exit 44 head south from

Idaho

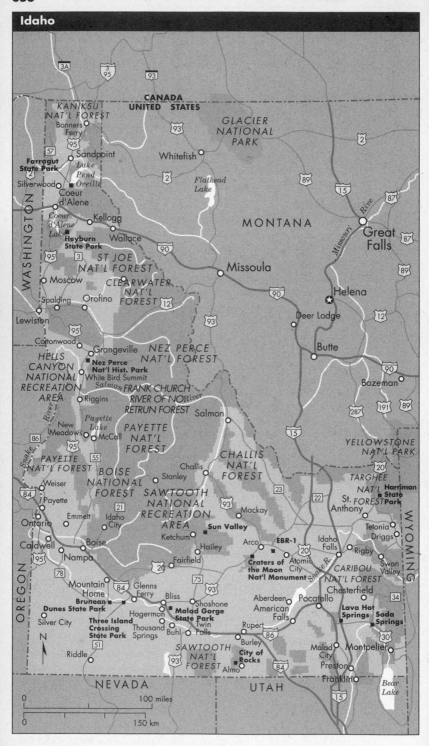

CANADA
UNITED STATES

WASHINGTON

MONTANA

WYOMING

OREGON

NEVADA

UTAH

KANIKSU NAT'L FOREST

GLACIER NATIONAL PARK

Bonners Ferry

Farragut State Park

Sandpoint

Whitefish

Flathead Lake

Silverwood

Lake Pend Oreille

Coeur d'Alene

Kellogg

Coeur d'Alene Lake

Heyburn State Park

Wallace

Great Falls

Helena

ST JOE NAT'L FOREST

CLEARWATER NAT'L FOREST

Moscow

Missoula

Spalding

Orofino

Deer Lodge

Lewiston

Cottonwood

Butte

HELLS CANYON NATIONAL RECREATION AREA

Grangeville

NEZ PERCE NAT'L FOREST

Nez Perce Nat'l Hist. Park

White Bird Summit

Bozeman

Riggins

FRANK CHURCH RIVER OF NO RETRUN FOREST

Salmon

New Meadows

Payette Lake

McCall

PAYETTE NAT'L FOREST

CHALLIS NAT'L FOREST

YELLOWSTONE NAT'L PARK

PAYETTE NAT'L FOREST

Weiser

BOISE NATIONAL FOREST

Challis

Stanley

TARGHEE NAT'L FOREST

Harriman State Park

Payette

Emmett

Idaho City

SAWTOOTH NATIONAL RECREATION AREA

Mackay

St. Anthony

Tetonia

Driggs

Ontario

Boise

Sun Valley

Ketchum

Arco

EBR-1

Idaho Falls

Rigby

Caldwell

Nampa

Hailey

Fairfield

Craters of the Moon Nat'l Monument

Atomic City

Swan Valley

CARIBOU NAT'L FOREST

Mountain Home

Glenns Ferry

Bliss

Shoshone

Aberdeen

Pocatello

Chesterfield

Bruneau Dunes State Park

Hagerman

Malad Gorge State Park

American Falls

Lava Hot Springs

Soda Springs

Silver City

Three Island Crossing State Park

Thousand Springs

Buhl

Twin Falls

Rupert

Burley

SAWTOOTH NAT'L FOREST

City of Rocks

Almo

Malad City

Montpelier

Preston

Riddle

Franklin

Bear Lake

0   100 miles

0   150 km

the town of Meridian to Kuna, then take Swan Falls Road south into park), the **Snake River Birds of Prey National Conservation Area** (☎ 208/384–3300) encompasses 483,000 acres along 80 mi of the Snake River. In spring cliffs towering 700 ft above the river host 15 species of migratory raptors.

The largest concentration of Basque people in the United States has called Idaho's Snake River plain home since the late 1800s. Visit a restored 1864 former boardinghouse; then go next door to the **Basque Museum and Cultural Center** and see colorful costumes, relics, and exhibits on Basque culture. ⊠ *611 Grove St.,* ☎ *208/343–2671. Closed Sun.–Mon.*

The Owyhee Uplands and the South-Central Region

South of Boise, from the Owyhee Mountains and arid Uplands east along the verdant Snake River canyon to Twin Falls, you'll find Oregon Trail wagon ruts, rocky gorges, hushed waterfalls, and springs trickling from canyon walls behind a veil of moss and ferns. Just south of Murphy a 25-mi gravel road off Route 78 leads to the onetime queen

★ of Idaho's mining region, **Silver City** (☎ 208/495–2319), now a ghost town with 70 rustic buildings. **Three Island Crossing State Park** (⊠ Rte. 78 off I–84 near Glenns Ferry, ☎ 208/366–2394) marks an important Oregon Trail wagon-train fording sight on the Snake River. At **Malad Gorge State Park** (⊠ Off U.S. 30 north of Hagerman, ☎ 208/837–4505) a suspension footbridge spans a 250-ft chasm as a 60-ft waterfall gushes into the Devil's Washbowl below. Warmed by geothermal springs, Idaho's "banana belt," the **Hagerman Valley**—a patchwork of melon fields, orchards, and trout farms off U.S. 30—is the gateway to the **Thousand Springs Scenic Byway.** Five miles north of the town of Twin Falls (take Fells Avenue east from U.S. 30 and head north on 3300 East Road), the **Shoshone Falls** (☎ 800/255–8946 or 208/736–2240), best viewed in the spring, cascade 212 ft (52 ft farther than Niagara Falls).

Blackfoot, Bear Lake, and Lava Hot Springs

Billionaire J. R. Simplot made Idaho famous for its potatoes beginning in the 1940s. Today much of southeastern Idaho's fertile Snake River crescent, stretching from Burley to Idaho Falls, is devoted to agriculture.

★ A must-see is the **World Potato Exposition** (⊠ 130 N. Main St., ☎ 208/785–2517), in Blackfoot. Exhibits explain potato production and display spud oddities. The gift shop sells potato cookbooks and fudge and hands out "free 'taters for out-of-staters." Fishing for cutthroat trout and using dip nets for Bonneville cisco and wildlife watching are big draws at **Bear Lake State Park** (☎ 208/945–2790), which is south of the town of Montpelier off U.S. 89 at St. Charles. Stop at the **Bear Lake National Wildlife Refuge** (☎ 208/847–1757) visitor center in Montpelier for maps before heading into the refuge, which surrounds 80,000-acre **Bear Lake** (roughly half of which is in Utah). A continuous flow of warm spring water at the base of lava cliffs has spawned the charming resort community of **Lava Hot Springs** (☎ 208/776–5500), 21 mi west of Soda Springs on U.S. 30.

Yellowstone/Teton Territory

Sixty miles of interconnecting scenic byways offer breathtaking views of the backsides of the Grand Tetons and Yellowstone Park. The **Mesa Falls Scenic Byway** (Route 47) travels through a 23-mi-wide caldera (volcanic crater). The byway travels through the Idaho portions of the **Targhee National Forest** (☎ 208/624–3151), which shelters pristine Upper and Lower Mesa Falls. The **Teton Scenic Byway** (Routes 32, 33, and 31 as the byway heads south from Ashton) passes through the small farming communities of Tetonia, Driggs, and Victor, all dwarfed by

the Tetons just to the east. In winter hundreds of inches of dry, pow-
dery snow draws skiers to the **Grand Targhee Ski & Summer Resort**
near Driggs.

Dining and Lodging

For price ranges *see* Chart 1 (B) *in* On the Road with Fodor's.

Boise

$$$ ✕ **Gamekeeper Restaurant.** Cut-glass chandeliers, fine paintings, and
★   historic architectural details create a refined setting for dining on veni-
      son, duck, halibut, prime rib, and table-side flambéed dishes. ⊠
      Owyhee Plaza Hotel, 1109 Main St., ☎ *208/343–4611. AE, D, DC,*
      MC, V. Closed Sun.

$$–$$$ ✕ **Peter Schott's New American Cuisine.** Many regard this small restau-
★   rant run by a local cooking-show celebrity as Idaho's best. Fresh fish
        dominates the menu, and the wine list is complete but not extravagant.
        ⊠ *Idanha Hotel, 928 Main St.,* ☎ *208/336–9100. AE, D, DC, MC,*
        V. Closed Sun. No lunch.

$$ ✕ **Onati–The Basque Restaurant.** Set in the back of a casual bar, this
      roomy eatery serves authentic Basque dishes and is known for its sa-
      vory lamb stew, chorizo sausage and rice, and squid in tomato sauce.
      ⊠ *3544 Chinden Blvd.,* ☎ *208/343–6464. MC, V.*

$$ ✕ **Sandpiper.** High ceilings, oak tables, river views, and live music on
      weekends make this a popular gathering place for dining on steak,
      seafood, and prime rib. ⊠ *1100 W. Jefferson St.,* ☎ *208/344–8911.*
      AE, D, DC, MC, V.

$ ✕ **Bar Gernika.** This cozy pub and restaurant is known for its mari-
      nated pork, sweet-red-pepper sandwiches, and other Basque special-
      ties, as well as traditional American sandwich fare. Beef Tongue
      Saturdays are a local tradition. ⊠ *202 S. Capitol Blvd.,* ☎ *208/244–*
      2175. MC, V. Closed Sun.

$ ✕ **Tablerock Brewpub & Grill.** Boise's first microbrewery has a south-
      western decor, with white pine, cacti, and prints by Native American
      artists. The diverse menu has something for everyone. ⊠ *705 Fulton*
      St., ☎ *208/342–0944. AE, D, DC, MC, V.*

$$$ ▥ **Idanha Hotel.** Close to business and shopping areas, this French
★   château–style bed-and-breakfast, with distinctive turrets and antiques-
      filled rooms, opened in 1901. ⊠ *928 Main St., 83702,* ☎ *208/342–*
      3611, 𝔽𝔸𝕏 *208/383–9690. 45 rooms. Restaurant. AE, D, DC, MC, V.*

$$–$$$ ▥ **Owyhee Plaza.** The glory of this hotel, built in 1910, can still be
        seen in its giant light fixtures and dark-wood paneling. Prices are
        lower at an adjacent motel. ⊠ *1109 Main St., 83702,* ☎ *208/343–*
        4611 or 800/233–4611, 𝔽𝔸𝕏 *208/381–0695. 100 rooms. 2 restaurants,*
        bar, beauty salon, meeting rooms. AE, MC, V.

$$ ▥ **Idaho Heritage Inn.** Tom and Phyllis Lupher operate this B&B in a
★   former governor's mansion about a mile east of downtown. Antiques,
      wallpaper, and old-style bed frames evoke an early 1900s mood. ⊠
      109 W. Idaho St., 83702, ☎ *208/342–8066. 6 rooms. AE, D, MC, V.*

Lava Hot Springs

$–$$ ▥ **Riverside Inn and Hot Springs.** This restored 1914 inn has mineral
      hot tubs and an immaculate interior. ⊠ *255 Portneuf Ave., 83246,* ☎
      208/776–5504 or 800/773–5504, 𝔽𝔸𝕏 *208/776–5504. 16 rooms, 12*
      with bath. 5 Hot springs, library. Continental breakfast. D, MC, V.

Twin Falls

$$–$$$ ✕ **Rock Creek.** Steak, prime rib, and seafood are the specialties at this
        restaurant with a massive salad bar and a wide selection of wine, vin-

tage ports, and single-malt whiskeys. ⊠ *200 Addison Ave. W,* ☎ *208/ 734–4154. AE, MC, V.*

$ ✕ **Buffalo Café.** Ask anybody in town where to go for breakfast, and
★ you'll get the same answer: this tiny café. The house specialty is the Buffalo Chip, a concoction of eggs, fried potatoes, cheese, bacon, peppers, and onion. ⊠ *218 4th Ave. W,* ☎ *208/734–0271. No credit cards. No dinner.*

Motels

🏨 **Best Western Canyon Springs Inn** (⊠ 1357 Blue Lakes Blvd. N, Twin Falls 83301, ☎ 208/734–5000 or 800/727–5003, 𝔽𝔸𝕏 208/734–5000), 112 rooms, restaurant, bar, pool; $$. 🏨 **Best Western–Apollo Motor Inn** (⊠ 296 Addison Ave. W, Twin Falls 83301, ☎ 208/733–2010 or 800/528–1234), 50 rooms, hot tub; $. 🏨 **Comfort Inn** (⊠ 2526 Airport Way, Boise, ☎ 208/336–0077, 𝔽𝔸𝕏 208/342–6592), 60 rooms, indoor pool, hot tub; $.

Wilderness Camps and Lodges

For price range *see* Chart 2 (A) *in* On the Road with Fodor's.

$$$$ 🏨 **Teton Ridge Ranch.** West of the Tetons on a 4,000-acre spread atop a 6,800-ft knoll, the ranch accommodates just 14 guests. The ranch's lodge has cathedral ceilings, stone fireplaces, an inviting lounge, and a library with comfy sofas. The lodge and guest suites have majestic views of the Tetons; the suites are equipped with woodstoves, hot tubs, and steam showers. Outdoor activity programs include hiking, horseback riding, fishing, cycling, and shooting. ⊠ *200 Valley View Rd., Tetonia 83452,* ☎ *208/456–2650,* 𝔽𝔸𝕏 *208/456–2218. No credit cards. Closed Nov.–Dec. 25, Apr.–May.*

Nightlife and the Arts

The **Idaho Shakespeare Festival** holds performances in the open-air theater in Boise's Park Center (⊠ 412 S. 9th St., ☎ 208/336–9221) from June through September. The **Boise River Festival** (☎ 800/635– 5240 or 208/344–7777), held the last Thursday–Sunday in June, includes more than 300 events, a huge nighttime parade, and entertainment on six stages.

Outdoor Activities and Sports

Fishing

The **Silver Creek Preserve** (⊠ Box 624, Picabo 83348, ☎ 208/788– 2203), northeast of Shoshone in south-central Idaho, has rainbow, brown, and brook trout catch-and-release fishing. Eastern Idaho's **Henry's Fork of the Snake River** (☞ State Parks, *above*) is a renowned fly-fishing stream, with enormous rainbow and cutthroat trout. The **Targhee National Forest** (⊠ 420 N. Bridge St., St. Anthony 83445, ☎ 208/624–3151) watershed is home to Big Springs, spawning grounds for rainbow trout, which can be viewed from a bridge. **Bear Lake** (☞ Blackfoot, Bear Lake, and Lava Hot Springs, *above*), in the southeast corner of the state, is the only place where fishing for ciscoes with dip nets is allowed.

Ski Areas

DOWNHILL

Bogus Basin (⊠ 2405 Bogus Basin Rd., Boise 83702, ☎ 208/332–5100), 48 runs, 6 lifts, 1,800-ft drop. **Grand Targhee** (⊠ Driggs 83422, ☎ 800/827–4433), 46 runs, 3 lifts, 2,200-ft drop. **Kelly Canyon** (⊠ Box 367, Ririe 83443, ☎ 208/538–6261), 23 runs, 4 lifts, 1,000-ft vertical drop. **Pebble Creek** (⌧ Box 370, Inkom 83245, ☎ 208/775–4452), 24 runs, 3 lifts, 2,000-ft drop.

CENTRAL IDAHO

Idaho's midsection is a dense mosaic of rugged wilderness terrain so impenetrable that even cartographers find it difficult to sketch some of the roadways that traverse the region. A teeming waterway system fed by the **Snake** and **Salmon rivers** spins a lacy web across the bumpy landscape and has been the favored mode of transportation since the days of Lewis and Clark. The 420-mi Salmon is the longest undammed river in the lower 48 states.

Visitor Information

Hells Canyon and Lewiston-Clarkston: North Central Idaho Travel Association (⌧ 2207 E. Main St., Lewiston 83501, ☎ 208/743–3531 or 800/473–3543). **McCall:** Visitors Information (⌧ Box D, McCall 83638, ☎ 208/634–7631). **Ketchum–Sun Valley:** Chamber of Commerce (⌧ Box 2420, Sun Valley 83353, ☎ 208/726–3423 or 800/634–3347). **Sawtooth Mountains:** Stanley/Sawtooth Chamber of Commerce (⌧ Box 8, Hwy. 75, Stanley 83278, ☎ 208/774–3411).

Exploring Central Idaho

Sun Valley–Ketchum

The legendary Sun Valley resort opened in 1935. It's located at the precise point where alpine and desert climes converge. The resort's signature pedestrian mall is patterned after an Austrian village. **Ketchum,** a mile from Sun Valley, is an old mining town with shops and restaurants. Just outside Ketchum, beside Trail Creek, the **Ernest Hemingway Memorial** commemorates the writer's last years there.

The **Sawtooth National Recreation Area** (☞ National Parks, *above*), home to the jagged gray-granite peaks of the Sawtooth Mountains, begins about 20 mi north of Ketchum on Route 75. At the northern end of the 30-mi range, the rough-and-tumble town of Stanley serves as a launching point for rafting trips on the Salmon River (☞ Rafting *in* Outdoor Activities and Sports, *below*). On Saturday night river rafters, cowboys, and fishers unwind doing the Stanley Stomp at local saloons in town.

McCall

The 108-mi drive north from Boise on Route 55 to the summer/winter resort town of McCall runs along the shore of the Payette River as it jumps down mountains, over boulders, and through alpine forests. The arid plains of the Snake River give way to higher and higher mountains covered by tremendous stands of pines.

Hells Canyon and Lewiston-Clarkston

The ragged Seven Devils Range stands at 9,000 ft, rimming the southeastern lip of the Snake River Canyon, a deep, dark basalt abyss within the **Hells Canyon National Recreation Area** (☞ National Parks, *above*). Route 71 traces a portion of the gorge, but the best way to take in the scenery is by jet boat or raft (☞ Rafting *in* Outdoor Activities and Sports, *below*). North of Hells Canyon, **Lewiston** and its sister city, **Clarkston, Oregon,** owe their lifeblood to the confluence of the Clearwater and Snake rivers. Ships ply the waters 470 mi from the ocean via the Columbia River to Lewiston's inland seaport. Route 12, among the few east–west motor routes in this part of the state, travels from Lewiston to **Lolo Pass** on the Montana border, following the route that

Sacagawea, Lewis and Clark's Native American guide, traced through the rugged wilderness. The **Nez Percé National Historic Park Headquarters** (☞ National Parks, *above*) displays Nez Percé artifacts and outlines the history of the Native American nation and its famous leader, Chief Joseph.

Dining and Lodging

For price ranges *see* Chart 1 (B) *in* On the Road with Fodor's.

McCall

$ ✕ **The Pancake House.** At the southern edge of town, this breakfast spot has become a favorite of skiers thanks to its massive pancakes. You may have a short wait since everybody in McCall seems to eat here. ⊠ *201 N. 3rd St.,* ☎ *208/634–5849. MC, V. No dinner.*

$$–$$$ 🏨 **The Shore Lodge.** Thanks to its lakefront location, the lodge has become almost synonymous with McCall. Lakefront suites are large, with high ceilings and excellent views, but street-side units are like small motel rooms. Game selections at the lodge's restaurant (no lunch, reservations essential) include elk, venison, and duck. The sharp-cheddar-and-beer soup with red pepper and potato is warming and smooth. ⊠ *501 W. Lake St., 83638,* ☎ *208/634–2244 or 800/657–6464,* 𝔽𝔸𝕏 *208/634–7504. 116 rooms. Restaurant, café, hot tub, sauna, exercise room. AE, D, MC, V.*

$$–$$$ 🏨 **Hotel McCall.** This hybrid between a hotel and a B&B is in the center of town. Rooms (and prices) vary widely; six are small, dark, and share a bath, while others are almost grand and have lots of light and antique furnishings. ⊠ *3rd and Lake Sts., Box 1778, 83638,* ☎ *208/634–8105. 22 rooms, 16 with bath. Dining room. Continental breakfast. AE, MC, V.*

Sun Valley–Ketchum

$$$ ✕ **Lodge Dining Room.** The dramatic, circular, two-level restaurant at the Sun Valley Resort is the area's signature establishment. The Continental menu showcases fresh fish, and there is an extensive wine list. Sunday brunch is a mammoth affair. ⊠ *Sun Valley Rd., Sun Valley,* ☎ *208/622–2150. Reservations essential. AE, D, DC, MC, V.*

$$$ ✕ **Michel's Christiania Restaurant.** Among the highlights at this Sun Valley classic are roast lamb in a parsley crust, sautéed ruby Idaho trout with hazelnuts and cream, and savory tenderloin of venison. ⊠ *Sun Valley Rd. and Walnut Sts., Ketchum,* ☎ *208/726–3388. AE, MC, V.*

$ ✕ **Desperado's.** Huge burritos, black beans, and four kinds of salsa headline the menu at this popular Mexican restaurant in the heart of Ketchum. ⊠ *4th St. and Washington Ave.,* ☎ *208/726–3068. MC, V.*

$$$$ 🏨 **Idaho Country Inn.** Log beams and a river-rock fireplace in the roomy lounge and dining room lend a western feel to this quiet lodging in a residential neighborhood. Guest rooms are spacious and luxurious. ⊠ *134 Latigo La. (Box 2355), Sun Valley 83353,* ☎ *208/726–1019,* 𝔽𝔸𝕏 *208/726–5718. Lounge. AE, MC, V.*

$$$$ 🏨 **Knob Hill Inn.** Rooms at this modern luxury hotel with an alpine decor have large tubs, wet bars, and balconies with mountain views. Intermediate rooms, suites, and penthouses have fireplaces. ⊠ *960 N. Main St., Box 800, Ketchum 83340,* ☎ *208/726–8010 or 800/526–8010,* 𝔽𝔸𝕏 *208/726–2712. 25 rooms. 2 restaurants, indoor pool, hot tub, sauna, exercise room. Full breakfast. AE, MC, V.*

$$$ 🏨 **Sun Valley Lodge and Inn.** Accommodations at the lodge range from luxury suites to family units. The formal lodge dining room serves French cuisine; the restaurant that overlooks the ice rink has more casual fare.

✉ *Sun Valley Resort, Sun Valley 83353,* ☎ *208/622–4111 or 800/786–8259,* ⨎ *208/622–3700. 560 units. 3 restaurants, 3 bars, lounge, 3 pools, sauna, 18 tennis courts, horseback riding, ice-skating, children's program. AE, D, DC, MC, V.*

$$ 🏨 **Bald Mountain Lodge.** On the National Register of Historic Places and right in the center of town, this 1929 one-story log hotel has tastefully decorated rooms, many in knotty pine. ✉ *151 S. Main St. (Box 426), Ketchum 83340,* ☎ *208/726–9963. 10 rooms, 20 apartments. Pool. AE, D, DC, MC, V.*

Motel

🏨 **Sacajawea Motor Inn** (✉ 1824 Main St., Lewiston 83501, ☎ 208/746–1393 or 800/333–1393, ⨎ 208/743–3620), 94 rooms, restaurant, lounge, pool, hot tub, exercise room, laundry; *$$.*

Wilderness Camps and Lodges

For price ranges *see* Chart 2 (A) *in* On the Road with Fodor's.

$$$ 🏨 **Idaho Rocky Mountain Ranch.** The ranch's 8,000-square-ft lodgepole-pine lodge remains much the same as when it was constructed in the 1930s. Period photographs hang on the walls, and animal trophies, rustic artifacts, and a massive rock fireplace immediately catch the eye. Lodge rooms and most of the duplex cabins have Oakley stone showers and handcrafted log furniture. Breakfast, lunch, and dinner are served in the lodge dining room. ✉ *HC 64, off Rte. 75 (Box 9934), Stanley 83278,* ☎ *208/774–3544. 2 lodge rooms, 8 duplex cabins. Dining room, pool, hot springs, hiking, horseback riding, horseshoes, volleyball. D, MC, V. Closed May, Oct.*

$$$ 🏨 **Twin Peaks Ranch.** This 2,300-acre ranch 2 mi off U.S. 93 is nestled in a mile-high valley between the Salmon River and the Frank Church–River of No Return Wilderness Area. Cabins, the original ranch house, and an apple orchard are set on several acres of lawn. Learn horsemanship from experienced wranglers in the full-size rodeo arena; then venture out for a guided day ride or an overnight pack trip. Stocked trout ponds attract anglers, and guided fishing and white-water rafting trips can be arranged. ✉ *Box 774, Salmon 83467,* ☎ *208/894–2290 or 800/659–4899. 13 cabins. Dining room, pool, hot tub. MC, V.*

Outdoor Activities and Sports

Fishing

Steelhead fishing is a major attraction in the **Frank Church–River of No Return Wilderness Area** (☞ National Parks, *above*). The 20-pound fish swim 1,800 mi to the ocean and back again to spawn in the Salmon River.

Hiking and Backpacking

The **Sawtooth National Recreation Area** (☞ National Parks, *above*) is popular with hikers and backpackers. During the winter several yurts (tents made of skins) in the Boulder, Smoky, and Sawtooth mountains are accessible for day ski trips or backcountry multiday trips. Extensive trail systems run through the **Selway Bitterroot Wilderness Area,** the **Frank Church–River of No Return Wilderness Area,** and the **Gospel Hump Wilderness Area.**

Rafting

Salmon and Riggins are launching points for trips on the **Salmon River** and the **Middle Fork of the Salmon River.** The Middle Fork is the state's most famous stretch of water, spanning 100 mi with 100 rapids. Reserve well ahead for summer. The **Salmon** and **Selway,** both federally protected as "wild and scenic" rivers, and the **Clearwater,** are choice rafting waterways.

Ski Areas

Cross-Country

The central Idaho mountain valleys and backcountry are ideal for Nordic skiing. The **North Valley Trails** (⊠ Blaine County Recreation District, 308 N. Main, Hailey 83333, ☎ 208/788–2117) system in the Ketchum–Sun Valley area grooms more than 100 mi of trails.

Downhill

Brundage (⊠ Box 1062, McCall 83638, ☎ 208/634–4151), 38 runs, 4 lifts, 1,800-ft drop. **Sun Valley** (⊠ Sun Valley 83353, ☎ 800/635–8261 or 800/786–8259), 80 runs, 18 lifts, 3,400-ft drop. **Soldier Mountain** (⊠ Box 465, Fairfield 83327, ☎ 208/764–2526), 42 runs, 3 lifts, 1,400-ft vertical drop.

NORTHERN IDAHO

With more than 140 lakes (the highest concentration of any other region in the western United States) and 2,000 mi of streams and rivers, water reigns supreme over lush, wooded northern Idaho. Six major lakes, including **Coeur d'Alene** and the state's largest, **Pend Oreille,** dominate the Panhandle of Idaho.

Visitor Information

Coeur d'Alene: Convention & Visitors Bureau (⊠ Box 1088, 83816, ☎ 208/664–0587). **North Idaho Travel Association:** Greater Sandpoint Chamber of Commerce (⊠ Box 928, Sandpoint 83864, ☎ 208/263–2161). **Silver Valley:** Wallace Visitor Information Center, Wallace Chamber of Commerce, (⊠ 10 River St., Wallace 83873, ☎ 208/753–7151).

Arriving and Departing

By Bus

Greyhound (⊠ 1527 Northwest Blvd., Coeur d'Alene, ☎ 800/231–2222).

By Car

The major highways serving northern Idaho are I–90 (east–west) and U.S. 95 (north–south).

By Plane

The nearest airport is **Spokane International** (☎ 509/455–6455), 20 mi from Coeur d'Alene in eastern Washington.

By Train

Amtrak (☎ 800/872–7245) serves Sandpoint, about 40 mi north of Coeur d'Alene.

Exploring Northern Idaho

Coeur d'Alene and the Silver Valley

Nestled in a pine green mantle beside a gem of a lake of the same name, the city of **Coeur d'Alene** boasts perhaps the most idyllic setting of any town in the state. Restaurants with waterfront dining, a 3,300-ft floating boardwalk, and resort hotels cluster along the water's edge. The American bald eagle and the largest population of osprey in the western United States make this setting home; the watery playground attracts sailors and water-skiers as well. Cruises aboard the sightseeing craft **Mish-An-Nock** (☎ 800/688–5253) pass by the floating 14th hole of the golf course at the Coeur d'Alene Resort (☞ Dining and Lodging, *below*).

Silver Valley, the world's largest silver-mining district, is centered in the towns of Kellogg and Wallace along I–90. The entire town of **Wallace** is listed on the National Register of Historic Places. The **Sixth Street Melodrama** (☎ 208/753–7151) recalls the Wallace's colorful past. The **Wallace District Mining Museum** (☎ 208/753–7151) contains a mother lode of mining history. The **Sierra Silver Mine Tour** (☎ 208/752–5151) provides a peek into an old mine.

The Northern Lakes

The resort town of **Sandpoint,** on the northwestern shores of Lake Pend Oreille, is completely surrounded by mountains; it has been a railroad depot and a mining town but now survives on tourism and lumber. Many buildings here date to the early 1900s. The **Festival at Sandpoint** (☎ 208/263–2161) presents a mix of classical, jazz, and pop concerts from July to September. At the southern end of Lake Pend Oreille, the 4,000-acre **Farragut State Park** (☎ 208/683–2425) supports a diverse wildlife population.

Route 57 provides access to remote **Priest Lake,** with 70 mi of densely wooded shoreline, and the **Upper Priest Lake Scenic Area,** just a jump from the Canadian border. The **Grove of Ancient Cedars,** on the west side of Priest Lake, is a virgin forest with trees up to 12 ft across and 150 ft high.

Dining and Lodging

For price ranges *see* Chart 1 (B) *in* On the Road with Fodor's.

Coeur d'Alene

$$$ ✕ **Cedars Floating Restaurant.** This restaurant is actually *on* the lake, giving it wonderful views. Beer-garden steak is a specialty. ✉ *U.S. 95, ¼ mi south of I–90,* ☎ *208/664–2922. AE, DC, MC, V. No lunch.*

$$ ✕ **Jimmy D's.** The menu here—chicken pastas, steaks, and fish—is uncomplicated but well done, and there's a good wine list. ✉ *320 Sherman Ave.,* ☎ *208/664–9774. AE, D, MC, V.*

$ ✕ **Hudson's Hamburgers.** These folks have been in business since 1907—even rivals admit that Hudson's serves the town's favorite burgers. ✉ *207 Sherman Ave.,* ☎ *208/664–5444. No credit cards. Closed Sun. No dinner.*

$$$$ ✕🏨 **Coeur d'Alene Resort.** The plush rooms at this lakeside resort have fireplaces or balconies with terrific views of the water. Beverly's, one of the hotel's two restaurants, is known for its fine Northwest cuisine and superb wine cellar and also delivers incomparable views of the lake and the mountains. ✉ *2nd and Front Sts., 83814,* ☎ *208/765–4000 or 800/688–5253,* FAX *208/667–2707. 337 rooms. 2 restaurants, 3 lounges, 2 pools, sauna, 18-hole golf course, bowling, exercise room, beach. AE, D, DC, MC, V.*

$$$ 🏨 **Blackwell House.** This B&B in a Victorian jewel of a house is close to the lake and shopping. Its quaintly elegant rooms have wing chairs and antique beds, and the bathtubs are big and old-fashioned. ✉ *820 Sherman Ave., 83814,* ☎ *208/664–0656 or 800/899–0656. 8 rooms, 2 share bath. AE, D, MC, V.*

Priest Lake

$$$ 🏨 **Hill's Resort.** Cabins or condos here all have kitchenettes, and some have fireplaces. The restaurant serves steaks and oysters, and there's dancing in the summer. ✉ *HCR 5, Box 162A, 83856,* ☎ *208/443–2551,* FAX *208/443–2363. 48 units. Restaurant. D, MC, V.*

Wallace

$$ 🏨 **Jameson Inn.** An 1889 redbrick building in downtown Wallace houses this inn. Six small guest rooms (which share two baths) are furnished with miniature wood dressers, mirrored vanity tables, and other Victorian-style touches. The inn's Jameson Restaurant serves casual fare in a setting reminiscent of an Old West saloon. ⊠ *314 6th St., 83873,* ☎ *208/556–1554 or 800/643–2386. 6 rooms. MC, V.*

Outdoor Activities and Sports

Fishing

Lake Pend Oreille is famous for kamloops (large rainbow trout), Priest Lake for mackinaw, Lake Coeur d'Alene for cutthroat trout and chinook salmon. The St. Joe and Coeur d'Alene rivers are good for stream angling.

Ski Areas

DOWNHILL

Schweitzer (⊠ Box 815, Sandpoint 83864, ☎ 208/263–9555 or 800/ 831–8810), 48 runs, six lifts, 2,400-ft vertical drop. **Silver Mountain** (⊠ 610 Bunker Ave., Kellogg 83837, ☎ 208/783—1111), 52 runs, six lifts, 2,200-ft drop.

MONTANA

By Ellen Meloy

Updated by
Kristin Rodine

Capital	Helena
Population	879,400
Motto	Oro y Plata (Gold and Silver)
State Bird	Western meadowlark
State Flower	Bitterroot
Postal Abbreviation	MT

Statewide Visitor Information

Travel Montana (⊠ Dept. of Commerce, 1424 9th Ave., Helena 59620, ☎ 406/444–2654 or 800/847–4868).

Scenic Drives

Beartooth Highway, the stretch of U.S. 212 from Red Lodge to Yellowstone National Park, is a slow but spectacular 68-mi route over a 10,947-ft mountain pass; it's open from June to mid-October. For 187 mi—between Helena and East Glacier—**I–15** and **U.S. 287** and **U.S. 89** run parallel to the Rocky Mountain Front as it rises from the eastern plains. The 50-mi-long **Going-to-the-Sun Road** runs through Glacier National Park (☞ Exploring the Flathead and Western Montana, *below*).

National and State Parks

Millions of acres of Big Sky Country—Montana's nickname for its vast wide-open spaces—are public reserves, including national parks, monuments, and recreation areas. There are eight national wildlife refuges, 10 national forests, and 15 wilderness areas. Yellowstone National Park is also a logical part of a Montana itinerary.

National Parks
Glacier National Park (☞ Exploring the Flathead and Western Montana, *below*) crowns the Continental Divide on the Montana-Canada border. **Little Bighorn Battlefield National Monument** (☞ Bighorn Country, *below*) preserves the battle site in southeastern Montana.

State Parks
The **Montana Department of Fish, Wildlife and Parks** (⊠ 1420 E. 6th Ave., Helena 59620, ☎ 406/444–2535) manages 41 state parks, including **Bannack State Park,** west of Dillon, a ghost town of homes, saloons, and a gallows; **Missouri Headwaters State Park,** near Three Forks, where Lewis and Clark came upon the confluence of the three rivers that form the Missouri; and **Makoshika State Park,** northeast of Billings near Glendive, which contains dramatic badlands formations and dinosaur fossils.

THE FLATHEAD AND WESTERN MONTANA

The northwestern, or Flathead, region is a destination resort area, with such attractions as Flathead Lake and Glacier National Park. In western Montana south of the Flathead, forests, lakes, and meadows mix with ranch country and small valley towns.

Visitor Information

Glacier Country: Regional Tourism Commission (✉ Box 1396, Dept. 507–10–21, Kalispell 59903, ☎ 406/756–7128 or 800/338–5072).

Arriving and Departing

By Bus
Intermountain Bus Co. (☎ 406/755–4011) stops in Kalispell. **Greyhound Lines** (☎ 800/231–2222) serves Missoula.

By Car
I–90 and U.S. 93 pass through Missoula. U.S. 93 and Route 35 lead off I–90 to Kalispell, in the Flathead; from there U.S. 2 leads to Glacier National Park. From Great Falls take I–15 and then U.S. 89 to St. Mary, at the east entrance to Glacier's Going-to-the-Sun Road, which is open June–September, depending on snowfall. During West Glacier off-season, take U.S. 2 west from U.S. 89 at Browning.

By Plane
Glacier Park International Airport (☎ 406/257–5994), in Kalispell, and **Missoula International Airport** (☎ 406/728–4381) are served by major domestic airlines.

By Train
Amtrak (☎ 800/872–7245) stops in Essex, Whitefish, West Glacier, and East Glacier.

Exploring the Flathead and Western Montana

The Flathead
The relatively close proximity of Flathead's towns is atypical of Montana. Bigfork, Kalispell, and Whitefish make good touring bases.

★ **Glacier National Park** (✉ West Glacier 59936, ☎ 406/888–5441) preserves more than a million spectacular acres of peaks, waterfalls, lakes, and wildlife best seen from a hiking trail (☞ Outdoor Activities and Sports, *below*) or on horseback. The 52-mi **Going-to-the-Sun Road,** the park's only through road, is a cliff-hanger and unsuitable for oversize vehicles. A shuttle service is available (☎ 406/862–2539), and guided bus tours (☎ 406/226–5551) leave from either end. Most of the park, including this road, is closed to vehicles in winter.

South of Kalispell is **Flathead Lake,** the largest freshwater lake west of the Mississippi. An 85-mi loop drive around it takes in cherry orchards, parks, sweeping views of the Mission and Swan ranges, and the arts community of **Bigfork,** which has a repertory theater company.

Western Montana
Missoula, 60 mi south of Kalispell via U.S. 93, is home to the **University of Montana** (☎ 406/243–5874 to arrange a free guided tour) and to a thriving community of writers and artists. The Clark Fork, Bitterroot, and Blackfoot rivers converge here—it's not unusual to see anglers casting just downstream of the movie theater. The **Missoula Museum of the Arts** (✉ 335 N. Pattee St., ☎ 406/728–0447) exhibits contemporary works. Hand-carved steeds circle 'round **A Carousel for Missoula** (☎ 406/549–8382) in downtown Caras Park, along the Clark Fork River.

The **Rocky Mountain Elk Foundation Wildlife Visitor Center** (✉ 2291 W. Broadway, ☎ 406/523–4545 or 800/225–5355) has natural history, art, and wildlife displays and information. At **Smokejumper Visitor Center** (✉ W. Broadway/Old Hwy. 10, ☎ 406/329–4934) guides conduct summer tours and provide firsthand accounts of forest fires and smoke jumping. View bison, elk, deer, antelope, and bighorn sheep

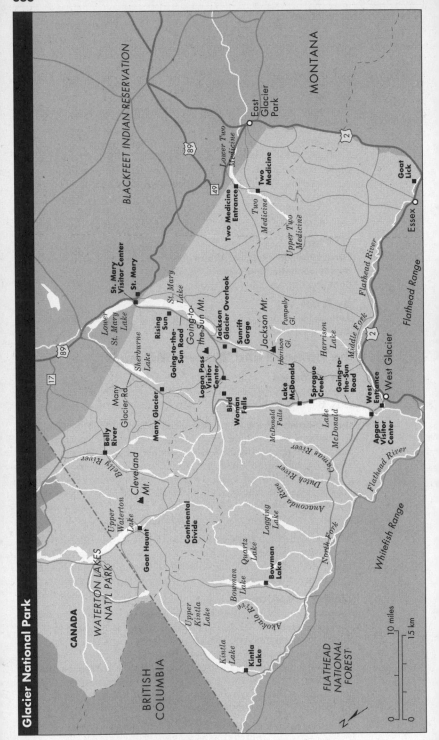

Glacier National Park

CANADA

BRITISH COLUMBIA

WATERTON LAKES NAT'L PARK

BLACKFEET INDIAN RESERVATION

MONTANA

East Glacier Park

89

49

Lower Two Medicine

Two Medicine Entrance

Two Medicine

Upper Two Medicine

Two Medicine

Goat Lick

Essex

St. Mary Visitor Center

St. Mary

St. Mary Lake

Lower St. Mary Lake

Rising Sun

Going-to-the-Sun Road

Going-to-the-Sun Mt.

Jackson Glacier Overlook

Jackson Mt.

Sunrift Gorge

Pumpelly Gl.

Flathead River

Flathead Range

89

17

Sherburne Lake

Logan Pass Visitor Center

Harrison Gl.

Harrison Lake

Middle Fork

Going-to-the-Sun Road

2

West Glacier

Many Glacier Rd.

Many Glacier

Bird Woman Falls

Lake McDonald

Sprague Creek

West Entrance

Belly River

Belly River

Cleveland Mt.

McDonald Falls

Lake McDonald

Apgar Visitor Center

Flathead River

Upper Waterton Lake

Goat Haunt

Continental Divide

Camas River

Dutch River

Anaconda River

Logging Lake

Quartz Lake

Bowman Lake

North Fork

Whitefish Range

Upper Kintla Lake

Bowman Lake

Kintla Lake

Kintla Lake

Akokala River

FLATHEAD NATIONAL FOREST

10 miles

15 km

N

★ through your car window at the **National Bison Range** at Moiese, north of Missoula en route to the Flathead.

East of town, Route 200 leads to **Seeley-Swan Valley,** densely forested and studded with lakes. View loons and other waterfowl from turnouts along the scenic 18-mi **Clearwater Chain-of-Lakes** (⊠ Rte. 83, from Salmon Lake to Rainy Lake).

South of Missoula on U.S. 93, **Bitterroot Valley** stretches between the Sapphire Mountains and the Bitterroots, one of the northern Rockies' most rugged ranges. Jesuit missionaries founded **St. Mary's Mission** in 1841 at Stevensville.

Dining and Lodging

Reserve well in advance for Glacier and for Flathead's popular summer and ski seasons. For price ranges *see* Charts 1 (B) and 2 (B) *in* On the Road with Fodor's.

Bigfork

$$–$$$ ▦ **O'Duach'ain Country Inn Bed and Breakfast.** This log inn sits in a
★ quiet lodgepole-pine forest near Flathead Lake and the Swan River. The main house and log cabin next door are furnished with Old West antiques. *⊠ 675 Ferndale Dr., 59911, ☎ 406/837–6851, ℻ 406/837–4390. 5 rooms, 2 with bath. Hot tub, hiking trails. AE, MC, V.*

Glacier National Park

Glacier Park, Inc. runs Glacier's grand lodges, which date from the early 1900s. The rooms in all the lodges are rustic—no TVs—but comfortable. Make reservations at any of the lodges by calling the central Glacier Park office. *⊠ East Glacier 59434, ☎ 406/226–5551 (June–Labor Day); ⊠ Greyhound Tower, Station 1210, Phoenix, AZ 85077, ☎ 602/207–6000 (Labor Day–May).*

$$–$$$ ✕▦ **Glacier Park Lodge.** On the east side of the park across from the Amtrak station, this beautiful hotel is constructed of giant timbers. *154 rooms. Restaurant, bar, snack bar, pool, golf course, horseback riding. D, MC, V. Closed mid-Sept.-mid-May.*

$$–$$$ ✕▦ **Lake McDonald Lodge.** This former hunting refuge near West Glacier has cabins (that can sleep four people), motel units, and a lodge on the lake. *100 rooms. Restaurant, bar, coffee shop, horseback riding, boating, fishing. D, MC, V. Closed mid-Sept.–mid-May.*

$$–$$$ ✕▦ **Many Glacier Hotel.** The park's largest lodge, 12 mi west of Babb on the east side of the park, overlooks Swiftcurrent Lake and has commanding mountain views. *208 rooms. Restaurant, bar, horseback riding, boating, fishing. D, MC, V. Closed mid-Sept.–mid-May.*

Hot Springs

$–$$ ▦ **Chico Hot Springs Lodge.** Built at the turn of the century, this resort is nestled against the Absarokee Mountains 29 mi north of Yellowstone. The dining room is famous, as are the mineral hot springs. Accommodations are in condominiums or the old lodge, as well as in cabins and two small motels. *Drawer D, Pray 59065, ☎ 406/333–4933 or 800/468–9232, ℻ 406/333–4694. 85 rooms. Restaurant, pools. D, MC, V.*

$–$$ ▦ **Lost Trail Hot Springs Resort.** Hot springs feed the swimming pool and a hot tub at this resort 90 mi south of Missoula in the Bitterroot National Forest. RV spaces are available. *⊠ Off U.S. 93 (Box 8321), Sula 59871, ☎ 406/821–3574, ℻ 406/821–4012 or 800/825–3574. 18 rooms, 7 cabins. Restaurant, bar, pools, casino. AE, MC, V.*

Missoula

$$
★ ✕ **Alley Cat Grill.** A subtle feline motif graces this bistrolike eatery that serves French, Indonesian, and seafood specials. ⊠ *125½ Main St.,* ☎ *406/728–3535. MC, V.*

$–$$ ✕ **Guy's Lolo Creek Steak House.** This quintessentially Montana restaurant, 8 mi south of Missoula, serves sirloin and other meats cooked over an open fire in a massive log structure. ⊠ *6600 U.S. 12 W, Lolo,* ☎ *406/273–2622. AE, D, MC, V.*

$$–$$$ 🏨 **Goldsmith's Inn.** This restored B&B, built in 1911 as the residence of the University of Montana's first president, was moved to its present riverside location in 1989. The large front deck overlooks the river. ⊠ *809 E. Front St., 59801,* ☎ *406/721–6732. 7 units. AE, D, MC, V.*

Ranches

Montana's guest ranches range from working ranches to deluxe spreads with nary a cow in sight; check Travel Montana's directory (☞ Statewide Visitor Information, *above*). Those listed throughout this chapter are categorized as either $$ (less than $1,000 per person per week) or $$$ ($1,000–$1,900 per person based on double occupancy). Meals and recreation are included.

$$$ 🏨 **Flathead Lake Lodge.** Reserve at least a year in advance for this deluxe 2,000-acre dude ranch on the shores of Flathead Lake. The decor is rustic western. Each lodge holds a big stone fireplace. Rates are American Plan, with a one-week minimum. ⊠ *Box 248, Bigfork 59911,* ☎ *406/837–4391,* 𝔽𝔸𝕏 *406/837–6977. 18 rooms, 20 cottages. Dining room, tennis, hiking, horseback riding, boating, waterskiing, fishing. MC, V. Closed Oct.–Apr.*

Motels

🏨 **Village Red Lion Inn** (⊠ 100 Madison St., Missoula 59801, ☎ 406/728–3100 or 800/237–7445, 𝔽𝔸𝕏 406/728–2530), 172 rooms, restaurant, bar, coffee shop, pool, hot tub; *$$–$$$.* 🏨 **Best Western Outlaw Inn** (⊠ 1701 Hwy. 93S, Kalispell 59901, ☎ 406/755–6100 or 800/237–7445, 𝔽𝔸𝕏 406/756–8994), 220 rooms, restaurant, bar, 2 indoor pools, casino; *$$–$$$.*

Campgrounds

Glacier National Park's 10 campgrounds are available first-come, first-served; they fill by noon. Other public campgrounds are in national forests and state parks. Look for private campgrounds with RV services near towns or check Travel Montana's directory (☞ Statewide Visitor Information, *above*).

Outdoor Activities and Sports

Biking

Glacier's Going-to-the-Sun Road is a challenging ride. **Backcountry Bicycle Tours** (⊠ Box 4029, Bozeman 59772, ☎ 406/586–3556) organizes five- to seven-day trips in Glacier National Park as well as the rest of the state.

Fishing

In the Flathead Valley, fish for cutthroat and bull trout in the Flathead River or perch, whitefish, and lake trout in Flathead Lake. **Pointer Scenic Cruises** (⊠ Bigfork, ☎ 406/837–5617) operates custom charter tours on Flathead Lake. For western Montana waterways, fish the Clark Fork, Bitterroot, and Blackfoot rivers; Rock Creek, a blue-ribbon trout stream; or Seeley Lake. Local stores sell fishing licenses.

Golf

Eagle Bend Golf Club (⊠ Box 960, Bigfork 59911, ☎ 406/837–7300 or 800/255–5641), 18 holes.

Hiking and Backpacking

Glacier National Park has 730 mi of trails. **Glacier Wilderness Guides** (⊠ Box 535, West Glacier 59936, ☎ 406/888–5466 or 800/521–7238) leads backcountry trips. The **Great Bear, Bob Marshall,** and **Scapegoat wilderness areas** (⊠ Flathead National Forest, 1935 3rd Ave. E, Kalispell 59901, ☎ 406/755–5401) constitute a million-acre refuge along the Continental Divide. The **Jewel Basin Hiking Area,** 13 mi east of Bigfork off Route 83, is a short, minimal-ascent trail to high-country lakes and superb views. For information on backcountry hiking, contact the **U.S. Forest Service Northern Region Office** (⊠ 2000 E. Broadway Ave., Missoula 59807, ☎ 406/329–3511).

Rafting and Canoeing

Rafting outfitters include **Glacier Raft Co.** (⊠ Box 218M, West Glacier 59936, ☎ 406/888–5454 or 800/332–9995). Canoes take the calmer waters of Glacier Park's Lake McDonald. For canoe rentals try **Glacier Park Boat Company** (⊠ Box 5262, Kalispell 59903, ☎ 406/888–5727 May–Sept. or 406/752–5488 Oct.–Apr.).

Most stretches of the Clark Fork and Bitterroot can be run by raft or canoe; the Blackfoot is more difficult. Outfitters include **Western Waters** (⊠ 5455 Keil Loop, Missoula, ☎ 406/543–3203). Northeast of Missoula near Seeley Lake, the **Clearwater River Canoe Trail** follows an easy 4-mi stretch.

Water Sports

Flathead Lake supports a large sailing community, countless water-skiers and windsurfers, and cruises on the *Port Polson Princess* (⊠ Polson, ☎ 406/883–2448 or 800/882-6363).

Ski Areas

For **ski reports** call 406/444–2654 or 800/847–4868.

Cross-Country

Trails are found at Glacier National Park, in the Flathead National Forest, and in Lolo National Forest near Missoula. On Glacier's southern border, the **Izaak Walton Inn** (⊠ U.S. 2, Essex 59916, ☎ 406/888–5700, ℻ 406/888–5200) has 18 mi of groomed trails.

Downhill

Big Mountain (⊠ Box 1400, Whitefish 59937, ☎ 406/862–1900 or 800/858–5439) has 63 runs, 9 lifts, and a 2,300-ft vertical drop.

SOUTHWESTERN MONTANA

Montana's pioneer history began here, and the full range of the early mining frontier—from rough-and-tumble camps to the mansions of the magnates—is still evident. In the high country north and west of Yellowstone National Park you'll find world-class fishing and some of the state's best ski terrain.

Visitor Information

Gold West Country: Regional Tourism Commission (⊠ 1155 Main St., Deer Lodge 59722, ☎ 406/846–1943 or 800/879–1159). **Yellowstone Country:** Regional Tourism Commission (⊠ Box 1107, Red Lodge 59068, ☎ 406/446–1005 or 800/736–5276).

Arriving and Departing

By Bus
Intermountain Bus Co. (☏ 406/442–5860) stops in Helena and Butte (☏ 406/723–3287). **Greyhound Lines** serves Bozeman (☏ 800/231–2222). In summer **Karst Stages** (☏ 800/332–0504) runs between Bozeman, Livingston, and Yellowstone.

By Car
I–15 passes through Helena. Use I–90 for Butte and Bozeman. U.S. 191, 89, 287, and 212 link the region with Yellowstone.

By Plane
Major domestic airlines fly to Helena, Bozeman, and Butte.

Exploring Southwestern Montana

The humble mining origins of **Helena,** Montana's capital, are visible in its earliest commercial district, **Reeder's Alley.** By 1888, the "Queen City of the Rockies" boasted major gold rushes and 50 resident millionaires. The mansions on the **West Side** and commercial buildings on the main street, **Last Chance Gulch,** preserve the era's opulence.

Helena's vibrant arts scene includes dramatic performances and movies in the two auditoriums within the **Myrna Loy Theater** (✉ 15 N. Ewing St., ☏ 406/443–0287). The **Archie Bray Foundation** (✉ 2915 Country Club Ave., ☏ 406/443–3502), a nationally known center for ceramic arts, offers tours. The **Montana Historical Society Museum** (✉ 225 N. Roberts St., ☏ 406/444–2694) and **Holter Museum of Art** (✉ 12 E. Lawrence Ave., ☏ 406/442–6400) showcase valuable collections of folk and western paintings and historic memorabilia.

The millionaires may have resided in Helena, but the miners lived in **Butte,** a tough, wily town with a rich ethnic mix. The **Berkeley Pit,** a mile-wide open-pit copper mine, sits at the edge of the **Butte National Historic District,** a downtown area of ornate buildings with an Old West feel. On the northern edge of Deer Lodge, the **Grant-Kohrs Ranch National Historic Site** (✉ 316 Main St., ☏ 406/846–2070) preserves the home and outbuildings of a 19th-century ranch, still worked by cowboys and draft horses. The **Towe Ford Museum** (✉ 1106 Main St., ☏ 406/846–3111) is a car buff's delight, with more than 100 vintage Fords and Lincolns dating from 1903 to the 1970s.

★ Montana's oldest state park, **Lewis and Clark Caverns** (✉ Rte. 2, off I–90, ☏ 406/287–3032), lies 40 mi east of Butte. Two-hour tours lead through narrow passages and vaulted chambers past colorful, intriguingly varied limestone formations. The park is closed from mid-October through mid-April.

Bozeman, 50 mi east of Butte on I–90, is a regional trade center, a place crazy for food, art, and the outdoors. At Montana State University, the
★ **Museum of the Rockies** (✉ 600 W. Kagy Blvd., ☏ 406/994–3466) presents paleontology exhibits, a hands-on dinosaur playroom, planetarium shows, and western art and history exhibits.

South of town, U.S. 191 follows the Gallatin River to West Yellowstone, the gateway to **Yellowstone National Park** (☞ Wyoming). On the U.S. 89 approach to Yellowstone, **Livingston**—former home of Calamity Jane and now a haven for hiking, fishing, and other outdoor activities—sits at the head of Paradise Valley, which is bisected by the Yellowstone River. Another route to Yellowstone, U.S. 212, leads to **Red Lodge.** The coal mines here drew immigrants from Great Britain, Italy, Finland, Yugoslavia, and other nations at the turn of the century.

The town celebrates its diverse heritage each August with a weeklong celebration. Late summer is rodeo season in Livingston, Red Lodge, and Big Timber, 35 mi east of Livingston.

Dining and Lodging

For price ranges *see* Charts 1 (B) and 2 (B) *in* On the Road with Fodor's.

Big Sky

$$–$$$ ✕⌂ **Big Sky Ski and Summer Resort.** After enjoying outdoor activities, come back to large, bright rooms in the ski lodge or condominiums of this resort in Gallatin Canyon, 43 mi south of Bozeman and 18 mi from Yellowstone National Park. ✉ *Box 160001, 59716,* ☎ *406/995–5000 or 800/548–4486,* FAX *406/995–5001. 298 rooms. Restaurants, pool, golf, health club, horseback riding, fishing, skiing. AE, D, DC, MC, V. Closed mid-Apr.–early June, late Sept.–mid-Dec.*

Bozeman

$ ✕ **Mackenzie River Pizza Co.** This casual, upbeat eatery prepares pies with innovative toppings. ✉ *232 E. Main St.,* ☎ *406/587–0055. Reservations not accepted. AE, MC, V.*

$$ ⌂ **Voss Inn.** This 1883 Victorian house in Bozeman's historic district is furnished with period antiques. ✉ *319 S. Willson Ave., 59715,* ☎ *406/587–0982,* FAX *406/585–2964. 6 rooms. AE, MC, V.*

Butte

$$ ✕ **Uptown Cafe.** Fresh seafood, steaks, and pasta are served in this informal café. ✉ *47 E. Broadway,* ☎ *406/723–4735. AE, MC, V.*

Helena

$$ ✕ **The Windbag.** This saloon was named in honor of the hot political debates you're likely to overhear while dining on burgers and seafood. ✉ *19 S. Last Chance Gulch,* ☎ *406/443–9669. AE, D, MC, V.*

$$–$$$ ⌂ **The Sanders.** Wilbur Fisk Sanders, frontier politician and vigilante,
★ once lived in this 1875 mansion, now a centrally located B&B on the National Register of Historic Places. ✉ *328 N. Ewing St., 59601,* ☎ *406/442–3309,* FAX *406/443–2361. 7 rooms. AE, MC, V.*

Motels

⌂ **Bozeman Inn** (✉ 1235 N. 7th Ave., Bozeman 59715, ☎ 406/587–3176 or 800/648–7515, FAX 406/585–3591), 49 rooms, restaurant, bar, pool, hot tub, sauna; *$–$$.* ⌂ **War Bonnett Inn** (✉ 2100 Cornell Ave., Butte 59701, ☎ 406/494–7800), 134 rooms, restaurant, bar, pool, hot tub, sauna, exercise room; *$$.* ⌂ **Jorgenson's Holiday Motel** (✉ 1714 11th Ave., Helena 59601, ☎ 406/442–1770 or 800/272–1770 in MT, FAX 406/449–0155), 117 rooms, restaurant, bar, indoor pool, laundry; *$$–$$$.*

Ranch

For price ranges *see* Lodging *in* The Flathead and Western Montana, *above.*

$$ ⌂ **Lazy K Bar.** This working ranch, built in 1880, sits on 22,000 acres below the Crazy Mountains. Guests can do a lot of riding, including actual cattle moving and other ranch work, if they choose. Rates include everything except gratuities, with a one-week minimum stay. ✉ *Box 550M, Big Timber 59011,* ☎ FAX *406/537–4404. Horseback riding, fishing. No credit cards. Closed Oct.–May.*

Campgrounds

Public campgrounds are in national forests and state parks; private ones with RV services are near towns, or check Travel Montana's directory (☞ Statewide Visitor Information, *above*). In peak season campgrounds near Yellowstone fill early in the day.

The Arts

The String Orchestra of the Rockies performs at the **Big Sky Arts Festival** at the Big Sky Ski and Summer Resort (☞ Dining and Lodging, *above*) in July. Big Timber hosts August's **Montana Cowboy Poetry Gathering** (⊠ Sweet Grass Chamber of Commerce, ☎ 406/932–5131).

Outdoor Activities and Sports

Fishing

Few trout streams rival the Missouri, Beaverhead, and Big Hole rivers; one outfitter is the **Complete Fly Fisher** (⊠ Wise River ☎ 406/832–3175). Livingston, Ennis, and West Yellowstone are base towns for the superb fly-fishing on the Yellowstone, Madison, and other local rivers; **Dan Bailey's Fly Shop** (⊠ 209 W. Park St., Livingston, ☎ 406/222–1673 or 800/356–4052) is a Montana legend. Licenses are sold at local stores.

Golf

Big Sky Golf Course (⊠ Rte. 64, Big Sky, ☎ 406/995–4706), 18 holes.

Hiking and Backpacking

Wilderness areas include the **Gates of the Mountains** (☎ 406/449–5201), near Helena; the **Anaconda-Pintler Wilderness** (☎ 406/496–3400), near Anaconda; the **Lee Metcalf Wilderness** (☎ 406/587–6701), near Bozeman; and **Absarokee-Beartooth Wilderness** (☎ 406/587–6701), near Livingston.

Rafting and Canoeing

The Missouri River north of Helena is easy for rafts and canoes. Bear Trap Canyon, on the Madison River near Ennis, and Yankee Jim, on the Yellowstone near Gardiner, require white-water experience or an outfitter, such as the **Yellowstone Raft Co.** (☎ 406/848–7777 or 800/858–7781).

Ski Areas

For **ski reports** call 406/444–2654 or 800/847–4868.

Cross-Country

In winter many national forest roads and trails become backcountry ski trails. **Lone Mountain Ranch** (⊠ Box 160069, Big Sky 59716, ☎ 406/995–4644 or 800/514–4644, ₣ₐₓ 406/995–4670) has 45 mi of groomed and tracked trails, food, lodging, and such extras as sleigh-ride dinners and guided cross-country ski tours of nearby Yellowstone National Park.

Downhill

Big Sky Resort (☞ Dining and Lodging, *above*) has 75 runs, 15 lifts, and a 4,180-ft vertical drop.

BIGHORN COUNTRY

Cowboy culture seems overpowering in southeastern Montana, but this is truly Native American land. A stunning country of rimrock, badlands, wide-open grasslands, and rugged mountains, it is still the home of the Northern Cheyenne and the Crow. Billings is a convenient base for touring.

Visitor Information

Custer Country: Regional Tourism Commission (⊠ Rte. 1, Box 1206A, Hardin 59034, ☎ 406/665–1671 or 800/346–1876).

Arriving and Departing

By Bus
Greyhound Lines (☎ 800/231–2222) and **Rimrock Stages** (☎ 406/549–2339 or 800/255–7655) serve Billings.

By Car
The main routes between Yellowstone and Broadus, in the southeastern corner of the state, are I–94, I–90, U.S. 212, and Route 59.

By Plane
Major domestic airlines fly to **Logan International Airport** (☎ 406/657–8495), in Billings.

Exploring Bighorn Country

Booms in coal, oil, and gas made **Billings** Montana's largest town. Sprawled between steep-face rimrocks and the Yellowstone River, it has big-city services and a stockman's heart. In summer the town puts on a nightly rodeo. The **Moss Mansion** (⊠ 914 Division St., ☎ 406/256–5100) is an elegantly restored 1903 dwelling. Tours are offered. A broader view of the social history of the Yellowstone Valley can be found in the varied exhibits of the **Western Heritage Center** (⊠ 2822 Montana Ave., ☎ 406/256–6809). The **Yellowstone Art Center** (⊠ 401 N. 27th Ave., ☎ 406/256–6804) showcases regional art in the old county jail.

Southeast of Billings on I–94 lie the Crow and Northern Cheyenne Indian reservations. **Crow Fair** (☎ 406/638–2601), held in Crow Agency for five days in August, draws visitors from all over the West for parades, rodeos, traditional dancing, and horse races.

On the Montana-Wyoming border is **Bighorn Canyon National Recreation Area** (⊠ Fort Smith 59035, ☎ 406/666–2412). **Ok-A-Beh Marina** (⊠ 604 S. 1st St., Hardin 59034, ☎ 406/665–2216) rents boats for exploring the canyon.

★ Fifteen miles southeast of Hardin on I–90, **Little Bighorn Battlefield National Monument** (⊠ National Park Service, Crow Agency 59022, ☎ 406/638–2621) preserves the site where in 1876 the Cheyenne and Sioux defended their lives and homeland in a bloody battle with General George Armstrong Custer. Visit the museum or take a guided tour.

Dining and Lodging

For price ranges *see* Charts 1 (B) and 2 (B) *in* On the Road with Fodor's.

Billings

$–$$ ✕ **CJ's Restaurant.** Juicy mesquite-grilled ribs, steaks, chicken, and seafood dominate the fare at this popular spot, where the barbecue sauces range from mild to three-alarm. ⊠ *2456 Central Ave.,* ☎ *406/656–1400. AE, D, DC, MC, V.*

$$$ ✕▥ **Radisson Northern Hotel.** Room decor at this historic hotel follows an American West theme; views are glorious. The Golden Belle restaurant serves fine Continental cuisine in an atmosphere that's fancier than usual for Montana. ⊠ *Broadway at 1st Ave. N (Box 1296), 59101,* ☎ *406/245–5121 or 800/333–3333,* ℻ *406/259–9862. 160 rooms. Restaurant, bar. AE, D, DC, MC, V.*

Motel

Ponderosa Inn Best Western (⊠ 2511 1st Ave. N, Billings 59101, ☎ 406/259–5511 or 800/628–9081, FAX 406/245–8004), 130 rooms, restaurant, bar, pool, hot tub, sauna, exercise room; $$.

Campgrounds

Public campgrounds are in **Custer National Forest** and **Bighorn Canyon National Recreation Area**; for private campgrounds check Travel Montana's listing (☞ Statewide Visitor Information, *above*).

Outdoor Activities and Sports

Fishing

Trout anglers fish the Yellowstone River above Columbus. Downriver, expect walleye, bass, and warmer-water fish. The Bighorn River below Yellowtail Dam near Pryor is trout heaven; lake species inhabit the reservoir above the dam.

Hiking and Backpacking

The northern region of the arid Pryor Mountains, south of Billings, is on the Crow Reservation; permits for backcountry travel are issued by the **Crow Tribal Council** (⊠ Crow Agency 59022, ☎ 406/638–2601). The southern Pryors are in **Custer National Forest** (⊠ 2602 1st Ave. N, Billings 59103, ☎ 406/657–6361).

Rafting and Canoeing

Canoes, rafts, and drift boats suit the Yellowstone River and the Bighorn River below Yellowtail Dam.

Ski Area

Red Lodge Mountain (⊠ Box 750, Red Lodge 59068, ☎ 406/446–2610 or 800/444–8977), an hour southwest of Billings, has 45 runs, 8 lifts, and a 2,350-ft vertical drop.

ELSEWHERE IN MONTANA

Central and Eastern Montana

Arriving and Departing

I–15 and U.S. 89 traverse the region north–south; U.S. 2 and I–94 run east–west.

What to See and Do

Montana's heartland is open grasslands and, rising abruptly from the plains, the sheer escarpment of the Rocky Mountain Front. In **Great Falls,** the **C. M. Russell Museum** (⊠ 400 13th St. N, ☎ 406/727–8787) has a formidable collection of works by the cowboy artist, along with his original log cabin studio. Cowboy life thrives in **Miles City,** which in May hosts the **Miles City Bucking Horse Sale,** three days of horse trading, rodeo, and street dances. For more information on the region, contact the **Russell Country Regional Tourism Commission** (⊠ Box 1366, Great Falls 59403, ☎ 406/761–5036 or 800/527–5348) and the **Custer Country Regional Tourism Commission** (⊠ Rte. 1, Box 1206A, Hardin 59034, ☎ 406/665–1671).

WYOMING

By Geoffrey
O'Gara

Updated by
Candy
Moulton

Capital	Cheyenne
Population	481,000
Motto	Equal Rights
State Bird	Meadowlark
State Flower	Indian paintbrush
Postal Abbreviation	WY

Statewide Visitor Information

Wyoming Division of Tourism (⊠ I–25 at College Dr., Cheyenne 82002, ☎ 307/777–7777 or 800/225–5996 for recorded ski reports). **Information centers** in Cheyenne, Evanston, Jackson, and Sheridan are open year-round; those in Pine Bluffs, Chugwater, and near Laramie close in winter.

Scenic Drives

North of Cody and east of Yellowstone is the 60-mi **Beartooth Highway,** U.S. 212. Switchbacking across Beartooth Pass at 10,947 ft, it's the state's highest highway and open only in summer. Add a few miles to your drive and take the **Chief Joseph Scenic Highway** (Route 296, south from Beartooth Highway toward Cody) to see the gorge carved by the Clarks Fork of the Yellowstone River. There is more scenery than service on these roads, so gas up in Cody or at the northeastern end of the route, in Red Lodge or in Cooke City, Montana.

National and State Parks

National Parks

Yellowstone National Park (☞ Exploring Yellowstone, Grand Teton, Jackson, and Cody, *below*) is widely considered the crown jewel of the national park system. **Grand Teton National Park** (☞ Exploring Yellowstone, Grand Teton, Jackson, and Cody, *below*) contains the jagged Teton Range, the Snake River, and, in between, a string of pristine lakes. **Devils Tower National Monument** (☞ Elsewhere in Wyoming, *below*) contains a site that is sacred to Native Americans.

State Parks

Wyoming's state parks are listed on the Division of Tourism's state road map. Historic sites include **South Pass City** (⊠ 125 South Pass Main, ☎ 307/332–3684), a history-rich gold camp near the Oregon Trail, and **Fort Bridger State Historic Site** (⊠ Fort Bridger, ☎ 307/782–3842), the pioneer trading post started by Jim Bridger and later used by the military. **Hot Springs State Park** (☎ 307/864–2176), in Thermopolis on U.S. 20, has the world's largest hot spring.

YELLOWSTONE, GRAND TETON, JACKSON, AND CODY

When John Colter's descriptions of **Yellowstone** were reported in St. Louis newspapers in 1810, most readers dismissed them as tall tales. Colter had left the Lewis and Clark expedition to trap and explore in a region virtually unknown to whites, and his reports of giant elk roaming among fuming mud pots, waterfalls, and geysers in a wilderness of evergreens and towering peaks were just too farfetched to be taken seriously. Sixty years and several expeditions later, however, the nation was convinced, and in 1872 Yellowstone became the country's first national park.

Yellowstone and Grand Teton National Parks

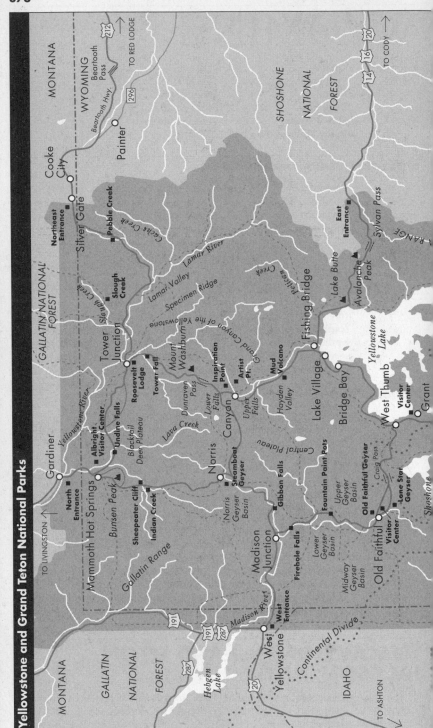

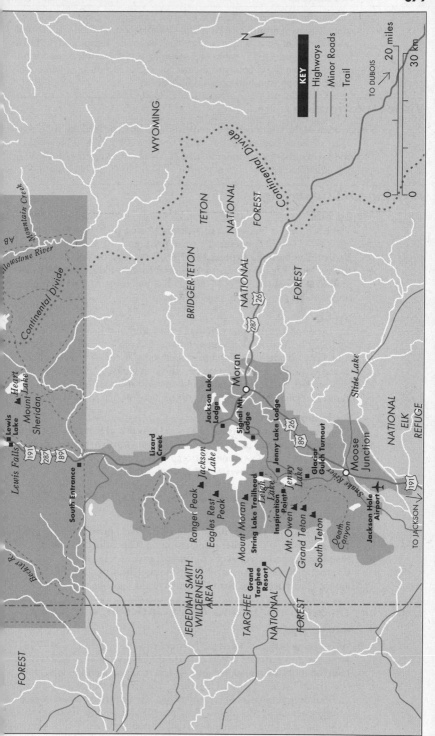

The **Snake River** runs through Jackson Hole Valley, making its way south and west along the foot of the Grand Tetons and through **Grand Teton National Park,** which is nestled between the Tetons and the Gros Ventre Mountains. The town of **Jackson** was first a rendezvous for fur trappers, then the gateway to the nearby parks and dude ranches, and later the center of a booming ski industry.

Visitor Information

Jackson Hole: Chamber of Commerce (⊠ Box E, 83001, ☎ 307/733–3316); Visitors Council (⊠ Box 982, Dept. 8, 83001, ☎ 800/782–0011). **Cody:** Chamber of Commerce (⊠ 836 Sheridan Ave., 82414, ☎ 307/587–2297).

Arriving and Departing

By Bus

There is no direct bus service to Jackson. During ski season **START** buses (☎ 307/733–4521) operate between town and the Jackson Hole Ski Resort. The **Targhee Express** (☎ 307/733–3101 or 800/827–4433) crosses Teton Pass on its way to the Grand Targhee Ski Resort. **TW Recreational Services** (☎ 307/344–7901) has bus tours of Yellowstone in summer and snow-coach tours in winter.

By Car

To reach Yellowstone through the Teton Valley and Jackson Hole, turn north off I–80 at Rock Springs and take U.S. 191 the 177 mi to Jackson; Yellowstone is 60 mi farther north on U.S. 191/89. You can also approach Yellowstone from the east through Cody, 52 mi from Yellowstone on U.S. 14/16/20; for north and west entrances *see* Montana. Grand Teton National Park is 10 mi north of Jackson on U.S. 191/89.

By Plane

Several airlines have daily service from Denver and Salt Lake City into **Jackson Hole Airport** (☎ 307/733–7682), 9 mi north of town and about 40 mi south of Yellowstone National Park. Major car rental agencies serve the airport. **Yellowstone Regional Airport** (☎ 307/587–5096), at Cody on the park's east side, is served by commuter airlines out of Denver. For information on additional services, *see* Montana.

By Train

The **Amtrak** *Pioneer* (☎ 800/872–7245) travels three times per week across Wyoming's southern tier, stopping (depending on the day) in Evanston, Green River, Rock Springs, Rawlins, Laramie, and outside Cheyenne. Rock Springs and Evanston are the stops for those heading to Yellowstone; cars can be rented at the stations.

Exploring Yellowstone, Grand Teton, Jackson, and Cody

Yellowstone

Yellowstone National Park (⊠ Mammoth 82190, ☎ 307/344–7381) preserves and provides access to natural treasures such as **Yellowstone Lake,** with its 110-mi shoreline and lake cruises, wildlife, waterfowl, and trout fishing; **Grand Canyon of the Yellowstone,** 24 mi long, 1,200 ft deep, in shades of red and ocher surrounded by emerald-green forest; spectacular **Mammoth Hot Springs;** and 900 mi of horse trails, 1,000 mi of hiking trails, and 370 mi of public roads. Visitor centers throughout the park are the departure points for guided hikes and are the sites of evening talks and campfire programs (check the park newsletter *Discover Yellowstone* for details). Park service literature and warnings about interaction with the wildlife—grizzly bears and bison, especially—should be taken seriously.

Roads from all five Yellowstone entrances eventually join the figure-8 that is **Grand Loop Road,** which makes many areas accessible by vehicle. If you enter from the south, start in the Old Faithful area. The best-known geyser is, of course, **Old Faithful,** the crowd pleaser that erupts every hour or so. Wooden walkways wind by other geysers, mud pots, and colorful springs and along nearby Firehole River. Stay on the walkways—geysers can be dangerous. Elk and bison frequent this area. Near the west park entrance is **Norris Geyser Basin;** among its hundreds of springs and geysers is the unpredictable Steamboat Geyser, which shoots water more than 300 ft into the air.

A short hike from **Canyon,** at the intersection of the loops, are Inspiration, Grandview, and Lookout points, where the vistas confirm Colter's accounts. The **North Rim Trail** leads to views of the 308-ft Upper Falls and 109-ft Lower Falls. In the northeast corner of the park is beautiful **Lamar Valley,** which attracts bison in the summer.

Grand Teton

Grand Teton National Park (⊠ Moose 83012, ☎ 307/739–3300 or 307/739–3399) was established in 1929 and expanded to its present size when the Rockefeller family donated land it owned in Jackson Hole. The park is south of Yellowstone and linked to it by the John D. Rockefeller Memorial Parkway (U.S. 89).

Technical climbers rope up and drag themselves to the 13,770-ft summit of the **Grand,** but day hikers find many rewards, too—from a journey up Cascade Canyon to a lakeshore ramble. Jenny, Leigh, and Jackson lakes, strung along the base of the Tetons, are popular with fishers and canoeists, who are joined on Jackson Lake by windsurfers and sailors. For rafters, the **Snake River** offers smooth and fast-moving water and the possibility of seeing moose or bison. Willow Flats and Oxbow Bend are excellent places to see waterfowl, and Signal Mountain Road affords a top-of-the-park view of the Tetons.

Jackson

With its raised wooden sidewalks and old-fashioned storefronts, the town of **Jackson** may look like a western-movie set, but it's the real thing. Residents hotly debate whether and how much to control development, with most locals determined to avoid what they call Aspenization. For the time being the town remains compact and folksy, a place where genuine cowboys rub shoulders with the store-bought variety and where the antler-arched square, the whoop-it-up nightlife, and the surrounding wilderness are pretty much intact.

Jackson is walk-around size and easy to relax in after white-water rafting, hiking, or skiing. Whether your idea of relaxation is enjoying an epicurean meal, lolling in a hot tub, or two-stepping at the Cowboy Bar (⊠ 25 N. Cache Dr., ☎ 307/733–2207), Jackson is a good host.

Cody

Most people use Cody as a way station en route to or from Yellowstone's east entrance, but the town's museum is a must-see for anyone interested in the history of the American West. The **Buffalo Bill Historical Center** (⊠ 720 Sheridan Ave., ☎ 307/587–4771) has a **Plains Indian Museum,** the **Cody Firearms Museum,** the **Buffalo Bill Museum,** and the **Whitney Gallery of Western Art.**

What to See and Do with Children

Granite Hot Springs, south of Jackson off U.S. 191 and 10 mi into Bridger–Teton National Forest along a gravel road, has a creekside campground, a hot-springs pool, hiking trails, and scenery. From December 15 through March the **National Elk Refuge** (⊠ 675 E. Broadway, Jackson 83001, ☎ 307/733–0277) operates horse-drawn sleigh trips through the herd of more than 7,000 elk in their winter preserve.

Dining and Lodging

You can make reservations for a stay in Jackson or Jackson Hole Ski Resort through **Central Reservations** (☎ 800/443–6931). **Bed & Breakfast Rocky Mountains** (⊠ 906 S. Pearl St., Denver, CO 80209, ☎ 303/744–8415) handles bed-and-breakfasts throughout the region. For information about the many guest ranches between Cody and Yellowstone, contact the **East Yellowstone Valley Lodges** (⊠ 1231 Yellowstone Hwy., Cody 82414, ☎ 307/587–9595).

For price ranges *see* Charts 1 (B) and 2 (B) *in* On the Road with Fodor's.

Grand Teton

Grand Teton Lodge Company operates three of the park's lodges—Jackson Lake, Jenny Lake, and Colter Bay Village (☞ *below*). ⊠ *Box 240, Moran 83013,* ☎ *307/543–3100,* FAX *307/543–3143. AE, DC, MC, V.*

$$$ ✕🏨 **Jackson Lake Lodge.** This brown stone edifice has huge windows overlooking Willow Flats. Guest rooms in the adjacent buildings are larger and more appealingly decorated than those in the main lodge. The Mural Room's menu sometimes features local game such as venison or antelope. ⊠ *Off U.S. 89 north of Jackson Lake Junction. 385 rooms. 2 restaurants, pool. Closed late-Oct.–early May.*

$$$ ✕🏨 **Jenny Lake Lodge.** Set amid pines and a wildflower meadow, this
★ lodge has cabins and rooms that are rustic yet luxurious, with sturdy pine beds covered with handmade quilts and electric blankets. The restaurant emphasizes Rocky Mountain cuisine, including roast prime rib of buffalo or breast of pheasant. ⊠ *Jenny Lake Rd. 37 cabins. Restaurant, bar. Closed mid-Oct.–late May.*

$$–$$$ ✕🏨 **Signal Mountain Lodge.** The lodge's main building, on the shore
★ of Jackson Lake, was constructed of volcanic stone and pine shingle; inside is a cozy lounge with a fireplace, a piano, and Adirondack furniture. Guest rooms are in a separate cluster of cabinlike units, some with kitchenettes. The Aspens restaurant serves such dishes as shrimp linguine and medallions of elk. ⊠ *Park Inner Teton Rd., Moran 83013,* ☎ *307/543–2831. 79 rooms. Restaurant, bar, marina. AE, DC, MC, V. Closed mid-Oct.–early May.*

$$ ✕🏨 **Colter Bay Village.** Log cabins and less expensive tent cabins (canvas-covered wood frames) are the accommodations at this resort near the shore of Jackson Lake. The Chuckwagon restaurant serves lasagna, trout, and barbecued spare ribs. ⊠ *Off U.S. 89. 250 cabins, 66 tent cabins, 113 RV spaces. 2 restaurants, bar, coin laundry. Closed late Sept.–early June.*

Jackson

$$$ ✕ **Blue Lion.** The fare served in this homey light-blue clapboard house
★ ranges from rack of lamb to fresh seafood. ⊠ *160 N. Milward St.,* ☎ *307/733–3912. AE, D, MC, V.*

$$ ✕ **Nani's.** The ever-changing menu at this cozy restaurant may include
★ braised veal shanks with saffron risotto and other regional Italian dishes. ⊠ *240 N. Glenwood St.,* ☎ *307/733–3888. DC, MC, V.*

$ ✕ **The Bunnery.** This pine-paneled whole-grain bakery and restaurant serves irresistible breakfasts, from omelets with blue cheese and sautéed spinach to home-baked pastries. Lunch or dine on sandwiches, burgers, and Mexican fare. ⊠ *130 N. Cache St.,* ☎ *307/733–5474. Reservations not accepted. MC, V.*

$$–$$$ ✕▦ **Spring Creek Ranch.** This luxury resort atop Gros Ventre Butte,
★ near Jackson, has beautiful views of the Tetons. Thirty-six hotel rooms
are complemented by a changing mix of studios, suites, and condos
with lofts. Rooms with kitchenettes are available. Native American art
decorates the fine Granary restaurant, where reservations are essential. Try Dungeness crab and Havarti cheese wrapped in phyllo dough
followed by poached salmon in cucumber-dill sauce. ⊠ *1800 Spirit
Dance Rd., 83001,* ☎ *307/733–8833 or 800/443–6139,* ℻ *307/
733–1524. 117 units. Restaurant, pool, 2 tennis courts, horseback riding, sleigh rides, cross-country skiing. AE, D, DC, MC, V.*

$$ ▦ **Painted Porch Bed & Breakfast.** This 1901 farmhouse 8 mi north
of Jackson has rooms decorated with antiques; some have Japanese soak-
ing tubs. ⊠ *Teton Village Rd. (Box 3965), 83001,* ☎ *307/733–1981.
4 rooms. MC, V.*

$$ ▦ **Cowboy Village Resort.** Each of the pine-log cabins in this quiet complex has bunk beds and a kitchenette, making it a popular spot for fam-
ilies and groups of friends who don't mind close quarters. ⊠ *120 S.
Flat Creek Dr., 83001,* ☎ *307/733–3121,* ℻ *307/739–1955. 82 cabins. Hot tubs. AE, D, MC, V.*

MOTELS
▦ **Antler Motel** (⊠ 43 W. Pearl St., Jackson 83001, ☎ 307/733–2535
or 800/522–2406), 107 rooms, hot tub; $$$. ▦ **Days Inn** (⊠ 350 S.
Hwy. 89, Jackson 83001, ☎ 307/739–9010, ℻ 307/733–0044), 74
rooms, Continental breakfast, whirlpool, sauna; $$$. ▦ **Virginian
Motel** (⊠ 750 W. Broadway, Jackson 83001, ☎ 307/733–2792, ℻
307/733–9513), 159 rooms, restaurant, pool; $$. ▦ **Motel 6** (⊠ 1370
W. Broadway, Jackson 83001, ☎ 307/733–1620, ℻ 307/734–9175),
155 rooms, pool; $.

Teton Village

$$ ✕ **Mangy Moose.** Folks pour in here off the ski slopes with big appetites
★ and a lot to gab about. It's noisy, but the trendy American fare is de-
cent. ⊠ *South end of Teton Village,* ☎ *307/733–4913. AE, MC, V.*

$$$ ✕▦ **Alpenhof.** This European-style hotel is the lodge closest to Jack-
★ son Hole Ski Area's lifts. The restaurant, which serves veal, wild game,
and seafood, is small, quiet, and comfortable. ⊠ *Box 288, 83025,* ☎
307/733–3242, ℻ *307/739–1516. 41 rooms. Restaurant, bar, pool,
hot tub, sauna. AE, D, MC, V.*

Yellowstone

The lodgings and restaurants within Yellowstone are operated by **TW
Recreational Services.** There are gas stations, snack bars, and other ser-
vices throughout the park. ⊠ *Yellowstone National Park, 82190,* ☎
307/344–7311, ℻ *307/344–2456. AE, D, DC, MC, V.*

$$–$$$ ✕▦ **Lake Yellowstone Hotel.** The park's oldest (late 1800s) and most
★ elegant resort, at the north end of the lake, has a pale-yellow neoclas-
sical facade. The lobby's tall windows overlook the water, and some
rooms have brass beds and vintage fixtures. The cabins are compara-
tively rustic. The restaurant (☎ 307/242–3701) prepares such items
as Thai curried shrimp or fettuccine with smoked salmon and snow
peas; reservations are essential. ⊠ *Lake Village. 296 units. Restaurant.
Closed late Sept.–mid-May.*

$$–$$$$ ✕▦ **Old Faithful Inn.** You can loll in front of the lobby's immense stone
★ fireplace and look up six stories at wood balconies that seem to dis-
appear into the night sky. Guest room decor ranges from brass beds
to Victorian cherry wood to inexpensive motel-style furniture. The dining room (☎ 307/344–7901, ext. 4999), a huge hall centered on a fire-

place of volcanic stone, serves shrimp scampi and other delights; dinner reservations are essential. ⊠ *Old Faithful. 327 rooms. Restaurant, bar. Closed late-Oct.–early May.*

$–$$ ✕🏨 **Mammoth Hot Springs Hotel.** The smallish cabins here are arranged around "auto courts"; four have hot tubs. The dining room (☎ 307/344–7901) serves regional American fare, including prime rib and chicken with Brie and raspberry sauce. The cafeteria-style Terrace Grill, across from the lodge, has large windows that seem to bring in the outdoors. ⊠ *Mammoth. 126 cabins, 96 rooms. 2 restaurants, bar, horseback riding. Closed mid-Sept.–mid-Dec., early Mar.–late May.*

$–$$ ✕🏨 **Old Faithful Snow Lodge.** This compact, drab-looking motel off to one side of the Old Faithful complex is one of only two park lodgings open in winter. Rooms are nondescript, but the lobby has a welcoming wood-burning stove. ⊠ *Old Faithful. 65 units. Restaurant. Closed mid-Oct.–mid-Dec., mid-Mar.–mid-May.*

$ ✕🏨 **Roosevelt Lodge.** Near the Lamar Valley in the park's northeast
★ corner, this simple, homey log lodge is more ranch house than resort. The dining room serves barbecued ribs, Roosevelt beans, and other western fare. Accommodations are in nearby cabins. ⊠ *Tower-Roosevelt. 86 cabins. Restaurant, bar. Closed early Sept.–early June.*

Cody

$ ✕ **Proud Cut Saloon.** This popular downtown eatery has authentic western decor and what it bills as "kick-ass cowboy cuisine": steak, prime rib, fish, and chicken. ⊠ *1227 Sheridan Ave.,* ☎ *307/527–6905. AE, D, DC, MC, V.*

$$–$$$ 🏨 **Irma Hotel.** This hostelry has an ornate cherry-wood bar; some rooms are decorated in turn-of-the-century western style. ⊠ *1192 Sheridan Ave., 82414,* ☎ *307/587–4221. AE, D, DC, MC, V.*

$$ 🏨 **Pahaska Teepee Resort.** Buffalo Bill's original getaway in the high country is 2 mi east of Yellowstone's East Entrance. ⊠ *183 Yellowstone Hwy., 82414,* ☎ *307/527–7701 or 800/628–7791,* 𝖥𝖠𝖷 *307/527–4019. 52 cabins. Restaurant, horseback riding, snowmobiling. MC, V.*

Campgrounds

In Grand Teton the **National Park Service** (⊠ Drawer 170, Moose 83012, ☎ 307/739–3300) has five campgrounds, none with RV hookups, but all with fire grates and rest rooms. The privately run **Colter Bay Trailer Village** (⊠ Grand Teton Lodge Co., Box 240, Moran 83013, ☎ 307/543–3100) has 113 full RV hookups.

Among the **Yellowstone National Park** (☎ 307/344–7381) campsite areas, **Bridge Bay** (420 sites and a marina) is the largest, and **Slough Creek** (32 tent-trailer sites) is the smallest. There are also 300 backcountry campsites, for which you need a permit from the park rangers.

Outdoor Activities and Sports

The **Jackson Hole Chamber of Commerce** (☞ Visitor Information, *above*) has lists of outfitters and news about winter and summer activities. For sporting opportunities in the parks—including skiing, horseback riding, hiking, and climbing—contact the visitor centers.

Boating

Hire boats on Jackson Lake through **Colter Bay Marina** (☎ 307/543–3100). **Signal Mountain Marina** (☎ 307/543–2831) also rents boats.

Climbing

Two options for climbers are **Jackson Hole Mountain Guides** (☎ 307/733–4979) and **Exum Mountain Guides** (☎ 307/733–2297).

Fishing

Blue-ribbon trout streams thread through northwestern Wyoming, and Jackson Lake has set records for Mackinaw trout. The license for fishing in Yellowstone and Grand Teton costs $10 for seven days or $20 for the season and is payable at entrance gates or park offices. For fishing elsewhere, buy licenses at sporting goods or general merchandise stores; or contact **Wyoming Game and Fish** (⊠ 5400 Bishop Blvd., Cheyenne 82002, ☎ 307/777–4600). Fly shops in Jackson include **Jack Dennis Sporting Goods** (⊠ 50 E. Broadway, ☎ 307/733–3270) and **High Country Flies** (⊠ 165 N. Center St., ☎ 307/733–7210).

Golf

Jackson Hole Golf and Tennis Club (⊠ Off U.S. 89, 8 mi north of Jackson, ☎ 307/733–3111) and **Teton Pines Golf Club** (⊠ 3450 N. Clubhouse Dr., ☎ 307/733–1733) have 18 holes.

Rafting and Canoeing

Peaceful, scenic floats on the Upper Snake include the beautiful Oxbow, which you can navigate by canoe or kayak. Guided rafting trips are available from **Barker-Ewing Scenic Float Trips** (⊠ Moose, ☎ 307/733–1000 or 800/365–1800), **Snake River Kayak & Canoe School** (⊠ Jackson, ☎ 307/733–3127 or 800/824–5375), and **Triangle X** (⊠ Moose, ☎ 307/733–5500). For guided white-water trips in Snake River Canyon, try **Dave Hansen Whitewater** (⊠ Jackson, ☎ 307/733–6295), **Barker-Ewing Float Trips** (⊠ Jackson, ☎ 800/448–4202), or **Lewis & Clark Expeditions** (⊠ Jackson, ☎ 307/733–4022 or 800/824–5375). Rent canoes and kayaks in Jackson from **Leisure Sports** (⊠ 1075 S. U.S. 89, ☎ 307/733–3040) and **Teton Aquatics** (⊠ 155 W. Gill St., ☎ 307/733–3127).

Ski Areas

Cross-Country

Cross-country skiing and snowshoeing are permitted in parts of both Yellowstone and Grand Teton national parks and surrounding forests. **Cowboy Village Resort at Togwotee** (⊠ Box 91, Moran 83013, ☎ 307/543–2847), at Togwotee Pass within Bridger–Teton and Shoshone national forests (U.S. 26/287), operates 13½ mi of groomed tracks. **Spring Creek Ranch Resort** (⊠ 1800 Spirit Dance Rd., Box 3154, 83001, ☎ 307/733–8833 or 800/443–6139) has 8 mi of trails. **Jackson Hole Nordic Center** (⊠ Box 290, Teton Village 83025, ☎ 307/733–2292) has 12 mi of trails.

Downhill

Grand Targhee Ski Resort (⊠ Box SKI, Alta 83422, ☎ 307/353–2300 or 800/827–4433), 64 runs, 3 lifts, 1 rope tow, 2,200-ft vertical drop. **Jackson Hole Ski Resort** (⊠ Box 290, Teton Village 83025, ☎ 307/733–2292 or 800/443–6931), 58 runs, 9 lifts including a high-speed quad, 4,139-ft drop (the longest of any U.S. ski area), some snowmaking. **Snow King** (⊠ Box SKI, Jackson 83001, ☎ 307/733–5200 or 800/522–5464), 400 acres of slopes, 3 lifts, 1,571-ft drop.

Shopping

Shopping in Jackson is centered on the town square. Western wear and outdoor clothing, some of it locally made, dominate in such stores as **Wyoming Outfitters** (⊠ 165 N. Center St., ☎ 307/733–3877), **Jackson Hole Clothiers** (⊠ 45 E. Deloney St., ☎ 307/733–7211), and **Hideout Leather** (⊠ 40 N. Center St., ☎ 307/733–2422). Specialists in the latest outdoor equipment include **Teton Mountaineering** (⊠ 170 N. Cache St., ☎ 307/733–3595) and **Skinny Skis** (⊠ 65 W. Deloney

St., ☎ 307/733–6094). **Trailside Americana** (✉ 105 N. Center St., ☎ 307/733–3186) features western jewelry and art. For photographic art try **Tom Mangelsen Images of Nature Gallery** (✉ 170 N. Cache St., ☎ 307/733–9752).

ELSEWHERE IN WYOMING

Cheyenne

Arriving and Departing

Both I–80 and I–25 pass through Cheyenne. Commuter airlines fly between Denver and **Cheyenne Municipal Airport** (☎ 307/634–7071). **Greyhound** (☎ 800/231–2222) provides bus service. **Amtrak** stops 10 mi outside the city; a shuttle bus takes passengers into town.

What to See and Do

The **Frontier Days** rodeo (☎ 800/227–6336), held the last week of July, is a reminder that the state's capital city was once nicknamed Hell on Wheels. Outside the gold-domed **state capitol** is a statue of Esther Hobart Morris, who helped gain equal rights for Wyoming women, who got the vote in 1869, 51 years before the rest of the nation. Morris was the first woman to hold U.S. public office and was appointed a justice of the peace in 1870. (In 1924 Nellie Taylor Ross became the nation's first elected female governor.)

The **Frontier Days Old West Museum** (✉ Frontier Park, 4501 N. Carey Ave., ☎ 307/778–7290 or 800/778–7290) displays buggies, stagecoaches, and buckboards.

Lodging

$$–$$$ 🏨 **Hitching Post Inn.** This hotel near the capitol is a favorite with travelers and state legislators. The Hitch, as locals call it, books country-western performers into its lounge. ✉ *1700 W. Lincolnway,* ☎ *307/638–3301 or 800/528–1234,* 🖷 *307/638–3301. AE, D, DC, MC, V.*

$$–$$$ 🏨 **Rainsford Inn.** Elegant surroundings and a bed-and-breakfast atmosphere welcome you on historic Cattleman's Row. ✉ *219 E. 18th St.,* ☎ *307/638–2337,* 🖷 *307/634–4506. AE, D, DC, MC, V.*

Devils Tower Area

Arriving and Departing

Devils Tower is 6 mi off U.S. 15 on Route 24.

What to See and Do

Native American legend has it that the corrugated Devils Tower was formed when a tree stump turned into granite and grew taller to protect some stranded children from a clawing bear. Geologists say that the rock tower, rising 1,280 ft above the Belle Fourche River, is the core of a defunct volcano. It was a tourist magnet long before a spaceship landed on top of it in the movie *Close Encounters of the Third Kind,* and the tower is still a significant site for Native Americans. During the month of July a voluntary ban on rock climbing allows Native Americans an opportunity to conduct spiritual activities here. For information contact **Devils Tower National Monument** (✉ Devils Tower 82714, ☎ 307/467–5283).

Lodging

$–$$ 🏨 **Best Western Inn at Sundance.** This quiet location has western charm. ✉ *26 Hwy. 585 (I–90, Exit 187), Sundance 82729,* ☎ *307/283–2800 or 800/238–0965,* 🖷 *307/283–2727. 37 rooms. Indoor pool, hot tub. AE, D, DC, MC, V.*

$–$$ 🏨 **Bear Lodge Motel.** The lobby at this downtown motel is cozy, with a stone fireplace and wildlife mounts on the walls. ✉ *218 Cleveland St.,* ☎ *307/283–1611,* 📠 *307/283–2537. 33 rooms. Hot tub. AE, D, DC, MC, V.*

Saratoga

Arriving and Departing
Saratoga is in south-central Wyoming, 20 mi south of I–80, and is also accessible via Wyoming 130 (the Snowy Range Road) in summer only or via Wyoming 230 year-round.

What to See and Do
Recreational opportunities abound in the **Medicine Bow National Forest,** and excellent white-water floating, kayaking, rafting, and fishing can be found on the North Platte and Encampment rivers. The **Grand Encampment Museum** (✉ Box 43, Encampment 82325, ☎ 307/327–5308), 18 mi south of Saratoga, has a complete historic town and a modern interpretive center. For information on hunting and dude ranch opportunities, contact the **Saratoga Platte Valley Chamber of Commerce** (✉ Box 1095, 82331, ☎ 307/326–8855).

Dining and Lodging
$$ ✕ **Hotel Wolf.** The restaurant here has the best prime rib and steak in town. ✉ *101 E. Bridge St.,* ☎ *307/326–5525.*

$$$$ 🏨 **Saratoga Inn.** The decor is decidedly western here, with pole-frame furniture and luxurious leather couches. The North Platte River runs through the inn's property, so fishing is literally right out the back door. ✉ *E. Pic-Pike Rd. (Box 869), 82331,* ☎ *307/326–5261. 58 rooms. Pool, 9-hole golf course, tennis courts. AE, DC, MC, V.*

Sheridan

Arriving and Departing
Commuter airlines fly from Denver to **Sheridan County Airport** (☎ 307/674–4222). **Powder River Transportation** (☎ 800/237–7211) buses connect with national carriers. Sheridan is 130 mi south of Billings, Montana, via I–90 and 140 mi north of Casper via I–25.

What to See and Do
This is authentic cowboy country, with a touch of dudish sophistication. The **Equestrian Center** (☎ 307/674–5179) holds polo matches on summer weekends, as well as horse shows and a steeplechase. Mosey into **King's Saddlery and Ropes** (✉ 184 N. Main St., ☎ 307/672–2702 or 800/443–8919) to view hundreds of lariats, as well as hand-tooled leather saddles. Or see western collectibles, saddles, and tack in the store's museum. For information contact the **Sheridan Chamber of Commerce** (✉ Box 707, 82801, ☎ 307/672–2485).

Lodging
$$$ 🏨 **Eaton's Guest Ranch.** West of Sheridan on the edge of the Bighorn National Forest, this working ranch can accommodate up to 125 guests (make summer reservations by March). ✉ *270 Eaton Ranch Rd., Wolf 82844,* ☎ *307/655–9285. Dining room, pool, horseback riding, fishing, hiking. MC, V. Closed Oct.–May.*

11 The West Coast

California, Oregon, Washington

By Bonnie
Engel

Some visitors from the East picture the West Coast as America's frontier, but the shoreline of California, Oregon, and Washington presents no barrier to the region's businesspeople, who carry the pioneering spirit to the Pacific Rim. West Coast "fusion" chefs create fresh dishes with Asian accents, and its high-tech entrepreneurs generate products and services the world will take for granted in the next millennium.

The area that is now California was first settled by several Native American peoples, followed by the gold-hungry Spanish, who built missions and huge ranchos. Modern treasure hunters head for California's Silicon Valley to find the computing and networking wizards who are leading the nation's communications, information, and technology revolution.

Washington and Oregon are similar in topography and climate, cooler than California, and are bisected by the Cascade Mountains. Rain-soaked Seattle, Washington, is home to one of the world's busiest container ports as well as the legendary Bill Gates, chairman of Microsoft. Portland, in Oregon's lush Willamette River valley, is known for its calm curtain of fog, rain, and pine trees.

Despite development, nature continues to provide a critical perspective on human pursuits. The ragged edges of Washington's Olympic Peninsula and the Oregon coast illustrate the power of the ocean; the mountains surrounding Seattle offer a sobering sense of scale, as does the view from Yosemite's valley floor; and tremors along the San Andreas Fault remind California residents that the earth is an unstable place. Every town along the West Coast sits amid some grand gesture of nature.

The great West Coast cities—Seattle, Portland, San Francisco, San Jose, Los Angeles, and San Diego—continue to attract a hopeful, worldly mix of immigrants in search of personal freedom and economic opportunity. In contrast to the urban areas, the extraordinary landscapes of these states feature wild climatic changes and altitudes—deserts, forests, a 1,500-mi seashore, mountains, and rich agricultural valleys. In addition to the athletic attractions of rock climbing, deep-sea fishing, wilderness camping, surfing, skiing, and snowboarding, tourists and residents enjoy five-star resorts, historic western towns, Disneyland, Hollywood studios, world-class museums, and top-notch art and entertainment from grunge to opera.

When to Go

You can take a West Coast vacation any time of the year. Weather in coastal areas is generally mild year-round, with the rainy season running from October through March. Expect to encounter heavy coastal fog throughout the summer. Inland areas such as Napa Valley, the Columbia Gorge, and the High Sierra can be hot in summer, with temperatures reaching up to 90°F in the plains and mountains; in California's Central Valley and desert regions, summer temperatures can soar to 110°F. The ski season in the High Sierra and Cascades runs from October through March, occasionally into April and May. Those who want to enjoy the sun-drenched delights of the desert should plan a trip between October and May; the wildflowers are at their peak in April. Whenever you visit the West Coast, expect temperatures to vary widely from night to day, sometimes by as much as 40°. Most West Coast attractions are open daily year-round, but summer is the busiest tourist season, when you can expect the most congestion and the highest prices.

Festivals and Seasonal Events

Winter
JAN. 1➤ The **Tournament of Roses** (☎ 626/449–4100), in **Pasadena, California,** features a parade of more than 50 floral floats, equestrian units, and marching bands and is followed by the Rose Bowl football game.

LATE JAN.–EARLY FEB.➤ California's **AT&T Pebble Beach National Pro-Am** (☎ 408/649–1533) pairs 180 top professional golfers with amateurs from the business, sports, and entertainment worlds.

FEB.➤ **Chinese New Year** celebrations are held in **San Francisco** (☎ 415/982–3000) and **Los Angeles** (☎ 213/617–0396), complete with dragon parades, fireworks, and sumptuous feasts.

Spring
EARLY MAR.➤ The **Mendocino Whale Festival** (☎ 707/961–6300), in **Mendocino, California,** combines whale-watching with art viewing, wine tasting, lighthouse tours, music, and merriment.

LATE MAR.–EARLY APR.➤ Washington's **Skagit Valley Tulip Festival** (☎ 360/428–8547) showcases millions of colorful tulips and daffodils in bloom.

MEMORIAL DAY WEEKEND➤ The **Sacramento Jazz Jubilee** (☎ 916/372–5277) brings more than 100 jazz bands to **Sacramento, California,** for four days of jamming.

LATE MAY➤ The **Northwest Folklife Festival** (☎ 206/684–7300) lures musicians and artists to Seattle for one of the largest folk festivals in the United States.

Summer
MID-FEB.–LATE OCT.➤ The **Oregon Shakespeare Festival** (☎ 541/482–4331), held in **Ashland,** presents four plays by Shakespeare—plus seven

West Coast (Northern)

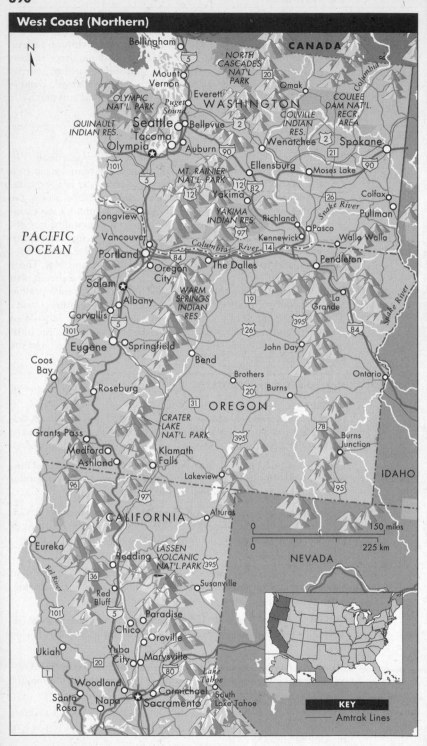

West Coast (Southern)

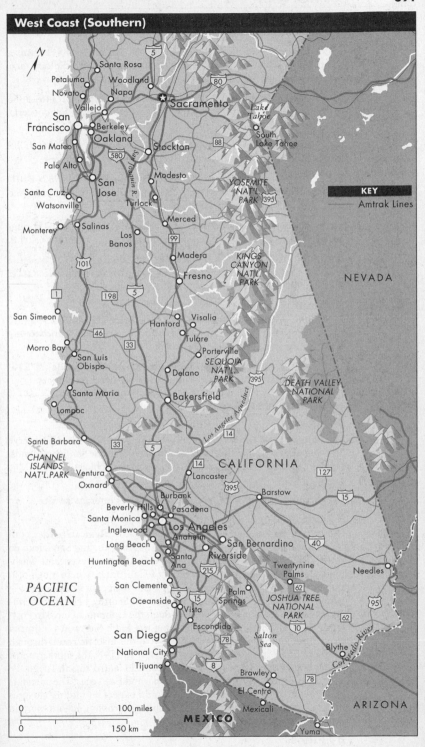

Santa Rosa
Petaluma
Novato
Woodland
Napa
Vallejo
San Francisco
Berkeley
Oakland
San Mateo
Palo Alto
San Jose
Santa Cruz
Watsonville
Monterey
Salinas
Los Banos
San Simeon
Morro Bay
San Luis Obispo
Santa Maria
Lompoc
Santa Barbara
Ventura
Oxnard
Sacramento
Stockton
Modesto
Turlock
Merced
Madera
Fresno
Hanford
Visalia
Tulare
Porterville
Delano
Bakersfield
Lancaster
Barstow
Burbank
Pasadena
Beverly Hills
Santa Monica
Inglewood
Los Angeles
Anaheim
Long Beach
Santa Ana
Riverside
Huntington Beach
San Bernardino
San Clemente
Oceanside
Vista
Palm Springs
Twentynine Palms
Needles
Escondido
San Diego
National City
Tijuana
Blythe
Brawley
El Centro
Mexicali
Yuma

Lake Tahoe
South Lake Tahoe
YOSEMITE NAT'L PARK
KINGS CANYON NAT'L PARK
SEQUOIA NAT'L PARK
DEATH VALLEY NATIONAL PARK
CHANNEL ISLANDS NAT'L. PARK
JOSHUA TREE NATIONAL PARK
Salton Sea
San Joaquin R.
Los Angeles Aqueduct
Colorado River

NEVADA
CALIFORNIA
ARIZONA
MEXICO
PACIFIC OCEAN

KEY
Amtrak Lines

0   100 miles
0   150 km

other plays by both classical and contemporary playwrights—in repertory in three theaters; tours, concerts, and lectures are also offered.

EARLY JUNE➤ The **Portland Rose Festival** (☎ 503/227–2681) features a rose show, carnivals, celebrity entertainment, a hot-air balloon race, two parades, an air show, bands, and a world-class auto show.

MID-JUNE–EARLY JULY➤ The **Oregon Bach Festival** (☎ 541/346–5666 or 800/457–1486) brings stellar musicians to **Eugene** for concerts, recitals, lectures, chamber music, and opera.

LATE JULY➤ The **Pacific Northwest Arts & Crafts Fair** (☎ 206/454–4900) brings the work of Northwest artists to **Bellevue, Washington.**

EARLY AUG.➤ In California, **Old Spanish Days Fiesta** (☎ 805/962–8101) is **Santa Barbara**'s biggest event, with parades, a carnival, a rodeo, and dancers in the Spanish marketplace.

EARLY AUG.➤ The **Mt. Hood Festival of Jazz** (☎ 503/231–0161) brings acclaimed jazz musicians to **Gresham, Oregon,** for a tuneful weekend.

LATE AUG.–EARLY SEPT.➤ **Bumbershoot** (☎ 206/281–8111), a Seattle festival of the arts, presents more than 450 performers in music, dance, theater, comedy, and the visual and literary arts.

Autumn

LATE AUG.–OCT.➤ **Renaissance Pleasure Faire** (☎ 800/523–2473) draws revelers in Elizabethan-style costumes to the **San Francisco Bay Area** for weekends of music, merriment, and theater.

LATE NOV.–EARLY DEC.➤ The **Hollywood Christmas Parade** (☎ 213/469–2337) features celebrities riding festively decorated floats.

Getting Around the West Coast

By Boat
Washington State Ferries (☎ 206/464–6400 or 800/843–3779) serve 20 destinations around the Puget Sound, including the San Juan Islands. Ferries can accommodate cars and recreational vehicles.

By Bus
Greyhound Lines (☎ 800/231–2222) provides intercity service.

By Car
I–5 runs north–south from the Canadian to the Mexican border, connecting Seattle, Portland, Sacramento, Los Angeles, and San Diego en route. The coastal route is designated U.S. 101 in Oregon and Washington; it's called Highway 1 in most of California, where much of it travels through coastal valleys. Major east–west routes include I–90, which bisects Washington from Spokane to Seattle; I–84, which traverses eastern Oregon and travels through the Columbia Gorge to Portland; I–80, the main highway crossing the High Sierra in California from Lake Tahoe to San Francisco; I–10, the historic route through southern California's desert to Los Angeles; and I–8, the southernmost route, hugging the Mexican border from El Centro to San Diego. I–15 is the route between southern California and Las Vegas. The interstate highways are open all year, but you should expect temporary closures during severe winter storms. State highways crossing high mountain passes are normally closed in winter.

By Plane
The West Coast is served by all major domestic airlines and most international carriers. Major airports in California include **Los Angeles International Airport** (☎ 310/646–5252), plus John Wayne Orange County Airport and other regional airports at Burbank, Long Beach,

and Ontario; **San Diego International Airport Lindbergh Field** (☎ 619/231–2100); and **San Francisco International Airport** (☎ 650/876–2377), plus regional airports at Oakland and San Jose. The region's other major airports are Oregon's **Portland International Airport** (☎ 503/335–1234) and Washington's **Seattle-Tacoma International Airport** (☎ 206/433–4645).

By Train

Amtrak (☎ 800/872–7245) serves rail passengers in the region. Trains run daily between Seattle and Los Angeles; the trip takes 35 hours. Commuter trains serve Los Angeles from San Diego and Santa Barbara. **CalTrain** (☎ 650/508–6200 or 800/660–4287) brings passengers to San Francisco from peninsula locations. Transcontinental trains serve Los Angeles, San Francisco/Oakland, Portland, and Seattle.

CALIFORNIA

Capital	Sacramento
Population	31,878,234
Motto	Eureka
State Bird	Valley quail
State Flower	Golden poppy
Postal Abbreviation	CA

Statewide Visitor Information

California Division of Tourism (⊠ 801 K St., Suite 1600, Sacramento 95814, ☎ 800/862–2543, ℻ 916/322–3402).

Scenic Drives

The land- and seascapes along the nearly 400 mi of coastline between San Francisco Bay and the Oregon border are beautiful and rugged; switchbacked **Highway 1** is punctuated by groves of giant redwood trees, tiny coastal towns, and secluded coves and beaches. **U.S. 395** north from San Bernardino rises in elevation gradually from the Mojave Desert to the Sierra foothills and on past the east entrance to Yosemite National Park. **Highway 49** winds 325 mi through northern California's historic Gold Country.

National and State Parks

National Parks

California has eight national parks: Death Valley, Joshua Tree, Lassen Volcanic, Redwood, Sequoia, Kings Canyon, Yosemite, and the Channel Islands. National monuments include Cabrillo, in San Diego, and Muir Woods, north of San Francisco. For information contact the western regional office of the **National Park Service** (⊠ Fort Mason Center, Bldg. 201, San Francisco 94123, ☎ 415/556–0560).

State Parks

The **California State Park System** (⊠ Box 942896, Sacramento 94296, ☎ 916/653–6995) includes more than 200 sites; many are recreational and scenic, others historic or scientific.

SAN FRANCISCO

San Francisco is a relatively small city, with slightly more than 750,000 residents nested on a 46.6-square-mi tip of land between San Francisco Bay and the Pacific Ocean. Its residents cherish the city's colorful past, and many older buildings have been spared from demolition and nostalgically converted into modern offices and shops. First-time visitors won't want to miss Golden Gate Park, the Palace of Fine Arts, Chinatown, the Golden Gate Bridge, or a cable car ride on Nob Hill.

Much of the city's neighborhood vitality comes from the distinct borders provided by its hills and valleys, for which many areas are named: Nob Hill, Twin Peaks, Eureka Valley. Experiencing San Francisco means visiting its neighborhoods: the colorful Mission District, the gay-friendly Castro, countercultural Haight Street, serene Pacific Heights, bustling Chinatown, and still-bohemian North Beach.

Visitor Information

Convention and Visitors Bureau (⊠ 201 3rd St., Suite 900, San Francisco 94103, ☎ 415/391–2000); send $1 for booklet or pick one up at the lower level of Hallidie Plaza, at the corner of Market and Powell streets.

Arriving and Departing

By Bus

Greyhound Lines (☎ 800/231–2222) serves San Francisco's **Transbay Terminal** (⊠ 1st and Mission Sts.).

By Car

I–80 comes into San Francisco from the east, crossing the Bay Bridge from Oakland. U.S. 101 runs north–south through the city and across the Golden Gate Bridge.

By Plane

San Francisco International Airport (SFO; ☎ 415/876–2377), 20 minutes south of the city off U.S. 101, is served by most major airlines. **Oakland Airport** (☎ 510/577–4000), across the bay but not much farther from the city, provides additional air access through several domestic airlines. The **SFO Airporter** (☎ 415/495–8404) bus runs every 15–30 minutes between various downtown hotels and SFO; it's $9 one-way, $15 round-trip. For $12 the **SuperShuttle** (☎ 415/558–8500) will take you from SFO to anywhere within the city limits in 30–50 minutes, depending on traffic and your destination. **Taxis** between downtown and either airport take 20–30 minutes and cost about $30.

By Train

Amtrak (☎ 800/872–7245) trains stop in Oakland (⊠ Jack London Sq., 245 2nd St.) and Emeryville (⊠ 5885 Landregan St.); shuttle buses connect the Emeryville station and San Francisco's Ferry Building, on the Embarcadero. **CalTrain** serves the southern peninsula from San Francisco's Southern Pacific depot (⊠ 4th and Townsend Sts., ☎ 800/660–4287).

Getting Around San Francisco

By Car

Driving in the city is a challenge. Watch out for one-way streets, curb your wheels when parking on hills, and check street signs for parking restrictions—of which there are many. Public parking garages or lots tend to be expensive, as are hotel parking spaces. Except at a few marked intersections, a right turn at a red light is legal.

By Public Transportation

Cable cars, buses, and trolleys can take you to or near many attractions. Most of the light-rail and bus lines of the Municipal Railway System, called **Muni** (☎ 415/673–6864), operate continuously; standard fare is $1, and exact change (coins or a dollar bill) is required. If you'll be changing buses, get a **transfer** when you board; it is good only for a specified time. Three **cable car** lines crisscross downtown; information and tickets ($2)—and multiday tourist passes—can be obtained at the main turnaround, at Powell and Market streets, and at major stops. **BART** (Bay Area Rapid Transit; ☎ 800/817–1717) trains service the East Bay and beyond to Daly City, Concord, and Richmond; wall maps list destinations and fares. Trains run Monday–Saturday 4 AM–midnight, Sunday 8 AM–midnight.

By Taxi

Rates are high—$1.70 just to get in—and it can be difficult to hail a cab in some neighborhoods. For a radio-dispatched taxi, try **Yellow Cab Co.** (☎ 415/626–2345).

Orientation Tours

Gray Line (⊠ 350 8th St., ☎ 415/558–9400 or 800/826–0202) offers a variety of city tours on buses and double-deckers ranging in price from $16 to $39. Tickets can be purchased at Union Square and Pier 39; hotel pickups are available. The **Great Pacific Tour** (⊠ 518 Octavia St., ☎ 415/626–4499) lasts 3½ hours at a cost of $29; German-, French-, Spanish-, and Italian-speaking guides are available. Pickups are available at many downtown hotels.

Walking Tours

Trevor Hailey's **Cruising the Castro** (☎ 415/550–8110) tour focuses on the history and development of the city's gay and lesbian community. The **Chinese Cultural Heritage Foundation** (☎ 415/986–1822) offers a Heritage Walk and a Culinary Walk through Chinatown. Elaine Sosa's highly caffeinated **Javawalk** (☎ 415/673–9255) visits some of San Francisco's more than 400 cafés.

Exploring San Francisco

Touring San Francisco is best done one neighborhood at a time and on foot—although the hills are a challenge. Dependable walking shoes are essential. You'll need a jacket for the dramatic temperature swings, especially in summer, when fog rolls in during the afternoon.

Union Square

The landmark of Union Square is the grand **Westin St. Francis Hotel** (⊠ 335 Powell St., ☎ 415/397–7000), San Francisco's second oldest hostelry, on the southeast corner of Post and Powell streets. After a day exploring the stores of this major shopping district (☞ Shopping, *below*), you can relax over tea in the Westin's dramatic Art Deco **Compass Rose** lounge.

Maiden Lane, directly across Union Square from the St. Francis, is a quaint two-block alley lined with pricey boutiques and sidewalk cafés. The **Circle Gallery** at 140 Maiden Lane is said to be the model for New York's Guggenheim museum.

Chinatown

The dragon-crowned **Chinatown Gate,** at Bush Street and Grant Avenue, is the main entrance to this eponymous neighborhood. Join the residents as they shop for fresh fish, vegetables, and baked goods. Almost 100 restaurants are squeezed into these 14 blocks.

Among the many interesting architectural examples here is the **Chinese Six Companies** building (⊠ 843 Stockton St.), with curved roof tiles and elaborate cornices. The **Old Chinese Telephone Exchange** (now the Bank of Canton; ⊠ 743 Washington St.), a three-tier pagoda, was built just after the '06 earthquake.

To learn about the area's rich immigrant history, go to the **Chinese Culture Center,** which exhibits the work of Chinese-American artists. *See* also Walking Tours, *above.* ⊠ *Holiday Inn, 750 Kearny St.,* ☎ *415/986–1822. Closed Mon.*

Nob Hill

Nob Hill, north of Union Square, is home to the city's elite as well as some of its finest hotels. The 1906 earthquake destroyed the neighborhood mansions that had been built by gold rush millionaires and the later railroad barons. The shell of railroad magnate James Flood's **brownstone mansion** (⊠ 1000 California St.) managed to survive the quake. The Episcopal **Grace Cathedral** (⊠ 1051 Taylor St.) has bronze doors cast from Ghiberti's *Gates of Paradise* in Florence. The **Mark Hopkins Inter-Continental Hotel** (⊠ 1 Nob Hill, ☎ 415/392–3434), atop Nob Hill, is known for the view from its **Top of the Mark** lounge.

Civic Center

City hall (⊠ Polk St. between Grove and McAllister Sts.), a granite-and-marble masterpiece modeled after the Capitol in Washington, faces the long **Civic Center Plaza,** which has a fountain, walkways, and flower beds. Many transients frequent the plaza, and caution is advised after dark. If all goes as planned, city hall will reopen in late 1998 after a seismic upgrade is completed. The **Performing Arts Center** complex, on Van Ness Avenue between McAllister and Hayes streets, includes the **War Memorial Opera House** and the **Louise M. Davies Symphony Hall.**

In the Western Addition, a neighborhood due west of the Civic Center area, is the much-photographed row of six identical Victorian houses along **Steiner Street,** at the east end of Alamo Square. If you're walking, the safest route is up Fulton Street to Steiner Street; avoid the area at night.

The Financial District and the Heart of the Barbary Coast

Bounded by the Union Square area, Telegraph Hill, Mission Street, and the Embarcadero, San Francisco's Financial District is distinguished from the rest of town by its cluster of steel-and-glass high-rises and older, more decorative architectural monuments to commerce. The city's signature high-rise is the 853-ft **Transamerica Pyramid** (⊠ Clay and Montgomery Sts.). Dominating the Financial District skyline is the 52-story **Bank of America** (⊠ California and Kearny Sts.).

Other notable structures in the Financial District include the **Pacific Stock Exchange** (⊠ 301 Pine St.). The ceiling and entry are black marble in the **Stock Exchange Tower** (⊠ 155 Sansome St.), an Art Deco gem. **Jackson Square** is at the heart of what used to be called the Barbary Coast, a late-19th-century haven for brawling, boozing, and whoring. The old redbrick buildings and narrow alleys in the area bordered by Pacific Avenue and Washington, Sansome, and Montgomery streets recall the romance and rowdiness of early San Francisco.

The Embarcadero and South of Market (SoMa)

The beacon of the port area is the **Ferry Building,** at the foot of Market Street on the Embarcadero. The clock tower is 230 ft high and was modeled after the campanile of Seville's cathedral. A **waterfront promenade** that extends from the piers north of the Ferry Building to the San Francisco–Oakland Bay Bridge is great for watching sailboats on the bay or enjoying a picnic.

Take-out food for a waterfront picnic is available at the five-block **Embarcadero Center,** across the Embarcadero from the Ferry Building. The **Hyatt Regency Hotel** (⊠ 5 Embarcadero, ☎ 415/788–1234) is noted for its lobby and 20-story hanging garden. In front of the Hyatt Regency is **Justin Herman Plaza,** site of frequent arts-and-crafts shows and political rallies.

The **Center for the Arts at Yerba Buena Gardens** (⊠ 701 Mission St., ☎ 415/978–2787), in the SoMa (South of Market Street) area, hosts some of the city's most ambitious, multiethnic work—dance, music,

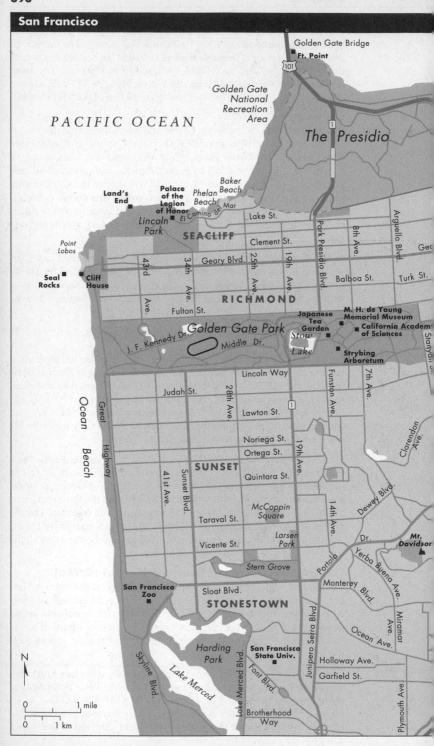

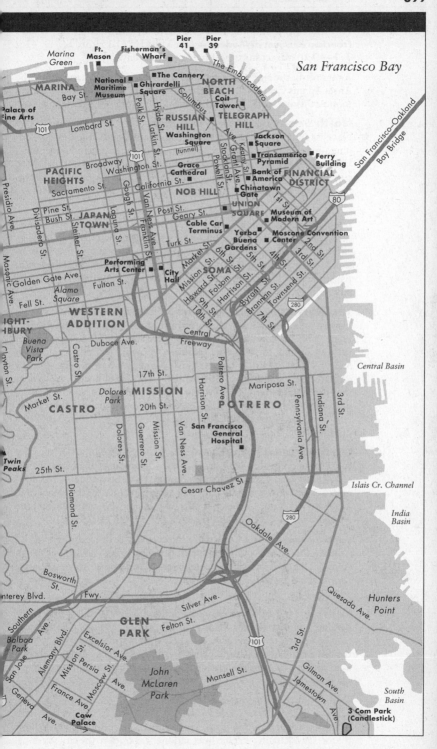

performance, theater, visual arts, film, video, and installations. The adventurous programming and fine permanent collection of the **San Francisco Museum of Modern Art** (SFMOMA; ⊠ 151 3rd St., ☎ 415/357–4000) attract hordes of patrons every day.

A number of the city's best **galleries** are near SFMOMA, including the Ansel Adams Center (⊠ 250 4th St., ☎ 415/495–7000) and the **Cartoon Art Museum** (⊠ 814 Mission St., ☎ 415/546–3922).

North Beach and Telegraph Hill

★ Novelist and resident Herbert Gold calls **North Beach** "the longest-running, most glorious American bohemian operetta outside Greenwich Village." The streets are packed with Italian delicatessens and bakeries, coffeehouses, and, increasingly, Chinese markets. Grant and Columbus avenues contain intriguing postcard, record, and new and vintage clothing shops.

Telegraph Hill, which rises to the east of North Beach, provides some of the best views in town. From Filbert Street, the Greenwich Stairs climb to **Coit Tower,** a monument to the city's volunteer firemen. Inside are the works of 25 muralists, most notably the great Mexican painter Diego Rivera. From the top there's a panoramic view of the bay, bridges, and islands.

The Northern Waterfront and Fisherman's Wharf

Fisherman's Wharf and the waterfront are at the end of the Powell-Hyde cable car line from Union Square. From the Hyde Street cable car turnaround, the **National Maritime Museum** (⊠ Polk St. at Beach St., ☎ 415/556–3002) and Ghirardelli Square are to the west; Fisherman's Wharf and Pier 39 are to the east. Several historic vessels at the **Hyde Street Pier** (⊠ Hyde St. at Jefferson St., ☎ 415/556–3002), one of the wharf's best sightseeing bargains, are a delight to explore. Bay cruises leave from Piers 39 and 41 (☎ 415/705–5555 or 415/546–2628).

Ghirardelli Square (⊠ N. Point St. between Polk and Larkin Sts.) is a complex of renovated 19th-century factory buildings filled with shops, restaurants, and galleries. Just east of the Hyde Street Pier is the **Cannery** (⊠ Leavenworth and Beach Sts.). Built in 1894 for the Del Monte Fruit and Vegetable Cannery, it now houses shops, restaurants, and the Museum of the City of San Francisco (☎ 415/928–0289).

Lombard Street, better known as "the crookedest street in the world," is just south of the waterfront area, between Hyde and Leavenworth streets. This series of sharp switchbacks was designed to compensate for the steep grade.

Pier 39 is the most popular of San Francisco's waterfront destinations for its shopping and entertainment options. Moving walkways at **Underwater World at Pier 39** transport visitors through a space surrounded on three sides by water filled with marine life indigenous to the Bay Area—from fish and plankton to sharks. Above ground, there's a carousel, roving entertainment, food stalls, and a population of noisy sea lions that basks on the north side of the pier.

To the west of the waterfront area, at the edge of the Marina District, is the rosy, rococo **Palace of Fine Arts** (⊠ Baker and Beach Sts.), with massive columns, an imposing rotunda, and a swan-filled lagoon. Built for the 1915 Panama-Pacific International Exposition, the city's semiofficial celebration of its rebuilding after the earthquake, the palace is a cherished San Francisco landmark. Inside is the **Exploratorium** (☎ 415/561–0360), whose imaginative, interactive exhibits have made it one of the best science museums in the world.

To reach the **Golden Gate Bridge,** walk along the bay from the Marina District or take Muni Bus 28 to the toll plaza. Nearly 2 mi long, the bridge looks serene and airy, yet it's tough enough to withstand winds of 100 mph. Even when conditions are gusty and misty (as they frequently are), a walk across the bridge offers unparalleled views of the skyline, the bay, the Marin Headlands, and the Pacific Ocean.

Golden Gate Park and the Western Shore

★ **Golden Gate Park,** in the northwestern part of town, is ideal for strolling, especially on Sunday, when many of its streets are closed to car traffic. A cluster of museums in the park's eastern section includes the **M. H. de Young Memorial Museum** (☎ 415/863–3330), with American art; adjoining it are the galleries of the **Asian Art Museum** (☎ 415/668–8921). The **California Academy of Sciences** (☎ 415/750–7145), a natural history museum, is one of the park's best attractions. Inside the Academy, the **Steinhart Aquarium** (☎ 415/750–7145) features a 100,000-gallon tank; the Fish Roundabout, home to hundreds of creatures; and a coral reef. The **Strybing Arboretum and Botanical Gardens** (☎ 415/661–0668) features Californian, Australian, Mediterranean, and South African plants.

At the west end of the park, the **Beach Chalet** holds a visitor center (with some fine depression-era murals) and a brew-pub restaurant with views of Ocean Beach. At the north end of Ocean Beach is the **Cliff House** (✉ 1066 Point Lobos Ave., ☎ 415/386–3330), a restaurant where you can dine to the sound of crashing surf. The **San Francisco Zoo** (✉ Sloat Blvd. at Great Hwy., ☎ 415/753–7083), at the south end of Ocean Beach, has fine exhibits and a petting corral for children.

Dining

For price ranges *see* Chart 1 (A) *in* On the Road with Fodor's.

$$$ ✕ **Aqua.** Chef-owner Michael Mina has a talent for creating contemporary versions of French, Italian, and American seafood classics. ✉ *252 California St. (downtown),* ☎ *415/956–9662. Reservations essential. AE, DC, MC, V. Closed Sun. No lunch Sat.*

$$$ ✕ **Boulevard.** The American menu at this restaurant in a historic building along the Embarcadero juxtaposes aristocratic fare with homey comfort foods like maple-cured pork loin and wood-roasted fowl. ✉ *1 Mission St. (Embarcadero),* ☎ *415/543–6084. AE, DC, MC, V. No lunch weekends.*

$$$ ✕ **Garden Court.** The stained-glass ceiling, Ionic columns, and crystal chandeliers make for the ultimate Old San Francisco dining experience. The Sunday brunch is extravagant. ✉ *Palace Hotel, Market and New Montgomery Sts. (downtown),* ☎ *415/546–5000. Jacket required. AE, D, DC, MC, V.*

$$$ ✕ **Postrio.** In Wolfgang Puck's open kitchen and stunning three-level
★ bar and dining area, the food is Californian with Mediterranean and Asian overtones and emphasizes pastas, grilled seafood, and freshly baked breads. ✉ *545 Post St. (Union Sq.),* ☎ *415/776–7825. AE, D, DC, MC, V.*

$$$ ✕ **Stars.** This huge dining room with a clublike ambience is the culi-
★ nary temple of Jeremiah Tower, an acknowledged co-creator of California cuisine. The menu ranges from grills to ragouts to sautés—some daringly creative and some classical. ✉ *150 Redwood Alley (Civic Center),* ☎ *415/861–7827. AE, DC, MC, V. No lunch weekends.*

$$ ✕ **Harbor Village.** Classic Cantonese cooking, dim sum breakfasts and lunches, and fresh seafood from its own tanks are the hallmarks of this restaurant with great bay views. ✉ *4 Embarcadero Center,* ☎

415/781–8833. Reservations not accepted for weekend lunch. AE, DC, MC, V.

$$ ✗ **Rose Pistola.** Chef Reed Hearon celebrates North Beach's Ligurian roots with a wide assortment of small antipasti plates, such as roasted peppers and house-cured fish, in addition to pizzas from a wood-burning oven and cioppino, the classic San Francisco Italian seafood stew. ⊠ *532 Columbus Ave. (North Beach),* ☏ *415/399–0499. Reservations essential. AE, MC, V.*

$$ ✗ **Scala's Bistro.** Smart leather-and-wood booths, an extravagant mural along one wall, and an appealing menu of Italian plates make this one of downtown's most attractive destinations. ⊠ *432 Powell St. (Union Sq.),* ☏ *415/395–8555. AE, DC, MC, V.*

$ ✗ **Café Claude.** Order a *croque monsieur, salade niçoise* or simple daube from the French-speaking staff at this café in a Financial District alley, and you might forget what country you're in. Order a *pastis,* and you'll soon be whistling the "Marseillaise." ⊠ *7 Claude La. (downtown),* ☏ *415/392–3505. AE, DC, MC, V. Closed Sun.*

$ ✗ **Helmand.** Authentic Afghani cooking, elegant surroundings, and amazingly low prices are Helmand hallmarks. Look for the leek-filled ravioli served with yogurt and ground beef and the exceptional lamb dishes. There's free validated parking at night at Helmand Parking, 468 Broadway. ⊠ *430 Broadway (North Beach),* ☏ *415/362–0641. AE, MC, V. No lunch weekends.*

$ ✗ **Mifune.** Bowls of thin brown *soba* (buckwheat) and thick white *udon* (wheat) are the traditional Japanese specialties served at this North American outpost of an Osaka-based noodle empire. ⊠ *Japan Center Bldg., West Wing, 1737 Post St. (Japantown),* ☏ *415/922–0337. Reservations not accepted. AE, D, MC, V.*

Lodging

For free assistance with hotel reservations try **San Francisco Reservations** (☏ 800/333–8996). For price ranges *see* Chart 2 (A) *in* On the Road with Fodor's.

$$$$ 🏨 **Campton Place Hotel.** Rooms here, small but well appointed, are
★ decorated with Asian touches in tones of gold and brown, with double-pane windows, Chinese armoires, and good-size writing desks. ⊠ *340 Stockton St. (Union Sq.), 94108,* ☏ *415/781–5555 or 800/235–4300,* ℻ *415/955–5536. 117 rooms. Restaurant, bar, in-room safes, minibars, no-smoking rooms, room service, laundry service and dry cleaning, concierge, meeting rooms, parking (fee). AE, DC, MC, V.*

$$$$ 🏨 **The Clift.** Its dark paneling and enormous lobby chandeliers lend this Grand Heritage Hotel property a note of grandeur. Rooms, some rich with dark woods and burgundies, others refreshingly pastel, all have large writing desks, plants, and flowers. ⊠ *495 Geary St. (Union Sq.), 94102,* ☏ *415/775–4700 or 800/652–5438,* ℻ *415/441–4621. 329 rooms. Restaurant, bar, in-room modem lines, minibars, no-smoking floor, room service, exercise room, laundry service and dry cleaning, concierge, meeting rooms, parking (fee). AE, DC, MC, V.*

$$$$ 🏨 **Ritz-Carlton, San Francisco.** The Ritz-Carlton is a stunning tribute
★ to beauty, splendor, and warm, sincere service. Rooms are elegant and spacious, and every bath is appointed with double sinks, hair dryers, and vanity tables. ⊠ *600 Stockton St. (Nob Hill), 94108,* ☏ *415/296–7465 or 800/241–3333,* ℻ *415/296–8261. 336 rooms. 2 restaurants, bar, 2 lounges, laundry service and dry cleaning, concierge, business services, meeting rooms, parking (fee). AE, D, DC, MC, V.*

$$$ 🏨 **Hotel Majestic.** One of San Francisco's original grand hotels, the Majestic offers romantic rooms with a mix of French and English antiques.
★ ⊠ *1500 Sutter St. (north of Civic Center), 94109,* ☏ *415/441–1100*

or 800/869–8966, FAX *415/673–7331. 57 rooms. Restaurant, bar, laundry service and dry cleaning, parking (fee). AE, DC, MC, V.*

$$ 🏨 **Hotel Rex.** Literary and artistic creativity are celebrated at the stylish Hotel Rex, where thousands of books, largely antiquarian, line the clubby, 1920s-style lobby. Rooms have writing desks and lamps with whimsically hand-painted shades. Striped bedspreads and carpets and restored period furnishings evoke the spirit of 1920s salon society. ✉ *562 Sutter St. (Union Sq.), 94102,* ☎ *415/433–4434,* FAX *415/433– 3695. 94 rooms. Bar, lobby lounge, in-room modem lines, minibars, no-smoking rooms, laundry service and dry cleaning, concierge, parking (fee). AE, D, DC, MC, V.*

$$ 🏨 **Petite Auberge.** Rooms are small at this B&B with a country-French
★ flair, but each has a teddy bear, brightly flowered wallpaper, an old-fashioned writing desk, and an armoire. ✉ *863 Bush St. (Union Sq.), 94108,* ☎ *415/928–6000 or 800/365–3004,* FAX *415/775–5717. 26 rooms. Breakfast room, no smoking floors, parking (fee). AE, DC, MC, V.*

$ 🏨 **Adelaide Inn.** The bedspreads don't match the curtains, but the rooms are clean and cheap at this friendly small hotel popular with Europeans. ✉ *5 Isadora Duncan Ct., off Taylor St. between Geary and Post Sts. (Union Sq.), 94102,* ☎ *415/441–2474,* FAX *415/441–0161. 18 rooms. Breakfast room, refrigerators. AE, MC, V.*

$ 🏨 **Marina Inn.** B&B accommodations in English country–style rooms are offered here at motel prices. ✉ *3110 Octavia St. (Marina), 94123,* ☎ *415/928–1000 or 800/274–1420,* FAX *415/928–5909. 40 rooms. Lobby lounge, no-smoking floor, barbershop, beauty salon. Continental breakfast, afternoon sherry. AE, MC, V.*

$ 🏨 **San Remo Hotel.** This Italianate Victorian just a couple of blocks
★ from Fisherman's Wharf has reasonably priced rooms and a down-home, slightly tatty elegance. Rooms share six tiled shower rooms, one bathtub chamber, and six scrupulously clean toilets. ✉ *2237 Mason St., 94133,* ☎ *415/776–8688 or 800/352–7366,* FAX *415/776–2811. 62 rooms. No-smoking rooms, parking (fee). AE, DC, MC, V.*

Nightlife and the Arts

The best guide to arts and entertainment events in San Francisco is the pink Datebook section of the Sunday *Examiner-Chronicle*. The *Bay Guardian* and *S.F. Weekly,* free weeklies available throughout the city, list more neighborhood, avant-garde, and budget-priced events and clubs. **BASS** (☎ 510/762–2277 or 415/776–1999) offers charge-by-phone ticket service. Half-price same-day tickets to many stage shows go on sale at 11 AM Tuesday–Saturday at the **TIX Bay Area** (☎ 415/433– 7827) ticket booth, on the Stockton Street side of Union Square. Credit cards are not accepted.

Nightlife

COMEDY CLUBS

Cobb's Comedy Club (✉ 2801 Leavenworth St., at Beach St., ☎ 415/ 928–4320) books stand-up comedians. The **Punch Line** (✉ 444 Battery, ☎ 415/397–7573) launched comics Jay Leno and Whoopi Goldberg.

DANCE CLUBS

DJs at tiny **Nickie's Barbeque** (✉ 460 Haight St., ☎ 415/621–6508) spin a different genre of music—from hip-hop to soul to funk—every day of the week. The **Metronome Ballroom** (✉ 1830 17th St., ☎ 415/ 252–9000) is a lively yet mellow smoke- and alcohol-free Friday–Sunday spot for ballroom dancing.

MUSIC CLUBS

Bottom of the Hill (✉ 1233 17th St., ☎ 415/621–4455) showcases alternative rock and blues. **Cafe Du Nord** (✉ 2170 Market St., ☎ 415/979–6545) is a former speakeasy that presents jazz, blues, and alternative music. The **Great American Music Hall** (✉ 859 O'Farrell St., ☎ 415/885–0750), one of the country's great eclectic nightclubs, has top blues, folk, jazz, and rock entertainers. **Julie Ring's Heart and Soul** (✉ 1695 Polk St., ☎ 415/673–7100), a '40s-style club, hosts talented vocalists and small jazz combos, featuring music of the '30s and '40s. **Slim's** (✉ 333 11th St., ☎ 415/522–0333) specializes in basic rock, jazz, and blues.

SAN FRANCISCO'S FAVORITE BARS

Cypress Club (✉ 500 Jackson St., off Columbus Ave., ☎ 415/296–8555) is an eccentric restaurant-bar where sensual, '20s-style opulence clashes with Fellini/Dali frivolity. There's live jazz seven nights a week. The famous **Tonga Room** (✉ Fairmont Hotel, 950 Mason St., at California St., ☎ 415/772–5278), with its fake palm trees, grass huts, lake (combos play pop standards on a floating barge), and sprinkler-system rain—complete with simulated thunder and lightning—is the height of Polynesian kitsch. **Vesuvio Cafe** (✉ 255 Columbus Ave., ☎ 415/362–3370) recalls the heyday of the beat poets, with memorabilia from the era covering nearly every surface.

GAY AND LESBIAN NIGHTLIFE

San Francisco's large and active gay/lesbian community supports a multitude of bars, comedy clubs, cabarets, and discos. Check *Odyssey* (☎ 415/621–6514) for the latest one-night-a-week clubs. The Stud (✉ 399 9th St., ☎ 415/252–7883), one of the city's oldest gay bars, hosts a gender-bending mix of straight, lesbian, gay, and bisexual urbanites and suburbanites. Wednesday is always packed for oldies night. Many lesbians and some gay men hang out at the **Café** (✉ 2367 Market St., ☎ 415/861–3846.)

The Arts

DANCE

The **San Francisco Ballet** (✉ War Memorial Opera House, 301 Van Ness Ave., ☎ 415/865–2000) performs classical and contemporary works from February through May. (Note: If repairs to the opera house aren't completed in time for the ballet's 1998 season, performances will take place at several venues.)

FILM

The **San Francisco International Film Festival** (☎ 415/931–3456), the city's largest, takes place late April–early May. The city's second largest, the **San Francisco International Lesbian and Gay Film Festival** (☎ 415/703–8650) takes place in late June.

MUSIC

The **San Francisco Symphony** plays from September to June in the Louise M. Davies Symphony Hall (✉ 201 Van Ness Ave., ☎ 415/431–5400).

OPERA

Productions of the **San Francisco Opera** (✉ War Memorial Opera House, 301 Van Ness Ave., ☎ 415/864–3330), presented from September through December, are often sold out; standing-room tickets are usually available.

THEATER

The American Conservatory Theater, a repertory company that specializes in classics and contemporary dramas, performs at the historic

Geary Theater (⊠ 415 Geary St., ☎ 415/749–2228). The **Curran** (⊠ 445 Geary St., ☎ 415/474–3800) hosts touring companies.

Spectator Sports

Baseball: San Francisco Giants (⊠ 3Com Park, off U.S. 101, ☎ 415/467–8000). **Oakland A's** (⊠ Oakland Coliseum, off I–880 at 66th Ave., ☎ 510/638–0500).

Basketball: Golden State Warriors (⊠ Oakland Coliseum, ☎ 510/762–2277).

Football: San Francisco 49ers (⊠ 3Com Park, ☎ 415/468–2249).

Oakland Raiders (⊠ Oakland Coliseum, ☎ 510/639–7700 or 510/762–2277).

Shopping

Shopping Districts
Union Square is flanked by the Macy's, Saks Fifth Avenue, and Neiman Marcus department stores. Also on or near the square are Tiffany & Co., Disney, Border's Books and Music, Niketown, and Virgin Megastore. **Fisherman's Wharf,** the **Embarcadero Center,** and **Chinatown** (☞ Exploring San Francisco, *above*) are three shopping areas near tourist attractions. The **SoMa** area, between 2nd, 10th, Townsend, and Howard streets, contains many clothing, record, and other discount outlets. Gentrification has altered the fabled **Haight-Ashbury District,** but there are some interesting shops, particularly on the 1500 block of Haight Street.

Antiques
Brand X (⊠ 570 Castro St., ☎ 415/626–8908) sells estate jewelry and objets d'art. **Telegraph Hill Antiques** (⊠ 580 Union St., ☎ 415/982–7055) stocks fine china and porcelain, crystal, cut glass, Victoriana, and bronzes.

Art
Art Options (⊠ 372 Hayes St., ☎ 415/252–8334) specializes in contemporary crafts and one-of-a-kind nonprecious jewelry from local and nationally known artists. There are more galleries nearby.

Books
City Lights (⊠ 261 Columbus Ave., ☎ 415/362–8193), stomping ground of the 1950s beat poets, is well stocked with poetry, contemporary literature and music, and translations of Third World literature.

Clothing
Designers Club (⊠ 3899 24th St., ☎ 415/648–1057), in Noe Valley, carries natural-fiber fashions. **Solo** (⊠ 1599 Haight St., ☎ 415/621–0342) sells women's clothes made of luxurious fabrics.

Gifts
Gordon Bennett (⊠ 2102 Union St., ☎ 415/929–1172; ⊠ Ghirardelli Square, ☎ 415/351–1172) carries housewares, dried-flower arrangements, ceramics, and other creations, many by local artists.

Side Trip to Berkeley and Oakland

Berkeley is the home of the 178-acre **University of California at Berkeley.** Along Telegraph Avenue south of the campus is a student-oriented business district with a dog-eared counterculture ambience.

Food lovers will want to head for that cradle of California cuisine,
★ **Chez Panisse Cafe & Restaurant.** Alice Waters masterminds the culi-

nary wizardry, and Jean-Pierre Moullé performs as head chef. ⊠ *1517 Shattuck Ave.,* ☎ *510/548–5525. Closed Sun.*

Oakland has the second-largest port in California. The revitalized Jack London Square area along the waterfront has attracted long-overdue attention to the city. The **Oakland Museum** (⊠ 1000 Oak St., ☎ 510/ 238–3401) displays California art, history, and natural sciences through engaging exhibits and films.

Arriving and Departing

By car, follow I–80 across the Bay Bridge; exit at University Avenue for Berkeley or pick up I–580 and exit at Grand Avenue for Oakland. By BART, Berkeley is 45 minutes to an hour from the city; exit at the downtown Berkeley stop, then take the shuttle to the campus. Oakland is a 45-minute BART ride from San Francisco; exit at the Lake Merritt station for the museum.

Side Trip to Sausalito and Muir Woods

Sausalito, a hillside town on Richardson Bay, an inlet of San Francisco Bay in Marin County, has usually sunny weather and superb views. The main street, **Bridgeway,** has waterfront restaurants, shops, and hotels.

★ **Muir Woods National Monument** is a 550-acre park that contains majestic redwoods, some nearly 250 ft tall and 1,000 years old. The park is open daily from 8 AM until sunset, but visit before 10 AM or after 4 PM to avoid traffic congestion.

Arriving and Departing

To get to Sausalito by car, cross the Golden Gate Bridge and drive north a few miles to the Sausalito exit. **Golden Gate Ferry** (☎ 415/923–2000) and the **Red and White Fleet** (☎ 415/546–2628) cruise regularly from the Embarcadero and Fisherman's Wharf to Sausalito. To drive to Muir Woods, continue north on U.S. 101 to the Highway 1–Stinson Beach exit and follow the signs.

THE WINE COUNTRY

California's beautiful **Napa and Sonoma counties** produce some of the world's finest wines. The Napa Valley becomes crowded on weekends, when visitors jam the gift shops and restaurants. In Sonoma County the pace is less frenetic.

Visitor Information

Napa Valley: Conference and Visitors Bureau (⊠ 1310 Napa Town Center, 94559, ☎ 707/226–7459). **St. Helena:** Chamber of Commerce (⊠ 1080 Main St., Box 124, 94574, ☎ 707/963–4456 or 800/799–6456). **Sonoma County:** Convention and Visitors Bureau (⊠ 5000 Roberts Lake Rd., Rohnert Park 94928, ☎ 707/586–8100 or 800/326–7666). Sonoma Valley Visitors Bureau (⊠ 453 1st St. E, Sonoma 95476, ☎ 707/996–1090).

Arriving and Departing

By Bus

Greyhound Lines (☎ 800/231–2222) runs buses from the Transbay Terminal at 1st and Mission streets in San Francisco to the cities of Sonoma and Santa Rosa. **Sonoma County Area Transit** (☎ 707/585–7516) and **Napa Valley Transit** (☎ 707/255–7631) provide local transportation.

By Car

Although traffic on the two-lane country roads can be heavy, the best way to get around the Wine Country is by car. There are three major paths through the area: U.S. 101 north from Santa Rosa, Highways 12 and 121 through Sonoma County, and Highway 29 north from Napa. From San Francisco cross the Golden Gate Bridge and follow U.S. 101 to Santa Rosa and head north, or take the exit east onto Highway 37 and then north on Highway 121 into Sonoma. Another route runs over San Francisco's Bay Bridge and along I–80 to Vallejo, where you can pick up Highway 29 north to Napa.

By Train

The **Napa Valley Wine Train** (☎ 707/253–2111 or 800/522–4142, 800/427–4124 in CA) serves lunch, dinner, and a weekend brunch on a restored Pullman car as it runs between Napa and St. Helena.

Exploring the Wine Country

The Napa Valley

Along Highway 29 north of the town of **Napa** and parallel to the highway on the Silverado Trail are some of California's most important wineries. **Domaine Chandon** (✉ California Dr., Yountville, ☎ 707/944–2280) is owned by Moët-Hennessey and Louis Vuitton. Call ahead for tour hours. **Stag's Leap** (✉ 5766 Silverado Trail, Yountville, ☎ 707/944–2020) produces the highest-ranking chardonnay in the world.

The largest wine caves in America are below **Rutherford Hill** (✉ 200 Rutherford Hill Rd., Rutherford, ☎ 707/963–7194). **Beaulieu Vineyard** (✉ 1960 St. Helena Hwy., Rutherford, ☎ 707/963–2411) utilizes the same wine-making process it did in the last century. At **Robert Mondavi** (✉ 7801 St. Helena Hwy., Oakville, ☎ 707/259–9463), the 60-minute tour is encouraged before imbibing. Architect Michael Graves designed the postmodern **Clos Pegase** (✉ 1060 Dunaweal La., Calistoga, ☎ 707/942–4981) winery. Visitors ride up the side of a hill in a gondola to reach **Sterling Vineyards** (✉ 1111 Dunaweal La., Calistoga, ☎ 707/942–3344).

Calistoga, at the Napa Valley's north end, was founded as a spa and remains notable for its mineral water, hot mineral springs, mud baths, steam baths, and massages. **Indian Springs** (✉ 1712 Lincoln Ave., ☎ 707/942–4913) has full spa amenities. **Old Faithful Geyser of California** (✉ 1299 Tubbs La., 1 mi north of Calistoga, ☎ 707/942–6463) blasts its 60-ft tower of steam and vapor about every 40 minutes.

The Sonoma Valley

East of U.S. 101 and west of the Napa Valley, Highway 12 runs through the hills of Sonoma County. The historic central plaza in the town of Sonoma is the site of **Mission San Francisco Solano** (✉ 114 Spain St. E, ☎ 707/938–1519), now a museum with a fine collection of 19th-century watercolors.

California's wine-making industry got its start at the landmark **Buena Vista Carneros Winery** (✉ 18000 Old Winery Rd., Sonoma, ☎ 707/938–1266) in 1857. The **Benziger Family Winery** (✉ 1883 London Ranch Rd., Glen Ellen, ☎ 707/935–3000) specializes in premium estate and Sonoma County wines. The beautifully rustic grounds at **Kenwood Vineyards** (✉ 9592 Sonoma Hwy., Kenwood, ☎ 707/833–5891) complement the attractive tasting room and artistic bottle labels. The well-conceived tour at **Korbel Champagne Cellars** (✉ 13250 River Rd., west of U.S. 101, Guerneville, ☎ 707/887–2294) explains the process of making sparkling wine.

Dining and Lodging

For price ranges *see* Charts 1 (A) and 2 (A) *in* On the Road with Fodor's.

Calistoga

$$–$$$ ✕ **Catahoula Restaurant and Saloon.** Chef Jan Birnbaum employs a
★ large wood-burning oven at this homey restaurant to churn out such
California-Cajun dishes as spicy gumbo with andouille sausage and oven-
braised lamb shank with red beans. ⊠ *1457 Lincoln Ave.,* ☎ *707/942–*
2275. Reservations essential. MC, V. Closed Tues. and Jan.

$$$–$$$$ 🏨 **Mount View Hotel.** This full-service European spa offers state-of-
the-art pampering, and three cottages are each equipped with a pri-
vate redwood deck, Jacuzzi, and wet bar. ⊠ *1457 Lincoln Ave., 94515,*
☎ *707/942–6877,* ﬀ *707/942–6904. 33 rooms. Restaurant, pool, spa.*
MC, V.

Rutherford

$$$ ✕ **Auberge du Soleil.** The dining terrace of this hilltop inn, looking down
★ across groves of olive trees to the Napa Valley vineyards, is the clos-
est you can get to the atmosphere, charm, and cuisine of southern France
without a passport. ⊠ *180 Rutherford Hill Rd.,* ☎ *707/963–1211.*
AE, D, MC, V.

St. Helena

$$$$ 🏨 **Meadowood Resort.** Set on 256 wooded acres, this rambling country lodge has individual five-suite bungalows and smaller lodges clustered on the hillside. ⊠ *900 Meadowood La., 94574,* ☎ *707/963–3646*
or 800/458–8080, ﬀ *707/963–3532. 85 rooms. 2 restaurants, bar,*
room service, 2 pools, spa, 9-hole golf course, 7 tennis courts, croquet.
D, DC, MC, V.

Santa Rosa

$$$ ✕ **John Ash & Co.** The chef emphasizes presentation, innovation, and
★ freshness and uses mainly seasonal foods grown in Sonoma County.
This is a favorite spot for Sunday brunch. ⊠ *4430 Barnes Rd.,* ☎ *707/*
527–7687. AE, MC, V. Closed Mon.

Sonoma

$$$ 🏨 **Thistle Dew Inn.** Half a block from Sonoma Plaza, this Victorian inn
has Arts and Crafts furnishings and antique quilts. ⊠ *171 W. Spain*
St., 95476, ☎ *707/938–2909 or 800/382–7895. 6 rooms. Hot tub,*
bicycles. AE, MC, V.

Yountville

$$$$ ✕ **French Laundry.** This intimate, cottage-style restaurant, surrounded
★ by lush gardens, offers exquisite prix-fixe French menus of four or five
courses. ⊠ *6640 Washington St.,* ☎ *707/944–2380. Reservations es-*
sential. AE, MC, V. Closed Mon. and 1st 2 wks in Jan. No lunch Tues.
and Sun.

Outdoor Activities and Sports

Hot-Air Ballooning

Many hotels arrange excursions, or contact **Napa Valley Balloons** (☎
707/944–0228 or 800/253–2224). For Sonoma trips try **Sonoma**
Thunder Wine Country Balloon Safaris (☎ 707/538–7359 or 800/
759–5638).

ELSEWHERE IN NORTHERN CALIFORNIA

The Gold Country

Arriving and Departing

Sacramento Metro Airport (☎ 916/648–0700) is served by major domestic airlines. **Greyhound** (☎ 800/231–2222) serves Sacramento, Auburn, Grass Valley, and Placerville from San Francisco. The most convenient way to see the area is by car. I–80 intersects with Highway 49, the main route through the region, at Auburn; U.S. 50 intersects with Highway 49 at Placerville.

What to See and Do

When gold was discovered at **Coloma** in 1848, people came from all over the world to search for the treasure. Today, clustered along Highway 49 are restored villages and ghost towns, antiques shops, crafts stores, and vineyards. The heart of the Gold Country lies on Highway 49 between Nevada City and Mariposa.

★ **Empire Mine State Historic Park** (⊠ 10791 E. Empire St., Grass Valley, ☎ 530/273–8522) has exhibits on gold mining. The **Marshall
★ Gold Discovery State Historical Park** (⊠ Hwy. 49, Coloma, ☎ 530/622–3470) has a replica of Sutter's Mill, where the gold rush started.

★ In **Columbia State Historic Park** (⊠ Hwy. 49, ☎ 209/532–4301) you can ride a stagecoach, pan for gold, or watch a blacksmith working at his anvil. At the **California State Mining and Mineral Museum** (⊠ Mariposa County Fairgrounds, Hwy. 49, Mariposa, ☎ 209/742–7625) a glittering 13-pound piece of ore vividly illustrates what the Gold Rush was all about.

Sacramento, the California state capital, is also the largest Gold Country city. The Visitor Information Center (⊠ 1101 2nd St., ☎ 916/442–7644) has the latest on key attractions, plus lodging, reservations, and other services. The kid-friendly **Discovery Museum** (⊠ 101 I St., ☎ 916/264–7057) presents a streamlined introduction to Sacramento's his-
★ tory. The **California State Railroad Museum** (⊠ 125 I St., ☎ 916/448–4466) displays restored locomotives and railroad cars.

Lake Tahoe

Arriving and Departing

Reno-Tahoe International Airport, 35 mi northeast of the lake, is used by national and regional airlines (☞ Nevada). The smaller **Lake Tahoe Airport** on Highway 50, 3 mi south of Tahoe's lakeshore, is not served by commercial airlines. **Amtrak** (☎ 800/872–7245) and **Greyhound Lines** (☎ 800/231–2222) also serve the Tahoe area. **South Tahoe Area Ground Express** (☎ 916/573–2080) and **Tahoe Area Regional Transit** (☎ 530/581–6365) are the local bus companies. Lake Tahoe is 198 mi northeast of San Francisco, and you drive there in about four hours. The major route is I–80 through the Sierra Nevada; U.S. 50 from Sacramento is the direct route to the south shore. Tire chains are sometimes necessary in winter.

What to See and Do

Visitors to Lake Tahoe's California side—where gambling isn't legal—come here to ski, hike, fish, camp, and boat in the spectacular Sierra Nevada range, 6,000 ft above sea level. Ski resorts, such as Incline Village and Squaw Valley, open at the end of November and operate as late as May. Tourist information is provided by the **Lake Tahoe Visi-
★ tors Authority** (☎ 530/544–5050 or 800/288–2463). Ride the **Heav-**

enly Tram (⊠ North on Ski Run Blvd. off U.S. 50 and follow signs, ☎ 702/586–7000) for a view of the lake from 8,200 ft.

The 72-mi Lake Tahoe shoreline is best seen along a route through wooded flatlands and past beaches, climbing to vistas on the rugged west side of the lake. It should take about three hours but can be slow going in summer and on holiday weekends.

West of South Lake Tahoe on Highway 89 is the **Pope-Baldwin Recreation Area** (☎ 530/541–5227), where three grand century-old mansions are open to the public. The **Lake Tahoe Visitors Center** (☎ 530/573–2674), on Taylor Creek, is near the site of a onetime Washoe Indian settlement; there are trails through meadow, marsh, and forest.

★ Tahoe's **Emerald Bay** is famed for its shape and color.

The *Tahoe Queen* (☎ 530/541–3364), a glass-bottom stern-wheeler, cruises on the lake and swings by Emerald Bay year-round from the Ski Run marina, off U.S. 50 in South Lake Tahoe. Beyond Emerald Bay is **D. L. Bliss State Park** (☎ 530/525–7277), with 6 mi of shorefront and 168 family campsites. At Tahoe City Highway 89 turns north to **Squaw Valley,** site of the 1960 Winter Olympics.

YOSEMITE NATIONAL PARK

Yosemite's U-shape valleys were formed by the action of glaciers during recent ice ages. A pass to the park, good for a week, costs $20 per car or $10 per person if you don't arrive in a car. A reservation system for entrance to Yosemite Valley during peak visiting times (mainly summer) may be in force in 1998; call ahead.

Visitor Information

Yosemite National Park (⊠ Box 577, Yosemite National Park 95389, ☎ 209/372–0264 or 209/372–0200 for 24-hr information).

Arriving and Departing

By Bus
Yosemite VIA (☎ 209/384–2576 or 800/369–7275) runs three daily buses from Merced to Yosemite Valley. Greyhound serves Merced from the California coast.

By Car
Yosemite is four to five hours from San Francisco (take I–80 to I–580 to I–205 to Highway 120) and a six-hour drive from Los Angeles (take I–5 north to Highway 99 to Fresno, and Highway 41 north to Yosemite). Highways 41, 120, and 140 all intersect with Highway 99, which runs north–south through California's Central Valley.

By Plane
Fresno Air Terminal (☎ 209/498–4095), the nearest major airport, is served by national and regional carriers.

Exploring Yosemite National Park

★ The highlights of **Yosemite Valley** include **Yosemite Fall,** the highest waterfall in North America; the famous **El Capitan** and **Half Dome** granite peaks; misty **Bridalveil Fall;** and **Glacier Point,** which affords a phenomenal bird's-eye view of the entire valley. Near **Wawona** at the park's south entrance are the historic **Wawona Hotel** and the **Mariposa Grove of Big Trees.** A free **shuttle bus** runs around the east end of Yosemite Valley year-round. A summer shuttle runs from Wawona to the Mariposa Grove of Big Trees.

Dining and Lodging

Besides the Ahwahnee Hotel's classy restaurant, dining options in Yosemite Valley include fast food and picnic fixings from a grocery store. **Yosemite Concession Services Corporation** (☎ 209/252–4848) handles reservations for the park's fancy hotels, modest lodge rooms, and Yosemite Valley tent cabins and tent sites. **Destinet** (☎ 619/452–8787 or 800/436–7275 in the U.S.) handles other camping sites within the park.

THE CENTRAL COAST

Raging surf, rugged rocks, hidden tidal pools, and wind-warped trees mark the coastline south from San Francisco. Several towns provide entertainment, but the Pacific Ocean dominates. Coast-hugging Highway 1, sometimes precariously narrow, is the route of choice; it's slow and winding, but the views are worth the extra time.

Visitor Information

Monterey Peninsula Chamber of Commerce (⊠ 380 Alvarado St., Monterey 93942, ☎ 408/649–1770). **Santa Barbara Tourist Information Center** (⊠ 1 Santa Barbara St., at Cabrillo Blvd., 93101, ☎ 805/965–3021).

Arriving and Departing

By Car
Highway 1 heads south from San Francisco through the region. U.S. 101 can be taken to Salinas, from which Highway 68 goes to Monterey. From San Francisco I–280 connects with Highway 17 just south of San Jose and gets you to the coast near Santa Cruz.

By Plane
Monterey Peninsula Airport (☎ 408/648–7000) and **Santa Barbara Municipal Airport** (☎ 805/683–4011) are served by airlines including America West, American Eagle, United, United Express, and Skywest/Delta.

By Train
Amtrak's *Coast Starlight* makes stops in Santa Barbara, San Luis Obispo, and Salinas on its run from Los Angeles to Seattle.

Exploring the Central Coast

About 75 mi south of San Francisco is the seaside and college town of **Santa Cruz,** with an old-time boardwalk and an amusement park where one of the last clackety wooden roller coasters still dips and dives.

About an hour south of Santa Cruz, the town of **Monterey** is rich in California's history. The Path of History is a 2-mi self-guided tour through ★ **Monterey State Historic Park** (☎ 408/649–7118). **Custom House,** built by the Mexican government in 1827, and the **Pacific House** (☎ 408/649–2907), a former hotel and saloon that is now a museum of early California life, are two highlights.

Monterey's barking sea lions are best seen along **Fisherman's Wharf,** an aging and touristy pier. A footpath leads from Fisherman's Wharf to **Cannery Row,** where the old tin-roof canneries made famous by John Steinbeck's eponymous book have been converted into restaurants, art ★ galleries, and minimalls. The outstanding **Monterey Bay Aquarium** (⊠ 886 Cannery Row, ☎ 408/648–4800 or 800/756–3737 in CA) is a window on the sea waters beyond.

Pacific Grove recalls its Victorian heritage in tiny board-and-batten cottages and in stately mansions. For years migrating monarch butterflies from Canada and the Pacific Northwest have made Pacific Grove their winter home. **Monarch Grove Sanctuary** (⊠ 1073 Lighthouse Ave.) is a good viewing spot.

★ The celebrated **17-Mile Drive** offers a chance to explore an 8,400-acre microcosm of the Monterey Peninsula's coastal landscape. You'll find the weather-sculpted **Lone Cypress** tree here. At **Seal Rock** and **Bird Rock,** just offshore, you can watch the creatures sunning themselves en masse. Also along the drive is the famous **Pebble Beach Golf Links.**

Before it became an art colony in the early 20th century and long before it became a shopping mecca, **Carmel** was an important religious center for Spanish California. The stone buildings and tower dome of the 1770 **Carmel Mission** (⊠ Rio Rd. and Lasuen Dr., ☎ 408/624–3600) have been beautifully restored. Another example of Carmel's architectural heritage is the late poet Robinson Jeffers's **Tor House** (⊠ 26304 Ocean View Ave., ☎ 408/624–1813).

Carmel's greatest beauty is in the rugged coastline and surrounding cypress forests, best seen at **Carmel River State Park,** off Scenic Road and south of Carmel Beach, and the larger **Point Lobos State Reserve** (☎ 408/624–4909 for both), a 1,250-acre headland just south of Carmel. At the latter, the Sea Lion Point Trail is a good spot to observe sea lions, otters, harbor seals, and seasonally migrating whales.

You can catch the quintessential view of California's coast from the elegant concrete arc of **Bixby Creek Bridge,** 13 mi south of Carmel. **Big Sur** begins at the Point Sur Light Station, atop a sandstone cliff just south of Bixby Creek. At Pfeiffer Big Sur State Park (☎ 408/667–2315) a trail leads up a small valley to a waterfall. One of the few places where you can actually reach the water is **Pfeiffer Beach** (follow the road just past the Big Sur Ranger Station for 2 mi).

★ **Hearst Castle** reigns in solitary splendor a few miles north of Cambria. William Randolph Hearst's grandiose mansion contains extravagant marble halls, ornate swimming pools, and an extensive European art and antiquities collection. A film ($6) at the new giant-screen theater details Hearst's life and the castle's construction. Tour reservations are usually required and may be made up to eight weeks in advance. ☎ *805/927–2020 or 800/444–4445.* ⊠ *$14 day tours ($25 sunset).*

The coastal ribbon of Highway 1 ends at **Morro Bay.** Morro Rock, with the sheltered harbor on one side and the Pacific surf on the other, is a preserve for peregrine falcons. At **San Luis Obispo,** just south of Morro Bay, halfway between San Francisco and Los Angeles, are such historic sites as the 1772 **Mission San Luis Obispo de Tolosa** (☎ 805/543–6850) downtown. Drop by the garish, goofy **Madonna Inn** (⊠ 100 Madonna Rd., off U.S. 101, ☎ 805/543–3000) if only for a drink and a look at the kitschy accoutrements.

Temperate **Santa Barbara** seems like the most relaxed place in the world. It retains its Spanish character with wide tree-shaded streets, red-tile-roof arcades downtown, and courtyards filled with upscale boutiques and restaurants. Scenic murals adorn the interior walls of the Spanish-
★ Moorish-style **Santa Barbara County Courthouse** (⊠ 1100 Anacapa St., ☎ 805/962–6464), well worth a visit. The Spanish built what is now **El Presidio State Historic Park** (⊠ 123 E. Cañon Perdido St., ☎ 805/966–9719) as a military stronghold in 1782. Along the Santa Barbara waterfront, not far from downtown, is **Stearns Wharf** (⊠ Cabrillo Blvd. at State St.), a pier holding shops, eateries, and the Museum of

★ Natural History's Sea Center. The landmark **Mission Santa Barbara** (✉ 2201 Laguna St., ☎ 805/682–4713) lies a bit north of Stearns Wharf. In the Santa Ynez foothills, the **Santa Barbara Botanic Garden** (✉ 1212 Mission Canyon Rd., ☎ 805/682–4726) contains 65 acres of native plants.

Dining and Lodging

For price ranges *see* Charts 1 (A) and 2 (A) *in* On the Road with Fodor's.

Big Sur

$–$$ ✕ **Nepenthe.** On an 800-ft cliff overlooking lush meadows and the ocean, the house now occupied by this restaurant was once owned by Orson Welles. The food—from roast chicken to sandwiches and hamburgers—is only adequate; it's the location that warrants a stop. ✉ *Hwy. 1 at south end of town,* ☎ *408/667–2345. AE, MC, V.*

$$$$ ✕▣ **Post Ranch Inn.** Each unit at this clifftop resort has its own spa
★ tub, stereo, private deck, fireplace, and massage table. The inn's restaurant, serving cutting-edge American fare, is the best in the area. ✉ *Hwy. 1 (Box 219), 93920,* ☎ *408/667–2200 or 800/527–2200,* 𝔽𝔸𝕏 *408/667–2512. 30 rooms. Restaurant, bar, 2 pools, hot tub, exercise room, library. Continental breakfast. AE, MC, V.*

$$$ ▣ **Big Sur Lodge.** Motel-style cottages at this lodge within Pfeiffer Big Sur State Park—some with fireplaces or kitchens—are set around a meadow surrounded by redwood and oak trees. ✉ *Hwy. 1 (Box 190), 93920,* ☎ *408/667–2171 or 800/424–4787,* 𝔽𝔸𝕏 *408/667–3110. 61 rooms. Restaurant, grocery, pool. AE, MC, V.*

Cambria

$–$$ ✕ **Hamlet at Moonstone Gardens.** This patio in the middle of 3 acres
★ of luxuriant gardens is perfect for lunch. An upstairs dining room overlooks the Pacific. Salmon comes poached in white wine; meat entrées range from hamburgers to rack of lamb. ✉ *Hwy. 1 on east side,* ☎ *805/927–3535. MC, V.*

Carmel

$$$ ✕ **Crème Carmel Restaurant & Cafe.** Dinner specialties at this California-French restaurant include charbroiled Muscovy duck and beef tenderloin. Lunch, served in the adjacent café, is less pricey and more casual. ✉ *San Carlos St. near 7th Ave.,* ☎ *408/624–0444. AE, MC, V.*

$$$$ ▣ **Highlands Inn.** The hotel's setting, on high cliffs above the Pacific,
★ gives it outstanding views in a region famous for them. The plush spa suites and condominium-style units have wood-burning fireplaces and ocean-view decks; some also have full kitchens. ✉ *Hwy. 1 (Box 1700), 93921,* ☎ *408/624–3801 or 800/538–9525, 800/682–4811 in CA;* 𝔽𝔸𝕏 *408/626–1574. 142 rooms. 2 restaurants, pool. AE, D, DC, MC, V.*

$–$$ ▣ **Carmel River Inn.** Clean and safe, this great value near area beaches is across the street from a supermarket (some rooms have kitchenettes). ✉ *Hwy. 1, at the Carmel River Bridge (Box 221609), 93922,* ☎ *408/624–1575 or 800/882–8142,* 𝔽𝔸𝕏 *408/624–0290. 43 rooms. Pool. MC, V.*

Monterey

$$$ ✕ **Fresh Cream.** Locals love this spot for French cuisine with light, imag-
★ inative Californian accents. Dishes include rack of lamb Dijonnaise and roast duck in black-currant sauce. ✉ *100 Pacific St.,* ☎ *408/375–9798. AE, DC, MC, V. Closed Mon. No lunch.*

$–$$ ✕ **Paradiso Trattoria.** Cal-Mediterranean specialties and pizzas from a wood-burning oven are the luncheon fare at this bright beachfront restaurant; seafood is a good choice for dinner. ⊠ *654 Cannery Row,* ☎ *408/375–4155. AE, D, DC, MC, V.*

$–$$ ✕ **Tarpy's Roadhouse.** The kitchen at this renovated roadhouse cooks everything Mom used to make, only better. ⊠ *2999 Monterey–Salinas Hwy. (Hwy. 68), at Canyon Del Rey Rd.,* ☎ *408/647–1444. MC, V.*

$$$–$$$$ 🛏 **Spindrift Inn.** This Cannery Row hotel has a private beach and
★ rooftop garden. Rooms are spacious, with hardwood floors, featherbeds, fireplaces, canopied beds, down comforters, and other luxuries. ⊠ *652 Cannery Row, 93940,* ☎ *408/646–8900 or 800/841–1879,* 𝖥𝖠𝖷 *408/646–5342. 42 rooms. AE, D, DC, MC, V.*

$$ 🛏 **Del Monte Beach Inn.** The reasonably priced rooms at this small bed-and-breakfast are decorated à la Martha Stewart. Be sure to check in before the office closes at 9 PM. ⊠ *1110 Del Monte Ave.,* ☎ *408/649–4410,* 𝖥𝖠𝖷 *408/375–3818. 18 rooms. AE, D, MC, V.*

$–$$ 🛏 **Monterey Motor Lodge.** Its location near El Estero Park gives this motel an edge over similarly priced competitors. A large, secluded courtyard with pool is another plus. ⊠ *55 Aguajito Rd., 93940,* ☎ *408/372–8057 or 800/558–1900,* 𝖥𝖠𝖷 *408/655–2933. 45 rooms. Restaurant, pool. AE, D, DC, MC, V.*

Morro Bay

$$–$$$$ 🛏 **Inn at Morro Bay.** Inside a state park and across from a heron rookery, this upscale hotel complex contains a variety of romantic country French–style rooms. Some have fireplaces, hot tubs, and bay views; others look out on extensive gardens. ⊠ *60 State Park Rd., 93442,* ☎ *805/772–5651 or 800/321–9566,* 𝖥𝖠𝖷 *805/772–4779. 96 rooms. Restaurant, bar, pool. AE, D, DC, MC, V.*

Pacific Grove

$$$ 🛏 **Old Bath House.** This romantic converted bathhouse overlooks the
★ water at Lovers Point. The menu makes the most of local seafood and produce. ⊠ *620 Ocean View Blvd.,* ☎ *408/375–5195. AE, D, DC, MC, V. No lunch.*

Santa Barbara

$$$ ✕ **Citronelle.** The accent at this offspring of Los Angeles's famed Cit-
★ ron is on French Riviera–style dishes: light and delicate but loaded with intriguing good tastes. Sweeping harbor views can be had from the dining room. ⊠ *901 E. Cabrillo Blvd.,* ☎ *805/963–0111. AE, D, DC, MC, V.*

$ ✕ **Roy.** This downtown storefront is a real bargain. Owner-chef Leroy Gandy serves a $12.50 prix-fixe dinner that includes a small salad, fresh soup, and a tempting roster of Cal-Mediterranean main courses. Expect a wait on weekends. ⊠ *7 W. Carrillo St.,* ☎ *805/966–5636. AE, DC, MC, V. Closed Mon.*

$ ✕ **La Super-Rica.** Fans of this food stand with a patio drive for miles
★ to fill up on soft tacos and incredible beans. ⊠ *622 N. Milpas St., at Alphonse St.,* ☎ *805/963–4940. No credit cards.*

$$$$ 🛏 **Four Seasons Biltmore.** This grande dame of Santa Barbara hostel-
★ ries is more formal than other city accommodations, with lush gardens and palm trees galore. ⊠ *1260 Channel Dr., Montecito 93108,* ☎ *805/969–2261 or 800/332–3442,* 𝖥𝖠𝖷 *805/969–5715. 234 rooms. 2 restaurants, bar, pool, hot tub, putting green, 3 tennis courts, health club, shuffleboard. AE, DC, MC, V.*

$$–$$$ 🛏 **Ambassador by the Sea Motel.** Near the harbor and Stearns Wharf, this place has a real California beach feel. Sundecks overlook the ocean and bike path. ✉ *202 W. Cabrillo Blvd., 93101,* ☎ *805/965–4577,* FAX *805/965–9937. 32 rooms. Pool. AE, D, DC, MC, V.*

$ 🏨 **Motel 6.** Low price and great location near the beach are the pluses for this no-frills place. ✉ *443 Corona Del Mar Dr., 93103,* ☎ *805/ 564–1392,* FAX *805/963–4687. 51 rooms. Pool. AE, D, DC, MC, V.*

Santa Cruz

$$ ✕ **India Joze.** Southeast Asian, Indian, and Persian specialties are prepared here with organic ingredients, exotic spices, and tantalizing sauces. ✉ *1001 Center St.,* ☎ *408/427–3554. AE, D, MC, V.*

$$$ ✕ **Stagnaro Brothers.** You'll find 20 different seafood choices at this casual family-style restaurant. ✉ *Municipal Wharf,* ☎ *408/423–2180. AE, D, MC, V.*

$$ 🏨 **Harbor Inn.** The lived-in furniture and wooden beds at this clean, friendly inn are reminiscent of a stay at grandma's. Many rooms have kitchenettes. ✉ *645 7th Ave.,* ☎ *408/479–9731. 19 rooms. MC, V.*

Nightlife and the Arts

The Carmel-Monterey area's top performing arts venue is the **Sunset Community Cultural Center** (✉ San Carlos St. between 8th and 10th Aves., Carmel, ☎ 408/624–3996), which presents concerts, lectures, and headline performers. The **Arlington Theater** (☎ 805/963–4408) is home to the Santa Barbara Symphony.

Outdoor Activities and Sports

Biking

The Monterey Peninsula is prime biking territory, with paths following parts of the shoreline; rentals are available from **Bay Bikes** (✉ 640 Wave St., Monterey, ☎ 408/646–9090). In Santa Barbara the **Cabrillo Bike Lane** passes the city zoo, a bird refuge, beaches, and the harbor. Rent bikes, quadricycles, and skates from **Beach Rentals** (✉ 22 State St., ☎ 805/966–6733).

Fishing

Charter boats leave from Monterey, Morro Bay, and Santa Barbara. Most fishing trips—from such outfits as **Monterey Sport Fishing and Whale Watching** (✉ 96 Fisherman's Wharf, Monterey, ☎ 408/372–2203) or **Sea Landing Sportfishing** (✉ Cabrillo Blvd. at Bath, Santa Barbara, ☎ 805/963–3564)—include equipment rental, bait, fish cleaning, and a one-day license.

Golf

Pebble Beach Golf Links (✉ 17-Mile Dr., ☎ 408/625–8518), with its sweeping ocean views, is one of the world's most famous courses; reservations are essential. At **Spyglass Hill** (✉ Spyglass Hill Rd., ☎ 408/ 624–3811), the holes are unforgiving, but the views offer consolation. The **Santa Barbara Golf Club** (✉ Las Positas Rd. and McCaw Ave., ☎ 805/687–7087) and **Sandpiper Golf Course** (✉ 7925 Hollister Ave., Goleta, ☎ 805/968–1541) are two options farther south.

Surfing

Steamer's Lane between the Boardwalk and the lighthouse is the site of several summer competitions. **Beach 'n' Bikini Surf Shop** (✉ Beach and Front Sts., ☎ 408/427–2355) rents surfboards and wet suits by the day.

Whale-Watching

On their annual migration between the Bering Sea and Baja California, 45-ft gray whales can be spotted at many points not far off the coast. The migration south takes place from December through February; the journey north, from March to mid-May. Other species of whales can be seen in the summer and autumn.

Beaches

In general, the shoreline north of San Luis Obispo is rocky and backed by cliffs, the water rough and often cold, and sunbathing limited to only the warmest hours of the early afternoon. Still, the **boardwalk at Santa Cruz, Point Lobos State Reserve** in lower Monterey Bay, **Big Sur,** and **Morro Bay** provide unparalleled beach experiences. **Pismo Beach** marks the first of the classic southern California beaches, with long, low stretches of sand. From Point Concepción down through Santa Barbara and into Ventura County are some fine beaches. Santa Barbara's **East Beach** has lifeguards, volleyball courts, a jogging-and-biking trail, a jungle-gym play area, and a bathhouse with a gym, showers, and changing rooms. **Arroyo Burro County Beach,** near Santa Barbara, is a state preserve, with a small grassy area that has picnic tables and with sandy beaches below the cliffs. **El Capitan, Refugio,** and **Gaviota state beaches** near Santa Barbara have campsites, picnic tables, and fire pits.

LOS ANGELES

Los Angeles is a wholly 20th-century city, created, defined, dependent on, and thrust into prominence by the advances of the modern age: automobiles, airplanes, and the movies. It is among the nation's most ethnically diverse cities, with thriving Hispanic, Korean, Chinese, Japanese, and Middle Eastern communities.

Visitor Information

Convention and Visitors Bureau (✉ 633 W. 5th St., Suite 6000, 90071, ☎ 213/624–7300).

Arriving and Departing

By Bus
Greyhound Lines (✉ 1716 E. 7th St., at Alameda St., ☎ 800/231–2222).

By Car
I–5 (called the Golden State or Santa Ana Freeway here) runs north–south. I–10 heads east cross-country. I–15 comes into the area from the northeast and continues down to San Diego.

By Plane
Los Angeles International Airport (LAX; ☎ 310/646–5252), about 25 mi west of downtown and 10 mi from Beverly Hills, is served by more than 85 major airlines. Four smaller regional airports—in **Burbank, Long Beach, Orange County,** and **Ontario**—also serve the greater L.A. area. Taxis to downtown cost $24–$30 (request a flat fee—metered fares are more) and take 20–60 minutes, depending on traffic. **SuperShuttle** (☎ 310/782–6600) services downtown hotels for about $12 ($13 to Disneyland hotels); fares to private residences vary. **Airport Bus** (☎ 714/938–8900 or 800/772–5299) provides service from LAX to the Pasadena ($12 one-way, $20 round-trip) and Anaheim ($14 and $22) areas.

By Train
Amtrak (☎ 800/872–7245) serves Los Angeles's Union Station (✉ 800 N. Alameda St.).

Getting Around Los Angeles

Freeways, whose names can change along the route, are the most efficient way to get from one end of the city to another.

By Public Transportation

The **Southern California Metropolitan Transit Authority** (MTA; ☎ 213/626–4455) provides bus service and is expanding with the Metrorail Blue Line, which runs daily, 5 AM–10 PM, from downtown Los Angeles to Long Beach. The Metro Red Line runs from Union Station to MacArthur Park. The line will extend to Hollywood by 1998. Bus fare is $1.35 plus 25¢ for a transfer. **DASH** (Downtown Area Short Hop; ☎ 213/626–4455) is a system of minibuses serving the downtown area. DASH runs weekdays 6 AM–7 PM, Saturday 10–5. Stops are every two blocks or so, and you pay 25¢ every time you get on, no matter how far you go.

By Taxi

All cabs must be ordered by phone; companies include **Independent Cab. Co.** (☎ 213/385–8294 or 310/569–8214) and **United Independent Taxi** (☎ 213/653–5050). The metered rate is $1.90 at the flag drop and $1.60 per mile thereafter.

Orientation Tours

Starline Tours of Hollywood (☎ 213/463–3333 or 800/959–3131) offers tours of movie stars' homes, Disneyland, Universal Studios, the *Queen Mary*, Santa Catalina Island, and other attractions.

Exploring Los Angeles

Downtown

★ Pyramidal skylights mark the **Museum of Contemporary Art** (✉ 250 S. Grand Ave., ☎ 213/626–6222), which was designed by renowned Japanese architect Arata Isozaki. The permanent collection includes works from the 1940s to the present; artists represented include Mark Rothko, Franz Kline, and Susan Rothenberg.

On weekends especially, **Chinatown**'s colorful shops, exotic markets, and restaurants attract crowds of shoppers. The historic buildings of the 44-acre **El Pueblo de Los Angeles Historical Monument** (Sepulveda House visitor center, ✉ 622 N. Main St., ☎ 213/628–1274) celebrate the birthplace of Los Angeles (no one knows exactly where the original 1780 settlement was). Fiestas are held nearly every weekend on **Olvera Street,** a genuine Mexican-style marketplace with shops, stalls, restaurants, and the oldest downtown building (1818).

City hall (✉ 200 N. Spring St.), south of Olvera Street, is recognizable from its role as a backdrop for *Dragnet*. Farther south, along 1st and San Pedro streets, stretches **Little Tokyo,** with Japanese shops, restaurants, and sushi bars.

Amid shops and sidewalk vendors along **Broadway** catering to the Hispanic community, **Grand Central Market** (✉ 317 S. Broadway, ☎ 213/624–2378) has exotic produce, herbs, and meats. The gentrified Victorian-era **Bradbury Building** (✉ 304 S. Broadway, ☎ 213/626–1893) has a filigreed, glassed-in courtyard and open balconies.

A few miles south of Broadway is **Exposition Park** (✉ Figueroa St. at Exposition Blvd.), site of 1932 and 1984 Olympics events and home to the impressive **California Science Center** (☎ 213/744–7400) and **Natural History Museum** (☎ 213/744–3414).

Los Angeles

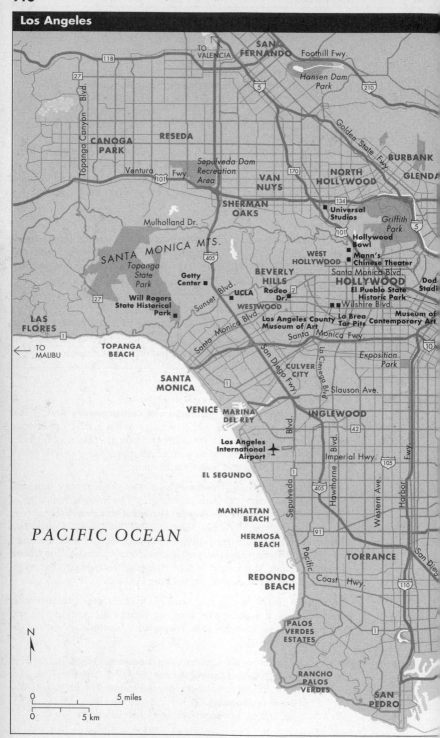

PACIFIC OCEAN

N

0 _____ 5 miles
0 _____ 5 km

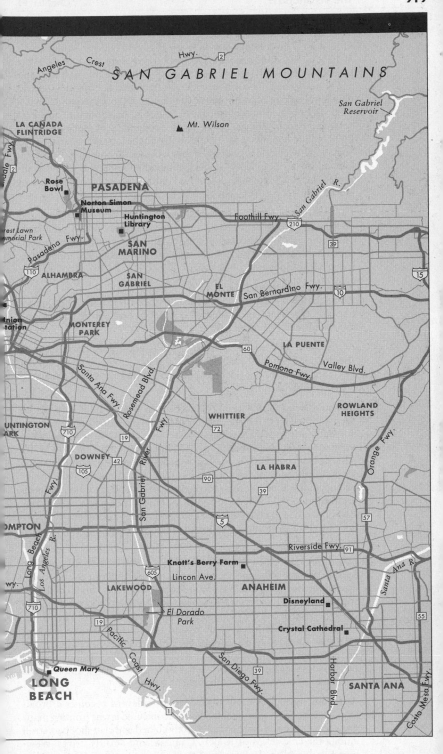

Hollywood

The cradle of the movie industry is rife with landmarks of its glamorous past. The **Capitol Records Tower** (✉ 1750 N. Vine St.) was built in 1956 to resemble a stack of records. The **Palace** (✉ 1735 N. Vine St., ☎ 213/467–4571) for years presented vaudeville shows; it was later a TV studio and now hosts rock concerts and late-night weekend dancing. The Art Deco **Pantages Theater** (✉ 6233 Hollywood Blvd.), originally a movie house, hosted the Oscars in the 1950s and now presents large-scale Broadway musicals. **Frederick's of Hollywood** (✉ 6608 Hollywood Blvd., ☎ 213/466–8506), the famous name in risqué

★ lingerie, also has a bra museum. **Mann's Chinese Theatre** (✉ 6925 Hollywood Blvd., ☎ 213/464–8111), originally Grauman's Chinese, invented the gala premiere; its famous courtyard holds the footprints of more than 160 movie celebrities.

The **Hollywood Walk of Fame** immortalizes the names of movie and other entertainment greats on brass plaques embedded in pink stars along the city's sidewalks. Marlon Brando is at 1765 Vine Street, Clark Gable at 1608 Vine, John Wayne at 1541 Vine, and Marilyn Monroe at 6774 Hollywood Boulevard.

Wilshire Boulevard

Along the 16-mi Wilshire Boulevard are many of the city's best museums and tallest office buildings, the heart of both Beverly Hills, and the seaside cliffs of Santa Monica.

At the southeast corner of Wilshire and Western Avenue sits the **Wiltern Theatre** (✉ 3790 Wilshire Blvd.), one of the city's best examples of Art Deco architecture. The 1930s zigzag design was restored to its splendid turquoise hue in 1985.

★ **Hancock Park** (✉ Wilshire Blvd. at Curson Ave.) is built atop the La Brea Tar Pits, from which more than 100 tons of fossils have been removed. Many fossils are on view next door at the **George C. Page Museum of La Brea Discoveries** (✉ 5801 Wilshire Blvd., ☎ 213/936–2230). Also in Hancock Park is the **Los Angeles County Museum of Art** (✉

★ 5905 Wilshire Blvd., ☎ 213/857–6000), containing collections of paintings and decorative arts, a sculpture garden, and Japanese art. **Farmers Market** (✉ 6333 W. 3rd St., ☎ 213/933–9211), north of Hancock Park (near the CBS television studios), is a partly covered marketplace with food stalls, produce vendors, and a few boutiques.

The Westside

L.A.'s Westside—encompassing West Hollywood, Beverly Hills, Bel Air, and Westwood—epitomizes what most people think of as the southern California good life: palatial hilltop homes, chic shops, and star-studded restaurants. **West Hollywood** is trendy, stylish, and home to both the bizarre and the beautiful. **Melrose Avenue** is a test kitchen for the avant-garde, with quirky shops and a clutch of great eateries. **Sunset Strip**—the stretch of Sunset Boulevard through West Hollywood—became a movie-star stomping ground in the 1930s, headquarters to the suave TV detectives of *77 Sunset Strip* in the 1950s, and today is the center of a lively rock club scene.

As it runs through **Beverly Hills,** Sunset Boulevard becomes a broad tree-shaded avenue, with immaculately manicured lawns fronting mansions of every conceivable style. Perfectly coiffed and clad shoppers stroll among the chic shops of Rodeo, Camden, and Beverly drives. **Westwood,** home to the **University of California at Los Angeles,** straddles the hillsides between Wilshire and Sunset boulevards west of Beverly Hills. UCLA has sculpture and botanical gardens and offers walking tours of the campus (☎ 310/206–0616). On weekends the surrounding area offers lively nightlife. Northwest of Beverly Hills in the Santa

★ Monica Mountains is the Richard Meier–designed **Getty Center** (⊠ 1200 Getty Center Dr., ☎ 310/440–7300), the new home of most of oil billionaire J. Paul Getty's extensive art collection.

Santa Monica and the Beach Cities

Wilshire Boulevard ends at Ocean Avenue in **Santa Monica.** The **Santa Monica Pier** (☎ 310/458–8900) has a 46-horse antique carousel, an amusement park, gift shops, arcade, cafés, and a psychic adviser. A sandy beach stretches north and south of the pier. Palm-shaded **Palisades Park** overlooks the beach from the cliffs above. North from Santa Monica along the Pacific Coast Highway is **Malibu,** site of the beachfront homes of many stars.

Venice, immediately south of Santa Monica, is known for its active scenes—street vendors, musicians, in-line skaters, guys and gals pumping iron, and folks simply tanning—on **Ocean Front Walk** and the **Venice Boardwalk.**

Long Beach

To the south, in Long Beach, is the *Queen Mary* (⊠ Pier H, ☎ 562/435–3511). The famous ocean liner now houses a hotel, shops, and restaurants.

Pasadena

The communities northeast of downtown L.A. were the first suburbs of the city, established by wealthy Angelenos in the 1880s. In **Highland Park** the **Southwest Museum** (⊠ 234 Museum Dr., ☎ 213/221–2163) houses a collection of Native American art and artifacts. In **San Marino** the **Huntington Library, Art Gallery, and Botanical Gardens** (⊠ 1151 Oxford Rd., ☎ 626/405–2100) is spread over 207 hilly acres. The complex's collections number more than 4 million items, including a Gutenberg Bible, the Ellesmere manuscript of Chaucer's *Canterbury Tales,* and first editions by Shakespeare.

In **Pasadena** the **Norton Simon Museum** (⊠ 411 W. Colorado Blvd., ☎ 626/449–6840) houses Impressionist paintings, as well as masterpieces by Rembrandt, Goya, and Picasso. **Gamble House** (⊠ 4 Westmoreland Pl., ☎ 626/793–3334), built by Charles and Henry Greene in 1908, is the ultimate in California Craftsman–style architecture.

San Fernando Valley

★ **Universal Studios and CityWalk,** 5 mi north of Hollywood in the San Fernando Valley off U.S. 101 (the Hollywood Freeway), has tremendously popular five- to seven-hour tram tours of its back lot, which feature special effects and stage shows. ⊠ *100 Universal City Pl.,* ☎ *818/508–9600.* ⊡ *$34 adults, $25 children. AE, MC, V.*

At **Warner Bros. Studios** you can observe the day-to-day action of movie making on a two-hour walking tour (weekdays 9–3) of whatever is being filmed at the time. Reserve tickets one week in advance. ⊠ *4000 Warner Blvd., Burbank,* ☎ *818/954–1744.* ⊡ *$29. No children under 10. AE, MC, V.*

Outside Los Angeles

Santa Catalina Island, 26 mi offshore, is a good day trip or weekend getaway from Los Angeles. From San Pedro and Long Beach, **Catalina Express** provides boat service (☎ 310/519–1212 or 800/995–4386). No private cars are permitted on the island (golf carts can be rented), but the main town of Avalon is easily explored on foot. **Santa Catalina Island Co.** (☎ 310/510–8687) and **Catalina Adventure Tours** (☎ 310/510–2888) offer escorted bus tours of the interior, coastal cruises, and glass-bottom-boat rides.

Parks and Gardens

★ **Griffith Park** (⊠ Ventura and Golden State Fwys., ☎ 213/665–5188)
has acres of picnic areas, hiking and bridle trails, a carousel, and pony
rides. Also in the park are the **Los Angeles Zoo** (☎ 213/666–4090);
Travel Town (⊠ 5200 Zoo Dr., ☎ 213/662–5874), with railcars,
planes, and classic cars; and the **Planetarium and Observatory** (⊠
Enter at Los Feliz Blvd. and Vermont Ave., ☎ 213/664–1191).

Dining

Parking can be difficult; most restaurants listed here offer valet parking. For price ranges *see* Chart 1 (A) *in* On the Road with Fodor's.

$$$$ ✕ **L'Orangerie.** French specialties at this elegant restaurant include duck
★ with foie gras, John Dory with roasted figs, rack of lamb for two, and
an unbeatable apple tart served with a jug of double cream. ⊠ *903 N.
La Cienega Blvd. (West Hollywood),* ☎ *310/652–9770. Reservations
essential. Jacket and tie. AE, D, DC, MC, V. Closed Mon. No lunch.*

$$$ ✕ **Campanile.** Faves at this restaurant in Charlie Chaplin's former of-
★ fice complex include any of the lamb dishes, the crisp flattened chicken
with mashed potatoes and garlic confit, and the crusty sourdough-based
breads. ⊠ *624 S. La Brea Ave. (Hollywood),* ☎ *213/938–1447. Reser-
vations essential. AE, D, DC, MC, V. No lunch weekends. No dinner
Sun.*

$$$ ✕ **Citrus.** One of L.A.'s most prominent chefs, Michel Richard, cre-
★ ates superb dishes by blending French and American cuisines. You can't
miss with the delectable tuna burger, the impossibly thin angel-hair pasta,
or the carpaccio salad. ⊠ *6703 Melrose Ave. (Hollywood),* ☎ *213/
857–0034. Jacket required. AE, MC, V. Closed Sun.*

$$$ ✕ **Dining Room.** The California cuisine here is wonderful—try the
★ loin of Colorado lamb accompanied by eggplant and sweet-pepper
lasagna. Adjoining the Dining Room is a cocktail lounge, with romantic
lighting and a pianist playing show tunes. ⊠ *Regent Beverly Wilshire
Hotel, 9500 Wilshire Blvd. (Beverly Hills),* ☎ *310/275–5200. Jacket
and tie. AE, D, DC, MC, V.*

$$$ ✕ **La Cachette.** Owner-chef Jean-François Meteigner's modern French
★ cuisine manages to be both light and sublimely delicious. ⊠ *10506 Lit-
tle Santa Monica Blvd. (West Los Angeles),* ☎ *310/470–4992. Reservations essential. AE, MC, V. Closed Sun. No lunch Sat.*

$$$ ✕ **Restaurant Katsu.** A stark, simple, perfectly designed sushi bar with
★ a small table area is the stage for exquisite and delicious Japanese del-
icacies. ⊠ *1972 N. Hillhurst Ave. (Los Feliz),* ☎ *213/665–1891.
Reservations essential. AE, DC, MC, V. Closed Sun. No lunch Sat.*

$$$–$$$$ ✕ **Valentino.** The light, modern Italian dishes at this top-notch restau-
★ rant include fried calamari, lobster cannelloni, fresh broiled porcini mush-
rooms, and osso buco. Order from the lengthy list of daily specials. ⊠
3115 Pico Blvd. (Santa Monica), ☎ *310/829–4313. Reservations es-
sential. AE, DC, MC, V. Closed Sun.*

$$–$$$ ✕ **Eclipse.** Chef Serge Falesitch's memorable Cal-Mediterranean fare
★ injects just a hint of Provençal magic in dishes like the salmon in
parchment with fresh herbs, served on a bed of citrus and bay leaves.
⊠ *8800 Melrose Ave. (West Hollywood),* ☎ *310/724–5959. Reser-
vations essential. AE, D, DC, MC, V. No lunch.*

$$–$$$ ✕ **Granita.** The menu at this Wolfgang Puck eatery favors seafood items.
★ There's also a spicy shrimp pizza with sun-dried tomatoes and herb
pesto and a roasted Chinese duck with dried fruit chutney. ⊠ *23725
W. Malibu Rd. (Malibu),* ☎ *310/456–0488. Reservations essential. D,
DC, MC, V. No lunch Mon.–Tues.*

$$–$$$ ✕ **Spago.** At this restaurant that propelled Wolfgang Puck into the culinary spotlight, the proof is in the tasting: grilled baby Sonoma lamb, pizza with Santa Barbara shrimp, and baby salmon. ⊠ *1114 Horn Ave. (West Hollywood),* ☎ *310/652–4025. Reservations essential. Jacket required. D, DC, MC, V. No lunch.*

$$–$$$ ✕ **Yujean Kang's Gourmet Chinese Cuisine.** Start with the tender slices
★ of veal on a bed of enoki and black mushrooms and topped with a tangle of quick-fried shoestring yams or the sea bass with kumquats and a passion-fruit sauce; then finish with poached plums or with watermelon ice under a mantle of white chocolate. ⊠ *67 N. Raymond Ave. (Pasadena),* ☎ *818/585–0855. AE, D, DC, MC, V.*

$$ ✕ **Ca'Brea.** The divine Italian fare includes roast leg of lamb with black-
★ truffle-and-mustard sauce, whole boneless chicken marinated and grilled with herbs, and the ever-popular osso buco. ⊠ *346 S. La Brea Ave. (Hollywood),* ☎ *213/938–2863. AE, D, DC, MC, V. Closed Sun. No lunch weekends.*

$$ ✕ **Cafe Pinot.** The Pinot menu is rooted in the traditional French bistro
★ standards—steak *frites,* roast chicken encrusted with five mustards, lamb shank—but it also includes some superb light spa dishes and a few worthy pastas. ⊠ *700 W. 5th St. (downtown), 213/239–6500. Reservations essential. DC, MC, V. No lunch Fri.–Sat.*

$–$$ ✕ **Border Grill.** The eclectic menu here ranges from grilled tandoori
★ skirt steak marinated in garlic and cilantro to Yucatán seafood tacos to vinegar-and-pepper-grilled turkey. ⊠ *1445 4th St. (Santa Monica),* ☎ *310/451–1655. AE, D, DC, MC, V. No lunch.*

$–$$ ✕ **Broadway Deli.** Whatever you feel like eating at this brasserie-cum-
★ upscale-diner, you will probably find it on the menu, from a platter of assorted smoked fish or Caesar salad to shepherd's pie, carpaccio, steak, and broiled salmon with creamed spinach. ⊠ *1457 3rd St. Promenade (Santa Monica),* ☎ *310/451–0616. Reservations not accepted. AE, MC, V.*

$–$$ ✕ **Chan Dara.** Try any of the Thai noodle dishes here, especially those with crab and shrimp. Also tops on the extensive menu are *satay* (skewered meat appetizers with peanut sauce) and barbecued chicken and catfish. ⊠ *310 N. Larchmont Blvd. (Hollywood),* ☎ *213/467–1052. AE, D, DC, MC, V. No lunch weekends.*

$ ✕ **Art's Delicatessen.** One of the best Jewish-style delicatessens in the
★ city serves mammoth sandwiches. ⊠ *12224 Ventura Blvd. (Studio City),* ☎ *818/762–1221. Reservations not accepted. AE, D, DC, MC, V.*

$ ✕ **Dive!** Only Steven Spielberg could have created such a restaurant— it's as much a theme park as a place to eat. The kitchen's specialty is submarine sandwiches; good ones include the Parisian chicken sub and the brick oven–baked Tuscan steak sub. ⊠ *10250 Santa Monica Blvd.,* ☎ *310/788–3483. Reservations not accepted. AE, D, DC, MC, V.*

$ ✕ **El Cholo.** This restaurant serves zesty margaritas and tacos (includ-
★ ing some you make yourself), along with first-rate L.A.-Mex versions of chicken enchiladas, *carnitas,* and other standards. ⊠ *1121 S. Western Ave. (Mid-Wilshire),* ☎ *213/734–2773. AE, DC, MC, V.*

Lodging

Because of L.A.'s sprawl, select a hotel that is close to where you'll be touring. For price ranges *see* Chart 2 (A) *in* On the Road with Fodor's.

$$$$ 🏨 **The Mondrian.** Each apartment-size accommodation at this Ian
★ Schrager–run property, done in white with industrial gray carpeting, has floor-to-ceiling windows, slip-covered sofas, marble-top coffee tables, and a kitchen with sleek Philippe Starck–designed accessories. ⊠ *8440 Sunset Blvd., West Hollywood 90069,* ☎ *213/650–8999 or*

800/525–8029, FAX 213/650–5215. *245 rooms. Restaurant, 2 bars, outdoor café, picnic area, snack bar, tapas bar, in-room modem lines, kitchenettes, no-smoking rooms, refrigerators, room service, pool, hot tub, massage, sauna, steam room, health club, laundry service and dry cleaning, concierge, business services, meeting rooms, car rental, parking (fee). AE, D, DC, MC, V.*

$$$$ 🏨 **Regal Biltmore Hotel.** Many historic details at this recently upgraded classic, built in 1923, remain. Guest rooms are done in pastels, with contemporary furniture and armoires. Executive-floor accommodations have in-room coffeemakers and desks with larger-than-usual work space. ⊠ *506 S. Grand Ave., Los Angeles (downtown) 90071,* ☎ *213/624–1011 or 800/245–8673,* FAX *213/612–1545. 683 rooms. 2 restaurants, 2 bars, no-smoking floors, minibars, room service, in-room VCRs, indoor pool, hot tub, health club, baby-sitting, laundry service and dry cleaning, concierge, business services, travel services, car rental, parking (fee). AE, D, DC, MC, V.*

$$$$ 🏨 **Regent Beverly Wilshire.** This landmark property has Italian Renaissance–style architecture with a French neoclassic influence; guest rooms have appropriate period furnishings in subtle hues and glorious marble bathrooms with deep tubs. ⊠ *9500 Wilshire Blvd., 90212,* ☎ *310/275–5200 or 800/421–4354, 800/427–4354 in CA;* FAX *310/ 274–2851. 275 rooms. 2 restaurants, bar, lobby lounge, in-room modem lines, in-room safes, minibars, no-smoking floors, room service, in-room VCRs, pool, beauty salon, hot tub, massage, health club, piano, baby-sitting, children's program, laundry service and dry cleaning, concierge, business services, travel services, car rental, parking (fee). AE, D, DC, MC, V.*

$$$$ 🏨 **Shutters on the Beach.** This is the only Los Angeles hotel that sits
★ directly on the beach. Amenities in the luxurious rooms include Frette linens and bathrobes, clock radios, hair dryers, three telephones, and complimentary classic movies for the VCR. ⊠ *1 Pico Blvd., Santa Monica 90405,* ☎ *310/458–0030,* FAX *310/458–4589. 186 rooms. 2 restaurants, bar, lobby bar, in-room modem lines, in-room safes, minibars, no-smoking floors, room service, in-room VCRs, pool, hot tub, massage, sauna, spa, steam room, health club, beach, windsurfing, mountain bikes, baby-sitting, laundry service and dry cleaning, concierge, business services, meeting rooms, travel services, car rental, parking (fee). AE, D, DC, MC, V.*

$$$ 🏨 **Barnabey's Hotel.** The hotel's deluxe rooms (still in the same price
★ range) are the way to go, as they have more light and exude more charm. ⊠ *3501 Sepulveda Blvd. (at Rosecrans), Manhattan Beach 90266,* ☎ *310/545–8466 or 800/552–5285,* FAX *310/545–8621. 122 rooms. Restaurant, pub, in-room modem lines, no-smoking rooms, in-room VCRs, pool, hot tub, bicycles, nightclub, video games, baby-sitting, laundry service and dry cleaning, concierge, business services, meeting rooms, travel services, airport shuttle, car rental, parking (fee). AE, D, DC, MC, V.*

$$$ 🏨 **Westin LAX.** This luxurious three-wing hotel is a good place to stay
★ if you want to be pampered but also need to be close to the airport. ⊠ *5400 W. Century Blvd., Los Angeles 90045,* ☎ *310/216–5858,* FAX *310/670–1948. 720 rooms. Restaurant, bar, minibars, no-smoking rooms, refrigerators, in-room modem lines, pool, 3 hot tubs, sauna, exercise room, laundry service and dry cleaning, business services, meeting rooms, airport shuttle, car rental, parking (fee). AE, D, DC, MC, V.*

$$ 🏨 **Carlyle Inn.** The contemporary four-story hotel gives guests several extras such as a buffet breakfast in the morning and a glass of wine in the late afternoon. Modern rooms are done in peach with light-pine furniture; amenities include bathrobe, hair dryer, and turndown ser-

vice. ✉ *1119 S. Robertson Blvd. Beverly Hills 90035,* ☎ *310/275–4445 or 800/322–7595,* FAX *310/859–0496. 32 rooms. Restaurant, in-room modem lines, minibars, no-smoking rooms, room service, in-room VCRs, hot tub, exercise room, laundry service and dry cleaning, business services, travel services, parking (fee). AE, D, DC, MC, V.*

$$ 🖼 **Clarion Hotel Hollywood Roosevelt.** Most rooms at this local landmark are done in a pastel decor with pine furniture and have irons and ironing boards, hair dryers, and coffeemakers. ✉ *7000 Hollywood Blvd., Hollywood 90028,* ☎ *213/466–7000 or 800/950–7667,* FAX *213/466–9376. 359 rooms. 3 restaurants, bar, lobby lounge, in-room safes, in-room minibars, no-smoking rooms, room service, pool, exercise room, nightclub, laundry service, baby-sitting, travel services, car rental, parking (fee). AE, D, DC, MC, V.*

$$ 🖼 **Kawada Hotel.** Akin to a small European hotel, this property near the Music Center and local government buildings offers good service, immaculate (if smallish) rooms, and an excellent restaurant. ✉ *200 S. Hill St., Los Angeles (downtown) 90012,* ☎ *213/621–4455 or 800/752–9232,* FAX *213/687–4455. 117 rooms. Restaurant, bar, deli, kitchenettes, no-smoking rooms, refrigerators, room service, in-room VCRs, coin laundry, laundry service and dry cleaning, concierge, business services, meeting rooms, car rental, parking (fee). AE, DC, MC, V.*

$$ 🖼 **Sportsmen's Lodge.** An English country–style structure, this hotel has attractive grounds and rooms done in soft colors. Studio suites with private patios are available. ✉ *12825 Ventura Blvd., Studio City 91604,* ☎ *818/769–4700 or 800/821–8511,* FAX *213/877–3898. 191 rooms. 3 restaurants, bar, no-smoking floors, room service, pool, barbershop, beauty salon, hot tub, exercise room, baby-sitting, coin laundry, laundry service and dry cleaning, travel services, airport shuttle, car rental, free parking. AE, D, DC, MC, V.*

$–$$ 🖼 **Ocean View Hotel.** With a coveted location in the heart of Santa Monica facing the ocean, this Best Western hotel offers a breath of fresh air—literally. Rooms have ocean or courtyard views. ✉ *1447 Ocean Ave., Santa Monica 90401,* ☎ *310/458–4888 or 800/452–4888,* FAX *310/458–0848. 72 rooms. In-room modem lines, no-smoking rooms, refrigerators, in-room VCRs, laundry service and dry cleaning, business services, free parking. AE, D, DC, MC, V.*

$–$$ 🖼 **Wyndham Hotel at Los Angeles Airport.** Done in greens and yellows, the rooms are small (250 square ft) but have plenty of amenities, such as fax machines, voice mail, and movies. ✉ *6225 W. Century Blvd., Los Angeles 90045,* ☎ *310/670–9000 or 800/996–3426,* FAX *310/670–8110. 591 rooms. 2 restaurants, bar, in-room modem lines, in-room safes, minibars, no-smoking floors, refrigerators, pool, hot tub, sauna, exercise room, baby-sitting, laundry service and dry cleaning, concierge, car rental, parking (fee). AE, D, DC, MC, V.*

$ 🖼 **Banana Bungalow Hotel and International Hostel.** You'll get good value for your money at this friendly, no-smoking inn, which is popular with international backpackers and college students. ✉ *2775 Cahuenga Blvd. W, Hollywood 90068,* ☎ *213/851–1129 or 800/446–7835,* FAX *213/851–1569. 45 rooms. Restaurant, pool, exercise room, billiards, recreation room, theater, coin laundry, travel services, airport shuttle, car rental, free parking. MC, V.*

$ 🖼 **The InnTowne.** This contemporary three-story hotel just 1½ blocks from the convention center offers large rooms with a beige-and-white or gray-and-white color scheme. ✉ *913 S. Figueroa St., Los Angeles (downtown) 90015,* ☎ *213/628–2222 or 800/457–8520,* FAX *213/687–0566. 170 rooms. Bar, coffee shop, room service, pool, laundry service and dry cleaning, concierge, car rental, free parking. AE, D, DC, MC, V.*

Nightlife and the Arts

The Calendar section of the *Los Angeles Times* is the best source of information for local events. Tickets can be purchased by phone from **TeleCharge** (☎ 800/762–7666), **Ticketmaster** (☎ 213/480–3232), or **Good Time Tickets** (☎ 213/464–7383).

Nightlife

COMEDY

The **Comedy Store** (✉ 8433 Sunset Blvd., Hollywood, ☎ 213/656–6225) showcases comedians, including top names. The **Improvisation** (✉ 8162 Melrose Ave., West Hollywood, ☎ 213/651–2583) features comedy and some music. The **Laugh Factory** (✉ 8001 Sunset Blvd., Hollywood, ☎ 213/656–8860) offers stand-up comedy and improvisation.

DANCE CLUBS

Coconut Teaszer (✉ 8117 Sunset Blvd., Hollywood, ☎ 213/654–4773) has dancing to live music, a great barbecue menu, and pool tables. The spacious **Love Lounge** (✉ 657 N. Robertson Blvd., West Hollywood, ☎ 310/659–0472) opens its doors Tuesday–Friday, with a different theme—from drag shows to retro new wave—each night. **Roxbury** (✉ 8225 Sunset Blvd., West Hollywood, ☎ 213/656–1750) presents live music, from hip-hop to '70s oldies, and is known for its gourmet pizza. **Sunset Room** (✉ 9229 Sunset Blvd., Beverly Hills, ☎ 310/271–8355) is a hot and hip dance club.

LIVE MUSIC

Studio musicians often sit in at the **Baked Potato** (✉ 3787 Cahuenga Blvd. W, North Hollywood, ☎ 818/980–1615), a club near Universal Studios. At the **Lighthouse** (✉ 30 Pier Ave., Hermosa Beach, ☎ 310/372–6911) you'll hear everything from reggae to big band. **Marla's Jazz Supper Club** (✉ 2323 W. Martin Luther King Jr. Blvd., Los Angeles, ☎ 213/294–8430) swings with blues and jazz.

The **Roxy** (✉ 9009 Sunset Blvd., West Hollywood, ☎ 310/276–2222), classy and comfortable, is L.A.'s premier rock club, though it presents stage productions as well. The **Viper Room** (✉ 8852 Sunset Blvd., West Hollywood, ☎ 310/358–1880) presents pop, rock, blues, and jazz/fusion performers. For the most current alternative sounds, **Spaceland** (1717 Silverlake Blvd., Silverlake, ☎ 213/413–4442), a former tacky disco in Silverlake, is now the place to go.

The Arts

MUSIC

The **Dorothy Chandler Pavilion** (✉ 135 N. Grand Ave., ☎ 213/972–7211) is home to the Los Angeles Philharmonic Orchestra and presents other large-scale productions. The **Hollywood Bowl** (✉ 2301 Highland Ave., Hollywood, ☎ 213/850–2000) offers an outdoor summer season of classical and popular music. The outdoor **Greek Theater** (✉ 2700 N. Vermont Ave., ☎ 213/665–1927) presents summer jazz, popular, and Pops concerts.

THEATER

Plays are presented at two of the three theaters at the **Music Center** (✉ 135 N. Grand Ave.): the Ahmanson Theatre (☎ 213/972–7211) and the Mark Taper Forum (☎ 213/972–7353). The **Center Theatre Group at Mark Taper Forum** is a resident company that also books its shows into other theaters. The **James A. Doolittle Theatre** (✉ 1615 N. Vine St., Hollywood, ☎ 213/462–6666) presents dramas. The **Geffen Playhouse** (✉ 10886 Le Conte Ave., Westwood, ☎ 310/208–6500 or 310/208–5454) presents musicals and comedies year-round.

Spectator Sports

Baseball: Los Angeles Dodgers (⊠ Dodger Stadium, 1000 Elysian Park Ave., downtown, ☎ 213/224–1400).

Basketball: Los Angeles Lakers (⊠ The Forum, 3900 W. Manchester Ave., Inglewood, ☎ 310/419–3182). **Los Angeles Clippers** (⊠ L.A. Sports Arena, 3939 S. Figueroa St., downtown, ☎ 213/748–8000).

Hockey: Los Angeles Kings (⊠ The Forum, 3900 W. Manchester Ave., Inglewood, ☎ 310/673–6003).

Horse Racing: Santa Anita Race Track (⊠ Arcadia, ☎ 626/574–7223); late December–April, October–mid-November; **Hollywood Park** (⊠ Century Blvd. and Avenue of Champions, Inglewood, ☎ 310/419–1500) April–mid-July, mid-November–December 24.

Soccer: Galaxy (⊠ Rose Bowl, Arroyo Blvd., Pasadena, ☎ 213/817–5425).

Beaches

Los Angeles County beaches (and state beaches operated by the county) have lifeguards. Public parking (for a fee) is widely available, most state beaches have picnic and rest-room facilities, and most city beaches (some local favorites are listed below from north to south) are lined with a boardwalk that has plenty of services.

Leo Carrillo State Beach (⊠ 35000 block of Pacific Coast Hwy. [PCH], Malibu, ☎ 818/880–0350) is fun at low tide, when tide pools emerge. There are hiking trails, sea caves, and tunnels; and you can often see whales, dolphins, and sea lions.

Zuma Beach Park (⊠ 30050 PCH, Malibu, ☎ 310/457–9891), Malibu's largest and sandiest beach, is a favorite surfing spot and teen hangout.

Westward Beach/Point Dume State Beach (⊠ South end of Westward Beach Rd., Malibu, ☎ 310/457–9891) has tide pools and sandstone cliffs. It's a favorite surfing spot among older surfers because of its slow, long-breaking waves.

Paradise Cove (⊠ 28128 PCH, Malibu, ☎ 310/457–9891), with its pier and equipment rentals, is a mecca for sportfishing boats.

Surfrider Beach/Malibu Lagoon State Beach (⊠ 23200 PCH, Malibu, ☎ 818/880–0350), north of Malibu Pier, has steady 3- to 5-ft waves that make it a great long-board surfing spot. The International Surfing Contest is held here each September. The lagoon is a sanctuary for many birds.

Topanga State Beach (⊠ 18700 block of PCH, Malibu, ☎ 310/394–3266), rocky but a favorite with surfers, stretches from the mouth of the canyon down to Coastline Drive.

Will Rogers State Beach (⊠ 15800 PCH, Pacific Palisades, ☎ 310/394–3266) is a wide, sandy beach with a steady, even surf. There's plenty of beach, volleyball, and bodysurfing action parallel to the pedestrian bridge. Parking is limited.

Santa Monica State Beach (⊠ Santa Monica Blvd. and Ocean Ave., Santa Monica, ☎ 310/394–3266), the widest stretch of beach on the Pacific coast, is also one of the most popular, with bike paths, facilities for people with disabilities, playgrounds, and volleyball.

Manhattan State Beach (⊠ West of the Strand, Manhattan Beach, ☎ 310/372–2166), 44 acres of sandy beach, offers swimming, diving, surfing, fishing, and picnic facilities.

Redondo Beach (⊠ Foot of Torrance Blvd., Redondo Beach, ☎ 310/372–2166) is usually packed in summer, and parking is limited.

Shopping

You can find anything you want in Los Angeles's shops: brand names in department stores at any mall; one-of-a-kind items along Melrose Avenue; designer originals on Rodeo Drive; art in galleries on La Cienega Boulevard; and specialty foods at ethnic neighborhood shops and the Farmers Market.

Shopping Districts

Rodeo Drive, in Beverly Hills, is the world-famous street with such pricey shops as **Fred Hayman** (⊠ 273 N. Rodeo Dr., ☎ 310/271–3000), for designer men's and women's fashions, and **Bijan** (⊠ 420 N. Rodeo Dr., ☎ 310/273–6544), where you shop by appointment for designer men's fashions. The **Cooper Building** (⊠ 860 S. Los Angeles St., ☎ 213/622–1139), in downtown L.A., contains four floors of outlet shops. For vintage styles or the just plain weird, go to **Melrose Avenue** between La Brea and Crescent Heights. The stylish **Beverly Center** (⊠ Beverly Blvd. at La Cienega Blvd.) has more than 200 upscale stores and boutiques. The **Santa Monica Promenade** and **Montana Avenue** feature boutique after boutique of quality goods.

Department Stores

Los Angeles has branches of many national and regional chains, including Neiman Marcus, Saks Fifth Avenue, Sears, Macy's, Nordstrom, and Robinsons-May.

Gifts and More

Tesoro (⊠ 319 S. Robertson Blvd., Beverly Hills, ☎ 310/273–9890) stocks trendy ceramics, southwestern blankets, and contemporary art.

Star Wares on Main (⊠ 2817 Main St., ☎ 310/399–0224) carries sample costumes from movies like *Independence Day* and celebrity memorabilia of stars from Loretta Swit to Liz Taylor.

Music

Aron's Records (⊠ 1150 N. Highland Ave., Hollywood, ☎ 213/469–4700) carries new releases and an extensive selection of old records.

Vintage Clothing

Wasteland (⊠ 7428 Melrose Ave., ☎ 213/653–3028) is a fun place to shop for '50s bowling shirts, '40s rayon dresses, funky ties, worn jeans, and leather jackets. It's also a good place to spot young celebrities.

ORANGE COUNTY

Orange County sits between Los Angeles to the north and San Diego to the south. Though primarily suburban, it is one of the top tourist destinations in California, with attractions such as Disneyland, pro sports, and miles of beaches.

Visitor Information

Anaheim Area: Convention and Visitors Bureau (⊠ Anaheim Convention Center, 800 W. Katella Ave., 92802, ☎ 714/999–8999); Visitor Information Hot Line (☎ 714/635–8900).

Arriving and Departing

By Bus
Greyhound Lines (☎ 800/231–2222) serves Santa Ana and Anaheim.

By Car
I–405 (San Diego Freeway) and I–5 (Santa Ana Freeway) run north–south through Orange County. I–405 merges into I–5 south of Laguna.

By Plane
John Wayne Orange County Airport (✉ Santa Ana, ☎ 714/252–5252) is served by a number of major carriers.

By Train
Amtrak (☎ 800/872–7245) has nine trains daily with stops in Fullerton, Anaheim, Santa Ana, Irvine, San Juan Capistrano, and San Clemente.

Exploring Orange County

Inland Orange County

★ Anaheim is the home of **Disneyland.** Visitors enter the Magic Kingdom by way of Walt Disney's idealized turn-of-the-century Main Street. In late 1997 Disneyland was scheduled to close down Tomorrowland to build a bigger and better futuristic play area to debut in 1998. **Fantasyland** features rides based on children's stories. **Frontierland** depicts the Wild West. The highlight of **Adventureland** is the Indiana Jones thrill ride. New Orleans Square is the setting for **Pirates of the Caribbean,** a boat ride through a scene lavish with animated characters, and the Blue Bayou restaurant. The nearby **Haunted Mansion** is full of holographic ghosts. In Critter Country is **Splash Mountain,** a flume ride that drops 52 ft at 40 mph. **Mickey's Toontown** is a child-size interactive community that gives kids the feeling of being inside a cartoon with Mickey and other characters. Along with the various thrill rides and high-tech wizardry are the strolling Disney characters, a daily parade on Main Street, and fireworks nightly in summer. ✉ *1313 Harbor Blvd.,* ☎ *714/999–4565.* ◈ *$34 adults, $26 children.*

★ **Knott's Berry Farm,** a 150-acre complex of food, shops, rides, and other attractions, is near Disneyland, in Buena Park. **Ghost Town** re-creates an 1880s mining town; the **Gold Mine** ride descends into a replica of a working gold mine. **Camp Snoopy** is a kid-size High Sierra wonderland where Snoopy and the *Peanuts* gang hang out. At **Wild Water Wilderness** riders can brave white water in an inner tube in the **Big Foot Rapids** or commune with Native peoples of the northwest coast in the spooky **Mystery Lodge.** Thrill rides are placed throughout the park, including the **Wind Jammer, Boomerang, Jaguar!** and **Montezooma's Revenge** roller coasters. **X-K-1** is a living version of a video game. The **Boardwalk** includes dolphin and sea lion shows at the Pacific Pavilion, along with the Good Time and 3-D Nu Wave theaters. And don't forget what made Knott's famous: the fried chicken dinners and boysenberry pies at **Mrs. Knott's Chicken Dinner Restaurant,** just outside the park gates in Knott's California MarketPlace. ✉ *8039 Beach Blvd., Buena Park,* ☎ *714/220–5200.* ◈ *$28.50.*

The **Movieland Wax Museum** (✉ 7711 Beach Blvd., Buena Park, ☎ 714/522–1155) re-creates the famous in wax.

Garden Grove is the site of the **Crystal Cathedral** (✉ 12141 Lewis St., Garden Grove, ☎ 714/971–4013), the domain of televangelist Robert Schuller.

The Coast

Pacific Coast Highway (Highway 1) is the main thoroughfare for all the beach towns along the Orange County coast. **Huntington Beach** is a popular surfer hangout; you can watch the action from the Huntington Pier. South of Huntington Beach is **Newport Beach,** a Beverly-Hills-by-the-sea. Nearly 10,000 boats bob in the U-shape Newport Harbor, which arcs around eight small islands. **Balboa Peninsula,** with its Victorian Balboa Pavilion and active Fun Zone, is a popular visitor area. The **Orange County Museum of Art** (⊠ 850 San Clemente Dr., ☎ 714/759–1122) holds a collection of works by California artists.

★ Farther south is the town of **Corona del Mar,** a small jewel of a town with exceptional beaches. You can walk clear out onto the bay on a rough-and-tumble rock jetty, or you can wander about tide pools and hidden caves. Protected by small cliffs, the beaches here resemble those of northern California's coastline. In **Laguna Beach** art galleries in town coexist with volleyball games and sun worship on nearby Main Beach; in July and August the **Pageant of the Masters** (☎ 714/494–1147) features living models re-creating famous paintings. Below Laguna the small harbor town of **Dana Point** is reminiscent of northern California's beaches. In March migrating swallows and spectacle-loving tourists flock to **Mission San Juan Capistrano** (⊠ Camino Capistrano and Ortega Hwy., ☎ 714/248–2048).

Dining and Lodging

For price ranges *see* Charts 1 (A) and 2 (A) *in* On the Road with Fodor's.

Anaheim

$$$ ✕ **JW's.** This upscale steak house specializes in aged beef but also serves seafood, lamb, and chicken. ⊠ *Anaheim Marriott, 700 W. Convention Way,* ☎ *714/750–8000. AE, D, DC, MC, V. Closed Sun. No lunch.*

$$–$$$ ✕ **White House.** The northern Italian menu features a good selection from pasta to scallopini, with a heavy emphasis on seafood. Vegetarian entrées are available. A three-course lunch for $16 is served weekdays from 11:30 to 2. ⊠ *887 S. Anaheim Blvd.,* ☎ *714/772–1381. AE, DC, MC, V. No lunch weekends.*

$–$$ ✕ **The Catch/Hop City Blues and Brew.** Hearty portions of steak, seafood, and salads are served at the Catch. Over at Hop City, it's California-cajun cuisine and blues tunes. ⊠ *1929 and 1939 S. State College Blvd.,* ☎ *714/634–1829. AE, DC, MC, V. No lunch weekends.*

$$$$ 🖫 **Disneyland Hotel.** This 60-acre resort is connected to the theme park by a monorail. The towers and tropical village make for unique accommodations. On most days hotel guests receive admission to the park before the general public. ⊠ *1150 W. Cerritos Ave., 92802,* ☎ *714/778–6600,* ℻ *714/956–6582. 1,136 rooms. 6 restaurants, 5 lounges, 3 pools, hot tub, exercise room, beach, concierge floor, business services. AE, D, DC, MC, V.*

$$$ 🖫 **Disneyland Pacific Hotel.** Part of the Disneyland Resort, the Pacific offers many of the benefits of the adjacent Disneyland Hotel (☞ *above*), in slightly quieter and more modern surroundings. There's also tram service to Disneyland. ⊠ *1717 S. West St., 92802,* ☎ *714/999–0990,* ℻ *714/776–5763. 502 rooms. 2 restaurants, 2 lobby lounges, pool, hot tub, health club, recreation room, concierge floor. AE, D, DC, MC, V.*

$$$ 🖫 **Inn at the Park Hotel.** This longtime favorite of conventioneers has large rooms, all with balconies and views of Disneyland. The pool area is especially attractive and spacious. ⊠ *1855 S. Harbor Blvd., 92802,* ☎ *714/750–1811 or 800/353–2773,* ℻ *714/971–3626. 500 rooms.*

Restaurant, coffee shop, lounge, pool, hot tub, exercise room, video games. AE, D, DC, MC, V.

$$ 🏨 **Ramada Maingate/Anaheim.** This reliable member of the Ramada chain is across the street from Disneyland. Guests are provided a free shuttle and early admission to the parks. ⊠ *1460 S. Harbor Blvd., 92802,* ☎ *714/772–6777 or 800/447–4048,* FAX *714/999–1727. 465 rooms. Restaurant, pool. AE, D, DC, MC, V.*

$–$$ 🏨 **Best Western Stovall's Inn.** This well-kept facility's charms include its topiary gardens, room decor in soft desert colors, and friendly staff. Ask about discounts for several-night stays. ⊠ *1110 W. Katella Ave., 92802,* ☎ *714/778–1880 or 800/854–8175,* FAX *714/778–3805. 290 rooms. Restaurant, lounge, 2 pools. AE, D, DC, MC, V.*

Brea

$$$ ✕ **La Vie en Rose.** A reproduction of a Norman farmhouse with a large
★ turret, this restaurant across from the Brea Mall attracts visitors and locals for its artfully prepared French food. ⊠ *240 S. State College Blvd., 91621,* ☎ *714/529–8333. AE, DC, MC, V. Closed Sun.*

Dana Point

$ ✕ **Proud Mary's.** The best burgers and sandwiches in southern Orange County are enjoyed alfresco, overlooking the fishing boats and pleasure craft in Dana Point Harbor. ⊠ *34689 Golden Lantern,* ☎ *714/ 493–5853. AE, D, MC, V. No dinner.*

$$$$ ✕🏨 **Ritz-Carlton Laguna Niguel.** One of California's most highly respected
★ hotels, the Ritz offers beach access, a spectacular ocean view, the Dining Room restaurant, a lavishly decorated lobby, and spacious rooms. ⊠ *1 Ritz-Carlton Dr., 92677,* ☎ *714/240–2000 or 800/241–3333,* FAX *714/240–0829. 393 rooms. 3 restaurants, lounge, 2 pools, beauty salon, 4 tennis courts, health club, concierge. AE, D, DC, MC, V.*

Irvine

$$–$$$ ✕ **Bistango.** Sleek, stylish, and art-filled Bistango serves first-rate California cuisine: crab cakes, salads, seafood pasta, Mediterranean pizzas, and grilled ahi tuna. ⊠ *19100 Von Karman Ave.,* ☎ *714/752–5222. Reservations essential. AE, D, DC, MC, V. Valet parking.*

$$ ✕ **Prego.** Try the spit-roasted meats and chicken or the charcoal-
★ grilled fresh fish. Also try one of the reasonably priced Californian or Italian wines. ⊠ *18420 Von Karman Ave.,* ☎ *714/553–1333. AE, DC, MC, V. No lunch weekends.*

$$$ 🏨 **Irvine Marriott.** Despite its size, the hotel has an intimate feel about it, due in part to the cozy lobby, the friendly staff, and the repeat guests. Asian-style rooms all have small balconies. ⊠ *1800 Von Karman Ave., 92715,* ☎ *714/553–0100,* FAX *714/261–7059. 513 rooms. 2 restaurants, sports bar, indoor-outdoor pool, hot tub, massage, 4 tennis courts, health club, concierge floors, business services. AE, D, DC, MC, V.*

Laguna Beach

$$$–$$$$ ✕ **Five Feet.** Here you'll find delicate pot stickers, wontons stuffed with
★ goat cheese, a salad featuring sashimi, plus steak and fresh fish. ⊠ *328 Gleneyre St.,* ☎ *714/497–4955. AE, D, DC, MC, V. No lunch Sat.– Thurs.*

$$ ✕ **Beach House.** A Laguna tradition, the Beach House has a water view from every table. Fresh fish, lobster, and steamed clams are the drawing cards. It's open for breakfast, lunch, and dinner. ⊠ *619 Sleepy Hollow La.,* ☎ *714/494–9707. AE, MC, V.*

$–$$ ✕ **Ti Amo.** Laguna's newest Italian eatery quickly became its best, justifiably acclaimed for the refinement of its pastas and creativity of its main courses. All the nooks and crannies are charming, but to maximize the romance, request a table in the lush garden in back. ✉ *31727 S. Pacific Coast Hwy.,* ☎ *714/499–5350. AE, D, DC, MC, V. No lunch.*

$$$–$$$$ 🏨 **Inn at Laguna Beach.** Set on a bluff overlooking the ocean, this ocean-
★ front Mediterranean-style inn has luxurious amenities and many rooms with views. ✉ *211 N. Pacific Coast Hwy., 92651,* ☎ *714/497–9722 or 800/544–4479,* FAX *714/497–9972. 70 rooms. Pool. AE, D, DC, MC, V.*

Newport Beach

$$$ ✗ **Aubergine.** A few Californian touches influence the otherwise purely
★ modern French menu at this worthy recent addition to the Orange County culinary scene. ✉ *508 29th St.,* ☎ *714/723–4150. AE, MC, V. Closed Sun.–Mon. No lunch.*

$ ✗ **Crab Cooker.** This shanty serves fresh fish grilled over mesquite at low, low prices. ✉ *2200 Newport Blvd.,* ☎ *714/673–0100. Reservations not accepted. No credit cards.*

$ ✗ **El Torito Grill.** The just-baked tortillas, turkey mole enchilada, and
★ miniature blue-corn duck tamales are good choices here. The bar serves hand-shaken margaritas and 20 brands of tequila. ✉ *Fashion Island, 941 Newport Center Dr.,* ☎ *714/640–2875. AE, D, DC, MC, V.*

$$$$ 🏨 **Four Seasons Hotel.** Marble and antiques fill the airy lobby. The guest
★ rooms, decorated in southwestern colors, have spectacular views. ✉ *690 Newport Center Dr., 92660,* ☎ *714/759–0808 or 800/332– 3442,* FAX *714/759–0568. 285 rooms. 2 restaurants, lounge, pool, massage, sauna, steam room, 2 tennis courts, health club, mountain bikes, concierge, business services. AE, D, DC, MC, V.*

$$$$ 🏨 **Sutton Place Hotel.** This ultramodern hotel has an eye-catching zig-gurat design. The luxuriously appointed rooms all have minibars. ✉ *4500 MacArthur Blvd., 92660,* ☎ *714/476–2001 or 800/810–6888,* FAX *714/476–0153. 435 rooms. 2 restaurants, lounge, pool, hot tub, 2 tennis courts, health club, concierge. AE, D, DC, MC, V.*

Nightlife and the Arts

The **Orange County Performing Arts Center** (✉ 600 Town Center Dr., Costa Mesa, ☎ 714/556–2787) presents symphony orchestras, opera companies, and musicals. Next door to the performing arts center is the award-winning **South Coast Repertory Theater** (✉ 655 Town Center Dr., Costa Mesa, ☎ 714/957–4033), which presents traditional and contemporary works. Summer concert series are presented at the **Irvine Meadows Amphitheater** (✉ 8800 Irvine Center Dr., ☎ 714/855– 4515).

Outdoor Activities and Sports

Biking

A **bike path** runs from Marina del Rey down to San Diego with only minor breaks. For rentals try Rainbow Bicycles (✉ Laguna, ☎ 714/ 494–5806) or Team Bicycle Rentals (✉ Huntington Beach, ☎ 714/ 969–5480).

Water Sports

Water-sports equipment rentals are near most piers, including **Hobie Sports** (✉ Dana Point, ☎ 714/496–2366; ✉ Laguna, ☎ 714/497– 3304). **Balboa Boat Rentals** (☎ 714/673–7200), in Newport Harbor, and **Embarcadero Marina** (☎ 714/496–6177), at Dana Point, rent sail- and powerboats.

Spectator Sports
Baseball: Anaheim Angels (⊠ Anaheim Stadium, 2000 Gene Autry Way, ☎ 714/634–2000).

Hockey: Mighty Ducks of Anaheim (⊠ The Arrowhead Pond of Anaheim, 2695 E. Katella, ☎ 714/740–2000).

Beaches

The beaches along Highway 1 in Orange County are among the finest and most varied in southern California, offering fine swimming, great surfing, and many services. Posted warnings about undertow should be taken seriously.

Huntington Beach State Beach is a long stretch of flat, sandy beach with changing rooms, concessions, fire pits, and lifeguards. **Lower Newport Bay** is a sheltered 740-acre preserve for ducks and geese. **Newport Dunes Resort** offers picnic facilities, changing rooms, and a boat launch. **Corona del Mar State Beach** has sandy beaches backed by rocky bluffs and tide pools and caves. **Laguna** has the county's best spot for scuba diving—the **Marine Life Refuge**, which runs from Seal Rock to Diver's Cove. **Main Beach,** a sandy arc just steps from downtown Laguna, is a popular picnic and volleyball venue. In South Laguna **Aliso County Park** has recreational facilities and a fishing pier. **Doheny State Park,** near Dana Point Harbor, has food stands, camping, and a fishing pier. **San Clemente State Beach** has camping facilities and food stands and is renowned for its surf.

SAN DIEGO

San Diego is the birthplace of Spanish California. Its combination of history, pleasing climate, outdoor recreation and sports, and cultural life makes it a popular destination.

Visitor Information

International Visitor Information Center (⊠ 11 Horton Plaza, 92101, ☎ 619/236–1212). **Mission Bay Visitor Information Center** (⊠ 2688 E. Mission Bay Dr., off I–5, 92109, ☎ 619/276–8200).

Arriving and Departing

By Bus
Greyhound Lines (⊠ 120 W. Broadway, ☎ 800/231–2222).

By Car
I–5 runs north–south. I–8 comes into San Diego from the east, I–15 from the northeast.

By Plane
San Diego International Airport Lindbergh Field (☎ 619/231–2100) is 3 mi northwest of downtown and is served by most domestic and many international air carriers. The **Cloud 9 Shuttle** (☎ 619/278–8877 or 800/974–8885) has door-to-door service to anywhere in San Diego County, often for less than a taxi. **San Diego Transit** (☎ 619/233–3004) Bus 2 leaves the airport every 10–15 minutes and costs $1.50. Taxi fare is $7–$9 (plus tip) to most center-city hotels.

By Train
Amtrak (☎ 800/872–7245) trains arrive at **Santa Fe Depot** (⊠ Kettner Blvd. and Broadway, ☎ 619/239–9021).

Getting Around San Diego

It's best to have a car, but avoid the freeways during rush hours. The **San Diego Trolley** (☎ 619/233–3004) travels the 20 mi from downtown to within 100 ft of the Mexican border; other trolleys on the line serve Seaport Village, the Convention Center, and inland areas. **San Diego Harbor Excursion** (☎ 619/234–4111) provides water-taxi service from Seaport Village to Coronado.

Exploring San Diego

Central San Diego

★ **Balboa Park** encompasses 1,400 acres of cultural, recreational, and environmental delights, including a theater complex and public gardens. Among the park's several museums are the **Mingei International Museum** (☎ 619/239–0003), devoted to folk art; the **San Diego Museum of Art** (☎ 619/232–7931), which hosts major traveling shows; and the **San Diego Aerospace Museum and International Aerospace Hall of Fame** (☎ 619/234–8291). Wide-format films are shown on the Omnimax screen of the **Reuben H. Fleet Space Theater and Science Center** (☎ 619/238–1233). Across from the Museum of Man, the **Alcazar Garden** is an impressive horticultural display.

★ Balboa Park's most famous attraction is the **San Diego Zoo** (⊠ 2920 Zoo Dr., ☎ 619/234–3153), where more than 4,000 animals of 800 species roam in habitats built around natural canyons. The zoo is also an enormous botanical garden with one of the world's largest collections of subtropical plants.

Coronado is a city of numerous Victorian houses whose most prominent landmark is the historic **Hotel Del Coronado,** all turrets and gingerbread. **Silver Strand Beach State Park** is one of San Diego's nicest. You can reach Coronado via the 2¼-mi San Diego–Coronado Bridge, which yields a stunning view of the San Diego skyline, or by ferry (☎ 619/234–4111) or water taxi (☎ 619/235–4111).

The **Embarcadero** is a waterfront walkway lined with restaurants and cruise-ship piers. The **Maritime Museum** (⊠ 1306 N. Harbor Dr., ☎ 619/234–9153) has a collection of restored ships, including the windjammer *Star of India*.

Seaport Village, a bustling array of specialty shops, snack bars, and restaurants, spreads out across 14 acres and connects the harbor with the hotel towers and the convention center.

The **Gaslamp Quarter** is a 16-block National Historic District containing most of San Diego's Victorian-era commercial buildings. At the fringe of the redeveloped quarter, the **William Heath Davis House** (⊠ 410 Island Ave., ☎ 619/233–4692), one of the first residences in town, serves as the information center for the Gaslamp Quarter.

San Diego's monument to sports and fitness, **Mission Bay** is a 4,600-acre aquatic park dedicated to action and leisure.

The traditional favorite at **Sea World** theme park is the Shamu show, with giant killer whales entertaining the crowds, but performing dolphins, sea lions, and otters at other shows also delight. ⊠ *1720 South Shores Rd., Mission Bay,* ☎ *619/226–3901.* ☎ *$30.95 adults, $22.95 children.*

San Diego's Spanish and Mexican history and heritage are most evident in **Old Town San Diego State Historic Park** (☎ 619/220–5422), a six-block district north of downtown. **Old Town Plaza** contains many historic buildings. **Bazaar del Mundo** is a shopping complex with

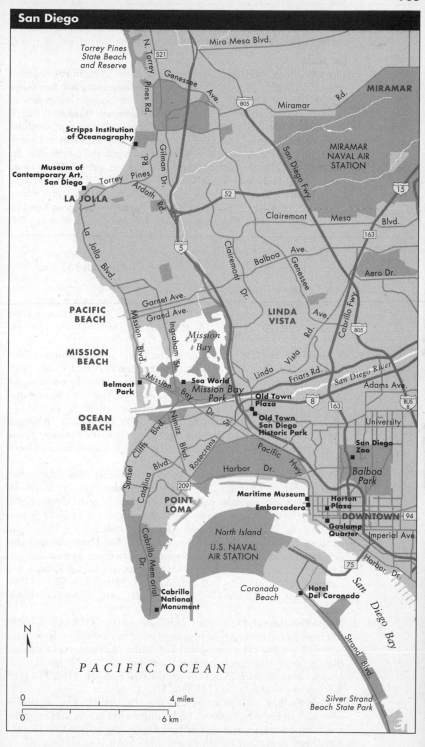

Torrey Pines
State Beach
and Reserve

N. Torrey Pines Rd.

S21

Mira Mesa Blvd.

Genessee Ave.

805

Miramar Rd.

MIRAMAR

Miramar

MIRAMAR
NAVAL AIR
STATION

Scripps Institution
of Oceanography

Gilman Dr.

15

Museum of
Contemporary Art,
San Diego

Torrey Pines Rd.

Ardath Rd.

52

Clairemont

Mesa

Blvd.

LA JOLLA

5

163

La Jolla Blvd.

Clairemont Dr.

Balboa Ave.

Genessee Ave.

Aero Dr.

Cabrillo Fwy.

**PACIFIC
BEACH**

Garnet Ave.

Grand Ave.

Ingraham St.

Mission Bay

**LINDA
VISTA**

Linda Vista Rd.

805

**MISSION
BEACH**

Mission Blvd.

Mission Bay Dr.

Friars Rd.

San Diego River

Adams Ave.

8

BUS 8

Belmont
Park

Sea World

Mission Bay
Park

Old Town
Plaza

163

University

**OCEAN
BEACH**

Nimitz Blvd.

Sunset Cliffs Blvd.

Catalina Blvd.

Rosecrans

Old Town
San Diego
Historic Park

San Diego
Zoo

Harbor Dr.

Pacific Hwy.

**Balboa
Park**

**POINT
LOMA**

209

Maritime Museum

Embarcadero

Horton
Plaza

DOWNTOWN

94

Cabrillo Memorial Dr.

North Island

U.S. NAVAL
AIR STATION

Gaslamp
Quarter

Imperial Ave.

75

Harbor Dr.

San Diego Bay

Cabrillo
National
Monument

Coronado
Beach

Hotel
Del Coronado

N

Strand Blvd.

PACIFIC OCEAN

0   4 miles

0   6 km

Silver Strand
Beach State Park

gardens, exotic shops, and outdoor restaurants, built to represent a colonial Mexican square. **Robinson-Rose House,** once the commercial center of San Diego, is now park headquarters.

La Jolla

The attractions in the upscale village of La Jolla, 13 mi north of downtown San Diego, include the **Museum of Contemporary Art, San Diego** (⊠ 700 Prospect St., ☎ 619/454–3541). The Scripps Institution of Oceanography operates the **Stephen Birch Aquarium-Museum** (⊠ 2300 Expedition Way, ☎ 619/534–3474), the largest oceanographic exhibit in the United States. Tanks filled with colorful saltwater fish and a simulated submarine ride are among the attractions. Palm trees line the
★ sidewalk on Coast Boulevard where it runs along scenic **La Jolla Cove. Torrey Pines State Beach and Reserve** (☎ 619/755–2063), north of La Jolla, has hiking trails with dramatic ocean views. Farther north, Highway 76 east of I–5 leads to the well-preserved **Mission San Luis Rey** (⊠ 4050 Mission Ave., Oceanside, ☎ 760/757–3651), built in 1798.

Dining

For price ranges *see* Chart 1 (A) *in* On the Road with Fodor's.

$$$$ ✕ **Mille Fleurs.** Long established as one of San Diego's premier restaurants, this gem of a French auberge offers a setting as romantic as its contemporary French cuisine is exquisite. ⊠ *6009 Paseo Delicias (Rancho Santa Fe),* ☎ *619/756–3085. AE, DC, MC, V. No lunch weekends.*

$$$–$$$$ ✕ **Marius.** Invariably ranked one of San Diego's best restaurants, this refined dining room serves an impressive menu of French dishes ranging from Parisian haute cuisine to Provençal country cooking. ⊠ *2000 2nd St. (Coronado),* ☎ *619/435–3000. Reservations essential on weekends. AE, D, DC, MC, V. Closed Sun.–Mon. No lunch.*

$$$ ✕ **Dobson's.** The perennial favorite here is mussel bisque. Fish, veal,
★ fowl, and beef entrées are menu highlights. ⊠ *956 Broadway Circle (downtown),* ☎ *619/231–6771. AE, DC, MC, V. Closed Sun. No lunch Sat.*

$$$ ✕ **George's at the Cove.** Service is excellent at this art-filled dining room
★ with a view of La Jolla Cove. The imaginative menu is heavy on seafood but also includes pasta, beef, and veal. Casual dining and a sweeping view are available on the rooftop terrace. ⊠ *1250 Prospect St. (La Jolla),* ☎ *619/454–4244. AE, D, DC, MC, V.*

$$$ ✕ **Laurel.** A local hit, the stylish restaurant of San Diego culinary star
★ Douglas Organ spotlights the cooking of southern France and the Mediterranean. The ambience is sophisticated yet casual: Guinea hen confit, risotto, and roast fish are among the best dishes. ⊠ *505 Laurel St. (uptown),* ☎ *619/239–2222. AE, D, DC, MC, V. No lunch weekends.*

$$$–$ ✕ **The Fish Market.** Downstairs, families enjoy fresh fish in a bustling, informal dining room whose enormous windows look directly onto the harbor. Upstairs, the more formal Top of the Market serves a distinctive menu of exquisitely prepared seafood. ⊠ *750 N. Harbor Dr. (downtown),* ☎ *619/232–3474 for the Fish Market, 619/234–4867 for Top of the Market. AE, D, DC, MC, V.*

$$ ✕ **Café Pacifica.** This charming café serves eclectic California cuisine with an emphasis on seafood. Light, interesting sauces and imaginative garnishes are teamed with perfectly cooked, very fresh fish. ⊠ *2414 San Diego Ave. (Old Town),* ☎ *619/291–6666. AE, D, DC, MC, V. No lunch Sat.–Mon.*

$$ ✕ **Fio's.** Contemporary variations on traditional Italian cuisine are served in a high-ceiling, brick-and-wood dining room overlooking the 5th Avenue street scene. The menu includes a range of imaginative pizzas baked in the wood-burning oven and classic Italian dishes. ⊠ *801 5th Ave. (downtown),* ☎ *619/234–3467. AE, D, DC, MC, V. No lunch weekends.*

$$ ✕ **Palenque.** This family-run restaurant in Pacific Beach serves a won-
★ derful selection of regional Mexican dishes, including chicken with mole, served in the regular chocolate-based sauce or with a green-chili version, and *camarones con chipotle,* large shrimp cooked in a chili-tequila cream sauce (an old family recipe of the proprietor). ⊠ *1653 Garnet Ave. (Pacific Beach),* ☎ *619/272–7816. AE, D, DC, MC, V. No lunch Mon.*

$$ ✕ **Piatti Ristorante.** Local singles and families alike flock to this neighborhood trattoria for the country-style Italian food. A wood-burning oven turns out excellent pizzas, and the pastas are delicious. Lunch features tasty salads and sandwiches; the tree-shaded patio is pleasant. ⊠ *2182 Avenida de la Playa (La Jolla),* ☎ *619/454–1589. AE, DC, MC, V.*

$–$$ ✕ **Bayou Bar and Grill.** Seafood gumbo and fresh Louisiana Gulf
★ seafood dishes are among the Cajun and creole specialties served here. Desserts include praline cheesecake and an award-winning bread pudding. ⊠ *329 Market St. (downtown),* ☎ *619/696–8747. AE, D, DC, MC, V.*

$ ✕ **Hob Nob Hill.** The French toast, pot roast, and fried chicken here taste truly homemade. The place has been under the same ownership since 1944, and its dark-wood booths lend a vintage feel. ⊠ *2271 1st Ave. (uptown),* ☎ *619/239–8176. AE, D, MC, V.*

$ ✕ **Mission Coffee Cup Cafe.** This colorful coffeehouse serves tasty American, Latino, and Chino-Latino breakfasts and lunches. Try the cinnamon-bread French toast with berries, the tamales with eggs and green chili salsa, or the Asian quesadilla. The original Mission Cafe and Coffeehouse serves a similar menu in a funkier setting and stays open for dinner. *Coffee Cup Cafe:* ⊠ *1109 Wall St. (La Jolla),* ☎ *619/ 454–2819. Original Mission Cafe:* ⊠ *3795 Mission Blvd. (Mission Beach),* ☎ *619/488–9060. AE, MC, V.*

Lodging

For price ranges *see* Chart 2 (A) *in* On the Road with Fodor's.

$$$–$$$$ ▥ **Hotel Del Coronado.** Rooms and suites in the 1888 original Victorian building are charmingly quirky. A newer high-rise has more standard accommodations. ⊠ *1500 Orange Ave. (Coronado), 92118,* ☎ *619/435–6611 or 800/468–3533,* ℻ *619/522–8262. 692 rooms. 3 restaurants, deli, pool, sauna, steam room, 8 tennis courts, croquet, beach, bicycles. AE, D, DC, MC, V.*

$$$–$$$$ ▥ **Hyatt Regency La Jolla.** The warm and fluffy down comforters and
★ cushy chairs and couches at this postmodern complex make you feel right at home. Rates are lower on the weekends at this business-oriented hotel. ⊠ *3777 La Jolla Village Dr. (La Jolla), 92122,* ☎ *619/ 552–1234 or 800/233–1234 for central reservations,* ℻ *619/552–6066. 425 rooms. 4 restaurants, bar, pool, hot tub, 2 tennis courts, aerobics, basketball, health club, jogging, meeting rooms, business center. AE, D, DC, MC, V.*

$$$–$$$$ ▥ **La Valencia.** This centrally located pink-stucco hotel is a La Jolla
★ landmark. It has a courtyard for patio dining and an elegant lobby where guests congregate to enjoy the ocean view. Rooms have a romantic European ambience. ⊠ *1132 Prospect St. (La Jolla), 92037,* ☎ *619/454–0771,* ℻ *619/456–3921. 100 rooms. 3 restaurants, bar, pool, hot tub, sauna, exercise room. AE, D, DC, MC, V.*

$$$–$$$$ ★   ▣ **Westgate Hotel.** Antiques, Italian marble counters, and bath fixtures with 24-karat-gold overlays typify the opulent furnishings here. High tea, breathtaking views, and nearby Horton Plaza are other highlights. ✉ *1055 2nd Ave. (downtown), 92101, ☎ 619/238–1818 or 800/221–3802, 800/522–1564 in CA;* FAX *619/557–3737. 223 rooms. 3 restaurants, lounge, barbershop, exercise room. AE, D, DC, MC, V.*

$$–$$$ ▣ **Heritage Park Bed & Breakfast Inn.** This romantic 1889 Queen Anne mansion is decorated with 19th-century antiques. ✉ *2470 Heritage Park Row (Old Town), 92110, ☎ 619/295–7088 or 800/995–2470. 9 rooms. Continental breakfast. AE, MC, V.*

$$ ▣ **Lodge at Torrey Pines.** This easygoing resort on a bluff between La Jolla and Del Mar commands an expansive coastline view. ✉ *11480 Torrey Pines Rd. (La Jolla), 92037, ☎ 619/453–4420 or 800/995–4507,* FAX *619/453–0691. 74 rooms. Restaurant, 2 bars, coffee shop, pool. AE, D, DC, MC, V.*

$–$$ ★   ▣ **Vacation Inn.** At this cheerful property rustic colors and reproduction furnishings lend rooms an old-country-inn feel. ✉ *3900 Old Town Ave. (Old Town), ☎ 619/299–7400 or 800/451–9846,* FAX *619/ 299–1619. 133 rooms Pool, hot tub, airport shuttle, parking. Continental breakfast, afternoon snacks. AE, D, DC, MC, V.*

$ ★   ▣ **La Pensione.** This budget hotel in a quiet downtown neighborhood has a pretty central courtyard and rooms with harbor views; some also have kitchenettes. ✉ *1700 India St. (downtown), 92101, ☎ 619/ 236–8000 or 800/232–4638,* FAX *619/236–8088. 81 rooms. Laundry service. AE, MC, V.*

$ ▣ **Mission Bay Motel.** A half block from the beach, this motel on the main drag offers modest units within walking distance of restaurants and nightlife. ✉ *4221 Mission Blvd. (Mission Beach), 92109, ☎ 619/ 483–6440. 50 rooms. Pool. MC, V.*

$ ▣ **TraveLodge Point Loma.** For far less money, you'll get the same view here as at the higher-price hotels. The rooms are adequate and clean. ✉ *5102 N. Harbor Dr. (Point Loma), 92106, ☎ 619/223–8171 or 800/ 578–7878,* FAX *619/222–7330. 45 rooms. Pool. AE, D, DC, MC, V.*

Nightlife and the Arts

The daily *San Diego Union-Tribune* and weekly *Reader* have nightlife and cultural-event listings. Half-price tickets to most theater, music, and dance events can be bought on the day of performance at the **TIMES ARTS TIX Ticket Center** (✉ Horton Plaza, ☎ 619/497–5000). Only cash is accepted. **TicketMaster** (☎ 619/220–8497) sells tickets to many San Diego cultural and entertainment events.

Nightlife

San Diego's nightlife ranges from quiet piano bars to cutting-edge rock. The **Casbah** (✉ 2501 Kettner Blvd., ☎ 619/232–4355) showcases rock, reggae, and funk bands every night. **Humphrey's** (✉ 2241 Shelter Island Dr., ☎ 619/523–1010) presents outdoor concerts in the summer. **Leo's Little Bit O' Country** (✉ 680 W. San Marcos Blvd., San Marcos, ☎ 619/744–4120) hosts country-and-western dancing. The **Comedy Store** (✉ 916 Pearl St., La Jolla, ☎ 619/454–9176) books local and national talent. The best local Latin, jazz, and blues bands alternate appearances during the week at the classy bar at the **U. S. Grant Hotel** (✉ 326 Broadway, downtown, ☎ 619/232–3121).

The Arts

The **Old Globe Theatre** (✉ Simon Edison Centre, Balboa Park, ☎ 619/ 239–2255) presents classics, experimental works, and a summer Shakespeare festival. The **San Diego Opera** (☎ 619/232–7636) performs at the Civic Theatre (✉ 202 C St., ☎ 619/236–6510) from January to April.

Outdoor Activities and Sports

Baseball: San Diego Padres (✉ Qualcomm Stadium, 9449 Friars Rd., ☎ 619/283–4494).

Football: San Diego Chargers (✉ Qualcomm Stadium, ☎ 619/280–2111).

Horse Racing: Del Mar Thoroughbred Club (✉ 2260 Jimmy Durante Blvd.; take I–5's Via de la Valle exit, ☎ 619/755–1141); July–September.

Beaches

The following beaches are listed geographically from north to south.

La Jolla Cove is a favorite of rough-water swimmers, but Children's Pool, a shallow lagoon at the south end, is a safer haven. Follow Coast Boulevard north to the signs; or take the La Jolla Village Drive exit from I–5, head west to Torrey Pines Road, turn left and drive down the hill to Girard Avenue, then turn right and follow the signs.

Mission Beach/Pacific Beach has a boardwalk that's popular with strollers, roller skaters, and cyclists. The south end is full of surfers, swimmers, and volleyball players. Pacific Beach is a teen hangout; it's crowded in summer, and parking is a challenge. Exit I–5 at Garnet Avenue and head west to Mission Boulevard.

Ocean Beach is a haven for volleyball players, sunbathers, and swimmers. You'll find food vendors and fire rings; limited parking is available. The municipal pier at the south end is open to the public for fishing and walking and has a restaurant at the end. Take I–8 west to Sunset Cliffs Boulevard and head south; turn right on Santa Monica Avenue.

Coronado Beach is perfect for sunbathing or Frisbee throwing. There are rest rooms and fire rings; parking can be difficult on busy days. From the bridge turn left on Orange Avenue; then follow signs.

Silver Strand State Beach Park, on Coronado, has relatively calm water, an RV campground ($12–$16 per night), and other facilities. Parking is $4 per car, but collection is lax from Labor Day through February. Take the Palm Avenue exit off I–5 west to Highway 75; turn right and follow signs.

Shopping

Horton Plaza (✉ Broadway and G St. from 1st to 4th Aves., ☎ 619/238–1596), occupying several square blocks downtown, is a multilevel postmodern mall. The Macy's, Nordstrom, and Neiman-Marcus department stores anchor the also huge **Fashion Valley** mall (✉ 452 Fashion Valley Dr., ☎ 619/297–3386).

The **Gaslamp Quarter** holds art galleries, antiques shops, and other specialty stores. Trendy boutiques and galleries line **Girard Avenue** and **Prospect Street** in La Jolla. Old Town has the **Bazaar del Mundo, La Esplanade,** and the **Old Town Mercado,** with international goods, toys, souvenirs, and arts and crafts. Gay and funky **Hillcrest** is home to many gift, book, and music stores.

ELSEWHERE IN SOUTHERN CALIFORNIA

Palm Springs

A desert playground for Hollywood celebrities since the 1930s, Palm Springs has plenty of attractions: luxurious resorts, nearly year-round golf and tennis, and fine upscale and outlet shopping.

Visitor Information

Palm Springs Desert Resorts Bureau (⊠ 69–930 Hwy. 111, Suite 201, Rancho Mirage 92270, ☎ 760/770–9000 or 800/967–3767). **Palm Springs Visitor Information Center** (⊠ 2781 N. Palm Canyon, Palm Springs 92262, ☎ 800/347–7746). Both have lists of golf courses in the area that are open to the public.

Arriving and Departing

Palm Springs is about a two-hour drive east of Los Angeles and a three-hour drive northeast of San Diego. From L.A. take I–10 east to Highway 111. From San Diego take I–15 north to Highway 60, then I–10 east to Highway 111. **Palm Springs Regional Airport** is served by national and regional airlines.

What to See and Do

For an overview of the area, ride up the ★**Palm Springs Aerial Tramway** (⊠ 1 Tramway Rd., ☎ 760/325–1391). The region's natural attrac-
★ tions include **Joshua Tree National Park** (⊠ Hwy. 62 northeast from Hwy. 111, ☎ 760/367–7511). Its oddly shaped trees, with their branches raised like arms, and its weather-sculpted rocks are entrancing. Come eyeball to eyeball with coyotes, mountain lions, cheetahs, and golden eagles at the **Living Desert Wildlife and Botanical Park** (⊠ 47-900 Portola Ave., Palm Desert, ☎ 760/346–5694). Easy to challenging trails traverse desert gardens populated with plants of the Mojave, Colorado, and Sonoran deserts.

The **Palm Springs Desert Museum** (⊠ 101 Museum Dr., ☎ 760/325–0189) has a fine collection that emphasizes natural science and 20th-century art. The museum's Annenberg Theater presents plays, concerts, lectures, operas, and other cultural events. The hottest ticket in the desert
★ is the **Fabulous Palm Springs Follies** (⊠ Plaza Theater, 128 S. Palm Canyon Dr., ☎ 760/864–6514), a vaudeville-style revue that stars extravagantly costumed retired (but very much in shape) showgirls, singers, and dancers.

Dining and Lodging

For price ranges *see* Charts 1 (A) and 2 (A) *in* On the Road with Fodor's.

$$–$$$ ✕ **Blue Coyote Grill.** Diners sit under blue umbrellas and munch on burritos, tacos, fajitas (or more unusual items, such as Yucatan lamb or orange chicken) at this casual restaurant with several flower-decked patios in addition to inside dining rooms. ⊠ *445 N. Palm Canyon Dr.,* ☎ *760/327–1196. AE, DC, MC, V.*

$$ ✕ **Palomino Euro Bistro.** One of the hot spots in the desert, this restaurant specializes in grilled and roasted entrées: spit-roasted garlic chicken, oak-fired thin-crust pizza, and oven-roasted prawns. ⊠ *73–101 Hwy. 111, Palm Desert,* ☎ *760/773–9091. AE, D, DC, MC, V. No lunch.*

$$$$ ✕▥ **Ritz-Carlton Rancho Mirage.** The gem of the desert has rooms that
★ are comfortably furnished in 18th- and 19th-century style. The restaurant here is superb. ⊠ *68–900 Frank Sinatra Dr., Rancho Mirage 92270,* ☎ *760/321–8282,* ℻ *760/321–6928. 240 rooms. 3 restaurants, bar, pool, hot tub, outdoor hot tub, 9-hole pitch-and-putt golf, 10 tennis*

courts, basketball, croquet, health club, hiking, volleyball, children's programs, business services. AE, D, DC, MC, V.

$$–$$$$ 🖫 **Ingleside Inn.** Many rooms at this 1920s hacienda-style inn have antiques, fireplaces, and private patios; all have two-person whirlpool tubs and steam showers. ✉ *200 W. Ramon Rd., 92264,* ☎ *760/325–0046 or 800/772–6655,* FAX *760/325–0710. 30 rooms. Restaurant, bar, pool, outdoor hot tub. AE, D, DC, MC, V.*

$–$$ 🖫 **Hampton Inn.** Appointments here are basic but clean. There are barbecues available for guest use. Room rates include Continental breakfast. ✉ *200 N. Palm Canyon Dr., 92262,* ☎ *760/320–0555 or 800/732–7755,* FAX *760/320–2261. 96 rooms. Pool, outdoor hot tub, meeting rooms. AE, D, DC, MC, V.*

Death Valley

Arriving and Departing

To reach Death Valley from the west (about 300 mi from Los Angeles), exit U.S. 395 at either Highway 190 or 178. From the southeast (about 140 mi from Las Vegas), take Highway 127 north from I–15 and Highway 178 past Badwater and Artists Palette to Highway 190 at Furnace Creek. Zabriskie Point and Dante's View are off Highway 190 heading back southeast to Highway 127. Reliable maps are a must.

What to See and Do

★   **Death Valley National Park** (visitor center: ✉ Furnace Creek, Hwy. 190, ☎ 760/786–2331) is a desert wonderland of sand dunes, crusty salt flats, 11,000-ft mountains, and hills and canyons of many hues. In the northwestern section is **Scotty's Castle** (✉ Hwy. 190, north from Furnace Creek), a Moorish-style mansion built by a onetime performer in Buffalo Bill's Wild West Show. **Harmony Borax Works** (✉ Hwy. 190, near Furnace Creek) illustrates the mining history of the valley, from which the 20-mule teams hauled borax to the railroad at Mojave. **Dante's View** (✉ Hwy. 190, south of Furnace Creek), 5,000 ft up in the Black Mountains, has views of the lowest (Badwater) and highest (Mt. Whitney) points in the continental United States.

OREGON

By Jeff Kuechle

Updated by
Donald S.
Olson

Capital	Salem
Population	3,203,735
Motto	She Flies with Her Own Wings
State Bird	Western meadowlark
State Flower	Oregon grape
Postal Abbreviation	OR

Statewide Visitor Information

Oregon State Welcome Center (✉ 12348 N. Center Ave., Portland 97217, ☎ 503/285–1631). **Oregon Tourism Commission** (✉ 775 Summer St. NE, Salem 97310, ☎ 800/547–7842).

Scenic Drives

The **Crown Point Scenic Highway** twists and turns its way above I–84 through the heavily wooded, waterfall-laced Columbia Gorge east of Portland. **U.S. 101** hugs the largely unspoiled Oregon coastline. **Highway 138** from Roseburg to Crater Lake is a National Scenic Byway and goes through rugged canyons and past waterfalls, mountain lakes, and camping areas.

National and State Parks

National Parks

Crater Lake National Park (✉ Box 7, Crater Lake 97604, ☎ 541/594–2211) has guided boat trips of the pristine lake, as well as a variety of nature trails (☞ Ashland/The Rogue Valley *in* Elsewhere in Oregon, *below*). **Newberry National Volcanic Monument,** administered by the Deschutes National Forest (✉ 1645 Hwy. 20E, Bend 97701, ☎ 541/388–2715), provides recreation for cross-country skiers, snowmobilers, fishers, and hikers. **Oregon Caves National Monument** (✉ 19000 Caves Hwy., Cave Junction 97523, ☎ 541/592–3400) conducts guided tours of the Marble Halls of Oregon. **Oregon Dunes National Recreation Area** (✉ 855 Highway Ave., Reedsport 97467, ☎ 541/271–3611) contains 40 mi of undulating camel-color sand (☞ Exploring the Oregon Coast, *below*).

State Parks

Oregon's 225 state parks run the gamut from sage-scented desert to mountains to sea. The **Oregon State Parks and Recreation Department** (✉ 1115 Commercial St. NE, Salem 97310, ☎ 800/551–6949) has information on the parks and facilities.

PORTLAND

Portland, one of America's most important gateways to the Pacific Rim, has earned a reputation as a well-planned, relaxing city. Straddling the banks of the wide, salmon-filled Willamette River, the town has flower-filled parks, efficient mass transit, and restored historic buildings.

Visitor Information

Portland/Oregon Visitors Association (✉ World Trade Center 3, 26 S.W. Salmon St., 97204, ☎ 503/222–2223 or 800/962–3700, 800/345–3214 in OR). Portland Guides in green jackets walk the sidewalks downtown; they can assist with directions, answer questions about the city, and even recommend top spots to eat, drink, or rest your feet.

Arriving and Departing

By Bus
Greyhound Lines (✉ 550 N.W. 6th Ave., ☎ 800/231–2222).

By Car
I–84 (Banfield Freeway) and Highway 26 (the Sunset) run east–west; I–5 and I–205 run north–south.

By Plane
Portland International Airport (☎ 503/335–1234), in northeast Portland about 10 mi from the city center, is served by major domestic carriers. Portland Taxi (☎ 503/256–5400), Broadway Cab (☎ 503/227–1234), as well as buses (Raz Transportation, ☎ 503/246–3301) and hotel shuttle services, connect the airport to downtown. A taxi ride downtown costs about $22; the bus is $8.50.

By Train
Amtrak serves Union Station (✉ 800 N.W. 6th Ave., ☎ 503/273–4865 or 800/872–7245).

Getting Around Portland

The metropolitan area is laid out in a grid system, with numbered avenues running north–south and named streets running east–west. The **MAX light-rail line** links eastern and western Portland suburbs to the downtown core, the Lloyd Center District, the Convention Center, and the Rose Quarter, which includes the Memorial Coliseum and the new sports arena. A new western extension to Hillsboro, scheduled to open in the fall of 1998, will include a stop at the Washington Park Zoo. At 260 ft below ground, the transit station will be the deepest in the nation. The **Tri-Met bus system** covers the metro area extensively. Call 503/238–7433 for schedules and routes for both Tri-Met and MAX.

Exploring Portland

Downtown
Pioneer Courthouse Square (✉ S.W. Broadway and S.W. Morrison St.) is the city's main gathering place and people-watching venue.

The **Portland Art Museum,** the Northwest's oldest arts facility, is one of several interesting buildings that line the South Park Blocks, a tree-lined boulevard of statues and fountains. The museum contains 35 centuries of Asian, European, and Native American art. ✉ *1219 S.W. Park Ave.,* ☎ *503/226–2811. Closed Mon.*

Across from the art museum, towering murals of Lewis and Clark and the Oregon Trail frame the entrance to the **Oregon History Center** (✉ 1200 S.W. Park Ave., ☎ 503/222–1741), where the state's history from prehistoric times to the present is documented.

The **Old Church,** built in 1882, is a prime example of Carpenter Gothic architecture, complete with rough-cut lumber, tall spires, and the original stained-glass windows. Free concerts on one of the few existing Hook and Hastings pipe organs are presented on Wednesday at noon. ✉ *1422 S.W. 11th Ave.,* ☎ *503/222–2031. Closed Sun.*

Architect Michael Graves's **Portland Building** (✉ 1120 S.W. 5th Ave.) was one of the country's first postmodern designs. *Portlandia,* the second-largest hammered-copper sculpture in the world (after the Statue of Liberty), kneels on the second-story balcony. Inside is the **Metropoli-**

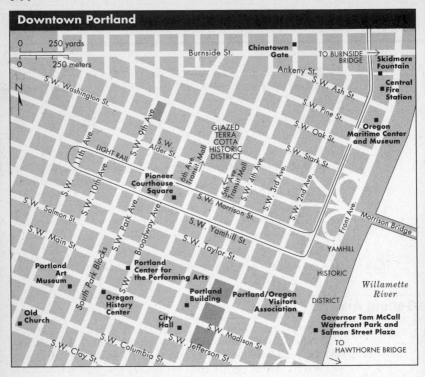

Downtown Portland

Burnside St.
Chinatown Gate
TO BURNSIDE BRIDGE
Skidmore Fountain
Central Fire Station
Ankeny St.
S.W. Ash St.
S.W. Pine St.
S.W. Washington St.
S.W. 9th Ave
S.W. Alder St.
11th Ave.
LIGHT RAIL
Oregon Maritime Center and Museum
S.W. Oak St.
S.W. Stark St.
GLAZED TERRA COTTA HISTORIC DISTRICT
6th Ave. Transit Mall
5th Ave. Transit Mall
S.W. 4th Ave.
S.W. 3rd Ave.
S.W. 2nd Ave.
Pioneer Courthouse Square
10th Ave.
S.W. Salmon St.
Park Ave.
Broadway Ave.
S.W. Morrison St.
Front Ave.
Morrison Bridge
S.W. Main St.
S.W. Yamhill St.
S.W. Taylor St.
YAMHILL
Portland Art Museum
Portland Center for the Performing Arts
South Park Blocks
HISTORIC
Willamette River
Oregon History Center
Portland Building
Portland/Oregon Visitors Association
DISTRICT
Old Church
City Hall
Governor Tom McCall Waterfront Park and Salmon Street Plaza
S.W. Clay St.
S.W. Columbia St.
S.W. Jefferson St.
S.W. Madison St.
TO HAWTHORNE BRIDGE

0 250 yards
0 250 meters
N

tan **Center for Public Art** (☎ 503/823–4196). Across Madison Avenue from the Portland Building is the classically styled **city hall,** built in 1895, with columns on two of its faces and high ceilings, marble hallways, and pillars inside.

Across Front Avenue along the Willamette River you'll find **Governor Tom McCall Waterfront Park,** a grassy 2-mi expanse (a former expressway) that is a popular venue for festivals, concerts, picnics, jogging, and biking. From the park you can see some of the many distinctive bridges that have earned Portland the name Bridgetown.

Many fine examples of 19th-century cast-iron architecture are preserved in the **Yamhill and Skidmore National Historic districts,** which begin on Front Avenue across from the waterfront park. The former commercial waterfront of Portland is now a district of galleries, fountains, and shops that is particularly lively on weekends.

The main mast of the battleship *Oregon,* which served in three wars, stands at the foot of Oak Street. The exterior of the **Oregon Maritime Center and Museum** (⊠ 113 S.W. Front Ave., ☎ 503/224–7724) incorporates fine street-level examples of cast-iron architecture. Inside are models of ships that once plied the Columbia River. The admission price allows you to board the last operating stern-wheeler tug in the United States, docked across the street. Inside the Central Fire Station is the **Jeff Morris Memorial Fire Museum** (⊠ 111 S.W. Front Ave.), which houses antique pumps and other equipment.

The **Portland Saturday Market** (☎ 503/222–6072), underneath the west end of the Burnside Bridge and open weekends from March through Christmas, has live entertainment and 300 merchants selling ethnic foods, arts, and crafts.

The official entrance to Portland's **Chinatown** is the ornate **Chinatown Gate** (⊠ N.W. 4th Ave. and W. Burnside St.). In the 1890s Portland's Chinese community was the second largest in the United States. Today it is compressed into several blocks in the northwestern part of town, with popular restaurants, shops, and grocery stores.

Other Neighborhoods

In an attempt to ward off suburban sprawl, fast-growing Portland has put a new emphasis on "urban density" and revitalization of its inner-city neighborhoods. As a result, several areas have been transformed. Many of the storefronts and warehouses in the formerly industrial **Pearl District,** bordered by Burnside and Marshall streets and N.W. 8th and N.W. 15th avenues, have been converted over the past 10 years into lofts, art galleries, furniture and design stores, and restaurants. A few blocks west of the Pearl District, grand old Portland houses, some dating back 100 years, line the streets of **Nob Hill,** one of the city's oldest neighborhoods. At the heart of Nob Hill are the 20 fashion-conscious blocks of **N.W. 23rd Avenue** between Burnside and Vaughn streets—now a citywide destination for dining, café sitting, and general hanging out. Several of the avenue's old homes have been turned into upscale boutiques, where you'll find everything from women's clothing to antique linens. Across the Willamette River, **S.E. Hawthorne Boulevard** between 30th and 39th avenues has become the east side's most popular stomping ground. More down-to-earth than N.W. 23rd and still countercultural around the edges, S.E. Hawthorne has an eclectic array of bookstores, coffeehouses, taverns, restaurants, antiques stores, and unusual boutiques.

Outside Portland

The **Pittock Mansion** (⊠ 3229 N.W. Pittock Dr., ☎ 503/823–3624), perched 1,000 ft above the city about 2 mi from downtown, yields superb views of the skyline, rivers, and Cascade Mountains. The 1914 mansion was built for Henry Pittock, former editor of the *Oregonian*. Set in its own scenic park, the opulent manor has been restored and is filled with art and antiques of the 1880s.

★ **Washington Park** (⊠ 611 S.W. Kingston Ave., ☎ 503/223–5055), covering 322 acres in the west hills, is the site of the renowned **International Rose Test Garden** and, directly above it, the serene **Japanese Gardens,** considered one of the most authentic outside Japan.

What to See and Do with Children

The **Children's Museum** (⊠ 3037 S.W. 2nd Ave., ☎ 503/823–2227) offers hands-on play with interactive exhibits. The **Oregon Museum of Science and Industry** (⊠ 1945 S.E. Water Ave., ☎ 503/797–4000), in a restored steam plant on the Willamette's east bank, has touring exhibits, permanent displays, a planetarium, and an Omnimax theater.

Dining

Bounteous local produce from land and sea receives star billing at many Portland dining establishments, and recent Pacific Rim immigrants have added depth and spice to the restaurant scene. For price ranges *see* Chart 1 (B) *in* On the Road with Fodor's.

$$$ ✕ **Genoa.** Small, crowded, and intimate, Genoa seats 35 people for
★ sumptuous four- and seven-course prix-fixe northern Italian dinners. The menu changes to take advantage of seasonal bounty. ⊠ *2832 S.E. Belmont St.,* ☎ *503/238–1464. Reservations essential. AE, D, DC, MC, V. Closed Sun. No lunch.*

$$$ ✕ **Heathman Restaurant and Bar.** Master chef Philippe Boulot assembles Pacific Northwest products and ingredients in a classical style. Salmon with pesto crust is a signature dish here, and local free-range game dishes—venison, veal, rabbit—are also on the menu. The Heathman has one of the finest wine cellars in Oregon. ✉ *1001 S.W. Broadway,* ☎ *503/790–7752. AE, DC, MC, V.*

$$$ ✕ **Zefiro.** The sophisticated menu at this chic and popular neighbor-
★ hood eatery applies Southeast Asian and Mediterranean cooking principles to local ingredients such as wild mushrooms and salmon. ✉ *500 N.W. 21st Ave.,* ☎ *503/226–3394. AE, DC, MC, V. Closed Sun.*

$$ ✕ **Bima Restaurant and Bar.** Housed in a restored warehouse in Portland's arts-filled Pearl District, Bima takes its cues from the cuisines of the Gulf of Mexico coast. Pecan-crusted catfish, assorted fish and meat skewers, fish tacos, and luscious ribs are some of the specialties. There's a bar menu as well. ✉ *1338 N.W. Hoyt,* ☎ *503/241–3465. AE, MC, V. Closed Sun.*

$$ ✕ **Jake's Famous Crawfish.** White-coated waiters at Portland's best-known restaurant serve up fresh Northwest seafood, selected from a lengthy sheet of daily specials, in a warren of old-fashioned wood-paneled dining rooms. Alder-smoked salmon, crab cakes, and baked halibut stuffed with bay shrimp and Brie are consistent standouts. ✉ *401 S.W. 12th Ave.,* ☎ *503/226–1419. AE, D, DC, MC, V. No lunch weekends.*

$$ ✕ **Montage.** Spicy Cajun is the jumping-off point for the menu at this sassy bistro under the Morrison Bridge, on Portland's east side. Jambalaya, blackened pork and catfish, Hoppin' Jon, rabbit sausage, and macaroni dishes are some of the specialties served from 6 PM until the wee hours in an atmosphere that's loud, crowded, and casually hip. ✉ *301 S.E. Morrison,* ☎ *503/234–1324. No lunch weekends. No credit cards.*

$ ✕ **Saigon Kitchen.** Consistently good Vietnamese and Thai food and extrafriendly service have made this a neighborhood gem. Fried and salted calamari, *chazio* rolls, and fiery chili noodles with prawns or chicken are delectable standouts on the wide-ranging menu. ✉ *835 N.E. Broadway,* ☎ *503/281–3669. AE, D, MC, V.*

$ ✕ **Yen Ha.** The vibrant flavors of Vietnam find full expression here. Superb rice-paper rolls (filled with shrimp, pungent bean threads, and fresh mint and dipped in peanut sauce) and exquisite noodle dishes are among the star attractions. ✉ *6820 N.E. Sandy Blvd.,* ☎ *503/287–3698. MC, V. Closed Mon.*

Brew Pubs

Portland is the microbrewery mecca of North America. Its dozen-odd small breweries and affiliated pubs offer both satisfying dining and good value. Among the standouts are the **B. Moloch Heathman Bakery and Pub** (✉ 901 S.W. Salmon St., ☎ 503/227–5700) and the **Pilsner Room** (✉ 0309 S.W. Montgomery St., ☎ 503/220–1865), which showcase local brews and inexpensive nouvelle pub cuisine. The **Bridgeport Brew Pub** (✉ 1313 N.W. Marshall St., ☎ 503/241–7179) serves thick hand-thrown pizzas; wash them down with creamy pints of Bridgeport real ale. **McMenamins Edgefield** (✉ 2126 S.W. Halsey St., Troutdale, ☎ 503/492–4686) is the showpiece of the vast microbrewing empire of the Mc-Menamin brothers; the 12-acre estate has its own pub, restaurant, movie theater, 105-room inn, winery, and brewery. The McMenamin brothers' newest venture, **Ringlers Pub** (✉ 1332 W. Burnside St., ☎ 503/225–0047), occupies the first floor of a historic Portland building that houses the Crystal Ballroom (☞ Nightlife, *below*).

Lodging

You'll find many national and regional chains near the airport. The city center and waterfront support both elegant new and historic hotels. Bed-and-breakfasts cluster in the West Hills and across the river in the Lloyd Center/Convention Center area. **Northwest Bed & Breakfast** (☎ 503/243–7616) is a good source for information and reservations in Portland and the entire coastal region. For price ranges *see* Chart 2 (B) *in* On the Road with Fodor's.

$$$ ▦ **The Benson.** Portland's grandest hotel, built in 1912, has maintained its turn-of-the-century grandeur. Elegance is everywhere, from walls paneled in Russian walnut to the opulent guest rooms to the muted tinkling of the lobby's grand piano. ⊠ *309 S.W. Broadway, 97205,* ☎ *503/228–2000 or 800/426–0670,* ℻ *503/226–4603. 287 rooms. 2 restaurants, 2 lounges, exercise room, concierge, airport shuttle. AE, D, DC, MC, V.*

$$$ ▦ **Doubletree Hotel/Lloyd Center.** At Portland's second-largest hotel (formerly part of the Red Lion chain), service runs like a well-oiled machine. Many of the large rooms with balconies have views of the mountains or the city center. Lloyd Center shopping and MAX light-rail are across the street. ⊠ *1000 N.E. Multnomah St., 97232,* ☎ *503/281–6111 or 800/547–8010,* ℻ *503/284–8553. 476 rooms. 3 restaurants, 2 lounges, pool, exercise room, airport shuttle. AE, D, DC, MC, V.*

$$$ ▦ **The Governor.** Thanks to its recent renovation, the Governor is now Portland's most distinctive old hotel. The lobby, with its mahogany walls and mural of Northwest Indians fishing in Celilo Falls, feels like a clubroom. Guest rooms, painted in soothing earth tones, have large windows, whirlpool tubs, and, in some cases, fireplaces and balconies. ⊠ *611 S.W. 10th Ave., 97205,* ☎ *503/224–3400 or 800/554–3456,* ℻ *503/241–2122. 100 rooms. Restaurant, concierge, airport shuttle. AE, D, DC, MC, V.*

$$$ ▦ **The Heathman.** Superior service, an award-winning restaurant, an
★ elegant tea court, and a library of signed first editions by authors who have been guests here have earned the Heathman a reputation for quality. The guest rooms have original artwork by Northwest artists. ⊠ *1009 S.W. Broadway, 97205,* ☎ *503/241–4100 or 800/551–0011,* ℻ *503/790–7110. 151 rooms. Restaurant, bar, exercise room. AE, D, DC, MC, V.*

$$$ ▦ **Hotel Vintage Plaza.** From the names of the rooms to a complimentary wine hour each evening, this luxury hotel takes its theme from Oregon's wine country. Top-floor rooms have skylights and wall-to-wall conservatory-style windows. ⊠ *422 S.W. Broadway, 97205,* ☎ *503/ 228–1212 or 800/243–0555,* ℻ *503/228–3598. 107 rooms. Restaurant, piano bar, exercise room, concierge, business services. AE, D, DC, MC, V.*

$$$ ▦ **Shilo Inn Suites Hotel.** Each suite has three TVs, a VCR, a microwave, four phones, a refrigerator, a wet bar, and two oversize beds. ⊠ *11707 N.E. Airport Way, 97220,* ☎ *503/252–7500 or 800/222– 2244,* ℻ *503/254–0794. 200 rooms. Restaurant, lounge, indoor pool, hot tub, steam room, exercise room, business services, airport shuttle, free parking. AE, D, DC, MC, V.*

$$ ▦ **Best Western Inn at the Convention Center.** Rooms are done in pleasing creams and rusts at this property across the street from the convention center. ⊠ *420 N.E. Holladay St., 97232,* ☎ *503/233–6331,* ℻ *503/233–2677. 97 rooms. Restaurant, laundry, free parking. AE, D, DC, MC, V.*

$$ ▦ **MacMaster House.** Less than 10 minutes by foot from fashionable N.W. 23rd Avenue, this 17-room Colonial Revival mansion, built in 1886, is comfortable and funky. Its parlors are stuffed with a Victorian furniture and antiques. The seven guest rooms on the second and third floors are charming in a subtle way. ⊠ *1041 S.W. Vista Ave., 97205,* ☎ *503/223–7362. 7 rooms. AE, D, MC, V.*

$ ☑ **Mallory Hotel.** The rooms in this Portland stalwart, eight blocks from the city center, are on the small side and about half haven't been refurbished since the 1970s. But the hotel is clean and friendly. Pets are allowed. ☒ *729 S.W. 15th Ave., 97205,* ☎ *503/223–6311 or 800/228–8657,* ⅏ *503/223–0522. 144 rooms. Restaurant, lounge, free parking. AE, D, DC, MC, V.*

$ ☑ **Portland Guest House.** This northeastern Portland 1890s B&B has dusty-heather exterior paint and original oak floors. Rooms are done in white on white with Victorian walnut furniture and original Pacific Northwest art. ☒ *1720 N.E. 15th Ave., 97212,* ☎ *503/282–1402. 7 rooms. AE, DC, MC, V.*

Motels
☑ **Riverside Inn** (☒ 50 S.W. Morrison St., 97204, ☎ 503/221–0711, ⅏ 503/274–0312), 141 rooms, restaurant, lounge, health club; *$$–$$$.* ☑ **NW Portland Silver Cloud Inn** (☒ 2426 N.W. Vaughn St., 97210, ☎ 503/242–2400 or 800/205–6939, ⅏ 503/242–1770), 81 rooms, hot tub, exercise room, laundry; *$–$$.*

Nightlife and the Arts

The Oregonian (on newsstands) and *Willamette Week* (available free in the metro area) list arts and entertainment events. *Just Out* (available free in the metro area) is the city's gay newspaper.

Nightlife and the Arts
Rock 'n' Rodeo (☒ 220 S.E. Spokane St., ☎ 503/235–2417) remains a hot spot for country-and-western music and line dancing. The **Crystal Ballroom** (☒ S.W. 14th and Burnside, ☎ 503/225–0047), dating from 1914 and completely restored in 1997, hosts dancing to live bands on its huge "elastic" floor, built on ball bearings. The top jazz spots in Portland are **Brasserie Montmartre** (☒ 626 S.W. Park Ave., ☎ 503/224–5552) and **Jazz De Opus** (☒ 33 N.W. 2nd Ave., ☎ 503/222–6077). For comedy try **Harvey's Comedy Club** (☒ 436 N.W. 6th Ave., ☎ 503/241–0338), which presents headliners with a national reputation. **Embers** (☒ 110 N.W. Broadway, ☎ 503/222–3082), a full-throttle disco, is popular with both straights and gays. Several gay bars line S.W. Stark Street downtown, including **C.C. Slaughters** (☒ 1014 S.W. Stark, ☎ 503/248–9135).

The **Portland Center for the Performing Arts** (☒ S.W. Broadway and S.W. Main St., ☎ 503/796–9293), which includes the 2,776-seat Arlene Schnitzer Concert Hall and (across the street) the Performing Arts Building, presents rock concerts, symphony orchestra performances, theater, dance, lectures, and touring Broadway musicals. **Portland Center Stage** performs from November to April at the Performing Art Building's Intermediate Theater (☒ 1111 S.W. Broadway, ☎ 503/274–6588). The **Oregon Symphony** (☎ 503/228–1353) performs more than 40 concerts each season at the Arlene Schnitzer Concert Hall. The **Portland Opera** (☎ 503/241–1802) and the **Oregon Ballet Theater** (☎ 503/222–5538) perform at the **Civic Auditorium** (☒ S.W. 3rd Ave. and Clay St. downtown). **Portland Repertory Theatre** (☒ 24 S.W. Salmon, ☎ 503/224–4491) presents a full season of plays in the city's World Trade Center.

Spectator Sports

Basketball: Portland Trail Blazers (☒ Rose Garden Arena, 1 Center Court, east end of Broadway Bridge, ☎ 503/234–9291).

Shopping

For local products try the several **Made In Oregon** shops, at Portland International Airport, Lloyd Center, the Galleria, Old Town, Washington Square, and Clackamas Town Center. Merchandise ranges from books to smoked salmon, hazelnuts, honey, dried fruits, local wines, and Pendleton woolen products.

Pioneer Place (⊠ 700 S.W. 5th Ave., ☎ 503/228–5800) is the jewel in the city's shopping crown. More than 80 specialty shops are anchored by a gleaming Saks Fifth Avenue store. The original **Meier & Frank** (⊠ 621 S.W. 5th Ave., ☎ 503/223–0512) department store, a Portland landmark since 1857, sits across the street from Pioneer Place. **Nordstrom** (⊠ 701 S.W. Broadway, ☎ 503/224–6666), across from Pioneer Courthouse Square, has quality apparel and accessories and a large shoe department. High-tech **Niketown** (⊠ 930 S.W. 6th Ave., ☎ 503/221–6453) is part sports shrine, part sales outlet.

With more than 1 million new and used volumes, **Powell's City of Books** (⊠ 1005 W. Burnside St., ☎ 503/228–4651) is one of the largest bookstores in the world. **Norm Thompson** (⊠ 1805 N.W. Thurman St., ☎ 503/221–0764) features clothing and one-of-a-kind Northwest gifts. The **Portland Pendleton Shop** (⊠ 900 S.W. 4th Ave., ☎ 503/242–0037) carries men's and women's wear, including the Oregon mill's famous Pendleton shirts and blankets.

THE OREGON COAST

Oregon has 400 mi of white-sand beaches, not a grain of which is privately owned. U.S. 101 parallels the coast from Astoria south to California, past monoliths of sea-tortured rock, brooding headlands, hidden beaches, haunted lighthouses, tiny ports, and, of course, the tumultuous Pacific.

Visitor Information

Astoria–Warrenton area: Chamber of Commerce (⊠ 111 W. Marine Dr., 97103, ☎ 503/325–6311 or 800/875–6807). **Coos Bay/North Bend area:** Chamber of Commerce (⊠ 50 E. Central St., Coos Bay 97420, ☎ 541/269–0215 or 800/824–8486). **Cannon Beach:** Chamber of Commerce (⊠ 2nd and Spruce Sts., 97110, ☎ 503/436–2623). **Florence area:** Chamber of Commerce (⊠ 270 Hwy. 101, 97439, ☎ 541/997–3128). **Lincoln City:** Visitors Center (⊠ 801 S.W. Hwy. 101, Suite 1, 97367, ☎ 541/994–8378 or 800/452–2151).

Arriving and Departing

By Bus
Greyhound Lines (☎ 800/231–2222) serves coastal communities such as Coos Bay, Florence, and Lincoln City.

By Car
The best way to see the coast is by car, following twisting, slow-paced, two-lane U.S. 101. Highway 26 (the Sunset) is the main link to Portland.

Exploring the Oregon Coast

Astoria, founded in 1811 at the site where the mighty Columbia River meets the Pacific Ocean, is believed to be the first official settlement established by the United States on the West Coast. Here Lewis and Clark wept with joy when they first saw the Pacific. The Victorian houses once owned by fur, timber, and fishing magnates still dot the flanks of Coxcomb Hill; many are now inviting B&Bs. The **Astor Column,** a 125-ft monolith atop Coxcomb Hill and patterned after Trajan's Column in Rome, rewards a climb up 164 spiral stairs with breathtaking views over Astoria, the Columbia, the Coast Range, and the ocean.

The **Columbia River Maritime Museum** (⊠ 1792 Marine Dr., ☎ 503/ 325–2323) has exhibits ranging from the fully operational lightship *Columbia* to poignant personal belongings from some of the 2,000 ships that have been wrecked at the mouth of the river since 1811.

★ Five and a half miles southeast of Astoria is the **Fort Clatsop National Memorial** (⊠ U.S. 101, ☎ 503/861–2471), a replica of the log stockade depicted in Clark's journal, commemorating the achievement of Lewis and Clark. Farther south, at the north end of Cannon Beach, **Ecola State Park** (☎ 503/436–2844) is a playground of sea-sculpted rock, sandy beach, tide pools, green headlands, and panoramic views.

Thirty miles south of Astoria and close enough to Portland to make it
★ a popular weekend getaway, **Cannon Beach** draws visitors to its long, sandy beach, restaurants, and weathered-cedar shopping district. **Haystack Rock,** a 235-ft offshore sea stack with tide pools at its base, is one of the most photographed sites on the coast.

South of Tillamook Bay, on the lush coastal plain that is Oregon's dairy country, Tillamook invites travelers to taste the cheese that has made the area world famous, at the **Tillamook Cheese factory** (⊠ 4175 Hwy. 101, ☎ 503/842–4481). The **Three Capes Scenic Loop,** west of Tillamook, encompasses magnificent coastal scenery, a lighthouse, offshore wildlife refuges, sand dunes, camping areas, and hiking trails.

Bustling **Lincoln City,** 43 mi south of Tillamook on U.S. 101, is known for its excellent seafood restaurants, lodgings, and proximity to some of the Oregon coast's most scenic landscapes.

Twenty-five miles south of Lincoln City, **Newport,** with its fishing fleet, art galleries, and seafood markets along a charming old bay front, is a fine place for an afternoon stroll. **Mariner Square** (⊠ 250 S.W. Bay Blvd., ☎ 503/265–2206) has undersea gardens and a wax museum. Across Yaquina Bay, the **Oregon Coast Aquarium** (⊠ 2820 S.E. Ferry Slip Rd., ☎ 541/867–3474) has more than 4 acres of outdoor pools, cliffs, and caves for frolicking sea otters, sea lions, and other marine creatures; fascinating indoor galleries are devoted to Oregon's coastal habitats and native marine life. Keiko, the orca whale featured in the *Free Willy* movies, now makes his home in a 150-ft-long pool with viewing windows.

South of Newport, the coast takes on a very different character— slower paced, less touristy, far less crowded, but just as rich in scenery and outdoor sporting activities. The peaceful village of Florence is the northern gateway to the **Oregon Dunes National Recreation Area** (☞ *National and State Parks, above*), a remarkable 40-mi swath of tawny sand. The dunes, some more than 500 ft high, are popular with campers, hikers, mountain bikers, dune-buggy enthusiasts, and even dogsledders. Children particularly enjoy the sandy slopes surrounding cool Cleawox Lake.

Umpqua River Lighthouse State Park (⊠ 460 Lighthouse Rd., 1 mi west of U.S. 101, ☎ 541/271–4118) adjoins an operating lighthouse and encompasses a small freshwater lake and campground. Also in the park are a whale-watching station, 500-ft-high sand dunes, and the **Douglas County Coastal Visitors Center** (☎ 541/271–4631), which has local history exhibits.

Western Oregon

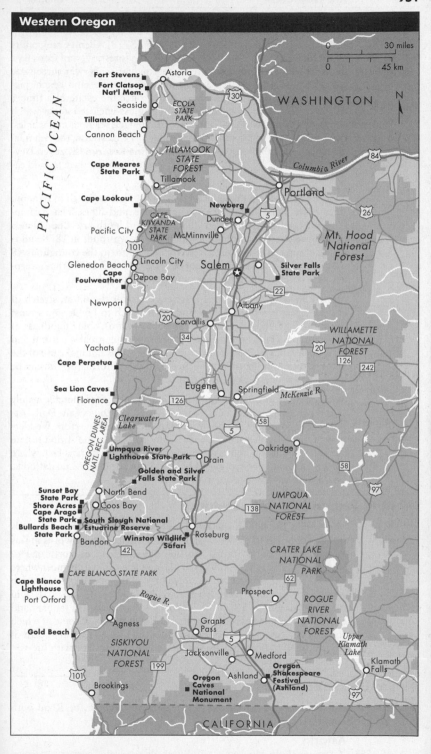

WASHINGTON

PACIFIC OCEAN

Fort Stevens
Fort Clatsop Nat'l Mem.
Astoria
ECOLA STATE PARK
Seaside
Tillamook Head
Cannon Beach

TILLAMOOK STATE FOREST

Cape Meares State Park
Tillamook

Cape Lookout

CAPE KIWANDA STATE PARK

Newberg
Dundee
McMinnville

Pacific City

Portland

Mt. Hood National Forest

Columbia River

Glenedon Beach
Lincoln City
Cape Foulweather
Depoe Bay

Salem

Silver Falls State Park

Newport

Albany

Corvallis

WILLAMETTE NATIONAL FOREST

Yachats

Cape Perpetua

Eugene
Springfield
McKenzie R.

Sea Lion Caves
Florence

Clearwater Lake

OREGON DUNES NATL. REC. AREA

Oakridge

Umpqua River Lighthouse State Park
Drain

Golden and Silver Falls State Park

UMPQUA NATIONAL FOREST

Sunset Bay State Park
North Bend
Shore Acres
Cape Arago State Park
Coos Bay
South Slough National Estuarine Reserve
Bullards Beach State Park
Bandon
Winston Wildlife Safari
Roseburg

CRATER LAKE NATIONAL PARK

Cape Blanco Lighthouse
Port Orford

CAPE BLANCO STATE PARK

Rogue R.

Prospect

ROGUE RIVER NATIONAL FOREST

Upper Klamath Lake

Gold Beach
Agness

Grants Pass

Klamath Falls

SISKIYOU NATIONAL FOREST

Jacksonville
Medford

Ashland
Oregon Shakespeare Festival (Ashland)

Brookings

Oregon Caves National Monument

CALIFORNIA

30 miles
45 km

N

Coos Bay is the Oregon coast's largest metropolitan area. At the end of a gravel road in **Golden and Silver Falls State Park** (⊠ 24 mi northeast of Coos Bay off U.S. 101, ☎ 541/888–3778), Glenn Creek pours over a high rock ledge deep in the old-growth forest. West of Coos Bay, the Cape Arago Highway presents spectacular scenery at three state parks (☎ 541/888–4902). **Sunset Bay** has a white-sand beach, picnicking, and campgrounds. **Shore Acres,** once the estate of a timber baron, has a 7.5-acre formal garden and a glass-enclosed storm-watch viewpoint. **Cape Arago** is a prime site for viewing sea lions and whales. Four miles south of the small fishing village of Charleston, the rich tidal estuaries of **South Slough National Estuarine Reserve** (⊠ Seven Devils Rd., ☎ 541/888–5558) support life ranging from algae to bald eagles and black bears.

Bullards Beach State Park (☎ 541/347–2209), 2 mi north of Bandon, spreads over miles of shoreline and impressive sand dunes. It has a campground as well as the restored Coquille River Lighthouse. **Cape Blanco Lighthouse,** west of the community of Sixes, was built in 1878 and is still operating. It is the most westerly lighthouse in the contiguous 48 states. Adjacent **Cape Blanco State Park** (☎ 541/332–6774) has sweeping views of rocks and beaches plus a campground.

Many knowledgeable coastal travelers consider the 63-mi stretch of U.S. 101 between Port Orford and Gold Beach to be Oregon's most beautiful. The highway soars up green headlands, some hundreds of feet high, past awesome scenery: caves, towering arches, natural and man-made bridges. Take time to admire the views but make use of the many turnouts along the way—this close to California, traffic can be heavy, and rubbernecking dangerous.

Gold Beach, about 30 mi north of the California border, is notable mainly as the place where the wild Rogue River meets the ocean. Daily jet-boat excursions roar up the scenic, rapids-filled Rogue from Wedderburn, Gold Beach's sister city across the bay, from late spring to late fall. Gold Beach also marks the entrance to Oregon's banana belt, where milder temperatures encourage a blossoming trade in lilies and daffodils. You'll even see a few palm trees here.

What to See and Do with Children

May brings the **Cannon Beach Sandcastle Contest,** when thousands throng the beach to view imaginative and often startling works in this most transient of art forms. **Sea Lion Caves** (⊠ 11 mi north of Florence, off U.S. 101, ☎ 541/547–3111) is a huge vaulted chamber where kids can get a close view of hundreds of sea lions, the largest of which weigh a ton or more. **West Coast Game Park Safari** (⊠ U.S. 101, 7 mi south of Bandon, ☎ 541/347–3106), closed weekdays in January and February, keeps animals of more than 75 exotic species, some of which children can pet. At **Prehistoric Gardens** (⊠ U.S. 101, 14 mi north of Gold Beach, ☎ 503/332–4463) kids come face to face with life-size dinosaur replicas.

Dining and Lodging

For price ranges *see* Charts 1 (B) and 2 (B) *in* On the Road with Fodor's.

Astoria

$$–$$$ ✕ **Cannery Café.** Housed in a 100-year-old renovated cannery on a pier, this bright, contemporary restaurant has windows that look onto the Columbia River. Fresh salads, large sandwiches, clam chowder, and crab cakes are lunch staples. The varied dinner menu emphasizes fresh seafood, including cioppino and oyster stew, as well as homemade southern Italian pasta dishes. ⊠ *1 6th St.,* ☎ *503/325–8642. AE, D, MC, V. Closed Mon. No dinner Sun.*

$–$$ ⚏ **Franklin Street Station Bed & Breakfast.** The ticking of clocks and
★ the mellow marine light shining through leaded-glass windows set the tone at this B&B, built in 1900. Breakfasts are huge, hot, and satisfying. ⊠ *1140 Franklin Ave., 97103,* ☎ *503/325–4314 or 800/448–1098. 6 rooms. MC, V.*

Brookings

$$ ✕ **Starboard Tack.** Fishing vessels docked in the adjacent boat basin and picture windows looking out to the sea lend a salty ambience to this pleasant, low-key restaurant. The fresh daily seafood specials—usually halibut and salmon—are the best choices, along with the prime rib. ⊠ *16011 Boat Basin Rd.,* ☎ *541/469–6006. MC, V.*

$$ ⚏ **Chetco River Inn.** Acres of private forest surround this modern fish-
★ ing lodge 15 mi up the Chetco River from Brookings. Fishing guides are available on request, as are eclectic dinners cooked by the B&B's owner, Sandra Burgger; she's also a font of information on the many hiking trails in the area. Quilts and fishing gear decorate the comfortable bedrooms. ⊠ *21202 High Prairie Rd., 97415,* ☎ *541/670–1645 or 800/327–2688. 4 rooms. MC, V.*

Cannon Beach

$$$ ✕ **The Bistro.** Cannon Beach's most romantic restaurant is candlelit and intimate. The four-course prix-fixe menu features imaginative Continental-influenced renditions of fresh local seafood dishes. It's best to reserve ahead for weekend dining. ⊠ *263 N. Hemlock St.,* ☎ *503/436–2661. MC, V. Closed most of Jan. and Tues.–Wed. in winter.*

$–$$ ✕ **Dooger's.** This comfortable family-style eatery's fresh, well-prepared seafood, exquisite clam chowder, and low prices keep 'em coming back for more. ⊠ *1371 S. Hemlock St.,* ☎ *503/436– 2225. AE, MC, V.*

$$$$ ✕⚏ **Stephanie Inn.** The impeccably maintained rooms at this three-
★ story premier oceanfront hotel have sophisticated country-style furnishings, fireplaces, large bathrooms with Jacuzzi bathtubs, and balconies commanding outstanding oceanfront views of Haystack Rock. Here you can also enjoy four-course prix-fixe dinners of innovative Pacific Northwest cuisine; reservations are essential. Room rates include generous country breakfasts and evening wine and hors d'oeuvres. ⊠ *2470 S. Pacific, 97110,* ☎ *503/436–2221 or 800/633–3466,* 𝔽𝔸𝕏 *503/436–9711. 46 rooms. Dining room, minibars, refrigerators, massage, library. AE, D, DC, MC, V.*

$$–$$$$ ⚏ **Hallmark Resort.** This oceanfront resort has cozy rooms—many with fireplaces, kitchens, and/or whirlpool baths—and some of the best views in Cannon Beach. ⊠ *1400 S. Hemlock St., 97110,* ☎ *503/436–1566 or 888/448–4449. 132 rooms. Restaurant, lounge, refrigerators, indoor pool, wading pool, hot tub, sauna, exercise room. AE, D, DC, MC, V.*

Coos Bay

$$ ✕ **Blue Heron Bistro.** You'll get subtle preparations of local seafood, chicken, and homemade pasta with an international flair at this busy bistro. There are no flat spots on the far-ranging menu; the innovative soups and desserts are also excellent. ⊠ *100 Commercial St.,* ☎ *541/267–3933. D, MC, V. Closed Sun. in winter.*

$$ ✕ **Portside Restaurant.** This unpretentious spot with picture windows overlooking the busy Charleston boat basin buys directly from the fishermen moored outside. Try the steamed Dungeness crab with drawn butter, a local specialty, or the all-you-can-eat seafood buffet on Friday night. ⊠ *8001 Kingfisher Rd. (follow Cape Arago Hwy. from Coos Bay),* ☎ *541/888–5544. AE, DC, MC, V.*

$$–$$$ ☷ **Coos Bay Manor.** Built in 1912 on a quiet residential street in Coos Bay, this 15-room Colonial Revival manor is listed on the National Register of Historic Places. An unusual open balcony on the second floor leads to the large, comfortable guest rooms. Innkeepers Patricia Williams and David Roth serve an extended Continental breakfast in the wainscoted dining room or on the upper balcony. ⊠ *955 S. 5th St., 97420,* ☎ *541/269–1224 or 800/269–1224 outside OR. 5 rooms. MC, V.*

Florence

$$ ✕ **Bridgewater Seafood Restaurant.** The salty ambience of Florence's photogenic Old Town permeates this spacious fish house. Steaks, salads, and, of course, plenty of fresh seafood are the mainstays at this creaky-floored Victorian-era restaurant. ⊠ *1297 Bay St.,* ☎ *541/997–9405. MC, V.*

Gleneden Beach

$$$$ ✕☷ **Salishan Lodge.** Nestled into a 750-acre hillside forest preserve, Salishan embodies a uniquely Oregonian elegance—from the soothing silvered-cedar tone of its guest rooms (all with fireplaces) to its collections of original art. The dining room is famous for its seasonal Northwest cuisine. ⊠ *7760 N. Hwy. 101, 97388,* ☎ *541/764–3600 or 800/547–6500. 205 rooms. 2 restaurants, bar, indoor pool, beauty salon, hot tub, massage, saunas, 18-hole golf course, tennis courts, exercise room, hiking, playground. AE, D, DC, MC, V.*

Gold Beach

$$$$ ✕☷ **Tu Tu Tun Lodge.** This lavishly appointed fishing resort perches above
★ the clear blue Rogue River, 7 mi upstream from Gold Beach. The units have an upscale rustic charm; private decks overlook the river. Meals are simple and satisfying American fare. ⊠ *96550 North Bank Rogue, 97444,* ☎ *541/247–6664,* ⅋ᾹⅩ *541/247–0672. 18 rooms, 1 2-bedroom house, 1 3-bedroom house. Restaurant, bar, pool, hiking, dock, fishing. D, MC, V. Dining room closed Nov.–Apr.*

$–$$ ☷ **Ireland's Rustic Lodges.** Original one- and two-bedroom cabins filled with rough-and-tumble charm plus newer motel rooms and three new houses are set amid spectacular landscaping. Most units have a fireplace and a deck overlooking the sea. ⊠ *29330 Ellensburg Ave. (U.S. 101), 97444,* ☎ *541/247–7718. 7 cabins, 30 motel rooms, 2-, 3- and 4-bedroom houses. No-smoking rooms. MC, V.*

Lincoln City

$$–$$$ ✕ **Bay House.** This bungalow serves meals to linger over while you enjoy
★ views across sunset-gilded Siletz Bay. The seasonal Northwest cuisine includes Dungeness crab cakes with roasted-chili chutney, fresh halibut Parmesan, and roast duckling with cranberry compote. The wine list is extensive, the service impeccable. ⊠ *5911 S.W. Hwy. 101,* ☎ *541/996–3222. AE, D, MC, V. Closed Mon.–Tues., Nov.–Apr. No lunch.*

$–$$ ✕ **Kyllos.** Perched on stilts beside the world's shortest river (the D) and bestowing views of Pacific surf and sand, Kyllos is a spacious, light-filled aerie. It's also one of the best places in Lincoln City to enjoy a casual but well-prepared seafood, meat, or pasta meal. ⊠ *1110 N.W. 1st Ct.,* ☎ *541/994–3179. AE, D, MC, V.*

$$-$$$ 🎦 **Ester Lee Motel.** Perched on a seaside bluff, this small whitewashed motel attracts repeat guests through value and simplicity. For the price, there are some nice amenities, including wood-burning fireplaces, full kitchens, and cable TV in all rooms. ⊠ *3803 S.W. Hwy. 101, 97367,* ☎ *503/996–3606. 53 rooms. D, MC, V.*

Newport

$$ ✕ **Canyon Way Restaurant and Bookstore.** The best dining in Newport is just up the hill from the center of the Bay Front. Cod, Dungeness crab cakes, bouillabaisse, and Yaquina Bay oysters are served inside or on the outdoor patio, next to a well-stocked bookstore. There's also a deli counter for take-out. ⊠ *S.W. Canyon Way,* ☎ *541/265–8319. AE, DC, MC, V. Closed Sun. No lunch Tues.–Sat.*

$$ ✕ **Whale's Tale.** Fresh local seafood, thick clam chowder, fish-and-chips, burgers, and sandwiches are all on the menu of this Bay Front eatery. The atmosphere is casual and family oriented. ⊠ *452 S.W. Bay Blvd.,* ☎ *541/265–8660. AE, D, DC, MC, V. Closed Wed. Nov.–Apr.*

$$–$$$$ ✕🎦 **Sylvia Beach Hotel.** Each of the phoneless, TV-less, antiques-filled
★ guest rooms at this restored 1912 B&B is named for a famous writer and decorated accordingly. For example, a pendulum swings over the bed in the Poe Room. Upstairs is a well-stocked library with a fireplace, a slumbering cat, and too-comfortable chairs. Breakfast is a hearty buffet. ⊠ *267 N.W. Cliff St., 97365,* ☎ *541/265–5428. 20 rooms. Restaurant. AE, MC, V.*

Yachats

$$$$ 🎦 **Ziggurat.** It's hard to miss this terraced, pyramid-shape inn just south of Yachats, one of the most charming small communities on the coast. Two large suites opening onto a grassy cliff are on the first floor; a third guest room, with two balconies and outstanding views, is on the fourth level. ⊠ *95330 Hwy. 101,* ☎ *541/547–3925. 3 rooms. Library. No credit cards.*

Campgrounds

Nineteen state parks along the coast include campgrounds. Most feature full hookups and tent sites. Many are near the shore, and some contain group facilities and hiker/biker or horse camps. The **Oregon State Parks and Recreation Department** (☞ National and State Parks, *above*) has details. **Honeyman State Park** (⊠ 84505 Hwy. 101, Florence 97439, ☎ 541/997–3641) adjoins the Oregon Dunes National Recreation Area. Reserve well ahead.

Outdoor Activities and Sports

Biking
The **Oregon Coast Bike Route** parallels U.S. 101 and the coast from Astoria south to Brookings.

Fishing
Huge salmon, delectable Dungeness crab, and dozens of species of bottom fish are the quarry here, accessible from jetties, docks, and riverbanks from Astoria to Brookings. Charter boats and guides are plentiful; contact local chambers of commerce (☞ Visitor Information, *above*) for information on seasons, rates, and schedules.

Golf
The Oregon coast has about 20 public and private courses, including **Salishan Golf Links** (⊠ 7760 N. Hwy. 101, Gleneden Beach, ☎ 541/764–3632), the coast's most challenging course, with 18 holes. Newport has the nine-hole **Agate Beach Golf Course** (☎ 541/265–7331). In Florence the 18-hole **Ocean Dunes Golf Links** (☎ 541/997–3232)

draws amateurs and professionals. Gold Beach's **Cedar Bend Golf Course** (☎ 541/247–6911) has nine holes.

Beaches

Virtually the entire 400-mi coastline of Oregon consists of clean white-sand beaches, accessible to all. Thanks to its sea-sculpted stone, **Face Rock Wayside,** in Bandon, is thought by many to have the most beautiful walking beach in the state. The placid semicircular lagoon at **Sunset Bay State Park,** on Cape Arago, is Oregon's safest swimming beach. Fossils, clams, mussels, and other eons-old marine creatures embedded in soft sandstone cliffs make **Beverly Beach State Park,** 5 mi north of Newport, a favorite with young beachcombers.

Shopping

Hemlock Street, the main drag of **Cannon Beach,** is the best place on the coast to browse for unusual clothing, souvenirs, picnic supplies, books, and gifts. **Newport**'s Bay Boulevard is a good place to find local artwork, gifts, and fresh seafood. You'll find bargains galore at the **Lincoln City Factory Stores** (⊠ 1510 E. Devils Lake Rd., ☎ 541/996–5000). Particularly good deals on vintage items can be found in the antiques malls in Astoria, Seaside, and Lincoln City.

ELSEWHERE IN OREGON

Mt. Hood and Bend

Arriving and Departing

Mt. Hood lies about an hour east of Portland on U.S. 26; the only way to get there is by car. Continue east on U.S. 26, then south on U.S. 97 for the resort town of Bend, two hours beyond Mt. Hood. **Redmond Municipal Airport** (☎ 541/548–6059), about 14 mi north of Bend, is served by Horizon Airlines (☎ 800/547–9308) and United Express (☎ 800/241–6522).

What to See and Do

Mt. Hood, 11,245 ft and surrounded by the 1.1-million-acre **Mt. Hood National Forest** (⊠ 16400 Champion Way, Sandy 97055, ☎ 503/668–1700), is an all-season playground that attracts more than 7 million visitors annually for skiing, camping, hiking, fishing, or day-tripping to breathe the mountain air. Historic **Timberline Lodge,** off U.S. 26 a few miles east of Government Camp (⊠ Timberline 97028, ☎ 503/272–3311 or 800/547–1406), has withstood howling winter storms on the mountain's flank for more than 60 years; it's a popular spot for romantic getaways.

Hood River, a town 60 mi east of Portland on I–84 in the spectacular Columbia Gorge, is the self-proclaimed sailboarding capital of the world. **Columbia Gorge Sailpark** (⊠ Port Marina, ☎ 541/386–2000), on the river downtown, contains a boat basin, a swimming beach, jogging trails, and picnic tables.

The skiing is excellent in **Bend,** which occupies a tawny high-desert plateau in the very center of Oregon, framed on the west by three 10,000-ft Cascade peaks. With its plentiful dining and lodging options, Bend makes a fine base camp for skiing at nearby **Mt. Bachelor,** white-water rafting on the **Deschutes River,** world-class rock climbing at **Smith Rocks State Park,** and other outdoor activities. Don't miss the archaeological and wildlife displays at the **High Desert Museum** (⊠ 59800 S. Hwy. 97, 3½ mi south of Bend, ☎ 541/382–4754). **Newberry**

National Volcanic Monument (☞ National and State Parks, *above*), 25 mi southeast of Bend, contains more than 50,000 acres of lakes, lava flows, and spectacular geological features.

Willamette Valley/Wine Country

Arriving and Departing

I–5, the state's main north–south freeway, runs straight down the center of the Willamette Valley from Portland.

What to See and Do

Oregon's **wine country** occupies the wet, temperate trough between the Coast Range to the west and the Cascades to the east. More than 40 wineries dot the hills between Portland and Salem, and dozens more are scattered from Newport to as far south as Ashland, on the California border. Although tiny in comparison with California's, Oregon's wine industry is booming. Cool-climate varietals such as pinot noir and Johannisberg Riesling have gained the esteem of international connoisseurs.

Most vineyards welcome visitors. The best way to tour is by car. *Discover Oregon Wineries,* an indispensable map and guide to the wine country, is available free at wine shops and wineries or by calling the Oregon Wine Advisory Board (☎ 800/242–2363). **Northwest Bed & Breakfast** (☎ 503/243–7616) is a good source of reservations for the Willamette Valley's extensive B&B network.

Newberg is a graceful old pioneer town at a broad bend in the Willamette River southwest of Portland. The boyhood home of President Herbert Hoover, the circa-1881 **Hoover-Minthorne House** (⊠ 115 S. River St., ☎ 503/538–6629), is a beautifully preserved frame house with many original furnishings. South of Newberg, the idyllic orchard land around **Dundee** produces 90% of America's hazelnut crop.

Salem, the state capital, makes a good base for exploring; in addition to its hotels, B&Bs, and restaurants, there are some fine gardens and museums. A gilded 23-ft-high bronze statue of the Oregon Pioneer atop the 106-ft capitol dome is the centerpiece of Salem's **capitol** (⊠ 900 Court St., ☎ 503/986–1388), where Oregon's legislators convene every two years. Near the capitol are the tradition-steeped brick buildings of **Willamette University,** the oldest college in the West, founded in 1842. Just south of downtown Salem, **Bush's Pasture Park** (⊠ 600 Mission St. SE) includes **Bush House** (☎ 503/363–4714), a Victorian mansion with 10 fireplaces and original furnishings, and **Bush Barn,** an art center with two exhibition rooms and a sales gallery. **Deepwood Estate** (⊠ 1116 Mission St. SE, ☎ 503/363–1825), on the National Register of Historic Places, encompasses 5½ acres of lawns, formal English gardens, and a fanciful 1894 Queen Anne mansion with splendid interior woodwork and original stained glass. **Silver Falls State Park** (⊠ Hwy. 214, 26 mi east of Salem, ☎ 503/873–8681) covers 8,700 acres and includes 10 waterfalls accessible to hikers.

At **Albany,** 24 mi south of Salem on I–5, visitors can take self-guided driving tours of three historic districts that encompass 350 homes and every major architectural style popular in the United States since 1850. Tour maps are available at the Albany Chamber of Commerce (⊠ 435 W. 1st St., 97321, ☎ 541/926–1517).

Liberal-minded **Eugene** is Oregon's second-largest city and the home of the University of Oregon. In town the **Willamette Science and Technology Center** (⊠ 2300 Leo Harris Pkwy., ☎ 541/687–3619) has imaginative hands-on scientific exhibits and a planetarium.

South of Eugene, the sleepy farming community of **Roseburg** is on the Umpqua River, famous among fishers. West of town are a dozen of the region's wineries. The **Douglas County Museum** (⊠ 125 Museum Dr., I–5 Exit 123, ☎ 541/440–4507) has an exceptional fossil collection. **Wildlife Safari** (⊠ 3 mi west of I–5 Exit 119, Winston, ☎ 541/679–6761) is a 600-acre drive-through wildlife park with a petting zoo, elephant rides, a restaurant, and a seasonal RV park.

Ashland/The Rogue Valley

Arriving and Departing

Ashland is midway between Portland and San Francisco on I–5, about 15 mi north of the California border. **Jackson County Airport** (☎ 541/772–8068), in nearby Medford, is served by Horizon Airlines, United, and United Express.

What to See and Do

Ashland is home to the Tony Award–winning **Oregon Shakespeare Festival** (⊠ 15 S. Pioneer St., 97520, ☎ 541/482–4331), which annually attracts more than 350,000 visitors to this relaxing Rogue Valley town. The local arts scene, a warm climate, and opulent B&Bs and sumptuous restaurants make this a pleasant place for a holiday. You'll find excellent downhill and Nordic skiing atop 7,523-ft **Mt. Ashland.** West of Ashland, the famous Rogue River boils and churns through the rugged, remote Kalmiopsis Wilderness in **Siskiyou National Forest** (☎ 541/471–6516). The local wineries are also worth a visit.

Jacksonville, in the eastern part of the state, preserves the look and feel of an Old West pioneer settlement; the entire town is a National Historic Landmark. Each summer from mid-June to Labor Day Jacksonville hosts the **Peter Britt Festival** (☎ 503/773–6077 or 800/882–7488), a concert series featuring some of the world's best jazz and

★ classical musicians. The main attraction at **Crater Lake National Park** (☞ National and State Parks, *above*) began 6,800 years ago, when Mt. Mazama decapitated itself in a huge explosion. Rain and snowmelt eventually filled the caldera, creating a sapphire blue lake so clear that sunlight penetrates to a depth of 400 ft. Visitors can drive or hike the park's 25-mi **Rim Drive,** explore a variety of nature trails, and (in summer) take guided boat trips around the lake itself. The park is about 80 mi northeast of Jacksonville along Highway 62.

WASHINGTON

By Tom Gauntt

Updated by
Susan English

Capital	Olympia
Population	5,447,720
Motto	By-and-by
State Bird	American goldfinch
State Flower	Rhododendron
Postal Abbreviation	WA

Statewide Visitor Information

Washington Tourism Development Division (✉ Box 42500, Olympia, 98504-2500, ☎ 360/586–2088 or 800/544–1800).

Scenic Drives

About 90 mi north of Seattle, starting from just south of Bellingham on I–5, Highway 11 loops 25 mi around **Chuckanut Bay.** On one side of Highway 11 is the steep, heavily wooded Chuckanut Mountain and on the other are sweeping views of Puget Sound and the San Juan Islands. The area is also dotted with fine restaurants. Near the Oregon border, Highway 14 winds east from Vancouver into the **Columbia River National Scenic Area.** The road clings to the steep slopes of the gorge and traverses several tunnels and picturesque towns such as Carson, known for its hot springs, and White Salmon, renowned for windsurfing.

National and State Parks

National Parks

Mt. Rainier National Park (✉ Tahoma Woods, Star Rte., Ashford 98304, ☎ 360/569–2211), about 85 mi southeast of Seattle, comprises 14,411-ft Mt. Rainier—the fifth-highest mountain in the lower 48 states—and nearly 400 square mi of surrounding wilderness. The visitor center has exhibits, films, and a 360-degree view of the summit and surrounding peaks. For a vision of the apocalypse, head for the **Mount St. Helens National Volcanic Monument** (✉ 42218 N.E. Yale Bridge Rd., Amboy 98601, ☎ 360/750–3900). The visitor center (☎ 360/247–3900) is on Highway 504, 5 mi east of the Castle Rock exit off I–5, and the monument is 45 mi east of Castle Rock. Although the crater still steams and small earthquakes are common, excellent views are available within 10 mi of the mountain. **Olympic National Park** (✉ 600 E. Park Ave., Port Angeles 98362, ☎ 360/452–4501) is one of the most outstanding pieces of natural beauty in the United States, with such diverse areas as its jagged wilderness coastline; a lush, temperate rain forest; 60-odd active glaciers; and Hurricane Ridge, with its alpine contours. **North Cascades National Park** (✉ 2105 Hwy. 20, Sedro Woolley 98284, ☎ 360/856–5700), a little-known park about 120 mi northeast of Seattle, holds some of the state's most rugged mountains, craggy peaks, and jewel-like lakes. Heavy snows in the Cascades close Highway 20 through the park most winters from October through April.

State Park

Leadbetter Point State Park (✉ Robert Gray Dr., 2 mi south of Ilwaco, Box 488, 98624, ☎ 360/642–3078), at the northernmost tip of the Long Beach Peninsula, is a wildlife refuge that's good for bird-watching. The dunes at the very tip are closed from April to August to protect the nesting snowy plover. Black brant, sandpipers, turnstones, yellowlegs, sanderlings, knots, and plovers are among the 100 species known to inhabit the point.

SEATTLE

Whether it's a double, tall, decaf nonfat latte with a dash of nutmeg or a standard cup of java, coffee has transformed Seattle's reputation from soggy and mossy to rich, dark, and steamy. Since 1971, when three enterprising young men first started Starbucks, the city's premier coffee company, Seattle has claimed its place as the nation's coffee capital. Espresso carts are on nearly every block downtown, and coffee bars dot Seattle's neighborhoods.

Seattle has become a major cultural center, its sophistication evident in its architecture, food, fashion, and arts. The city is a magnet for people drawn by its blend of urban sophistication, easygoing charm, and ready access to spectacular outdoor recreation. The arts are strong and innovative, and the restaurants—from tiny International District dumpling stands to world-class dining rooms—serve a steady supply of visitors, longtime residents, and newcomers, all caught up in the act of simultaneously discovering and celebrating this place. Surrounding it all are those old familiars: the mountains and the water.

Visitor Information

Seattle/King County: Stop by Convention and Visitors Bureau (⊠ 800 Convention Pl., at Pike St., 98101, ☎ 206/461–5840) or the street-level visitor center (☎ 206/467–1600) at the Westlake Center (⊠ 5th Ave. and Pine St.). Or write to the Visitor Information Center (⊠ 520 Pike St., Suite 1300, 98101, ☎ 206/461–5840).

Arriving and Departing

By Bus
Greyhound Lines (⊠ 8th Ave. and Stewart St., ☎ 800/231–2222).

By Car
I–5 enters Seattle from the north and south, I–90 from the east.

By Plane
Seattle-Tacoma International Airport (Sea-Tac) is 20 mi south of downtown and is served by major American and some foreign airlines. A cab ride to downtown takes about 30 to 45 minutes and costs about $25. **Gray Line Airport Express** (☎ 206/626–6088) buses run to and from major downtown hotels; the fare is $7.50 one-way, $13 round-trip. A taxi ride costs about $25 from the airport to downtown.

By Train
Amtrak (⊠ 303 S. Jackson St., ☎ 800/872–7245).

Getting Around Seattle

A car is the handiest way to cover metropolitan Seattle, but bus service is convenient and efficient, too. Despite occasional steep hills, downtown is good for walking.

By Car
Hills, tunnels, reversible express lanes, and frustrating rush hours can make driving a chore. Main thoroughfares into downtown are Aurora Avenue (called the Alaskan Way Viaduct through town) and I–5.

By Public Transportation

Metropolitan Transit (☎ 206/553–3000) provides free rides in the downtown-waterfront area until 7 PM; fares to other destinations range from 85¢ to $1.70, depending on the zone and time of day. The elevated **monorail** runs the 2 mi from the Seattle Center to Westlake Center; the fare is $1.

By Taxi

Hailing a cab is not always easy; it's sometimes quicker to get one at a downtown hotel taxi stand. Fare is $1.80 at the flag drop and then $1.80 per mi. Major companies are **Farwest** (☎ 206/622–1717) and **Yellow Cab** (☎ 206/622–6500).

Orientation Tours

Bus Tour

Gray Line Tour (⊠ Sheraton Hotel, 1400 6th Ave., ☎ 206/626–5208) provides guided bus tours of the city and environs ranging from a daily 2½-hour spin to the six-hour Grand City Tour, offered in spring, summer, and fall.

Boat Tour

Argosy Cruises (⊠ Pier 55, ☎ 206/623–1445) operates one-hour tours of Elliott Bay, the port of Seattle, Lake Union, Hiram M. Chittenden Locks, and Lake Washington.

Exploring Seattle

Downtown

Downtown Seattle is bounded by the Kingdome to the south, the Seattle Center to the north, I–5 to the east, and the waterfront to the west. You can reach most points of interest by foot, bus, or monorail. But remember that Seattle is a city of hills, so wear your walking shoes.

★ The five-story **Seattle Art Museum** (⊠ 100 University St., ☎ 206/654–3100), by postmodern theorist Robert Venturi, is a work of art in itself, with a limestone exterior and vertical fluting accented by terra cotta, cut granite, and marble. Inside are extensive collections of Asian, Native American, African, Oceanic, and pre-Columbian art, a café, and a gift shop.

The **Out to Lunch** series (☎ 206/623–0340) of free outdoor concerts is held weekdays at noon in various downtown parks, plazas, and atriums from mid-June to early September.

Pike Place Market (⊠ 1st Ave. at Pike St., ☎ 206/682–7453) got its start in 1907, when the city issued permits allowing farmers to sell produce from their wagons parked at Pike Place. Urban renewal almost closed the market, but citizens rallied and voted it a historical asset. Sold here are fresh seafood (which can be packed in dry ice for your flight home), produce, cheese, Northwest wines, bulk spices, teas, coffees, and arts and crafts.

At the base of the Pike Street Hillclimb at Pier 59 is the **Seattle Aquarium** (☎ 206/386–4320), showcasing Northwest marine life. Sea otters and seals swim and dive in their pools, and the State of the Sound exhibit shows aquatic life and the ecology of Puget Sound.

A couple of blocks east of Pier 51, at the foot of Yesler Way, is **Pioneer Park,** where an ornate iron-and-glass pergola stands. This was the site of Henry Yesler's pier and sawmill and of Seattle's original business district. An 1889 fire destroyed many of the wood-frame buildings in

★ the area now known as **Pioneer Square,** but the residents rebuilt them

Seattle

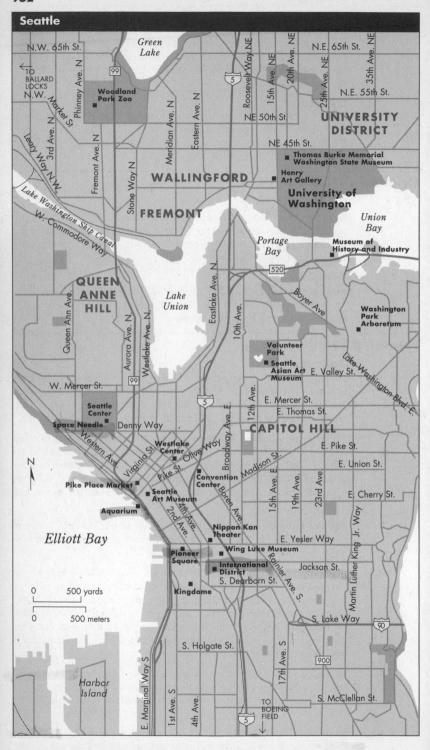

N.W. 65th St.

Green Lake

N.E. 65th St.

Phinney Ave. N

TO BALLARD LOCKS N.W.

Market St.

3rd Ave. N

99

Woodland Park Zoo

Fremont Ave. N

Meridian Ave. N

Eastern Ave. N

Roosevelt Way NE

15th NE

20th Ave. NE

25th Ave. NE

35th Ave. NE

N.E. 55th St.

UNIVERSITY DISTRICT

NE 50th St.

NE 45th St.

Thomas Burke Memorial Washington State Museum

WALLINGFORD

Stone Way N

Henry Art Gallery

University of Washington

Leary Way N.W.

Lake Washington Ship Canal

FREMONT

Union Bay

W. Commodore Way

Portage Bay

Museum of History and Industry

QUEEN ANNE HILL

Queen Ann Ave.

Aurora Ave. N

Westlake Ave. N

Lake Union

Eastlake Ave. N

10th Ave.

520

Boyer Ave

Washington Park Arboretum

Volunteer Park

Seattle Asian Art Museum

E. Valley St.

Lake Washington Blvd. E.

W. Mercer St.

99

5

12th Ave.

E. Mercer St.

E. Thomas St.

CAPITOL HILL

Seattle Center

Space Needle

Denny Way

Western Ave.

Virginia St.

Westlake Center

Olive Way

Pike St.

Broadway Ave. E.

Madison St.

E. Pike St.

E. Union St.

15th Ave. E.

19th Ave.

23rd Ave.

E. Cherry St.

N

Pike Place Market

Seattle Art Museum

4th Ave.

2nd Ave.

Convention Center

Boren Ave.

Aquarium

Elliott Bay

Nippon Kan Theater

Pioneer Square

Wing Luke Museum

International District

S. Dearborn St.

E. Yesler Way

Jackson St.

Martin Luther King Jr. Way

Rainier Ave. S.

Kingdome

0   500 yards

0   500 meters

S. Lake Way

90

S. Holgate St.

17th Ave. S

900

Harbor Island

E. Marginal Way S

1st Ave. S

4th Ave.

5

TO BOEING FIELD

S. McClellan St.

with brick and mortar. This area was in a state of decline from the Depression until the 1970s, when buildings were restored and stores and cafés moved in. Some older saloons remain, giving the area a historical flavor. College kids party hearty here at night; during the day you can browse through the art galleries and the several dozen stalls and shops at the **Downtown Antique Market** (⊠ 2218 Western Ave., ☎ 206/448–6307). **Gallery Walk** (☎ 206/587–0260) is a free open house hosted the first Thursday of every month by Seattle's art galleries, most of them in Pioneer Square.

Southeast of Pioneer Square is the **International District** (known locally as the ID), where a third of the residents are ethnic Chinese, a third Filipino, and a third from elsewhere in Asia. The ID began as a haven for Chinese workers after they'd finished building the transcontinental railroad. Today the district includes many Chinese, Japanese, and Korean restaurants, as well as herbalists, massage parlors, and acupuncturists. The **Nippon Kan Theater** (⊠ 628 S. Washington St., ☎ 206/224–0181) was historically the focal point for Japanese-American activities, including Kabuki theater. Renovated and reopened in 1981 as a national historic site, it presents many Asian-oriented productions.

North of Downtown

From **Westlake Center** (☞ Shopping, *below*), a shopping complex completed in 1989, you can catch the monorail to **Seattle Center,** a 74-acre complex built for the 1962 Seattle World's Fair. It includes an amusement park, theaters, a new coliseum, exhibition halls, museums, and shops. Within Seattle Center is the **Space Needle** (☎ 206/443–2111), a Seattle landmark that is visible from almost anywhere in the downtown area and looks like something from *The Jetsons*. Take the glass elevator to the observation deck for an impressive view of the city.

From downtown or the Seattle Center head north on Highway 99 (Aurora Avenue North), across the Aurora Bridge to the 45th Street exit, to the 92-acre **Woodland Park Zoo** (⊠ N. 50th St. and Fremont Ave., ☎ 206/684–4800). Animals here roam freely within "bioclimatic" zones that re-create their native habitats.

A short drive east of the zoo is the **University of Washington.** On the northwest corner of the campus is the **Thomas Burke Memorial Washington State Museum** (⊠ 17th Ave. NE and N.E. 45th St., ☎ 206/543–5590), Washington's natural history and anthropological museum. South of the University of Washington's Husky Stadium, across the Montlake Cut, is the **Museum of History and Industry** (⊠ 2700 24th Ave. E, ☎ 206/324–1125).

Parks and Gardens

Near the university at the **Washington Park Arboretum** (⊠ 2300 Arboretum Dr. E, ☎ 206/543–8800), Rhododendron Glen and Azalea Way are in bloom from March through June. The Hiram M. Chittenden Locks, better known as the **Ballard Locks** (⊠ 3015 N.W. 54th St., west of the Ballard Bridge, ☎ 206/783–7059), control the 8-mi-long Lake Washington Ship Canal, which connects freshwater Lake Washington to Puget Sound. Alongside the canal is a 7-acre **ornamental garden** of native and exotic plants, shrubs, and trees.

What to See and Do with Children

The **Children's Museum** (⊠ Seattle Center, 305 Harrison St., fountain level, ☎ 206/441–1768) has an infant/toddler area with a giant, soft ferryboat for climbing and sliding. The museum also offers intergenerational programs, special exhibits, and workshops. **Seattle Children's**

Theater (✉ 2nd Ave. N and Thomas St., at the Seattle Center, ☎ 206/441–3322) presents several plays each year.

Dining

For price ranges *see* Chart 1 (A) *in* On the Road with Fodor's.

$$$$ ✕ **Canlis.** This sumptuous restaurant—renovated to maximize the views
★ of Lake Union—is a Seattle institution famous for its steaks, fresh fish, and (in season) Quilcene Bay oysters. ✉ *2576 Aurora Ave. N,* ☎ *206/283–3313. AE, DC, MC, V. Closed Sun. No lunch.*

$$$ ✕ **Campagne.** Overlooking Pike Place Market and Elliott Bay, Campagne is intimate and urbane, with white walls, picture windows, and colorful modern prints setting the tone. The flavors of Provence pervade the menu in such dishes as salmon in a cognac-and-champagne butter sauce. ✉ *Inn at the Market, 86 Pine St.,* ☎ *206/728–2800. Jacket required. AE, MC, V.*

$$ ✕ **Place Pigalle.** Despite its French name, this popular restaurant is very American. Large windows overlook Elliott Bay and in good weather admit the salt breeze. The menu includes seasonal meals of seafood and local ingredients. ✉ *Pike Place Market, 81 Pike St.,* ☎ *206/624–1756. MC, V. Closed Sun.*

$$ ✕ **Wild Ginger.** The specialty is Pacific Rim cookery, including tasty
★ southern Chinese, Vietnamese, Thai, and Korean dishes served in a warm, clubby dining room. Daily specials are based on seasonally available products. ✉ *1400 Western Ave.,* ☎ *206/623–4450. AE, D, DC, MC, V. No lunch Sun.*

$ ✕ **Emmet Watson's Oyster Bar.** This small seafood place is hard to find
★ (it's in the back of Pike Place Market's Soames-Dunn Building and faces a small courtyard), but it's worth the effort. The oysters are fresh and offered in several varieties. The beer list, too, is ample, with 25 or more selections, from local microbrews to fancy imports. ✉ *Pike Place Market, 1916 Pike Pl.,* ☎ *206/448–7721. Reservations not accepted. No credit cards. No dinner Sun.*

Lodging

Seattle has an abundance of lodgings, from deluxe downtown hotels to less expensive digs in the University District. For information on bed-and-breakfasts, contact the **Pacific Bed & Breakfast Agency** (✉ 701 N.W. 60th St., Seattle 98107, ☎ 206/784–0539 or 206/782–4036). For price ranges see Chart 2 (A) in On the Road with Fodor's.

$$$–$$$$ 🏨 **Alexis.** At this intimate hotel in a restored 1901 building near the
★ waterfront, guest rooms are decorated in contemporary, subdued colors. Some suites have whirlpool baths, others wood-burning fireplaces. The hotel has a no-tipping policy. ✉ *1007 1st Ave., 98104,* ☎ *206/624–4844 or 800/426–7033,* 🆋 *206/621–9009. 74 rooms. Restaurant, bar, café. AE, DC, MC, V.*

$$$–$$$$ 🏨 **Edgewater.** The only hotel on Elliott Bay has rooms decorated in a comfortably rustic style, with unfinished wood furnishings and plaid fabric in red, green, and blue. ✉ *Pier 67, 2411 Alaskan Way, 98121,* ☎ *206/728–7000 or 800/624–0670,* 🆋 *206/441–4119. 235 rooms. Restaurant, bar. AE, D, DC, MC, V.*

$$$–$$$$ 🏨 **Four Seasons Olympic Hotel.** Restored to its 1920s grandeur, the
★ Olympic is Seattle's most elegant hotel. Its public rooms are furnished with marble, thick rugs, wood paneling, and potted plants. The less luxurious guest rooms have a homey ambience with comfortable reading chairs and floral-print fabrics. ✉ *411 University St., 98101,* ☎ *206/621–1700 or 800/223–8772,* 🆋 *206/682–9633. 450 rooms. 3 restaurants, indoor pool, health club. AE, DC, MC, V.*

$$$–$$$$ ⊞ **Inn at the Market.** Adjacent to the Pike Place Market, this hotel com-
★ bines the best aspects of a small, deluxe hotel with the informality of
the Pacific Northwest. Rooms are spacious, with contemporary fur-
nishings and ceramic sculptures, and offer views of the city, Elliott Bay,
the Pike Place Market, and the hotel courtyard. ⊠ *86 Pine St., 98101,*
☎ *206/443–3600,* FAX *206/448–0631. 65 rooms. No-smoking rooms,
room service. AE, D, DC, MC, V.*

$$ ⊞ **Edmond Meany Tower Hotel.** Built in 1931 and remodeled several
times, this pleasant hotel a few blocks from the University of Wash-
ington campus has a contemporary ambience. Nearly all the rooms have
views of the Cascades or the Olympic Mountains, the University of Washington, or Lake Union. ⊠ *4507 Brooklyn Ave. NE, 98105,* ☎ *206/
634–2000,* FAX *206/547–6029. 155 rooms. Restaurant, lounge, no-smoking rooms. AE, DC, MC, V.*

$ ⊞ **Seattle YMCA.** A member of the American Youth Hostels Associa-
tion, this Y has single and double rooms that are clean and plainly furnished with bed, phone, desk, and lamp. Ten dollars extra gets you a
room with a private bath; another $3 and your room will have a view
of Elliott Bay. ⊠ *909 4th Ave., 98104,* ☎ *206/382–5000. 198 beds,
3 rooms with baths. Pool, health club. MC, V.*

Motels

⊞ **Doubletree Suites** (⊠ 16500 Southcenter Pkwy., Tukwila 98188, ☎
206/575–8220, FAX 206/575–4743), 221 suites, restaurant, bar, indoor
pool, hot tub, sauna, health club, racquetball; *$$$.* ⊞ **Doubletree Inn**
(⊠ 205 Strander Blvd., Tukwila 98188, ☎ 206/246–8220, FAX 206/575–
4749), 200 rooms, coffee shop, dining room, bar, pool; *$$.* ⊞ **University Plaza Hotel** (⊠ 400 N.E. 45th St., 98105, ☎ 206/634–0100, FAX
206/633–2743), 135 rooms, restaurant, bar, pool, exercise room; *$.*

Nightlife and the Arts

Nightlife

For a relatively small city, Seattle has a strong and diverse music scene.
On any given night you can hear high-quality sounds at a wide variety of nightspots.

BARS AND NIGHTCLUBS

Pescatore (⊠ 5300 34th Ave. NW, ☎ 206/784–1733), in Ballard, has
large windows overlooking the Ship Canal. **Adriatica** (⊠ 1107 Dexter Ave. N, ☎ 206/285–5000), a Mediterranean restaurant and lounge,
sits above Lake Union's west side. **Arnie's Northshore Restaurant** (⊠
1900 N. Northlake Way, ☎ 206/547–3242) has a lounge with giant
windows overlooking Gas Works Park and Lake Union. A Seattle favorite, **Ray's Boathouse** (⊠ 6049 Seaview Ave. NW, ☎ 206/789–3770)
is perched on the shore of Shilshole Bay, a perfect spot for watching
the sun set behind the Olympic Mountains.

BLUES/R&B CLUB

The **Ballard Firehouse** (⊠ 5429 Russell St. NW, ☎ 206/784–3516) is
a music mecca in Ballard, with an emphasis on the blues.

COMEDY CLUB

Comedy Underground (⊠ 222 Main St., ☎ 206/628–0303), a Pioneer
Square club that's literally underground, beneath Swannie's, presents
stand-up comedy and open-mike nights.

DANCE CLUBS

Fenix Underground (⊠ 323 2nd Ave. S, ☎ 206/467–1111) is one of
several popular clubs in Pioneer Square. **Fenix** (⊠ 315 2nd Ave. S,
☎ 206/467–1111) pulsates with recorded dance music. On Capitol

Hill **Neighbours** (⊠ 1509 Broadway E, ☎ 206/324–5358) attracts a good mix of gay men and everyone else.

JAZZ CLUB

Dimitriou's Jazz Alley (⊠ 2037 6th Ave., ☎ 206/441–9729) downtown books nationally known performers every night except Sunday. Excellent dinners are served before the first show.

ROCK CLUBS

Central Saloon (⊠ 207 1st Ave. S, ☎ 206/622–0209) an often crowded club in Pioneer Square, presents local and national rock acts. **Crocodile Cafe** (⊠ 2200 2nd Ave., ☎ 206/448–2114) rocks with live local groups from Tuesday through Saturday. **Mo'Roc' N Cafe** (⊠ 925 E. Pike St., ☎ 206/323–2373) presents punk rock, alternative, and other music. At the **OK Hotel** (⊠ 212 Alaskan Way S, ☎ 206/621–7903) you'll find grunge, acoustic, jazz, and even poetry readings.

The Arts

Friday's editions of the *Seattle Times* and the *Post-Intelligencer* list the coming week's events. *Seattle Weekly,* which hits newsstands on Wednesday, has detailed arts coverage.

To charge tickets, call **TicketMaster** (☎ 206/628–0888). **Ticket/Ticket,** with two locations (⊠ 401 Broadway E; and 1st Ave. and Pike St.; ☎ 206/324–2744), sells half-price same-day tickets for cash only.

DANCE

The **Pacific Northwest Ballet** (⊠ Opera House, Seattle Center, ☎ 206/441–2424) is a resident company and school that presents 60–70 performances annually.

MUSIC

The **Seattle Symphony** (⊠ Opera House, Seattle Center, ☎ 206/443–4747) presents some 120 concerts September–June in and around town. A new $99 million Symphony Hall at Second Avenue and University Street is set to open for the 1998–99 season. **Northwest Chamber Orchestra** (☎ 206/343–0445), the Northwest's only professional chamber orchestra, presents a full spectrum of music, from Baroque to modern, at various venues.

OPERA

The **Seattle Opera** (⊠ Opera House, Seattle Center, ☎ 206/389–7600), considered one of the top companies in America, presents five productions during its August–May season.

THEATER

The **Seattle Repertory Theater** (⊠ Bagley Wright Theater, Seattle Center, 155 Mercer St., ☎ 206/443–2222) presents high-quality programming from classics to new works in nine productions during its October–May season. The **New City Arts Center** (⊠ 1634 11th Ave., ☎ 206/323–6800) is home to experimental performances by the resident company in conjunction with national and international artists. The **Empty Space Theater** (⊠ 3509 Freemont Ave. N, ☎ 206/547–7500) has a strong reputation for introducing new playwrights. The **Group Theatre** (⊠ Seattle Center, Center House, lower level, ☎ 206/441–1299) presents socially provocative works by both old and new artists of varied cultures and colors. **A Contemporary Theater** (ACT; ⊠ 7th Ave. and Union St., ☎ 206/292–7676) develops works by new playwrights.

Outdoor Activities and Sports

Spectator Sports

Baseball: Seattle Mariners (✉ Kingdome, 201 S. King St., ☎ 206/628–3555).

Basketball: Seattle SuperSonics (✉ Key Arena, 1st Ave. N, ☎ 206/281–5850).

Football: Seahawks (✉ Kingdome, ☎ 206/827–9777).

Shopping

Shopping Centers

City Centre (✉ 1420 5th Ave., ☎ 206/467–9670), a gleaming marble tower, houses upscale shops such as Ann Taylor and Barneys of New York. **Westlake Center** (✉ 1601 5th Ave., ☎ 206/467–1600) is a three-story steel-and-glass building with 80 upscale shops and covered walkways that connect it to branches of Seattle's major department stores, Nordstrom and the Bon.

Food Market

Pike Place Market (☞ Exploring Seattle, *above*), a partially open-air market, has a wide selection of fresh meat, seafood, produce, flowers, and crafts available from vendors' stalls.

Specialty Stores

ANTIQUES AND JEWELRY

Antique Importers (✉ 620 Alaskan Way, ☎ 206/628–8905) carries mostly English oak and pine antiques. **Fourth & Pike Building** (✉ 4th Ave. and Pike St.) houses many retail-wholesale jewelers. **Turgeon-Raine Jewelers** (✉ 1407 5th Ave., ☎ 206/447–9488) is an exceptional store with a sophisticated but friendly staff.

MEN'S APPAREL

Mario's (✉ 1513 6th Ave., ☎ 206/223–1461) carries a good mix of trendy and designer fashions for men.

OUTDOOR WEAR AND EQUIPMENT

Eddie Bauer (✉ 5th Ave. and Union St., ☎ 206/622–2766) specializes in classic sports and outdoor apparel. **REI** (✉ 222 Yale Ave. N, ☎ 206/223–1944) sells clothing and outdoor equipment in an 80,000-square-ft renovated warehouse that includes a climbing wall, an outdoor bicycle trail, an indoor foot trail and a rain room.

TOYS

Magic Mouse Toys (✉ 603 1st Ave., ☎ 206/682–8097) has two floors stuffed with toys, from small windups to giant plush animals.

WOMEN'S APPAREL

Boutique Europa (✉ 1420 5th Ave., ☎ 206/587–6292) carries sophisticated European clothing. On the edge of the Pike Place Market, **Local Brilliance** (✉ 1535 1st Ave., ☎ 206/343–5864) showcases fashions by local designers. **Nubia's** (✉ 1507 6th Ave., ☎ 206/622–0297) is a small shop with an excellent selection of unconstructed knits for women's business and casual wear as well as belts, beads, and other accessories.

Side Trip to Whidbey and the San Juan Islands

Whidbey Island and the San Juan Islands are the jewels of Puget Sound. Except for Whidbey, they are reachable only by ferry, airplane, or private boat; so the islands beckon souls longing for a quiet change of pace, whether kayaking in a cove, walking a deserted beach, or nestling by the fire in an old farmhouse. Bicycling, boating, fishing, and camping are favored activities on the islands, but the small villages also teem with antiques shops and art galleries. The **San Juan Tourism Cooperative** (✉ Box 65, Lopez 98261, ☎ 360/468–3663) can provide information.

Arriving and Departing

BY PLANE

From Seattle-Tacoma International Airport, **Harbor Airlines** (☎ 800/359–3220) flies to San Juan Island and Whidbey Island. **Kenmore Air** (☎ 206/486–1257 or 800/543–9595) flies sea planes from Lake Union in Seattle to the San Juan Islands. **West Isle Air** (☎ 360/293–4691 or 800/874–4434) flies to San Juan Island from Anacortes and Bellingham.

BY CAR

By car from Seattle, drive north on I–5 to La Conner; go west on Route 536 to Route 20 and follow signs to Anacortes; then pick up the ferry for the San Juan Islands. Whidbey Island can be reached by ferry from Mukilteo, or you can drive from Seattle along I–5, then head west on Highway 20 and cross the dramatic Deception Pass via the bridge at the north end of the island.

BY FERRY

The **Washington State Ferry System** (☎ 206/464–6400 or 800/843–3779) provides car and passenger service from Mukilteo, on Highway 525 30 mi north of Seattle, to Clinton, on Whidbey Island, and from Anacortes, about 90 mi north of Seattle, to the San Juan Islands. The **San Juan Islands Shuttle Express** (✉ Alaska Ferry Terminal, 355 Harris Ave., No. 105, Bellingham 98225, ☎ 888/373–8522 or 360/671–1137) provides daily passenger service from Bellingham to Orcas Island and San Juan Island's Friday Harbor along with a narrative talk on the wildlife and natural history of the area. You can also take a three-hour whale-watching trip out of Friday Harbor.

What to See and Do

Whidbey Island is mostly rural, with undulating hills, gentle beaches, and little coves. **Langley** is a quaint town that caters to locals and tourists with a number of inviting bed-and-breakfast inns and a handful of good restaurants, shops, and galleries. It sits atop a 50-ft bluff overlooking the southeastern shore. A little over halfway up 50-mi-long Whidbey Island is **Coupeville**, site of many restored Victorian houses and one of the largest National Historic Districts in the state. The town was founded in 1852 by Captain Thomas Coupe, whose house, built the next year, is one of the state's oldest.

Ebey's Landing National Historic Reserve (☎ 360/678–4636), headquartered in Coupeville, is a 17,000-acre area including Keystone, Coupeville, and Penn Cove. Established by Congress in 1978, the reserve is the first and largest of its kind, dotted with 91 nationally registered historic structures along with farmland, parks, and trails. At **Deception Pass State Park** (☎ 360/675–2417), at the north end of Whidbey Island, take in the spectacular view and stroll among the madrona trees, with their peeling reddish-brown bark.

The other major islands are **Lopez Island,** with old orchards, weathered barns, and sheep and cow pastures; **Shaw Island,** where Franciscan nuns in traditional habits run the ferry dock; **Orcas,** a large, mountainous horseshoe-shape island with marvelous hilltop views and several good restaurants; and **San Juan Island,** with the colorful, active waterfront town of Friday Harbor. Lopez, Orcas, and San Juan all feature a number of excellent bed-and-breakfast accommodations.

Dining

For price ranges *see* Chart 1(B) *in* On the Road with Fodor's.

$$–$$$ ✕ **Christina's.** Some of the best salmon entrées in Washington compete for diners' attention with romantic water views at this Orcas Island favorite. ⊠ *N. Beach Rd. and Horseshoe Hwy., Eastsound,* ☎ *360/376–4904. AE, DC, MC, V. Closed Tues. Oct.–mid-June. No lunch.*

$$$ ✕ **Duck Soup Inn.** Everything served at this San Juan Island restaurant along a country road is made from scratch—fresh bread, Mediterranean-inspired entrées, vegetarian dishes, and delicious ice cream. ⊠ *3090 Roche Harbor Rd., near town of Roche Harbor,* ☎ *360/378–4878. Closed Mon.–Tues. Apr.–Oct., and Nov.–Mar. No lunch.*

$$ ✕ **Garibyan Brothers Café Langley.** You'll find Greek fare in a casual atmosphere at this Whidbey Island eatery. ⊠ *113 1st St., Langley,* ☎ *360/221–3090. MC, V. Closed Tues. in winter. No lunch Tues.*

Side Trip to Tacoma

Seattleites often make fun of the industrial aromas emanating from Tacoma, but the city has a strong cultural scene, some renovated historical theaters, wonderfully restored residential neighborhoods, fine bay views, and a world-class zoo.

Visitor Information

Tacoma–Pierce County Visitors and Convention Bureau (⊠ 906 Broadway, Tacoma 98402, ☎ 253/627–2836).

Arriving and Departing

Tacoma is about 35 mi south of Seattle via I–5. Sea-Tac Airport is about a 30-minute drive away. The city is served by major bus, train, and air carriers.

What to See and Do

Union Station (⊠ 1717 Pacific Ave., ☎ 253/343–7932) is an heirloom from the golden age of railroads, when Tacoma was the western terminus for the transcontinental Northern Pacific Railroad. Built by Reed and Stem, the architects of New York City's Grand Central Station, the massive copper-domed Beaux Arts depot was opened in 1911. It now houses federal district courts. The rotunda is open to the public and displays a large exhibit of Dale Chihuly art glass. The **Washington State Historical Society Museum** (⊠ 1911 Pacific Ave., ☎ 253/272–3500) near Union Station houses exhibits on the natural, Native American, pioneer, maritime, and industrial history of the state.

Downtown on Broadway is **Antique Row,** with antiques shops, two restored theaters, and funky boutiques. The **Tacoma Art Museum** (⊠ 1123 Pacific Ave., ☎ 253/272–4258) contains a rich collection of American and French paintings, as well as Chinese jades and imperial robes. **Wright Park** (⊠ 6th and Division Sts., I and J Sts.) is a 30-acre park just north of downtown. Within the park is the **W. W. Seymour Botanical Conservatory** (⊠ 316 S. G St., ☎ 253/591–5330), a Victorian-style greenhouse with an extensive collection of exotic flora.

Northeast of Tacoma, the 700-acre **Point Defiance Park** is one of the largest urban parks in the country. The **Point Defiance Zoo and Aquarium,** founded in 1888, is now one of the top zoos in America. ⊠ *5400 N. Pearl St.,* ☎ *253/591–5337.*

Dining

For price ranges *see* Chart 1(B) *in* On the Road with Fodor's.

$ ✕ **Swiss.** You'll find good pub fare and Northwest microbrews at this restaurant in a distinctive 1913 building that was once Tacoma's Swiss

Hall. ⊠ *1904 S. Jefferson Ave.,* ☎ *253/572–2821. Reservations not accepted. No credit cards.*

Side Trip to Olympia

Arriving and Departing
Olympia is on I–5, about 60 mi southwest of Seattle and 25 mi southwest of Tacoma.

What to See and Do
Olympia, Washington's state capital, is fairly quiet except when the legislature is in session. You can tour the **Legislative Building** (⊠ Capitol Way between 10th and 14th Aves.), a handsome Romanesque structure with a 287-ft dome that closely resembles the capitol in that *other* Washington. Southeast of the Legislative Building is the modern **State Library,** with collections of works by Northwest authors and art by Mark Tobey and Kenneth Callahan.

Dining
For price ranges *see* Chart 1(B) *in* On the Road with Fodor's.

$$$ ✕ **La Petite Maison** serves imaginative Pacific Northwest cuisine with a European touch in a converted 1890s farmhouse. ⊠ *2005 Ascension Way,* ☎ *360/943–8812.*

THE OLYMPIC PENINSULA

The rugged Olympic Peninsula forms the northwest corner of the continental United States. Much of it is wilderness, with the Olympic National Park and National Forest at its heart. The peninsula has tremendous variety: the wild Pacific shore, the sheltered waters along the Hood Canal and the Strait of Juan de Fuca, the rivers of the Olympic's rain forests, and the towering Olympic Mountains.

Visitor Information

North Olympic Peninsula Visitor & Convention Bureau (⊠ Box 670, Port Angeles 98362, ☎ 360/452–8552 or 800/942–4042). **Port Angeles:** Visitor center (⊠ 121 E. Railroad Ave., 98362, ☎ 360/452–2363).

Arriving and Departing

By Bus
Olympic Van Tours and Bus Lines (☎ 360/452–3858) serves the Olympic Peninsula.

By Car
U.S. 101 loops around the Olympic Peninsula, which can be reached from Olympia via Routes 8 and 101 and from Tacoma, 50 mi away, via Highway 16.

By Ferry
The **Washington State Ferry System** (☎ 206/464–6400 or 800/843–3779) provides car and passenger service from downtown Seattle to Bremerton. The **Black Ball Ferry Line** (☎ 360/457–4491) operates between Port Angeles, on the Olympic Peninsula, and Victoria, British Columbia.

By Plane
Horizon Air (☎ 800/547–9308) flies into Port Angeles from the Seattle-Tacoma airport. Private charter airlines fly into Port Angeles, Forks, and Hoquiam.

Exploring the Olympic Peninsula

From Olympia go west along Highway 101 and Routes 8 and 12 to **Gray's Harbor** and the twin seaports of **Hoquiam** and **Aberdeen.** From Hoquiam you can drive north on **Route 109,** which sticks to the coast and passes through resorts and ample beach areas such as Copalis Beach, Pacific Beach, and Moclips. Route 109 eventually leads to the Quinault Indian Reservation and the tribal center of **Taholah,** whose main draw is pristine, expansive scenery.

Route 109 dead-ends at Taholah, and you must backtrack to return to U.S. 101. About 20 mi north of Aberdeen on U.S. 101, 1½ mi north of the Hoh River Bridge, is Hoh River Rainforest Road, which goes

★ east to the **Hoh Rain Forest** (☎ 360/374–6925 or 360/452–4501), part of the Olympic National Park. This complex ecosystem of conifers, hardwoods, grasses, mosses, and other flora shelters such wildlife as elks, otters, beavers, salmon, and flying squirrels. The average annual rainfall here is 145 inches. The Hoh Visitor Center (often unstaffed September–May) at the campground and the ranger station at road's end (18 mi east of U.S. 101) have interpretive displays and information on nature trails.

On U.S. 101 north of Hoh River Rainforest Road is the small logging town of **Forks,** renowned for its three-day Fourth of July celebration, which features logging-truck parades, fireworks, and a demolition derby. From Forks, La Push Road leads west about 15 mi to **La Push,** a coastal village and the tribal center of the Quileute Indians. Several points along this road have short trails with access to the ocean, fabulous views of nearby islands, and dramatic rock formations.

Returning to U.S. 101, which swings to the east as you go north from Forks, you go through the **Sol Duc River Valley,** famous for its salmon fishing. The **Soleduck Fish Hatchery** (☎ 360/327–3246) has interpretive displays on fish breeding. A few miles past the tiny town of Sappho are the deep azure waters of **Lake Crescent.** The area has abundant campsites, resorts, trails, canoeing, and fishing. The original lodge buildings (☞ Dining and Lodging, *below*)—constructed in 1915 and now well worn but comfortable—are still in use.

Twelve miles south of Lake Crescent on Soleduck Road (which meets U.S. 101 1 mi west of the western tip of Lake Crescent) is an entrance to Olympic National Park and to **Sol Duc Hot Springs,** where you can dip into three hot sulfur pools ranging from 98°F to 104°F. ☎ 360/327–3583. *Closed Oct.–mid-May.*

On the northern tip of the Olympic Peninsula, on U.S. 101E, is **Port Angeles,** a bustling commercial fishing port and a ferry access route to Canada. The town hosts the visitor center for Olympic National Park (☞ National Parks, *above*), at 3002 Mt. Angeles Road. A bus will take you or you can drive up the road to **Hurricane Ridge,** 17 mi south of Port Angeles, which rises nearly a mile above sea level as it enters the park and yields spectacular views of the Olympics, the Strait of Juan de Fuca, and Vancouver Island.

Seventeen miles east of Port Angeles on U.S. 101 is the charming town of **Sequim** (pronounced *squim*). Animal life present and past can be found at the **Museum and Arts Center** (✉ 175 W. Cedar St., ☎ 360/683–8110) in the Sequim–Dungeness Valley, where you can view the remains of an Ice Age mastodon and exhibits on the early Klallam Indians and the town's pioneer history. In the fertile plain at the mouth of the Dungeness River, 4 mi northwest of Sequim, the **Dungeness Na-**

Western Washington

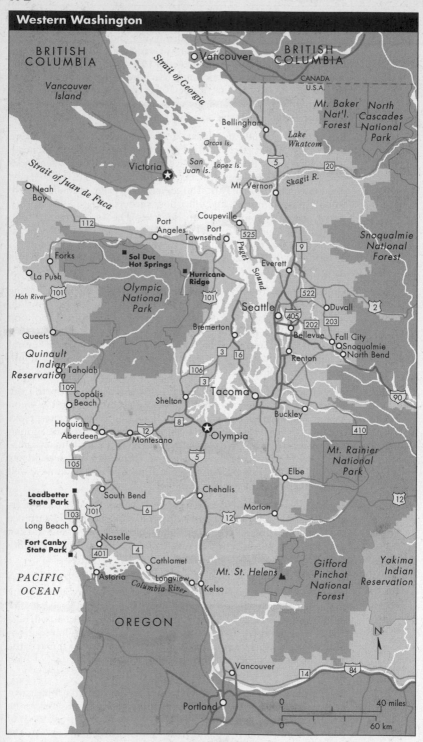

tional Wildlife Refuge (☎ 360/457–8451) is home to thousands of migratory waterfowl, as well as clams, oysters, and seals.

About 10 mi east of Sequim, Route 20 turns northward 12 mi to **Port Townsend.** Its waterfront is lined with carefully restored brick buildings from the 1870s that house shops and restaurants. High on the bluff are large gingerbread-trim Victorian homes, many of which have been turned into B&Bs. Driving south on U.S. 101 through the sawmill town of **Shelton** will bring you back to Olympia.

Shopping

Confirmed shoppers head for the waterfront boutiques and stores of **Port Townsend,** all of which feature Northwest arts and crafts.

Outdoor Activities and Sports

Biking

Biking is popular in the flatter parts of Port Townsend and within Olympic National Park. There are bike-rental shops in Port Townsend and other resort areas on the peninsula.

Fishing

Trout and salmon are abundant in rivers throughout the peninsula. Contact the area tourist office (☞ Visitor Information, *above*) for details.

Hiking

Ocean and mountain areas contain hiking trails for all levels. Contact the **Olympic National Forest** (☎ 360/288–2525) or **Olympic National Park Visitor Center** (⊠ 3002 Mt. Angeles Rd., Port Angeles 98362, ☎ 360/452–0330).

Skiing

Hurricane Ridge (☞ Exploring the Olympic Peninsula, *above*) has 25 mi of cross-country ski trails.

Beaches

Beaches abound on the Olympic Peninsula, though the ones on tribal or private lands are not generally accessible. Remember that the North Pacific is not for swimming—unless you wear a wet suit. For walking and exploring, the main beaches are Copalis and Pacific, north of Hoquiam; a series of scenic, unnamed beaches north of Kalaloch; and Rialto Beach, near La Push.

Dining and Lodging

For price ranges *see* Charts 1 (B) and 2 (B) *in* On the Road with Fodor's.

Gig Harbor

$$ ✕ **Neville's Shoreline.** This pleasant marina restaurant specializes in
★ seafood—try the pan-fried oysters—and serves a Sunday brunch. ⊠ *8827 N. Harborview Dr.,* ☎ *206/851–9822. AE, DC, MC, V.*

$$–$$$ ☷ **Sandpiper Beach Resort.** The four-story Sandpiper complex has at-
★ tractive suites; most have a sitting room, a dining area, a fireplace, a small kitchen, and a porch. With no in-room phones, no pool, no TVs, and no restaurant, this is the place to get away from it all. ⊠ *4159 Rte. 109, 1½ mi south of Pacific Beach (Box A), 98571,* ☎ *360/276–4580 or 800/567–4737,* ℻ *360/276–4464. 30 rooms. MC, V.*

Port Angeles

$$$ ✕ **C'est Si Bon.** This locally famous spot run by a French couple is probably the most elegant restaurant on the decidedly informal Olympic Peninsula. The walls are adorned with art, the tables with fine linen, and windows offer a good view of the flower-laden terrace and the Olympic Mountains. The cuisine, of course, is French. ⊠ *23 Cedar Park Dr. (4 mi east of town),* ☎ *360/452–8888. Reservations essential. AE, D, MC, V. Closed Mon. No lunch.*

$$–$$$ ▥ **Sol Duc Hot Springs Resort.** This casual resort dates from the turn of the century. Some of the minimally outfitted cabins are rustic, while others are more modern. There are plenty of hiking trails in the area. ⊠ *12 mi south of U.S. 101 on Soleduck Rd. (Box 2169), 98362,* ☎ *360/327–3583,* FAX *360/327–3398. 32 units, camping and RV facilities. Restaurant, pool, 3 hot springs. AE, D, MC, V. Closed mid-Oct.– mid-May.*

$–$$ ▥ **Lake Crescent Lodge.** This old but comfortable accommodation with a big main lodge and small cabins overlooks the beautiful deep-blue Lake Crescent. Units in the lodge are minimal—some are dimly lighted, with bathrooms down the hall—but the setting makes up for sparse amenities. ⊠ *416 Lake Crescent Rd., Port Angeles, 98363,* ☎ *360/928–3211,* FAX *360/928–3253. 52 rooms, 47 with bath. Restaurant, boating, fishing. AE, DC, MC, V. Closed mid-Nov.–Apr.*

Port Townsend

$$ ✕ **Fountain Café.** This small café off the main tourist drag is one of
★ the best restaurants in town. You can count on seafood and pasta specialties with imaginative twists, such as oysters in an anchovy wine sauce. ⊠ *920 Washington St.,* ☎ *360/385–1364. MC, V.*

$ ✕ **Salal Café.** Featuring home-style cooking and daily specials, this restaurant shines among early morning breakfast joints. Try one of many variations on the blintze, crepe, or omelet for lunch. Seafood and regional American-style meals are good, portions ample, and prices reasonable. ⊠ *634 Water St.,* ☎ *360/385–6532. Reservations not accepted. MC, V. No dinner Tues.–Wed.*

$$$ ▥ **James House.** Commanding a spot on the bluff overlooking downtown and the waterfront, this antiques-filled Victorian B&B provides visitors with a great sense of how the well-heeled lived in the late 1800s. ⊠ *1238 Washington St., 98368,* ☎ *360/385–1238 or 800/385–1238. 12 rooms. AE, MC, V.*

$$ ▥ **Palace Hotel.** This friendly hotel in the historic section of downtown is pleasingly decorated to reflect its 1889 construction date and its one-time history as a bordello. The rooms have no phones, but they do have cable TV. ⊠ *1004 Water St., 98368,* ☎ *360/385–0773 or 800/962–0741,* FAX *360/385–0780. 15 units. Kitchenettes. AE, D, MC, V.*

Quinault

$$$ ▥ **Lake Quinault Lodge.** This deluxe lodge is set on a perfect glacial lake in the midst of the Olympic National Forest. Built in 1926 of cedar shingles, the lodge has delightfully decorated public rooms with antique reproductions and a fireplace. ⊠ *S. Shore Rd. (Box 7), 98575,* ☎ *360/288–2571,* FAX *360/288–2901. 92 rooms. Restaurant, bar, indoor pool, hot tub, sauna, recreation room. AE, MC, V.*

Campgrounds

Some of the best campgrounds within the Olympic National Park are **Hoh River** (☎ 206/220–7450), **Mora** (☎ 360/374–5460), and **Fairholm** (☎ 360/452–0330). Elsewhere on the peninsula are **Bogachiel State Park** (☎ 360/374–6356), near Forks (closed after dusk in winter); **Fort**

Flagler State Park (☎ 360/385–1259), near Port Townsend (closed for overnight camping November–February); **Ocean City State Park** (✉ 148 Rte. 115, Hoquiam 98550, ☎ 360/289–3553); and **Pacific Beach State Park** (☎ 360/276–4297). There is also camping at **Sol Duc Hot Springs Resort** (☞ Port Angeles, *above*).

LONG BEACH PENINSULA

If the waters of the Pacific and the Columbia River met in a less turbulent manner, a huge seaport might sit at the river's mouth. Instead, the entrance to the Columbia is sparsely populated, dotted with fishing villages and cranberry bogs. Although only a 3½-hour drive southwest of Seattle and two hours northwest of Portland, Long Beach Peninsula is worlds away from either city. Just north of the river's mouth, the peninsula separates the Pacific Ocean and Willapa Bay and is known for excellent bird-watching, beachcombing, hiking, and a handful of gourmet restaurants.

Visitor Information

Visitors Bureau (✉ Intersection of Hwys. 101 and 103, Seaview 98631, ☎ 360/642–2400 or 800/451–2542).

Arriving and Departing

By Car
Long Beach is accessible from the east via Highway 4, which connects with I–5 near Longview, and from the north and south via U.S. 101.

Exploring Long Beach Peninsula

U.S. 101 crosses the broad Columbia River between Astoria, Oregon, and Megler, Washington, in a high, graceful span. Just beyond, on Highway 103, is **Ilwaco,** a small fishing community of about 600. The **Ilwaco Heritage Museum** (✉ 115 S.E. Lake St., ☎ 360/642–3446) uses dioramas to present the history of southwestern Washington.

A couple of miles south of Ilwaco is the **Cape Disappointment Lighthouse,** first used in 1856 and one of the oldest lighthouses on the West Coast. The cape was named by an English fur trader in 1788 in honor of his unsuccessful attempt to find the Northwest Passage.

Fort Canby State Park (✉ 3 mi west of Ilwaco, off U.S. 101, ☎ 360/642–3078) was an active military installation until 1957, when it was turned over to the Washington State Parks and Recreation Commission. Now it is best known for great views of the Columbia River Bar during winter storms. The **Lewis & Clark Interpretive Center** (☎ 360/642–3029 or 360/642–3078) documents the 8,000-mi round-trip journey of the famous pair, from Wood River, Illinois, to the mouth of the Columbia.

The town of **Long Beach** has beach activities and an old-fashioned amusement park with go-carts and bumper cars. About halfway up the peninsula is **Ocean Park,** the area's commercial center. A few miles north of Ocean Park is **Oysterville,** established as an oystering town in 1854. When the native shellfish were fished to extinction, a Japanese oyster was introduced, but the town never made a comeback. Tides have washed away homes, businesses, and a Methodist church, but the village still exists. Maps inside the vestibule of the restored **Oysterville Church** direct you through town, which is now on the National Register of Historic Places. At the northern tip of the peninsula is **Leadbetter State Park** (☞ National and State Parks, *above*).

Shopping

The **Bookvendor** (⊠ 101 Pacific Ave., Long Beach, ☎ 360/642–2702) stocks children's books, classics, and travel books. **North Head Gallery** (⊠ 600 S. Pacific Ave., Long Beach, ☎ 360/642–8884) has the largest selection of Elton Bennett originals, plus Bennett reproductions and works from other Northwest artists.

Outdoor Activities and Sports

Biking

Good areas for bicycling on the peninsula include Fort Canby and North Head roads, Sandridge Road to Ocean Park and Oysterville, U.S. 101 from Naselle to Seaview, and Route 103 along Willapa Bay. There are rentals available in virtually every town.

Fishing

Salmon, rock cod, lingcod, flounder, perch, sea bass, and sturgeon are popular and plentiful for fishing. A guide is available from the **Port of Ilwaco** (⊠ Box 307, 98624, ☎ 360/642–3145). The clamming season varies depending on the supply; for details call the **Washington Department of Fisheries** (☎ 360/902–2250) or the **fisheries' shellfish lab** (☎ 360/665–4166). There are tackle shops all over Long Beach Peninsula, and most sell the necessary fishing licenses.

Golf

Peninsula Golf Course (☎ 360/642–2828) has nine holes at the north end of Long Beach. **Surfside Golf Course** (☎ 360/665–4148), 2 mi north of Ocean Park, has nine holes.

Hiking

Hiking trails are available at **Fort Canby State Park** (☞ Exploring Long Beach Peninsula, *above*) and **Leadbetter State Park** (☞ National and State Parks, *above*).

Dining and Lodging

For price ranges *see* Charts 1 (B) and 2 (B) *in* On the Road with Fodor's.

Ilwaco

$$$ 🏨 **Chickadee Inn.** This B&B is set in a renovated New England–style church. Guest accommodations—most of them upstairs in the old Sunday-school rooms—are cozily furnished with antiques, armoires, and eyelet or printed chintz curtains and coverlets. ⊠ *120 Williams St. NE, 98624,* ☎ *360/642–8686. 8 rooms, 7 with bath. AE, MC, V.*

Long Beach

$ ✕ **My Mom's Pie Kitchen.** Though this place in a mobile home keeps limited hours, it's worth dropping by for such pies as banana whipped cream, chocolate almond, sour-cream raisin, and fresh raspberry. Also on the menu are clam chowder and quiche. ⊠ *Hwy. 103 and 12th St. S,* ☎ *360/642–2342. MC, V. Closed Mon.–Wed. No dinner.*

Seaview

$$$ ✕ **Shoalwater Restaurant.** The dining room at the Shelburne Inn (☞
★ Lodging, *below*) has been acclaimed by *Gourmet* and *Bon Appétit.* Seafood brought from the fishing boats to the restaurant's back door is as fresh as it can be; mushrooms and salad greens are gathered from the peninsula's woods and gardens. ⊠ *Pacific Hwy. and N. 45th St.,* ☎ *360/642–4142. AE, MC, V.*

$$ ✕ **42nd Street Cafe.** The daily-changing fare here runs the gamut from deep-fried seafood to expensive gourmet dishes—the iron-skillet-fried chicken is especially popular. ⊠ *Hwy. 103 and 42nd St.,* ☎ *360/642–2323. MC, V.*

$$$ ⊞ **Shelburne Inn.** This bright and cheerful, antiques-filled inn built in 1896 is on the National Register of Historic Places. It is also right on the highway, which can make it noisy, so the best picks are rooms on the west side. ⊠ *4415 Pacific Way (Box 250), Seaview 98644,* ☎ *360/642–2442 or 800/466–1896,* ℻ *360/642–8904. 15 rooms. Restaurant, pub. AE, MC, V.*

$ ⊞ **Sou'wester.** A stay here is a bohemian experience. Choose from rooms and apartments in a historic lodge, in cabins, or in classic mobile-home units on the surrounding property just behind the beach. The lodge was built in 1892 as the summer retreat for a wealthy businessman and politician from Portland. ⊠ *Beach Access Rd. (Box 102), 98644,* ☎ *360/642–2542. 3 rooms share bath, 4 cabins, 8 trailers. D, MC, V.*

Campgrounds

Camping is available at **Fort Canby State Park** (⊠ Box 488, Ilwaco 98624; ☞ Exploring Long Beach Peninsula, *above*).

ELSEWHERE IN WASHINGTON

The North Cascades

Visitor Information

Leavenworth Chamber of Commerce (⊠ 894 Hwy. 2, 98826, ☎ 509/548–5807).

Arriving and Departing

Only two highways pierce the Cascade Range in northern Washington and one—the North Cascades Highway (Highway 20) through the North Cascades National Park—is closed winters. Highway 2 from Spokane crosses Stevens Pass at Leavenworth and continues west to I–90. There is no passenger train or air service to the North Cascades, but the area is served by Greyhound buses, which stop at Leavenworth.

What to See and Do

Cross-country skiers flock to the eastern slopes of the North Cascades for high dry-powder snow from early November until May. The small Bavarian-theme town of Leavenworth is especially popular; trails on the local golf course are groomed for skiers. Mission Ridge downhill ski area is nearby. In summer rafters can run the rapids of the Wenatchee River, or there's hiking above the tree line in the nearby **Wenatchee National Forest** to Enchantment Lakes; an advance permit is required from the Leavenworth Ranger Station (☎ 800/452–4687).

Yakima Valley

Visitor Information

Yakima Valley Visitor and Convention Bureau (⊠ 10 N. 8th St., Yakima, 98901-2515, ☎ 509/575–1300).

Arriving and Departing

The valley is along I–82 between Yakima and the tri-city area of Richland, Kennewick, and Pasco. From Seattle drive east on I–90 to Ellensburg and south on Highway 97 (about 180 mi). Yakima has a small airport with limited service from Seattle, Spokane, and Portland on United Airlines. There is no passenger train service, but the area is served by Greyhound buses, which stop in Yakima, Toppenish, Sunnyside, Wapato, and Prosser.

What to See and Do

Aside from the views of 12,688-ft Mt. Adams and 14,410-ft Mt. Rainier to the west, the main attractions here are the dozens of small wineries that dot this fertile area. Some of the best-known vineyards are **Hogue Cellars, Château Ste. Michelle,** and **Covey Run Winery.** The **Yakima Valley Wine Growers Association** (⊠ Box 39, Grandview 98930, ☎ 509/882–1223) publishes maps of the region and a brochure that lists local wineries with tasting-room tours.

Spokane

Spokane (pronounced Spo-*can*) seems like a bit of the Midwest dropped into the Northwest. The 400,000 residents of the area don't necessarily embrace Seattle as the state's cultural capital or Olympia as the seat of government. Wedged against the Idaho border (which locals cross regularly in search of outdoor recreation), Spokane is separated from Seattle by a good 300 mi and the formidable Cascade Range.

Arriving and Departing

Spokane International Airport is served by Horizon, Northwest, Alaska, Delta, and United airlines. Amtrak and Greyhound both serve Spokane. By car Spokane can be reached by I–90 (east–west) and Highway 195 (north–south).

What to See and Do

In town the main attraction is **Riverfront Park** (⊠ 507 N. Howard St., ☎ 509/625–6600), 100 acres covering several islands in the Spokane River and including a spectacular falls, especially during spring runoff in March. Developed from old downtown railroad yards to be the site of the Expo '74 world's fair, Riverfront Park retains one of the ultra-modernist buildings from that exposition, which houses an IMAX theater, a skating rink (winters only), and exhibition space. At the southern edge of the park, the 1909 carousel hand-carved by master builder Charles Looff is a local landmark. In sharp architectural contrast to Riverfront Park's Expo '74 building is the 1902 **Great Northern Railroad Station,** nearly at the center of the park near Washington Street, with its tall stone clock tower.

Two miles south on Grand Boulevard at 18th Avenue, **Manito Park** has a formal English garden, a conservatory, rose and perennial gardens, a Japanese garden complete with ponds stocked with koi, and a duck pond; it's a pleasant place to stroll in summer; in winter bring ice skates for a turn or two on the frozen duck pond.

Cheney Cowles Museum (⊠ 2316 W. 1st Ave., ☎ 509/456–3931) displays pioneer and mining relics. Open for viewing next door is the museum-run Campbell House, a mining-era residence.

Dining

$$$ ✕ **Patsy Clark's.** This elegant restaurant is housed in one of Spokane's finest mansions. Its marble was shipped in from Italy, wood carvings and clocks from England, a mural from France, and a spectacular stained-glass window from Tiffany & Co. Diners eat at Patsy Clark's as much for the ambience as for the mostly American cuisine, which includes a New York steak with a sour-mash-whiskey demiglace. ⊠ *2208 W. 2nd Ave.,* ☎ *509/838–8300. AE, D, DC, MC, V.*

$$$ ✕ **Luna.** The seasonal cuisine here has strong southwestern and Californian influences. The focus on fruits and vegetables is natural, as the

building used to be a produce market. ⊠ *5620 S. Perry St.,* ☎ *509/ 448–2383. AE, D, MC, V.*

$$ ✕ **Clinkerdagger's.** In a building that housed a flour mill in Spokane's early days, Clinks, as it's known locally, has a fine view of the Spokane River and Riverfront Park to the south. When fresh seafood is available, there might be four or five specials. ⊠ *621 W. Mallon Ave.,* ☎ *509/328–5965. AE, DC, MC, V.*

Lodging

$$–$$$ ⊞ **Cavanaugh's Inn at the Park.** This hotel's greatest asset is its location, adjacent to Riverfront Park and a two-block walk from the downtown shopping district. All five stories in the main building open onto the spacious central-atrium lobby; more guest rooms are in two newer wings. ⊠ *303 W. North River Dr., 99201,* ☎ *509/326–8000 or 800/843–4667,* ☎ *509/325–7329. 402 rooms. Restaurant, bar, café. AE, D, DC, MC, V.*

The Arts

The **Spokane Symphony,** under the direction of Brazilian-born conductor Fabio Mechetti, plays a season of classical and pops concerts from September to April in the Opera House (⊠ 601 W. Riverside Dr., ☎ 509/624–1200). **Interplayers Ensemble** (⊠ 174 S. Howard St., ☎ 509/455–7529) is a professional theater company with productions October–June.

Outdoor Activities and Sports

Just 30 mi east of Spokane on I–90 is Idaho's **Lake Coeur d'Alene** (☞ Idaho), which has fishing, camping, hiking, water sports, and resort accommodations. A walking path named the Centennial Trail flanks the Spokane River continuously from west of downtown Spokane to east of Coeur d'Alene.

GOLF

The most challenging Spokane golf course is the 18-hole **Creek at Qualchan** (⊠ 301 E. Meadow La., ☎ 509/448–9317).

SKIING

Skiers flock to **Mt. Spokane** (⊠ Hwy. 206, 31 mi north of Spokane, ☎ 509/238–6281 or 509/238–6845 for cross-country ski area), which holds the modest 49 Degrees North (⊠ Hwy. 395, 58 mi north of Spokane near Chewelah, ☎ 509/935–6649) downhill resort and 11 mi of groomed cross-country ski trails. A state Sno-Park pass, available at the resort or numerous outlets throughout the state, is required at the cross-country ski areas.

SPECTATOR SPORTS

Baseball: Spokane Indians (⊠ Seafirst Stadium, Broadway and Havana St., ☎ 509/535–2922) play in the Class A Northwest League.

Hockey: Spokane Chiefs (⊠ Spokane Arena, 701 Mallon Ave., at N. Howard St., ☎ 509/328–0450) play in the Western Hockey League.

The Palouse

Visitor Information

Walla Walla: Chamber of Commerce (⊠ 29 E. Sumach St., 99362, ☎ 509/525–0850). **Pullman:** Chamber of Commerce (⊠ 415 N. Grande Ave., 99163, ☎ 509/334–3565).

Arriving and Departing

From Spokane drive south on Highway 195 to Pullman or at Colfax take Highways 26, 127, and then 12 to Walla Walla. Pullman has a small airport that it shares with Moscow, Idaho, 8 mi to the east, with

limited service from Lewiston, Idaho. There is no passenger-train service, but the area is served by Greyhound buses, which stop in Pullman and Walla Walla.

What to See and Do

Those interested in Northwest history will find the Palouse particularly rich. The Lewis and Clark expedition passed through in 1805,
and in 1836 missionary Marcus Whitman built a medical mission 7
mi west of present-day Walla Walla. A band of Cayuse Indians mas-
sacred Whitman and more than a dozen other settlers in 1847; a **visitor center** (✉ Off U.S. 12, 7 mi west of Walla Walla, ☎ 509/529–2761)
now marks the site. Nearby **Fort Walla Walla Park** (✉ 755 Myra Rd.,
☎ 509/525–7703) has 14 historic buildings and a pioneer museum.

The U.S. Calvary lost an important battle to the Indians on the site of
the **Steptoe Battlefield,** north of Pullman on Highway 195 near Ros-
alia. On Highway 12 between Colfax and Walla Walla, **Dayton** is
worth a stop just to see the impressive 88 Victorian buildings there listed
on the National Register of Historic Places. A brochure with two self-
guided walking tours of Dayton is available from the Dayton Chamber of Commerce (✉ 166 E. Main St., ☎ 509/382–4825).

History buffs can take a walking or bicycle tour of Walla Walla, one
of the earliest settlements in the Inland Northwest. Maps are available
from the Chamber of Commerce (☞ Visitor Information, *above*). **Pioneer Park** (✉ E. Alder St.), which has a fine aviary, was landscaped
by sons of Frederick Law Olmsted, who designed New York City's Central Park.

In winter skiers head southeast of Walla Walla to the Blue Mountains
and two small downhill and cross-country ski resorts, **Ski Bluewood**
(✉ Touchet River Rd., 21 mi south of Dayton, ☎ 509/382–4725) and
Spout Springs (✉ Hwy. 204, 3 mi south of Milton-Freewater, OR,
☎ 541/566–2164), in the Umatilla National Forest in Oregon.

Just north of the confluence with the Snake River, the Palouse River
gushes over a basalt cliff higher than Niagara Falls and drops 198 ft
into a steep-walled basin. Those who are sure-footed can hike to an
overlook above the falls, which are at their fastest during spring runoff
in March. Just downstream from the falls is the **Marmes Rock Shelter,**
where remains of the earliest-known inhabitants of North America,
dating back 10,000 years, were discovered by archaeologists.

12 Alaska and Hawai`i

Updated by
Steve Crohn
and Bill
Sherwonit

The two youngest states in the union, Alaska and Hawai`i, have more in common than their images might suggest. Both are thousands of miles from the U.S. mainland, both have dramatic landscapes, and both have significant populations of indigenous people. The two states also share a reliance on water—rivers, lakes, and the Pacific Ocean—which supplies a means of transportation, a source of food, and a host of recreational possibilities. Humpback whales also forge a link, summering in Alaska's Inside Passage and Prince William Sound, then swimming the 4,000 mi to Hawai`i to mate, calve, and nurse their young in the warm waters off Maui, the Big Island, and O`ahu. Although Alaskan and Hawaiian stores are stocked with the same goods found on the mainland, each state retains its unique exotic flavor.

Alaska, with its vast, austere wilderness and extreme weather, is demanding, but it rewards exploration with temperate summers, a frontier atmosphere, and flora and fauna rarely accessible elsewhere. From the nation's highest mountain, Mt. McKinley, to the islands, glaciers, and fjords of the southeast, the state provides superb hiking, boating, and fishing—and scenery as majestic and unspoiled as any in North America.

Hawai`i's gentle climate and tremendous diversity make it welcoming and endlessly fascinating. Each of the eight major volcanic islands has its own character—from lush tropical scenery and stunning white beaches to towering dramatic cliffs and rugged volcanic terrain. If you enjoy rampant commercialism in a spotlessly clean environment, O`ahu's

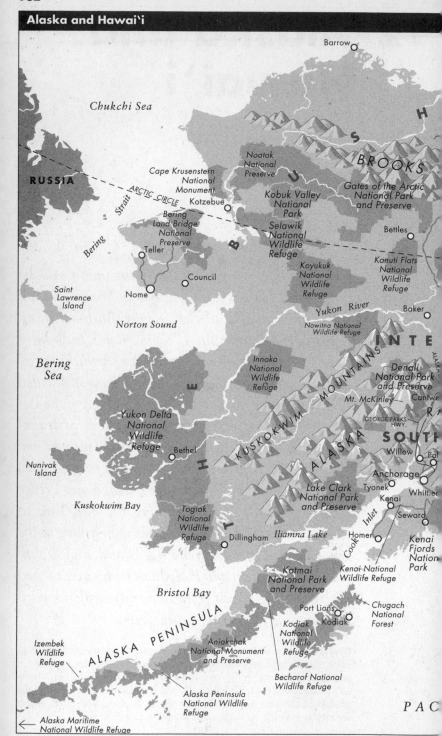

Barrow

Chukchi Sea

BROOKS

Noatak
National
Preserve

Cape Krusenstern
National
Monument

Gates of the Arctic
National Park
and Preserve

ARCTIC CIRCLE

Kotzebue

Kobuk Valley
National
Park

RUSSIA

Bering Strait

Bering
Land Bridge
National
Preserve

Selawik
National
Wildlife
Refuge

Bettles

Teller

Koyukuk
National
Wildlife
Refuge

Kanuti Flats
National
Wildlife
Refuge

Council

Nome

Saint
Lawrence
Island

Yukon River

Baker

Norton Sound

Nowitna National
Wildlife Refuge

INTE

Innoko
National
Wildlife
Refuge

Denali
National Park
and Preserve

*Bering
Sea*

Mt. McKinley

Cantwe

KUSKOKWIM MOUNTAINS

GEORGE PARKS
HWY.

SOUTH

R

Yukon Delta
National
Wildlife
Refuge

Willow

ALASKA

Bethel

Anchorage

Pal

Nunivak
Island

Tyonek

Whittier

Kenai

Kuskokwim Bay

Lake Clark
National Park
and Preserve

Seward

Togiak
National
Wildlife
Refuge

Cook Inlet

Homer

Kenai
Fjords
Nation
Park

Dillingham

Iliamna Lake

Katmai
National Park
and Preserve

Kenai National
Wildlife Refuge

Izembek
Wildlife
Refuge

Bristol Bay

Port Lions

Chugach
National
Forest

Kodiak
National
Wildlife
Refuge

Kodiak

ALASKA PENINSULA

Aniakchak
National Monument
and Preserve

Becharof National
Wildlife Refuge

PAC

Alaska Peninsula
National Wildlife
Refuge

Alaska Maritime
National Wildlife Refuge

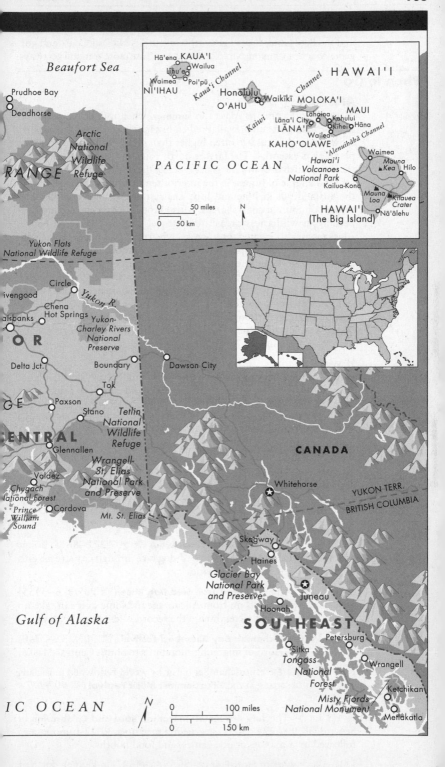

Beaufort Sea

Prudhoe Bay
Deadhorse

Arctic
National
Wildlife
RANGE   Refuge

Yukon Flats
National Wildlife Refuge

Circle
ivengood
Chena
airbanks   Hot Springs
Yukon R.
Yukon-
Charley Rivers
National
Preserve

O R

Delta Jct.   Boundary   Dawson City

Tok

G E   Paxson
Slano   Tetlin
National
Wildlife
ENTRAL   Refuge
Glennallen   Wrangell-
St. Elias
Valdez   National Park
Chugach   and Preserve
National Forest   Cordova
Prince   Mt. St. Elias
William
Sound

CANADA

Whitehorse   YUKON TERR.
BRITISH COLUMBIA

Skagway

Haines

Gulf of Alaska   Glacier Bay
National Park
and Preserve   Juneau

Hoonah   SOUTHEAST

Petersburg

Sitka   Tongass
National   Wrangell
Forest
Ketchikan
IC OCEAN   N   0   100 miles   Misty Fjords
National Monument   Metlakatla
0   150 km

KAUA'I
Hā'ena   Wailua
Waimea   Poi'pū   Kaua'i Channel   HAWAI'I
NI'IHAU
Honolulu   MOLOKA'I
O'AHU   Waikīkī   Channel
Kaiwi   MAUI
Lāna'i City   Lahaina
Kahului
LĀNA'I   Kīhei   Hāna
KAHO'OLAWE   Wailea
·Alenuihāhā Channel
PACIFIC OCEAN   Waimea
Hawai'i   Mauna
Volcanoes   ▲Kea   Hilo
National Park
Kailua-Kona   Mauna▲   Kilauea
Loa   Crater
0   50 miles   HAWAI'I   Nā'ālehu
0   50 km   N   (The Big Island)

Waikīkī is the place for you, but for pineapple plantations and active volcanoes, cheerful towns, and remote natural refuges, head for Maui and the Big Island. Kaua`i is worthwhile for its Na Pali Coast and gorgeous Waimea Canyon; Moloka`i and Lānai`i are more tranquil getaways.

When to Go

Alaska

Most visitors come to Alaska in **summer,** when milder temperatures and the midnight sun prevail. Predictably, hotels and campgrounds are crowded, and prices are often higher than in the off-season: Advance planning is essential. The farther north you go in summer, the longer the days; Fairbanks in June is never really dark, although the sun does set for a couple of hours. In the interior temperatures can easily reach the 80s and 90s in June and July. The rest of the state is cooler, and rain is common in coastal areas. Mosquitoes are fierce in summer, especially in wilderness areas; never travel without repellent. **Fall** in Alaska is an abbreviated three weeks, when trees and bushes blaze with color and daytime temperatures are still pleasant. It comes as early as late August in the interior and in September farther south. **Winters** are extremely cold in the interior (daytime temperatures of 0°F or lower), but many Alaskans prefer that season, because it opens up most of the state for travel by snowmobile and dogsled. In the southeast's temperate maritime climate, though, temperatures rarely dip below freezing. **Spring** is often a month-long soggy period of thawing and freezing, starting at the beginning of April.

Hawai`i

Hawai`i's long days of sunshine and fairly mild year-round temperatures allow for 12 months of pleasurable island travel. In resort areas near sea level the average afternoon temperature during the coldest months of December and January is 80°F; during the hottest months of August through October, temperatures can reach the low 90s. The northern shores of each island usually receive more rain than those in the south. Mid-December through mid-April and July through August are peak travel times, which means accommodation rates can be 10%–15% higher than those in other seasons.

Festivals and Seasonal Events

Alaska

MID-FEB.➤ The **Anchorage Fur Rendezvous** (☎ 907/277–8615) brings a three-day world-championship sled-dog race through city streets, plus hundreds of other winter activities.

EARLY MAR.➤ The **Iditarod Trail Sled Dog Race** (☎ 907/376–5155) officially covers 1,049 mi from Anchorage to Nome and can take up to two weeks to complete, though the record is less than 10 days.

EARLY MAY➤ **Kachemak Bay Shorebird Festival** (☎ 907/235–7740) celebrates the return of migrating shorebirds to South Central Alaska.

EARLY–MID-JUNE➤ Enjoy chamber music by world-renowned musicians in a beautiful setting at the **Sitka Summer Music Festival** (☎ 907/277–4852).

EARLY JULY➤ The **July 4th Mount Marathon Race and Celebration** in Seward (☎ 907/224–8051) is grueling race up a 3,022-ft mountain, followed by a parade, crafts, games, and food booths.

LATE AUG.➤ **Alaska State Fair** (☎ 907/745–4827) in Palmer, north of Anchorage, is a traditional celebration complete with cooking, handicrafts, livestock, and brewing competitions.

EARLY NOV.➤ Dancing, guitar playing, and fiddling are all part of the **Athabascan Fiddling Festival** (☎ 907/456–7491) in Fairbanks.

Hawai'i

LATE MAR.–EARLY APR.➤ Reserve tickets months in advance for the **Merrie Monarch Festival** (☎ 808/935–9168) in Hilo on the Big Island—a full week of hula competitions beginning Easter Sunday.

MAY 1➤ The statewide **Lei Day** is an annual flower-filled celebration with lei-making competitions and exquisite leis for sale.

JUNE➤ Body- and skim-board surfing steal the show at the **Pro Surf Championships** held at Sandy Beach on O'ahu.

Honoring the king who united Hawai'i's various islands, **King Kamehameha Day** brings parades and fairs, and twin statues of the king—in Honolulu, O'ahu, and Hāwī on the Big Island—are draped in giant leis.

AUG.➤ Billed as the world's leading international marlin fishing tournament, the **Hawaiian International Billfish Tournament,** in Kailua-Kona on the Big Island, includes a parade with amusing entries.

SEPT.–OCT.➤ **Aloha Festivals** celebrate Hawaiian culture with street parties, canoe races, craft exhibits, music, and dance events statewide.

OCT.➤ Watch 1,250 of the world's fittest athletes swim, run, and cycle in the **Ironman Triathlon World Championships.**

NOV.➤ The **Hawai'i International Film Festival** (☎ 808/944–7007), on O'ahu and Neighbor Islands, showcases films from the United States, Asia, and the Pacific and includes seminars with filmmakers and critics.

Getting Around

Alaska

The **Alaska Pass** (☎ 800/248–7598 or 800/89–82–85 from the U.K.) provides discounted one-price travel on trains, buses, and boats throughout Alaska, British Columbia, and the Yukon.

BY PLANE

Alaska's major gateway airports are **Anchorage International Airport** (☎ 907/266–2437), **Fairbanks International Airport** (☎ 907/474–2500), and **Juneau International Airport** (☎ 907/789–7821). Carriers include Alaska Airlines, Northwest, Delta, and United.

BY CAR

Alaska has few roads for its size, and most are concentrated between Anchorage, Fairbanks, and the Canadian Yukon. In southeast Alaska travel between communities is almost exclusively by boat or airplane. In the South Central area and the interior most highways have only two lanes, and a few are dirt roads. The following are paved highways that are open year-round: The **Alaska Highway** enters the state from Canada near Tok and continues west to Fairbanks. The **Glenn Highway** begins at Tok and travels south and then west to Anchorage. The **Richardson Highway** runs north–south between Valdez and Delta Junction, where it meets the Alaska Highway. The **Seward Highway** heads south from Anchorage through the Kenai Mountains to Seward, with the branch **Sterling Highway** heading southwest to Soldotna, Kenai, and Homer. The **George Parks Highway** runs north from Anchorage, past Denali National Park to Fairbanks.

BY TRAIN

The **Alaska Railroad** (☎ 907/265–2494 in Anchorage, 907/456–4155 in Fairbanks, 800/544–0552 for individual reservations, 800/895–7245 for group reservations) runs mainline service from Seward through Anchorage to Fairbanks. A secondary line links Portage, southeast of Anchorage, and Whittier on Prince William Sound. Travel to Seward is in the summer only; the rest of the route operates year-round, with reduced services September–May.

The **White Pass and Yukon Route** (☎ 907/983–2217 or 800/343–7373) operates between Skagway and Fraser, British Columbia, following the route that gold seekers took into the Yukon.

BY BUS
Gray Line of Alaska (✉ 745 W. 4th Ave., Anchorage 99501, ☎ 907/277–5581, 907/456–7741 in Fairbanks) conducts seasonal tours between and within Alaskan cities.

Alaska Direct Bus Lines (✉ Box 501, Anchorage 99510, ☎ 907/277–6652 or 800/770–6652) operates year-round service between Fairbanks, Anchorage, Skagway, and Whitehorse and will customize tours.

BY BOAT
The **Alaska Marine Highway System** (✉ Box 25535, Juneau 99802, ☎ 907/465–3941 or 800/642–0066) is a state-operated ferry system that serves ports in the southeast, South Central, and southwest regions of the state. You cannot get from southeast to South Central Alaska by ferry; the boats do not cross the Gulf of Alaska.

Hawai`i
BY PLANE
Honolulu International Airport (☎ 808/836–6411), on O`ahu, is served by American, Continental, Delta, Northwest, TWA, United, and Hawaiian Airlines. Aloha and Hawaiian airlines fly interisland between Honolulu and the four major neighbor island airports: **Ke-ahole–Kona International Airport** (✉ The Big Island, ☎ 808/329–2484), also served by United; **Hilo International** (✉ The Big Island, ☎ 808/934–5801); **Kahului** (✉ Maui, ☎ 808/872–3800), also served by American, Delta, Hawaiian, and United; and **Līhu`e** (✉ Kaua`i, ☎ 808/246–1400).

BY CAR
No Hawaiian island can be circumnavigated by car. The Big Island's roads are well maintained, although lava has closed the road from Kalapana to just east of Kamoamoa in Hawai`i Volcanoes National Park. On Maui, highways are in fairly good shape—though often crowded—and a four-wheel-drive vehicle may be necessary for the road south of Hāna. Kaua`i's main route runs south from Līhu`e and west to Polihale Beach; a narrower northern route runs to Hā`ena, the beginning of the roadless Nā Pali Coast. Moloka`i's main route becomes narrow and potholed as it nears Hālawa Valley in the east. Lāna`i's few paved roads are fine, but a four-wheel-drive vehicle is essential for exploring. On O`ahu's Wai`anae Coast the paved road ends just before Ka`ena Point.

BY BUS
Honolulu is the only city with a municipal service, the **Bus** (☎ 808/848–5555). The county-run **Hele-On Bus** (☎ 808/935–8241) operates between Hilo and Kailua-Kona, and to other points on the Big Island. The other islands have no public bus system, although shuttles run between the airports and major shopping centers and hotels.

BY BOAT
An alternative way to tour the islands is with **American Hawaii Cruises** (✉ 2 North Riverside Plaza, Chicago, IL 60606, ☎ 312/466–6000 or 800/765–7000). Its 800-passenger ship, the S.S. *Independence,* leaves Honolulu year-round on seven-day cruises that visit the O`ahu, the Big Island, Maui, and Kaua`i.

ALASKA

By Barbara
Hodgin and
Mary Engel

Updated by
Bill Sherwonit

Capital	Juneau
Population	607,000
Motto	North to the Future
State Bird	Willow ptarmigan
State Flower	Forget-me-not
Postal Abbreviation	AK

Statewide Visitor Information

The **Alaska Division of Tourism** (✉ Box 110801, Juneau 99811, ☎ 907/ 465–2010, FAX 907/465–2287) provides general visitor information. The **Alaska Public Lands Information Center** (✉ 605 W. 4th Ave., Suite 105, Anchorage 99501, ☎ 907/271–2737) is a clearinghouse of information on state and federal lands, including hiking trails, cabins, and campgrounds inside and outside the parks. The **Department of Fish and Game** (✉ Box 25526, Juneau 99802, ☎ 907/465–4180 for seasons and regulations, 907/465–2376 for licenses) can answer questions about sportfishing. The **Alaska Native Tourism Council** (✉ 1577 C St., Suite 304, Anchorage 99501, ☎ 907/274–5400, FAX 907/263–9971) represents the state's Native-run attractions. **Alaska Bed and Breakfast Association** (✉ 369 S. Franklin St., Suite 200, Juneau 99801, ☎ 907/586–2959, FAX 907/463–4453 or 800/493–4453) can set you up at a B&B.

Cruising

About a third of Alaska's visitors arrive by cruise ship. Most cruises leave from Vancouver, British Columbia, on a weeklong itinerary up the Inside Passage of Alaska's Southeast Panhandle, visiting Ketchikan, Sitka, Juneau, and either Haines or Skagway. Many include a day in Glacier Bay National Park, but check to find out which cruises schedule such a visit. The major cruise tour operators serving Alaska are **Princess Cruises and Tours** (✉ 2815 2nd Ave., Suite 400, Seattle, WA 98121, ☎ 206/728–4202 or 800/426–0442) and **Holland America Line/Westours** (✉ 300 Elliott Ave. W, Seattle, WA 98119, ☎ 206/281–3535 or 800/426–0327). For a small-ship cruise tour, contact **Alaska Sightseeing/Cruise West** (✉ 2401 4th Ave., Suite 700, Seattle, WA 98121, ☎ 206/441–8687 or 800/426–7702). State ferries provide year-round budget service for passengers and vehicles (☞ Arriving and Departing *in* Southeast, *below*) on similar routes.

National and State Parks

Alaska has more land in national parks, wilderness areas, and national wildlife refuges than all the other states combined.

National Parks

Denali National Park and Preserve (☞ The Interior, *below*) is home to North America's tallest peak, Mt. McKinley. **Glacier Bay National Park and Preserve** (☞ Southeast, *below*) is a marine preserve where 17 spectacular glaciers meet tidewater and seals float on icebergs. **Katmai National Park and Preserve** (☞ Southwest, *below*), a mixture of volcanic moonscape, rugged coast, large lake systems, mountains, and forested lowlands on the Alaska Peninsula, is home to huge coastal brown bears that fish for salmon in the Brooks River. On the Kenai Peninsula south of Anchorage is **Kenai Fjords National Park** (☞ South Central, *below*). The country's largest national park, **Wrangell–St. Elias** (☞ South Central, *below*), east of Anchorage, is six times the size of Yellowstone.

The nation's largest national forest, the **Tongass** (☞ Southeast, *below*), stretches the length of the Panhandle. **Chugach National Forest** (☞ South Central, *below*) encompasses much of the Kenai Peninsula and Prince William Sound.

State Parks

Chugach State Park (✉ HC 52, Box 8999, Indian 99540, ☎ 907/345–5014), near Anchorage, has scores of hiking trails, excellent wildlife viewing, and easily accessible wilderness. **Denali State Park** (✉ HC 32, Box 6706, Wasilla 99654, ☎ 907/745–3975) has some of the best views of Mt. McKinley, as well as a popular ridge-top trail and public-use cabins.

SOUTHEAST

Southeast Alaska is a maritime region of thousands of islands blanketed by old-growth spruce forest. The waters abound in Pacific salmon (five species) and sea mammals. The shore is home to deer, bears, and coastal communities that cling to the mountainsides. The wet climate inspires locals to call galoshes "Juneau tennis shoes," although summer does bring some breathtakingly beautiful sunny days. The villages of Tlingit, Haida, and Tsimshian, as well as museums and cultural centers in the region's larger communities, offer insights into Native American cultures.

Visitor Information

Southeast: Tourism Council (✉ Box 20710, Juneau 99802, ☎ 907/586–4777 or 800/423–0568 for a travel planner, FAX 907/463–4961). **Ketchikan:** Visitors Bureau (✉ 131 Front St., 99901, ☎ 907/225–6166 or 800/770–3300, 800/770–2200 for brochures, FAX 907/225–4250). **Sitka:** Visitors Bureau (✉ Centennial Bldg., Box 1226, 99835, ☎ 907/747–5940, FAX 907/747–3739) provides brochures and advice. **Juneau:** Log Cabin Information Center (✉ 134 3rd St., 99801, ☎ 907/586–2201, FAX 907/586–6304).

Arriving and Departing

Southeast Alaska is mainly accessible by air or water. The mainland road system (from Anchorage, through the Canadian Yukon) connects only with tiny northern communities after hundreds of miles of wilderness road. Cruise ships (☞ Cruising, *above*) and state ferries are the most common means of visitor transportation.

By Car

Ferries to Southeast Alaska leave from Bellingham, Washington, and from Prince Rupert, British Columbia. From the north, the Alaska and Haines or Klondike highways lead to Skagway and Haines, and ferries continue south through the region.

By Ferry

The **Alaska Marine Highway System** (✉ Box 25535, Juneau 99802, ☎ 907/465–3941 or 800/642–0066, FAX 907/277–4829) is an extensive network of large and small vessels that link most Southeast communities. All ferries take cars (reservations necessary in summer) and have cafeterias or restaurants; most also have staterooms, but many Alaskans camp on deck in tents or on the lounges' floors. The system makes connections with **BC Ferries** in Prince Rupert, British Columbia.

By Plane

Regular jet service is available from Pacific Coast and southwestern U.S. cities to Ketchikan, Wrangell, Petersburg, Sitka, and Juneau (**Juneau International Airport,** ☎ 907/789–7821). The Southeast is served year-round by **Alaska Airlines** (☎ 800/426–0333). In summer **Delta Airlines** (☎ 800/221–1212) also provides service. Flight service to the villages is available from the region's larger communities.

Exploring the Southeast

Ketchikan

Ketchikan is a fishing and logging town at the southern end of the Panhandle. Its centerpiece is **Creek Street,** the historic red-light district, now home to quaint shops built on stilts over Ketchikan Creek. Ten miles ★ north of town, **Totem Bight State Historical Park** (⊠ N. Tongass Hwy., ☎ 907/247–8574) displays beautiful totem poles—many date only from the 1930s but replicate much older totem poles. The village of **Saxman** (☎ 907/225–5163), 2½ mi south of Ketchikan, also has many totem poles. Original totem poles, some 200 years old, can be seen at the **Totem Heritage Center** (⊠ 601 Deermont St., ☎ 907/225–5900). The city, in fact, contains the largest collection of totem poles in the world.

Sitka

This historic town was the capital of Russian America before Alaska was sold to the United States in 1867. Russian cannons still crown **Castle Hill,** and the flagpole where the Stars and Stripes replaced the czarist Russian standard still stands. **St. Michael's Cathedral** (⊠ Lincoln St., ☎ 907/747–8120) is a 1976 replica of the 1848 church. During the 1966 fire that destroyed the original, townspeople entered the burning building to rescue precious icons and other religious objects, which are now on display.

The **Russian Bishop's House** (⊠ Lincoln St.) is a log structure built in 1842 and restored by the National Park Service. The **Sheldon Jackson Museum** (⊠ Lincoln St., ☎ 907/747–8981) has a fine collection of priceless Native American, Aleut, and Eskimo items. In **Sitka National Historical Park** (⊠ Box 738, 99835, ☎ 907/747–6281), Tlingit carvers still work at the venerable craft of carving totems; a forest trail winds among 15 totems, both old and new.

Juneau

The state capital clings to the mountainside along a narrow saltwater channel. It was born as a gold rush town in 1880 and remained an active gold-mining center until World War II. Today its number one employer is the state government, with transportation and tourism important runners-up.

Although Juneau's hills are steep, most visitors can explore the charming town on foot. Houses downtown date from the gold rush. On South Franklin Street, the **Red Dog Saloon** preserves the rough-and-tumble spirit of '98. The Victorian **Alaskan Hotel** is a more genteel relic of the gold rush era. The tiny, onion-domed **St. Nicholas Russian Orthodox Church** (⊠ 5th and Gold Sts., ☎ 907/586–1023), constructed in 1894, is the oldest original Russian church in Alaska. The **Alaska State Museum** (⊠ 395 Whittier St., ☎ 907/465–2901), near the waterfront, highlights the state's rich cultural heritage, with Eskimo and Native American artifacts, gold rush memorabilia, and natural history displays.

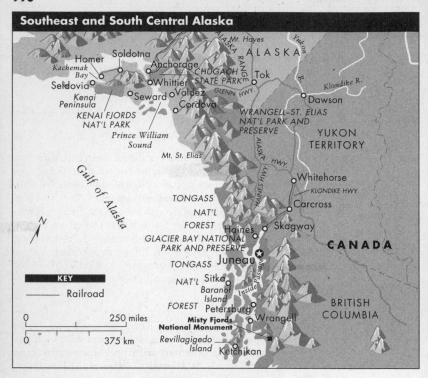

Southeast and South Central Alaska

Glacier Bay National Park and Preserve

★ Whales, porpoises, sea otters, sea lions, seals, and seabirds inhabit the 62-mi-long **Glacier Bay** (⊠ Box 140, Gustavus 99826, ☎ 907/697–2230), a remote and wild marine park wilderness accessible only by boat. In addition to wildlife, the bay has 17 tidewater glaciers and about a dozen inlets or arms to explore, making it a favorite destination for sea kayaking as well as wildlife viewing from charter boats and cruise ships. Visitor services are available in the nearby community of Gustavus, 30 minutes by plane from Juneau.

Tongass National Forest

The largest of the nation's forests, the **Tongass** (⊠ Centennial Hall, 101 Egan Dr., Juneau 99801, ☎ 907/586–8751) encompasses 16.8 million acres, or nearly three-fourths of Southeast Alaska. Mostly covered by old-growth temperate rain forest, the Tongass is a breeding ground for a wide variety of animals, including black and brown bears, bald eagles, Sitka black-tailed deer, mountain goats, and wolves. **Misty Fjords** (☎ 907/225–2148) and **Admiralty Island** (☎ 907/586–8790), two national monuments, both feature old-growth rain forest and rugged shorelines.

Dining and Lodging

For price ranges *see* Charts 1 (B) and 2 (B) *in* On the Road with Fodor's.

Ketchikan

$$$ ✕ **Salmon Falls Resort.** Fresh local seafood is served in a lovely log build-
★ ing overlooking the Inside Passage. Just 17 mi north of Ketchikan, it's a good choice after a visit to Totem Bight Park. ⊠ *Mile 17, N. Tongass Hwy.,* ☎ *907/225–2752. AE, MC, V.*

Sitka

$$$ ✕ **Channel Club.** Fine steaks and seafood are served in nautical surroundings, including glass and fishnet floats and whalebone carvings. ⊠ *2906 Halibut Point Rd.,* ☎ *907/747–9916. AE, DC, MC, V.*

$$–$$$ ▥ **Westmark Shee Atika.** The lobby and rooms in this Westmark chain outpost re-create the feeling of a rustic lodge. Many rooms overlook Crescent Harbor and the islands beyond; others have mountain and forest views. ⊠ *330 Seward St., 99835,* ☎ *907/747–6241 or 800/544–0970,* FAX *907/747–5486. 100 rooms. Restaurant, bar. AE, D, DC, MC, V.*

Juneau

$$–$$$ ✕ **Silverbow Inn.** Alaskan seafood and steaks are served in the oldest
★ operating bakery in the state (circa 1890). The fare is complemented by wine from an award-winning wine list. ⊠ *120 2nd St.,* ☎ *907/586–4146. AE, D, DC, MC, V.*

$$–$$$ ✕ **The Summit.** Housed in a converted turn-of-the-century brothel, this restaurant serves its meals in a small, candlelighted room. Diners have their choice of nearly two dozen excellent local fish and shellfish dishes. ⊠ *455 S. Franklin St.,* ☎ *907/586–2050. AE, D, DC, MC, V.*

$$ ✕ **The Fiddlehead.** Healthy, eclectic food ranging from black beans with rice to pasta with smoked salmon is served in a comfortable setting of light wood and stained glass, with a view of Mt. Juneau. The homemade bread is delicious. ⊠ *429 Willoughby Ave.,* ☎ *907/586–3150. AE, D, DC, MC, V.*

$–$$ ✕ **Giorgio at the Pier.** This elegant trattoria with a view of the harbor
★ gives an authentic Italian twist to fresh Alaskan seafood. Try anything from Alaskan clam chowder to pasta *e fagioli* (with beans). ⊠ *544 S. Franklin St.,* ☎ *907/586–4700. AE, MC, V.*

$$$ ▥ **Baranof Hotel.** This grande dame of Juneau hotels has been refurbished over the years to match the decor of its 1930s origins. Guest rooms are furnished in a simple, contemporary style. ⊠ *127 N. Franklin St., 99801,* ☎ *907/586–2660 or 800/544–0970,* FAX *907/586–8315. 194 rooms. Restaurant, bar, coffee shop. AE, D, DC, MC, V.*

$$–$$$ ▥ **The Prospector.** A short walk west of downtown, this small, mod-
★ ern hotel has very large rooms with contemporary furnishings and views of the channel, mountains, or city. In the McGuires' dining room and lounge you can enjoy outstanding prime rib. ⊠ *375 Whittier St., 99801,* ☎ *907/586–3737 or 800/331–2711,* FAX *907/586–1204. 60 rooms. Restaurant, lobby lounge. AE, D, DC, MC, V.*

$–$$ ▥ **Alaskan Hotel.** This historic 1913 hotel is 15 mi from the ferry ter-
★ minal and 9 mi from the airport (city bus service is available). Rooms are on three floors and have turn-of-the-century antiques. ⊠ *167 S. Franklin St.,* ☎ *907/586–1000 or 800/327–9347,* FAX *907/463–3775. 40 rooms. Bar. D, DC, MC, V.*

Wilderness Camps and Lodges

Accommodations range from spartan bunkhouses to luxury lodges where guests dress for candlelight dinners. One agency that books area sportfishing lodges is **Alaska Sportfishing Packages** (⊠ Box 9170, Seattle, WA 98109, ☎ 206/216–2920 or 800/426–0603, FAX 206/216–2973).

Campgrounds

State and national forest campgrounds are available near all Southeast communities (☞ Alaska Public Lands Information Center *in* Statewide Visitor Information, *above*). The *Milepost,* available in most Alaska and Washington bookstores, lists campgrounds throughout the state.

Outdoor Activities and Sports

Fishing

Southeast Alaskans are blessed with great salmon fishing off city docks and on beaches where creeks meet saltwater. Another option is to take an air taxi to a remote spot for a day's fishing or an extended stay (☞ Wilderness Camps and Lodges, *above.*). Fishing licenses are available in most grocery and sporting goods stores.

Kayaking and Rafting

You can bring your own kayak aboard state ferries or hire a local outfitter—such as **Alaska Discovery Wilderness Adventures** (✉ 5449 Shaune Dr., Suite 4, Juneau 99801, ☎ 907/780–6226 or 800/586–1911)—for a guided Inside Passage or Glacier Bay excursion; the company also guides canoe trips on Admiralty Island and floats the Tatshenshini and Alsek rivers. For rafting on the Mendenhall River as well as glacial travel, canoe and kayak trips, and hiking, contact **Alaska Travel Adventures** (✉ 9085 Glacier Hwy., Suite 301, Juneau 99801, ☎ 907/789–0052 or 800/478–0052 in AK). Guided sea-kayaking tours of nearby Misty Fjords National Monument in Tongass National Forest are available from **Southeast Exposure** (✉ Box 9143, Ketchikan 99901, ☎ 907/225–8829).

Wildlife Viewing

Southeast Alaska is renowned for its abundance of whales, eagles, and brown bears (the coastal cousins of grizzlies). **Glacier Bay National Park** is a prime viewing area for several species of whales, including humpbacks and orcas. Alaska Discovery Wilderness Adventures (☞ Kayaking and Rafting, *above*) also leads whale-watching tours at **Icy Strait,** near Chichagof Island. Popular bear-viewing areas are **Pack Creek,** within Admiralty Island National Monument (☞ Glacier Bay National Park and Preserve, *above*) and **Anan Creek,** in the Tongass Forest near Wrangell (☎ 907/874–2323). The **Alaska Chilkat Bald Eagle Preserve** (☎ 907/766–2292), near Haines, hosts the world's largest gathering of bald eagles: Between 1,000 and 4,000 eagles gather here each November and December.

Ski Areas

The **Eaglecrest** ski area, across the channel from Juneau on Douglas Island, has 31 trails, three lifts, a ski school, and equipment rental. ✉ *155 S. Seward St., Juneau 99801,* ☎ *907/586–5284 or 907/586–5330 for recorded ski conditions. Closed May–Nov.*

Cross-country skiing is popular in all Southeast communities. Check with local visitor centers for the location of trails groomed for either diagonal or skate skiing.

Shopping

Silver Lining Seafoods (✉ 1705 Tongass Ave., ☎ 907/225–9865), north of Ketchikan's city dock, has excellent locally smoked seafood and fish-motif postcards and T-shirts by local artist Ray Troll.

In Juneau the **Alaska Steam Laundry Building,** on South Franklin Street, has shops and a good coffeehouse downstairs. The **Senate Building Mall,** also on South Franklin, houses a charming Christmas store and other import shops. In the Senate Building Mall, **Taku Smokeries** has two retail outlets selling locally smoked seafood.

SOUTH CENTRAL

South Central Alaska is home to most of the state's population and many of its most popular attractions. Many visitors start their trips in Anchorage, then continue south to the fishing and artists' communities of the Kenai Peninsula.

Visitor Information

Anchorage: Convention and Visitors Bureau (✉ 524 W. 4th Ave., 99501, ☎ 907/276–4118 or 907/276–3200 for events hot line, ℻ 907/278–5559), Log Cabin Information Center (✉ W. 4th Ave. and F St., ☎ 907/274–3531). **Kenai Peninsula:** Tourism Marketing Council (✉ 150 N. Willow, Kenai 99611, ☎ 907/283–3850 or 800/535–3624, ℻ 907/283–2838). **Soldotna:** Visitor Information Center (✉ 44790 Sterling Hwy., 99669, ☎ 907/262–1337, ℻ 907/262–3566). **Homer:** Visitor Center (✉ Box 541, 99603, ☎ 907/235–7740, ℻ 907/235–8766). **Seward:** Visitor Information Center (✉ Mile 2, Seward Hwy., Box 749, 99664, ☎ 907/224–8051, ℻ 907/224–5353).

Arriving and Departing

By Bus

Gray Line of Alaska (☎ 907/277–5581 in Anchorage, 907/456–7741 in Fairbanks) serves Anchorage, Denali, and Fairbanks.

By Car

To get to Anchorage from Tok, on the Alaska Highway near the Canadian border, head southwest on the Glenn Highway. From Fairbanks travel south on the George Parks Highway. From Anchorage, the Seward and Sterling highways lead south to the Kenai Peninsula.

By Ferry

The South Central section of the **Alaska Marine Highway** ferry system (☞ Southeast, *above*) links communities on Prince William Sound, the Gulf of Alaska, and Cook Inlet. Road connections to and from Anchorage can be made in Whittier and Seward. There is no ferry service between the South Central and Southeast regions.

By Plane

Anchorage International Airport (☎ 907/266–2437), about 6 mi from downtown, is served by Alaska Airlines, American West, Continental, Northwest, Delta Airlines, Reno Air, and United. Commuter plane service is available to Denali National Park, Homer, Kenai, and other destinations within the region. A cab from the Anchorage airport to downtown costs about $15 plus tip. Some hotels have shuttles.

By Train

The **Alaska Railroad** (☎ 800/544–0552, 907/265–2494 in Anchorage, 907/456–4155 in Fairbanks, ℻ 907/265–2323) offers mainline service between Seward, Anchorage, Denali National Park, and Fairbanks and secondary service between Portage and Whittier.

Exploring South Central

Anchorage

Anchorage is a young, spirited city in a spectacular setting between mountains and sea. Nearly half the state's population resides here, which may explain why you can find everything from oil industry high-rises to backwoods cabins with resident sled-dog teams.

The **Anchorage Museum of History and Art** (✉ W. 7th Ave. and A St., ☎ 907/343–6173) has an outstanding exhibit on Native Alaskan life

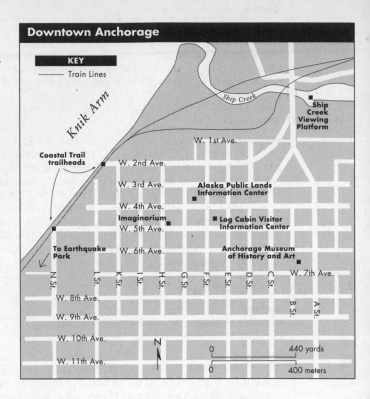

Downtown Anchorage

KEY
— Train Lines

Knik Arm

Ship Creek

Ship Creek Viewing Platform

W. 1st Ave.

Coastal Trail trailheads

W. 2nd Ave.

W. 3rd Ave.

Alaska Public Lands Information Center

W. 4th Ave.

Imaginarium

W. 5th Ave.

Log Cabin Visitor Information Center

To Earthquake Park

W. 6th Ave.

Anchorage Museum of History and Art

N St. L St. K St. I St. H St. G St. F St. E St. D St. C St.

W. 7th Ave.

W. 8th Ave.

B St. A St.

W. 9th Ave.

W. 10th Ave.

N

W. 11th Ave.

0   440 yards

0   400 meters

and a permanent display of artwork depicting Alaska as seen by explorers, resident painters, and latter-day visitors. The **Imaginarium** (⊠ 737 W. 5th Ave., ☎ 907/276–3179) is an interactive science museum with a shop that sells educational toys. At **Ship Creek,** just north of downtown, you can see salmon jump in summer as they head upstream to spawn; there's a platform for easy viewing.

Earthquake Park, at the west end of Northern Lights Boulevard, shows the damage wrought by the 1964 quake, when houses tumbled into the ocean. Trees have claimed the earth mounds and ponds created by the quake's force. The floatplane base at **Lake Hood,** near the Anchorage International Airport, is the world's largest and busiest. For a scenic walk stroll the **Coastal Trail,** which runs along Cook Inlet. Plan a sunset visit, when the sun moves slowly across the horizon and bathes the trail in golden light. There are several trailhead access points in mid- and downtown.

The Kenai Peninsula

Thrusting into the Gulf of Alaska south of Anchorage, the **Kenai Peninsula** is a glacier-hewn landscape offering magnificent wildlife viewing and fishing from its spectacular coastline. In summer the Alaska Railroad runs a passenger train daily to **Seward,** a small fishing and timber town on Resurrection Bay, but most people drive the three hours from Anchorage. Tour boats leave Seward's busy downtown harbor for excursions that include visits to sea lion rookeries and bird rookeries and close-up views of tidewater glaciers.

Seward is the jumping-off point for **Kenai Fjords National Park** (☞ *below*). **Mariah Tours** (☎ 907/243–1238 or 800/270–1238) has wildlife and glacier tours of the park.

At the southern terminus of the Seward Highway, 225 mi from Anchorage, lies **Homer,** in a breathtaking setting that includes a sand spit jutting into Kachemak Bay. The town's buildings are picturesque, and you can comb the beach, fish off the docks, or charter a boat for halibut fishing (☞ Outdoor Activities and Sports, *below*). Wildlife abounds in the bay, and most fishing charters give you a close-up view of seals, porpoises, birds, and, more rarely, whales. If you walk along the docks at the end of the day, you can see fishermen unloading their catch. Across from the end of the Homer spit is **Halibut Cove,** one of the prettiest spots in South Central Alaska and reachable by water taxi. **Seldovia,** on the other side of Kachemak Bay from Homer, has an onion-domed Russian church and excellent fishing.

Kenai Fjords National Park

★ One of only three national parks connected to Alaska's highway system, the 670,000-acre **Kenai Fjords** (⊠ Box 1727, Seward 99664, ☎ 907/224–3175) is known for its abundant marine wildlife, deep-blue tidewater glaciers, waterfalls, and coastal fjords: long and steep-sided glacially carved valleys now filled with seawater. People come here by boat to see whales, porpoises, seals, and seabirds, fish for salmon, and hear the booming echoes of calving tidewater glaciers. Yet the park's most popular visitor attraction is on land: **Exit Glacier** is a short walk from the one gravel road that leads into the park.

Wrangell–St. Elias National Park and Preserve

Bridging the Canadian border, 13-million-acre **Wrangell–St. Elias** (⊠ Box 29, Glennallen 99588, ☎ 907/822–5234) could fit six Yellowstones within its borders. Known to some as Alaska's Mountain Kingdom, the park encompasses four major mountain ranges and six of the continent's 10 highest peaks, including the 18,008-ft **Mt. St. Elias.** Here, too, is North America's largest subpolar ice field, the Bagley, which calved several gigantic glaciers; one of them, the **Malaspina,** is larger than Rhode Island. The park has two main entryways: On the north side is Nabesna Road, while on its eastern border is 60-mi-long McCarthy Road, which leads to the historic town of **McCarthy** and neighboring **Kennicott Mine** (now closed), two of the park's key attractions for those who don't want to venture far from the road system.

Chugach National Forest

Second only to the Tongass in size, **Chugach National Forest** (⊠ 3301 C St., Anchorage 99503, ☎ 907/271–2500) encompasses much of Prince William Sound, the Kenai Peninsula, and the Copper River Delta region. Its 5.8 million acres include forested hills and valleys, rugged coastal mountains, one of the world's largest tidewater glaciers, and wetlands that support migrating waterfowl and shorebirds. About an hour's drive south of Anchorage, **Portage Glacier** and the **Begich-Boggs Visitor Center** are two of Alaska's premier visitor attractions.

Dining

For price ranges *see* Charts 1 (B) and 2 (B) *in* On the Road with Fodor's. For information on wilderness camps and lodges, *see* Southeast, *above*. For bed-and-breakfast reservations, call **Alaska Private Lodgings: Stay With a Friend** (⊠ Box 200047, Anchorage 99520, ☎ 907/258–1717, 𝖥𝖠𝖷 907/258–6613).

Anchorage

$$–$$$ ✕ **Marx Brothers Cafe.** The second-oldest house in Anchorage was orig-
★ inally constructed for the engineers who built the Alaska Railroad.
Within, you can sample wild game, caramelized rack of lamb and the
like. There are more than 500 selections on the wine list. ⊠ *627 W.
3rd Ave.,* ☎ *907/278–2133. AE, DC, MC, V. No lunch.*

$$–$$$ ✕ **Double Musky.** It's worth the 40-mi trip south of town and the wait
★ once you arrive. The little building set among spruce trees is casually
decorated with Mardi Gras memorabilia, the better to prepare you for
the fine Cajun dishes and huge, tender steaks to come. ⊠ *Crow Creek
Rd., Girdwood,* ☎ *907/783–2822. Reservations not accepted. AE, D,
DC, MC, V. Closed Mon. No lunch.*

$$–$$$ ✕ **Sacks Cafe.** A favorite before- or after-show dining spot of those
attending concerts and plays at Anchorage's Performing Arts Center,
this downtown restaurant serves fresh seafood, pasta, and dinner salads. It also has take-out service for sandwiches, salads, and espresso.
⊠ *625 W. 5th Ave.,* ☎ *907/276–3546. Reservations not accepted (except some holidays). AE, MC, V.*

$$–$$$ ✕ **Seven Glaciers Restaurant.** Perched high on a mountain at 2,300
ft, this restaurant has a setting that ensures a scenic adventure—diners arrive by high-speed tram. It's a culinary adventure as well: Meat,
fish, and fowl dishes are served "architecturally." Translation: Your
steak may arrive standing on its side. ⊠ *Alyeska Resort, Girdwood,*
☎ *907/754–2237. Reservations essential. AE, D, MC, V. Closed
Sun.–Thurs. in winter. No lunch.*

$$–$$$ ✕ **Simon and Seafort's Saloon and Grill.** Large windows overlook
Cook Inlet at this brass-and-wood restaurant. Fresh local seafood and
rack-roasted prime rib are the specialties. ⊠ *420 L St.,* ☎ *907/274–
3502. AE, MC, V. No lunch Sun.*

$–$$ ✕ **Downtown Deli.** This classic delicatessen serves sandwiches, salads,
and local fish in a casual atmosphere. ⊠ *525 W. 4th Ave.,* ☎ *907/276–
7116. AE, D, DC, MC, V.*

$$$ ▥ **Anchorage Hotel.** Many original details have been restored in this
centrally located small hotel, built in 1916. Rooms are decorated in
pastel colors. ⊠ *330 E St., 99501,* ☎ *907/272–4553 or 800/544–0988,*
FAX *907/277–4483. 26 rooms. Pub. AE, D, DC, MC, V.*

$$$ ▥ **Hotel Captain Cook.** This three-tower hotel takes up a full city
★ block. The South Pacific decor includes teak paneling in public spaces
and teak furniture in the rooms. ⊠ *W. 5th Ave. and K St. (Box 102280),
99501,* ☎ *907/276–6000 or 800/843–1950; 800/478–3100 in AK;*
FAX *907/278–5366. 643 rooms. 3 restaurants, indoor pool, health club.
AE, D, DC, MC, V.*

$$–$$$ ▥ **Voyager Hotel.** This small four-story hotel has full kitchens in all
rooms as well as bathrooms with pedestal sinks and wainscoting.
Some rooms have views of the Cook Inlet. ⊠ *501 K St., 99501,* ☎
907/277–9501 or 800/247–9070, FAX *907/274–0333. 38 rooms.
Restaurant, lounge. AE, D, DC, MC, V.*

$ ▥ **Anchorage International Hostel.** Guests share dorm-style rooms
and a kitchen on each floor in this cinder-block building downtown.
⊠ *700 H St., 99501,* ☎ *907/276–3635,* FAX *907/276–7772. 95 beds.
MC, V.*

The Kenai Peninsula

$$–$$$ ✕ **Harbor Dinner Club.** Run by the same family since 1958, this reno-
vated and expanded eatery serves local halibut and salmon in a simply appointed dining room with a view of Resurrection Bay and the
mountains. ⊠ *220 5th Ave., Seward,* ☎ *907/224–3012. AE, D, DC,
MC, V.*

$$ ✕ **The Saltry.** A half-hour water-taxi ride from Homer Harbor takes
★ you to this restaurant with a deck over the water. Once there, sample
some of South Central Alaska's best seafood dishes, including fine sushi.
⊠ *Halibut Cove*, ☎ *907/235–7847 or 800/478–7847 in AK. Boat and
dining reservations through Central Charter Booking Agency. MC, V.*

$$–$$$ ⊡ **Land's End.** The three wings of this hotel have a contemporary nau-
tical theme. All rooms facing the bay have small balconies for watch-
ing the sunset. ⊠ *4786 Homer Spit Rd., Homer 99603*, ☎ *907/
235–2500 or 800/478–0400 in AK*, ℻ *907/235–0420. 61 rooms.
Restaurant, lounge. AE, D, DC, MC, V.*

$$ ⊡ **Van Gilder Hotel.** This aging but dignified three-story stucco building is listed on the National Register of Historic Places. Brass beds,
pedestal sinks, and claw-foot tubs give the guest rooms an ersatz look.
The staff is friendly. ⊠ *308 Adams St., Seward 99664*, ☎ *907/224–
3079 or 800/204–6835 outside AK*, ℻ *907/224–3689. 25 rooms. Travel
services. AE, D, DC, MC, V.*

Campgrounds

In Anchorage, the city-operated **Centennial and Lions Campground** (⊠
Box 196650, 99519, ☎ 907/333–9711) has 88 spaces and showers;
it's closed mid-October through April. Near Anchorage, **Chugach State
Park** (⊠ HC52 Box 8999, Indian, 99540, ☎ 907/345–5014) has
three public campgrounds. For **Kenai Peninsula** and other area campgrounds, contact the Alaska Public Lands Information Center (☞
Statewide Visitor Information, *above*).

Nightlife and the Arts

The **Alaska Center for the Performing Arts** (⊠ 621 W. 6th Ave., ☎ 907/
263–2900) is home to a local symphony orchestra and theater companies and also presents operas, symphonies, and performances by national and international touring companies. The **Fly-by-Night Club** (⊠
3300 Spenard Rd., ☎ 907/279–7726) stages popular revues with lots
of good boogie-woogie music and tacky jokes. The *Anchorage Daily
News* publishes a weekend activity guide every Friday.

Outdoor Activities and Sports

Biking

Most South Central highways are suitable for biking on the shoulder.
Anchorage has more than 125 mi of bike trails. The **Matanuska Valley** is an increasingly popular place for farm-road rides. Bikes are
available for rent at many hotels and at **Downtown Bicycle Rental** (⊠
5th Ave. and C St., Anchorage, ☎ 907/279–5293) and **Adventure Café**
(⊠ 414 K St., Anchorage, ☎ 907/276–8282).

Fishing

All South Central coastal communities have fishing charters, outfitters,
and guides. Although Anchorage does not have good saltwater fishing—glacial runoff makes the water too murky—the freshwater lakes
are stocked and a hatchery-enhanced run of salmon returns to Ship Creek,
in the city's downtown area, each summer. In Homer, **Central Charter
Booking Agency** (⊠ 4241 Homer Spit, 99603, ☎ 907/235–7847 or
800/478–7847 in AK) arranges salmon and halibut charters. **Alaska
Wildland Adventures** (⊠ Box 389, Girdwood 99587, ☎ 800/334–8730
or 800/478–4100 in AK) offers a variety of float and fish packages on
the Kenai River, world famous for its huge salmon runs. Licenses are
sold in most grocery and other retail stores.

Hiking and Backpacking

There are public cabins for rent along many hiking trails in South Central Alaska (☞ Alaska Public Lands Information Center *in* Statewide Visitor Information, *above*). **Chugach State Park** (☎ 907/345–5014), just east of Anchorage, has nearly 30 trails totaling more than 150 mi. Several popular trails are maintained within **Chugach National Forest** on the Kenai Peninsula as well.

Kayaking and Rafting

Floating is available on hundreds of rivers within a small area. **Nova River Runners** (⊠ Box 1129, Chickaloon 99674, ☎ 907/745–5753 or 800/746–5753 in AK) offers guided day trips on the Chickaloon, Matanuska, and Six-Mile rivers and overnighters on the Talkeetna and Copper rivers. **Ketchum Air Service** (⊠ Box 190588, Anchorage 99519, ☎ 907/243–5525 or 800/433–9114) provides drop-off and pickup service and gear for wilderness float trips.

Sled-Dog Racing

On winter weekends the **Alaska Sled Dog and Racing Association** (☎ 907/562–2235) hosts races. The three-day **Fur Rendezvous World-Championship Sled Dog Race** is staged in downtown Anchorage in mid-February. March brings the famous, 1,049-mi **Iditarod,** which begins in Anchorage and ends in Nome.

Wildlife Viewing

Some of Alaska's best wildlife viewing is possible right outside Anchorage in **Chugach State Park:** Moose, Dall sheep, bears, and a wide variety of smaller mammals and bird life can be found in this accessible wilderness. The coastline of the **Kenai Peninsula** offers excellent viewing opportunities for whales, sea lions, sea otters, seals, and seabirds.

Ski Areas

The **Alyeska Resort** (⊠ Box 249, Girdwood 99587, ☎ 907/754–1111 or 800/880–3880, 907/754–7669 for recorded ski conditions), about 40 mi south of Anchorage, is the largest in the state, with 470 acres of skiable terrain, a 3,125-ft vertical drop, 61 trails, seven lifts, and a 60-passenger tram. It also has a 307-room hotel, a ski school, and a mountaintop restaurant (☞ Seven Glaciers *in* Dining, *above*). **Hilltop Ski Area** (⊠ 7015 Abbott Rd., Anchorage 99516, ☎ 907/346–1446 or 907/346–2167 for recorded ski conditions), 10 mi from downtown Anchorage, has one lift and one rope tow, nine trails, a vertical drop of 300 ft, ski instruction, cross-country trails, and a national-grade half-pipe for snowboarders. **Alpenglow at Arctic Valley** (☎ 907/563–2524 or 907/428–1208, 907/249–9292 for recorded ski conditions) is in the Chugach Mountains about 15 mi northeast of downtown Anchorage. It has three double-chairs, a T-bar, a pony tow, open-bowl skiing with a 1,300-ft vertical drop, two day lodges, a rental shop, and a ski school.

Anchorage also is home of a vast and diverse Nordic ski-trail system, with more than 70 mi of groomed trails. The **Nordic Ski Club of Anchorage** (☎ 907/561–0949) has a ski hot line (☎ 907/248–6667) that provides grooming and trail condition updates.

Shopping

The shops along 4th and 5th avenues sell T-shirts, trinkets, and Alaskan arts and crafts. At the **Alaska Native Arts and Crafts Association** (⊠ 333 W. 4th Ave., ☎ 907/274–2932) you'll find genuine, if pricey, local baskets, carvings, and beadwork.

THE INTERIOR

The Alaska and George Parks highways offer access to this diverse area, a vast wilderness of birch and spruce forest, high mountains, tundra valleys, and abundant wildlife. Its crown jewel is **Denali National Park,** 240 mi north of Anchorage. En route here from Anchorage, visitors travel through green Matanuska Valley farm country. North of Fairbanks, two hot springs retreats welcome visitors year-round.

Visitor Information

Denali National Park and Preserve (⊠ Superintendent, Box 9, Denali National Park 99755, ☎ 907/683–2294 year-round or 907/683–1266 in summer, FAX 907/683–9612 year-round). **Fairbanks:** Convention and Visitors Bureau Information Cabin (⊠ 550 1st Ave., 99701, ☎ 907/456–5774 or 800/327–5774, 907/456–4636 for events hot line, FAX 907/452–2867).

Arriving and Departing

By Car

Much of the Interior is inaccessible by road, but some major roadways do pass through the region. Fairbanks is connected to Anchorage in South Central Alaska by the George Parks Highway, while the Steese, Elliot, and Dalton highways provide access north of Fairbanks. Hardy RVers and campers drive the Alaska Highway through British Columbia and the Yukon to Fairbanks; it takes at least a week.

By Plane

Year-round, Alaska Airlines, Delta, and United have daily nonstop jet service between Anchorage and the **Fairbanks International Airport** (☎ 907/474–2500). In summer Alaska Airlines flies nonstop between Seattle and Fairbanks. Also in summer Northwest flies to Fairbanks from Minneapolis. A number of bush carriers originate in Fairbanks and will take you to otherwise inaccessible destinations in the region.

By Train

The **Alaska Railroad** (☎ 800/544–0552, 907/265–2494 in Anchorage, 907/465–4155 in Fairbanks; FAX 907/265–2323) offers service between Anchorage and Fairbanks via Denali.

Exploring the Interior

Denali National Park

Denali is 6 million acres of wilderness, including the majestic **Mt. McKinley**—at 20,320 ft, the highest peak in North America. Along with panoramic vistas of unspoiled taiga and tundra, the park is the natural habitat of bears, wolves, moose, Dall sheep, and caribou. The only road through the park is closed, with few exceptions, to private vehicles beyond Mile 12. Visitors ride shuttle buses (☎ 800/622–7275), which cost $12–$30 depending on turnaround point, on the 11-hour round-trip excursion to **Wonder Lake,** famous for its views of wading moose and Mt. McKinley. If you tire of the ride, you can get out and walk, then catch another bus (they leave from the park entrance every half hour starting at 5 AM) in either direction. Check with the **Visitor Access Center,** near the park entrance, for the day's schedule of naturalist walks and sled-dog demonstrations. Denali is open year-round, but services and accommodations are limited from September to May. For information on camping *see* Campgrounds *in* Dining and Lodging, *below.*

Fairbanks

Built on the banks of the Chena River, Fairbanks was founded by gold miners early in the century and later became a transportation hub for all the Interior. Today it's the state's second-largest city, although its atmosphere is more that of a frontier town. Its residents—who cope with incredible winter temperatures (lows reach −50°F) and darkness or twilight almost around the clock—consider themselves the hardiest of Alaskans.

One of Fairbanks's main attractions is the **University of Alaska** (⊠ 501 Yukon Dr., ☏ 907/474–7211). On its grounds are the **Large Animal Research Station** (☏ 907/474–7207), home to live musk ox and caribou, and the **University of Alaska Museum** (☏ 907/474–7505), whose collection includes a 36,000-year-old mummified steppe bison. The **Geophysical Institute** (☏ 907/474–7558) shows a free video on the aurora borealis on Thursday afternoon from June through August. The west ridge of the campus affords an excellent view of the Alaska Range to the south.

Another big draw in Fairbanks is the **Alaskaland Park** (⊠ Airport Way and Peger Rd., ☏ 907/459–1087), on the Chena River near downtown. Among its numerous free attractions are museums, a theater, an art gallery, a native village, and a reconstructed gold rush town. The park is closed Labor Day through Memorial Day.

Hot Springs Retreats

The discovery of natural hot springs in the frozen wilderness just north of Fairbanks sent early miners scrambling to build communities around this heaven-sent phenomenon. Today, Fairbanks residents come to soak in pools filled with hot spring water and to enjoy excellent fishing, hiking, and cross-country skiing. The springs are also a favorite spot to view the famed northern lights.

Dining and Lodging

For price ranges *see* Charts 1 (B) and 2 (B) *in* On the Road with Fodor's.

Denali

$ ✕ **Lynx Creek Pizza & Pub.** This funky frame building just outside Denali is popular with young park workers for after-work beer and pizza; try the reindeer-sausage topping. ⊠ *Parks Hwy., 1½ mi north of park entrance,* ☏ *907/683–2548. Reservations not accepted. AE, D, MC, V. Closed Sept.–May.*

$$$ 🏨 **Denali National Park Hotel.** The main attractions of this hotel—the only one inside the park—are its location near the railroad station and its auditorium, where there are free naturalist films and ranger talks daily. Rooms are simple, some in old Pullman cars. ⊠ *241 W. Ship Creek Ave., Anchorage, 99501,* ☏ *907/276–7234 year-round or 907/683–2215 in summer,* 🖷 *907/258–3668. 100 rooms. Cafeteria, snack bar, lounge. AE, D, MC, V. Closed mid-Sept.–May.*

$$$ 🏨 **Denali Princess Lodge.** This large log complex above the Nenana River, just 1 mi north of Denali, is the park's most luxurious hotel. Suites have whirlpools, and the lounge has a fireplace. ⊠ *Parks Hwy., 1 mi north of park entrance (Reservations: 2815 2nd Ave., Suite 400, Seattle, WA 98121),* ☏ *907/683–2282,* 🖷 *907/683–2545 in summer;* ☏ *800/426–0500 or* 🖷 *206/443–1979 for reservations. 280 rooms. 2 restaurants, bar, lounge, outdoor hot tubs, meeting rooms, travel services. AE, DC, MC, V. Closed mid-Sept.–mid-May.*

$ ▢ **Denali Hostel.** A log building with two bunkhouses, the hostel offers shared accommodations and bus service to and from the park. It's 10 mi north of the park entrance, near Healy. ⊠ *Box 801, Denali National Park 99755,* ☎ *907/683–1295. No credit cards. Closed mid-Sept.–mid-May.*

WILDERNESS CAMPS AND LODGES

$$$$ ✕▢ **Camp Denali.** This rustic compound in the heart of the park has
★   cabins lighted by gaslight. Its authentic charm and delicious home cooking make it a popular place to stay in Denali. A knowledgeable staff and naturalist programs will acquaint you with the surrounding wilderness. ⊠ *Box 67, Denali National Park 99755,* ☎ *907/683–2290,* FAX *907/683–1568. 17 cabins. Closed early Sept.–early June.*

$$$$ ✕▢ **Denali Wilderness Lodge.** Built as a hunting camp to supply gold rush–era miners, this complex of more than two dozen log buildings is reachable only by bush plane. Activities include horseback riding, hiking, bird-watching, and nature walks. ⊠ *Box 50, Denali National Park 99755; Box 71784, Fairbanks 99707;* ☎ *907/683–1287 in summer or 800/541–9779 year-round;* FAX *907/479–4410 in winter, 907/683–1286 in summer. 13 cabins. Closed Sept.–late May.*

CAMPGROUNDS

There are seven campgrounds in Denali. Three are open to private vehicles for tent and RV camping; three are reached by shuttle bus and are restricted to tent camping; and one is for backpackers only. For reservations call **Denali Park Resorts** (☎ 907/272–7275 or 800/622–7275). For more information contact the park superintendent (☞ Visitor Information, *above*). Several private campgrounds are outside the park along the highway, such as **Grizzly Bear Cabins and Campground** (⊠ Box 7, Denali National Park 99755, ☎ 907/683–2696 in summer, 907/683–1337 in winter). For general campsite information and availability, contact the **Alaska Public Lands Information Center** (☞ Statewide Visitor Information, *above*).

Fairbanks

$$–$$$ ✕ **Two Rivers Lodge.** Once a wilderness homestead, this rustic log building is now a full-service restaurant with award-winning cuisine. In summer guests may sit on a deck that overlooks a pond and sample tapas, appetizer-size portions of Spanish dishes cooked in a wood-fired oven. The wine list is one of Alaska's largest. ⊠ *Mile 16, Chena Hot Springs Rd., Fairbanks,* ☎ *907/488–6815. AE, D, MC, V. No lunch.*

$$$ ▢ **Sophie Station.** Every room has a kitchen at this all-suite hotel near
★   Fairbanks International Airport. ⊠ *1717 University Ave., Fairbanks, 99709,* ☎ *907/479–3650 or 800/528–4916,* FAX *907/479–7951. 147 rooms. Restaurant, bar. AE, D, DC, MC, V.*

$$–$$$ ▢ **Westmark Fairbanks.** Close to downtown, this full-service member of Alaska's biggest chain is built around a courtyard on a quiet street. Rooms are contemporary and comfortable. ⊠ *813 Noble St., Fairbanks 99701,* ☎ *907/456–7722 or 800/544–0970 for central reservations,* FAX *907/451–7478. 238 rooms. Restaurant, lounge. AE, D, DC, MC, V.*

Hot Springs

$$–$$$ ✕▢ **Chena Hot Springs Resort.** This resort, just 60 mi from Fairbanks on Chena Hot Springs Road, is the local favorite. There's a campground with RV hookups, as well as hotel rooms furnished with antique wardrobes and rustic cabins with electricity but no water. Nonguests can pay to use the heated pool and eat in the restaurant. ⊠ *Box 73440, Fairbanks 99707,* ☎ *907/452–7867 or 800/478–4681 in AK,* FAX *907/456–3122. 47 rooms, 8 cabins. Restaurant, lounge, pool, 3 hot tubs, spa. AE, D, DC, MC, V.*

$$–$$$ ✗⌂ **Circle Hot Springs Resort.** A 2½-hour drive from Fairbanks on the Steese Highway, this four-story spa-hotel dates from 1930. There are also one- and two-bedroom cabins with whirlpool baths and kitchenettes. The entire complex is naturally heated by the hot springs. ⊠ *Box 254, Central 99730,* ☎ *907/520–5113,* ℻ *907/520–5442. 24 rooms, 10 cabins. Restaurant, lounge, pool. MC, V.*

Outdoor Activities and Sports

Canoeing
The Chena River is popular for canoeing, both in Fairbanks and out in the wilderness. Entry points are marked along Chena Hot Springs Road. Avoid the Tanana River because of its swift and tricky current and hidden sandbars.

Fishing
Char, grayling, and pike are abundant in the lakes and rivers of the Interior. The Chena River between Fairbanks and Chena Hot Springs is especially popular for grayling fishing.

Hiking and Backpacking
Skilled wilderness travelers can hike anywhere in Denali National Park, except for areas occasionally closed because of bear-related dangers. There are well-marked beginner trails near the park entrance.

Rafting
Several companies offer white-water trips on the thrilling **Nenana River,** which parallels the George Parks Highway near the Denali entrance. Try **Denali Raft Adventures** (⊠ Drawer 190, Denali National Park 99755, ☎ 907/683–2234) or **McKinley Raft Tours** (⊠ Box 138, Denali National Park 99755, ☎ 907/683–2392).

Sled-Dog Racing
The **North American Open Sled Dog Championship** is held in downtown Fairbanks in March. Check with the visitor center (☞ Visitor Information, *above*) for details.

Wildlife Viewing
Few places in North America can equal the wildlife-viewing opportunities at Denali National Park, where most visitors see grizzly bears, caribou, moose, and Dall sheep. Wolves and golden eagles can also sometimes be spied.

Spectator Sports
The **Gold Kings** (☎ 907/456–7825) and the **University of Alaska Nanooks** (☎ 907/474–7205) draw big crowds of ice hockey fans.

SOUTHWEST

Visitor Information

Southwest Alaska Municipal Conference (⊠ 3300 Arctic Blvd., Suite 203, Anchorage 99503, ☎ 907/562–7380, ℻ 907/562–0438).

Arriving and Departing

Alaska Airlines (☎ 800/426–0333) has a daily nonstop jet service to Kodiak Island from Anchorage. For packages to Kodiak contact **Alaska Airlines Vacations** (⊠ SEARV, Box 68900, Seattle, WA 98168, ☎ 800/468–2248).

Commuter planes serve the town of King Salmon, which is just a short floatplane ride from Katmai National Park and Preserve, 290 mi southwest of Anchorage. Airlines serving King Salmon include **Alaska Airlines** (☞ *above*), **PenAir** (☏ 907/243–2323 or 800/448–4226), and Reeve Aleutian Airways (☞ *below*).

Contact **Reeve Aleutian Airways** (✉ 4700 W. International Airport Rd., Anchorage, ☏ 907/243–4700 or 800/544–2248) for flight and package-tour information on the Aleutian and Pribilof islands, in the remote Bering Sea region.

Getting Around

The **Alaska Marine Highway System** (☞ Southeast, *above*) serves some Alaska Peninsula and Aleutian Islands communities in summer.

Exploring the Southwest

Kodiak

The largest island in the United States, Kodiak is home to the brown bear, North America's largest land mammal. Before the seat of colonial government was moved to Sitka, Kodiak was the original capital of Russian Alaska. Today the town is a commercial fishing center: Visitors can go halibut fishing, sea kayaking, or flightseeing for bears. Much of the rain-forest-covered island lies within 1.6-million-acre **Kodiak Island National Refuge** (☏ 907/487–2600).

Katmai National Park and Preserve

Katmai National Park and Preserve (✉ Box 7, King Salmon 99613, ☏ 907/246–3305) is a more remote and less developed park than Denali, but therein lies its charm. A lush valley within what is now the park became a land of steaming fumaroles after the 1912 eruption of Mt. Novarupta and the collapse of nearby Mt. Katmai's peak. The residents fled the area, which is now dubbed the Valley of Ten Thousand Smokes. These days trophy rainbow trout and abundant salmon attract serious fishing types, and the **Brooks River** features one of the world's largest gatherings of brown bears. Hiking, boat tours, and coastal kayaking are other Katmai attractions. **Katmailand Inc.** (✉ 4550 Aircraft Dr., Suite 2, Anchorage, ☏ 907/243–5448 or 800/544–0551) offers tours and backcountry lodging.

The Aleutian and Pribilof Islands

For most people package tours are the only practical way to see these areas. Schedules are flexible, as weather often delays flights to and from the islands.

The **Aleutian Islands,** a volcanic, treeless archipelago of 20 large and several hundred smaller islands, stretch 1,000 mi from the Alaska Peninsula toward Japan. The Aleut natives who live in the tiny settlements here work in canneries or as commercial fishermen and guides; many continue to lead subsistence lifestyles. Out here, where the wind blows constantly and fog is common, you can find some of the most spectacular bird-watching opportunities in the country, with abundant terns, guillemots, murres, and puffins, as well as species unique to the islands. The Japanese invaded the Aleutian Islands during World War II, and at Dutch Harbor on Unalaska Island visitors can still see concrete bunkers, gun batteries, and a partially sunken ship. **The Grand Aleutian Hotel** (✉ Box 9221169, Dutch Harbor, 99692, ☏ 800/891–1194, FAX 907/581–7157), in Dutch Harbor, offers a variety of guided activities and tours as well as lodging.

Every spring the largest herd of northern fur seals in the world—nearly 1 million seals—comes to the tiny, volcanic **Pribilof Islands,** in the Bering Sea about 200 mi northwest of Cold Bay. Most tours fly to

St. Paul Island, largest of the Pribilofs and home to the world's largest Aleut community (about 600 of the island's 750 year-round residents are Aleuts). The island is also the summer home of legions of birds, making it a favorite with birders. Contact **Reeve Aleutian Airways** (☞ Arriving and Departing, *above*) for tour information.

Next to St. Paul Island, **St. George Island** is the only other island in the Pribilof chain to be inhabited by humans. It is also a birder's paradise; more than 1.5 million seabirds nest here each summer. Contact **Joseph Van Os Photo Safaris** (⊠ Box 655, Vashon Island, WA 98070, ☎ 206/463–5383) for tour information.

THE ARCTIC

Visitor Information

Barrow and **Kotzebue:** Alaska Native Tourism Council (☞ Statewide Visitor Information, *above*). **Nome:** Convention and Visitors Bureau (⊠ Box 240, Nome 99762, ☎ 907/443–5535, ⨎ 907/443–5832).

Arriving and Departing

Nearly all destinations in the Arctic are accessible only by plane because only one public highway leads there—the Dalton Highway, which is open to traffic all the way to Deadhorse, on the North Slope, but is impassable in winter due to snow conditions. **Alaska Airlines Vacations** (⊠ SEARV, Box 68900, Seattle, WA 98168, ☎ 800/468–2248) runs air tours of the Arctic from Anchorage and Fairbanks. **Princess Tours** (⊠ 2815 2nd Ave., Suite 400, Seattle, WA 98121, ☎ 800/835–8907) offers packages.

Exploring the Arctic

Gold was discovered in 1898 in **Nome,** just below the Arctic Circle. Colorful saloons and low-slung, ramshackle buildings help perpetuate its vintage gold camp aura. **Kotzebue** is a proud Eskimo community north of Nome where salmon dries on wooden racks and Eskimo boats rest in yards. The **Living Museum of the Arctic** (☎ 907/442–3301) preserves Nome's Eskimo heritage, as does a cultural camp where elders pass on traditions to the next generation. At the top of the state, tours of the **Prudhoe Bay** area explore the oil industry life there, as well as the wildlife and tundra surrounding it. In **Barrow,** the northernmost community in the United States, the sun rises on May 10 and doesn't set for nearly three months.

In the northernmost portion of the Brooks Range, the 18-million-acre ★ **Arctic National Wildlife Refuge** (☎ 907/456–0250) contains the United States' only protected Arctic coastal lands as well as millions of acres of mountains and alpine tundra. The refuge is home to one of the world's largest groups of caribou, the 160,000-member Porcupine Caribou Herd. Other residents are grizzly and polar bears, Dall sheep, wolves, musk ox, and dozens of varieties of birds. Accessible only by boat, plane, or foot, the refuge can be explored by backpacking or river running.

HAWAI'I

By Marty
Wentzel

Updated by
Steve Crohn

Capital	Honolulu
Population	1,184,000
Motto	The Life of the Land Is Perpetuated in Righteousness
State Bird	Nēnē (Hawaiian goose)
State Flower	Hibiscus
Postal Abbreviation	HI

Statewide Visitor Information

Hawai'i Visitor and Convention Bureau (⊠ Royal Hawai'ian Shopping Center, 2201 Kalākaua Ave., Suite A 401-A, Honolulu 96815, ☎ 808/923–1811 or 800/464–2924 for brochures).

Scenic Drives

On the eastern tip of Oahu, the 10-mi stretch of **Kalaniana'ole Highway** from Hanauma Bay to Waimānalo is a cliff-side road resembling U.S. 1 up the California coast. On the Big Island **Highway 19** north out of Hilo runs along the lush and rugged Hāmākua Coast to Waipi'o Valley, past sugarcane fields and spectacular ocean views. From Pā'ia to Hāna, Maui's **Hāna Highway** (Highway 36) is a winding 55-mi coastal route that spans rivers and passes tropical waterfalls. From the town of Waimea, Kauai's **Waimea Canyon Drive** meanders upward past panoramas of Waimea Canyon, culminating at the 4,120-ft Kalalau Lookout.

National and State Parks

National Parks

Some of Hawai'i's best National Park Service attractions are **Hawai'i Volcanoes National Park, Pu'uhonua o Hōnaunau National Historic Park,** and **Pu'ukoholā National Historic Site** (☞ The Big Island, *below*); **Haleakalā National Park** (☞ Maui, *below*); **Kalaupapa** (☞ Elsewhere in Hawai'i, *below*); and the **USS Arizona Memorial** (⊠ 1 Arizona Memorial Pl., Honolulu 96818-3145, ☎ 808/422–0561). A 20-minute drive west from downtown Honolulu, the memorial bridges the hulk of the USS *Arizona,* which sank with 1,102 men aboard during the attack on Pearl Harbor on December 7, 1941.

State Parks

Popular state parks include **Hāpuna Beach State Recreation Area** (☞ The Big Island, *below*), **Kōke'e State Park** (☞ Kauai, *below*), and **Wailua River State Park** (⊠ Wailua Marina, Kapa'a, Kauai 96746, ☎ 808/822–5065), where you can see the sites of ancient villages and an enormous fern-laced lava tube. For information write to the **District Office of the Hawaii Department of Land and Natural Resources,** Division of State Parks (⊠ Box 621, Honolulu 96809, ☎ 808/587–0300).

HONOLULU AND WAIKIKI

Honolulu, on the island of Oahu, is the urban metropolis of the Aloha State. Here the salad of cultures is artfully tossed in a blend that is harmonious yet allows each culture to retain its distinct flavor and texture. Its downtown sector contrasts royal history with the modern-day action of a major government and business capital. Just 3½ mi from downtown is the tourist mecca of Waikīkī. Set on the sunny, dry side of O'ahu, Waikīkī provides a stunning physical setting along with the buzz of international hotel and shopping destinations.

Arriving and Departing

By Plane

Honolulu International Airport (☎ 808/836–6411) is only 20 minutes from Waikīkī. U.S. carriers serving Honolulu include American, Continental, Delta, Hawaiian, Northwest, TWA, and United. A cab from the airport to downtown costs about $20 plus tip. **TransHawaiian Services** (☎ 808/566–7300) runs a shuttle service to Waikīkī for $7. Some hotels also provide pickup and shuttle service; ask when you make reservations.

Getting Around Honolulu and Waikīkī

By Car

Don't bother renting a car unless you're planning to travel outside Waikīkī. When making hotel or plane reservations, ask if there's a car tie-in. Driving in rush hour (6:30 AM–8:30 AM and 3:30 PM–5:30 PM) is frustrating because of traffic, parking limitations, and numerous one-way streets. At peak times—summer, Christmas vacation, and February—reservations are a must. **Avis** (☎ 800/331–1212), **Hertz** (☎ 800/654–3131), and **Budget** (☎ 800/527–0700) are among the many national agencies with locations in Honolulu.

By Public Transportation

You can ride the **bus** (☎ 808/848–5555) all around O'ahu for a mere $1—either exact change or a dollar bill.

By Taxi

You can usually get a cab outside your hotel. Meter rates are $1.50–$2 at the drop of the flag, plus $1.95 for each additional mile. The two biggest cab companies are **Charley's** (☎ 808/531–1333) and **SIDA of Hawai'i** (☎ 808/836–0011).

Orientation Tours

The **Pearl Harbor and Punchbowl Tour** offered by Polynesian Adventure Tours (☎ 808/833–3000) includes a Navy launch out to the **Arizona Memorial.** In downtown Honolulu the **Chinatown Walking Tour** (☎ 808/533–3181) provides a look at O'ahu's oldest neighborhood.

Exploring Honolulu and Waikīkī

In Hawai'i directions are often given as *mauka* (toward the mountains) and *makai* (toward the ocean), or they may refer to Diamond Head (east, toward the famous volcanic landmark) and *ewa* (west).

Downtown Honolulu

Aloha Tower Marketplace is a two-story conglomeration of shops, kiosks, indoor and outdoor restaurants, and live entertainment next to Honolulu Harbor, with the landmark 10-story Aloha Tower as its anchor. To view the harbor, take the free ride up to the observation deck or go for a cruise on the *Abner T. Longley,* a restored fireboat. ⊠ *101 Ala Moana Blvd., at Piers 8, 9, and 10,* ☎ *808/528–5700 or 800/378–6937.*

The **Hawai'i Maritime Center** is at the far side of the marketplace. Look for the century-old sailing vessel *Falls of Clyde,* a four-masted, square-rigged tall ship moored out front. Lively, informative exhibits trace the history of Hawai'i's love affair with the sea. ⊠ *Pier 7,* ☎ *808/536–6373.*

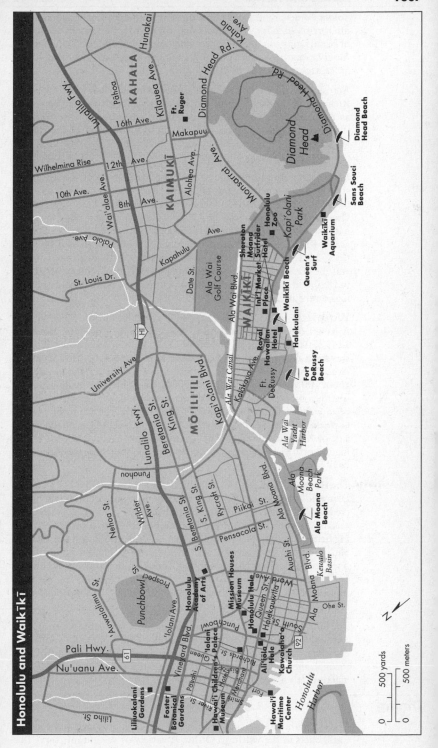

Honolulu and Waikīkī

KAHALA

Hunakai Ave.
Pāhoa
Kīlauea Ave.
Ft. Ruger
16th Ave.

Kahala Ave.

Diamond Head Rd.

Diamond Head

Diamond Head Rd.

Diamond Head Beach

Makapuu
12th Ave.
Wilhelmina Rise
10th Ave.
8th Ave.

Alohea Ave.

KAIMUKĪ

Monsarrat Ave.

Sans Souci Beach

Ala Wai Golf Course

Honolulu Zoo

Kapiʻolani Park

Waikīkī Aquarium

Pali Hwy.

Waiʻalae Ave.
Palolo Ave.
St. Louis Dr.

Kapahulu Ave.

Date St.

Sheraton Moana Surfrider Hotel

WAIKĪKĪ

Waikīkī Beach

Queen's Surf

University Ave.

Lunalilo Fwy.

MŌʻILIʻILI

Kapiʻolani Blvd.

Ala Wai Blvd.

Ala Wai Canal

Intʼl Market Place

Royal Hawaiian Hotel

Kalakaua Ave.

Ft. DeRussy

Halekulani

Fort DeRussy Beach

Lunalilo Fwy.
Beretania St.
King St.

Punahou

Nehoa St.

Wilder Ave.

S. Beretania St.
S. King St.
Rycroft St.

Piikoi St.

Ala Moana Blvd.

Ala Moana Beach Park

Ala Wai Yacht Harbor

Ala Moana Beach

Pensacola St.

Prospect St.

Punchbowl

Punchbowl St.
ʻIolani Ave.

Honolulu Academy of Arts

Mission Houses Museum

Honolulu Hale

Ward Ave.

Auahi St.

Keawalo Basin

Ohe St.

Pali Hwy.
Nuʻuanu Ave.
61

Vineyard Blvd.
Queen St.
Hotel St.
Beretania St.
Pauahi
Smith St.
Bishop
Fort

ʻIolani Palace

Halekauwila St.

Kawaiahaʻo Church

Aliʻiolani Hale

South St.

Ala Moana Blvd.

92

Liliha St.
ʻAuwaiolimu St.

Liliuokalani Gardens

Foster Botanical Gardens

Hawaiʻi Children's Museum

River St.

Hawaiʻi Maritime Center

Honolulu Harbor

N

0   500 yards
0   500 meters

'Iolani Palace, built in 1882 on the site of an earlier palace and beautifully restored today, is America's only royal palace. It contains the thrones of King Kalākaua and his successor (and sister) Queen Lili'uokalani. Reservations are essential. Children under 5 are not allowed. ⊠ *King St. at Richards St.,* ☏ *808/522–0832. Closed Sun.–Tues.*

Across the street from 'Iolani Palace is **Ali'iōla Hale** (⊠ King St. at Richards St., ☏ 808/539–4919), the old judiciary building that served as parliament hall under the monarchy and now houses the state supreme court. In front is the gilded statue of Kamehameha I, the Hawaiian chief who unified the islands.

Honolulu Hale (⊠ 530 S. King St., at Punchbowl St., ☏ 808/527–6666 for concert information), the city hall, is a Mediterranean Renaissance–style building constructed in 1929. Free live concerts take place here in the evenings. Built in 1842 of massive blocks of solid coral, **Kawaiaha'o Church** (⊠ 957 Punchbowl St., ☏ 808/522–1333) witnessed the coronations, weddings, and funerals of generations of Hawaiian royalty; it's across King Street from Honolulu Hale. The **Mission Houses Museum** (⊠ 553 S. King St., ☏ 808/531–0481), next door to Kawaiaha'o Church, was the home of the first U.S. missionaries to Hawai'i after their arrival in 1820. The mission's three main structures are among the oldest buildings on the islands.

Waikīkī

A paved ocean walk leads up to the pink **Royal Hawaiian Hotel** (⊠ 2259 Kalākaua Ave., ☏ 808/923–7311), built in 1921 when Waikīkī was still a sleepy paradise. **International Market Place** (⊠ 2330 Kalākaua Ave., ☏ 808/923–9871) is on the mauka side of Kalākaua Avenue, about 100 yards east of the Royal Hawaiian. With its spreading banyan tree, the outdoor bazaar retains a little authentic flavor among the dozens of souvenir stands. The oldest hotel in Waikīkī, the **Sheraton Moana Surfrider** (⊠ 2365 Kalākaua Ave., ☏ 808/922–3111), is on the makai side of Kalākaua Avenue. The beautifully restored Beaux Arts building is worth visiting to get a sense of what Hawai'i was like before the days of jet travel.

The **Honolulu Zoo** (⊠ 151 Kapahulu Ave., ☏ 808/971–7171), at the Diamond Head end of Waikīkī, is home to thousands of furry and finned creatures. It's not the biggest zoo in the country, but its 40 lush acres certainly make it one of the prettiest. **Kapi'olani Park,** a vast green playing field adjoining the Honolulu Zoo, is where you'll find the **Waikīkī Shell** (⊠ 2805 Monsarrat Ave., ☏ 808/521–2911), Honolulu's outdoor concert arena. Next door, the **Kodak Hula Show** (☏ 808/833–1661) has been wowing crowds for more than 50 years. The **Waikīkī Aquarium** (⊠ 2777 Kalākaua Ave., ☏ 808/923–9741) harbors more than 300 species of marine life.

The hike to the summit of **Diamond Head** (⊠ Monsarrat Ave. near 18th Ave., ☏ 808/971–2525) offers a marvelous view of O'ahu's southern coastline. The entrance is about 1 mi above Kapi'olani Park. Drive through the tunnel to the inside of the crater, and then park and start walking. It's a steep climb to the top.

Dining

The strength of Hawai'i's tourist industry has attracted some of the finest chefs in the world to O'ahu. A variety of restaurants serve fine ethnic food, especially Chinese, Japanese, and Thai. No matter what or how you eat, you'll probably pay higher prices in Waikīkī than in the rest of Hawai'i. For price ranges *see* Chart 1 (A) *in* On the Road with Fodor's.

$$$$ ✕ **La Mer.** In the exotic, elegant atmosphere of a Mandalay mansion,
★ you'll be served a blend of French and fresh Hawaiian cuisine that might
include fillet of duck crusted with goat cheese and olives. For dessert,
the soufflé with *liliko'i* (passion fruit) sauce is a must. ⊠ *Halekūlani,
2199 Kālia Rd.,* ☎ *808/923–2311. Reservations essential. Jacket required. AE, MC, V. No lunch.*

$$$ ✕ **Bali by the Sea.** The glorious ocean-side views of Waikīkī Beach might
★ be upstaged here by entrées such as roast duck with black-currant-and-
litchi glaze or *kiawe 'ōpakapaka* (mesquite-grilled snapper). Pastry chef
Gale O'Malley has been decorated by the French government for his
culinary expertise, and the sommelier is one of the wisest and wittiest
in Waikīkī. ⊠ *Hilton Hawaiian Village, 2005 Kālia Rd.,* ☎ *808/941–
2254. Reservations essential. AE, D, DC, MC, V. No dinner Sun.*

$$$ ✕ **Nick's Fishmarket.** It's a little old-fashioned, perhaps—with its
★ black booths, candlelight, and formal table settings—but for seafood
it's hard to beat Nick's. ⊠ *Waikīkī Gateway Hotel, 2070 Kalākaua
Ave.,* ☎ *808/955–6333. Reservations essential. AE, D, DC, MC, V.*

$$ ✕ **Golden Dragon.** Local Chinese people consider this the best. The
★ tasty bill of fare primarily focuses on Cantonese and unconventional
nouvelle Chinese cuisine. Signature dishes include stir-fried lobster
with *haupia* (coconut pudding), and Szechuan beef. ⊠ *Hilton Hawai-
ian Village, 2005 Kālia Rd.,* ☎ *808/946–5336. Reservations essential.
AE, D, DC, MC, V. No lunch.*

$$ ✕ **Hau Tree Lāna'i.** Right beside the sand at Kaimana Beach you can
dine under graceful hau trees and hear the whisper of the waves at break-
fast, lunch, or dinner. At breakfast try the Belgian waffle or salmon
omelet. ⊠ *New Otani Kaimana Beach Hotel, 2863 Kalākaua Ave.,* ☎
808/921–7066. Reservations essential. AE, D, DC, MC, V.

$$ ✕ **Keo's Thai Cuisine.** Hollywood celebrities have discovered this or-
★ chid-filled nook, where the Evil Jungle Prince (chicken, shrimp, or veg-
etables in a sauce of fresh basil, coconut milk, and red chili) is tops.
⊠ *625 Kapahulu Ave.,* ☎ *808/737–8240. Reservations essential. AE,
D, DC, MC, V. No lunch.*

$ ✕ **California Pizza Kitchen.** A glass atrium showcases designer pizzas
with such toppings as Thai chicken, Peking duck, and Caribbean
shrimp. There's another branch (☎ *808/955–5161*) on Ala Moana
Boulevard in Waikīkī. ⊠ *Kahala Mall, 4211 Wai'alae Ave.,* ☎ *808/737–
9446. Reservations not accepted. AE, D, DC, MC, V.*

$ ✕ **Eggs 'N Things.** Late-night revelers often stop at this breakfast-only
eatery after a night on the town. Omelets are as huge as your plate and
come with a variety of fillings; chili and cheese is a favorite. ⊠ *1911
Kalākaua Ave.,* ☎ *808/949–0820. Reservations not accepted. No
credit cards. No dinner.*

Lodging

O'ahu's best accommodations are in or near Waikīkī, with a few places
of note in Honolulu. Except for the peak months of January, Febru-
ary, and August, you'll have no trouble getting a room if you call first.
For bed-and-breakfasts in the area contact **Bed and Breakfast Hawai'i**
(⊠ Box 449, Kapa'a 96746, ☎ 808/822–7771 or 800/733–1632, 🖷
808/822–2723). For price ranges *see* Chart 2 (A) *in* On the Road with
Fodor's.

$$$$ 🏨 **Halekūlani.** This serene and elegantly modern hotel has beautifully
★ detailed marble-and-wood rooms, some with breathtaking ocean views,
plus two of the finest restaurants in Honolulu. ⊠ *2199 Kālia Rd., 96815,*
☎ *808/923–2311 or 800/367–2343,* 🖷 *808/926–8004. 456 rooms.
3 restaurants, 3 lobby lounges, refrigerators, pool, exercise room,
beach, meeting rooms. AE, DC, MC, V.*

$$$$ ▣ **Hilton Hawaiian Village.** Waikīkī's largest resort includes four tow-
  ★ ers, a botanical garden, and a pond with penguins. Rooms are done
     in raspberry or aqua, with rattan and bamboo furnishings. ☒ *2005
     Kālia Rd., 96815,* ☎ *808/949–4321 or 800/445–8667,* ☒ *808/947–
     7898. 2,542 rooms. 6 restaurants, 5 lobby lounges, 3 pools, exercise
     room, beach. AE, D, DC, MC, V.*

$$$$ ▣ **'Ihilani Resort and Spa.** This sleek 15-story hotel is the first of a
     new resort development west of Honolulu that provides a Neighbor
     Island atmosphere only 25 minutes from the airport. Rooms have
     marble bathrooms and private lānai. ☒ *92–1001 'Ōlani St., Kapolei
     96707,* ☎ *808/679–0079 or 800/626–4446,* ☒ *808/679–0295. 387
     rooms. 4 restaurants, 2 pools, spa, 18-hole golf course, 6 tennis courts,
     baby-sitting. AE, DC, MC, V.*

$$$$ ▣ **Kahala Mandarin Oriental Hawai'i.** Minutes away from Waikīkī,
     on the quiet side of Diamond Head, this elegant oceanfront hotel is an
     oasis of sybaritic comfort away from the madding crowds. As the Ka-
     hala Hilton it was a celebrity getaway; it reopened in 1996 after a $75
     million renovation. Guest rooms are in off-white hues, with touches
     of Asia and old Hawai'i in the art and furnishings. ☒ *5000 Kahala
     Ave., Honolulu 96816,* ☎ *808/734–2211 or 800/367–2525,* ☒ *808/
     737–2478. 370 rooms. 2 restaurants, bar, beach, pool, sauna, steam
     room, exercise room, shops, business services, meeting rooms. AE, D,
     DC, MC, V.*

$$$ ▣ **Outrigger Waikīkī Hotel.** At this beachfront property in the heart
     of the best shopping and dining action, rooms have a Polynesian motif,
     and each has a lānai. ☒ *2335 Kalākaua Ave., 96815,* ☎ *808/923–0711
     or 800/688–7444,* ☒ *800/622–4852. 530 rooms. 6 restaurants, 5 bars,
     lobby lounge, kitchenettes, pool, beach. AE, D, DC, MC, V.*

$$$ ▣ **Waikīkī Joy.** In the heart of Waikīkī, this gem has some rooms with
     refrigerators, others with kitchens, wet bars, or king-size beds. Every
     room has a whirlpool, a deluxe stereo system, and a bedside control
     panel. ☒ *320 Lewers St., 96815,* ☎ *808/923–2300 or 800/922–
     7866,* ☒ *808/924–4010. 93 rooms. Restaurant, lobby lounge, pool,
     sauna. AE, D, DC, MC, V.*

$$$ ▣ **Waikīkī Parc.** Despite having its main entrance down a narrow side
  ★ street, this hotel's location, just one block from Waikīkī's beach, is a
     real plus. Guest rooms are done in cool blues and whites, with lots of
     rattan and plush carpeting. ☒ *2233 Helumoa Rd., 96815,* ☎ *808/921–
     7272 or 800/422–0450,* ☒ *808/923–1336. 298 rooms. 2 restaurants,
     in-room safes, refrigerators, pool. AE, D, DC, MC, V.*

$$–$$$ ▣ **Manoa Valley Inn.** Tucked away in a lush valley 2 mi from Waikīkī,
  ★ this inn was built in 1919 and renovated when it was converted into a
     B&B in 1982. Rooms have antique four-poster beds, marble-top dressers,
     and period wallpaper. ☒ *2001 Vancouver Dr., 96822,* ☎ *808/947–6019
     or 800/634–5115,* ☒ *808/946–6168. 8 rooms, 1 cottage. AE, MC, V.*

$$–$$$ ▣ **New Otani Kaimana Beach.** Polished to a shine, the New Otani sits
  ★ on the beach across from Kapi'olani Park. Rooms are small but nicely
     appointed, with soothing pastels and off-white furnishings. ☒ *2863
     Kalākaua Ave., 96815,* ☎ *808/923–1555 or 800/356–8264,* ☒ *808/
     922–9404. 125 rooms. 2 restaurants, lobby lounge, beach, meeting
     rooms. AE, D, DC, MC, V.*

$$–$$$ ▣ **Outrigger Reef Hotel.** A beachfront location and moderate rates are
     this hotel's selling points. Rooms are done in mauves and pinks; many
     have lānai. ☒ *2169 Kālia Rd., 96815,* ☎ *808/923–3111 or 800/688–
     7444,* ☒ *808/924–4957. 885 rooms. 2 restaurants, 4 lobby lounges,
     pool, beach, nightclub, meeting rooms. AE, D, DC, MC, V.*

$ ▣ **Continental Surf.** This budget Waikīkī high-rise is two blocks from
     the ocean and convenient to shopping and dining. Rooms are com-

fortable, with standard modern decor but limited views; some have kitchenettes. ⊠ *2426 Kūhiō Ave., 96815,* ☎ *808/922–2803,* 𝔽𝔸𝕏 *808/923–9487. 140 rooms. Kitchenettes. No credit cards.*

$ 🖭 **Royal Grove Hotel.** A flamingo pink Waikīkī landmark, this hotel has a family atmosphere. Rooms have no decorative theme nor views worth noting. ⊠ *15 Uluniu Ave., 96815,* ☎ *808/923–7691,* 𝔽𝔸𝕏 *808/922–7508. 87 rooms. Kitchenettes, pool. AE, D, DC, MC, V.*

Nightlife and the Arts

Cocktail and Dinner Shows

Don Ho (⊠ Waikīkī Beachcomber Hotel, 2300 Kalākaua Ave., ☎ 808/931–3009). Waikīkī's old pro still packs them in to his Polynesian revue with its cast of attractive Hawaiian performers. There's a candlelight dinner show Tuesday–Friday and Sunday at 7 and a cocktail show at 9.

Magic of Polynesia (⊠ Hilton Hawaiian Village Dome, 2005 Kālia Rd., ☎ 808/949–4321). Magician John Hirokawa displays mystifying sleight-of-hand in this entertaining show, which also includes the requisite hula dancers and island music. Shows are nightly at 6:30 and 8:45.

Dinner Cruises

Patterned after an ancient Polynesian vessel, **Ali'i Kai Catamaran**'s (⊠ Pier 8, Honolulu, ☎ 808/524–6694) *Ali'i Kai* takes 1,000 passengers on a deluxe dinner cruise, complete with two open bars and a Polynesian show. **Windjammer Cruises** (⊠ Pier 7, Honolulu, ☎ 808/537–1122) ferries you along O'ahu's south shores on the 1,000-passenger *Kulamanu,* done up like a clipper ship.

Lū'au

Royal Hawaiian Lū'au (⊠ 2259 Kalākaua Ave., Waikīkī, ☎ 808/923–7311) takes place at the venerable Royal Hawaiian and is a notch above many other commercial lū'au offerings on the island.

Music

The **Honolulu Symphony Orchestra,** led by a young and dynamic conductor named Samuel Wong, is a top-notch ensemble. International guest artists are often headlined, and pops programs are featured as well. Shows take place at the Blaisdell Center and the Hawai'i Theatre. ⊠ *677 Ala Moana Blvd., Honolulu* ☎ *808/524–0815.* 🎟 *$10–$50.*

Nightclubs

Lewers Lounge (⊠ Halekūlani, 2199 Kālia Rd., ☎ 808/923–2311) features contemporary jazz and standards sung by Loretta Ables, Tuesday–Saturday 9 PM–12:30 AM. A vocalist-pianist sits in Sunday and Monday 9 PM–12:30 AM. A dessert menu is offered. The **Paradise Lounge,** at Hilton Hawaiian Village (⊠ 2005 Kālia Rd., ☎ 808/949–4321), showcases a variety of acts (Friday–Saturday 8–midnight), including the band Olomana.

Rumours (⊠ Ala Moana Hotel, 410 Atkinson St., ☎ 808/955–4811) provides videos and disco dancing with high-tech lights. A two-story smoky dive called **Anna Bannana's** (⊠ 2440 S. Beretania St., ☎ 808/946–5190) has fresh, loud, and sometimes avant-garde live music.

Theater

The **Diamond Head Theater** (⊠ 520 Makapu'u Ave., ☎ 808/734–0274) is in residence five minutes away from Waikīkī, right next to Diamond Head. Its repertoire includes a little of everything: musical comedies as well as experimental, contemporary, and classical dramas.

The **John F. Kennedy Theater** (⊠ 1770 East–West Rd., ☎ 808/956–7655) at the University of Hawai'i's Manoa campus is the setting for eclectic dramatic offerings—everything from Kabuki, Noh, and Chinese opera to contemporary musical comedy.

Outdoor Activities and Sports

Golf

O'ahu has more golf courses than any other Hawaiian island. **Ala Wai Golf Course** (⊠ 404 Kapahulu Ave., ☎ 808/733–7387), on Waikīkī's mauka end, is quite popular; call ahead. Advanced reservations are also recommended at the 6,350-yard **Hawai'i Kai Championship Course** and the neighboring 2,386-yard **Hawai'i Kai Executive Course** (⊠ 8902 Kalaniana'ole Hwy., Honolulu, ☎ 808/395–2358 for either.)

Tennis

In the Waikīkī area there are four free public courts at **Kapi'olani Tennis Courts** (⊠ 2748 Kalākaua Ave., ☎ 808/971–2525); nine at the **Diamond Head Tennis Center** (⊠ 3908 Pākī Ave., ☎ 808/971–7150); and 10 at **Ala Moana Park** (⊠ Makai side of Ala Moana Blvd., ☎ 808/522–7031).

Water Sports

Seemingly endless ocean options—from sailing to surfing—can be arranged through any hotel travel desk or beach concession. Try the **Waikīkī Beach Center,** next to the Sheraton Moana Surfrider, or the **C & K Beach Service,** by the Hilton Hawaiian Village (no phones).

Sailing lessons may be arranged through **Tradewind Charters** (☎ 808/973–0311). For scuba diving, **South Seas Aquatics** (☎ 808/922–0852) offers two-tank boat dives for $75. **Ocean Works, Inc.** (☎ 808/926–3483) offers a four-day scuba-diving course.

The most famous snorkeling spot in Hawai'i is Hanauma Bay. **Hanauma Bay Snorkeling Excursions** (☎ 808/941–5555) runs to and from Waikīkī. **Hanauma Bay Snorkeling Tours & Rentals** (☎ 808/944–8828) has a half-day Hanauma Bay excursion.

Beaches

Honolulu

Ala Moana Beach Park, across from Ala Moana Shopping Center, is the most popular beach for families because the protective reef keeps waters calm. Facilities include bathhouses, indoor and outdoor showers, lifeguards, concession stands, and tennis courts. At **Hanauma Bay,** a 30-minute drive (or a $1 bus ride) east of Waikīkī, the main attraction is snorkeling. Coral reefs are clearly visible through the turquoise waters of this designated marine preserve. Food and snorkel-equipment-rental concessions, changing rooms, and showers are among the facilities.

Waikīkī

Fort DeRussy Beach, the widest part of Waikīkī Beach, has volleyball courts, picnic tables, showers, dressing rooms, and food stands. A favorite with sunbathers, the beach is also frequented by military personnel. **Queen's Surf,** across from the Honolulu Zoo, is named for Queen Lili'uokalani's beach house, which once stood here. Sand is soft, and there are plenty of shade trees and picnic tables, as well as a changing house with showers. The beach attracts a mixture of families and gays.

Shopping

Just outside Waikīkī is the **Ala Moana Shopping Center** (⊠ 1450 Ala Moana Blvd., ☎ 808/946–2811), a 50-acre open-air mall with a host of major department stores, including Liberty House, Hawai'i's home-grown department store chain. **Ward Centre** (⊠ 1200 Ala Moana Blvd.,

☎ 808/591–8451) has upscale boutiques and eateries. **Ward Warehouse** (✉ 1050 Ala Moana Blvd.) is a two-story mall with 65 shops and restaurants. **Aloha Tower Marketplace** (☞ Exploring Honolulu and Waikīkī, *above*) bills itself as a festival marketplace. Along with food and entertainment, it has shops and kiosks selling mostly visitor-oriented merchandise, from expensive sunglasses to refrigerator magnets.

In Waikīkī shopping options include the **International Market Place** (☞ Exploring Honolulu and Waikīkī, *above*). The **Royal Hawaiian Shopping Center** (✉ 2201 Kalākaua Ave., ☎ 808/922–0588) is three stories high and three blocks long, with 120 stores.

Side Trip to the North Shore

Arriving and Departing
From the Diamond Head end of Waikīkī go toward the mountains on Kapahulu Avenue and follow the signs to the Lunalilo Freeway (H–1). Take H–1 northwest to H–2 through Wahiawa. Then follow the signs to Haleʻiwa, which marks the official beginning of the north shore.

What to See and Do
The **North Shore** of Oʻahu is the flip side of Honolulu. Instead of highrises there are old homes and stores, some converted into businesses catering to tourists, surfers, and beach bums. The area's wide, uncrowded beaches, rural countryside, and slower pace are reminiscent of Hawaiʻi's other islands.

Haleʻiwa is a sleepy plantation town that has come of age with contemporary boutiques and galleries. Northeast of Haleʻiwa the road continues past such beaches as **Waimea Bay,** where winter waves can crest at 30 ft. **Waimea Valley,** home of **Waimea Valley Park** and once an ancient Hawaiian community, is a lush garden setting with wildlife, walks, and cliff-diving shows. You can have a free hula lesson here. ✉ *59-864 Kamehameha Hwy., Haleʻiwa,* ☎ *808/638–8511.*

 East of Haleʻiwa is the **Polynesian Cultural Center,** 40 acres containing lagoons and seven re-created South Pacific villages, where a spectacular evening lūʻau and revue are offered. ✉ *55–370 Kamehameha Hwy., Laie,* ☎ *808/293–3333 or 808/923–1861.* ☜ *$55, includes dinner. Closed Sun.*

THE BIG ISLAND OF HAWAI`I

Nearly twice as large as all the other Hawaiian Islands combined, this youngest of the chain is still growing: Since 1983 lava flowing from Kīlauea, the world's most active volcano, has added more than 70 acres to the island. In a land of South Seas superlatives, the Big Island is also the Aloha State's most diverse region. You can hike into volcanic craters, catch marlin, visit *paniolo* (cowboy) country, tour orchid farms and waterfalls, or simply sunbathe along 266 mi of coastline.

Visitor Information

Hawai`i Visitors and Convention Bureau (✉ 250 Keawe St., Hilo 96720, ☎ 808/961–5797).

Arriving and Departing

Visitors to the west side of the island fly into Kona's **Ke-āhole–Kona International Airport** (☎ 808/329–2484). Those staying on the east side fly into **Hilo International Airport** (☎ 808/934–5801). Both air-

ports are served by Aloha and Hawaiian airlines; Mahalo Airlines and
United fly into Ke-āhole–Kona.

Exploring the Big Island

The Big Island is so large and varied that it's best to split up your exploring itinerary. Spend a night in the county seat of Hilo, visit the town
of Waimea, head to Volcanoes National Park for some hiking, then wind
up on the west coast, home of the best beaches, weather, and nightlife.

Hilo and the Hamakua Coast

Hilo is nicknamed the City of Rainbows because of its frequent showers, but rain or shine, this east coast town is truly beautiful. In the last
few years refurbishment of some older buildings has revitalized the downtown area while maintaining Hilo's unique charm and relaxed air. Historic **Lyman House** was built in 1839 by missionaries from Boston. The
collection at adjacent **Lyman Museum** (⊠ 276 Haili St., ☎ 808/935–
5021) includes carved wooden cuspidors and historical costumes. A
walking-tour map of historic sites and buildings in Old Hilo is available in the museum's gift shop.

'Akaka Falls State Park, where two waterfalls provide dramatic photo
opportunities, is about 10 mi north of Hilo and 5 mi inland off Highway 19. **Honoka'a,** one of the sleepy little towns along Highway 19
north of Hilo, is where the first macadamia trees were planted in
Hawai'i in 1881. **Waipi'o** lies 8 mi west of Honoka'a on Highway 240.
Arrange here for a four-wheel-drive tour of **Waipi'o Valley** (☎ 808/
775–7121)—the least strenuous way to visit the valley's dramatic
2,000-ft cliffs and 1,200-ft waterfalls. The view from an overlook at
the end of the highway is spectacular. **Waimea** (also known by its older
name, Kamuela) is home to the Parker Ranch Visitor Center and Museum (⊠ Parker Ranch Shopping Center, off Hwy. 19, ☎ 808/885–
7655). A video and life-size dioramas detail the growth of the ranch;
several residences are open on the property and a prestigious art collection is on display. It's a 90-minute drive from Hilo on Highway 19.

Hawai'i Volcanoes National Park

Hawai'i Volcanoes National Park, a 344-square-mi park established
in 1916, features an abundance of attractions inspired by Kīlauea. Just
beyond the park entrance, 30 mi southwest of Hilo on Highway 11,
is Kīlauea Visitor Center (☎ 808/967–7184), open daily 7:45–5,
where displays and a movie focus on past eruptions. The **Volcano Art
Center** (☎ 808/967–7511) was built in 1877 as a lodge and features
the work of local artists. **Volcano House** (☎ 808/967–7321), dating
from 1941, is a charming lodge with a huge stone fireplace. Windows
in the restaurant and bar provide picture-perfect views of Kīlauea
Caldera and its steaming fire pit, Halema'uma'u Crater. Drive around
the caldera to see the **Thomas A. Jaggar Museum** (☎ 808/967–7643),
with seismographs and filmstrips of current and previous eruptions.
Park Headquarters: ⊠ *Box 52, Volcano 96718,* ☎ *808/967–7311.*

Kailua-Kona

Kailua Pier, where the fishing fleet arrives each evening, is the center
for much of the action in this touristy seaside village on the island's
west coast. During the big-game tournaments each summer, daily
catches are weighed in here. A short walk from the pier, **Hulihe'e
Palace** (⊠ 75–5718 Ali'i Dr., ☎ 808/329–1877) served as King
Kalākaua's summer residence in the 1880s.

A boat shuttles passengers from Kailua Pier to the 65-ft *Atlantis IV* submarine, which feels more like an amusement park ride than the real

thing. A large glass dome in the bow and 13 viewing ports on the sides allow up to 48 passengers clear views of the watery world outside. ⊠ *75–5669 Ali'i Dr.,* ☎ *808/329–6626.* ◺ *$79.*

Waterfront Row (⊠ 75–5770 Ali'i Dr., ☎ 808/329–8502) is a trendy assemblage of shops and restaurants, which you'll get to if you walk the 1-mi-long main street of Kailua town from north to south. There are plenty of T-shirt emporiums and art galleries along the way to keep you entertained.

Pu'uhonua o Hōnaunau is a 180-acre national historic park. In early times fugitive *kapu* (taboo) breakers, criminals, and prisoners of war who reached this refuge were allowed to escape further punishment by remaining here after they were purified by local priests. Tide pools and a picnic area with bathrooms are part of the complex. ⊠ *Follow Hwy. 11 south of Kailua-Kona to Kēōkea, turn right and follow Hwy. 160 3½ mi to the park,* ☎ *808/328–2326.*

Kohala Coast

If you're staying in Kona, you can tour the Kohala Coast by driving north from Kailua-Kona on Highway 19, past luxury resorts and sweeping stretches of old lava flows. The **Pu'ukoholā National Historic Site** (☎ 808/882–7218) is worth a stop as you head north on Highway 19 from Kailua-Kona. The visitor center tells the story of the three stone temples (one of them is submerged just offshore) built here by King Kamehameha's men in 1791.

Dining and Lodging

With so many good restaurants on the scene, choosing a place to eat in the western part of the Big Island is difficult. The Kohala Coast is somewhat pricey, although Hilo dining has remained fairly inexpensive and family oriented. The same is true of accommodations. You can find good deals on charming accommodations by contacting **Hawai'i's Best Bed and Breakfasts** (⊠ Box 563, Kamuela 96743, ☎ 808/885–4550 or 800/262–9912). For price ranges *see* Charts 1 (A) and 2 (A) *in* On the Road with Fodor's.

Volcano

$$ ✕ **Ka Ohelo Room.** What makes this restaurant so special is its mountain lodge setting at the edge of Kīlauea Crater. Try the fresh catch of the day or the prime rib. ⊠ *Volcano House, Hawai'i Volcanoes National Park,* ☎ *808/967–7321. AE, D, DC, MC, V.*

$–$$ ✕ **Kīlauea Lodge.** Built in 1938 as a scouting retreat, the restaurant still has the original stone Friendship Fireplace, embedded with coins from around the world. Owner-chef Albert Jeyte is known for entrées such as venison, duck à l'orange, and *hasenpfeffer* (braised rabbit with herbs). ⊠ *Old Volcano Rd., Volcano Village,* ☎ *808/967–7366. MC, V. No lunch.*

Hilo

$$ ✕ **Café Pesto.** Even folks who don't like pizza like the the kind made here. Sample pizza *al pesto,* with sun-dried tomatoes, eggplant, and fresh basil pesto, or the popular seafood risotto made with sweet Thai chili, Hawaiian spiny lobster, jumbo scallops, and tiger prawns. ⊠ *308 Kamehameha Ave.,* ☎ *808/969–6640. AE, D, DC, MC, V.*

$$ ✕ **Harrington's.** A popular and reliable steak-and-seafood restaurant,
★ Harrington's has a dining lānai that extends out over the water. The mahimahi meunière and the Slavic steak (thinly sliced and slathered with garlic butter) are outstanding. ⊠ *135 Kalaniana'ole St.,* ☎ *808/ 961–4966. MC, V.*

$$$–$$$$ 🏨 **Hawai'i Naniloa Hotel.** New carpets and basic repainting and re-decorating in 1996 have helped maintain this attractively modern hotel. There's a glass-walled exercise room with wraparound ocean-front views inside the new health club. ⊠ *93 Banyan Dr., 96720,* ☎ *808/969–3333 or 800/367–5360,* 🖷 *808/969–6622. 325 rooms. 2 restaurants, lobby lounge, bar, pools, health club. AE, DC, MC, V.*

$ 🏨 **Arnott's Lodge.** This plain, tidy dwelling in a wilderness setting has dorm rooms for up to four people plus semiprivate rooms and suites. It's best for active visitors who don't mind sharing a kitchen and a TV room. ⊠ *98 Apapane Rd., 96720,* ☎ *808/969–7097 or 800/368–8752,* 🖷 *808/961–9638. 9 units. AE, DC, MC, V.*

Kailua-Kona

$$ ✕ **Jameson's by the Sea.** Sit outside next to the ocean or inside by the picture windows for glorious sunset views over Magic Sands Beach. The co-owner and chef serves three or four island fish specials daily plus a tasty baked shrimp stuffed with crab and garnished with hol-landaise sauce. ⊠ *77–6452 Ali'i Dr.,* ☎ *808/329–3195. AE, D, DC, MC, V. No lunch weekends.*

$$$ 🏨 **King Kamehameha's Kona Beach Hotel.** Although its rooms are not
★ particularly special, this is the only centrally located Kailua-Kona hotel—right next to the pier—with a white-sand beach. There's a shopping mall in the lobby. ⊠ *75–5660 Palani Rd., Kailua-Kona 96740,* ☎ *808/329–2911 or 800/367–6060,* 🖷 *808/329–4602. 460 rooms. 2 restaurants, 2 bars, pool, sauna, tennis courts, beach, shops. AE, D, DC, MC, V.*

$$ 🏨 **Kona Islander Inn.** Turn-of-the-century plantation-style architecture in a setting of palms and torchlit paths makes this older apartment hotel across the street from Waterfront Row a good value. ⊠ *75–5776 Kuakini Hwy., Kailua-Kona 96740,* ☎ *808/329–3181 or 800/922–7866,* 🖷 *808/326–9339. 60 rooms. Pool. AE, D, DC, MC, V.*

Kohala Coast and Waimea

$$ ✕ **CanoeHouse.** This open-air beachfront restaurant surrounded by fish
★ ponds serves Pacific Rim cuisine, such as pesto-seared scallops with roasted taro and guava sauce and grilled Korean-style chicken with red Thai curry-coconut sauce and pineapple salsa. ⊠ *Mauna Lani Bay Hotel, 68–1400 Mauna Lani Dr., Kohala Coast,* ☎ *808/885–6622. AE, D, DC, MC, V.*

$$ ✕ **Merriman's.** Peter Merriman earns rave reviews for his imaginative
★ Hawaiian cuisine using fresh local ingredients, including vegetarian se-lections. Wok-charred *ahi* fish is a favorite entrée. ⊠ *Opelo Plaza II corner of Rte. 19 and Opelo Rd., Kamuela,* ☎ *808/885–6822. AE, MC, V.*

$$$$ 🏨 **Kona Village Resort.** Accommodations at this resort 15 mi north
★ of Kailua-Kona are in thatched-roof bungalows by the sea or around fish ponds. The extralarge rooms have no telephones, TVs, or radios but do come with ceiling fans and bright tropical prints. Full Ameri-can plan includes activities as well as meals. ⊠ *Box 1299, Kailua-Kona 96745,* ☎ *808/325–5555 or 800/367–5290,* 🖷 *808/325–5124. 125 units. 2 restaurants, 2 bars, 2 pools, 2 hot tubs, massage, tennis courts, shuffleboard, volleyball, beach, snorkeling, boating, meeting rooms, airport shuttle. AE, DC, MC, V. Closed 1 wk in Dec.*

$$$$ 🏨 **The Orchid at Mauna Lani.** On 32 acres of secluded beachfront prop-
★ erty, this former Ritz-Carlton property changed hands in 1996, but its spacious rooms with marble baths and ocean views are still comfortable and luxurious. As at most other Hawai'i resort destinations, there is a host of recreational facilities—on both land and sea. The tennis com-

plex is the best on the island. ⊠ *1 N. Kaniku Dr., Kohala Coast 96743,* ☎ *808/885–2000 or 800/845–9905,* FAX *808/885–5778. 596 rooms. 2 restaurants, bar, pool, 2 hot tubs, massage, sauna, spa, 2 18-hole golf courses, 10 tennis courts, beach, snorkeling. AE, D, DC, MC, V.*

$$ ⊞ **Waimea Country Lodge.** In the cool upcountry, the lodge has rustic rooms that look out on green pastures. All units have heaters, and some have kitchenettes. The lodge has no restaurant, but a number of good Waimea establishments are nearby. ⊠ *Box 2559, Kamuela 96743,* ☎ *808/885–4100,* FAX *808/885–6711. 21 rooms. AE, MC, V.*

Nightlife

In Kailua-Kona the **Eclipse Restaurant** (⊠ 75–5711 Kuakini Hwy., ☎ 808/329–4686) has a DJ and disco music from 10 PM Wednesday through Saturday. Sunday features a big-band sound. The hottest place on the island is the **Second Floor,** about half an hour out of town, a disco at the Hilton Waikoloa Village (⊠ 425 Waikoloa Beach Dr., off Queen Ka'ahumanu Hwy., ☎ 808/885–5737). This is a high-energy club for the young at heart. Tuesday through Saturday you might be able to find some easy listening jazz at the **Honu Bar,** in the Mauna Lani Bay Hotel and Bugalows (⊠ 68-1400 Mauna Lani Dr., Kohala Coast, ☎ 808/885–6622).

In Hilo there is live music at **Fiascos** (⊠ 200 Kanoelehua Ave., Hilo, ☎ 808/935–7666) on Friday and Saturday nights. **D'Angoras Restaurant and Nightclub** (⊠ Hilo Lagoon Center, 101 Aupuni St., ☎ 808/ 934–7888) serves reasonably priced dinners until the music (alternating live jazz bands and DJs) starts at about 9:30 PM from Thursday through Sunday.

Outdoor Activities and Sports

Camping and Hiking
Popular areas are the 13,796-ft **Mauna Kea,** in the northeast, and **Hawai'i Volcanoes National Park.** For more information contact the Department of Parks and Recreation (⊠ 25 Aupuni St., Hilo 96740, ☎ 808/961–8311).

Fishing
More than 50 charter boats are available for hire, most of them out of Honokohau Harbor, just north of Kailua. For bookings call the **Kona Activities Center** (☎ 808/329–3171 or 800/367–5288).

Golf
On the Kohala Coast the **Mauna Kea Beach Resort** (⊠ 1 Mauna Kea Beach Dr., ☎ 808/882–7222) has a well-regarded 18-hole course, and there are another great 36 holes to be played on the North and South courses of the **Francis I'i Brown Golf Course** (⊠ Mauna Lani Resort, ☎ 808/885–6655) nearby.

Sailing/Snorkeling
Captain Zodiac Raft Expedition (☎ 808/329–3199) offers a four-hour snorkel cruise off the Kona Coast. From January through April you may see humpback whales.

Scuba Diving
The Kona Coast has calm waters for diving. Outfitters include **Big Island Divers** (☎ 808/329–6068 or 800/488–6068). Many Kohala Coast resorts, such as Waikoloa Resort, hold scuba diving classes for guests.

Beaches

Onekahakaha Beach Park, a protected white-sand beach 3 mi south of Hilo, is a favorite of local families. Close to Kailua-Kona the most popular beach is **Kahalu'u Beach Park,** where the swimming, snorkeling, and fine facilities attract weekend crowds. Currents can pull swimmers away from the beach when the surf is high. On the Kohala Coast **Anaeho'omalu Beach** (⌧ Royal Waikoloan Resort) is an expanse perfect for water sports. Equipment rentals and instructors are available at the north end. The long, white **Kauna'oa Beach** (⌧ Mauna Kea Beach Resort) is one of the most beautiful on the island, but beware of the high surf that pounds the shore during winter months. Amenities here are hotel owned. Between the Mauna Kea Beach and Mauna Lani resorts, **Hāpuna State Recreation Area** is a half-mile crescent of sand flanked by rocky points. The surf can be hazardous in winter, but calmer summer water makes it ideal for swimming, snorkeling, and scuba diving.

Shopping

Prince Kūhiō Shopping Plaza (⌧ 111 E. Puainako, Hilo, 808/959–8451) has specialty boutiques and larger stores. The upscale hotels of the **Kohala Coast** have shops off their main lobbies that provide quality goods at high prices. **Parker Square** (⌧ Kawaihae Rd., Waimea, ☎ 808/885–7178) houses many shops and boutiques including the popular **Gallery of Great Things** (☎ 808/885–7706), which sells fine art and handicrafts.

MAUI

Maui is known for its perfect beaches, heady nightlife, and sophisticated resorts. The island offers a range of experiences, from the sun and fun of the western Maui Gold Coast to the laid-back lifestyle of Hāna, on the east side. Presiding over it all is a 10,023-ft dormant volcano, Haleakalā, from whose peak you can see a sunrise like none other on earth.

Visitor Information

Maui Visitors Bureau (⌧ 1727 Wili Pa Loop, Wailuku 96793, ☎ 808/244–3530).

Arriving and Departing

Maui's major airport, **Kahului Airport** (☎ 808/872–3800 or 808/372–3830), at the center of the island, is served by United, American, Delta, Hawaiian, Mahalo, and Aloha airlines. If you're staying in West Maui, you might be better off flying into **Kapalua–West Maui Airport** (☎ 808/669–0623), served by Aloha and Mahalo airlines. The landing strip at **Hāna Airport** (☎ 808/248–8208) is served by Aloha Airlines.

Exploring Maui

West Maui

The road that follows the island's northwest coast passes through the beach towns of **Nāpili, Kahana,** and **Honokōwai,** which are all packed with condos and have a few restaurants. To the south is **Lahaina,** former capital of the islands and a 19th-century whaling town, where many old buildings have been renovated. On the ocean side of Lahaina's **Front Street** is a **banyan tree** planted in 1873 and the largest of its kind in Hawai'i. Docked at Lahaina Harbor is the brig **Carthaginian II** (☎ 808/661–3262), built in Germany in the 1920s and now open as a mu-

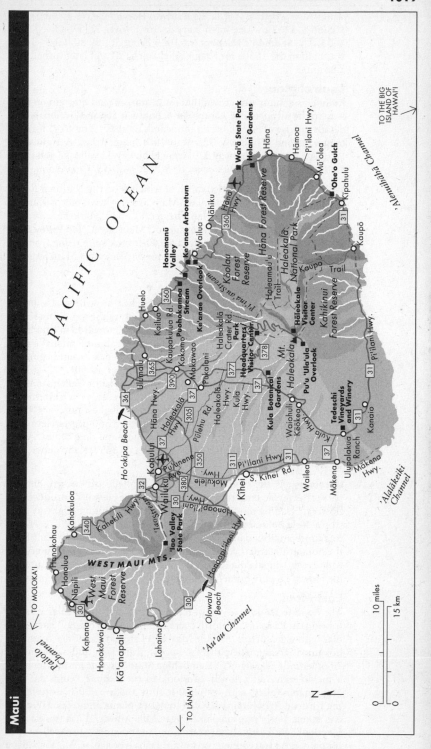

Maui

PACIFIC OCEAN

TO MOLOKA'I

Pailolo Channel

TO LĀNA'I

'Au'au Channel

'Alalakeiki Channel

'Alenuihāhā Channel

TO THE BIG ISLAND OF HAWAI'I

WEST MAUI MTS.

West Maui Forest Reserve

Kō'olau Forest Reserve

Hāna Forest Reserve

Haleakalā National Park

Kahikinui Forest Reserve

Honolua
Honokōhau
Kahakuloa
Nāpili
Kahana
Honokōwai
Kā'anapali
Lahaina
Olowalu Beach
Kahului
Wailuku
Pu'unēnē
Kīhei
Wailea
Mākena
'Īao Valley State Park
Ho'okipa Beach
Pā'ia
Huelo
Ulumalu
Kailua
Ha'ikū
Makawao
Pā'uwela
Pukalani
Kōkō
Keōkea
Waiohuli
Kanaio
Kula
Ke'anae Arboretum
Ke'anae Overlook
Honomanū Valley
Wailua
Nāhiku
Wai'ō State Park
Helani Gardens
Hāna
Hāmoa
Mū'olea
Pi'ilani Hwy.
Kīpahulu
'Ohe'o Gulch
Kaupō
Puohokamoa Stream
Haleakalā Crater Rd
Park
Headquarters/Visitor Center
Kula Botanical Gardens
Pu'u 'Ula'ula Overlook
Haleakalā Visitor Center
Mt. Haleakalā
Tedeschi Vineyards and Winery
Ulupalakua Ranch
Haleamau'u Trail
Haleakalā Trail
Kaupō Trail
Kahikinui Trail
S. Kīhei Rd.
Waikamoi Stream
Pi'ina'au Stream

36
340
30
32
30
36
365
360
360
350
380
390
305
37
377
378
37
31
31
31

'Īao Stream
Kahekili Hwy
Honoapi'ilani Hwy
Hāna Hwy
Haleakalā Hwy
Kaupakalua Rd.
Kula Hwy
Haleakalā Hwy
Pūlehu Rd
Piʻilani Hwy
Mokulele Hwy
Kula Hwy
Pi'ilani Hwy
Mākena Hwy

N

0   10 miles
0   15 km

seum. Also worth a visit is the **Baldwin Home** (✉ 696 Front St., ☎ 808/661–3262), where missionary doctor Dwight Baldwin lived from 1836. The **Seamen's Hospital** (✉ 1024 Front St., ☎ 808/661–3262) was built in the 1830s for King Kamehameha III and later turned into a hospital.

Central Maui

Kahului is an industrial town that most tourists pass through on their way to the airport. The **Alexander & Baldwin Sugar Museum,** which details the rise of sugarcane on the islands, is about 2 mi from Ka'ahumanu Avenue (Highway 32), Kahului's main street. A right onto Pu'unēnē Avenue (Highway 350) from Highway 32 will take you there. ✉ *3957 Hansen Rd., Pu'unēnē,* ☎ *808/871–8058. Closed Sun.*

Wailuku's Historical District, much of which is on the National Register of Historic Places, centers on Main Street—drive out of Kahului on Kahumanu Avenue. The '**Īao Theater** (✉ 68 N. Market St., ☎ 808/242–6969), dating from 1927, is right off Main Street. '**Īao Valley State Park** is the home of 'Īao Needle, a 1,200-ft rock spire rising from the valley floor. Drive toward the mountains on Wailuku's Main Street to reach the park.

Haleakalā and Upcountry

Haleakalā has terrain and views unmatched anywhere else in the world; bring a sweater or jacket since it's chilly at the top. From Kahului, drive on Haleakalā Highway (Highway 37) toward Haleakalā. At the fork veer to the left on Highway 377. After about 6 mi make a left onto Haleakalā Crater Road where the switchback ascent begins. At 7,000 ft is **Haleakalā National Park headquarters** (☎ 808/572–9306), with a gift shop and rest rooms. At **Haleakalā Visitor Center,** at about 9,800 ft, a ranger gives lectures on Haleakalā geology each afternoon. The road ends at **Pu'u 'Ula'ula Overlook,** the highest point on Maui, where you'll find a glass-enclosed lookout with a 360-degree view. Sunrise begins between 5:45 and 7, depending on the time of year. On a clear day you can see the islands of Moloka'i, Lāna'i, Kaho'olawe, and Hawai'i.

Upcountry, as the western slopes of Haleakalā are known, encompasses the fertile land responsible for much of Hawai'i's produce and flowers. Heading down from the volcano's summit on Highway 377, stop at **Kula Botanical Gardens** (✉ Upper Kula Rd., ☎ 808/878–1715) to admire an abundance of beautiful tropical flora. About 8 mi from the botanical garden you'll reach **Tedeschi Vineyards and Winery** (✉ Kula Hwy., Ulupalakua Ranch, ☎ 808/878–6058), where you can sample Hawai'i's only homegrown wines.

East Maui

The **Road to Hāna** is 55 mi of hairpin turns and spectacular scenery. It begins in Pā'ia on the north coast and passes Ho'okipa Beach, popular with windsurfers. At Mile Marker 11 stop at the bridge over Puahokamoa Stream, where there are pools, waterfalls, and picnic tables. Another mile takes you to **Kaumahina State Wayside Park,** which has a picnic area and a lovely overlook to the Keanae Peninsula. Past Honomanū Valley, with its 3,000-ft cliffs and a 1,000-ft waterfall, is the Ke'anae Arboretum, devoted to native plants and trees. Here you can take a fairly rigorous hike. Near Mile Marker 17 is the Ke'anae Overlook, with views of taro farms and the ocean; it's an excellent spot for photos. As you continue on toward Hāna, you'll pass Wai'ānapanapa State Park (☎ 808/248–8061), with state-run cabins and picnic areas. Closer to Hāna is Helani Gardens (☎ 808/248–8274), a 60-acre enclave of tropical plants and flowers, such as ginger and bird-of-paradise, grown by Hāna native Howard Cooper.

Hāna is just minutes from Helani Gardens. On the hill above town is a cross erected in memory of rancher Paul Fagan, who built the Hotel Hāna-Maui and stocked the surrounding pasture with cattle. **'Ohe'o Gulch** and its famous pools are about 10 mi past Hāna on a bumpy stretch of road called Pi'ilani Highway; swimming is hazardous here, but it's a popular spot for sunning and picture taking.

Dining and Lodging

Maui attracts fine chefs who combine fresh Hawaiian produce with classic preparations. Some of the best restaurants are at resort hotels. West Maui is the center of tourism, while central Maui's choices are limited; eastern Maui is a mixed bag in terms of rates and comfort. For B&B accommodations contact **Bed & Breakfast Maui-Style** (⊠ Box 98, Kīhei 96784, ☎ 808/879–7865 or 800/848–5567). For price ranges *see* Charts 1 (A) and 2 (A) *in* On the Road with Fodor's.

East Maui

$$$ ✕ **Hali'imaile General Store.** It was a camp store in the 1920s, and
★ now its white, green, and peach tin exterior looks a little out of place in an Upcountry pineapple field. Inside you'll find a fine smoked duck with pineapple chutney and dynamite barbecued ribs. ⊠ *900 Hali'imaile Rd., 2 mi north of Pukalani,* ☎ *808/572–2666. MC, V.*

$$$ ✕ **A Pacific Cafe.** Kaua'i's superstar chef, Jean-Marie Josselin, serves
★ up foods from lands bordering the Pacific: smoked and grilled island chicken with Thai black rice, pineapple, lemon-jalapeño marmalade, and green curry, to name one example. ⊠ *Azeka Place II, Kīhei,* ☎ *808/879–0069. AE, DC, MC, V. No lunch.*

$$ ✕ **Makawao Steak House.** This popular Upcountry restaurant is arguably one of the best steak joints on the island—a tender New York strip goes for less than $25. The fresh fish and fresh-baked bread are just as good. ⊠ *3612 Baldwin Ave.,* ☎ *808/572–8711. No lunch. AE, D, DC, MC, V.*

$$$$ ▥ **Four Seasons Resort.** Low-key elegance defines this stunning prop-
★ erty with open-air public areas and access to one of Maui's best beaches. Nearly all rooms have ocean views and elegant marble bathrooms with high ceilings. ⊠ *3900 Wailea Alanui, Wailea 96753,* ☎ *808/874–8000 or 800/334–6284,* ℻ *808/874–6449. 380 rooms. 3 restaurants, 4 bars, pool, health club, beach. AE, D, DC, MC, V.*

$$$$ ▥ **Hotel Hāna-Maui.** The trellised verandas here look out onto lush
★ ranch lands. Rooms feature bleached-wood floors, overstuffed furniture in natural fabrics, and local art. ⊠ *Box 9, Hāna 96713,* ☎ *808/248–8211 or 800/321–4262,* ℻ *808/248–7264. 96 rooms. Restaurant, bar, 2 pools, spa, tennis courts, horseback riding, shops, library. AE, D, DC, MC, V.*

$ ▥ **Aloha Cottages.** Two-bedroom units and one studio are sparsely furnished but clean and equipped with kitchens. A special touch is the view of papaya, banana, and avocado trees on the neighboring property. ⊠ *Hāna 96713,* ☎ *808/248–8420. 4 cottages. No credit cards.*

West Maui

$$$ ✕ **Gerard's.** One of Hawai'i's most talented chefs, owner Gerard Re-
★ versade changes the French menu daily: You might find confit of duck or shiitake and oyster mushrooms in puff pastry. Prepare to do some stargazing, as this is a celebrity favorite. ⊠ *Plantation Inn, 174 Lahainaluna Rd., Lahaina,* ☎ *808/661–8939. AE, D, DC, MC, V. No lunch.*

$$-$$$ ✕ **Avalon.** Ethnic influences give rise to eclectic dishes such as giant
★   prawns in garlic-and-black-bean sauce. The only dessert, caramel Mi-
       randa, is made of fruit and caramel sauce. ⊠ *Mariner's Alley, 844 Front
       St., Lahaina,* ☎ 808/667–5559. *AE, D, DC, MC, V.*

$$ ✕ **Lahaina Coolers.** This surf bistro serves unusual dishes, such as Evil
       Jungle Pasta (chicken and linguine with peanut sauce) and a spinach-
       and-feta quesadilla. ⊠ *180 Dickenson St., Lahaina,* ☎ 808/661–
       7082. *AE, MC, V.*

$$$$ 🛏 **Ritz-Carlton.** This Kapula resort has spacious, comfortable rooms
★   with oversize marble bathrooms and lānai, a manicured golf course,
       panoramic ocean views, a three-level pool, and all the elegance and ser-
       vice that this hotel chain is known for. ⊠ *1 Ritz-Carlton Dr., Kapalua,*
       ☎ 808/669–6200 *or* 800/262–8440, 𝖥𝖠𝖷 808/669–3908. *550 rooms.
       4 restaurants, lobby lounge, pool, beauty salon, 18-hole golf course,
       tennis courts, health club, shops, children's program, business ser-
       vices, meeting rooms, travel services. AE, D, DC, MC, V.*

$$$–$$$$ 🛏 **Kapalua Bay Hotel.** This resort hotel has a real Maui feel to it: The
★   exterior is all understated white and natural wood. The open lobby,
       filled with flowering vanda and dendrobium orchids, has a fine view
       of the ocean beyond. Guest rooms are spacious and appealing. ⊠ *1
       Bay Dr., Kapalua 96761,* ☎ 808/669–5656 *or* 800/367–8000, 𝖥𝖠𝖷 808/
       669–4694. *194 rooms, 135 condo units. 3 restaurants, 2 pools, 6 ten-
       nis courts, beach. AE, D, DC, MC, V.*

$$ ✕🛏 **Lahaina Hotel.** This 12-room Maui property is stocked with an-
       tique beds and wardrobes and decked out with country print curtains
       and spreads. Downstairs is David Paul's Lahaina Grill, where you can
       enjoy evening wine tastings, along with fruit and cheese, before a
       unique new American meal. ⊠ *127 Lahainaluna Rd., Lahaina 96761,*
       ☎ 808/661–0577 *or* 800/669–3444, 𝖥𝖠𝖷 808/667–9480. *12 rooms.
       Restaurant. AE, D, MC, V.*

Nightlife

The best options are in resort areas and Lahaina. **Moose McGilly-
cuddy's** (⊠ 844 Front St., Lahaina, ☎ 808/667–7758) offers live
music Wednesday, Friday, and Saturday nights. **Molokini Lounge** (⊠
Maui Prince Hotel, Makena Resort, ☎ 808/874–1111) is a pleasant
bar with live Hawaiian music, a dance floor, and an ocean view. The
best lū'au on Maui is the small, personal, and authentic **Old Lahaina
Lū'au** (⊠ 505 Front St., Lahaina, ☎ 808/667–1998), which takes place
from Monday to Saturday, 5:30–8:30.

Outdoor Activities and Sports

Fishing
You can fish year-round in Maui for such catch as tuna, bonefish, Pacific blue marlin, and wahoo. Plenty of fishing boats run out of Lahaina and Mā'alaea harbors, including *Finest Kind* (⊠ Lahaina Harbor,
Slip 7, ☎ 808/661–0338).

Golf
Kapalua Golf Club (⊠ 300 Kapalua Dr., Lahaina, ☎ 808/669–8877)
has three 18-hole golf courses. The **Wailea Golf Club** (⊠ 120 Kaukahi
St., Wailea, ☎ 808/875–5100) also has three courses.

Sailing
Most companies combine their sailing tours with a meal, snorkeling,
or whale-watching. Try **Genesis Charters** (⊠ Box 10697, Lahaina, ☎
808/667–5667).

Snorkeling and Scuba Diving

Lahaina has numerous dive shops—including **Dive Maui** (⊠ Lahaina Market Place, ☎ 808/667–2080)—which rent equipment and offer diving trips and lessons. Many dive companies offer snorkeling tours as well; the **Ocean Activities Center** (⊠ 1325 S. Kīhei Rd., Kīhei, ☎ 808/879–4485) offers an enjoyable trip to the nearby island of Molokini.

Tennis

The finest facilities are at the **Wailea Tennis Club** (⊠ 131 Wailea Ike Pl., Kīhei, ☎ 808/879–1958), often called Wimbledon West because of its grass courts.

Windsurfing

Ho'okipa Bay, 10 mi east of Kahului, is the windsurfing capital of the world. Rent a board or take lessons from **Kā'anapali Windsurfing School** (⊠ 104 Wahikuli Rd., Lahaina, ☎ 808/667–1964).

Beaches

If you start at the northern end of West Maui and work your way down the coast, you'll find numerous beaches. **D. T. Fleming Beach,** 1 mi north of Kapalua, is a sandy cove better for sunbathing than swimming. **Nāpili Beach,** a secluded crescent, is right outside the Nāpili Kai Beach Club. **Kā'anapali Beach** is best for people-watching; cruises, Windsurfers, and parasails launch from here. Farther south of Kā'anapali are **Wailea**'s five crescent-shape beaches, which stretch for nearly 2 mi with little interruption. South of Wailea are **Big Beach,** a 3,000-ft-long, 100-ft-wide strand, and **Little Beach,** popular for nude sunbathing (officially illegal here).

Shopping

You can have fun browsing through the stores of Front Street in Lahaina or the boutiques in the major hotels. Maui also has several major shopping malls. **Ka'ahumanu Center** (⊠ 275 Ka'ahumanu Ave., Kahului, ☎ 808/877–3369) has nearly 100 shops and restaurants, including Liberty House and the Japanese retailer Shirokiya. Also in Kahului is the **Maui Mall Shopping Center** (⊠ Corner of Ka'ahumanu and Pu'unēnē Aves., ☎ 808/877–7559), with 33 stores. The **Lahaina Cannery Shopping Center** (⊠ 1221 Honoapiilani Hwy., Lahaina, ☎ 808/661–5304), resembling an old pineapple cannery, has some 50 shops, including Dolphin Galleries, which offers sculpture, paintings, and other Maui artwork. **Whalers Village** (⊠ 2435 Kā'anapali Pkwy., Kā'anapali, ☎ 808/661–4567) has grown into a major West Maui shopping center, with a whaling museum and 65 restaurants and classy shops such as Louis Vuitton.

KAUA'I

The oldest of the Hawaiian Islands, Kaua'i is rich with natural splendor, history, and the reflections of past cultures. The cooler, damper north shore has lush landscaping and award-winning golf courses in startling contrast to Kaua'i's western side, where Waimea Canyon—the Grand Canyon of the Pacific—displays its vivid, rich colors of copper, rust, and gold in the tropic sun.

Visitor Information

Hawai'i Visitors and Convention Bureau (⊠ 3016 Umi St., Suite 207, Līhu'e 96766, ☎ 808/245–3971). **Kaua'i Visitor Center** (⊠ Coconut Plantation Marketplace, Kapa'a 96746, ☎ 808/822–5113; ⊠ Kaua'i Village, Kapa'a 96746, ☎ 808/822–7727).

Arriving and Departing

Līhu'e Airport (☎ 808/246–1400) handles most of Kaua'i's air traffic; 3 mi east of the county seat of Līhu'e, it is served by Aloha, Hawaiian, and Mahalo. Aloha Airlines flies to **Princeville Airport** (☎ 808/826–3040), a tiny strip to the north of the island.

Exploring Kaua'i

A coastal road runs around the rim of Kaua'i and dead-ends on either side of the rugged 15-mi coast called Nā Pali (the Cliffs). If you're looking for sunshine, head to the southern resort of Po'ipū; for greener scenery and a wetter climate, try Hanalei and Princeville to the north. For a bird's-eye view of the whole island, consider a helicopter excursion.

The Road North

Kīlauea Lighthouse (☎ 808/828–1413), built in 1913, is now part of a wildlife refuge near the former plantation town of Kīlauea, north of Wailua on Highway 56. The **Hanalei Valley Overlook** encompasses a view of more than a half mile of taro, the staple plant of the Hawaiian diet, plus a 900-acre endangered-waterfowl refuge. **Hanalei** is the site of the **Waioli Mission** (⊠ Kūhiō Hwy., ☎ 808/245–3202), founded by Christian missionaries in 1837 and open Tuesday, Thursday, and Saturday.

Smith's Tropical Paradise (⊠ 174 Wailua Rd., Kapa'a, ☎ 808/822–4654) is a 30-acre expanse of jungle, exotic foliage, tropical birds, and lagoons. From Wailua Marina, on the east coast, boats depart for **Fern Grotto,** a yawning lava tube with enormous ferns and an 80-ft waterfall. ⊠ *Smith's Motor Boat Service, 174 Wailua Rd., Kapa'a, ☎ 808/821–6892.*

To the South and West

Kaua'i Museum (⊠ 4428 Rice St., Līhu'e, ☎ 808/245–6931) is chock-full of exhibits about the island's history. **Kilohana** (⊠ 3–2087 Kaumuali'i Hwy., ☎ 808/245–5608), a historic sugar-plantation house dating from 1935, is now a 35-acre visitor attraction with agricultural exhibits, local arts-and-crafts displays, and more. **Po'ipū** is the premiere resort of Kaua'i's south shore and a mecca for body surfers. **Spouting Horn,** a waterspout that shoots up through an ancient lava tube, lies west of Po'ipū along Highway 52.

Waimea, a sleepy little town, marks the first landfall of British captain James Cook to the Sandwich Islands in 1778. **Waimea Canyon,** created by an ancient fault in the earth's crust, stretches inland from Waimea. The canyon, 3,600 ft deep, 2 mi wide, and 10 mi long, is known as the Grand Canyon of the Pacific. At 4,000 ft Waimea Canyon Drive passes through **Kōke'e State Park** (☎ 808/335–5871), a 4,345-acre wilderness. The drive ends 4 mi above the park at the **Kalalau Lookout.** At 4,120 ft above sea level, it offers the best views on Kaua'i.

For a helicopter flightseeing adventure with aerial views you won't easily forget—the rugged splendor of the Nā Pali coast or the hidden waterfalls of Waimea Canyon—call the **South Sea Tour Company** (⊠ Main Terminal, Līhu'e Airport, ☎ 808/245–2222 or 800/367–9214). The spectacular Nā Pali coast is not accessible by land, so this may be your best way to have a good look.

Dining and Lodging

On Kaua'i you can enjoy almost any style of cuisine. Accommodations range from swanky resorts to bare-bones cabins. For an insider's look at Kaua'i, book with **Bed & Breakfast Hawai'i** (⊠ Box 449, Kapa'a 96746, ☎ 808/822–7771 or 800/733–1632). For price ranges *see* Charts 1 (A) and 2 (A) *in* On the Road with Fodor's.

East and North Kaua'i

$$$ ✕ **La Cascata.** Terra-cotta floors and trompe l'oeil paintings give the restaurant the feel of an Italian villa. The tastes of southern Italy are showcased in the grilled Hawaiian swordfish with balsamic vinegar and pancetta. ⊠ *Princeville Hotel, Princeville,* ☎ *808/826–9644. Reservations essential. Jacket required. AE, D, DC, MC, V. No lunch.*

$$–$$$ ✕ **Casa di Amici.** Dine on the porch of the House of Friends and
★ choose your own combination of pasta with such sauces as pesto or *salsa di noci* (walnut cream sauce with Romano cheese and marjoram). ⊠ *2484 Keneke St., at Lighthouse Rd., Kīlauea,* ☎ *808/828–1555. AE, DC, MC, V. No lunch.*

$$–$$$ ✕ **Roy's Po'ipū Bar & Grill.** Hawai'i's culinary superstar, Roy Ya-
★ maguchi's serves first-rate Euro-Asian-Pacific cuisine. Who but Roy could team fresh-seared 'ōpakapaka with orange shrimp butter and Chinese black bean sauce? ⊠ *Po'ipū Shopping Village, 2360 Kiahuna Plantation Dr., Po'ipū Beach,* ☎ *808/742–5000. AE, D, DC, MC, V.*

$$ ✕ **Bull Shed.** This A-frame restaurant is rustic, with exposed wood, ocean views, and family-style tables. Menu highlights include Alaskan king crab and prime rib. ⊠ *796 Kūhiō Ave., Kapa'a,* ☎ *808/822–3791. AE, D, DC, MC, V. No lunch.*

$$$$ ▥ **Princeville Hotel.** This splendid cliff-side property has breathtaking
★ views of Hanalei Bay. Bathrooms have gold-plated fixtures and picture windows that cloud up for privacy at the flick of a switch. The setting and service here are unmatched. ⊠ *Box 3069, Princeville 96722,* ☎ *808/826–9644 or 800/826–4400,* ℻ *808/826–1166. 252 rooms. 3 restaurants, 3 lobby lounges, pool, 2 18-hole golf courses, 8 tennis courts, cinema. AE, D, DC, MC, V.*

$$ ▥ **Kapa'a Sands.** Furnishings in this intimate condominium are bungalow style, with rustic wood and ceiling fans. Ask for an oceanfront room with open-air lānai and Pacific views. ⊠ *380 Papaloa Rd., Kapa'a 96746,* ☎ *808/822–4901 or 800/222–4901. 21 units. Kitchenettes, pool. AE, D, DC, MC, V.*

South and West Kaua'i

$$ ✕ **Brennecke's Beach Broiler.** At this veteran restaurant with picture windows overlooking the ocean, the chef specializes in mesquite-broiled foods and homemade desserts. ⊠ *Hoone Rd., Po'ipū,* ☎ *808/742–7588. AE, MC, V.*

$ ✕ **Camp House Grill.** Down-home food in a down-home setting is what you'll get at this restaurant on the road to Waimea Canyon: burgers, chicken, ribs, fish, and a host of barbecued specialties. ⊠ *Kaumuali'i Hwy. (Hwy. 50), Kalāheo,* ☎ *808/332–9755. MC, V.*

$ ✕ **Green Garden.** In business since 1948, this family-run no-frills restau-
★ rant is brightened by an assortment of hanging and standing plants. Local fare includes breaded mahimahi fillet and passion-fruit chiffon pie. ⊠ *Hwy. 50, Hanapēpē,* ☎ *808/335–5422. AE, D, DC, MC, V. Closed Tues.*

$$$$ ▥ **Hyatt Regency Kaua'i.** Low-rise, plantation-style architecture with
★ dramatic open-air courtyards, lush tropical landscaping, and spectacular rock-enclosed swimming lagoons make this the most Hawaiian of Hyatts—and one of the most striking hotel resorts anywhere. Rooms have comfortable furnishings; two-thirds have ocean views. The 25,000-square-ft spa offers the works, including aromatherapy facials and massages. ⊠ *1571 Po'ipū Rd., Koloa 96756,* ☎ *808/742–1234 or 800/233–1234,* ℻ *808/742–6229. 600 rooms. 4 restaurants, 3 lobby*

lounges, 3 pools, saltwater pool, spa, 18-hole golf course, 4 tennis courts, beach, shops, nightclub. AE, D, DC, MC, V.

$ ⊞ **Kōke'e Lodge.** Twelve mountaintop cabins are surrounded by pine ★   trees and hiking trails. Furnishings are rustic (prices vary according to quality), but each is cozy, with a fireplace and fully equipped kitchen. ⊠ *Box 819, Waimea 96796,* ☎ *808/335–6061. 12 cabins. Restaurant. AE, MC, V.*

Nightlife

Locals enjoy **Kūhiō's Nightclub** (⊠ Hyatt Regency Kaua'i, ☎ 808/742–1234), a south-shore hot spot. **Legends Nightclub** (⊠ Pacific Ocean Plaza, 3501 Rice St., 2nd floor, Nawiliwili, ☎ 808/245–5775) delivers Top 40 tunes in a garden setting. Of Kaua'i's lū'au options, **Kaua'i Coconut Beach Resort Lū'au** (⊠ Coconut Plantation, Kapa'a, ☎ 808/822–3455, ext. 651) is regarded by many as the best on the island.

Outdoor Activities and Sports

Fishing
For deep-sea fishing, **Sportfishing Kaua'i** (⊠ Box 1195, Koloa, ☎ 808/742–7013) has a 28-ft, six-passenger custom sportfisher.

Golf
Best known are the Makai and Prince courses at **Princeville Resort** (⊠ Princeville, ☎ 808/826–3580).

Hiking
Kōke'e State Park has 45 mi of hiking trails. The **Department of Land and Natural Resources** (⊠ Līhu'e, ☎ 808/241–3444) provides hiking information.

Snorkeling and Scuba Diving
Explore spectacular underwater reefs with **Dive Kaua'i** (⊠ 4–976 Kūhiō Hwy., Suite 4, Kapa'a, ☎ 808/822–0452). **Hanalei Sea Tours** (⊠ Box 1437, Hanalei, ☎ 808/826–7254) has a four-hour snorkeling cruise off the Nā Pali coast.

Tennis
Princeville Tennis Center (⊠ Box 3040, Princeville 96722, ☎ 808/826–9823) has six courts.

Beaches

The waters that hug Kaua'i are clean, clear, and inviting, but be careful where you go in: The south shore sees higher surf in the summer, while north-shore waters are treacherous in winter.

North Shore
On the winding section of Highway 56 west of Hanalei is **Lumahai Beach,** flanked by high mountains and lava rocks. There are no lifeguards here, so swim only in summer. **Hanalei Beach Park** offers views of the Nā Pali coast and shaded picnic tables, but swimming here can be treacherous. Near the end of Highway 56, **Ha'ēna State Park** is good for swimming when the surf is down in summer. Highway 56 dead-ends at **Kē'ē Beach,** a fine swimming beach in summer.

South and West Shores
Kalapak Beach, a sheltered bay ideal for water sports, fronts the Marriott in Līhu'e. Small- to medium-size waves make **Brennecke's Beach** in Po'ipū a bodysurfer's heaven, and there are showers, rest rooms, and lifeguards. At the end of Highway 50W is **Polihale Beach Park,** a long,

wide strand flanked by huge cliffs. Swim here only when the surf is small; there are no lifeguards.

Shopping

In Līhu'e is **Kukui Grove Center** (✉ 3–2600 Kaumuali'i Hwy., ☎ 808/ 245–7784), Kaua'i's largest mall. **Coconut Plantation Marketplace** (✉ 4–484 Kūhiō Hwy., Kapa'a, ☎ 808/822–3641) is a standout among east-coast malls. **Kaua'i Village** (✉ 4–831 Kūhiō Hwy., Kapa'a, ☎ 808/ 822–4904) has 19th-century plantation-style architecture and 25 shops. **Princeville Center** (✉ 5–4280 Kūhiō Hwy., Kapa'a, ☎ 808/826– 3040), in the north end of the island, has interesting shops.

ELSEWHERE IN HAWAI'I

Moloka'i

With its slow pace and emphasis on Hawaiiana, Moloka'i drowses in another era. There are no high-rises, no traffic jams, and no stoplights on the 10- by 38-mi island. The fanciest hotels are bungalow style, and there's plenty of undeveloped countryside.

Arriving and Departing

Ho'olehua Airport (☎ 808/567–6140), a tiny strip just west of central Moloka'i, is served by Hawaiian, Aloha, Air, Moloka'i, and Mahalo airlines.

What to See and Do

The **Meyer Sugar Mill** was built in 1878 and reconstructed to teach visitors about sugar's importance to the local economy. ✉ *Rte. 470, Kala'e, 2 mi below Pala'au State Park,* ☎ *808/567–6436. Closed weekends.*

Purdy's Natural Macadamia Nut Farm, Moloka'i's only such farm still in operation, is a family business where you can learn all about the delectable nuts. ✉ *Lihipali Ave., Ho'olehua,* ☎ *808/567–6601 or 808/567–6495. Closed Sun.*

Kalaupapa National Historic Park (✉ Box 222, Moloka'i 96742, ☎ 808/567–6102) was a leper colony until 1888. The pretty little town is now a National Historic Landmark. It's most accessible via Damien Tours (☎ 808/567–6171) or Moloka'i Mule Ride (✉ 100 Kala'e Hwy., Kualapu'u 96757, ☎ 808/567–6088).

The **Moloka'i Ranch Wildlife Conservation Park** is a 400-acre preserve and home to nearly 1,000 animals such as the oryx and the eland. Comfortable 14-passenger touring vans depart from Kaluakoi Resort. Reservations are essential. ✉ *Box 259, Maunaloa 96770,* ☎ *808/552– 2681.* 🎟 *$35. Closed Sun.–Mon.*

For more information, including advice on accommodations, contact the **Moloka'i Visitors Association** (✉ Box 960, Kaunakakai 96748, ☎ 808/553–3876 or 800/800–6367) or the **Maui Visitors Bureau** (✉ 1727 Wili Pa Loop, Wailuku, Maui 96793, ☎ 808/244–3530).

Lāna'i

Arriving and Departing

Hawaiian and **Aloha** airlines serve this tiny island, whose airport (☎ 808/565–6757) is a 10-minute drive from Lāna'i City.

What to See and Do

For decades Lāna'i was known as the Pineapple Island, with hundreds of acres growing the golden fruit. Today this 140-square-mi island has been dubbed Hawai'i's Private Island, as developers replace pineapples with people. There are now two upscale hotels and two championship golf courses, but despite these new additions, Lāna'i—the third smallest of the islands—still remains remote.

Lāna'i is for those who love the outdoors, because the island has no commercial attractions other than those offered at the two resorts. You can visit such sights as the **Garden of the Gods,** where rocks and boulders are scattered across a crimson landscape; spend a leisurely day at **Hulopo'e Beach,** where the waters are brilliantly blue and clear; or hike or drive to the top of **Lāna'ihale,** a 3,370-ft perch with a view of every inhabited Hawaiian island except Kaua'i and Ni'ihau. For visitor information contact **Destination Lāna'i** (⊠ Box 700, Lāna'i City 96763, ☎ 808/565–7600).

INDEX

.

Fodor's Travel Publications

Available at bookstores everywhere, or call 1–800–533–6478, 24 hours a day.

Gold Guides

U.S.

Alaska	Florida	New Orleans	Seattle & Vancouver
Arizona	Hawai'i	New York City	The South
Boston	Las Vegas, Reno, Tahoe	Pacific North Coast	U.S. & British Virgin Islands
California		Philadelphia & the Pennsylvania Dutch Country	USA
Cape Cod, Martha's Vineyard, Nantucket	Los Angeles		Virginia & Maryland
	Maine, Vermont, New Hampshire	The Rockies	Walt Disney World, Universal Studios and Orlando
The Carolinas & Georgia	Maui & Lāna'i	San Diego	
Chicago	Miami & the Keys	San Francisco	Washington, D.C.
Colorado	New England	Santa Fe, Taos, Albuquerque	

Foreign

Australia	Europe	Montréal & Québec City	Scotland
Austria	Florence, Tuscany & Umbria	Moscow, St. Petersburg, Kiev	Singapore
The Bahamas	France		South Africa
Belize & Guatemala	Germany	The Netherlands, Belgium & Luxembourg	South America
Bermuda	Great Britain		Southeast Asia
Canada	Greece	New Zealand	Spain
Cancún, Cozumel, Yucatán Peninsula	Hong Kong	Norway	Sweden
Caribbean	India	Nova Scotia, New Brunswick, Prince Edward Island	Switzerland
China	Ireland		Thailand
Costa Rica	Israel	Paris	Toronto
Cuba	Italy	Portugal	Turkey
The Czech Republic & Slovakia	Japan	Provence & the Riviera	Vienna & the Danube
Eastern & Central Europe	London	Scandinavia	
	Madrid & Barcelona		
	Mexico		

Special-Interest Guides

Adventures to Imagine	Fodor's Gay Guide to the USA	Halliday's New Orleans Food Explorer	Rock & Roll Traveler USA
Alaska Ports of Call	Fodor's How to Pack	Healthy Escapes	Sunday in San Francisco
Ballpark Vacations	Great American Learning Vacations	Kodak Guide to Shooting Great Travel Pictures	Walt Disney World for Adults
Caribbean Ports of Call	Great American Sports & Adventure Vacations	National Parks and Seashores of the East	Weekends in New York
The Official Guide to America's National Parks	Great American Vacations	National Parks of the West	Wendy Perrin's Secrets Every Smart Traveler Should Know
Disney Like a Pro	Great American Vacations for Travelers with Disabilities	Nights to Imagine	
Europe Ports of Call		Rock & Roll Traveler Great Britain and Ireland	
Family Adventures			

CNN✈
Airport Network

Your
Window
To The
World
While You're
On The
Road

Keep in touch when you're traveling. Before you take off, tune in to CNN Airport Network. Now available in major airports across America, CNN Airport Network provides nonstop news, sports, business, weather and lifestyle programming. Both domestic and international. All piloted by the top-flight global resources of CNN. All up-to-the-minute reporting. And just for travelers, CNN Airport Network features intriguing segments such as "Travel Facts." With an information source like Fodor's this series of fascinating travel trivia will definitely make time fly while you're waiting to board. SO KEEP YOUR WINDOW TO THE WORLD WIDE OPEN. ESPECIALLY WHEN YOU'RE ON THE ROAD. TUNE IN TO CNN AIRPORT NETWORK TODAY.

WHEREVER YOU TRAVEL, *H*ELP IS NEVER FAR AWAY.

From planning your trip to

providing travel assistance along

the way, American Express®

Travel Service Offices are

always there to help

you do more.

For the office nearest you, call
1-800-AXP-3429

do more AMERICAN EXPRESS

Travel

http://www.americanexpress.com/travel

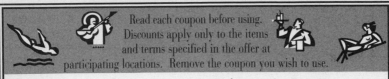

Las Vegas TRAVEL

Advance reservations required. For show, wedding, or casino information call
900-RESORT CITY. Valid Sunday thru Thursday only, except holidays and during city-wide
conventions. May not be used in conjunction with any other discount or promotion.

1-800-449-4697 – One toll-free call gives you all these:

Luxor • Monte Carlo • Tropicana • Circus Circus • Caesar's Palace • New York-New York • Bally's
The Orleans • Rio Suite Hotel • Plaza • Stardust • Stratosphere • Boomtown • Sahara • Westward Ho
Holiday Inn Board • Excalibur • Flamingo Hilton • Las Vegas Hilton • Lucky Lady • The Plaza • San Remo
And so many more.

TASTE PUBLICATIONS INTERNATIONAL

≋ National Car Rental.

TERMS AND CONDITIONS: Valid for one weekend day with the purchase of two consecutive weekend days on car classes indicated on front at participating National locations in the U.S. (Not valid in Manhattan, NY.) • Subject to availability, blackout dates and capacity control. • Weekend rate and time parameters, local rental and minimum rental day requirements apply. • Cannot be used in multiples or with any other certificate, special discount or promotion. • Standard rental qualifications apply. • Minimum rental age at most locations is 25.

In addition to rental charges, where applicable, renter is responsible for: Optional loss Damage Waiver, up to $15.99 per day; a per mile charge in excess of mileage allowance; taxes; surcharges; additional charges if car is not returned within a prescribed rental period; drop charge and additional driver fee; optional refueling charge; optional insurance benefits.

RENTAL AGENT INSTRUCTIONS: 1. Rental Screen 1: • Key Promo Coup # from the front side. **2.** Rental Screen 3: • Key Discount # from the front side in "RATE RECAP #" field. • Key applicable rate for one weekend day in "DEP: ORIG" field. • Key 7 in "TYPE" field. **3.** Write RA# and rental date below. **4.** Retain certificate at rental. Send certificate to Headquarters, Attn: Travel Industry Billing.

RA# _____ Rental Date ___/___/___

TASTE PUBLICATIONS INTERNATIONAL

ASTROLAND AMUSEMENT PARK
"Home of the World Famous CYCLONE"

Not valid with other discount offers or on holidays.
Valid Monday-Friday in season.

TASTE PUBLICATIONS INTERNATIONAL

ONE HOUR MOTOPHOTO®

TASTE PUBLICATIONS INTERNATIONAL

Fodor's
The name that means smart travel.

 **1-800-354-2322**

Save An Additional $25.00 Off
Certificate is valid for $25.00 off Alamo's low weekly basic rate.

Just reserve a compact through a minivan for 4 or more days in the U.S.A. or Canada. For reservations, call your travel agent, access us at **http://www.goalamo.com** or call Alamo at **1-800-354-2322**. Be sure to require **ID 422325**, Rate Code **BY** and Coupon Code **D86B** at time of reservation.

Offer expires December 15, 1998 | D86B |

  SUPER 8 MOTELS   **1-800-800-8000**

10% Off
Receive a 10% discount at all Super 8
Motel locations, over 1,500 motels.

Mentioning **8800/101852** when calling Superline® at **1-800-800-8000** to make reservations. E-Mail Address: **http://www.super8motels.com**

Offer expires August 31, 1998

          1-800-327-7799

10% Off
Receive a 10% discount off all time and mileage charges
on Cruise America or Cruise Canada vehicles only.

For reservations call: **1-800-327-7799** U.S. and Canada.

Offer expires August 31, 1998

 Empire State Building Observatories   **New York**

Up To Four Admissions
Enjoy $1.00 off adult admissions and $1.00 off children admissions.

Offer good for up to four admissions upon presentation of coupon at ticket office. Open daily 9:30 a.m. - midnight. Last elevator to the top at 11:30 p.m.

Offer expires August 31, 1998